THE CAMBRIDGE HISTORY OF

THE FIRST WORLD WAR

Volume II of *The Cambridge History of the First World War* offers a history of the war from a predominantly political angle, and concerns itself with the story of the state at war. It explores the multi-faceted history of state power and highlights the ways in which different political systems responded to, and were deformed by, the near-unbearable pressures of war. Every state involved faced issues of military-civilian relations, parliamentary reviews of military policy and the growth of war economies; and yet their particular form and significance varied in each national case.

Written by a global team of historical experts, this volume sets new standards in the political history of the waging of war in an authoritative new narrative which addresses problems of logistics, morale, innovation in tactics and weapons systems, and the use and abuse of science; all of which were ubiquitous during the conflict.

JAY WINTER is Charles J. Stille Professor of History at Yale University and Distinguished Visiting Professor at Monash University. He is one of the founders of the Historial de la Grande Guerre, the International Museum of the Great War, in Péronne, Somme, France. In 1997, he received an Emmy award for the best documentary series of the year as co-producer and co-writer of *The Great War and the Shaping of the Twentieth Century*, which was an eight-hour series broadcast on PBS and the BBC, and shown subsequently in twenty-eight countries. His previous publications include *Sites of Memory, Sites of Mourning: The Great War in European Cultural History* (1995); *Remembering War* (2006) and *Dreams of Peace and Freedom* (2006).

THE HISTORIAL MUSEUM OF THE

GREAT WAR

PÉRONNE, SOMME

The Historial is an internationally acclaimed museum that presents the First World War in a unique way. Located on the battlefields of the Somme, the museum presents and compares the presence of the three main belligerent nations on the Western Front – Great Britain, France and Germany. It unfolds the story both of the front and of civilians under the pressure of war. The Battle of the Somme in 1916 caused over a million casualties in less than five months of fighting. The ground would be fought over again in 1918. By the end of the war, combatants from well over twenty-five nations had fought on the Somme, making it the place where the war truly became a World War.

Historial de la Grande Guerre / Thiepval
Château de Péronne
B. P. 20063
80201 Péronne Cedex
www.historial.org

JOHN HORNE
Trinity College Dublin

HEATHER JONES
London School of Economics and Political Science

GERD KRUMEICH
Heinrich-Heine-Universität Düsseldorf

PHILIPPE NIVET
Université de Picardie Jules Verne

ANNE RASMUSSEN
Université de Strasbourg

LAURENCE VAN YPERSELE
Université Catholique de Louvain

ARNDT WEINRICH
Deutsches Historisches Institut, Paris

JAY WINTER
Yale University

THE CAMBRIDGE HISTORY OF THE FIRST WORLD WAR

*

VOLUME II
The State

*

Edited by

JAY WINTER

Charles J. Stille Professor of History, Yale University

and

The Editorial Committee of the International Research Centre of the Historial de la Grande Guerre

CAMBRIDGE
UNIVERSITY PRESS

University Printing House, Cambridge CB2 8BS, United Kingdom

Cambridge University Press is part of the University of Cambridge.

It furthers the University's mission by disseminating knowledge in the pursuit of education, learning, and research at the highest international levels of excellence.

www.cambridge.org
Information on this title: www.cambridge.org/9780521766531

First published 2014
Reprinted 2014
Paperback edition first published 2016
3rd printing 2018

Printed and bound in Great Britain by Clays Ltd, Elcograf S.p.A.

A catalogue record for this publication is available from the British Library

Library of Congress Cataloguing in Publication data
The Cambridge History of the First World War / general editor, Jay Winter, Charles J. Stille Professor of History, Yale University.
pages cm
Includes bibliographical references and index.
ISBN 978-0-521-76385-1 (v. 1) – ISBN 978-0-521-76653-1 (v. 2) – ISBN 978-0-521-76684-5 (v. 3)
1. World War, 1914–1918. 2. World War, 1914–1918 – Political aspects.
3. World War, 1914–1918 – Social aspects. I. Winter, J. M., editor.
II. Title: History of the First World War.
D521.C36 2013
940.3–dc23
2013007649

ISBN 978-0-521-76653-1 Hardback
ISBN 978-1-316-50499-4 Paperback
ISBN 978-1-316-60066-5 Paperback set

Contents

PART II
ARMED FORCES

PART III
THE SINEWS OF WAR

Illustrations

Plate section I

All illustrations are from the collection of the Historial de la Grande Guerre, Péronne (Somme), unless otherwise stated.

Photography: Yazid Medmoun (Conseil Général de la Somme), unless otherwise stated.

Plate section II

Every effort has been made to contact the relevant copyright-holders for the images reproduced in this book. In the event of any error, the publisher will be pleased to make corrections in any reprints or future editions.

The colour plates can be found between pages 334 and 335 and pages 654 and 655.

Maps

Contributors

Stéphane Audoin-Rouzeau is Directeur d'études at the École des Hautes Études en Sciences Sociales (EHESS), Paris, and President of the Centre International de Recherche de l'Historial de la Grande Guerre, Péronne, Somme.

Jean-Jacques Becker is Professor Emeritus at the University of Paris, Nanterre, and founding president of the Centre International de Recherche de l'Historial de la Grande Guerre, Péronne, Somme.

Richard Bessel is Professor of Twentieth-Century History at the University of York in the United Kingdom.

Ian M. Brown holds a Ph.D. in War Studies from King's College London.

Martin Ceadel is Professor of Politics at the University of Oxford and a Fellow of New College.

Dittmar Dahlmann is Professor of East European History at Rheinische Friedrich-Wilhelms-Universität, Bonn.

Stig Förster is Professor of Modern History at the University of Bern and President of the 'Arbeitskreis Militärgeschichte'.

Robert Gerwarth is Professor of Modern History at University College Dublin and Director of its Centre for War Studies.

Stefan Goebel is Senior Lecturer in Modern British History at the University of Kent, Canterbury.

Frédéric Guelton is Editor-in-Chief of the *Revue historique des Armées*, and teaches military history at the École spéciale militaire de Saint-Cyr and the history of international relations at the Institut d'études politiques de Paris.

Heather Jones is a Senior Lecturer in International History at the London School of Economics and Political Science.

Helmut Konrad is Professor of History at the University of Graz.

Alan Kramer holds the chair of European History at Trinity College Dublin.

SAMUËL KRUIZINGA is Assistant Professor in Contemporary History at the University of Amsterdam.

GERD KRUMEICH is Professor Emeritus of Contemporary History at the Heinrich-Heine-Universität, Düsseldorf, and Vice-President of the Centre International de Recherche de l'Historial de la Grande Guerre (Péronne, Somme).

ROY MACLEOD is Professor Emeritus of (Modern) History at the University of Sydney, and an Honorary Associate in the History and Philosophy of Science.

ANTOINE PROST is Professor Emeritus of History at the University of Paris I, Panthéon-Sorbonne. He directed the Centre for the Social History of the Twentieth Century for twenty years. He is President of the French Scientific Committee of the Centenary of 1914.

LEONARD V. SMITH is Frederick B. Artz Professor and Chair of the History Department at Oberlin College, Ohio, United States.

GEORGES-HENRI SOUTOU is Professor Emeritus at Paris-Sorbonne (Paris IV) and member of the Institut de France.

DAVID STEVENSON is Stevenson Professor of International History at the London School of Economics and Political Science.

BARRY SUPPLE is Professor Emeritus of Economic History at the University of Cambridge.

HANS-PETER ULLMANN is Professor of Modern History at the University of Cologne.

ALEXANDER WATSON is Lecturer in History at Goldsmiths College, University of London.

ARNDT WEINRICH is a researcher at the German Historical Institute in Paris.

JAY WINTER is Charles J. Stille Professor of History at Yale University and Distinguished Visiting Professor at Monash University.

BENJAMIN ZIEMANN is Professor of Modern German History at the University of Sheffield.

Acknowledgements

The completion of this three-volume history of the First World War would not have been possible without the support and assistance of the staff of the Historial de la Grande Guerre, Péronne, Somme, France. This museum, opened in 1992, was the first international museum of the 1914–18 conflict to give equal treatment to both sides and to its global character. The fruit of a generation of work in cultural history, the Historial was designed and its museography developed through its Research Centre, which began its work in 1989. We historians were at the heart of the project throughout its inception and remain so today.

The Historial is funded by the Conseil Général de la Somme. It reflects local pride and a commitment to the preservation of the traces of the Great War embedded in the landscape and cultural life of the Department of the Somme and of the wider world that shared the catastrophe of the Great War. In the Conseil Général, we are indebted to Christian Manable, Président, and Marc Pellan, Directeur de la Culture. At the Historial itself, thanks are due to Pierre Linéatte, Président, Historial de la Grande Guerre; Marie-Pascale Prévost-Bault, Conservateur en chef; Hervé François, Directeur; and the following staff members: Christine Cazé (a very large vote of thanks); Frederick Hadley; Catherine Mouquet; Séverine Lavallard. In addition, Yazid Medmoun was of essential help in providing us with photographs of the Historial's unique collection, visible in the illustrations selected for this three-volume history.

This transnational account of the history of the Great War was assembled through an editorial board composed of the members of the Comité directeur of the Research Centre of the Historial. As editor-in-chief of this project, I simply could not have even begun the task of creating this history without being part of a collective of historians with whom I have worked for more than two decades. Their shared vision is at the heart of these three volumes, and it is to these people and numerous other colleagues in the field of Great War studies working alongside us that the deepest vote of thanks is due. May I add a special note of gratitude for Rebecca Wheatley for her help in preparing the maps we have used?

Our work took the following form. After the table of contents was set, and authors' assignments distributed, each section of the book was placed in the hands of section editors, who were responsible for the development and completion of individual chapters and bibliographical essays for each chapter in their sections. The chapters they approved were sent to the editorial board as a whole, and I, as editor-in-chief, ensured their completeness, and the compatibility of their style and approach with our global and transnational objective. Helen McPhail and Harvey Mendelsohn did yeoman's work and more in translating French and German draft chapters into English, respectively. An essential part of the coordination of this vast project rested on the shoulders of Caroline Fontaine, Director of the International Research Centre of the Historial de la Grande Guerre at Péronne. For any errors that still remain, I take full responsibility.

Introduction to Volume II

JAY WINTER

The First World War was a test of the legitimacy of the states which waged it. They had to provide the weapons and manpower needed to win the war, and at the same time ensure that the war effort did not reduce the population to hunger, misery and despair. With the major exception of Russia, the Allies passed the test of legitimacy, winning the war on the battlefields while maintaining adequate standards of living among the civilians whom the armies were purportedly defending. The Central Powers failed that test, and as a consequence, the major imperial powers in that alliance – Germany, Austria-Hungary and Ottoman Turkey – collapsed.

This volume tells the story of the First World War as a test of state and imperial power, but it also considers ways in which the structure of the state and its relationship to civil society were transformed by the conflict. Carl Schmitt defined the sovereign as he who has the right to declare a state of exception, a time when normal legal, bureaucratic and political rules are suspended.[1] The greatest, most catastrophic, state of exception to date in world history was the First World War, and the radical concentration of power in the hands of an array of executive and military leaders in wartime had lasting effects on the history of all combatant states thereafter.

One implication of Schmitt's view, which he developed in the immediate aftermath of the war, was the collapse of parliamentarianism as a way of waging war, either external or internal. 'The pinnacle of great politics is the moment in which the enemy comes into view in concrete clarity as the enemy', Schmitt wrote in 1927.[2] That 'moment' occurred during the Great

1 Carl Schmitt, *Political Theology. Four Chapters on the Concept of Sovereignty* (1922), trans. by G. Schwab (University of Chicago Press, 2005), pp. 5, 10, 12–13; Andrew Norris, 'Sovereignty, exception, and norm', *Journal of Law and Society*, 24:1 (2007), pp. 31–45.

2 Carl Schmitt, *The Concept of the Political* (Berlin: Duncker Humblot, 1963, 1st edn, 1927), as cited in Richard Wolin, 'Carl Schmitt: the conservative revolutionary habitus and the aesthetics of horror', *Political Theory*, 20:3 (1992), p. 425.

War, and deformed both domestic political conflict and the terms in which the war against external enemies was understood. War was the state of the permanent 'abnormal', that moment when legal, parliamentary, and bureaucratic rules had to be set aside in the effort to ensure the survival of the state. So much for dissent, for divisions of opinion, for the division of powers in states. It is hardly surprising that Schmitt's 'state of exception' continued long after the Armistice in a vast number of countries where violence followed the war in Ireland, Poland, Russia, Turkey, Egypt, India, Korea and China. Blood continued to flow long after the peace treaties were formally concluded.

This volume shows the ways in which the different functions of the state – political, military, economic, diplomatic – were changed by and during the war. In some cases, this transformation was radical and permanent, as in Russia; in others, it was temporary and transient, as in Great Britain. In all countries, though, the state after the war was very different from the state before the war. What economists refer to as the threshold and concentration effects of war reflected the way in which armed conflict brought more and more of the resources of the nation under the direct or indirect control of the state. In 1914, the 'threshold' was passed whereby the percentage of gross domestic product occupied by the state was limited to single figures. In 1918, despite demobilisation, the share of the state in the nation's economy never returned to pre-1914 levels. The 'concentration' of services and functions in the central institutions of the state, providing pensions, social insurance and education in wartime, continued after the Armistice. It was the cost of maintaining these services alongside servicing war debt which ensured that the 'threshold effect' would be irreversible.[3] In effect, the state grew in size, in its multiple functions and in its authority in wartime: this history is at the core of this, the second volume of the *Cambridge History of the First World War.*

These developments were truly transnational, happening everywhere, but their coloration and significance varied in every national case. Issues of military-civilian relations, or of parliamentary review of military policy, of the growth of war economies, were shared by all states at war. Problems of logistics, morale, innovation in tactics and weapons systems, the use and abuse of science in wartime, problems of indiscipline or mutiny: all were ubiquitous during the conflict. Armies went home, but to a degree, the state never fully demobilised.

This volume therefore explores the multi-faceted history of state power under the terms of Schmitt's 'state of exception', and shows the ways in which

3 Alan T. Peacock and Jack Wiseman, *The Growth of Public Expenditure in the United Kingdom* (Princeton University Press, 1961).

different political systems responded to and were deformed by the almost unbearable pressures of war. To understand the crisis of interwar liberalism, the survival of parliamentary regimes in some states and their displacement by dictatorships elsewhere in the 1920s and 1930s, we must fully understand a war which transformed the limits of state power and first enforced and then subverted its monopoly on the legitimate use of physical force.

PART I

★

POLITICAL POWER

Introduction to Part I

JEAN-JACQUES BECKER AND GERD KRUMEICH

Had the war lasted as long as contemporaries thought it would – a few weeks or a few months at most – this section would not have been necessary to write. Instead, an account of military operations, soldiers and commanders would have sufficed. But reflecting on a war which lasted longer than four years requires us to pose the question differently. It took considerable time for many people to understand or to admit the difference between the war they had anticipated and the war they were forced to endure.

General Joffre, Commander-in-Chief of the French army, believed that everything depended on him and on the army; he held this view virtually until he was relieved of his command on 26 December 1916. The two men who ran the German war effort from 29 August 1916 until the autumn of 1918, Hindenburg and Ludendorff, shared this view, at least until Ludendorff asserted that civil authorities had to take the responsibility for arranging an Armistice when he saw that the war was lost.

The lever which enabled civil authorities, in Britain and with greater difficulty in France, to seize the reins of power was the combination of the economic effort and in particular an industrial effort unimaginable before the conflict, to equip and re-equip the armies without impoverishing the civilian population. This view constituted a recognition of the significance of home-front mobilisation, without which the military effort would have ground to a halt.

Consequently, in some places, the war enabled civilians to reaffirm their authority over the military. This was true certainly of Clemenceau in France, but also of Orlando in Italy and, to a debatable extent, of Lloyd George in Britain. In a mixed parliamentary and imperial regime as in Germany, in contrast, the military dominated civilian authorities. In all combatant countries, there was friction and at times open conflict between the civilian and the military leadership. But there was conflict on this matter within the civilian leadership itself. The overt hostility between Poincaré and Clemenceau in France, between the head of state and the head of government, is a case in point. Strife was constant between parliaments and governments too, for instance in the case of the German Reichstag, issuing its own peace terms in July 1917, a peace without conquests or indemnities, much to the chagrin of some civilian and military leaders alike. There were other patterns of conflict in countries less well able to meet the challenges of war, for instance in Russia and Austria-Hungary, where the ruling authorities lost legitimacy and power in 1917 and 1918 respectively.

The pressure of war transformed diplomacy too. Ambassadors were entrusted with the important task of bringing new allies into the war, maintaining the links between allies and preventing them going over to the other side.

We use the terms 'the First World War' and 'the first total war' not only because they describe a conflict which straddled the globe, taking in vast colonial empires, but also because the war mobilised societies and the social and political structures which ran them. Perhaps it would be more accurate to say that the war was almost global, since the key theatre of operations was in Europe, and almost total, since apart from the Armenian genocide, the difficulties posed by the German occupation of Belgium and France, by the Austrian occupation of Serbia and the German occupation of parts of the Russian Empire, most civilians worldwide were outside the primary theatres of military operations. But in any case, the history of political power in wartime, told in this section, is a vital part of the history of the war.

I

Heads of state and government

JEAN-JACQUES BECKER

One of the central questions of the history of the First World War is whether autocracies or democracies were better at waging war. Political philosopher Carl Schmitt saw the merits of a sovereign who solely had the right to declare and manage what he termed the state of exception. The parallel between such a conception of politics and the vertical structure of the military chain of command would suggest that in wartime, autocrats hold the trump card. They have the information and the authority needed to decide the fate of nations on their own. They can act with speed and remain unencumbered by civilian committees or delegates or representatives. And yet, the opposite case can be made. Yes, democracy is slow, but when finally geared into action, it can move decisively and stay the course whatever the price. The mobilisation required in the First World War was so vast that it required the consent of the governed to be realised effectively. In this chapter I survey the way in which very different political structures responded to the challenge of war.

The First World War was essentially a European event, but how was the world governed, politically, in 1914? Apart from Switzerland, Europe's only republics were France, which developed gradually after the fall of Napoleon III in 1870, and Portugal, from 1910. All other European states were headed by a monarch.

In North America, the most powerful country, the United States, had been a republic since the American Revolution and was governed under the Constitution of 1787, while Canada was still linked to Great Britain as a self-governing dominion. Most Latin American states were republics, including the largest, Brazil, which had become a republic in 1891 after a long period of monarchy; but constitutional principles were seldom respected in these nations. Political life was marked by violent eruptions, 'pronunciamentos', which generally overthrew one dictatorship in order to install another. The great states of the south – Argentina, Brazil and Chile – were republics. Their

Helen McPhail translated this chapter from French into English.

political institutions were more European in character, and the role of the military was weaker. Social conflicts resembled those in Europe; Argentina's Socialist Party was indeed a member of the Second International.

Gradually, sympathy for the Allies won over the countries which were not directly concerned by the European war, despite moderately strong British and Italian influence in Argentina and German influence in Chile and Bolivia; but when the United States entered the war, its influence brought in a large part of Latin America – Cuba, Panama, Bolivia from April 1917, and Brazil, Peru, Uruguay and Ecuador later in the year. Others were content to break off diplomatic relations, but the role of South and Central America remained marginal during the Great War. There were, though, important effects on this region in the long term (see Volume I Chapter 20). The indirect economic effects of the war, in encouraging import substitution and in weakening the British economic hold on Latin America, were more significant, although the political repercussions of these changes were muted in the short term.

Most of Africa was wholly or almost wholly under European imperial control, as well as the greater part of Asia, except to some extent the Far East. Japan, a monarchy, had opened up and modernised since the Meiji era at the end of the 1860s as it moved from feudal conditions to modern statehood, but it was constitutional in appearance only. Even though the powers of the Emperor Mutsuhito (1867–1912) and then of his son Yoshihito had been much weakened, the Parliament (the Diet), with a small number of electors, played a very limited role despite the efforts of liberal or progressive parties to win a greater share. Power belonged to the five members of the Genro, a sort of Council of Elders, who held their places for life. Two clans, heirs of feudal ancestry, the Choshu and the Satsuma, controlled the land army and navy respectively. The latter designated prime ministers. From 1914 to 1916, this was Marquis Shigenobu Okuma (1838–1922), a Samurai and much earlier a leader of the progressive party. For some forty years he had occupied numerous ministerial posts, including Foreign Affairs on several occasions.

China became a republic in 1911–12 after overturning the Manchu dynasty, but its main feature was a considerable state of anarchy. Supported by the bourgeoisie of Shanghai, the revolutionary Sun Yat Sen at the head of the Kuo Mintang became President of the Republic in October 1911 in Nanking, but stood down at the end of a few weeks in favour of Yuan Shikai, the leader of the imperial army. In his turn, the new leader was elected President in October 1913 and sought to establish his dictatorship over China, with little success. With the exception of Japan, the Far East's opening into the modern world was still too recent for it to be able to confront Europe either politically or militarily.

Talk of a 'world war' made sense mainly because of the existence of the European colonial empires. The global character of military conflict was limited, except with respect to Japan and to the United States at a late stage, both with great consequences.

Heads of state and governments at the outbreak of war

When the war broke out, five European states were at the centre of events: Russia, Germany, Austria-Hungary, France and, after a slight delay, the United Kingdom. The emperors of Germany, Austria-Hungary and Russia in theory still held substantial power, but in reality their effective roles depended to a large extent on their personalities – weak in the case of Nicholas II of Russia, diminished by age for Franz-Joseph in Austria-Hungary, and very active and highly interventionist in the case of Wilhelm II in Germany.

In 1914, Wilhelm was 55 years of age and in the prime of life. He came to imperial power unexpectedly in 1888 when his elder brother, Frederick II, died of cancer after a few months' reign. He plunged into great activity and was soon in conflict with Chancellor Bismarck, whom he forced to resign in 1890. His subsequent actions ensured that successive chancellors were weaker personalities. His great enthusiasm was for stormy declarations, spectacular voyages and military display, and the birth defect in his left arm may have led him to exaggerate this character trait. In 1900, as the German contingent set off to take part in the international expedition against the Boxer Revolt in China, he wrote a note for himself: 'Act so that for a thousand years a Chinaman will not dare look a German in the face.' As one of the important German diplomats of this time, Fritz von Holstein, was to say: 'He had a taste for theatre, not for politics . . .' Intelligent, the Kaiser loved talking. In reality, he was thoroughly unstable and also quite cautious, despite his deliberately bellicose speeches. As a grandson of Queen Victoria, he had confidence in the stabilising effects of family links between the European sovereigns. He was close to Archduke Franz-Ferdinand, whose assassination initially led him to support the violent reaction of the Austro-Hungarian Government. Following Serbia's conciliatory response, however, Wilhelm considered the affair settled. He was in the habit of annotating diplomatic documents, and on this occasion he wrote: 'brilliant success obtained in less than 48 hours! It was more than one could hope. A great moral victory for Vienna'.

The Russian Emperor, Tsar Nicholas II, came to power in 1894 at the age of 26, on the premature death of his father Alexander III. He was thus 40 years old in 1914, the youngest of the three emperors. Limited in intelligence, he had received very little intellectual education and was completely unprepared to lead his Empire. In Pierre Renouvin's words, he was:

> a weak man, who seeks to hide his hesitations behind an appearance of authority; the stubbornness of which he gave frequent proof was merely one aspect of this weakness. In all, a man of narrow ideas and irritable temper, a leader without clear-sightedness and without energy.[1]

He held one strong conviction; he was an autocrat, and he was totally unaware of how Russia was changing. Leading a very retired life in his palace of Tsarskoye-Selo and loving only family life, he knew neither the people he was supposed to rule nor even the aristocracy. He was under the influence of his wife, Alexandra of Hesse, a superstitious and mystical German princess who attracted adventurers and charlatans. The most famous of these was Rasputin, who from 1905 onwards exercised great influence over the imperial couple, particularly because Alexis, their son and heir to the throne, born in 1904, suffered from the then-incurable disease of haemophilia.

Wilhelm II and Nicholas II, who were both very reluctant to see the European crisis turn into a general war, famously exchanged telegrams at the end of July 1914, signed Nicky and Willy. Nicolas's ministers and generals had the greatest difficulty in convincing him to accept war, and for a long time he resisted the arguments of his Minister for Foreign Affairs, Sazonov: 'Think of the responsibility that you are advising me to take! Think of the thousands and thousands of men who will be sent to their death.' It was only on 30 July that he agreed to give the order for general mobilisation.

Of the three emperors, the most senior and the oldest was the Austro-Hungarian Emperor Franz-Joseph. Nephew of the Emperor Ferdinand I, who was forced to abdicate in 1848, in 1914 Franz-Joseph was 84 years old and recovering from illness at the moment of the July crisis. After his accession to the throne at the age of 18, his interminable reign had been marked only by a succession of family and political misfortunes: his brother Maximilian executed by firing squad in Mexico; his sister-in-law Charlotte mad with grief; his only son Rudolph's suicide at Mayerling; his wife Elizabeth assassinated by an Italian anarchist in Geneva. On the political level, the Austrian Empire had been chased out of Germany and Italy and had been forced to accept the

1 Pierre Renouvin, *La crise européenne et la première guerre mondiale* (Paris: Presses Universitaires de France, 1962), vol. XIX, p. 102.

dualism which gave birth to Austria-Hungary. It is not certain that these personal misfortunes affected this somewhat insensitive monarch, but political problems had made him cautious and hostile to any foreign venture.

Further, at the time of his great-nephew's assassination, he was in his summer residence 200 kilometres from Vienna, which reduced his influence on events. He was, however, more cautious than his Minister for Foreign Affairs since 1912, Count Leopold von Berchtold, one of the richest aristocrats in the Empire (and famous for his dilettante attitudes). Both he and Franz Conrad von Hötzendorf, in command of Franz-Joseph's army, whose military abilities were very mediocre, favoured immediate action against Serbia – indeed, as Conrad had wanted long before Sarajevo. Franz-Joseph did not believe it was possible to leave the murder of his heir unpunished, even if he had disliked him, but since the military defeats of the first part of his reign – about half a century earlier – he was averse to any military venture of any kind. He considered above all that, even if action was decided on, it could not be undertaken without the agreement of Germany, which at the end of the Balkan wars, the preceding year, had been against Austrian intervention.

Yet none of these three emperors, despite their way of talking and their beliefs, like Nicholas II, was an autocrat. All the empires had constitutional regimes: in Russia since the laws of 1906; in Germany under the Reich Constitution of 1871; in Austria-Hungary following the establishment of dualism in 1867. All of these states had assemblies elected according to various forms of franchise – the Duma in Russia, the Reichstag and the Bundesrat in Germany, and different assemblies in Austria-Hungary – but apart from Hungary to some extent, they were still not parliamentary assemblies. The executive was not held responsible to the assemblies, and heads of government were nominated by the sovereign and subject to his recall. In practice, day-to-day governing was difficult without the agreement of the assemblies, even if only for budgetary matters, but questions of war or peace were not part of their role. Neither the Austrian Parliament, in recess at this time, nor the Hungarian Parliament played any part at all in the war crisis.

The Austrian Government was directed by Count Karl von Stürgkh from 1911 to 1915, when he was assassinated by Friedrich Adler, son of the socialist leader Victor Adler. Stürgkh was a somewhat listless bureaucrat, always preferring to await the results of enquiries. The Hungarian Prime Minister from 1911 to 1917 was Count Istvan Tisza, who had already held the post from 1902 to 1905; he was to be killed by revolutionary soldiers in 1918. Tisza was a strong personality, firmly against military intervention, particularly since he considered that there were more than enough Slavs in the Empire.

In Germany, the Chancellor since 1909 – as he would be until 1917 – was Theobald von Bethmann Hollweg. At the same time as being Chancellor of the Empire, he was the Prussian Prime Minister and Minister of Foreign Affairs. Coming from a family of bankers, jurists and university academics, his friendship with the Emperor with whom he had been a student had facilitated a rapid career in Prussian and imperial administrative circles. As François Roth put it: 'Just as his predecessor [von Bülow] was brilliant, but adequate and lightweight, Bethmann Hollweg was serious, applied, somewhat bureaucratic and professorial.'[2]

Conservative, calm, hardworking and efficient, he was not much concerned with external ventures. During the crisis, in the absence of the Secretary of State Gottlieb von Jagow, he was assisted by the Under-Secretary of State for Foreign Affairs, Arthur Zimmermann, whose attitudes were similar to his own. Zimmermann was later to be Secretary of State and directed Foreign Affairs from November 1916 until August 1917.

On 5 July 1914, the German leaders received a hand-written letter from the Emperor Franz-Joseph, but in fact prepared by Berchtold, and delivered by Count Alexandre Hoyos, the chief aide to the Austro-Hungarian Minister for Foreign Affairs. Contrary to their attitude a year before, Kaiser Wilhelm II and his ministers agreed to allow Austro-Hungarian intervention against Serbia, convinced that the conflict was bound to remain localised, in view of its circumstances, and that in particular Russia would not get involved.

Russia had been governed in recent years by two energetic political personalities, Serge de Witte – dismissed by Nicholas II in 1906 because he had forced him to accept certain institutional reforms – and Pyotr Stolypin, Prime Minister from 1906 until his assassination in 1911. Both men were opposed to external ventures. Stolypin was succeeded by Vladimir Kokotsov, a Prime Minister of quality, even though inferior to Stolypin; but he was replaced in January 1914 by Ivan Goremykin, who was to remain until 1916. A weak character, highly conservative, Goremykin would play only a very minor role. Sergei Sazonov, Minister of Foreign Affairs (and Stolypin's brother-in-law), then became Chief Minister. With a good appreciation of international affairs, he had been ambassador in Rome and London, and directed foreign affairs since 1910, but he was nervous and changeable.

The reactions of the Russian Government after the Sarajevo attack had been cautious and reserved, but they changed when, on 23 July, Austria-Hungary

2 François Roth, 'Bethmann-Hollweg', in François Lagrange (ed.), *Inventaire de la Grande Guerre* (Paris: Universalis, 2005).

addressed its ultimatum to Serbia. The reaction in urban Russian opinion was very strong, and it seemed to the government that it must act, in the hope that this reaction was aimed only at Austria-Hungary, leaving Germany out of the matter; hence the idea that partial mobilisation was preferable to general mobilisation. But for the leaders of the Russian army, partial mobilisation was technically impossible and, in truth, militarily useless because in their view it was impossible to avoid a general war.

Among the four front-rank continental powers, France was alone in having a parliamentary regime. Its main political personality at the time was Raymond Poincaré. A native of Lorraine, born in Bar-le-Duc in 1860, he was 11 years old when the city was occupied by Prussian troops in the war of 1870–1; this was an experience that marked him for life. Barrister, republican, secular, patriot, elected Deputy for La Meuse in 1887, when he was 27 years old, he was a rising star of the 'new' Republic, in Philippe Nivet's words.[3] Minister for the first time in 1893, at the age of 33, Senator for La Meuse in 1903 at an unusually early age, he was called to form a government in January 1912 following the Agadir Incident in the previous year. This eminent specialist in financial matters took on the Ministry of Foreign Affairs, since he judged the international situation to be dangerous. Poincaré expected to strengthen ties with Russia, which had kept its distance from French policy at the time of Agadir, but he was concerned by what was stirring in the Balkans under Russian protection. France was not informed of Russian views on this matter. He decided to visit Russia (by sea in order to avoid having to cross Germany) and left Dunkirk on 5 August 1912. As soon as he arrived in St Petersburg, he demanded to see the documents on the formation of the Balkan League and its objectives.

Contrary to previous information, Poincaré understood that this alliance was not defensive, but offensive. 'It is a treaty which leads to war', he observed. The Russian Minister for Foreign Affairs, Sazonov, wanted to reassure him, asserting that the Balkan states would not move into action without authorisation from Russia. In reality, even the Russian Government was short-circuited by its representatives on the spot, Anatol Nékloudoff in Bulgaria and Nicolas Hartwig in Serbia. He could do no more than slightly delay Balkan actions as they launched what became known as the 'First Balkan War' in October 1912. Much irritated, Poincaré still did not wish to oppose the action, which would have risked breaking the Franco-Russian alliance. This was extremely risky behaviour: Russia now knew that for Poincaré the

3 'Poincaré', by Philippe Nivet, in *Inventaire de la Grande Guerre*.

Franco-Russian alliance was so fundamental that they had no need to consult France before launching an adventurous operation, which is what was to happen less than two years later.

In 1913, during the Second Balkan War (June to August 1913), Germany prevented Austria from getting involved, which might have unleashed a general war. But one consequence of the Balkan wars was that the head of the German army (Helmuth von Moltke, the younger, nephew of the victor of 1870) obtained from the Chancellor Bethmann Hollweg reinforcements for the army, despite Bethmann Hollweg's financial worries. The French command immediately decided that their troop numbers had to be augmented without delay: for this purpose, military service had to be extended from two to three years. Supported by a minority on the left and by the right as a whole, the Three Years' Law was voted through on 19 July 1913.

Raymond Poincaré had been elected President of the Republic on 17 January 1913. Generally classed as 'Centre-Left', he had needed support from the right to gain election. For the past thirty years the Presidents of the Republic had played a minor role, but Poincaré fully expected to take the lead in international politics, in particular to do everything in his power to protect the Three Years' Law in the face of violent protest from the socialist and radical left. The elections in May 1914 had been a success for the left, but a section of the left supported the Three Years' Law, thereby balancing the number of electors who favoured it and those who were against it. In order to ensure that the Three Years' Law would not be challenged, Poincaré tried to impose a government headed by Alexandre Ribot, a man of the Centre-Right who also favoured the law; but the Chamber of Deputies overturned him immediately, simply because a leftist assembly could not support a government of the right! Poincaré resigned himself to calling René Viviani to head the government. He was hardly a specialist in foreign affairs, despite having held this ministry. A lawyer, an eloquent and somewhat hollow character, Viviani was a socialist-republican – a group located between socialists and radicals. He was personally hostile to the Three Years' Law, but his government included a majority of ministers or secretaries of state who had voted in favour of the law. His was therefore a government which expected not to return to the matter, at least not in the immediate future.

Installed in mid-June 1914, a month later Viviani was on his way to Russia, accompanying the President of the Republic. In principle this was a routine voyage – it was customary for the newly elected Presidents of the Republic to visit Russia – but this trip, following so closely on Poincaré's visit as Prime

Minister, took on a different meaning so soon after the Sarajevo attack. The two national leaders stayed in Russia from 21 to 23 July 1914; they did not return to France until 29 July, abandoning some of the intended programme of stop-overs in Scandinavian capitals.

What had happened in Russia, while the Austrian ultimatum to Serbia on 23 July was not yet known, even though it was felt that something was in preparation? Nothing, apparently, except that Raymond Poincaré had spoken about the strength of the Franco-Russian alliance. He restated the firmness of the French, further convincing the Russians that they had no need to consult France before acting in case of necessity.

A fifth country dominated the European scene, the United Kingdom, but it had so many internal problems – the Irish question, labour problems, the suffragette movement – and a kind of free trade pacifism was so strongly developed that continental problems were of little interest. Moreover, the assassinations in Sarajevo had done nothing to dispel feelings of distaste for the Serbs in some quarters.

In practice, King George V had scarcely any power, although during the war he was not without influence on his military leaders. Real power lay with the government. In 1906, a thorough electoral landslide had driven out the Conservatives and put the Liberals in power. In 1914, the Prime Minister was Herbert Asquith, while Foreign Affairs was the preserve of Edward Grey, Minister from 1905 until 1916. Entirely hostile to being drawn into Balkan affairs, he could not, however, accept any change in the balance of power in favour of Germany. The German incursion into Belgium was its manifestation, and the consequence was British entry into the war on 4 August 1914.

In total, in a paradox which has been insufficiently appreciated, a war which concerned the greater part of Europe began in the early part of August 1914 when most of the heads of state and governments were against it. They had been the victims of an escalation process for which many of the military leaders must share responsibility. In Austria-Hungary and Russia too they had taken some part, but, still more significantly, they were also usurping the civil authorities in Germany. For General Moltke, while the Russian mobilisation was getting under way, to wait was to endanger the operation of a variant on the Schlieffen Plan, which required a rapid conclusion with France before turning all forces against Russia. This fear of 'delay' haunted all the military leaders. In France, for example, the Chief of the General Staff, General Joffre, literally snatched the order for general mobilisation from the government on 31 July at 3.30 pm to avoid taking the risk of further uncertainty.

Heads of state and the extension of the war

Expected to last but a few weeks or months, the war was to last for more than four years and to extend to far reaches of the world. The first non-European state to enter the war when it had barely begun was, paradoxically, Japan. A British ally, from 23 August 1914 Japan considered itself as being at war with Germany. Its aim was to seize the German possessions in China, but after the capture of Tsingtao on 7 November, the Japanese war effort halted. To the French Government which, in particular, wanted Japanese troops to be sent west, Baron Kato, Minister for Foreign Affairs, responded on 19 November: 'I am against sending troops to Europe.'

The Ottoman Empire came next. Since 1909 it had in principle been led by the Sultan Mehmet V. In reality, this peacable old man of 70 had no power, like his Grand Vizier Saïd Halim Pasha, who held the post from 1913 to 1917, and was no more than a sort of head of administration. The masters were the 'Young Turks', officers who had put Mehmet on the throne after overthrowing his brother Abduhamid II, the 'red sultan'. His nickname reflected his cruelty, particularly towards the Armenians in 1894 to 1896, but his zeal did not prevent a gradual dissolution of the Empire in the Balkans. A first revolution, which began in the Army of Salonica in 1908, was followed by a troubled period. There had even been an attempt at the restoration of the Sultan's powers, but from 1913, members of the Union and Progress movement, 'The Young Turks' governed absolutely. Originally a modernist and liberal movement, it had gradually become a nationalist movement which intended to achieve homogeneity in the whole of the Ottoman Empire, that is to 'turkify' the whole population. The movement was not united over the outbreak of war in Europe. It is possible to distinguish at least three factions: those who wanted to stay out of the war; those who wanted to be involved on the side of the Entente; and those who were on the German side. The three main leaders in 1914, Enver Pasha, Minister for War, Talat Pasha, Minister for the Interior, and Dejemal Pasha, Minister for the Navy (Enver and Dejemal were former officers in the Army of Salonica), finally came down in favour of the Germans, probably on the grounds of traditional hostility to Russia. They concluded a secret treaty with Germany on 30 July, then forced the hand of their colleagues by unleashing war on 29 October by using the two German ships of Admiral Souchon, which had taken shelter in the Straits, the *Goeben* and the *Breslau*, to attack Russian ships in the Black Sea. War between the Ottoman Empire and Russia was officially declared on 2 November 1914.

The war then took over the whole of the Balkans, where all the states had territorial ambitions at the expense of their neighbours or of Austria-Hungary.

Serbia, where the war had first begun, was the only one of the Balkan states to have a national royal dynasty. Two families had disputed power during the nineteenth century: the Karadjordjević and the Obrenovic. The last Obrenovic king, Alexander, who followed a policy of submission towards Austria, had been assassinated by Serb nationalists with his wife in 1903. Peter I (Karadjordjević), who then became king, was a former cadet at the French military academy at Saint-Cyr and had fought as a French officer during the war of 1870 – but he was old (70 years of age in 1914) and ill, and did not play a significant part. Indeed, in July 1914, he had given up most of his power to his son Alexander, who in turn left his Prime Minister, Nicola Pasic, to rule. Pasic, the chief Serbian (later Yugoslav) personality of this period, was not to give up power until shortly before his death in 1926. Energetically nationalist and anti-Austrian, he had directed national politics towards the Russian alliance and showed very strong opposition to Austria, not least over the annexation of Bosnia-Herzegovina in 1908. He was prudent, and despite hearing rumours of the assassination plot in advance, he had not succeeded in preventing the Sarajevo attack.

Romania, Bulgaria and Greece all had dynasties of German origin. King Carol I of Romania was from the Hohenzollern family; King Ferdinand I of Bulgaria from the Saxe-Coburg-Gotha family – he became Tsar of the Bulgarians in 1908 – and King Constantine I of Greece from the Holstein family. In addition, the King of Greece had married a sister of Kaiser Wilhelm II. They all, therefore, and particularly the King of Greece, had Germanophile sympathies. All of these states had constitutional regimes, but the monarch's powers remained considerable.

Bulgaria had the closest interest in taking revenge for the Balkan wars, but lacked the financial means and was traditionally close to Russia. King Ferdinand was convinced by a large financial donation from Austria-Hungary and Germany, and declared war on Serbia on 14 October 1915.

The King of Romania, Carol I, favoured the Central Powers, but he died in October 1914, and his successor, his nephew Ferdinand, tended to favour the Allies; yet until 1915 he hesitated to become involved. Seen from France, this delay gave the impression that the Romanian Government was above all following a 'carpet-bagger' policy, seeking the alliance of greatest benefit. This, according to Catherine Durandin, was a false impression:[4] it was merely the reflection of the deep divisions in political circles and public opinion. Those in favour of the Entente were numerous in Bucharest, in both the

4 Catherine Durandin, *Histoire de la nation roumaine* (Paris: Editions Complex, 1994), pp. 66 ff.

Liberal Party and Democratic-Conservative Party. They made themselves heard in Parliament, in the government, the university, the press, while against them, there were also conservatives, Germanophiles and representatives of a 'peasant' left, heirs to a large peasant revolt in 1907. In addition, among the peasant mass of the nation, for the great majority, the chief wish was for peace. The head of government, Ionel Bratianu, son of Ion Bratianu who had led Romania to independence in 1878, had undertaken his advanced studies in Paris (the École Polytechnique) and was generally in favour of entering the war on the side of the Allies. He judged the moment favourable at the time of the Russian victories in 1916, and Romania declared war on Austria-Hungary on 27 August 1916.

Greece was equally divided, between a Germanophile court and a Prime Minister, Eleftherios Venizelos, who favoured the Entente – and who dreamed of reconstituting the Byzantine Empire. The result was a very chaotic policy. Venizelos encouraged the landing of Allied troops at Salonica in October 1915, then forced King Constantine to abdicate in 1917 in favour of his son Alexander, and took Greece into the war on 29 June 1917.

Two more European states were still to join the Allied cause in the war. First was Italy. It belonged to the Triple Alliance (with Germany and Austria-Hungary) at the moment of the outbreak of war, but the great majority of its political parties and public opinion favoured neutrality. This was also the opinion of the most important politician in Italy, the Liberal Giovanni Giolitti. In May 1914, another Liberal, Antonio Salandra, became Prime Minister. He was to remain in this post until May 1916 and was personally in favour of joining the war – on the Allied side, with the aim of taking back from Austria-Hungary the 'irredentist' (unrecovered) territories, consisting principally of the Trentino, Trieste and Fiume. His Minister for Foreign Affairs, Sidney Sonnino, signed the Treaty of London (26 April 1915) with the French and the British, which promised Italy these acquisitions in return for its participation in the war. In May, great nationalist demonstrations were fomented with the complicity of King Victor Emmanuel (the interventionists' 'radiant king') and Salandra took Italy into the war on 24 May 1915.

Finally, Portugal. Suffering substantial political instablilty, Portugal had become a republic in 1910, following the overthrowing of King Manuel. Despite the caution of Portugal's close ally, Britain, the most advanced democratic section of the Republicans wanted to take part in a war which would legitimise the republic. After an attempted coup d'état in 1915 by General Pimenta de Castro – who favoured Germany – the 'strong man' of the advanced republicans, Bernadino Machado, became President of the Republic in August

1915. Facing the hostile attitude of Portugal, it was indeed Germany which took the initiative itself and declared war on it on 9 March 1916.

The United States enters the war

Profiting from divisions within the Republican Party, it was a Democrat, Woodrow Wilson, who was elected President of the United States in 1912. When the war broke out in Europe, no one, either European or American, imagined that the United States might take part in it, particularly since the war was expected to last a few months at most. From 4 August 1914, Wilson had proclaimed the complete neutrality of the United States, and in 1916 he was triumphantly re-elected: he had managed to 'keep America at peace in a world at war'. From the beginning of the European war, he had imagined the creation of international organisations which would ensure the maintenance of world peace, but there were circumstances which would push the United States on to the side of the Allies. Because of the British blockade, only the Entente powers could trade with the United States, and loans from American banks had facilitated substantial purchases. In order to be repaid, the American banks had an interest in an Entente victory, an attitude which was strengthened by German actions. For Germany, it was essential to try to interrupt trade between the United States and the Entente states. To this end, on 31 January 1917, it proclaimed unrestricted submarine warfare, against neutral as well as enemy shipping, and therefore American shipping if the occasion arose. After further hesitation, following publication of the 'Zimmermann Telegram' which sought to push Mexico into a war against the United States, the sinking of three American ships by torpedo and also the fall of tsarism in Russia, Wilson engaged the United States in the war for the freedom of the seas and the survival of democracy in the world. On 6 April 1917, Congress voted to enter the war.

Political development among nations at war

Each nation at war faced several problems – the ability to maintain national unity, political stability and cordial and effective relations between the civil and military powers. The automatic reflex of the military powers everywhere was to consider that the only role of the civil powers was to supply them with the means that they needed; everything else was their responsibility.

In France, where political instability was more or less the rule, it did not disappear. In a little over four years of war, France had six governments.

Yet only one of these governments was voted out of office, that of Painlevé in 1917; the other six resigned. Following the elections in May 1914, France had been surprised by the war. The government in power was on the left, and its symbol was the Prime Minister, René Viviani. Initially, Raymond Poincaré, who considered himself entirely capable of leading the nation, did not think it necessary to change the composition of the government, but his own proclamation of the political truce, the *union sacrée*, made it necessary for a country such as France – this did not seem to be the case in other nations – to have a government which reflected this commitment. Here is the explanation for the establishment of a second government, still presided over by René Viviani, on 26 August 1914. In the circumstances, Poincaré could have called for a new Prime Minister. Among the first rank of politicians, there was one who stood out and would not have refused – Georges Clemenceau – but Poincaré did not want this, because he would have been immediately rejected, and because Clemenceau had refused to accept a post, even as important as that of Justice. Although there was no change of Prime Minister, the government itself was considerably modified. Even then, in a secular France, it did not seem possible to call on representatives of the Catholic Right, but it did seem conceivable to call on the left. The socialists agreed to join the government, in the form of Jules Guesde as Minister without Portfolio and Marcel Sembat as Minister for Public Works. Another socialist, Albert Thomas, was named as Under-Secretary of State for Artillery and Military Equipment. Although Jules Guesde and Marcel Sembat seemed somewhat background figures, the role of Albert Thomas grew steadily. A certain number of front-line personalities were also summoned: at Justice (Aristide Briand), Foreign Affairs (Théophile Delcassé) and War (Alexandre Millerand). Finance was handed to a man of the Republican Right, Alexandre Ribot.

The problem still remained, whatever its composition, to work out the role of governments in a nation at war. For the head of the army, General Joffre, the response was one of the greatest simplicity. Everything must depend on the High Command, the role of the government was at best simply to supply the army with what it needed. The President of the Republic soon complained that he was not even kept informed about the military situation. Indeed, at the beginning of September 1914, he and his government were even forced to leave Paris under the threat of the German advance, and settle in Bordeaux. When they wished to return to Paris, once the danger had passed, the High Command was very firm in its opposition. It was not until 10 December, three months after victory in the Battle of the Marne, that they managed to return. The Assemblies also returned, first for an extraordinary session at the end of 1914, and then sat as normal from 1915. The commissions of the two chambers of government had the right to scrutinise military and civilian policy, and in particular the army commissions expected to play their part. This was particularly true of the senatorial commission of the army, under the chairmanship of Clemenceau from November 1915.

The return of the government and the Assemblies to Paris was not reflected in governmental stability. Alexandre Millerand, Minister for War since 26 August 1914, saw his role as being spokesman and filter for the High Command. To change this situation, the second Viviani government resigned on 28 October 1915 after fourteen months in office. The new government under Aristide Briand claimed to follow in the line of his predecessor; in reality, he extended the composition of the government, bringing in a representative of the Catholic Right, Denys Cochin, and his assumptions about the role of government were very different. Briand had already plunged into the management of the war and of diplomacy; he had been an active partisan for the despatch of an Allied contingent to Salonica, against Joffre's advice. Although he chose a general – Gallieni – as his Minister of War, this was a general who understood how to contain the General Headquarters within its customary powers and who had very stormy relations with General Joffre. However, when on 7 March 1915, Gallieni had read in the Council of Ministers a note which appeared to be an indictment of the High Command and the intervention of the General Headquarters in diplomatic, political or economic matters, this matter received little attention from the Prime Minister. Already in poor health, Gallieni resigned nine days later, only a few weeks before his death. He was replaced by General Roques, a friend of Joffre, who allowed the General Headquarters to recover the full powers which it had previously taken upon itself.

This did not prevent many parliamentary figures from being wearied by the ineffectiveness of the action of the High Command, as they showed at the secret committee sessions which Briand had not wanted but was forced to accept. To avoid being forced out of power, he had to reorganise command. General Joffre was replaced by General Nivelle on 13 December 1916. On 12 December, Briand had also been forced to reshuffle his government. The socialists left it, apart from Albert Thomas, who in contrast, was promoted. From being Under-Secretary of State, he was named as Minister for Armaments and War Manufacturing. But this new Briand government was very short-lived; his War Minister, General Lyautey, who had no confidence either in the new Commander-in-Chief nor in the parliamentarians with whom he was in conflict, resigned on 4 March, soon followed by the government as a whole. Briand had thus stayed in power during seventeen months of the war.

The Briand governments were succeeded by a government led by Alexandre Ribot, who was to remain in power for a little over five months, from late in March 1917 until the beginning of September. His political formula was the same: a socialist on one side, Albert Thomas, a representative of the Catholic Right on the other, Denys Cochin. Ribot was forced to resign following a major speech by Clemenceau on 22 July on 'defeatism', accusing Louis Malvy, the immovable Minister for the Interior since the outbreak of the war, of not having fought sufficiently hard against defeatist propaganda.

The new government, under Paul Painlevé, was the first government not to be part of the *union sacrée* – the socialists had refused to support it; he was overturned after barely two months by a coalition of socialists and the right who in their turn reproached him for not having tackled the many current rumours of treason.

There had already been three governments in 1917. President Poincaré could do nothing now but call on Clemenceau, whose government can be considered as the first 'war government'. He stated firmly that his only concern was to make war. The leader was at the same time War Minister – true, Painlevé had already combined the two roles, but above all, with Clemenceau, the question of the pre-eminence of military power, which had indeed already been considerably nibbled away, or of civil power, was no longer applicable. He was the only 'war leader'; and the generals, whether it was Pétain at the head of the French army since Nivelle's removal on 15 May 1917 (following the disastrous Chemin des Dames offensive), or Foch, who had step by step become Commander-in-Chief of the Allied forces after the Doullens conference in March 1918, were merely his subordinates who occasionally muttered in dissent. It was this Clemenceau government which was to lead France to victory, and would then conduct the peace negotiations. This government finally tendered its resignation in January 1920 after 26 months in power. In sum, France was the only country to have had six governments during the four years of war without any challenge to its political system.

When the war broke out, the British Prime Minister, Herbert Asquith, a Liberal, did not feel it necessary to make more than very marginal changes in his Cabinet. He offered a post to the socialist Ramsay MacDonald – who refused since he was against the war. Asquith kept his government virtually unchanged because he anticipated a very short war, although he was very soon forced to accept that, contrary to general expectations, it would not be finished by Christmas. Nonetheless, in August he had appointed Britain's most famous general, Lord Kitchener, the Minister for War. He knew the war would last for years. It was immediately apparent that the British army was entirely inadequate, but for the Liberals, for reasons of principle, there was still no question of introducing conscription to raise an army. It was Kitchener's great merit that he created a powerful movement for voluntary enlistment, symbolised by the poster showing him pointing his finger: 'Your country needs you' or 'I want you to enlist in the British Army'. Almost 2 million British men enlisted during the first year of the war, before the wave of volunteers declined. By January 1916, it was impossible to avoid a gradual move to compulsory military service, although exemptions remained numerous.

Despite the successful creation of a large British army, the government very quickly attracted press criticism on the conduct of the war; Asquith was not a very effective war leader, and in May 1915 the government became one of National Unity with twelve Liberals, eight Conservatives and even a Labour member, Arthur Henderson, the new leader of the Parliamentary Labour Party. Like Ramsay MacDonald, still opposed to the war, other Labour MPs and activists in the smaller socialist parties remained outside this national coalition.

The arguments remained very lively, however, between the Commander-in-Chief Sir John French – who was indeed less than entirely competent – and the Minister for War, Lord Kitchener, who died at sea en route to Russia in June 1916, as well as with the rest of the government. The Kitchener aura had diminished considerably; he did not recognise how the war had to be managed in a democratic regime. In a way, his death could be seen as fortunate: some thought that it was not entirely accidental, although there is no evidence to support this assertion.

Within the government itself, disagreements also accumulated with Asquith, accused of running the war too lethargically (many reproached him for having mismanaged the munitions supplies to the army). This criticism worked to the advantage of the Chancellor of the Exchequer, Lloyd George, who had been Minister of Munitions in 1915 and had replaced Kitchener as Minister for War. In December 1916, Asquith was obliged to resign and gave way to Lloyd George who, although a Liberal, was supported by all the Conservatives and only a section of the Liberal and Labour parties. From that time on, the war was managed by a War Cabinet of only five members led by Lloyd George, sometimes accused of dictatorship, but also sometimes seen as the 'British Clemenceau'. He led the nation to victory, while still on fairly bad terms with the new Commander-in-Chief, Sir Douglas Haig, who had replaced French in December 1915.

Italy was no more ready than the United Kingdom for the war; this related particularly to its army. Antonio Salandra's Liberal government was without authority in the face of the army chief General Luigi Cadorna, who would have preferred to fight alongside the Central Powers, and who considered himself completely independent of the government. He was also the butt of a trend against the war, animated in particular by the great Liberal politician Giolitti. Defeated in June 1916 following an Austrian offensive in the Trentino which threatened to break through into the plain of the River Po, the Salandra government was replaced by an even weaker government led by the ageing Paolo Boselli. His Minister of Justice, the Sicilian and great professor of law Vittorio Orlando, was first accused by the nationalists of weakness towards pacifists, before he turned to firmness in the face of defeatist or subversive propaganda. At the rout after Caporetto, the Boselli government was thrown out (25 October 1917) and Orlando was summoned to replace him. His government included representatives of virtually all the parties, but Orlando still refused to be bound by any one political group. He started by dismissing General Cadorna, seen as responsible for the disaster, and discredited for his bloody and useless offensives and his brutality towards the soldiers whom he had accused of cowardice in the throes of battle. Cadorna was replaced by General Diaz, a strong personality but one general who wished to stay on good terms with the government.

Once the Italian front was established 100 kilometres to the west of the Isonzo, Orlando devoted himself to re-establishing internal order and managed to help forge a national consensus around the order of the day, 'Resist, resist, resist'. He had defeatists energetically pursued, condemned and imprisoned, and the great majority of the Chamber of Deputies, including Giolitti, gathered round him. Orlando was to lead Italy to victory. There was also something of Clemenceau about him. As Pierre Milza has stressed, it is to him that Italy owed the victory of Vittorio-Veneto at the very end of the war, when he commanded General Diaz to go on the offensive against the advice of the High Command and most ministers.[5]

With variations and even some important differences – France being highly distinctive – the three parliamentary nations, France, the United Kingdom and Italy, showed a similar pattern of development. The statesmen, Clemenceau, Lloyd George and Orlando, who led their nations to victory, appeared to represent the same kind of leader, with firmness towards defeatists or pacifists, a gift for creating unity of political or public opinion around them, and a degree of success in asserting civilian power over military power.

5 'Orlando', by Pierre Milza, in *Inventaire de la Grande Guerre.*

Matters were different in Germany, which did not have a parliamentary regime. Initially, all political forces (including the majority of the Social Democratic party members of the Reichstag accepting group discipline) had rallied behind the Kaiser, convinced that the war was defensive, in particular against Russia. This was the 'political truce', the *Burgfrieden*; but from the first days of the war the military conduct of the war had totally eluded Bethmann Hollweg. He was barely kept informed of operations, particularly as the army was convinced of a very rapid victory. In this war, which he had considered an impossibility, Bethmann Hollweg was persuaded by his belief in a quick victory to accept the programme of 9 September 1914, inspired by the army and the pan-germanists who foresaw large annexations in the west and east. The defeat on the Marne soon dispelled his hopes.

On 14 September, Moltke yielded his place at the head of the German army to the Prussian Minister for War, Eric von Falkenhayn. Relations between Bethmann Hollweg and the new Commander-in-Chief had always been difficult; they did not improve. The Chancellor saw Falkenhayn as a political competitor and disapproved of his military vision. Falkenhayn's belief that victory lay in the West led him, after limited successes in the east, to launch the Battle of Verdun. Faced with failure here, Falkenhayn found his position further weakened by Romania's entry into the war on the side of the Allies. Bethmann Hollweg, in agreement with Hindenburg and Ludendorff, who commanded in the East and sought total victory against Russia, persuaded the Kaiser to replace Falkenhayn. On 29 August 1916, Hindenburg took command of the whole of the German army, with Ludendorff, his Quartermaster General, holding effective power. But their relations with Bethmann Hollweg very quickly deteriorated; in their view, victory in the west depended on total victory in the east, while Bethmann Hollweg no longer believed this to be realistic and favoured a search for other solutions and negotations with Russia, an apparent possibility after the February Revolution in 1917. In reality, increasingly isolated and impotent, Bethmann Hollweg's role was simply to gain a majority in the Reichstag to vote on war credits. Kaiser Wilhelm II himself retained barely greater importance. Bethmann Hollweg therefore had to submit to the decision to engage in total submarine warfare (9 January 1917), despite his conviction that this would bring the United States into the war, and sink any chances of a negotiated peace.

Faced with the prolongation of the war, two groups formed in the Reichstag. In July 1917, a majority of the Reichstag, behind the Catholic deputy Matthias Erzberger, Catholics of the *Zentrum*, progressives and socialists, called for peace talks to end the war. They were opposed by Conservatives and Nationalists, representing a 'Patriotic Front' which wanted to resist defeatism. Chancellor Bethmann Hollweg was caught between two sides. Seen as too soft by the generals, he was forced to resign on 13 July 1917, and was replaced by individuals of lesser abilities. Georg Michaelis came first, a simple instrument of Hindenburg and Ludendorff, who survived for only three months. Next was Count Georg von Hertling, who belonged to the right wing of the *Zentrum* and, like the majority of the Reichstag, supported the search for a 'just peace'; but he was old and ill and played virtually no part in formulating war policy. Although it is altogether exaggerated to speak of a Clemenceau dictatorship in France – he was on the contrary the symbol of the pre-eminence of civil power – in Germany, Hindenburg and Ludendorff did indeed install a 'quasi-dictatorship' by further intensifying and accelerating the mobilisation of economic and human resources according to their own war plans.

The military were solely responsible for the terms of the Treaty of Brest-Litovsk, much harsher than those sought by Richard von Kühlmann, the Minister for Foreign Affairs from 6 August 1917 to 9 July 1918. It was the military and the military alone which imposed extremely harsh conditions in preparation for a vast German expansion in the rest of Europe. This required large numbers of troops to be retained in the East – which in turn helped weaken the thrust for victory in the west in the last major German offensives in the spring of 1918.

Primacy of civil power in the parliamentary democracies of the west and primacy of military power in Germany, with Austria-Hungary on the side of the Central Powers, and Russia on the side of the Entente, were ill-matched. It appeared very quickly that military powers alone both achieved and were incapable of making effective use of the powers they held in such a war.

There were signs that some in power recognised this dilemma, and tried to take steps to forestall disaster. In Austria-Hungary, change was signalled by the death in November 1916 of the 86-year-old Emperor Franz-Joseph. He was succeeded by his very young great-nephew, Charles (aged 29). The new Emperor was convinced that the war could not be won and that moreover a dazzling victory for Germany, even if it were possible, would lead to her domination over Austria-Hungary. Defeat must, however, be avoided if possible, since it would precipitate the disintegration of the Empire. Emperor Charles intended to lead a complete reversal of Austro-Hungarian policy, internally and externally. He recalled Parliament and dismissed the Chief of the Army, Conrad von Hötzendorf, accused of being incapable of preventing the Austro-Hungarian army from passing under German authority on 28 February 1917. Reducing the pressure of the army on the nation, Charles in reality wanted if possible to take Austria-Hungary out of the war. As he said, 'the duty of the Austro-Hungarian government was to seek peace' . . . 'if necessary against the wishes of Germany'. Indeed, secret conversations took place between France and Austria-Hungary, but without any chance of success for several reasons: among others, because Austria-Hungary, whose Minister for Foreign Affairs, Count Czernin, undoubtedly wanted peace but had rejected a separate peace (contrary to what has been thought in France), and because the Balkan and Italian allies of the Entente had no wish to give up their ambitions to occupy Austro-Hungarian territories. Further, the 'promise' to return Alsace and Lorraine to France was wholly unrealistic, since they were German possessions and Germany was totally opposed to ceding them. Too inexperienced beside his powerful German ally, Emperor Charles's initiatives came to nought. In fact, Austria-Hungary was adrift.

In Russia, after a fairly short period of political union, power was rapidly split. Very quickly, some governmental functions had been transferred to other bodies, the Pan-Russian Union of Zemstvos or the Pan-Russian Union of Cities. During 1915 and 1916, the political, economic and military situation deteriorated steadily, forcing the Duma to reassemble, although it had no effective power. Government ministers came and went; there were four Prime Ministers and six Ministers of the Interior in 1915 and 1916, all equally incompetent or impotent. Among them was Boris Stürmer, Prime Minister during 1916, a Rasputin man – and under suspicion of being a German agent. On 5 September 1915, the Tsar – entirely without authority – took command of the army, which led him to live in General Headquarters at Mohilev, several hundred kilometres from his capital. This left power more or less in the hands of the Tsarina under the influence of Rasputin. His assassination during the night of 30–31 December 1916 did not improve matters; this killing could have initiated an attempt at recovery, but the reverse occurred. The chaos grew, uninterrupted. Indeed, as Nicholas II commented: 'Just consider whether *I*, personally, must win back the confidence of my people or that *they* must win back mine.'[6] Before such incompetence bordering on stupidity, *coups d'état* were in the works.

End of the war, and revolutions

In these circumstances, it is understandable that the first state to see its regime swept away by the war was the Russian Empire. A first revolution, in

6 Quoted by Renouvin, *La crise*, p. 397.

February/March 1917, had forced Nicholas II to abdicate (16 March in the modern calendar). Provisional governments then followed one another, presided over by a liberal prince, George Lvov, then, from July, by the socialist Alexander Kerensky. They had to share power, however, with the soviets of soldiers, workers and peasants, forming more or less everywhere. They were above all caught in an impossible contradiction: they did not want to leave the war, but it was impossible for them to carry on waging it.

They were in their turn to be swept away by a second revolution led by the Bolsheviks on 7 November 1917 (25 October in the Russian calendar). Lenin, Prime Minister of the People's Commissars, was convinced, unlike the other Bolshevik leaders, that getting out of the war as fast as possible, whatever the conditions, was essential to the survival of the new regime. Negotiations began on 3 December in Brest-Litovsk, which after a Soviet walk-out producing a massive German advance, ended in a peace treaty on 3 March 1918.

In this same year, 1918, having been within a hair's breadth of victory in the spring, the Central Powers crumbled one after the other. First was Bulgaria: following the abdication of King Ferdinand on 3 October, an armistice was signed on 30 October. On the same day, the Ottoman Empire capitulated in the Moudros armistice signed with the British, and its dismemberment began. The principal leaders of the Young Turks, Talaat, Djemal and Enver, fled and initially took refuge in Germany.

Also on the same day, the Austro-Hungarian Empire signed the armistice at Villa Giusti with the Italians – but there was already no more empire: national councils had proclaimed the independence of the Czechs on 18 October, the Serbo-Croats and the Slovenes on 29 October, the Hungarians on 30 October. Without abdicating formally, the Emperor Charles could only abandon power, and an Austrian Republic was proclaimed on 2 November.

There was still Germany – the last to fall. While the Secretary for Foreign Affairs, Richard von Kühlmann, had been forced to resign for having engaged in secret negotiations designed to seek a balanced armistice during the summer of 1918, by the end of September Ludendorff insisted that the Armistice must be sought immediately, to save the army. To persuade the Allies that this was no ruse, he wanted a liberal prince, Max von Baden, who had the support of a parliamentary majority, to be called to the Chancellery. Not without reluctance, Max von Baden accepted on 1 October. It was under the orders of the general staff that he resigned himself to seeking the Armistice without delay.

On 9 November, Kaiser Wilhelm II was forced to abdicate both as King of Prussia and as German Emperor. On the same day, Chancellor Max von Baden yielded his powers to the socialist Friedrich Ebert. Also on the same day, another socialist, Philipp Scheidemann, proclaimed the Republic. The Armistice was signed on 11 November, and the Kaiser sought and received sanctuary in the Netherlands, where he died twenty years later.

Conclusion

In 1913, one of the most important French socialist leaders, Marcel Sembat, had published a pamphlet entitled 'Make a king, or make a peace'. Paradoxically, Minister for Public Works in the war governments of René Viviani and then of Aristide Briand, from August 1914 to December 1916, he had wanted to say then that only a monarchical and authoritarian regime was capable of conducting a war. Disavowing this unfortunate prognostication, when the war ended, in all the nations or almost all where monarchs had retained sufficiently broad powers to 'conduct the war', regimes had tottered or collapsed and their sovereigns forced to flee or abdicate. To cite only the most important, the German Kaiser Wilhelm II, the Tsar of Russia Nicholas II and the Emperor Charles I of Austria-Hungary (Franz-Joseph having died in the meantime) had been swept away in the defeat. Some sovereigns had certainly survived in Europe or elsewhere in the world – the kings of England, Italy and Belgium, the Japanese Mikado – but their shared characteristic was that they no longer held more than symbolic powers and could not wage war (except perhaps the King of the Belgians).

Practically everywhere, sometimes for not very long of course, representative regimes were established and the victory camp was one of democracy. Does this mean that a representative authority was more capable of leading a nation to victory than an autocratic or authoritarian regime and that the victory had been the result of what the victorious nations had claimed they were fighting for, democracy?

It is always possible to imagine that matters could have evolved differently: but we cannot entirely ignore that it was a very finely balanced outcome as to whether the eventually victorious nations would be defeated or the reverse. Initially, more or less everywhere, men had fought for their country, had fought out of patriotism, and in this struggle for the nation at a time when military service had become the rule (although not initially in the United Kingdom), it may be considered that finally the representative regimes were the more capable of calling on the support of all their citizens and to compensate for a certain initial weakness. And yet it was only after nearly three years of war that the United States, in the voice of President Wilson – as he made clear on 2 April 1917 – joined the war for democracy. It would have been more than ironic if Wilson was forced to become a brother in arms of the Tsar, but very opportunely Nicholas II had been forced to abdicate a fortnight earlier.

Even if we avoid belief in the systematic and inescapable nature of historic change, it is still the fact that it was the most representative regimes which won the war and that everywhere in Europe, after the war, democracy was predominant, even when it was not entirely wholly respected, or was even ridiculed or treated as a form of political hypocrisy.

Was the parliamentary form of political power ultimately strengthened by the Great War? Unquestionably, yes: both where it had already existed and where it was able to adapt. Consider for example the 'secret committees' of the French National Assembly and the '*Ausschüsse*' of the Reichstag in Germany, and then consider where no such voices existed to challenge the domination of the military in matters of life and death. So much had been demanded of the peoples during the war, that the peoples of the world were bound to expect governments after the war to express their will and their voice. After all, that is the essence of democracy.

2

Parliaments

DITTMAR DAHLMANN

Introduction

Both older and modern conceptions of parliaments see them as consisting of two chambers, an Upper House and a Lower House, or in the case of Germany a *Reichstag* or Imperial Diet and a *Bundesrat* or Federal Council respectively. In this chapter, however, only the lower houses will be dealt with, which – with the exception of the Russian Duma and the British House of Commons – were elected by universal suffrage, although this comprised – with only few exceptions – exclusively male suffrage. Whenever, therefore, I refer to 'Parliament', what is meant is only the Lower House.

The existing parliamentary institutions had very different historical traditions, which we can only describe very briefly here. The English Parliament goes back to the mid thirteenth century. In the late fourteenth and early fifteenth centuries, the Commons were accorded the sole right of assenting to and raising taxes. The French 'Parlement', too, goes back to the Middle Ages, as do the diets of the Holy Roman Empire. A consultative assembly of the higher nobility, the *Duma of the Boyars*, was also known to the Kievan Rus' and the Muscovite Empire, but this institution disappeared in the course of the seventeenth century at the latest.

On the outbreak of the First World War at the beginning of August 1914, there was a parliament consisting of an upper and lower chamber in all European Great Powers. However, only in the United Kingdom, a constitutional monarchy, and in France, the only republic among the warring powers, did they play a decisive political role, due to historical developments. In the Russian Empire and the Austrian half of the Habsburg monarchy, the parliaments played a largely subordinate role, even if they assumed a certain amount of political leadership at the time of the monarchies' collapse. In the German Empire, it was not until the middle of 1917 that the Reichstag gained greater importance. The final section of this chapter briefly examines the parliaments of the United States and Japan by way of comparison.

Russia

In the Russian Empire, there had only been a parliament since the revolution of 1905 to 1907: the Imperial Diet (*Gosudarstvennyj Soviet*) as Upper House, which was partly composed of appointed members and partly persons chosen by institutions; and the Imperial Duma (*Gosudarstvennaya Duma*) as Lower House. The deputies of the Duma were elected by a complicated indirect census suffrage, which bore a certain similarity to Prussia's three-class franchise. Although about 80 per cent of the country's male population was eligible to vote, the peasant majority had been massively under-represented since 1907.[1] In a putsch-like act, Prime Minister Pyotr A. Stolypin changed the franchise to the advantage of the nobility and the clergy on 3 June 1907, when the Second Duma was dissolved. The Fourth Duma, elected in 1912, consisting of 442 deputies with a majority of right-wing liberal Octobrists and Nationalists, began its legislative life in mid November 1912 for a term of five years. The Duma had the right to initiate laws, and no law could be passed without its agreement, but the conservative Imperial Diet also had to give its assent and the Tsar had to sign the law. Specific areas of the national budget, among them that of the Imperial Household and part of the military budget, were immune from parliamentary scrutiny and were thus not subject to debate in the Duma. As in the German Empire and in Austria, the Prime Minister and the ministers were not answerable to Parliament, being appointed and dismissed by the Tsar. However, the Duma did have the right of interpellation, of which it made frequent use.[2]

After the revolutionary events of 1905 to 1907, there was initially a phase of consolidation, with rapid economic growth in the Russian Empire. However, when it became increasingly apparent that the government of Tsar Nicholas II was scarcely amenable to reform, from 1912 there was an increasing number of strikes and unrest in the country. In foreign policy, too, Russia was forced to accept several setbacks, so that the situation both within the country and abroad was escalating more and more in 1914. The Imperial Duma met jointly with the Upper House, the Imperial Diet, on 8 August 1914[3] for a historic

1 On the franchise and the four legislative periods in total of the Duma, generally known as the First to Fourth Dumas, cf. Dittmar Dahlmann, *Die Provinz wählt. Russlands Konstitutionell-Demokratische Partei und die Dumawahlen 1906–1912* (Cologne: Böhlau Verlag, 1996), pp.106–8, 289–92, 447–50.

2 *Ibid.*, pp. 353–7.

3 All the dates in Russian history are given in the Gregorian calendar customary in Western Europe, not in the Julian calendar then in operation in the Russian Empire, which in the twentieth century was thirteen days behind the Gregorian calendar.

session to announce a political truce, so as to demonstrate outward national unity. At the same time, the two houses approved the required war credits.

In the events leading up to this vote, the Russian Government had considered no longer convening Parliament, but a deputy of the right-wing party of the Nationalists had convinced Prime Minister Ivan L. Goremykin that in this hour of need it was urgently necessary to demonstrate publicly to the other European countries that all of Russia's classes and parties were united in solidarity and at the same time to demonstrate the willingness of the whole country to support the monarchy and the mother country. After the Council of Ministers had given its assent, Tsar Nicholas II used the opportunity to 'be united with my people'.[4] In his address to the deputies of both houses, he said: 'The great wave of patriotism, of love for the country and the loyalty to the throne, which swept through our country like a tornado, serves in my eyes, and I think not only in my eyes, as a guarantee that our Mother Russia will see a victorious end to this war which was sent to us by God.'[5] The President of the Duma, the right-wing Octobrist Mikhail V. Rodzyanko, and Pavel N. Milyukov, leader of the largest opposition party, the Constitutional Democrats,[6] emphasised the unity of the Russian fatherland. The talk was no longer of nationalities and different classes, but only of a family of brothers, which in this moment of peril for the fatherland had to stand together. Milyukov refused to make political demands at a time like this: 'Whatever our attitude to the government's policies may be, it remains our prime duty to keep our country united and undivided and to retain that rank among the world powers which our enemies wish to deny us.' Nevertheless, Milyukov had stated previously that internal peace was only temporary and the parliamentary battle would only be postponed until the danger to the fatherland had passed.

On the eve of the session of the Duma, Alexander F. Kerensky, the leader of the socialist Trudoviks, had proposed in the parliamentary advisory committee that the Duma should only support the government if it assented to domestic reforms during the course of the war. His proposal had found some support among the deputies of the Mensheviks, the Constitutional Democrats and the Progressivists, but Milyukov had made it clear that the Duma should trust the

4 Dittmar Dahlmann, 'Russia at the outbreak of the First World War', in Jean-Jacques Becker and Stéphane Audoin-Rouzeau (eds.), *Les sociétés européennes et la guerre de 1914–1918* (Paris: Université de Nanterre, 1990), p. 55; Raymond Pearson, *The Russian Moderates and the Crisis of Tsarism 1914–1919* (London: Macmillan, 1997), p. 16.

5 See Sergei S. Oldenburg, *Last Tsar. Nicholas II. His Reign and His Russia* (Gulf Breeze, FL: Academic International Press, 1978), vol. 4, p. 10.

6 Known as *Kadety* after their initials in Russian, from which the term used abroad, 'Cadets', was derived.

government and not make such demands in times of war. As an example of such attitude, he mentioned the British Parliament, and years later in his memoirs he gave the *union sacrée* in France as an additional example of which path the Duma ought to have taken.

Yet the session of the Duma on 8 August 1914 already revealed the first cracks in the country's united front, for the socialist parties, the Bolsheviks, Mensheviks and Trudoviks abstained during the vote on war credits. Although they could not agree on a joint statement, their speakers stated unanimously that they regarded the war as the beginning of a process that would liberate the country.

These, however, were for the moment the only voices among the ranks of the Russian deputies who spoke out firmly against the war.

By contrast, the President of the Duma took the view in this session that the Duma should be dissolved for the duration of the war, since it was of no consequence for the country and would only impede the work of the government. In this session, too, the representatives of the many nationalities in the territory of the Russian Empire, which had often been violently oppressed by the Tsarist Government, declared their support for the unity of the country. At first, the government wanted to prorogue the Duma until November 1915, and only reluctantly agreed to its meeting on 1 February 1915.

However, the support which the moderate parties offered to the government at the outbreak of war was not only due to the external threat to the country, but also to the state of the parties, which were being shaken by internal dissension. Furthermore, an attitude of rejection of the Tsarist Government would have implied, in the eyes of the general public, that party politics were more important than patriotic support. In view of this dilemma, the Octobrists split into right- and left-wing groups, while the Constitutional Democrats and the Progressives scarcely had any other option than to support the Imperial Government. The Cadets and Progressives, particularly, were firmly convinced that the Russian Government would have to grant domestic reforms during, or at the latest after, the war. One of the leaders of the entrepreneurial party of the Progressivists, the multi-millionaire Pavel P. Ryabushinsky, had not minced his words when he plainly stated shortly before the outbreak of war that a war 'would shake the entire Russian organism to such an extent' that a return to the old order would be impossible. A Russian victory, in the view of the Progressives, would lead to reforms which would be demanded by society. A defeat, by contrast, would ultimately lead to revolution.[7]

7 James L. West, 'The Rjabušinskij Circle: Russian industrialists in search of a bourgeoisie, 1909–1914', *Jahrbücher für Geschichte Osteuropas*, N. F. 32 (1984), pp. 376 ff.

For this reason, the consenting attitude of the bourgeois parties in the Duma to the war can be regarded more as a ceasefire than as a truce or a *union sacrée*. There was undoubtedly patriotic fervour in bourgeois circles, which, however, was radically different from the position of those close to the Tsar, the aristocratic military circles and the government. Eventually, the moderate socialist parties also bit the bullet, agreeing to limited assent to the war, whereas the Bolsheviks, led by Vladimir I. Lenin, rejected any support for the war. Their deputies were arrested in November 1914 and banished to Siberia.

It was already becoming clear soon after the outbreak of war that the Russian Government would not be able to cope with the problems it faced. As a result, various groups and institutions in society assumed increasing levels of responsibility. As early as late summer 1914, the municipal administrations and autonomous rural associations (*zemstvos*) combined as the *zemgor*,[8] and were soon coordinating supplies for the army.[9] In May 1915, the Moscow industrialists followed suit by setting up the War Industry Committee, in order to build up a consistent and planned organisation of the war industry.[10]

In early February 1915, the Duma met again for several days before being sent home once more. When in April 1915 the progress of the war took a turn for the worse with the collapse of the South-Western Front, the domestic situation visibly worsened. When the Duma reconvened in late July and early August, the deputies of the moderate bourgeois parties demanded the establishment of a 'government of confidence'. When elderly Prime Minister Ivan L. Goremykin rejected this demand, in early September almost all the parties in the Duma and members of the Upper House, the Imperial Diet, combined to form what became known as the Progressive Bloc at the instigation of Pavel Milyukov, the leader of the Cadets, with only the radical left and right declining to join. A total of 236 of the 422 Duma deputies joined the Progressive Bloc, together with 64 members of the Imperial Diet, the Centre, the Academic Group and the Independents.[11] Just as there was a broad spectrum of parties in the united

8 Formed from the first syllable of the word 'zemstvo' and the first syllable of the word 'gorod' ('town, city').

9 Manfred Hildermeier, *Die russische Revolution 1905–1921* (Frankfurt am Main: Suhrkamp, 1989), pp. 128 ff.

10 Heiko Haumann, *Geschichte Russlands* (Zurich: Chronos Verlag, 2003), p. 321.

11 Michael F. Hamm, 'Liberal politics in wartime Russia. An analysis of the Progressive Bloc', *Slavic Review*, 33 (1974), pp. 453–68; Thomas Riha, 'Miliukov and the Progressive Bloc in 1915. A study in last chance politics', *Journal of Modern History*, 32 (1960), pp. 16–24; V. Ju. Černjaev, 'Pervaja mirovaja vojna i perspektivy demokratičeskogo preobrazovanija Rossijskoj Imperii', in N. N. Smirnov *et al.* (eds.), *Rossija i pervaja mirovaja vojna. Materialy meždunarodnogo naučnogo Kollokviuma* (St Petersburg: Dmitrij Bulanin, 1999), pp. 189–201.

opposition, so the programme of the Bloc was to a large extent non-committal. It urged in particular the formation of a government enjoying the confidence of society and strict adherence to legality in the administration, a policy which aimed to ensure the maintenance of domestic peace and the elimination of conflict among the 'nationalities and classes'. The Progressive Bloc programme included demands for the autonomy of Poland, concessions in the Jewish question, the restoration of the Ukrainian press, the restitution of trade unions and the equal status in law for the peasants. Essentially, the demands aimed to pacify the troubled domestic situation in the Russian Empire, which was to be achieved by an amnesty for political prisoners, greater scope for the rule of law and increased tolerance. So as not to alienate the right wing of the Bloc, the Octobrists and moderate Nationalists, a demand for responsible government was not made.[12]

The Progressive Bloc was able to find support outside Parliament in the union of towns and zemstvos (*zemgor*), and was also supported by some ministers of the Imperial Government. However, the leadership of the state ignored the Opposition Bloc in Parliament and once more sent the Duma into a compulsory recess. At the same time, several of the 'liberal' ministers were dismissed. This was a lethal blow to the *union sacrée*, which from the outset had stood on shaky ground. Although the tide seemed to be turning in early 1916, when Nicholas II announced that the Duma would be recalled on 9 February for four months and that he would be present in person at the reopening of Parliament, this changed little. The new Prime Minister, Boris V. Stürmer, proved to be a dyed-in-the-wool conservative and an anaemic favourite of the Tsarina and her spiritualist entourage.[13] The Progressive Bloc did not even succeed in introducing into the Duma those reform projects which had been prepared in parliamentary commissions.[14] Parliament continued to remain without influence on how ministerial posts were filled. In the phase between September 1915 and February 1917, the Tsarist Empire went through four Prime Ministers, five Ministers of the Interior, three War Ministers, three Transport Ministers and four Ministers of Agriculture. Contemporaries spoke of 'ministerial leapfrog'.

The confidence of the people in the ruling elite had been rapidly declining since the second half of 1916. This was also true for the Progressive Bloc, which had little with which to counter the growth of popular anger. The Duma was

12 The programme is set out in: Vestnik Evropy, 1916, No. 9, pp. 367–9; English translation: Frank Golder (ed.), *Documents of Russian History, 1914–1917* (Gloucester, MA: Peter Smith, 1964), pp. 134–6.

13 Hildermeier, *Russische Revolution*, pp. 129 ff.

14 Hamm, 'Progressive Bloc', p. 459.

again convened for 1/14 November. Although Pavel N. Milyukov, the leader of the Opposition Bloc, made the most famous parliamentary speech in the short period of the Duma's existence, he was unable to guide the unruly masses back to a peaceful and loyal path.[15]

Milyukov repeatedly asked the question, which was certainly not meant rhetorically, whether the guiding principle of Tsarist Government policy was 'stupidity or treachery'. Of course, this was a piece of demagoguery, but it revealed the deep-seated mistrust of government by large parts of the Russian people. Nevertheless, the party led by Milyukov, the Constitutional Democrats, like the Progressive Bloc, continued to behave legalistically, and meekly acquiesced in another prorogation of Parliament until 14 February 1917. The reasons for this lay, on the one hand, in concerns about the revolutionary violence of the streets and, on the other hand, in the national conviction that continuing the war was a necessity.

Despite the silence of the Duma, the growth of a revolutionary movement within the country could no longer be halted. In the winter of 1916/17, there were rumours about a conspiracy to topple the autocracy, in which even members of the Imperial family were involved. In mid December 1916, the 'miracle monk', Rasputin, was murdered. In this murder, too, members of the aristocracy and the Tsar's family were involved.[16] When the supply crisis worsened enormously that harsh winter, revolutionary rioting began in Petrograd on 23 February/8 March 1917. The President of the Duma, the Octobrist Mikhail V. Rodzyanko, informed Nicholas II of the catastrophic situation in the capital, urging him to install a new government. Instead, the Tsar dissolved the Duma once more on 26 February/11 March 1917 and sent it into recess until April.[17]

In view of the alarming situation in the capital, where by now units of the military were refusing to obey orders, the Progressive Bloc and deputies of the left-wing parties summoned the members of the Duma on 27 February/12 March 1917 for a private meeting at which, at Pavel Milyukov's initiative, the 'Provisional Committee of the Imperial Duma' (*Vremenny komitet Gosudarstvennoy dumy*) was set up, consisting of 12 (later 13) persons. It declared itself to be the government of the country, from which a short time later the 'Provisional Government' emerged, following the abdication of Nicholas II

15 Thomas Bohn, '"Dummheit oder Verrat?" – Did Milyukov fire the "starting shot" for the February Revolution?', *Jahrbücher für Geschichte Osteuropas*, N. F. 41 (1993), pp. 361–93.

16 Dittmar Dahlmann and Gerhard Hirschfeld, *Vergangenes Russland. Bilder aus dem Zarenreich* (Essen: Klartext Verlag, 1995), pp. 158–60.

17 Hildermeier, *Russische Revolution*, pp. 137 ff.

(in his name and that of his son) on 2/15 March 1917 in favour of his brother Mikhail.

It was on that same 27 February that the Council of Workers and Soldiers (*Soviet*) was also set up in Petrograd, which in contrast to the Provisional Government had real power, since it could rely on the support of the soldiers. In the subsequent months, the Duma only met rarely, and on 6/19 October 1917, it was dissolved by a Provisional Government decree.

In sum, the semi-autocratic system of the Russian Empire – its parliament, the Duma – did not play a decisive role during the First World War. However, the Progressive Bloc, which emerged from the ranks of the Duma, was an important force in the domestic clashes in wartime and in the revolutionary upheaval of 1917.

Austria

After the Austro-Hungarian Compromise (*Ausgleich*) of 1867, the Reichsrat or Imperial Council formed the Lower House of the Parliament of the Cisleithanian (Austrian) half of the Empire, which consisted of two chambers, the *Herrenhaus* or House of Lords and the *Abgeordnetenhaus* or House of Deputies. The convening, proroguing and closure always applied to both houses. They were also obliged to approve any legislation jointly which the Emperor had signed and the ministers responsible had countersigned.[18] The government was not responsible to Parliament, being only answerable to the Emperor, who appointed and dismissed the government without the Imperial Council having any influence on the matter. The initiative on legislation lay normally with the government, but the Imperial Council also had the right to introduce bills. Budgetary and financial bills had to first be presented to the Imperial Council; alternatively, a government bill could be presented to either the Imperial Council or the House of Lords. After a first reading, the bills were then sent to the relevant committees. For a law to be passed – after three readings – the agreement of both houses and the monarch was required. For financial legislation and in military recruitment matters, the

18 This section is based on Berthold Sutter and Ernst Bruckmüller, 'Der Reichsrat, das Parlament der westlichen Reichshälfte Österreich-Ungarns (1861–1918)' in Ernst Bruckmüller (ed.), *Parlamentarismus in Österreich* (Vienna: Österreichischer Bundesverlag, 2001), pp. 60–109; and Lothar Höbelt, 'Parlamente der europäischen Nachbarn II: Die Vertretung der Nationalitäten im Wiener Reichsrat', in Dittmar Dahlmann and Pascal Trees (eds.), *Von Duma zu Duma. Hundert Jahre russischer Parlamentarismus* (Göttingen: Vandenhoeck & Ruprecht, 2009), pp. 339–59.

rule was that where there was dissension between the two houses, the lower figure was taken as approved.

After the Social Democrats staged mass demonstrations in 1905, the principle of universal, direct, equal, free and secret ballot for all men over the age of 24 was introduced in Austria in 1906 in elections to the House of Deputies, which consisted of 516 members. At the elections in 1907 and 1911, the trend to the new mass parties became obvious. In 1907, the Christian Democrats won; in 1911, the Social Democrats won. In the House of Deputies, many parties and groupings were represented, since the political parties were organised separately among the various nationalities. The friction between the nationalities determined both the deliberations of the House of Lords and the House of Deputies, where the debates were dominated not only by questions of principle, but were also the forum for local conflicts which occasionally got out of hand. Consequently, the government was only able to achieve a majority with great difficulty, so that the Imperial Council was often prorogued by the Emperor at the suggestion of the government because of these conflicts.

The rules of procedure of the House of Deputies were a contributory factor in making parliamentary work difficult, and sometimes impossible. The deputies could speak in their native language, and there was no provision for interpreters, with no limits on speaking time. This led to filibustering when members wanted to prevent a vote. An additional factor was unseemly behaviour, such as using instruments to make a noise, and even scuffling between members was not a rarity. One of the most embittered points of contention was the refusal by the Czech deputies to recognise the authority of the Imperial Council for Bohemia and Moravia.

Several months before the outbreak of the First World War, in March 1914, Emperor Franz-Joseph had approved the request by Prime Minister Karl Graf von Stürgkh to prorogue Parliament once more. It was not reconvened until the end of May 1917. This led to a situation where the domestic press could be censored without restrictions, special courts could be set up in political matters in contravention of the Constitution, meetings were banned and the basic rights of the peoples of Austria were restricted. For this reason, it is certainly legitimate to claim that Austria in that phase of the war was ruled along absolutist lines by a war government.

Only when voices in the country had grown louder against the use of martial law, death sentences, prison sentences and the conviction of political leaders, and when the food situation had become worse because Hungary refused to send food to Austria, did the situation change. Before this, in October 1916, the Minister-President, Karl Graf Stürgkh, had been shot dead by the left-wing socialist Friedrich Adler, son of the party leader Viktor Adler. In a radical departure from what had been the customary practice during the war, Friedrich Adler received a public trial, which was given extensive and comprehensive coverage in the press. Adler used this to make a sweeping indictment of the regime. Although he was sentenced to death, Emperor Charles I pardoned him, his sentence being commuted to life imprisonment.

A few weeks after Stürgkh's assassination, the elderly Emperor Franz-Joseph died on 21 November 1916, succeeded by his great-nephew Charles I. Recognising the difficult situation in the Habsburg monarchy, Charles attempted to portray himself as a constitutional monarch, advocating an early reconvening of Parliament. After the appointment of Ottokar Graf Czernin as Foreign Minister and Heinrich Clam-Martinic as Minister-President, Parliament was convened for 30 May 1917. In this session, the deputies representing the different nationalities declared their political intentions after the end of the war. In essence, this anticipated the break-up of the Empire in October and November 1918.

Clam-Martinic was not successful in persuading any of the nationalities represented in Parliament to accept his programme, which amounted to limited national autonomy. Both the German and Slav members rejected it: the former because it did not reflect their historical leadership role; the latter because it was completely non-committal. However, for the radicals the time for reforms was over.

In mid June 1917, Clam-Martinic resigned. He was followed by Ernst von Seidler, an official from the Ministry of Agriculture, who had the reputation of being a narrow-minded German centralist. At the request of Emperor Charles, an amnesty for political prisoners was proclaimed, which, however, completely failed to have the desired effect on the representatives of the Slav nationalities in Parliament. Seidler demonstrated his inability to achieve a compromise between the nationalities in Austria when he attempted to solve the national problems in Bohemia in mid 1918 by dividing up the administration into national areas, a plan which the Czechs decisively rejected.

In its session from June 1917 to November 1918, in addition to making the necessary decisions on the budget and war taxes, in summer 1918 Parliament above all passed legislation on accident insurance and social welfare. Such was the limit of its horizons.

When the end of the Habsburg monarchy was approaching in October 1918, it was the representatives of the nationalities, particularly, who took the initiative. For example, the members of the Imperial Council of the predominantly German areas of what would become Austria met on 21 October as a

'Provisional National Assembly', electing a German-Austrian Government on 30 October, thereby establishing a new state.

On 24 October 1918, the Polish deputies of the Imperial Council declared that any further participation in Parliament was pointless. Four days later, Czech politicians established the Czechoslovak Republic in Prague, with the South Slavs also proclaiming their separation from Austria the following day. The last session of the House of Deputies took place on 12 November 1918, one day after Emperor Charles had resigned and the government of Heinrich Lammasch was relieved of its duties. As no provision was made in the Constitution for Parliament to dissolve itself, the deputies accepted the proposal of the acting President of the Parliament not to fix a date for a new meeting of Parliament. Several hours later, the 'Provisional National Assembly of German-Austria' took the decision to declare the state a republic forming part of the German republic. Three months later, in February 1919, elections were held in Austria for the constituent National Assembly.

Germany

After the establishment of the German Empire in 1871, the deputies of the Imperial Diet or *Reichstag* were elected in equal, secret, universal and direct ballot, using a first-past-the-post voting system. All men above the age of 25 were eligible to vote. The Reichstag initially comprised 382, and from 1874, 397, members. All of the deputies enjoyed immunity and indemnity. The Reichstag jointly made up the legislative arm together with the *Bundesrat* or Federal Council, but the Imperial Chancellor was only partly answerable to the Reichstag. The Imperial Chancellor enjoyed the right of a personal audience, an *Immediatvortrag*, with the emperor and king. Only the emperor could appoint and dismiss the Imperial Chancellor and it was only to him that the latter was answerable. Since there were no independent ministers in the structure of the 'Imperial leadership', the heads of department were permanent secretaries, who were obliged to follow instructions from a higher level and were thus not responsible to Parliament; this was only true to a limited extent of the Imperial Chancellor, since the Reichstag could certainly pass a motion of no confidence in him, although this had no repercussions for him.[19]

19 A standard source on the constitutional history of the German Empire is Ernst Rudolf Huber, *Deutsche Verfassungsgeschichte seit 1789*, vol. III, *Bismarck und das Reich*, 3rd rev. edn, chs. 15–17; vol. IV, *Struktur und Krisen des Kaiserreichs*, 2nd edn, chs. 2 and 4; and vol. V, *Weltkrieg, Revolution und Reichserneuerung 1914–1919*, 2nd rev. edn (Stuttgart: Kohlhammer, 1988).

Constitutionally, it was the Bundesrat, to which the twenty-five constituent states, i.e., the Federal States of the German Empire, sent their representatives, which was the supreme body of the Empire. How many votes each state had was set out in the Imperial Constitution. Prussia had the most votes (seventeen). The President of the Federal Council was the Imperial Chancellor. The representatives of the federal states voted under instructions from their governments. There was a veto, which required fourteen votes, with the result that Prussia on its own could veto decisions. The assent of the Federal Council was required for any legislation and for specific decisions of the emperor, particularly the dissolution of the Imperial Diet and a declaration of war.

However, what is known as the *Dreiklassenwahlrecht* or three-class franchise was in operation in the largest federal state of the German Empire, Prussia, from 1849 up until autumn 1918. This divided voters on the basis of the taxes they paid into three classes, or more accurately divisions. In this ballot, which was neither direct nor secret, about 4 per cent of voters of the first class (division) were electing, around the early twentieth century, just as many electors as the 82 per cent of men eligible to vote in the third class. These electors then voted for the deputies in the Prussian House of Deputies. Electoral reform in Prussia as the most important federal state was one of the salient demands of the progressive parties in Prussia before and during the First World War.

At the last Reichstag elections before the outbreak of the First World War, the Social Democrats (SPD) gained just under 35 per cent of the votes, forming, with its 110 deputies, the largest parliamentary party among the 397 Members of Parliament; the second largest party was the Centre Party with 16.5 per cent of the votes and ninety-one seats. Yet all the attempts to formulate the Imperial Chancellor's accountability more precisely and carefully or to strengthen the position of Parliament in comparison with that of the Emperor and Imperial government remained fragmentary. Even the first acceptance of a motion of no confidence against an Imperial Chancellor – in this case Theobald von Bethmann Hollweg – after a heated debate in connection with the Zabern Affair in 1913 did not lead to his resignation.[20]

When the international crisis increasingly escalated in July 1914, and the SPD and trade unions called for demonstrations against the 'imperialist war', hundreds of thousands responded. However, at these meetings too it was

20 Ernst-Albert Seils, *Weltmachtstreben und Kampf für den Frieden. Der deutsche Reichstag im Ersten Weltkrieg* (Frankfurt am Main: Peter Lang, 2011), p. 73.

emphasised that Social Democracy was prepared to defend the nation against aggression, in other words to fight a defensive war against the Russian Empire. In the SPD newspaper *Vorwärts*, it was stated on 31 July 1914: 'If the hour of destiny arrives, the "unpatriotic riff-raff" will do their duty and will not allow themselves to be outstripped by the "patriots".'[21]

Thus, the SPD too was impressed by the Emperor's speech to his people on 4 August 1914, in which he emphasised that the German Empire was engaged in a defensive war against Russia, adding the famous words: 'I no longer see different parties, all I see is Germans.'[22] And this is also why the Social Democrats voted to approve war credits. Two days earlier, the trade unions had already declared that they would abstain from 'wage demands and strikes' for the duration of the war. In addition, the Reichstag decided not to hold new elections when the legislative period expired in 1917, or to hold by-elections or any more plenary sessions in public. At the same time, the deputies of the Imperial Diet transferred the right to the Federal Council to pass emergency legislation on economic, financial and other matters of the civil administration while a state of war existed. The Reichstag thereby ceded large parts of its responsibility to the Bundesrat, which had far less democratic legitimacy than the former. Initially, the Reichstag only met every six months to approve additional war credits. Part of the political truce was also the state of war and the state of siege which had been proclaimed as early as 31 July.[23]

Only a few weeks after this 'patriotic sense of unity', the first cracks appeared. The political left demanded a democratic reform of the franchise, the recognition of trade unions by the state and above all constitutional reform. Among these were accountability of the Chancellor to Parliament and the parliamentary right to propose legislation. One of the leaders of the SPD, Eduard David, stated that the party 'expected a democratic reform of the franchise as the price for the war effort which the working class was supporting'.[24] Soon afterwards, the domestic debate on war aims, which

21 *Vorwärts* of 31 July 1914, quoted in Susanne Miller, 'Die SPD vor und nach Godesberg', in Susanne Miller and Heinrich Potthoff, *Kleine Geschichte der SPD. Darstellung und Dokumentation 1848–1983*, 5th rev. edn (Bonn: Dietz, 1983), p. 73; cf. also Jean-Jacques Becker and Gerd Krumeich, *Der Große Krieg. Deutschland und Frankreich 1914–1918* (Essen: Klartext Verlag, 2010), pp. 82 ff.

22 Sten. Berichte der Verhandlungen des Reichstages, Berlin 1914/16, vol. 306, 1 ff, quoted in Becker and Krumeich, *Der Große Krieg*, p. 83.

23 Ludger Grevelhörster, *Der Erste Weltkrieg und das Ende des Kaiserreiches. Geschichte und Wirkung* (Münster: Aschendorff Verlag, 2004), p. 40.

24 Becker and Krumeich, *Der Große Krieg*, p. 83. The quotation is from Hans-Ulrich Wehler, *Deutsche Gesellschaftsgeschichte* (Munich: C. H. Beck, 2003), vol. IV, p. 45.

began in autumn 1914 and became increasingly fierce, led to the crumbling of the political truce.[25]

After the 'hunger winter' of 1916/17 and the 1917 February Revolution in Russia, the domestic political situation in the German Empire deteriorated rapidly. In April 1917, 'hunger strikes' broke out among workers in many German cities, which also involved demands being made for an early negotiated peace and political reforms. In winter 1915, a split had already developed within the SPD, when Social Democratic deputies had refused to approve the war credits once more, which led to them being excluded from the parliamentary party. These 'dissenters' now set up, at Easter 1917, the USPD (Unabhängige Sozialdemokratische Partei Deutschlands, i.e., the Independent Social Democratic Party of Germany), thereby splitting the party.

In view of the escalating social and political situation during this period and the splits in the party, the Majority Social Democrats (MSPD) demanded an intensification of reforms in mid March in *Vorwärts*. First, this involved strengthening the political influence of the Reichstag, but secondly the aim was primarily to change the situation in Prussia, where the House of Deputies was still elected according to the three-class franchise and was therefore under the control of the conservative forces. In general, the SPD had assumed since the outbreak of war that this franchise would be abolished in return for supporting the policy of a political truce.[26]

The Imperial Chancellor, Bethmann Hollweg, now also felt, particularly in view of the public debate in the conservative press, that it was urgently necessary to act so as to still the troubled domestic waters, to save the monarchy as a form of government and to be able to continue the war until an acceptable negotiated peace was possible.[27] He succeeded in persuading Emperor Wilhelm II to give an 'Easter message', in which, on 7 April 1917, he publicly declared that after the war the three-class franchise would be replaced by a more modern electoral system. However, the Emperor did not explain what exactly was meant by that, leaving open whether it implied a universal, free, equal and secret ballot. Social Democrats, particularly, were profoundly disappointed by these vague statements. Thus, the Easter message, which was supposed to represent a significant step forward, proved instead to be

25 Seils, *Weltmachtstreben*, pp. 161–75. 26 Grevelhörster, *Der Erste Weltkrieg*, p. 101.

27 Cf. on this the articles or letters to the editor by Max Weber in the *Frankfurter Zeitung*, the 'Europäische Staats- und Wirtschaftszeitung' and 'Die Hilfe', in Wolfgang J. Mommsen and Gangolf Hübinger (eds.), *Max Weber. Zur Politik im Weltkrieg. Schriften und Reden 1914–1918*, vol. xv, *Max Weber-Gesamtausgabe* (Tübingen: Mohr Siebeck, 1984), pp. 204 ff (referred to below as *MWG* 15).

counterproductive, even though previously, on the initiative of the National Liberal Party, a parliamentary committee, generally known as the Constitutional Committee, had been set up, whose remit was to examine and deliberate upon constitutional questions, beginning its work in early May 1917.[28]

These first signs of a change in the political system had been apparent since the end of October 1916. Their source was, on the one hand, the National Liberal Gustav Stresemann, and, on the other hand, the Social Democrats. Stresemann advocated the setting up of parliamentary committees for the most important departments, with the SPD demanding in the main committee, which had emerged from the budgetary committee, that the government's real aims should be made public, thereby pressing for the Reichstag to have more say in foreign policy.[29] The main committee met even when Parliament was not sitting, convening regularly and in secret, but some remarks were repeatedly leaked, which fed the rumour mill even more. Increasingly, foreign policy and the conduct of the war became its main focus. In addition, it had the right to demand information and accountability from the imperial leadership. It soon took on the 'character of an executive committee for the whole Reichstag'.[30]

One of the fiercest critics of delays in implementing electoral, parliamentary and constitutional reforms was Max Weber, who since spring 1917 had been arguing the case for early reforms in a whole series of publications and other contributions to the debate, since he 'saw the question of the Prussian franchise as directly linked to the problem of reforming the Empire's constitution, which should bring about a strengthening of the influence of the parties on the Imperial leadership, which was absolutely imperative'.[31] He was essentially arguing in favour of a parliamentarisation of the Empire on Western, i.e., British, lines. He levelled his criticism in particular at the existing 'unchecked ascendancy of the civil service'.[32]

A further crisis opened in July 1917, when the Centre Party's Matthias Erzberger unleashed in the main committee scathing criticism of the Admiralty and the policy of all-out submarine warfare, demanding a public declaration by

28 Mommsen and Hübinger, Editorischer Bericht zu 'Parlament und Regierung im neugeordneten Deutschland', *MWG* xv, p. 422.

29 Wolfgang J. Mommsen, *Bürgerstolz und Weltmachtstreben. Deutschland unter Wilhelm II. 1890–1918* (Berlin: Propyläen Verlag, 1995), pp. 746–8.

30 Roger Chickering, *Das Deutsche Reich und der Erste Weltkrieg* (Munich: C. H. Beck, 2002), p. 201.

31 Mommsen and Hübinger, *Einleitung zu MWG* xv, p. 11.

32 Wolfgang J. Mommsen, *Der Erste Weltkrieg. Anfang vom Ende des bürgerlichen Zeitalters* (Frankfurt am Main: Fischer Taschenbuch Verlag, 2004), p. 83.

the Reichstag in favour of a compromise peace, action on the question of the electoral system and closer cooperation between the government and Parliament. On the one hand, this resulted in the formation of an inter-party committee to which the Social Democrats, the Centre Party, the Progressive People's Party and the National Liberals belonged, in other words the overwhelming majority of the Reichstag. Its objective was to coordinate parliamentary activities and monitor the work of the government.[33] It was here that, for the first time, there was now a majority in the Reichstag which was prepared to act jointly and independently of the Imperial Government and was capable of doing this. This committee aimed to share power in the Empire and can be viewed as an initial attempt at parliamentary democracy in Germany.[34] It also discussed the matter of passing a peace resolution in the Reichstag.

At the insistence of the Supreme Military Command, Emperor Wilhelm II then dismissed the Chancellor, Bethmann Hollweg, replacing him by Georg Michaelis, a high-ranking Prussian state official. Only a few days later, on 19 July 1917, a peace resolution was passed which talked of a 'peace promoting understanding and reconciliation between the peoples' and rejected 'transfers of territory under duress' with the votes of the Majority Social Democrats, the Centre Party and the Progressive People's Party against the opposition of the Supreme Military Command and the new Imperial Chancellor.[35] However, this did not result in any profound changes in the relationship between the Imperial Government and the Reichstag. The new Chancellor declared that he would treat the resolution 'as I interpret it' and that 'any peace' could be made with it which was desired.[36]

The developments first of all led to the 'German Fatherland Party' (Deutsche Vaterlandspartei) being set up in Germany in September at the instigation and with the support of the Supreme Military Command, primarily Erich Ludendorff, as a movement encompassing a variety of national groups, whose aim was to prepare the public mood patriotically for a victorious peace. As a counterweight to this, the 'Popular Association for Freedom and Fatherland' (*Volksbund für Freiheit und Vaterland*) was founded, which pressed for internal political reforms and moderate war aims.

In the Reichstag, the National Liberals had been supporting the policies of the majority parties since autumn 1917. They joined forces in a parliamentary resolution demanding a democratisation of the Prussian franchise. This

33 Mommsen, *Bürgerstolz*, pp. 752 ff; Seils, *Weltmachtstreben*, pp. 331–7.
34 Grevelhörster, *Der Erste Weltkrieg*, pp. 106 ff.
35 Chickering, *Das Deutsche Reich*, p. 199. 36 *Ibid.*, p. 200.

resulted once again in the Imperial Chancellor being dismissed; Michaelis was replaced by the Bavarian Centre Party politician Georg von Hertling, who was 74 years of age when he took office. The subsequent months to spring 1918 are frequently described as a 'semi-parliamentary system' in the literature. Both in the Imperial Diet and in many regional diets there were bitter debates about the franchise, ministerial responsibility and other aspects of constitutional reform, in the course of which it became evident that the conservative forces were not prepared to give up their positions.[37]

The whole dilemma of German domestic politics and thus also of the Reichstag was revealed in March 1918, when, six months after the Russian October Revolution, the Central Powers imposed a dictated peace on the young Soviet state and the newly emergent Ukraine, which also had severe repercussions on Poland and the Baltic area. This dilemma consisted in the fact that any change in the domestic circumstances, any move towards parliamentarisation and democratisation of the German Empire, was invariably bound up with the progress of the war. A large majority in the Reichstag agreed to this dictated peace, which included the annexation of territory; only the USPD voted against it, with the Majority SPD being split. It could only manage to agree to abstain.

In many German cities in January 1918, there were large-scale strikes and demonstrations due to the poor food and fuel situation, indignation at the absence of reforms and the lack of a desire for peace, and also sympathy with the Russian workers, which made clear that the support for the war among the workers had declined substantially and that the policy of a political 'truce' no longer had much backing.[38] Despite this, after the dictated Peace of Brest-Litovsk, the Supreme Military Command beat the drum for a decisive last battle on the Western Front, which opened in March. Ludendorff declared this offensive to be a failure in late September 1918.

The majority parties in the Reichstag had disagreed about the Peace of Brest-Litovsk. It was only when defeat became evident that the inter-party committee became active again on 12 September, where once more the parliamentarisation of the Empire came up for debate. Yet it was not until the Supreme Military Command urged, on 29 September 1918, the commencement of immediate negotiations aimed at an armistice and peace that the majority parties again acted in unison. Now Wilhelm II also acceded to the demands of the Supreme Military Command and favoured a parliamentary government. On 3 October 1918, Prince Max von Baden, who did not have

37 *Ibid.*, p. 202. 38 Grevelhörster, *Der Erste Weltkrieg*, pp. 118 ff.

much political experience, but was regarded as a liberal reformer, became the new Imperial Chancellor. The prince's first Cabinet was now appointed in line with parliamentary practice, even though the majority parties largely left the selection of the ministerial candidates to the new Chancellor.

As a result of these October reforms, the German Empire was turned into a constitutional parliamentary monarchy. On 28 October, the changes to the Imperial Constitution took effect, in accordance with which the government had to have the confidence of Parliament, which now also had to approve declarations of war and the conclusion of peace.

A few days later, revolutionary unrest broke out which brought the collapse of the Empire. On 9 November 1918, Wilhelm II abdicated, and Max von Baden handed over power to Friedrich Ebert, the chairman of the SPD, stipulating that a national assembly be convened without delay which should decide the future shape of the country. Shortly afterwards, the SPD deputy Philipp Scheidemann proclaimed the Republic, followed by the leader of the Spartacus League, Karl Liebknecht; the Reichstag did not meet again.[39] On 30 November 1918, the Council of People's Deputies issued a decree with regard to the election of a national constitutional assembly, fixing the date of the election for 16 February 1919, which the Imperial Congress of Workers' and Soldiers' Councils brought forward to 19 January.[40]

France

In France, ever since the 1848 Revolution, all men over the age of 21 had had the right to vote for the Chamber of Deputies. During the Third Republic from 1875 onwards, three laws had in essence determined the competences of the Chamber, Senate and the President of the Republic.[41] The legislative bodies were the Chamber and Senate, with the Chamber being constituted on the basis of universal manhood suffrage. Both institutions joined forces in the National Assembly to elect the President, who de jure had wide-ranging powers – the introduction of legislation, dissolution of the Chamber with the consent of the Senate and removal from office only in the event of treason. However, after 1877, when a conflict developed between President MacMahon

39 Mommsen, *Bürgerstolz*, pp. 819–27.

40 Ernst Rudolf Huber (ed.), *Dokumente zur deutschen Verfassungsgeschichte*, vol. III, *Dokumente der Novemberrevolution und der Weimarer Republik* (Stuttgart: Kohlhammer, 1966), p. 32.

41 Cf. in the following: Jean-Jacques Chevallier and Gérard Conac, *Histoire des institutions et des régimes politiques de la France* (Paris: Dalloz, 1991), pp. 236 ff.

and Parliament, the President had to content himself de facto with purely representational functions, even though he formally retained the right to choose ministers and dissolve the Chamber (with the Senate's consent).[42] An additional important factor is that the state adopted a policy of laïcité, or indifference to religion, with an objective of rolling back the influence of the Catholic Church. In the wake of the Dreyfus Affair, from 1894 onwards there was a trend to increasing anti-clericalism, and in 1905 a law was passed on the separation of church and state, which inter alia provided for the removal of all religious symbols from public buildings and abolished religious education in state schools.

In the course of time, the Chamber gained preponderance over the Senate, although they formally enjoyed equal status. Thus, legislation and resolutions were normally first debated in the Chamber before going to the Senate. The ministers were answerable to both Houses. It was a characteristic feature of French parliamentarianism that political parties were not very important until the late nineteenth and early twentieth centuries. The deputies represented their voters and the nation, even though there were parliamentary parties (*groupes politiques*) in the Chamber, where, however, use of the parliamentary whip was unknown. This can also be explained by the existence in France of the simple majority voting system with individual candidates, in which the strong position of local dignitaries and the independence of those elected from the party organisations played an important role. Thus, it was only after 1905 as a consequence of the Dreyfus Affair that parties became more prominent. From 1910, the deputies had to register with the parliamentary parties, with the parties being given the right to a proportionate representation in parliamentary committees and legalised as organs of constitutional life.[43] In 1875, 533 deputies were elected to the Chamber, with this figure rising to 602 by 1914. From 1902, Parliament was dominated by a 'Bloc des gauches', which at times held up to 70 per cent of the seats; however, after 1906, several cracks appeared in this bloc when the electoral system was being debated, but in the May 1914 elections it was successful, continuing to have a majority. The most important parties or groupings in Parliament were the Right, the Centre, the bourgeois left ('radicaux' and 'radicaux-socialistes') and the socialists.[44]

42 Leslie Derfler, *President and Parliament. A Short History of the French Presidency* (Boca Raton, FL: Florida University Press, 1983).

43 Klaus Burkhardt and Gottfried Niedhart, 'Frankreich', in Frank Wende (ed.), *Lexikon zur Geschichte der Parteien in Europa* (Stuttgart: Alfred Kröner Verlag, 1981), p. 174.

44 *Ibid.*

At the same time, the Chamber of Deputies and the Senate exercised important regulatory functions. These included the setting up of commissions of enquiry, written questions and requests. Whereas the Chamber met in public and the minutes of parliamentary proceedings were published, for the meetings of the commissions only their members were admitted, with not even other deputies having access; nor were the minutes published.[45] In principle, there were twenty large commissions or committees with forty-four members, whose work was in theory assigned to a ministry. This was laid down by the Chamber's rules of procedure, whose composition was decided on at the beginning of every legislative period. In addition, there were a large number of temporary commissions. The commissions always met on Wednesdays and received all the projected legislation and bills together with all the relevant material, so that they were able to exercise their appropriate function of monitoring legislation. Furthermore, they could summon ministers to a hearing and question them accordingly.[46]

Intense internal divisions dominated political and social life in France before the outbreak of the First World War. The socialist and pacifist left, especially the revolutionary 'Confédération générale du travail' (CGT), decisively rejected an 'imperialist' war and even in late July was threatening to mount a general strike. On 31 July 1914, the most prominent socialist leader, Jean Jaurès, was then shot dead in a Paris café by a nationalist assassin. There was also alienation between the French Catholics and the anti-clerical bourgeois and socialist parties. Despite this, after the German declaration of war on France on 3 August 1914, it was quite plain that there were no serious reservations either on the part of the socialists or the Catholics against forging a *union sacrée*. Quite the contrary: the result was an astonishing unanimity, 'the concentration of all the forces for the defence of the Fatherland'.[47]

One day after the declaration of war by the German Empire on France, the French President Raymond Poincaré's message was read out in the Chamber of Deputies and the Senate, in which he spoke of France being defended heroically by all its sons, 'whose sacred unity in face of the foe is unshakeable, they are all fraternally united in indignation at the aggressor and in their patriotic faith'.[48]

In France, there was an almost universal and deeply felt conviction that only German aggression had led to this war and that France was its victim.

45 In the Senate, commissions were not introduced until 1920.

46 Jean-Marie Mayeur and Madeleine Rebérioux, *The Third Republic. From its Origins to the Great War* (Cambridge University Press, 1984), ch. 8.

47 Becker and Krumeich, *Der Grosse Krieg*, p. 79. 48 *Ibid.*

However, more recent research emphasises that *union sacrée* is not to be understood as 'total unity' among the French, but rather as being of a pragmatic nature; it had not been able conclusively to overcome the 'profound gulf between the clerical side and their opponents'. There was a truce between the political parties 'for as long as was needed for national defence'.[49] However, the *union sacrée*, just as the *Burgfriede* ('political truce') in Germany and Russia, was certainly vulnerable, since each side understood quite different things by the term.

Unlike in Russia, the German Empire and the Austrian part of the Habsburg monarchy, in the French Republic the Chamber of Deputies was not prorogued for an indefinite period or sent into an enforced recess. It was vitally necessary for the functioning of the political and social system.[50] Parliament had initially suspended its activities indefinitely, when the government moved to Bordeaux on 4 August. And the government side saw no need to have recourse to Parliament in the foreseeable future, since it regarded its duty as virtually being to follow the military unconditionally, since the Germans were only 40 kilometres from Paris.

However, once the fronts had stabilised, Parliament came into its own again. On 22 August, it was already being recalled to Paris for an extraordinary meeting. In January 1915, this was followed by regular meetings, at which it was decided to meet 'permanently' from then on. Nevertheless, there was a danger that information from Parliament might also reach the enemy, and for this reason it was resolved to hold Parliament only in the form of '*comités secrets*', with the public excluded and without the minutes being published. In June 1916, the first of these '*comités secrets*' met to discuss the Battle of Verdun and the manner in which the army command had allowed itself to be surprised by the attack. A total of eight *comités secrets* of the Chamber of Deputies and four *comités secrets* of the Senate were formed. Normal parliamentary life therefore essentially took place in these committees and commissions.[51]

In the French parliamentary system of the Third Republic, commissions and temporary committees were part of 'normal' procedure. Their main functions were to take part in the legislative process and in political review of the government.[52] Since approximately the 1880s, what had been intended to be

49 *Ibid.*, pp. 80–2.

50 Fabienne Bock, *Un parlementarisme de guerre, 1914–1919* (Paris: Editions Belin, 2002).

51 Cf. Jean-Jacques Becker, 'France' in G. Hirschfeld *et al.* (eds.), *Brill's Encyclopedia of the First World War* (Leiden and Boston: Brill, 2012), pp. 22–3.

52 Inge Saatmann, *Parlament, Rüstung und Armee in Frankreich 1914/18* (Düsseldorf: Droste Verlag, 1978), p. 9.

'special commissions' had been developing into standing commissions, which were known as '*grandes commissions*'. There was therefore a distinction between the permanent '*grandes commissions*' – such as the Army Commission – and the commissions set up for special problems.[53] There were commissions in both the Senate and the Chamber of Deputies. After the composition of the commissions had long been fixed according to a permanent lottery system, so as to strengthen the freedom of the individual deputy and prevent the formation of self-contained groups, from early 1915 a different system was put into operation which had already been agreed on in November 1913, in which the allocation of seats in the commissions was dependent on the strength of the parties.[54]

During the First World War there were, in the Chamber of Deputies, nineteen permanent or standing commissions (*grandes commissions permanentes*) and eleven special commissions, which in normal cases had between forty-three and forty-six members. Only the Army Commission as the most important commission was expanded in April 1916 by sixteen new members to about sixty. The three most important and longest serving commissions were the Army Commission, the Commission for Selected Affairs and the Finance Commission.

In the Third Republic, the Army Commission was involved in all legislation affecting the army.[55] During the First World War, it formed a large number of sub-commissions, which among others were responsible for staff, weapons, the air force, equipment, transport and the medical service.[56] The '*contrôle aux armées*' became the most important component of the commission's work. This constant and efficient monitoring of the executive by a legislative body meant that the parliamentary system was ultimately successful in the face of tendencies in the War Ministry and general staff to assume an autonomous life of their own. The Chamber's large commissions, but also those of the Senate, had constant contact with each other because their members were on two or more commissions, which facilitated the flow of information.[57]

What is important to note is that there was a substantial increase in the power wielded by commissions, probably not only of the Army Commission, although the commission evidently experienced this to a particular extent. It managed to smuggle its reports into the ministries, especially into the ministerial bureaucracy. Apparently, during the course of the war, the ministries, too,

53 Bock, *Un parlementarisme*, p. 124. 54 *Ibid.*, pp. 11 ff.

55 Saatmann, *Parlament*, p. 82.

56 *Ibid.*, p. 86. The other commissions also formed several sub-commissions, some of which only consisted of a few people or sometimes only had five members present at their meetings.

57 *Ibid.*, p. 112.

preferred direct cooperation with the commissions to that with the whole Parliament. In this way, the power of Parliament as a whole was specifically weakened, and also the principle of the separation of powers undermined. But the Parliamentary Commissions put the legislature in a central position on the decisive questions of how to win the war. Thus, we can concur with Jean-Jacques Becker's assessment: 'Even though in the first few weeks of the war democracy was, so to speak, wrongfooted by events, France's parliamentary system was strengthened rather than weakened during the course of the war.'[58]

United Kingdom

The United Kingdom is a constitutional monarchy. Technically speaking, the king or queen rules via parliament and appoints the ministers, bishops, judges and leading military staff, although this is only after these have been proposed by the Prime Minister, who is elected by the largest party in Parliament. Similarly, the king or queen gives the speech at the opening of Parliament (the king's or queen's speech) – although this is held in the House of Lords, since the head of state is not allowed to enter the House of Commons. This speech is written by the Prime Minister. The Crown as the head of state has representative, ceremonial and integrative functions.

The British Parliament consists of two Houses: the House of Commons as Lower House and the House of Lords as Upper House. The House of Lords comprised the lords temporal, the peers, who were members for life, and the lords spiritual, two archbishops and twenty-four bishops of the Anglican Church, for as long as they held office. Up until the beginning of the nineteenth century, about 2 per cent of the population was eligible to vote for the House of Commons. In the course of the nineteenth century and in the early twentieth century after the Great Reform Bill of 1832, there were further changes to the franchise, until the 1884 Act, which extended the franchise to around 60 per cent of all adult males. One year later, the constituency boundaries were changed, with the result that there was now only one MP in any given constituency, elected on the first-past-the-post majority voting system.[59] At this point, the

58 Becker, 'France', in *Brill's Encyclopedia*, p. 23.

59 On structural changes to Parliament in the second half of the nineteenth century, cf. Herbert Döring, 'Britischer Parlamentarismus um 1900 zwischen Bewunderung und Krisenbewußtsein', in Dahlmann and Trees, *Von Duma zu Duma*, pp. 12–15; Hans Setzer, *Wahlsystem und Parteienentwicklung in England. Wege zur Demokratisierung der Institutionen 1832–1948* (Frankfurt am Main: Suhrkamp, 1973); the standard work on British parliamentarianism in the nineteenth century is the very comprehensive and detailed book by Josef Redlich, *Recht und Technik des englischen Parlamentarismus. Die Geschäftsordnung des*

House of Commons consisted of 670 MPs.[60] In 1911, the Liberal government under Prime Minister Herbert Henry Asquith curtailed the rights of the House of Lords, which henceforth could only delay legislation for a maximum of three parliamentary sessions. This act also introduced payment of MPs and reduced the length of parliamentary sessions from seven to five years. The House of Commons which was elected in 1910 remained for eight years, as no elections were held during the war. Universal male suffrage was not introduced until 1918, with universal female suffrage following ten years later, after an initial period, beginning in 1918, when only women who were 30 years of age or older had the right to vote.[61]

In the House of Commons elected in December 1910, Conservatives and Liberals had 272 seats each, the Irish Nationalists 84 and the Labour Party 42 seats. At by-elections up until the outbreak of war, the Liberals lost eleven and Labour five seats, which were all won by the Conservatives.[62] The ruling Liberal Party remained in office due to the support of the two minority parties.

In the years leading up to the First World War, Britain was shaken by several internal crises. First, it was hit by a massive wave of strikes which lasted until the summer of 1914, the aims of which were to achieve recognition and to press for higher wages. Social reform was at the top of the agenda of the Liberals and the Labour Party, and they managed to secure passage of the path-breaking National Insurance Act in 1911. The second big crisis concerned votes for women. The suffragettes used mass demonstrations and acts of violence to attempt to impose their demands for equal voting rights. A third focus of disaffection was the campaign for Home Rule in Ireland, as a solution to the intractable division between Irish nationalists and those in the north of Ireland who wanted to remain within the United Kingdom.[63]

At the outbreak of war in 1914, Asquith's Liberal government remained in power. When war broke out, the trade unions declared their willingness to

House of Commons in ihrer geschichtlichen Entwicklung und gegenwärtigen Gestalt (Leipzig: Duncker & Humblot, 1905); cf. also Harold R. G. Greaves, *Die britische Verfassung* (Frankfurt am Main: Metzner, 1951), pp. 12–33.

60 465 MPs representing England, 103 from Ireland, 72 from Scotland and 30 from Wales. Ireland, which only became independent after the end of the First World War, was clearly over-represented. An MP in England represented 67,000, in Ireland approx. 44,000 voters.

61 Peter Wende, 'Großbritannien', in Wende, *Lexikon zur Geschichte der Parteien*, pp. 236 ff; Hans-Christoph Schröder, *Englische Geschichte*, 2nd edn (Munich: C. H. Beck, 1997), pp. 18 ff, 55–9, 64–6.

62 Karsten Schröder, *Parlament und Außenpolitik in England 1911–1914* (Göttingen: Musterschmidt, 1974), pp. 16 ff.

63 John Turner, *British Politics and the Great War. Coalition and Conflict 1915–1918* (New Haven, CT and London: Yale University Press, 1992), pp. 16 ff.

renounce the use of strikes, which, however, was not universally adhered to. There was no or hardly any parliamentary or extra-parliamentary opposition to the war.[64] In March 1915, the trade union movement accepted what was termed 'the Treasury agreement', granting recognition to unions in return for the suspension for the duration of the war of the right to strike and restrictive practices at work. In January 1916, conscription was introduced, initially for unmarried men, followed in May 1916 by the 'Military Service Act', which ushered in general conscription for all males.

In May 1915, a national coalition led by Asquith was formed with the support of the Conservatives and the Labour Party. It was followed in December 1916 by a new coalition government under the Liberal David Lloyd George, again with the support of the Conservatives and the Labour Party led by Arthur Henderson. A. J. P. Taylor called this 'more than a change in government: a revolution British-style'.[65] Lloyd George, who had been Chancellor of the Exchequer since 1908, was the only one of the 'radical pacifist' wing of the Liberals who had remained in the Cabinet after the declaration of war. He became Minister of Munitions in May 1915, a newly created ministry, and in June 1916 Secretary of State for War. In December 1916, Lloyd George forced out Prime Minister Asquith, thereby splitting the Liberal Party. Asquith's demise took place not only with the support of the Conservatives, the Labour Party and sections of the press, but also with the help of backbenchers in Parliament.[66] Lloyd George formed an inner Cabinet consisting of six, later only five, ministers, his 'War Cabinet', which also included Arthur Henderson as the leading Labour politician, and Andrew Bonar Law as the leader of the Conservatives in the House of Commons.[67]

It was characteristic of the British Government's policy during the war that important decisions were made in a small circle, where intrigues and personal animosities played a not insignificant part. Again and again, usually in times of crisis, new ministries were also set up: in 1915, the Munitions Ministry after a crisis in the supply of munitions, later the Ministries of Shipping, Labour, Food, National Service and Food Production. Aside from Munitions, they

64 Catriona Pennell, *A Kingdom United. Popular Responses to the Outbreak of the First World War in Britain and Ireland* (Oxford University Press, 2012), p. 45.

65 Alan J. P. Taylor, *English History 1914–1945* (Oxford University Press, 1965), p. 73.

66 *Ibid.*

67 Kurt Kluxen, *Geschichte Englands: Von den Anfängen bis zur Gegenwart*, 4th edn (Stuttgart: Kröner, 1991), p. 732; a standard text on British domestic politics during the Great War is Turner, *British Politics and the Great War* (see fn. 63).

were not led by politicians, usually being run by businessmen without political ambitions, but with the relevant expertise.

By contrast, the House of Commons was only marginally involved in these decisions, which occasionally led to expressions of extreme irritation, but these were usually fought out in secondary theatres of confrontation. During the war, the Commons continued to hold their meetings without interruption. The number of times legislation was voted on was noticeably less because the government introduced considerably fewer bills. From autumn 1914, the 'Private Members' Days' were scrapped, yet the number of questions directed at the government increased substantially.[68] From 1915, there were exhaustive debates repeatedly in the Commons on electoral reform, Home Rule, customs tariffs, agricultural problems and colonial issues or, as in November 1916 in the 'Nigeria Debate', on whether confiscated German palm-oil factories in West Africa should be sold to the highest non-German bidder, as the Colonial Office proposed.[69] This led to frequent absences by MPs, who felt ignored by the government.[70] Although commissions were also a feature of the British Lower House, it was mostly individual parties or wings of these parties which set up their own enquiries.

These splits of the parties into wings or factions, whether it was the Liberals, Conservatives or Labour Party, were one of the repercussions for the parties and thus also for the British Parliament. The Great War marked, on the one hand, a massive decline in the Liberals as a political force, and, on the other hand, the rise of the Labour Party and the trade unions. Whether this would have happened anyway is an open question.

On 9 May 1918, one of the few parliamentary interventions in the conduct of the war took place. It is known as 'the Maurice debate', following the dismissal of General Sir Frederick Maurice as Director of Military Operations, and the publication of a letter he wrote to *The Times* claiming that the Prime Minister had lied to Parliament about the disposition of British forces on the Western Front, following Lloyd George's decision to redeploy troops to Palestine. Lloyd George won the vote, but the bitterness of the debate showed that the division of the Liberal Party was irreversible.

In the last year of the war, 1918, the franchise was again reformed, since many soldiers who had fought in the war were still not allowed to vote, likewise the women who had worked in the factories during the war. By the

68 David Butler and Anne Sloman, *British Political Facts 1900–1979*, 5th edn (London: Macmillan, 1980), p. 169.

69 Turner, *British Politics and the Great War*, pp. 115 ff.

70 *Ibid*., pp. 227 and 239.

'Representation of the People Act', all male citizens of 21 years of age and over and women aged 30 and over were given the right to vote, which resulted in the number of those eligible to vote trebling compared to the previous elections in December 1910. Plural votes were also abolished, double constituencies were dissolved and constituency boundaries redrawn so that they contained approximately 70,000 voters. Moreover, elections now took place on a single day and everywhere at the same time.[71]

After the Armistice was announced in the House of Commons on 11 November 1918, the government proclaimed the dissolution of Parliament, fixing the date of the election as 14 December. In these elections, the parties of the Coalition Government under Lloyd George won an overwhelming majority. However, the turnout of 60 per cent was considerably lower than at previous elections, in which over 80 per cent of the registered voters had taken part.[72] This was mainly due to the low turnout among women and soldiers, most of the latter being still at the front. These elections to the House of Commons, which the Liberals entered as a divided party, were certainly the shape of things to come for the country's future. Neither at this nor at subsequent elections did the Liberal Party gain a majority to form a government; furthermore, the Labour Party succeeded in getting almost 2.4 million votes, compared with the less than 400,000 votes in December 1910.[73]

United States

The American Constitution created a presidential system of government with Congress, a parliament consisting of two chambers, the Senate and the House of Representatives, with terms of six and two years respectively. Until 1860, the suffrage was restricted to white males over the age of 21. At that time, it was dependent on property or taxation level, with the exact details being left to the individual states. Each individual state sent approximately as many representatives as corresponded to its proportion of the total population. In principle, black American males were also given the franchise in 1870, but in practice this was repeatedly obstructed by legislative manipulation in many states until 1965. The first state to introduce female suffrage was Wyoming in 1869, and by 1900 ten more states had followed suit. It was introduced throughout the country in August 1920. In 1914, the House of Representatives consisted of 435

71 Kluxen, *Geschichte Englands*, pp. 739 ff; Taylor, *English History*, pp. 125–30.
72 Butler and Sloman, *British Political Facts*, p. 206. 73 *Ibid.*

members; in the 1916 elections, the first woman, Jeannette Rankin from Montana, took her seat for the Republicans.

Each federal state sends two senators to the Senate, irrespective of its size and population, which up to 1913 were chosen by the state legislatures and since 1913 have been directly elected by the people.[74] In contrast to the House of Representatives, the Senate has the right to be involved in the appointment of high-ranking officials (simple majority) and likewise when concluding foreign treaties (where a two-thirds majority is required).

At the outbreak of the First World War, President Woodrow Wilson declared US neutrality. He asked the nation to behave impartially.[75] In the first two years of the war, the US banking sector supported Britain and France, with grants, loans and credits, particularly in order to export weapons, munitions and food to the countries of the Entente. In these years, there was a heated debate between the opponents and advocates of US entry into the war.[76] In the Senate and House of Representatives, between 1913 and 1917, the Democrats had a large majority. In the House of Representatives, after the 1916 elections, there was a stalemate, with 215 Democrats, 217 Republicans and 2 Progressives; in the Senate, however, the Democrats dominated by 54 to 42 seats.

In the election year of 1916, a majority of Americans continued to support neutrality and hope for peace. President Wilson stated that he wanted to keep the country out of the war, but that despite this, the nation should prepare for all eventualities. Even before the presidential election, Congress had passed several laws which enabled the United States to expand its modest military forces, engaged in an extended and futile police action in Mexico.[77]

After his narrow election victory in November 1916, Wilson argued in favour of a 'peace without victory', urging the countries at war to state their terms. When the German Empire resumed all-out submarine warfare in 1917, the President broke off diplomatic relations. Even so, the United States did not enter the war until after a telegram sent by the German Permanent Secretary in the Foreign Ministry, Arthur Zimmermann, had been made public. In it he had urged the German ambassador in Mexico to approach the Mexican President with a view to offering several southwestern American states to

74 Hartmut Wasser and Werner Kremp, 'Politische Institutionen einst und jetzt', in Horst Wasser (ed.), *USA. Wirtschaft – Gesellschaft – Politik* (Opladen: Verlag Leske und Budrich, 1996), pp. 102 ff.

75 Jürgen Heideking and Christof Mauch, *Geschichte der USA*, 4th edn (Tübingen and Basel: Francke Verlag UTB, 2006), p. 219.

76 *Ibid.*, pp. 219–21. 77 *Ibid.*, p. 221.

Mexico should she join a German-Mexican alliance. British intelligence had provided Wilson with the text of the telegram, which Zimmermann acknowledged to be valid.

One group of senators in particular opposed America's entry to the war. However, when German U-boats sank several US ships, killing hundreds of American citizens, their opposition melted away. On 2 April 1917, Wilson requested Congress to declare war on the German Empire. The declaration of war followed four days later, with fifty members of the House of Representatives, among them the first woman member, and six senators voting against in the Senate.[78] What was initially controversial was the bill presented by Wilson's government on the introduction of general conscription, which, however, was then passed by both houses in May.[79]

Since the declaration of war, Congress had supported the reinforcement of the war effort by passing the 1917 Espionage Act, which banned any attempts to obstruct recruitment and rearmament and made censorship of the press and the US mail possible. This formed part of the 'Crusade for Democracy' which Woodrow Wilson had declared. In 1918, the Sedition Act was passed, which enabled anyone to be prosecuted who disparaged the government, the uniform or the national symbols.[80] These laws substantially contributed to the hysterical and xenophobic climate which spread throughout the United States both during and even more virulently after the war.

On 8 January 1918, Wilson also put before Congress his Fourteen Points, with which he intended to end the war. After the Armistice had been signed, in December 1918 he travelled to Europe as the first US President while still in office, taking part in the Versailles Peace Conference. In November 1918, his Democratic Party had lost the elections for the House of Representatives and the Senate, because foreign affairs were again being eclipsed by the country's domestic problems, particularly by rising levels of inflation.[81]

The role of the Senate after the war was decisive in breaking Wilson's dream of creating a new international system surrounding the League of Nations. Twice he failed to secure the support of two-thirds of the Senate

78 David M. Kennedy, *Over Here. The First World War and American Society* (Oxford University Press, 1980), pp. 15–24.

79 Robert H. Ferrell, *Woodrow Wilson and World War I 1917–1921* (New York: Harper & Row, 1985), pp. 16 ff.

80 Heideking and Mauch, *Geschichte der USA*, pp. 224 ff; on the enemy within, cf. Jörg Nagler, 'Pandora's box. Propaganda and war hysteria in the United States during World War I', in Roger Chickering and Stig Förster (eds.), *Great War, Total War: Combat and Mobilization on the Western Front, 1914–1918* (Cambridge University Press, 2000), pp. 485–500.

81 *Ibid.*, pp. 226 ff.

for the Peace Treaty of 1919, thereby destroying his presidency and his dream of constructing a mechanism for avoiding future wars. Among all the combatant powers, it was only in the United States that the parliamentary struggle decided matters of war and peace in a way which altered the international political landscape.

Japan

As part of the Meiji Restoration, beginning in the late 1860s, in which Japan transformed itself into a great imperial power and a constitutional monarchy, there was much discussion of the introduction of a modern system of separation of powers and the establishment of a 'national Parliament'.[82] In 1879, regional parliaments were then set up in all the prefectures in which all men over the age of 20 were eligible to vote and who paid a minimum specified amount of property tax. These institutions organised the payment of regional taxes to support budgets.[83]

After lengthy debates and studies, eventually in 1889 a constitution was adopted which also provided for the establishment of a parliament. According to the provisions of the Constitution, this Imperial Diet consisted, on the British model, of an Upper and a Lower House. The Upper House largely consisted of the aristocracy of the Meiji oligarchy, which controlled the state. For the elections of the 300 deputies of the Lower House, which took place for the first time in 1890, all men over the age of 25 were eligible to vote who paid taxes of at least 15 yen. This corresponded to a proportion of just under 1.2 per cent of the total population. The election was won by the liberal opposition, which had joined forces in Parliament to form one party.[84]

The Diet could initiate legislation and voted, after a debate, on the bills proposed by the government, particularly on the budget and the introduction of new taxes. In addition, it gave 'its assent' to the emperor's official duties. However, the approved legislation was only deemed valid after being signed by the emperor (the Tenno), who in emergencies could issue decrees without Parliament, which, however, de facto were all approved. According to the

82 Reinhard Zöllner, *Geschichte Japans. Von 1800 bis zur Gegenwart* (Paderborn: Ferdinand Schöningh, 2006), pp. 207, 217–19; cf. also Marius B. Jansen, 'The Meiji Restoration', in M. B. Jansen (ed.), *The Cambridge History of Japan*, vol. v, *The 19th Century* (Cambridge University Press, 1989), pp. 308–66.

83 Zöllner, *Geschichte Japans*, p. 235.

84 *Ibid.*, pp. 260–2; see also Stephen Vlastos, 'The Popular Rights Movement', in Jansen, *Cambridge History of Japan*, vol. v, pp. 402–25.

Constitution, in which the conservative German legal expert Lorenz von Stein had also been involved in an advisory capacity, Emperor, government and Parliament were linked through the separation of powers. In principle, the emperor stood above the Constitution, for example with regard to his supreme command of the military, the imperial household and the Privy Council.[85] The ministers were answerable to the Lower House, but were mainly recruited from the ranks of the civil service and military. Although, in March 1911, the Lower House voted in favour of the introduction of universal male suffrage, the Upper House opposed it, which meant that the bill was rejected. However, it is worth noting that between 1905 and 1918 – with one exception – all Cabinets had the support of the majority party or a coalition of parties in the Lower House.[86]

At the outbreak of the First World War, Japan took the side of the Entente, declaring war at the request of the British on 23 August, and by October had conquered the German possessions in East Asia and the Pacific. At the same time, Japan took advantage of the opportunity to impose its own interests on China.[87]

As Japan was scarcely affected by the Great War, in March 1915 a new Lower House was elected, which resulted in the 'Constitutional Association of Friends' (Rikken Dōshikai), a grouping set up in 1913 which was fairly liberal, winning the election.[88]

During the war, Japan benefited from the export of armaments to the Entente states, and was able to continue to expand into Asian markets. Thus, exports trebled between 1915 and 1918, with Japan achieving large trade surpluses. It went from being a debtor to a creditor nation.[89]

At the end of the First World War, the first Cabinet emerged, which consisted of a majority of deputies, whereas previously it was predominantly the military and high-ranking civil servants who had been appointed. It was headed for the first time by a politician from a political party, Prime Minister

85 Zöllner, *Geschichte Japans*, pp. 247 ff.

86 Peter Duus, 'Domestic politics: from instability to stability', in P. Duus (ed.), *The Cambridge History of Japan*, vol. VI, *The 20th Century* (Cambridge University Press, 1988), p. 35. A detailed description of the rise of parties during the First World War is given in Frederick R. Dickinson, *War and National Reinvention. Japan in the Great War, 1914–1919* (Cambridge University Press, 1999).

87 Louis Michael Cullen, *A History of Japan* (Cambridge University Press, 2003), pp. 239–44.

88 *Ibid.*, pp. 224 ff; cf. also Duus, *The Cambridge History of Japan*, vol. VI, pp. 80–4; *Kodansha Encyclopedia of Japan* (Tokyo and New York: Kodansha, 1983), vol. VI, pp. 314 ff.

89 Zöllner, *Geschichte Japans*, p. 333.

Hara Kei.[90] Despite this, the Diet did not have much influence, even though the political parties, basically supported by a prosperous entrepreneurial class, continued to develop. Political power rested with the deeply rooted paternalistic structures, which continued to dominate. Even so, in 1925 the franchise for the Lower House was extended to all adult males.[91]

Conclusions

When comparing the structures and activities of parliaments during the First World War between different countries, the first point to note is that it was not only the parliaments of the 'semi-democratic' or 'semi-parliamentary' states, i.e., the Russian Empire, the German Empire and the Austrian part of the Habsburg monarchy, which played what was more of a minor role in important decision-making processes in the conduct of the war and in domestic and economic policy. This was also true of the British Parliament. Ingeborg Saatmann is no doubt correct to observe that when comparing France and Britain what is striking is that in France there was greater formal stability both in the legislative and the executive arms. In France, there were only a few new ministries and hardly any new permanent commissions. Furthermore, the pattern was more one of an informal shift in competences, resulting from the growth in power of the Army Commission, which just like other large commissions ignored the separation of powers between legislative and executive.[92] The US Congress, too, was certainly involved in decisions about war aims and wartime policy, but did not participate decisively in them; its role in rejecting the Peace Treaty, though, was decisive. The young Japanese Parliament played a negligible role.

Whereas the Austrian Parliament played an insignificant role, only being recalled from its 'enforced recess' at the end of May 1917, the parliaments in the other two 'semi-parliamentary' monarchies tried to expand their power during the war years and to decide problems of the franchise and constitution in their favour or to strengthen their position in these fields particularly. This was most successful in the German Empire, albeit not until the end of the war, when it was too late.

By contrast, after the war the British and French Parliaments succeeded in a relatively short space of time in once more playing a decisive role in the

90 Hans H. Baerwald, *Japan's Parliament: An Introduction* (Cambridge University Press, 1974), pp. 3 ff.

91 *Ibid.* 92 Saatmann, *Parlament*, pp. 461 ff.

political system, with the British Parliament now representing a completely different electorate, which was reflected in an entirely new composition of the House of Commons. In all the victorious countries, with the exception of Italy, parliamentary government was strengthened by the war. The view of many Italians that they had won the war but lost the peace helped to undermine the parliamentary regime and lead to the fascist seizure of power in 1922.

In the defeated countries, including Russia, the post-war parliamentary system remained weak, and proved incapable of mediating the increasingly bitter economic and social conflicts which emerged out of the war. This weakness could be observed in the pre-war period too, where imperial power trumped parliamentary power, but the costs of the war, human, material and political, weakened parliament further still. The disaster of totalitarian rule meant the effective end of parliamentary rule in many parts of Europe, leading Mark Mazower to term it the 'dark continent'. This darkness, partly derived from a war which vastly enhanced the power of the executive, cast a pall over parliaments in many countries between the wars.[93]

93 Mark Mazower, *Dark Continent. Europe's Twentieth Century* (New York: Knopf, 1999).

3
Diplomats

DAVID STEVENSON

The formative histories of the origins of the First World War were written from diplomatic documents. When the Bolsheviks seized power, among their first priorities was to publish the tsarist foreign ministry records. After Germany's 1918 Revolution, the Republican Government commissioned the veteran socialist Karl Kautsky to edit the files on the outbreak of hostilities. As an international furore mounted over the Versailles Treaty's 'war guilt' clause, the Weimar foreign ministry produced a forty-volume compilation of pre-1914 material, to which Britain, France, Russia, Belgium, Austria and Italy published multi-volume counterparts. Unprecedented quantities of confidential documentation became public unprecedentedly quickly, and scholars such as Bernadotte Schmitt, Pierre Renouvin and Luigi Albertini could access a wealth of material. Unsurprisingly, their attention focused on the pre-war crises and alignments and on the diplomacy of July–August 1914.[1]

In contrast, wartime diplomacy remained neglected until Fritz Fischer's *Griff nach der Weltmacht*.[2] His work was not a conventional diplomatic history, as it was written from one country's viewpoint, but it treated peace feelers in conjunction with war aims and it drew on German foreign ministry records. It set the pattern for similar studies of the other belligerents.[3] The opening of the pre-1914 archives also enabled new research into war origins, again now

1 Pierre J. E. Renouvin, *Les Origines immédiates de la guerre (28 juin–4 août 1914)* (Paris: A. Cortes, 1927); Bernadotte E. Schmitt, *The Coming of the War, 1914* (New York and London: Scribner, 1930); Luigi Albertini, *The Origins of the War of 1914*, Engl. edn, 3 vols. (Oxford University Press, 1952–7).

2 Albert Pingaud, *Histoire diplomatique de la France pendant la Grande Guerre*, 3 vols. (Paris: Alsatia, 1938–40); Zbynek A. B. Zeman, *A Diplomatic History of the First World War* (London: Weidenfeld & Nicolson, 1971); Fritz Fischer, *Griff nach der Weltmacht: die Kriegszielpolitik des kaiserlichen Deutschland, 1914/18* (Düsseldorf: Droste Verlag, 1961), Eng. edn, *Germany's Aims in the First World War* (London: Chatto & Windus, 1967).

3 Victor H. Rothwell, *British War Aims and Peace Diplomacy, 1914–1918* (Oxford University Press, 1971); David Stevenson, *French War Aims against Germany 1914–1919* (Oxford University Press, 1982); Horst G. Linke, *Das Zarische Rußland und der Erste Weltkrieg: Diplomatie und Kriegsziele,*

written from national perspectives, and drawing on insights from political science.[4] In contrast to the historiography on war aims, which since the 1980s has tailed off, that on war origins continues to grow, has reverted to the international system as the unit of analysis, and has placed diplomacy in its strategic and economic context.[5] It has also scrutinised the diplomats themselves: both the personalities and their institutional environment.[6] With the approach of the centenary, new work is challenging Fischer by reasserting the responsibilities of the Triple Entente.[7] This chapter will draw on all of these bodies of literature to retrace the role of diplomats in the war's onset and development. The story it presents is one of diminishing influence. It will take the discussion through the three sub-periods of pre-1914, 1914–16 and 1917–18.

Pre-1914

We owe the terms 'diplomacy' and 'diplomat' to the French Revolution.[8] But regular and permanent diplomatic representation began between the states of fifteenth-century Italy.[9] French kings had secretaries for foreign affairs from

1914–1917 (Munich: Wilhelm Fink, 1982); David French, *British Strategy and War Aims, 1914–1916* (London: Allen & Unwin, 1986); Georges-Henri Soutou, *L'Or et le sang: les buts de guerre économiques de la Première Guerre mondiale* (Paris: Fayard, 1989).

4 Fritz Fischer, *War of Illusions: German Policies from 1911 to 1914* (London: Chatto & Windus, 1975); Volker R. Berghahn, *Germany and the Approach of War in 1914* (London: Macmillan, 1973); Zara S. Steiner, *Britain and the Origins of the First World War* (London: Macmillan, 1977); John F. V. Keiger, *France and the Origins of the First World War* (London: Macmillan, 1983); Dominic C. B. Lieven, *Russia and the Origins of the First World War* (London: Macmillan, 1983); Richard J. Bosworth, *Italy and the Approach of the First World War* (London: Macmillan, 1983); Samuel R. Williamson, *Austria-Hungary and the Origins of the First World War* (Basingstoke: Macmillan, 1991).

5 David G. Herrmann, *The Arming of Europe and the Making of the First World War* (Princeton University Press, 1996); David Stevenson, *Armaments and the Coming of War: Europe, 1904–1914* (Oxford University Press, 1996); J. Dülffer (ed.), *Vermiedene Kriege: Deeskalation von Konflikten der Grossmächte zwischen Krimkrieg und Erstem Weltkrieg, 1865–1914* (Munich: R. Oldenbourg Verlag, 1997).

6 Zara S. Steiner, *The Foreign Office and Foreign Policy, 1898–1914* (Cambridge University Press, 1969); M. B. Hayne, *The French Foreign Office and the Origins of the First World War, 1898–1914* (Oxford University Press, 1993); Peter Jackson, 'Tradition and adaptation: the social universe of the French Foreign Ministry in the era of the First World War', *French History*, 24 (2010), 164–96; Thomas G. Otte, *The Foreign Office Mind: The Making of British Foreign Policy, 1865–1914* (Cambridge University Press, 2011).

7 Stefan Schmidt, *Frankreichs Außenpolitk in der Julikrise 1914* (Munich: R. Oldenbourg Verlag, 2009); Sean McMeekin, *The Russian Origins of the First World War* (Cambridge, MA and London: Harvard University Press, 2009); and Christopher Clark, *The Sleepwalkers: How Europe Went to War in 1914* (London: Allan Lane, 2012).

8 Amédée Outrey, 'Histoire et principes de l'administration française des affaires étrangères', *Revue française de science politique*, 3 (1953), 298.

9 Matthew S. Anderson, *The Rise of Modern Diplomacy, 1450–1919* (London and New York: Longman, 1993), pp. 6 ff.

the 1620s, Russia had a foreign ministry from 1720 and Britain's Foreign Office dated from 1782.[10] In 1814–15, the European Great Powers introduced a 'congress system' of regular summit meetings, but from the 1830s a more flexible machinery of periodic ambassadorial conferences replaced it. Such gatherings were convoked at times of crisis and extended their scope to the Near East and to Africa. They continued until the London conference during the First Balkan War in 1912–13.

By the twentieth century, 'diplomats' can be used as an umbrella term for diplomatic services, consular services and foreign ministry officials. Generally, the diplomatic postings – embassies under ambassadors in the European Great Powers, legations under ministers plenipotentiary in the smaller and extra-European states – were the most prestigious and most costly for their holders, who were paid too little to cover their expenses. This was a small and snobbish world, which kept the imprint of its courtly origins. Royal patronage was not uncommon in appointments,[11] and most diplomatic services were distinctly aristocratic and recruited from exclusive schools. 55 per cent of senior diplomats in the leading British embassies between 1855 and 1914 were of noble birth, as were all German ambassadors. Men from middle-class backgrounds did reach top positions in the Berlin foreign ministry, but prejudice against them was endemic and Jews were almost everywhere excluded.[12] Foreign ministries functioned secretively, opening their archives only at their discretion and often decades after the events concerned.[13] Men such as Palmerston and Bismarck ran their portfolios with little interference from other ministers or from legislatures, and treated their civil servants as clerks: the Quai d'Orsay juniors served daily tea to their superiors at 5.00 pm.[14]

Nonetheless, a complex of changes in the pre-war period marked the most significant transformation in the system since its origins. Most obviously, it

10 Zara S. Steiner (ed.), *The Times Survey of Foreign Ministries of the World* (London: Times Books, 1982).

11 Steiner, *Foreign Office and Foreign Policy*, pp. 71, 73; Lamar Cecil, *The German Diplomatic Service, 1871–1914* (Princeton University Press, 1976), p. 217.

12 Markus Mosslang and Torstan Riotte (eds.), *The Diplomats' World: A Cultural History of Diplomacy, 1815–1914* (Oxford: German Historical Institute London and Oxford University Press, 2008), pp. 23–57. Cf. William D. Godsey, Jr, *Aristocratic Redoubt: The Austro-Hungarian Foreign Office on the Eve of the First World War* (West Lafayette, IN: Purdue University Press, 1999).

13 Keith M. Wilson (ed.), *Forging the Collective Memory: Government and International Historians through Two World Wars* (Providence, RI and Oxford: Berghahn, 1996), chs. 1, 2, 7.

14 Jackson, 'Tradition and adaptation', 171. Following convention, ministries will be referred to by their addresses: the Ballhausplatz (Vienna), the Quai d'Orsay (Paris), the Wilhelmstraße (Berlin) and the Choristers' Bridge (St Petersburg). The Italian ministry was known as the Consulta.

was becoming more global. In 1893, a law authorised the US President to appoint ambassadors to powers that raised their Washington legations to embassies, which over the ensuing decade they did.[15] Yet during the later nineteenth century, when America faced no plausible external threat, the State Department had second-rate chiefs and Congress starved diplomacy of funds. The United States owned no properties in foreign capitals – its envoys having to rent accommodation – and ambassadorial postings were sucked into the 'spoils system' of partisan appointments.[16] In Tokyo, by contrast, legations were raised to embassy status after the Russo-Japanese War. The promotion reflected not only Japan's military prowess, but also its adaptability after centuries of shunning external representation. Japanese diplomats (unlike Chinese) adopted Western dress and sat European-style examinations. The foreign ministry (Kasumigaseki) was also organised along Western lines, although up until 1914 American advisers provided international legal training and helped to draft treaties, while a group of elder statesmen (the *genro*) shared in key decisions.[17] The other biggest extra-European powers – the Ottoman Empire and China – experienced more painful transitions. From the 1830s, Ottoman Turkey maintained permanent postings in the European capitals, and a foreign ministry whose working language was French. But traditionally it had confined relations with Christian countries to making demands and waging war on them, and its integration into European diplomacy accompanied decline.[18] Similarly, Chinese emperors were used to a deferential regime and to receiving tribute from their neighbours. They tried to keep relations with the Europeans at arm's length. Defeat in the Second Opium War forced them to accept Western missions in Beijing and to station their own overseas, but a modern foreign ministry had to await the Republican Revolution of 1911–12.[19]

A second force for change was technological. The submarine telegraph crossed the English Channel in 1851 and the Atlantic in 1866.[20] Steamships and railways facilitated summit meetings such as the 1878 visit by Benjamin Disraeli

15 Warren F. Ilchman, *Professional Diplomacy in the United States, 1789–1939: A Study in Administrative History* (University of Chicago Press, 1961), p. 72.

16 Ilchman, *Professional Diplomacy*, pp. 19–32; David J. Reynolds, *Summits: Six Meetings that Shaped the Twentieth Century* (London: Allen Lane, 2007), p. 25; Steiner, *Times Survey*, p. 576.

17 Steiner, *Times Survey*, pp. 328–31; Ian H. Nish, *Japanese Foreign Policy, 1869–1942: Kasumigaseki to Miyakezaku* (London: Routledge and Kegan Paul, 1977), pp. 1, 16, 28.

18 Steiner, *Times Survey*, pp. 494–505.

19 Steiner, *Times Survey*, pp. 1, 20–30, 136.

20 Daniel R. Headrick, *The Invisible Weapon: Telecommunications and International Politics 1851–1945* (Oxford University Press, 1991), pp. 15–19.

to the Congress of Berlin.[21] Although conferences of ambassadors remained – with bilateral diplomacy – the customary mechanism for crisis management, diplomats could now be guided more closely. Cables were costly and their terseness gave little scope for detailed exposition, although dispatches, conveyed by courier (diplomatic bag), continued alongside them. Moreover, as telegrams were sent via public channels, they had to be encrypted and might be intercepted. By the 1890s, the Quai d'Orsay was decrypting Italian, Spanish, British, Turkish and German cables. It read German telegrams during the 1905–6 and 1911 Moroccan crises, although French politicians' indiscretions then deprived them of this prime intelligence source until 1914, and whereas the Russians also practised decryption the British and Americans did not.[22] Nonetheless, the telegraph contributed to a vast increase in correspondence, which outpaced the growth in personnel.[23] To cope with it, diplomats needed to be more professional, and their chiefs needed to delegate.

Much research has focused on ministers' relations with their officials, whose influence grew as that of the ambassadors waned. Zara Steiner identified a break in continuity in the Edwardian Foreign Office as a new generation of Germanophobe officials exploited more devolved procedures and took senior positions alongside a relatively inexperienced Foreign Secretary, Sir Edward Grey.[24] Nonetheless, Grey remained his own man: with time he grew more independent, and from 1912 relations with Germany improved as fear of Russia revived.[25] In France, Raymond Poincaré, as Premier and Foreign Minister in 1912 and President from 1913, tried to rein in similarly Germanophobe subordinates.[26] The role of Russian officials is murkier, but many shared Foreign Minister Sergei Sazonov's determination to uphold the balance of power by deterrence and if necessary by war.[27] In contrast, the Wilhelmstraβe was more deferential, and the Reich Chancellor overshadowed the State Secretary for Foreign Affairs, but at the Ballhausplatz Count Leopold Berchtold as Foreign Minister drew ideas from a group of younger hawks (including his private office chief, Count Alexander Hoyos), who feared Austria-Hungary's disintegration and sought to check it through resolute action.[28]

21 Reynolds, *Summits*, pp. 21–4.

22 Christopher M. Andrew and David Dilks (eds.), *The Missing Dimension: Governments and Intelligence Communities in the Twentieth Century* (Basingstoke: MacMillan, 1984), ch. 2.

23 Steiner, *Foreign Office and Foreign Policy*, pp. 3–4. 24 *Ibid.*, chs. 2–3.

25 Otte, *Foreign Office Mind*, pp. 365–88. 26 Keiger, *France and the Origins*, pp. 53, 165.

27 Lieven, *Russia and the Origins*, pp. 83–101.

28 Cecil, *German Diplomatic Service*, pp. 7, 320 ff; J. Leslie, 'The antecedents of Austria-Hungary's war aims: policies and policy-making in Vienna and Budapest before and during 1914', *Wiener Bieiträge zur Geschichte der Neuzeit*, 20 (1993), 375 ff.

A further sign of professionalisation was that other government departments appointed specialised attachés.[29] From the 1850s, military attachés proliferated as the powers established Prussian-style general staffs, which expected technical updates on foreign developments. Unlike generalist diplomats, military attachés often engaged in espionage, and their reports are a neglected mine of information.[30] During the naval enthusiasm of the later nineteenth century, naval attachés also multiplied, and commercial attachés joined them.[31] As trade and investment expanded, business lobbies expected greater activism in promoting exports.[32] America's consular service was modernised between 1906 and 1915,[33] and foreign ministries recognised the growing interdependence of economic and political affairs. The Ballhausplatz established a trade policy department, while the Quai d'Orsay in 1907 merged its political and commercial subdivisions.[34]

Pressure from business formed part of a trend towards public scrutiny. In Germany, the Reichstag lobbied for a less socially exclusive diplomatic corps, and in Britain Edmund Dene (E. D.) Morel launched a campaign for democratic control over foreign policy.[35] *The Times* intoned: 'Who then, makes war? The answer is to be found in the Chancelleries of Europe, among the men who have too long played with human lives as pawns in a game of chess, who have become so enmeshed in formulas and the jargon of diplomacy that they have ceased to be conscious of the poignant realities with which they trifle.'[36] Foreign ministries had long used certain newspapers as quasi-official mouthpieces – for example, the *Norddeutsche Allgemeine Zeitung* in Germany. The 1907 Quai d'Orsay reform created a press bureau, and on the eve of war the Russian foreign ministry did likewise.[37] Ministries also subsidised organisations that

29 Alfred Vagts, *The Military Attaché* (repr. Princeton University Press, 1967).

30 Matthew S. Seligmann, *Spies in Uniform: British Military and Naval Intelligence on the Eve of the First World War* (Oxford University Press, 2006), chs. 2–4.

31 Jack W. T. Gaston, 'Trade and the late Victorian Foreign Office', *International History Review*, 4 (1982), 317–38.

32 Paul G. Lauren, *Diplomats and Bureaucrats: The First Institutional Responses to Twentieth-Century Diplomacy in France and Germany* (Stanford University Press, 1976), p. 64; Ilchman, *Professional Diplomacy*, pp. 35–8.

33 Ilchman, *Professional Diplomacy*, ch. 3.

34 Mösslang and Riotte, *Diplomats' World*, p. 76; Lauren, *Diplomats and Bureaucrats*, p. 88.

35 Cecil, *German Diplomatic Service*, pp. 324–7; Alan J. P. Taylor, *The Trouble Makers: Dissent over Foreign Policy, 1792–1939* (London: Panther, 1969), pp. 109–10.

36 *The Times*, 26 November 1912, p. 13.

37 Lauren, *Diplomats and Bureaucrats*, p. 191; George Bolsover, 'Isvolsky and the reform of the Russian Ministry of Foreign Affairs', *Slavonic and Eastern European Review*, 63 (1985), 36.

spread the national language and culture, such as the Quai d'Orsay with the Alliance française and the Consulta with the Dante Alighieri Society.[38]

A final change was the growth of international organisation. Despite the impression in retrospect that pre-1914 international politics resembled a Hobbesian state of nature, economically the European countries were more interdependent than they would be again until the 1960s, and inter-state cooperation assisted this process.[39] New bodies based on inter-governmental agreements included the International Telegraphic and the Universal Postal Unions, while the Paris and London Declarations and the Hague Conventions codified the rules of war. International law became an academic discipline, with journals, conferences and chairs, and foreign ministries strengthened their legal departments. Alliances and arms control conventions were dressed up as legal instruments, and governments did not sign them simply intending to break them.[40]

Nonetheless, the system failed. According to A. J. P. Taylor: 'In nearly all European countries the forces making for war were much what they had always been – silly old generals who had never seen any fighting, pedantic diplomats who had been told by someone or other that they should guard the national honour, hack journalists who could pull in an odd penny by writing a jingoistic piece.'[41] In actual fact, the role of diplomats and foreign ministries in July 1914 was greatest early on. Nikolai Hartwig, Russia's Belgrade representative, encouraged Serbian intransigence.[42] At the Ballhausplatz Franz von Matscheko had prepared a memorandum urging a Balkan diplomatic offensive, which after the Sarajevo assassinations was revised into a demand for war against Serbia. Hoyos conducted the mission that secured Germany's promise of support in the Potsdam 'blank cheque', taking with him the modified Matscheko text. Berchtold and his officials drafted the 23 July ultimatum to Serbia. Nonetheless, the Austro-Hungarian Council of Ministers had authorised Hoyos's démarche, which emerged from a broader governmental consensus in favour of forcing the issue.

38 Lauren, *Diplomats and Bureaucrats*, pp. 91, 114.

39 Carl Strikwerda, 'The troubled origins of European economic integration: international iron and steel and labor migration in the era of World War I', *American Historical Review*, 98 (1993), 1106–42.

40 S. A. Keefer, 'Great Britain and Naval Arms Control: International Law and Security, 1898–1914' (unpublished PhD thesis, London School of Economics and Political Science, 2012).

41 Alan J. P. Taylor, *War by Timetable: How the First World War Began* (London: MacDonald & Co, 1969), p. 42.

42 McMeekin, *Russian Origins*, pp. 48–9; cf. Lieven, *Russia and the Origins*, pp. 41–2.

In Germany, the blank cheque similarly resulted from high-level conversations, principally between Wilhelm II, his entourage and military advisers, and Chancellor Theobald von Bethmann Hollweg. The foreign ministry then managed the crisis during the interim period from 5 to 23 July. It tried to lull the Entente while urging Austria-Hungary to strike quickly, though on the grounds that speed offered the best chance of localising a Balkan conflict. But Foreign Minister Gottlieb von Jagow and his officials resisted compromise, and when Grey proposed a conference, Berlin encouraged Vienna to reject it. Having secretly encouraged aggression, Germany obstructed a diplomatic solution.[43]

After Austria-Hungary delivered its ultimatum, telegraph traffic swelled across Europe, but diplomats served primarily as conduits of information. The major exception was in St Petersburg, where Poincaré's influence slackened while he and French Premier / Foreign Minister René Viviani sailed back from a state visit. They left the initiative to Maurice Paléologue, the former Political Director at the Quai d'Orsay and now ambassador, who encouraged the Russians to act firmly and assured them they could count on the French alliance. How far he acted in harmony with Poincaré's wishes remains disputed.[44] In Russia's and Britain's deliberations, in contrast, the Foreign Minister took the lead. Sazonov was Nicholas II's principal adviser in the crisis, and in his view Germany stood behind Austria-Hungary and giving way would not preserve peace. He bears much of the responsibility for Russia's recourse to mobilisation measures. In London, after mediation failed, Grey warned Germany that Britain was likely to intervene. He brought the issue to the Cabinet and would have resigned over it, although for his more hawkish officials he moved too cautiously. Having done much to shape the contours of the crisis, in its final phases foreign ministries became more marginal.

1914–1916

The outbreak of hostilities plunged diplomats into a new and disturbing world.[45] Except for matters such as prisoner exchanges, contact between

43 On the foreign ministry's role, see Imanuel Geiss, *July 1914: The Outbreak of the First World War* (London: Batsford, 1967), docs. 15, 18, 24, 30, 33, 101. On the conference system, see Richard J. Crampton, 'The decline of the concert of Europe in the Balkans, 1913–14', *Slavonic and Eastern European Review*, 52 (1974), 393–419.

44 Schmidt, *Frankreichs Außenpolitik* argues that Paléologue followed a line set by Poincaré, although questions his influence on Russia's decisions.

45 On wartime diplomacy, see Chapter 19 by Georges-Henri Soutou.

belligerents ceased, and diplomacy was harnessed to the war effort.[46] Grey commented that it was not his job to play the strategist, and negotiating success depended on military fortunes.[47] Many diplomats enlisted and were wounded or killed.[48] Nonetheless, the Foreign Office trebled its staff by 1916, and it merged its Eastern and Western Departments into a new War Department.[49] Its German counterpart, in contrast, maintained its peacetime structure.[50] But for all the ministries their more traditional functions – adding new and retaining existing allies – became more difficult, and they had to take on new ones – such as propaganda, economic warfare and defining war aims – which other departments contested.

Wartime relations between allies became so complex that foreign ministries and embassies lost their monopoly over managing them. High commands liaised directly over strategy; finance and armaments ministries over war production; and summit meetings – between the French and British and the Austrians and Germans – became frequent.[51] But in the first half of the conflict, much activity was expended on finding new partners. The Allies were more successful, although generally not because more skilful diplomacy gave them the edge. Germany and Austria-Hungary gained two allies – the Ottoman Empire and Bulgaria – and in the first of these adhesions the German ambassador at Constantinople, Hans Freiherr von Wangenheim, figured prominently. Wangenheim was an experienced diplomat who had good relations with Enver Pasha, the Turkish War Minister. In August 1914, Berlin authorised him to sign a secret alliance if its terms satisfied him, but the Ottomans did not join the war immediately as Wangenheim had wished, and discussions dragged on for months. The British, underestimating Turkish military effectiveness, came up with no attractive counter-offer, and the Allies operated at a fundamental disadvantage, given that the Turks thought Germany militarily stronger yet feared Russia, and that Britain and France failed to reassure Constantinople.[52]

46 In 1918, the Foreign Office created the Political Intelligence Department (including seconded academics) to report on countries with which Britain had broken off relations.

47 Edward Grey, *Twenty-Five Years, 1892–1916*, 2 vols. (London: Hodder & Stoughton, 1925), vol. II, pp. 70, 153–4.

48 John Fisher, 'The Impact of military service on the British Foreign Office and Diplomatic and Consular Services 1914–18', *International History Review* 34 (2012), pp. 431–48.

49 Rothwell, *British War Aims*, pp. 10 ff; Public Record Office, *The Records of the Foreign Office, 1782–1939* (London: HMSO, 1969), p. 14.

50 Zbyněk A. B. Zeman (ed.), *Germany and the Revolution in Russia, 1915–1918: Documents from the Archives of the German Foreign Ministry* (Oxford University Press, 1958), p. 153.

51 Elizabeth Greenhalgh, *Victory through Coalition: Britain and France during the First World War* (Cambridge University Press, 2005), chs. 2, 4.

52 Mustafa Aksakal, *The Ottoman Road to War in 1914: The Ottoman Empire and the First World War* (Cambridge University Press, 2008), chs. 4, 6.

Similarly, the key factors in bringing in Bulgaria were that during 1915 the military balance moved in the Central Powers' favour and they could outbid the Allies in offering territory.[53]

At first sight, Allied diplomacy was more fruitful. Yet wartime circumstances circumscribed its freedom of action. Thus, Japan's declaration of war on Germany was actually an embarrassment for the Foreign Office, which had made a limited request for naval assistance and not intended to invoke the Anglo-Japanese alliance. The driving force in Tokyo was Foreign Minister Kato Takaaki, who had been looking to strengthen Japan's position in China. That his policy prevailed reflected a decline in the *genro*'s moderating function: although the armed forces remained less influential than a generation later.[54]

In 1915–16, competition for new allies centred on the Mediterranean and the Balkans. The biggest development was Italy's entry in May 1915. The Italian side of this process was driven by Premier Antonio Salandra and Foreign Minister Sidney Sonnino, assisted by the Consulta's Secretary-General, Giacomo de Martino. Its timing too was largely governed by military developments: Germany's defeat on the Marne suggested that the Allies were more likely to win, and the attack on the Dardanelles suggested that action was urgent before Italy lost its bargaining leverage. Negotiations centred in London, where Italy's demands dismayed the Foreign Office (and the Rome ambassador, Sir Rennell Rodd, lost credibility for supporting them), but Britain and France saw no alternative to agreeing. The role for their diplomacy was largely one of reconciling Russia to Italy's claims to South Slav lands.[55] But the price paid complicated the Allies' next task, of heading off Bulgarian intervention by urging further sacrifices on Serbia, the Russians having already sent a senior foreign ministry official, Count G. N. Trubetskoi, to Belgrade for this purpose.[56] Even if Premier Nikola Pašić and the Serbian diplomats were willing to consider concessions, King Alexander and his circle were not. The entire episode was intensely frustrating for those involved in it;[57] and the ensuing debacle when

53 Gerard E. Silberstein, *The Troubled Alliance: German-Austrian Relations, 1914 to 1917* (Lexington, KY: University of Kentucky Press, 1970), ch. 6; Richard J. Crampton, *Bulgaria, 1878–1918: A History* (Boulder, CO and New York: East European Monographs, 1983).

54 Ian H. Nish, *Alliance in Decline: A Study in Anglo-Japanese Relations, 1908–1923* (London: Athlone Press, 1972), ch. 7.

55 Wilhelm W. Gottlieb, *Studies in Secret Diplomacy during the First World War* (London: Allen & Unwin, 1957), ch. 22; C. Jay Smith, *The Russian Struggle for Power, 1914–1917: A Study of Russian Foreign Policy during the First World War* (New York: Philosophical Library, 1956), pp. 247 ff.

56 Smith, *Russian Struggle for Power*, pp. 158 ff.

57 Cedric J. Lowe, 'The failure of British diplomacy in the Balkans, 1914–1916', *Canadian Journal of History*, 4 (1969), pp. 73–100.

Serbia was overrun harmed the Foreign Office's and Quai d'Orsay's reputations. But to Romania, in contrast, in negotiations led by Russia, the Allies could offer Bulgarian and Austro-Hungarian territory. Even so, although the terms of the deal were settled months beforehand, it was once again a military development – the 1916 Brusilov offensive – that impelled Romania to intervene.[58]

America's war entry differed fundamentally, not least because Washington had no territorial price. Its intervention did not result from bargaining like that with Italy, Bulgaria and Romania, although diplomacy still played a role. In 1914–15, the State Department and the Foreign Office swapped notes over the Allied blockade, but fundamental was President Woodrow Wilson's determination to avoid a repetition of the war of 1812 and Britain's to get as much blockade as possible without a breach with the United States.[59] Hence, neither government took positions that would set them on a collision course, in contrast with the Washington-Berlin exchanges over U-boats. In the latter, Wilson also set the tone and drafted the key messages, but believed that firmness was essential for his credibility in eventual peace negotiations.[60]

In these proceedings the ambassadors played minor parts. It is true that the German ambassador in Washington, Johann Count von Bernstorff, helped postpone a confrontation by exceeding his instructions during the 1915 *Lusitania* and *Arabic* crises. He overstated American goodwill towards Germany and the chances of American mediation.[61] But Sir Cecil Spring-Rice, the British ambassador, got on poorly with the President,[62] while Walter Hines Page, the American ambassador in London, was a friend of Wilson, but identified excessively with the Allied cause.[63] The President bypassed both men as well as Secretary of State Robert Lansing, and used as his principal envoy the Texan businessman 'Colonel' Edward Mandell House, whom he sent to Europe in 1915 and 1916 and via whom he negotiated the secret 'House-Grey memorandum' for possible American intervention. This episode was uncharacteristic, however, and the President preferred public diplomacy,

58 V. N. Vinogradov, 'Romania in the First World War: the years of neutrality, 1914–1916', *International History Review*, 14 (1992), 452–61.

59 Charles M. Seymour (ed.), *The Intimate Papers of Colonel House*, 4 vols. (London: Benn, 1926–8), vol. I, pp. 309–10; Grey, *Twenty-Five Years*, vol. II, p. 103.

60 Seymour, *House*, vol. I, p. 437.

61 Reinhard R. Doerries, *Imperial Challenge: Ambassador Count von Bernstorff and German-American Relations, 1908–1917* (Chapel Hill and London: University of North Carolina Press, 1989).

62 Stephen Gwynn (ed.), *The Letters and Friendships of Sir Cecil Spring Rice*, 2 vols. (London: Constable, 1924), vol. II, pp. 215 ff.

63 Burton J. Hendrick, *The Life and Letters of Walter H. Page* (London: Heinemann, 1950).

most prominently in his 18 December 1916 peace note asking both sides to declare their war aims. The Quai d'Orsay inclined to refuse, but the Foreign Office insisted on responding, which helped win Wilson's sympathy at a critical moment. In the final stages the Allies played a successful waiting game, whereas Arthur Zimmermann, the energetic (and non-aristocratic) diplomat who replaced Jagow in late 1916, took up the idea of Arthur von Kemnitz, a foreign ministry official (opposed by most of Kemnitz's colleagues) to offer an alliance to Mexico.[64] The result was the Zimmermann Telegram, decrypted like much of the correspondence between Berlin and Washington by British intelligence, forwarded to the Americans, and released by Wilson to the press.[65]

The telegram's publication was an Allied propaganda triumph, and manipulating public opinion had become a major diplomatic responsibility. The most ambitious departure was the Quai d'Orsay's Maison de la presse (1916), the brainchild of Briand's private office chief, Philippe Berthelot. Its 300 employees (who were abused as draft-dodgers) cultivated journalists, analysed foreign newspapers, delivered books and pamphlets, and arranged lectures abroad.[66] Propaganda spread to many neutrals (the Foreign Office subsidising newspapers in Greece and South America),[67] but the United States was the primary target. Germany's efforts there, financed by its foreign ministry, proved clumsy and counter-productive, but their biggest handicap was the Berlin government's own actions.[68] Conversely, the Foreign Office oversaw the secret agency known as Wellington House, which engaged leading British writers and worked through books and pamphlets (more than 7 million distributed by 1916), films and press articles in a more subtle assault on elite American views.[69] Yet although the Allies generally worked with the grain of

64 Doerries, *Imperial Challenge*, pp. 225–7.

65 Barbara Tuchman, *The Zimmermann Telegram*, new edn (New York: Macmillan, 1966); Christopher M. Andrew, *Secret Service: The Making of the British Intelligence Community* (London: Heinemann, 1985), pp. 108–14.

66 Jean-Jacques Becker and Stéphane Audoin-Rouzeau (eds.), *Les Sociétés européennes et la guerre de 1914–1918* (Paris: Publications de l'université de Nanterre, 1990), pp. 135–43; George Bruntz, *Allied Propaganda and the Collapse of the German Empire in 1918* (Stanford University Press, 1938), pp. 14–15.

67 Michael L. Sanders, 'Wellington House and British propaganda during the First World War', *Historical Journal*, 18 (1975), 132.

68 Hans-Jürgen Schroeder (ed.), *Confrontation and Co-operation: Germany and the United States in the Era of World War I, 1900–1924* (Providence, RI and Oxford: Berg, 1993), chs. 7, 8.

69 Sanders, 'Wellington House', pp. 129 ff; D. G. Wright, 'The Great War, government propaganda, and English "men of letters", 1914–1916', *Literature and History*, 7 (1978), pp. 70–100.

American opinion and the Germans against it, during 1916 the Dublin Easter Rising and new clashes over the blockade rekindled anti-Allied feeling. Wellington House's impact remains hard to assess.

Propaganda formed one element in wider enterprises of subversion. Zimmermann was the leading advocate of a pan-Islamist strategy, and the German foreign ministry supported a Middle Eastern propaganda bureau and sent a mission to Afghanistan. It tried to arm Irish Republicans and Indian secret societies, as well as subsidising the Bolsheviks.[70] In contrast, the Allies were at first more cautious in assisting the Austro-Hungarian subject nationalities, and their principal success was the Arab Revolt. The correspondence preceding it between Sir Henry McMahon (the British High Commissioner in Cairo) and Sharif Hussein of Mecca was conducted under Foreign Office direction, although McMahon exceeded his instructions and used vague and grandiloquent wording to get Hussein into the conflict.[71]

Blockade and economic warfare were additional new activities, and claimed much higher-level diplomatic energies than had peacetime trade promotion. Pre-eminently they were an Anglo-French concern. The British Admiralty had planned to paralyse Germany by severing its communications and excluding it from financial service markets, as well as halting imports and exports, but the Cabinet backed off from implementing the scheme, not least because the repercussions might damage Britain itself. Instead, the Foreign Office improvised a less draconian regime.[72] The biggest challenge was not naval, but diplomatic: to inhibit the neutrals adjoining Germany from expanding their re-exports to the Central Powers. The Quai d'Orsay led the French Government's administration of the blockade, particularly in Switzerland; but plans for 'preclusive purchase' of Swiss livestock fell foul of lack of finance.[73] In London, the Admiralty assailed the Foreign Office for being too lenient.[74] In February 1916, a ministry of blockade took over, headed by Sir

70 Hew Strachan, *The First World War*, vol. 1, *To Arms* (Oxford University Press, 2001), pp. 697, 707, 771, 800; Fischer, *Germany's Aims*, pp. 122–55.

71 Elie Kedourie, *In the Anglo-Arab Labyrinth: The McMahon-Husayn Correspondence and its Interpretations, 1914–1939* (Cambridge University Press, 1976); Isaiah Friedman, *The Question of Palestine, 1914–1918: British-Jewish-Arab Relations* (London: Routledge & Kegan Paul, 1973), ch. 3.

72 Nicholas A. Lambert, *Planning Armageddon: British Economic Warfare and the First World War* (Cambridge, MA and London: Harvard University Press, 2012), chs. 5, 6.

73 Marjorie M. Farrar, *Conflict and Compromise: The Strategy, Politics, and Diplomacy of the French Blockade, 1914–1918* (The Hague: Martinus Nijhoff, 1974), pp. 95 ff, 142, 193.

74 Lambert, *Planning Armageddon*, ch. 9; M. R. P. Consett, *The Triumph of Unarmed Forces (1914–1918)* (London: Williams & Northgate, 1923), pp. vii–xv, 253.

Robert Cecil, who remained as Foreign Office Parliamentary Under-Secretary.[75] In July, a major new agreement curtailed Dutch exports and exacerbated Germany's food supply crisis, encouraging its gamble on the 1917 unrestricted submarine offensive.[76] But until then, the blockade's effects were limited.

A final new activity was defining war aims and extending peace feelers. In 1914 to 1916, such feelers were few, and rarely entrusted to professional diplomats, partly because unofficial intermediaries were easier to repudiate. Germany sent the Danish merchant, Hans Andersen, to sound out Russian interest in a separate peace; Count Törring to meet Professor Waxweiler, representing the Belgian King Albert; and the steel magnate, Hugo Stinnes, to Stockholm to explore a change of sides by Japan.[77] After the 1914 Western Front campaigning failed to deliver victory, Bethmann Hollweg hoped to split the Allies by enticing one of them into a separate agreement.[78] Conversely, Britain, France and Russia rejected contact before achieving victory, and in the September 1914 Pact of London they pledged not to negotiate independently.[79]

Both camps drew up war aims on the assumption of military triumph. Germany moved earliest to defining its objectives, but the 'September Programme' of 9 September 1914 was drafted not in the foreign ministry, but by the Chancellor's circle, the biggest contributions coming from Bethmann Hollweg's private secretary, Kurt Riezler, and the head of AEG and now chief of the *Kriegsrohstoffabteilung* in the War Ministry, Walther Rathenau.[80] Subsequent discussions on the future of Belgium and on a Central European customs association were taken forward not by Jagow, but by the Deputy Chancellor, Clemens von Delbrück.[81] The foreign ministry became more involved in autumn 1915, when Jagow and Bethmann Hollweg proposed to Austria-Hungary a set of political, military and economic agreements that would perpetuate the two countries' alliance and – Jagow hoped – strengthen

75 *Records of the Foreign Office*, p. 24.

76 Roger Chickering and Stig Förster (eds.), *Great War, Total War: Combat and Mobilization on the Western Front, 1914–1918* (Cambridge: German Historical Institute Washington/ Cambridge University Press, 2000), pp. 235–6.

77 Fischer,*Germany's Aims*, pp. 189–97, 216–22, 230–6.

78 Lancelot L. Farrar, Jr, *Divide and Conquer: German Efforts to Conclude a Separate Peace, 1914–1918* (New York: Columbia University Press, 1978), pp. 7, 105.

79 Stevenson, *French War Aims*, p. 12; Linke, *Zarische Rußland*, p. 237.

80 Rathenau letter, 11 September 1914, Bundesarchiv, Akten der Reichskanzlei, R/43/2476; Wayne C. Thompson, *In the Eye of the Storm: Kurt Riezler and the Crises of Modern Germany* (Iowa City: University of Iowa Press, 1980), pp. 98 ff.

81 Soutou, *L'Or et le sang*, p. 32.

the Dual Monarchy's German-speakers. The Germans proposed to place their newly conquered Polish territories under Habsburg sovereignty in return for Vienna binding itself to Berlin.[82] Austria-Hungary shied away from this arrangement, and negotiations stalled. The Germans therefore switched to favouring a nominally independent Poland that would become a German buffer state, and after being defeated in the Brusilov offensive the chastened Austrians acquiesced. By this point, however, Paul von Hindenburg and Erich Ludendorff had taken over the High Command (*Oberste Heeresleitung* – OHL), and the foreign ministry and chancellery faced a more assertive military, it being partly to placate the OHL that Zimmermann replaced Jagow.[83] The new balance of influence became evident in the discussions preceding the Central Powers' peace note of 12 December 1916, which was meant to prepare the ground for unrestricted submarine warfare.[84] It necessitated a negotiation with the OHL, which insisted on expanding German objectives.[85]

In the other belligerents, foreign ministries defended themselves more successfully. The Ballhausplatz, in which Stephen Burián had now replaced Berchtold, also faced an assertive High Command, which demanded sweeping Balkan annexations. But in the key phase of war aims formulation in the winter of 1915–16, the ministry maintained support for a moderate solution based on buffer states.[86] Similarly, the Kasumigaseki under Kato formulated the notorious Twenty-One Demands presented by Tokyo to Beijing.[87] And in Russia, led by Sazonov, the Tsarist Government was quicker than Britain and France to formulate war aims. In September 1914, Sazonov unveiled a programme to the Allied ambassadors, although Paléologue (characteristically) made this out to be firmer than it was.[88] In any case, Russia's defeats in Poland made it impracticable, whereas Turkey's war entry opened the alternative possibility of controlling Constantinople. In November 1914, Sazonov received a memorandum from one of his officials, N. A. Bazili, who recommended

82 André Scherer and Jacques Grunewald (eds.), *L'Allemagne et les problèmes de la paix pendant la Première Guerre mondiale*, 4 vols. (Paris: Presses Universitaires de France, 1966–78), vol. 1, docs. 146, 165.

83 Karl E. Birnbaum, *Peace Moves and U-Boat Warfare: A Study of Imperial Germany's Policy towards the United States, April 18, 1916–January 9, 1917* (Stockholm: Almqvist och Wiksell, 1958), p. 216.

84 Birnbaum, *Peace Moves*, ch. 8.

85 Scherer and Grunewald, *L'Allemagne*, vol. 1, docs. 361, 365, 367, 369.

86 M. B. Fried, 'War Aims and Peace Conditions: Austro-Hungary's Foreign Policy in the Balkans, July 1914–May 1917' (unpublished PhD thesis, London School of Economics and Political Science, 2011).

87 Nish, *Japanese Foreign Policy*, ch. 5; Peter Lowe, *Great Britain and Japan, 1911–1915: A Study of British Far Eastern Policy* (London and New York: Macmillan, 1969), ch. 5.

88 William A. Renzi, 'Who composed "Sazonov's Thirteen Points"? A re-examination of Russia's war aims of 1914', *American Historical Review*, 88 (1983), pp. 347–57.

annexing as much as possible on both shores of the Straits; and he commissioned a second, from the head of the foreign ministry legal section, Baron Boris Nolde, who set out maximum and minimum options. Sazonov went for the maximum, chiding Nolde for circumspection, and a paper from Captain A. V. Nemitz, the navy official responsible for foreign ministry liaison, reinforced the minister's ambitions.[89] In the first big wartime secret treaty, the Straits agreement of March–April 1915, Russia obtained promises that it could annex Constantinople and the Straits. The British yielded quickly, the French more reluctantly, although London and Paris did obtain a Russian counter-promise to support their own demands against the Ottomans.[90]

Russia became more passive as its military fortunes deteriorated. Foreign ministry memoranda envisaged dismembering Austria-Hungary, but remained think pieces.[91] The Quai d'Orsay and Foreign Office were slower to discuss European war aims, as Grey and Théophile Delcassé (French Foreign Minister in 1914–15) feared undermining diplomatic unity and domestic consensus. By summer 1916, however, the military prospects seemed brighter, and at this point Sir Charles Hardinge, who had been Foreign Office Permanent Under-Secretary in 1906–10, returned to the post. He feared that the French were defining their objectives, whereas Britain had not, and he set up a war aims committee. From it resulted a memorandum by two officials, Sir William Tyrrell and Sir Ralph Paget, which was circulated to the Cabinet. It prompted further papers but not a Cabinet discussion before David Lloyd George replaced Herbert Asquith as Premier. Indeed, the Tyrrell-Paget recommendations that France should regain Alsace-Lorraine and an independent Poland be created at Germany's expense exceeded what the government was willing to adopt.[92] In Paris, however, firmer conclusions were reached. In November 1915, Aristide Briand became both Premier and Foreign Minister. His administrative laxity created opportunities for the Quai d'Orsay officials: most notably for Berthelot, but also for Berthelot's rival, Jules Cambon, who took the new post of Secretary-General, while Cambon's brother Paul remained ambassador in London. In summer 1916, Paul requested guidelines for conversations with the British, while Paléologue

89 Ronald P. Bobroff, *Roads to Glory: Late Imperial Russia and the Turkish Straits* (New York: I. B. Tauris, 2006), pp. 118–22.

90 Bobroff, *Roads to Glory*, pp. 131–8.

91 Alexander Dallin (ed.), *Russian Diplomacy and Eastern Europe, 1914–1917* (New York: King's Crown Press, 1963), pp. 100–13.

92 Rothwell, *British War Aims*, pp. 39–52. Printed in David Lloyd George, *The Truth about the Peace Treaties*, 2 vols. (London: Gollancz, 1938), vol. 1, pp. 31–50.

warned that Russia might make peace. The Cambons drafted a programme that in January 1917 the council of ministers approved. It asserted France's right to the 'preponderant voice' in the future of the west bank of the Rhine. However, discussions followed not with the British, but with the Russians – a mission to Petrograd headed by the Colonial Minister, Gaston Doumergue, concluding an agreement for French buffer states in the Rhineland and Briand promising support for whatever Russia demanded in Poland. In contrast with the letter to Paul Cambon, the council of ministers never discussed this correspondence, which would cause great embarrassment. An outstanding example of foreign ministry assertiveness, it was about to become symbolic of a bygone era.[93]

1917–1918

Conditions for the foreign ministries now further deteriorated. The spring of 1917 and the subsequent winter marked two turning points, centred on developments in Petrograd and Washington.[94] Nicholas II's abdication brought to office a Russian Provisional Government that inherited his annexationism, but in May street demonstrations forced its Foreign Minister, Paul Miliukov, to resign. His successor, Mikhail Tereshchenko, relinquished the Constantinople claim. The new government uneasily shared authority with the Petrograd Soviet of workers' and soldiers' deputies, led by the Menshevik and Socialist Revolutionary Parties, which called for a peace without annexations and indemnities and supported the Socialist International's proposal for a conference of neutral and belligerent socialist parties in Stockholm.[95] Simultaneously, America's intervention brought in a power that had no secret treaties and heartily disliked the Allied ones, and distanced itself from its new partners. Given that both Page and Spring Rice were discredited, Britain maintained contact with Wilson via liaison between House and the Washington head of MI6, Sir William Wiseman.[96] In this new context, support for progressive parties spread across Europe, and even the more patriotic socialist leaders became radicalised. Until now, anti-war protest had

93 Stevenson, *French War Aims*, ch. 2.

94 Generally, Arno J. Mayer, *Political Origins of the New Diplomacy, 1917–1918* (New Haven, CT: Yale University Press, 1959).

95 David Kirby, 'International socialism and the question of peace: the Stockholm Conference of 1917', *Historical Journal*, 25 (1982), 709–16; Rex A. Wade, *The Russian Search for Peace, February–October 1917* (Stanford University Press, 1969).

96 Wilton B. Fowler, *British-American Relations, 1917–1918: The Role of Sir William Wiseman* (Princeton University Press, 1969), ch. 2.

been muted and Britain's Union of Democratic Control (UDC), founded with Morel as secretary, was unusual in demanding that '[a]dequate machinery for democratic control of foreign policy shall be created'.[97] More moderate critics advocated a League of Nations, and in 1916 Wilson endorsed this idea.[98] But in August 1917, a Labour Party conference adopted much of the UDC programme, while the French socialists came out in favour of the Stockholm conference and were aghast when their Russian counterparts revealed the Doumergue agreement.[99]

A second feature of 1917 was a concentration of peace initiatives. Pope Benedict XV appealed for a return to the pre-war status quo. Secret feelers went via amateur go-betweens or bypassed foreign ministries altogether. Thus, the new Austrian Emperor Karl sent his brother-in-law, Prince Sixte de Bourbon, to Paris without informing his Foreign Minister, Ottokar Czernin.[100] But Czernin also resorted to 'paradiplomacy', exploiting his connections with the Catholic Centre Party in the Reichstag to press the German Government to moderate its peace terms.[101] The Germans too used unorthodox methods, Zimmermann approving the arrangements made to transport Lenin from Switzerland to Petrograd.[102] They employed the Centre Party deputy Matthias Erzberger to sound out the Provisional Government about a separate peace. But their most important démarche followed the Pope's peace appeal. Richard von Kühlmann, who replaced Zimmermann in July, had served before the war in the London embassy. For a while he recaptured the initiative within the Berlin bureaucracy, and he attempted, like Bethmann Hollweg earlier, to probe the opposing coalition's fault lines.[103] He pursued a feeler from an official in the German administration in Brussels, the Baron von der Lancken, via Belgian middlemen, the Baron Coppée and his son, to Briand, who was now out of government. But Kühlmann's principal quarry was Britain, which he contacted via the Marquis de Villalobar, the Spanish

97 Marvin Swartz, *The Union of Democratic Control in British Politics during the First World War* (Oxford: Clarendon Press, 1971), p. 42.

98 George W. Egerton, *Great Britain and the Creation of the League of Nations: Strategy, Politics, and International Organization, 1914–1919* (Chapel Hill: University of North Carolina Press, 1978), ch. 1.

99 Lawrence W. Martin, *Peace without Victory: Woodrow Wilson and the British Liberals* (New Haven, CT: Yale University Press, 1958), p. 133.

100 Prince Sixte de Bourbon, *L'Offre de paix séparée de l'Autriche (5 décembre 1916–12 octobre 1917)* (Paris: Plon-Nourrit, 1920).

101 Robert F. Hopwood, 'Czernin and the fall of Bethmann-Hollweg', *Canadian Journal of History*, 2 (1967), 49–61.

102 Philip W. Dyer, 'German support of Lenin during World War I', *Australian Journal of Politics and History*, 30 (1984), 45–55.

103 Farrar, *Divide and Conquer*, p. 105.

representative in the Low Countries. Lloyd George's foreign secretary, Arthur Balfour, guessed that the approach came from his German counterpart, and insisted that any reply must come from the Allies collectively, a crucial principle that the premier at first resisted. But whereas Lloyd George contemplated making peace at Russia's expense, his Cabinet disagreed. After the Allies responded collectively, Kühlmann abandoned his initiative, while the French Foreign Minister, Alexandre Ribot, vetoed a Lancken-Briand meeting. Foreign ministries still played their customary roles: in Berlin seeking to sow division, in London and Paris to uphold coalition solidarity.[104] Ironically, within weeks, the Russians would split from their partners anyway.

For the next shock was the Bolshevik coup in Petrograd on 7/8 November. Lenin and Trotsky envisaged that Russia would become the headquarters of a global insurgency rather than conduct inter-state diplomacy. Trotsky took on reluctantly the role of People's Commissar for Foreign Affairs as he expected to have little to do: his Decree on Peace called for an immediate settlement without annexations and indemnities.[105] It promised to conduct all diplomacy in public and it denounced the inter-Allied secret treaties.[106] These latter the Bolsheviks proceeded to publish, though with difficulty as the foreign ministry's staff refused to work with them, most of Russia's diplomats abroad were sacked and the Allied ambassadors boycotted the new regime. Liaison continued via unofficial agents, Robert Bruce Lockhart being sent for the purpose from Britain, while through an understanding reached at the Lyons Corner (coffee) House Maxim Litvinov became the contact in London.[107]

Once revolution failed to spread, Lenin changed tack. The Bolsheviks signed a ceasefire with the Central Powers and opened peace negotiations at Brest-Litovsk, insisting that the proceedings were in public. Initially, Kühlmann and Czernin set the Central Powers' line, playing the Bolsheviks along in order to divide them from the Allies and paying lip service to self-determination in order to detach Russia's Polish, Baltic and Ukrainian territories. This approach failed when Trotsky walked out of the proceedings, and at the Bad Homburg

104 Farrar, *Divide and Conquer*, ch. 4; David R. Woodward, 'David Lloyd George, a negotiated peace with Germany, and the Kühlmann Peace Kite of September 1917', *Canadian Journal of History*, 4 (1971), pp. 75–93; Stevenson, *French War Aims*, pp. 88–92.

105 John W. Wheeler-Bennett, *Brest-Litovsk: The Forgotten Peace, March 1918* (London: Macmillan, 1938), pp. 375–8; Richard K. Debo, *Revolution and Survival: The Foreign Policy of Soviet Russia, 1917–1918* (University of Toronto Press, 1979), pp. 18–20.

106 Wilson, *Forging the Collective Memory*, pp. 64–6.

107 Robin H. Bruce Lockhart, *Memoirs of a British Agent: Being an Account of the Author's Early Life in Many Lands and of His Official Mission to Moscow in 1918* (London: Macmillan, 1974), pp. 198–202.

conference on 13 February 1918 Wilhelm II and Chancellor Georg Hertling backed Hindenburg and Ludendorff's insistence on a renewed advance to force the Bolsheviks to sign a treaty.[108] Kühlmann considered resigning, but stayed, and was obliged to acquiesce in a succession of faits accomplis as the army moved into the Russian interior. In June 1918, he incautiously suggested in the Reichstag that the war could not be won by military means, and OHL pressure forced his resignation. By this stage, Czernin had also lost office, after the 'Czernin incident' in April when the French disclosed Karl's secret contacts via Prince Sixte. Karl had to sign up to new long-term agreements with Berlin, and Austria-Hungary lost much of its remaining independence. Both German and Austro-Hungarian diplomacy were now in eclipse.

Yet their opponents' foreign ministries were scarcely better placed. Until the Bolsheviks signed the Brest-Litovsk peace treaty, the Allies still hoped to keep Russia in. This hope lent impetus to Woodrow Wilson's Fourteen Points address on 8 January, with its commitment in Point One to 'open covenants of peace, openly arrived at, after which there shall be no private international understandings of any kind but diplomacy shall always proceed frankly and in the public view', and in Point Fourteen to a League of Nations.[109] The President spoke out unilaterally after failing to secure an Allied war aims declaration, despite the public relations disaster of the publication of the secret treaties. He drafted his speech in conjunction with House and in the light of reports from William Buckler in the London embassy (bypassing Page) about the mood of British progressives, whereas Lansing made only minor changes.[110] But the Quai d'Orsay and Foreign Office were also being sidelined. In the new French Government that took office in November 1917, Georges Clemenceau held the premiership and the war ministry. His Foreign Minister, Stephen Pichon, deferred to him.[111] The Maison de la presse was cut down to size, and a ministry of blockade took over economic warfare.[112] In Britain,

108 Winfried Baumgart and Konrad Repgen (eds.), *Brest-Litovsk* (Göttingen: Vandenhoeck & Ruprecht, 1969), pp. 57–62.

109 James B. Scott (ed.), *Official Statements of War Aims and Peace Proposals, December 1916–November 1918* (Washington, DC: Carnegie Endowment for International Peace, 1921), pp. 234–9.

110 Seymour, *House*, vol. III, ch. II; Klaus Schwabe, *Woodrow Wilson, Revolutionary Germany, and Peacemaking, 1918–1919: Missionary Diplomacy and the Realities of Power*, Eng. edn (Chapel Hill and London: University of North Carolina Press, 1985), pp. 12–17.

111 Robert K. Hanks, '"Generalissimo" or "skunk": the impact of Georges Clemenceau's leadership on the Western Alliance in 1918', *French History*, 24 (2010), pp. 210–11; Jackson, 'Tradition and adaptation', p. 183.

112 Becker and Audoin-Rouzeau, *Sociétés européennes*, pp. 140–1; Bruntz, *Allied Propaganda*, p. 16; Farrar, *Conflict and Compromise*, p. 55.

Lloyd George truncated the Foreign Office's propaganda role on the grounds that it had been insufficiently aggressive. A new Department of Information took over Wellington House, first under the author, John Buchan, and then under the newspaper proprietor, Lord Northcliffe.[113] The premier had little respect for diplomats, and he replaced Spring Rice and Sir Francis Bertie (the ambassador in Paris) by non-professionals. Lloyd George had alternative sources of foreign policy advice from his 'Garden Suburb' staff in 10 Downing Street, the Cabinet Secretariat under Maurice Hankey and the War Cabinet itself. Summit conferences became more frequent, and in the final year the Allied premiers met each month in the Supreme War Council. In April 1917 at Saint-Jean-de-Maurienne, the premier assigned the Turkish territory round Smyrna to Italy, disregarding an appalled Foreign Office, and in February 1918 the War Cabinet overrode Balfour by approving a meeting between Count Mensdorff (the former Austro-Hungarian ambassador in London) and Philip Kerr from the Garden Suburb.[114] Although the Balfour Declaration in favour of a Jewish national home in Palestine bore the foreign secretary's name, it originated as a Zionist draft to which the Foreign Office made minor amendments, but was then very substantially modified by the War Cabinet.[115] Similarly, Cecil, Jan-Christian Smuts and Lloyd George himself were mainly responsible for the war aims statement in the premier's 5 January 1918 Caxton Hall speech.[116] The speech did not call for open diplomacy and was more guarded than Wilson about the League. But even as the Bolsheviks and the American President railed against traditional diplomacy, foreign ministries' influence reached its lowest ebb.

After Brest-Litovsk and the Czernin incident, little scope remained for peace talks. On 21 May 1918, the Foreign Office (with Lloyd George's approval) informed its ambassador in Paris that attempts to detach Vienna from Berlin must be abandoned as 'inopportune and impracticable', and 'all possible support' be given to the Austro-Hungarian nationalities.[117] In Berlin, however, the Wilhelmstraβe recovered ground under Kühlmann's successor, Paul von Hintze, although partly because Hintze was not a career diplomat, but a naval officer and former attaché who spoke to Hindenburg and

113 Philip M. Taylor, 'The Foreign Office and British propaganda during the First World War', *Historical Journal*, 23 (1980), pp. 886–90.
114 Roberta M. Warman, 'The erosion of Foreign Office influence in the making of foreign policy, 1916–1918', *Historical Journal*, 15 (1972), pp. 133–59.
115 Friedman, *Question of Palestine*, ch. 16.
116 Rothwell, *British War Aims*, pp. 145–53, 162.
117 Kenneth J. Calder, *Britain and the Origins of the New Europe, 1914–1918* (Cambridge University Press, 1976), p. 182.

Ludendorff in their own language.[118] Even after the German ambassador in Moscow was assassinated, Hintze successfully defended his ministry's policy of doing business with the Bolsheviks.[119] But he also recognised that the war was going badly, and with his officials such as Wilhelm von Stumm he prepared a plan to liquidate it by appealing to Wilson for a ceasefire based on the President's principles and by launching a 'revolution from above' or stage-managed democratisation.[120] This was the manoeuvre that the Germans tried to execute in October 1918, although only after Ludendorff and Hindenburg accepted that the military prospects were hopeless.

In Allied and American policy towards the Armistice, the foreign ministries had an advisory role. Wilson consulted House and at one point his Cabinet before responding to the Germans, but again he drafted his replies himself. He sent House rather than Lansing to the Paris conference of 29 October to 4 November that determined the ceasefire terms.[121] In London, the Foreign Office headed off French suggestions of a common front against Wilson, but the Cabinet took the decision to accept an armistice if the terms were right.[122] Although several French ambassadors wanted to rebuff the German appeal, Pichon and Clemenceau authorised the Allied generalissimo, Ferdinand Foch, to draft ceasefire conditions that would enable the victors to occupy the left bank of the Rhine. The foreign ministry had initially expected Wilson to reject an armistice, and Foch rather than the Quai d'Orsay salvaged the French position.[123]

Conclusion

The peace conference offered the foreign ministries an opportunity to reclaim influence, but they largely failed to do so.[124] The exception was again Germany, where the foreign ministry under Ulrich Graf Brockdorff-Rantzau devised a strategy of playing for US sympathy and targeting Allied public

118 Johannes Hürter (ed.), *Paul von Hintze: Marineoffizier, Diplomat, Staatssekretär. Dokumente einer Karriere zwischen Militär und Politik, 1903–1918* (Munich: Harald Boldt, 1998).

119 Fischer, *Germany's Aims*, pp. 571–3.

120 Hürter, *Paul von Hintze*, pp. 103–5; Schwabe, *Woodrow Wilson*, pp. 35–8.

121 Schwabe, *Woodrow Wilson*, pp. 43–6, 58–67.

122 Cecil minute on Crowe note, 18 October 1918, TNA, FO 371/3444; War Cabinet, 26 October 1918, TNA CAB 23/14.

123 René M. M. Lhopital, *Foch, L'Armistice et la paix* (Paris: Plon, 1938), pp. 33–9.

124 For the peace conference, see Chapter 22 by Helmut Konrad.

opinion.[125] The strategy failed, although it shook the confidence of many in the British and American delegations, and laid the basis for anti-Versailles revisionism. Among the victors, such American preparations as were made for the conference were largely due to House, who worked with Wilson on an initial draft for the League Covenant and helped to establish the Enquiry, an agency composed largely of academics that investigated the issues in the settlement, although remaining dependent on State Department expertise. House had ambitions to be the principal orchestrator of the conference, but in fact the American delegation comprised a mixture of State Department officials, Enquiry members, House loyalists and economic experts.[126] The upshot, given that Wilson himself had little flesh to place on the bare bones of the Fourteen Points, was that the Americans arrived singularly ill prepared.

If the French and British were better placed, it was little thanks to their foreign ministries. The Quai d'Orsay tried to draft an overall negotiating position, but Clemenceau transferred the task to André Tardieu, the wartime French high commissioner in the United States, who pulled France's claims together and presented them at the conference. The Quai d'Orsay's officials had most influence on the Eastern European territorial arrangements.[127] Similarly, the Foreign Office commissioned background briefings in the so-called 'peace handbooks', and submitted papers on the principles of the settlement. It organised the Phillimore Committee of officials, lawyers and historians, which first drafted what became the collective security clauses in the League Covenant.[128] However, the peace conference organisation copied the Supreme War Council,[129] and Lloyd George used Hankey rather than Hardinge as his principal administrator.[130] Whereas at first the supreme conference body was the Council of Ten, which foreign ministers as well as heads of government attended, after March 1919 the key security and economic provisions were settled in the Council of Four, where Wilson, Lloyd

125 Manfred F. Boemeke, Gerald D. Feldman and Elisabeth Glaser (eds.), *The Treaty of Versailles: A Reassessment after 75 Years* (Cambridge: German Historical Institute Washington/Cambridge University Press, 1998), pp. 43–52.

126 Inga Floto, *Colonel House in Paris: A Study of American Policy at the Paris Peace Conference, 1919* (Aarhus: Universitetsforlaget i Aarhus, 1973), pp. 73, 96–7; Lawrence E. Gelfand, *The Inquiry: American Preparations for Peace, 1917–1919* (New Haven, CT and London: Yale University Press, 1963), pp. 316–22.

127 Stevenson, *French War Aims*, pp. 151–8, 170.

128 Egerton, *Great Britain*, chs. 4–6; Michael L. Dockrill and Zara S. Steiner, 'The Foreign Office at the Paris Peace Conference in 1919', *International History Review*, 2 (1980), pp. 71–2.

129 Frank S. Marston, *The Peace Conference of 1919: Organization and Procedure* (repr. Westport, CT: Greenwood Press, 1981), p. 1.

130 Dockrill and Steiner, 'Foreign Office', 58–9.

George, Clemenceau and the Italian premier, Vittorio Orlando, called in experts, but deliberated in secret and alone apart from minute-takers and interpreters. 'Open diplomacy' fell at the first hurdle, and although the Council of Four delivered a result, many of the professional diplomats in the British and American – and indeed French – delegations doubted the Versailles Treaty's wisdom and practicality.[131]

After the war, major reforms took place in many foreign services and foreign ministries. The Wilhelmstraße was restructured on lines similar to those adopted by the Quai d'Orsay in 1907, and assumed an aggressive propaganda role.[132] In Britain, the Foreign Office and the diplomatic service were amalgamated.[133] In the United States, the professionalisation of the consular service was extended to its diplomatic counterpart.[134] In Soviet Russia, Trotsky's successor, Georgy Chicherin, built up a new diplomatic machinery.[135] Pressures for change that had long been building now culminated. But traditional diplomacy was still blamed for having contributed to the war, for secretly negotiating annexationist treaties and for failing to update its practices. Lloyd George continued working through summit conferences in 1919 to 1922, and he and his advisers such as Kerr and Hankey saw them as the modern and efficient way to conduct business.[136] By 1925, when the British, French and German foreign ministers met at Locarno, it seemed that foreign service professionals were recovering influence, but they still had to grapple with a new style of diplomacy, in which international institutions, public opinion and economic considerations were all more prominent. Locarno proved to be an Indian summer.

Like other state institutions, foreign ministries between 1914 and 1918 underwent an exceptional test. Already under growing criticism before the war, they were forced to develop in new directions in which they lacked experience and expertise. During and after the conflict, many foreign ministries were restructured, and some consular and diplomatic services professionalised with modified career tracks, although their social composition altered little. The UDC, Woodrow Wilson, and the Bolsheviks, however, called also for deeper changes,

131 James W. Headlam-Morley, *A Memoir of the Paris Peace Conference, 1919* (London: Methuen, 1972), pp. 161–3; Harold Nicolson, *Peacemaking 1919* (London: Constable, 1933).

132 Lauren, *Diplomats and Bureaucrats*, ch. 4; Steven E. Miller *et al.* (eds.), *Military Strategy and the Origins of the First World War* (Princeton University Press, 1991), pp. 202 ff.

133 *Records of the Foreign Office*, pp. 9, 26.

134 Steiner, *Times Survey*, p. 580.

135 Edward H. Carr, *The Bolshevik Revolution, 1917–1923*, 3 vols. (Harmondsworth: Pelican, 1966), vol. III, pp. 77 ff.

136 Dockrill and Steiner, 'Foreign Office', 85.

even if their aspirations were vague. In practice, neither the revolutionary demand for abolishing bourgeois diplomacy nor the radical one for transparent international transactions had much impact, and the reformist demand for stronger international institutions proved most influential. For all the League's deficiencies, the machinery for conducting international politics was permanently altered, and the acceleration of that process ranked not least among the legacies of the war.

4

Civil-military relations

STIG FÖRSTER

Reflections on civil-military relations in the 'age of total war'

'La guerre! C'est une chose trop grave pour être confiée à des militaires.' Or in English translation: 'War is too serious a matter to leave to soldiers.'[1] This remark by Georges Clemenceau is perhaps the most famous comment on the troubled relationship between civilian and military authorities in modern warfare. By the mid nineteenth century, monarchs and other rulers could not keep political and military leadership in their own hands. Society and economy became ever more differentiated, while political developments necessitated the establishment of an increasingly large and complex machinery of government. Under the strains of war, political leadership developed into an extremely demanding business, which could only succeed with the support of a sophisticated bureaucracy.

On the other hand, the character of war itself had changed. It no longer consisted of one or two campaigns and a few battles. Geographically, the theatre of war became too large for a single commander to keep control of all military activities. Even more important was the tendency towards totalisation that implicated all aspects of society, economy and politics in the war effort. Under such circumstances, who, then, was to lead and organise the war effort – the civilian politicians in government or the generals and admirals in charge of the armed forces? If war was becoming ever-more total, was it to be conducted according to the needs and wishes of society as a whole, or was everything to be subjected to alleged military necessities?

Some believed that the Prussian General Carl von Clausewitz knew the answers. In his famous book, *On War*, he wrote: 'The political object – the

1 Quoted in John Hampden Jackson, *Clemenceau and the Third Republic* (London: Hodder & Stoughton, 1946), p. 228.

original motive of the war – will thus determine both the military objective to be reached and the amount of effort it requires.' From this, he concluded: 'We see, therefore, that war is not merely an act of policy but a true political instrument, a continuation of political intercourse, carried on with other means.'[2] The French philosopher Raymond Aron mistook these statements as a postulate for the primacy of civilian political leadership over military command.[3] General Erich Ludendorff, who will figure prominently in this chapter, fell into the same intellectual trap when he denounced Clausewitz's theory as completely useless in modern warfare. To Ludendorff, total war was the order of the day, and the military leadership had to take control of state, economy and society and thereby maximise the war effort.[4]

But Clausewitz's reflections on the relationship between policy and war were far more complex than what Aron and Ludendorff made of them. He did not allude to certain forms of government or even the primacy of civilians over the military. To him, every war was ruled by policy. In reality, war was not possible without political issues, which determined its character. War, therefore, may have its own grammar, but certainly not its own logic.[5] And yet this particular grammar matters. In Clausewitz's words:

> If we keep in mind that war springs from some political purpose, it is natural that the prime cause of its existence will remain the supreme consideration in conducting it. That, however, does not imply that the political aim is a tyrant. It must adapt itself to its chosen means, a process which can radically change it; yet the political aim remains the first consideration. Policy, then, will permeate all military operations, and, in so far as their violent nature will admit, it will have a continuous influence on them.[6]

This is the core of the problem and was the bone of contention of all civil-military disputes during the First World War. It was policy that started the war and decisively influenced its course. But policy could not fight this war alone. Even if generals took control of the state, they naturally pursued their own political

2 Carl von Clausewitz, *On War*, edited and trans. by Michael Howard and Peter Paret (Princeton University Press, 1976), pp. 81 and 87.

3 Raymond Aron, *Penser la guerre. Clausewitz*, 2 vols. (Paris: Gallimard, 1976), vol. 1, pp. 427–8.

4 Erich Ludendorff, *Der totale Krieg* (Munich: Ludendorffs Verlag, 1935), pp. 3–10.

5 Clausewitz, *On War*, p. 605. See also Panajotis Kondylis, *Theorie des Krieges. Clausewitz – Marx – Engels – Lenin* (Stuttgart: Steiner, 1988), pp. 28–48; and Stig Förster, '"Vom Kriege". Überlegungen zu einer modernen Militärgeschichte', in Thomas Kühne and Benjamin Ziemann (eds.), *Was ist Militärgeschichte?* (Paderborn: Ferdinand Schöningh, 2000), pp. 265–82.

6 Clausewitz, *On War*, p. 87.

ends. It was still policy. But what happened on the battlefields had an enormous influence on the development of policy. Political and military conduct of the war thus underwent a complex process of interaction, as Clausewitz would have called it. Things became even more complicated, as the home front developed into the backbone to the whole war effort. Facing this fact, political and military considerations were quite often at odds. It is interesting to see how the nations involved in that war and their rather different political and social systems reacted to this challenge. On the extremes stood Ludendorff and Clemenceau. The former lost all confidence in civilian politicians, whom he regarded as mere obstacles to his quest for victory. The latter had always mistrusted the military men and was determined to limit their influence to their profession alone.

Civil-military relations comprise certainly more aspects than just the question of leadership in war. As civilian life during the Great War was increasingly affected by the war effort, military influence on all levels became increasingly apparent. In particular, the introduction of martial law in parts or even the whole of the countries involved meant military rule over much of society. This affected industrial relations, agricultural production, gender relations and the whole of the economy.[7] Conscription, introduced even in Britain in 1916, subjected young men to military law and left few families untouched. The presence and power of the military was also felt on a local level, especially when the fighting front was not too far away.[8] And, of course, there was the influence of war and the military on culture. However, it would carry things too far for this chapter to address all of the issues mentioned above. Instead, the focus will be laid on civil-military relations at the top level. One may regard this as an old-fashioned approach. So be it. But even in this rather limited field, matters are rather complicated, particularly on a comparative level. Moreover, as will be shown, the decision-making process at the top level impacted the lower echelons of society and the fate of the nation quite directly. After all, this war was waged by stratified societies and the top level ruled. But those elites who took the wrong decisions were doomed.

Troubled civil-military relations were not just a problem during the First World War. The problem is as old as the division of labour between civilian

7 As an interesting overview of several countries, see Stephen Broadberry and Mark Harrison (eds.), *The Economics of World War I* (Cambridge University Press, 2005). For Germany, see: Gerald D. Feldman, *Army, Industry, and Labor in Germany 1914–1918* (Princeton University Press, 1966); and Jürgen Kocka, *Klassengesellschaft im Krieg* (Göttingen: Vandenhoeck & Ruprecht, 1973).

8 See, e.g., the case study by Roger Chickering, *The Great War and Urban Life in Germany: Freiburg, 1914–1918* (Cambridge University Press, 2007).

authorities and military leadership. In modern times, its roots reached well back into the nineteenth century. A particularly interesting case in this context is Prussia. Prussia's constitutional development created a triangle of leadership that was in charge of affairs especially during wartime. At the head of this triangle stood the king, who had the last word in foreign affairs and all military matters. At the two lower ends stood the Prime Minister (later on the North German Chancellor) and the commander of the field army (since 1866 the Chief of the General Staff). Prime Minister Otto von Bismarck was to run diplomacy and political affairs, whereas Helmuth von Moltke, who headed the general staff, conducted military operations. This system of leadership appeared to be rather reasonable in theory. But in reality it worked badly, particularly when political and military difficulties resulted in mounting stress. In addition, Bismarck and Moltke were two strong-willed men, who were not very fond of each other and had little taste for compromise.

During the Franco-Prussian War of 1870/71, things came to a head. From the beginning of the campaign military authorities did their best to keep Bismarck on the sidelines. Bismarck was not amused, but he kept a stiff upper lip, as long as the German armies proceeded from victory to victory. With the siege of Paris, however, differences escalated. Bismarck, afraid of intervention by neutral powers, wanted to end the war quickly. He therefore demanded the storming of the city. But Moltke, for good military reasons, refused. Then Bismarck asked him to shell Paris with heavy artillery – Moltke procrastinated. Meanwhile, the armies in the French provinces ran into serious trouble. The new French Government had proclaimed 'guerre à outrance' and mobilised all available resources for the continuation of the war. The Germans had to face several new armies and at Orléans they suffered their first defeat. Behind German lines, 'francs tireurs' fought a guerrilla war. The campaign had turned into an ugly affair with no end in sight. Now Moltke lost his nerve and suggested that the army occupy the whole of France and annihilate her forces. This time, Bismarck pleaded for reason and with the help of the crown prince and the king, he stopped Moltke's extreme schemes. Throughout these disputes, King Wilhelm I found it rather difficult to take sides and to make decisions. Only the sudden collapse of France saved the Prussian triangle of leadership from further trouble. But the mutual distrust between Bismarck and the military leadership lingered on for years to come.[9]

9 Stig Förster, 'The Prussian triangle of leadership in the face of a people's war: a reassessment of the conflict between Bismarck and Moltke, 1870–71', in Stig Förster and Jörg Nagler (eds.), *On the Road to Total War: The American Civil War and the German Wars of Unification, 1861–1871* (Cambridge University Press, 1997), pp. 115–40.

Moltke drew his own conclusions from this experience. In 1871, he wrote in a short article on strategy: 'Policy uses war to achieve its own goals. It influences decisively the beginning and the end of war. During war it reserves the right to alter its aspirations or to accept more limited results. Due to this uncertainty strategy must always aim at the best results possible on the basis of existing means. In this way strategy works best for the ends of policy, but must act totally independent of it.'[10] But – alas – this approach was no solution. Policy and strategy (in fact, Moltke rather meant the conduct of military operations) could not be separated. They were intertwined. During the First World War, some tried to follow Moltke's advice, with fearsome results. There was no escaping it: some decision was to be made as to which principles should be paramount: political considerations or military necessities.

What made matters worse was the fact already evident in Moltke's times that warfare involved the whole population. The concept of short, sharp wars conducted by a small ruling elite was out of date. On 14 May 1890, in his last speech in the Reichstag (the Imperial German Parliament), Moltke issued a serious warning:

> The time of cabinet's war is behind us – now we have only people's war . . . Gentlemen, if this war, that for ten years like the sword of Damocles hovers over our heads, – if this war breaks out, its duration and its end are unforeseeable. The greatest powers of Europe, armed as never before, will enter the struggle. None of them can be defeated decisively in one or two campaigns, surrender, and accept hard terms. They will rise again to renew the fighting, even if it takes a year. Gentlemen, it could be seven years', it could be thirty years' war . . .[11]

Moltke was a good prophet. The First World War came close to his expectations or even exceeded them. Between 1914 and 1918, the tendency towards total war – the first signs of it had become apparent during the American Civil War and the Franco-Prussian War – gained momentum. This tendency never materialised in full, as 'total war' was a propaganda catchphrase and an ideal type. But the implications of this tendency meant nothing but the erosion of the dividing-line between civilians and soldiers.[12] Civil-military relations during the Great War should be seen within this context.

10 Helmuth von Moltke, 'Über strategie', in Stig Förster (ed.), *Moltke: Vom Kabinettskrieg zum Volkskrieg: Eine Werkauswahl* (Bonn: Bouvier, 1992), p. 630 (translation by S. Förster).

11 Helmuth von Moltke's speech in the Reichstag, 14 May 1890 in Förster, *Moltke*, pp. 638–4.

12 Roger Chickering and Stig Förster (eds.), *Great War, Total War: Combat and Mobilization on the Western Front, 1914–1918* (Cambridge: German Historical Institute Washington/ Cambridge University Press, 2000). For further reading on the concept of total war, see

The following analysis will focus on the Great Powers. In each of these cases, civil-military relations took a specific course. This was due to their different political, social and constitutional situation. With the exception of France and the United States, all of them were monarchies. The influence and role played by the respective monarchs varied widely. Some of them were mere figureheads, while others were at least in theory supreme commanders and capable of taking important decisions, especially in regard to appointing and sacking leading personnel. In some countries, the influence of parliament was not to be underestimated. Social, economic and military developments had of course great impact on changing civil-military relations. Above all, the long duration of the war and the catastrophic losses on the battlefields exerted enormous pressure on the societies involved and shifted civil-military relations in one way or another.

Perhaps the most interesting case was Imperial Germany. It was perhaps the only country where the power of the military became overbearing. After Hindenburg and Ludendorff took over High Command in 1916 and intervened directly in the process of political decision-making, many contemporaries spoke of a military dictatorship. Several historians later on argued in similar fashion. But, as will be shown, this view is an exaggeration. Yet, there can be no doubt that many German officers felt nothing but contempt for civilian politicians, as the structural and mental legacy of the conflict between Bismarck and Moltke lingered on. Inside Germany, however, the officers never managed to rid themselves completely of, as they saw it, weak, hesitant and meddling politicians. And far away from the homeland one general – Lettow-Vorbeck – succeeded in staging an outright military coup.

France

The Dreyfus Affair in the 1890s and early twentieth century severely damaged the reputation of the French army leadership. Public opinion, politicians on the left and the staunch Republican Georges Clemenceau deeply mistrusted the military. Conservative politicians and many officers

the rest of the series of conferences we organised as a team: Förster and Nagler, *On the Road to Total War*; Manfred F. Boemeke *et al.* (eds.), *Anticipating Total War: The German and American Experience, 1871–1914* (Cambridge University Press, 1999); Roger Chickering and Stig Förster (eds.), *The Shadows of Total War: Europe, East Asia, and the United States, 1919–1939* (Cambridge University Press, 2003); Roger Chickering *et al.* (eds.), *A World at Total War: Global Conflict and the Politics of Destruction, 1937–1945* (Cambridge University Press, 2005).

felt humiliated and held a grudge against democracy in general and the left in particular. This was not a good basis for balanced civil-military relations in times of war.

A decree of 28 October 1913 attempted to solve the problem of leadership in war. The government was to conduct the war in general, whereas High Command should be limited to the conduct of military operations. But when war broke out in August 1914, things ran less than smoothly. On 2 August, President Raymond Poincaré issued a decree that put the whole of France under a state of siege. On 6 September, the government even went so far as to declare a state of war for the whole country. In effect, this meant that France was under martial law. The military took over police functions from civil authorities and received powers to bring civilians before military tribunals. As parliament had adjourned on 4 August, General Joseph Joffre, Head of High Command, gained almost dictatorial powers. Joffre was convinced that the fate of France now depended entirely on the army. He did not even find it necessary to keep President Poincaré informed about developments. Joffre and some other officers apparently also regarded the emergency of war and their new powers as an opportunity to take revenge for their defeat in the Dreyfus Affair. Part of the problem was the government of Prime Minister René Viviani and particularly his Minister of War, Alexandre Millerand. They made no attempt to hold the army in check and instead regarded it as their duty to support the military in every way possible.

In the years before 1914, France suffered a series of domestic crises. The socialists and the trade unions found themselves in a more or less open class struggle against the ruling elites. On 31 July 1914, Jean Jaurès, the leader of the socialist movement, was murdered by a nationalistic fanatic. Yet, under the looming threat of a German invasion, the majority of the working class movement entered the *union sacrée*, the alliance of all patriots to save the fatherland.

This certainly helped the ascendancy of the military at first. But military rule was unpopular and drew public criticism. After the Battle of the Marne, when the gravest danger was over and the government had returned to Paris from Bordeaux, parliament reconvened on 22 September. From now on, the generals and their supporters in government had to face strong opposition. The inability of the army to liberate the parts of the country under enemy occupation, the mounting casualties on the front and the fact that no end to this murderous war was in sight further strengthened the opposition. As the war dragged on, an influential peace movement emerged, but it remained a minority. Within the socialist movement, however, it gained momentum, particularly after the Russian Revolution in February 1917. When in May 1917 the government, under pressure from the army and nationalistic circles, did not allow socialist delegates to participate in a peace congress in Stockholm, the *union sacrée* was finished. Strikes by workers and mutinies in the army both reflected and increased social tensions and brought to the surface older conflicts.

In the meantime, parliament demonstrated its strength. Since October 1915, when Viviani stepped down, changing governments went from crisis to crisis. But the happy days for the military were over. Government and parliament increasingly restricted their powers and strengthened civilian authorities. Already in April 1915 martial law for civilians was abolished. In December 1916, stubborn General Joffre was elevated to Marshal of France, but lost his position as Commander-in-Chief. His successor – General Robert Nivelle – proved to be a disaster. In spring 1917, he started a huge offensive at the Chemin des Dames, which ended in catastrophe. The French army lost 140,000 men and Nivelle was fired. Now Henri-Philippe Pétain took over and abandoned the idea of costly and futile offensives.

In the autumn of 1917, prospects for France were bleak. In this situation, Poincaré saw no alternative but to appoint his old enemy, strong-willed Georges Clemenceau, as head of government. It was a good choice. Clemenceau succeeded in re-establishing a modicum of lost national unity. But he also saw to it that government and parliament finally established control over the military. General Pétain and Marshal Ferdinand Foch, who in spring of 1918 became commander of all Allied forces on the Western Front, were told to mind their own business as military men and to no longer interfere in politics.[13]

In the end, France was victorious. But it had suffered incredible casualties, its economy was severely damaged, and its financial situation was disastrous. But the real winner was French democracy. Class struggle from below and above was not over and caused very serious problems in the years to come. Nevertheless, parliament had strengthened its control over government and the military. This was a strange success. At the beginning of the war, France was on the brink of military dictatorship. But as the war progressed, the power of the generals gradually waned. Towards the end, the staunch parliamentarian

13 For France during the Great War, see among many others: Jean-Jacques Becker, *Les Français dans la Grande Guerre* (Paris: Robert Laffont, 1972); Jean-Baptiste Duroselle, *La France et les Français, 1914–1920* (Paris: Editions Richelieu, 1972); Patrick Fridenson (ed.), *The French Home Front, 1914–1918* (Providence, RI: Berg, 1992); Fabienne Bock, *Un parlementarisme de guerre: Recherches sur le fonctionnement de la IIIème République pendant la Grande Guerre*, 3 vols. (Paris: Editions Belin, 1998).

Clemenceau pushed the military back to their places. There were many reasons for this outcome. But perhaps most important among them was the inability of military leaders to offer anything more than mass casualties. Clemenceau was right: war was indeed too serious a matter to be left to the military alone. But in other countries, the outcome was very different.

United Kingdom

Prior to the Great War, the army in Britain was in a difficult position. It consisted of a relatively small body of professional soldiers, most of whom were drawn from the lowest echelons of society. The army was rather unpopular, and many politicians were happy to see the forces out of the country. But the mostly noble officers could become heroes and start a brilliant career, if they were victorious in battle. Since 1906, however, Secretary of State for War Richard Haldane, a liberal parliamentarian, remedied some of the weaknesses of the British army with a reform project bearing his name and created the foundations of the British Expeditionary Force. Thus, Britain was able to enter the war in 1914 not just with the largest navy in the world, but also with a small but strong army. The army's popular standing was high at the outbreak of hostilities.

Because of his alleged sympathies with Germany, Haldane nevertheless had to resign in this first period of the war. His successor was a true war hero: Horatio Herbert Kitchener, First Earl of Khartoum and Broome. From now on, the army was solely in the hands of generals. Kitchener, who expected a long war, immediately began with the build-up of a huge volunteer force. He and the commanders of the British Expeditionary Force on the continent, Field Marshal John French and General Douglas Haig, insisted on separating military matters from politics and quite successfully resisted all attempts by politicians to interfere. Kitchener and the generals did not hesitate, however, to meddle in politics when they thought it convenient for military purposes. After catastrophic losses on the Western Front, it was pressure from military quarters that convinced the government to start a revolution in British military history: the introduction of conscription in 1916. This serious measure, which broke with British traditions and affected the whole of society, demonstrated the enormous influence the military had gained in British politics. From 1915 onwards, even before conscription, other steps into the direction of total war, such as government regulation of the war economy, were taken. On the other hand, Haig, the new commander of the Expeditionary Force, continued to block all government interference in his operations. Thus, nobody – not even

David Lloyd George, Prime Minister from December 1916 until the end of the war – stopped him from sacrificing hundreds of thousands of soldiers in futile offensives. After the victory over Germany in 1918, Haig became a celebrated hero. But his leadership had been disastrous for the British army.

The reluctance of the government to intervene in the way in which operations were conducted certainly had something to do with Gallipoli. The offensive against the Straits held by the Ottomans was the only case when British politicians meddled directly with military operations. The First Lord of the Admiralty, Winston Churchill, was the mastermind behind this adventure. The whole operation was misguided and bungled. Between April 1915 and January 1916, thousands of soldiers from many parts of the British Empire died in vain on the beaches and hills of Gallipoli. Churchill had to step down, and from then on generals and admirals alone took over the military conduct of the war.

In British affairs, parliament played a distinctive role. But during the Great War it lost much of its influence. Foreign Secretary Sir Edward Grey never informed the Cabinet or Parliament as to commitments he had entered into from 1906 onwards to come to the aid of France in the event of war. In 1915, an all-party government was formed and continued to run the country, albeit with changing personnel and a changing balance of power within the Cabinet. Under these circumstances, there was little opposition in parliament. Government could carry out its duties without much consideration for the rights of parliament. This also meant, however, that parliament was in no position to control the military.

Outside parliament, there was some anti-war opposition in the general public and especially in Ireland. But against the united front of the established parties – including the majority of Labour – these movements stood no chance. If need be, the army intervened with brutal force, as in Ireland during Easter Week 1916. This constituted another serious breach with British traditions.

In the end, British democracy survived and was even strengthened by the introduction of a more general suffrage that also gave women over the age of 30 the right to vote. But during the war the military ran the war without parliamentary control and at the expense of too many young lives. In a way, it was strange that Britain became the country whose conduct of war came closest to Moltke's idea 'on strategy'.[14]

14 John M. Bourne, *Britain and the Great War, 1914–1918* (London: Edward Arnold, 1989); Francis L. Carsten, *War against War: British and German Radical Movements in the First World War* (London: Batsford Academic and Educational, 1982); Niall Ferguson, *The Pity*

Italy

This country was a constitutional monarchy, but King Vittorio Emanuele III retained important powers, particularly with regard to foreign policy. Parliament had much influence in Italy's political system. But the country was not a true democracy. In spite of electoral reform in 1912, the majority of Italy's poor and the vast rural population did not have the right to vote. The political parties – liberals, conservatives, Catholics and socialists – were involved in almost constant struggle, against each other and among themselves. Against this background, Prime Minister Antonio Salandra, Foreign Minister Sidney Sonnino, and the king in spring 1915 plotted the entry of Italy into the war. Their motive was 'sacro egoismo'. Italy was to have a share in the spoils of victory and thus to become a great power. But the majority of parliament, under the leadership of Giovanni Giolitti, at first opposed the abandonment of neutrality. Public opinion, however, swung in favour of the war party. Especially the writer Gabriele D'Annunzio and the journalist Benito Mussolini stood at the forefront of a war-mongering nationalistic campaign. Giolitti, who was afraid to alienate the king, finally gave in. On 20 May 1915, parliament voted to declare war on Austria-Hungary and gave the government far-reaching powers for the duration. From now on, the government and the king conducted the war without much interference from parliament.

But it was the Chief of the General Staff, General Luigi Cadorna, who took control of operations. Cadorna steadfastly refused to give the politicians any say in military matters. On the home front, vast parts of the country were in effect under military rule. By September 1917, martial law had been introduced in one-third of Italy's provinces. There was much reason to doubt that the population were in any sense enthusiastic about the war effort, especially when things on the fighting front went badly. Regardless of criticism, Cadorna waged one offensive after the other near the Isonzo River. Human casualties were catastrophic, but no ground could be gained. The army consisted largely of peasants with few political rights. They were allowed to die for a fatherland in which they had little say. Mass desertions and military strikes followed, but

of War: Explaining World War I (London: Penguin, 1998); David French, *British Economy and Strategic Planning, 1905–1915* (London: Allen & Unwin, 1982); David French, *British Strategy and War Aims, 1914–1916* (London: Allen & Unwin, 1986); Peter Simkins, *Kitchener's Army: The Raising of the New Armies, 1914–1916* (Manchester University Press, 1988); Trevor Wilson, *The Myriad Faces of War. Britain and the Great War, 1914–1918* (Cambridge: Polity Press, 1986); Jay M. Winter, *The Great War and the British People* (London: Macmillan, 1985).

were brutally suppressed. About 750 soldiers were executed and, in addition, army command reverted to the practise of decimation, arbitrarily choosing individuals for the punishment of the group. Yet, the morale of the soldiers sank ever lower. Incompetent leadership and bad equipment added to the worsening situation of the army. In October 1917, at Caporetto, the front collapsed. The numerical weakness of the enemy, a remobilisation of forces under new leadership and Allied reinforcements saved Italy from total disaster.

Caporetto was the final straw that cost Cadorna his command. His successor, Armando Diaz, changed the conduct of operations. The time of useless mass offensives was over. General Diaz and the new Prime Minister Vittorio Emanuele Orlando introduced some reforms that lightened the burden of the ordinary soldier. This helped to stabilise the army. In the end, the collapse of Austria-Hungary handed Italy victory. But it was a bitter victory for which the country paid an extremely high price.[15]

Russia

The revolution of 1905 weakened Russia's political system. Tsar Nicholas II had to cede some powers to the Duma, the Russian Parliament. But he and his wife, Alexandra Feodorovna, still hoped to re-establish autocratic rule. The Great War provided them with an opportunity to do so, or so they believed. As the war began, the Tsar's uncle, Grand Duke Nikolay Nikolayevich, was Commander-in-Chief of the Russian army. The generals, however, were often less than competent military leaders. Intrigues and squabbling characterised much of the officer corps. Moreover, this huge army was badly equipped, not always well trained and hampered by an inadequate transport infrastructure. The Russian economy was in no position to support years of all-out war. After the Ottoman Empire entered the war, Russia was largely cut off from Western supplies. Under these circumstances, the war did not go well for Russia. Even initial success against the forces of Austria-Hungary could not be exploited, as Russia also faced the powerful German armies. A series of defeats and the loss of much territory followed.

According to law, the army took control of certain military zones and subordinated all civil authorities to its orders. In fact, much of the country

15 Howard J. Burgwyn, *The Legend of the Mutilated Victory: Italy, the Great War, and the Paris Peace Conference, 1915–1919* (Westport, CT: Greenwood Press, 1993); Mario Isnenghi, *Il mito della grande guerra* (Bologna: Il Mulino, 1997); Volker Reinhard, *Geschichte Italiens. Von der Spätantike bis zur Gegenwart* (Munich: C. H. Beck, 2003).

was under military rule since August 1914. As the war continued and the incompetence of military authorities as well as the central government became ever-more apparent, local government and private entrepreneurs took matters into their own hands. They did much good to the country's war effort, but could not remedy the general confusion. In occupied enemy territory, military commanders ruled unchecked. They created chaos. General Yanushkevich, for instance, ordered the brutal mass deportations of Jews in Galicia. The Tsar wanted him removed from his command, but his uncle refused. Hence, Nicholas II decided to sack the Grand Duke as well and send him to the Caucasus front. It was August 1915. The military situation was difficult and the enemy was on the march. Much of Poland and parts of the Baltic region had been lost. But who was to succeed Nikolay Nikolayevich? The Tsar took a fateful decision. He believed that at this time of crisis it was his duty to stay with his soldiers. Therefore, Nicholas II himself took command of his troops. His advisers and members of government were dismayed. They suspected the Empress and the influential faith-healer Rasputin to have masterminded this decision. But above all, they feared that any military setback would from now on damage the Tsar's personal reputation. Yet, no one could stop Nicholas II from this autocratic act.

The government in Petrograd was weak anyway. Ministers came and went. None of them was competent enough to control the war effort. Many decisions were taken behind the backs of ministers, as Alexandra Feodorovna and her circle of friends tried to keep the autocratic regime of the Tsar intact. This caused much opposition in the Duma. But the government and Alexandra's cronies blocked all attempts by parliamentarians to initiate reforms and to put an end to military despotism.

By autumn 1916, the initially successful offensive of General Brusilov had collapsed, and the army showed signs of dissolution. The country was in uproar and was soon hit by a widespread strike movement. Food shortages aggravated the situation. In Central Asia, a rebellion broke out and was brutally suppressed. Several hundred thousand people were killed. On 29 December 1916, a group of right-wing officers murdered Rasputin. Finally, in March 1917, revolution broke out. On 15 March, Nicholas II abdicated and Russia became a republic. But the new government continued the war, only to suffer further defeats on the battlefields. The revolution radicalised, the army fell apart, and in the end power went to the Bolsheviks, who promised to take Russia out of the war.

Under the Tsar, Russia's political and social system proved unable to cope with modern industrialised mass warfare. As in other countries, civil-military relations in Russia were filled with strife under the impact of this terrible war, a war that would not end, caused enormous numbers of casualties and only led to defeats. But those who clung to autocratic rule left little room to sort matters out. Neither the generals nor politicians had the power to tilt the balance in their favour. There was only one way out of the stalemate: revolution.[16]

Japan

In the complex history of civil-military relations, the case of modern Japan is particularly interesting. The overbearing influence in politics exerted by army officers from 1930 onwards led to disastrous results during the Second World War. But in the First World War, developments in Japan were very different. After all, Japan only briefly participated in the fighting. On 23 August 1914, Japan declared war on Germany. On 2 September, Japanese forces attacked Tsingtau, the German colony in China. The siege lasted until 7 November, on which day the Germans surrendered. During these weeks, Japanese soldiers also occupied several German-held islands in the Pacific. They met with no resistance. By the end of 1914, the shooting war was over for Japan. Japan lost less than 2,000 men. There was only one more military operation. The Allies asked Japan to send destroyers to the Mediterranean, but they were ordered to avoid any engagement with the enemy. Against this background, civil-military relations never came under stress due to the war. And yet, the Great War was of much significance for Japan too. In the long run, this war set developments into motion leading to catastrophe.

In the second half of the nineteenth century, Japan had been a victim of Western informal imperialism. But as the country underwent a process of rapid modernisation, it became a power to be reckoned with in East Asia. Victories over China (1894/5) and, more significantly, over Russia (1904/5), as well as the establishment of colonies on the mainland, set Japan on a course to great-power status. Japan's armed forces and in particular its commanders gained considerable political influence. Former Prime Minister Marshal Yamagata Aritomo, the father of the modern Japanese army, pulled many strings. But as in other countries, the army and navy were envious of each

16 Dominic C. B. Lieven, *Russia and the Origins of the First World War* (London: Macmillan, 1983); Hugh Seton-Watson, *The Russian Empire, 1801–1917* (Oxford University Press, 1967), pp. 698–727; Norman Stone, *The Eastern Front, 1914–1917* (London: Hodder & Stoughton, 1975); Allan K. Wildman, *The End of the Russian Imperial Army*, 2 vols. (Princeton University Press, 1980).

other and often pursued different interests. Civilian politicians in parliament and government could therefore find ways to block the ascendancy of the soldiers. Moreover, powerful clans played a major role in Japanese politics. And of course there was the emperor, who at least in theory held the balance. But *Tenno* Taisho, who inherited the throne in 1912 from his father *Tenno* Meiji, was ill and weak. At this time, Japanese politics was in turmoil. The Cabinets of General Katsura Taro and Admiral Yamamoto Gombei fell in quick succession. Rioting in several cities broke out and was quelled only by the use of military force. In the spring of 1914, the civilian politician Okuma Shigenobu became the new Premier. Contrary to all expectations, he cooperated closely with the military and the clans. Hence, the expansionist aspirations of the military and of radical nationalists were never distant from government policy. Okuma did not hesitate, therefore, to honour the alliance with Britain (concluded in 1902) and enter the war against Germany. After all, Japan was to have a share in the spoils of victory.

Japan's conquests of German colonies in the autumn of 1914 were a promising start. But it was not clear whether Japan would be allowed to hold onto them in a peace settlement. The Chinese Government was entitled to reclaim Tsingtau, over which it still held formal sovereignty. In January 1915, Foreign Minister Kato Takaaki presented the Chinese with his 'Twenty-One Demands'. China was to accept Japanese rule over the former German colonies and to allow the enlargement of Japan's sphere of influence in Manchuria and elsewhere. Above all, Japanese 'advisers' were to be employed in all leading military and civilian offices. This would, in fact, have turned China into a Japanese protectorate.

Okuma and Kato believed that Japan had a free hand in China, while the European powers were distracted by the war. But there remained the United States and her traditional open-door policy in China. Washington objected and forced the Japanese Government to drop their demand for control of Chinese authorities. From then on, US-Japanese relations turned sour, with serious long-term consequences.

Military circles in Japan, particularly Yamagata, were incensed by the clumsy way in which Okuma and Kato had handled Chinese affairs. Both had to resign and Marshal Terauchi Masatake became Premier. But this did not mean that the military had finally taken power. Terauchi governed with the support of the principal parties in parliament. Regarding China, he pursued a more cautious course. Instead of threats and coercion, he used bribes, but the course of policy remained the same.

Before 1914, Japan was a relatively poor country and suffered repeated financial difficulties. But the war changed all this. As the European powers engaged in their deadly struggle and mobilised their economies for war, Japanese products filled the resulting gaps in the world market. In addition, Japan supplied the Allies with all kinds of goods they needed. Naturally, this also led to a boom in Japan's financial market. Old and new businessmen benefited enormously and the middle class began to expand. But there was also much speculation and graft in the market. Real wages for workers declined as inflation set in. The result was increasing wealth and mounting social tension.

After the Bolshevik Revolution in Russia, the army saw another opportunity for imperial expansion. This time, they aimed at Siberia. The Allies worried that the Bolsheviks might expand their power to East Asia and therefore decided to intervene militarily. Japan promised to participate with 12,000 men. But, instead, the general staff and the war ministry sent 73,000 soldiers to occupy much of Russia's eastern territory. In the end, this intervention led to nothing. But at home there was much public outcry about this controversial operation, which ordered many thousand conscripts into the Siberian wilderness.

In the meantime, inflation went through the roof. The poor were particularly hit by a doubling of the price for rice in summer 1918. Speculation and the hoarding of rice by the army authorities exacerbated the situation. This was too much. In August 1918, rice riots affected large parts of the country. For three weeks, Japan was in uproar. Finally, the army intervened. More than 100 people died and many thousands were arrested.

On 29 September 1918, the new Premier, Hara Takashi, a commoner, formed the first government based on party support. This led to a certain amount of liberalisation. For a few years, Japan appeared to be on its way towards democratisation and recognition as a major international power.

But the army remained powerful. Radical nationalism gained momentum, as the Allies curtailed Japan's share of the spoils of victory. Economic crisis destabilised the social and political structures in the following years. In September 1931, officers of the Japanese Kwantung Army plotted the Mukden Incident. This marked the beginning of Japan's fateful road to expansion, war and dominance by the military.[17]

17 Frederick R. Dickinson, *War and National Reinvention: Japan in the Great War, 1914–1919* (Cambridge, MA: Harvard University Press, 1999); Richard Storry, *A History of Modern Japan* (London: Penguin, 1960).

United States

'He kept us out of war': on this ticket, President Woodrow Wilson ran for re-election in 1916 and won. Even by American standards, a campaign slogan was rarely rendered obsolete as quickly as this one. Only a few months later, the United States entered the war on the side of the Allies as an 'associated' power. The German decision to reopen unrestricted submarine warfare, the subsequent sinking of neutral American ships and above all the Zimmermann Telegram made this move inevitable.

But even before that absurd episode, the United States were already deeply involved in the war. American supplies and loans kept the Allied war effort going. The US economy and the financial sector thrived on this business. American entrepreneurs would have loved to do business with the Central Powers as well, but the British naval blockade prevented that. Hence, in economic terms the United States were less than neutral in this war. In all fairness, it should be mentioned, however, that Wilson and his adviser 'Colonel' Edward M. House did their best to mediate peace before America was sucked into the conflagration, but to no avail.

However, once the US Government and Congress decided to become directly involved in the fighting, the American war effort became very serious indeed. Ludendorff and the German military, who had taken the American entry into the war lightly, were in for a nasty surprise.

As far as mobilisation was concerned, the US authorities were ready to move into the direction of total war. But in contrast to other powers, this endeavour remained firmly in the hands of civilian administrators. Nobody questioned the authority of the President and the constitutional rights of Congress. Wilson's Democrats for the most part enjoyed a majority in both houses and let the administration do their job. Army command was far away in France and more concerned with gaining some form of independence within Allied supreme command than to quarrel with civilian authorities at home. The navy got most of what it needed and had little to complain about. Thus, civil-military relations appeared to be in good shape and the future of American democracy seemed to be safe. But were they?

Traditionally, the US army was a small professional force that led a rather mediocre existence on the fringes of society. Only during the Civil War did governments on both sides find it necessary to introduce some form of conscription. In 1914, the army consisted of only 90,000 regulars. Against much opposition, Wilson worked to increase the army in the following years. On 3 June 1916, Congress voted in favour of the National Defence

Act, which allowed the army to grow to 175,000 men. But compared to the mass slaughter on the European battlefield, these numbers were still ridiculously small. When the United States entered the war, something much greater had to be done.

On 26 May 26 1917, Secretary of War Newton D. Baker signed the order appointing General John J. Pershing as Commander of the American Expeditionary Forces. After his arrival in France with just 14,500 men, Pershing toured the Allied armies and talked to their commanders. His findings were devastating. The French had lost their ability to embark on larger offensives and the British were also in terrible shape. Only the provision of new mass armies made victory at all possible, and they could only come from America. In July 1917, Pershing submitted a General Organization Project to Washington in which he demanded at least 1 million men to be sent to France. As the war continued, he raised that number to 3 million!

Congress had already laid the foundations for this huge undertaking, when in May 1917 it passed the Selective Service Act – the introduction of conscription on a scale as never seen before in American history. There would be sufficient men to fill Pershing's army. It proved to be much more difficult to train this huge mass of recruits well and to find enough able officers to lead them. On the battlefields of Europe, the 'doughboys' paid a high price for the improvised nature of the expeditionary force. But their sheer numbers and their élan sufficed to help bring final victory to the Allies.

In Europe, Pershing was given almost a free hand by the authorities at home. Neither President Wilson nor Secretary of War Baker interfered with his military decisions. Baker regarded it as his duty to cover Pershing's back and to provide him with everything he needed. But at home the army had little say in the development of the war effort. The War Ministry and all the other military authorities were simply unable to organise America for war. They lacked the manpower, experience and knowledge. Even the draft was administered by local boards composed of citizens. The provision of arms, munitions and equipment certainly exceeded the abilities of the military administration. Several newly created boards took control of the necessary measures. Their members came mostly from the private sector.

To top it all, the War Industries Board led by the financier Bernard Baruch became the central institution to gear up the American economy for war. Their achievements were impressive. But the capacities of American industry and of shipping remained insufficient to provide the expeditionary force with all the weapons and equipment necessary to fight a modern war. For artillery, machine-guns and aviation, the US army in

Europe depended heavily on deliveries from France and Britain. Again, improvisation was the order of the day. There could be little doubt, however, that the American war economy gave the Allies a decisive advantage in the final months of the war.

Although Pershing could act like a proconsul in Europe, the mobilisation of the American economy and society for war remained firmly in the hands of civilians. That was certainly also true for the formulation of war aims. In this sphere, the President and his advisers had the decisive word.

The military victory had its political costs at home. Civil liberties suffered severely. In contrast to several European powers, civilian authorities in the United States were at the forefront of a clampdown on any resistance to the war on the home front. A Committee for Public Information embarked on a huge propaganda campaign and intimidated journalists from raising any impertinent questions. Congress passed laws against espionage and sedition, which provided the ground for arrests, witch hunts and general mistrust. Vigilante groups harassed suspected dissidents, and these extra-legal measures were tolerated by the authorities. So-called enemy aliens, mostly of German origin, who had lived for generations in the country, fell victim to oppression, persecution and even murder.

The country went through a preposterous phase of war hysteria. It was the Wilson administration and not some military strong men who presided over the erosion of democratic values. The American example demonstrated that civilian control over the war effort did not necessarily guarantee civil rights and the rule of law.[18]

The Ottoman Empire

On 11 June 1913, Grand Vizier Mahmud Shevket was shot dead in Constantinople. Military Governor Ahmed Cemal blamed the murder on the liberal opposition. Many of their leaders were arrested and some of them sentenced to death. The Committee of Union and Progress (CUP), of which Cemal was a leading member, seized power. Military oppression made sure that in

18 Edward M. Coffman, *The War to End All Wars: The American Military Experience in World War I* (Madison, WI: University of Wisconsin Press, 1986); David M. Kennedy, *Over Here. The First World War and American Society* (Oxford University Press, 1980); Jörg Nagler, *Nationale Minoritäten im Krieg: 'Feindliche Ausländer' und die amerikanische Heimatfront während des Ersten Weltkriegs* (Hamburg: Hamburger Edition, 2000); Russel F. Weigley, *History of the United States Army* (Bloomington, IN: Indiana University Press, 1967); Robert H. Zieger, *America's Great War: World War I and the American Experience* (Lanham, MD: Rowman & Littlefield, 2000).

the election for parliament in early 1914 only the CUP was allowed to run. The Ottoman Empire was now firmly in the hands of the Young Turks. It was to remain that way until November 1918.

From its beginning, many of the leading members of the Young Turk movement were army officers. After 1913, they filled the highest military ranks and were in charge of the armed forces. But it would be too simplistic to regard the CUP's rule during the Great War just as a military dictatorship. There were always civilian politicians and intellectuals in important positions. Mehmed Said Halim Pasha, who succeeded the murdered Mahmud Shevket as Grand Vizier and remained in office until 1917, and Mehmed Talat Pasha, Minister of Interior and 1917/18 Grand Vizier, were both civilians. There were also many civilian deputies who sat for the CUP in parliament. Moreover, serious disagreements inside the CUP existed over politics and in particular over the course the internal reforms of the Empire should take.

But parliament had little say during the war. In fact, for the most part, an inner circle – a triumvirate – was in charge of affairs. It consisted of Cemal, Talaat and War Minister General Ismail Enver Pasha. Sultan Mehmed V as constitutional monarch was only a figurehead. Thus, civil-military relations were of a complex nature during the Great War, made even more complicated by the presence of German officers in high-ranking military positions as advisers to their allies the Turks.

When the CUP took power, the Empire was in dire straits. The war against Italy (1911) and the Balkan wars (1912/13) had demonstrated the weakness of the armed forces and cost the Empire huge stretches of territory. The Ottoman Empire was economically backward, financially under the supervision of Western powers and suffered from having a disastrous infrastructure. Even after the loss of most of the European possessions, the Empire still contained a multitude of peoples and creeds: Turks, Arabs, Kurds, Armenians, Jews, Greeks, etc. Many of these groups loathed each other and were deemed by ardent patriots to be less than loyal to the Empire.

As the CUP propagated Turkish nationalism, domestic tensions were on the rise. The Empire was in urgent need of reform, but since the nineteenth century such reforms had made little headway. At least there was now a constitution, and the power of the *ulema* of Muslim authorities had been largely broken. Some progress was made in other areas as well. Work on the railroad to Baghdad continued with German aid, and Enver reorganised the army. Several incompetent officers were fired. In many of their projects, the Ottoman Government received help from Germany. But relations were not always easy. General Otto Liman von Sanders, head of the strong German military mission, tended to be arrogant and overbearing. Many Ottoman officers were disgusted by the 'German tyranny'. Enver himself was infuriated by Liman's efforts to secure key positions for German officers. Trouble was in the making.

When war broke out in Europe, the Ottoman Government hesitated as to how to react. Remaining neutral appeared to be dangerous, as there were fears that the victorious side might proceed to carve up the Empire. Some circles wanted to join the Allies, although there was Turkey's geographically driven conflict with Russia to consider. But neither France nor Britain were interested. Instead, the British Admiralty in highhanded manner seized two battleships, which had been built in Britain and paid for by the Ottomans. There was a public outcry in the Empire. This gave Enver the chance to bring his own ideas to bear. On 2 August 1914, he and Said Halim concluded a secret treaty with the Germans. The two powers were to form an alliance: Germany promised military and financial support, and in return German officers were to obtain key positions in the Ottoman army. The treaty was so secret that even the inner circle of the CUP was not informed. When two German warships arrived in Constantinople and were sold to the Ottoman navy, Enver's scheme had won. By November, the Empire was at war on the side of the Central Powers.

It was almost a miracle that the Ottoman Empire was able to stay in the war for four years. Certainly, without financial aid and material provisions from Germany the Ottoman war effort would have collapsed rather quickly. But the Ottoman authorities managed to put a large army in the field. In spite of mass desertions, there were 800,000 men under arms by 1916. And they fought well. However, at first, things went badly. Enver and his German Chief of Staff, Friedrich Bronsart von Schellendorf, committed a terrible blunder when they ordered an offensive against the Russians through the Caucasus Mountains in the winter of 1914/15. Almost the whole army of 90,000 men was lost. In January 1915, an offensive against the Suez Canal, led by General Ahmed Cemal and his Chief of Staff, Friedrich Kress von Kressenstein, failed too. But defensively the Ottoman army fared better. Throughout 1915, Ottoman forces vigorously defended the Gallipoli peninsula against British attacks. Liman von Sanders was in command, but it was the Turkish officer, Mustafa Kemal, who became a war hero.

In spring of 1916, another triumph occurred. At Kut-al-Amarah, 250 miles south of Baghdad, a British-Indian army surrendered after several months of siege. Khalil Pasha and Field Marshal Colmar von der Goltz, who died during the siege, achieved another famous victory. It was to be the last. In the following two years, the Ottoman armies were forced back by the Allies.

Arab territories were lost to the British and the Arab Revolt. By the end of October 1918, the Empire collapsed.

The population suffered terribly during the war. Food shortages led to hunger and on occasion to famine. Diseases spread and malnutrition caused widespread scurvy. More than 400,000 soldiers died of illness, more than the 350,000 killed in action. Many of these problems were exacerbated by the weak transportation infrastructure and bad management. This also caused dissatisfaction, dissent and violent resistance. As the war dragged on and the Ottoman army suffered ever-more defeats, the Empire began to unravel.

During the Great War, censorship, police control and martial law were standard procedure in almost all belligerent powers. But a high degree of organisation, a well-functioning bureaucracy and good communication were necessary to put such measures into effect. In many parts of the Ottoman Empire, such conditions did not exist. Hence, the authorities reverted to more traditional means of keeping control over the population: brutal force and massacre.

Throughout 1915, Ahmed Cemal, as regional Commander-in-Chief, used drastic measures to stamp out Arab nationalism in Syria. People were hanged, put in prison or deported. Christians and Jews also suffered violence. But much worse was the fate that awaited the Armenians. Some Armenian nationalists had welcomed invading Russian troops in Eastern Anatolia. There had been difficulties with this Christian minority, which was suspected of disloyalty, in previous decades. Now, in spring 1915, the inner circle of the CUP decided to put an end to this problem forever. Hundreds of thousands of Armenians were to be deported into the Syrian Desert. In fact, most men were killed instantly, while women and children were forced on death marches. Army and civilian authorities cooperated in this operation, while Kurdish fighters were allowed to rape, plunder and murder the deportees. More than 1 million people perished. It was the first genocide in the twentieth century.

Some of the German officers serving in the Middle East looked on in horror. But others, like Goltz, sympathised with the removal of the Armenians or even, like Bronsart, positively encouraged this murderous undertaking. Not only for this reason, Goltz and Bronsart were popular with the Young Turks. There was a long tradition of Prussian and German officers serving as advisers in the Ottoman army. Goltz spent many years in the Empire and had gained admiration as a moderniser and someone who paid respect to his Ottoman comrades. He was, therefore, more than welcome when he arrived in Constantinople to help his old friends in the war. But others, notably Liman, were deeply disliked due to their arrogant behaviour. Nobody, however, drew as much hatred as Erich von Falkenhayn, who took over command of a new army group in 1917. Falkenhayn despised and mistrusted all Turks and made no attempts to hide his feelings. Some Ottoman officers simply refused to work with him – most prominently General Mustafa Kemal. In the end, Falkenhayn was recalled.

There were certainly clashes of personality and cultural differences that let to trouble. But the roots of the problem lay deeper. The Ottoman leadership wanted to keep the war effort in their own hands and jealously rejected all tendencies that would reduce them to the status of auxiliary forces. In this respect, Enver and his men were ultimately successful, even if Germans were appointed to High Command positions. Enver demonstrated his independence when, towards the end of the war, he ordered his troops to occupy Baku against German opposition. But this was only a quixotic operation, because the Empire had already lost the war.[19]

Austria-Hungary

One thing is certain: in July 1914, the top-ranking men in the monarchy wanted to have their war. Only the Hungarian Prime Minister Istvan Tisza hesitated for a time. But old Emperor Franz-Joseph, the Austrian ministers and certainly the military commanders were keen to have a go at Serbia. Whether they were also ready for an all-out European war is doubtful, but they did not shy away from that ultimate challenge. Franz Conrad von Hötzendorf, Chief of the General Staff of the Austro-Hungarian army, was a flagrant warmonger anyway. His favourite enemy was Italy, in spite of the fact that, until August 1914, this country was officially an ally of Austria-Hungary and Germany. And it was Conrad who commanded the army of Austria-Hungary for most of the war. But his successes remained limited. At the beginning, he bungled the deployment of his forces in such a way as to weaken them considerably in the face of the Russian invasion. His armies did better than expected by many. But none of the offensives he masterminded led to any lasting

19 Holger Afflerbach, *Falkenhayn. Politisches Denken und Handeln im Kaiserreich* (Munich: R. Oldenbourg Verlag, 1994); Edward J. Erickson, *Ordered to Die. A History of the Ottoman Army in the First World War* (London: Greenwood Press, 2001); Carl A. Krethlow, *Generalfeldmarschall Colmar Freiherr von der Goltz Pascha. Eine Biographie* (Paderborn: Ferdinand Schöningh, 2012); Alan Palmer, *The Decline and Fall of the Ottoman Empire* (London: John Murray, 1992); Jehuda L. Wallach, *Anatomie einer Militärhilfe. Die preussisch-deutschen Militärmissionen in der Türkei, 1835–1919* (Düsseldorf: Droste Verlag, 1976).

positive results. Instead, the army suffered catastrophic losses and became increasingly dependent on German support. In 1916, German generals took in effect supreme command on the Eastern Front. The Austro-Hungarians were reduced to the status of junior partners – to Conrad's dismay.

Conrad was more successful on the home front. For decades, Austria-Hungary had been a tottering Empire. Its many nations were drifting apart. The division between Austria and Hungary, the two halves of the Empire, made a united government and a concerted policy difficult, if not impossible. In Austria, the government was weak. Parliament was divided by nationalistic aspirations and ideological controversy. Since March 1914, parliament had been adjourned. Hungary appeared to be more united and better governed. In reality, however, this meant nothing but the exclusive dominance of Hungarian nationalism over all other minorities. Large parts of the Empire were economically backward, whereas important industrial zones existed in politically less reliable regions such as Bohemia. Against this background the Empire was in danger of breaking up under the strains of war. Political and military leaders therefore held the conviction that only the establishment of an authoritarian regime could hold the Empire together and support the war effort.

The Austrian Prime Minister Karl von Stürgkh saw no alternative than to remain subservient to the military. Stürgkh became a close ally of Conrad. With the help of the Emperor, Stürgkh suspended the rights of citizens, introduced martial law in much of the Empire and allowed the army to take control over civilian bureaucracy. Strict censorship made the public expression of critical opinion next to impossible. Austria came close to a military dictatorship that was barely concealed by a civil dictatorship. Yet, the military still criticised the Austrian Prime Minister for not being efficient enough in mobilising all available resources for the war effort.

Material problems were indeed severe. Foot shortages became so extreme as to lead to widespread unrest. The production of weapons and ammunition, as well as clothes for the army, failed to fill requirements by far. As the war went on, casualties mounted, and people began to go hungry. Stürgkh became one of the most hated men in the Empire. On 21 October 1916, he was shot dead in a hotel in Vienna. But this murder did nothing to remedy the situation. Behind the front, thousands of Polish and Czech soldiers deserted. Army commanders reacted with brutality. Many executions followed. By the end of 1916, Austria-Hungary was on the brink of collapse.

Conrad did not allow the government to interfere in any way with his operations. Emperor Franz-Joseph was too old anyway to act as supreme commander. At least Conrad kept him informed about developments. But Conrad did not desist from meddling in political affairs. He demanded time and again the enforcement of martial law. He pushed for an increase of industrial production and the widening of state control over the economy. The general staff even formulated war aims and came up with plans for the creation of a more centralised Empire after final victory. In Austria-Hungary, civil-military relations clearly tilted in favour of the army.

On 21 November 1916, Franz-Joseph died. Crown Prince Karl, who was just 29 years old, succeeded him. Karl had a military education and served as a high-ranking officer in the army. But Conrad saw to it that Archduke Karl was made to leave High Command. These two men were less than friends. There existed more serious reasons, however, for disagreements. Whereas Conrad was still striving for victory at all costs, Karl felt pity for the suffering of his people and feared for the existence of the Empire. Karl wanted peace as quickly as possible. He also intended to introduce some reforms to ensure the survival of the monarchy. In order to achieve these aims, Karl had to break the overbearing power of the military and their supporters in government. He sacked several ministers, including Istvan Tisza. On 1 March 1917, the young Emperor relieved Conrad of his duties as Chief of General Staff and transferred him to the Italian Front. There, Conrad failed with yet another offensive and was finally sent into retirement on 15 July 1918.

Karl had won an important victory over the military. The civilian government regained control. Already on 30 May 1917, the Emperor had recalled the Austrian Parliament, which now remained in session until the end of the war. Parliament did indeed vote for some reforms, but this was too insufficient to have any lasting effect. Moreover, members were still divided by nationality and were therefore unable to exert much influence. Worst of all, however, Karl's peace initiatives came to nothing. The powerful German ally wanted nothing of it. The Allies refused Karl's overtures and instead made it clear that the dissolution of the Dual Monarchy was one of their major war aims. In April 1918, the Sixtus Affair blew up. Clemenceau publicised Karl's clandestine attempts to come to terms with France. A huge scandal erupted, and the German leaders were outraged by what they saw as Karl's treacherous activities. Foreign Minister Ottokar Count Czernin, who supported Karl's peace policy, was sacked. From now on, Austria-Hungary was in an extremely weak position vis-à-vis Germany.

In effect, the Empire had lost most of its sovereignty. At home, the already serious food shortage became even worse. In several parts of the Empire, strikes broke out. Some army units were hit by mutinies. In February 1918, sailors waged a rebellion at the naval base of Cattaro in Montenegro. The military authorities hit back and executed several of the alleged ringleaders. The victory over Russia did little to alleviate the crisis. On 1 November, Austria-Hungary had to ask for peace terms. The Empire was finished and fell apart.

Until the succession of Emperor Karl, Austria-Hungary was largely in the hands of the military. But with all their enormous powers, the generals never managed to wage anything like total war and mobilise all resources of the Empire. There was far too much opposition in many parts of the monarchy. Military blunders on the battlefields and the inability even to organise sufficient food supplies demonstrated that the army leadership and their civilian helpers were not capable of conducting the war efficiently. Instead, they increasingly lost ground to the overbearing German ally. Clearly, military rule was a failure. But Karl's attempt to turn the tide in civil-military relations came too late and could not save the Empire. Ultimately, the strains of all-out war were too much for Austria-Hungary.[20]

Imperial Germany

Theoretically, the Prussian triangle of leadership was still intact when Imperial Germany went to war in 1914. But this time things were different. In contrast to his grandfather, Emperor Wilhelm II was erratic, less than hardworking and not always abreast of developments. Chancellor Theobald von Bethmann Hollweg was an intelligent man and quite capable of making his point of view heard, but he was no Bismarck. Helmuth von Moltke the younger, Chief of the General Staff and the man to conduct Germany's military operations in war, was an able strategist and got on well with his subordinates, even with the stubborn Erich Ludendorff. But Moltke was a nervous man and certainly not of the same calibre as his famous uncle.

20 Holger H. Herwig, *The First World War: Germany and Austria-Hungary, 1914–1918* (London: Edward Arnold, 1997); Günther Kronenbitter, '"Nur los lassen". Österreich-Ungarn und der Wille zum Krieg', in Johannes Burkhardt *et al.*, *Lange und kurze Wege in den Ersten Weltkrieg. Vier Augsburger Beiträge zur Kriegsursachenforschung* (Munich: Ernst Vögel, 1996), pp. 159–87; Manfried Rauchensteiner, *Der Tod des Doppeladlers: Österreich-Ungarn und der Erste Weltkrieg*, 2nd edn (Graz: Styria, 1994); Max-Stephan Schulze, 'Austria-Hungary's economy in World War I', in Broadberry and Harrison, *Economics of World War I*, pp. 77–111; Graydon A. Tunstall, Jr, 'Austria-Hungary', in Richard F. Hamilton and Holger H. Herwig (eds.), *The Origins of World War I* (Cambridge University Press, 2003), pp. 112–49.

Since 1871, Germany had grown not only in size, but also in economic power. Next to the United States, it possessed the most advanced economy in the world. Consequently, society had become much more differentiated, urbanised and dynamic. The army had increased enormously and had developed into a modern force, depending on sophisticated weaponry and equipment provided by heavy industry. But the army competed for resources, finance and influence with the new and powerful navy.

In this context, it was certainly much more complicated to wage war than in 1870/1. If this was not difficult enough, the triangle of leadership was further challenged by the Reichstag – the German Parliament. In the decades before 1914, parliament increasingly gained ground in German public affairs. After the election of 1912, the Social Democrats became the strongest party in the national assembly and began to cooperate with the parties of the political centre. In Germany – in contrast to other countries – parliament remained in session throughout the war. Even in the darkest hours during the war, the leaders of the German war effort could not ignore the presence of the Reichstag entirely. In the long run, the Reichstag turned out to be the most important stumbling block against the establishment of full military dictatorship. But this did not mean that parliament did not go very far indeed in compromising with the demands of High Command, as long as there was any hope for victory. In any case, after 1916, the traditional triangle of leadership was shattered by the attempt to wage total war.

In Imperial Germany, the officer corps did its best to remain aloof from the rest of society. There was not much love lost between civilians and professional soldiers, and certainly not among soldiers for politicians who attempted to meddle in military affairs. The constitution provided some ground for the distinct position of the military, as the emperor was supreme commander and had the last word in matters concerning the army and the navy. In reality, however, as recruitment for the armed forces was based on conscription, the military could not afford to live an entirely separate life from civilian society. In addition, the Reichstag possessed the right to vote on the military budget. This frequently led to much controversy and made civil-military relations complicated even before 1914.

Most officers displayed or purposed to display a warlike attitude. Several prominent officers, especially the members of the general staff, over the decades openly advocated pre-emptive war against France, Russia and possibly even against Britain. But during the July crisis of 1914, it was Chancellor Bethmann Hollweg who played the decisive role in pushing Europe over the brink into general war. Moltke, who expected the war to be long and catastrophic for the whole continent, hesitated, to the dismay of War Minister Erich von Falkenhayn. The Kaiser, as usual, vacillated.

Moltke was right to be nervous about this war. By September 1914, the German offensive against France had failed. From now on, there was no end to this war in sight. The Kaiser sacked Moltke from High Command and appointed Falkenhayn as his successor. On the Eastern Front, however, there was some reason to celebrate. Generals Paul von Hindenburg and Erich Ludendorff, who in an emergency had taken over command, managed to stop and partly destroy the invading Russian armies in East Prussia. The glorious victory at the Battle of Tannenberg, planned by others, turned these two men into Germany's greatest war heroes.

According to law, the army had to take over supervision of local and regional administration in times of war. This they did. Deputy commanding generals, who answered solely to the Kaiser, became something of regional rulers and there was no one to control them. But these military officials depended on their respective civil administration. The result was a bureaucratic nightmare, with negative effects on the efficiency of the war effort. Of course censorship was introduced. But civil rights were not entirely scrapped. Civilian courts continued to function. Above all, the Reichstag, where even the majority of the Social Democrats had voted in favour of funding the war, remained in session and reconvened every six months. Parliament delegated its legislative powers to the Bundesrat, the assembly of representatives from the state governments. And although the Reichstag retained the right to review the laws issued by the upper house, it never vetoed them. Yet, the potential existed for parliament to play a more prominent role in Germany's conduct of war.

The conduct of operation was left to the military commanders. But the Chancellor still had sufficient influence to intervene with the Kaiser, if he regarded military actions to be counterproductive for political reasons. In 1915 and 1916, Bethmann Hollweg succeeded twice in stopping the navy from waging unlimited submarine warfare, as it risked provoking the intervention of hitherto neutral powers, namely the United States. This led to the resignation of the father of Germany's navy, Admiral Alfred von Tirpitz.

The Kaiser, however, lost ground in the battle for power between the political and military leadership. Wilhelm II was not the man to keep matters in hand. But until the summer of 1916, one important tool of power remained his: the power to appoint and to dismiss high-ranking officials both in government and the military. He had appointed Erich von Falkenhayn to lead the

German armies and he was determined to hold on to him, regardless of opposition.

But the opposition was strong. Arrogant Falkenhayn had not many friends in the army. In the autumn of 1914, he failed to make headway on the Western Front and lost many soldiers in unsuccessful offensives. Bethmann Hollweg tried to convince the Kaiser to replace him with Ludendorff. But Wilhelm II refused. At the same time, controversy arose over strategy. Hindenburg and Ludendorff strongly demanded to put the emphasis on the Eastern Front, where victory over Russia seemed possible. But Falkenhayn was only prepared to send limited forces east. This controversy continued well into 1916.

In February 1916, Falkenhayn ordered a huge offensive against the French fortress of Verdun. This led to one of the most dramatic battles of the war. Casualty figures on both sides were gruesome. More than 300,000 men died. Falkenhayn had little to show for this disaster, as no ground could be gained. At the same time, Hindenburg and Ludendorff grew immensely popular by their victories in the East. Again, Bethmann Hollweg sided with them and exerted pressure on the Kaiser to remove Falkenhayn. In the end, Wilhelm II had to give in. The final straw was Romania's entry into the war, against Falkenhayn's predictions. On 28 August 1916, the Kaiser relieved Falkenhayn of his duties at the Head of High Command and sent him to the Romanian Front. Hindenburg was appointed as his successor, with Ludendorff as deputy. Public opinion was relieved and hopes were high that these two heroes would save the country.

Falkenhayn had warned Wilhelm II that by appointing Hindenburg and Ludendorff he would cease to be emperor. Indeed, aggressive and stubborn Erich Ludendorff was suspected by many to be the true leader of the war effort, sidelining the Kaiser and even Hindenburg. But there was still Bethmann Hollweg, who soon ran into trouble with Ludendorff.

The new High Command had to deal with a crisis of major proportions. Verdun was a catastrophe, at the Somme German armies stood in desperate defence against a huge Allied onslaught, and on the Eastern Front the Brusilov offensive brought the Germans and Austro-Hungarians to disarray and close to collapse. The German armies faced numerically vastly superior enemies, which – at least in the cases of Britain, France and Italy – enjoyed the additional advantage of having direct access to supplies on the world market. By contrast, the Central Powers suffered badly under Allied naval blockade. If there should be any hope to win the war, the German war economy had to grow almost to breaking point or beyond. But so far, the war economy was hampered by many shortcomings. The production of ammunitions, weaponry and equipment was insufficient to supply the armies. Shipbuilding, especially submarines, lagged behind expectations. But problems in regard to raw materials as well as competing interests and insufficient coordination in the private sector amounted to serious obstacles to the increase of war production. Above all, there were not enough workers, as millions of men had been called up to the armed forces.

Hindenburg and Ludendorff therefore aimed at bringing the economy under centralised military control. By aiming at the mobilisation of all material and human resources, they took major steps towards total war. Shortly after taking High Command, the field marshal and the general launched the Hindenburg Programme, which was meant to boost the war economy. Stores of ammunitions were to be doubled, the supply of artillery pieces and machine guns were to be tripled and 3 million additional workers were to be recruited for the arms industry. All factories that were of no importance to the war economy should be shut down and their workers transferred to the arms sector.

In order to put these extraordinary plans into practice, High Command brought the war ministry under its control and created a Supreme War Office, which in effect answered only to Ludendorff. This new department was to control and organise the whole economy. Employers were dismayed and looked for ways to sabotage military rule over industry wherever they could.

Most controversial of all was the intention to introduce a civilian draft for the workforce. The High Command was determined to mobilise every able-bodied man and even women for the war economy. For Bethmann Hollweg, these measures went too far. In autumn 1916, he fought a rearguard battle against the introduction of military control over the economy and particularly against the draft of women. He was partly successful, as the draft of women was dropped. Hence, the government submitted a watered-down version of the Auxiliary Service Law to parliament. It stipulated that all men between the ages of 17 and 60 were to be conscripted for war service. The freedom of workers to change employment would be drastically restricted. But due to the privations of war, the mood in the Reichstag was critical. After intense debates, parliament nevertheless passed the bill on 2 December 1916. But deputies made significant changes in the Act. Trade unions received the right to participate in overseeing the enactment of the law. For the first time in German history, collective bargaining was allowed too.

Ludendorff was, to say the least, less than happy with these developments, and bore a grudge against Bethmann Hollweg. In the end, the Hindenburg Programme failed. Some improvements could be made, but its illusionary aims were never achieved. Resistance by government, parliament, employers and organised labour was too strong. Mass strikes further hampered the programme. Above all, the Hindenburg Programme exceeded Germany's industrial capacity.

The High Command took its revenge on Bethmann Hollweg. At issue were two matters: the reform of suffrage in Prussia and Bethmann Hollweg's peace initiative. But dominating policy discussion was another matter entirely: submarine warfare. Traditionally, the army and the navy were jealous of each other. Generals and admirals rarely cooperated on military matters. But in autumn 1916, they suddenly found common ground. The navy promised to bring Britain to her knees within a few months, if the new submarines were allowed to sink enemy and neutral ships en route to the British Isles without any restrictions. The idea appealed to Ludendorff, who hoped that a decisive blow against Britain might open the way to victory. He was aware, though, that such a ruthless course could provoke the entry of the United States into the war. But if the admirals were right, this risk was worth a try.

Bethmann Hollweg fought tooth and nail against this plan. On 26 December 1916, Hindenburg wrote a harshly worded letter to Bethmann-Hollweg, rejecting all government interference in military operations and particularly on the question of unrestricted submarine warfare. On 5 January 1917, the Allies officially rejected German overtures for peace, putting an end to one of Bethmann Hollweg's initiatives. Now High Command had the stronger arguments, drawing the Kaiser to its side. Bethmann Hollweg was forced to agree to let the submarines loose. On 9 January 1917, Wilhelm II ordered the resumption of unrestricted submarine warfare. On 6 April 1917, the United States declared war on Germany.

Bethmann Hollweg's standing was shattered. In summer 1917, he also lost support in parliament. Ludendorff took the opportunity to issue an ultimatum to Wilhelm II to fire the Chancellor. On 13 July 1917, Bethmann Hollweg resigned. His successors were weak and no match for the generals. The Kaiser too had been reduced to a mere figurehead. Now Ludendorff appeared to be fully in charge. But his power depended on military success. As the German constitution was still intact and the centre-left parties in the Reichstag were about to form a coalition in favour of peace and domestic reform, failure on the battlefields could bring down Ludendorff's reign at any time. If it was a dictatorship at all, its power and duration were more than shaky.

In 1917, Ludendorff's plans had mixed outcomes. The submarine offensive caused significant damage, but not enough to change the course of the war. But Ludendorff could blame hesitant Bethmann Hollweg. On the Western

Front, Allied offensives were beaten back with great losses. After that, the French and British armies lost their ability to launch any further general attack. Italy was dealt a hard blow at Caporetto. It took the United States more than a year to mobilise a sizeable army.

Most important, Russia was on its way out of the war. When the Bolsheviks took power in Petrograd, the chances for final victory in the East were excellent. On 9 December 1917, German, Austro-Hungarian, Ottoman and Russian delegates met at Brest-Litovsk to start peace negotiations. It was in Germany's interest to bring these negotiations quickly to a successful conclusion in order to be able to transfer their forces from the East to the Western Front. But the Bolsheviks intended to gain time. Ludendorff was also dissatisfied with the rather lenient attitude of the German diplomats in these negotiations. In February 1918, he therefore gave orders to resume hostilities.

Lenin saw no alternative other than to sign the peace treaty regardless of the cost. The final meetings at Brest-Litovsk turned into a German diktat handed out by Ludendorff's right-hand man, General Max Hoffmann. When peace was signed on 3 March, Russia lost an enormous amount of territory. Still, Ludendorff's appetite for conquest was not yet satisfied. In the following weeks and months, he pushed his troops ever further to the East. He eventually even intended (and failed) to take Baku. The peace negotiations at Brest-Litovsk demonstrated that Ludendorff by now was determined to formulate war aims himself and therefore sidelined the diplomats in the process. But Germany paid a high price for Ludendorff's expansionist course. A million men remained in the East and were missing in the decisive battles on the Western Front.

Here it came to the crunch. Ludendorff prepared with great skill for a huge final offensive, which, he hoped, would break Allied morale before the Americans would appear in full force on the continent. But after initial success, 'Operation Michael' and subsequent attacks failed. In July, French, British and American forces went on the counter-offensive and forced the Germans into retreat. The army and the home front began to disintegrate. The war was lost.

On 29 September Ludendorff admitted as much, blaming his 'unreliable' troops. High Command now handed power to the politicians in government and parliament, who were left with the task of liquidating the war and carrying the burden of defeat. By the end of October, the new Chancellor Prince Max von Baden demanded that the Kaiser get rid of Ludendorff. On 26 October, in an angry meeting with Wilhelm II and Hindenburg, Ludendorff resigned. He fled into temporary exile in Sweden.

From summer 1916 until autumn 1918, Hindenburg and to a greater extent Ludendorff were the strongmen of Germany. They destroyed the traditional triangle of leadership. But they failed to establish military dictatorship. The constitution, the Reichstag and opposition in the general public prevented them from taking full control. The attempt to completely mobilise all resources overburdened state, society and the economy. Total war proved to be impossible. But it was defeat in the West that finally brought these strongmen down. With them, the monarchy went soon afterwards. In defeat and revolution, Germany faced a bleak future.[21]

The arrogant attitude of the German military to anything civilian certainly contributed to the rise of Hindenburg and Ludendorff, but they never managed to rid themselves completely of civilian interference. On the periphery of the German Empire militarist inclinations bore more radical fruits. In German East Africa, the governor was in charge of the colony and supervised the running of affairs. He was also supreme commander. The commander of the colonial armed force (*Schutztruppe*) was limited to immediate military duties. In case of general war, the military prospects for the colony appeared to be almost hopeless. The authorities in Berlin therefore forbade the defence of the coastline and ordered the retreat of all armed forces into the interior to protect valuable goods and above all the civil population of European origin. Governor Heinrich Schnee was determined to execute this plan.

In January 1914, the new commander of the colonial force, Paul von Lettow-Vorbeck, arrived in Dar es Salaam. He had different ideas and very little respect for civil authorities. In case of war, Lettow-Vorbeck intended to fight aggressively and tie up as many Allied forces as possible in East Africa in order to help the fatherland in its struggle in Europe. And certainly he had little taste for sitting on the sidelines somewhere in the bush, while other officers gained glory on the battlefield.

Lettow-Vorbeck toured the colony to drum up support for his plans among German settlers, several of whom were retired officers. When war did indeed

21 Robert B. Asprey, *The German High Command at War: Hindenburg and Ludendorff and the First World War* (New York: W. Morrow, 1991); Roger Chickering, *Imperial Germany and the Great War, 1914–1918* (Cambridge University Press, 1998); Stig Förster, 'Ein militarisiertes Land? Zur gesellschaftlichen Stellung des Militärs im Deutschen Kaiserreich', in Bernd Heidenreich and Sönke Neitzel (eds.), *Das Deutsche Kaiserreich, 1890–1914* (Paderborn: Ferdinand Schöningh, 2011), pp. 157–74; Martin Kitchen, *The Silent Dictatorship: The Politics of the German High Command under Hindenburg and Ludendorff, 1916–1918* (London: Croom Helm, 1976); Manfred Nebelin, *Ludendorff. Diktator im Ersten Weltkrieg* (Munich: Siedler Verlag, 2010); Markus Pöhlmann, 'Der "moderne Alexander" im Maschinenkrieg. Erich Ludendorff. 1865–1937', in Stig Förster *et al.* (eds.), *Kriegsherren der Weltgeschichte: 22 historische Portraits* (Munich: C. H. Beck, 2006), pp. 268–85.

break out, Schnee and Lettow-Vorbeck were at loggerheads. As Schnee retreated into the interior and issued orders not to resist British landings on the coast, Lettow-Vorbeck sent his officers to countermand them. This led to a military confrontation with British forces. Lettow-Vorbeck went even further and authorised attacks into British East Africa. Schnee was outraged and threatened Lettow-Vorbeck with court-martial; Lettow-Vorbeck simply ignored him. Instead, he prepared for battle. In early November 1914, numerically superior British forces landed at Tanga. Lettow-Vorbeck, who had assembled almost all his troops in the area, beat them decisively. Now the man was a war hero. Schnee had no choice but to succumb to Lettow-Vorbeck, who continued the fight until the end of the war. Schnee joined his camp in retreat in the latter years of the war and was treated almost as a prisoner. East Africa suffered severely from Lettow-Vorbeck's adventure. The whole story was an extreme example of distorted civil-military relations. In fact, Lettow-Vorbeck's behaviour constituted nothing but a military coup.[22]

Conclusion

Lettow-Vorbeck's adventure in East Africa was just a sideshow, albeit an interesting one. In other theatres, civil-military relations proved to be a much more complicated affair. Political, social and economic structures were far too complex to allow for simple solutions. Naturally, the military gained power in the initial stages of the war. But this was a war of long duration; hence, all major powers underwent significant changes, as the war went on. Developments were different, according to the respective social and political systems. In some cases, the results were surprising. Who would have expected that in Britain parliament played almost no role at all, whereas in Imperial Germany the Reichstag became a major stumbling block to the establishment of military dictatorship?

Outside Europe, things were different. Within the Ottoman Empire, civil-military relations were somewhat in harmony, as civilian politicians and generals of the CUP were firmly in control. These men closely cooperated and achieved some positive results in the face of extremely difficult odds. But their greatest 'achievement' was the mass murder of the Armenians. Even so, the collapse and destruction of the Empire could not be prevented. Japan

22 See Tanja Bührer, *Die Kaiserliche Schutztruppe für Deutsch-Ostafrika: Koloniale Sicherheitspolitik und transkulturelle Kriegführung, 1885 bis 1918* (Munich: R. Oldenbourg Verlag, 2011), pp. 401–77.

never came close enough to danger to have to wage total war. Civil-military relations in that country had since the Meiji Restoration been problematical, with the army and the navy being in very powerful positions. But the war itself did not put these relations to test. Yet, expansionist policy and domestic difficulties demonstrated that the armed forces were always ready to make their influence felt. For the time being, however, all this resulted in compromise and some liberal reforms. Upon entering the war, the United States was more than ready to mobilise the whole country. The results were impressive. But in contrast to all other powers, civilian administrators, mostly drawn from the private sector, were firmly in control of the war effort on the home front. Interestingly enough, however, this did not result in protection of civil liberties. Quite to the contrary, the ruthless rule of the majority allowed brutal suppression of all opposition. Civilian control of the war effort, therefore, is not necessarily good news for ordinary people.

The turning point in the European theatre came in 1916/17. By then, the means of traditional, almost conservative, warfare had been exhausted. It would have been reasonable to find ways at this time to end this terrible conflagration. But neither side was ready to compromise. The numbers of casualties were already too high and the hatred generated everywhere was too deep for any leadership to give in. Therefore, the war effort was intensified, regardless of the consequences. The attempt to wage total war became the order of the day. The problem was that no power was prepared for this extreme measure. Some of the countries involved simply collapsed before this challenge. This was certainly true of Russia and Austria-Hungary. Italy only escaped by chance. France, Britain and Germany were in a stronger position to wage war in the extreme. The Western Allies were lucky to withstand the consequences, as eventually the United States bailed them out. But nobody came to the rescue of Germany.

The tendency to wage total war presented new problems in the configuration of civil-military relations. If all available resources were to be mobilised, the overall question as to who was to run the war became all the more important. Britain, typically, compromised. France, in the end, handed power over to a strong-willed politician. In Germany, the military attempted to take control, but failed to achieve its aims.

Civil-military relations under the impact of the slide towards total war produced different outcomes. In some cases, the efforts of those in charge of the war ended in collapse and revolution. In others, they resulted in victory, in part by sheer luck. But the central questions raised by Clausewitz and Moltke found no lasting answers. They linger on to the present day.

5

Revolution

RICHARD BESSEL

> These two phenomena, world war and world revolution, are much more closely inter-related than a first glance would indicate. They are two sides of an event of cosmic significance, whose outbreak and origins are interdependent in numerous respects.[1]

> Arising from the war, the social revolution did not emerge so much from the factory as from the barracks.[2]

> A war of the masses ends with the triumph of the masses ... The bourgeois revolution of 1789 – which was revolution and war in one – opened the gates of the world to the bourgeoisie ... The present revolution, which is also a war, seems to open the gates of the future to the masses, who have served their apprenticeship of blood and death in the trenches.[3]

> All around us madness and danger rules, [. . .] a thickening dark cloud is gathering above us, and a great black abyss opens before us.[4]

The First World War was the great catalyst for revolution in the twentieth century. Not only did it lead directly to political revolution, understood as 'the destruction of an independent state by members of its own society and its replacement by a regime based on new political principles';[5] it also led to revolution in a deeper sense, if we understand revolution more broadly as the erosion and dissolution of established hierarchies and the reconstruction of

1 Ernst Jünger, 'Total mobilization', in Richard Wolin (ed.), *The Heidegger Controversy: A Critical Reader* (New York: Columbia University Press, 1991), p. 123.

2 Otto Bauer, *Die österreichische Revolution* (Vienna: Volksbuchhandlung, 1923), p. 96.

3 Benito Mussolini, *Opera omnia*, ed. E. and D. Susmel, 35 vols. (Florence: La Fenice, 1951–63), speech at Bologna, 19 May 1918, vol. XI, p. 87; *Il Popolo d'Italia*, 5 and 8 March 1919, vol. XII, pp. 268, 310. Quoted in Christopher Seton-Watson, *Italy from Liberalism to Fascism* (London: Methuen, 1967), p. 517.

4 Solomon Grigor'evich Gurevich, quoted in Michael C. Hickey, 'Revolution on the Jewish street: Smolensk, 1917', *Journal of Social History*, 31:4 (1998), p. 838.

5 Stephen M. Walt, 'Revolution and war', *World Politics*, 44:3 (1992), p. 323.

societies as well as polities on the basis of new concepts, allegiances and structures of power and authority. The First World War spread destruction over wide swathes of territory; it triggered vast campaigns of forced removal; it shattered communities; it strengthened the hand of those who sought the end of old dynastic regimes; it undermined the legitimacy of states that seemed to offer their populations never-ending privation and ever-rising casualties. In short, the war created the conditions for revolution.

The aim of this chapter is not so much to sketch a history of revolution in 1917 or 1918 as to focus on the causal relationship between the First World War and the revolutionary transformations that took place towards its end. The revolutionary upheaval that was a consequence of military defeat for the great European empires – those of the Romanovs, Hohenzollerns and Habsburgs – together with the political challenges that shook Allied and neutral countries around the world, led to what many at the time were convinced was the dawn of a new revolutionary age. Yet that revolutionary age did not take the shape envisaged by those who had looked forward to the birth of a brave new socialist world. For revolution during and after the First World War was inspired not just by socialism, but also by nationalism; it was driven not just by political conviction, but also by anger over hardships caused by war; and it involved not just the destruction of old power structures, but also the erosion of norms of civilised behaviour.

The contrast with the pre-1914 world was profound. While it may not have seemed so at the time, Europe on the eve of the First World War appears at least in hindsight to have been remarkably stable. The ruling systems of the major European powers appeared strong; social and economic hierarchies appeared firmly in place; European domination around the globe appeared to be secure. In Russia, revolution had been beaten back after the outburst of 1905; and it was the – now largely forgotten – ostentatious celebration of the tercentenary of the Romanov dynasty in 1913 rather than memories of the Petrograd Soviet that seemed to express the spirit of the age.[6] Germany too saw self-congratulatory celebrations in the 'festive year' 1913, commemorating the centenary of the Battle of the Nations and the silver jubilee of Kaiser Wilhelm II, staged to celebrate a quarter of a century of peace and progress.[7] The Hohenzollern state appeared strong and confident, certainly not without political and social tensions, but with an increasingly large number of people

6 See Orlando Figes, *A People's Tragedy: The Russian Revolution, 1891–1924* (London: Jonathan Cape, 1996), pp. 3–6.

7 Jeffrey R. Smith, *A People's War: Germany's Political Revolution, 1913–1918* (Lanham, MD: University Press of America, 2007), pp. 25–49.

participating in the political system (as evidenced by voting) and with a growing Socialist Party set on a reformist rather than revolutionary path.

The impression of peaceful progress rather than revolutionary upheaval was underpinned by substantial growth among Europe's industrial economies in the years before the First World War, most notably those of Germany and Russia – the two most prominent states whose governments soon would be overthrown through revolution. Economic development fuelled the growth of industrial workforces, and consequently of political organisations that aimed to represent working-class interests, as well as rising incomes and living standards. In 1913, therefore, Europe did not appear to be on the verge of a revolutionary transformation. Had it not been for the outbreak of war in 1914, it is doubtful whether such a wave of revolution would have swept across Europe in the second decade of the twentieth century.

The picture of a largely peaceful pre-1914 Europe, of a continent seemingly on a path of gradual political, economic and social progress, excludes the Balkans. Yet the Balkans should not be excluded from the discussion. In South-Eastern Europe, war began not in 1914, but in 1912, and the revolutionary consequences of war were a matter not so much of socialist as of nationalist transformations that altered politics and society. The Balkan wars of 1912 to 1913, Richard Hall has written, 'represent the beginning of an era in European history dominated by nationalism and conflict' and 'introduced an age of modern warfare encompassing mass armies, machines, and entire civilian populations'.[8] What occurred in the Balkans – and one should not forget that the First World War began in the Balkans and that some of the areas most damaged by that war were in the Balkans – heralded nationalist upheavals across Eastern Europe; and the violence that was to dissolve the glue of civilisation across a continent already was undermining society and community in the Balkans before the outbreak of the Great War in August 1914.

There was no more ferocious assault on civilised values than the onslaught against the Armenians of eastern Anatolia that occurred in what Ronald Suny has described as 'the fierce context of the First World War'.[9] It began with administrative measures taken by the Ottoman Government between the autumn of 1914 and the summer of 1915 and culminated in the massacre and

8 Richard C. Hall, *The Balkan Wars, 1912–1913: Prelude to the First World War* (London: Routledge, 2000), pp. ix, 130.

9 Thus, Suny describes the radicalisation of Young Turk policies in the Ottoman Empire at the time. See Ronald Suny, 'Explaining genocide: the fate of the Armenians in the late Ottoman Empire', in Richard Bessel and Claudia Haake (eds.), *Removing Peoples. Forced Removal in the Modern World* (Oxford University Press, 2009), p. 220.

deportation of roughly 1 million people in 1916.[10] This first great 'ethnic cleansing' of the twentieth century was in its way a revolutionary product of the First World War. It occurred in the wake of a Russian military campaign against the Ottomans, resulted in hundreds of thousands of Armenians fleeing to the Russian Empire, where many stayed for years,[11] and constituted a key event in the wartime histories of two of the multi-national empires that would not survive into the post-war world.

When revolution broke out during the First World War, it broke out first in Russia. And it was war that generated the tensions and pressures that precipitated the Russian Revolution. The failure to pursue the war successfully, Russia's huge military losses (dead, wounded and soldiers taken prisoner) and the destruction of social and economic networks in the western provinces of the Russian Empire fuelled unrest and fostered revolution. Rapid turnover in the Russian army, which lost more men than any other army during the First World War, undermined discipline and morale. A huge 'army of the rear', which numbered some 2 million men in January 1917 and which was stationed in and around many towns including Petrograd, consisted in large measure of poorly trained, poorly led and poorly disciplined replacement units. At the same time, the Russian war economy had drawn large numbers of people into munitions and other factories, roughly a quarter of a million in Petrograd alone. And they had to be fed. So it was of critical importance that these changes took place against the background of what was described in Russian newspapers during 1916 as a wartime 'food-supply crisis', due in large measure to government mismanagement: 'A grain-rich country – the world's leading exporter of grain – had found itself facing grain shortages by the third winter of the war.'[12] Not surprisingly, there was substantial inflation, and the wages of most workers did not keep pace with the rising cost of food.

The food crisis was the catalyst for the revolution that brought down the tsarist regime in February/March 1917. The immediate spark, in March 1917, was provided by protests in Petrograd over bread shortages, coinciding with a

10 See Donald Bloxham, *The Great Game of Genocide: Imperialism, Nationalism, and the Destruction of the Ottoman Armenians* (Oxford University Press, 2005).

11 Joshua Sanborn, 'Unsettling the empire: violent migrations and social disaster in Russia during World War I', *Journal of Modern History*, 77:2 (2005), p. 313. On the conflict between the Ottoman and Russian empires, see Michael A. Reynolds, *Shattering Empires: The Clash and Collapse of the Ottoman and Russian Empires* (Cambridge University Press, 2011).

12 Peter Holquist, *Making War, Forging Revolution. Russia's Continuum of Crisis* (Cambridge, MA: Harvard University Press, 2002), pp. 30, 44. See also Norman Stone, *The Eastern Front 1914–1917* (London: Hodder & Stoughton, 1975), pp. 291–301.

lock-out at the Putilov armaments works. Within a few days, replacement troops around the city had mutinied, workers' stoppages had led to a general strike and protests over bread shortages had escalated into riots. Within the army, discipline disintegrated and the number of desertions rose steeply from March 1917. As replacement troops increasingly joined what in effect had become an uprising, armed groups began to take over the capital. Government buildings were seized and police disarmed, and with the 'soldiers' outbreak' of 12 March, in the words of P. N. Miliukov (Foreign Minister in the Provisional Government), 'a real revolution broke out'.[13]

The course of the Russian Revolution during 1917, a course that eventually led to the successful coup by Lenin's Bolsheviks in the autumn, was bound up with Russia's involvement in the First World War. The failure of the Provisional Government to maintain its grip on power was due in no small measure to its determination to continue Russia's participation in the war despite widespread war-weariness and popular demands that Russia exit from the conflict. The hope that the population of the Empire would unite behind the Provisional Government to pursue the war to a successful conclusion proved an illusion. Military failure, in the shape of the collapse of the July offensive in Galicia, led to the crumbling of the army itself and opened the door to the more radical politics of those who promised an early exit from the war. And it was only the Bolsheviks who advocated peace unequivocally. Revolution in Russia thus stemmed directly from war-related problems of provision, war-weariness and the disintegration of the army under the pressures created by an unsuccessful war.

Although the outcome was different, revolution in Germany also was a consequence of military disaster after the state had been weakened economically and socially; and the immediate causes also stemmed from war-related problems of provision, war-weariness and the disintegration of the armed forces. As in Russia, in Germany the revolutionary events were sparked by shortages, strikes among industrial workers and discontent among military personnel. The strains of war undermined the legitimacy of the imperial regime and the 'silent' military dictatorship into which it degenerated[14] – a regime that was able neither to mitigate the hardships of the civilian population nor to bring the war to the promised victorious conclusion. As the conflict dragged on, discontent mounted, and soldiers on leave contributed to the

13 Quoted in A. M. Nikolaieff, 'The February Revolution and the Russian Army', *Russian Review*, 6(1) (1946), 20.

14 Martin Kitchen, *The Silent Dictatorship. The Politics of the German High Command under Hindenburg and Ludendorff, 1916–1918* (New York: Holmes & Meier, 1976).

deterioration of civilian morale with their accounts from the front. In the summer of 1917, as the war was about to enter its fourth year, the army command in Karlsruhe reported:

> In so far as one is in a position to draw a picture of the morale of the soldiers from letters from the military post, conversations etc., one certainly would not be exaggerating if one were to prophesy a result with the next political elections that will open the eyes of certain statesmen. The men in field grey are angry and if they finally get the opportunity to express their feelings about what one justifiably can hope for from the new political orientation, the overt and covert opponents of that orientation would experience the shock of their lives.[15]

The shock arrived in 1918. In January 1918, roughly 400,000 workers in Berlin munitions and metal-working factories went out on strike. While the German military offensive in the spring of 1918 initially raised hopes for a positive and rapid conclusion to the war, after it stalled and then was reversed in the summer, civilian and military morale plummeted. As in Russia, military defeat led to revolution. With the military collapse in the autumn of 1918, support for the imperial state evaporated. The deterioration of military discipline, the crumbling of the authoritarian governing system, the external pressure from the Allies (in particular, the 'Fourteen Points' articulated by American President Woodrow Wilson) alongside extreme war-weariness at home, and the example of Russia that inspired the workers' and soldiers' councils that emerged in Germany in late 1918 – combined to create a crisis of legitimacy. What this meant within the German armed forces was summed up neatly in a conversation between two soldiers in a reserve military hospital in Bremerhaven in mid August 1918 (as overheard by a police spy): 'You see comrade [*Kamerad*], we've had it, no one believes in victory any more, what the newspapers write is all lies and deception. [. . .] If we quit now, we still can save a lot, money, people. [. . .] We are bringing our comrades to the point that they all get involved like in Russia, we have nothing more to lose.'[16]

The German Revolution itself began with a revolt by sailors and by soldiers stationed within the country. The immediate spark was the order of 28 October 1918 by the Imperial Naval Command to send out the fleet to confront the

15 Generallandesarchiv Karlsruhe, 456/E.V.8, Bund 86: Stellv. Gen. Kdo. XIV. A.K. [to the Kriegsamt, Abteilung für Volksernährungsfragen, Berlin], [Karlsruhe], 1.7.17.

16 'Aus einem belauschten gespräch zweier Soldaten im Reservelazarett Bremerhaven. Mitteilung des Kommandanten der Befestungen an der Wesermündung vom 14.8.1918', in Jörg Berlin (ed.), *Die deutsche Revolution 1918/19. Quellen und Dokumente* (Cologne: Pahl-Rugenstein, 1979), p. 110.

Royal Navy in a final battle. After having spent much of the war in port, German sailors had little enthusiasm to be sacrificed in a suicide mission for what, by this point, obviously was a lost cause and could serve only to scupper Armistice negotiations. Instead, they mutinied. Unrest spread, and by 30 October it had overwhelmed the naval base at Kiel and industrial workers joined in; a week later the rebellion had reached the port cities of Bremen, Lübeck, Wismar, Cuxhaven, Wilhelmshaven, Bremerhaven and Hamburg, and then spread to cities and towns in the interior. Revolutionary sailors and soldiers acted as missionaries for revolution, and workers' and soldiers' councils formed.[17] By 9 November, the old regime had been overwhelmed by protest, a republic was declared and the Kaiser abdicated. During the weeks and months that followed, what initially had been a remarkably peaceful political transition turned increasingly violent, not least with the intervention of Freikorps units (led by war veterans) that were used by Germany's provisional government to suppress left-wing revolutionary activity. The First World War bankrupted the old regime in every sense – militarily, politically, financially and morally – and paved the way for revolution in Germany, and for its suppression.

The end of the war and the revolutionary upheaval in Austria-Hungary bore similarities to those in Germany, but within a complicated multi-national and multi-ethnic context. It generally has been assumed that the collapse of the Austro-Hungarian Empire and the revolutionary transformations that occurred in its wake were due primarily to nationalism, to the long-term development of national consciousnesses and to nationalist movements that were able to seize their chance as the Habsburg state disintegrated at the end of the war.[18] There can be little doubt that Slav nationalisms eroded the ties that had bound the multi-ethnic state together and contributed to the upheavals that transformed the Habsburg Empire into a patchwork of smaller states in 1918 and 1919. However, the immediate consequences of Austro-Hungarian participation in the First World War were at least as important as long-term, nationalist undercurrents in fomenting revolution.

17 Ulrich Kluge, 'Militärrevolte und Staatsumsturz. Ausbreitung und Konsolidierung der Räteorganisation im rheinisch-westfälischen Industriegebiet', in Reinhard Rürup (ed.), *Arbeiter- und Soldatenräte im rheinisch-westfälischen Industriegebiet* (Wuppertal: Hammer, 1975), pp. 39–82.

18 Clifford F. Wargelin, 'A high price for bread: the first treaty of Brest-Litovsk and the break-up of Austria-Hungary, 1917–1918', *International History Review*, 19:4 (1997), pp. 757–8. Wargalin outlines this traditional position as an introduction to his attempt to offer a rather different perspective that privileges developments during the final stages of the war.

Prominent among these were the acute food shortages that affected the Austrian parts of the Empire in 1917 to 1918. According to Clifford Wargelin, 'by the end of 1917, the domestic food supply had shrunk so far that the inhabitants of Austria's cities faced starvation, confronting the government for the first time with the spectre of serious internal unrest.'[19] Increasingly, strikes in Austria took the form of protests against high food prices and poor food distribution. As in Russia in 1917 and in Germany in 1918, food shortages undermined the legitimacy of the state and demands for bread and peace fuelled unrest that eventually provided a spark for revolution. In January 1918, strikes broke out in various parts of the Habsburg Empire, with calls for the election of workers' and soldiers' councils and for 'immediate general peace', as well as for the end of the existing government; and on 14 January, after an announcement that the flour ration in Austrian cities would be halved, industrial workers at the Daimler-Motorenwerke in Wiener Neustadt downed tools. Within a few days, nearly 1 million workers had stopped work across Austria, Hungary, Galicia and Moravia; demands grew for 'the most speedy end to the war' and for national self-determination.[20] (News of the strikes in Austria also inspired workers to strike in Berlin at the end of January.) This was followed at the beginning of February by a short-lived sailors' mutiny, driven by demands for better food, democracy and an immediate peace on the basis of Wilson's Fourteen Points, at Cattaro (Kotor) in Montenegro, one of the main bases for the Austro-Hungarian navy.[21] Mutinies followed among army units in the Balkans, amidst calls for peace and a 'socialist revolution', as well as crude expressions of anti-Semitism.[22]

As in Germany, in Austria-Hungary the January strikes did not lead immediately to revolution, but, as in Germany, they provided a foretaste of what was to come later in the year. Central to the dissolution of the Habsburg Empire was the fate of its army. The fighting record of the Austro-Hungarian army during the First World War was not unblemished, having had to be

19 Wargelin, 'A high price for bread', p. 762.

20 Bauer, *Die österreichische Revolution*, p. 63; Reinhard J. Sieder, 'Behind the lines: working-class family life in wartime Vienna', in Richard Wall and Jay Winter (eds.), *The Upheaval of War: Family, Work and Welfare in Europe, 1914–1918* (Cambridge University Press, 1988), pp. 125–8; Wargelin, 'A high price for bread', p. 777. For the strikes, see Richard G. Plaschka *et al.*, *Innere Front. Militärassistenz, Widerstand und Umsturz in der Donaumonarchie 1918* (Munich: R. Oldenbourg Verlag, 1974), vol. 1, pp. 59–106, 251–74.

21 Bauer, *Die österreichische Revolution*, p. 66; Plaschka *et al.*, *Innere Front*, vol. 1, pp. 107–48; Clifford F. Wargelin, 'A high price for bread', p. 783. The sailors in question were nearly all South Slavs.

22 Plaschka *et al.*, *Innere Front*, vol. 1, pp. 148–58, 251–74, and on anti-Semitic outbursts, pp. 385–6.

rescued repeatedly by their German allies and losing enormous numbers of soldiers as prisoners. The release and return of soldiers who had been in Russian captivity in 1917 helped to spread the revolutionary message; and in the last months of the war the Austro-Hungarian army, once a main pillar of the multi-ethnic Empire, crumbled. By the autumn of 1918, the army was acutely short of supplies and its soldiers were going hungry; increasing incidence of desertion left the army in no position to fight effectively.[23] Once it became apparent, with the failure of the Austrian offensive in Italy and the German defeats in the West, that the war was lost, the Habsburg Empire's army fell apart as military discipline collapsed.[24] Non-Germans in the Habsburg armed forces no longer proved willing to fight and die for the Empire; towards the end of October 1918, Slav and Hungarian soldiers were refusing to obey their officers; on 23 October, Croatian troops in Fiume mutinied and on 28 October, Croatian sailors began to mutiny as well; one unit after another refused to obey orders; and in the end not even German-Austrian units could be counted on and military discipline had broken down even in barracks in Vienna.[25] As with their German allies, in the Austro-Hungarian army growing animosity was directed against officers by the men under their command, men who were increasingly less willing to follow orders that might lead to their deaths and seemed designed only to prolong a lost war.

The revolutionary upheavals in Central and Eastern Europe had some, rather more muted, parallels in the West. In France, waves of strikes occurred in the metal industry between July 1916 and May 1918, and in the spring of 1917 strikes spread through the French workforce, with calls for higher wages and an end to the war; and in May and June 1917, the French army suffered mutinies, a 'crisis of discipline' that affected perhaps half the French divisions on the Western Front, sometimes accompanied by calls of 'Vive la Révolution' as soldiers staged demonstrations and refused to go back to the front lines.[26]

23 Bauer, *Die österreichische Revolution*, pp. 71–2; Plaschka *et al.*, *Innere Front*, vol. II, pp. 62–103.

24 Karel Pichlík, 'Der militärische Zusammenbruch der Mittelmächte im Jahre 1918', in Richard G. Plaschka and Karlheinz Mack (eds.), *Die Auflösung des Habsburgerreiches. Zusammenbruch und Neuorientierung im Donauraum* (Munich: R. Oldenbourg Verlag, 1970), pp. 249–65.

25 Bauer, *Die österreichische Revolution*, pp. 79, 82, 90–2, 97; Manfred Reichensteiner, *Der Tod des Doppeladlers. Österreich-Ungarn und der Erste Weltkrieg* (Graz, Vienna and Cologne: Styria Verlag, 1993), pp. 612–14.

26 Guy Pedroncini, *Les Mutineries de 1917*, 3rd edn (Paris: Presses Universitaires de France, 1996); Leonard V. Smith *et al.*, *France and the Great War* (Cambridge University Press, 2003), pp. 113–45.

Nevertheless, worrying though the unrest was, it was contained, and did not develop into a fully-fledged French revolution. In northern Italy, too, the spring and summer of 1917 saw disturbances and protests (often by women) against rising prices, food shortages and the continuation of the war, culminating in major riots in Turin in August 1917 that had been triggered by a bread shortage. 'The shadow of revolution had fallen on Italy.'[27] But it remained only a shadow, and not until after the 'mutilated peace' did an explosion of unrest bring Italy to the brink of revolution during the *biennio rosso* ('the two red years'), and subsequently to fascism. In Britain, the extent and frequency of strikes increased during the war, but only in Ireland with the Easter Rising in Dublin, the nationalist urban insurrection launched on 24 April 1916 by the Irish Volunteers, did a revolutionary initiative really erupt in the United Kingdom during wartime, and subsequently develop into what William Kautt has termed a 'people's war'.[28] However, the Easter Rising had no real impact on Irish soldiers fighting in British uniform on the European continent, and was brutally suppressed; indeed, the rising was significant far more with regard to what followed in the coming years – Irish independence and civil war – than for the threat it may have posed to British rule at the time. Revolutionary unrest, if not successful revolution, also extended to neutral Spain, which witnessed its *Trienio Bolchevique* ('the three Bolshevik years') from 1918 to 1920, when unrest spread across the rural south.[29]

Unlike the imperial states of Central and Eastern Europe, the Western powers were not pushed across the threshold to revolution by the discontent that spread through soldiers' ranks and civilian workforces. Of course, it helped to have been on the winning side, although the prospect that France or Britain would emerge victorious was far from obvious in 1917. Furthermore, the problems of supplying food to the civilian population were more severe in Russia, Germany and Austria-Hungary than in the Western countries. But there was another important cause of the difference between France, Britain and even Italy, on the one hand, and Russia, Germany and Austria-Hungary, on the other. Unlike the former, the latter entered the war as autocratic political formations in which the majority of the population had limited, if any, input. Participation in the war, and the sacrifices that were demanded of the mass of the population,

27 Seton-Watson, *Italy from Liberalism to Fascism*, p. 471.

28 William H. Kautt, *The Anglo-Irish War, 1916–1921. A People's War* (Westport, CT and London: Praeger Press, 1999).

29 See Edward E. Malefakis, *Agrarian Reform and Peasant Revolution in Spain: Origins of the Civil War* (New Haven, CT: Yale University Press, 1970); and Gerald H. Meaker, *The Revolutionary Left in Spain 1914–1923* (Stanford University Press, 1974).

led to increasingly loud calls for popular participation in the political system. As casualties mounted, prices rose and food became scarce, economic and political demands inevitably were linked. Protest against deteriorating living conditions and bread shortages in Russia, Germany or Austria-Hungary spilled over into demands for a meaningful say in the political system, for democratic government and popular sovereignty, and thus posed a challenge to existing governing structures in a way that unrest in France, for example, did not.

This was one set of causes for the eruption of revolution in the East rather than the West during the First World War. The course of the war itself was another. As many men fought and died on the Eastern Front as on the Western Front during the First World War; the country that suffered the highest number of casualties overall was Russia (which mobilised roughly 15.8 million men in its armed forces and lost altogether roughly 3.5 million dead, military and civilian); and the country that suffered the highest number of casualties relative to its population was Serbia (with over 16 per cent of the entire population killed), followed by Romania. In the East, unlike in the West, the war was more a war of movement, as the military front moved back and forth across vast areas, and the conflict led to a crumbling of the social and economic cement that had held systems of rule together. A central element of that crumbling was the forced removal of large numbers of people. Perhaps because of the even greater scale of forced removal during and after the Second World War, we tend to forget the magnitude of what happened during the First. Nevertheless, during the First World War, millions of people were affected. 'Refugees', writes Pierre Purseigle, 'were in many ways the paradigmatic embodiment of the culture of warfare in 1914–1918'.[30]

Within Europe, at least 7.7 million people were displaced during the First World War,[31] and while all sides engaged in the practice, this was in large measure an Eastern European story, where communities were destroyed as their populations were violently uprooted. The worst of this coincided with the 'Great Retreat' from April to October 1915 (when the Russian army was driven from Galicia and Poland), when at least 300,000 Lithuanians, 250,000

30 Pierre Purseigle, '"A wave on to our shores": the exile and resettlement of refugees from the Western Front, 1914–1918', *Contemporary European History*, 16, Special Issue 4 (2007), p. 432.

31 Nick Baron and Peter Gatrell, 'Population displacement, state-building and social identity in the lands of the former Russian Empire, 1917–1923', *Kritika: Explorations in Russian and Eurasian History*, 4:1 (2003), p. 61; Peter Gatrell, 'Introduction: world wars and population displacement in Europe in the twentieth century', *Contemporary European History*, 16, Special Issue 4 (2007), p. 418; Alan Kramer, 'Deportationen', in Gerhard Hirschfeld *et al.* (eds.), *Enzyklopädie Erster Weltkrieg* (Paderborn: Ferdinand Schöningh, 2009), pp. 434–5.

Latvians, more than half a million Jews and between 750,000 and 1 million Poles were deported to the Russian interior.[32] The tally of human displacement in the Russian Empire was staggering: over 3.3 million refugees by the end of 1915, and more than 6 million – roughly 5 per cent of the Empire's entire population – by the beginning of 1917.[33] This in itself constituted a revolutionary upheaval, as 'mass population displacement [. . .] simultaneously became a cause and an effect of the collapse of the Russian Empire'.[34] It not only undermined loyalty to the Russian state among the minority groups on the receiving end of the violence, but it also effectively destroyed social and state structures over wide swathes of the western provinces of the Russian Empire.

The extent of the social upheaval brought by the First World War to Eastern Europe is illustrated well by the example of Riga. Before the war, Riga had been the fourth largest city in the Russian Empire, a multicultural metropolis with more than half a million inhabitants (including a substantial German minority, which still dominated the city's commercial life, as well as Latvians, Russians and Jews). During the conflict, it became a front city and lost much of its population, in large measure as a consequence of the evacuation of workers in war industries and their families.[35] Beginning in August 1915, Latvian volunteer units formed in the city, and fought against the German forces on the Riga front, with substantial losses. By 1916, the city had been transformed into a military camp; in July 1917, following the 'February Revolution' in Russia, various groups claimed Latvia's autonomy within the new Russian Republic; in September 1917, the Germans finally entered the city; and after the German defeat in the autumn of 1918, and a declaration of Latvian independence in Riga on 18 November, the German army left. Shortly thereafter, on 3 January 1919, Bolshevik forces entered the city and established a short-lived Latvian Soviet Government, until they in turn were driven out by

32 Alan Kramer, *Dynamic of Destruction. Culture and Mass Killing in the First World War* (Oxford University Press, 2007), p. 151; Kramer, 'Deportationen', pp. 434–5; Gatrell, 'Introduction', p. 420.

33 Sanborn, 'Unsettling the empire', p. 310; Joshua Sanborn, 'The genesis of Russian warlordism: violence and governance during the First World War and the Civil War', *Contemporary European History*, 19:3 (2010), esp. 198–208; Peter Gatrell, *A Whole Empire Walking: Refugees in Russia during World War I* (Bloomington, IN: Indiana University Press, 1999), p. 3. See also Mark von Hagen, *War in a European Borderland: Occupations and Occupation Plans in Galicia and Ukraine, 1914–1918* (Seattle, WA: University of Washington Press, 2008).

34 Baron and Gatrell, 'Population displacement', p. 99.

35 Julien Gueslin, 'Riga, de la métropole russe à la capitale de la Lettonie 1915–1919', in Philippe Chassaigne and Jean-Marc Largeaud (eds.), *Villes en guerre (1914–1945)* (Paris: Armand Colin, 2004), pp. 185–95.

German formations (*Landeswehr*) on 22 May. (Latvian units entered the city on the next day.) By the time the fighting in and around Riga was over, the city – now capital of an independent Latvia – had lost half its population; its industry (which had driven the rapid growth of the city in the decades before the First World War) largely had ceased to exist; its infrastructure was in tatters; unemployment was substantial. The history of Riga during the conflict is a history of a city transformed by war. The changes that it experienced – the devastation caused by fighting, occupation, the evacuation of industrial firms and their workforces, the flight of refugees trying to escape the worst of the war[36] – constituted a social revolution and created the stage for political revolution.

In Riga, after the transformation of society and economy through war, it was not socialism but nationalism that triumphed. Nationalism, as much as socialism, undermined dynastic loyalties, multi-national political formations and colonial empires. It was, Dominic Lieven has pointed out, 'the most powerful ideology of the day'.[37] However, context matters. The revolutionary potential of nationalism, like that of socialism, became revolutionary reality in the context of world war.

This was true not only in Europe. The defeat of the Ottoman Empire in the First World War was followed by its break-up, by nationalist revolts in its former Arab territories, by military campaigns launched against the newly established Democratic Republic of Armenia, by war with the Greeks and, in October 1923, by the proclamation of a nationalist, secular Turkish Republic. (The Caliphate was abolished formally in March 1924.) This – the transition from the Ottoman Empire to the Turkish Republic under the leadership of the former Ottoman General Mustafa Kemal (Atatürk), and the terrible intercommunal violence that accompanied that transition[38] – also numbers among the great revolutionary transformations to emerge from the First World War.

It was not only in Turkey that the break-up of the Ottoman Empire was followed by a revolutionary upsurge. In March and April 1919, Egypt, which nominally had been part of the Ottoman Empire before the First World War but was proclaimed a protectorate by the British in 1914, witnessed 'one of the great peasant revolts of her history and of the 20th century', a revolt that

36 Uldis Ģērmanis, *Oberst Vācietis und die lettischen Schützen im Weltkrieg und in der Oktoberrevolution* (Stockholm: Almqvist & Wiksell, 1974), pp. 147, 155.

37 Dominic Lieven, 'Dilemmas of empire 1850–1918. Power, territory, identity', *Journal of Contemporary History*, 34:2 (1999), p. 196.

38 See Ryan Gingeras, *Sorrowful Shores: Violence, Ethnicity, and the End of the Ottoman Empire, 1912–1923* (Oxford University Press, 2009).

'marks the emergence of Egyptian liberalism and the construction of the modern state'.[39] Against a background of food shortages, the 1919 revolt was triggered by the arrest and exiling of leaders of the Egyptian national movement (most prominent among them Sa'd Zaghoul), who wanted an Egyptian delegation to be recognised at Versailles in order to demand Egyptian independence. Here, a popular, anti-colonialist insurrection was sparked by demands for popular and national sovereignty, and could be suppressed only by the deployment of tens of thousands of British troops (which did not prevent Sa'd Zaghoul's populist Wafd movement from winning elections overwhelmingly in 1923).

Popular challenges to imperial rule in the wake of the First World War were by no means limited to Egypt. In Iraq, the British, the mandate power, suffered substantial casualties when suppressing the revolution that broke out in protest against British occupation in the summer of 1920. In India, where the British were fearful that the Russian Revolution had 'given an impetus to Indian political aspirations',[40] the political atmosphere was transformed in the wake of the First World War with the massacre of hundreds of people in the city of Amritsar in the Punjab. (There, in April 1919, the commanding British Brigadier General Reginald E. H. Dyer, fearing a revolt, ordered his troops to fire on a large unarmed crowd that had assembled for a traditional festival.) In response, in the summer of 1919, Gandhi launched the Indian National Congress's mass campaign of non-cooperation against the British authorities in support of the struggle for Indian independence.

This suggests that what happened in Dublin in 1916 and its aftermath needs to be understood not just in an Irish or European context, but in a broader, global framework. The First World War led to a wave of revolutionary nationalist and anti-colonialist agitation and unrest, whereby 'all sorts of self-appointed movements and spokesmen were demanding national independence' as 'the cry of self-determination spread far beyond Europe'.[41] The First World War stirred up revolutionary demands for popular and national sovereignty not only in Europe, but globally.

39 Ellis Goldberg, 'Peasants in revolt – Egypt 1919', *International Journal of Middle East Studies*, 24:2 (1992), p. 261.

40 The Montagu-Chelmsford Report, published on 8 July 1918, quoted in H Tinker, 'India in the First World War and after', *Journal of Contemporary History*, 3:4 (1968), p. 92.

41 Eric D. Weitz, 'From the Vienna to the Paris system: international politics and the entangled histories of human rights, forced deportations, and civilizing missions', *American Historical Review*, 113:5 (2008), p. 1315.

How can we summarise the relationship between the First World War, war on an unprecedented scale, and the revolutionary upsurge that came in its wake? It would appear that the war precipitated revolutionary politics and change as a consequence of a number of fundamentally destabilising factors:

1. *The increases in physical hardship, especially shortages of food that provoked popular discontent.* The hardships caused by a war that consumed vastly more resources than had been imagined possible before 1914 provoked anger and protest in numerous countries. The most sensitive area was food supply, and it was hardly coincidental that revolutionary upheavals in the Russian, German and Austro-Hungarian empires all were sparked by food shortages, rapid rises in food prices and dismay at the failure of governments to ensure an adequate and equitable food supply. From factory workers in Berlin to peasants in Egypt, it was food shortages resulting from war that provoked revolutionary unrest. This was particularly incendiary during a period of war-fuelled rapid inflation (after a long period of price stability), provoking anger when prices rose and a conviction that profiteering was rife. These reactions contributed mightily to the erosion of support for governments, particularly for the autocratic governments of Central and Eastern Europe.
2. *The growth of the state and its responsibilities, and the simultaneous undermining of the legitimacy of the state.* The scale of the First World War, of its human and material cost, led to the state being charged with new and enhanced responsibility for the welfare of its citizens. Increased state involvement in managing the war economy and compensating for wartime sacrifice undermined its legitimacy when it failed to deliver. The millions of people who had lost family members, whose property had been damaged or destroyed, who had been injured and suffered long-term physical consequences of combat, left the states of combatant countries with huge economic, political and moral liabilities. The wartime social contract between the state and its subjects, that the sacrifice of the population would be honoured through support by the state – neatly summed up in the phrase repeated in Germany during the First World War, 'You can be sure of the thanks of the Fatherland' – became a source of bitterness when the state could not make good on its promises. War vastly increased the size and responsibilities of the state, while it simultaneously reduced the resources available to meet those responsibilities, and enhanced popular expectations during a time of hardship undermined the legitimacy of the old regime.

3. *The expectations of political change as a result of mass popular participation in the war*. In the same way that those who sacrificed their health and well-being for their state expected that the wartime social contract be made good, those who contributed to the war effort generally expected that the state honour an implicit political contract: that those who fought for the nation ought to have a meaningful political voice. Mass participation in combat and in supporting the war effort fuelled demands for popular political participation, for the extension of the franchise, democratic republican government, and recognition of the right to national self-determination – demands that were by their nature revolutionary in autocratic, multinational and colonial empires.
4. *The interaction among soldiers and civilians of different nationalities and the spread of revolutionary ideas and sentiment*. The war brought soldiers into contact with other peoples and other lands and, particularly after the outbreak of revolution in Russia, exposed them to revolutionary ideas. During the First World War, unprecedented numbers of soldiers were taken captive. Altogether, between 6.6 and 8 million soldiers were captured during the First World War; the Russian army alone had between 2.5 and 3.5 million of its soldiers taken prisoner and captured roughly 2 million soldiers of opposing armies, and estimates of the numbers of soldiers of the Austro-Hungarian monarchy taken prisoner range from 2.2 to over 2.7 million.[42] Of the roughly 2.4 million prisoners taken by the Germans during the 1914–18 conflict, 1.4 million were from the Russian Empire.[43] Not only did this contribute to social upheaval, but it also spread the revolutionary message – for example, among the roughly 2 million soldiers of the Austro-Hungarian army who had been taken prisoner by the Russians, many of whom experienced the Russian Revolutions of 1917 at first hand; they were freed by the Bolsheviks at the time of the October

42 Uta Hinz, 'Kriegsgefangene', in Hirschfeld *et al.*, *Enzyklopädie Erster Weltkrieg*, p. 641; Sanborn, 'Unsettling the empire', p. 317; Matthew Stibbe, 'The internment of civilians by belligerent states during the First World War and the response of the International Committee of the Red Cross', *Journal of Contemporary History*, 41:1 (2006), p. 5; Niall Ferguson, *The Pity of War: Explaining World War I* (London: Penguin, 1998), p. 369; John Paul Newman, 'Post-imperial and post-war violence in the south Slav lands, 1917–1923', *Contemporary European History*, 19:3 (2010), pp. 251–2. Newman notes that for a large number of soldiers in Habsburg armies on the Eastern Front, 'the war was over by June 1916'.

43 Uta Hinz, *Gefangen im Großen Krieg. Kriegsgefangenschaft in Deutschland 1914–1921* (Essen: Klartext Verlag, 2006), p. 10; Mark Spoerer, 'The mortality of Allied prisoners of war and Belgian civilian deportees in German custody during the First World War: a reappraisal of the effects of forced labour', *Population Studies*, 60:2 (2006), p. 127.

Revolution, and upon their return refused to re-enlist in their regiments and instead proselytised revolution at home.[44]

5. *The crumbling of armed forces and the growing conviction that the only way to bring the war to an end was through revolution.* The apparent military stalemate that set in after the German offensive of 1914 in northern France had been stopped at the Marne gradually undermined support for governments that persisted in fighting. On the eve of revolution the conviction grew that 'it cannot go on this way' and that upheaval was imminent.[45] The fact that the fighting, with the huge numbers of casualties it generated and the miserable conditions that soldiers had to endure, had gone on for years and with no apparent end in sight led to a growing conviction that if the war was going to be brought to an end this had to be done through the overthrow of the governments that insisted on continuing the war. It was the government, and in the case of Germany the Kaiser himself, that came to be regarded as the obstacle to achieving the peace desired so passionately after years of hardship and death. Calls grew louder for 'peace at any price',[46] and the price was the abolition of the old regime. In all the countries where there was a revolutionary overthrow of the old regime, the armed forces cracked under the pressure of an unsuccessful pursuit of war. Riddled with discontent, plagued by lack of adequate supplies, faced with increasing incidence of desertion, the armed forces no longer were in a position to defend the state from revolutionary threats and instead came to constitute a revolutionary threat themselves. Thus, the last line of defence of the old regime disintegrated under the pressures created by the First World War. Where the armed forces held together – for example, those of France and Britain – revolution was avoided; where they did not – for example, in Russia, Germany and Austria-Hungary – revolution brought down the old regime.
6. *The weakening of the imperialist world order of the nineteenth century.* Not only did the war bring destruction to the three main continental European empires; it also shook the belief in the solidity of European global domination

44 Newman, 'Post-imperial and post-war violence', p. 253. Roughly half a million returned from Russian captivity during the first half of 1918. See Richard G. Plaschka *et al.*, *Innere Front. Militärassistenz, Widerstand und Umsturz in der Donaumonarchie 1918* (Munich: R. Oldenbourg Verlag, 1974), vol. I, pp. 278–80.

45 'So kanns nicht weitergehen!', quoted in V. Ulrich, 'Zur inneren Revolutionierung der wilhelminischen Gesellschaft des Jahres 1918', in Jörg Duppler and Gerhard P. Groß (eds.), *Kriegsende 1918. Ereignis, Wirkung, Nachwirkung* (Munich: R. Oldenbourg Verlag, 1999), p. 281.

46 Benjamin Ziemann, 'Enttäuschte Erwartung und kollektive Erschöpfung. Die deutschen Soldaten an der Westfront 1918 auf dem Weg zur Revolution', in Duppler and Groß, *Kriegsende 1918*, p. 176.

and created an international forum where demands for popular and national sovereignty could be articulated. Revolutionary calls for popular and national sovereignty were not limited to European peoples who lacked their own state, but were echoed around the world as the conviction grew that what was valid for Europeans should be valid for non-Europeans as well. This constituted a revolutionary challenge to imperial power, in Cairo no less than in Dublin.

Taken together, these observations suggest that the revolutionary nature of the First World War may not best be understood simply with reference to the ideologies and activities of self-proclaimed revolutionaries, who saw their opportunity to achieve their goals in the crucible of the war. There was nothing inevitable about the triumph of political movements inspired by socialist or nationalist visions, for in the end revolution is about power, and revolutionary transfers of power need to be understood in context. Contingency, as much if not more than ideology, made possible the revolutionary transformations that followed from the First World War, and it was war that framed contingency. Particularly in Eastern Europe, in the context of a vast war of movement, societies and communities already had undergone revolutionary transformations before political revolution arrived. It was there that hundreds of thousands of Europeans were forced from their homes, that communities were destroyed as populations were torn from their towns and villages, that normative constraints on behaviour that had taken decades to coalesce were eroded by war. It was there that the revolutionary breaking and remaking of European civilisation in the twentieth century occurred.

The revolution unleashed by the First World War thus needs to be seen in the context of the violence unleashed through war. At its most basic, the revolutionary element of the First World War was violence – the remaking of political, economic and social formations through violence. That was the fundamental link between war and revolution unleashed by a conflict that opened the floodgates to violence on an extraordinary scale and with an extraordinary intensity. Welcoming the new world of violence precipitated by the Great War, Ernst Jünger wrote in *Der Kampf als Inneres Erlebnis* the oft-quoted passage:

> This war is not the end but the beginning of violence. It is the forge in which the world will be hammered into new borders and new communities. New forms want to be filled with blood, and power will be wielded with a hard fist. The war is a great school, and the new man will bear our stamp.[47]

47 Ernst Jünger, *Der Kampf als inneres Erlebnis* (Berlin: Mittler, 1928), pp. 70–1.

The deep revolutionary character of the First World War was that it constituted, as Michael Geyer has observed, 'the beginning of a *Zivilisationsbruch*, a rupture in civility, that shook Europe to its foundations'; 'the general history of the twentieth century in Europe is the history of the aftershocks of World War I. It is the history of the trauma inflicted by fighting.'[48]

The First World War did not end with the Armistice of November 1918, or even with the peace conferences in 1919 and 1920. War and conflict continued – in the campaigns of paramilitary formations in Central and Eastern Europe, in anti-colonial struggles in the Arab world and beyond, in civil wars in Russia, Finland and Ireland, in inter-state wars from the Polish-Soviet War to the war between Turkey and Greece and British campaigns from Egypt to Afghanistan, and in the political violence committed by formations of war veterans across Europe. The First World War was indeed revolutionary, as a catalyst not only for the destruction of political and social systems and hierarchies, but also for the creation of a new world of violence.[49] At the time, the First World War indeed seemed to herald what Karl Kraus referred to as 'the last days of mankind'. In fact, the revolutionary violence and the violent revolutions of the First World War remade the modern world.

48 Michael Geyer, 'War and the context of general history in an age of total war: comment on Peter Paret, "Justifying the obligation of military service," and Michael Howard, "World War One: the crisis in European history"', *Journal of Military History*, 57:5 (1993), pp. 159–60.

49 On the violent legacy of the First World War in Europe, see Chapter 23 in this volume by Robert Gerwarth, 'The continuum of violence'.

PART II

*

ARMED FORCES

Introduction to Part II

STÉPHANE AUDOIN-ROUZEAU AND HEATHER JONES

At the heart of the Great War lies an important, if troubling, paradox – that the 'war to end all wars' in reality dramatically enhanced the capacity of armed forces to wage future conflict. The war marked the moment when the old truisms and practices of nineteenth-century warfare ended, to be replaced by something far more familiar and still with us: rapid, clinical and mechanised mass destruction. The role of the armed forces, the theme of this section, was central to this process. To understand the Great War is thus to understand the dramatic modernisation of warfare that it brought, the key lessons which would leave their imprint upon all later conflicts: the revelations of the power of artillery, mass conscription, aerial bombardment, grenades, mortars or machine-gunnery expertise to advantage a belligerent; the search to restore mobility which ultimately culminated in the development of the elite-trained storm trooper, the armoured train and the tank. All of these innovations would have later repercussions; all changed the nature of warfare forever. Indeed, far from the widespread popular image of the war in terms of a static, stagnant Western Front, the Great War was in reality all about change – constantly evolving weaponry, logistics and tactics, as well as the ongoing adaptation and development of the relationship between the individual combatant and the army in which he served. The aim of this section is to explore these changes which were so fundamental to the conflict, looking at both the technological and the human aspects that were central to how the war's armed forces functioned.

Above all else, the question of scale was fundamental to the way in which the First World War changed warfare. Between 1914 and 1918, in total, nearly 75 million men wore military uniform: never before in the history of armed conflict had such a vast number been mobilised in armed forces for such a long period of time. The war saw the creation of armies, on an unprecedented scale, the majority made up of European conscripts. Many never returned: the cumulative number of military war dead is estimated at 10 million. The wounded, many often mutilated or crippled for life, totalled 21 million. These figures testify to a profound militarisation of Western society which accepted the waging of war on this epic scale and which supplied and supported these armies and these casualties – a militarisation process which began before 1914, but which reached its apogee during the war years, when the means of mobilising, sustaining and technically waging war developed in ways that changed the face of battle forever.

The Great War had a dramatic, permanent impact on the nature of combat. At an operational level, some of the new trends that it developed, such as the use of heavy artillery or of trenches, had, in fact, already appeared during the American Civil War (1861 to 1865) and even more clearly during the conflicts at the turn of the nineteenth and twentieth centuries, in particular, the Boer War (1899 to 1902), the Russo-Japanese War (1904 to 1905) and the Balkan wars of 1912 to 1913. However, the First World War saw these trends applied on an entirely new scale – in particular, it marked a new departure in the scale of combat deployment, with fighting taking place along thousands of kilometers of front. The very essence of combat activity was transformed by the new intensity of firepower, the dramatic preponderance of the defensive over the offensive and by the extension of combat in terms of both timespan and space, as this section will highlight.

Yet while combat was obviously central, the study of the armed forces in the Great War extends well beyond the domain of purely military operations; given the duration and scale of the conflict, which involved all the major economic powers of the time, this was also a war that mobilised technological and scientific prowess to the utmost in order to arm the troops. A state's level of technological development is central here, as is the question of weaponry and how it evolved in each belligerent country in the face of the challenges brought by the conflict. Overall, between 1914 and 1918, the major belligerent powers often unleashed technological potential that had previously been under-utilised, experimenting with new ways of using weapons and increasing efficiency. Indeed, from the very outset of the war in 1914, a complex relationship developed between the use of the available arms already in existence and the development of additional weaponry from the adaptation of older armament forms in which new potential was now seen, which largely occurred through a process of retro-innovation. It was only surprisingly rarely, as this section will show, that the development of completely new, unprecedented weapons occurred – weapons that did not build upon pre-war armaments in any way. Technological advances were thus complex and highly interactive, linking scientists, soldier-experts, the state and industrialists.

Logistics were also a fundamental factor that determined the operation of the armed forces in a conflict that rapidly became a mass industrial war. The provisioning of the infantry increased fourfold between the outbreak of the conflict and its end. Often overlooked, the issues of transport and supply were far from mundane in 1914 to 1918; rather, the war saw the rapid and radical expansion of logistics and a reciprocal race between belligerents to ensure that their side was kept well resourced. Indeed, ultimately, the Allies' radical success at logistical management was key to their victory on the Western Front.

Morale was also key to how armed forces functioned: although the severity of military discipline varied according to the different belligerents, armies generally operated with strict, coercive legal codes that enforced obedience among the rank and file. Yet the ability of armies to endure the strain of the long duration of the Great War was never solely based upon military coercion or upon the level of training of the troops. As important was the extent of the support and emotional investment which the largely citizen soldiers of the Great War felt for their own side's war effort. As a result, the First World War marked the beginning of the era of psychological warfare – the mental attitudes of the troops were a factor that mattered in a new, and ever more professionally assessed, way.

In addition, as the war went on, an increasingly significant intermediary zone developed between the world of the combatants and that of civilians; there was no clear home front/front line divide during the conflict. Rather, a series of ubiquitous vectors linked the two worlds; there was constant connection between the armed forces and the civilian realm through logistics, morale issues and troops on leave. Indeed, certain wartime populations specifically existed within this intermediary 'grey zone', culturally suspended between the front line and the home front spheres. In some cases, these were actual members of the armed forces themselves: mutinying soldiers were one such grouping – often mutiny began on the home front in troop transports or among soldiers recalled from leave. In other cases, mutiny was sparked by the desire to return home. Perhaps the most spectacular example of mutiny is the case of Russia in revolution where, from autumn 1917 onwards, hundreds of thousands of combatants left the lines and sought to return home, often concomitantly spreading the violence of the front to the rear areas. Prisoners of war were another such intermediary population, totalling an estimated 8 to 9 million men by the end of the conflict. Long overlooked, this figure of 8 to 9 million prisoners is in the vicinity of the number of war dead, highlighting how central captivity was to the war. Prisoners were subject to radically new forms of captivity, in which nascent techniques of social engineering that would later mark the twentieth-century camp began to first appear. Indeed, this experience of managing the mass captivity of troops between 1914 and 1918, which saw the privileging of certain nationalities and an increasingly racialised view of the enemy, would leave a sinister legacy. Totalitarian regimes in the interwar period took from the Great War the idea of modernised captivity as a powerful tool for securing and reordering societies.

In sum, the role of the armed forces in 1914 to 1918 has to be understood in terms of its dramatic complexity, as this section will highlight – a complexity which stemmed from the presence of many, very different, combinations of factors. The evolutions in warfare brought by the conflict were constantly in flux, varying according to the front, according to the level of development and command system of the belligerent, and according to the precise moment of the war; there was no one static or homogeneous model of how armed forces adapted to the stresses of waging modern industrialised warfare. Rather, as this section will show, there were a series of, often interconnected, developments, which produced a wide variety of outcomes. Yet for all the heterogeneity visible within the dynamic changes and modernisations unleashed by the war, one thing is certain: in their extreme brutality, the new forms of combat in 1914 to 1918 left an indelible mark, still visible today, upon both warfare practices and our images of war.

6
Combat and tactics

STÉPHANE AUDOIN-ROUZEAU

The opening months of the First World War were marked by a major strategic setback: by the end of 1914, not one of the nations under arms had defeated its enemy. This disappointment was followed by three years of strategic stalemate, which was broken only in 1918. This situation was unprecedented, unforeseen at the outbreak of the war. The stalemate created unexpected operational conditions and shaped patterns of combat; in short, the stalemate dictated tactics. The means of engagement – tactics – were developing independently of strategy, the essential management of the war. The way in which the war was fought was detached from the objectives of the states waging it.

Patterns of engagement in battle evolved extremely rapidly between 1914 and 1918. In only four-and-a-half years, there was a seismic shift from one kind of war to another. Transformations on this scale redirected thinking about combat after 1918. Indeed, the profound effects on Western societies of combat during the Great War are still apparent today.

Combat was not one thing, but many things, which appeared in varying forms in different battle locations. Tactical innovation circulated from one front line to another (particularly from West to East, and vice versa), and thus elements of combat tended to converge in the various theatres of operation. It is striking to note how the specific conditions on each front reflected the technology deployed on them and shaped how that technology was used. Geographic variations in combat matched differences over time.

This variability has been insufficiently recognised and too little studied, because of the powerful sway exercised by the Western Front on historiography and on the collective memory of the Great Powers of Western Europe, among the principal belligerent nations in the Great War. And it remains true in one respect: the Western Front, established from the autumn of 1914, running for four years along a length of 700 kilometres, from the Belgian

Helen McPhail translated this chapter from French into English.

coast to the Swiss frontier, deserves to be seen as the 'decisive front' from the beginning to the end of the war. At the very least, it should be identified as the front line *perceived* as decisive, both by general staffs and by most contemporaries. This was the front where the three chief military powers of Europe confronted each other: France, Great Britain, Germany, with, in the case of the two Entente powers, the added support of troops from their dominions and empires. It was on this same front that American troops were to arrive and fight from 1917. This was the setting too for the heaviest losses – from the summer of 1914 – and up until November 1918: on no other front was the human, technological and logistical effort so massive. The vast battles of *matériel* of 1916 had no corresponding equivalent on the other fronts of the First World War. Above all, it was on this same Western Front that a decisive military defeat of one of the warring nations would inescapably mean the defeat of one of the two coalitions at war from the summer of 1914.

But no such event occurred. It is ironic to realise that the Russian front was the first to collapse, in late 1917 and early 1918, and that it was the rupture of the Bulgarian front, in September 1918, which marked the beginning of the strategic crumbling of the Central Powers. This confirms the need to rebalance the study of combat during the Great War by looking at the other fronts, each with a different configuration, but starting always from a shared technological, strategic and tactical orientation. In comparison with the Western Front, along the Austro-Italian front of the Isonzo, on the Gallipoli peninsula and in the Balkans, on the Austro-German-Russian front, and above all in the Near East or indeed in Africa, everything happened as if tactics and modes of combat were part of a differentiated process of 'demodernisation'. The reduced technology used by some at least of the enemies present, the sometimes insurmountable obstacles of landscape (mountains, the great length of the fronts, climatic constraints), finally the smaller number of soldiers involved, transformed the patterns of engagement, sometimes marginally, more often at every level and in every way. This *transformation* process in tactics and modes of combat as a function of location and moment was part of the variation in the intensity and character of violence deployed between 1914 and 1918.

From battle imagined to the battle of position

Until it became a concrete reality for the millions of Europeans thrown into the war in August 1914, battle had been imagined, and imagined most significantly by the general staffs of the different Western powers. Naturally, this expectation was largely the consequence of past wars – in this respect the war of 1870 to 1871 was the most recent example, in terms of battle, of a major conflict between great European powers. And yet the wars at the turn of the late nineteenth to early twentieth centuries offered endless lessons on the effect of modern weapons on tactics and modes of battle: the Boer War (1899 to 1902), the Russo-Japanese War (1904 to 1905) and the two Balkan wars (1912 to 1913) had been intensively scrutinised by the military observers of the great European powers, who had every opportunity to observe, in particular, the new effects of firepower on the armies engaged. In particular, the Battle of Mukden (February to March 1905) had shown on a small scale the tactical pattern that would be reproduced more extensively, on a far vaster scale, in the Great War: the superiority of defence over attack because of the possibilities of immobilising attacks through modern firepower (artillery, machine guns, etc.); the mirrored pattern of troops digging in, with the rapid development of a network of trenches; the extension of a battle over time, until it was transformed into a long siege in open country; and the weight of extremely heavy losses without any decisive strategic result in favour of one or other of the opposing armies.

It is less that recognition of these new conflicts was lacking in the summer of 1914, and more that contemporaries were incapable of interiorising recently observed facts – because they did not fit the accepted representations of what a future war *ought* to be. Precisely because firepower made the battlefield more deadly than ever before, the war somehow *had to be* short. Equally, tactics of attack *must* prevail, at the cost of pushing to or beyond limits the physical and emotional strain suffered by soldiers. Joffre, Haig and Moltke all worked on the general assumption that this would be a short war, a war of movement and thus of attack.

The test of combat for the soldiers engaged in a potential European conflict was imagined initially as very intense, no doubt, but also as relatively short-lived. Further, thinking about battle remained strongly imbued with an ancient ethos of combat which continued to colour strategic and tactical thinking, and consequently to frame the instruction of men as part of the mass armies of the beginning of the twentieth century. Also, and more broadly, this ethos continued to inform discussions about uniforms, weapons and logistics, through to the actual representations of leaders and fighting men. It was as part of this image of war and of battle that the great confrontations of August and September 1914 took place, in the East as well as the West. During this first phase of the war, the underestimation of the effects of firepower was particularly significant: it explains the terrible losses of the first weeks of combat.

Pre-war assumptions about war and battle clashed with the brutal counter-evidence inflicted by real-life experience of the real battlefield. On the Western Front, no later than the autumn of 1914, soldiers were often spontaneously burrowing into the ground. As this practice came to be prescribed systematically by the High Command, a conflict initially based on movement and speed was transformed into 'trench warfare'. Its origins can be found in the defensive measures improvised by the infantry after the Battle of the Marne in September 1914, and then at the end of the 'race to the sea', which extended into the autumn. Exhausted by their immense effort, the soldiers spontaneously dug 'fox-holes' to protect themselves from bullets or shells, as in Manchuria less than ten years earlier. As they gradually linked up, these individual holes formed the first trench lines. The German infantry, better trained in field fortifications, appear to have led the way in this systematic digging in – which cost them the indignant reproach of the Allies for ignoring traditional modes of battle. On the Western Front, the gradual hardening of existing positions was part of the autumn months of 1914, provoking a strategic *impasse* which would not be overcome for another four years. As the infantry practice of digging in came to be regular practice in the trenches, it became a recognised system on an unprecedented scale and degree of sophistication, at the cost of a complete transformation of tactical methods and modes of battle. The outcome was a fundamental development in the shape and topography of military activity.

As the attack unfolded on an unprecedented geographical scale, the trenches extended along almost the full length of the fronts: in the West, in the East, then in Italy and the Balkans. On the 'Eastern Front', however, they were established less systematically than in the West; the positions, less deep, less organised, were also more easily abandoned as the armies moved, and manoeuvre and movement remained daily activities. Indeed, in the East and, until 1917, for each side, movement remained a daily possibility. On the other fronts, however, the superiority of defence over attack provoked corresponding conditions of mutual obstruction, with the combatants well dug in and immobilised; on the Gallipoli peninsula from April 1915, on the Austro-Italian front from May of the same year, and even on the vast front of the Balkans from 1916, the trenches compelled recognition everywhere as the predominant mode of battle, if not immediately, at least after a more or less extended delay. It was only in the Near East, in an immense and fluid theatre of operations in desert conditions, that movement remained fully operational as a daily possibility until the end.

The effectiveness of firepower

The First World War contributed to the permanent transformation of 'bodily dispositions'[1] for the Western fighting man. The trench system, the tactical representation of the superiority of defence over attack, formed one of the major features of the Great War. First, the tactical ascendancy of the defensive showed itself in the new intensity of fire on the battlefield – a battlefield simultaneously more murderous than ever before and yet, despite this, apparently empty.

It is impossible to understand this without returning briefly to the weapons available. The magazine rifle of Western armies in the early twentieth century could fire off more than ten bullets per minute over a practical distance of around 600 metres. Along with the rifle, with its frequently awkward management in trench warfare, grenades became increasingly important in battle. Originally a siege weapon, used for the first time in their modern form during the Russo-Japanese War, grenades had sufficiently engaged the interest of the German High Command for them to be made available in large numbers at the beginning of the war. Their use then expanded rapidly on the Western Front. To deploy this weapon with its need for delicate handling, specially trained 'bombers' (infantry trained in the use of grenades) were increasingly used. Sent forward as part of a movement of attack, they came to be a major factor in infantry attacks from 1915 onwards: Ernst Jünger's eyewitness accounts[2] rightly stress the widespread use of grenades by assault troops. But this weapon of attack was also used as an instrument of close defence, in armed raids on enemy positions, or again as the tool for 'mopping up' enemy shelters during major offensives.

To this new effectiveness of *individual* weaponry was added the equally new power of *collective* weapons. The machine gun, the typical weapon of industrial warfare, threw out a wall of bullets at the rate of between 400 and 600 each minute: its firepower was equal to that of sixty or a hundred rifles, despite its shorter firing range. In 1914, the weapon was quite recent – the Boer War (1899 to 1902), the Russo-Japanese War of 1904 to 1905, followed by the Balkan wars of 1912 to 1913 were the first opportunities for its military use. 'The bursting fire of machine-gun fire is the only one not to spare a single

1 Following the expression of Marcel Mauss: 'Les techniques du corps', *Journal de psychologie*, 32:3–4 (15 March–15 April 1936), pp. 271–93. Reproduced in Marcel Mauss, *Sociologie et anthropologie* (Paris: Presses Universitaires de France, 1989), pp. 365–6.

2 Ernst Jünger, *In Stahlgewittern* (Hannover: private publisher, 1920); English edn: *Storm of Steel* (London: Chatto & Windus, 1929).

person, literally' was the accurate comment of the French historian Marc Bloch,[3] evoking in hindsight his experience of battle as an officer in the Great War. Indeed, when artillery bombardment had left machine guns intact, their firepower was capable of preventing any attacking forces from crossing no-man's-land. This happened on 1 July 1916, during the British offensive on the Somme: the waves of attacking troops were cut down immediately as they emerged from their front-line trenches.

Artillery, however, was the principal instrument for domination of the battlefield throughout the war, above all when it achieved the peak of its power, in 1916, also on the Western Front. This pre-eminent position arose from a series of technological innovations of prime importance during the final third of the nineteenth century. The first weeks of the war of movement brought into sharp perspective the role of heavy artillery in the destruction of the Belgian forts in August and September 1914. Subsequently, the emergence of the war of position confirmed the need for this same heavy artillery fire to reach shelters dug deep down into the ground, to destroy trenches and to strike at positions at the rear. Massive bombardment became the main tactical response to the prolongation of the strategic stalemate: heavy artillery, hitherto used to defend permanent positions, thus took on the offensive role which had hitherto been the task of field artillery. The war of position also demanded the urgent perfection of new models of guns capable of striking at positions deep underground and beyond the capacity of weapons designed for long-range fire. This was the role of howitzers, capable of firing shells on a steeply curving short range aimed at buried targets. Here, too, the demands of the war of position pointed towards the design and production of increasingly important and complex heavy guns.

Overall, heavy guns came to dominate the various forms of fire on the battlefield. Their role could vary considerably, depending on the tactical objectives in question: for reprisal, demonstration, concentration, destruction or obliteration, range-finding, barrage, box-barrage, harassment and so on; also to fire gas shells, which were used in steeply increasing proportions during the war and reached a quarter of all projectiles by the end of the war. In parallel with the development of heavy artillery, on the model of

3 Marc Bloch, *L'Etrange défaite* (Paris: Folio, 1990), pp. 84–8. *L'Etrange défaite* was edited by Marc Bloch between July and October 1940, immediately after the French defeat. The text, focused on the explanation for the defeat, also referred extensively to the author's experience of battle in 1914–18 (English edn: Marc Bloch, *Strange Defeat* (New York and London: W. W. Norton & Co., 1949)).

old-style siege gunnery for modern times, high trajectory *mobile* artillery was also used for bombardment over a very short distance.

After the serious munitions supply crisis, which struck the armies involved at the end of the battles of the summer and autumn of 1914, this new role for the artillery took the form of a spectacular increase in the number of guns and rounds fired. On the Somme, during the week-long Allied bombardment which preceded the offensive on 1 July 1916, 1.5 million shells were fired by the British artillery alone (with incalculable physical efforts on the part of the men and animals who carried the ordnance), representing on average some thirty strikes per 1,000 square metres. In 1918, the Allied offensives on the Western or Italian Fronts were regularly driven home by between 5,000 and 8,000 artillery guns.

This considerable expansion had many tactical consequences. The guns were more vulnerable confronted by different kinds of aerial observation, raising the corresponding need for better camouflaged positions. New forms of traction had to be developed. In this respect, as part of growing mechanisation, the tank came to feature as a form of artillery capable of independent mobility, as indicated by the French term for tank of 'assault artillery'. The main innovation of the war in matters of uniforms – the helmet – was also a direct response to this new artillery role. From 1915, in virtually all the nations at war, with the notable exception of the Russian army, helmets were recognised as essential to protect the skull and nape of the neck. They could not provide protection against a direct hit, but could deflect a bullet in certain circumstances and could resist small shell bursts. Above all, helmets prevented wounds from falling debris after shell bursts.

On the 'decisive front' in 1914 to 1918, the Western Front, the role of artillery in battle was therefore crucial: 70 to 80 per cent of war wounds were inflicted by artillery fire. Despite this, the impossibility of moving this weapon across a battlefield churned up by shell explosions was one of the main obstacles to artillery support for waves of attack by infantry troops once they arrived at the enemy lines. In this sense, the violence of bombardment in 1914 to 1918 set an intrinsic limit to the effective use of artillery in the great attempts at breakthrough – one of the greatest tactical contradictions in the war of position. Even at its most powerful, in fact, artillery soon reached its own limits. It always remained incapable of destroying shelters excavated at a great depth, above all if they were set in concrete, as on the Somme in 1916 or the Chemin des Dames in 1917, where the deeply buried German positions resisted all preparatory bombardments.

In sum, the growth and diversification of armaments and soldiers' equipment explains the immense development of combatant tactics between 1914 and 1918. Drawing lessons from his experience of the First World War over twenty years earlier, in 1940 the historian Marc Bloch summed up the never-ending interaction between the evolution of soldiers' kit and the transformation of patterns of combat during the four years of the Great War:

> At the beginning of 1918, General Gouraud, who was a zealous and ingenious teacher, one day presented various officers, including myself, with two companies of infantry: one armed in the style of 1914 and manoeuvring as such; the other, of the new type in its composition, weaponry and style of manoeuvre. The contrast was striking.[4]

Indeed, by the end of the war, in the most modern armies and on the decisive front, the soldiers had become *technicians*, highly trained as specialists in their own weapons, often operating as a team, with arms requiring complex handling in combat. In 1918, the tactical simplicity of the early stages of trench warfare was no more than a distant memory.

Battle and tactics on the Western Front took on the character of a war of position by September 1914. On the Eastern Front, the situation was more fluid, and the war of position overlapped or alternated with the war of movement. In the East, several factors contributed to continued movement and manoeuvre in battle. Here, the struggle unfolded along a front that was strikingly more open than the Western Front, primarily because of the relationship between the number of men available and the extended positions to be defended, twice as long as in the west.[5] In the East, for example, one-and-a-half German divisions were deployed to hold an area which, on the Western Front, would require five divisions. Similarly, the Austrians calculated that they lined up one rifle for every two metres of front line against the Russians, but six rifles for every two metres against the Italians.[6] When it came to artillery, the difference in density was even greater: at the end of 1916, the belligerents on the Eastern Front had 8,000 guns available in various locations, while on the Western Front 18,000 Allied guns faced 11,000 German guns.[7] In terms of shells available, the disproportion in ammunition between East and West was even sharper.

To this was added the much more uncertain nature of communication and transportation on the Russian side, and also among the Austro-Hungarians,

4 Bloch, *L'étrange défaite*, pp. 152–3.

5 Compared to Western Europe, the Eastern Front would have stretched from Rotterdam to Valence, and even from Rotterdam to Algeria after Romania joined the war (Norman Stone, *The Eastern Front, 1914–1917* (London: Penguin, 1998), pp. 93–4).

6 Stone, *Eastern Front*, pp. 93–4. 7 Stone, *Eastern Front*, p. 93.

whether these operated by rail or road; in consequence, retreats moved very slowly, increasing the number of prisoners taken and preventing the rapid and large-scale movement of reserves. In the case of Russia, movement was all the more compromised by tactical choices which, for both military and cultural reasons, left extensive space for the cavalry. Provisioning the horses created a further logistical burden.[8] In all, for both the Russian and the Austro-Hungarian armies, defensive weaknesses, combined with lesser firepower and lesser mobility of reserves (decisive in cases of breakthrough of their own lines or those of the enemy) explain the enduring relevance of movement on the Eastern Front. This applied notably to its southern reaches, where movement alternated with long periods of immobility in the trenches. In winter in this area, the intense cold and deep snow became determinant elements of battle, paralysing transport and even the weapons themselves. In the Carpathians, in January to February 1915, the Austro-Hungarian fighting strength was virtually eliminated by the harshness of the climate: to the 250,000 killed and wounded was added a vast mass of soldiers who were frozen or suffering from cold-induced illness.

In the East, the very weak initial quality of the Russian army's defensive measures helps account for the maintenance of the war of movement. While the Germans rapidly applied in the East the techniques of combat of position learned in the West (defence in depth, observation, camouflage, close cooperation between infantry and artillery, the insistence on accuracy of fire, economy in the use of infantry, intensive preparation of terrain, etc.), the Russian lines were characterised by very inadequate defence. The trenches were sketchy, often reduced to a shallow ditch protected by one or two lines of barbed wire. Communication with the rear was rarely protected, no reserve position was planned. Further, the then current tactics demanded the concentration of large numbers of troops in the front lines, to the detriment of the rear positions and the reinforcement of reserves.[9] The German attack of May 1915, which forced the Russian army into its Great Retreat, was symptomatic of this possibility of breakthrough remaining intact on the Eastern Front, at least at this time. The initial massive shelling pulverised the fragile Russian front line, cut communications and prevented reserve troops from moving

8 Russia maintained fifty cavalry divisions whereas the other nations at war had dismounted most of this arm (Stone, *Eastern Front*, pp. 93–4). One million horses were available to the Russian army, which mobilised 50 per cent of Russian railway capacity, against 20 per cent of German capacity (*ibid.*, pp. 134–5).

9 Stone, *Eastern Front*, p. 135.

forwards. The defenders were forced into an extremely deadly retreat over open ground.

However, after the deadlock of the winter of 1915/16 and the establishment of an effective war economy in Russia, it was the turn of the Russian army to restart movement with the Brusilov offensive of June/July 1916. Paradoxically, the major success achieved against the Austro-Hungarian troops in the southern part of the Eastern Front, where immobility continued to operate in the north until 1917, was achieved through improved mastery of the techniques of the war of position. Under Brusilov's personal drive, the Russian front lines had been brought considerably closer to the enemy positions; tunnels had been dug under the networks of barbed wire, reserves had been brought up to the front lines and protected in deep shelters, while a dense network of communications trenches had been established. The assault troops had also been trained in attack on model trenches constructed like those of the enemy. While the efficient use of aerial observation had provided a full appreciation of each enemy battery, tactical cooperation between artillery and infantry – hitherto unknown in the Russian army – had been established.

The success of the Brusilov offensive, obvious from the outset, developed along a broad front.The advantage was less in ground gained than in the breach forced in the Austrian line and in the losses inflicted on the Austro-Hungarian army, amounting to 260,000 men and 330 guns.[10] Nonetheless, the war of position took over again after August, with problems of maintaining the offensives at full strength appearing in the Russian army, in ways somewhat like those that prevailed in the West. These problems did not in fact allow the definitive redefinition of the balance of power on the Eastern Front, however, as seen in the vast strategic movements of the Romanian campaign at the end of 1916.

Tactics for trench fighting

Life in the trenches was depicted in vivid and terrifying terms by all veterans who wrote about it. Tactically speaking, however, the extreme conditions of the war of position, above all in bad weather, in cold and rain, often resulting in 'trench foot', were characteristic of the entire period from the end of the war of movement in the autumn of 1914 until the German

10 Stone, *Eastern Front*, pp. 232 ff.

offensive of spring 1918[11] – but this should not obscure the trench system's high degree of sophistication.

The Western Front presented endless nuances and specificities, according to local conditions, different in every sector. Overall, the prevailing situation was as follows. The opposing troops were separated by a zone of extreme danger, no-man's-land; its width could vary from tens to hundreds of metres, depending on circumstances. The immediate outlook was blocked by immense tangles of barbed wire – the passive weapon which was one of the most effective in the whole war – set up and constantly reinforced in the course of demanding nocturnal sorties. On each side of no-man's-land the trenches formed a series of successive lines of defence, more or less parallel, but never in straight lines, in order to prevent enfilading fire and to limit the effects of shell bursts. The first position was organised for battle, with its parapet of sandbags, crenellations and firing step. It was itself preceded by still more advanced positions: small observation posts designed for surveillance, and parallel jumping-off lines dug secretly out into no-man's-land before an attack, so that assault troops could assemble closer to the enemy positions: for at the terrifying moment of climbing out of the trench, every metre saved could make the difference between life and death.

Communication trenches running perpendicular to the front lines linked them to the support trenches which formed the second line, which was generally established on a reverse slope to avoid observation as well as enemy fire, and protected by fresh networks of barbed wire. This second line was in turn provided with a reserve trench, leading to yet further communication trenches which enabled the troops to move out to the rear and rest camps. This complex series of staging posts produced a subtle and gradual progress into or out of danger.

Mountain sectors, such as the Austro-Italian front, the Carpathians, the Balkans or the Vosges, provided a specific version of the war of position, intensifying the multiple tactical problems produced by this kind of combat. The superiority of defence over attack was further increased, and for this reason movement was virtually paralysed. In the mountains, the trenches (and sometimes the tunnels and mines, as in the Dolomites) had to be dug out of the rock, demanding extraordinary and prolonged effort. In some sectors, the opposing lines of trenches might be very close together; the slope made the movement of men and the transport of *matériel* and food

11 In warmer regions, on the other hand, such as Gallipoli or Mesopotamia, the trenches became particularly unhealthy places because of their insanitary conditions.

supplies extremely difficult, while the great cold, the snow and above all the wind, aggravating the harsh conditions of life for the combatants, very quickly wore down their powers of resistance. Such circumstances tended to 'demodernise' patterns of engagement and fighting in the mountains; motorised vehicles were largely paralysed, yielding to cable railways or mules, donkeys and human porterage; heavy artillery could not be brought up and artillery movement of any kind remained difficult, or impossible in certain cases, despite gunnery adapted for mountain use. In contrast, it is true, the effects of shell bursts were magnified by explosion on rock surfaces. In such a context, the role of heavy infantry supported by light weapons was primordial.

The 'decisive front' in the West, on the other hand, essentially ran across flat or undulating ground. In terrain that was close to sea level, as in Flanders, it was impossible to contemplate deep digging: defences had to be established at surface level, and it was often more practical to use shell-holes than to attempt the digging of real trenches. From Picardy to Champagne, on the other hand, the chalky sub-soil allowed for more secure installations, but at the cost of incessant labour. The often impermeable ground, and a humid climate for much of the year, demanded the massive use of materials designed to resist the effects of bad weather to maintain the lines in good condition. Timbering and fascines supported the sides of the trenches as well as the walls and roofs of shelters. In the front lines, these shelters were often a simple hole in the side of the trench: hollowed out well back, they were deeper and reached by ladders, while a thick roof, made of interlinked rough timbers, protected the occupants from shelling; at the bottom of trenches and communication lines, duckboards gave some protection from contact with stagnant water. But these measures soon reached their limits under continuous bombardment which was capable of destroying the skilfully organised positions, or during prolonged periods of very bad weather.

By the autumn of 1915, the Germans were pioneers in the use of concrete to create deep and secure underground shelters, sometimes linked in networks and often heated and lit with electricity. The trenches of the warring nations differed. For the Germans, who occupied almost the whole of Belgium, vast spaces of northern and eastern France and then the even greater areas gradually won from Russia, trench warfare could be seen as an acceptable compromise until the enemy was sufficiently worn down to bring about his definitive defeat. For Germany's enemies, on the other hand, the perspective of prolonged existence underground constituted an implicit renunciation of any territorial reconquest. The French and the British, therefore, tended to adopt a type of installation clearly more provisional in a form of warfare which, until 1917, remained overwhelmingly dominated by belief in a decisive offensive to restart movement and bring the war to a rapid conclusion. This belief was also responsible for the large number of useless and deadly assaults – particularly in 1915 – against the enemy's front lines. A further direct consequence was the tactic of systematic reconquest (at any cost) of front lines lost, which was not abandoned by headquarters until very late in the war.

In the higher ranks of command – Brigade, Division, Army Corps and Army – distance from the front lines undoubtedly favoured an abstract view of methods of combat on the ground. Even at regimental and battalion level, senior officers (colonels, majors) generally remained far from the front lines: their coordinating role in the conflict took precedence over any direct contact with danger. It was the junior officers – company commanders and section leaders – who directed the battle most closely: they paid a very high price for this when their hard-won tactical experience was not fully taken into account by their superior officers.

On the Western Front, the Germans were also responsible for the systematic application of the principle of 'defence in depth'. From 1916, their development of successive lines of trenches, two or three kilometres apart and flanked by concrete machine-gun positions, made it possible to yield ground to the enemy in case of attack, to regroup in well-prepared positions and then to counter-attack. On the Somme in 1916, and then on the Chemin des Dames in 1917, this plan proved its deadly effectiveness in the face of British and French assaults. Constructed from September 1916, the Hindenburg Line, composed of fortified zones (*Stellung*), installed along a front 15 kilometres deep, characterised the new system of German defence established from the North Sea to Verdun. From the summer of 1918, this contributed considerably to slowing down the Allied advance, until its main points of support finally yielded in the course of the autumn. The British, meanwhile, adopted 'defence in depth' only gradually, from the end of 1916. For the French, the change came even later: at the time of the first German attacks in March 1918 in Picardy, the French army was still far from giving up its routine defence of front-line positions.

Among the chief drawbacks to trench warfare were lack of mobility, the difficulty of moving equipment and problems of communication and supplies. Narrow-gauge railways, which were in general use in the West, could not release the infantry from transport duties to keep the front lines supplied. Even food deliveries to the men in the front line were frequently impossible without exhausting working-party duties. Field telephones ensured that most communications got through, but constant shelling during assaults meant that their fragile wires required constant repairs under fire: flares and liaison staff therefore had to make up for the shortage or absence of communications. Movement was punishing: the winding trench lines tripled the distance to be covered, compared to the true distance as the crow flies. The (deliberate) narrowness of the trenches and communication lines, the twists and pinch points, the state of the ground underfoot and the sides of the trench, the heavy burden of individual packs and equipment, the crossing-over of columns 'going up' or 'going down' on relief, the difficulties of finding the way by night; everything exhausted the infantryman, both physically and mentally.

Yet the trench system was only apparently provisional: in fact, the patterns of fighting there were characterised by their high level of technicality. The expanding techniques of observation, from the ground (by periscope), by balloon or aircraft (aerial photography), not to mention the development of camouflage and concealment or deception, were all proof of a growing tactical sophistication. Perfect familiarity with a sector was also of great value. All of these elements explain the high losses among soldiers who were novices or newly posted to an unfamiliar sector. Battlefield experience was central here: survival in the trenches demanded a very specialised range of knowledge. This explains, for example, the difficulty faced by French and British troops as they moved on to the offensive in the summer of 1918. Trained and accustomed to static warfare where they knew all the pitfalls, these men, unlike the more recently arrived American troops, found the return to fighting over open country a real challenge. The long-established experience of a particular kind of combat proved very difficult to overturn.

In the trenches, actual combat was intermittent and even at times unusual. For this reason, what has come to be known as 'fraternisation' occurred, essentially agreements or tacit truces designed to reduce localised levels of violence. Full-scale fighting was rare, and one of its major features was the fact that it mainly meant violence delivered over a long distance. Losses from fighting with improvised weapons at close quarters represented a tiny proportion of casualties on all fronts. And yet, this did not mean that close combat did not exist. The void of the battlefield, the invisibility of the adversary, the deaths inflicted from afar and anonymously by modern weapons, did not signify a total absence of contact between adversaries. Close combat could occur at times of attack, when some soldiers had no time to leave their positions or their shelters; or in raids carried out at night across no-man's-land, with the aim of seizing prisoners for interrogation; or again as part of a surprise raid on a point in the enemy lines. The demands of this type of engagement, which was particularly frightening for the soldiers involved, led to the development of hand-to-hand weapons. Settling into the war of position and the growing technical complexity of battle was marked by regressive developments, such as the use of daggers and bludgeons or even trench shovels with sharpened sides. Museum collections, photogaphs of soldiers taken at the front, formal texts and letters written at the time, as well as certain eyewitness accounts, indicate the very visible presence of weapons for hand-to-hand fighting at the front. This was true of all the armies. Seeing such weapons does not make it easy for us to reconstruct the precise signs and practices linked to close combat. Similarly, it is difficult to determine the frequency of the use of this type of weaponry, which could be seen as instruments of precaution and reassurance as well as being effective offensive weapons.[12]

Whatever the truth, this intimate face of battle in 1914 to 1918 has been persistently downplayed. It was denied by the social actors themselves, notably in the aftermath of the war, and later most historians continued this process of downplaying it. This is understandable: there is strong guilt attached to this directly interpersonal dimension of the experience of war, which contrasts so sharply with the anonymity of industrial warfare, excusing soldiers from all responsibility for administering violence during those years. And yet this interpersonal dimension must undoubtedly be recognised as part of the process of brutalisation of the soldiers of the Great War, so well identified by the historian George Mosse. His view was that the experience of battle in the war years had 'brutalised those who had suffered it and had been active in it'.[13] To identify the problem in this way is to pose the question of registering the experience of battle in the long term, and thus that of its reappearance in other areas of society after the war.

The end of traditional battle

In France, as in Italy and the Balkans, the systematisation of the trench system transformed the Great War into a vast and long-drawn-out siege which finally became an end in itself, as the trenches, like inverted city walls, extended for hundreds of kilometres across the open countryside. Faced with the

12 Stéphane Audoin-Rouzeau, *Les armes et la chair. Trois objets de mort en 1914–1918* (Paris: A. Colin, 2009).

13 George Mosse, *Fallen Soldiers. Reshaping the Memory of the World Wars* (New York: Oxford University Press, 1990).

redoubtable effectiveness of such a situation, deployed on such a vast scale, tactics of attack evolved to reflect the growing technicality of combat. The initial attempts at breakthrough without massive preliminary bombardment, during which the infantrymen threw themselves on to networks of barbed wire undamaged by gunfire and thus impassable, were succeeded by lengthy preliminary artillery bombardment designed to eliminate enemy defences and open the way for the infantry. Yet this meant that the enemy was warned of the imminence of an attack, and the infantry in their turn suffered the consequence. The tactic of the rolling barrage, generalised from 1916, represented a refinement of this tactic of preliminary bombardment: thanks to very precise planning, the infantry, henceforward widely spaced, attacked in sudden forward dashes under the umbrella of an artillery barrage which gradually moved ahead (although the Italian infantry maintained until 1917 their habit of attacking the Austro-Hungarian defences in formations that were unnecessarily dense). But although it limited losses, this innovation requiring perfect coordination between infantry and artillery was no more successful in breaking through the enemy front line.

In contrast, the tactics of infiltration perfected by the German army from the autumn of 1917, based on the attack of *Sturmtruppen* units trained to penetrate as far as possible through the enemy positions by attacking its rear units, proved to be formidably effective. These assault tactics had first been tried in 1916: by the Germans at Verdun, and by the Russians in Galicia during the Brusilov offensive, in which the attacking forces stepped up their attacks at several points along the Austro-Hungarian line. The German General von Hutier then perfected the system in September 1917 as part of the 8th Army battles in front of Riga. Afterwards – equally, a sign of the scale of tactical east-to-west transmission – this mode of attack was deployed on a vast scale at Caporetto in October 1917, in December for the counter-offensive outside Cambrai and in March 1918 in the breakthrough in Picardy. Companies and then battalions of elite troops, grouped round determined officers, armed with light machine guns, mortars and flame-throwers, infiltrated every area where resistance was weak, attacking the rear positions and artillery concentrations. Faced with the friction caused by men lined up in depth in the trenches, and in places where the Allied headquarters had tended to respond with increasingly detailed plans of attack, the German tactic of infiltration proved to be the most effective method. Generalised by Ludendorff, the tactic relied on a high degree of independence of base groups, linked to very rapid situation reports to the core of the chain of command.

This set of tactical innovations was not, however, decisive, since it did not allow for long-range exploitation – above all when the principle of defence in depth was well established, as Pétain had succeeded in doing in 1917 to 1918. In trench warfare on the Western Front, any offensive was inevitably bound to lose strength as it penetrated further towards the heart of the enemy dispositions. The exhaustion of the waves of assault, the impossibility of moving artillery forwards over churned-up terrain, the enemy's continuing capacity to move reinforcements by lorry and train, the inadequacy of communications – all of these factors meant the failure of every major attempt to break through the multi-tiered defensive systems, at least on the Western Front. These attacks degenerated into interminable, bloody and indecisive confrontations, sometimes stretching out over several months. It needed the triple conjunction of the exhaustion of German reserves, the new effectiveness of the tank-plus-aircraft combination, and the manpower contribution of the Americans before the Allies could finally emerge from the strategic impasse, in the second half of 1918. Even so, they did not truly achieve a 'breakthrough': in the face of Allied assaults, the retreat of the German army appeared to have all the features of a gradual withdrawal.

At this time, a tactic of 'peaceful penetration' in fact prevailed among the Allies, based on the belief that enemy positions would be totally destroyed through massive bombardment and the coordination of all arms (artillery, aircraft, tanks, etc.), ahead of the occupation of a limited portion of the battlefield. This tactic, with its economical use of manpower, lay behind the Allied successes of the second half of 1918: incapable of achieving a rapid breakthrough, it was very well suited to armies which had spent the past four years bogged down in a defensive war.

In these ways, and for these reasons, the tradition of 'The Battle' in the Western world, focused on the model of very violent but very brief confrontation unfolding in a tightly constrained space and time, was dealt a decisive blow.[14] Indeed, the 'battles' of the First World War, linked as they were to the superiority of defence over attack, pushed this change to the point of absurdity, to the extent that most engagements were 'battles' in no more than name. The situation was much more one of veritable siege warfare in open country, although it rendered ineffective the techniques (rediscovered and modernised) of the traditional siege war: lines of trenches – these inverted ramparts, in some ways – mines dug beneath enemy positions, grenades,

14 Victor-Davis Hanson, *The Western Way of War. Infantry Battle in Classical Greece* (Paris: Les Belles Lettres, 1989).

short-range artillery, etc. The consequence was that the 'battle' of Verdun lasted ten months, the Somme five months, the second and third battles of Ypres a month in 1915 and five months in 1917. After having visited the Somme front, General Ludendorff was so impressed by this new kind of confrontation, dominated by the crushing power of the artillery, that he invented the expression 'battle of matériel' (*Materialschlacht*) in an attempt to name the new configuration. The expression did not last.

Tactical renewals: gas, aircraft and tanks

Modes of combat during the Great War were profoundly transformed, reflecting the new technologies which would ultimately transform Western warfare itself. It was, once again, on the Western Front that these new methods were taken to their maximum degree and developed their full range.

In this respect, the use of gas as a battle weapon was undoubtedly one of the most spectacular innovations.[15] First introduced by the Germans on the Eastern Front in January 1915 – but unsuccessfully, because of the cold and a contrary wind – and then with marked although not decisive effect at Ypres in April 1915, its use spread relatively rapidly in two main ways: the appearance of new poisons (chlorine with the addition of phosgene in the autumn of 1915, yperite and mustard gas in 1917); and the replacement of the tactic of releasing gas from cylinders by the use of artillery to deliver toxic shells that were more effective, more reliable and much more flexible in their operation. In parallel, the use of gas spread to other fronts: the Austrians used it for the first time on the Carso in June 1916, stimulating a rapid Italian response.

Once past its initial surprise effect, battle gas proved to be a weapon of limited value. In the west, counter-measures, in particular protective masks, were in due course developed faster than the means of attack: in the gas war too, therefore, defence proved to be more effective than attack. Moreover, the losses caused by gas represented only a very small percentage of the total losses of the First World War (a maximum of between 3 and 4 per cent on the Western Front).

Unlike gas, combat aircraft were already being developed before the war; after 1914, however, there was a major change of scale in the war in the skies. The military potential of aircraft and balloons had been seen by the existing armies before 1914, but the aerial arm was still in its infancy at

15 Olivier Lepick, *La Grande Guerre chimique, 1914–1918* (Paris: Presses Universitaires de France, 1998).

the outbreak of the war. Aviation developed rapidly thereafter, above all on the Western Front which, in this domain as in others, constituted the largest field of operations. By the end of the war, each of the combatant nations possessed several thousand aircraft.

But it was qualitatively that the most spectacular technological transformations emerged. In 1914, aeroplanes were too fragile to take heavy loads, to struggle against contrary winds, or to fly by night. Their role was therefore limited to reconnaissance missions (as, for example, before the Battle of the Marne), liaison and artillery guidance. With the developing war of position, however, the role of aviation expanded: long-range reconnaissance missions became possible, as well as close aerial photography and support in locating and registering artillery fire – although at the cost of heavy losses. Most aircraft brought down on the Western Front between 1914 and 1918 were reconnaissance planes. In this respect, anti-aircraft measures were increasingly important, in addition to battle planes designed to achieve and retain air supremacy.

From 1916, aviation changed profoundly: increased speed, agility, the ability to climb rapidly, ease of flying and the development of more robust machines. These factors were matched by the growing specialisation of aircraft, moves to strengthen squadrons and a series of innovations which augmented their battle effectiveness. At the end of fierce technological competition, by the autumn of 1918, Allied aircraft held absolute domination in the air. From then on, they were deployed en masse, engaged in groups of several dozen in the aerial battles known as 'dogfights'. From March to November 1918, the attack on enemy trenches was the main tactical mission of aviation, enabling it to play a leading role in all the battles of the last year of the war. The losses were very heavy, however, above all because of the development of appropriate defences (anti-aircraft guns, protective nets, projectors, barrage balloons, incendiary ammunition and pursuit action).

From 1917, airborne action was linked increasingly closely to the use of tanks, the most direct response to the strategic blockade on the Western Front. After the British Admiralty had established the first specifications for tank models, they built prototypes, fabricated experimental models and then, in April 1916, embarked on the production of the first Mark I tanks under the code name of 'water tanks' (hence the name for this new weapon). They entered service on the Somme on 15 September 1916. French research into 'assault tanks' (*les chars d'assaut*) was stimulated by the British advances: experimental trials undertaken at the end of 1915 led to the first practical developments early in 1916, commissioned from Le Creusot's Schneider factories and the Saint-Chamond factories. These models went into action for the first time during the Nivelle offensive of April 1917.

The battle effectiveness of the heavy British and French tanks proved disappointing. In September 1916, on the Somme, the use of inadequately tested tanks driven by under-trained teams ended with losses of nearly 50 per cent and with very limited effectiveness. Deployed in small numbers in April 1917 during the attack on Arras, they still produced no conclusive results. This was followed by Messines in June 1917, then Ypres in the same summer, where the new models sent into action were neutralised by the mud. The heavy French tanks met with no greater success: in April 1917, engaged in terrain that was too churned up, the tanks suffered 60 per cent losses. The heavy tanks met with no real success until October 1917, in the French offensive at Malmaison on the Chemin des Dames. Similarly, the British attack on Cambrai of 20 November 1917 was led by nearly 380 heavy tanks, which plunged through the first two lines of defence before the German fire inflicted very heavy losses on the Tank Corps.

It was only very late in the war that the Germans took tanks seriously.[16] After the attack, ultimately checked, of the British tanks on Cambrai in November 1917, Ludendorff judged that 'the best weapons against tanks were solid nerves, discipline and boldness'. The Germans developed several effective tactics to deploy against tanks: support points with one or two field guns, ditches, large camouflaged pits, minefields consisting of concealed mortar bombs, fire from coordinated artillery and machine guns, and anti-tank rifles.

While searching for a lighter model of tank, at the end of 1917 the British army introduced the medium-sized Whippet tank, which became increasingly important in British armoured operations in 1918. Meanwhile, it did not abandon heavy tanks and, with the support of 1,000 French aircraft, a large number of the heavy models supported the attack of 8 August 1918 in Picardy, which met with little resistance. Meanwhile, the French army shifted its tank production towards light models, commissioned from Renault in October 1917. Deployed as a weapon of close infantry support and supported by hundreds of aircraft, nearly 500 tanks emerged from the forest of Villers-Cotteret during the successful counter-offensive on the Aisne on 16 July 1918. They were also

16 The *A7V Panzerkampfwagen* was thus the only tank produced in Germany. It was the heaviest of all models produced in 1914–18, which made it an easy target. During 1918, the Germans had only very few of these tanks available and, despite the contribution from British tanks captured in battle, their use on the battlefield remained entirely marginal.

used during the final assaults of 1918, notably in the combined Franco-American offensive on the Meuse–Argonne front on 26 September. At least in part, the tanks had resolved the tactical problem posed by the war of position: they finally made it possible to crush the barbed wire and to enable artillery and machine guns to advance in support of infantry.

This massive presence of aircraft and tanks on the Western Front at the end of the war signalled the definitive end of the role of traditional cavalry as a breakthrough force on the modern battlefield. Moreover, aircraft and tanks were deliberately used as substitutes for now-ineffective horses, part of a very ancient warrior ethos itself now vanished from the trenches. However, horses were still used on a very large scale on the Western Front. And a change of this kind, as much cultural as tactical, did not take place everywhere: on the Eastern Front, in the Balkans, and still more in the Near East and in Africa, traditional cavalry forces retained a major role to the end of the war. And even on the Western Front, the hope lingered on for a long time that cavalry divisions could be launched in pursuit of the enemy, once the breach was opened in enemy positions. The experience of modern battle in these four years of war thus only slowly and incompletely overturned the very ancient body of military values which, in Europe, was attached to warrior activity, much of which took place on horseback or alongside the cavalry.

Conclusion

The price of the fumblings and tactical wanderings of the First World War can be read in its human cost. This applies particularly on the Western Front, which was also the most deadly. Between 1914 and 1918, losses in battle reached levels beyond any historic precedent, anywhere. The total has been calculated at close to 10 million dead among the European and Western belligerent nations; the number of wounded was probably close to or above 21 million. The average losses each year from 1914 to 1918 rose to nearly 900 men killed *per day* for the French, more than 1,300 for the Germans; for Russia, the daily figure was close to 1,450. The most murderous days of battle recorded in the twentieth century indeed relate to the First World War and not to later conflicts: on 20 to 23 August 1914, the French army lost 40,000 men killed, including 27,000 on 22 August alone. On 1 July 1916, losses in the British army were 20,000 men dead and 40,000 wounded.

Between August 1914 and November 1918, the Great War transformed the conditions and patterns of Western war, in virtually all respects. The war introduced a new kind of soldier, lying flat under fire, as invisible as possible, in a dirty and muddy uniform, powerless in the face of shelling and machine-gun fire, physically exhausted, sometimes permanently traumatised. His tactical skills, the result of training, battle experience, acquired endurance and physical courage no doubt still played their part in his own survival, but from that time on they frequently weighed little against the effectiveness of the blind anonymous fire that is characteristic of modern warfare. The twentieth-century battlefield, deadly and empty, ceased to be the unquestioned 'field of honour' of nineteenth-century attitudes. Between 1914 and 1918, Western representations of the military-virile model suffered a decisive blow. A certain 'image of man'[17] undoubtedly never recovered from the experience of those four years.

The historian John Horne has very rightly stressed that the soldiers had lived through 'their own cognitive dissociation between the image of war that they had grown up with (and as it continued to be imagined) and the counter-evidence of the battlefield'.[18] Nonetheless, it should be noted that they did not resolve this dissociation by a rejection of battle and the tactical modes of attack, however deadly, in which they were simultaneously victims and actors. In three cases only did the will to continue the fight collapse on a large scale.[19] The disaster of Caporetto in October 1917 was followed by an episode of mass surrender (280,000 prisoners), with temporary desertions and mutiny, affecting an Italian army in full retreat, if not in panic, until the restoration of military order; in the Russian army, in the summer and autumn of 1917, 1 million deserters could initially be seen leaving the front, spontaneously and collectively. As they returned to the interior with their weapons, their combat violence was transferred to the rear;[20] in October to November 1918, finally, a very small element of the German army remained at their stations while whole groups surrendered to the enemy, with their junior officers as intermediaries.[21] Spectacular though these rejections of the war

17 George Mosse, *The Image of Man. The Creation of Modern Masculinity* (New York: Oxford University Press, 1995).

18 John Horne, 'De la guerre de mouvement à la guerre de positions: les combattants français', in John Horne *et al.* (eds.), *Vers la guerre totale. Le tournant de 1914–1915* (Paris: Tallandier, 2012), p. 91.

19 The French mutinies in the spring of 1917 constitute in this respect a much more limited phenomenon numerically, and much more controlled in the practices operated by the mutineers (Leonard V. Smith, *Between Mutiny and Obedience. The Case of the French Fifth Infantry Division during World War I* (Princeton University Press, 1994).

20 Nicolas Werth, 'Les déserteurs en Russie: violence de guerre, violence révolutionnaire et violence paysanne (1916–1921)', in Stéphane Audoin-Rouzeau *et al.* (eds.), *La violence de guerre, 1914–1945* (Brussels: Complexe, 2002), pp. 99–116.

21 Alexander Watson, *Enduring the Great War. Combat, Morale and Collapse in the German and British Armies, 1914–1918* (Cambridge University Press, 2008).

were, it is, however, striking to note how late in the war they occurred, even *in extremis* as in the final example cited here. For the war as a whole, the 70 million men mobilised between 1914 and 1918 resolved the cognitive dissociation between combat imagined and combat experienced in their acceptance, in their mass and in the long run, of the conditions of engagement which faced them, however ill-suited, however deadly, they may have been. The solidarity of the primary group and the severe constraints of military discipline cannot explain this alone: it must be remembered that the Great War marked the outcome of a long process of the 'nationalisation of the masses'[22] – certainly more advanced in Western Europe than in Eastern and Balkan Europe – which substantiated the *defensive* motivations (strongly present even at the core of the armies serving as occupying forces) and encouraged the processes of interiorisation of social constraints at the heart of the existing armies.

The great rejection of the forms of battle and the tactics in operation during the war thus relate above all to its aftermath. It was in this post-war period that the war of 1914 to 1918 lost all meaning and came to be seen as an absurdity. This particular experience has become ugliness par excellence, epitomised in expressions such as 'butchery' or 'abattoir' which emerged in the post-war writing of most eyewitnesses of the Great War. Although never unanimous, this new representation of battle asserted itself gradually, with growing strength. The image of war in the twentieth century has proceeded broadly from this discrediting of a set of ideas about battlefield tactics that was destroyed forever by the conditions and modes of battle between 1914 and 1918.

22 George Mosse, *The Nationalization of the Masses. Political Symbolism and Mass Movements in Germany from the Napoleonic Wars through the Third Reich* (New York: H. Fertig, 1975).

7
Morale

ALEXANDER WATSON

When, at the end of October 1918, General Erich Ludendorff complained that German defeat was imminent not due to numerical inferiority, but as a result of 'the spirit of the troops', he vindicated the widely held belief that morale would be decisive in the outcome of the First World War.[1] For wartime commanders, neither machines nor material, but troop psychology and, in contemporary parlance, 'spirit' were paramount in armed struggle. This conviction had already developed in peace, a reaction both to vast increases in firepower caused by the adoption of magazine rifles, machine guns and quick-firing artillery and to Social Darwinist fears of societal degeneration. To those who wished to believe that the attack was still possible in the new conditions of combat, it was convenient to stress that firepower was less decisive than the quality of an army's human material. Ferdinand Foch, who as supreme Allied commander would play a vital role in the German military defeat of 1918, famously declared in 1903 that: 'War = the domain of moral force. Victory = moral superiority in the victors; moral depression in the vanquished.'[2] Significantly, however, the industrial warfare of 1914 to 1918 did not challenge, but confirmed this formula. Field Marshal Franz Conrad von Hötzendorf, the Chief of the Habsburg General Staff until March 1917, for example, could still write with conviction in the conflict's aftermath that an army's effectiveness was determined by 'combatant strength, equipment, training, discipline and above all the moral value'.[3]

1 Report of the Saxon Militärbevollmächtigter to War Minister of a speech given by Ludendorff, 24 October 1918. Hauptstaatsarchiv Dresden, Militärbevollmächtigter 4216, fo. 114–15.

2 Ferdinand Foch, *The Principles of War*, trans. H. Belloc (New York: Henry Holt & Co., 1920), p. 287.

3 Franz Conrad von Hötzendorf, *Aus meiner Dienstzeit 1906–1918. 24. Juni 1914 bis 30. September 1914. Die politischen und militärischen Vorgänge vom Fürstenmord in Sarajevo bis zum Abschluß der ersten und bis zum Beginn der zweiten Offensive gegen Serbien und Rußland*, 4 vols. (Vienna: Rikola, 1923), vol. IV, p. 222.

Early-twentieth-century military professionals often referred to 'moral' rather than 'morale'; a usage reflecting the strong ethical connotations which the term possessed for them. As Friedrich Altrichter, a German officer, veteran of the First World War and scholar of military science, explained in the interwar period, morale 'encompasses all the martial virtues, among which courage and boldness, resolution, tenacity, the will to triumph and also the endurance of strain and privation stand in the first position'.[4] In an era of mass armies, however, it was unrealistic to suppose that every soldier would be a hero. The foremost pre-war thinker on morale, the French Colonel Ardant du Picq, warned that 'the mass always cowers at the sight of the phantom, death'. The challenge was to override individuals' self-preservation instinct, and Ardant du Picq saw the solution in military organisation. Self-confident leaders, 'iron discipline' and a cause, be it 'religious fanaticism, national pride, a love of glory' or 'a madness for possession', were all necessary. Above all, however, he stressed that armies should cultivate mutual trust among their men and foster self-supporting, self-supervising teams, thus promoting 'unity' and 'moral cohesion'.[5]

Modern research on morale has extended Ardant du Picq's insight. S. A. Stouffer's seminal study of the American soldier during the Second World War, for example, explained how 'the guidance and support of the formal Army system and the informal combat group, convictions about the war and the enemy' and 'personal philosophies of combat' all sustained men in battle.[6] Other sociologists, notably Morris Janowitz, Edward A. Shils and Roger W. Little, have deepened understanding of what today are called 'primary groups' – the bands of front-line soldiers whom Ardant du Picq saw as crucial in an army's resilience.[7] Yet, increasingly, researchers have argued that military organisation can provide only a partial explanation of morale – understood in this chapter not in terms of troops' mood or happiness (as combatants are frequently dirty, exhausted, frightened and miserable, while

4 Friedrich Altrichter, *Die seelischen Kräfte des Deutschen Heeres im Frieden und im Weltkriege* (Berlin: Mittler, 1933), p. 41.

5 Charles J. J. J. Ardant du Picq, *Battle Studies: Ancient and Modern*, trans. J. N. Greely and R. C. Cotton (n. pl.: Dodo Press, 1921, 2012), pp. 73–9.

6 Samuel A. Stouffer *et al.*, *The American Soldier. Combat and its Aftermath*, 2 vols. (Princeton, NJ: John Wiley & Sons, 1949, 1965), vol. II, pp. 105–91.

7 See Edward A. Shils and Morris Janowitz, 'Cohesion and disintegration in the Wehrmacht in World War II', *Public Opinion Quarterly*, 12 (1948), pp. 280–315; Roger W. Little, 'Buddy relations and combat performance', in Morris Janowitz (ed.), *The New Military. Changing Patterns of Organization* (New York: Russell Sage Foundation, 1964), pp. 195–223.

still continuing to perform their battlefield role), but functionally, as *the readiness of a soldier or a group of soldiers to carry out the commands issued by military leadership*. As Stephen D. Wesbrook has observed, soldiers in the twentieth century have needed wider loyalties beyond the 'primary group' to legitimise and elicit obedience to the orders – often highly detrimental to men's personal safety – issued by military authorities. For mass armies of citizen-soldiers, these allegiances have usually been to the society and state which they defend.[8]

Commanders were correct to expect morale to play a decisive role in the First World War. Their armies became nations in arms: over half of all military-aged men were mobilised in Britain and Italy, while four-fifths had served in the armed forces of France, Germany and Austria-Hungary by 1918. Upholding these citizen-soldiers' morale proved critically important for two reasons. The first was the unforeseen duration of the war. Ardant du Picq, Foch and other pre-war theorists had been principally preoccupied with how to motivate men in the extreme danger of the attack. Yet for all armies in 1914 to 1918, equally, if not more important, was sustaining their soldiers through extended periods of gruelling static warfare offering little prospect of victory. Secondly, the tactical methods developed to break the deadlock placed a new premium on high morale. The French in particular found to bloody cost in the conflict's opening campaign that neither impulsive *élan* nor unconditional obedience were alone sufficient to carry troops across the fire-swept battlefield. However, the most effective armies learned over the course of hostilities to devolve authority downwards to non-commissioned officers (NCOs) and junior officers, and employ open order, combined arms tactics dependent for their success on the men's own drive and determination. In their efforts to sustain and inspire their citizen-soldiers, armies employed not only traditional military motivational methods, but also innovated. Recognising that their wartime manpower's loyalties and the source of its combat motivation lay beyond the military organisation, they took their first faltering steps into psychological warfare, seeking to reinforce their own troops' commitment to society and state, while attacking that of the enemy.

8 Stephen D. Wesbrook, 'The potential for military disintegration', in Sam C. Sarkesian (ed.), *Combat Effectiveness. Cohesion, Stress and the Volunteer Military* (London: Sage Publications, 1980), pp. 244–78.

Morale and the military

The armies that fought the First World War possessed long and partially shared traditions of motivating soldiers. Centuries of European warfare had produced organisations similar in structure and appearance, highly adapted to withstand the immense psychological and physical stresses of battle. Training, discipline, cohesion, support and leadership were the five methods which were all used to underpin their men's morale. The forms in which these were applied, and the success, varied however according to armies' own traditions and doctrines, their officers and manpower, and also the dominant ideology of their parent societies and states.

Training was considered the foundation of high morale by professional officers across Europe in 1914. In peacetime, continental militaries had retained their conscripts for at least two years, while the British had maintained a force of long-service professional soldiers. War forced a drastic reduction in the training provided to recruits; in the German and British armies it was set at three months by 1918. However, its purposes and methods remained substantially unchanged. It had three goals. First, it was intended to raise men's physical strength through exercises and strenuous route marches. Secondly, good basic training would develop the skills and self-confidence needed to function in combat. It would teach fieldcraft and familiarise a soldier with his weapons. It was also supposed to provide him with a realistic idea of conditions on the battlefield. Finally, and most importantly, it was designed to socialise the recruit into the army, fostering, as the British army's infantry training manual of 1914 stated, 'the development of the soldierly spirit'.[9]

The first step in this process everywhere was to instil discipline. For Prussian Field Regulations, this was 'the keystone of the army' and 'precondition for every success'.[10] Discipline was imparted by assimilating the newcomer into the military organisation, teaching him to obey its rules and cultivating a collective martial identity. Recruits were clothed uniformly, their heads were shorn and they were introduced to the communal routines of barrack life. They practised close order drill, an exercise which accustomed men to act together and give instant obedience to superiors' commands. Off the parade ground, as well as on it, their conduct was regulated by watchful NCOs, and even tiny deviation from regulations was immediately punished. The aim of strict training regimes was to emphasise the army's absolute power and to

9 [British] General Staff, War Office, *Infantry Training. (4-Company Organization) 1914* (London: HMSO, 1914), p. 1.

10 [Prussian] Kriegsministerium, *Felddienst-Ordnung. (F.O.)* (Berlin: Mittler, 1908), p. 9.

socialise men into habits of obedience. Compliance should cease to be a conscious choice for soldiers and become an automatic reaction; defiance, even at times of intense stress and mortal danger, should be literally unthinkable.

Armies never allowed soldiers to forget these first lessons in discipline. Although men were less closely regulated and harassed beyond the recruit depot, the expectation of unconditional respect for the authority of NCOs and officers remained, and was backed by a vast range of sanctions. These varied in harshness from army to army. Thus, delinquents guilty of more minor offences in the British and, until it abolished the punishment in 1917, the German army might be bound for several hours in public to a wheel or post. The Austro-Hungarians went a step further, also until 1917, manacling petty offenders hand and foot and leaving them in discomfort for several hours. The Russian army sanctioned beatings and whippings. More serious crimes, such as desertion, cowardice or mutiny, were punished in most forces with long prison sentences. Armies also proved adaptive, however. The Ottoman military, reluctant to lose manpower from the front line, replaced some prison sentences with corporal punishment in 1916. Similarly, when German commanders began to suspect in 1917 that some soldiers regarded a prison term as preferable to active service, they established seventy-eight penal companies in which convicts were put to work performing dangerous tasks at the front.

Armies also possessed the ultimate power to sentence men to death during the First World War. Even in the most punitive forces, however, executions remained highly exceptional (see Table 7.1).

The Germans were most sparing in applying the death penalty because their justice system was staffed by professional legal personnel and influenced more than that of other forces by civilian norms. Their courts' concern with justice for the individual was bitterly criticised after the war by conservatives, who claimed wrongly that it had damaged discipline and morale. The lenience of the US military was solely due to President Wilson, who commuted all death sentences for military crime; only murderers and rapists were executed. Other forces embraced the death penalty as a deterrent more wholeheartedly. The French used exemplary executions to enforce order already during their troops' first morale crisis in August and September 1914. After the army was swept by mutinies in 1917, they were again employed on a lesser but significant scale as a symbolic restoration of the higher command's authority. In the British army, the punishment received by a deserter depended not only on the circumstances of his crime and past conduct, but also on whether his commanders believed that an exemplary execution might benefit his unit's

Table 7.1 *Military executions, 1914–18.*

Army	Manpower	Executions	% of men executed
German	13,380,000	48	0.00036
American (1917–18)	4,750,000	35*	0.00074
British Empire	5,250,000	346	0.00659
French	8,100,000	*c.* 600	0.00741
Austro-Hungarian	9,000,000	754	0.00838
Italian (1915–18)	5,600,000	729	0.01302

Sources: R. Overmans, 'Kriegsverluste' in G. Hirschfeld *et al.* (eds.), *Enzyklopädie Erster Weltkrieg*, 2nd edn (Paderborn: Ferdinand Schöningh, 2004), p. 664; C. Corns and J. Hughes-Wilson, *Blindfold and Alone. British Military Executions in the Great War* (London: Cassell, 2001), pp. 103–4; G. Lelewer, 'Die Militärpersonen' in F. Exner, *Krieg und Kriminalität in Österreich* (Vienna and New Haven, CT: Holder-Pichler-Tempsky and Yale University Press, 1927), p. 126; Nicolas Offenstadt, *Les fusillés de la Grande Guerre et la mémoire collective (1914–1999)* (Paris: Odile Jacob, 1999), p. 21; Jennifer D. Keene, *Doughboys, the Great War, and the Remaking of America* (Baltimore, MD and London: John Hopkins University Press, 2001), p. 65; V. Wilcox, 'Discipline in the Italian Army 1915–1918' in P. Purseigle (ed.), *Warfare and Belligerence. Perspectives in First World War Studies* (Leiden and Boston, MA: Brill, 2005), p. 80.
*America's executions were all for non-military crimes (murder and rape). Ten soldiers were executed in France and twenty-five in the United States.

discipline. The force's justice system did adjust to the influx of citizen-soldiers during the war and became more forgiving: the highpoint of executions was passed already in mid 1915. Nonetheless, commanders strove to magnify executions' deterrent effect, publicising them throughout the ranks as warnings of the dire fate that could befall those who defied authority.

The supervisory organs at armies' disposal were also potent deterrents against indiscipline, for they ensured that any serious flouting of military authority would most likely quickly be noticed and attract retribution. A man seeking to flee the front had not only to evade his comrades and immediate superiors, but also, behind the lines, military police. Their numbers swelled during the war, albeit due to increased traffic control as well as disciplinary duties: in the British army, the ratio of military policemen to soldiers soared from 1 to every 3,306 in 1914 to 1 to 292 in 1918.[11] They manned straggler posts, searched houses behind the front and, further back, patrolled

11 David Englander and James Osborne, 'Jack, Tommy and Henry Dubb. The armed forces and the working class', *Historical Journal*, 21 (1978), p. 595.

trains, stations and ports. The risk of capture, and the difficulty of covering sometimes vast distances to reach home, ensured that desertion was principally a problem in the rear and along the lines of communication, not at the front. This was the case even in very adverse circumstances. Thus, in the Russian army during the spring and early summer following the revolution of March 1917, desertions from combat units comprised less than 1 per cent of strength, despite the fact that across the whole force a fivefold increase was registered. The main leakage came from rear-line units, men overstaying leave and, above all, reinforcement battalions.[12] The same was true of Austria-Hungary and the Ottoman Empire, where 250,000 and 500,000 deserters respectively hid in cities or roamed the countryside as bandits by the war's end.[13] Similarly, in the German army, as many as 180,000 men may have absconded from railways en route to France in the summer and autumn of 1918. By contrast, on the Western Front, the most recent research has found that, although the Allies' final offensives shook the field army's disciplinary system, desertion was not a major phenomenon before the very last weeks of the war.[14]

Discipline, in its dual manifestations as both the socialisation of men into habits of obedience and an ever-present deterrent that threatened malcontents with capture and harsh punishment, was highly effective in ensuring a minimum of compliance from most soldiers. This was best demonstrated by the Italian army, which was run by its Chief of Staff up until 1917, General Luigi Cadorna, according to the precept 'without instilling fear in everyone, nothing is achieved'.[15] Its military law code was arbitrary and ruthlessly applied. Around one in every seventeen Italian soldiers was charged with offences, and 65 per cent were found guilty. Summary justice was sanctioned. At least

12 Allan K. Wildman, *The End of the Russian Imperial Army. The Old Army and the Soldiers' Revolt (March–April 1917)* (Princeton University Press, 1980), pp. 362–71.

13 See Mark Cornwall, *The Undermining of Austria-Hungary. The Battle for Hearts and Minds* (Basingstoke and New York: Macmillan and St Martin's Press, 2000), pp. 408–9; Erik-Jan Zürcher, 'Little Mehmet in the desert: the Ottoman soldier's experience', in Hugh Cecil and Peter H. Liddle (eds.), *Facing Armageddon. The First World War Experienced* (London: Leo Cooper, 1996), p. 234.

14 Alexander Watson, *Enduring the Great War. Combat, Morale and Collapse in the German and British Armies, 1914–1918* (Cambridge University Press, 2008), pp. 206–15; and Christoph Jahr, *Gewöhnliche Soldaten. Desertion und Deserteure im deutschen und britischen Heer 1914–1918* (Göttingen: Vandenhoeck & Ruprecht, 1998), pp. 166–7. A different but problematic portrayal of desertion and 'shirking' on the Western Front is Wilhelm Deist, 'The military collapse of the German Empire: the reality behind the stab-in-the-back myth', *War in History*, 3 (1996), pp. 186–207.

15 Cadorna, quoted in Vanda Wilcox, '"Weeping tears of blood": exploring Italian soldiers' emotions in the First World War', *Modern Italy*, 17 (2012), p. 179.

200 men were executed without trial, some the victims of decimation (in which one of every ten soldiers in a unit was chosen at random to be shot), which was used from January 1916 in cases where large numbers of men were to be punished or guilty parties could not be identified.[16] Terrible as it was, the system carried the Italian Army through eleven bloody battles on the Isonzo between May 1915 and September 1917. Yet it had clear limitations. First, fear did not inspire in soldiers initiative or aggression. Even allowing for the extraordinarily difficult mountainous terrain in which the army operated, its combat performance remained notably weak throughout its eleven offensives. Secondly, when the army was itself attacked at Caporetto, the twelfth Battle of the Isonzo, by an enemy employing innovative infiltration tactics and setting a pace of operations which overwhelmed its ability to react, fear of punitive discipline proved inadequate to deter Italian soldiers from retreating or capitulating. Almost 250,000 surrendered to advancing German or Austro-Hungarian troops, and in the general panic tens of thousands more deserted.

Sensibly, most armies sought not merely to subdue their soldiers, but also to provide them with new corporate identities which would support them in danger and provide positive reasons to fight. The British army's infantry training manual stressed in 1914 that instruction for the recruit should 'increase his powers of initiative, of self-confidence, and of self-restraint', 'give him confidence in his superiors and comrades' and 'teach him how to act in combination with his comrades in order to defeat the enemy'.[17] These goals became ever-more important during the war, as armies gradually recognised that devolving authority downwards and fostering and harnessing initiative and teamwork among the troops would be indispensable in breaking the deadlock. 'Tactics', Ludendorff remembered, 'became more and more individualized'.[18] The speed with which this process took place varied among, and even within, armies, but a key point in its development came about at the turn of 1916/17, when both the German and British armies published new tactical guidelines. The Germans' 'Principles of Leadership in the Defensive Battle in Position Warfare' of December 1916 put forward a more flexible defensive scheme, in which front-line officers and their men would have greater

16 Vanda Wilcox, 'Discipline in the Italian Army 1915–1918', in Pierre Purseigle (ed.), *Warfare and Belligerence. Perspectives in First World War Studies* (Leiden and Boston, MA: Brill, 2005), pp. 80–5.
17 [British] General Staff, War Office, *Infantry Training*, p. 2.
18 Erich Ludendorff, *My War Memories 1914–1918*, 2 vols. (Uckfield: The Naval & Military Press, 1919, 2005), vol. 1, p. 387.

autonomy. Much of the combat would be conducted by scattered 'primary groups' from shell holes, rather than whole companies fighting in line. 'Soldiers in the ranks with nerves as hard as steel' were, the pamphlet advocated, to 'become the main bearer of the fight'.[19] The British were thinking along similar lines at the lower tactical levels. Their army's 'Instructions for the Training of Platoons for Offensive Action' (February 1917) regarded the platoon (a unit of around fifty men under an officer) no longer as a line of riflemen under supervision, but as a dynamic, self-contained tactical unit. Each of its four sections had a speciality – rifles, grenades, rifle grenades and a light machine gun – and it was cooperation and mutual support among these differently armed soldiers which would enable the advance. Both the German and British tactical innovations relied on the troops' self-motivation and teamwork. As Ludendorff rightly recognised, they 'made demands on the men which could only be fulfilled by troops which, if no longer trained to perfection, were at any rate animated by a spirit of self-sacrifice and true discipline'.[20]

The 'primary group' at the centre of these new tactics was much more, however, than a mere combat team. It was a key support underpinning the resilience of both the individual and the army. As the American sociologist Samuel Stouffer explained after the Second World War, it 'served two principal functions: it *set and enforced group standards* of behaviour, and it *supported and sustained the individual* in stresses he would otherwise not have been able to withstand'.[21] Soldiers during the First World War greatly valued the security offered by membership of a trusted group of comrades. A study of German combatants' psychological coping strategies undertaken during the conflict identified 'social emotions' as the third most frequently named support in danger after 'religious feelings' and 'memories of home'. Autobiographical accounts offer insight into the relations between soldiers. In Frederic Manning's fictionalised account of his war service on the Somme, the men's social horizons are limited. His hero, Bourne, 'only knew a few of the men outside his own section by name'. Bourne's closest relations are with Shem, a fellow veteran, and Martlow, a younger soldier. While the men have little in common personally, the war makes their mutual support indispensable: there was, Manning writes, 'no bond stronger than the necessity which had bound them together'. Within the wider group there are tensions, divisions of rank – but also loyalties formed through communal life, the

19 See Matthias Strohn, *The German Army and the Defence of the Reich. Military Doctrine and the Conduct of the Defensive Battle 1918–1939* (Cambridge University Press, 2011), pp. 49–54.
20 Ludendorff, *War Memories*, vol. I, p. 387.
21 Stouffer *et al.*, *American Soldier*, vol. II, pp. 130–1.

pooling of food and reliance on one another in danger. As the soldier who, at the end of the book, brings Bourne's lifeless body back to British lines miserably asserts, ''ere we are, an' since we're 'ere, we're just fightin' for ourselves; we're just fightin' for ourselves, an' for each other'.[22]

The high casualty rates suffered by combatants between 1914 and 1918 might call into question whether comradeship could be sustained. Was the turnover caused by deaths or wounds such that soldiers were separated before they had a chance to build mutual bonds of trust? Certainly, fighting was sometimes so bloody that 'primary groups' were wiped out. On one day in the Battle of Arras in April 1917, for example, the combat strength of Bavarian Infantry Regiment 18 dropped from over 2,000 to 220 soldiers. Other evidence, however, taken from a typical British battalion, the 1/5th Durham Light Infantry (DLI), suggests that units could maintain a core of veterans, even in the lethal conditions of the Western Front. The 1/5th DLI were territorial soldiers who fought in Belgium and France from April 1915. They served in some of the worst fighting of the war: immediately upon its arrival at the front, the battalion was thrown into the Second Battle of Ypres, it then fought on the Somme in September 1916, participated in the British offensives at Arras and at Ypres in the spring and autumn of 1917 and was finally wiped out when facing German attacks in March, April and May 1918. The battalion's initial strength of 1,031 soldiers was but a third of its wartime losses of 3,285 killed, wounded and prisoners.[23] Nonetheless, examination of its casualty rolls demonstrates that the 1/5th DLI's original members maintained a significant presence for a surprisingly long time. A quarter of the men killed on the Somme in September 1916, after the battalion had spent nearly a year-and-a-half at the front, belonged to its initial complement. Original members comprised one-sixth of the unit's fatalities at Arras in April 1917. Even in March 1918, after three years on the Western Front, these veterans accounted for one-seventh of the battalion's dead in the first of the German spring offensives (see Figure 7.1).

The lifespan of 'primary groups' could be prolonged by returning the wounded, once they were healed, to their original units. The dead, by contrast, did leave the ranks of the 'primary group' permanently, yet, importantly, did not necessarily lose membership of it. Soldiers remembered fallen comrades, and the desire to avenge them or to ensure that their sacrifice was

22 Frederic Manning, *The Middle Parts of Fortune* (London: Penguin, 1930, 2000), pp. 20, 156, 232.

23 Alwyn L. Raimes, *The Fifth Battalion. The Durham Light Infantry 1914–1918* (n. pl.: Committee of Past and Present Officers of the Battalion, 1931), pp. 214–15, 222, 226.

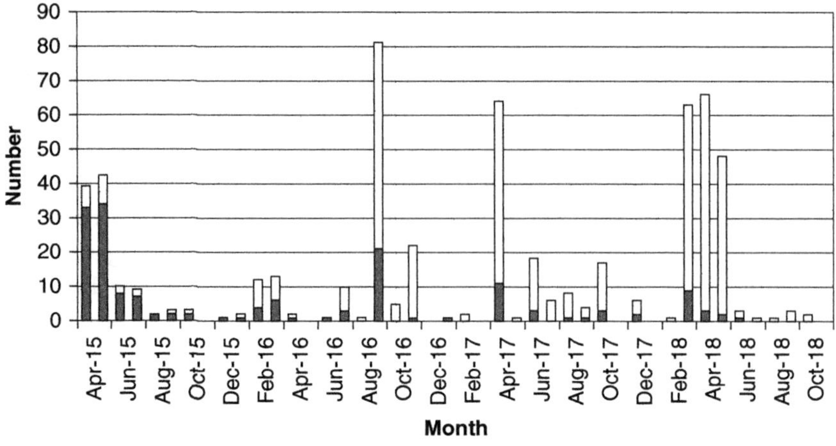

Figure 7.1 1/5th Durham Light Infantry (other ranks) killed in action, April 1915 – November 1918.
Source: A.L. Raimes, *The Fifth Battalion. The Durham Light Infantry 1914–1918* (no place: Committee of Past and Present Officers of the Battalion, 1931), pp. 204–12 and 216–22.

vindicated could strengthen survivors' will to fight through to victory. Such memories could also contribute beyond the 'primary group' to broader unit cohesion. *Esprit de corps*, which had been cultivated in peace by familiarising troops with their regiments' traditions and glorious martial deeds in past wars, came increasingly to rest on the shared memory of the battalion or regimental community's own sacrifices and ordeals in the 1914 to 1918 conflict. This was reflected in songs composed by soldiers. Germans in Reserve Infantry Regiment 30 still sung in 1915 about comrades killed in the unit's baptism of fire in August 1914. Infantry Regiment 114 had a song in 1916 which recalled its successful defence against French attack a year earlier at Loos. On the other side of the lines, British soldiers in the 16/King's Royal Rifle Brigade sang about 'the lads that we have left behind' and promised grimly that 'we will have our own back on the Allemands one day'.[24]

Armies took various measures to strengthen cohesion in 'primary groups' and larger units. The most common, employed by all but the Ottoman military, was to recruit territorially. Men hailing from the same region and speaking the same dialect would, it was believed, form attachments to one

24 'There's a battalion out in France', in Roy Palmer (ed.), *'What a Lovely War!' British Soldiers' Songs from the Boer War to the Present Day* (London: Michael Joseph, 1990), p. 115.

another more quickly and would fight for the same narrowly defined 'home'. The British took this idea furthest with their wartime 'Pals Battalions' filled with men from the same streets, associations or firms. More usually, however, wider regional identities were tapped. British regiments in peacetime were, in theory if often not in practice, recruited from one or two counties. During the war, regiments and even divisions raised in populous areas did maintain a shire identity, and those that could not were allocated men from neighbouring areas, so that at least a broader regional homogeneity was maintained. Continental armies focused on regional loyalties from the start. Austria-Hungary was divided into sixteen corps districts, while France had twenty-one military regions on the eve of war. The Germans raised regiments and drew reinforcements from twenty-four army corps districts covering the Reich. Both French and German units were, in addition, divided by age, thus making them even more homogeneous. Heavy casualties led already in 1915 to much mixing, as drafts were posted to whichever unit most needed them. French regiments' local and regional identities collapsed. The Germans, by contrast, strove to restore their units' homogeneity during the second half of the war. From August 1916, reinforcements were again allocated to units according to age and, in 1917, men and even regiments were transferred between divisions to strengthen their regional homogeneity.

While promoting 'primary group' bonds was relatively easy for nationally homogeneous armies, it presented a far greater challenge for multi-ethnic forces. In the US army, nearly one-fifth of soldiers were foreign-born and some formations extremely mixed: the 77th division, for example, contained men from over forty nationalities. Only through the adoption of an elaborate training programme were they turned into effective soldiers. All foreign-language-speaking recruits were assigned to special developmental units where they learned drill and attended intensive English-language courses. The platoons to which they were allocated, however, were composed of men who shared the same tongue. In this way, it was hoped that troops would gain sufficient English to understand commands and communicate with soldiers beyond their unit, yet would, through their own language and common cultural traditions, successfully build strong 'primary groups' within their own formations.

In other circumstances, homogeneity might be undesirable for a multi-ethnic force. In the Austro-Hungarian army, Czech, Serb and Ruthenian soldiers were regarded as deeply untrustworthy by the High Command. The force employed a territorial recruitment system at the war's opening which, although it did not remove ethnic diversity within units, did at least limit it: 142 of the 330 regiments in the Common Army and Austrian *Landwehr* were linguistically homogeneous, 164 used two languages, and a small minority of twenty-four were even more linguistically mixed. In May 1917, after a controversial surrender by a Czech regiment in April 1915 and the catastrophic Brusilov offensive in the summer of 1916, the army abandoned this structure, reorganising its regiments to make them much more ethnically mixed. This measure was designed to improve the performance of 'unreliable' groups by ensuring that they could no longer dominate units. Surrounding them with loyal troops placed them under closer supervision and ensured that peer pressure encouraged obedience, not defiance, to military orders. However, the new mixed composition also brought serious costs: it loosened the social bonds underpinning unit cohesion as troops could scarcely become comrades when communication was limited to the eighty German words comprising the army's language of command. The reorganisation was largely effective in obstructing front-line mutinies, but it probably also contributed to the mediocre combat performance of Habsburg units in 1918.

However an army chose to organise its men, it also had to support their basic needs. Soldiers' health, mood and, ultimately, morale was greatly influenced by how well fed, clothed and rested they were. The physiological was the most significant but far from the sole aspect of these needs. Food, which the German military postal censor found 'plays absolutely the most important role in the soldier's life', could promote 'primary group' bonding.[25] The sharing of food and, behind the lines, alcohol brought men in the same squad or section closer emotionally. Food was also highly influential for inter-rank relations. It might lubricate these relations: officers in every army went through the ritual of tasting their subordinates' rations in order to express paternalistic care. On the other hand, it could be deeply divisive. In the German army, the shortages that began after the spring of 1916 caused troops to regard their officers' nutritional privileges with bitterness. The decreasing quality of food was also interpreted by the Central Powers' soldiers as a predictor of defeat. As one man wrote home in July 1917, 'at midday there was a meal which was impossible to enjoy. If it continues this way, we cannot win'.[26]

Clothing also affected morale in ways that went beyond its basic functions of keeping troops warm, dry and capable of marching. A man's uniform was the external expression of his military identity and position in the army. It contributed to unit cohesion as the numbers and badges that it carried marked

25 German 5th Army censorship report, 12 July 1917, p. 14. Bundesarchiv-Militärarchiv Freiburg [hereinafter, BA-MA Freiburg]: W-10/50794.
26 *Ibid.*, p. 22. BA-MA Freiburg: W-10/ 50794.

out its wearer as a member of a particular regiment or division. Other additions were more personal, testifying to a soldier's own war service. Wound stripes, bars, chevrons and badges were introduced during the conflict, allowing troops to wear their sacrifices – in Britons' case, literally – on their sleeves. Medals were offered to encourage soldiers to act courageously, although armies' generosity varied greatly. While only around 5 per cent of personnel in the British Expeditionary Force received a distinction, the Central Powers' militaries were far more ready to distribute awards. Already by 1917, the Austro-Hungarians had given out more than 3 million medals. The Germans were no less profligate, awarding 5,209,000 Iron Cross Class IIs, one for almost every second soldier who served. Ultimately, however, such generosity proved counterproductive as the ubiquity of medals eroded their symbolic value and desirability.

Rest, as well as food and clothing, was a basic requirement of combat troops. Units left too long in the field became exhausted and apathetic, and their strength was eroded as men reported sick. Rotating troops in and out of the line frequently was critical in sustaining their fighting potential. Researchers found in the Second World War that soldiers who were regularly rested remained combat effective for up to twice as long (measured in days in action) as those given no relief. Additionally, the timely withdrawal of units helped to preserve their 'primary groups' and *esprit de corps*. At the Battle of Verdun in 1916, German practice was to keep units at the front until they suffered such heavy casualties that they could no longer hold their positions. The French under General Pétain were wiser, withdrawing their units once they lost more than half of their men. The policy was beneficial for troop morale, as it gave individuals embroiled in the battle more hope of survival and it preserved cadres of veterans on which units could be rebuilt.

Not only the frequency of rest periods but also the way in which they were spent was important. Troops left unoccupied might become morose and homesick, obsess about traumatic experiences or put themselves out of action, on purpose or unintentionally, by getting involved in bar brawls or contracting venereal disease in a brothel. Traditional methods of keeping peacetime conscripts and regulars busy such as endless kit polishing and parades antagonised wartime citizen-soldiers. Battle training could be helpful, improving men's combat skills and strengthening unit cohesion, but was not restful.

It was best if recreation was organised within the army. The British excelled in this field, as their regular battalions had often been posted to remote imperial garrisons during peacetime where the sole entertainment was that which they organised themselves. Formations arranged sports days, horse shows and excursions to the seaside. There were inter-regimental football tournaments, which subtly encouraged *esprit de corps*. Almost half of British divisions owned cinemas, and all benefited from the canteens, recreation rooms and libraries established behind the lines by private charities, such as the YMCA. By far the most popular entertainment among British troops was concert parties, organised at the initiative of units themselves and based on civilian music halls. Almost every division had its own troupe by the end of 1917, as did many brigades and even battalions. The shows' importance extended far beyond dispelling boredom; they gave soldiers a welcome reminder of their peacetime lives, their humour provided a useful safety valve for fears and grievances, and the in-jokes strengthened unit cohesion.

The final important military influence on morale was leadership. Commanders-in-Chief could be sources of inspiration; this was above all true in the German army, where troops placed considerable faith in Field Marshal Hindenburg. Divisional, regimental and battalion commanders, as middle-ranking officers who ordered men to their deaths from relative safety, were more vulnerable to bitter comment. They could be popular if they gained a reputation for skill, but plenty were despised, justly or not, as 'thrusters' who sacrificed soldiers wantonly in unnecessary raids. All were remote, however. For most troops, contact with the officer corps came in the form of their platoon or company commander. These junior officers were the keystones of any army: frontline soldiers who through their commissions were also tied to the leadership elite in the rear. They had two sets of duties. First, they were battle commanders, a task in which they would ideally not only display tactical skill, but were also expected to lead by example. Secondly, junior officers were responsible for their men's welfare. The best ensured that their soldiers received hot meals in the line and warm billets in rest areas, and even defended them from unfair demands made by higher commanders. Such care contributed greatly to prolonging troops' ability to endure. A British post-war official investigation into shell shock named 'good officers, especially as regards leadership and the care of their men' as among the most important factors protecting soldiers from psychiatric collapse.[27]

The success with which junior officers performed these duties varied among the armies. Casualty figures testify to the readiness of most, at least in Central and Western European forces, to lead by example and risk their lives in battle. In the British, French and German armies, officer fatalities were

27 [British] War Office (ed.), *Report of the War Committee of Enquiry into 'Shell-Shock'* (London: HMSO, 1922), p. 151.

around 2 to 3 per cent higher than those of other ranks during the war. Records in troop welfare were more mixed. The aristocratic and upper middle-class professional and reserve officer corps of the German, Austro-Hungarian and British forces, whose composition was predicated in part on the belief that socially elite men were naturally paternalistic, did effectively care for their soldiers in the first years of the war. Heavy casualties and rapid expansion forced these armies, however, to open up to new officer material. The British officer corps faced the greatest challenge, as its 12,738 pre-war regulars were joined by no fewer than 247,061 wartime commissions; the largest expansion undergone by any European corps. It responded remarkably effectively, accepting thousands of lower middle- and working-class men, whom it trained to lead and care like their upper-class forebears.[28] The German corps, which commissioned around 220,000 so-called 'war officers', was less successful. Committed to its aristocratic 'caste consciousness' as the surest means of guaranteeing politically reliable and paternalistic leaders, it preferred to limit officer numbers rather than commission working-class men. Youthful, hastily trained war officers were often overstretched by their responsibilities, and severe food shortages prompted troops to challenge their privileges. In rear-line units containing older men, inter-rank relations deteriorated sharply. However, in the crucial combat units, officers' proximity to their troops, conscientious paternalism and shared danger created much stronger officer-soldier bonds, which remained unbroken even at the war's end.

The French officer corps also experienced difficulties. Unique among its allies and enemies, it had a middle-class ethos and already in peacetime had recruited more than half of its membership by promotion from the ranks. Heavy losses in 1914 led to an exceptionally acute officer shortage, the effects of which were at first worsened by the inadequate training of replacement leaders. Nonetheless, despite these early problems, neither poor junior leadership nor inter-rank enmity contributed to the crisis of morale and mutinies of 1917. On the contrary, mutineers' actions indicate that they felt a good deal of trust towards their own officers, and were treated by them with understanding.

There was no similar closeness or respect between Russian officers and their men. The tsarist corps had begun the war collectively more aristocratic than any other officer corps in Europe, but with a poor reputation for taking interest in its troops' welfare. The desperate need for wartime leaders led to a

28 Gary Sheffield, *Leadership in the Trenches. Officer-Man Relations, Morale and Discipline in the British Army in the Era of the First World War* (Basingstoke: Macmillan, 2000), pp. 30–2.

radical change in its social composition. By 1917, many Russian officers were deferred students, skilled workers or prosperous peasants who were either unable or too much in sympathy with the rank and file to maintain discipline.

Morale became ever-more crucial between 1914 and 1918 in underpinning armies' resilience and combat performance. The training, discipline, 'primary group' and unit cohesion, supply of basic needs and conscientious leadership provided by belligerent forces proved extremely successful in enforcing compliance and supporting troops. Nonetheless, military incentives, positive and negative, were alone insufficient to sustain mass armies composed of nations' manhood. Behind them lay the primary sources of wartime troops' loyalty and obedience, their societies and states.

Patria and propaganda

The First World War was fought overwhelmingly by 'citizen-soldiers', men who served because they had a stake in the political communities that they were defending. The 'citizen-soldier' had originated in revolutionary France at the end of the eighteenth century, but by the early twentieth century the conception of military service as a civic duty had spread throughout Europe, as far afield as autocratic Russia. The legitimacy of mass armies' orders and demands for sacrifice ultimately rested on these soldiers' identification, however vague, with their society, state and the justice of their cause.

At its outbreak, all governments were thus careful to present the war as a defensive struggle. The draft was justified by the need to protect national (or, in the Habsburg Empire, multi-national) communities and, even more emotively for most men, their constituent parts, the family and local community. The threat of invasion, stories of terrible atrocities and the sight of devastation caused by the fighting provided powerful reasons for citizen-soldiers to fear the consequences of defeat for their communities.

Troops' allegiances to society, state and the cause proved durable. Even after the bloody Somme offensive of 1916, British soldiers' letters still expressed, according to the military postal censor, 'a splendid unity of purpose, a glowing sense of patriotism, and, above all, a spiritual idealism which is in strange contrast to the reality of the War'.[29] Moreover, although patriotic rhetoric did decline over the course of hostilities, men's affection for their families and their

29 3rd Army censorship report of 23 November 1916, p. 9 (Papers of M. Hardie, Imperial War Museum, London: 84/46/1).

desire to protect loved ones from harm maintained their commitment to the national cause. Soldiers sang about their families on the march, drew comfort from memories of them when under fire and yearned to see them again. So strong was the wish for leave that one French trench newspaper described it as 'the *poilu's* war aim'.[30] Visits home were rarely permitted, however, so troops kept in contact by writing. Billions of letters passed between soldiers and their families during the war, and played a crucial role in upholding morale. Letters and parcels were powerful tokens of the affection that families felt for their men in the field, and they provided those soldiers with a constant reminder of why they were fighting. As one German soldier wrote to his wife in 1915, 'I live and fight for you'.[31]

That commitment came under great strain during the conflict, however. Everywhere, soldiers grew weary due to the constant risk, loss of friends, homesickness and long duration of the war. Worse still, these stresses opened splits with home fronts. Combatants complained, largely unjustly, that civilians did not appreciate their sacrifice. There was bitter grumbling about war profiteers, shirkers and newspapers which printed 'eye-wash', trivialising the dangers of active service. Most ominously, in the Russian, German and Austro-Hungarian armies, disgruntlement with governments grew during the second half of the war. Partly, this was caused by troops' growing suspicions that their rulers were prolonging hostilities to pursue annexationist ambitions. There was also anger and dismay that families – the only people at home who escaped the opprobrium – were not being properly fed. Women wrote to their men at the front in growing numbers from 1916 to complain of hunger, hoarders and official incompetence. Food shortages and the suffering of civilians challenged governments' legitimacy and the purpose of the war.

These strains prompted armies to search for ways to reconnect soldiers to the causes for which they were fighting. Several turned for assistance to military chaplains; respected figures who, along with providing spiritual sustenance and psychological support, had traditionally been used to bolster soldiers' ideological motivation. The Habsburg army made extensive use of chaplains to minister to and inspire its largely Catholic manpower. Its divisions generally fielded at least twelve chaplains, twice as many as those allocated to

30 *Le Périscope*, August–September 1917, quoted in Stéphane Audoin-Rouzeau, *National Sentiment and Trench Journalism in France during the First World War* (Oxford and Washington, DC: Berg, 1992), p. 135.

31 E. W. Küpper [pseudonym], letter to wife, 25 March 1915, BA-MA Freiburg: MSg 2/ 5254.

German divisions.[32] Latin masses offered a shared reference point in an army which was multi-lingual and unable to appeal to national loyalties. Priests' sermons sought both to reassure troops that God guided the war for the best and warned that any breach of their oath to the Kaiser would attract not only earthly reprisals, but also divine punishment. The 25th Infantry Division used chaplains especially intensively in an experimental propaganda campaign of 'ethical instruction' in 1916: the formation's Czech troops were concentrated into two companies and subjected to religious and dynastic indoctrination by Czech priests. General Sir Douglas Haig, the pious and aggressive commander of the British Expeditionary Force, placed chaplains at the centre of a much wider, centrally sponsored effort to underpin his troops' morale. Haig desired that clergy explain to the men 'the *Great Cause* for which we are fighting' and, probably even more influentially for morale, encouraged them to deploy much closer than previously to the front, where they comforted the wounded, buried the dead and tended to soldiers' spiritual needs. The sacrifice demanded by the British army of its chaplains was great: whereas only eleven Habsburg priests were killed, no fewer than 166 of Haig's clergymen lost their lives in battle.[33]

It was the German and revolutionary Russian armies, however, which pioneered modern defensive and offensive programmes aimed at reinforcing or undermining troops' ideological motivation. In Russia, the revolutionary authorities which came to power in March 1917 moved quickly to cultivate support among the soldiery and by the summer, a 'Central Committee for Sociopolitical Enlightenment' was monitoring military morale and organising propaganda. In Germany, too, an innovative propaganda programme named 'Patriotic Instruction' was set up in July 1917. This aimed to innoculate troops against what Hindenburg and Ludendorff regarded as siren voices suggesting compromise peace, strengthen their morale – more crucial than ever in consequence of the army's new tactics – and steel their resolve to win total victory. Divisional 'Instruction Officers' rather than chaplains were tasked with leading the German programme. They not only received much institutional support, but also possessed a rich variety of means to identify troops' anxieties and grievances and assess their reactions to the propaganda. Postal

32 Patrick J. Houlihan, 'Clergy in the Trenches: Catholic Military Chaplains of Germany and Austria-Hungary during the First World War' (PhD dissertation, University of Chicago, 2011), p. 75.

33 Michael Snape, *God and the British Soldier. Religion and the British Army in the First and Second World Wars* (London and New York: Routledge, 2005), pp. 87–116. For Habsburg chaplain casualties, see Houlihan, 'Clergy in the trenches', p. 214.

censorship reports, discussions with company officers, military doctors and chaplains and information from so-called 'Vertrauensleute', soldiers tasked with reporting on their comrades' mood, allowed the Instruction Officers to tailor their material to their audiences. When it was recognised that troops received lectures poorly, new, more effective methods were introduced. Some officers won a listenership by combining talks with free beer at company evenings or before cinema outings. They also recognised that the entertainment itself could be exploited to strengthen soldiers' combat motivation: films showing city and landscapes in Germany were popular and served to remind troops of why they should hold out. The core message disseminated was in keeping with soldiers' own defensive reasons for fighting: guidelines stressed that 'everyone must hear time and again that in the case of an enemy victory not only the farther and nearer homeland but he himself and his relatives are lost'.[34]

The Germans' Patriotic Instruction inspired other armies to introduce similar programmes. The Italians acknowledged after their defeat at Caporetto that coercion alone was an inadequate basis for discipline and, in January 1918, established propaganda offices, the 'Sezioni "P"', tasked with assessing troop morale, improving soldiers' rest areas and organising propaganda. The Austro-Hungarians followed in March with an 'Enemy Propaganda Defence Agency'. In the West, the British army launched a programme in the same month, appointing divisional education officers and publishing a series of lectures intended to explain to troops their duties as British citizens and the cause for which they fought. Even the still fresh US army established a Morale Section, which began work in training camps in the autumn of 1918. These programmes, unlike that of the Germans which, arguably, helped to raise morale before the last great spring offensive on the Western Front, were too late to have much effect. They demonstrated, however, that armies everywhere were newly recognising the importance of ideological motivations for fighting power.

The scramble to set up propaganda programmes was motivated not just by concern about war-weariness or desire to imitate the German initiative. The collapse of the Russian army in 1917 appeared to provide a chilling warning of the need to defend troops against attacks on morale. A propaganda battle to influence neutral and enemy opinion had raged since the war's opening, but beyond the sporadic dropping of leaflets and the odd manifesto over enemy

34 Leitsätze für den Vaterländischen Unterricht der Armee-Abteilung A, 15 November 1917, pp. 5–6, BA-MA Freiburg: PH 5 IV/2.

lines, armies had played little part in it. What changed in the spring of 1917 was that the German army, seeking to take advantage of the Russian Revolution, conducted the war's first coordinated military propaganda campaign. The campaign had a number of original features. First, the German Foreign Ministry and military cooperated in formulating the arguments that would be used to undermine the Russian army. Secondly, the front propaganda was carefully coordinated and organised. Oral propaganda conducted in the trenches by intelligence personnel with loud hailers was followed by informal fraternisation, and when fighting resumed in the summer Russian troops were bombarded with propaganda materials before the Austro-Hungarian and German armies went into the attack. The campaign was considered successful. Valuable intelligence was gathered, enemy morale lowered and the fraternisation enabled the Central Powers to transfer much-needed troops to other fronts. Their propaganda reinforced that of the Bolsheviks, playing on the same fears and desires, and thus in a small way contributed to the October Revolution. The Austro-Hungarians were sufficiently impressed that at the end of 1917 they brought psychological warfare to the Italian Front.

The war's most notorious military propaganda campaign, however, was that launched by the Western Allies against the Germans themselves in 1918. Even before Ludendorff's spring and early summer offensives had been beaten off, an assault on his troops' morale commenced. Alone in May and June, the British scattered 4 million propaganda leaflets over the German front.[35] The Allies adopted three lines of psychological attack: they stressed the overwhelming material superiority faced by the enemy, promised good treatment for prisoners and exploited soldiers' growing disillusionment with their government by questioning the sense of fighting for the Kaiser and agitating for his overthrow. This propaganda was not the primary cause of the dramatic collapse of the German army's fighting performance during the second half of the year. The Kaiser's troops were intensely exhausted after months of constant fighting, depressed at their own offensive's failure, outnumbered on the battlefield and recognised the inevitability of defeat. Nonetheless, the news in Allied leaflets of US troops' arrival en masse in France and the good food and comfortable conditions in prisoner-of-war camps was skilfully chosen, increased despair and suggested a way out of the horror. In the summer and autumn of 1918, before the German army could be physically annihilated, its morale failed. Hundreds of thousands of fatigued soldiers,

35 Jahr, *Gewöhnliche Soldaten*, p. 165.

often following their despondent officers, surrendered, allowing the Allies to advance, destabilising their force's rear and hastening the war's end.[36]

Conclusion

Armies proved themselves extremely effective at upholding morale during the First World War. The methods at competing forces' disposal were similar, although how they were applied varied significantly. The most robust armies not only instilled discipline through socialisation and the threat of coercion, but provided for soldiers' basic needs at and behind the front, trained them to face battle and integrated them into cohesive 'primary groups' and larger military units led by conscientious officers. Success was crucial, for tactical innovation during the war tied combat effectiveness ever-more tightly to high morale. Coercive discipline, as the Italian army demonstrated, could hold troops to obedience for long periods. New tactics developed in Western armies by 1916 to 1917, however, placed a premium on individual drive, initiative and teamwork. Morale became more, not less, important in the conditions of industrial warfare.

The citizen-soldiers who were an integral part of this industrial war owed their primary loyalties not to the army, however, but to their families, communities and, through them, the states which they had enlisted to defend. Troops' growing weariness and disgruntlement with the home front, and the greater demands made on morale by tactical innovation, prompted armies to direct new attention to reinforcing these loyalties. The Germans, soon followed by other forces, pioneered propaganda programmes intended to reconnect soldiers with the homes and causes for which they fought. The final years of the war also witnessed the first organised efforts by armies to conduct campaigns of psychological warfare. These initiatives, belated and experimental, had only a very limited impact on the conflict's outcome. They held portentous lessons, however, especially for the war's losers. In the Soviet Red Army and Nazi *Wehrmacht* during the Second World War, unprecedentedly vicious discipline and, in the German case, a cult of comradeship, were key but not alone in underpinning morale. At the heart of both forces' motivational strategies were far-reaching indoctrination programmes, designed to bind troops closely to the home front and their leaders and to instil deep belief in the cause. Industrial war, by placing a premium on high morale, developed into ideological conflict.

36 Niall Ferguson, 'Prisoner taking and prisoner killing in the age of total war: toward a political economy of military defeat', *War in History*, 11 (2004), pp. 155–63. Also Watson, *Enduring*, pp. 184–231.

8
Mutiny

LEONARD V. SMITH

'Mutiny' here means collective resistance on the part of military personnel to recognised state authority. If we accept the formulation of Carl von Clausewitz that the military is simply that instrument of state bureaucracy authorised to use violence, any challenge from within the military constitutes a challenge to the state itself. This, among other things, distinguishes a mutiny from a strike. Paradoxically, in his classic *On War* (1832), Clausewitz pointedly ignored mutiny. He might have preferred to think of mutiny simply as a radical form of 'friction', that array of physical and metaphysical phenomena that can slow down the smooth functioning of any military machine. But, at some level, Clausewitz knew better:

> War is more than a true chameleon that slightly adapts its characteristics to the given case. As a total phenomena its dominant tendencies always make war a remarkable trinity – composed of primordial violence, hatred, and enmity, which are to be regarded as a blind natural force; of the play of chance and probability within which the creative spirit is free to roam; and of its element of subordination, as an instrument of policy, which makes it subject to reason alone.[1]

In other words, contingency and emotion are too much a part of war for any state to guarantee rational mastery over it. Indeed, under certain circumstances, armed forces can become the instrument of war itself rather than of the state endeavouring to wage it, particularly if the state no longer exercises full sovereignty or is in the process of disintegrating. One could thus argue that 'mutiny' occurs when the state loses control over the military, for a short or long period of time. Just what regains control over the military when the mutiny concludes demarcates, shapes or even replaces the state itself.

1 Carl von Clausewitz, *On War*, ed. and trans. Michael Howard and Peter Paret (Princeton University Press, 1976), p. 89.

During the Great War, mutiny challenged and sometimes overcame state authority. This explains why mutiny took so many forms, and had so many different outcomes. As I use the term here, 'mutiny' concerned more than 'morale'. Indeed, my argument rests on the notion that 'morale' exists at all only in functioning militaries, which by definition an army or a navy in mutiny is not. Morale may well be an issue before or after a mutiny, but not during it. For this reason, it makes sense to exclude for my purposes 'passive mutinies' connected to morale, such as chaotic retreat from the battlefield following a defeat, or a suspicious willingness on the part of defeated troops to be taken prisoner. 'Mutiny' here means active defiance of the state, and of organised military authority as its instrument.

When the state remained strong, mutiny served to articulate and in some cases even affirm it. Mutiny could also demarcate the limits of the wartime state. Other mutinies shook the wartime state to its core, and even overthrew it. Still other forms of resistance were 'mutinies' in a technical or legalistic sense, as they took place in the context of disintegrating state authority. Still other mutinies went beyond resisting discredited state authority to reconstituting it in the creation of a new state. Mutiny in the Great War thus tracked the authority of the wartime state. The form, content and outcome of a given mutiny thus shaped and was shaped by the state authority being resisted.

Some mutinies, fleeting and apparently highly localised in origins, are largely forgotten today. But they served to highlight basic fault lines in states and society during the Great War. Race constituted one such fault line. Societies at war mobilised race hierarchically. But mobilising different races differently could serve to undermine the preservation of hierarchies deemed essential to the war effort. For example, on 23 August 1917, some 75 to 100 armed African-American soldiers stationed near Houston, Texas, disobeyed their white officers by marching from their barracks towards the city.[2] A variety of provocative incidents preceded the mutiny, such as a local insistence that black soldiers in and out of uniform sit at the back of streetcars. Some 25 per cent of the black soldiers stationed in Houston were from the northern states, where racial discrimination assuredly existed, but was less overtly woven into the fabric of public behaviour.

Further enraged by untrue rumours that a white policeman had murdered a black soldier, as well as also untrue rumours of the approach of a white mob, the mutinous African Americans rioted, killing four civilian policemen and

2 Robert B. Haynes, *A Night of Violence: The Houston Riot of 1917* (Baton Rouge, LA: Louisiana State University Press, 1976).

wounding three others. Before it was over, the riot resulted in the deaths of nine more civilians (eight white, one latino), along with nine national guardsmen and two of the mutineers. Thereafter, the mutineers dispersed. Some returned to camp, while others unsuccessfully sought refuge in the African-American neighbourhoods of Houston. The largest court-martial in US military history certified the repression of the mutiny – 118 men tried, 110 of them found guilty. Nineteen soldiers were hanged, and twenty-two sentenced to life in prison.

At the heart of the matter lay a disparity between federal and regional constructions of African-American soldiers in the Jim Crow South, in the context of national mobilisation for the Great War. By the early twentieth century, it had become clear that the Civil War of 1861 to 1865 had ended in a compromise. The southern states accepted federal supremacy in exchange for the gradual defeat of Reconstruction, which to its most fervent adherents involved the full integration of former black slaves into American society. States in the South as in the North were permitted to regulate racial issues more or less as they saw fit. Jim Crow institutionalised racial segregation, enforced by the institutionalised atrocity of lynching. Yet federal institutions such as the US army remained, supported by the supremacy of the federal state.

Few except those oppressed by it found the compromise solution to the Civil War problematic – until the 'United States' as a nation had to mobilise for the European war. To be sure, the American military was becoming even more segregated in the early twentieth century, a development that accelerated during the presidency of Woodrow Wilson. But the federal government had called on all races to mobilise in a global crusade for democracy, increasingly identified with 'self-determination'. Black soldiers wore the uniform of the US army, which they believed afforded them not just social mobility, but a certain level of protection against the more overt forms of Jim Crow discrimination. Not unreasonably, they saw themselves as agents of federal authority rather than the subjects of the southern states.

The repression of the Houston mutiny through courts martial and executions appeared to certify that when the time came to choose, 'white' authority would close ranks – at the federal and state levels. But the incident had national repercussions. The Houston mutiny attracted considerable attention in the African-American press, notably in W. E. B. Du Bois's monthly *The Crisis*. The Houston mutiny revealed emerging African-American resistance to the structural outcome of the Civil War. With the 'Great Migration' of African Americans to the industrialised North well underway, Jim Crow and its political patrons could not control increasingly organised black opinion. Even President Wilson (assuredly no friend of racial equality) felt obligated to commute ten of the death sentences to life imprisonment. While such a gesture could only have comforted the convicted in relative rather than absolute terms, Wilson's 'clemency' did illustrate how mobilisation for the Great War had come to undermine the status quo of race relations in the United States.

Racial hierarchies within formal empires also came under strain through mobilisation for war. Mutinies based on race served to articulate the fault lines in the colonial state. Empires did not expect to mobilise all their subjects equally. Imperial armies in the Great War tended to resemble European armies under the Ancien Régime more than those of the twentieth century. Recruitment practices looked more like the exaction of feudal dues than systematic conscription, and relied on the influence and repressive capacities of local elites. White officers presided over stern discipline enforced by non-commissioned officers (NCOs) from the colonies. Physical punishments, often directed as much towards humiliation as the infliction of pain, were tolerated to a far greater degree than among white forces.

Mutiny could expose the thin veneer of white imperial authority. The largest mutiny in the British Empire during the Great War occurred among Indian troops in Singapore in February 1915.[3] Although thousands of miles from the Western Front, Singapore constituted a choke point in shipping lanes to East Asia, and thus a strategic outpost of British power. Like the Houston mutiny, the Singapore mutiny was more a riot based on racial resentment and rumour than a premeditated plot to overthrow the state. Untrue rumours persisted that the majority Muslim Indian garrison was to be dispatched to fight their co-religionists in the Ottoman Empire. Some 400 men from the 5th Light Infantry of the British Indian Army (approaching half the regiment) broke ranks and attacked a munitions truck. They dispersed thereafter, with many soldiers seeking to escape up the Malay Peninsula. In the process, they killed some thirty-two Europeans and fifty Singaporeans. They also gave the British authorities particular fright by releasing a small number of German prisoners, although exactly what threat the unarmed enemy could have posed in this situation remained unclear.

Within a few days, the British rounded up the mutineers, with the help of local volunteer militias and small contingents of foreign troops who happened

3 Ian F. W. Beckett, 'The Singapore Mutiny of February 1915', *Journal of the Society of Army Historical Research*, 62 (1984), pp. 132–53.

to be present. The British tried 202 men, handing out 47 death sentences and ultimately executing 23 in full public view. The colonial state imagined itself performing its traditional power of life and death over the bodies of those who had dared to defy it. In so doing, it could perform its ability to coerce mobilisation through racial subordination. It is difficult to imagine opinion in the United Kingdom or the Dominions tolerating the public execution of twenty-three white soldiers, whatever they had done.

In fact, the repression of the Singapore mutiny had illustrated the frailty of imperial rule. A few hundred angry men for a time held in their hands the fate of this strategic British outpost. Their mutiny, by calling into question norms of soldierly comportment, inevitably called into question norms of masculinity.[4] Inspired by generations of stories of the 1857 Sepoy rebellion in India, the British authorities played up the threat of sexual predation by the mutineers upon the white women of Singapore. They relied on this tried-and-true racialised menace, even though there were no recorded incidences of rape. Only one woman was killed, and she by selflessly leaping in front of fire directed towards her husband. Sexualising the mutiny in this way justified the ferocity of the repression, but also raised the uncomfortable question of just why white women had been left so vulnerable in the first place. As was so often the case in war, the mobilisation of gender proved a two-edged sword.

The Great War continued to crack the veneer of imperial rule. The imperial relationship could not rely on one-directional subordination, which in any event agreed poorly with the official explanation throughout the British Empire that the Great War was a global crusade for justice and against oppression. 'Mutiny' in the sense of resistance to military authority proved a form of resistance easily transferable to the civilian domain, and radically politicised along the way. At Amritsar, India on 13 April 1919, thousands of civilians gathered in defiance of martial law to celebrate the traditional festival of Baisakhi. The hideous suppression of this gathering became known as the Amritsar massacre, a turning point in the history of Indian nationalism. As Mohandas K. Gandhi and other nationalists understood, the use of wildly disproportionate physical force against those who resisted military authority showed not British strength, but weakness. Arch-imperialist Winston Churchill understood this as well, as he said in his famous speech in Parliament after the massacre: 'Our reign in India or

4 Christine Doran, 'Gender matters in the Singapore Mutiny', *Sojourn: Journal of Social Issues in Southeast Asia*, 17 (2002), pp. 76–93.

anywhere else has never stood on the basis of physical force alone, and it would be fatal to the British Empire if we were to try to base ourselves only upon it.'

Some mutinies blended race and class, and resembled strikes. Observers, particularly after the fact, could trace their origins to specific, identifiable grievances that seemed particularly unjust after the Armistice with Germany. A mutiny among Caribbean soldiers of the British West Indies Regiment in Italy in December 1918 stemmed from discontent at a combat unit being given tasks normally reserved for labour units, and from levels of compensation and promotion below those of white troops.[5] On 21 December 1918, soldiers from the Canadian Siberian Expeditionary Force refused point blank to board a ship to Vladivostok, to take part in the ill-advised Allied intervention against the Bolshevik regime.[6] Although 'white' in race, the Canadians were Québécois and working class in origin. The mutineers had little use for what they saw as a pointless campaign in the name of British imperialism. After some twenty hours of uncertainty, their obedient comrades broke the 'strike' by compelling them to board the ship at the point of a bayonet. Both the West Indies and Québécois mutinies achieved results. The British Government granted pay concession to the Caribbean soldiers. As the Siberian adventure came to look increasingly absurd from the dominion government point of view, efforts to punish men who resisted it became an embarrassment. All ten Québécois tried had their sentences suspended after the Canadian Government decided to withdraw their troops from Siberia.

The best-known mutiny in the armies of the British Empire took place in September 1917 at the training camp at Etaples in France. Dominion and British soldiers were housed in overcrowded tents, fed unappetising fare even by the low standards of military cuisine, and deprived of meaningful recreational facilities. Both novices and the most battle-hardened veterans had to endure the same demoralising and pointless military exercises, directed by NCOs who often had never seen combat themselves. Soldiers referred to them scornfully as 'canaries', because of their yellow armbands. The mutineers refused to carry out their duties, and demonstrated against poor treatment.

At Etaples, it appeared in the end as though military authority had carried the day. Field Marshal Sir Douglas Haig scorned a wartime British army

5 W. F. Elkins, 'Revolt of the British West India Regiment', *Jamaica Journal*, 11 (1978), pp. 72–5.

6 Benjamin Isitt, 'Mutiny from Victoria to Vladivostok, December 1918', *Canadian Historical Review*, 87 (2006), pp. 223–64.

diluted by uppity conscripts. In the Old Army, men knew their places. The Great War had called up men 'not satisfied with remaining quiet, they come from a class which like to air real or fancied grievances . . .'.[7] Nor did power content itself with whining about the bygone Old Army. The Etaples mutinies resulted in the court-martial of some fifty men (four of them for mutiny), and one execution. But beneath this veneer of unquestioned authority, the Etaples mutiny produced tangible results. Discreetly, the military authorities removed the officers responsible for discipline in the camp, opened up the town of Etaples for soldiers' recreation, and dispersed training to the less carceral conditions of the individual army corps.

Is there more to such episodes than what Julian Putkowski many decades later called 'collective bargaining in khaki'?[8] To some extent, the question implies its own answer. According to military authority as Clausewitz imagined it, soldiers are supposed to obey, not bargain, collectively or otherwise. When they do so, disobedience calls into question the relationship between the military and the state. In a strike, workers down tools, negotiate and eventually return to work, either satisfied or dissatisfied with the outcome. A mutiny has no such predetermined narrative. The discontented African Americans in Houston assuredly had no accepted model in 1917 for resisting Jim Crow. Likewise, the Indians in Singapore did not see themselves as in a position to bargain formally with the British Empire, any more than the Québécois headed to Vladivostok. Likewise, the mutinous soldiers at Etaples, some of them Dominion soldiers, leapt into the unknown at a time when British and Allied mastery of the battlefield was anything but certain. As the Great War dragged on, 'total' mobilisation seemed to have produced not total victory, but total stalemate. In all of these cases of mutiny, the state appeared to win the struggle for authority, and to perform its will on the mutinous soldiers. But in different ways, each case also demarcated the limits of state power over those who wore its uniform.

To whom were mutinous soldiers accountable in a republic in which they held full citizenship? Accountability lay at the heart of the French army mutinies of the spring of 1917, in the wake of the failed Chemin des Dames

7 Letter from Haig to Lord Derby, quoted in Douglas Gill and Gloden Dallas, *The Unknown Army* (London: Verso, 1985), p. 74.

8 Letter from Putkowski to *The Guardian*, 26 September 1986, quoted in Gary Sheffield, *Leadership in the Trenches: Officer-Man Relations, Morale and Discipline in the British Army in the Era of the First World War* (New York: St Martin's Press, 2000), p. 153.

offensive.[9] The most common form of mutiny involved soldiers collectively refusing to take up positions in the front lines when ordered to do so. They would then depart to open areas and hold demonstrations airing their myriad demands. In all, incidents of collective indiscipline occurred in nearly one-half of all of the divisions in the French army. In the short run, the command structure simply lacked the means to resolve the matter by physical force. Senior commanders deemed only the cavalry (particularly from colonial units) certain to fire on French soldiers if ordered to do so. These never numbered sufficiently to prevail over armed and angry infantry. To a great extent, the most extensive mutiny on the Western Front temporarily displaced external authority structure.

In the saturnalian situation of mutiny, discontented soldiers could vent their demands with little apparent accountability to anyone. In stating their demands, soldiers moved effortlessly from relatively mundane matters such as the quality of their food, to concern for their families behind the lines, to issues as abstract as 'injustice'. As mutiny inevitably interrogates military identity, mutiny inevitably interrogates masculinity. The concern for families was closely connected to traditional male roles as providers and protectors of families. Soldiers particularly fretted about untrue rumours that the authorities were using 'blacks' (*les noirs*, a common generic term for colonial troops) to break up women's strikes in the interior.

Above all, soldiers wanted 'peace'. Indeed, they wanted *both* peace and a reformed leave policy, even though the former would presumably have rendered the latter irrelevant. Of course, who in Europe in 1917 did not want peace? The devil, among mutinous French soldiers as among so many others, lay in the details. When pressed, soldiers seldom meant peace on any terms, or even on terms inconsistent with the war aims as the French government had articulated them since 1914. Most considered the return of Alsace and Lorraine consistent with a peace without annexations, and requiring Germany to pay for all damage caused by the war consistent with a peace without indemnities. The question of 'peace' joined the micro and macro elements of soldiers' demands, and posed the question of accountability, for the outcome of the mutinies and for the war itself. 'Peace', in a word, made the French army mutinies political.

9 Leonard V. Smith, 'Remobilizing the citizen-soldier through the French army mutinies of 1917', in John Horne (ed.), *State, Society, and Mobilization during the First World War* (Cambridge University Press, 1997), pp. 144–59.

In so doing, the mutinies brought to the surface a tension as old as French democracy itself between direct democracy and representative government. The mutinies had become became an exercise in direct democracy, as shown by the widespread demonstrations. Yet in difficult but essential partnership with direct democracy existed representative government. The republic, the organised community of the sovereign people, expressed itself in the constitution and the institutions of the French state. The people thus had delegated power to find expression through their representatives. In other words, the citizen-soldier served the army as a representation of the state, and the state as a representation of the people. Direct democracy thus had to find a way to express itself through this representative framework, as the soldiers themselves appeared to understand full well. Discontented soldiers returned again and again to the necessity of transmitting their concerns to their elected representatives in the Chamber of Deputies.

Both direct democracy and representative government drew their legitimacy from the French Republican tradition, that is, from the General Will of the sovereign people. That tradition proved a formidable instrument of coercion, precisely because of the success of the republican project in internalising a certain conception of power. Soldiers obeyed a source of authority accountable to themselves and their compatriots. Whether in obeying their commanders as the instrument of representative government or disobeying in claiming their rights as citizens to agitate against the war, soldiers remained accountable to the republic as a discursive structure. They had no solution for winning the war that had hitherto escaped their commanders. Eventually, they would have to decide whether to lose the war, or to endorse conventional military authority and their commanders' solutions for winning it. In the end, the French army mutinies of 1917 were more about consenting to the war than about rejecting it. In an agonised way, mutiny in France thus affirmed and articulated the mutineers' accountability to the wartime state, even as they challenged it.

What did 'mutiny' mean when the state itself foundered, as happened throughout Europe from Germany eastwards? In Austria-Hungary, the state and the armed forces of the Dual Monarchy seemed to be in a race towards mutual destruction almost since 1914. After the death of the aged Emperor-King Franz-Joseph in 1916, the 'Austrian' half of the Habsburg monarchy appeared likely to survive at all only as a German client, joined to a Kingdom of Hungary ruling over a non-Magyar majority. Of course, the defeats of the Habsburg forces at Galicia in 1916 and Vittorio Veneto in October and November 1918 had characteristics of 'passive' mutiny. But given the progressive enfeeblement of the two states joined by the Habsburg crown, the resilience of the royal and imperial forces is at least as surprising as their eventual disintegration.

In certain situations, mutiny could show that a military machine once in motion tends to remain in motion. Habsburg sailors mutinied at Cattaro naval base (now Kotor in Montenegro) on 1 February 1918.[10] The crew of the anchored cruiser *Sankt Georg*, it seems spontaneously, took over the ship. They hoisted the red flag, although the Austro-Hungarian colours remained in place and the discontented sailors even continued to salute them morning and evening as scheduled. Croats and Slovenes led the mutineers, although their complaints and demands had little to do with South Slav nationalism. Rather, they resented tedious training exercises and the unrealised benefits promised by the Treaty of Brest-Litovsk with the Bolsheviks (specifically, enhanced food deliveries). Ethnic Germans and Magyars by and large did not take part. The discontented Croat and Slovene sailors had little concept of what to do next, and loyal ground and sea forces quickly surrounded them. Some 392 sailors were charged in the incidents, although 348 of them were acquitted. In the end, four mutineers were shot. The Cattaro mutiny became a nationalist rebellion well after the fact, notably when Marshal Tito laid a wreath on the graves of the executed soldiers in 1968.

The most important form of mutiny among the Habsburg forces was somewhat theoretical, and took place in an unlikely setting – Allied prisoner-of-war (POW) camps. Italians, Serbs and particularly Russians all sought to convince over 1.5 million Habsburg prisoners in their charge to take up arms against Austria-Hungary in the name of what would become known as national self-determination. Well over 100,000 prisoners did so in Russia alone. While all of these soldiers in principle were 'mutineers' given their nominal status as the soldiers of Emperor-King Franz-Joseph, they saw themselves as appropriating and legitimising national sovereignty *in absentia*. In short, the war had given rise to national military formations without formal state control or, for that matter, national territory. As Istvan Deák has argued, 'the dissolution of the [Habsburg] monarchy into hostile national entities had begun in the POW camps'.[11]

The Imperial Russian army had tended to separate its Slav and non-Slav prisoners, precisely to foster mobilising the former according to pan-Slav

10 David Woodward, 'Mutiny at Cattaro, 1918: insurrection in the Austro-Hungarian fleet on February 1st', *History Today*, 26 (1976), pp. 804–10.

11 Istvan Deák, *Beyond Nationalism: A Social and Political History of the Habsburg Officer Corps, 1848–1918* (New York: Oxford University Press, 1990), p. 198.

sympathies. Throughout the war, Poles fought on opposite sides in the Imperial German, Austro-Hungarian, and Imperial Russian armies. In general, Poles were considered too politically volatile to recruit in large numbers from POW camps. But the tsarist regime courted Czech and Slovaks assiduously. The matter became more complicated after the February Revolution of 1917 in Russia. The Provisional Government continued to recruit Czechs and Slovaks. Various more dissident elements courted the Hungarians. The Czech Legion, the best-established and best-known unit among former POWs, rose from this effort.[12] The matter became still more complicated after the Treaty of Brest-Litovsk of January 1918. Theoretically, all POWs were freed, and their status became unclear. Under the best of circumstances, repatriating so many men would have presented a formidable logistical challenge. But their political situation back home had become complicated, and potentially fatal. Even a debilitated Dual Monarchy could still execute former POWs who had, in effect, deserted to the enemy. And many former POWs found themselves in locations not under the practical control of the Bolsheviks.

The emerging Czechoslovak government-in-exile led by Tomáš Masaryk and Edvard Bénès sought the transfer of the Czech Legion, then some 60,000 strong, to the Western Front. Given their ever-more desperate manpower situation, the French and the British offered their support. But the only feasible way to carry out such a transfer was through Siberia, by means of the Trans-Siberian Railway. During this process, the Czech Legion got caught up in the ill-conceived and ill-fated Allied intervention in Siberia, and became increasingly identified with the counter-revolutionary Whites.[13] By the summer of 1918, the ex-mutineers from the Habsburg Royal and Imperial Army were scattered across the vast railway to the Pacific. Essentially stateless, the dispersed Czech Legion operated as an Allied force under nominal French command. At the Armistice in 1918, 'Czechoslovakia' had a government-in-exile (operating in London) and an army (operating in Siberia), but no national territory.

Hungarian recruits, though never as well known as the Czech Legion, were actually more numerous. Béla Kun, a POW from the Honvéd (the national guard of the Kingdom of Hungary), got his start in serious politics recruiting comrades for the revolutionary Reds among some 600,000 Hungarian prisoners. Any Magyar fighting alongside the Reds put himself in rebellion against the successor to Franz-Joseph as King of Hungary, Charles IV (Charles I as

12 George F. Kennan, 'The Czechoslovak Legion', *Russian Review*, 16 (1957), pp. 3–16.
13 John Albert White, *The Siberian Intervention* (Princeton University Press, 1950).

Emperor of Austria). Nevertheless, an estimated 80,000 to 100,000 Hungarians ultimately fought for the Bolsheviks in the civil war, some in the Red Guards, others in the nascent Red Army.[14] Exactly how 'Red' this rendered them remains a matter of dispute. Soldiers, on whichever side, tended to be provisioned before civilians. Fighting meant food in an increasingly chaotic situation, as the former Imperial Russia descended into civil war. Some Magyar prisoners simply resented the favouritism showed by the tsarist, Provisional Government, White and Allied authorities to the Czechs and Slovaks. 'Czechoslovakia', after all, would depend on the annexation of Slovakia (since medieval times, part of the lands of the Hungarian crown). Kun would lead a short-lived Soviet regime in Hungary, from March to August 1919, his ambitions doubtless bolstered by the success of the Magyar mutineers in supporting the Bolsheviks.

In Russia itself, mutiny destroyed the wartime tsarist state. Imperial Russian soldiers entered the war fundamentally unincorporated into a Western-style national community.[15] Some 95 per cent being of peasant origin, the soldiers of the Tsar brought with them two ancient and intersecting images of authority, both drawn from the countryside. The officer simply replaced the landowner. This authority was as irresistible as it was capricious; the soldier could only submit and hope for better, most probably in the next world. Against this image of authority lay that of the Tsar, the distant, almost mythical 'little father' of his peoples who had his will constantly thwarted by evil subordinates.

As the strains of total war intensified, the 'little father' became very real and very fallible. By assuming personal command of his armies in 1916, Nicholas II undercut the mysticism so important to his own legitimacy. Despite a generally deteriorating military situation, the mutinies in the Imperial Russian armies beginning in March 1917 (February under the Julian calendar then in use in Russia) were not provoked by any particular calamity on the battlefield.[16] Rather, they began because of food riots in the large cities. Garrisons refused wholesale to fire on starving civilians. This provoked a political crisis that in a matter of days led to the Tsar's abdication. The authority of the 'little

14 Ivan Volgyes, 'Hungarian prisoners of war in Russia, 1916–1919', *Cahiers du Monde russe et soviétique*, 14 (1973), pp. 54–85.

15 Elise Kimmeling Wirthschafter, *From Serf to Russian Soldier* (Princeton University Press, 1990); John Bushnell, *Mutiny amid Repression: Russian Soldiers in the Revolution of 1905–1906* (Bloomington, IN: Indiana University Press, 1990).

16 Alan K. Wildman, *The End of the Russian Imperial Army*, 2 vols. (Princeton University Press, 1980, 1987).

father' simply vanished. External suasion ceased to exist as the Tsar's regime collapsed. Millions of peasant-soldiers lost overnight their notion of just what this war had to do with them. Mutiny thus bred further mutiny. The issue became whether anyone could instil the external or internal suasion necessary to regain control over this population.

Initially, the Russian forces directly engaged against Germany and Austria-Hungary did not disintegrate. Soldiers refused to attack, but generally proved willing to hold the line. As in France, soldiers were much more restive behind the lines than in them. But former subjects of the Tsar ceased to have any clear notion of to what or whom they were loyal. Whoever could remobilise their military and civilian identities would stand a good chance of gaining state power, both in the short and the long term.

Alexander Kerensky, the leader of the Provisional Government, had in mind the image of the armies of the Year II of the French Revolution. He tried to make history repeat itself by transforming the subject-soldier into the citizen-soldier of an emerging Russian republic in a matter of months. The Provisional Government placed exceptional demands on soldiers' military and political identities by ordering a new offensive in Austrian Galicia in July 1917, just as the French army mutinies were calming down. The French would not have dared to launch an offensive on this scale at this time, although they very much encouraged the Russians to do so. The Russians were joined by some 3,500 men from the technically mutinous Czechoslovak Rifleman Brigade, in the only significant engagement of the Czech Legion on the traditional Eastern Front. After initial success, the forces of the Provisional Government were beaten back not just from Galicia, but into the Ukraine. Thereafter, authority within the former imperial army began to crumble. As the Great War morphed into civil war in revolutionary Russia, desertion became chronic on all sides. Millions of brutalised, politically unmoored and armed peasant-soldiers struggled to make sense of it all.

This unintended slippage from one war to another in Russia illustrated Clausewitz's formulation of war as 'more than a true chameleon'. The blind natural force of war had created a structurally chaotic situation that 'rational' actors of varying political stripes struggled for years to master. An alternative source of authority emerged more or less simultaneously to that of the Provisional Government: the workers' and soldiers' councils, more commonly known as the soviets. In its famous Order No. 1 issued on 14 March 1917, the Petrograd Soviet explicitly called for the establishment of soviets throughout the former imperial armed forces:

> In all companies, battalions, regiments, depots, batteries, squadrons and separate branches of military service of every kind and on warships immediately choose committees from the elected representatives of the soldiers and sailors of the above-mentioned military units.

All units were expected to send representatives to the State Duma (parliament) the next day, although just how this was to be accomplished across the vast expanses of All the Russias was not clear. Military units were supposed to become overt political actors, although all activities were supposed to be subordinate to the Petrograd Soviet. No order coming from the State Duma was to be considered valid without the approval of the Petrograd Soviet.

The imperial ambitions of the Petrograd Soviet notwithstanding, the soviets began as a genuine grassroots institution. No party or faction controlled them. The soviets formalised the negotiation of military-authority relations. They dealt with matters as diverse as food distribution, military justice, and whether and how to take up positions in the front lines. The soviets thus constituted something of an institutionalised mutiny. The Provisional Government did everything it could to circumvent and undermine them, as a direct challenge to itself. But paradoxically, rather more than the ostensibly democratic Provisional Government itself, the soviets also began successfully inculcating the idea that sovereignty depended on some new variety of political identity. Ultimately, to control the soviets was to control the state.

In the meantime, however, millions of peasant-soldiers continued to leave the ranks.[17] Some were 'mutineers' who consciously abandoned the disintegrating Imperial Russian army. Some deserted for personal reasons, and some simply left units that no longer existed. With rail transport in chaos, most deserters struggled largely on foot to return to homes hundreds or even thousands of miles away. Peasants brutalised by three years of war in the East suddenly had the chance to act upon a primordial hatred of oppressive authority, witnessed by a great many atrocities committed against officers or landowners. Historically speaking, atrocity stories almost always get better with the telling. But what contemporaries described as *aziatscina*, meaning 'Asiatic' techniques such as cutting out tongues, eyes and even penises, surely took place, both as acts of revenge and as a means of terrorising those who stood by the Ancien Régime in Russia. Semi-organised bands of peasant-soldier deserters known as the 'Greens' constituted the third actor in the civil

17 Nicolas Werth, 'Les Déserteurs en Russie: violence de guerre, violence révolutionnaire et violence paysanne (1916–1922)', in Stéphane Audoin-Rouzeau *et al.* (eds.), *La Violence de guerre, 1914–1945* (Brussels: Éditions Complexe, 2002), pp. 99–116.

war alongside the Reds and the Whites.[18] While they remained the least coherent of the three actors, Green paramilitary units circulated throughout European Russia. The 'dictatorship of the proletariat' or even 'Russia' in the abstract had little meaning to the Greens. The Russia of the Tsar had been swept away, and no new Russia existed yet – at least not one responsive to their profoundly local concerns.

In the end, the Bolsheviks best figured out the delicate interplay between the micro-dramas of military authority and the macro-dramas of keeping, holding and recreating state power. The Bolsheviks saw that by promising land and peace immediately, they could gain what passed for state power immediately. Thereafter, they could mobilise a critical mass of soldiers, if not to support a workers' revolution, at least to resist a return of the Ancien Régime. Nominal state power, in time, could become real state power. Bolsheviks V. I. Lenin and Leon Trotsky had a rather more sophisticated understanding than the democrat Kerensky of popular sovereignty as an instrument of state rule over the military. The key lay not in repressing or circumventing the soviets, but in co-opting them. For in the soviets lay the means of constructing a soldier who would not just fight his former oppressors, but obey a source of authority of which he himself, at least in theory, was the source. Thereafter, the Bolshevik citizen-soldier could become the enforcer of the new civic order.

The Bolshevik state and the Red Army constructed each other over the course of the 1920s. Soldiers more than workers, let alone peasants, became the vanguard of the proletarian dictatorship. As early as 1921, the bloody suppression of the Kronstadt naval mutiny showed that the Bolshevik regime would not suffer even left-wing ideological unorthodoxy from those who wore its uniform. The demobilised soldier-peasants could be dealt with gradually. Lenin used the carrot, notably the New Economic Policy (NEP), which partly legitimised private property and profit.[19] The NEP largely completed the demobilisation of the 'Greens'. After 1928, Stalin would use the stick, notably the Five-Year Plans and the accompanying brutal collectivisation of agriculture. The Bolshevik citizen-soldier had learned his new cues well enough to enforce both policies.[20]

18 Vladimir Brovkin, 'On the internal front: the Bolsheviks and the Greens', *Jahrbücher für Geschichte Osteuropas*, 39 (1989), pp. 541–68.

19 Donald Raleigh, *Experiencing Russia's Civil War: Politics, Society, and Revolutionary Culture in Saratov, 1917–1922* (Princeton University Press, 2002).

20 Mark von Hagen, *Soldiers in the Proletarian Dictatorship: The Red Army and the Soviet Socialist State, 1917–1930* (Ithaca, NY: Cornell University Press, 1990).

In Germany, mutiny both invoked the destruction of the Kaiserreich and seriously undermined the formation of the Weimar Republic. Mutiny began in the German Imperial Navy – strictly speaking, at the highest levels of command.[21] By 29 October 1918, armistice discussions had been taking place for several weeks between the German Government and President Wilson. On that date, Admirals Franz Ritter von Hipper and Reinhard Scheer briefed their staffs on a scheme to stage an epic naval battle. The German fleet, U-boats and all, would first wreak havoc on British shipping in the Thames Estuary, then meet the British Grand Fleet in the English Channel. The German navy would either inflict a great defeat that would strengthen Germany's hand at the peace table, or would arrange its own Wagnerian exit from the conflict. The plan had received no sanction from the government, or even the real power in Germany by that time, the army High Command.

German sailors, first at Wilhelmshaven then at Kiel, refused to take up their duties, and their comrades refused to fire on them. Over the course of 1918, Germany's Great War had been nearly won, then lost, with very little input from them. The German Admiralty had hitherto declined to risk a decisive pitched battle to break the Allied blockade, relying instead on U-boats to inflict severe damage on enemy supply lines. The High Seas Fleet, built at vast expense, thus spent much of the war bottled up at harbour, its crews occupied by the most mundane and tedious of duties. By November 1918, sailors saw that the war plainly was being lost on land, after all, and that a grand naval battle won or lost would prove unlikely to make much difference one way or another. Indeed, carnage at sea could only exacerbate the international reputation for German 'frightfulness' that the Allies had constructed so skilfully since 1914. Few German sailors believed that the naval war deserved an operatic finish. Unlike the Habsburg mutineers at Cattaro, the German mutineers had close and sustained links to the civilian population. Sailors' resistance soon spread to the docks, transport and factories. Within a matter of days, a naval mutiny morphed into a general strike that brought down the Kaiserreich itself.

The abdication of Wilhelm II on 9 November 1918 made the definition of 'mutiny' a matter of political opinion.[22] At 2 p.m., Philip Schiedemann, of the Social Democratic Party (SDP), proclaimed a parliamentary republic. At 4 p.m., Karl Liebknecht declared a revolutionary socialist republic to be overseen by soviets. He had founded the Spartacist League with Rosa

21 Daniel Horn, *The German Naval Mutinies of World War I* (New Brunswick, NJ: Rutgers University Press, 1968).

22 Richard Bessel, *Germany after the First World War* (Oxford: Clarendon Press, 1993).

Luxemburg, and their version of revolution became known as the Spartacist uprising. Any person in uniform who took a side thus became mutinous in the opinion of the other. Moreover, for many months, lines between soldiers and civilians blurred, as soldiers demobilised and civilians armed themselves. It was not a coincidence that Max Weber coined in a January 1919 lecture 'Politics as a Vocation' his famous definition of sovereignty as a monopoly over the legitimate use of physical force over a given territory. With sovereignty in Germany lacking in this sense, just who was a loyal servant of the Fatherland and who was a mutineer proved highly situational.

Paradoxically, the formal end of the Great War in Germany thus created a situation in which war overwhelmed state power.[23] The first to ride the tiger of 'mutiny' in the sense of military personnel who had escaped state authority was Friederich Ebert, the SDP Chancellor called in to pick up the pieces after the abdication. Ebert, determined to escape the fate of Kerensky in Russia, immediately placed a famous call to General Wilhelm Groener, deputy chief of the Imperial General Staff. Ebert would leave intact the imperial officer corps in exchange for his help in restoring order in the streets. But with most of the regular army still on foreign soil on the Western Front or in the East, Groener lacked sufficient forces at his disposal to regain control on his own.

The government and the military would come to rely on the Freikorps, 'demobilised' soldiers self-organised into autonomous paramilitary bands.[24] We can think of them in some sense as professional mutineers in that they considered themselves a source of sovereignty – embodiments of a true 'Germany' beyond any regime that claimed to be in charge on a given day. The war had created them, and they would continue to create the war, Armistice or no. As one Freikorps veteran, Friederich Wilhelm Heinz, wrote in his memoirs:

> When they told us that the war was over, we laughed, because we ourselves were the war. Its flame continued to burn in us, it lived on in our deeds surrounded by a glowing and frightful aura of destruction. We followed our inner calling and marched on the battlefields of the post-war period just as we had marched toward the front: we were singing, full of recklessness and adventurism while marching; we were grim, silent and merciless in combat.[25]

23 Robert Gerwarth and John Horne, 'Vectors of violence: paramilitarism in Europe after the Great War, 1917–1923', *Journal of Modern History*, 83 (2011), pp. 489–512.

24 Mark Jones, 'Violence and Politics in the German Revolution of 1918–19' (PhD thesis, European University Institute, 2011).

25 Friedrich Wilhelm Heinz, *Sprengstoff* (1930), quoted in Robert Gerwarth, 'The Central European counter-revolution: paramilitary violence in Germany, Austria and Hungary after the Great War', *Past and Present*, 200 (2008), p. 185.

Individual Freikorps paramilitaries had an unsettling array of motivations – from a highly gendered terror of a lack of external boundaries, to perverse nostalgia for the front, to a bitter and generally irrational hatred of civilians (notably women), socialists, communists and Jews (in any order).[26] Paradoxically, 'defeat' provided a powerful means of mobilising Freikorps against the outcome of the war. Of course, not all veterans took such a nihilistically sanguine view of the war of the trenches. Of some 11 million Germans mobilised in the Great War, only about 400,000 would ever join a Freikorps formation. But these professional mutineers exercised an influence over interwar German politics far disproportionate to their numbers.

The SDP and the new republic indeed avoided the fate of Kerensky in Russia. The Freikorps and its military backers put down the Spartacist uprising in Berlin, and in 1919 put down a would-be Bavarian Soviet Republic based in Munich. But the new regime had prevailed at a steep price. In order to gain a monopoly over the legitimate use of force in Germany, the republic turned to people who despised it. Whatever their diverse political beliefs, the Freikorps fighters were united in their conviction that the socialists and communists had been behind the defeat, which happened in the interior rather than at the front – what became known as the 'stab in the back' myth. Moreover, most Freikorps fighters equated both socialism and communism with Jews, the latter increasingly tagged as a threatening racial 'other'. For the time being, the Freikorps simply hated communists, and particularly those they construed as communist Jews, just a little more than socialists. The Freikorps murdered Liebknecht, Luxemburg and thousands of other revolutionaries and dissenters with no pretense of a trial.

A policy of subcontracted terror provided an unpromising start for what became the Weimar Republic. The knowledge that they had 'saved' the republic from Russian-style revolution was hardly going to disrupt the Freikorps veterans' sense of themselves as the authentic source of sovereignty in Germany. Their ideological mutiny would thus prove permanent. Political murder, once sanctioned unofficially, was not easily abolished officially. Right-wing terrorists would assassinate Matthias Erzberger in 1921. Erzberger had signed the Armistice agreement in November 1918, and had later become Finance Minister. Walther Rathenau was similarly murdered in 1922. Although no one had done more to mobilise the German economy during the war, Rathenau was Jewish. As Foreign Minister, he had signed the Treaty of Rapallo,

26 Klaus Theweleit, *Male Fantasies*, trans. Stephan Conaway, 2 vols. (Minneapolis, MN: University of Minnesota Press, 1987–9).

which regularised relations with the Soviet Union. Freikorps ideology thus branded him twice a traitor.

The Treaty of Versailles contained strict provisions against irregular military organisations, and the persistence of the Freikorps became a cause of increasing Allied concern. Formally outlawed by Weimar in 1921, the Freikorps presence in German political life diminished during the interwar years, but never really disappeared. 'Paramilitary' proved a difficult concept to define, and the term itself was not coined until the 1930s. Name changes could provide a thin but effective veil for Freikorps sympathies. For example, in 1921, the early Nazi Party simply rechristened the Saalschutz Abteilung (more commonly known as the SA) the Turn- und Sportabteilung (Gymnastic and Sports Division) of the broader Nazi organization. Its mutinous attitude towards the Weimar Republic remained unaltered.

Perhaps 'mutiny' most successfully merged with state building in Anatolia, when rebellious soldiers around a charismatic individual built a new state in opposition to the old, and eventually overcame it. The Moudros Armistice of 30 October 1918 accorded the Allies vast but almost unenforceable powers. Article XVI ordered Ottoman garrisons throughout Anatolia, the Arabian Peninsula, Syria and Mesopotamia to surrender their weapons to the nearest Allied commanders (who could be hundreds of miles away). This foreshadowed a problem that would haunt peacemaking in the region down to the Treaty of Lausanne in 1923 – the disparity between the apparent Allied 'victory' and their sparse military capabilities on the ground. How could the Allied forces in the field enforce peace throughout the vast former Ottoman realm, even before the huge popular clamour for demobilisation that immediately followed the Armistice? A modest force of some 3,500 Allied (mostly British) troops entered Constantinople, as an unofficial occupying force. The sultan and the formal structures of the Ottoman Government remained in place. The Allied 'victory' over the Ottoman Empire depended on the persistence of a regime in Constantinople that accepted that victory.

Mutiny in the end game of the Ottoman Empire came to be personified in Mustafa Kemal, later known as Atatürk.[27] He had been a career officer in the Ottoman army who had served in the war with Italy over Libya in 1911, and in the Balkan wars (1912 to 1913). He made his reputation, however, by reorganising the Ottoman defences at Gallipoli in 1915 as commander of the 19th Infantry Division. He held a variety of other combat and staff positions through the Moudros Armistice. On 30 April 1919, Kemal took up the

27 When surnames became mandatory in 1934, Kemal became known as 'Atatürk'.

innocuous sounding title of inspector of the 9th Army, with a base in Samsun on the Black Sea. In fact, this placed him beyond the power of the sultan in semi-occupied Constantinople and, for that matter, beyond the practical military reach of the Allies. While nominally reporting to the War Ministry, Kemal in effect had become the senior military and civilian official for all of Anatolia east of Ankara. Yet he later claimed his new position had the blessing of Sultan Memhet VI, who told him upon departing:

> Pasha, you have already rendered many services to the state. They are now part of history. Forget about them, for the service you are about to render will be more important still. You can save the state.[28]

Kemal's 'mutiny' took shape gradually. Shortly after his arrival in Samsun, the Supreme Council of the Paris Peace Conference authorised a Greek occupation of Smyrna (later Izmir). In response, Kemal and a group of other senior officers issued the Amasya Circular on 22 June 1919. The circular proclaimed that the independence and territorial integrity of the nation had become imperilled, and a national conference was necessary to address the situation. This implied, of course, that the regime in Constantinople was no longer sufficiently able to protect national interests, increasingly defined as those of Muslim Turks in Anatolia. Under pressure from the British (itself an indication of where effective sovereignty lay in Constantinople), the Ottoman War Minister requested on 5 July that Kemal return to the capital. Kemal declined, responding that he now served 'the forces of the nation'. On 9 July, Kemal resigned from the army. This was at once his last act as a mutineer and his first act as founding father of a new state.

While the enfeebled regime of the sultan would eventually condemn Kemal to death *in absentia* for his rebellion, the actual disengagement between the old and the new state took place over several years. Unauthorised conferences of nationalists at Erzerum in July 1919 and at Sivas in September 1919 established the two most salient principles of what would become the Misak-i Millî (National Pact), which elaborated the principles of the Amasya Circular. The nationalists declared the lands of Anatolia an indivisible Turkish nation. Moreover, any regime that did not support this policy ipso facto lacked legitimacy. All the while, Kemal claimed that he was neither a mutineer nor a rebel, and that he wanted nothing more than to liberate the sultan from foreign domination.

28 Quoted in Andrew Mango, *Atatürk: The Biography of the Founder of Modern Turkey* (Woodstock: Overlook Press, 1999), p. 216.

The British permitted elections in December 1919 for what proved to be the last Ottoman Parliament. To the surprise perhaps only of the British, the elections returned a strong pro-Kemal majority. When this parliament adopted the Misak-i Millî on 12 February 1920, the British responded with formalising the occupation of Constantinople and dissolving the parliament. Shortly thereafter, the alternative Turkish Grand National Assembly in Ankara elected Kemal as its president. But only after Sultan Mehmet VI refused definitively to recognise the Ankara Government in November 1922 did the assembly depose him.

Of course, Kemal saw himself as the instrument, and indeed the servant, of the 'authentic' post-Ottoman Turkish nation. This proved a compelling argument for thousands of his followers, though a risky one. If one mutinous officer could proclaim himself the voice of the nation, why not another? Kemal became 'Atatürk' or 'father of the Turks' by building a new state that recaptured sovereignty in its Weberian sense, the monopoly of the legitimate use of physical force over the Anatolian peninsula. He came to monopolise 'legitimacy' in a discursive as well as material sense. It helped, of course, that Kemal could mobilise his post-imperial nation against a foreign threat – first against the Western Allied occupiers, then against Greece, which clearly intended to annex not just Constantinople, but at least the western third of Anatolia. But all of the enemies of the new Kemalist republic were not so clearly external.

Anatolia was far from the homogenous Turkish nation-in-waiting of Kemalist propaganda. Even after the frequently brutal 'Great Exchange' of some 1.5 million individuals following the settlement with Greece, Anatolia remained as ethnically and religiously diverse as any of the former battlegrounds of the Great War. Muslims, Christians, Jews, Turks, Greeks, Kurds, Armenians, Albanians, Circassians (North Caucasians) and many others had lived alongside each other for centuries. Diverse individuals by the thousands had taken diverse positions for diverse reasons as the Ottoman Empire morphed into Kemalist Turkey. Paramilitary violence continued, particularly in the Kurdish regions and in the hitherto ethnically mixed areas along the Sea of Marmara.[29] The Kemalist army bolstered its internal legitimacy through victories over the Greeks and the British following the Chanak affair of 1922. It would tolerate no further 'mutiny', on ethnic, religious or any other basis. Militarised assimilation became the order of the day. For better or worse,

29 Ryan Gingeras, *Sorrowful Shores: Violence, Ethnicity, and the End of the Ottoman Empire, 1912–1923* (Oxford University Press, 2009).

the military built by Atatürk and his followers would provide the backbone of political society in Turkey until the early twenty-first century.

As we have seen, mutinies in the Great War occurred across a wide spectrum. Mutiny, like the war itself, proved 'more than a true chameleon', with highly diverse patterns and outcomes. Mutiny meant so many things because state authority itself was in play. Resistance to military authority could articulate wartime race relations in Houston and Singapore. It could blunt the edges of traditional discipline at Etaples, so long as no one publicly admitted as much. Mutiny, in the end, could provide an agonised affirmation of the Republican project in France. The memory of the Cattaro mutiny could be re-engineered decades after the fact by a communist Yugoslav state that would not long outlive its founder. Technical or legalistic 'mutiny' in Russian POW camps could help build a successor state in Czechoslovakia and undermine the building of one in Hungary. The instrumentalisation of mutiny paved the way to Bolshevik power in Russia. Mutiny helped the founding of a republic in Germany, only to maim it at birth through the reliance of the republic on professional mutineers in the Freikorps. Mutiny became so successfully incorporated into state building in Kemalist Turkey that it ceased to be referred to as mutiny at all. Indeed, the term 'mutiny' is seldom applied when using the first person. 'We' resist in the name of the true interests of the national community. 'They' resist in order to destroy that community.

On balance, mutiny would matter much less in the Second World War than in the Great War. Certainly, soldiers committed 'mutiny' according to the definition used here – such as the flight of Charles de Gaulle and a small band of followers to London in June 1940, and the bomb plot of German officers to kill Adolf Hitler in 1944. But structurally, these 'mutinies' were similar to that of Mustafa Kemal. The perpetrators simply claimed to be speaking more authentically for the national interest than the recognised state authorities then in place. By the Second World War, the position of Hitler's Propaganda Minister Joseph Goebbels on national sovereignty had won out. The sovereign nation-state had indeed become lord in its castle – able to mobilise, repress and murder millions within the territories it ruled. This often relegated resistance to isolated acts of sabotage, most commonly in remote locations. The authority of the state had become so strong, few dared even to contemplate mutiny against it. Perhaps only after 1945, with the fracturing of the colonial state with the wars of decolonisation, and the chronic coups and mutinies that afflicted the post-colonial states, do we find authentic echoes of mutiny in the Great War.

9
Logistics

IAN BROWN

One student of logistics, Henry Eccles, wrote in 1959, '*economic* capabilities limit the combat forces which can be *created*. At the same time, *logistic* capabilities limit the forces which can be *employed* in combat operations."[1] This was as true in 1914 as it is today. The old truism that an army marches on its stomach is useful, but necessarily oversimplified. It does, however, encapsulate the essence of military logistics – meeting the subsistence requirements of soldiers in such a way that those soldiers can prosecute military operations. One could follow Jon Sumida's lead and examine what a military-industrial complex requires to produce weapons or take Avner Offer's approach and examine how food production and imports affect military-political decision-making, but focusing on what soldiers actually consume and how to get it to them in the field is at the heart of military logistics. The First World War marks a watershed as the first true, modern war, and the processes developed to resupply the soldiers that fought it laid the groundwork for many of the things, such as fresh mid-winter grapes in northern hemisphere supermarkets, that we now take for granted.

One can break the Great Powers of 1914 into two broad geographic categories based on their lines of supply and communication: continental and extra-continental. The litmus test is simply the answer to the question: could the armies of the power march to a war on the European land mass? Regardless of the number of overseas possessions, colonies or territories, if the answer is 'yes', then the power may be defined as continental. The others – the British Empire, Imperial Japan and the United States – comprised the extra-continental contingent. The continental powers, to a greater or lesser degree, had transportation networks consisting of railways and inland waterways for moving large quantities of material efficiently, backed by road networks that

1 Henry Eccles, *Logistics in the National Defense* (Harrisburg, PA: Stackpole, 1959), p. 41, emphasis in original.

enhanced their armies' ability to march. This raised the potential for each nation to deploy armies to their borders on relatively short notice along with the supplies those armies required. The threat from a rapidly mobilised and hostile neighbour meant all continental powers maintained sizeable standing armies backed by readily mobilised reserves. Further, the military-industrial complex in each of these powers had developed over time to support the needs of their largely land-based militaries. While both France and Germany maintained substantial navies to provide some ability to protect overseas colonies, their focus was each other (or in the German case both France and Russia) and armies had precedence.

Extra-continental powers maintained small armies and powerful navies. For centuries, Britain's security rested on the might of the Royal Navy, which had also been a factor in the growth of Britain's global trading empire. In 1914, Britain, the world's pre-eminent trading power, maintained a huge merchant marine devoted to maintaining that trading life-blood. Japan also relied on trade for both foodstuffs and mineral resources, while the United States, as a great power with what amounted to its own continent, did not have the same reliance on trade, although its businesses certainly traded on a global scale. While Japan initially confined her operations to the Pacific, both Britain and America committed to operations on the European land mass. For each, this meant creating mass expeditionary armies and figuring out how to provide for those armies at the end of an overseas supply chain.

When discussing the issue of logistics, overseas supply chains and naval forces, one must make a differentiation between pure naval power, the fighting strength of a nation's naval forces, and maritime power, which encompasses both naval power and the transport capability of that nation's merchant marine.[2] In July 1914, the British Empire had under its flag just over 45 per cent of the world's steam ships greater than 100 tons (10,123 vessels) comprising a total of 20.5 million tons of shipping.[3] This is deceptive and recent work indicates that Britain controlled in excess of 55 per cent of global shipping and trade (80 per cent when adding Allied vessels).[4] An additional complication is that shipping in 1914 was a very different prospect from what it is today

2 Keith Neilson, 'Reinforcements and supplies from overseas: British strategic sealift in the First World War', in Greg Kennedy (ed.), *The Merchant Marine in International Affairs, 1850–1950* (London and Portland, OR: Frank Cass, 2000), p. 31.

3 Charles Ernest Fayle, *The War and the Shipping Industry* (London: Humphrey Milford, 1927), pp. 2–3.

4 Nicholas A. Lambert, *Planning Armageddon: British Economic Warfare and the First World War* (Cambridge, MA and London: Harvard University Press, 2012), pp. 238–40.

as, of the world's roughly 45 million tons of shipping, *all* of it required labour-intensive loading and unloading. The container ships that ply modern sea lanes and carry a large percentage of global trade in a shrink-wrapped, palletised and containerised form are a relatively recent invention (the first, the *Ideal X*, sailed on 26 April 1956).[5] During the First World War, large numbers of stevedores physically loaded and unloaded ships, which slowed the pace of maritime trade. Additionally, Britain's maritime power was, in 1914, devoted to the maintenance of the British economy and could not simply be made available to support military operations overseas without adversely impacting that economy. Nonetheless, the sheer size of Britain's merchant marine and the scale of pre-war ship production (60 per cent of the world's total shipping output from 1910 to 1914, with 80 per cent of that being built for British owners) left considerable scope for supporting operations with minimal domestic impact.[6]

The British Empire's position as the world's paramount maritime power provided the Allied powers with tremendous flexibility and staying power. This allowed Britain to manage an historic logistic feat by creating and supplying a continental army of nearly 1 million men *overseas* from their sources of supply in roughly a year.[7] America later had to do this as well, but rather than the 50 or so kilometres of English Channel between home ports and French ports, she had to deal with 5,500 kilometres of the Atlantic Ocean. While many American troops moved to France in American hulls, the sheer magnitude of British maritime power played a huge role, and in 1918 alone just over 55 per cent of the 1.828 million troops shipped to France that year went in British hulls.[8] Further, British shipping provided the logistic backbone funnelling those troops' supplies into France. Finally, British shipping supported the British army in multiple war theatres (using an average of 1.75 million displaced tons of shipping, which moved a cumulative total of nearly 24 million men and over 46 million tons of military stores during the war), supported the British economy and carried 45 per cent of imports to both France and Italy in 1917 to 1918.[9]

5 Brian J. Cudahy, *Box Boats: How Container Ships Changed the World* (New York: Fordham University Press, 2006), pp. ix, 27–32.

6 Fayle, *Shipping*, p. 17.

7 Ian M. Brown, *British Logistics on the Western Front, 1914–1918* (Westport, CT: Praeger, 1998), pp. 75–104, *passim*.

8 David Stevenson, *With Our Backs to the Wall: Victory and Defeat in 1918* (Cambridge, MA: The Belknap Press of Harvard University Press, 2011), p. 345.

9 Neilson, 'Reinforcements and supplies', pp. 46–8.

The reach of Allied supply lines was truly global. South American produce and Canadian wheat moved over the South and North Atlantic to British and then European destinations. The Japanese navy provided substantial help in escorting troop carriers bringing soldiers and supplies from as far away as Australia and New Zealand to the Mediterranean fronts, and to the Western Front thereafter. The Second Special Squadron in the Mediterranean escorted over 700 ships, and 700,000 Allied soldiers to their destinations, and also rescued over 7,000 people from damaged or destroyed vessels. Supplies had to be provided for sailors and soldiers alike in this set of complex operations.

The First World War despite its name was not unique in its geographic scope. The Seven Years War had witnessed conflict on a global scale with land battles in Europe, North America and India. The unique nature of the First World War is that it had both a global scale and was fought between sides that were, in the main, modern, industrialised nation-states. As a result, the sheer magnitude of the forces engaged dwarfed prior conflicts. Further, technological changes in the late nineteenth century allowed those forces to use military consumables such as ammunition at a rate that had only been dimly imagined before the shooting began, and for all armies, figuring out how best to employ their formations with their new firepower while keeping them effectively resupplied took time. Modern weapons systems such as the French Soixante-Quinze (75 mm) field artillery piece could fire twenty shells per minute at targets up to 8 kilometres away; even the heavy artillery had a significantly higher rate of fire than their pre-1897 predecessors.[10] In discussing the American Expeditionary Forces' (AEF's) operational development, Mark Grotelueschen offers a cogent summary of what all armies ultimately learned on the Western Front, stating:

> . . . it took much more firepower and better coordinated firepower, as well as smaller, more flexible infantry formations to take smaller objectives than AEF leaders generally thought . . . but even the best infantry divisions . . . all earned their successes in large part by learning how to coordinate massive amounts of firepower, not by relying on the rifle and the bayonet or even solely on infantry auxiliaries.[11]

10 Jonathan B. A. Bailey, *Field Artillery and Firepower* (Annapolis, MD: Naval Institute Press, 2004), p. 209.

11 Mark Ethan Grotelueschen, *The AEF Way of War: The American Army and Combat in World War I* (New York: Cambridge University Press, 2007), p. 57.

One could easily substitute the words French, German or British in place of AEF without changing the accuracy or meaning of this statement and, indeed, the lesson could be applied to all of the war's major theatres. The combination of sheer numbers of combatants, global scale of operations and the ability to consume supplies at staggering rates placed unparalleled challenges in front of the logisticians of all nation-states.

August 1914 witnessed the continental powers fully utilising their transportation networks to rapidly fill their armies to wartime strength and those armies immediately began consuming supplies – munitions, food, soldiers, horses – at a frightening rate. The German Schlieffen Plan relied on rapid and precise rail movements coordinated by the Great General Staff's largest section, the Railroad Department,[12] and swung through Belgium into northwest France, while the French, following Plan XVII, launched a massive assault on the eastern side of their mutual border. In the East, Russia and Austria-Hungary followed suit. During August and early September, the Germans pressed forward into France's industrial heartland and moved far ahead of their railheads; troops in the First Army, for example, marched some 500 kilometres in the late summer heat. The German Second Army found itself in similar condition, though it had 'only' marched 440 kilometres to reach the River Marne.[13] Even hungry, thirsty and tired, German armies posed a threat to Paris; they were dangerous, but also at the absolute limits of resupply. This is an example of what is generally termed the 'logistic equaliser'; the paradox that means armies advancing from their sources of supply see their combat power weakened by the need to move supplies further and further, while those falling back effectively increase their combat power because their resupply routes are shortened. In this case, the French had access to interior lines of communication and were not advancing off their railheads. Indeed, prior to the First Battle of the Marne, and following evidence that Plan XVII had failed, General Joffre used those internal lines and moved four army corps from his right wing to his left – four corps moved in under six days with each corps using up to 118 trains; a 'feat of logistic brilliance' by the Directorate of Railways that had a significant impact on the outcome of the Battle of the Marne.[14] In the East, Russia mobilised more swiftly than anticipated, but superior German generalship and the skilful use of a dense

12 David Zabecki, *The German 1918 Offensives: A Case Study in the Operational Level of War* (London: Routledge, 2006), p. 84.

13 Holger Herwig, *The Marne, 1914: The Opening of World War I and the Battle that Changed the World* (New York: Random House, 2009), pp. 219–20, 250–1.

14 Herwig, *Marne*, p. 306.

railway network in East Prussia led to a Russian rout at Tannenberg.[15] While Russia found itself handicapped by a comparative lack of transportation infrastructure (roughly 5 per cent as much railway line per 100 square kilometres near the battle front), the Russian railways generally performed well.[16] Further, following Tannenberg, that very lack of rail lines handicapped the Central Powers as they sought to advance into Russian territory. Enormous casualties had ensued as armies confronted a basic reality – the combination of modern, quick-firing artillery, machine guns and bolt action rifles made the battle space a killing zone in which it was near-suicide to leave oneself exposed; as a result, the trench digging began.

Contrary to popular belief, the trenches proved the infantryman's friend as they provided cover, shelter and protection from the lethality of modern war.[17] Their advent, along with the static, continuous front also allowed logisticians on both sides to actually begin the long process of building the supporting infrastructure their armies required; a process that proved more difficult in the long run than ramping up production of military consumables, as infrastructure is inherently more difficult to build.[18] While parts of the various fronts fell at or close to the pre-war borders, significant portions did not, and no one had effectively planned for the circumstances that ensued. By the end of 1914, the Western Front had stabilised into what, outside of a significant German pull-back in early 1917, would be its general location until March 1918. The Eastern Front proved more fluid, but in places it also saw stability through the winter of 1914/15. Ironically, the presence of the trenches and a static front in the West helped both sides from a logistic angle. During 1915, the major powers suffered shell crises as their expenditures vastly exceeded even the worst pre-war forecasts.[19] By December 1914, for example, Russia had essentially depleted its entire pre-war ammunition reserve and the ongoing demand of some 45,000 shells per day was more than thirty times the actual daily production of roughly 1,300.[20] Factories simply could not

15 Christian Wolmar, *Engines of War: How Wars were Won and Lost on the Railways* (New York: Perseus, 2010), p. 190; Timothy C. Dowling, *The Brusilov Offensive* (Bloomington and Indianapolis, IN: Indiana University Press, 2008), pp. 18–20.

16 Dowling, *Brusilov*, p. 8.

17 Stephen Bull, *Trench: A History of Trench Warfare on the Western Front* (London: Osprey, 2010), p. 218.

18 Zabecki, *1918 Offensives*, pp. 83–4.

19 Cf. Dennis E. Showalter, 'Mass warfare and the impact of technology', in Chickering and Forster, *Great War, Total War*, pp. 79–80; Jay Luvaas, 'A unique army: the common experience', in Robert A. Kann *et al.* (eds.), *The Habsburg Empire in World War I* (New York: Columbia University Press, 1977), p. 97.

20 Dowling, *Brusilov*, p. 6.

produce enough ammunition to fill the demand, but this allowed concentrated efforts on building infrastructure and lines of communications – moving railheads as close as feasible to the front lines, building major depots and ammunition dumps near those railheads, laying light railways with horse-drawn or light engines for motive power and the like. Simultaneously, the dramatic expansion of the British Expeditionary Force (BEF) from an imperial constabulary into a continental army began in earnest. The BEF had the additional complication of having to ship almost everything their army required into France from Britain and other overseas sources of supply. By the end of 1915, however, the BEF had created its lines of communication in France and managed to increase its size over 300 per cent to just under 1 million soldiers. In an unusual paradox, the shell crisis in Britain actually eased the task of expanding the BEF because the lack of shells decreased the load on its lines of communication and allowed the expansion to proceed more swiftly.[21] Add several million French and German soldiers to the equation, all of whom had to be supplied with everything necessary to sustain health and combat power, and the logistic ramifications become clear.

The Western Front represented the largest number of men who had ever faced off in a wartime situation. At the same time, these millions of men were no longer employed in their home nations' workforces in a productive capacity; rather, they now filled inherently unproductive roles and had to be supported.

Outside of the obvious, weapons and munitions, what basics does it take to support and sustain soldiers in the field? First, food; while the current US Department of Agriculture (USDA) recommendations call for up to 3,000 calories per day for an active male between the ages of 19 and 30; the demands of life on active military service are considerably higher.[22] The main combatants on the Western Front all recognised this early on and adopted generous caloric goals ranging from the German 4,038 calories to the US 4,714 calories.[23] While laudable goals, meeting them proved difficult; the BEF, for example, had various ration scales in France during the war (see Table 9.1). While changes do not appear particularly significant in and of themselves, when multiplied by up to 2 million men they could be very significant. For example,

21 Brown, *British Logistics*, p. 78.

22 *Dietary Guidelines for Americans*, 2010, 7th edn (Washington, DC: US Government Printing Office, December 2010, US Department of Agriculture and US Department of Health and Human Services), p. 14.

23 *Statistics of the Military Effort of the British Empire during the Great War, 1914–1920* (London: War Office, 1922), p. 586.

Table 9.1 *British ration scales, 1914 to 1918, in grams*

Foodstuff	Initial	29/10/1915	4/4/1916	20/1/1917	1/7/1917	26/1/1918
Meat (fresh or frozen)	567	454	454	454	454	454
or meat (preserved)	454	340	340	340	255	255
Bread	567	567	567	454	454	454
or biscuit	340	340	340	340	283	283
Bacon	113	113	113	113	113	113
Cheese	85	85	85	57	57	57
Fresh vegetables	227	227	227	227	227	227
or dried vegetables	57	57	57	57	57	57
Tea	18	18	18	18	18	14
Jam	113	113	85	85	85	85
*Butter**	24	24	24	24	24	24
Sugar**	85	85	85	85	85	85
*Oatmeal**	24	24	24	24	24	24
Rice	12	12	12	12	12	12
Salt	14	14	14	14	7	7
Mustard	1.4	0.6	0.6	0.6	0.3	0.3
Pepper	0.8	0.8	0.8	0.8	0.3	0.3
Milk (condensed)***	21	21	28	28	28	28
Pickles*	12	12	12	12	12	12
Max. total mass (nearest gram)	1,884	1,770	1,749	1,608	1,601	1,597
Min. total mass (nearest gram)	1,374	1,259	1,238	1,210	1,061	1,057

Source: Statistics of the Military Effort of the British Empire during the Great War, 1914–1920 (London: War Office, 1922), p. 584.
Italics: issued as an 'extra' until January 1917
* Issued three times per week, number so adjusted.
** From 1 July 1917, if sweetened condensed milk issued, then sugar ration lowered to 71 g.
*** Prior to 20 January 1917, this is estimated based on data provided.

the reduction in the tea ration on 26 January 1918 by 4 grams appears trivial, but it meant a reduction of some 8 metric tons that needed to be distributed per day. Further, had the 1914 ration been maintained through 1918, the roughly 300 grams per day extra would have meant a need to distribute an additional 600 metric tons per day. Clearly, ration scales needed to be generous enough to provide soldiers with sufficient sustenance to maintain health and morale, without being so generous as to unnecessarily stress infrastructure.

In addition, armies had to feed and care for animals as they provided most of the actual motive power at the time. This had a significant impact. The British army employed over 800,000 animals worldwide as of the end of August 1917, including over 700,000 actually deployed in combat theatres (see Table 9.2). These animals consumed substantial amounts of food and water; indeed, during the war the BEF imported to France over 3 million deadweight tons of oats and nearly 2.7 million deadweight tons of hay, the combination being termed 'fodder'.[24] The fodder issue has been raised by David Kenyon and others in defence of British cavalry and its doctrine. The argument is cogent – the implicit assumption that cavalry used most of the fodder shipped to France is a false one; cavalry comprised a very small percentage of the BEF's horses in France.[25] Examining the fodder issue in more detail, however, on a pure cost-benefit basis, a given number of regular infantrymen provided more firepower at a lower tonnage cost per man than did the same number of cavalrymen (see Table 9.3). Only unrealistically maximising the infantry division's ration mass while minimising that of the cavalry division leaves the relative numbers anywhere close. Using more realistic assumptions indicates that from a basic ration perspective (human food and horse fodder combined), a cavalry division consumed essentially the same amount as an infantry division. Even allowing that cavalry could cover ground more quickly than infantry over a tactical time frame, in the conditions prevailing on the Western Front from late 1914 to at least early 1918, such calculations would always favour keeping infantry in France rather than cavalry. Once motorised transport began replacing the horse, this equation began to change, but even then, not in favour of the cavalry as motorised transport (trucks and tractors) began to take the place of the draft horses in divisions' artillery and supply echelons.

Nonetheless, equine power and the forage to 'fuel' it made up a very significant portion of the tonnage moved to France during the war because of the sheer number of horses on the lines of communication and in the artillery, not because of their presence in cavalry divisions. While all armies, and particularly Western ones, greatly increased the use of motorised transportation during the war, animals filled the role of prime movers forward of the railheads. It was not until 1917 that, on the Allied side at least, motorised transport began phasing out horse-drawn transport and both Mesopotamia

24 *Statistics*, p. 521 (3,250,243 deadweight tons of oats and 2,669,184 deadweight tons of hay from 9 August 1914 to 26 March 1920).

25 David Kenyon, *Horsemen in No Man's Land: British Cavalry & Trench Warfare 1914–1918* (Barnsley: Pen & Sword, 2011), pp. 7–8.

Table 9.2 *British army, animals employed by theatre, 1918*

Theatre	Riding horse	Lt draft horse	Hvy draft horse	Pack horse	Unclassified horse	Lt draft mule	Hvy draft mule	Pack mule	Unclassified mule	Camel	Oxen	Donkey	Grand total
United Kingdom	34,717	47,614	15,177	834	25,500	11,849	256	1,303	345				137,595
France	122,421	168,917	70,362	6,449		78,394		3,337					449,880
Egypt	31,566	11,632	1,207	1,428	4,696	15,636	613	4,977	1,192	44,502			117,449
Salonica	9,246	6,848	1,445	408	3,770	3,216		43,312	8,486				76,731
Mesopotamia					25,543				38,186	2,952	5,016		71,697
East Africa					1,544				2,219		6,033	6,810	16,606
Total	197,950	235,011	88,191	9,119	61,053	109,095	869	52,929	50,428	47,454	11,049	6,810	869,958
War theatres	163,233	187,397	73,014	8,285	35,553	97,246	613	51,626	50,083	47,454	11,049	6,810	732,363

Source: Statistics of the Military Effort of the British Empire during the Great War, 1914–1920 (London: War Office, 1922), p. 400.
Note: Mesopotamia numbers in *Statistics* are off by 27 in the total column.

Table 9.3 *Daily ration mass per soldier and horse, British infantry and cavalry divisions, 1914 establishments*

		Case 1		Case 2	
Infantry division		Per diem (kg)	Total (kg)	Per diem (kg)	Total (kg)
Soldiers	18,073	1.884	34,050	1.6	28,917
Horses (700 kg)	5,592	21	117,432	14	78,288
Total ration mass/day			151,482		107,205
Ration mass/day/soldier			8.4		5.9
Cavalry division		Per diem (kg)	Total (kg)	Per diem (kg)	Total (kg)
Soldiers	9,269	1.374	12,736	1.6	14,830
Horses (500 kg)	9,815	10	98,150	10	98,150
Total ration mass/day			110,886		112,980
Ration mass/day/soldier			12.0		12.2
Cavalry soldier/infantry soldier (%)			143%		205%

Sources: Horse consumption – Greg Lardy and Chip Poland, *AS-953 (Revised): Feeding Management for Horse Owners* (Fargo: NDSU Extension Service, February 2001), p. 4; *Statistics of the Military Effort of the British Empire during the Great War, 1914–1920* (London: War Office, 1922), p. 584.
Case 1: Cavalry horses, lightly worked, consume 2% of their body mass per day; infantry horses, heavily worked, consume 3%; infantry soldiers receive higher mass fresh/frozen rations; cavalry soldiers receive lower mass dried rations.
Case 2: All horses lightly worked, soldiers receive same basic ration with mix of fresh/frozen/dried.

and the East African theatre, for example, saw ever-increasing numbers of trucks, although animals remained crucial.[26] Finally, while the numbers of trucks employed increased over time and ultimately began to replace equine power, the fuel requirements ultimately provided little savings in tonnage; what they did was to allow armies to supply their soldiers at a greater distance from railheads than did horses.

26 Showalter, 'Mass warfare', p. 84. See also Kaushik Roy, 'From defeat to victory: logistics of the campaign in Mesopotamia, 1914–1918', *First World War Studies*, 1:1 (2010), pp. 51–2.

Water and associated basic sanitation was as critical as food, and unfortunately few firm figures are available to indicate how much was actually transported. It is, however, even more of a necessity to sustain life, and all armies had to devise ways to get it to their front-line troops. Given the current recommended intake of 1 US gallon per day (just under 4 litres) from all sources (including food), one might reasonably assume that soldiers, exerting themselves, would need to drink at least a couple of litres of water per day above that contained in their food (and often considerably more). Water needs for soldiers in the Middle East, Mesopotamia, Salonica and East African theatres were still higher because of the environment in which they fought. For the BEF in early 1918, 2 litres per man per day would have worked out to approximately 4,000 metric tons that had to be distributed simply to avoid dehydration, and establishments for formations certainly included provision for water transportation. In early 1916, the BEF had a specialised water purification barge in service capable of delivering 18,000 litres per hour with five more in the process of working up. In addition, they had settled on a motorised army water column which, to supply three army corps, used eighty-nine light trucks loaded with 680-litre water tanks, thirty-two 3-ton trucks each loaded with a 2,250-litre water tank and a number of additional vehicles carrying purification plants and chemicals – a combined capacity of 133,500 litres.[27] Such army water columns delivered water to the divisions, which then moved it to their troops. As another example, an American division's establishment included 101 water carts (each drawn by a mule) with another half-dozen 'trail-mobile' carts kept with the division's sanitary echelon.[28] While a large percentage of the various armies' manpower at any given time were not actively engaged in the front lines, for the men that were, the water had to be physically carried over the final stage of the journey often in rum jars, barrels or water carts and, at least on the German side of the line, frequently as bottled mineral water because it was readily available to them. The rum jars, barrels and bottles then sufficed to store the water in the trenches. Almost regardless of the source, water was always safest when boiled.[29] In extreme circumstances, soldiers might be forced to drink the polluted surface water available in shell holes, with dysentery being possibly

27 Q2811, Cubitt to War Office, 10 January 1916 and Q2811/1, Haig to War Office, 3 February 1916, WO95/29, QMG Branch, War Diary, British National Archives (BNA) (4.54 litres per imperial gallon).

28 *United States Army in the World War 1917–1919*, CD-ROM edn (Washington, DC: Center of Military History, 1948), vol. VI, p. 341 (hereinafter, *USOH*).

29 Bull, *Trench*, p. 82.

the least serious side-effect, because no-man's-land was an inherently unsanitary place.

While basic sanitation (washing and shaving) could be accomplished in the trenches without necessarily using potable water, some means had to be used to deal with excrement. Generally, some combination of latrines regularly disinfected and, ideally, a bucket system with the contents removed from the trenches on a daily basis proved the preferred method; pit systems also saw use.[30] The negative side to systems that did not physically evacuate excrement was that it was readily available for shell-fire to redistribute indiscriminately. Beyond this basic level, however, bathing and de-lousing could only be done outside of the trench zones in rear areas where wash houses and dedicated sanitary facilities could operate in reasonable safety. Grotelueschen illustrated the effects of poor sanitation combined with other supply issues using the US 26th Division's October 1918 sanitation report. In summary, the division suffered from a general lack of sanitation in the front lines and the interruption of the regular flow of supplies (such as potable water and clean clothing). The cumulative effect of the worn clothing, unsanitary conditions and just a single hot meal per day left the division in a parlous operational state.[31]

Next, armies need to provide clothing and shelter. Clothing, boots and other basic 'kit' breaks down rapidly when it is roughly used, and trench warfare was a very tough environment for natural fibres. Further, soldiers literally carried their possessions with them at all times. Once things got dirty or wet, they tended to stay that way until the soldier rotated out of the trenches into reserve where they had access to improved sanitation and quartering. At that time, they and their clothing would be cleaned and de-loused and replacements issued. This required all armies to keep vast stocks of replacement equipment in storage near enough to the front to allow issue without undue delay and, generally speaking, most succeeded well enough, although the winter of 1914/15 proved brutally harsh in places like the Carpathians.

Shelter was a somewhat trickier issue. Historically, armies in the field relied on tents and the like to shelter their troops, but a tent was not something that could be set up in the trenches, so 'shelter' took other forms. The trench itself could provide shelter, but most contained dugouts that used, at a minimum, timber support to provide overhead cover from the worst of the elements. In some cases, mostly on the German side of the lines, elaborate shelters were built using reinforced concrete and became comfortable at times. From the

30 Bull, *Trench*, p. 76. 31 Grotelueschen, *AEF Way of War*, pp. 193–5.

most mundane to elaborate, shelters consumed substantial quantities of timber and other building materials, such as stone and concrete for their construction; materials also in great demand for constructing the infrastructure that the armies required to store and move the supplies.

As soon as the war of movement on the Western Front broke down in 1914, the rear areas on both sides of the trenches saw a frenzy of infrastructure construction. Demand for timber, stone and coal in particular spiked dramatically as numerous rail sidings and depots had to be constructed to handle the flow of goods to the troops. Prior to the war, six main rail lines ran between Germany and France – two from Cologne to Paris, and one each from Coblenz to Verdun, Mayence to Nancy, Mayence to Metz and Mannheim to Colmar.[32] Each of these lines had obviously been cut by the trenches and both sides needed to determine the best locations for their railheads (generally in or very near to whichever major rail centre was closest to the trenches, without being so close as to be in danger), lay additional rail lines and sidings to expand them such that they could be effectively used, construct numerous depots and dumps within relatively close proximity to the railheads to store vast quantities of consumables, and finally improve or create roads and light railways to speed movement of supplies to the trenches. Such construction simply had to be undertaken because 'where the railways ran, the army could be moved and supplied. Once off the rail lines, the supply system was little improved over the ones extant at the time of Wellington.'[33] This all took vast quantities of building material: stone for road and rail beds; timber for buildings, rail sleepers, trench improvements and heat; concrete for foundations and trench improvements; coal to power industry, provide motive power for railways and for heat. During the war, the BEF shipped to France over 850,000 tons of timber, 4.5 million tons of coal (second only to ammunition in total shipments) and nearly 1.5 million tons of road and railway construction material such as stone.[34] In addition, the British and French governments created the Franco-British War Timber Commission in 1916, which allowed the BEF to commission battalions of loggers to begin actively logging selected French forests to supplement timber imports, as the BEF did not have the port capacity to handle all their needs.

32 John A. Porter, 'The German supply system as it affected operations in the offensive of March 21–27 against Amiens; the offensive of May 21 to July 15, 1918, in the Marne Salient' (Fort Leavenworth, KS: Command and General Staff School Papers, 1931), p. 1.

33 Roger G. Miller, 'The logistics of the British Expeditionary Force, 4 August to 5 September 1914', *Military Affairs* (1979), p. 137.

34 *Statistics*, p. 521.

All armies created massive storage facilities located on or near ports and major rail lines. Supplies then moved from such facilities by rail to both large storage facilities and smaller depots in closer proximity to the fighting area. From there, they moved on to railheads where formations from army down to division picked them up for storage and distribution by some combination of light railway (typically 60 cm gauge) and horse-drawn or motorised transport. This might include moving the supplies to depots and dumps in army and corps areas or it could be that divisional supply echelons picked the supplies up for direct distribution from the railheads to their troops. Once in the divisional areas, the divisions generally got the supplies to their soldiers by some combination of horse-drawn transport and in the final stages human carriage to the trenches. The AEF, for example, planned for a ninety-day stock of supplies immediately available in France with an additional thirty days continually in transit and had absolutely no infrastructure in place in France to store those supplies.[35] Bearing in mind plans to field a 4-million-man army in Europe in 1919, whether realistic or not, and a forecast requirement of nearly 92,000 metric tons of supplies per day for that army, the Americans had a vast array of construction projects under way even before 1917 drew to a close. This included work on eighty-nine berths in twenty-eight different ports and the use of over 8,000 kilometres of rail lines to deliver supplies to storage areas, depots and railheads. Their largest single project, the port storage yard under construction near Montoir, if fully completed, would have contained 378 kilometres of railway tracks and 1,025 associated turnouts, 180 warehouses with just over 4 million square feet of covered storage and an additional 10 million square feet of open storage on a footprint of 1,200 acres (roughly 2.5 miles by 1 mile). As of the Armistice, the yard was roughly half-completed. Five other smaller port storage yards covering an additional 2,600 acres were also under construction. The largest American depots, both roughly as large as Montoir, were under construction near Gievres and Montierchaume and, if fully completed, each would have held some 14 million square feet of covered and open storage space.[36] The British, French and German armies had facilities of similar scope.

While the French, British and Germans dug and built in the West, the Germans took advantage of their dense rail network in East Prussia to mount a major offensive. During the winter of 1914/15, the Austro-Hungarian and Russian armies suffered shocking privations in the Carpathians, and in spite of

35 *USOH*, vol. xv, p. 10. 36 *USOH*, vol. xiv, pp. 228–32 and *passim*.

this, both hammered away at each other in the brutal Carpathian Winter War.[37] The Germans suffered far fewer problems and illustrated at Gorlice-Tarnow in early May what happened when a comparatively well-equipped and supplied army attacks one that is poorly equipped and supplied. The Eleventh German Army poured fire from a total of 1,272 field and 334 heavy artillery pieces on the Russian Third Army at a time when the latter's gunners only had fifty shells per gun with which to reply. When combined with Russian rifle shortages, the end result could not be in doubt, and the Third Army shattered, leaving a gaping hole which the Germans could exploit. In spite of this, and the resulting advances that would, quite simply, not occur on the Western Front, the Eastern Front eventually stabilised, as railheads could not keep up and the logistic equaliser panned out. By mid August, German field railways (light railways using horses as motive power) were still 125 *kilometres* short of the front lines, to say nothing of the broad gauge railheads. Indeed, during the year the front moved up to 450 kilometres at its maximum, from west of Warsaw to Pinsk – had such a move occurred in the West, it would have shifted the front line from the Ypres area to near Rennes at the foot of the Brittany peninsula had it moved southwestwards, or to Munster had it gone in the other direction. Following the advance, German railway troops faced the task of re-gauging nearly 8,000 kilometrs of track and building many hundreds of kilometres of narrow-gauge track before further advances could be contemplated; a task that lasted into 1916.[38] The scope of the Eastern Front meant that all operations had to deal with the relative dearth of transportation infrastructure. Further, it is evident that the Habsburg Empire eventually suffered serious transportation issues that ultimately became its Achilles heel.[39]

Mountain warfare on the Italian Front presented logistical problems of staggering proportions. Hauling artillery and ordnance up to mountain galleries, carved out of the rock face itself, soldiers in the Dolomites suffered acutely from shortages of provisions. The same topographical difficulties made logistics at other points of the Italian-Austrian Front a nightmare for both sides.

The other Allied powers suffered similar, though less intractable, issues. The BEF, for example, witnessed a near collapse of their supply system during

37 Gordon A. Tunstall, *Blood on the Snow: The Carpathian Winter War of 1915* (Lawrence, KS: University Press of Kansas, 2010), pp. 21–2, 29, *passim*.

38 Dowling, *Brusilov*, pp. 25–6, 28–30, 32–3; Wolmar, *Engines*, pp. 194–5.

39 Robert J. Wegs, 'Transportation: the Achilles heel of the Habsburg war effort', in Kann *et al.*, *Habsburg Empire*, pp. 130–1 and *passim*.

the middle stages of the Somme offensive in 1916. They managed to avert the worst of the crisis and fixed their issues with considerable success by retaining the services of Eric Geddes, an experienced civilian railway man, who implemented a complete overhaul and rationalisation of the BEF's system over the winter of 1916/17. The AEF also suffered similar issues, related to their swift growth, and worked to resolve them by retaining the services of George Goethels, a military engineer best known for his work in constructing the Panama Canal. Goethals, like Geddes, worked to implement a mix of solutions and rationalise the AEF's administrative and transportation infrastructure and, while not completely successful prior to the end of the war, he laid much groundwork that would have paid dividends had the war continued.[40]

The Western Front in 1918 provides excellent logistic examples and lessons. By 1918, both sides (four major powers) had their infrastructure sufficiently constructed to fully support the forces involved; further, they had all come more or less to grips with the challenges of modern, industrial warfare and implemented doctrines that let them fight effectively. During the winter of 1917/18, the German High Command decided on a series of major offensives on the Western Front designed to win before the AEF became a significant factor there. German logisticians made tremendous efforts to create the supply conditions required to support these offensives and given the difficulties they faced succeeded admirably.

The Michael offensive of 21 March is a case study in this. In the build-up to Michael, the German High Command amassed an enormous artillery park and ensured its lavish supply. Tremendous emphasis went into preparations to repair infrastructure as the advance occurred and to link existing German infrastructure such as roads and light railways as quickly as possible to those they planned to capture.[41] Three full armies were used in the Michael offensive, supported by 10,000 artillery pieces and trench mortars whose sheer weight of metal effectively stunned and disorganised the defences of the British Fifth Army.[42] The opening day advances were astonishing; the kind of movement that had not been seen since 1914, but

40 See Keith Grieves, *Sir Eric Geddes: Business and Government in War and Peace* (Manchester University Press, 1989); Phyllis Zimmerman, *The Neck of the Bottle: George W. Goethals and the Reorganization of the US Army Supply System* (College Station, TX: Texas A & M University Press, 1992).

41 Zabecki, *1918 Offensives*, pp. 130–2.

42 Bailey, *Artillery*, p. 262, indicates 6,473 guns and 3,532 trench mortars.

there was no real operational direction to the offensive beyond breaking a hole and seeing what happened. In spite of the stunning advances, by 25 March the logistic equaliser began to punish the German formations at the sharp end. The Eighteenth Army, over 50 kilometres in advance of its railheads, had to try to continue to push against British troops that had fallen back much closer to theirs. As a result, while German formations found themselves forced to scale back their artillery use, they did so while attacking British formations that could and often did expend ammunition with reckless abandon.[43]

Despite correctly identifying the BEF as the crucial centre of gravity for the initial operations, the German High Command itself did not account for the vulnerabilities of *Allied* logistic networks and refused to make strategic or operational plans that emphasised those vulnerabilities. Had the German High Command taken the time to assess British positions, they should have easily realised that the railway centre of Amiens was critical to the BEF's entire supply infrastructure. Nearly half of the BEF's supplies arrived in the southern channel ports of Le Havre, Rouen and Dieppe, and most of it funnelled through Amiens on its way to the rear area depots and dumps maintained by the BEF. Had Michael been directed ruthlessly at Amiens, they almost certainly would have taken it and potentially *crippled* the BEF; at a minimum, they would have forced them to counter-attack and retake it. Failing that, the BEF could easily have found itself in an untenable position from which they would have either had to withdraw south of the River Somme or pull everything north of the Somme and create a defensive line on that right flank that ran back to the Channel. In either case, the BEF would have assumed a purely defensive position, and had to withdraw excess formations that they no longer had the port capacity to supply and simply hope for the best. Had the ensuing Georgette operation then been aimed directly at Hazebrouck, Amiens's analogue on the BEF's northern line of communications, the BEF might have been facing a Dunkirk situation, twenty-two years before it actually occurred. Yet, there is no evidence that Ludendorff understood Amiens's significance, except in the battles of the *ex post facto* memoirs. Indeed, the German spring offensives as a whole are notable for the general lack of emphasis on aiming at targets in Allied rear areas that would have hurt them. Finally, the offensives' primary success, if it can be so called, was to create a number of exposed salients at a substantial cost in highly trained manpower

43 Zabecki, *1918 Offensives*, pp. 151–2.

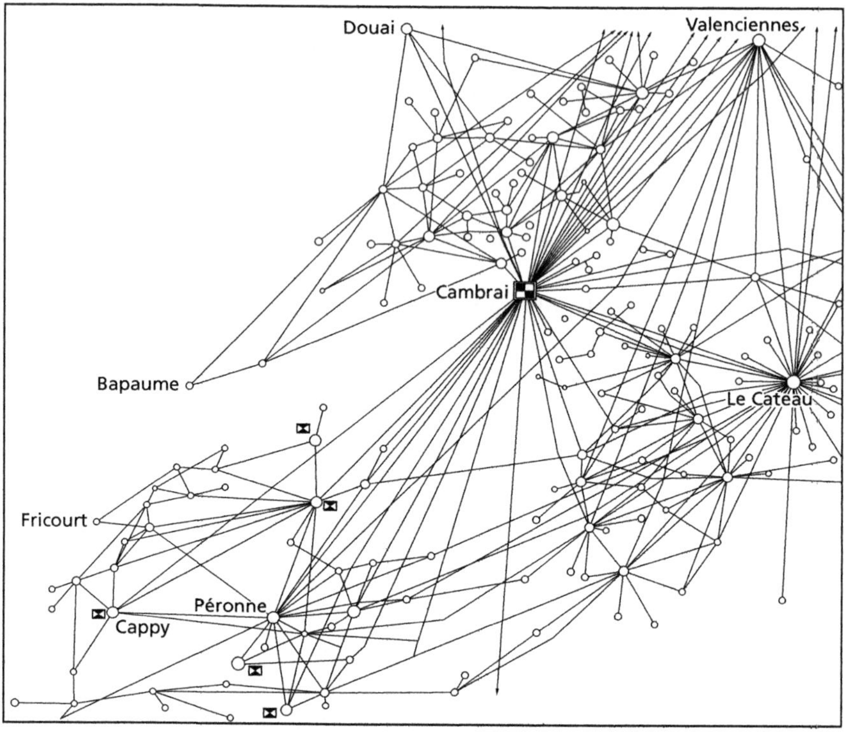

Map 9.1 German communications system 1915

from which they then refused to withdraw, leaving their armies vulnerable to counter-attack.[44]

The first Allied counter-attack duly fell on the salient created by the final German offensive; indeed, it began before that offensive ended as Franco-American armies attacked on 18 July. Unlike the Germans, the Franco-American assaults did take German logistics into account and the offensive's goals included specific efforts to sever German communications into the salient. Likewise, the second great Allied offensive fell near Amiens on 8 August, and had as one of its primary goals pushing the Germans back far enough that they no longer had the ability to interfere with rail operations in that vital rail centre. Allied advances in August were almost as dramatic as the German advances of the spring, and many of the same issues the Germans had

44 See Brown, *British Logistics*, ch. 8, *passim*; Zabecki, *1918 Offensives*, pp. 151–2, 314–15, 317–18.

faced with the logistic equaliser also caused problems for the Allied armies. Indeed, British formations sometimes had problems with artillery ammunition during 1918 because they were used to being close to their sources of supply and with the more mobile warfare that evolved they tended to be too profligate in their expenditures.[45] Further, during the operations later that year, having pushed well forward of the lines held in August, the sheer difficulty of resupplying multiple field armies at an extended distance from railheads while having to repair the damage caused by the retiring Germans meant that logistics became the main constraint on operational tempo.[46] Rather than attempting to advance recklessly, however, the Allied armies accepted pauses while their railheads advanced as much as possible. In addition, the Allied powers relied on motorised transport to provide an ever-increasing percentage of the supply lift forward of railheads and essentially began to replace their fodder needs with fuel requirements to service that growing fleet of vehicles. By 1918, British monthly imports to France included roughly 14,660 tons of forage, but 49,400 tons of fuel, although cumulative fuel imports only came to 15 per cent of the forage over the course of the war.[47] For example, the AEF used 274,000 vehicles of 219 different makes and models in part because of the relative scarcity of horses, and as of mid November 1918, the BEF employed 57,000 vehicles (including nearly 27,000 lorries) on active service in France, with some 24,000 additional vehicles (including nearly 6,000 lorries) in service in other theatres.[48]

Over the course of the summer and autumn, the Allied powers, under Ferdinand Foch's direction, carried out the precursor of Eisenhower's broad-front approach and demonstrated that the Allies not only had access to superb logistic support, but that they were finally in a position to exploit it. The best example of this is the period beginning on 26 September with the assault on the Hindenburg Line's Siegfried Stellung. Over the next several days, multiple Allied armies launched consecutive attacks on German positions until, by 29 September, multiple Allied armies were all simultaneously engaged in high-tempo active operations. By 10 October, in spite of at times crippling tactical resupply problems in the Meuse-Argonne, the Hindenburg Line had been shattered along its length. Indeed, the Meuse-Argonne is an example of

45 Andy Simpson, *Directing Operations: British Corps Command on the Western Front 1914–18* (London: Spellmount, 2006), p. 148.

46 Simpson, *Operations*, p. 172.

47 Stevenson, *Backs to the Wall*, p. 223; *Statistics*, p. 521.

48 Daniel R. Beaver, '"Deuce and a Half": Selecting U.S. Army Trucks, 1920–1945', in Lynn, *Feeding Mars*, p. 253; *Statistics*, p. 595.

both the Allied logistic strength at the operational level – in moving roughly 600,000 US soldiers from the Saint-Mihiel sector to the Meuse-Argonne sector in a timely manner – and the inherent weakness of all armies at the tactical levels exemplified by the American resupply crisis on the Meuse-Argonne.[49] The tempo of operations in late 1918 is yet another indicator of Allied logistic strengths. And to a degree that was not exceeded until the next world war.

From the war's opening salvoes with the rapid mobilisation of their forces, to the skilful deployment of formations by the French prior to the Marne to the German use of interior lines in the war's closing years, the physical movement of the materiel and men required to wage modern, industrial warfare is impressive. Continental powers moved millions of men and tens of millions of tons of supplies around and between the war's European theatres. Russia's problems were, in many ways, economic, but those economic problems had a logistic impact, which reduced the effectiveness of Russian forces while increasing casualties as Russian armies faced a German opponent who suffered comparatively few such troubles. Germany's logistic problems began to be seen in early 1918 as the blockade began to really cut into the German economy. The reduction of that economy had a knock-on effect at the front as it impacted Germany's logistic capability – by late 1918, while the Allied powers waged an early form of the next war's broad front strategy and launched high-tempo, materiel-intensive attacks, the German army in the West increasingly had to defend with fewer and fewer troops, and that defence became less and less capable.

The effort of the extra-continental powers, however, is even more impressive. Both Britain and America fielded continental scale armies in a European war with such success that, barring one major battlefield crisis each (the BEF's near-breakdown on the Somme and the AEF's on the Meuse-Argonne), both managed to prosecute twentieth-century industrial warfare at the end of an overseas supply chain. Further, Britain fielded armies in many other global theatres and supported it all with the shipping technology of the day in which everything was simply more cumbersome and bulky. It is all too easy in a modern era where one can get from London to any major city on the globe in under twenty-four hours, or when container ships carrying thousands of containers (containing 250,000 tons or more of cargo) can reach cruising speeds above eighteen knots, to forget just how much more difficult it was to move materiel a century ago. Regardless of the realism in the AEF's 4-million-man target, even at the end of a 5,500 kilometre overseas supply

49 Stevenson, *Backs to the Wall*, pp. 132–5.

chain, the over 2-million-man AEF would have been in a position to carry the bulk of the fighting had the war continued into 1919. The Great Powers involved in the First World War managed to move vast quantities of materiel efficiently enough and for a long enough period to bring modern, industrialised warfare into being. For good or ill, the logisticians of the Great Powers met the challenges thrown at them with considerable success and laid the groundwork for the logistic changes of the ensuing century.

10

Technology and armaments

FRÉDÉRIC GUELTON

Introduction

In 1914, the war began with weapons that were the result of each nation's synthesis of two elements: its level of technological development and its conception of the war to come, which included its conception of a future war's likely progress, intensity and duration. This synthesis characterised the initial relationship that existed in all the belligerent nations between the weapons at their disposal and the technological development of each country. As Fernand Gambiez and Maurice Suire have rightly pointed out,[1] this relationship between arms and technology was simple: 'the means that the belligerents had at their disposal [were] inferior to their immediate technical potential'. This gap between the types of weapons that were already in existence and the potential for new weaponry that was offered by technical progress, a gap which is normal in peacetime, is partly explained by the level of military budgets, which are always regarded as inadequate by the military, even during an arms race. However, above all, it was the result of the High Commands' refusal to accept the evolutions in technology with which they were presented. Technological evolution was firmly rejected for a number of reasons: it threatened a body of warlike traditions that was regarded as immutable; it tended to upset certainties about the nature of war, which at the time was regarded more as a Napoleonic activity than an industrial one; and it was likely to challenge pre-set doctrines and would force commanders to revise – to rewrite – the rules of engagement of their major units. Witticisms on this subject, which in this case have the value of historical evidence, abounded in the early years of the twentieth century. Around 1909 or 1910, the following well-known remark was attributed to Foch: 'Cars and

Helen McPhail translated this chapter from French into English.

1 General Fernand Gambiez and Colonel Maurice Suire, *Histoire de la Première Guerre mondiale*, vol. 1, *Crépuscule sur l'Europe* (Paris: Fayard, 1968), p. 139.

Ader's aeroplanes, all that stuff is very pretty, very enjoyable and sporty, but for the army it's zero!' Given the context of the major technological advances that were occurring, this highlights the military scepticism regarding technology – Around the same time: the French pilot, Léon Lemartin, was carrying six passengers aboard his Blériot XIII airplane; two Britons, Charles Stewart Rolls and Henry Royce, had started a company to build engines that bore their name; Léon Morane was breaking the world speed record at just over 106 kilometres an hour for horizontal flight; two Canadians, Frederick Baldwin and John McCurdy, had achieved the first 'air to ground' transmission from a Curtiss biplane; and the French army had officially been equipped with its first air units. Yet, in 1914, most European military chiefs still felt that the maxims of Catherine the Great's general, Alexander Suvorov, would be sufficient to win a war if, by chance, one should break out. They felt as he did, and as they had done for 200 years, that 'the bullet is foolish, the bayonet wise'.

This denial of both the realities of technology and the pace of technological change had, by virtue of its irrationality, a consequence which is of particular significance here. It ensured that in 1914 almost all the weapons destined to be used during the war already existed in a potential state, but still awaiting further development. Some were already in embryonic allocation, in the case of the machine gun, the aeroplane and truck, still subordinate to the infantry rifle, dirigible and horse-drawn transport which, for the time being, continued to be preferred. Others were practically still at an experimental stage, for example, the armoured car or the submarine. Despite the fact that it was not in competition with any existing weapon, the armoured car languished at the experimental stage; in 1914, France possessed only three armoured cars. The submarine also remained experimental, although it had attracted the interest of technically advanced naval powers and those ranked below Britain's Royal Navy, the model that all aspired to or dreamed of overtaking, as Germany did. Other weapons struggled to even move beyond the conceptual stage, as was the case with the assault tank, despite the fact that all of its future components (engine, caterpillar tracks, turret, weaponry) already existed, like so many pieces of a puzzle that nobody intended or wanted to put together.

All of these weapons, which were of recent date if not brand new, shared the fate of having their utility or lethality, in other words their warlike effectiveness, more often than not dismissed. They were condemned to give way to earlier, long-established weapons that staff officers judged to be both the best as well as the only necessary ones because they had proved themselves – in peacetime. Such weapons wholly prevailed until war broke out and, little by little, the reality of the battlefield overcame pre-war attitudes. A similar situation arose regarding the dreadnought and even the 75 mm field gun, which in their country of origin remained, to begin with, weapons whose symbolic character transcended their operational value. The dreadnought was the symbol of Great Britain's global naval and industrial power; the 75 mm gun was the embodiment of the revenge of French polytechnicien officers following the absolute supremacy of Prussian artillery over the French in 1870 to 1871. The corollary of this situation is that the invention of 'new' weapons in the course of the war – one thinks of the machine-pistol, the flame-thrower or poison gas – was rare, and even their claim to genuine novelty is open to debate.

The military chiefs' limited attitudes had further consequences, not only at a technological, but also at a logistical, level. This is clearly illustrated by a historical comparison between the so-called 'pounds per soldier per day' rates of 1870, 1914 and 1918. The 'pounds per soldier per day' of a combatant – the weight of everything with which he is supplied for twenty-four hours of war – was the same in 1914 as it had been in 1870, roughly 8 kg (17.6 lb) per day. By 1918 it had, on average, doubled, and quadrupled in the infantry divisions within which it exceeded, at times of combat, 30 kg (66.1 lb) per day. A similar comparison can be extended to the artillery. The planned French production of artillery shells of all calibres in time of war was a little over 7,000 per day, chiefly of 75 mm shells; this was thought to be sufficient. By 1917, production had exceeded 260,000 shells per day, of which more than 220,000 were for the field artillery. The production and consumption of shells had multiplied by a factor of forty, on average, compared to the initial forecast.

War and technology: a crucial encounter

For everyone, with the exception of Austria-Hungary and Serbia, the war that broke out at the end of July 1914 was a (relative) surprise. Austria-Hungary would have liked it to remain contained, a regional conflict. The speed of its spread, the pace and new violence that characterised its first weeks, and especially the consumption of weapons and ammunition that it brought about, rendered every forecast, every plan and doctrine, null and void. Existing weaponry, especially the available stocks of hardware, which matched both the financial capacity of each state and the a priori expectation of a short, mobile and swift war, in the event allowed none of the belligerents to end the war swiftly. Pre-war anticipations were key here. For example, widespread expectations regarding how a future war would unfold meant that no belligerent felt it necessary to protect its infantry soldiers in any way. Were they not all going out to win a rapid victory? To protect them – to weigh them down – would have made no sense given this context. The few heavy cavalrymen equipped with a helmet wore it less to protect themselves than out of respect for tradition. The infantry helmet was neither useful nor useless: it was simply not thought of. The German helmet was as much a martial and aesthetic item as a piece of protective equipment, except for its tip, which had formerly served to deflect sabre blows.

The same was true of numerous other items of equipment. But military ideologies were no more able to resist the reality of combat than a line of advancing infantry was able to challenge a couple of machine guns. By the time the first few months of fighting were up, the war's demands were forcing armies to adapt their armaments, equipment and industries, if they intended to succeed where so far all had failed, and win. This widespread adaptation of weapons and techniques to a new kind of war broke down into specific adaptations of many different kinds, ranging from 'retro-innovation', which became a general phenomenon, to the pure invention of new armaments, which remained exceptional. The pace of adaptation was determined by the ability of army staffs to reflect on the new situations that faced them, to understand them and adjust to them. It was a long process, which exposed all sorts of organisational deficiencies. It was likewise a function of each belligerent nation's state of industrial development and of the workload and the degree of destruction that a state's industrial fabric and productive apparatus had to face. In the end, three converging new and unexpected demands determined the success (or failure) of a state's adaptation process in response to the new realities of war: first, the need for the instantaneous production of large quantities of weapons and munitions in existing factories in order to replenish stocks following the war's initial destructive impact; secondly, the adaptation of systems of production to respond to demands for improvements to existing weaponry that was considered to be performing poorly; and thirdly, the necessity of creating new production lines from scratch in order to produce brand-new weapons.

This confrontation between the war's ever-increasing demands and the limitations of what belligerent states were technologically capable of achieving occurred haphazardly. The war's requirements overturned existing systems. Disorder reigned. It is, however, possible to identify four principal types of adaptation which occurred. These types are not 'pure models'. Grey areas of overlap exist between them. They nevertheless help us to disentangle a clear vision of broad trends from a confused overall situation.

The first form of adaptation, retro-innovation, was theoretically the most surprising, given that it occurred at a time when the advances of the Industrial Revolution were being applied to the manufacture of weapons. Retro-innovation was characterised by the industrial production of arms and equipment that seemed incontrovertibly out of date, items such as maces, infantry shields, breastplates, steel helmets, combat knives, trench artillery and even grenades. In reality, however, although the nature of this weaponry appeared to represent a form of regression, a process of innovation was also occurring in terms of how it was manufactured and in its physical and chemical make-up. Retro-innovation was the prime form of adaptation of weapons to the war via technology. It was rapid, practically instantaneous, and a process that continued throughout the conflict.

The second form of adaptation was paradoxical: we might call it technological stagnation. This technological stagnation applied to all weapons in existence at the outbreak of war that then continued to be produced as the war went on, but benefited from no noteworthy technical improvement. If these weapons stagnated, it was because they had already undergone their 'technological revolution'. Some, such as the French 75 mm gun, had been at the forefront of technical progress for more than ten years when war broke out. They were widely used, produced good results, and there was therefore no cause to modify them in a substantial way, only to go on producing more: a positive stagnation. Others, including for example the dreadnought, had likewise reached the peak of their effectiveness before the war. Unlike the 75 mm gun, however, its non-deployment during the war revealed the dreadnought's true nature and as a consequence the relative limitations of its military usefulness. The dreadnought thus appears in an unexpected light during the war, that of a weapon of diplomacy and deterrence, as it had been in the pre-war period. From 1914 onwards, its non-deployment perfectly expressed its deterrent function, while revealing the fears that its potential deployment aroused. Given how much it cost to manufacture, particularly in comparison with other aerial, naval and terrestrial battlefield weapons, its deployment was all the more limited because its destruction in combat would rob it of its deterrent character and make it a target for every kind of propaganda. No one can say how the war at sea would have developed if the dreadnought had not existed, but it has to be said that because it did exist, the war at sea remained limited: a stagnation by default.

The third form of adaptation was related to the capacity for innovation in wartime. This is technological innovation in the strict sense of the term. It can be described as the interaction between an existing but still marginal type of weapon and the demands imposed by the war, whereby, through a process of innovation, this weapon moves from a marginal or marginalised status to develop into an arm that is essential for all armies. The machine gun is a good example of this. However, such technological innovation also clearly revealed the different industrial levels of development between the belligerents. For example, if the importance of the aeroplane rapidly became obvious to everyone, only the great nations that were also first-division economic powers could innovate and adapt them to the war and make them in quantity. The same was true of aircraft carriers, submarines and heavy railway guns. Finally, technological innovation could be thrown off balance if a belligerent decided that a particular weapon would be deployed in a more strategic rather than tactical way, as was the case with the submarine.

The fourth form of adaptation was the invention of completely new weapons: the supreme stage of convergence between technology and war-making. It represents the quintessential culmination of the application of the fruits of the Industrial Revolution to armed conflict. During the Great War, however, actual inventions were rare, if only because the interval between inventing something and then producing it is long, even in times of war. Even if it is somewhat historically misleading to describe them as 'inventions' in the strict sense of the term, it is possible to identify the tank, flame-thrower, machine pistol and even poison gas as among the most interesting inventions of the conflict.

Time and the human factor

In order to assess the temporal dimension of the relationship between war and technology, with regard to the manufacture of weapons, it is necessary to consider an essential constituent: the human factor. Above all, it means considering the decisive individual – statesman or military chief – who plays a central role, to the extent that he has the sole power to determine at will the speed at which 'new' weapons are chosen, as well as to direct industrial effort towards realising and producing them. His role depends closely upon that of every other contributor involved in production, from the initial phase of scientific research right up to the final product emerging from the production chain. The fact that engineers, foremen and workers who had earlier been sent to the front were – more or less rapidly depending on which country one examines – returned to the factory to help the war economy provides indisputable evidence for this interdependence. France's mobilisation plans, for example, foresaw the assignment of some 50,000 special workers to its armament factories, but in fact almost 600,000 men were sent back from the front to work in weapons production, in which they were joined by 400,000 women and 100,000 foreign workers.

Above all, human intervention appreciably altered the pace of technological adaptation that occurred in response to the demands of the war. It operated on the basis of a threefold temporality that intersected with the four forms of adaptation described above. The first temporality was that of projected future time. The essential characteristic of projected time is to be, by its very nature, uncertain. It is the anticipation of a future time that it is expected will occur at the outbreak of a war – a war that sometimes seems probable, but is always unknown. Projected time is a constant feature of peacetime. A more specific, concrete example of projected time begins each time an army staff identifies a weapon that it considers it needs to equip its army despite being objectively incapable of defining the nature and the timing of any future war. Projected time spans a period that begins before the war; it continues into the conflict, covering the initial phase when combatants discover the realities of battlefield combat; and it ends when commanders, having apprehended the nature – new or not – of the war, decide upon the necessary technological adjustments in response to the conflict. The slow adoption of the steel helmet by different armies in the First World War, or the difficulty in choosing heavy artillery over field artillery, are examples of how projected time operated to affect technological responses.

Projected time is fundamental and the choices made during its period of pre-eminence are crucial. The initial military engagements generate interaction between the imagined, anticipated war and the reality of the effects of the weapons currently being issued. If the choices made during projected time closely match the reality of the war, then technological adaptation can occur very quickly, which leads to important tactical and strategic advantages. Conversely, the more distant those choices are from the reality of the war, the slower and more expensive the adaptation will be. Heavy artillery is a typical case in point. The different choices made by the German, British and French armies during the period of projected time influenced its technological development, weighed down the progress of operations and limited how it could evolve, in both tactical and strategic terms, for over half of the war.

The second temporality is that of real time. Real time is also what can be termed 'the moment of truth'. This temporality begins on the first day of the war. As soon as the fighting starts, weapons and ammunition that exist in limited quantities are destroyed, damaged, even abandoned, and ammunition is used up. These losses have to be replaced, and new weapons and ammunition produced, by mobilising industrial production for the benefit of the war. The ability or failure to renew or to increase the quantity of weapons and ammunition available influences the pace of technological adaptations to the war, slowing or accelerating it. This is clearly illustrated by the difficulties faced by all the armies on the Western Front in producing sufficient quantities of artillery shells for their guns or by the problems faced by the Russian army in producing sufficient quantities of rifles for its needs. When the first phase of the war ended with what the general historiography, symbolically but inappropriately, refers to as the 'race to the sea', the opposing belligerents 'stopped'. Yet the truth is that if they were forced to pause, it was not so much because they had reached the sea, or even because their men were exhausted, but because they lacked the ammunition necessary for the further pursuit of operations in a new form.

The third form of temporality is the time that follows confrontation, or in shorthand 'confronted time'. This is the phase when a belligerent 'confronts' enemy technology: it is defined by the ability of a belligerent to respond within a given time frame to the innovation or invention of an enemy, through a process of wartime action–reaction. The two most typical examples in the Great War are poison gas and the battle tank. Confronted with the use of poison gas in 1915, which could perhaps have revolutionised tactics and strategy, belligerents responded rapidly, and, as a result of their decisions during this period of 'confronted time', gas turned out to be ineffective, mainly because of the speed with which those who were first gassed adjusted to the situation and introduced simple counter-measures that reduced the impact of gas upon troops. In other words, during confronted time, the value of an innovation does not depend upon the impact of the use of a new weapon – positive or negative – but upon the nature and speed of the adaptation it produces. The same is true of the introduction of the battle tank to the British and French armies and the German reaction, which focused more on developing anti-tank weapons than upon symmetrical innovation. In this case, confronted time highlighted not only a tactical, but also a technical and economic, confrontation.

Retro-innovations

The steel helmet: an example of the relationship between projected time and retro-innovation

The use of the steel helmet by the various armies offers a clear example of how the interaction between projected time and retro-innovations functioned, as well as its determining characteristics: the demand grew out of a real need; manufacture was relatively simple; and yet technological differences and differing speeds of implementation are evident in how the belligerents responded. Initially, during the projected time period, the helmet received little attention: at the outbreak of war, in any army anywhere in the world, only certain units of heavy cavalry were equipped with a metal helmet. Issuing a similar helmet to any other arm had not been imagined; indeed, it was almost inconceivable – which prompts the historian to wonder about staff officers' peacetime reflections on the developments in artillery: in particular, field artillery in the case of the British and French, and field and heavy artillery in the case of the Germans. Contemporaries all had high expectations of artillery's effects on the enemy and all were aware of the existence of explosive and shrapnel shells,[2] both fused and percussion, but no one was studying the effects of the enemy's artillery on their own men; it was as if artillery would have no impact upon them. Real time, in the shape of the slaughter of the first months of the war that was mainly caused by artillery shelling, came as a 'surprise': the head wounds that resulted and were regularly fatal were a 'revelation' for all army staffs, a situation that reveals both a denial of intelligence and a refusal of reality. However, the growing realisation of the importance of head wounds was accentuated when contemporaries observed that when cavalry units were dismounted to fight alongside the infantry, they suffered lighter losses than the infantry each time helmets were worn.[3]

Faced with these facts, what solutions were adopted, how fast, and with what results? The first solutions – the first adaptations – were developed by the combatants themselves. Anyone who owned a hemispherical metal object put it underneath his existing headgear (cap, forage cap, képi) to protect himself. In France, Louis Adrian,[4] Assistant Quartermaster General, observing the

2 Shrapnel was a British invention by Lieutenant Henry Shrapnel (1761–1842) and was already 100 years old in 1914. When war broke out, roughly 50 per cent of 75 mm shells were loaded with shrapnel. See 'Histoire de l'artillerie de terre française', *Cahiers d'études et de recherches du Musée de l'armée*, hors-série no. 1 (2003).

3 Until steel helmets were issued as standard to the infantry, three-quarters of the wounded were wounded in the head and 88 per cent of such wounds were fatal. See: Philippe Richardot (ed.), *Le service de santé des armées entre guerre et paix* (Paris: Economica, 2003), p. 232; Alain Larcan and Jean-Jacques Ferrandis, *Le service de santé aux armées pendant la Première guerre mondiale* (Paris: LBM, 2008).

4 Louis Adrian, born in 1859, had retired in 1913 after a conventional career in the engineer corps. A year later he was called back to the auxiliary staff of the supply corps. On 20 August, he was named Assistant Quartermaster General at the French Ministry of War, responsible for clothing and equipment. See Jean-Pierre Verney, 'Adrian, un grand serviteur de l'état', *Le Magazine de la Grande Guerre*, 14–18:11 (December 2002–January 2003), pp. 34–41.

beneficial effects of the cavalry helmet, proposed equipping the French army with a steel helmet. His proposal was turned down by the general staff because it was still operating within projected time expectations: General Joffre felt that given the anticipated brevity of the war, French industry would not have the time to design and produce several million infantry helmets for which no model existed. Indeed, he only reluctantly accepted a suggestion made between November and December 1914 to equip soldiers with a steel 'skullcap', which began to be issued in February 1915.[5] However, from this point on, matters accelerated: on the twenty-first of that month, the French Ministry of War decided, at Joffre's request, to begin manufacture of a steel helmet. 1.6 million units of Louis Adrian's prototype, received in April, were ordered on 5 June 1915. The first helmets were issued in September. By the end of 1915, 3 million helmets had been produced, and by the first months of 1916 the whole French army had been equipped. In Britain, the War Office took the first steps in June 1915. The French helmet was tried and rejected, as it was thought to be too complicated to produce in view of the constraints being faced by industry in other areas. The War Office preferred the design of John L. Brodie: the first units produced from his design were delivered in November 1915 and it was first tested under fire near Arras in April 1916. However, production only reached 1 million helmets during the summer of 1916, and the entire British army was not equipped until the end of the year. As for the Germans, their efforts to produce a steel helmet began in early 1915 under the direction of Friedrich Schwerd of the Hanover Technical Institute. Trials, including those on the battlefield, lasted until the end of the year, and the model known as the Stahlhelm M1916 was officially adopted in January 1916. The first units received it on the Western Front in February, shortly before the Verdun offensive. During the same year, the whole German army was equipped.

To sum up, in the general staffs of all three armies the need to produce a steel helmet became clear between January and February 1915 (France, Germany) and June 1915 (Great Britain). The initial decision-making process was swift in France, fairly swift in Britain and slow in Germany. In contrast, the French and German production intervals were identical, while that of the British was slower. Finally, it is worth noting, in terms of retro-innovation, that the French helmet was inspired by the bourguignotte, a fifteenth-century

5 Considered uncomfortable to wear, the 'skullcap' was 0.5 mm thick. 700,000 units were produced and issued from February 1915 onwards. The Grand Quartier-Général claimed that it protected men from 60 per cent of shrapnel or other wounds.

helmet of Burgundian origin, the German helmet was inspired by the sallet of the fifteenth century and the British helmet was reminiscent of the thirteenth-century kettle hat.

The grenade, retro-innovation, and practically spontaneous adaptation in real time

From the very first weeks of the war, soldiers were quick to dig their own 'personal hole', described as a defensive fighting position, even though at the time the strategy was meant to be offensive. Before the end of 1914, these 'personal fighting positions' had gradually evolved into collective fighting positions, then lengthened into trenches. The birth of the trench did not rule out fighting: it merely modified its character. The pursuit of offensive combat from a trench required the infantry soldier to free himself from the double constraint of being in a semi-buried and narrow position. The individual soldier needed a projectile that was relatively easy to direct in order to be able to hit an enemy who was sometimes located tens of metres away and, like him, buried in a hole. Use of a rifle obliged a soldier to emerge partially from his hole, then wait for the enemy to do the same in order to have a target; however, as soon as he emerged from his protective hole, he in turn became the 'other's target'. Another solution was to attack collectively: the battalion, regiment, division or other unit mounted an attack together. Bound together in an immediate combat group of several dozens of men, the soldier could thus participate individually in the collective conquest of the enemy trenches. Once again, the weapon he was issued with – the rifle – was more awkward than effective: general-issue rifles such as the British Lee-Enfield, the German Mauser K98 and the Russian Mosin-Nagant were more than 150 cm long; the French Lebel rifle with its bayonet fixed was more than 180 cm long. To stop and shoot during an attack was almost impossible, to shoot while walking or running was ineffective if not useless, and once the enemy trench was reached using a rifle remained a tricky business because of its awkwardness. To attack through a tunnel was even more difficult. Faced with these difficulties, combatants used the few grenades then available (the German and Serbian armies had more than others) and then made what they needed on the spot, until industry caught up and began mass-producing grenades.

The grenade therefore developed in an unexpected way. As a weapon in 1914 it had only existed in limited quantities at the army level. The German army, among those armies that possessed the most, had only approximately 70,000 1913-model hand grenades. However, from 1915 onwards, the grenade was omnipresent on the battlefield. By the middle of 1915, European arsenals were producing more than a million a week or, to put it another way, every day they produced twice the total number that had been in existence in 1914.

How did this systematic re-appropriation by combatants of a weapon that had practically disappeared from Europe's military panoply happen? Since its invention, the grenade had enjoyed an erratic existence, largely used under another name and by the Chinese. Used in Europe under its current name from the fifteenth century onwards, it had become more widespread up to the eighteenth century, then fallen into disuse. It reappeared on several occasions in the nineteenth century when war took on new forms, in the Crimea and during the US Civil War. It nevertheless disappeared from regulation British armaments[6] by the end of the nineteenth century, before reappearing in improvised form during the Russo-Japanese War. The Japanese and Russians, as might be expected, learned necessary lessons for the future. In 1914, all the belligerents possessed grenades somewhere in their arsenal. But their usefulness was not considered sufficient to bring about either their general issue or specific regulations for their usage (although in 1914 the Russian army possessed a regulation grenade known as the '1912'). The French, who attentively observed the Russo-Japanese War and were allies of the Russians, had not drawn the same conclusions. For them, doctrine overruled critical reflection. In 1914, the French army only possessed a grenade known as the grenade pétard raquette or 'Third Republic grenade'. Archaic in design, it nevertheless continued in service throughout the Great War, as a result of its initial archaism. Shortly after its entry into the war, France then produced a '1914' grenade, which only began to be issued to French combat units in 1915. At the outbreak of war, the British army had a Mark I grenade, the product of lessons it had learnt in the Boer Wars. In service since 1908, its operation was delicate, and soldiers preferred their own makeshift grenades, which they called 'jam-tin bombs', after the materials they were made from.

Among the British and the French, the 'jam-tin bomb' and pétard raquette make it possible to measure the extent to which real time, in other words the soldiers' time, imposed its will on army staffs and overturned all preconceived doctrines. The situation was slightly different in the German army, the only

6 C. Collins, 'Lessons to be learnt from the siege of Port Arthur as regards RE work', *Journal of the United Service Institution of India*, April 1910, p. 303, quoted by James D. Sisemore, *The Russo-Japanese War, Lessons Not Learned* (Fort Leavenworth, KA: Master of Military Art and Science, Faculty of the US Army Command and General Staff College, 2003), p. 33.

Western force to benefit from its observation of the Russo-Japanese War,[7] although its stocks of grenades were still modest and it had no rules in place for their use. The army that possessed more grenades than any other was that of Serbia, which had used them in abundance during the two Balkan wars.

The stabilisation of the Western Front saw a rapid industrialisation of grenade production among all the belligerents. The main reason was simple. Having turned into the weapon of choice for the infantry in attack as much as defence, the grenade offered, from a technological point of view, the dual advantage of being easily produced in very large quantities and not being expensive to manufacture. It was widely, even systematically, used to 'clean' enemy trenches, and those who used it were in no doubt of its efficacy, which was far greater than that of a bayonet. It is worth noting here that this particular usage is often overlooked by the historiography of trench warfare, because its symbolic charge is far less potent than that of the knife. From 1915 onwards, the grenade began to gain ground in the culture of war at a national level: in the course of that year, the British equipped themselves with a 'modern' grenade developed by a Birmingham engineer, William Mills. Pineapple shaped, the Mills bomb was grooved and segmented, which in theory aided fragmentation and threw fragments further when it exploded. In fact this belief was false, but appearance won out over reality and segmentation became a feature of the 'British grenade', even when other armies imitated it. On the German side, the collective imagination seems to have registered only one grenade – the stick grenade or Stielhandgranate – although in fact from the pre-war period (1913) onwards the German army had equipped itself with a series of lightly segmented, round grenades, and the stick grenade only came into common use in 1915 with the war of position.

From 1915 to 1918, then, the grenade, an ancient weapon that had existed for hundreds of years, was subject to repeated improvements that resulted essentially from progress in the fields of war chemistry and metal physics. At a constant weight, its power grew, and at a constant power its weight diminished, allowing its thrown range to increase. The small German 'egg' grenade (Eierhandgranate) was a case in point: developed for assault troops in 1917, it could easily be thrown further than 50 metres. Defensive in its ability to scatter lethal fragments, offensive by virtue of its blast effect, the grenade became the subject of repeated studies, which led to the development of, among others,

7 'The Von Lobell Annual Reports on the Changes and Progress in Military Matters in 1905', quoted by Sisemore, *Russo-Japanese War*, p. 93.

the gas grenade, fragmentation grenade, anti-barbed wire grenade, stun grenade, smoke grenade and even the French message-carrying grenade.

The interest shown in grenade design was such that in a war in which artillery was daily increasingly present, the grenade evolved into the infantry soldier's own personal artillery with the development of the rifle grenade. This form of grenade, usually fixed at the end of the gun barrel with an immovable cup-shaped launcher, was launched with the energy supplied by the detonation of a blank cartridge. Its range, often less than 100 metres in 1914, easily reached 400 metres by 1918. The best-known and best-performing launch system was the French Vivien-Bessière.

In total, the belligerent nations developed roughly 100 models of grenade in the course of the war. As a weapon, it was one of the war's most interesting retro-innovations, its name inspired in the fifteenth century by the pomegranate and its cluster of seeds. Like the helmet, it had fallen into disuse prior to the conflict, and in 1914 was a marginal weapon; by 1918, it was ubiquitous.

Stagnant technologies

The dreadnought and technological stagnation resulting from projected time

The dreadnought,[8] capital ship of the early twentieth century, appeared in 1906 and thus was the result of projected time. Developed in a period during which globalisation was already a fait accompli, its initial justification grew out of diplomatic necessity and rivalries between powers. While the dreadnought's combat function existed in purely potential form only, its actual value lay in its twofold function as both a representatation of power and a deterrent: in other words, its value lay precisely in it not being employed in battle. Until 1914, it embodied the global ambitions of those nations that possessed it, especially if, as was the case with HMS *Dreadnought*, ordered by Admiral Sir John 'Jackie' Fisher, British First Sea Lord, in 1904 and launched by the Royal Navy in February 1906, it was at the forefront of technical progress.

It was above all the rivalry between sea powers and the maritime arms race that had brought about the disappearance of wooden-hulled warships, the construction of 'pre-dreadnoughts' around 1890, and the appearance of HMS *Dreadnought*, whose name became associated with an entire generation of

8 This discussion includes the 'super-dreadnoughts' launched immediately before the war.

battleships, incorporating as it did at its launch every aspect of contemporary modern technology in a single, unique war machine that rendered all others null and void in the context of the time.

Several characteristics made the dreadnought the *nec pluribus impar* of the technology of war during this period.[9] She was a warship of more than 20,000 tonnes that could reach a speed of 25 knots thanks to new steam turbines powered by coal- and oil-fired boilers. Her armament was both simplified and improved in range and accuracy in comparison with that of her predecessors – simplified because her artillery was limited to two calibres: that of her main guns varied between 280 and 381 mm, with a range that exceeded 17 kilometres, while her secondary guns varied between 120 and 150 mm. She had fewer double and triple turrets than the pre-dreadnoughts and her turrets were better protected. Her armour, concentrated on her quick work, reached thicknesses of 250 to 360 mm. Comparisons carried out with German dreadnoughts show that they were on average less well armed and less protected than their British counterparts, although their shells were superior to those used by the British navy.

When war broke out, the ramifications of peacetime rivalries emerged clearly. If the British dominated the other Great War navies with their twenty dreadnoughts, the Germans were beginning to compete with thirteen warships, while the Americans had nine. The French, lagging far behind, possessed four, the Austro-Hungarians three and the Russians only one. These figures reveal another key significant reality: dreadnoughts were expensive. In peacetime, this was only of relative importance, as there was little that physically threatened them: they paraded and acted as a deterrent, as was their function. War – in other words, real time – changed everything. The replacement cost of a dreadnought became a constraint: there could be no question of putting these warships in danger unless they were sure to destroy the enemy fleet. This explains the race at the outset of the First World War to confine the great fleets to their home ports and the rarity of naval battles thereafter, with the well-known exception of Jutland in May 1916, a major battle in which none of the twenty-five warships sunk was a dreadnought. Conversely, despite the long duration of the war, HMS *Dreadnought* sank only one German submarine in combat, in the North Sea in February 1915. To build a dreadnought was to invest heavily for an exceedingly light return, and in technological

9 See Richard Hough, *Dreadnought, A History of the Modern Battleship* (New York: MacMillan, 1975); Richard Hough, *The Great War at Sea, 1914–1918* (Oxford University Press, 1987).

terms the result was simple: costly and useless, the dreadnought found itself neglected. It is worth noting that Admiral Fisher, HMS *Dreadnought*'s sponsor, made sure that eight new dreadnoughts were planned between 1914 and 1916 (five were eventually launched). Yet efforts made to improve the dreadnought during the war were restricted, especially if we compare them with the efforts made by Great Britain and Germany before the war. For the principal war fleets, the technical progress achieved in peacetime had been amply adequate to meet the demands of wartime, especially from the moment when their warships were confined to port and relative non-use. Available funds were diverted elsewhere to the manufacture of terrestrial armaments within redeployed naval arsenals. This explains the technical stagnation of the dreadnought by default throughout the war, even though new vessels were being built.

An interesting comparison can be made here between the construction from scratch of new ships of this class and the construction of the earliest (or proto-) aircraft carriers. The Royal Navy built around twenty 'aircraft carriers' between 1913 (*Hermes*) and 1918 (*Vindictive*), but it did so only by the transformation of existing platforms, as in the case of, among others, HMS *Argus*. The *Argus*, the first aircraft carrier equipped with a single flat deck for take-off and landing, anticipating the Japanese aircraft carriers of the Second World War, was completed using as a base an Italian ferry, the *Conte Rosso*, built in Glasgow in 1914 and repurchased by the Royal Navy, then transformed into an aircraft carrier that only became operational in September 1918.

Technological innovations

The submarine

The dreadnought had reached its apogee before war began. The submarine, then still at the experimental stage, underwent its great technological revolution during the war. From its marginal status, it emerged, for reasons diametrically opposed to those that had led to the making of the dreadnought, as central for both camps. How best to understand this sudden evolution? Or, to put it another way, why did the submarine, a prototype that had never launched a torpedo in combat conditions before 1914, steal a march on the dreadnought, a capital ship that had ruled the oceans until the outbreak of the war?

Due to its nature, as a weapon that operated on the basis of surprise and secrecy, the submarine was not, had no need to be, and could not be an expression of power in projected time. In any case it was, for historical reasons, viewed with haughty condescension by the Admiralty, which at the turn of the century, in the words of Admiral Sir Arthur Wilson, considered it to be 'damned un-English'.[10] The Germans, in the shape of Admiral Tirpitz and the Kaiser, showed no more consideration than the British for a machine that, hiding beneath the waves, was inappropriate as a symbol of imperial *Weltpolitik*. The French, as a second-division naval power, reinforced these sentiments with Admiral Aube's[11] *poussière navale* theories and those later developed in the *jeune école* (Young School) concept of a naval strategy based on multiple numbers of fast warships of reduced tonnage. Predictably, the sums allocated to building submarines were directly related to each country's admiralty's perception of them, and, that perception being negative or at best hedged with reservations, those sums remained limited and concrete progress slow.

Given the British and German reservations regarding the submarine, it is therefore unsurprising that in the early years of the twentieth century it was the French and Americans who were at the forefront of submarine development. At that time, the most widely used form of propulsion was the steam engine, whose technology was well mastered but whose performance remained limited. The adoption of diesel power from 1904 onwards, barely ten years after its invention by Rudolf Diesel, revolutionised the concept of the submersible, but many continued to doubt the diesel engine's potential as a new method of propulsion. Simultaneously, submarine control fins began to be operated by electric motors, the gyrocompass replaced the magnetic compass, and the torpedo became the submarine's main weapon. By 1914, torpedoes had a potential range of around 10 kilometres at a speed of 30 knots, carrying an explosive charge of more than 100 kg. Certain submarines, such as the Russian Krabov, could carry mines, and all were armed with an artillery piece.

In other words, at some point between 1912 and 1913, all the technical constituents of the modern submarine came into existence and were assembled in a modern war machine, whose future power was not yet understood or imagined. Successful experiments were conducted during naval exercises: in 1912, the British submarine D2 penetrated the Firth of Forth without resistance and 'hit' a docked ship; shortly afterwards, her sister

10 The submarine was 'underhand, unfair, and damned un-English . . . treat all submarines as pirates in wartime . . . and hang all crews': Admiral Wilson quoted in Stephen Wentworth Roskill, *Naval Policy between the Wars* (New York: Walker, 1968), vol. I, p. 231.

11 French Navy Minister, 1886–7.

boat D6 'hit' two others. The following year, a German submarine, U9, on an exercise 'hit' three battleships with four torpedoes.

The progress achieved in the use of submarines was plain, but their impact on military minds remained slow. Admiralties still doubted their efficacy,[12] and plans for their use in wartime were quite limited and did not envisage using them to their full potential. Accidents at sea resulting from technical inadequacies remained a problem and occurred relatively frequently in all extant submarine fleets. Richard Compton-Hall has calculated that between 1904 and 1914 there were eight in the Royal Navy, eleven in the French navy, five in the Russian, and one each in the Italian, American, German and Japanese navies.[13] Thus, when war broke out the rise to importance of the submarine was unexpected: it proved valuable due to its nature as a weapon of stealth. It was a weapon of war whose potential was underrated and whose use as such had neither been considered nor analysed systematically; by and large, the significance of the submarine was not understood fully, although there were some exceptions, in particular, Winston Churchill, who realised its potential. It was the reality of war, the shock of real time and the successes delivered at low cost by submariners that would dictate the technical developments in submarine technology made by the various belligerents in the years that followed.

In 1914, the belligerent nations deployed approximately 290 submarines[14] in coastal defence and on the high seas. In Britain, the Royal Navy, having produced American submarines under licence at the beginning of the century, had started production of its own boats. In 1914, it possessed seventy-five, among them roughly forty for coastal defence (classes B and C), with limited operational ability, and half that number of modern submarines of classes D and E, classed as 'semi-ocean-going'. The French navy possessed more than 100 submarines, of which around fifty were modern Brumaire-type boats[15] that had entered service in 1912. Russia operated roughly forty submarines in coastal defence and built another dozen by 1917. Italy's submarine fleet numbered twenty-five in 1915, and the United States' thirty-six in 1914, forty-four in 1917 and eighty in 1918. On the eve of war, Germany was no better off

12 Richard Compton-Hall, *Submarines and the War at Sea, 1914–1918* (London: MacMillan, 1991).

13 *Ibid.*, p. 17.

14 Author's own calculations. The figures vary between 250 and 300, depending on whether they include older, less operational submarines, training submarines and submarines under construction.

15 Lt Jean-Michel Roche (ed.), *Dictionnaire des Bâtiments de la Flotte de Guerre française de Colbert à nos jours*, vol. II, *1870–2005* (Toulon: Net-Marine, 2005).

than the Allies. Its main support, Austria-Hungary, possessed only five submersibles, and the German naval dockyards had only begun serial production of modern 500-ton submarines from 1910, in other words only just before the French began production of their Brumaires. Their submarines were distinguished by being equipped with a forward-firing and a backward-firing torpedo tube. In 1914, the German navy still only possessed twenty-eight operational submarines, of which eighteen were old models used solely for coastal defence, and they had a further seventeen under construction. The manner of their deployment was still highly restrictive. Their principal mission was reconnaissance and intelligence for the main fleet. It was the successes achieved in 1914, and especially the struggle against the blockade and Allied supply routes, that would determine their future development and significance by 1917.

In technological terms, similar patterns of development occurred on both sides in the war at sea, even though Germany was the main mover in the submarine's modernisation. Germany's dominance can be explained by the individual successes achieved by German submarines in 1914 (eighteen warships and other ships sunk, five submarines lost), by the refusal to become involved in surface engagements after the Battle of Jutland, and by the outbreak of all-out submarine warfare in 1917. It reveals the link that the German High Command had made between submarine technological development – crucial given that the submarine was a weapon which was defined by its technical characteristics – and its immediately strategic possibilities. To optimise this link, German naval dockyards rationalised their manufacture of submarines by limiting the number of models and regularly updating them to minimise technical deficiencies.

Throughout the war, the German dockyards produced three main types of submarine: boats of 500 tons such as the U9 (these had been in production since 1910), of 850 tons, and lastly the Type U151 and U152 (1,550 tons) which were produced from 1916 onwards. These last were the most modern submarines of the war. Their ability to range autonomously for long distances – 46,000 kilometres on the surface, 120 kilometres underwater – combined technical sophistication with a new geostrategic role.

The Allies too rationalised their manufacture of submarines, but from a different perspective. Their rationalisation was achieved through a centralisation of production in British yards, which launched more than 130 vessels during the war, of which forty-six were recent E-class submarines, while France launched only twenty-eight in the same period. The Allies did not neglect submarines, but surface ships were more useful to them to guarantee the resupply of the British Isles, the blockade of the Central Powers, the successful transport of US troops and anti-submarine operations.

By 1918, the submarine was probably, along with the aeroplane, the weapon that had undergone the most significant changes during the conflict. Unlike the aeroplane, which remained a battlefield weapon, the submarine, initially perceived during the phase of projected time as an auxiliary weapon, became the focus of significant attention as soon as the German High Command realised that its capability far exceeded simple naval tactical use and made it a major weapon of total war.

Inventions

Weapons which were actually 'invented' from scratch during the course of the First World War are relatively rare, if by 'invent' we mean the definition given by the *Oxford English Dictionary* ('to find out in the way of original contrivance; to create, produce, or construct by original thought or ingenuity'). We can nevertheless consider the battle tank and poison gases as distinctly new weapons, in the sense that their appearance on the battlefield was, by contrast with weapons that were merely innovative, a genuine surprise to combatants – which leads us to consider whether the novelty of a weapon does not result from its intellectual creation, but from its operational realisation on the battlefield.

Poison gas, an example of adaptation to a new weapon in confronted time

The date of 22 April 1915 has gone down in history as that of the first use of gas in warfare. On that day in Flanders, to the north of the town of Ypres, along 6 kilometres of the front, German forces facing British and French troops released some 170 tons of chlorine in gaseous form, contained in roughly 6,000 canisters. In less than half an hour, the front had given way.

This April date is interesting because it illustrates how the Western historiography of the Great War generally ignores the use of shells filled with tear gas – around 20,000 of them – that were fired by General Mackensen's IXth Army at the Battle of Bolimov, near Warsaw, on the Eastern Front in January 1915. However, what is more important here, for the purposes of the discussion in this chapter, is what the use of gas reveals regarding the adaptation, in confronted time, of the opposing sides to the development of a new weapon. In January 1915, the Germans, the first to use gas, experienced clear problems in adapting to the use of gas in combat. On the Russian front they failed sufficiently to take into account the technical considerations of using gas at a range of temperatures. The very cold weather in January in the East of Europe had a significant operational consequence. It meant that the gas shells did not work as the gas hung low, remaining close to the ground rendering it almost harmless, to the point that the Russian soldiers were barely aware of the attack launched against them. The hoped-for tactical effect was not achieved. The same was true at Ypres three months later. The front line was certainly breached thanks to the gas, but the gap was not exploited because of the German soldiers' apprehension at the sight of the poisonous cloud in front of them and the relative lack of preparation for operationally following up such a breach, which allowed the British and French to plug it. At Ypres tactical success was on the cards, but its strategic exploitation did not take place.

In the confronted time of the first uses of poison gas, the enemy's adaptation to the new weapon was swift, effective and cheap. The first form of adaptation was the realisation that it was unwise to run away. This was the result of a cynical observation by combatants: all else being equal, poison gas, even though alarming, was less dangerous, less lethal, less wounding than classic explosive shells. And frantic flight was more dangerous than anything, because a man's accelerated breathing as he ran towards the rear would rapidly bring on asphyxiation. The second form of adaptation originated in the chemical qualities of the chlorine used in April 1915, which was soluble in water and whose effects on the respiratory tract were lessened by urea, which meant that immediate protection, although not totally effective, could be obtained from a cotton wad soaked in water or, even better, urine.

Thus, spontaneous, then local, and ultimately industrial adaptation was swift and less onerous than the development of new gases such as phosgene (developed by the French in 1915), mustard gas or yperite (introduced by the Germans in 1917) or even lewisite, developed by the Americans in 1918 in readiness for the anticipated 1919 offensives. To each of these technical developments, adaptation in response was almost instantaneous. The first cotton wads soaked in urine were rapidly replaced by goggles and official-issue pads, by the British hypo helmet, and finally, in every belligerent army, by full gas masks equipped with a face-piece and filter cartridge whose successive filters reacted to the characteristics of the different gases used.

Finally, we should note that even if the image of poison gas remains closely associated with its initial use by the Germans, the French used some tear-gas grenades from August 1914 onwards and, overall, throughout the war, the Allies used more poison gas than the Germans did. In this respect, poison gas reflects the link that existed during the conflict between technology and the economy. When the Germans developed their first gases, they did it as much to alleviate their lack of classic explosive munitions and free themselves from the early effects of the naval blockade as for other reasons; and when the Allies overtook the Germans in their use of poison gas, it was chiefly because the Germans, suffering from the blockade, could no longer equal the Allies' production rates despite their scientists being capable of making the chemical weapons that they produced increasingly lethal.

The tank, an example of divergent technologies of attack and defence

The battle tank is a complex machine. From a technical point of view, it is an internal combustion engine surrounded by resistant armour-plating, which carries one or more weapons mounted on a turret or from a casemate as well as their corresponding ammunition, transporting a crew and being able to manoeuvre comfortably over any ground thanks to caterpillar tracks. Up until 1914, all of the isolated ideas that had been put forward with a view to developing such a machine, like those of the Australian Lancelot de Mole, were rejected by army staffs. Any such new weapon was considered pointless, in the light of how contemporaries envisaged the future form of war. Real time changed the landscape entirely. However, the pace at which it changed was determined by two factors: first, the speedy recognition, which developed by the end of 1914, that there was a real need for such a new machine; and, secondly, the time industry required to produce it – due to the complex nature of its engine, the tank necessitated, on average, a three-year manufacturing cycle. The intellectual awareness that there was a need for the tank was a French and British realisation; no such realisation occurred on the German side. It did not come from the infantry, who would be the prime beneficiaries of tanks on the battlefield, nor from the cavalry who could have found in the tank a substitute for the horse, which, by 1915, had lost most of its effectiveness in combat. Why did this French and British recognition develop? Because from 1914 onwards, both the British and the French were constantly involved in offensives aimed at dislodging the Germans from ground where they had simultaneously established themselves defensively. An armoured vehicle was more use in attack than defence and thus would clearly be of greater interest to the Allies who were constantly planning offensives. To attack, to advance, the ground had to be prepared by shelling, then the infantry had to climb out of its trenches and face the machine guns, reach the enemy position, overrun it, and then exploit the breakthrough with more waves of infantry, or in some cases cavalry. Infantry soldiers died in their hundreds of thousands attacking this way, almost always in vain: the breakthrough did not occur. The landscape became so smashed by shelling that the speed of attack invariably became slower than that of defence.

Eventually another solution had to be found to traverse a battlefield that had become impassable by men. The solution lay in a machine that could protect the infantry soldier, destroy the machine guns, increase the speed of advance, allow artillery fire to be moved further forwards, beyond where even horses could pass, and which throughout the advance could ensure the 'mopping up' of the ground that had been taken. The technological challenge was immense. The constituent parts of the 'new' machine – engine, tracks, turret and so on – already existed, but the decision had to be taken to develop the tank idea and those elements then transformed into a coherent, technically viable and tactically useful fighting machine. The decision-making process that enabled a theoretical idea to become one of the major inventions of the war is worth following, from the French side as well as from the British. On the British side, the idea took root in the mind of a somewhat unusual lieutenant colonel of the Royal Engineers, Ernest Swinton. In 1914, Swinton, aged 46, was far from being on active service. Before hostilities broke out, he had closely followed the Russo-Japanese War with the intention of writing an official history, and when the First World War started in 1914 he was sent to France as a war correspondent. Thus, the idea of the tank first took root in the mind of this officer who had fought in the Boer War of 1899 to 1902, written a manual of tactics for small fighting units (*The Defence of Duffer's Drift*), and was removed from the main fighting force and only supposed to report the war as it happened. Swinton envisaged a machine that 'would utilise "petrol tractors on the caterpillar principle" and be "armoured with hardened steel plates proof against German steel-cored, armour-piercing and reversed bullets, and armed with – say – two maxims and 2-pounder gun"'.[16] In France, the same idea was born at around the same time on the battlefield, in the mind of an unusual gunnery officer, Colonel Jean-Baptiste Estienne, a pioneer of pre-war military aviation who announced to the officers of his regiment (the 22nd

16 The descriptions within double quotes are often repeated, although it has not been possible to discover their initial source. They are borrowed here from Robert Kershaw, *Tank Men* (London: Hodder & Stoughton, 2008).

Régiment d'Artillerie) on 25 August 1914 after the Battle of Charleroi that 'the victory will belong to him who will be the first to place a gun on a vehicle capable of moving over every kind of terrain'.[17] The idea having been conceived, it was necessary to get official approval to forge ahead with developing it. Colonel Swinton, only half-listened to by the British High Command, attempted to have his ideas accepted directly in London. The War Office demurred. However, Winston Churchill, First Lord of the Admiralty, was a keen supporter and in January 1915 wrote to Prime Minister Asquith, without result. Churchill then decided to create within the Royal Navy an ad hoc 'Landships Committee'. The cause was heard at last. British tanks were engaged for the first time on the battlefield in September 1916, a year and nine months after the first decision was taken.

In France, the objections were more numerous and the decision-making process slower. Initial attempts by Estienne, commanding at the front, to convince the French command throughout 1915 were without success. The turning point came when he wrote to Joffre on 1 December 1915: 'I regard it as possible to manufacture mechanically driven vehicles which will permit the transport of infantry with weapons and kit, and of artillery, across every obstacle and under enemy fire, at a speed greater than 6 kilometres an hour.'[18] His voice was finally heard and he was allowed to return to Paris to discuss his projects with manufacturers he already knew. There he came up against the hostility of both the Automobile Services Department, a technical service of the army, and the Armaments Ministry, who refused to accept that the tank could be developed without the involvement of their respective services. It required the intervention of Clemenceau to rule finally in Estienne's favour. However, the first French tanks were not deployed until April 1917, and the Renault FT tank (often wrongly described as the FT17), equipped with a 360-degree revolving turret and advocated by Estienne, only made its first appearance in combat on 31 May 1918, south of Soissons.

Faced by 6,500 tanks deployed by the Allied armies between 1916 and 1918, the Germans responded on the battlefield with only some twenty A7V tanks and 100 or so captured from the British. Why? Not because German

17 Quoted by Henri Ortholan, *La guerre des chars, 1916–1918* (Paris: Bernard Giovanangelis Éditeur, 2007), p. 24. See also Arlette Estienne Mondet, *Le général JBE Estienne, père des chars* (Paris: L'Harmattan, 2011), p. 65.

18 Letter of Col. Estienne, commander of artillery of the 6th division, to the Commander-in-Chief, Méricourt sur Somme, 1 December 1915, quoted by Ch. Menu, *Applications de l'industrie, la leçon d'une guerre, essai historique* (École supérieure de Guerre, December 1931), p. 148. See also Mondet, *Le général JBE Estienne*, p. 65.

technology was incapable of producing tanks in quantity, but because no German – scientist, officer, manufacturer or politician – decided to be the pioneer who promoted the cause. On the contrary, the German command believed that in the defensive position in which it found itself the tank was not 'the best enemy of the tank'. It shared Ludendorff's opinion that there was 'no reason to fear them, [for] if the defence is well organised, artillery and infantry should see their attacks coming with the greatest possible calm'.[19]

The result was a technological divergence that opened up between the main belligerents. As the Allies manufactured tanks in their thousands, German industry turned to making *sui generis* anti-tank weapons and adapting existing weapons and ammunition to anti-tank combat. They were successful with the 77 mm direct-fire field gun and developed a 13 mm anti-tank rifle whose rounds could penetrate 15 mm-thick armour-plate at 300 metres, enough in the majority of cases to go through the armour of Allied tanks. The cost-benefit ratio of such developments was favourable to the Germans, who likewise opposed Allied technology with new tactics, often carried out by assault troops, which aimed to separate tanks from their accompanying infantry and then to immobilise and neutralise them individually: an effective tactic in its way, but insufficient.

In the struggle between technology and tactics, the final victor was neither the tank nor the anti-tank rifle or field gun. The battle was won by the Allies' industrial mass production, against which by 1918 the Germans had nothing left to offer.

Conclusion

Why, in the end, did the relationship between war and technology turn out the way it did between 1914 and 1918? Why did certain weapons at the peak of their development in 1913 disappear in 1914? Why were others, neglected until that moment, so important for the outcome of the war? Why were so few new weapons invented during the first industrial war?

The first most obvious initial answer would be that these outcomes were due to the fact that the weapons that were used had already been in existence at varying levels of development for several years prior to the war and that no one could foresee the exact date when they would be used in combat rather than merely on exercises. Such reasoning prompts us to consider the concept of an 'arms race' in a new light. The arms race is generally, and wrongly,

19 Quoted by Gambiez and Suire, *Histoire de la Première Guerre mondiale*, p. 339.

studied retrospectively from 1914 backwards. This approach, as well as being erroneous, fails to concern itself with a fundamental dynamic reality of the beginning of the twentieth century. At this point, all industrialised societies were engaged in militarisation and rapid arming, but this was occurring in the context of a lack of vision regarding how weaponry would be used, as well as the near-total indifference of citizens to this process. In other words, all progress in scientific research was contributing and accelerating militarisation and armaments, but rare were the men who wondered what the possible consequences of such a dynamic might be.

Another possible answer to these questions is that the actions of individual decision-makers were ultimately key. We have seen for ourselves how progress made during the war – in terms of armaments – occurred each time an idea was nurtured by an individual endowed with a sufficient conviction to overcome all the obstacles that were put in his way. Among those mentioned here, let us remember Swinton and Estienne (tanks), Adrian and Brodie (helmets), Mills (grenades) and add, since he has not yet been mentioned, the German corvette captain Hermann Bauer (submarines). These protagonists shared another common feature: they were generally eccentric, and to some extent marginal characters, who did not belong to the civil or military establishment of the time and would very likely have remained unknown, if the war had not brought them to the fore in technological planning. This, in turn, raises further questions about the role of military elites in general: how they influenced the preparation for war during projected time; what was their capacity to deal with unexpected developments; what role their relationship with manufacturers and politicians played; and more generally what was the effect of their contact networks and interactions, their links with scientific research and industrial production. It also leaves us asking what ultimately they may have cost.

11

Prisoners of war

HEATHER JONES

The First World War revolutionised captivity practices in Europe in terms of both scale and militarisation. There were, in effect, two forms of mass army in each of the belligerent states in the First World War: the army of men who fought and the army of men who were held in captivity as millions of enemy troops were incarcerated indefinitely all across Europe and in parts of Asia and Africa, following their capture on the battlefield, along with a small minority of naval men taken prisoner at sea. Worldwide, with the outbreak of war, it became the norm for all states, regardless of whether they were democratic or authoritarian, to establish military-run prisoner-of-war camps. Older forms of dealing with captured enemy combatants, which had existed in previous wars, such as parole, ransom or exchange were largely abandoned in favour of what many contemporaries considered the epitome of the modern – the militarised prisoner-of-war camp.

It may appear provocative to declare that prisoners of war were indeed an 'army'. Yet prisoners of war were managed and confined in ways very similar to the structures and controls applied to the fighting armies: confined in camps, which were often barrack structures, or held in small working units lodged in improvised billets, they lived according to orders, issued by their guards. They were surrounded by barbed wire and subject to the same military law as operated in their captor army, subordinate to the same military discipline rules and hierarchies. Effectively they existed within a militarised space, an army in every structural sense, contained by the captor state through force. The key distinction between a state's captive army of prisoners of war and its own army in the field was that the prisoner of war was deprived of access to arms; in every other regard, he existed within a soldierly culture and, as under international law other-rank prisoners of war could be compelled to labour for the captor state, in many countries the prisoners proved as valuable, and integrated, a wartime labour resource as the captor state's own troops.

In fact, one of the key trends of the Great War was the increasing blurring of the lines between the fighting army of a state and its captive army of prisoners of war. One of the most significant developments of the war was that increasing numbers of other-rank prisoners were retained by captor armies at or near the front to work for them directly and were never evacuated to home front prisoner-of-war camps; this dual system of front area prisoner working units, labouring for the captor army, and home front prisoner-of-war camps, supplying workers to the home front war economy, occurred in the German, French, British, Austro-Hungarian and Russian cases. A systematised front line world of forced labour companies, housed in Spartan temporary billets or improvised 'camps', developed across European battlefields. For example, in 1915, the German army began using Russian prisoners as workers in prisoner-of-war labour companies at or near the front; by 1916, it was using numerous prisoner nationalities in this way – a front area workforce of some 250,000 men in 1916. The same year, the British and French armies instigated their own prisoner-of-war labour companies. The accommodation and food provided for these front line prisoner labourers were reasonable in the British army; in contrast, conditions for prisoner-of-war labour companies in the French army were frequently poor. In 1916, the French army made some of its German prisoner-of-war labourers work for months on the Verdun battlefield under shell-fire. In the German army, in 1918, prisoners of war labouring directly for the army on the Western Front suffered from malnutrition and very frequent beatings. The Austro-Hungarian army also used prisoners in prisoner-of-war labour companies: by January 1918, there were 309,772 prisoners working for it near the front.[1] The death rate for prisoners labouring directly for the Austro-Hungarian army appears to have been very high: as early as autumn 1915, the decision was taken not to allow information about these prisoners' death rates or sickness rates to be made public; by 1918, the Austro-Hungarian Ministry of War had itself stopped keeping a record of accurate statistics on prisoner deaths.[2] In the case of the Russian army, little is known about the working conditions of those prisoners who worked directly for it near the battle zone. It appears, however, that punishments for prisoners refusing to work for the Russian army at the front could be extreme: 'when 100 prisoners refused to dig trenches near Lublin in summer 1915, one in ten

1 Alan Kramer, 'Prisoners in the First World War', in Sibylle Scheipers (ed.), *Prisoners in War* (Oxford University Press, 2010), p. 78.

2 Hannes Leidinger and Verena Moritz, 'Verwaltete massen. Kriegsgefangene in der donaumonarchie', in Jochen Oltmer (ed.), *Kriegsgefangene im Europa des Ersten Weltkriegs* (Paderborn: Ferdinand Schöningh, 2006), p. 56.

was shot and the others were severely beaten'.[3] The advent of this prisoner-of-war labour system in close proximity to the front was a near universal trend and it marked a major deterioration in prisoner-of-war treatment. These prisoners suffered physically and psychologically: they were often hit by shells from their own side and forced to work directly on their captor's war effort, in breach of international law; front line camps were also often to be found in occupied territory, a fact which rendered prisoners more vulnerable to abuse.

In sum, by 1918, the majority of belligerent states were increasingly dependent upon two 'armies' – their fighting force and their captive army of prisoner-of-war labourers, working both at the front and at home. In the case of Germany, prisoners made up 16 per cent of the workforce in the Ruhr coal mines by 1918.[4] A technocratically managed dual system of captivity – home front and front line – had emerged across Europe and Russian Asia, driven by wartime labour needs. This particular wartime constellation which fused modern technology, mass captivity and militarisation was new in 1914 to 1918: it created and normalised incarceration that was completely unprecedented in both its scale and in the way that it combined both the most advanced aspects of contemporary modernity – in the form of state management, labour efficiency and technological expertise – with a militarised culture of control and coercion. The First World War has long been associated with innovative technological developments in battlefield killing, industrialised warfare and armaments production, themes which have dominated both public perception and historiographical scrutiny. Yet the fact that the war also marked the advent of mass industrialised, militarised captivity, a new phenomenon that instigated just as much of a technological leap forward and cultural caesura with the past, was largely overlooked until the last decade of the twentieth century, when historians began to turn their attention to the fate of men taken prisoner during the conflict. Captivity has since emerged as a fundamental wartime experience, deeply interwoven within both the front-line and home-front wartime worlds. General trends in captivity in Britain, France, Germany, Russia and Austria-Hungary have been subject to some historical research, although gaps remain: the Ottoman Empire and Italy have had less attention and unfortunately little is known regarding camps in Bulgaria and Romania.

3 Kramer, 'Prisoners', p. 83.

4 Kai Rawe, '*... wir werden sie schon zur Arbeit bringen!': Ausländerbeschäftigung und Zwangsarbeit im Ruhrkohlenbergbau während des Ersten Weltkriegs* (Essen: Klartext Verlag, 2005), pp. 73–9.

The scale of captivity was staggering: although total estimates vary, approximately 8 to 9 million men were taken prisoner in the whole war.[5] This was a significant proportion of all combatants: the historian Alon Rachamimov has estimated that roughly one out of every nine men in uniform experienced capture.[6] One-third of the total number of men mobilised by Austria-Hungary, 'about 11 per cent of the total male population of the Dual Monarchy', was taken prisoner.[7] The geographical spread of camps was also dramatic due to the imperial reach of the conflict: prisoner-of-war camps were established from Vladivostok and Siberia in Russia to Templemore in Ireland. German prisoners of war captured fighting in East Africa were sent to camps in Egypt, Malta and India at Ahmednagar.[8] British and dominion prisoners of war captured by the Ottoman Empire were held in camps in Anatolia, where conditions varied; German prisoners of war captured at the siege of Tsingtau were held in Japan where they received impeccably good treatment, in particular at Bando camp, and used the camp to showcase German culture to the local Japanese population.

For the first three years of the war, the vast majority of captives were taken on the Eastern Front where the war of movement lent itself to mass captures of thousands of men at a time. The prisoner totals for the Eastern Front are striking: Russia took 2.1 million Austro-Hungarian troops captive, while Austria-Hungary and Germany between them captured almost 50 per cent of the war's total prisoners of war, with Germany taking 2.4 million prisoners in total by October 1918 on both the Eastern and Western Fronts and Austria-Hungary taking between 1.2 and 1.86 million.[9] Western trench warfare did not lend itself so easily to capture tallies on this scale and it was only in 1914 and 1918, during the phases of mobile warfare, that it saw significant large-scale captures: the British army took more prisoners in 1918 than it had in the

5 Jochen Oltmer, 'Einführung, funktionen und erfahrungen von kriegsgefangenschaft im Europa des Ersten Weltkriegs', in Oltmer, *Kriegsgefangene im Europa*, p. 11. Other estimates put the figure between 6.6 and 8.4 million. See Kramer, 'Prisoners', p. 76.

6 Alon Rachamimov, 'The disruptive comforts of drag: (trans)gender performances among prisoners of war in Russia, 1914–1920', *American Historical Review*, 3:2 (2006), pp. 1–4.

7 Alon Rachamimov, *POWs and the Great War. Captivity on the Eastern Front* (Oxford and New York: Berg, 2002), pp. 4, 31.

8 Mahon Murphy, 'The geography of internment', unpublished paper. I am grateful to Mahon Murphy for providing me with this information.

9 For the statistic for Russia, see: Reinhard Nachtigal, *Kriegsgefangenschaft an der Ostfront. 1914 bis 1918* (Frankfurt am Main: Peter Lang, 2005), pp. 13–16. For the figures on the total numbers of prisoners captured by Austria-Hungary, see: Uta Hinz, *Gefangen im Großen Krieg. Kriegsgefangenschaft in Deutschland 1914–1921* (Essen: Klartext Verlag, 2006), p. 238; Leidinger and Moritz, 'Verwaltete massen', p. 54.

previous three years of the war combined. It is unlikely that exact figures for capture numbers for the whole war can ever be known: states often improvised new bureaucratic systems to keep statistical track of prisoner figures; however, the chaos caused by the war and the sheer numbers of prisoners meant this was an exercise in demographic record-keeping that proved a major challenge.

No one saw this phenomenon coming. The term 'prisoner of war' was itself ambiguous at the outset of the conflict – it was applied to civilian internees as well as to captured military combatants. The confusion surrounding the term illustrates well the initially improvised nature of Great War captivity: its scale and duration were not anticipated in the pre-war period; its very nomenclature remained uncertain. It emerged as a direct consequence of the introduction of mass conscription in the late nineteenth century which led to a significant increase in the size of armies. Within six months of the war's outbreak, there were between 1.3 and 1.4 million men in captivity throughout Europe, most initially shoddily housed in improvised camps; in Germany, thousands remained in the open air for several weeks while accommodation was found or built.[10] Few commentators anticipated these developments before 1914 or how captivity structures would have to adapt – and, in particular, how the labour needs of wartime economies and captor armies would drive the formation of technocratic captivity systems that served essentially as a means of managing and allocating a prisoner-of-war proletariat to those economic sectors where they were most required.

Instead, the focus before 1914 was on humanising captivity, with the belief widespread that increasing legal codification could standardise prisoner-of-war treatment in terms of a relatively liberal regime, with prisoners' legal status moving much closer to civilian rights and non-combatant status.[11] In the period 1864 to 1914, there was an increasing emphasis on new laws to regulate wartime captivity: following the Lieber code issued to the Union Army during the American Civil War, which set out that prisoners were to be treated humanely, the Geneva Conventions of 1864 and 1906, and the Hague Conventions of 1899 and 1907 contained significant clauses that were intended to protect prisoners of war from ill-treatment. The Geneva Conventions largely concerned the treatment of enemy wounded on the battlefield, stipulating that they should be given medical assistance and

10 Richard B. Speed III, *Prisoners, Diplomats and the Great War. A Study in the Diplomacy of Captivity* (New York: Greenwood Press, 1990), p. 6.

11 Speed, *Prisoners*, p. 5; Heather Jones, *Violence against Prisoners of War in the First World War: Britain, France and Germany, 1914–1920* (Cambridge University Press, 2011), pp. 33–7.

helped in the same way that the wounded from the captor's own side were treated. This, in effect, meant that wounded enemies on the battlefield had to be taken prisoner in order to receive this care. One of the most remarkable aspects of the Great War was the extent to which the Geneva Convention was largely respected by all belligerents for wounded prisoners once they had been removed from the battlefield. While prior to capture wounded men remained at risk of the coup de grâce – perhaps the most notorious incident of this being the order by General Stenger in 1914 to kill all French wounded who lay on the battlefield behind his German troops' advance – once a man had been evacuated from the front as a wounded prisoner he was usually treated reasonably well on both the Eastern and Western Fronts. Certainly, if compared with the Second World War, the First World War upheld the Geneva Conventions of 1864 and 1906 surprisingly successfully. In this sense, military prisoners were better protected than their civilian counterparts; the hundreds of thousands of Great War civilian internees had no protection in international law.

Yet the Geneva Conventions contained little to protect non-wounded prisoners of war, whose main safeguard in international law at the outbreak of the Great War was the Hague Conventions. These proved less effective once conflict broke out. The 1899 Hague Convention stated that 'prisoners of war are in the power of the hostile government, but not in that of the individuals or corps who capture them'.[12] This crucially established state control over prisoners of war. Prisoners were to be fed the same as the troops of the captor's own army and they were to be humanely treated. Both Hague Conventions set out that the state could use prisoners of war as labour 'according to their rank and aptitude'; however, the 1907 Hague Convention added wording that stated that officer prisoners were 'excepted' from labour. Both Conventions also stated that any work that prisoners were put to should have no connection with the captor state's war effort. This article had been deliberately breached by the majority of belligerents by 1916.

The two Hague Conventions, which all the war's belligerents had ratified, apart from Serbia and Montenegro, stipulated that prisoners of war were subject to the military law of the captor state – in matters of discipline, prisoners were legally subject to the forms of punishment that were legitimate in the domestic military law of the captor army.[13] This led to accusations of mistreatment as punishments allowed in the captor army could include forms

12 http://avalon.law.yale.edu/19th_century/hague02.asp; accessed 30 November 2011.
13 Rachamimov, *POWs and the Great War*, p. 69.

of corporal violence that were prohibited in a prisoner's home army. In sum, the Hague Conventions highlight the extent to which, prior to 1914, contemporaries envisaged prisoner-of-war captivity increasingly in terms of a relaxed interpretation of imprisonment which included the concept of allowing prisoners a certain freedom of movement within certain limits to which they would be bound on parole. Both Conventions stated that prisoners of war could be interned in a town, fortress or camp and 'bound not to go beyond certain fixed limits; but they could only be confined as an indispensable measure of safety'. The 1907 Convention also added further to this clause, stating that prisoners could be confined 'only while the circumstances which necessitate the measure continue to exist'.[14]

The mass incarceration systems that emerged in 1914 contrasted starkly with these pre-war expectations. Although there were a handful of incidents in France where officer prisoners were granted parole in the first weeks of the war, public hostility meant that parole was abandoned. As the realisation that the war would not be over by Christmas grew, states turned to constructing purpose-built camps. The Hague Conventions rapidly proved inadequate and, as the conflict progressed, belligerent states increasingly regulated prisoner treatment through bilateral agreements with the enemy, such as the agreements on prisoner treatment between Great Britain and Germany at The Hague in June 1917 and July 1918, the Stockholm Protocol signed in December 1915 between Eastern Front belligerents or the wartime Bern Accords between France and Germany; limited prisoner exchange agreements were also sporadically agreed throughout the war between belligerents and the Netherlands and Switzerland accepted small numbers of prisoners in ill-health from belligerent states for internment as a humanitarian gesture. States also increasingly relied upon reports by neutral powers or humanitarian organisations to monitor prisoner treatment. Indeed, neutral countries were assigned as 'protecting powers' to particular prisoner nationalities and sent delegations to inspect prisoner-of-war camps: for example, the treatment of French prisoners in Germany was monitored in this way by Spain. The International Red Cross at Geneva also inspected prisoner-of-war camps and monitored prisoner treatment through the work of its prisoner-of-war agency. However, such inspections were restricted to the home front: no neutral power or humanitarian agency was allowed access to prisoners of war working directly for armies at or near the front line.

14 http://avalon.law.yale.edu/20th_century/hague04.asp; accessed 4 December 2011.

The shift away from pre-war expectations is clearly evident in how the question of responsibility for feeding prisoners evolved. At the outset of war, the Hague Conventions set the norm, stating that prisoners of war should be fed the same rations as troops in the captor army. However, in 1915, with the Central Powers faced with Allied blockade at sea, Germany decided to feed prisoners of war at the same level as German civilians. The blockade, in turn, led the Allies to fully utilise the right of prisoners of war to receive parcels in order to supply their men held prisoner by Germany with foodstuffs to protect them from their blockade's impact. This rapidly became a new norm: across Europe, a complex food parcel scheme developed whereby prisoners of war received food aid by post.

In Western Europe, this was extremely effective: British, French, American and Belgian prisoners received crucial food parcels from their home state. These men received both individual parcels sent by their families and charities, as well as government-sponsored aid packages, often sent via the International Red Cross in Geneva, and bread and biscuit deliveries paid for by the British and French governments and sent via Copenhagen and Bern. German prisoners held in Britain and France also received parcels sent from home. However, as the war progressed and the blockade's impact tightened, it became more difficult for their families to send individual parcels; increasingly they received care packages purchased direct from the International Red Cross. Supplying parcels proved more difficult in Eastern Europe; in some cases bulk deliveries of aid were brought to camps in Russia by individual aid workers, such as the Swedish campaigner Elsa Brändström; in more accessible camps parcels did arrive by post. Many prisoners of war across Europe could also receive money sent by bank mandate to purchase food locally, where allowed. The impact of parcels was key to sustaining prisoners' health: the high Italian prisoner death rates are partly attributable to the fact that the Italian Government did not send state aid parcels to Italian prisoners held in Germany and Austria-Hungary and discouraged individual parcels sent by families, which, due to postal inefficiency, accumulated at the border.

Overall, prisoners of war were the subject of a mammoth charitable aid effort during the war which encompassed both domestic and international organisations such as the International Committee of the Red Cross at Geneva, the Vatican and the Young Men's Christian Association. This process drove a rapid modernisation of wartime humanitarian aid delivery and charity lobbying techniques. What this humanitarian aid to prisoners of war masked, however, was the tacit acceptance by all belligerents that it was not possible to adhere to the Hague Convention's stipulations and that responsibility for feeding prisoners was no longer solely that of the captor state; prisoners' access to food became a lottery, based on how well served their location was by rail and how much food either charities or their home state could provide. However, overall the parcel aid system to prisoners of war was one of the biggest humanitarian achievements of the war and saved many lives.

Fundamental to this wartime charitable intervention was the growth in size and status of the International Committee of the Red Cross (ICRC). At the start of the war it established a prisoner-of-war agency at Geneva dedicated to helping families find information about the whereabouts of their loved ones. Many prisoners of war had not been reported as captured, leaving their families only with the information that they were 'missing'. To help solve this problem, the ICRC compiled a gigantic card catalogue system that recorded details of men whose families reported them missing and matched these with information coming from captor regimes to identify individual prisoners. This work was helped by the growth within states of national red cross organisations and their equivalents operating under the red crescent in Islamic areas and by the fact that the Hague Conventions stipulated that each belligerent state had to establish a Prisoner of War Bureau to inform prisoners' home states of their whereabouts. These groups liaised with the ICRC to provide prisoner information. In contrast to national red cross societies and prisoner-of-war bureaux which were part of state war efforts, the ICRC adopted a strictly neutral stance during the war. As a result, by 1915, it had been granted the right to inspect prisoner-of-war camps in key belligerent states. It published frequent reports on conditions in the camps and by the end of the war it had established itself as the foremost international charitable organisation assisting prisoners.

The utilisation of bilateral agreements, neutral inspections or charitable interventions on an ad hoc basis during the First World War to humanise captivity could only go so far, however: much additional regulation of prisoner treatment during the Great War adopted innovative coercive measures as well. Belligerents turned increasingly to reprisals against prisoners in their own hands as a way of forcing the enemy to improve its treatment of captives. Reprisals in many ways were an intermediary form of violence, situated halfway on the spectrum of prisoner mistreatment that occurred during the war that ran from the random killing of prisoners at the moment of capture by individuals, to widespread prisoner deaths in captivity due to state or army negligence. Reprisal violence was deliberate, often officially ordered by the captor state and carefully controlled; moreover, it was nearly always made public. It took a variety of forms, ranging from withholding privileges, such as access to food parcels or exercise, to punitive labour or even human shield actions. Reprisal behaviour differed between countries: Britain's main reprisal took place in 1915 when it placed thirty-nine captured U-boat submarine personnel in solitary confinement in reaction to unrestricted submarine warfare, a reprisal that rapidly ended with Britain abandoning the action when the Germans responded in kind, placing the same number of British officers in solitary imprisonment. After this humiliation, Britain largely avoided carrying out any further reprisal action against prisoners of war. The Director of the Department of Prisoners of War at the War Office even viewed reprisals as un-British: 'our national characteristics are opposed to the ill-treatment of a man who has no power to resist and this especially in the case of one who is not personally responsible for the acts complained of'.[15] In contrast, Germany and France were more ruthless. Germany employed French prisoners from middle-class intellectual professions in marshland drainage work in a reprisal action in 1915; France put German officers on hospital ships as human shields as a response to U-boat attacks.

Yet it was the German army which carried out the most extreme reprisals of the Western Front belligerents. In 1916, it sent thousands of French and British prisoners of war to work on the Eastern Front, near the front line, in sub-zero temperatures in reprisal for the French decision to send German prisoners of war to camps in France's North African territories and the British decision to use German prisoner labourers in France, a break with earlier policy which was to evacuate them to UK camps. This German reprisal action saw prisoners die in emaciated conditions in the East, beaten and frozen, in an action that was closer to Second World War patterns of atrocity against prisoners than First World War ones. This 1916 action was followed by an additional German reprisal in 1917, when, in response to the British and French use of German prisoner labour near the front, including the French long-term use of German prisoners to work under shell-fire on the Verdun battlefield, the German High Command ordered that all newly captured British and French other ranks, taken prisoner unwounded, were to be held near the front line, without shelter and inadequately fed. In several cases, they were deliberately held as human shields at positions that were frequently shelled. The reprisal action was deliberately made public to pressurise the Allies. These two reprisal actions by the German army in 1916 and 1917 cost

15 TNA, FO 369/1450, Maj. Gen. Sir Herbert Belfield, 'Report on Directorate of Prisoners of War', September 1920, pp. 57–8.

British and French prisoner lives, before both governments ultimately ceded to the German ultimatum that the reprisals would end if they restricted German prisoner-of-war labour to a distance of 30 kilometres from the front.

Reprisals offer the clearest example of state-sanctioned violence against prisoners and they were innovative in terms of how states used the media to publicise and legitimise them. In contrast, the other extremes on the spectrum of First World War prisoner mistreatment – the killing of prisoners at the moment of capture and deaths due to poor living conditions caused by state or military negligence – were more in keeping with the kinds of practices that had occurred in late-nineteenth-century wars. However, the nature of trench warfare particularly facilitated battlefield killing at capture as it was difficult to evacuate prisoners back down the line during periods of intense bombardment and it was possible to kill large numbers of surrendering men by machine gun or grenade.

Historians continue to debate the frequency of incidents of prisoner killing at the moment of surrender. There is evidence to suggest that some units of the British army on the first day of the Battle of the Somme were ordered not to take prisoners and also that there was a policy of no quarter in some units of the German army during the 1914 invasion of France.[16] Joanna Bourke and Niall Ferguson have contended that prisoner killing was widespread, with Ferguson even arguing that this led to a fear of surrender among troops that prolonged the war; in contrast, Alan Kramer suggests that, in fact, it was relatively rare.[17] In any case, it was largely taboo – a fact that meant that few witnesses were prepared to write or speak about it and there is little historical evidence to gauge it: on the Western Front, it was never sanctioned by army high commands in official orders and where lower level orders were issued to take no prisoners these were usually verbal only.

However, despite official reticence on the subject, it appears to have been accepted practice in some armies to kill badly wounded enemies on the battlefield by giving the coup de grâce, particularly at moments where evacuating prisoners was militarily difficult; indeed, the French army even established specific units known as '*nettoyeurs des tranchées*' (trench cleaners)

16 John Horne and Alan Kramer, *German Atrocities, 1914. A History of Denial* (New Haven, CT: Yale University Press, 2001).

17 Joanna Bourke, *An Intimate History of Killing: Face-to-Face Killing in Twentieth-Century Warfare* (London and New York: Granta Press, 1999); Niall Ferguson, *The Pity of War: Explaining World War I* (London: Penguin, 1998); Niall Ferguson, 'Prisoner taking and prisoner killing in the age of total war: towards a political economy of military defeat', *War in History*, 11:2 (2004), pp. 148–92; Kramer, 'Prisoners', p. 85.

whose task it was to do this. On the Western Front, it also appears to have been common in the heat of battle to refuse quarter to men trying to surrender, particularly where their surrender required a leap of trust, or the suspension of the desire for vengeance or of prejudice on the part of the captor, such as when the men surrendering emerged from a dugout en masse, when a machine-gun nest surrendered or where the troops surrendering were black or Asian. Far rarer were incidents of killing prisoners *after* they had been taken prisoner on the Western Front; although these did occur, they appear to have been unusual and soldiers often criticised those who carried out such killings.

During the conflict, all belligerents accused the enemy of killing prisoners on the battlefield; such allegations were pivotal to the propaganda war.[18] Yet the moment of capture remains strangely under-researched, despite the fact that capture was utterly integral to the war combat experience, a key determining factor in whether or not an army won or lost a battle. Mass captures, such as those of Caporetto in 1917, when an estimated 250,000 Italians surrendered, or the German surrenders during the Hundred Days campaign in 1918, affected the outcome of the war.

One reason capture was such a highly sensitive issue was because of its association with cowardice. In a war fought by citizen armies, shame at surrender was not restricted to the officer class, but often permeated the other ranks as well. Prisoners often feared that they were seen as deserters; yet while desertion obviously occurred, it was a taboo issue among prisoners in captivity and captor armies were often careful to ensure that deserters were held with men who did not know the circumstances of their surrender. Overall, however, most men appear to have been captured due to reasons beyond their own control, such as being wounded or cut off by enemy advances. In 1914, a large number of men from the 1st Gordon Highlanders were captured at Bertry when their officers got lost; in 1918, whole German units surrendered in an orderly fashion following the orders of their officers; the Russians captured at Tannenberg in 1914 were surrounded due to command errors.

If battlefield prisoner killing illustrates one key extreme of violence against captives, the other key cause of prisoner deaths was negligence. Negligence leading to poor captivity conditions was frequent during the war, particularly in Eastern Europe and the Middle East theatres. This raises the paradox that while the First World War saw the most modern technologically developed

18 Jones, *Violence against POWs*, pp. 70–87.

camps that had ever been constructed, these advances were not uniform and in some theatres prisoners endured appallingly rudimentary living conditions. Moreover, in certain countries, such as Germany, the modern camp developed because initial negligence in preparing for large numbers of prisoners had led to poor captivity conditions and an international outcry when it was revealed that prisoners had died from exposure in 1914 while waiting in fields, without shelter, for their camps to be ready to accommodate them or from disease caused by poor hygiene conditions. Thus, at the heart of First World War captivity there is a negligence-modernisation paradox. The more cases of negligence came to light, the greater the striving to modernise camps. Negligence was not absent from First World War camp modernity: it was its very raison d'être and in a symbiotic relationship with the modernisation process.

This relationship between modernisation and negligence becomes particularly clear if we consider the typhus epidemic that broke out in 1915 in home front prisoner-of-war camps in Germany, Austria-Hungary and Russia, largely because of overcrowded conditions and inadequate delousing facilities. In total, in the whole epidemic, some 44,732 prisoners of war in Germany caught typhus. The epidemic was also severe in Austria-Hungary: in Mauthausen camp in January 1915, up to 186 prisoners a day died of typhus. Typhus also broke out in many camps in the Russian Empire: in the winter of 1915/16, typhus ravaged Totskoe camp where 'at least 10,000 men died out of 25,000'.[19] In the German case, the uncontrolled spread of the disease rapidly throughout thirty German prisoner-of-war camps caused panic and fear of contagion spreading to the home front population, and led to a rapid and radical modernisation of prisoner-of-war camp sites. This included the installation of modern disinfection vats to delouse prisoners' clothing and also the construction of shower blocks in many camps, practices already in evidence in some other wartime states. To reduce the risk of lice, in Germany prisoners also often had all hair on their bodies cut short or shaved upon arrival at a camp. Medical advice was sought and quarantine measures introduced as standard for all newly arriving prisoners coming from the front. In the Russian case, both neutral power and Central Power nurses carrying out inspections of the camps in Russia successfully pressurised the Russian Government to improve hygiene in the camps in the wake of the epidemic.

The technical and logistical modernisation of prisoner-of-war camps was therefore driven by the perceived need both to segregate prisoners of war in

19 Kramer, 'Prisoners', p. 80.

order to protect home front populations from contagion and danger, as well as to sustain prisoners of war so that they could serve as an effective, healthy workforce for the captor state. The need to rapidly accommodate and control large numbers of prisoners thus led to large purpose-built camps being constructed on the home front, mainly between 1914 and 1916 – often states used the prisoners themselves for this labour. Germany built such camps from 1914; Russia, in contrast, kept prisoners in small, improvised internment sites for most of 1915, and adapted slowly to using large, purpose-built camps.[20] Some of these camps were enormous: prisoner-of-war camps in Siberia, such as Berezovka, Krasnoyarsk and Nikolsk Ussurisk, at times housed 25,000 to 35,000 captives.

The same technological advances that had led to a preponderance of the defensive upon the battlefield were adapted in the construction of prisoner-of-war camps to ensure prisoners could not escape – barbed or electrified wire, sentry towers with machine guns, floodlights and guard dogs. Sophisticated railway delivery systems ensured that food supplies regularly reached camps and ever-improving forms of tinned foodstuffs enabled camps to stockpile supplies; even in Russia where systems were most backward at the outset of war, food delivery improved. Railways were also important for transporting prisoners, often in cattle trucks in the West or teplushki (a box waggon with a stove) in the East. In Germany and Austria-Hungary, wooden barracks were built to a standard model, often containing two or three tiered bunk beds. Across Europe, camps often also had purpose-built latrine, laundry and sanitary blocks; in several Western European states prisoners were immunised on arrival against typhoid. This increasingly technological mastery of mass captivity was one of the new forms of 'totalisation' of war produced by the conflict. The very industrial advances that led to total war on the front line also provided total 'security' methods against captives within the home state – the legacy of this was that in the interwar years, states would continue to see these new technologies of captivity as a way to provide 'total' internal state security. This was closely linked to sophisticated forms of intelligence gathering. An impressive postal service operated in camps in Western Europe: prisoners could send and receive a fixed monthly quota of postcards and letters for free. This correspondence with home was absolutely crucial to prisoners' mental well-being; it was also a vital source of intelligence information. Prisoners' mail was read and censored by the captor state and also by the

20 Rachamimov, *POWs and the Great War*, pp. 88–9.

home state: in particular, it was one of the principal forms of information about the enemy's home front morale and living conditions. In some cases, captor states eager to acquire intelligence from prisoners even placed agents in camps, posing as prisoners, to obtain information.

Moreover, during the Great War this modernisation of captivity was generally lauded as positive and progressive; totalised captivity was seen as providing a more humane environment for prisoners. Indeed, how well a state managed mass captivity and whether it implemented a technologically advanced, 'modern' captivity regime came to be seen as a test of its own competence and scientific advancement. Captor state propaganda often focused upon this issue – using images and accounts from prisoners of war to highlight that they were being well treated and hence the captor state was a model of compliance with international law and modern, civilised obligations to its captives. The large, purpose-built home front prisoner-of-war camp provoked enormous public curiosity: postcard photographs of camps were sold to the civilian population; in 1914, civilians often visited the vicinity of camps in an attempt to see the enemy captives. Film footage of large numbers of captured prisoners was also frequently used in propaganda. In this way, the prisoner of war became an iconic trope in home front propaganda – either as a well-treated captive of one's own side or as a victim of the enemy's brutality.

Prisoners themselves assisted the development of the image of the home front camp as the epitome of the modern. In many large home front camps, cultural practices flourished that used the latest available technology; this was particularly the case in officers' camps where prisoners had both money and time, allowing them to pursue cultural activities, such as constructing a theatre or printing press, although similar cultural activities also appear in some of the large home front camps for other-rank prisoners.

Prisoners often produced their own prison camp newspapers, for example, a phenomenon that thrived during the war throughout camps in Britain, Germany and Russia and also after the war in France and Egypt, as prisoners awaited repatriation. In the large home front camps, prisoners organised their own aid committees to distribute any surplus food from parcels to needy fellow captives. Prisoners also organised impressively professional concerts and theatrical performances, often using the skill sets of fellow captives to construct elaborate theatre sets and produce professional programmes, pursuits reflecting the leisure activities of the home front world. Sport was similarly well organised in the large camps, which, in some cases, had their own internal football leagues. In many large camps, prisoners also organised religious services and often built churches and synagogues. The Jewish community of Berlin even provided Mazzoth for Passover to Jewish prisoners held in nearby camps. Religion provided a refuge for many men in the face of the strain of captivity. Educational classes were also established, with prisoners in large home front camps across Europe able to avail of language, history, literature or politics classes by their peers. In some camps in Germany, British captives could even sit examinations for UK qualifications – the exam papers were delivered and returned by post and marked in the United Kingdom. Local professional photographers even visited some camps to take prisoners' pictures for a fee; prisoners then sent these pictures home by post to their loved ones, often made into postcards. In sum, the technological advances in communication, urbanisation and logistics allowed for captivity to evolve during the war into a new form of modern mass incarceration and prisoners were not the passive receptors of this process but interacted with it, co-opting the technology available to them to act as historical agents who modernised their lives in the camp as much as possible. There was a close symbiotic relationship between these endeavours of prisoners and the development of the camp as a site capable of sustaining new forms of long-term incarceration by states.

Yet much of this modernisation was aimed at facilitating the most efficient labour use of the captive, as states strained to find adequate manpower for industry and agriculture in the wake of the growing demand for soldiers. When, by 1916, it became clear to most captor states that prisoner labour was best exploited in small working units, the large home-front, other-rank prisoner-of-war camps were adapted into logistical bases from which small units of prisoners were sent out to work locally and the home front camp system was rapidly decentralised into smaller labour units in most belligerent states. Prisoners were increasingly moved within the system, frequently between different home front camps and between camps and temporary working units according to where their labour was required; officers, however, remained in larger camps for the whole war, as did prisoners who were disabled by war wounds and unable to work outside the camp as a result. Thus, the idea of the massive home front camps, sometimes described as segregated, single-sex 'towns', was mythologised well beyond their real role: in reality, the majority of prisoners of war across Europe had been relocated from them to work elsewhere from 1916 onwards, or 1917 to 1918 in the case of Britain. By 1916, 90 per cent of prisoners held by Germany were working, mainly in agriculture, as well as industry, quarrying and mining. As early as the second half of 1915, 60 to 70 per cent of Austria-Hungary's prisoners of war were no longer held in camps, but were living in work *Kommandos* – small units of prisoners sent to work in agriculture or industry.[21] In some cases, small working units, which often held fewer than fifteen men, were officially registered as attached to a large home front camp, but in reality were accommodated at their site of labour, which could be long distances away, particularly in the cases of Germany and Russia.

Working units were subject to far less international scrutiny and their prisoners often suffered from beatings, poor food provision and improvised accommodation, such as barns for those doing agricultural work or factories for those working in industry. These prisoners had no access to the superior 'modernised' living conditions of the larger home front camps. Mining or quarrying work was particularly difficult, where accidents were frequent; forestry, another economic sector which used large amounts of prisoner labour across Europe, was a slightly less onerous employment.

Perhaps the most psychologically demanding labour was working in industry as many prisoners felt that such employment aided the captor state's war effort. In some states, such as France and Germany, prisoners were employed directly in munitions-related industries; Britain proved the exception, where, in part due to the strength of trade union opposition, prisoners were not used in mining nor directly on making munitions, although they were used in small working units in agriculture and quarrying in the last two years of the war.

In Russia, working conditions varied very widely, with the worst occurring during the construction of the Murman railway, during which an estimated 25,000 out of the 70,000 mainly Austro-Hungarian and German prisoner-of-war workforce died; Germany initiated reprisals against Russia for its use of German prisoners on this task, even though only a minority of the prisoner workers were German; most of the dead were Austro-Hungarian.[22]

Prisoners were unable to refuse work allocated to them and, although they were theoretically entitled to a subsistence wage, in accordance with international law, due to be paid to them at the end of the conflict, most never received it because of chaotic conditions at the war's end. All of this marked a sophisticated contemporary recognition of the logistical value of a camp system for moving decentralised labour around a state. It also normalised the omnipresence of forced prisoner labour for home front civilian populations. Driven primarily by the ever-increasing need for prisoner manpower, this process introduced new forms of 'forced labour' under the aegis of public discourses that captivity was being modernised and humanised during the war.

21 Leidinger and Moritz, 'Verwaltete massen', p. 48. 22 Kramer, 'Prisoners', p. 83.

In contrast, for the large numbers of prisoners employed in small working units in the agricultural sector across Europe, conditions were generally relatively tolerable – although the work was demanding, the food available to prisoners working on farms was usually good and farming families often regarded the prisoner as they would a peacetime 'hired hand'. By January 1918, 490,931 prisoners of war were working in home front agriculture in Austria-Hungary. In some countries, particularly where prisoners were assigned to agriculture, individual prisoners were lodged with employers, although this never occurred in Britain. This was a frequent practice in parts of Russia. It led to considerable interaction between the prisoner and the family for whom he worked. In Russia, in several cases, this close proximity even led to marriage between local women and prisoners of war.[23] More generally, throughout captor states the idea of sexual relationships between prisoners of war and local women was of concern to both governments and soldiers alike. Such relationships did undoubtedly occur, but to a far lesser extent than the cultural alarm attributed to them in wartime discourses would suggest.

Overall, the modernisation of captivity helps to explain the fact that most prisoners of war survived. In particular, this was because there was only a limited number of epidemics in prisoner-of-war camps in the First World War in Western Europe compared to earlier conflicts – largely due to the implementation of better prison camp hygiene. In fact, apart from the major typhus epidemic in 1915, incidents of mass illness in prisoner-of-war camps were relatively limited. German prisoners sent by the French to North Africa in 1914 to 1915 almost all caught malaria; tuberculosis was also a frequent illness among prisoners of war. However, in general the main home front camps saw little disease in the First World War, with the exception of the 1918 influenza epidemic which struck prisoners of war, civilian and soldier populations alike. Holding camps for new captures on the Western Front, where conditions were poor, saw outbreaks of dysentery, such as that at Souilly camp in France in 1916; however, here again, the war saw surprisingly little contagious disease among prisoners.

However, although overall most prisoners survived captivity, their chances of doing so varied by nationality and between Western, Southern and Eastern Europe. Maximum death rates for British and French prisoners in Germany were around 7 per cent, Germans held in France had maximum death rates of 6.4 per cent and Germans held in Britain had maximum death rates

23 Rachamimov, *POWs and the Great War*, p. 152.

of 3 per cent.[24] Between 17,000 and 38,000 French prisoners died in German captivity; in comparison, approximately 25,000 German prisoners died in France and 9,349 in British captivity.[25] In contrast, 100,000 of the 600,000 Italians taken prisoner by Germany and Austria-Hungary died in captivity. Between 55,000 and 72,586 Russians died in German captivity. A total of 385,000 Austro-Hungarians are estimated to have perished in captivity in Russia, a death rate of 18 per cent.[26] Serbs in Austro-Hungarian captivity also endured particularly poor conditions: at least 30,000 to 40,000 had died of starvation by January 1918.[27] Thus, death rates suggest captivity conditions were worse in Eastern Europe than in the West. However, it is also important to note that there were significantly high death rates for certain nationalities held by Western powers: Romanians held by Germany, for example, had a disproportionately high death rate (29 per cent) compared to other nationalities in German captivity.[28] Turkish prisoners taken by the British army in the Middle East were held in Egypt, where many of them suffered from pellagra due to vitamin deficiencies caused by poor food; their death rates were sufficiently high to warrant a medical enquiry.

With the exception of Japan, which has a well-developed historiography on its efficiently run and humane First World War prisoner-of-war camps, the history of captivity in the non-European theatres of the war, particularly Africa, Palestine and Mesopotamia, remains to be written. One of the worst captivity death rates of the war occurred on the Mesopotamian front among British troops captured by the Ottomans at Kut-al-Amara in modern-day Iraq, which fell to Ottoman forces in April 1916 after a long siege. Here, the Ottoman army captured approximately 2,962 white British officers and other ranks, of whom

24 Jones, *Violence against POWs*, pp. 23–4.

25 The higher figure for French prisoner deaths in Germany is that given by the former head of the French Service des Prisonniers de Guerre, Georges Cahen-Salvador. See Georges Cahen-Salvador, *Les Prisonniers de Guerre (1914–1919)* (Paris: Payot, 1929), pp. 281, 284, 291; the lower figure comes from the German interwar history by Wilhelm Doegen, *Kriegsgefangene Völker*, vol. 1, *Der Kriegsgefangenen Haltung und Schicksal in Deutschland* (Berlin: D. Reimer, 1919), pp. 28–9. The figure for German deaths in France comes from *Völkerrecht im Weltkrieg, Das Werk des Untersuchungsausschusses der Verfassungsgebenden Deutschen Nationalversammlung und des Deutschen Reichstages, 1919–1928*, p. 715. See also Hans Weiland and Leopold Kern, *In Feindeshand. Die Gefangenschaft im Weltkriege in Einzeldarstellungen* (Vienna: Bundesvereinigung der ehemaligen österreichischen Kriegsgefangenen, 1931), vol. 2, statistical appendix. The figure for German deaths in British captivity is from War Office, *Statistics of the Military Effort of the British Empire during the Great War 1914–1920* (London: HMSO, 1922), pp. 329, 352, 632–5.

26 Rachamimov, *POWs and the Great War*, p. 39.

27 Alan Kramer, *Dynamic of Destruction. Culture and Mass Killing in the First World War* (Oxford University Press, 2007), p. 67.

28 Kramer, *Dynamic of Destruction*, p. 65.

1,782 would go on to die in Ottoman captivity.[29] Alongside these men, the Ottoman army also captured an unknown number of Indian prisoners who, along with their white comrades, experienced a horrific death march from Kut-al-Amara to the northern railhead at Ras-el-Ain via Baghdad. In total, in the whole of the Mesopotamian campaign, some 10,686 colonial soldiers from India, including 200 Indian army officers, were captured by the Ottoman army: of these, 1,708 were reported to have died in captivity and another 1,324 were recorded as untraced at the end of the war, a very high death rate.[30] The other most infamous death march of the conflict endured by prisoners of war occurred within Europe, when Austro-Hungarian prisoners of war held by the Serbian army were forced to retreat on foot with the Serbian army over the mountains into Albania and ultimately to the coast, from where the Serbian army was evacuated. The death rate on this march was extremely high. However, in contrast to the Kut-al-Amara march, where the Ottoman guards enjoyed reasonably good conditions while meting out terrible violence upon the captives, the Serbian army had no choice but to evacuate and its own men suffered high casualties on the march, alongside their prisoners due to the poor conditions.

The most frequent causes of death in captivity were old battlefield wounds, illness and malnutrition. Although some states such as Britain, France and the United States succeeded in feeding captives adequately for the whole conflict, malnutrition was a major problem for many prisoner nationalities, particularly those not receiving food parcels in Germany, Russia and Austria-Hungary. Yet overwork and violent treatment also played key secondary roles in certain countries in exacerbating the risk of death which by 1916, as Alan Kramer has stated, was almost certainly as great in captivity for some nationalities, in particular, Italians and Serbs in Austro-Hungarian captivity; Romanians and Italians in German captivity; and Germans and Austro-Hungarians in Russian hands, 'as it was at the front'.[31] In many states violence was used to enforce prison camp discipline; in Germany, until 1917 captives were tied to a post for several hours, or randomly beaten for misdemeanours; in French-run camps in North Africa prisoners were exposed to the sun as a punishment. The Austro-Hungarian army had special punishment camps for prisoners of war in occupied Albania and Montenegro, where conditions were

29 Heather Jones, 'Imperial captivities: colonial prisoners of war in Germany and the Ottoman empire, 1914–1918', in Santanu Das, *Race, Empire and First World War Writing* (Cambridge University Press, 2011), pp. 177–8.

30 *Ibid.* 31 Kramer, 'Prisoners', p. 86.

particularly bad. In sum, other-rank Great War captives often lived with the constant physical and psychological fear of violence, threatened or enacted.

Most significantly, too, the above death rate figures were almost entirely other-rank prisoner deaths. Central to how captivity was structured in 1914 to 1918 was the dominant belief that captured officers should receive a better standard of treatment than other-rank prisoners of war. This overwhelmingly led to captured officers being held in separate officers' prisoner-of-war camps, where they were allocated other-rank prisoners from their own country as orderlies and where conditions were generally far better than in the men's camps; in particular, airmen were privileged and treated according to old chivalric honour codes, as depicted in the most famous film on First World War captivity, *La Grande Illusion*. Officer prisoners were also paid a salary and were exempt from working. This special treatment of officer prisoners held true for all belligerent states for the whole war, with the exception of Russia, where the outbreak of revolution in 1917 led to general chaos, which affected supplies to all camps and, following the Bolshevik Revolution, less respect for officers.

All this shows that prisoner-of-war life was far from easy or comfortable, particularly for other ranks. Even in the main purpose-built home front camps with their cultural activities, prisoners were subject to depression and war-weariness. The term 'barbed wire disease' was coined during the war by a Swiss doctor to describe the psychological problems that afflicted men who faced an indeterminate length of time in captivity. Officer prisoners who were not forced to work suffered particularly from apathy, depression and a sense of shame at spending the war in captivity. Sexual frustration and fears regarding the fidelity of wives and sweethearts back home also afflicted prisoners, although this was largely a taboo subject. There were also cultural fears more broadly among contemporaries that prisoners would lose their virility or return after the war with homosexual tendencies. For many of these reasons, captivity was often unbearable; although suicide remained relatively uncommon, nervous breakdown was a real danger.

As a result, for some men, escape was an attractive option, despite the risks it entailed. For officer prisoners, such as Charles de Gaulle, whose multiple escape attempts from German captivity failed, escape was often a question of honour. Indeed, British officer prisoners in Germany were prohibited as the war went on from giving their word of honour that they would not try to escape, which was a prerequisite for being allowed to go on guarded group walks outside the prison camp, because the British army felt that escape was a military imperative for the officer prisoner. For other-rank prisoners across

Europe, escapes were provoked by a range of motives: from the desire to escape a violent or badly fed captivity to homesickness, to the wish to rejoin the home side's war effort. What is clear is that escapees who were recaptured were punished within the remits of the captor state's domestic military law and were in general not harshly abused in comparison with the Second World War – escape was also often a collaborative team effort involving several prisoners working together. Some of the more elaborate wartime escape plans involved tunnelling out of a camp – most famously at Holzminden camp which would go on to be mythologised in the interwar period.

If escaping offered one means of liberation from captivity, another was to join the captor side's war effort. This option was generally only open to a relatively limited number of prisoners of war – those who were part of an ethnic minority which the captor state was trying to convert to its side. German-speaking Russian prisoners in German captivity were offered the option of becoming naturalised German citizens; prisoners from Alsace-Lorraine captured by France were granted a privileged captivity and also the option of changing sides. Those who refused were treated harshly. Indeed, prisoners from Alsace-Lorraine captured fighting on the Eastern Front by Russia were privileged and some transferred to French captivity. As early as November 1914, the Russian Stavka ordered that Slav and Alsatian prisoners be given the best available lodgings, food and clothing and more freedom; the better camps of European Russia were intended for Slavs and 'friendly' nationalities, while Magyars, ethnic Germans and Jews were placed lowest in the Russian prisoner-of-war hierarchy. However, the disorganisation and decentralisation of the prisoner-of-war system in Russia meant that in reality these privileges were not uniformly implemented.[32] Both sides also sought, largely unsuccessfully, to recruit Poles from among their prisoner populations, although the Allies only began this late in the war.

In fact, most such recruitment attempts were failures. Early in the conflict, Irish prisoners of war fighting in the British army who were captured by Germany were gathered in a special prisoner-of-war camp at Limburg and attempts were made by the Irish nationalist Roger Casement to convert them to join a rebellion against Britain in Ireland. Very few prisoners were actually recruited despite German coercion, and ultimately Casement decided against bringing any to Ireland in 1916. Germany also tried unsuccessfully to recruit Muslims, captured fighting for the French, Russian and British armies, to support the Central Powers and to volunteer to fight in the Ottoman army:

32 Rachamimov, *POWs and the Great War*, pp. 93–4.

some 4,000 non-white colonial prisoners of war were centralised for this purpose at a camp at Wünsdorf near Zossen, which became known as the *Halbmondlager* (crescent moon camp), even though not all its inmates were Muslim – there were Sikhs, Hindus and Christians among the captives there. Wünsdorf was a propaganda show camp where a mosque was built for the Muslim prisoners and they were provided with Halal food preparation facilities. In total, 1,084 Arab prisoners and forty-nine Indian prisoners from the camp were sent to join the Ottoman army between 1916 and 1917; some volunteered; others were coerced. Many of these men found themselves fighting for the Ottomans on the Mesopotamian front.[33] However, overall the policy failed. The prisoner-volunteers resented the very harsh, brutal military conditions in the Ottoman army; some deserted to the British lines in Mesopotamia as soon as they could. In 1917, the remaining prisoners at Wünsdorf were moved by the German authorities to camps in occupied Romania.

In fact, ultimately the only truly successful example of prisoners of war becoming fighters for the captor side was the case of the Czech Legion. This consisted of Austro-Hungarian citizens of Czech or Slovak origin who, captured by Russia, had volunteered to support the Entente, forming a Czechoslovak Legion in Russia. When the October Revolution broke out, the Legion continued to support the Entente. At its peak in 1918, numbering some 60,000 men, it vehemently opposed the Bolsheviks and seized control of the Trans-Siberian railway, partly in response to the Bolsheviks reneging on their promise to repatriate it to fight for France in the West.[34] Eventually, after playing a major role fighting in conjunction with the Whites in the Russian civil war, and following a deal with the Bolsheviks, the Legion was evacuated via Vladivostok; its members would form the core of the army of the newly independent post-war Czechoslovakia. Overall, however, captor states were largely unable to 'turn' prisoners of war. Indeed, it is significant that only ethnic minorities were considered for such targeting. Prisoners ethnically from the majority belligerent nationalities were increasingly perceived as racial enemies, representatives of their nation-state in arms, and also as citizen-soldiers, rather than forced conscripts or mercenaries, and thus honour-bound to remain loyal to their own side, in contrast to earlier European conflicts.

Ultimately few prisoners escaped, were exchanged or changed sides; the majority remained in captivity until the end of the war and, in many cases, even after hostilities had ended. In the East, after the signing of the Brest-Litovsk Treaty, it proved impossible to repatriate all Central Power

33 Jones, 'Imperial captivities', p. 176. 34 Rachamimov, *POWs and the Great War*, p. 115.

prisoners from Russia, with many trapped by the chaos of the civil war. Those who returned were suspected of Bolshevism, often with good reason: returning prisoners played a significant role in disseminating communism in Hungary; Bela Kun was a former prisoner of war. While Allied prisoners returned from Germany rapidly in late 1918, released under the terms of the Armistice, German prisoners remained in British and American captivity until mid 1919 and in French captivity until 1920, retained by France as human reparations to help reconstruct the war-devastated regions. The most difficult repatriation was that of Russian prisoners from Germany and Austria-Hungary, many of whom were shot by the Bolsheviks upon their return or abandoned at the Russian border by their captor states, with no means of transport or food for the journey into Russia. There was also no agreement on what to do with those Russian prisoners who no longer wished to return home due to the revolution; indeed, France even interned the volunteer Russian brigades that had fought for it, in camps, effectively turning them into post-war prisoners of war. Prisoners held in far-flung locations such as Japan or Siberia only returned home in 1921 to 1922. Great War captivity was thus as much part of the violent aftershocks of the war as of the war itself. Debates about prisoner-of-war rights also marked this period: Polish mistreatment of Bolshevik Russian prisoners of war during the Polish-Soviet War of 1920 to 1921 outraged the Soviets, as did killings in Finnish prison camps of socialists and communists in the Finnish Civil War of 1919.

After the war, the Allies initially demanded the extradition from Germany of fifty-two suspects for the killing of captured soldiers and 151 suspects for killings and other mistreatment in German camps, 'for prosecution in war crimes trials'.[35] Ultimately, however, only a handful of these cases ever came to court in the Leipzig trials of 1921. Soviet Russia did not pursue punishment for crimes against Russian prisoners held by the Central Powers. The second attempt to respond to the prisoner mistreatment which had occurred in the Great War was the 1929 Geneva Convention on Prisoners of War. The negotiation and agreement of the 1929 Geneva Convention reveals that for post-war contemporaries, the Great War was seen as a caesura – one that required a new global response to radically reimpose humanitarian norms upon prisoner treatment.

Conclusions

The legacy of Great War captivity developments remains widely debated among historians. Some argue that the 1914 to 1918 period showed continuities

35 Horne and Kramer, *German Atrocities, 1914*, App. 4, pp. 448–9.

with the treatment of prisoners of war during the wars of the late nineteenth century, while others see the Great War as initiating precedents for forms of prisoner mistreatment that would later burgeon into the worst horrors of Second World War captivity. It seems likely that certain key trends did serve as precedents: in particular, the development of prisoner-of-war labour companies at or near the front, which blurred the distinction between the prisoner and the soldier labourer, with the prisoner increasingly integrated into the captor army and seen as an expendable military forced labour resource on the battlefield, undermining pre-war international law; the cult of the modern home front prisoner-of-war camp as a technological scientific advance; and the increasing racialisation of how prisoners of war were viewed by contemporary societies which sought to identify the captured enemy in racial terms, with anthropological studies carried out in some camps in Germany, Austria-Hungary and, on at least one occasion, in Britain. The camp by the end of the First World War was increasingly becoming a site of Foucauldian social engineering – a location where men were segregated, educated, observed and subject to hygienic controls and inspection as well as technological innovation. The home front captivity systems that developed, with their sophisticated exploitation of prisoner labour and cult of 'modernisation' of the camp, normalised the idea of mass wartime incarceration in belligerent states.

However, these precedents were still on a limited scale in 1914 to 1918. Most prisoners of war survived Great War captivity to return home. Humanitarian efforts were substantial and largely respected by belligerents. Prisoners of war taken captive wounded on the Western Front were given medical treatment. And, although they had little effect, belligerent states continued to try to agree bilateral exchange agreements throughout the war that were constructed on humanitarian terms: prisoners who were very ill, badly disabled, suffering from depression or over the age of 48 were all categories who at various points in the conflict were defined as eligible for exchange. Moreover, the increasingly racialised view of captive ethnicities in popular cultural discourse did not have a significant impact on state policy: policies of privileging specific prisoner ethnicities were grounded in a state's realpolitik strategic interest, not in pure ideological racial discrimination. Thus, ultimately, while the Great War set key precedents, these had a limited impact in 1914 to 1918. It was only with the later rise of totalitarian regimes that the true horrific potential of some of the Great War innovations in captivity would become clear.

PART III

*

THE SINEWS OF WAR

Introduction to Part III

JAY WINTER AND JOHN HORNE

The economic and social history of the First World War was marked by the unprecedented role played by the state in the production of munitions and arms for the front and essential supplies for the civilian populations. In this effort, the Allies were better able to distribute scarce goods and resources as between military and civilian claimants. To a degree, this was due to favourable factor endowments and to the worldwide network of shipping which, despite submarine warfare, brought supplies to the Allied war effort in substantially greater quantities than to the Central Powers. But the Allied economic advantage was also due to the strength of their blockade, and the greater degree to which military needs were met without sacrificing the well-being of the civilian populations for which the soldiers were fighting. After Russia withdrew from the war, it was evident that the democracies were better able to manage the difficult task of waging industrialised war than the autocratic Central Powers.

The chapters in this section show the enormous strain under which war economies were placed on both sides. The massive military mobilisation required huge shifts in the skill and sexual composition of the labour force of every combatant nation. The cities, like the agrarian hinterlands beyond them, became feminised. Women pulled ploughs and drove trams, and found ways to compensate for the loss of manpower and animal power. The re-gearing of economic effort to wartime conditions was an astonishing achievement, though after three years of war, anger at inequalities of sacrifice and profiteering appeared everywhere. What is astonishing is not that some war economies broke down, but that others survived the imposition on them of crushing targets of production and sixty-plus hour work-weeks.

Everywhere, the state's role politicised economic problems, ensuring that the inevitable social tensions of wartime would take on an ominous political character. For each side retained the loyalty of its population only as long as food supplies were maintained. In this respect, the advantage of the Allies was undeniable. For the Central Powers, defeat on the home front was just as decisive as defeat on the battle front in determining the outcome of the war. This section tells the story as to how this was so.

12

War economies

BARRY SUPPLE

In the economic historiography of the modern world, the Great War is frequently seen as a great transformation – destabilising the global economy, transforming the balance of international economic and financial power, and radically changing the economic and social role of the state.

Such trends certainly characterised twentieth-century history and were clearly related to the destructive upheavals of 1914 to 1918. At the same time, however, they must be seen in a longer perspective. On the one hand, some of the relevant institutional and geopolitical shifts – the growth of large-scale capitalist enterprises, the need for governments to respond to an assertive labour movement and the welfare needs of a restless working class, the presence of international instability and the emergence of the United States as a world economic power – were already prefigured in the world before 1914. On the other hand, the potential embodied in wartime innovations and expectations did not always endure, as peace brought a revival of orthodoxy in economic and financial policy and in government and business institutions – at least until the pressure for far-reaching social and economic change emerged again when global recession and then renewed war struck in the 1930s.

Nevertheless, the global economy did enter a new and dramatically destabilised stage after the war. Instability and disruption, together with chronic depression, although certainly not unknown in the late nineteenth and very early twentieth centuries, attained crippling levels of intensity. And perhaps the most important root of these tragic processes lay in the material destruction and financial and economic dislocations of 1914 to 1918.[1]

The war itself therefore had a substantial and abrupt influence on economic performance and global stability. It also impinged on institutional

1 Barry Eichengreen, *Golden Fetters: The Gold Standard and the Great Depression, 1919–1939* (Oxford University Press, 1992).

arrangements and attitudes, although its impact at these levels was more ambiguous. The normal, market-based operations of private-enterprise capitalism were subsumed by the state into war effort and mobilisation, but the basic economic system, and the dominance of big business, survived the conflict and essentially regained power and influence. At the same time, however, while (outside the Soviet Union) business institutions regained something of their pre-war role after 1918, over the longer run the war helped re-shape the course of world economic and social history and, therefore, the evolution of capitalist institutions.

Hence, no matter how much the post-war political economy of the world's leading nations had been partially anticipated before 1914, nor how enthusiastically governments and business attempted to return to the economic arrangements of the pre-war world, the nature of the war and the ideological and state reactions to it give it a prominent place in the evolution of political and economic structures and thinking.

The scale and perceptions of war

The war of 1914 to 1918 was an unprecedented economic event. Earlier conflicts had loomed large in their time and place. But even compared with the American Civil War – the first modern industrial war – the Great War was extraordinary in its intensity, geographic scope, and the mustering of men and wealth to an extent not hitherto known.

The likely impact of war had been seriously considered before 1914 as it became clear that a major international conflict was possible. Even so, the imagination of most observers had rarely envisaged the nature and extent of the problems that were to arise. One view was that the global economic system was so delicately balanced that large-scale military conflict might provoke universal losses and be economically irrational for victors as well as the defeated.[2] Some analysts, like the German military commander, Count von Schlieffen, even thought that prolonged wars 'are impossible in an age when the existence of the nation is founded upon the uninterrupted continuation of trade and industry . . . A strategy of exhaustion cannot be conducted where the maintenance of millions requires the expenditure of

2 This was the argument of Norman Angell in *The Great Illusion* (London: Heinemann, 1910) – although this was frequently misinterpreted as the view that war was therefore impossible. See Martin Caedel, *Living the Illusion: Sir Norman Angell, 1872–1967* (Oxford University Press, 2009), p. 2.

billions'[3] – an argument which, when combined with the fact that Germany's prospective enemies would have a long-run superiority in resources, led to the advocacy of a short war: 'we must try to overthrow the enemy quickly and then destroy him'.[4]

That view lay behind the German strategy in 1914 – to take the initiative in the West and overcome French resistance in a matter of weeks. And it was the failure of that assault which meant that the outcome of the war would be determined by the relative economic strengths of nations.

What most observers failed to foresee was that the reality of modern manufacturing production and mass conscription might lock the combatants into a prolonged and costly stalemate without the military means of resolving or the ability to abandon it. This had profound implications for the economics of the war. The prolonged immobilisation of mass armies in the battlefield led to insatiable demands for labour and munitions. And these involved grave threats to the war effort if the allocation of resources were left to competition. The market became the enemy of national survival.

The need for utterly unprecedented supplies of munitions was illustrated within a few weeks of the outbreak of hostilities. The German armies, for example, expended more munitions daily in the Battle of the Marne (5 to 12 September 1914) than they had during the ten months of the entire Franco-Prussian War (1870 to 1871).[5] The French found that their dependence on shell production was some ten times their pre-war estimate.[6] And in Britain, whereas pre-war planners had estimated that the first six months of a major war would necessitate the production of 162,000 rounds of 18-pounder shrapnel ammunition, by January 1915 that was the *monthly* total.[7] Indeed, a near-crippling shortfall of artillery shells in the spring of 1915 was to be a critical factor in the beginning of very far-reaching interventions of the British Government in the wartime economy.[8]

3 Gerald Feldman, *Army, Industry, and Labor in Germany, 1914–1918* (Providence, RI and Oxford: Berg, 1992), p. 6. [NB: there are some unimportant wording differences in his use of the same quotation in 'Mobilizing economies for war', in Jay Winter *et al.*, (eds.), *The Great War and the Twentieth Century* (New Haven, CT: Yale University Press, 2000), p. 169.]

4 Hew Strachan, *The First World War*, vol. 1, *To Arms* (Oxford University Press, 2001), p. 1008.

5 Roger Chickering, *Imperial Germany and the Great War, 1914–1918* (Cambridge University Press, 1998), p. 35.

6 Eric Hobsbawm, *Age of Extremes* (London: Abacus, 1995), p. 45.

7 David French, 'The rise and fall of "business as usual"', in Kathleen Burk (ed.), *War and the State: The Transformation of British Government, 1914–1919* (London: Allen & Unwin, 1982), p. 12.

8 Below, p. 696.

More generally, severe imbalances quickly emerged between demand and supply for a wide range of war materials and civilian goods. And to that extent it seemed possible that pre-war pessimists might have been right in doubting the ability of modern economic systems to cope with the priorities of a major war. But it also became apparent that they were wrong in not anticipating that even a vast continent-wide conflict could be sustained, however painfully – first, by adaptations of those systems and, secondly, by the levels of economic development and productive capacity already achieved. The war demonstrated that the potential for the prolonged concentration of resources and attention on war efforts had been underestimated.

National statistics for the early twentieth century are necessarily approximate, but indicate the startling impact of the war on the role of the state. Between 1913 and 1918, government shares of gross domestic product (GDP) rose from about 10 per cent to between 50 and 53 per cent in France and Germany, from 8 to 35 per cent in the United Kingdom, and from just under 2 per cent to just under 17 per cent in the case of the United States (which, of course, entered the war late and was relatively much wealthier).[9] In more human terms, whereas the standing armies of the belligerents and their overseas possessions had been less than 6 million in August 1914, the total mobilised by November 1918 was about 66 million.[10] Expending resources and marshalling manpower to this extent, governments were bound to assume much more explicit roles in the organisation and management of economic activity.

The absolute size and actual performance of different economies were obviously relevant to the course and outcome of the war. In November 1914, for example, the combined GDP of the United Kingdom, France and Russia exceeded that of their opponents, Germany, Austria-Hungary and the Ottoman Empire, by about 55 per cent. In terms of performance, the German GDP fell to roughly 82 per cent of the 1913 level for most of the war; Austria's averaged about 75 per cent of its pre-war level; and the UK economy, after an initial dip, actually grew and by 1918 stood at about 14 per cent above its pre-war level. Admittedly, France and Russia had much worse experiences,

9 Stephen Broadberry and Mark Harrison, *The Economics of World War I* (Cambridge University Press, 2005), p. 15.

10 Kevin D. Stubbs, *Race to the Front: The Material Foundations of Coalition Strategy in the Great War* (London: Praeger, 2002), Table 2.1.

but the balance of economic strength – especially with the entry of the United States – remained firmly on the side of the Allies.[11]

Beyond such aggregates, the economic history of the war was characterised by multiple transformations – of the mechanisms that allocated labour and capital, of traditional market arrangements for production and distribution, and of the established role of the state and interest groups. As a result, the very sophistication of industrial systems which had persuaded some people that large-scale hostilities were almost impossible, enabled the belligerents to sustain 'total' warfare for years on end.

Nevertheless, the cost was enormous and the process could not be maintained indefinitely. Russia (the least economically sophisticated and the worst organised of the principal belligerents) was the first casualty. Dependent on its allies for military supplies and finance almost from the outset, it began to collapse in 1916 and was brought to its knees in 1917 as economic disaster interacted with social discontent. The Austro-Hungarian Empire disintegrated under the strain of conflict; and after three years of vast effort, even the stability of mighty Germany was undermined. Indeed, in the absence of the United States' entry into the war, and its contributions of loans, men, munitions and civilian goods, the economic autonomy of France and possibly even the United Kingdom might have been threatened. Hence, although those who took a pessimistic view of the possibility of prolonged conflict were wrong about the war as it was actually experienced, they might ultimately have been proved right if hostilities had lasted much longer – just as (at another level) they were proved right in terms of indirect outcomes. Nevertheless, from the present viewpoint they undoubtedly underestimated the potential of industrial, political and social systems to undertake the huge productive efforts needed for massive conflicts. In the words of the General Editor of the History of the War sponsored by the Carnegie Endowment for International Peace, the war released:

> complex forces of national life, not only for the vast process of destruction but also for the stimulation of new capacities for production . . . This new economic activity, which under normal conditions of peace might have been a gain to society, and the surprising capacity exhibited by the belligerent nations for enduring long and increasing loss – often while presenting the

11 Broadberry and Harrison, *Economics of World War I*, Tables 1.1, 1.2, 1.4. The entry of the United States into the war in 1917 completely overshadowed the exit of Russia. When the United States joined the Allies, its GDP was more than twice that of the United Kingdom at the outset of the war.

> outward semblance of new prosperity – made necessary a reconsideration of the whole field of war economics.[12]

This chapter is primarily concerned with those 'war economics' in terms of the relationships between governments, markets and business associated with the mobilisation of vast resources and manpower, the creation and allocation of the 'new capacities for production', and the uncertain outcomes of economic and institutional change over the long run.

The immediate impact of war

The Great War's insatiable appetite for men and resources had almost immediate consequences for markets and mechanisms of supply. Traditionally, governments had acquired resources for war through a mixture of commercial purchases and state-owned factories. In this mix, commercial enterprises remained essential. They supplied almost all the uniforms, food, transport and accommodation needed by the forces, as well as the raw materials and intermediate products (chemicals, fuel, iron and steel) needed by the state or the private firms which produced war munitions. It was this situation which first forced governments into an often reluctant relationship with private business. Markets alone – whether for military or civilian goods, raw materials or final or intermediate products, capital or labour, transport services or investment funds – could not make effective contributions to war efforts without the intervention of official agencies, concerned with the continuity and costs of essential goods. This was the case even though, as happened almost universally, the resulting interventions needed the cooperation of the businessmen who were most closely involved in profit-seeking in those markets in peacetime.

In any case, the sheer scale of the war swamped the public sector of munitions production. (By 1918, for example, barely 18 per cent of France's 1.65 million munitions workers were public employees.[13]) But even private munitions factories needed extensive official oversight, while governments could not ignore the private supply of railways and shipping services, coal and steel, chemicals and metal products, textiles and food. All needed some degree

12 James T. Shotwell, Preface to Edward M. H. Lloyd, *Experiments in State Control at the War Office and the Ministry of Food* (Oxford: Clarendon Press, Carnegie Endowment for International Peace, Economic and Social History of the World War, 1924), p. v.

13 For the German and French statistics, see: Feldman, *Army, Industry, and Labor*, p. 58; and Gerd Hardach, 'Industrial mobilization in 1914–1918: production, planning and ideology', in Patrick Fridenson (ed.), *The French Home Front, 1914–1918* (Providence, RI: Berg, 1992).

of management if shortages or excessive costs were not to undermine the flow of essential supplies to armies and civilians.

Of course, it took time and experience, even for governments which were reasonably effective, to tackle the multiple aspects of the process of economic supply.[14] Officialdom was led from one function to another: from coordinating the supply of raw material and intermediate products to the control of transport and distribution; from recruiting soldiers to the allocation of manpower between fighting and producing; from dealing with shortages of strategic output to a direct concern with the processes of manufacturing and services; from responding to scarcity-induced profiteering, wage inflation and bottlenecks in labour supply to a more interventionist labour policy and price- and wage- and profit-determination.

These interventions were in the main ad hoc and responsive. State initiatives were piecemeal reactions to economic, and ultimately social, problems as they emerged. And although they were most often adopted with a sensitivity to existing market arrangements and business interests, it soon became clear that war on this scale meant that none of the essential economic processes (production, distribution, consumption) could be based solely on the operations of traditional economic mechanisms. Decentralised markets and price mechanisms could not coordinate supplies according to national and military priorities. Market incentives and opportunities had to be amended and supplemented in order to attain 'non-economic' (or, rather, non-profit) ends. Change had to occur not only in the ways in which governments marshalled resources, but also (and as a consequence) in the structures, operations and outlook of businessmen and workers, and their relationships with the state.

The wartime readjustment of inherited relationships between government institutions and private interests was perhaps most apparent in the markets for and organisation of labour supply and material production, supply and distribution. But the scale and necessities of the war also had a far-reaching impact on national fiscal and monetary policies, and on the institutional and ideological development of trade unions and labour movements. These receive detailed consideration in other chapters of this study.[15] However,

14 Not all states were capable of even modest effectiveness. Thus, the Russian system was unable to arrange for the systematic reordering of production or the management of its transport network, with the result that in terms of military and civilian supply, its performance was disastrous. See Michael T. Florinsky, *The End of the Russian Empire* (New Haven, CT: Yale University Press, Carnegie Endowment for International Peace, Economic and Social History of the World War, 1931).

15 See Chapters 13 and 16 of this volume.

given the central role of private financial activity in market capitalism, it is worth mentioning three aspects of wartime financial management.

First, the fact that government expenditure rose to between some 40 and 60 per cent of the national income of the principal European powers necessitated substantial increases in both public borrowing and taxes. These had far-reaching effects on the performance of and situation in the participant countries during the war. But they also shaped an inheritance of unrealistic post-war expectations and painful policies, while the inability to return to pre-war levels of taxes and debt meant that the war was the platform from which government fiscal policy emerged as an integral aspect of economic activity and development.[16]

The second notable aspect of wartime finance was the need to ensure that private investment (the raising of capital) was managed so as to focus on the creation of assets according to official wartime priorities. Capital markets therefore came under unprecedented control, or at least influence, by governments.

Thirdly, the imminence and then the formal outbreak of war in the late summer of 1914 so threatened the stability of monetary, equity and currency markets that massive state intervention was unavoidable. The gold standard was abandoned; stock markets were closed; rates of interest rose dramatically; and temporary moratoria were declared on the payment of bills of exchange. Such interventions, although unprecedented in degree, were hardly surprising or revolutionary. Market institutions and traditional policies could not maintain stability in the new circumstances. But financial markets have always deferred to the state and, within limits, welcome its intervention as soon as their stability and systemic profitability are threatened. Hence, after August 1914, financial and fiscal interventions by government were less contentious than the departures from 'traditional' systems and relationships in the 'real' economy of the markets for goods and service, labour and entrepreneurship.

Initial manpower needs and their impact

The basic resource for any war is manpower – and for most modern warfare, manpower in huge numbers. This presented few immediate problems in 1914.

16 Even in the United States, where government expenditure was a lower proportion of national income, national debt rose dramatically from $1 billion in 1915 to $20 billion in 1920, and post-war taxes were never to be less than five times the pre-war level. See David M. Kennedy, *Over Here: The First World War and American Society* (New York: Oxford University Press, 2004), p. 112.

In July, Russia had conscripted almost 4 million men in anticipation of the conflict (it ultimately mobilised some 15 million). In Britain, 300,000 men volunteered in August 1914 (and a further 700,000 by the end of the year). France mobilised 2.9 million men in the first two weeks of August, Germany some 3.8 million in the first month.[17] And the number of combatants continued to mount into the tens of millions over the next four years, as military necessity interacted with demographic change.

But in successfully mobilising so many men, the principal belligerents soon encountered the fundamental problem of economics – the allocation of scarce resources between alternative uses. As armies sucked up manpower, so they drained civilian production and services of their labour force. The inverse link between recruitment and production was most immediately apparent in the mass movement of skilled or essential labour out of strategic industries. In Britain's coal-mining industry, for example, some 250,000 men, or 20 per cent of the workforce (40 per cent of those aged 29 to 38), joined the army in the first year of the war. France and Germany experienced comparable diversions, with a critical scarcity of labour as a crisis of munitions supply emerged in the autumn of 1914.[18]

Unexpectedly, shortages of goods proved more immediately pressing than shortages of soldiers, and labour scarcities rather than the anticipated unemployment became national problems. Hence, the British authorities now attempted to dissuade miners from volunteering; and in both France and Germany industrialists, under pressure from the state to increase munitions production, brought irresistible counter-pressure on their governments to restrict recruitment and recall soldiers to the factory. In France, industrialists themselves were even empowered to recall men from front-line units; and by the end of 1915, against the protests of the generals, about 500,000 former soldiers had been brought back to the French munitions industries.[19]

These resource problems were bound up with the war's grand strategy. Failing to deliver a decisive blow, Germany had to organise its economy to a long war of attrition. And in Britain, the concept of 'business as usual' had to be abandoned together with the erroneous assumption that the country

17 Jay M. Winter, *The Great War and the British People* (London: Macmillan, 1985), p. 30; Arthur Fontaine, *French Industry during the War* (New Haven, CT: Yale University Press, 1926), pp. 29–30; Stubbs, *Race to the Front*, pp. 34–8. In the relatively short period of the United States' participation in the war (between the spring of 1917 and the Armistice in November 1918), it mobilised almost 4 million men, of whom about half were in France at the end of the hostilities. Kennedy, *Over Here*, p. 169.

18 Feldman, *Army, Industry, and Labor*, pp. 64–5.

19 Hardach, 'Industrial mobilization', p. 61.

could fight a major war by relying on its maritime power, economic strength and subsidies to the economies and land forces of its allies. Once it was recognised that Britain needed a large army, the distorting tension between the need for soldiers and the need for workers demanded government attention and oversight. Hence, as with all the major European powers, some control of economic activity by the state was an inevitable consequence of the movement of millions of men into the armed forces. The fact was that competitive markets in goods could not achieve the desirable levels of production or the adequate distribution of essential products to the military as well as the civilian sectors of the economy.[20] Conflict had become 'total war', and for all belligerents that implied the need to oversee priorities and to control or at least influence production, distribution and labour supplies.

Distribution, supply and coordination

Although manpower was ultimately the most sensitive issue of wartime political economy, commodity production, supply and distribution, and collateral issues of prices and profits, were also subject to significant official interventions in conventional markets and business activity.

One urgent candidate for such intervention was in transport. As early as 1871, the British Government had provided for state control or even the nationalisation of railways in the event of war. And on 4 August 1914, the day Britain declared war, the government took control of the nation's thirteen regional rail networks. Anticipating other wartime interventions, the new institution was a hybrid: authority lay with the government, but the execution lay with the businessmen who had been associated with the controlled enterprises: the wartime British rail network was managed by a board consisting of the general managers of the constituent companies. Pre-war profits were guaranteed, competition ceased, there were no charges for official traffic and passenger traffic was radically curtailed. As so often happened, oversight had to be associated with gestures towards the rewards of, as well restrictions on, business and labour. Control depended on cooperation, and cooperation had to be purchased. Even so, it was sometimes lacking: attempts to introduce a national scheme to pool the country's 1.4 million privately owned coal wagons and rationalise the distribution of coal were handicapped by the

20 The extent to which the recruitment of men outpaced the acquisition of goods for their support even in the short run is indicated by the fact that the initial volunteers for the British army were asked to bring their own blankets and toiletries to their induction camps. Lloyd, *Experiments in State Control*, p. 1.

fragmentation of ownership and bargaining pressures and resistance from railway and coal-mine companies.[21]

Unified control of transport proved even more problematic in Germany. For one thing, the various states administered their publicly owned railways separately, and the patchwork system proved significantly more difficult to coordinate than did the British network – especially given Germany's size, its multiple war fronts and the dispersed geography of its manufacturing. The problem was aggravated by the diversity of central organisations (the War Office, the Field Railway Service, the Ministry of Public Works). And it was in large part because of mounting crisis in transport that Germany encountered serious and threatening disruptions of coal. Even when the transport situation eased in the spring of 1917, the problem of inadequate coal supplies remained.[22] In the United States, supply bottlenecks and confusion led to the nationalisation of the rail network. And the anarchic disruption of Russia's railway system played an important part in the collapse of its war effort.

Allowing for the differences in organisation, comparable – indeed, more extensive – measures were introduced to control merchant shipping in the two principal maritime nations (the United Kingdom and the United States). The United States provided for this eventuality a year before it entered the war, and Britain imposed controls in 1917, as the German submarine campaign mounted. In Britain, freight rates, profits, cargoes and the movement of ships were now matters of 'official' decision. Licensing and the control of routes ensured that the distances and time involved in maritime transport were minimised: exports were curtailed and essential goods and routes were given priority irrespective of the costly need to use government credit to make 'uneconomic' commercial arrangements possible.[23] The state assumed power in return for adequate (many said more than adequate) financial compensation to ship-owners. And, as happened with the railways, where only those with a direct economic interest had the necessary managerial expertise, shipping interests naturally played a vital role in the new regimes.

Moreover, intervention in transport was not always restrictive: there were potential business advantages in the new oversight: profit levels were guaranteed; the control of freight rates was frequently welcomed by businesses (especially shippers of coal and agricultural goods) which had to use transport

21 Barry Supple, *The History of the British Coal Industry*, vol. IV, *1913–1946: The Political Economy of Decline* (Oxford University Press, 1987), p. 90.

22 Feldman, *Army, Industry, and Labor*, pp. 254–66.

23 Charles Ernest Fayle, *The War and the Shipping Industry* (London: Humphrey Milford, 1927), pp. 276 ff.

systems; and railway companies welcomed a cap on costs, even if the freight rates they could charge were also limited.

As far as international transport was concerned, national efforts were supplemented by international cooperation. In shipping, for example, confronted by huge losses of Allied shipping in 1917, the Allies established the Allied Maritime Transport Committee, and a parallel Executive, which (following the lead of the Allied Wheat Executive) allocated shipping to routes and cargoes, thereby controlling virtually all traded goods and materials on a global scale. 'National control and market forces were suspended simultaneously.'[24] On land on the continent, transport and the supply and allocation of crucial commodities (coal and wheat, for example) were also coordinated by official committees.

In every sphere of transport, however, official policy criteria were mediated by committees of businessmen, and the resulting market structures were managed privately.

Similar, or even more explicit, examples of market replacement re-shaped commodity trade. There, shortages and the threat to national priorities led to much more direct official intervention in 'normal' commercial arrangements. Yet in these areas, too, representatives of private enterprise had to play a central role in that intervention. Nor was the issue confined to the supply of finished goods. The manufacturers of shells, guns, uniforms, sandbags or tents were *themselves* dependent on others for the supply of iron and steel, semi-fabricated goods, coal, chemicals, jute, cotton, wool, etc. And it soon emerged that private market systems might well divert such supplies to higher bidders and other users than firms contracted to supply governments. Hence, governments were drawn into a concern not only with the output of final products for war activity, but with the availability and cost of the raw materials and intermediate goods needed to produce that output.

Significantly, private suppliers of finished goods were not averse to some oversight of the price and availability of intermediate supplies. For, by mitigating scarcities and high prices, that could ensure that they could continue in production (and profit). This situation diluted the ideological overtones and eased the process by which the state moved to assume a far-reaching role in market mechanisms. As a result, the new arrangements were less adversarial or ideologically fraught than might have been predicted: while governments were dependent on business expertise to help them in their

24 Frank Trentmann, *Free Trade Nation* (Oxford University Press, 2008), pp. 259–60.

new role, businessmen recognised that their supplies and orderly profit-making were also dependent on official intervention.

The initial reaction was most systematic in Germany,[25] which, because of its economic geography and relative strategic isolation and susceptibility to naval blockade, was more vulnerable to interruptions of industrial supplies. It also had a strong tradition of business collaboration, especially in heavy industry. As a result, market forces in important German industries were circumvented by collaboration between public and private interests. Within a few days of the outbreak of war, the Prussian War Ministry, which took the lead in German war planning and management, discovered that there was less than six months' supply of raw materials in stock. It therefore created a mechanism for the central control of their acquisition and distribution. This was the Raw Materials Section (*Kriegsrohstoffgesellschaften* or 'KRA') of the ministry, to which were subordinated a series of more specialised government-sponsored private stock companies known as War Raw Material Corporations and War Boards, charged with the actual fixed-price purchase, storage and use of raw materials. Although overseen by relevant ministries, they were quasi-independent and self-governing. Ultimately, there were some 200 of such corporations (each identified with a specific branch of industry, and each offering the government a single point of contact and negotiation for its acquisitions programmes). Investment in them facilitated profitable access to materials and contracts for private companies. Open competition was an early casualty of the war.

Significantly, the initiative for this system came from business itself: its proponent was Walther Rathenau, the chief executive of a giant industrial enterprise, AEG. And the authorities and corporations which managed it were mostly representative of the large companies which were customers for the very materials being managed – chemicals, metals, cotton and other textiles, rubber, etc. Hence, in a manner characteristic of almost all examples of the new political economy of control and regulation, the outcome was far from the minatory control, let alone repression, of business by the state. Rather, it harnessed business experience and expertise to oversee the management of markets. In effect, it was a form of administered capitalism, which aimed at greater continuity of industrial supply, and possibly more secure profit margins, than (at least in the circumstances) purely market forces could ensure. Supplies were to be rationed according to strategic need rather than through the price system, profits were guaranteed, competition was avoided, and

25 Feldman, *War, Industry, and Labor*, pp. 41 ff.

Germany resisted (at least in the initial years) any substantial top-down mobilisation of resources, preferring industrial self-government for as long as possible.[26]

In France, too, industry was adapted to war needs – in the main through private initiatives. There, the government organised an industrial conference in September 1914 and offered subsidies to boost productive capacity for munitions firms. (In 1915, it was to create a fully fledged Under-Secretariat of State for Artillery and Munitions – a parallel move to the United Kingdom's contemporaneous creation of a Ministry of Munitions.[27]) At the same time, however, in response to raw material shortages and changing markets, enterprises in different branches of the emerging war economy themselves moved to coordinate their activities. They formed independent associations to subcontract munitions orders. At first these groups proliferated, but the system was ultimately rationalised and the common interests of munitions manufacturers came to be represented by a central committee. Competition was substantially diluted. Moreover, as happened universally, when industrialists accepted that they would now have to produce to official order, they did so in return for longer contracts and higher prices for their products.[28]

In Britain, the government's initial reactions to the deficiencies of the market was less concerned with heavy industry. Direct official involvement with munitions industries came later. Nevertheless, given its tradition of competitive markets, the British example was equally striking. The best-known instance stemmed from the extraordinary demand for uniforms and sandbags in the first months of the war. This drove up prices and led to speculation in the linked markets for the principal intermediate products, primarily jute, as well as for the finished articles themselves. The government's response (managed by the War Office, which was the purchasing authority) was to amend the traditional system of competitive tendering and, in the case of uniforms, to recruit firms profitably involved in manufacture to 'manage' supply, enforce flat-rate prices and divide orders among themselves.

Intervention in Britain was advanced even further early in 1915, when the continued shortage and high price of sandbags led the War Office to requisition supplies at officially fixed prices. More flexible price and margin agreements and controls followed – as did regulatory intervention in

26 Gerald Feldman, 'Mobilizing economies for war', in Jay Winter *et al.*, *Great War*, pp. 168–70.

27 Below, p. 696.

28 Hardach, 'Industrial mobilization', pp. 67–8.

international trade (the import of jute and the export of coal, for example), and the necessary use of commercial firms as agents for the management of trading arrangements that demanded expertise and experience. Schemes for the control and safeguarding of supplies in industries such as boots, leather, linen, wool and food were also introduced. And by February 1916, in an indirect echo of earlier events in Germany, the Army Contracts Department created a 'Raw Materials Section' to sift information and prepare schemes for the control and safeguarding of basic supplies.

The system of control boards and agencies (often involving wholesale purchase of consumer goods) was extended in Britain, for example, to cover sugar, cotton, wheat, meats and fats. And Germany had about forty corporations performing the same function – purchasing and allocating supplies of essential commodities.

The central characteristic of the apparently dramatic changes in government-business relationships during the initial stages of the war led not to a command economy, but to a system of elaborate partnerships with a large degree of officially sanctioned self-regulation. It had become clear that conventional markets and profit incentives would not best serve national economic, let alone strategic, objectives. But it was also clear that those objectives would have to be pursued in conjunction with private interests and the maintenance of private enterprise.

The state and wartime production

Much of the economic activity of governments in the first months of the war could be interpreted as managing markets at one remove. But once the intensity of hostilities mounted, the ever-increasing appetite for war supplies drove some governments *behind* the facade of demand and supply to a more explicit concern with output. And ensuring the continuity of strategic *production* could lead to a much more diffuse socio-economic role for the state: with regard to investment and product development, manufacturing organisation, labour supply, the levels of profits and wages. At the same time, however, the precise role of the state and its relationship with industry varied from country to country.

The vitally important coal-mining industry provides a good example of the extension of government intervention beyond supplies and distribution into production itself in the two principal belligerents.

In Germany, critical difficulties with coal supply had initially led the War Office to establish a Coal Adjustment Bureau in the KRA, advised by a committee of coal producers. But shortages meant that central control was tightened in February 1917 by the appointment of an Imperial Coal Commissar. And in May the War Office secured the release of some 40,000 miners from the front. Even so, the situation was so grave that the government was driven to introduce compulsory plant closures and consolidation in order to economise on the use of coal, as well as to relieve the crippling burden on the transport system.[29] Market forces could not deal with the confusions and shortages implied in such inter-relationships. However imperfectly, the state had to step in.

In the British coal industry, change was provoked by problems of industrial relations rather than a direct imbalance of 'normal' supply and demand. A foretaste of the new dynamic had come early in 1915 with pressure for higher wages in South Wales. In spite of the illegality of the resulting strike, the government felt obliged to enforce an unconditional acceptance by the coal-mine owners of the miners' sweeping demands.[30] Subsequently, further threatening industrial disputes (stemming from wage demands and resentment at high prices and profits) led to official control first of the South Wales coal industry in November 1916, and then, in March 1917, of the nation's entire coal-mining industry. The timing almost precisely matched that of the German moves to a tighter official administration of the industry. In the event, the Coal Control was the largest example of industrial oversight by the state in Britain. Once again, it involved the direct participation of experienced businessmen. In the coal industry, as elsewhere, the new political economy was a departure in terms of structures and mechanisms rather than public power and personnel.[31]

Supply and production problems were more diffuse in the United States. But after it had entered the war in July 1917, Food and Fuel Administrations were created; commodity supplies and prices, together with industrial and agricultural production, trade and investment, were overseen by overarching boards, agencies and committees. At the apex of this system was the War Industries Board, with an autonomous Price Fixing Committee. Priorities and contracts were allocated, and prices controlled. And all involved very substantial business representation. The system also extended to direct intervention in industry, sometimes giving official blessing to wage increases in order to maintain production, and attempting to encourage mass production as well as setting output quotas and allocating raw material supplies. Under

29 Feldman, *Army, Industry, and Labor*, pp. 273–83.
30 Supple, *British Coal Industry*, pp. 62–7. 31 Below, p. 697.

the umbrella of national policy, output in the United States grew enormously during the war – although vast fortunes were also made in the war industries, with apparently only limited restraint by the board, which as a result came under severe criticism.

In British manufacturing more generally, as we have seen,[32] economic policy was determined by the need to abandon the initial strategic assumptions that the country could rely on its naval strength and subsidising allies. By the spring of 1915, it was obvious that the country needed much larger land forces and a more purposeful marshalling of strategic economic activity – especially more focused attention to production in the engineering as well as the coal industry. The proximate cause of direct state intervention in manufacturing industry was a combination of strategic and political pressures, as shortages (especially, but not only, of shells) were exposed on the Western Front. Scarcity of labour had driven up costs and increased the bargaining strengths of the trade unions, while employers were concerned at the enhanced power of their workers and the political pressure on their profits. The politics of ensuring industrial effectiveness for war needs became a balancing act between these forces.

The first systematic manifestation of a new stage in British policy came in March 1915 in the form of the so-called 'Treasury Agreement', with the unions in the munitions and engineering industries. This was designed to ease the shortage of labour by permitting the employment of unskilled workers, including women, and limiting the freedom to strike, in return for a guarantee to return to existing practices after the war and secure some limit on profits. But the agreement proved inadequate and it became necessary to institutionalise controls. Lloyd George's vision of a Ministry of Munitions to extend state control therefore became a reality, and in July 1915 the recently created ministry secured the passage of the Munitions of War Act – which greatly augmented the range of what were now to be 'controlled establishments'. In such firms the supply and mobility of labour were to be strictly regulated, skills were to be 'diluted', strikes and lockouts banned, disputes compulsorily settled and profits limited. In effect, the state now controlled the munitions and related industries – and was therefore involved in decisions about production methods and investment, as well as labour relations. Control was subsequently extended to embrace such activities as aircraft factories and plants for the production of agricultural machinery, sulphuric acid and fuel oils. By early 1918, there were some 20,000 'controlled establishments'.

32 See note 7.

These were extreme measures. But they did not amount to nationalisation, nor even state enterprise. Production still depended on privately employed business experience and expertise, output was still managed by private enterprise, and the limits on profits were generously based on a supplement to the best-performing pre-war years, as chosen by the businesses themselves.

Specific arrangements in other European countries naturally varied, but comparable circumstances orchestrated the emergence of common and familiar themes – notably pressure for an increasing intrusion of governments into decisions about the organisation, investment and location of industry. Russia – where ineffective governance and ambitious businessmen sustained a greater but still inadequate role for private enterprise – was an exception. But more generally governments assumed new and significant roles, which exemplified some common features, which were nevertheless far from constraining on business: a relaxed control of profits, favourable tax treatment of capital investment, and an unavoidable reliance on the principal economic actors, labour as well as business. But the forms and arrangements varied from country to country. In Germany and Italy, industrial firms were given a good deal of latitude in determining contracts and prices. In contrast, in Britain and France representatives of the state had more influence and authority over the terms of supply – although even there, the expertise and experience of businessmen could not be neglected.

Indeed, just as compromise with a new role for the state was recognised by erstwhile defenders of laissez-faire, so compromise with private enterprise in the 'management' of wartime production could extend to those notionally hostile to market capitalism. In France, for example, a crucial role was played by a socialist politician, Albert Thomas, who was appointed Under-Secretary of State in the War Ministry in May 1915, at a time when, as in the United Kingdom, the grave shortage of munitions threatened disaster. Thomas, desperate to increase production, secured the cooperation of labour by acceding to minimum wages and compulsory arbitration, while overseeing the collaboration between government and business, delegating a far-reaching authority to large-scale manufacturers, and resisting pleas for the requisition of factories or even the introduction of controlled establishments along British lines. On the other hand, as the production problems of the war mounted in 1916–17 (a Ministry of Armaments was created in December 1916), he appreciated the political need to expand capacity by fostering investment while restraining profits – and began to articulate the concept of a controlled capitalism, which he argued would help revitalise the post-war French economy.[33]

In Germany, there were disruptive tensions between military and civil interests, but a recognition that the timeless economic problem of allocating scarce resources was no longer susceptible to an acceptable market solution. Intervention was necessary – at the levels of both labour supply and the management of production. Moreover, the debilitating experience of the costs of war were much more manifest. Although Germany succeeded in mobilising about 60 per cent of its national income for the war effort by 1917,[34] by that time the economy was in severe difficulties. The Battle of the Somme in the summer of 1916 had demonstrated Germany's marked inferiority in available resources and the costs and likely duration of hostilities. The army response was to bypass or override the politicians, issue orders directly to manufacturing, and enforce ambitious (and unrealistic) objectives for increased munitions output, while introducing a system of labour control potentially parallel to that devised for military conscription.[35] Further, a War Industries Administration was created to oversee production, prices and priorities through a complex structure that was an enfeebling and tension-dogged compound of military, civil-service, political and industrial interests.[36]

In the event, for all the belligerents (except Russia, where ineptitude was succeeded by massive intervention by the Bolsheviks), the new role of the state in its concern with manufacturing proved relatively transient. And in some cases that role proved nugatory even at the time. In Russia, for example, manufacturers were expected to behave almost autonomously; and in Italy, which created a government post for 'arms and munitions' (June 1915) and a ministry in 1917, the state failed to exercise the far-reaching power that had been laid down. Instead, it relied on businessmen not merely to help with the administration of production, but even to set manufacturing standards and prices. Nor was the Italian war effort much improved by the existence of almost 300 government bodies reporting to different under-secretaries in

33 Alain Hennebicque, 'Albert Thomas and the war industries', in Fridenson, *French Home Front*, pp. 89–132; Pierre-Cyrille Hautcoeur, 'Was the Great War a watershed? The economics of World War I in France', in Broadberry and Harrison, *Economics of World War I*, p. 192.

34 Albrecht Ritschl, 'The pity of peace: Germany's economy and war, 1914–1918 and beyond', in Broadberry and Harrison, *Economics of World War I*, p. 45.

35 Notably in the Patriotic Auxiliary Services Act.

36 Feldman, *Army, Industry, and Labor*, pp. 168 ff.

six different ministries.[37] This was an extreme case. But no country succeeded in coordinating economic activity in any comprehensive way.

War and business structures

The war had manifold influences on business practice and organisation. At one level, the drive to increase productivity, with the blessing of the state, introduced a much more explicit, and economically successful, managerial and technocratic thrust into industry – indeed, into a range of economic activities. The application of science and scientific method increased in importance. Improved techniques and organisation were adopted.

At the same time, although the war introduced unprecedented measures of state intervention, it also resulted in an increase in the authority and, frequently, the power of business interests. As has been seen, the adaptation of market capitalism to wartime ends was in the main managed by various institutional forms of government-business collaboration. Officialdom used – indeed, depended on – business expertise and therefore businessmen. The inevitable outcome was to strengthen the position (and often the profits) of commercial companies as well as individuals.

There were few alternatives. In the circumstances of 1914 to 1918, regulation necessitated extensive cooperation between government principals and business agents. Profits, commercial position and investment funds had to be guaranteed. Irrespective of any ideological sympathies for business interests on the part of those in political power, the state could not impose its will without ensuring that businessmen were prepared to cooperate. Hence, in spite of the widespread introduction of special taxes on the high profits of wartime, a substantial issue of 'profiteering' remained to muddy the political waters and disturb the relationships between governments and trade unions.

'Institutionalising the inside track', or 'regulatory capture', in later American phrases – that is, recruiting interest groups into regulatory mechanisms to which they are subject – was the price that had to be paid for mitigating scarcity and the profits of scarcity while ensuring continuity of production. And this reflected and intensified a particular pattern of business enterprise and association. The very nature of control and the oversight and allocation of supplies in Germany and France, for example, gave an even more pre-eminent role to the large-scale companies which already occupied leading positions

37 Francesco Galussi and Mark Harrison, 'Italy at war, 1915–1918', in Broadberry and Harrison, *Economics of World War I*, pp. 279–80, 295.

in the principal industrial sectors. Their needs and market positions made them indispensable in the regulatory systems that were hurriedly devised. And this, in turn, encouraged the growth of large firms and further collaboration between big firms.[38]

The political economy of war therefore involved a balance (and by no means always an equitable balance) of private and public interests. And the outcome was a new distribution of power – or, more accurately, the solidification of evolving nodes of power and influence. For the evolution of business structures in 1914 to 1918 was in large part rooted in the organisational experience of the late nineteenth and early twentieth centuries, when large-scale firms were beginning to dominate entire industrial sectors. This was especially the case with Germany, but was also exemplified in the United States and to some extent in the United Kingdom, albeit less so in France, although even there – as in Italy – the national economy emerged from the war with more large-scale firms.[39]

The growth of large corporations and cartels was particularly stimulated by wartime developments in Germany. There, the traditional state encouragement of giant enterprises and the tolerance of cartels converged with the urgent demands for munitions and associated goods. The results were the strengthening of vast combinations – of which Siemens and AEG were pre-eminent examples – in the heavy industries (electro-technical, chemical, iron and steel, coal), and the stimulation of similar if new developments in mechanical engineering.[40] More indirectly, the war also generated *concerted* action on production, distribution and prices. It reduced competition and encouraged consultation and coordinated decision-making by individual firms in the same, or even loosely allied, fields. And it therefore opened up at least the possibility not only of enhanced efficiency, but of continuing collusion. These trends were accentuated in the post-war years: by 1922, there were some 1,500 cartels and industrial syndicates in Germany.[41]

38 Perhaps for this reason, not all businessmen welcomed this oversight. Some were excluded from the privileged circles, and few welcomed profit controls.

39 See Alfred D. Chandler, *Scale and Scope: The Dynamics of Industrial Capitalism* (Cambridge, MA: Harvard University Press, 1990), Pt IV; Barry E. Supple (ed.), *The Rise of Big Business* (Aldershot: Edward Elgar, 1992); John F. Godfrey, *Capitalism at War: Industrial Policy and Bureaucracy in France, 1914–1919* (Leamington Spa, UK: Berg, 1987); Galussi and Harrison, 'Italy at war'.

40 Wielfred Feldenkirchen, 'Concentration in German industry, 1870–1939', in Supple, *Big Business*, pp. 474 ff.

41 Jurgen Kocka, *Facing Total War: German Society, 1914–1918* (Leamington Spa and Cambridge, MA: Berg and Harvard University Press, 1984), p. 30.

Another, and more visible, business outcome of government initiative during the war was the creation of more formal trade associations of individual firms. Such associations were obviously concerned with conventional business issues: the management or manipulation of markets, the exchange of technical and commercial information, concerted responses to the actions (or even the existence) of trade unions. But they were also involved in the representation of opinion (and pressure) in the politics of national decision-making. Indeed, governments encouraged the formation of such groupings – as with the Federation of British Industries (1916) – in part to ease the process of cooperation in war production and in part as a counterweight to the enhanced influence of trade unions.[42] But their significance and roles far transcended the needs of wartime production and political persuasion. Companies turned towards more – or even more – collaboration in pursuit of their own long-term business interests. Managed markets and 'control' had given them not only the prospect of greater economic success, but the instructive experience of being active players in economies where the view that the state was going to have a greater role was now widely accepted. Associational activity was also a matter of seeking a counterpoise to what was seen as an accretion of power to labour during, and as a result of, the war. But whatever the origins of such institutional developments, they, too, involved a step away from traditional ideas of competitive market structures.

Economic strains: resources, manpower planning and civilian economy

As the war progressed, it became increasingly apparent that both the weight and the allocation of resources were critical considerations for the prospects of military success. Indeed, in the latter stages of the war, macroeconomic pressures, in the shape of economic crises in supply, manpower and civilian morale, became determining factors. On the Allied side, Russia was an extreme case, even though the aggregate figures of output were not disastrously lower than those of some other belligerents. It was brought low by structural as well as economic factors: inadequate official oversight of manufactured and mining output, the disruption of civil society, rampant inflation and the severe dislocation of the transport network. Weakened by 1916, it was bundled out of the war by the virtual disintegration of its economy

42 Keith Middlemas, *Politics in Industrial Society: The Experience of the British System since 1911* (London: Andre Deutsch, 1979), pp. 112–13.

combined with revolution in the course of 1917. And France, where the industrial sectors had performed reasonably well up to the spring of 1917, subsequently encountered increasingly critical shortages of labour, basic industrial supplies and transport services. However, the Allied cause found adequate compensation in the vast resources of the United States, when it declared war in April.

It was in Germany that the vulnerability of the national economic system was to prove decisive. The Allied superiority in men and war material provoked the army into desperate policies that succeeded in disrupting the war effort even further.[43] By 1917, the country was staggering towards collapse under the weight of blockade, economic exhaustion and the social and political unrest produced by severe food shortages, dislocations in the transport system and the supply of coal and other crucial materials, falling output, and the associated decline in living standards.

But Germany was only the most extreme case of a developed capitalist economy undermined by the prolonged cost of military stalemate. In fact, the war was destroying Europe's economies. And by 1918 the gloomy warnings of the pre-war pessimists about the impossibility of sustaining modern warfare appeared to be justified. However, experience suggested that their pessimism had been misdirected in two important respects: first, because economic and social efforts proved more tenacious than had been predicted; and, secondly, and more importantly, because the basic cause of the undermining of war efforts was not so much the disruption of normal trade and industry and economic structures, as the social and economic strain imposed by the unprecedented scale of the hostilities. The war simply absorbed too many resources.

The war's seemingly insatiable economic appetite led to urgent attempts to control the total allocation of human resources and to alleviate the shortages suffered by an increasingly pressed civilian population, whose despair began to overcome patriotic enthusiasm. Wartime policy had to be extended in two directions. One was the pursuit of overarching government control of *all* manpower. This was exemplified in hitherto liberal Britain by the extreme step of military conscription in 1916, followed by manpower budgeting in 1917 to 1918; and in beleaguered Germany by minatory controls under the Patriotic Auxiliary Services Law passed at the end of 1916 (which, however, reflected confusion and conflict among various authorities, and acceded

43 See note 3.

to pressure from labour unions).[44] The other wartime novelty was the systematic oversight and maintenance of civilian living standards – the circumvention of market forces by price and rent controls, the provision of welfare services, and the allocation and rationing of essentials (coal and basic foods such as bread, meats, fats and sugar).[45] Once again, the necessities of war overcame the inhibitions of free-market ideology.

Political economy

The exigencies of the war enforced a much more 'forward' role for government in production, distribution and the markets for goods and labour. Against this background, there emerged debate about the balance of government (or collaborative) and private economic activity in capitalist societies.[46]

The war obviously produced a variety of institutional departures from the traditional model of market competition. These included: the regulation (and self-regulation) of distribution and supply; price and profit controls; informal and formal collaboration between enterprises; national and international government agencies to coordinate economic activity; bureaucratic decision-making; and negotiated arrangements for working conditions, profits and wages. All of these suggested alternative models for post-war political economy. But in the aftermath of the war few of these models were adopted: they were widely seen as experiments suitable to war, not peace, and in any case their very variety and specificity meant that different interest groups and commentators could be highly selective in their choice of items from the menu of wartime experience. There was little consensus about the political-economy 'lessons' of the war. The core of the conventional model of capitalism survived in a form adapted to its own trends.

Of course, as has been seen, for many businessmen the war indicated the advantages of industrial collaboration and associations, as well as the potential for participating in, and sometimes welcoming, state-initiated regulation. As a result, the events of 1914 to 1918 encouraged the continued growth and legitimation of large-scale enterprises and trade associations – not merely

44 Feldman, *Army, Industry, and Labor*, pp. 197–249. Feldman argues that just as other policies failed to control industrialists' profits, so the compromises of the Auxiliary Services Act strengthened the position of labour and facilitated wage demands.

45 See Jay Winter and Jean-Louis Robert, *Capital Cities at War: Paris, London, Berlin 1914–1919* (Cambridge University Press, 1997).

46 Russia was, of course, a special case – but even there debate flared up as the initial experiments with state control were diluted by the 'New Economic Policy' in 1921.

as a source of immediate profit, but as a means of facilitating cooperation between business and government. And this trend was intensified insofar as innovation or depression persuaded governments of the need to stimulate and control structural change in both new and traditional staple industries. In a fairly narrow range of well-defined areas, ideological inhibitions about state activity, and fundamentalist views of private enterprise, were partially eroded, even though commitments to financial and fiscal orthodoxy remained strong. Corporatism – the pursuit of decisions about economic activity by interactions between groupings of business, labour and the state – emerged as a potential, if unspecific, quasi-collective alternative to the liberal state and economy. It found its most explicit form in the rise of fascism in Italy in the 1920s and Germany in the 1930s.

Wartime thinking about the economic role of the state was only patchily radical. It was, of course, natural that socialist politicians and commentators should interpret the war as a justification for state enterprise. But, apart from the Russian case, 'pure' nationalisation was rarely advocated by those in or near power. In France, Albert Thomas, at the War Ministry, contemplating the wartime collaboration between the state and manufacturing, argued that this experience might be a prelude to 'controlled capitalism' – a system conjoining government and business. But little of such a sweeping proposal survived the war. Most capitalist societies responded along more or less orthodox lines to the macroeconomic vicissitudes that accompanied the peace. The Russian Empire, of course, went its own way from 1917.

On the other hand, during the war itself, there were *some* expressions of unconventional views of the role of the market as a result of wartime experience. In Britain, for example, some unlikely commentators argued that a new basis for state activity might be justified. Thus, the *Economist* advocated a modest degree of collectivism, while *The Times* published articles which entertained the idea of 'one national plan', albeit on a partial basis.[47] And commentators were quick to argue that where profits were generated by reduced competition, the community had some entitlement to a share.[48] Aspects of such conclusions were discussed by 'mainstream' economists – like A. C. Pigou at Cambridge, who could contemplate a more 'forward' role for the state, especially in curbing monopolistic practices and instituting

47 Arthur Marwick, *Britain in the Century of Total War: War, Peace and Social Change, 1900–1967* (London: Bodley Head, 1968), p. 76.

48 This was argued by a Liberal Member of Parliament, Sir Joseph Compton-Rickett, in a chapter on 'Organisation of the national resources', in William H. Dawson (ed.), *After-War Problems* (London: Allen & Unwin, 1917), p. 119.

controls for the protection of consumers.[49] Indeed, on a more general level, some economists argued that the war had made manifest the need and potential for 'social'[50] – i.e., collective – interventions. But little came of these debates, or of liberal arguments in favour of international coordination of trade along wartime lines.[51]

In the event, while there was contemporary debate about government and the economy, the war did little to alter practice, or widely accepted and deeply ingrained views of the economic role of the state in 'normal' circumstances.

On the other hand, while direct economic intervention by the state was broadly avoided, after 1918 governments were more ready to play an indirect role in economic performance by stimulating scientific and technical research, and educational provision. Vital issues of national survival had been raised by the experience of 1914 to 1918, which provided a persuasive precedent for state interventions when – during major wars or, by extension, in a depression or amid global crises – national integrity was under threat. The Great War had brought home the manifest fact that market forces alone could not guarantee the strength or security of the economy and society. As a result, the military potential of a country as well as critical aspects of its well-being came to be identified with the structural balance and performance of its economy. And related to that, it was recognised that fighting a prolonged war with modern technology and on an industrial scale necessitated security of supply of crucial products and strategic materials (food, chemicals, explosives, motor vehicles, aircraft, scientific instruments, etc.).

Sometimes these needs were clear and urgent, and led to official responses almost from the outbreak of war – as when the German Government, moved by the blockade-induced shortages of vital resources, spurred the production of artificial cellulose (essential for munitions) and the process of nitrogen fixation (for agricultural fertilisers); or when the British Government, responding to domestic shortages, established a committee to ensure the supply of chemicals, and then a department to promote scientific and industrial research. In other circumstances, the economic aspects of the national interest were seen to be more general and long term. The issues of competitiveness and strategic industries were discussed, for example, in the conclusions of a

49 Arthur C. Pigou, *The Political Economy of War* (London: Macmillan, 1921), pp. 235–7.

50 John M. Clark, 'The basis of war-time collectivism', *American Economic Review*, 7:4 (1917), pp. 772–90.

51 Frank Trentmann, *Free Trade Nation: Commerce, Consumption and Civil Society in Modern Britain* (Oxford University Press, 2008), pp. 263 ff.

British Government committee on post-war economic policy.[52] Its report hesitantly but significantly argued that government had a role in sustaining Britain's competitive strength (especially vis-à-vis Germany) by facilitating the replacement of 'individualistic methods' by 'cooperation and coordination'; encouraging combinations, especially in 'the more modern branches of industrial production'; and providing targeted support for 'key' or 'pivotal' industries shown to be vulnerable to foreign competition or dependent on foreign origins or 'essential to national safety'. Among other examples, the committee listed synthetic dyes, spelter and tungsten for munitions, magnetos, optical and chemical glass, some drugs and specialist chemicals, and screw gauges. It even contemplated government ownership in extreme cases.

Admittedly, the committee drew back from advocating serious reform in the peacetime economic role of the state. But even modest proposals from such a quarter were unusually radical. They assumed a degree of market failure and envisaged state intervention in business structures as well as advocating a degree of public subsidy for broadly defined strategic industries.[53] And at a more general level, such arguments implied, and ultimately served to justify, government support for scientific research and higher education as well as for industries such as chemicals and drugs, aircraft and specialist motor vehicles, wireless production and agricultural output.

Nevertheless, such endeavours were limited in scope, strictly targeted and explicitly concerned with strategic considerations. And the consequences for the competitive standing of British companies were therefore modest.

Historical perspectives: war, institutions and economic performance

During the Great War, governments sought to allocate national manpower between strategic uses, and to maintain the production and distribution of goods and services in amounts and at prices which would not seriously handicap the war effort or generate political problems among the civilian population. The policies adopted in order to pursue these ends were in many ways imperfect and on the whole restricted in scope and duration. Governments

52 Final report of the committee on commercial and industrial policy after the war (Cd. 9035, 1918, XIII). The committee had been appointed in 1916, and coordinated a network of committees on different industries.

53 The committee also emphasised more traditionally orthodox policies – notably, government encouragement of private savings and investment and the reduction of the burden of taxation.

operated without much prior experience or relevant knowledge, and were in any case reliant on the economic agents they were hoping to regulate, and on interest groups that often saw the war as an opportunity to further and institutionalise their own aims and policies. Perhaps above all they had to try to control and manoeuvre unwieldy and diffused national economies with only rudimentary planning and administrative mechanisms and under the stress of national emergencies.

And yet, bearing in mind the unprecedented extent of these handicaps and the huge strain resulting from the war, the performance of some countries for much of the time was impressive. Until persistent and pervasive pressures began to threaten internal stabilities after three years of mass warfare, the conflict demonstrated the abundance and flexibility that had been attained by the market economies of the West by 1914 – as well as the adaptive potential of political and bureaucratic structures in the more successful economies. Nevertheless, this was far from the 'war socialism' posited by some historians.[54] With the exception of a few examples (notably in some aspects of manpower allocation), such planning tended to be sectoral or industrial rather than general or macroeconomic.

At the other extreme, while state agencies – or state-influenced agencies – were often dominant influences, the wartime experience was far from an example of even an attenuated form of the advocacy of a rather vague 'state capitalism' (although it was the term used by Lenin to describe the New Economic Policy in the USSR). In spite of the extreme nature of the challenges, the resulting instrumental changes were contained within the broad outlines of the existing economic, social and political power structures. Under wartime pressures, and the pressing need to boost production, in most countries those structures proved capable of a degree of systematic improvements in technical and organisational methods – even while suffering from severe shortages of supply and manpower. The essence of capitalism as it had been inherited in 1914 survived and evolved throughout the war – although the form of that survival was not irrelevant to the destabilising forces that threatened to undermine it in the interwar years.

It was, however, still the case that, while hostilities lasted, the Great War had a substantial and unprecedented impact on the structures and control of the economic and business systems of the leading belligerents. The state (most often through the medium, or with the direct help, of business agents) had arrogated a vastly greater share of national output and finances to itself,

54 Stubbs, *Race to the Front*, p. 17.

and assumed an explicit role in markets and production. It had exercised varying degrees of oversight, whether directly or through surrogates, of prices, profits, business structures and labour supply. Governments had also adopted equally unprecedented policies towards manpower planning, even while labour interests – often for the same reasons of expediency that had led to the accommodation of business during the war – were awarded more influence, if only briefly. And in response to wartime needs, social welfare was given greater priority on government agendas.

In sum, the capitalist system had only temporarily accepted state intervention. And insofar as it had adjusted its forms, it did so without substantially changing (and, indeed, in some respects by reinforcing) its core character. The more novel or dramatic transformations of wartime political economy in 1914 to 1918 were therefore not directly carried over into the challenging world of peacetime.[55] Only with the harrowing experience of the Great Depression was the conventional political economy of Western societies brought into serious question.

The war did have some positive consequences: the state extended its support of education and research and development; industrial technology and organisation were advanced; technical industries – synthetic chemistry, aircraft and motor-car manufacture, optics and medical instrumentation and techniques – were encouraged; and productivity through the growing scale of operations was stimulated. Moreover, the Allies had, for a while, fended off the threat of an expansionist Germany. They had done so in large part through the abundance of their resources and economic systems which, although imperfect as well as unfair, just about managed to sustain the terrible stalemates of mass warfare in the early twentieth century.

Nevertheless, the economic balance-sheet was profoundly negative, and victory, quite apart from its cost in terms of the pitiable destruction of human life, was pyrrhic. The draining effort and commitments of the war and the punitive peace imposed on the defeated meant that Germany fell into a mire of profound economic difficulties and vicious political tragedy; the Russian Empire imploded; Austria-Hungary was dismembered; France was profoundly weakened; and the United Kingdom lost its financial pre-eminence and trading strength and entered a prolonged and slow period of imperial twilight and relative economic decline.

55 Such a view depends on perspective and the definition of 'political economy'. Looked at in terms of such measures as the size of government (levels of taxation and expenditure), welfare systems, and overt roles in education and scientific research, the war did indeed generate long-lasting transformations.

More than this, devastation was global as well as national. The costs and material destruction of war and the peace settlement, the huge overhang of public debt, and the consequent dislocation of trade, money and capital flows – all helped to destroy the bases of the pre-war global economic and financial system.[56] Aggravated by economic nationalism and commercial protection, depression and mass unemployment shook the world from the late 1920s. The profound misery of humanity's economic and social experience between the wars flowed more or less directly from the Great War. And the even more dreadful consequences of that misery in terms of vicious political extremisms and the savage wars and millions of deaths which they provoked could trace much of their origin to 1914 to 1918.

56 Eichengreen, *Golden Fetters*.

13

Workers

ANTOINE PROST

Workers have vanished from the landscape of the Great War. Historiography bears this out, for there has been no book-length study of workers and labour movements in the First World War for about a generation.[1] Yet, in 1930, in three well-received lectures given at Oxford, Elie Halévy stressed the limits of a political and military history of the war that failed to show what a real social earthquake it had been, in particular in the world of labour. In his view, its most important features were collective forces, the shifts of popular opinion which had upset societies and led to revolution in 1917. The war was the introduction to the age of tyrannies, which he characterised in these terms:

(a) From the economist's point of view, the extreme nationalisation of all the means of production, distribution and exchange; in addition, governmental appeals to the leaders of worker organisations for their help in this work of nationalisation, in other words unionisation and corporatism at the same time as nationalisation;

Helen McPhail translated this chapter from French into English.

1 See the dates of the principal titles: James Hinton, *The First Shop Steward's Movement* (London: Allen & Unwin, 1973); Bernard Waites, *A Class Society at War. England 1914–1918* (Leamington Spa: Berg, 1987); John Horne, *Labour at War. France and Britain 1914–1918* (Oxford: Clarendon Press, 1991); Jay M. Winter, *Socialism and the Challenge of War: Ideas and Politics in Britain, 1912–18* (London: Routledge, 1974); Arthur Marwick, *The Deluge. British Society and the First World War*, 2nd edn (London: Macmillan, 1991); Jürgen Kocka, *Facing Total War, German Society, 1914–1918* (Leamington Spa and Cambridge, MA: Berg and Harvard University Press, 1984); Gerald D. Feldman, *Army, Industry and Labor in Germany, 1914–1918* (Princeton University Press, 1966); Patrick Fridenson (ed.), *1914–1918: l'autre front* (Paris: Ed. Ouvrières, 1977) (*Cahier du Mouvement social* no. 2); Jean-Louis Robert, *Les Ouvriers, la Patrie et la Revolution. Paris 1914–1918* (Besançon: Annales littéraires de l'Université de Besançon no. 392, série historique no. 11, 1995); Giovanna Procacci, *Stato e classe operaia in Italia durante la primo guerre mondiale* (Milan: Franco Angeli, 1983). The major works on strikes are: Léopold H. Haimson and Charles Tilly, *Strikes, Wars and Revolutions in an International Perspective* (Cambridge and Paris: Cambridge University Press, Ed. de la MSH, 1989); and then Léopold H. Haimson and Giulio Sapelli, *Strikes, Social Conflict and the First World War. An International Perspective* (Milan: Feltrinelli, 1992).

(b) From the intellectual point of view, nationalisation in thinking, this nationalisation itself taking two forms . . .[2]

This silence in the contemporary literature need not be maintained. The war demanded total mobilisation in the nations engaged, and in particular in the industries which fed the furnace. The war was also won in the factories, the ports and the transport systems. Every nation was therefore forced to mobilise its industries: all faced the same demands, and often adopted the same solutions in response. But national particularities, and the specific characteristics of what we will call their working classes (although the outlines of this social formation were not clearly defined), introduced differences which call for a comparative approach.

At the front or in the factory?

The First World War was indeed the first of its kind: no one had imagined anything like it, and there was no previous point of reference to deal with the situations that it created. Politicians in the nations at war had to improvise within their own nation's political, administrative and cultural frameworks.

As everyone expected a short war, no one anticipated the need for industrial mobilisation. In continental countries, the conscript armies mobilised men fit for service, whatever their employment. There were a few exceptions: in France, certain railway workers were essential to the smooth running of the mobilisation process.[3] By the end of September, Paris had lost 30 per cent of its male workforce in this way, and Berlin scarcely less.[4] In the United Kingdom, which had no conscription and depended on volunteers until 1916, the outbreak of war made its effects felt more gradually, but during the first year of the war, one-quarter of its workers in chemicals, electrical construction and explosives enlisted, and one-fifth of miners.

2 Elie Halévy, *The World Crisis of 1914–1918, An Interpretation* (Oxford: Clarendon Press, 1930), issued in French in *L'ère des tyrannies* (Paris: Gallimard, 1990, 1st edn 1938).

3 William Oualid and Charles Piquenard, *Salaires et tarifs; conventions collective et grèves. La politique du ministère de l'Armement et du ministère du Travail* (Paris: Presses Universitaires de France, 1924), publication of the Carnegie Endowment for International Peace, p. 45. 11,000 skilled workers were exempt from service, of whom 7,000 were in state factories, but Le Creusot, for example, lost half its workers. See Gerd Hardach, 'La mobilisation industrielle en 1914–1918: production, planification et idéologie', in Fridenson, *1914–1918*, pp. 81–109.

4 Thierry Bonzon, 'The labour market and industrial mobilization, 1915–1917', in Jay Winter and Jean-Louis Robert (eds.), *Capital Cities at War. London, Paris, Berlin 1914–1919* (Cambridge University Press, 1997), pp. 164–95.

These sudden departures as nations joined the war disorganised production completely. For lack of workers or markets, businesses closed. The result was a brief but intense unemployment crisis, lasting around two or three months in Germany and Great Britain, but longer in France, where the enemy occupation of the highly industrialised zones of the north intensified the disruption. But the armies very rapidly felt the lack of munitions, and it was realised that success or failure in battles would depend on the production of arms and ammunition. The choice had to be made between workers being sent to the trenches, which were beginning to appear, or to the factories. From September, the Vickers arms manufacturer, aware of the dangers of 'too much' patriotism, had the forethought to create a badge for workers whom they wanted to protect from zealous recruiting sergeants.[5] Both the French and the German armies began to send individual workmen back to the industrialists, who named the men they needed. The next step was to make skilled workers available by withdrawing them from the fighting units. From 11 October 1914, the French army brought metalworkers to a special depot in Paris; their skills had been identified at home and the men were shared between factories.[6]

To be posted to the front or to a factory mattered to workers, and however patriotic they might be – as indeed they were, as we shall see – many preferred to work rather than fight. An increasingly complex game developed between the army, industrial employers and the workers, giving rise to abuse, but also to recurrent conflict.

In France, Russia, Germany, the Austro-Hungarian Empire and later in Italy, the norm was that workers were mobilised; exemption was an exception, recognised everywhere as necessary, and sometimes on a large scale. Russia seems to have made the most exemptions, which were not without consequences for worker cohesion: only 40 per cent of workers may have been mobilised, although this figure was no doubt an overestimation.[7] In these lands of conscription, the army held records of men of mobilisation age and by name. The worker service of the French Secretariat of State (later the Ministry) for Artillery and Munitions was thus able to coordinate industrialists' demands with soldiers whose skills were needed in a war factory to which they could be returned. The outcome was a reference list with 700,000 entries. The service decided on what were known as 'special postings', and named

5 Marwick, *The Deluge*, p. 96. 6 'Depots' were the bases at the rear of regiments.

7 Diane P. Koenker, *Moscow Workers and the 1917 Revolution* (Princeton University Press, 1981), p. 79, estimates that only one-quarter of workers would have been mobilised; in Moscow, the figures are 28 per cent in metals and 18 per cent in textiles.

officers inside the large factories for local supervision of how these men were employed. In 1915, half a million workers were sent back to factories under this scheme, more than 60 per cent in the metal industries. Almost all were aged at least 23: the army retained the youngest men.[8] These engagements were regulated under a lengthy circular from the Minister for Ammunitions,[9] Albert Thomas, backed by the Dalbiez Law of 17 August 1915. The employers could not return men to the army on this special posting, nor could these men leave their work without the agreement of the supervisor. They could not go on strike and had the right to one day off per fortnight; it was part of the supervisor's duty to establish a detailed wage rate. The special posting man must be paid like a civilian worker, but he was subject to military discipline and could not leave the town where he was working without permission. The supervision system tried to post married men and the relatively older men to factories, while the industrial employers preferred younger men, often unmarried. In the general improvisation, these conditions were evidently not always respected; these men created irregularities, even trading in special postings, denounced by general opinion. Many conflicts broke out in factories, notably over wages, as some employers paid lower wages to men on special postings than to civilian workers. In general, however, this system of workforce management operated reasonably well.

The German Empire faced a different situation, primarily because of its federal structure. The 1815 law on the state of emergency still applied in 1914 (as in France, with the law of 1849 on the state of siege), and gave very extensive powers to the twenty-four generals commanding the army corps, with each army corps (CA) corresponding to a territorial district. Nominated by the appropriate local authority, they had a certain degree of autonomy from the War Ministry. From May 1915, a special ministry bureau shared out requests for workers between the army corps, but individual decisions depended on the generals in command.

This organisational structure created considerable disorder. In effect, the commanding officers of the twenty-four CAs were very close to the High Command, which was in constant conflict with the War Ministry – indeed, together with Hindenburg, it managed to create a parallel central administration, the *Kriegsamst* (War Office). But the High Command was closely linked to the major industrialists, who demanded their skilled workers back

8 Jean-Louis Robert, 'Ouvriers et mouvement ouvrier parisiens pendant la grande guerre et l'immédiat après-guerre. Histoire et anthropologie' (Thesis, Université de Paris I, 1989), ch. 13.

9 Circular dated 15 July 1915, Oualid and Piquenard, *Salaires et tarifs*, pp. 70–6.

from the army to fulfil orders for weapons and munitions. They did not consider that their need for workers could be satisfied by training new employees or by taking on women. The generals commanding the CAs failed to relocate unemployed workers from other branches of industry in munitions factories. The factories squabbled over skilled workers, who became excessively mobile. As applied by the CA commanding officers, the Patriotic Auxiliary Service Law of 2 December 1916, designed to promote the twin objectives of control over worker mobility and the organisation of employment, failed to put an end to this disorder; some workers with special exemption for one form of employment were engaged in another.[10] This was a significant wartime victory for the major industrialists, as the balance between front line and factory tilted quite strongly towards the latter. From September 1916 to July 1917, while battalion numbers dropped from 750 to 713 men, the total number of workers returned to factories rose from 1.2 to 1.9 million.[11] Overall, in January 1918, no fewer than 2.3 million men were exempted for work, of whom 1.2 million were recognised as 'fit for the front',[12] compared with the 518,000 specially posted French workers in 1917.

Without compulsory national service, the United Kingdom held no combined records of servicemen and no administration capable of directing the workforce as a whole. Further, as the government appealed for volunteer recruits to increase the size of the armies, it had even less authority over directing workers into war factories. Finally, it had to deal with the powerful unions – 2.2 million members in 1913 – which, unlike those in Germany and France (2.5 million and 250,000 members respectively) – had effectively taken local control of employment. The rules of trade which they imposed particularly implied respect for the worker hierarchy: a skilled task could not be handed over to an unskilled worker who had not completed his apprenticeship.

These three conditions meant that the British Government had to proceed with caution and pragmatism. Step by step it developed a policy which it negotiated with the unions. The first discussions bore on questions other than the management of employment, but the persistent lack of munitions in May 1915 entailed a ministerial reshuffle and the creation of a Ministry of Munitions, headed by Lloyd George. The Munitions of War Act, adopted on 3 July 1915, was designed to limit the turnover which was disrupting

10 Feldman, *Army, Industry and Labor*, p. 310. Feldman annexes the text of this law.
11 Feldman, *Army, Industry and Labor*, p. 301.
12 Feldman, *Army, Industry and Labor*, p. 417.

production in the war factories. First, it defined 'controlled' industrial establishments and made it illegal for workers in these factories to leave them without the employers' agreement, supported by a leaving certificate. To dissuade workers from changing employment without a leaving certificate in search of better wages, a six-month delay was imposed before they could be taken on, a period which was shortened and finally suppressed after 1917. Special tribunals were instituted to settle refusals of leaving certificates and to sanction workers who did not respect these obligations.

The Munitions Act, which directly inspired the German law on auxiliary service, did not enable the government to take overall control of the workforce. Yet volunteers to go out and be killed were increasingly rare, and conscription became necessary. Its introduction required first a record of men aged between 15 and 65 years, and to know what they were doing. These data were collected under the National Registration Act (15 July 1915). Next, the government sounded out the unions, which insisted that military conscription should not lead to industrial conscription, which would destroy their role in regulating conditions of labour. Next, the government attempted to settle matters with a form of limited voluntary service, the Derby Scheme, named after its creator Lord Derby (16 October 1915): men who volunteered under the scheme could either enrol immediately in the army – this produced 215,000 soldiers – or promise to respond to the call as soon as it was demanded of them. Out of 5 million men who were not enrolled, 1.2 million worked in protected businesses. A little over 2 million attested to this engagement, which confirmed the limitations of the volunteer system.

Conscription was established in January 1916 under the Military Service Act, and strengthened in May. It was less rigorous than in France or Germany. Workers in controlled factories were exempt by law, and those who considered themselves unfairly enrolled for conscription could call on the tribunal to gain exemption. The result was more than 750,000 requests. Many appeals came to nothing, which created additional discontent. In October 1916, a fitter in the Vickers factory in Sheffield, named Hargreaves, was mobilised because his employer had refused him the certificate which would have exempted him: this angered his comrades, and the union called for a strike if Hargreaves was not back at work by 15 November. On 16 November, 12,000 workmen downed tools. The government gave way and granted the main metalworkers' union, the Amalgamated Society of Engineers (ASE), which essentially recruited skilled workers, the right to give exemption cards to its members. Introduced in February 1917, this privilege was demanded by other unions and extended to them. The government yielded to the unions the right to designate those who would not be forced to face military service and death in action.

The war dragged on, however, and management of the workforce became increasingly critical. The figures drawn up by the Ministry of National Service in July 1917 showed that it could not meet both the needs of the armed forces and those of the factories. Unlike Germany, Great Britain finally gave priority to the army over industry. Exemption cards, frequently misused, were suppressed in May 1918. This gave rise to one of the most significant events of the war in Britain: between 30 April and 12 May, some 200,000 men went on strike in several cities – Manchester, Sheffield, Rotherham, Coventry and even London. The government held firm, and henceforward held overall control over the management of the workforce. By the end of the war, however, the lack of adequate worker numbers meant that the war factories were no longer able to work at full strength.[13]

Entering the war on 23 May 1915, Italy benefited from the example of the other warring nations, and until 1918 it made few changes in the organisation of its 'industrial mobilisation'. Under the responsibility of the Ministry of Armaments and Munitions, two royal decrees of 26 June and 22 August 1915 created the *Ufficio mobilitazione industriale* and eleven regional committees for industrial mobilisation (CRMI). Representatives of employers and unions were included on level terms, but under the aegis of the military administration. It was the CRMI which decided on special postings and worker mobility, as in France, but with a greater degree of decentralisation.

Clearly, the division of the workforce between army and industry varied considerably between nations. The centralised French administration and the less-centralised Italian administration both proved efficient. The German administration never succeeded in overcoming its internal struggles between the centre and the periphery – the network of employers, High Command and civil servants. Finally, by means of multiple compromises with the unions, the United Kingdom gradually succeeded in negotiating, imposing and managing full military conscription, without offending the unions through instituting industrial conscription. But nowhere were there sufficient numbers of men to supply both factories and armies at the same time. It was therefore necessary both to enlarge the workforce and find ways to intensify production.

13 Chris J. Wrigley, *David Lloyd George and the British Labour Movement: Peace and War* (Hassocks: Harvester, 1976), pp. 70–6.

Evolution or re-composition of the working classes?

The workforce

The nations attempted to remedy the lack of available labour by recruiting foreigners, prisoners of war, adolescents and women. Unlike Germany, whose colonial domain was reduced and rendered inaccessible by the blockade, both France and the United Kingdom called extensively on the populations of their empires and on foreigners, although union opposition in Britain prevented their industrial employment there. In France, however, in 1918, the armaments industries were employing 108,000 foreign workers and 61,000 colonial workers.[14] German industry also appealed to many foreign workers in Central Europe: it had around 250,000 active in industry overall in 1917, and 306,000 in 1918.[15] Most of these workers were very badly treated, overworked, very badly paid and above all very badly housed in improvised dormitories, where mattresses were sometimes used in constant succession by night-shift and day-shift workers.

The Hague Convention (1907) authorised the employment of prisoners of war, with the exception of officers, provided that the work was not excessive and was unconnected to military operations. This did not formally ban their use in war factories in the interior. The British were alone in not using this resource.[16] France made moderate use of its prisoners of war, but still had 40,000 of them in its war factories in 1917. Germany, which took prisoners on both fronts, and particularly on the Eastern Front,[17] went much further: in 1917, German industry had more than 390,000 prisoners of war in its factories.[18]

Young people, under the age of 18, were another potential source of labour. Their employment expanded greatly during the war, but in this case the state of the labour market was much more significant than governmental encouragement. There was never any shortage of vacancies, and the attraction

14 Pierre-Cyrille Hautecoeur, 'Was the Great War a watershed? The economics of World War I in France', in Stephen Broadberry and Mark Harrison, *The Economics of World War I* (Cambridge University Press, 2005), p. 175.

15 Albrecht Ritschl, 'The pity of peace: Germany's economy at war', in Broadberry and Harrison, *Economics of World War I*, p. 53.

16 Heather Jones, *Violence against Prisoners of War in the First World War. Britain, France and Germany, 1914–1920* (Cambridge University Press, 2011), p. 226. Out of 30,500 prisoners at work in Great Britain in May 1918, more than 2,500 were in weapons factories.

17 Ritschl, 'The pity of peace', gives a total figure of 1,703,500 prisoners in 1917. According to estimates collated by Jones, *Violence against POWs*, pp. 20 and 22, Germany held 175,000 British and 520,000 French prisoners, while France held 400,000 Germans captive and Great Britain a little over 300,000.

18 Ritschl, 'The pity of peace', p. 53. Agriculture employed 835,000.

of an immediate wage turned many young people away from apprenticeship. Indeed, British union leaders proclaimed a real crisis in the apprenticeship system. In France, in 1918, war industries employed 133,000 young people under the age of 18 – representing 8 per cent of the workforce, while in Russia the proportion in January 1917 was higher in the factories of Petrograd, and above all in Moscow.[19]

The real reserve of labour, however, consisted of the female population. In Germany, for example, out of a total labour force reduced by 8 per cent, the reduction of 25 per cent of men was partially balanced by a growth of 46 per cent in the number of women and 10 per cent of young people.[20] In all countries, industrial development in the manufacture of weapons and munitions depended on the mass employment of women. The 'munitionette', as she became known in France and Britain, was a widely recognised figure everywhere and a novelty in public opinion. It is difficult to know whether this general phenomenon reached the same scale everywhere: the figures come from official authorities which vary in their definitions of the various branches of industrial activity; it is not always clear, for example, whether transport is included in 'industry'. Female employment varied very considerably in different branches of work, and in addition the war reduced the reliability of the data assembled.[21] The figures shown in Table 13.1 below should therefore be treated with great caution.

The proportions are very similar: 37.7 per cent in Great Britain against 23.6 per cent before the war; 35.6 per cent in Germany against 20.6 per cent; 40.5 per cent in France against 32 per cent; and in Russia, 41.2 per cent against 31.8 per cent. In Vienna, the figure grew from 22.3 per cent of women in the workforce to 36.2 per cent between 1914 and 1918.[22] Everywhere, however, these averages conceal considerable differences according to region and industrial sector. Wartime magazine readers above all retained images of

19 For France, Gerd Hardach, 'La mobilisation industrielle in 1914–1918: production, planification et idéologie', in Fridenson, *1914–1918*, p. 86; for Petrograd, David Mandel, *The Petrograd Workers and the Soviet Seizure of Power: From the February Revolution to the July Days, 1917* (London: Macmillan, 1983), p. 46, gives a proportion of 8.6 per cent and for Moscow, Koenker, *Moscow Workers*, shows the figure of 13 per cent as children of 12–16 years old.

20 Kocka, *Facing Total War*, p. 17.

21 See in Jean-Louis Robert, 'Women and work in France during the First World War', in Richard Wall and Jay Winter (eds.), *Upheaval of War: Family, Work and Welfare in Europe, 1914–1918* (Cambridge University Press, 1988), p. 252, the very great differences in seven enquiries of inspection of work in France during the war. They do not even agree on the numbers employed in 1914.

22 Reinhard J. Sieder, 'Behind the lines: working-class family life in wartime Vienna', in Wall and Winter, *Upheaval of War*, p. 119.

Table 13.1 *Proportion of women in the workforce*

	1913 (%)	1914 (%)	1915 (%)	1916 (%)	1917 (%)	1918 (%)	1919 (%)	1920 (%)
Germany (1)	20.6					35.6		
France (2)		32.0	39.8	30.3	40.2	40.5	37.0	32.0
Great Britain (3)		23.6				37.7		
Vienna, metals industry (4)	18.5	22.3	26.6	34.8	36.2			
Russia (5)	30.7	31.8	36.0	39.6	40.2	41.2		

1 Richard Bessel, *Germany after the First World War* (Oxford: Clarendon Press, 1993), p. 16.
2 Robert, 'Women and work in France during the First World War', in Wall and Winter, *Upheaval of War*, p. 252.
3 Thom, 'Women and work in wartime Britain', in Wall and Winter, *Upheaval of War*, p. 320.
4 Reinhard J. Sieder, 'Behind the lines: working-class family life in wartime Vienna', in Walls and Winter, *Upheaval of War*, p. 119.
5 Peter Gatrell, *Russia's First World War. A Social and Economic History* (Harlow: Longman, 2005), p. 68. USSR territory, major companies. First half-year, 1918.

vast workshops where hundreds of women machined shells, as in the Citroën's Quai de Javel factory in Paris, where by the end of 1917, 13,000 women were producing 10,000 shells per day. The very large factories, such as Siemens in Berlin (47,000 workers in August 1917), with 46.2 per cent women, or the Woolwich Royal Arsenal in London (28,000 women and 6,500 'boy workers' alongside 4,200 men) formed unprecedented concentrations of women in the world of mechanical and electrical construction or metalworking. By the time of the Armistice, Krupp, which had employed no women among its 41,000 workers before the war, now had 38,000 women in its factories out of a total of 110,000 workers.[23] Many more examples could be cited; a new industrial landscape was emerging, which still awaits pictorial exploration.

However spectacular it may have been, this novelty was not as radical as it appeared. The war of 1914 did not bring women into the world of industrial labour for the first time: many were already present, and in some cases in large numbers, particularly across the full range of spinning and weaving factories.

23 For Siemens: Ilse Costas, 'Management and labor in the Siemens plant in Berlin (1916–1920)', in Haimson and Sapelli, *Strikes*, p. 275; for Woolwich, in November 1917: Angela Woollacott, *On Her Their Lives Depend. Munition Workers in the Great War* (Berkeley: University of California Press, 1994), p. 29; for Krupp, Richard Bessel, *Germany after the First World War* (Oxford: Clarendon Press, 1993), p. 19.

Figure 1 Masques de guerre.
Caricatures of (from left to right) Top row: General Joffre, General Gallieni, George V, Victor Emmanuel III, General Foch, Delcassé; Bottom row: Venizelos, Field Marshal French, Pope Benedict XV, Grand Duke Nicholas, General von Kluck, General von Hindenburg.

Figure 2 Hindenburg image.
A Christmas decoration with the face of General von Hindenburg, the hero of the Battle of Tannenberg in 1914.

Figure 3 'J'ai vu', 8 July 1916.
A collage of five Allied commanders – Haig, Broussiloff, Joffre, Sarrail and Cadorna – preparing to crush the Kaiser, the Ottoman Sultan, Crown Prince Wilhelm, and Emperor Franz-Ferdinand, 8 July 1916.

Figure 4 Revolutionary flag being sewn (ceramic).
Weaving the revolutionary flag: a woman weaving the Red flag, announcing the new age launched by the Bolshevisk Revolution, in a ceramic figure of 1918.

Figure 5 Revolutionary plate: *assiette révolutionnaire*.
A ceramic plate in the style of Russian constructivism, bringing abstract design into useful objects, as a revolutionary bridge between artists and artisans after the Great War.

Figure 6 French soldier's gear.
Presentation in a *fosse* or shallow dug-out in the Historial de la Grande Guerre, Péronne, Somme, of a French soldier's uniform, helmet, weapons and kit. The life soldiers shared on both sides of the line is portrayed vividly here. Anti-lice powder, toothpaste and cooking utensils all made life a little less miserable for the millions of men living in trenches or underground for extended periods of time.

Figure 7 German soldier's gear.
Presentation in a *fosse* or shallow dug-out in the Historial de la Grande Guerre, Péronne, Somme, of a German soldier's uniform, helmet, weapons and kit. German soldiers sometimes benefited from well-built deep trenches, but most of the time they lived in conditions just as miserable as their enemies on the other side.

Figure 8 Tank up a tree at Clapham junction, Ypres salient.
Photograph of the mud and detritus of war near Ypres which rendered tanks useless in the sodden summer of 1917.

Figure 9 Jean-Émile Laboureur, *Estaminet*.
A British soldier waving to waitresses in a café near the front, announcing invitingly that it serves English beer. Laboureur was a well-known popular artist, and a friend of the avant-garde.

Figure 10 Mandolin.
The ingenuity of troops in constructing and using musical instruments and other objects to while away the time in quiet sectors of the front was striking in all armies.

Figure 11 Cigarette lighter 'Somme Oise Marne Aisne'.
An engraved cigarette lighter with the names of the sectors on which its owner 'L R' served in the French artillery during the war.

Figure 12 German café concert.
Troops organised their own entertainments, including orchestras, melodramas and cross-dressing among the all-male company.

Figure 13 'Dernier Né d'Albert Thomas'.
The French socialist Minister of Armaments in 1916, welcoming the latest addition to his munitions stockpile.

Figure 14 Toy model of heavy gun on rail.
The artillery war was translated into children's toys, as in this French model of a French gun and its railway carriage.

Figure 15 Plate of Erfurt POW camp.
A German ceramic plate recalled with pride German military service at the Erfurt prisoner-of-war camp in 1914 and 1915.

Figure 16 German prisoners of war.
A photograph of a large number of German prisoners of war, some still wearing their helmets, suggests that this is Allied propaganda to document the widespread surrender of German troops in the summer of 1918 on the Western Front.

Figure 17 French prisoners of war.
A German photograph of French prisoners of war shows men far removed from combat. Notice the seven men astride a climbing bar in the centre.

Figure 18 'Keep these off the USA'.
All combatants tried to bolster war finance by soliciting from civilians contributions in the form of war loans. This American appeal followed the line of atrocity propaganda in the form of blood-stained German boots.

Figure 19 'Shoot ships to Germany': US war effort.
Charles Schwab, president of Bethlehem Steel, became head of the US Shipping Board Emergency Fleet Corporation, which oversaw all US shipyard construction for the war. Here is his pitch to workers to 'do their bit' for the war.

Figure 20 Logistics: African troops and horses.
There were approximately 500,000 Africans serving in British and French forces during the war. Alongside Asian labourers, many Africans in uniform did the hard logistical work of supplying the front. Unlike the Chinese, Africans and Indians engaged in heavy combat; all suffered the ravages of the Spanish flu epidemic of 1918.

Figure 21 Women moving shell casings.
Belgian women doing the heavy lifting of shell casings behind Allied lines. In occupied territories, the use of women for such work was a breach of the Hague Conventions. Nevertheless, they formed an essential part of the supply chain for the German army as well.

SOUVENIR

In ✻ Loving ✻ Memory

OF THE

MEN, WOMEN AND CHILDREN

KILLED IN

The London Air Raid

ON WEDNESDAY, JUNE 13TH 1917,

Killed—104. Seriously injured—154. Slightly injured—269. Total—527.

The casualties include 120 children either killed or injured.

Some of the Small Victims.

Name		Age	Name		Age
Louise Annie Acampora	Aged	5	Rose Martin	,,	11
Alfred Ernest Bart	,,	5	George Morris	,,	6
Leonard Charles Barford	,,	6	Edwin Cecil William Powell	,,	12
John Percy Brennan	,,	6	Robert Stimson	,,	5
William Thomas Henry Challen	,,	5	Elizabeth Taylor	,,	5
Vera Margaret Clayson	,,	4	Rose Tuffin	,,	5
Alice Maud Cross	,,	5	Frank Winfield	,,	5
William Hollis	,,	5	Florence Lilian Wood	,,	5
George Albert Hyde	,,	5			

"SUFFER LITTLE CHILDREN TO COME UNTO ME,
FOR OF SUCH IS THE KINGDOM OF HEAVEN."

Those tiny school babes, our little ones,
Had ceased their tasks and were listening with bated breath,
For the blotting out of the glorious sun
By the broken thunder of the German Death.

"IN THE MIDST OF LIFE, WE ARE IN DEATH."

Printer, E. Burgess, 4, York Place, Strand, London, W

Figure 22 Remembrance of London Air Raid, 1917.
An embroidered souvenir of the German air raid on London which killed over 100 civilians on 13 June 1917, including five-year-old children listed by name.

Bombardement de Paris
par canons à longue portée. "Berthas"
23 mars 1918 - rue Charles V.

Figure 23 Paris bombarded.
The Germans' heavy gun, dubbed the *Pariskanone*, with a 118 ft barrel demolished a housing district close to the Bastille in Paris on 23 March 1918. This attack preceded by six days a direct hit on the church of Saint-Gervais just next to the Paris City Hall on Good Friday, killing eighty-eight worshippers.

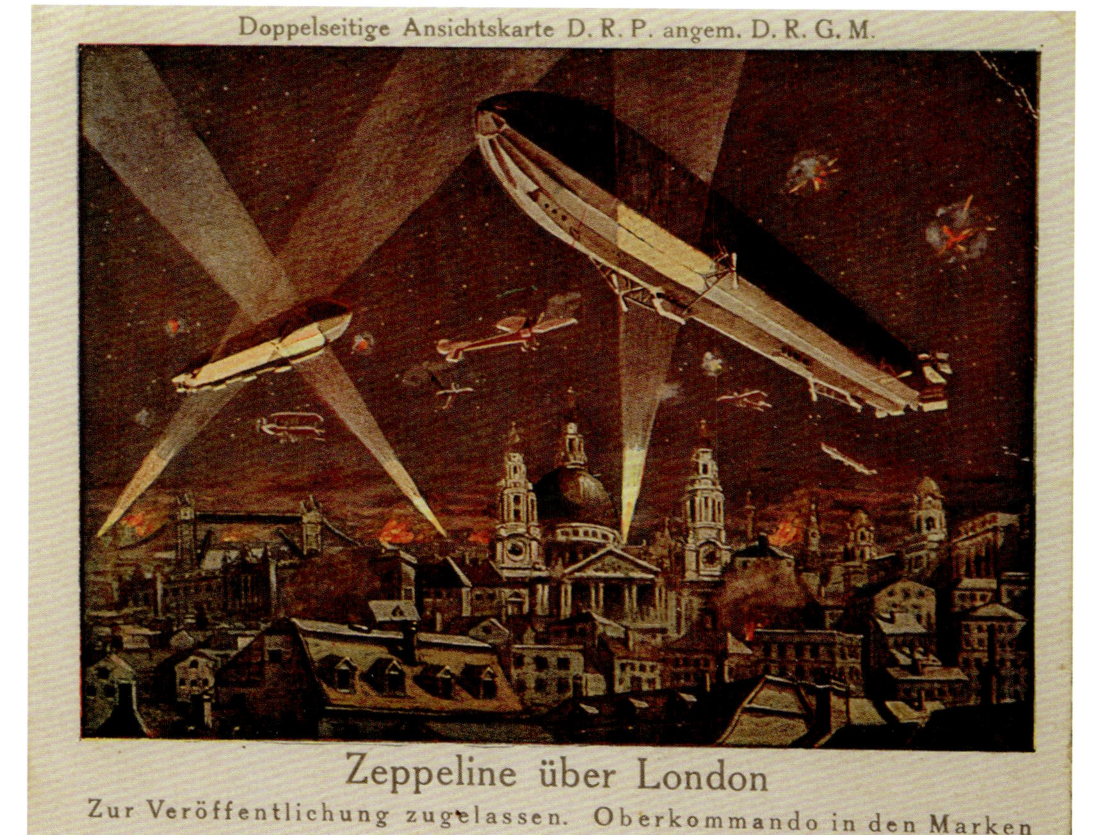

Doppelseitige Ansichtskarte D. R. P. angem. D. R. G. M.
Zeppeline über London
Zur Veröffentlichung zugelassen. Oberkommando in den Marken

Figure 24 Zeppelins over London.
A postcard of the bombardment of London by Zeppelins, with St Paul's Cathedral in the centre, officially approved by the German High Command.

Figure 25 Russian medieval image in war loan poster.
The Russian propaganda effort drew on medieval Christian images to promote financial support for the war. Anyone who answered the call lost every penny with the Revolutions of 1917 and Russia's withdrawal from the war.

Figure 26 Peace with Russia.
An Austrian insignia, with medieval profiles, celebrating the peace with Russia on 3 March 1918, concluded at what it terms the Lithuanian city of Brest-Litovsk. This refers to the part of the treaty in which the Bolsheviks renounced all territorial claims to Lithuania and their other western neighbours.

Figure 27 *Gueules cassées à Versailles.*
These disfigured soldiers were chosen by French premier Clemenceau to be at the entrance to the Hall of Mirrors in Versailles, and thus present an accusation of responsibility for the suffering of the war at the very moment when the German delegation signed the Peace Treaty on 28 June 1919.

28-Juin 1919
11. - Palais de VERSAILLES
Signature du Traité de Paix - Sortie de MM. Clémenceau, Wilson, Lloyd George sur la Terrasse du Château

Figure 28 Statesmen at Versailles.
A photograph of the victors emerging from the Hall of Mirrors at Versailles, with the Peace Treaty signed by Allied leaders and the German delegation, 28 June 1919.

Figure 29 Lost *Heimat* (Trentino)
A popular drawing by an anonymous artist, showing two young Austrian women, bereft over the loss of the Trentino, which was ceded by Austria to Italy in the Treaty of Saint-Germain-en-Laye on 10 September 1919.

Figure 30 'Too late': inaugurating a Peace Palace.
A pre-war critique of the creation of a Peace Palace in the Hague, completed in 1913, too late to stop the Balkan wars. In 1919, under Article 14 of the Covenant, the League of Nations established a Permanent Court of International Justice in the Peace Palace in the Hague. The court had its first sitting in 1922.

Figure 31 Anti-Bolshevik poster, 1919.
'Bolshevism means the drowning of the world in blood.' This is the message from the Berlin-based Organization for the Struggle against Bolshevism, at the time of the Sparticist revolt and its bloody suppression in January 1919.

Figure 32 *Freiwilliger Brigade Reinhard*.
Commanded by Colonel Wilhelm Reinhard, this right-wing paramilitary organisation of volunteers fought against the Sparticists in Berlin and against communists in Silesia.

Figure 33 *Sturmbataillon Schmidt*

This 1919 poster encouraging German men to volunteer for the 'Sturmbataillon [Assault Batallion] Schmidt' was the work of the Berlin artist Leo Impekoven. This group drew junior officers who never accepted the defeat of 1918 into armed conflict with revolutionaries.

The novelty was not that the women were in the factories, but that they were in the armaments factories, moving from textiles to metalwork. Use of a female labour force in the war factories was in fact balanced by its reduction in other sectors. In Germany, for example, mechanical construction employed 419,000 more women in 1918 than in 1913, but in textiles the figure fell by 195,000. In total, the female labour force grew by one-half, a considerable increase – but one which shows clearly that the pre-war base was by no means zero.[24] Of the 1,458,289 women workers listed in Bavarian factories in December 1916, only 6.9 per cent had not been working before the war.[25] In Britain, the increase in the number of women working in the weapons and munitions sectors was spectacular, rising in one year (July to July), from 212,000 in 1914 to 256,000, then 520,000 and 819,000 in 1917,[26] of whom 225,000 were in establishments under direct governmental management.[27] In 1918, British industry (including transport) was employing nearly 3 million women – but in 1914, the figure was already over 2 million: the real figure for the increase was 36 per cent. However incontestable, it should not be exaggerated: the shift towards war industries was greater than the move into paid manual labour.

In all the countries concerned, the efforts to develop female labour appear to have been hindered by similar but unequal obstacles. First came growing difficulties with food, with rationing and above all queues, which took up increasing amounts of time. Doing the shopping became an expedition lasting many hours and led to claims for reduced working hours. This was why French women won 'the English week' – half time on Saturdays.[28] In Great Britain, the queues became a major social phenomenon in the winter of 1917–18, beginning before dawn, particularly on Saturdays. This led to strikes, with accompanying demonstrations, on Saturdays. In Sheffield and Coventry, it was reported that workers left their workshops to take over their wives' places in the queue. In January 1918, the police counted half a million people queuing each week.[29] In Petrograd, the workers had to queue for between four and five hours every day as they left their factories in the summer of 1917, and the situation grew steadily worse.[30] But it was in Germany that the

24 Bessel, *Germany after WWI*, p. 16.
25 Ute Daniel, 'Women's work in industry and family: Germany, 1914–18', in Wall and Winter, *Upheaval of War*, p. 272.
26 Marwick, *The Deluge*, p. 131.
27 Woollacott, *On Her Their Lives Depend*, p. 25.
28 Law of 29 May 1917.
29 Hinton, *First Shop Steward's Movement*, ch. 9; Waites, *Class Society at War*, pp. 224–30.
30 Mandel, *Petrograd Workers: From the July Days to July 1918*, p. 217.

difficulties appeared first: from 1916, the disappointment of housewives who, after hours of standing in a queue, found that the tradesmen had nothing left to sell, set off riots and strikes.[31] It was very difficult for women, in such conditions, to work for up to ten or twelve hours a day in a factory.

Secondly, wages were competing with various forms of military allowance from all the governments, paid to women whose partners were mobilised. In France, these grants were shared out by local committees, which rejected them if the wage exceeded a certain level.[32] In Germany, the compensation could not exceed 60 per cent of the husband's wage, but if the wife was working, the indemnity was set at half her wages – which hardly encouraged women to go out to work for wages that were already very low.[33] Overall, comparison between Paris, London and Berlin shows that the pattern of military allowances was clearly more generous in Great Britain than in France, and above all than in Germany. Price indexation was better in Berlin, while support for large families was greater in Paris and above all in London.[34]

In effect, national and employers' policies introduced appreciable differences into the development and status of female work. On several occasions, the German Government wished to make it obligatory, particularly as part of the law on auxiliary service. The employers were opposed to this, just as they had resisted ministerial pressure to take on women. Above all, they insisted on retaining their skilled workers, and in some cases women who had been taken on were dismissed when the workers whom the employers wanted back returned.[35] They had no wish to train them or arrange cloakrooms and toilet facilities, still less to adapt work stations for their benefit.

In France, official policy did not encounter the same resistance. Industrialists viewed women's work more favourably, and public opinion saw no conflict between work and maternity; it was understood that mothers were working to feed their children. As Table 13.1 shows, pre-war female employment was already 50 per cent greater in France than in Germany or the United Kingdom. But the very strong fear of demographic decrease in France inspired

31 Feldman, *Army, Industry and Labor*, *passim*; Sean Dobson, *Authority and Upheaval in Leipzig, 1910–1920* (New York: Columbia University Press, 2001), ch. 6.

32 Thierry Bonzon, 'Transfer payments and social policy', in Winter and Robert, *Capital Cities at War*, p. 292.

33 Dobson, *Authority and Upheaval*, p. 126, Daniel, 'Women's work', pp. 285–6.

34 Bonzon, 'Transfer payments', p. 296.

35 Feldman, *Army, Industry and Labor*, pp. 301–2.

protective measures to ensure that women's family responsibilities, current or future, were compatible with their work. The minister, Albert Thomas, created a Committee for Female Work to deal with these questions in April 1916, and undertook concrete measures: a maximum of ten working hours, no night work for women under the age of 18 and time off each week; these were listed in his circular of 1 July 1917. The creation of female factory superintendents at the end of the war was a response to the same concern. The law of 5 August 1917 required industrial employers with more than 100 women workers to arrange breastfeeding rooms on their premises and to allow young mothers to breastfeed their baby twice a day. Citroën was very proud of their Javel nursery, with its sixty cradles and 150 child-minding places, and gave it wide publicity. Of course no general rule can be drawn from this exceptional case, and protective regulations were by no means always respected, but the 1918 enquiry discovered that three-quarters of establishments affected by the law had applied it and that pregnant women were very generally not employed on night work.[36] The war seems here to have established women workers as a specific category, defined by men and appreciated by them, employers or foremen, as part of their so-called 'natural' functions of endurance, discipline and close attention to detail.[37]

The British Government pushed industrial employers hard to replace men with women, who were encouraged with posters: 'Do your bit. Replace a man for the front'. Many women were employed in government-run establishments, and the management took pains to watch over their working conditions, with pragmatic concern for improving productivity. By the end of the war, these government-run establishments were employing 1,000 women as welfare supervisors to inspect canteens, sick rooms and toilets, and pay close attention to women's working conditions. Many factories opened crèches, but few troubled to organise work to make it possible for pregnant women or young mothers.[38] Employers appreciated women's work, but saw it as a short-term expedient. The image of the 'male breadwinner' was as strong for them as for the unions: the normal place of a woman with children was at home. This was very clear when the war ended – while the French dismissed unmarried women first, because they

36 Mathilde Dubesset *et al.*, 'Les munitionnettes de la Seine', in Fridenson, *1914–1918*, pp. 189–219.

37 Laura Lee Downs, *L'inégalité à la chaîne. La division sexuée du travail dans l'industrie métallurgique en France et en Angleterre* (Paris: A. Michel, 2002).

38 Woollacott, *On Her Their Lives Depend*, ch. 3; Thom, in Wall and Winter, *Upheaval of War*, p. 312.

thought that those with families needed to work, the British laid off their married workers first.[39]

The main resistance to female work in Britain came from the unions, and particularly the powerful union of skilled metal and construction workers, the ASE. But this was a matter above all of resistance to the new organisation of work.

Work

Developments in manual labour evolved in very similar ways in the United Kingdom and on the continent – with the difference that in Britain, these matters were much more conflictual because they raised issues which were incompatible with union achievements over control of the labour market, achievements they expected to keep. The British established terms, without equivalent in other countries, to define this evolution and those who were both the instruments and the victims of these changes: *dilution, the diluted labour force* and *dilutees*.

At the heart of this process was the major demand of industrial warfare: the increasingly rapid production of weapons and munitions. On average, between March 1917 and March 1918, the *daily* production of shells was 261,000 in France, 229,000 in the United Kingdom and 42,600 in Italy. Every day, the three countries together produced 10,000 rifles and 324 machine guns.[40] These prodigious quantities were programmed from the first months of the war. By 24 September 1914, the industrialists were already receiving demands from the French War Minister for 100,000 shells per day for the army's 75 mm field guns. This was mass production such as had never been known before and which, further, demanded total standardisation. Last but not least, cost constraints vanished since the governments, initally at least, did not discuss prices. Sometimes, indeed, they financed the necessary investment for the production process itself.[41]

Mass production, standardised products, freedom of pricing: the conditions were particularly favourable for the scientific organisation of work. 'Taylorism', or scientific management, had already begun to penetrate industries when the war provided a further incentive. Production-line work was appearing, still cautiously, sometimes in order to ease women's work. At Citroen's Javel factory, conveyor lines on rollers were established so that

39 Susan Pedersen, *Family, Dependence, and the Origins of the Welfare State. Britain and France 1914–1945* (Cambridge University Press, 1993).
40 Hardach, 'La mobilisation industrielle', p. 87.
41 Hardach, 'La mobilisation industrielle', p. 84.

women workers would not have to move heavy boxes of shells from one working area to another in the course of fabrication.

But the assembly line was only one way among others in managing factory work scientifically. Its fundamental principle was to break work down into distinct operations, carried out in succession by specialised machines which did not require highly skilled operators. The work could be learned in the actual workshop. In France, the phrase 'specialised workers', *manoeuvres spécialisés*, was used to designate those who serviced the machines, as opposed to those recognised as 'skilled', *qualifiés*; in Great Britain, the opposition was between *unskilled* and *skilled* workers. The new unskilled labour force, consisting of women and young men, was given repetitive work which required no training, thereby enabling them to replace skilled workers.

In Britain, however, the unions had succeeded in protecting skilled workers. In particular, they had obtained the commitment that any skilled worker would continue to be paid at the same rate even if he was undertaking work which did not require his level of qualification. Dilution was not compatible with these union rules, since it was designed to replace skilled workers systematically with the unskilled, whose job from this time on above all was the regulation and maintenance of a group of machines or tools. Dilution was inevitably extremely contentious.

The problem emerged very early. In discussion with the unions on 10 December 1914, the Engineering Employers' Federation insisted that skilled workers must be appointed to oversee several machines, and that women or semi-skilled workers who were not members of the union would be recruited to undertake this kind of work. A strike for increased wages along the River Clyde, which lasted from 16 February to 3 March 1915, led the government to create a Committee on Production to promote dilution, although its initial activities were confined to exhortation. The Treasury Conference of 17 to 19 March between unions and government proposed an agreement which was accepted a little later by the ASE: union rules were set aside, but the government undertook to re-establish them after the war, and not to leave employers with the benefits gained from their temporary abeyance. The struggle continued, however – particularly on Clydeside, where Lloyd George was severely challenged. On a visit to Glasgow immediately before Christmas 1915, he was booed by militants who made the establishment of workers' control over business the condition of their acceptance of dilution. In the end, he imposed it during the spring of 1916, factory by factory, but not without opposition, strikes and arrests.

Other nations encountered less opposition over dilution, but everywhere it was difficult to assess clearly. To what extent did the demands of war production entail the 'taylorisation' of manual labour? It profoundly transformed certain sectors, such as the Solingen knife-making industry in Germany, which changed the artisan skill of knife-making for export into mass production of bayonets.[42] Everywhere, the number of skilled workers dropped as a proportion of the labour force. But how far? In Great Britain, the most extreme example of this shift, 'dilutees' were officially recorded at 41 per cent of male workers and 45 per cent of women workers in chemical and metal industries, and 60 and 54 per cent respectively[43] in manufacturing explosives, in October 1917. But entire sectors of industry escaped this development. Naval shipbuilding, with its importance accentuated by submarine warfare, escaped dilution. Shipbuilding on Clydeside took on only 1,000 women, and thirteen shipyards had none. The employers protected their skilled workers, and in some cases they were paid to do nothing. When pneumatic riveting was introduced in 1917, the union won the argument that only its members could do it, with no change in wage rates.[44] The Admiralty had protected its 936,000 workers from the controls of the Munitions Act. Electricity, heavily and widely used, resisted dilution and the Electrical Trades Union (ETU) succeeded in maintaining its closed shop.[45] In France, only 7 per cent of the workforce employed in Le Creusot's Schneider factory were women;[46] the iron and steel industries ignored Taylorism. Visibly, the scale of the new scientific organisation of work should not be overestimated: it did not change everything in all factories.

In fact, the chief way of expanding production – not only arms and weapons, but all war supplies and munitions, from shell cases to equipment – was to accept partial redevelopment of old tooling and make better use of the workforce. The working day was extended everywhere, up to thirteen hours in Vienna,[47] and factory work days of fifteen to sixteen hours in Italy.[48]

42 Rudolf Boch, 'Changing patterns of labor conflict and labor organization in the German cutlery industry. Solingen 1905–1926', in Haimson and Sapelli, *Strikes*, pp. 253–68.

43 Waites, *Class Society at War*, p. 196.

44 Alastair Reid, 'Dilution, trade unionism and the state in Britain during the First World War', in Steven Tolliday and Jonathan Zeitlin, *Shop Floor Bargaining and the State: Historical and Comparative Perspective* (Cambridge University Press, 1985), pp. 45–74.

45 Waites, *Class Society at War*, pp. 150–1.

46 Jean-William Dereymez, 'Les usines de guerre (1914–1918): le cas de la Saône-et-Loire', Lyon, *Cahiers d'histoire*, 1 (1981), 151–81.

47 Hans Hautmann, 'Vienna: a city in the years of radical change', in Chris Wrigley, *Challenges of Labour. Central and Western Europe 1917–1920* (London and New York: Routledge, 1993), pp. 87–104.

48 Alessandro Camara, 'Salari, organizzazion et condizioni de lavoro', in Procacci, *Stato e classe operaia*, pp. 163–80.

In British detonator factories, the seventy-seven-hour week with one Sunday off each month was normal in 1915 and 1916.[49] Everywhere, night work became general, including for women. Faced with the claims of working women, this over-exploitation was somewhat reduced at the end of the war, particularly in Great Britain where studies showed that it diminished productivity. To intensify productivity, wage policies substituted piecework rates for hourly or daily wages. To make hours and production aims respected, discipline was strengthened, becoming semi-military in Germany and in state-controlled establishments in France, the United Kingdom and Italy. The range of sanctions available of course in some countries was strengthened with a particularly dissuasive novelty: despatch to the front. To quote the leader of the Italian metalworkers' union, the FIOM, industrial mobilisation ended in militarisation of the workers.[50] The social tensions created by this over-exploitation, reflected in the doubling or tripling of the number of accidents at work,[51] were all the more serious since they were part of the daily circumstances of societies profoundly challenged by the war.

Living conditions

The first question is to know whether the workers' standard of living improved, was maintained or reduced during the war in the various countries. This is very difficult to establish, because statistical series are not clear. The development of hourly wages has little meaning: the number of hours worked increased greatly, and hourly wage rates dropped considerably in comparison with pay by results. The latter increased much more because it favoured productivity. The policy of the French armaments ministry favoured very low base wages, with premiums for raised production.[52] In Turin, the increase in piecework pay exceeded the hourly wage by between 50 and 100 per cent.[53] In Great Britain, as we have seen, unskilled workers paid at piece rates gained more than the skilled workers, paid on a time basis, who maintained or adapted their machinery, so that some skilled workers did

49 Waites, *Class Society at War*, p. 136.

50 Luigi Tomassini, 'Mobilitazione industriale e classe operaia', in Procacci, *Stato e classe operaia*, p. 80. Proposal sustained at the congress of November 1918.

51 Waites, *Class Society at War*, pp. 134–9; Noel Whiteside, 'Concession, coercion or cooperation? State policy and industrial unrest in Britain, 1915–1920', in Haimson and Sapelli, *Strikes*, pp. 107–22.

52 Robert, *Les Ouvriers*, p. 109.

53 Stefano Musso, 'Political tension and labor union struggle: working-class conflicts in Turin during and after the First World War', in Haimson and Sapelli, *Strikes*, pp. 213–43.

take the jobs of the unskilled to earn more.[54] Elsewhere, sectors essential for the pursuit of the war were privileged, since governments were prepared to make concessions to avoid even short-lived strikes. Finally, employers and governments often preferred to grant indemnities against the raised cost of living, or 'war bonuses', rather than offer increased basic wages, in the hope that once the war was over the advantages conceded could be recovered. The result was a great lack of order in pay scales; reconstructed charts of wage indexation are therefore generally unreliable.

In all countries faced with rising claims, however, governments imposed wage increases on employers. Amounts therefore depended on power relations between the government and the employers, which were much more favourable to workers in Great Britain than in France and above all in Germany or Russia. In all countries, wage hierarchies were reduced: unskilled wages increased more than those for the skilled; for identical work, women's wages remained appreciably lower than those of their male counterparts, but the gender gap in wages diminished.

These facts sketch out an important change in the very concept of fair wages. Qualification and responsibility, the nobility of skill, counted less in the definition of wages than their principal function, which was to make life possible. That wages should follow the cost of living was a new idea. It led the British Government to re-examine wages every three months from February 1917. Does this mean that workers' wages in effect followed the rise in prices during the war?

The answer is no less difficult, since product prices did not all evolve at the same rate, and what is known as 'the cost of living' depends on what is selected to put in the housewife's hypothetical basket. Following the composition of indices, their evolution differs. Further, the base data details for 1914 to 1918 are often scanty or incomplete. But there is a more serious aspect: they are silent on the black market which, in Germany and Austria particularly, played a decisive role, since it is thought to have provided one-third of food consumption.[55] Employers, with the complicity of the authorities and the army, turned to the black market for supplies of food which they gave their workforce, to the extent that at the end of their war, town councils were also using the black market to purchase for their soup kitchens.[56] The cost of living was in fact far higher than appeared in the official published price lists.

54 Waites, *Class Society at War*, pp. 143–9; Whiteside, 'Concession, coercion or cooperation', pp. 107–22.

55 Kocka, *Facing Total War*, pp. 21–5.

56 Feldman, *Army, Industry and Labor*, pp. 389, 443.

Despite these uncertainties, it is impossible to avoid the question: how did the workers' standard of living evolve during the war? Table 13.2 shows some elements of response, despite all the uncertainties involved. These data show, first, important differences between the warring nations. The standard of living for German workers seems to have deteriorated profoundly, particularly because these figures do not include the effect of the black market. Italian workers also experienced a drop of one-third. In contrast, the cost of living for Russian workers seems to have been maintained until the revolution of February 1917, which provoked a sharp drop. British and French workers, meanwhile, or more precisely their least skilled workers, suffered less from the war. In 1918, real wages for the unskilled in Great Britain on the one hand, and for women workers in Paris metal industries on the other, rose slightly – but this was a strongly favoured sector in the French capital. The particularly rigorous study by Jean-Louis Robert, unfortunately unpublished, proves that in Paris construction workers, carpenters and railway workers were losers in terms of their purchasing power by 29, 39 and 45 per cent respectively. British railwaymen, miners and building workers, and still more those in the cotton industry, also lost out, although less, it seems, than did their French counterparts.

These statistics pose a question: they do not correspond to representations at the time. In France, as in Britain and even in Germany or Italy, the concept that workers were winning the war against rising prices was very widely accepted. This was true for the character, Maillecotin, in *Les Hommes de bonne volonté*, by Jules Romains: a shell-turner and his wife, paid six times their pre-war wages, who were enjoying the good life. Yet this was a myth, at least where it concerned wages. In the case of Great Britain, various indices offer a degree of consistency. There was the drop in infant mortality, as demonstrated by Jay Winter, which was noticed by school inspections: never before had the children in the poorest districts been so well clothed and fed – their health had never been better.[57] How can this paradox be explained?

By full employment, as Waites responded. After two months of very high unemployment, the war had finally put an end to seasonal unemployment depending on casual work, which was the bane of the British working classes. He sees here the origin of a unifying element in the consumption patterns of skilled workers, who were proud of their respectability, particularly as drink, a not inconsiderable expense, was severely restricted in 1915. In Britain, the sale of alcohol was authorised from midday to 2.30 p.m. only, while absinthe was

57 Waites, *Class Society at War*, p. 163.

Table 13.2 *Wages and cost of living (1913/14 = 100)*

	1913	1914	1915	1916	1917	1918	1919
Germany							
Cost of living (1)	100	103	129	170	253	313	415
True wages in real terms (2)			103	88	79	65	66
Great Britain							
Wages (1)		100	105/10	115/20	137/40	175/80	210/15
Engineering, skilled (3)		100	110	111	134	173	199
Engineering, unskilled (3)		100			154	213	255
Cost of living (January) (1)		100	110/15	135	165	185/90	220
True wages		100	96	117	120	106	105
France							
Wages (4)		100	110	125	130	175	250
True metalworking wages Paris (5)							
Male worker		100		93	105	92	100
Female worker		100		110	137	119	126
Turner		100		94	88	76	100
Fitter		100		91	82	70	89
Italy							
True wage (6)	100	99.7	93.5	85.0	73.1	64.6	93.1
Russia							
True wage (7)	100	105	106	107	83		

1 Jürgen Kocka, *Facing Total War, German Society, 1914–1918* (Leamington Spa and Cambridge, MA: Berg and Harvard University Press, 1984), p. 21.
2 Albrecht Ritschl, 'The pity of peace: Germany's economy at war, 1914–1918 and beyond', in Stephen Broadberry and Mark Harrison (eds.), *The Economics of World War I* (Cambridge University Press, 2005), p. 54.
3 'Weekly wages', in Bernard Waites, *A Class Society at War. England 1914–1918* (Leamington Spa: Berg, 1987), p. 137.
4 John Horne, *Labour at War. France and Britain 1914–1918* (Oxford: Clarendon Press, 1991), appendix.
5 Jean-Louis Robert, *Ouvriers et mouvement ouvrier parisien pendant la grande guerre, et l'immédiat après-guerre, historie et anthropologie* (unpublished thesis, Unversité Paris I, 1989), ch. 3.
6 Bordogna *et al.*, 'Labour conflicts in Italy before the rise of fascism, 1881–1923, a quantitative analysis', in Léopold H. Haimson and Charles Tilly, *Strikes, Wars and Revolutions in an International Perspective* (Cambridge and Paris: Cambridge University Press, Ed. de la MSH, 1989), p. 225.
7 Gatrell, 'Poor Russia, poor show: mobilising a backward economy for war, 1914–1917', in Broadberry and Harrison, *Economics of World War I*, p. 254.

completely banned in France. Above all, the mobility of the labour force was invoked. One of the most striking features of the period was in fact the high rate of worker turnover in the factories, sometimes running at five or six times the pre-war level. All governments struggled against this work-force mobility, and its limitation was a governmental aim in addition to leaving certificates. These were insisted on by Berlin employers from January 1915, imposed in Britain by the Munitions Act of 1915, generalised by the German Auxiliary Service Law in 1916, applied by Italian industrial mobilisation and the regime of special postings in France. The statistics registered the pattern of increasing wages for a given position, but workers continued to leave their position for a better paid post. Here is one of the explanations for contemporary impressions, which are contradicted by wage statistics.

Yet these remarks, valid for Great Britain and, to a lesser degree for France, are not relevant to Germany, Russia or even Italy, where the deterioration in working conditions was undeniable. Before seeing this contrast as a reason for revolutionary developments in certain countries and not others, we should examine the actions of those directly involved, since revolt does not emerge either spontaneously or automatically from over-exploitation and poverty.

Changes in the labour movement

Organisations: structure and foundation

On the eve of the war, labour movements differed greatly from one country to another. German employers had chosen to ignore the socialist unionism of the *Generalkommission der Gewerkschaften* as well as the Christian and liberal unions. To stifle them, unofficial unions, sometimes representing more than half the workers, had developed in the factories.[58] Similarly, Italian unions were on the defensive. The CGIL (Confederazione Generale Italiana dei Lavoro) was challenged, as in Germany, by the Christian unions. In France, trade-unionist-revolutionary agitation diminished after showing its great strength in 1906 to 1910, and the Confédération Générale du Travail had fewer than 300,000 members. In contrast, British trade unions were in full expansion; the powerful railways, transport and mining unions had formed a threatening triple alliance. The employers negotiated regularly with union representatives in their factories, but did not talk collectively with the trade

58 Friedhelm Boll, 'Reformist and revolutionary strike practice in Germany. Labor disputes in Hanover and Braunschweig 1906–1919', in Haimson and Sapelli, *Strikes*, pp. 351–66.

unions themselves. In Russia, strikes broke out very frequently, unceasingly and repeatedly.

From the very beginning of the war, the unions renounced their previous internationalism and proclaimed their support for their nation. In France and Britain, they formed committees with the political parties to which they were close to coordinate their activities and claims. In France, from September 1914, the CGT/socialist action committee was soon extended to worker cooperatives, and in Britain the War Emergency Workers National Committee was founded on 5 August 1914 and represented the TUC, the Labour Party and various other groups or unions.[59] Everywhere, strikes ceased. The most spectacular case was Russia, where the pattern of activity shifted from 2,404 strikers with 887,000 strikers in 1913 and 3,493 strikes with 1,328,000 strikes in the first seven months of 1914, to a mere 41 strikes involving 9,451 strikers for the final five months of the year.[60]

Apart from Russia, where unionism was forbidden and governmental repression was severe (thirty dead and fifty-three wounded in a strikers' demonstration at Ivanovo-Vosnesensk in August 1915), nations generally negotiated with the unions to avoid or halt strikes which interrupted production. The unions focused on the situation, in exchange for material advantages for the workers. They also hoped that their active loyalty would win them official recognition, and in this respect were partially successful.

The French Government first engaged in this process in August 1914, when it gave an official role to the Secretary General of the CGT, Léon Jouhaux. In February 1915, he established inter-departmental commissions for the return to work, a move greeted by a very confrontational unionist as 'a victory for the organised working class, in the sense that this was the first time that the public authorities deliberated and took action with the confederated organisations'.[61] The Ministers for the Interior and Munitions always supported each other over the unions. When he banned strikes and made arbitration on work conflicts obligatory (decree of 17 January 1917), Albert Thomas gave the responsibility to mixed departmental commissions in which employer and worker representatives met on equal terms. In Great Britain, in February 1915,

59 On the CA, CGT/PS and the WEWNC, see Horne, *Labour at War*. Further, on the WEWNC, see Roden Harrisson, 'The War Emergency Workers' National Committee', in Asa Briggs and John Saville (eds), *Essays in Labour History, 1886–1923* (London and Basingstoke: Macmillan, 1971).

60 Diane P. Loenker and William G. Rosenberg, *Strikes and Revolution in Russia* (Princeton University Press, 1989), p. 58.

61 Unions of Stone-masons, 25 April 1915, Robert, *Les Ouvriers*, p. 90.

the railway companies – which had hitherto opposed the move – granted the unions full recognition in wage negotiations.[62] Government and unions together negotiated the Munitions of War Act, leaving certificates and conscription. In Italy, union representatives met on equal terms with those of the employers in the CRMIs. In Germany, in 1916, the unions won the right not to be considered as political organisations, thereby legalising the right of young people to become members and take part in union meetings.[63] The German Patriotic Auxiliary Service Law forced the government to make substantial concessions to the unions, to the great displeasure of employers and the High Command. There was more: the German unions had the satisfaction of winning a longstanding claim, the ending of the very inegalitarian census-based electoral system. The Kaiser announced its abandonment in his speech at Easter 1917.

The unions hoped for this recognition to become permanent and that the gains won in wartime would become accepted rights. John Horne and Jean-Louis Robert have shown how the war changed the status of the state in the eyes of trade union leaders. A simple repressive tool in the eyes of pre-war French revolutionary-unionists, the state was now a partner open to arbitration in favour of the workers, and had shown proof of its effectiveness in the organisation of the economy. A reformist union programme emerged in 1916, including notably the nationalisation of the mines, railways and electricity. The same pattern developed in Britain, even though the move towards reform was taken on by the Labour Party rather than the unions, which reflected trade-union thinking in most respects. Its 1917 programme, *Labour and the New Social Order*, was also based on a still broader policy of nationalisation. In Italy, although the CGIL did not go as far as nationalisation, in May 1917 it adopted a reformist programme.[64]

Beyond doubt the war stimulated contacts between the labour movement and the state. The experience of industrial mobilisation had made fresh horizons of expectation conceivable. They were disappointed in 1920 to 1921, which has led John Horne to suggest that the heritage of this reformism should be sought not in the aftermath of 1918, but after 1945.[65]

Collaboration with the public authorities, which also developed over matters of housing and food supplies, distanced the unions from their base. The workers were torn: they appreciated the gains obtained, but always

62 Waites, *Class Society at War*, p. 140. 63 Feldman, *Army, Industry and Labor*, p. 222.
64 Tomassini, 'Mobilitazione industriale', p. 89.
65 'Should be sought not in the first but in the second *après-guerre*', Horne, *Labour at War*, p. 394.

considered them inadequate because local situations were never fully taken into account. Certain measures, such as restrictions on mobility which were accepted by the organisers in the name of the war effort, were not well received in the workshops. In any case, the procedures of union negotiation were too long-drawn-out for the resolution of urgent problems.

This context gave fresh vitality and a new function to bodies which already existed in certain factories, such as Italy's internal commissions, Germany's mixed commissions or work chambers (*Arbeitskammer*), which were challenged but more or less tolerated by the employers and managers. Berlin had 246 of these bodies in 1902, representing approximately one factory in four.[66] In both countries, the unions pushed for recognition of the commissions, their institutionalisation and the extension of their powers. The employers opposed such moves, but the governments forced their hand. In Italy, the decree of 23 June 1918 recognised the internal commissions, although it specified that they were temporary and purely consultative. Still, they had a legal existence.[67] In Germany, the Patriotic Auxiliary Service Law of December 1916 provided for worker committees (*Arbeiter Ausschusse*) in all businesses with more than fifty employees. Elected proportionally, they could hold meetings if one-quarter of their members were in favour. These worker committees were an effective creation: in the Düsseldorf area, out of 922 factories subject to the law, only 144 still did not have them in place by August 1917.[68]

In Great Britain, the shop steward's role was to be transformed by the war. Generally rising from the ranks of the skilled workers, they were charged by the unions to collect membership fees in the workshops; but as they became the spokesmen for the workers, the most militant among them organised protests and became genuine leaders, poorly controlled by the unions. They were particularly active on Clydeside and in the naval shipyards, with a first substantial strike involving 10,000 strikers which lasted for two weeks in February 1915. In October 1915, it gave birth to the Clyde Workers' Committee, which represented between 250 and 300 factory delegates. On the occasion of the Hargreaves affair, a similar committee was formed in Sheffield, another great centre of factories engaged in war production. These two bastions constituted a form of union counter-power, but the government refused to meet and discuss issues with them.

66 Dirk H. Müller, 'Trades unions, workers' committees and workers' councils in Berlin's wartime industry, 1914–1918', in Haimson and Sapelli, *Strikes*, pp. 287–301.

67 Simonetta Ortaggi, 'Dalle commssioni interni al consigli di fabrica', in Procacci, *Stato e classe operaia*, pp. 212–29.

68 Feldman, *Army, Industry and Labor*, p. 318.

In France, the worker movement was too weak and too indifferent to the problems of organisation to have created any pattern of continuity in the factories. Union sections which already existed had been dissolved by mobilisation. Active militants did exist, and were known and recognised, but no true structure emerged. Albert Thomas, who instigated the creation of workshop delegates, was reproached for it by industrialists and politicians on the right, but the decision of 16 January 1917[69] required all war factories employing more than fifty workers to nominate workshop delegates. Some employers chose these delegates, but election became the rule. At Renault, the electors, men and women, had to be French and aged at least 21: to be elected, the minimum age was 25, with a minimum of one year in the factory.[70] These delegates played the same role as the shop stewards in Britain, and the unions had the same problems in controlling them.

The wartime social movement: an interpretation

The institution of these commissions and delegates accompanied the return of strikes, and Table 13.3 displays the appreciable differences between the nations. Because of its very strict military supervision, Italy had very few strikes during the entire war, but the United Kingdom suffered considerably from strikes in 1915 and 1916, with more numerous episodes in the following years. In France and Germany, the number and scale increased strongly from 1917. Two very different reasons lay behind this: the first was the terrible winter of 1916–17, with four months of below-average temperatures, barges blocked by ice on the River Seine in Paris in February, and in Germany, where it became known as the 'turnip winter', devastating shortages of coal and potatoes. The second was the February Revolution in Russia, which raised hopes because it showed that change was possible in this state of stalemate.

These strikes, however, had features in common. Initially, they occurred spontaneously, starting from the bottom up, sometimes against union advice. The only strike which arose in response to a call to action was the action launched in Germany against the prosecution of Karl Liebknecht on 28 June 1916. Strong in Berlin (55,000 strikers) and in several other cities (Braunschweig, Bremen, Leipzig, Stuttgart), the strike did not become general and remained an isolated incident.

69 Oualid and Piquenard, *Salaires et tariffs*, p. 186, stress that this was a decision, not a decree or official order. Its legal foundation was a decree of 10 April 1899 on the working conditions in business which had an agreement with the state.

70 Gilbert Hatry, 'Les délégués d'atelier aux usines Renault', in Fridenson, *1914–1918*, pp. 221–35.

Table 13.3 *Trade union members, strikes and strikers*

	1913	1914	1915	1916	1917	1918	1919
Germany							
Union members (thousands) (1)	2,525	1,503	995	945	1,278	2,866	7,337
Strikes (2)			137	240	561	531	3,700
Strikers (thousands) (3)			61	14	129	667	391
Great Britain							
Union members (thousands) (4)	2,232		2,682	2,851	3,082	4,532	5,284
Strikes (5)	1,497	972	672	532	730	1,116	1,352
Strikers (thousands) (5)	516	326	401	235	575	923	2,401
France							
Union members (federations, thousands) (6)	355	257	50	101	296	599	1,230
Strikes (7)			19	102	336	161	171
Strikers (thousands) (7)			0.38	11.6	247	207.1	401
Italy							
Union members Confederazione Generale del Lavoro (thousands) (8)	327	321	234	201	238	249	1,159
Strikes (9)	810	752	539	516	442	303	1,663
Strikers (thousands) (9)	385	173	132	124	169	158	1,049
Russia							
Strikes (10)		3,534	1,034	1,161			
Strikers (thousands) (10)		1,337	553	878			

1 Dietmar Petzina *et al.*, *Materialen sur Statistik des deutschen Reichs 1914* (Munich: C. H. Beck, 1978), p. 111. Free unions (*Generalkommission*) only.
2 Kocka, *Facing Total War*, ch. 2.
3 Ritschl, 'The pity of peace', p. 57.
4 Horne, *Labour at War*, appendices.
5 Cronin, 'Strikes and power in Britain, 1870–1920', in Haimson and Tilly, *Strikes, Wars and Revolutions*, pp. 82–3.
6 Jean-Louis Robert, *La scission syndicale de 1921, essai de reconnaissance des formes* (Paris: Publ. de la Sorbonne, 1980), p. 159, dues paid to the federations.
7 Jean-Louis Robert, *Les Ouvriers, la Patrie et la Revolution. Paris 1914–1918* (Besançon: Annales littéraires de l'Université de Besançon no. 392, série historique no. 11, 1995), p. 12. Figure for 1919 for the period January–July only.
8 Bordogna, pp. 220, 225.
9 Musso, 'Political tension and labor union struggle: working-class conflicts in Turin during and after the First World War', in Léopold H. Haimson and Giulio Sapelli, *Strikes, Social Conflict and the First World War. An International Perspective* (Milan: Feltrinelli, 1992), p. 214.
10 Diane P. Koenker and William G. Rosenberg, *Strikes and Revolution in Russia* (Princeton University Press, 1989), p. 58.

These strikes were characterised later by strong participation on the part of the young, and above all of women, who had no fear of being sent to the front. The strikes of May to June 1917 in Paris were a spectacular example, for no one had ever seen such a large wave of strikes in the capital: starting with the 'cousettes', the dressmaking apprentices, they expanded to bring in the 'munitionettes' and mobilised at least 133,000 strikers, of whom 80 per cent were women.[71] At the same moment, the Petrograd laundry women went on strike for several weeks. At the beginning of the Russian Revolution, it was women who launched the strike of 23 February/8 March. In the summer of 1917, young people and women were prominent in the strikes in Leipzig.

Regional differences persisted in all countries. Some industrial areas were more strike-prone than others, for a host of reasons. Industrial concentration mattered in some places, and the presence of minority groups mattered in others. In France, areas of militancy included the Paris region and the Loire valley; in Italy, the triangle Genoa-Turin-Milan; in Germany, Berlin and Leipzig; in Great Britain, Clydeside and the Sheffield area. The harsh rules of German occupation stifled strike action in the industrial regions of Belgium and the north of France. In other areas, for reasons not at all clear, there was a kind of surprising calm in industrial relations. Freiburg-im-Breisgau in the Black Forest, for instance, had no strikes at any time during the war.[72]

In the end, these were short strikes, lasting for a day, sometimes two or three, rarely more than a week. Anxious above all to avoid any break in production, the governments responded very promptly. As the employers were making large profits from government orders, the latter could not condone any rejection of higher wages when the cost of living was manifestly increasing. The first reaction of the governments was therefore that the strikers must be satisfied, without delay. Lloyd George, for example, granted immediate satisfaction to the 200,000 miners on strike in South Wales on 14 July 1915, against the advice of the Minister of Labour. But it was impossible for conflicts to be managed rapidly from the centre as they broke out: all the governments set up a system for obligatory arbitration and banned strikes. This was the purpose of the Munitions Act of 1915 in Great Britain, the Auxiliary Service Law in Germany, the decree of January 1917 in France, and the CRMI in Italy.

71 Robert, *Les Ouvriers*, pp. 125 ff.

72 Roger Chickering, *The Great War and Urban life in Germany. Freiburg, 1914–1918* (Cambridge University Press, 2007).

Arbitration did not suppress strikes: it made them illegal and thus gave governments the legal right to a level of repression which was otherwise very difficult to apply. Overall, they responded case by case, balancing concessions with repression. Faced with the large-scale strike of May 1916 in Manchester, Rotherham, Coventry and Sheffield, Lloyd George agreed not to mobilise any skilled worker as long as any 'dilutees' remained unmobilised, but he ordered the arrest of seven leaders whom he liberated at the end of the strike. He responded very firmly, notably over the introduction of dilution on Clydeside in the spring of 1916, arresting shop stewards and posting them elsewhere.

The situation became strained at the end of the war, since governments were anxious to avoid strikes turning to revolution, as in Russia. The great strike which broke out on 28 January 1918 in Berlin (with 200,000 strikers), and expanded notably in Leipzig, Mannheim, Danzig and Frankfurt, was very severely repressed. The leader was condemned by court-martial to five years in a state prison, and many leaders were sent to the front, with a formal note on their file to ensure that they remained there.[73] The strikes in Silesia at the end of the summer were also quelled by the army. In France, similarly, the Clemenceau government, which initially extended the conciliatory policy of Albert Thomas, came round to strong-arm tactics ahead of the Parisian metalworkers' strike of May 1918 (105,000 strikers), which spread to the armaments factories of the Isère and the Loire. He had the main leaders arrested, and sent to the front 140 workshop delegates who were 'special postings' men.

The evolution of the labour movement broadly explains the hardening of repression. Russia, where strikes were politicised by 1915, was a special case: here, the absence of unions gave political parties a role in calling strikes, which very quickly acquired a pacifist character, as in the Ivanova area in August 1915. Further, the memory of 'Red Sunday', symbol of the rupture between the Tsar and his people, was very strong. The killings in 1905 were commemorated by major strikes on its anniversary on 9/22 January, with 100,000 strikers in Petrograd in 1916 and 200,000 to 300,000 strikers in 1917. The strike committees which developed in the factories called for solidarity against repression in February 1917 and sent delegates to a council: in consequence, in Petrograd and then in Moscow and other cities, soviets of workers' and soldiers' deputies were created which, following the abdication of the Tsar (2/15 March), formed a power parallel to and in competition with that of the provisional government.

The strikes became politicised in other countries from the spring of 1917. By now the strikers were no longer calling only for increased wages or better

73 Feldman, *Army, Industry and Labor*, p. 450.

working conditions, but for worker control and the end of the war. The scandal of employers' profits and the opacity of wage scales explained the demand for worker control and was particularly strong in Italy, where it was supported by the metalworkers' federation (FIOM). But it could be seen everywhere, notably among the Clydeside shop stewards, in Russia in 1917 and in Germany. Here, in 1917, the unions proposed to the government joint chambers operating on equal terms in factories which employed more than twenty workers, in particular to discuss wages. Opposition from the industrialists and the High Command brought the project to a halt in the Reichstag in May 1918.[74]

The major turning point was the development of pacifist claims, which can be explained not by the Russian Revolution, since the provisional government continued the war until the October Revolution, but by the context. Fatigue and the attritional effects of the war were making themselves felt; victory became more distant and problematic; the lists of the dead grew longer, as did the numbers of widows and orphans. The workers – who were not alone – expressed doubts. Since they rejected a peace of annexation and conquest, they demanded a public statement from the governments, stating their war aims. Peace without annexation headed the list of demands in the German strike of January 1918, and the 200,000 Viennese workers who were on strike at the same time, because of a reduction in the bread ration, said clearly that they no longer wished to fight to make the emperor the King of Poland.[75] The French strikes of May 1918 advanced pacifist slogans. The Peace of Brest-Litovsk (3 March 1918) aroused anger among French and Austrian workers, for its terms were proof of the German will to expand. In Russia, after the February Revolution, protest strikes were called over the Note from the Minister of Foreign Affairs which affirmed his government's intention to remain faithful to Allied war aims.

Jean-Louis Robert has used the term 'patriotic pacifism' to characterise this aspiration. This should not be misunderstood. For the immense majority, workers' pacifism did not mean an absolute rejection of the war. The position defined by the socialists in all the warring nations who met at Zimmerwald (5 to 8 September 1915), then at Kienthal (24 to 30 April 1916), of a peace without either annexations or indemnities, was for a long time very much a minority claim. It became generalised in 1917, although the announcement of a

74 Feldman, *Army, Industry and Labor*, pp. 473–5.
75 Arthur J. May, *The Passing of the Hapsburg Monarchy, 1914–1918* (Philadelphia, PA: University of Pennsylvania Press, 1968), pp. 654 ff.

third conference at Stockholm in September 1917 raised hopes that were rapidly disappointed; none of the governments at war authorised its nationals to attend. This was interpreted as an admission that the states had not rejected annexations. To the workers, therefore, to continue fighting for this unjust objective – which was contrary to the national right to self-determination – appeared outrageous. They did not want anyone to go on having men killed to achieve this. 'We will go to the front and we will consent to all the sacrifices which may be necessary', declared a Parisian striker in 16 May 1918, 'but we want to know why we are fighting'.[76]

However, the Leninist position of transforming the 'imperialist war' into a 'revolutionary war' was not supported by the vast majority of workers. In all the countries, the paradox was that the workers who went on strike for peace simultaneously supported the need for national defence. In London, in the middle of the all-out submarine war of April to May 1917, the strikers at the Crayford Works decided that those who were manufacturing anti-submarine weapons should not go on strike. During the German offensives of the spring of 1918, German, British and French workers gave up their strikes.[77] Through close chronological study, Jean-Louis Robert has shown that the Paris strikes stopped as soon as the Germans broke through the front line.[78] They did not want to be responsible for potential defeat. Dumoulin, although a 'pacifist', admitted this to the CGT conference in 1918: 'Myself, I have the honesty to declare here that one should not go on strike when there is a German offensive, though I am not for national defence at all costs.'[79] Even in Russia, the Soviets in Petrograd and Moscow initially adopted a defensist-revolutionary position: they refused any annexation, but intended to continue defending their freedom.

From the summer of 1918, the pursuit of a war without further hope of victory weakened German unions which remained faithful to the commitments made in 1914. The influence of the USPD, the minority Socialist Party hostile to the war, was growing. In November 1918, the *Oberleute* – the men of confidence – who emerged from the factory workers' commissions set up Worker Councils (*Arbeiterräte*) like the soviets. They joined with the councils of sailors and soldiers to use their parallel power in transforming the abdication of the Kaiser on 9 November into a revolution. The same thing

76 Robert, *Les Ouvriers*, p. 221.
77 Waites, *Class Society at War*, p. 232; Dobson, *Authority and Upheaval*, p. 221.
78 Robert, *Les Ouvriers*, p. 220.
79 Bernard Georges and Denise Tintant, *Léon Jouhaux, cinquante ans de syndicalisme*, vol. 1, *Des origines à 1921* (Paris: Presses Universitaires de France, 1962), p. 308, no. 1.

happened in Vienna, although here the worker committees did not join with the soldiers' committees. The employers then capitulated and granted the unions everything that they had previously refused them. In Russia, on 10/23 March 1918, the industrialists of Petrograd had signed an agreement with the Soviet which accepted the eight-hour day and increased the powers of the factory committees. German employers did the same: the agreement on 12 November 1918 between the employers' leader Stinnes, and Legien, secretary of the General Commission of Unions, included the eight-hour day, collective agreements and the creation of a central permanent commission for all industries, charged with supervision of the collective conventions. But the employers, like their Russian colleagues, had not made an active decision to respect this agreement – it was imposed on them by circumstances. They signed it to avoid the worst. All would depend on the revolution that was erupting.

In the other countries, the post-war period was marked by an outburst of very violent strikes. The most spectacular of these were in France, with the strike of Paris steel workers in June 1919 and railway workers in May 1920, which ended with the dismissal of 23,000 workers; in Britain, the strike on Clydeside for the forty-hour week, which was repressed by troops (30 January to 20 February 1919, with 60,000 demonstrators in Glasgow on 31 January), the miners' strike in November 1919 and the dockers' strike and refusal to load a boat with weapons for Poland, under Soviet attack in April 1920; in Italy, the major strikes of November to December 1919, which ended in a first strike in April 1920 (100,000 strikers) throughout the steel industry and the occupation of the Fiat factories in September 1920. The accumulated claims pushed aside during the war, notably through the threat of being sent to the front, exploded. Lloyd George, a well-placed witness, was fully aware of this when he declared to the Peace Conference on 25 March 1919:

> The whole of Europe is in a revolutionary mood. The workers have a deep feeling of dissatisfaction with conditions of life as they existed before the war; they are full of anger and indignation. The whole of the existing social, political and economic order is being called in question by many of the people from one end of Europe to the other.[80]

And yet it was only in Russia and Germany that revolution broke out. Why?

80 Quoted by Julius Braunthal, *History of the International, 1914–1964* (London: Nelson, 1967), p. 168.

Conclusion

Sociological changes in the working classes are not a sufficient explanation, although they were not without their effect. Within the British shop stewards' movement, a revolt took place led by the most highly skilled workers against union structures and the government and in defence of their status, as James Hinton argued. In Germany, a working class profoundly rooted in German society seems to have been submerged by a new working class made up of uprooted country people, as Ritter argued. These analyses have been influential, but they are in any case too closely focused on the working world to account for the radicalisation of a social movement. It arose out of the prolongation of a war of which the outcome could not be seen, and which still imposed excessive suffering and hardship on society.

In addition, the suffering and the hardships were profoundly unjust. The scandal lay first in war profits, which were enormous, and which were the result of over-exploitation of war workers. German employers had been particularly rapacious: the most spectacular case was that of Daimler, which wished to increase its prices at the end of 1917. The minister asked for the calculations of costs behind the demand: Daimler refused, and threatened to stop all overtime and night shifts, which they said were loss-making. This went too far: it was militarised.[81] The brutality of these industrialists who increased their prices and refused any increase in wages was a matter of public knowledge: they did not even respect the decisions of arbitration commissions. Employers in other countries were scarcely less greedy, but their governments had greater control over them. Under the pressure of the British trade unions, His Majesty's government had apparently been stricter than Albert Thomas in France. The latter acknowledged this in a meeting held with British industrialists in February 1918, explaining that he could not have developed in 'his' industrialists 'the taste for enterprise and risk' if he had not tolerated 'the protection of their profits for unusual production'.[82] Whatever the background, such scandalous profits enraged the workers.

But the feeling of injustice was much stronger. 'Profiteering', a new word, and war profiteers – who were also 'shirkers' – stirred up anger. Wartime sacrifices were not being shared. In Germany and Austria-Hungary, where the blockade, economic disorganisation and the black market led to poverty, hunger and sometimes famine, it was unbearable that the table of the rich

81 Feldman, *Army, Industry and Labor*, p. 480.
82 Hardach, 'La mobilisation industrielle', p. 106.

remained well laden. The spectacle of the well-supplied officers' mess was intolerable to soldiers and sailors who were hungry. The workers' revolt was not rooted only in the factory: it was the very functioning of society which nourished it.

In this suffering, this mourning, this injustice, it was the state which bore central and unavoidable responsibility. When they declared war, the nations had staked their legitimacy on victory. France, Great Britain and Italy had indeed not been capable of remedying wartime injustices; they had, at least, ensured acceptable conditions of life, uninterrupted food supplies, a normal functioning of public services for their people. In Germany and Austria-Hungary, because of the Allied blockade, administrative disorganisation and the black market, there was hunger and disease; the number of civilians who died due to war-related conditions in Central and Balkans Europe was estimated at 2 million. These states had proved their inability to cope with the elementary needs of daily life. Their arrogance and authoritarianism led to disaster.

But there was worse: they had lost the war. Victory would to some extent have legitimised *a posteriori* the sacrifices and injustices that had been imposed on the populations. If these had served a good outcome, they would have been forgiven. But the populations affected realised that their hardships had been to no purpose. Here was defeat and, with it, not only the ruin of so much effort, but the humiliation of being conquered. A state which engages in a total war and is defeated loses all legitimacy.

The Allied nations retained their legitimacy because they had won the war on the home front and on the battle front. More or less successfully they went through the difficult years of the return to peace. The Central Powers and Russia could not resist the revolutionary movement created by their negligence and their defeat.

14
Cities

STEFAN GOEBEL

Between 1924 and 1926, the French committee of the *Histoire économique & sociale de la Grande Guerre* series sponsored by the Carnegie Endowment for International Peace oversaw the publication of a remarkable run of volumes on cities at war: Bordeaux, Bourges, Lyon, Marseille, Paris, Rouen and Tours. The themes covered – industry and commerce, food and transport, housing and employment – were also dealt with in the other national series published under the auspices of the Carnegie Endowment, but what distinguished the French volumes was that they identified the urban experience of modern industrialised war as a significant and distinct story. Written by a combination of public officials and academics, these volumes are characterised by a top-down approach to urban history and a rather disembodied perspective on urban life. To be sure, here and there, the authors break out of the official-history mode. The volume on Paris, for instance, contains – albeit as a kind of afterthought – a chapter on the changing cityscape.[1]

The advance made by the French committee was of little immediate consequence to the historiography of the First World War until the 1990s. Two generations later, though, there was a critical mass of scholars who endeavoured to conceptualise the war in terms of urban history. A comparative study of wartime Paris, London and Berlin, written by a multi-national collective, led the way.[2] A host of studies on individual cities – ranging from total panoramas of urban life to micro-histories of particular groups or sites – has followed. Arguably, the sum of these works is greater than its constituent

1 Three volumes in particular are still indispensable: Henri Sellier *et al.*, *Paris pendant la guerre* (Paris: Presses Universitaires de France, 1926); Édouard Herriot, *Lyon pendant la guerre* (Paris: Presses Universitaires de France, 1924); Paul Masson, *Marseille pendant la guerre* (Paris: Presses Universitaires de France, 1926). For a reassessment of the series, see Jay Winter and Antoine Prost, *The Great War in History: Debates and Controversies, 1914 to the Present* (Cambridge University Press, 2005), pp. 153–5.

2 Jay Winter and Jean-Louis Robert (eds.), *Capital Cities at War: Paris, London, Berlin 1914–1919*, 2 vols. (Cambridge University Press, 1997–2007).

parts; we can see here the contours of a new field emerging: the urban or metropolitan history of total war, integrating the histories of social relations and cultural representations.[3]

Citizens and outcasts

In June 1915, the city of Essen, home to a massive steelworks, unveiled its 'war landmark', sponsored by the Krupp family. The statue of a powerfully muscular figure of a blacksmith equipped with a shield and sword celebrated the war worker as a new type of warrior bearing witness to total, mass-industrialised warfare. It was during this period that – in Germany and elsewhere in urban Europe – the metalworker became the emblematic representation of the labourer. Similarly, martial figures of blacksmiths sprang up in cities throughout the Ruhr industrial basin in 1915 and 1916. Designed to crystallise local pride into a coherent vision of the industrial/urban home front as a genuine second front in the war, these figures also highlighted the new hierarchy of urban citizenship that appeared after 1914.[4]

Before the war, it would have been unthinkable for local dignitaries to put a working man on a pedestal; but the civic stratifications of wartime departed in significant ways from pre-1914 notions of social class. The social upheaval of war enhanced the standing in the urban community of those who contributed directly to the survival of the nation. The symbolic elevation of those workers at the heart of the war economy was matched by the unintended redistribution of incomes. In the industrial cities of Western Europe, the war gave bargaining power to labourers in strategically important sectors such as armaments or shipyards. Here not only the skilled but sometimes also the unskilled – notably, women and young men – were among the economic and symbolic winners. Labourers in key industries enjoyed social recognition, steady employment and wage increases. However, they were the material winners in a relative sense only: their nominal pay rises were eaten up by

3 Stefan Goebel and Derek Keene, 'Towards a metropolitan history of total war: an introduction', in Goebel and Keene (eds.), *Cities into Battlefields: Metropolitan Scenarios, Experiences and Commemorations of Total War* (Farnham: Ashgate, 2011), pp. 1–46; see also Marcus Funck and Roger Chickering (eds.), *Endangered Cities: Military Power and Urban Societies in the Era of the World Wars* (Leiden: Brill, 2004).

4 Stefan Goebel, 'Forging the industrial home front: iron-nail memorials in the Ruhr', in Jenny Macleod and Pierre Purseigle (eds.), *Uncovered Fields: Perspectives in First World War Studies* (Leiden: Brill, 2004), pp. 159–78. On the emblematic figure of the metalworker, see Jean-Louis Robert, *Les Ouvriers, la Patrie et la Révolution: Paris 1914–1919* (Paris: Les Belles Lettres, 1995).

inflation (although some – especially skilled workers – lost less than others), and many (especially the munitionettes) were driven out of employment in industry again after 1918.[5]

The war years saw a levelling up of incomes and an inversion of pre-war privileges – a temporary one in the British and French capitals, but a longer lasting one in German metropolises. Particularly hard-pressed were the property-owning, non-manual working populations uninvolved with the war economy. The salariat, professionals, as well as rentiers dependent on incomes from property or investments were forced to live off their accumulated resources – a serious dilemma for a group whose notion of respectability had traditionally been linked to economic prudence. People that had been the backbone of urban society before 1914 faced the prospect of marginalisation. While their material hardship can be measured with some accuracy, the question of how (or, indeed, if) the war affected middle-class identity and aspirations is more difficult to answer. Did the war trigger a crisis of *Bürgerlichkeit* (bourgeois civility) as has been posited by a comparative study of Leipzig and Edinburgh? The practice of erecting 'war landmarks' as well as a host of other propaganda spectacles and war charities, whose organisation rested firmly in the hands of the bourgeoisie, suggest not. Although perilously close to economic disaster, the middle classes continued their involvement in the major spheres of urban public life.[6]

It is important to note the war's differential impact on sectors within the war economy and on sub-groups within social classes – and not only in the cities of the major belligerents, but also in those 'neutral' European countries whose economies thrived on the extra demand from abroad. In German cities, large-scale heavy industry enjoyed unparalleled prosperity, whereas big shipping lines, small merchant houses and corporate banks went into decline. Thus, in a commercial hub like Hamburg, with its global business interests and trade

5 Jonathan Manning, 'Wages and purchasing power', in Winter and Robert, *Capital Cities*, vol. 1, pp. 255–85; Niall Ferguson, *Paper and Iron: Hamburg Business and German Politics in the Era of Inflation, 1887–1927* (Cambridge University Press, 1995), pp. 126–8, 135; Mary Nolan, *Social Democracy and Society: Working-Class Radicalism in Düsseldorf, 1890–1920* (Cambridge University Press, 1981), pp. 253–4, 266; Elizabeth H. Tobin, 'War and the working class: the case of Düsseldorf 1914–1918', *Central European History*, 18 (1985), pp. 268–75.

6 Jon Lawrence, 'Material pressures on the middle classes', in Winter and Robert, *Capital Cities*, vol. 1, pp. 229–54; Martin H. Geyer, *Verkehrte Welt: Revolution, Inflation und Moderne; München 1914–1924* (Göttingen: Vandenhoeck & Ruprecht, 1998), pp. 152–5; Michael Schäfer, *Bürgertum in der Krise: Städtische Mittelklassen in Edinburgh und Leipzig 1890 bis 1930* (Göttingen: Vandenhoeck & Ruprecht, 2003); Dietmar Molthagen, *Das Ende der Bürgerlichkeit? Liverpooler und Hamburger Bürgerfamilien im Ersten Weltkrieg* (Göttingen: Wallstein, 2007).

networks, the economy contracted. Here even the upper echelons of the middle classes felt the pressure. By contrast, in Barcelona, the war years saw accelerated industrial development and the emergence of a class of nouveau riche.[7]

The (perceived) rise of the parvenu capitalist signalled the arrival of a new adversarial language of class in metropolitan life in the era of the Great War. After 1914, the fault line ran no longer between capital and labour per se, but between the 'war profiteer' and the patriotic citizen. In wartime representations (notably, in those fashioned by the satirical press), the big city appeared as a hotbed of licentious pleasures, conspicuous consumption and unchecked speculation – the natural habitat of the shameless speculator and shirker who was typically identified as a munitions maker, a trader on the black market or a bureaucrat in a cushioned job. The image of the profiteer not only drove a wedge between different groups within urban communities, but also between different cities. To residents of Munich, Berlin appeared the capital of profiteering; Antwerpians suspected the people of Brussels of faring well; and starving Viennese imagined Bratislava's residents feasting on strudel.[8]

In the polarised climate of finger-pointing within urban communities, the image of the profiteer and shirker often blended with the ideas about 'the Jew'. The upsurge of anti-Semitism was most striking in cities such as Breslau (Wrocław) that had been previously governed by a liberal consensus about pluralism in urban life. Between 1860 and 1914, Jews and other Breslauers had been close and anti-Semitism confined to the fringes of respectable society. The high degree of Jewish integration in that city eroded in the aftermath of the 'Jew count' of 1916. Ranging from subtle discrimination to open riots, anti-Semitism was part of a witch-hunt on imagined internal enemies within urban communities: profiteers, Jews and foreigners. European city-dwellers waged remarkably local wars against perceived enemies from within. In Vienna, the city's resident population of Jews, Czechs, Hungarians and Poles were a thorn in the German-speaking citizens' side, in fact, to such a degree that the authorities worried that the people had failed to grasp the seriousness of the external threat.[9]

7 Ferguson, *Paper and Iron*, pp. 108, 135; Chris Ealham, *Class, Culture and Conflict in Barcelona 1898–1937* (London: Routledge, 2005), pp. 4, 20.

8 Jean-Louis Robert, 'The image of the profiteer', in Winter and Robert, *Capital Cities*, vol. 1, pp. 104–32; Robert, *Les Ouvriers*, pp. 310–12; Maureen Healy, *Vienna and the Fall of the Habsburg Empire: Total War and Everyday Life in World War I* (Cambridge University Press, 2004), pp. 49, 64–8, 269–70; Geyer, *Verkehrte Welt*, pp. 273–7.

9 Till van Rahden, *Jews and Other Germans: Civil Society, Religious Diversity, and Urban Politics in Breslau, 1860–1925* (Madison, WI: University of Wisconsin Press, 2008), pp. 231–8; Maureen Healy, 'Local space and total war: enemies in Vienna in the two world wars', in Goebel and Keene, *Cities into Battlefields*, pp. 119–32.

The capital city of the Habsburg Empire was a Central European potpourri of people; just under half of its pre-war population had been recent arrivals. In the era before the war, large conurbations and, particularly, capital cities like Vienna had acted as magnets for migrants. In the age of industrialisation and urbanisation, foreign communities had increased exponentially and left their imprint on urban economies and cultural life. Even if they were not fully integrated or assimilated, migrant workers were at least tolerated. Yet, after 1914, certain expatriates became 'enemy aliens' and were subjected to discrimination, internment or violence; they were now at the very bottom of that new hierarchy of urban citizenship (by contrast, refugees from friendly nations, notably Belgians in London and Paris, were received into urban society, initially at least, with much compassion).[10] In effect, a xenophobic climate undermined the essence of metropolitan life. Before the war, transnational contacts and exchanges had been seen as an intrinsic part of what constituted a metropolis. The big cities often prided themselves for being *weltoffen* (literally, open to the world), but in the process of mobilisation the once-cherished cosmopolitanism was done away with, and, in a sense, metropolises became less metropolitan.

Consider the case of the German populations of London and Moscow, which had risen substantially during the second half of the nineteenth century. In London, the 27,000-strong German community was hit by five waves of riots during the war. Most notorious was the disorder of May 1915, which left 257 people injured, including many police officers. Even though the use of violence was sometimes indiscriminate – naturalised Germans and Russian Jews also became targets – the riots were neither unrestrained nor purposeless. Rather, the rioting was about the redefinition of local community and thus a battle over the symbolically charged public space in the capital. At the same time as the London mob was ravaging German property in the city, anti-alien riots broke out in Moscow. Both the London and Moscow riots followed a similar trajectory, but the disorder in the Russian metropolis was more violent (involving a number of deaths) and raised more serious questions about the stability of the polity as a whole.[11]

10 Winter and Robert, *Capital Cities*, vol. II, pp. 31–3, 95, 206–9, 212–14, 410.

11 Panikos Panayi, 'Anti-German riots in London during the First World War', *German History*, 7 (1989), pp. 184–203; Jon Lawrence, 'Public space, political space', in Winter and Robert, *Capital Cities*, vol. II, pp. 293–4; Eric Lohr, *Nationalizing the Russian Empire: The Campaign against Enemy Aliens during World War I* (Cambridge, MA: Harvard University Press, 2003), pp. 31–54.

The riots of May 1915 show how the global conflict brought about a climate of suspicion of a relatively small group of foreigners. By comparison, in the multi-ethnic and multi-religious cities of Eastern and South-Eastern Europe and Asia Minor, the experience of war and occupation aggravated more deep-rooted fissures with more far-reaching consequences for the social fabric of urban life. In Riga, relations between national and religious groups had begun to deteriorate since the 1860s. The fragile local community fell eventually to pieces after 1914. Under the eyes of the Russian authorities, the German language was driven to the margins of public life, and German denizens became fair game for their Latvian neighbours. The German seizure of the city in 1917 did nothing to restore local cohesion, and the multi-ethnic city disintegrated fully in the civil war of 1919 to 1920, which added the dimension of 'class' to the older ethnic and religious antagonisms. Compare to this the case of Lemberg (Lvov) in Austrian Galicia, where again the world war and the ensuing civil war became catalysts for radical nationalism. Yet, in pre-war Lemberg, radical nationalism seems to have been less virulent and divisive than in Riga. Until 1914, Poles, Ukrainians and Jews had lived under Austrian supervision in familiar juxtaposition. It was only during the war that 'nationality' became a dominant issue for many citizens.[12]

Even more dramatic was the wholesale uprooting of urban communities in Greece and Asia Minor in the aftermath of the Greco-Turkish War of 1919 to 1922. In the wake of the Turkish recapture of Smyrna (Izmir) in 1922, the cosmopolitan port of the eastern Mediterranean, some 30,000 Greek and Armenian Christians were killed and three-quarters of the city destroyed by fires, including the Armenian, Greek and Levantine districts. The killing and forced removal of its non-Muslim population rid Smyrna of its Ottoman cosmopolitanism and paved the way for the construction of a Turkish city. Many Greeks who escaped the conflagration found a new home in Salonica, driving out in their turn that city's remaining Muslim population – the group that had dominated urban life for the previous five centuries. The demographic shake-up of Salonica in the period between the Balkan wars and the 1923 population exchange was paralleled by a reconstruction of its urban space. The Ottoman town and its Jewish core had been consumed in a fire in 1917,

12 Ulrike von Hirschhausen, *Die Grenzen der Gemeinsamkeit: Deutsche, Letten, Russen und Juden in Riga 1860–1914* (Göttingen: Vandenhoeck & Ruprecht, 2006), pp. 367–70; Christoph Mick, 'Nationalisierung in einer multiethnischen Stadt: Interethnische Konflikte in Lemberg 1890–1920', *Archiv für Sozialgeschichte*, 40 (2000), pp. 128–46.

and after the war the city was rebuilt along modernist principles, where little remained of its Ottoman past.[13]

Bread-and-butter issues

In August 1914, Parisian crowds staged attacks on a number of stores owned (or believed to be owned) by Germans or Austrians. Initially, it was anti-alien sentiment alone which explained these spontaneous outbursts of violence; but later on in the war, equally important was resentment of increasing (food) prices and the merchants who raised them. No other issue preoccupied and often polarised urban populations as much as the food question. The city-dweller, notably in Central Europe, seemed to live in a 'world turned upside down', where money alone could no longer secure one's daily bread.[14] Burghers went to the countryside to barter ignominiously one-time status symbols such as rugs and jewellery for necessities like eggs and milk.

Calculating farmers, fraudulent traders (often imagined as Jews) and also wasteful war workers were blamed for the shortage of foodstuffs and the ensuing crisis of value in the cities. In Germany, popular opinion and the local press condemned the seller not the buyer of black-market goods and, from early 1915 onwards, pitted the image of the (male) profiteer against that of the *minderbemittelte Frauen* (women of lesser means). An explicitly urban collective persona, the 'women of lesser means' recast social categories in patterns of consumption, thereby reconfiguring pre-war conceptions of (working and lower-middle) classes. Similarly, in Paris, the official *union sacrée* did not terminate, but transformed class conflict, channelling it into a consumer struggle in which women took centre stage.[15]

The provisioning of urban centres with foodstuffs was hampered by several factors: the severance of international trade, reduced agricultural production at home, the lack of transport, the migration of additional population attracted by employment opportunities in war industry, and a policy that prioritised the army and set cities at the end of the erratic supply chain. Initially, many a

13 Mark Mazower, *Salonica: City of Ghosts: Christians, Muslims and Jews 1430–1950* (London: Harper Perennial, 2005), pp. 332–70; Biray Kolluoğlu Kırlı, 'Forgetting the Smyrna fire', *History Workshop Journal*, 60 (2005), pp. 25–44.

14 Geyer, *Verkehrte Welt*.

15 Belinda J. Davis, *Home Fires Burning: Food, Politics, and Everyday Life in World War I Berlin* (Chapel Hill, NC: University of North Carolina Press, 2000); Tyler Stovall, *Paris and the Spirit of 1919: Consumer Struggles, Transnationalism, and Revolution* (Cambridge University Press, 2012), pp. 25–79; Antoon Vrints, *Het theater van de straat: Publiek geweld in Antwerpen tijdens de eerste helft van de twintigste eeuw* (Amsterdam University Press, 2011).

city-dweller proved receptive to appeals for patriotic austerity and self-denial. It was not the shortages of critical foodstuffs as such, but their perceived unequal distribution that caused much friction. True to the spirit of a 'total' war, ordinary consumers expected the national government and local administration to intervene in the market economy in an unprecedented way by rationing and imposing price ceilings on necessities. Recognising the combined nutritional and symbolic relevance of bread and its place in popular Parisian memory, the authorities not only banned fancy bakery products, but also revived a law of 1791 fixing the price of bread at the pre-war level throughout the war. In the German capital, calls for a benevolent 'food dictator' were heard as early as 1915 and grew louder in 1916. Everywhere, the procurement and allocation of food became a – or, in many places, the – main business of city government. A system of food rationing was introduced in Berlin and Vienna in early 1915; in Paris, towards the middle of the war; but, in London, not until February 1918. Stability in London was in part achieved at the expense of a drain of resources from the colonies and dominions, and spiralling food prices in cities such as Calcutta or Melbourne.[16]

Market conditions were controlled, but never completely suspended. Relatively successful in quelling discontent in the Allied capitals, regulation failed to prevent chronic shortages, galloping inflation and illicit trading in Berlin. The authorities were well meaning; the main obstacle was not bureaucratic, but lay in the volatility of deliveries. Precarious from the start of the war, the food situation developed into a full-blown crisis from 1916 onwards. The turnip winter of 1916/17 saw not only supplies of all staples plummet, but humiliatingly forced Berliners and other Germans to eat a vegetable considered to be animal fodder. To be sure, there were significant variations between cities in Central Europe. Thus, a town like Freiburg in Baden with a significant agricultural hinterland fared comparatively better than the major conurbations. But did the inhabitants of the fifty or so German and Austrian *Großstädte* with a population of over 100,000 really starve? Contemporary experts were divided. Viennese physicians claimed that malnourishment was the direct cause in 7 to 11 per cent of deaths and a contributing cause in 20 to 30 per cent of cases. By contrast, a survey of food consumption in Leipzig concluded that, apart from the winter of 1916/17 and the summer of 1918, the

16 Thierry Bonzon and Belinda Davis, 'Feeding the cities', in Winter and Robert, *Capital Cities*, vol. 1, pp. 305–41; Healy, *Vienna*, pp. 43–4; Stovall, *Paris*, pp. 52–3; Herriot, *Lyon*, pp. 39–43; Suchetana Chattopadhyay, 'War, migration and alienation in colonial Calcutta: the remaking of Muzaffar Ahmad', *History Workshop Journal*, 64 (2007), pp. 214–16.

wartime diet was adequate, if short in meats and fats, and that the human body adapted to wartime conditions by losing weight.[17]

The food crisis left its mark not only on the physical appearance of the emaciated city-dweller, but also on the city itself. Urban space became partly re-ruralised as empty plots and sports grounds were converted into arable or pasture land: by 1917, nearly 3,000 war gardens were cultivated in Paris, and cows grazed the converted Longchamp racecourse. Marketplaces which had once been buzzing with activity grew deserted. Instead, long queues formed outside grocers' shops. The near-stationary food queue (formed by women) rather than the (male) *flâneur* freely traversing the city was to become a dominant and lasting image of the city at war. Mostly concentrated in the crowded, working-class districts, food lines highlighted the socio-spatial dimension of inequality over access to victuals. Approximately half a million were queuing in the streets of the British capital, principally in the East End, on one Saturday in January 1918. In the event, rationing helped reduce such bottlenecks in London, but not in Vienna. There, on an average day in 1917, an estimated 250,000 people were waiting in nearly 800 queues. These were not customers patiently waiting their turn. Rudeness, envy and violence marked people's behaviour in the food lines, effectively undermining any pretence of a home front united in purpose.[18]

The dissatisfaction of consumers sent away empty-handed after hours of queuing could ignite serious public disorder. Berlin saw tumultuous street scenes over potatoes in early 1915, riots over butter in autumn 1915, and a series of street protests-cum-strikes in the February and April of 1917 and again in January 1918. Police reports noted with alarm that 'an enormous portion of the population doesn't care about the war at all any more'.[19] The daily battle for food eclipsed interest in news from the military front; civilians at the home front, it appeared, were no longer engaged in the same conflict as soldiers at the front. Significantly, the authorities did not revert to the pre-war habit of stamping out unrests, but intimated that they were listening to the legitimate demands of 'women of lesser means'. This conciliatory stance might have

17 Healy, *Vienna*, pp. 41–2; Avner Offer, *The First World War: An Agrarian Interpretation* (Oxford: Clarendon Press, 1989), pp. 45–53.

18 Roger Chickering, *The Great War and Urban Life in Germany: Freiburg, 1914–1918* (Cambridge University Press, 2007), pp. 185, 221; Bonzon and Davis, 'Feeding the cities', pp. 323, 330; Reinhard J. Sieder, 'Behind the lines: working-class family life in wartime Vienna', in Richard Wall and Jay Winter (eds.), *The Upheaval of War: Family, Work and Welfare in Europe, 1914–1918* (Cambridge University Press, 1988), p. 127; Healy, *Vienna*, pp. 80–2.

19 Cited in Davis, *Home Fires Burning*, p. 193.

staved off revolution in the short term, but ultimately convinced city-dwellers that the existing regime was unreformable. In Vienna, the administration even arranged for emergency deliveries to demonstration sites, but in doing so only added fuel to the fire, increasing suspicion that profiteers were withholding vital supplies from the market.[20]

Women spearheaded the food protests in cities from Barcelona to Melbourne in 1917 and 1918. Demonstrations against the soaring cost of living had traditionally been legitimate areas of protests for mothers and housewives, allowing them to step out of the domestic sphere into the public domain. Yet some historians have argued that the bread riots in the era of the Great War empowered women in a new way. While a general strike of Barcelona's (male) workers in 1916 had not frightened the authorities into action, women's direct action against points of distribution – supported by anarchist women – in January 1918 did. The reason was that here the ritual of 'moral-economy' riots became fused with the ideology and organisation of new social movements. The same point has been argued about Paris, where the consumer struggle of the war years was on the brink of spilling over into a consumers' revolution in 1919. Rioters resorted to primitive violence such as overturning the carts of sellers in Les Halles and neighbourhood marketplaces, but they also set up more sophisticated organisations, vigilance committees, to ensure that the public protection of buyers enacted in wartime was not lost with the peace.[21]

The 'food revolution' in Paris that would have forced France to exit the war, predicted by the French Minister of Commerce in autumn 1917, did not happen.[22] The minister in his gloomy outlook might have been influenced by events in Russia's capital earlier in that year. In Petrograd, clashes between women – female textile workers and lower-class housewives – and shopkeepers on International Women's Day triggered the February Revolution. Born and raised in villages, the majority of the urban lower-class women had not only retained a peasant's expectations concerning the right to affordable subsistence, but also acquired a modern sense of entitlement derived from their status as soldiers' wives. Bread riots had sporadically occurred during the

20 Healy, *Vienna*, p. 83.

21 Lester Golden, 'The women in command: the Barcelona women's consumer war of 1918', *UCLA Historical Journal*, 6 (1985), pp. 5–32; Stovall, *Paris*, pp. 182–237; Judith Smart, 'Feminists, food and the fair price: the cost of living demonstrations in Melbourne, August–September 1917', in Joy Damousi and Marilyn Lake (eds.), *Gender and War: Australians at War in the Twentieth Century* (Cambridge University Press, 1995), pp. 274–301.

22 David Stevenson, *With Our Backs to the Wall: Victory and Defeat in 1918* (London: Penguin, 2012), p. 396.

war, but the anger over escalating prices for necessities in February 1917 was the last straw. Nevertheless, the revolutions of 1917 did not solve the cost-of-living crisis, and as Russia slid into civil war, food deliveries to the great industrial cities of the north plummeted, turning once bustling urban centres into depopulated sites of hunger pervaded by an eerie stillness.[23]

We know less about the food crisis accompanying the end of the Ottoman Empire. Jerusalem went hungry before Allenby arrived, and many other cities were in chaos as Turkish troops departed and Allied troops arrived.[24] In the harsh climate of the Middle East, disease spread easily, especially in these times of military and political upheaval. City life in wartime had its risks, which grew more alarming and lethal the further east in Europe and Asia the war travelled.

Stages for propaganda

With urban-dwellers increasingly preoccupied with obtaining basic goods, cultural life in cities throughout Central Europe lost its swagger, particularly in the second half of the war. There is a striking symmetry between the material and cultural adaptation to war in cities. The turnip winter marked a watershed not only in the Central Powers' ability to satisfy urban consumers, but also in urban populations' appetite for propaganda spectacles. Before the winter of 1916/17, urban dwellers had witnessed an invasion of public space by representations of war. In fact, they themselves had been often in the vanguard of the cultural (self-)mobilisation for war. From 1917 onwards, however, only the residents of the Allied metropolises, especially the British capital, had energy reserves to enjoy the pleasure culture of war. Thus, the relative success of the authorities in London and, to a lesser extent, Paris in containing the instabilities of food supply was paralleled in the field of cultural (re-)mobilisation.

The term 'propaganda' often connotes a moral pollution of innocent minds initiated from above. Yet the most powerful propaganda was not choreographed by the state or its subsidiary organisations, but emerged from within civil society in the first half of the conflict. The metropolitan populace was the principal target group as well as the facilitator of propaganda spectacles, and the

23 Barbara Alpern Engel, 'Not by bread alone: subsistence riots in Russia during World War One', *Journal of Modern History*, 69 (1997), pp. 696–721; Orlando Figes, *A People's Tragedy: A History of the Russian Revolution* (London: Jonathan Cape, 1996), pp. 603–11.

24 Bernhard Wasserstein, *Divided Jerusalem: The Struggle for the Holy City* (New Haven, CT: Yale University Press, 2001), pp. 71, 77; Abigail Jacobson, *From Empire to Empire: Jerusalem between Ottoman and British Rule* (New York: Syracuse University Press, 2011), pp. 37–8, 48.

city became its stage. In the summer of 1914, crowds filled the public squares from London to Petrograd (St Petersburg). The apparent 'war enthusiasm' of the crowds came to embody a new sense of unity. However, the meaning of the street scenes of July and August 1914 was more complex and ambivalent than acknowledged at the time. The crowds were motivated by sentiments ranging from excitement and curiosity to panic and depression. Moreover, the patriotic crowds that would acquire a new centrality to the iconography of the nation at war were concentrated in large cities and university towns. Although confined to a section of the urban population, they were capable of making a great deal of noise amplified by the nationalist press.[25]

With the crowds gathering in the boulevards, public life in the metropolis took on a distinctly carnivalesque air in the summer of 1914. Particularly in Berlin, the new theatricality of urban life was enhanced by the colonisation of semi-public places such as cafés and restaurants by artists presenting both patriotic and classical pieces. These were not only the usual street performers, but often established artists, driven partly by patriotic feelings and partly by the need to make ends meet. The outbreak of war prompted a crisis in one of the metropolis's core industries. The brightly lit entertainment district with its theatres, concert and music halls that had hitherto encapsulated a key feature of metropolitan life faced the prospect of insignificance and even closure in wartime. In an effort to keep the show going on, theatre managers and directors turned towards patriotic themes. Over half of the plays put on in Berlin in the second half of 1914 re-enacted the 'war enthusiasm' of the summer. Likewise, Parisian theatres felt compelled to shed their risqué image and to put on more sombre plays.[26]

The seriousness of the situation demanded an equally serious repertoire. To be sure, the moral regeneration of the metropolitan entertainment districts proved short-lived. After only a few months, moralistic pieces gave way to amusing productions in Paris. In Berlin, laughter returned to the stages and auditoria in the guise of the *Berliner Schnauze* (Berlin gob) as early as December 1914. The quick-wittedness of Berliners that had once connoted disrespect of authority was reinvented as a distinctly metropolitan source of patriotism and endurance in wartime. The longer the war lasted, the more

25 Jeffrey Verhey, *The Spirit of 1914: Militarism, Myth, and Mobilization in Germany* (Cambridge University Press, 2000); Winter and Robert, *Capital Cities*, vol. II, pp. 27–30, 282–8; Adrian Gregory, *The Last Great War: British Society and the First World War* (Cambridge University Press, 2008), pp. 9–39.

26 Martin Baumeister, *Kriegstheater: Großstadt, Front und Massenkultur 1914–1918* (Essen: Klartext, 2005), pp. 23–51.

awkward it became to suppress amusement. By the end of 1916, overtly propagandistic shows had virtually disappeared. Theatres (and cinemas, too) began to turn away from the war and to offer again pure diversion, often of a nostalgic and sentimental kind. And yet it was not back to business as usual. The works of 'Boche' composers such as Wagner, Strauss or Schoenberg were no longer performed by Parisian orchestras (although an exception was made for Mozart, Beethoven and Schumann). The war turned the clock back on transnational contacts, notably those connected with cultural experimentation. Avant-garde entertainments that had caused much excitement before 1914 became associated with a tainted cosmopolitanism.[27]

The severance of cosmopolitan ties went hand in hand with the rise of patriotic cultures. The fusion of popular entertainment, show business and war propaganda was pioneered in the large cities and rooted in urban civic culture.[28] Nowhere, perhaps, is this more palpable than in the field of exhibitions, an integral part of the metropolitan environment since the Great Exhibition of 1851. After 1914, visual displays continued to be a powerful medium, even though the war disrupted the cosmopolitan nature of pre-war exhibitions in Europe (as was most noticeable in the case of the discontinued series of Universal Exhibitions). In the German and Austrian capitals, huge war exhibitions opened in January and November 1916 respectively, sending predominantly civilian audiences on imaginary tours through space to the battlefields. These shows had the backing of the war ministries, but their organisation was in the hands of civilian notables. In London, Trafalgar Square became the headquarters of the 'tank bank' (where war bonds were sold) in 1917 and 1918 and was temporarily turned into a model battlefield with guns, trenches and debris in autumn 1918. In Paris, it was inconceivable to open a war exhibition at the Champs-de-Mars in the shadow of the Eiffel Tower, but the privately funded *Panthéon de la Guerre*, a giant panorama of the Great War, was inaugurated on a site near the Hôtel des Invalides in October 1918.[29]

27 Jan Rüger, 'Entertainments', in Winter and Robert, *Capital Cities*, vol. II, pp. 105–40 and 'Laughter and war in Berlin', *History Workshop Journal*, 67 (2009), pp. 23–43; Esteban Buch, '"Les Allemands et les Boches": la musique Allemande à Paris pendant la Première Guerre mondiale', *Le Mouvement Social*, 208 (2005), pp. 45–69; Judith R. Walkowitz, 'The "vision of Salome": cosmopolitanism and erotic dancing in central London, 1908–1918', *American Historical Review*, 108 (2003), pp. 337–76.

28 Hubertus Jahn, *Patriotic Culture in Russia during World War I* (Ithaca, NY: Cornell University Press, 1995), p. 172.

29 Stefan Goebel, 'Exhibitions', in Winter and Robert, *Capital Cities*, vol. II, pp. 143–87; Healy, *Vienna*, pp. 87–121; Mark Levitch, *Panthéon de la Guerre: Reconfiguring a Panorama of the Great War* (Columbia, MO: University of Missouri Press, 2006).

War exhibitions inscribed new meanings on existing cityscapes and transformed older sites of memory throughout Europe's metropolises. Timing, though, was different. In Berlin, patriotic spectacles for a mass audience flourished in the mid-war years. By contrast, in London, the 'tank banks' got rolling in the final year of the conflict. By then, German reserves had been eaten up, the cost of living spiralled out of control, and civilian morale reached low ebb. The spectacle in London mobilised financial and symbolic resources that had already dried up in the German capital.

The word city

The paucity of bread and other staples in Central European cities provided, however, rich fodder for journalists. Newspapers printed running critiques of the mounting shortages, regulatory breakdowns and illicit commerce. The Social Democratic *Vorwärts* featured a regular column entitled 'The Daily Bread', while reporters of the liberal *Vossische Zeitung* invoked the collective identity of 'we consumers'.[30] The Berlin press across the political spectrum lent a voice to the deprived consumer, regularly citing poor urban women directly in their articles. Press coverage of the food crisis relied heavily on hearsay and, in turn, accelerated the rumour mill. Thus, the boundary between 'news' and 'rumour', between printed and orally transmitted information, became progressively blurred after 1914. As a result, the urban public sphere underwent a significant shift. The free availability of information through sophisticated media is one distinguishing feature of the modern city, but in wartime news became increasingly a rationed and unreliable commodity.

In the age of urban mass literacy before the war, the city-dweller had transmuted into a city-browser: 'Reading about Berlin cannot be separated from being in Berlin.' According to Peter Fritzsche, it was the interplay between the 'built city' and the 'word city' that constituted the modern metropolis around 1900.[31] Increased censorship notwithstanding, the 'word city' did not disappear in Western Europe with the outbreak of war. On the contrary, from the days of the July crisis to the food protests during the war, the press continued to rework the city on a daily basis, creating an image of the streets for millions of readers. In the summer of 1914, curiosity drove large numbers of people to gather in the public squares or in front of the newspaper

30 Davis, *Home Fires Burning*, pp. 2, 60.
31 Peter Fritzsche, *Reading Berlin 1900* (Cambridge, MA: Harvard University Press, 1996), p. 47.

buildings where extra editions were sold and sandwich-men posted; these crowds became the stuff of myth ('the spirit of 1914') created in the newsrooms. Public commotion in places where breaking news about the war was made available was more noticeable in Berlin and Paris than in London. The main Paris newspapers, concentrated around the Grands Boulevards, became a hotspot for news-seekers, whereas Fleet Street retained the subdued atmosphere of a business district.[32]

Censorship might have been stricter in Berlin than in London, but that did not hinder Berliners from 'reading' the city at war. Coverage of the food riots was, in fact, so extensive that it even incited further disturbances in some quarters of the city.[33] In Munich, the censor proved even unable to control the influx of foreign-language newspapers. As late as summer 1918, copies of *The Times* and *Le Figaro* were on open sale at some book shops.[34] Occasional white spaces or, more rarely, the temporary suppression of entire newspapers (as in the case of the socialist *Forward* in Glasgow), made the Western 'word city' shrink, but only marginally so; in cities under military rule in the East, by contrast, it vanished altogether, leaving the city-browser in a state of disorientation. In Ottoman Jerusalem, the combined suspension of all foreign postal services and most of the Hebrew and Arabic newspapers led to a feeling of isolation from the outside world and of disconnection from fellow citizens. The stranglehold on news was even more severely felt in Belgrade under Austrian occupation, for it effectively undermined a quintessential metropolitan function of the Serbian capital. The military government understood that manipulating information was essential to controlling the population and, therefore, banned all of the city's twenty-four newspapers except for its own official daily, *Beogradske novine*. Published in German, Hungarian and Serbo-Croatian, the organ of the occupiers became a key weapon in the campaign to win over the population's support, representing the occupied city as a peaceful and thriving metropolis.[35]

32 Emmanuelle Cronier, 'The street', in Winter and Robert, *Capital Cities*, vol. II, pp. 74–5; Verhey, *Spirit of 1914*, pp. 1, 27, 73. On the provincial press, see Helen B. McCartney, *Citizen Soldiers: The Liverpool Territorials in the First World War* (Cambridge University Press, 2005), pp. 103–17.

33 Davis, *Home Fires Burning*, p. 103; cf. Florian Altenhöner, *Kommunikation und Kontrolle: Gerüchte und städtische Öffentlichkeiten in Berlin und London 1914/1918* (Munich: R. Oldenbourg, 2008), p. 84.

34 Adam R. Seipp, *The Ordeal of Peace: Demobilization and the Urban Experience in Britain and Germany, 1917–1921* (Farnham: Ashgate, 2009), p. 112.

35 Jovana Knežević, 'Reclaiming their city: Belgraders and the combat against Habsburg propaganda through rumours, 1915–18', in Goebel and Keene, *Cities into Battlefields*, pp. 101–18; Jacobson, *Empire to Empire*, pp. 24–5.

Although they read the official newspaper, Belgraders recognised that it was a dubious source of information. Yet the mail was equally inadequate for it was censored and arrived irregularly. In an effort to overcome this state of darkness, people rediscovered traditional word-of-mouth channels of communication. In informal gatherings in cafés, marketplaces and, above all, in private homes, they exchanged and discussed 'news', mostly about the prospects for peace. The military government constructed the unofficial procurement of information as a subversive act in itself. Nevertheless, there is little evidence to suggest that those spreading rumours understood it as covert resistance. Rather, rumours were a coping strategy that allowed the occupied people to 'reclaim their city', to regain a sense of agency by creating an ersatz public sphere. Rumours became the glue of social places of interaction, strengthening civic cohesion in the occupied city. By contrast, in cities that were not under military rule, the black market of information (in particular, stories about saboteurs and profiteers) fractured community solidarity just as much as the illicit market for foodstuffs.[36]

Rumours were not necessarily transmitted verbally. In their struggle against the unregulated counter-discourse in the Austrian capital, the police prosecuted the creators of anonymous posters, leaflets and graffiti. Yet the most prolific rumour-monger was, in fact, the metropolitan press. The atrocity stories told by the refugees on arrival at the railway stations – the hubs of rumour in Paris and London during the summer and autumn of 1914 – were re-narrated and magnified in the newspapers. Journalists recognised that the truth of these stories became distorted in the act of telling; but, without direct access, the refugees' tale was the only source available to them. Photographic images of destroyed buildings published in the mass-circulation *Daily Mail* and other London dailies and weeklies in August and September 1914 seemed to verify stories about German frightfulness. The result of the intense coverage of the sack of the Belgian city of Louvain was that, for the British reading public, the dominant image of German atrocities became an urban one: of property damage in a devastated university town.[37]

36 Knežević, 'Reclaiming their city', pp. 104, 118; Healy, *Vienna*, pp. 141–8; Chickering, *Urban Life*, pp. 317, 418.

37 Gregory, *Last Great War*, pp. 49–53; Adrian Gregory, 'Railway stations: gateways and termini', in Winter and Robert, *Capital Cities*, vol. II, p. 32; John Horne and Alan Kramer, *German Atrocities, 1914: A History of Denial* (New Haven, CT: Yale University Press, 2001).

War from the air

When cities came under attack, notably from the air, the instinct of those in charge of official information policy was more often than not to withhold essential details. Yet the restrictions placed on the local press backfired, as rumours about the scale of death and destruction and the negligence of the authorities flooded into this vacuum. Censorship could also cause intense frustration among the inhabitants of cities who felt that their suffering and endurance went unrecognised. The fact that the French Government encouraged limited media coverage of the stoic heroism of Parisians under fire while, at the same time, censoring information about air raids on Calais, Boulogne, Dunkirk or Nancy, created tension between the national capital and provincial cities.[38]

While terse about actual incidents, official propaganda frequently raised the spectre of a war from the air. An Australian recruitment poster showing a Zeppelin caught in the beams of two searchlights warned the viewer 'ZEPPELINS OVER YOUR TOWN'.[39] There was, of course, not the slightest danger of a German airship ever reaching Melbourne or Sydney. This poster is, however, indicative of the mental association of aerial warfare with the modern city; while no place was considered safe, cities were expected to bear the brunt of bombing. After the turn of the century, the invention of the Zeppelin had fuelled popular anxieties about the fate of the metropolises (and, by extension, civilisation itself) in a future conflict – anxieties that had been both echoed in and heightened by writers such as H. G. Wells. In *The War in the Air* (1908),[40] the scientist-turned-writer had painted a lurid picture of German airships smashing New York City.[41]

The arrival of the airship seemed to open up the possibility of inflicting major destruction on vital centres without a preliminary battle and without actually conquering them. Germans, notably exuberant civilians, had high hopes of what their miracle weapon could achieve. Urban spectacles involving Zeppelins stirred the imagination further. In Berlin, the unveiling of the statue of the 'Iron Hindenburg' in September 1915 (whose proceeds went partly to the airmen's benevolent fund) culminated in an air show with two Zeppelins

38 Susan R. Grayzel, '"The souls of soldiers": civilians under fire in First World War France', *Journal of Modern History*, 78 (2006), pp. 602, 621; Chickering, *Urban Life*, p. 107.

39 'Zeppelins over Your Town', n.d., PST 12259, IWM.

40 H. G. Wells, *The War in the Air* (London: Penguin, 2005).

41 Susan R. Grayzel, '"A promise of terror to come": air power and the destruction of cities in British imagination and experience, 1908–39', in Goebel and Keene, *Cities into Battlefields*, pp. 49–50.

overflowing the figure. A few days later, a single airship inflicted considerable damage on London and caused much excitement at the home front.[42] Air power bore the promise of bringing the war directly to the enemy population. In practice, though, the airship proved a costly failure; it was an expensive weapon that rarely hit its target. A powerful symbol rather than an effective weapon, Zeppelin hangars were, however, the principal target of the first proper bombing missions carried out by the Allies in the autumn of 1914. The earliest German civilian casualties occurred when British planes attacked the Zeppelin shed at Düsseldorf in October 1914. This was still collateral damage, but by mid 1915 non-combatants were identified as targets.[43]

The threat of a sudden attack from the air brought about significant changes to urban life. The lamps did not go out all over Europe, but they did in those cities within reach of the enemy's air forces. Gas lighting and electricity had transformed cities in the second half of the nineteenth century; this progress was now reversed as blackout procedures covered city centres in darkness again. In the university town of Freiburg, the streetlights went off after 10 p.m. – a measure that had the additional benefit of cutting down on the city's consumption of coal. While some visitors found that the darkness made the medieval beauty of the city newly visible, local residents began to understand the nocturnal precautions as a 'war on the senses'.[44] The loss of orientation was even stronger felt in the metropolises. In Paris, street lamps were turned off at night within a radius of 2 kilometres of the Eiffel Tower. Since the erstwhile 'city of lights' was highly vulnerable to air strikes, the military envisioned a gigantic urban camouflage: the construction of a *Faux* Paris on the River Seine northwest of the ancient capital, made up of an elaborate system of lights as a false target for enemy aircraft. Military strategists came close to realising their urban fantasy until work on the site was brought to a halt in 1918.[45]

Air raids led to a new use and understanding of urban space. They altered the physical city at a stroke, and, at the same time, opened up new spaces of thinking about the metropolis. In particular, the underground began to evolve

42 Goebel, 'Exhibitions', pp. 154–5; Peter Fritzsche, *A Nation of Fliers: German Aviation and the Popular Imagination* (Cambridge, MA: Harvard University Press, 1992), pp. 43–58.

43 Christian Geinitz, 'The first air war against non-combatants: strategic bombing of German cities in World War I', in Roger Chickering and Stig Förster (eds.), *Great War, Total War: Combat and Mobilization on the Western Front, 1914–1918* (Cambridge University Press, 2000), pp. 208–13.

44 Chickering, *Urban Life*, pp. 299–302.

45 Cronier, 'The street', p. 68; Roxanne Panchasi, *Future Tense: The Culture of Anticipation in France between the Wars* (Ithaca, NY: Cornell University Press, 2009), pp. 43–5.

into a safe area, affording protection that the over-ground city could no longer offer. It has been estimated that up to 300,000 Londoners took shelter in Tube stations each evening at the height of the Gotha raids in 1917. The looming danger of air raids gave birth to 'one of the century's distinctive urban rites', that is civil defence, 'the disciplined retreat of urban residents into underground sanctuaries'.[46] To be sure, these sanctuaries were largely improvised, and so too was the system of air-raid warnings that shepherded city-dwellers into them. In Paris, private cellars that were deemed to afford sufficient protection were requisitioned and lists of their location posted in public buildings. It is not difficult to discern here the makings of what Lewis Mumford would later, in his *The Culture of Cities*, come to recognise as the 'war capital', a place where the emergency had become a ritualised part of everyday life.[47]

In the First World War, strategic bombing was still in its infancy, and the physical destruction wrought on the urban fabric was uneven, but mostly limited. In Venice, several churches were damaged by bombs, while in Treviso almost all churches suffered hits; and in both cities, murals by Tiepolo were among the much-lamented losses. In Paris, by contrast, most of the bombs fell in the suburbs, although some came perilously close to Notre Dame. The town centre of Freiburg, too, notably its cathedral, escaped major damage. Even so, the accumulated cost of repairs to damaged buildings was immense, and since bombs threatened property values, the home-owning middle classes suffered yet another blow to their fortune. And yet the legacy of the air war was not entirely destructive everywhere. In interwar Britain, planners sought to boost the urban infrastructure by converting military airfields into a network of key aerodromes linked to the major conurbations.[48]

Air raids were not only not nearly as destructive as some of the darker scenarios had suggested, but also less lethal. In Germany, bombs caused the death of about 740 people, most of them civilians; in Italy, 984 people were killed; and in Britain, 1,239 civilians died. To be sure, casualties were geographically concentrated in cities near the front line. However, even in Germany's most frequently attacked town, Freiburg, the death toll amounted

46 Chickering, *Urban Life*, p. 105.

47 Lewis Mumford, *The Culture of Cities* (London: Martin Secker & Warburg, 1938), p. 275. Paul K. Saint-Amour, 'Air war prophecy and interwar modernism', *Comparative Literature Studies*, 42 (2005), 130–61.

48 Alan Kramer, *Dynamic of Destruction: Culture and Mass Killing in the First World War* (Oxford University Press, 2007), pp. 55–7; Chickering, *Urban Life*, pp. 109–10; Lynn Hollen Lees, 'Urban networks', in Martin Daunton (ed.), *The Cambridge Urban History of Britain*, vol. III, *1840–1950* (Cambridge University Press, 2000), pp. 89–90.

to 'only' thirty-one people, while air raids on Paris and its suburbs produced 275 dead. Yet the mere figures cannot reveal the social and psychological impact of the bombs. City-dwellers were not yet hardened to the idea of death from the air that could strike anyone at any moment. The fact that innocent 'women and children' were among the dead caused much public outcry, but it forced people to come round to the idea of a total war. Characteristically, the distinction between people in and out of uniform became sometimes blurred at the funerals of civilian air-raid casualties that elevated them to victim status on a par with the soldiers.[49]

The experience of air raids attracted a mixture of emotions ranging from shock and panic to curiosity. Above all, it created a sense of belonging to the community of those at risk of personal loss. In effect, the endurance of air raids became a source of civic pride that distinguished the (female) city-dweller above other civilians and enhanced his, or more particularly her, status vis-à-vis the combatants. The organ of the London teachers' union, for instance, claimed that its members – predominantly women – had gained 'first-hand experience of the perils of modern warfare': 'We share now, at any rate in some small degree, the fortunes in the field of our husbands, brothers, sons and comrades.'[50]

Commemorative cityscapes

Spared aerial bombardment, Dublin suffered havoc in the course of the rebellion, the war of independence and the civil war. A new model of urban insurrection, the Easter Rising left a scene of devastation that reminded contemporaries of images they had seen of war-ravaged Louvain and Ypres. In particular, the destruction inflicted on three Dublin landmarks – the General Post Office, Custom House and the Four Courts – between 1916 and 1922 impressed contemporary observers with the conviction that this was indeed a metropolis in peril. This goes some way to explain the resolve of the new Irish leadership to reconstruct these buildings despite their association with British rule.[51]

49 Stefan Goebel, 'Schools', in Winter and Robert, *Capital Cities*, vol. II, pp. 226–7; Geinitz, 'First air war', pp. 207–8, 225; Grayzel, 'Souls of soldiers', 596, 618; Kramer, *Dynamic of Destruction*, p. 56; Chickering, *Urban Life*, p. 98.

50 'Under fire!', *London Teacher and London Schools Review*, 34 (1917), p. 369.

51 Yvonne Whelan, *Reinventing Modern Dublin: Streetscape, Iconography and the Politics of Identity* (University College Dublin Press, 2003); Clair Wills, *Dublin 1916: The Siege of the GPO* (London: Profile, 2009).

In the post-revolutionary city, the task of physical rebuilding was complicated by the political need for a re-signification of urban space. Petrograd in 1920 appeared like a ghost town populated by emaciated figures. Yet, on the third anniversary of the October Revolution, the city became the scene of a gigantic spectacle watched by an audience of 100,000 when the soldiers and sailors returned to Palace Square to re-enact (a distilled and improved version of) the storming of the Winter Palace. Participants of the revolution became performers in a pageant, and the historic site became their stage. Material and imagined space fused together to create a commemorative cityscape. The performance marked the culmination of a campaign by the Soviets to re-signify the ceremonial centre of the city they had inherited from the previous regimes. Moreover, the re-enactment highlighted Petrograd's special status as the epicentre of the revolution, thus symbolically compensating the city for the loss of status following the move of the capital to Moscow.[52]

The grandest post-1918 commemoration was a thrilling festival with an uplifting message, held in a city that had no official war memorials, no recognised sites of mourning. Yet, with the exception of Soviet Russia, cityscapes became dotted with markers of memory and loss and also provided platforms for sombre rituals of war remembrance during the interwar period. Arguably, the Great War left its most lasting mark on urban space only after the guns had fallen silent. Nowhere is the legacy of war more visible than in some of the major cities furthest removed from the main theatres of war. The Anzac memorial in Sydney, the Shrine of Remembrance in Melbourne and, above all, the Australian War Memorial in what was then the new federal capital, Canberra, became landmarks that transformed these cities by placing the commemoration of war physically at the heart of urban life. The same could be said about the National War Memorial at Ottawa, which gave purpose and coherence to the construction of the Canadian capital.[53]

By contrast, it proved more difficult to integrate the war and its memory into the complex cultural fabric of the capitals of the old world. The *Panthéon de la Guerre* in Paris was sold off to American businessmen and exhibited in New York, Washington, Chicago, Cleveland and San Francisco during the

52 James von Geldern, *Bolshevik Festivals, 1917–1920* (Berkeley, CA: University of California Press, 1993), pp. 194–207; Katerina Clark, *Petersburg, Crucible of Cultural Revolution* (Cambridge, MA: Harvard University Press, 1995), pp. 122–34.

53 Ken S. Inglis, *Sacred Places: War Memorials in the Australian Landscape* (Melbourne University Press, 1998), ch. 7; David L. A. Gordon and Brian S. Osborne, 'Constructing national identity in Canada's capital, 1900–2000: Confederation Square and the National War Memorial', *Journal of Historical Geography*, 30 (2004), pp. 618–42.

interwar years. In London, the Imperial War Museum had to move twice before finding a permanent home on the fringe of the city centre. One ambitious but doomed scheme of autumn 1918 envisaged the rebuilding of central London as a war memorial (with the war museum taking over Banqueting House). The overall plan would have literally imposed the memory of the war on the cityscape of Westminster, but in a manner unacceptable to most Londoners. Inconceivable in London, the transformation of a city into a necropolis, an urban landscape dedicated to the memory of the war dead, was, however, what the British had in mind for the Belgian town of Ypres – somewhat to the consternation of many local inhabitants determined to revive the place. Hitherto a provincial town, war-torn Ypres matured into a hub of commemoration attracting tens of thousands of visitors from Britain and the Empire every year. In addition, British ex-servicemen employed as gardeners by the Imperial War Graves Commission became resident there in considerable numbers.[54]

Since the war dead lay mostly buried in military cemeteries abroad, war memorials at home functioned as substitute graves that triggered memories in the absence of bodies. The exception was the symbolic repatriation of Unknown Soldiers. This new institution represented a quintessentially metropolitan form of commemoration that spread from London and Paris in 1920 throughout the capitals of Europe from Brussels to Warsaw during the interwar period (with the exception of Berlin). As the tombs tended to be inconspicuously designed, it was the symbolism of the chosen location and its ceremonial use that infused the signifier with meaning. Britain's Unknown Warrior in Westminster Abbey invoked the glory of a medieval past. The grave in the monarch's church was paired with a secular empty tomb, the Cenotaph, in the street of the ministries. In Rome, the Unknown Soldier was interred in the monument to modern Italy's founding monarch, itself meaningfully situated at the junction between the ancient fora, the medieval and baroque city, and the building projects of the post-Risorgimento capital. The French *Soldat inconnu* also punctuated prominent points in the Parisian cityscape. Interred under the Arc de Triomphe, the funeral cortege through the capital, however, mapped out republican traditions.[55]

54 Goebel, 'Exhibitions', pp. 168–9; Mark Connelly, 'The Ypres League and the commemoration of the Ypres Salient, 1914–1940', *War in History*, 16 (2009), pp. 51–76.

55 Ken S. Inglis, 'Entombing unknown soldiers: from London and Paris to Baghdad', *History & Memory*, 5:2 (1993), pp. 7–31; Stefan Goebel, *The Great War and Medieval Memory: War, Remembrance and Medievalism in Britain and Germany, 1914–1940* (Cambridge University Press, 2007), pp. 32–5; David Atkinson and Denis Cosgrove,

In all three cases, Unknown Soldiers added another cultural layer to symbolically saturated spaces. Paradoxically, the desire to take the Unknown Soldier to the very heart of the capitals went hand in hand with efforts to insulate him – architecturally or ritually – from the hustle and bustle of metropolitan life. That was the effect of the two-minute silence on Armistice Day which brought urban life to a complete halt. Wherever it was held, the silence proved a powerful marker of loss, but in no other place was it as powerful as in the restless capitals.[56]

Despite the plans of other cities to bury local Unknown Soldiers, the institution remained confined to national capitals or their environs (as in the case of the United States and Yugoslavia). The Cenotaph, however, set a trend for similar structures in cities throughout Britain and the Empire, for instance in Glasgow and Toronto. In second and provincial cities, cenotaphs were signifiers of both public mourning and civic pride. London, by contrast, seemed wanting in local patriotism, for no metropolitan war memorial per se was ever built. The same is true of Paris and Berlin and also the Scottish capital. Edinburgh Castle houses the Scottish National War Memorial, but the city lacks a single, collective memorial dedicated to its fallen soldiers. This might indicate that the inhabitants of capital cities did not perceive a difference between the metropolitan and the national war memorial or that their horizon did not extend beyond the neighbourhood. Below the national and metropolitan levels, capital cities were distinguished by a high density of war memorials: mostly small and medium-sized structures, typically erected by local people for local people.[57]

The evidence of metropolitan commemorations suggests that the identities of districts were never completely subsumed by the rapidly expanding city as a whole. Certain building projects further strengthened the role of the neighbourhood as the basic cell of collective memory in the metropolis. From Hamburg to Melbourne, planners envisaged the building of new blocks of houses and sometimes entire wards whose identity rested firmly on the

'Urban rhetoric and embodied identities: city, nation, and empire at the Vittorio Emanuele II Monument in Rome, 1870–1945', *Annals of the Association of American Geographers*, 88 (1998), pp. 28–49.

56 Adrian Gregory, *The Silence of Memory: Armistice Day 1919–1946* (Oxford: Berg, 1994), p. 13.

57 Winter and Robert, *Capital Cities*, vol. II, pp. 450–1, 470; Elise Julien, *Paris, Berlin: La mémoire de la guerre 1914–1933* (Presses Universitaires de Rennes, 2009), pp. 221–60; Jenny Macleod, 'Memorials and location: local versus national identity and the Scottish National War Memorial', *Scottish Historical Review*, 89 (2010), pp. 73–95; Mark Connelly, *The Great War, Memory and Ritual: Commemoration in the City and East London, 1916–1939* (Woodbridge: Boydell, 2002).

experience of the Great War. The construction of war service homes or garden cities for disabled veterans and war widows was principally a response to longstanding concerns about urban housing conditions. The secondary effect was, however, that here family stories of loss and bereavement became embedded within the socio-spatial conditions of the city. To be sure, the most ambitious schemes for 'homes fit for heroes' remained paper dreams, and those that were realised did not generally facilitate durable communities of remembrance. In Western Europe, often only street names evocative of battles or explicit about their former designation (the ubiquitous *Heimstättenweg* in German towns) are all that remain. By contrast, many settlements for Greek expellees from Asia Minor constructed in the Athens-Piraeus metropolitan region after the 1923 population exchange retained their social cohesion for another two generations.[58]

The 'memory boom' of the 1990s breathed new life into the commemorative cityscapes dating from the era of the Great War. In Britain's cities, the restoration of the two-minute silence (which had been moved to Remembrance Sunday in 1946) on Armistice Day 1995 proved a powerful and popular marker of memory, bringing urban life to a temporary halt again. The institution of the Unknown Soldier, too, was reinvented and its metropolitan character restated. On 11 November 1993, an Unknown Australian Soldier exhumed from a war cemetery in France was interred in the Australian War Memorial at Canberra; seven years later, Ottawa followed suit. These were impressive affirmations of the presence of the dead of the First World War (and, expressedly or implicitly, all subsequent conflicts) in these two capital cities. However, the remaking of commemorative cityscapes was not everywhere a smooth process. In Berlin, the ill-conceived revamp of the Neue Wache in 1993 showed that, in terms of urban history, the scars of the Great War pale into insignificance when juxtaposed with the 'Topography of Terror' of an even greater war.[59]

58 Alex King, *Memorials of the Great War in Britain: The Symbolism and Politics of Remembrance* (Oxford: Berg, 1998), p. 75; Stefan Goebel, '"Kohle und Schwert": zur Konstruktion der Heimatfront in Kriegswahrzeichen des Ruhrgebietes im Ersten Weltkrieg', *Westfälische Forschungen*, 51 (2001), pp. 266–9; Renée Hirschon, *Heirs to the Greek Catastrophe: The Social Life of Asia Minor Refugees in Piraeus*, 2nd edn (New York: Berghahn, 1998).

59 Brian Ladd, *The Ghosts of Berlin: Confronting German History in the Urban Landscape* (University of Chicago Press, 1997).

15

Agrarian society

BENJAMIN ZIEMANN

For decades, writing on the social and economic history of the Great War has been dominated by a consideration of industrial production. The focus was and in many ways still is on the attempts to maximise factory output, to deliver cannon and ammunition to the fronts, and to manage industrial labour relations through collective bargaining and state interference. In that perspective, the key to the social history of the war is the triangular relation between 'army, industry and labour', so masterfully described for Germany in Gerald D. Feldman's pioneering study.[1] But as the Russian businessman Ivan Bloch noted in his reflections on *The Future of War*,[2] 'you cannot fight unless you can eat'. Agrarian resources were as crucial to sustain war over an extended period as any industrial output or financial mechanism to fund it. In that sense, the Great War was 'not only a war of steel and gold, but a war of bread and potatoes'.[3] In this chapter, however, we are not exploring the agrarian contribution to the overall war effort. We are rather concerned with the state of the rural economy, with the attempts of the state to regulate the production and pricing of agrarian produce, and with the unintended side-effects of these interventions.

Yet, such an analysis is only the first step to a broader understanding of changes in village societies under the impact of the Great War. For the first time since the Napoleonic Wars, peasants across Europe were deeply affected by the upheaval of war. Conscription and other forms of population movement fundamentally altered the demographic structure of village communities, changed labour relations and afffected the agency of villagers vis-à-vis the state. If not combat and military occupation itself, then media reports and

1 Gerald D. Feldman, *Army, Industry and Labor* (Princeton University Press, 1966).

2 Ivan Bloch, *The Future of War in its Technical, Economic and Political Relations: Is War Now Possible?* (New York: Doubleday & McClure, 1899).

3 Avner Offer, *The First World War. An Agrarian Interpretation* (Oxford: Clarendon Press, 1991), p. 1, the quote by Bloch, *ibid.*, p. 11.

propaganda efforts about it reached even remote stretches of countryside. There is no doubt that the Great War was a watershed moment in the history of European village societies in the sense that tightly knit parochial structures were opened up and peasants became more intensively involved in the broader framework of their national polities than ever before. Less clear and highly diverse, however, are the precise nature and the immediate political outcomes of this upheaval amidst a wave of agrarian politicisation in many belligerent countries. Any attempt to gauge the impact of the war on the countryside is faced with the relative neglect of peasants in research on the Great War. As Antoine Prost and Jay Winter have remarked in 2004 – and that remark is still valid – the state of historiography in this field is 'very poor'.[4] One further disclaimer is necessary. In the following, I will analyse changes and make comparisons mostly at the level of the nation-state. Such an approach, however, is bound to do injustice to the sheer diversity of farming patterns, economic strategies of the peasantry and rural politics across all European countries and beyond. Even among the 22,500 villages of one single part of the Russian Empire, Viatka province, which was situated hundreds of miles away from Moscow in the remote north-east of European Russia, differences abounded.[5] Wherever possible, it is hence prudent to study the impact of the Great War on agrarian society at the regional level.[6] All statements about the national level are usually – unavoidable – generalisations.

Agrarian economy and state intervention

In all belligerent countries, the war had a tremendous impact on the agrarian economy. Core resources of peasant farmers such as manpower, livestock, fertiliser and machinery were either reallocated to the military or were no longer available, most often due to import restrictions. In addition, the foreign military occupation of large swathes of territory interrupted traditional trade routes for the marketing of grain and other produce, most severely, but not exclusively, in Russia. It was soon obvious that the ensuing disruption

4 Antoine Prost and Jay Winter, *Penser la Grande Guerre. Un essai d'historiographique* (Paris: Seuil, 2004), p. 222.

5 See Aaron Retish, *Russia's Peasants in Revolution and Civil War. Citizenship, Identity, and the Creation of the Soviet State, 1914–1922* (Cambridge University Press, 2008), figure on p. 25.

6 Benjamin Ziemann, *War Experiences in Rural Germany, 1914–1923* (Oxford: Berg, 2007); Robert G. Moeller, *German Peasants and Agrarian Politics, 1914–1924. The Rhineland and Westphalia* (Chapel Hill, NC and London: University of North Carolina Press, 1986).

required state intervention not only into the distribution of food, but also into the pricing and the production of agricultural goods.

The first major effect of the war was an unprecedented presence of state policies and state officials in the countryside. State control of the agrarian economy did not only trigger angry responses and organisational realignment among the regional and national pressure groups that defended agrarian interests. In differing degrees, it also alienated the peasant population and undermined the legitimacy of the state.

The most important external factor that affected agricultural production among the Central Powers Austria-Hungary and Germany was the Allied blockade, which effectively sealed off imports of both agricultural produce and fertiliser. Before the war, Germany had been heavily depending on imports of agricultural produce, with up to one-third of consumption coming from abroad. Despite the fact that Germany was one of the two leading industrial nations in Europe, it had retained a strong agricultural sector, with 35 per cent of all gainfully employed persons in 1913 working in farming and forestry. But the German agrarian economy was far from self-sufficient. It heavily depended on imports, mostly of artificial fertilisers and of labour. In 1913, 364,000 foreign seasonal labourers entered Prussian agriculture alone, most of whom were Poles from Russia who worked on the large estates in the provinces east of the River Elbe.[7] Wartime circumstances and policies further exacerbated these external factors. Although reliable statistics are difficult to come by, there can be no doubt that considerable amounts of arable land were left fallow, and that others were turned into pasture. Thus, peasants responded to the shortage of available farmhands, but also to the idiosyncrasies of the state-controlled economy, which introduced maximum prices for grain in October 1914, but those for pigs and cattle only in late 1915 and March 1916 respectively, effectively offering a premium on the expansion of pasture. All factors taken together explain the drastic decrease in German agricultural production during the war. Compared to the level in 1913, total grain output in 1918 had dropped by 36 per cent, livestock production by 40 per cent and potato yields by 35 per cent.[8]

The war not only damaged the output of German agriculture, more than anything else it entailed a massive shift in agrarian policy. Since the passing of tariff legislation in 1879, German agriculture had enjoyed comprehensive

7 Gerhard A. Ritter and Klaus Tenfelde, *Arbeiter im Deutschen Kaiserreich 1871 bis 1914* (Bonn: J. H. W. Dietz, 1992), p. 182.

8 Figures in Hans-Ulrich Wehler, *Deutsche Gesellschaftsgeschichte*, vol. IV, *1914–1949* (Munich: C. H. Beck, 2003), p. 58.

protection from foreign imports of cereal and meat. This shielded the domestic market from the price pressures of imports, as the world market prices were markedly lower. It also allowed agricultural producers to boost their profits at the expense of consumers. This privileged position was shaken by the seminal switch to a 'consumption-oriented food policy' in the autumn of 1914.[9] This complex set of measures was set in motion in October 1914 with the introduction of maximum producers' prices for the wholesale trade in bread-making cereals. Fodder, cereal and potatoes, among other things, were soon subjected to the same kind of price restrictions. From January 1915 onwards, stocks of cereals for bread making and flour were confiscated. At the local level, the acquisition of cereals and all the other products later subject to state control, seizure of stocks, checks to ensure that farmers delivered everything they were supposed to, occasional expropriation and, finally, storage were down to the municipal syndicates (*Kommunalverbände*) set up in towns and by district authorities. By 1916 at the latest, peasants across Germany had come to the conclusion that the whole system of maximum prices, delivery quotas and outright confiscation of products amounted to nothing more than a 'programme of affirmative action for consumers'. The resentment of rural producers against this shift in state policy was accompanied by a growing rift between urban dwellers and village folk more generally. As the black market grew, growing numbers of hoarders roamed the villages near the cities, demonstrating an increasingly aggressive attitude in their readiness to buy food, to beg for it, or to simply steal it from the fields. By the end of 1916, the conflict between agrarian producers and urban consumers was the most important cleavage in German society.[10] This letter written by the wife of a peasant from southern Bavaria in December 1917 offers a vivid insight into the perceptions feeding into peasant discontent:

> The producers have it no better. The officials waste no time in confiscating cattle, poultry, cereals, potatoes, hay and straw. They work it out in such a way that you get the most meagre quantity possible. We're left with just six centners of oats for two horses until harvest. They've left us with too few seeds per *Tagwerk* [amount of land that can be sown in a day's work, in Bavaria slightly less than an acre]. We in agriculture have to slave away and worry ourselves sick in order to feed all. Yet you're still now and later the stupid peasant.[11]

9 Martin Schumacher, *Land und Politik. Eine Untersuchung über politische Parteien und agrarische Interessen 1914–1923* (Düsseldorf: Droste Verlag, 1978), p. 271.

10 Moeller, *German Peasants*, pp. 43–67, quote on p. 44.

11 Quoted in Ziemann, *War Experiences*, p. 174.

As the letter indicates, not only the lack of resources agitated peasants, but even more so the ways in which the state had curtailed their freedom of economic decision-making, conjuring up the image of 'slaves' who were bound to feed the hungry city-dwellers. Long-established stereotypes in the cultural encounter between town and countryside added insult to injury, as peasants were sure that the rest of society looked down on them as being vastly inferior in terms of civilisation and education.

In the case of the Dual Monarchy, the most important problem was the imbalance of food production between its two parts, cis-leithanian Austria and trans-leithanian Hungary. Whereas 64.5 per cent of the gainfully employed persons in the latter half of the Empire worked in the agrarian sector in 1910, the same figure for the former half stood at only 48.5 per cent. In addition, the physical conditions of the mountainous territory in the Alpine regions of Austria where not conducive to intensive farming. Hence, less intensive dairy farming on grasslands prevailed there. During peacetime, the resulting shortages of food production in the Austrian lands could easily be equalised through imports from Hungary. In the years before the war, slightly less than one-third of all flour and about two-thirds of all beef consumed in Austria came from Hungary. Yet, during the war, the lack of a unified economic administration for the whole Empire and the rivalries between its two halves made an effective agrarian policy impossible. Hungarian exports of most agricultural products to Austria had dwindled to less than one-tenth of their pre-war level by 1916. Without the availability of substantial grain imports from Romania in 1916 and 1917, which had joined the Entente in August 1916, but was within months largely occupied by German and Austrian troops, Austrian food supply would have collapsed at that point.[12]

In November 1914, the government in Vienna followed the German example in establishing maximum prices for agrarian produce, starting with grain. Like their counterparts north of the Alps, this decision motivated Austrian peasant farmers to shift production to those products which were not yet regulated by a price ceiling, thus forcing the state to roll out a comprehensive system of maximum prices on all produce by 1916. Effectively, though, these maximum prices soon established themselves as a minimum, as no reasonable farmer would demand less than the ceiling price. As scarcity of agrarian produce was a severe problem in the cis-leithanian parts of the Dual Monarchy from 1916 onwards, even the maximum price could not motivate farmers to

12 Hans Loewenfeld-Russ, *Die Regelung der Volksernährung im Kriege* (Vienna: Holder, 1926), pp. 5, 31, 61.

sell, and a substantial black market for agricultural produce emerged. Civil servants had anticipated at an early stage that state interference in price regulation would not suffice, and that a comprehensive system of state control of the agrarian economy would have to be established. The first decisive step in that direction was the founding of the Kriegs-Getreide-Verkehrsanstalt or 'War Grain Agency' in February 1915. It effectively acquired overall responsibility for the registration, if necessary the requsition, and for the distribution of all grain produced in Austria. In the process, it divided the population into three categories: 'self-suppliers', i.e., the farmers as producers, who could retain a certain daily quota of flour, and two groups of consumers, 'non-self-suppliers' and 'hard workers', the latter of whom could claim a slightly higher quota than the former. What is more, as it curtailed the freedom of their economic decision-making and aimed to source and control virtually all grain at the level of the individual producer, the agency turned grain-producing peasant farmers effectively into its own 'employees', causing a wave of deep-felt resentment among them about this loss of independence in economic decision-making.[13] Systematic state control of the pricing, requisition and distribution of food was again required to cover all forms of agricultural produce, with a comprehensive system of similar state agencies rolled out by 1916.[14] When an increasing number of producers could not meet their delivery quotas, state authorities responded with the forced requisition of cattle and grain. In 1917 and 1918, an increasing number of 'revisions' took place, and individual house searches for undeclared reserves of grain were conducted by a group of district officials, the village mayor and the gendarmerie. Peasants, who were used to taking pride in the independence of their own property and household, reacted furiously when policemen snooped around their houses, searching for grain not only in barns and stables, but also in bedchambers and under the house altar.[15] When a constable checked in a Tyrolian village whether grain mills had been sealed off as required, a disabled veteran who had already returned to his farm threatened him with violence, and was left alone.[16]

Overall, state intervention in the agrarian economy in Austria and Germany had similar effects. The piecemeal introduction of maximum prices did nothing to foster or balance production. Together with the following elements of the

13 Josef Lackner, 'Bauern in Salzburg 1914–1918' (PhD dissertation, University of Salzburg, 1980), pp. 72–86, quote on p. 79.

14 Loewenfeld-Russ, *Regelung*, pp. 71–4.

15 Lackner, *Bauern in Salzburg*, pp. 132 ff.

16 Oswald Sint, *'Buibm und Gitschn beinando is ka Zoig!' Jugend in Osttirol 1900–1930*, ed. Peter Paul Kloss (Vienna: Böhlau Verlag, 1986), p. 264.

controlled economy, though, it gave peasants and estate owners a clear signal that the interests of the military and of urban consumers were driving state policy in this field. Since the existing agrarian pressure groups were integrated in the corporatist arrangements of food policy, discontent with the established framework of agrarian representation grew among peasants at the grassroots level. War weariness and often radical discontent with state intervention in the agrarian economy did not turn Austrian and German peasants into revolutionaries. Only in parts of southern Bavaria, the left wing of the independent and anti-clerical 'Bavarian Peasants League' (Bayerischer Bauernbund) supported the revolutionary government of socialist Kurt Eisner and the formation of local peasant councils in 1918 and 1919.[17] Yet, while their associations still paid lip service to the monarchy in the dying days of the Austrian and German Empire, they also vented their exasperation about the situation of the peasantry in stark language. In 1917, the Catholic Peasants League in the province of Salzburg expressed its fears that the peasants might be turned into 'helots'.[18] When the revolution came in the autumn of 1918, most of the Austrian and German peasants did not regret the downfall of their respective *Kaiser*.

Among the Entente powers, Russia faced the most severe crisis of food supply during the war. This was all the more surprising as Russia had been one of the largest exporters of grain before 1914. And even during the war, the output of key products remained relatively stable. By 1917, the index of the combined Russian cereal harvest had only dropped 13 points to 87, if we set the average for the years 1909 to 1913 at 100.[19] Yet, three key factors compounded to turn a relatively stable agrarian output into a major disaster. The first of these factors was the reversal of transport routes, combined with the chronic insufficiency of the Russian railway system. A large surplus of wheat and barley was produced in the richly fertile lands of the Black Soil region, in the Ukraine and the North Caucasus in particular. Before the war, up to one-third of the yield was transported down south to the Black Sea ports on rivers and railway links, and then shipped to other countries. During the war, these exports came to a halt. But the main transport routes were now reversed to supply the domestic market, in order to meet the increasing demands of the vast Russian army – which consumed 50 per cent of all marketable grain by 1916 – and of the industrial regions in central Russia. Yet, rail transport of grain took only second place behind the operational demands of the army, and the

17 Ziemann, *War Experiences*, pp. 181–4.
18 Cited in Lackner, *Bauern in Salzburg*, p. 154.
19 Peter Gatrell, *Russia's First World War. A Social and Economic History* (Harlow: Longman, 2005), p. 159.

'dualism in food supply', which lasted until 1915 and was heavily biased in favour of the army, made an already difficult situation worse.[20]

The second factor was a shift in administrative responsibility, which led to provincial rivalries and created substantial regional imbalances. Problems started in 1914 when the acquisition of grain was laid in the hands of the Ministry of Agriculture, instead of the Ministry of the Interior. At the same time, the export of grain from some regions close to the front line was prohibited. Some provincial governors in the grain-producing regions took this as a licence to interrupt any export of grain from their territory. During the winter of 1915/16, a comprehensive system of fixed prices for all major produce was rolled out, and grain commissioners tried to procure grain on this basis. At the local level, they relied on the help of zemstvos, bodies of self-administration run by an educated elite of provincial officials. Yet, while government officials discussed the most appropriate level for these fixed prices and other implications of this substantial state intervention, peasant producers withheld grain from the market in expectation of a major price hike.[21] State intervention during the old imperial system reached a climax in November 1916, when the Ministry of Agriculture introduced a levy that required each province and district (*volost*) to deliver a certain amount of grain. While based on the idea that the zemstvos would cooperate in assigning and procuring the appropriate amount, the use of force was implied. When a village in Viatka province refused to hand over oats in December 1916, pointing out the vast discrepancy between the delivery price and the market rate, the provincial governor sent an armed detachment to the village.[22] Meanwhile, the problems of matching and equalising supply and demand between consumer and producer regions increased. The 'delicate interregional balance of grain production and utilisation came under intense pressure before 1916 and collapsed completely in 1917', causing severe food shortages and popular unrest among the urban population.[23]

The third factor in the emergence of a food crisis despite relatively stable output related to the economic preferences of the peasant farmers. During the war, a 'scissors crisis' between the prices for agricultural produce and industrial goods opened up, with the latter increasing much faster than the former. In addition, the wartime prohibition on alcohol, the price of which included a substantial amount of duty, cut peasant expenditure, while the

20 Lars T. Lih, *Bread and Authority in Russia, 1914–1921* (Berkeley, CA: University of California Press, 1992), pp. 7–32, quote on p. 16.

21 Gatrell, *Russia's First World War*, pp. 160–4.

22 Retish, *Russia's Peasants*, pp. 59 ff.

23 Gatrell, *Russia's First World War*, p. 167.

family allowance paid by the state to wives of mobilised soldiers brought additional cash into peasant households. In this situation, peasants had no incentive to sell all their produce, or to invest surplus money into their own household or farm, buying machinery or consumer articles. Rather, they withheld produce from the market and used it for their own consumption. According to some estimates, peasant families – many of whom had lived on a very meagre and monotous diet before the war – increased their consumption of food by one-quarter during the war.[24] The share of wheat that was marketed dropped, to give one example, from 25 per cent in the pre-war years to a mere 10 per cent already by 1915. To understand the rationality of this behaviour, it is necessary to view the average small peasant farmer in Russia not as an entrepreneur, whose core interest lay in the maximisation of revenue, but rather as part of a family-centred economic unit that tried to balance the relation between the workload of its individual members – including those who would usually not be fully employed in farm work – and the reproduction of the family unit through consumption. This does not mean that Russian peasants were detached from the national war effort and hence less interested in striving for maximum output, but implies that their economic behaviour did not conform to the abstract principles that underpinned a liberal market economy. In his seminal 1923 book on the *Theory of Peasant Economy*, the Russian economist Alexander Chayanov tried to understand the economic preferences of these peasant farmers, also building on insights he had gathered during the Great War.[25]

For France, the agricultural sector was of crucial significance. In 1911, 44 per cent of all gainfully employed persons still worked in farming, most of them on smallholdings of up to 25 acres that constituted about 85 per cent of all French farms. Large landed estates as in Eastern Europe, including East-Elbian Germany, were virtually absent in France. Due to the prevalence of smallholdings, the mechanisation and intensification of production had not made much progress by 1914, making French agriculture comparatively vulnerable to the lack of key resources. The biggest blow to production was conscription, which deprived many of the smallholdings of their only

24 Peter Holquist, *Making War, Forging Revolution. Russia's Continuum of Crisis, 1914–1921* (Cambridge, MA: Harvard University Press, 2002), pp. 32 ff.

25 Alexis N. Antsiferov *et al.*, *Russian Agriculture during the War* (New Haven, CT: Yale University Press, 1930), pp. 130–41, figure on p. 140; see Daniel Thorner *et al.* (eds.), *A. V. Chayanov on the Theory of the Peasant Economy* (Homewood, IL: Richard D. Irwin, 1966); Günther Schmitt, 'Ein bedeutender Agrarökonom ist wieder zu entdecken: Alexander Tschjanow', *Zeitschrift für Agrargeschichte und Agrarsoziologie*, 36 (1988), pp. 185–216.

full-time worker. Accurate statistics are impossible to obtain, but the best estimate puts the overall decrease of the male farming workforce through the draft at 43 per cent.[26] The second major detrimental factor was the German occupation of ten *départements* in the north of France. They represented only 6 per cent of the agricultural territory, but were on fertile ground and had thus produced one-fifth of all wheat and one-quarter of all oats in 1913. On both sides of no-man's-land, the situation was worst in those villages that were directly affected by continuous military occupation and, in addition, the relation between the British Expeditionary Force and French and Belgian farmers was never an easy one.[27]

The consequences for output were disastrous. Setting pre-war levels at 100, yields of wheat had dropped to 41 points in 1917, rye to 47 points, and those of sugar-beet to a mere 34 points. Production of livestock, mainly pigs, sheep and goats, held up much better, but the decline in overall production was substantial. State attempts to offer incentives to farmers or to intensify production had little relevance. Thus, as in Austria and Germany, the main focus of state intervention was the introduction of a system of maximum prices and requisitions in an attempt to shield urban consumers from a rapid inflation of grocery prices. It started in October 1915 with a cap on the price of wheat, and expanded into a comprehensive system by 1917, as farmers used increasing amounts of grain as fodder, despite a ban introduced in April 1915. This system was completed through the inspection and – if necessary – forced requisition of available stocks.[28] Like their counterparts in other countries, French peasants felt that these state controls disadvantaged them vis-à-vis urban consumers. Peasants serving at the front were damning in their disregard for 'those idlers in the city' who 'should work the land that has been left fallow' themselves, rather than asking for cheap food provision, and they advised their wives to hide stocks of grain whenever state inspections were imminent.[29]

In the United Kingdom, the agrarian economy was a less problematic aspect of the war effort, as only slightly more than 10 per cent of the male workforce

26 Michel Augé-Laribé and Pierre Pinot, *Agriculture and Food Supply in France during the War* (New Haven, CT: Yale University Press, 1927), pp. 10 ff; on conscription – Pierre Barral, 'Les campagnes', in Stéphane Audoin-Rouzeau and Jean-Jacques Becker (eds.), *Encyclopédie de la Grande Guerre 1914–1918* (Paris: Bayard, 2004), p. 652.

27 Augé-Laribé and Pinot, *Agriculture*, pp. 55–62; Craig Gibson, 'The British army, French farmers and the war on the Western Front 1914–1918', *Past & Present*, 180 (2003), pp. 175–239.

28 Augé-Laribé and Pinot, *Agriculture*, pp. 33, 69–99.

29 Letters from March 1917, cited in Martha Hanna, *Your Death would be Mine. Paul and Marie Pireaud in the Great War* (Cambridge, MA: Havard University Press, 2009), p. 198.

was employed in farming on the eve of the war. The absence of conscription meant that farms were not immediately depleted of labour, and the steady supply of imports from the United States and good harvests meant that agricultural policy was 'essentially laissez-faire' up until 1916. This changed when the government of Lloyd George came to power in 1916. Alarmed by a poor harvest in the United States and the prospect of German U-boat warfare, it changed tack and inaugurated a 'highly interventionist' agrarian policy.[30] The key element of this U-turn was the 'plough policy'. Overseen by a newly founded Food Production Department and implemented by County Agricultural Exceutive Committees, the policy forced farmers to turn permanent grassland into tillage, based on the – sound – assumption that production of wheat and oats provided much more calories for human consumption than the low-intensity finishing industry, prevalent in the north of England, Scotland and Wales, which produced cattle and sheep on pasture. This was indeed a 'revolutionary' form of state intervention into agriculture, although it was based on a widespread consensus among farmers, landowners and local officials, and was supported by an additional supply of labour, fertiliser and machinery, including the import of first generation petrol-powered Fordson tractors from the United States to help with the ploughing. The policy came into full effect only for the 1918 harvest, and its actual contribution to British food supply was ultimately limited, as it just helped to restore production to its pre-war level. Nevertheless, tillage in 1918 had risen by 20.8 per cent of its 1916 level. Thus, the plough policy did contribute to the overall stability of British farming during the Great War, and encouraged policymakers to roll out a similar scheme, yet on a much larger scale, during the Second World War.[31]

As our brief survey indicates, all major European countries had introduced substantial state intervention into the agrarian economy by 1916, usually through a system of maximum prices for all major produce, which was accompanied by delivery quotas or by the forced requisition of grain and livestock, and – in the case of the United Kingdom – direct intervention into farming decisions. In most countries, including Austria-Hungary, France, Germany and the United Kingdom, these measures included the existing private institutions for the marketing and trade of produce, i.e., they relied on the services of cooperatives, wholesalers and commercial warehouses to

30 Peter E. Dewey, *British Agriculture in the First World War* (London: Routledge, 1989), p. 23.

31 Dewey, *British Agriculture*, pp. 91–105, 148–63, quote on p. 95, figure on p. 201.

obtain and shift grain and livestock. Agrarian policy during the Great War was thus based on 'some kind of corporatism', a close, concerted cooperation between private and state actors, as historian Peter Holquist has observed. The only exception from this rule was Russia. Here, both the government and leading experts used state intervention 'to supplant, rather than incorporate, existing market structures', and tried to replace the services of wholesalers and other businessmen with the work of state officials.[32] This decision not only contributed to the disastrous performance of Russian food policy, it also directly undermined the legitimacy of the state and contributed to the collapse of the tsarist regime in February 1917. In Germany and Austria, on the other hand, peasant discontent with the state-controlled economy was to some degree deflected from the state through the visibility of private traders. Not only in the Austrian province of Salzburg many farmers were convinced that the Kriegs-Getreide-Verkehrsanstalt and other state agencies were 'verjudet', i.e., corrupted by the significant presence of Jewish merchants who were involved in the marketing of grain. Tapping into and further exacerbating existing anti-Semitic stereotypes among village folk, many peasants blamed the Jews rather than the state for the restrictions imposed on them by agrarian policy.[33]

At the end of the First World War, the agricultural sector in most European countries was depleted of key resources and suffered from an extended lack of investment, while the remaining workforce was exhausted. The war had shifted the international division of labour in the production of food. While the production on the European continent decreased, farmers in the United States benefited from the increasing demand on the global market and the need to export food to their British and French allies. For American agriculture, the Great War entailed prosperity, before the recovery of production in Europe since the early 1920s brought flattening prices.[34] However, the lack of key resources and the grievances about unprecedented state intervention into the agrarian sector were only two important aspects of the European peasant economy during the war. For an overall balanced view, it must be noted that many – but not all – peasants with medium-sized farms, and to a lesser degree smallholders, also benefited from the war. State allowances paid to the wives

32 Holquist, *Making War*, pp. 34 ff.

33 Lackner, *Bauern in Salzburg*, quote on p. 134; see Ziemann, *War Experiences*, pp. 186–90; for East-Elbian Prussia, cf. Elke Kimmel, *Methoden antisemitischer Propaganda im Ersten Weltkrieg. Die Presse des Bundes der Landwirte* (Berlin: Metropol, 2001).

34 David Danborn, *Born in the Country. A History of Rural America* (Baltimore, MD: Johns Hopkins University Press, 1995), pp. 161–87.

of soldiers and the rapid inflation of prices for produce that was sold on the black market brought disposable cash income on a scale that was unprecedented for smallholders, and still exceptional for those who owned larger plots of land. While the overall amount of additional cash income depended on the nature of the produce and the proximity to urban consumers – to name the two most important factors – the phenomenon itself was noted across Europe. In various French departments, teachers and officials reported, with characteristic exaggeration, that farmers were 'stuffed with gold'. It was indicative of a newly gained sense of taste, and of a penchant for conspicuous consumption, that French peasant wives and their daughters started to display a preference for fashionable clothes during the war. In 1918, the wife of a smallholder from the Dordogne ordered a new blouse not from a local fair, but from the catalogue of a department store in Paris, more than 300 kilometres away.[35] Wartime inflation also allowed peasants in all belligerent countries to write down existing mortgage debt. This process was particularly pronounced in Austria and Germany, where the inflationary process extended into the post-war period, at a vastly accelerated pace. On the peak of German hyperinflation in 1922/23, luxury items such as expensive bespoke cupboards, pianos and motorcycles found a place in the houses of medium-sized Bavarian peasants.[36]

As the Italian example demonstrates, even smallholders, leaseholders and sharecroppers (*mezzadri*) – who had to hand over a certain amount of the harvest crop to their landlord, who provided land, housing and stables in return – could benefit economically from the war. The agreements between sharecroppers and landlords were usually reviewed annually, but government legislation fixed the terms for the duration of the war. This allowed those *mezzadri* who marketed any surplus produce properly to benefit from price inflation, and to increase their net income by up to 500 per cent over the course of a few years. Towards the end of the war, an increasing number of leasehold farmers and *mezzadri* began to purchase their own land. In the wake of the war, the Italian countryside thus saw the 'emergence of a new class of small peasant proprietors'.[37] Statistical evidence stresses the significance of

35 Jean-Jacques Becker, *The Great War and the French People* (Leamington Spa: Berg, 1985), pp. 119–24, quote on p. 121; see Hanna, *Your Death*, p. 298; Michel Gervais *et al.*, *La fin de la France paysanne, de 1914 à nos jours* (Paris: Seuil, 1976), pp. 51 ff.

36 See Henri Gerest, *Les populations rurales du Montbrisonnais et la Grande Guerre* (Saint Étienne: Centre d'Études Foréziennes, 1977), pp. 183–94; Ziemann, *War Experiences*, pp. 179–81, 197–202.

37 Anthony L. Cardoza, *Agrarian Elites and Italian Fascism. The Province of Bologna, 1901–1926* (Princeton University Press, 1982), pp. 16–22, 230–2, quote on p. 232.

this phenomenon. Between the censuses conducted in 1911 and 1921, the overall number of agricultural proprietors in Italy had risen from 2.25 to 4.17 million. As the share of all full-time workers in the agrarian economy, that was an increase from 19 to 33.6 per cent, while the percentage of sharecroppers had dropped from 17.5 to 15.6 per cent, and that of leaseholders from 8.1 to 6.8 per cent, with labourers accounting for the rest.[38] In the tumultuous social struggles that erupted in the Italian countryside during the *biennio rosso*, the years of mass strikes, upheaval and socialist mobilisation in 1919/20, these 'petty bourgeois' landowners were increasingly drawn to the fascist movement that 'promised to defend their recently acquired propertied status'.[39]

The changing social fabric of the village community

The war not only drained the rural economy of vital resources and brought state intervention into farming on an unprecedented scale. It also affected the social fabric of rural society, exacerbated or transformed existing social fault lines within village communities, while at the same time bringing new forms of conflict to the fore. It is one of the arguments of this chapter that these conflicts were not always defined in terms of social class, even where rural wage labourers and farmers were two distinctive groups.[40] In many ways, cohesion and conflict in the countryside cut across the issue of class, creating a crisis of collective morality and realigning groups and individuals along different lines. The first major theme in this respect is the reaffirmation and subsequent unravelling of neighbourhood ties in the village community. Overall, peasants responded with mixed emotions to the declaration of war and to military mobilisation. In Austria-Hungary, France and Germany as well as in Russia, they displayed a similar set of reactions.[41] In the private sphere of the family, or in the groups of workers who were out on the fields to harvest wheat and barley, the prevalent feeling was one of despair and grief, as it was

38 See Arrigo Serpieri, *La guerra e le classi rurali italiane* (Rome: Laterza, 1930), pp. 360 ff; Francesco Bogliari, 'Le campagne italiane nella prima guerra mondiale', in Paolo Alatri *et al.* (eds.), *Storia della societa italiana*, vol. xxi, *La disagregazione dello stato liberale* (Milan: Teti, 1982), pp. 103–23, here p. 109.

39 Cardoza, *Agrarian Elites*, p. 322; 'piccola borghesia' is the term used by Bogliari, 'Le campagne italiane', p. 109.

40 For Russia, see Mark Baker, 'Rampaging soldatki, cowering police, bazaar riots and moral economy. The social impact of the Great War in Kharkiv Province', *Canadian-American Slavic Studies*, 35 (2001), pp. 137–55, 142.

41 On Austria, see Oswald Überegger and Matthias Rettenwander, *Leben im Krieg. Die Tiroler 'Heimatfront' im Ersten Weltkrieg* (Bozen: Verlagsanstalt Athesia, 2004), pp. 80 ff.

clear that the call-up of men for the draft would not only disrupt the ongoing harvest, but would also lead to fatalities. Yet after a church service had brought the village together and had strengthened their resolve, and when the reservists made their way to the train station, the mood changed and the fact that peasants supported the national war effort in principle became visible. Even for Russia, for which the contrary has often been stated, it would be wrong to assume that the peasants lacked involvement in the national polity only because their economic interests and interactions were mostly parochial. Mostly out of a sense of duty, Russian peasants initially supported the war. Only a minority of Russian peasants took part in draft riots, mainly fuelled by the belief of young conscripts that they were entitled to free alcohol.[42]

The first major test for the cohesion of village communities came in August 1914, with the immediate challenge to bring in the grain harvest. For all major countries, contemporary reports by local elementary schoolteachers and parish priests as well personal testimony point in the same direction: in these extraordinary circumstances, everyone rose to the occasion, and the mutual help and practical solidarity among peasants made it possible to bring in the harvest in time. Both farmhands and peasants who had stayed behind went to great lengths to help those families who had been robbed of their male workers.[43] Not only necessity dictated these reactions, but also goodwill. In tightly knit village communities, in which everyone lived close to the other, strife and acrimonoius relationships between neighbours could poison the whole atmosphere. It seems that at least on some occasions, peasants who had fallen out in the past used the start of the war to bury the hatchet. They reached out to their neighbour and wished him the best for his front-line duty.[44] Yet this reaffirmation of the village community was only a short-lived moment of mutual recognition, and quickly collapsed under the strains of the war. Already by the summer of 1915, the wife of a smallholder in the French department of Dordogne complained in a letter that 'nobody helps anyone now', that it was very difficult to solicit the help of male neighbours, and that if the wife of a peasant suffered 'a misfortune then the others laugh behind her back'.[45] As the war dragged on and deprived an increasing number of peasant families of their fathers and sons, it was almost impossible to rely on the practical solidarity of neighbors even in those French villages where most

42 Joshua Sanborn, 'The mobilization of 1914 and the question of the Russian nation: a reexamination', *Slavic Review*, 59 (2000), pp. 267–89; Retish, *Russia's Peasants*, pp. 24–9.

43 Becker, *The Great War*, pp. 13–17; Ziemann, *War Experiences*, p. 27; Sint, *Buibm*, p. 173.

44 Sint, *Buibm*, p. 171.

45 Hanna, *Your Death*, p. 52.

peasants owned a similar amount of land, let alone in countries with significant differences between smallholders and large farmers.

State intervention into the agrarian economy exacerbated these problems, and brought a new set of differences to the fore. As the state was setting maximum prices for agrarian produce, imposing the forced requisition of certain items and was sending gendarmes to verify the quantity of stocks or whether grain mills had been actually disabled in order to prevent peasants from milling their own flour, it had to rely on the cooperation of local officials. In France, as in Austria and Germany, the village mayor was responsible for filling in the necessary paperwork, and he liaised with the police about inspections. Yet the village mayor was usually himself a farmer and had family ties with others, and his position thus invited the charge of favouritism. Even if the mayor conducted his business in the controlled economy in an impartial manner, the whole system itself 'weighed most heavily on the honest people who obeyed it', i.e., those who declared all their stocks of grain and who delivered their produce for the maximum price, and not for the considerably higher black-market rates. Those peasants, on the other hand, who 'evaded' the controls 'in their own interests could not all be discovered, and the spectacle of their impunity spread dissatisfaction and demoralisation among their neighbors'.[46] It has been argued with regard to the German case that the 'war did not erase economic differences in the countryside, and in some respects [. . .] even underlined them', as a small farmer who had one of his two cows confiscated was hit harder than a largeholder who had one of his ten cows confiscated.[47] Yet these differences were overshadowed by the much more important conflict between urban consumers and rural producers of food. Within village communities, more important was the fact that those peasants who obeyed the rules of government interference were not only disadvantaged in economic terms. Not only did they get a lower return on their delivery, they also had to observe that their honesty was not respected and honoured within the village community. In the German case, this problem was more significant than in Austria, France or other countries as elements of the controlled economy continued here into the post-war period, and were only disbanded amid hyperinflation in 1922.[48]

46 Augé-Laribé and Pinot, *Agriculture*, quote on pp. 93 ff; on the charge of favouritism in Austria, see Lackner, *Bauern in Salzburg*, p. 95.

47 Robert G. Moeller, 'Dimensions of social conflict in the Great War: the view from the German countryside', *Central European History*, 14 (1981), p. 168.

48 Ziemann, *War Experiences*, pp. 174–6.

The second major theme in the social history of village communities during the war is the changing relations between the sexes and generations. In the wake of the mass conscription of male farmheads, the patterns of women's work in agriculture changed substantially, as did the overall presence of women in the village community. It would be wrong, however, to associate these shifts with terms such as emancipation or liberation. That was the perspective of some contemporary observers, such as in a newspaper article in 1918 that concluded for the rural province of Apulia in southern Italy that 'feminism triumphed' during the war.[49] Such rhetoric was mirrored by newspaper articles in Tyrolia that painted, in somewhat pathetic language, the image of those 'stout women' who worked in service for the Austrian fatherland as they brought in the potato harvest on their own.[50] Yet the reality on the ground and the subjective experiences of peasant women were much more complicated than these standard tropes of progressive or nationalist rhetoric suggest. With the absence of so many male peasants – an estimate for Bavaria puts the number of female farmheads in 1916 at 44 per cent – their wives not only had to take on physically extremely demanding tasks such as driving a plough pulled by a harnessed oxen or horse. In addition, their overall working hours were even longer than during peacetime, as the usual chores in the household and garden still required their attention.[51] By 1916 at the latest, the wives of most smallholders and medium-sized farmers were continually overworked, physically exhausted and also emotionally strained through the prolonged absence or even death of their sons and husbands. In their letters to the front, they minced no words about the feelings of despair, fatigue and also anger at the relative comfort and perceived laziness of the urban dweller. It was these feelings that shaped the overall self-perception of peasant women in the first instance, in Austria, France and Russia, as well as in Italy and Germany.[52] Male youth were employed for the most demanding tasks wherever possible, but they also faced limits of their physical abilities, for instance when it came to moving heavy carriages with fodder or manure.[53]

49 Cited in Frank M. Snowden, *Violence and Great Estates in the South of Italy. Apulia, 1900–1922* (Cambridge University Press, 1986), p. 154.

50 Überegger and Rettenwander, *Leben im Krieg*, p. 121.

51 Ziemann, *War Experiences*, pp. 156–8.

52 For Italy, see Matteo Ermacora, 'Women behind the lines. The Fríuli region as a case study of total mobilisation, 1915–1917', in Christa Hämmerle *et al.* (eds.), *Gender in the First World War. Topics and Perspectives* (Basingstoke: Palgrave, 2014); for France, see Hanna, *Your Death*.

53 See the example given by Oswald Sint, born in 1900: Sint, *Buibm*, p. 249.

Physical exhaustion not only added emotional strain to the lives of peasant women, it had further effects on peasant families. Together with the absence of farmers and delayed marriages, it was one factor contributing to the declining rural birthrate during the war, with an increased number of miscarriages adding to the problem. Yet the physical and emotional strains of taking on work that had been previously done by men were only one aspect of the changing role of peasant women. Smallholders and sharecroppers as well as largeholders also had to take important decisions during the annual cycle of farming, from determining the appropriate crop for each plot to timing the sowing and harvesting properly. In these roles, many female farmheads relied on the advice their husbands at the front provided in often daily conversation through letters. But they also took decisions on their own, and positively acknowledged the new set of skills they acquired in the process. Much more complicated was a third element of women's work in the countryside: their position in the village community. As the state interfered in the agrarian economy, female farmheads were confronted with decisions taken and implemented by males, from the delivery quotas imposed by state officials and scrutinised by village mayors to the requisitions and searches conducted by gendarmes and sometimes soldiers. The existing evidence on Austria, France and Germany suggests that female farmheads were usually not able to challenge the patriarchal power structures that prevailed in the village community, and that state interference not only relied upon, but also reaffirmed, these structures.[54] In that sense, the departure of their husbands to the front had left peasant women in a very vulnerable position. Scattered evidence that farmwomen and war widows were sexually harassed by military personnel during the requisition of their produce brings the underlying problem into sharp relief.[55]

However, it would be wrong to assume that peasant women were always only passively enduring the strains of war, and that they lacked a voice of their own vis-à-vis wartime mobilisation and the increasing state interference in the villages. At least in two belligerent countries, female farmheads developed a considerable sense of collective agency, and challenged the authorities in an unprecedented fashion. These two examples, however, have to be situated in the specific social and political context of the respective wartime society. In the Italian case, the general backdrop was provided by the huge social and political gap between the liberal urban elites and the rural population, a gap that had

54 For Germany, see Ziemann, *War Experiences*, pp. 159–66.
55 See Überegger and Rettenwander, *Leben im Krieg*, p. 93.

been widened further in the wake of the *intervento* in May 1915 when Italy had joined the war on the side of the Entente. The main social classes in Italian rural society, the *fittavoli*, leaseholders who rented their land from a landlord, the *mezzadri*, sharecroppers who gave part of their harvest crop to the owner of the land, the very large group of rural labourers and farm-hands, and the smallholders all had no substantial stake in the war effort and resented Italian participation in the war more or less from the beginning. The outright 'hostility' of the male peasants towards the war found a vivid expression in many letters they wrote to their relatives at home, but also in written submissions to King Vittorio Emanuele III, whom the peasants addressed in a rather strange mixture of subaltern deference and bold aggression, demanding him to intervene immediately and withdraw Italy from the war.[56]

Amid rapidly worsening economic conditions, however, the wives of these peasants took direct action. In the province of Lazio as well as in other regions, groups of peasant women started in 1915 to squat land that they thought they needed to sustain their livelihood. Mostly smallholders, they acted on the basis of a 'moral economy', in their view only restoring the legitimate rights of the collective through the occupation. For the period from December 1916 to April 1917 alone, the Italian authorities counted about 500 incidents of spontaneous collective protest across the country, many of which took place in the countryside, bringing groups of peasant women as active participants to rural towns. During these incidents, mainly in the south of Italy, the offices of district prefects and mayors were stormed and lists of conscripts destroyed, barricades were erected and police stations of the *carabinieri* were showered with a hail of stones. While state officials were thus the main target, the rage and anger was sometimes also directed at the houses of rich people. These protests of peasant women had a political dimension insofar as they not only demanded the return of their husbands from the front, but also voiced concerns about the instability of their livelihood due to the war, and often called for an immediate peace.[57] It has been argued that an important factor for

56 Bogliari, 'Le campagne italiane', p. 117; Livio Vanzetto, 'Contadini e grande guerra in aree campione del Veneto (1910–1922)', in Mario Isnenghi (ed.), *Operai e contadini nella grande guerra* (Bologna: Capelli, 1982), p. 78; see Angelo Bazzanella, 'Die Stimme der Illiteraten. Volk und Krieg in Italien 1915–1918', in Klaus Vondung (ed.), *Kriegserlebnis. Der Erste Weltkrieg in der literarischen Gestaltung und symbolischen Deutung der Nationen* (Göttingen: Vandenhoeck & Ruprecht, 1980), pp. 334–51.

57 Bogliari, 'Le campagne italiane', p. 120; Giovanna Procacci, *Dalla rassegnazione alla rivolta. Mentalità e comportamenti popolari nella Grande Guerra* (Rome: Bulzoni, 1999), pp. 207–50; see Giovanna Procacci, 'A "latecomer" in war: the case of Italy', in Frans Coetzee and Marilyn Shevin-Coetzee (eds.), *Authority, Identity and the Social History of the Great War* (Providence, RI and Oxford: Berg, 1995), pp. 19 ff.

quelling this wave of popular unrest was the fact that the government embarked on a systematic propaganda campaign and promised the distribution of land under the slogan *'la terra ai contadini'* (the land to the peasants). Other scholars, however, have raised doubts with regard to the actual reception of such proganda among smallholders, sharecroppers and rural labourers. When some of the latter returned home in early 1919, they found that POWs had been employed instead of them.[58]

However, Italian peasant wives displayed their collective agency not only in public protests, but also in other acts of solidarity that demonstrated the extent to which women were part and parcel of a rural culture of disengagement from and hostility towards the national war effort. Early on, the Italian army was substantially undermined by widespread acts of individual refusal mainly by rural soldiers, predominantly self-mutilation, desertion and draft-dodging. Exact figures are difficult to obtain, but the number of draft-dodgers alone has been put at 470,000.[59] Many of the deserters and draft-dodgers with a rural background were seeking refuge from court-martial procedures in the barns and houses of peasant women whose husbands were still at the front. On many occasions, these peasant women integrated them into their household, providing shelter in return for work on the fields, and offered protection from the police. In some village communities, whole bands of deserters were accepted and integrated. Yet the example of these deserters also demonstrates the fact that Italian peasant wives whose men served at the front were still in a very vulnerable situation, as the number of acts of sexual violence and rape against them increased significantly. A similar ambivalence characterised the so-called 'unioni liberi', free sexual relationships which some married women started with soldiers or deserters. Despite new female work patterns and acts of collective agency, the established gender hierarchy in the Italian countryside remained intact.[60]

In Russia, many village communities saw what historian Mark Baker has described as the 'rise of the *soldatki*'. These were the wives of those men who had been called up to military service. They had already been a distinctive social

58 Bogliari, 'Le campagne italiani', p. 121; see the sceptical remarks by Bernd Kölling, *Familienwirtschaft und Klassenbildung. Landarbeiter im Arbeitskonflikt: Das ostelbische Pommern und die norditalienische Lomellina 1901–1921* (Vierow: SH-Verlag, 1996), pp. 117, 136.

59 Bazzanella, 'Stimme der Illiteraten', p. 342; on self-mutilation, see Leonardo Raito, *Gaetano Boschi. Sviluppi della neuropsichiatria di guerra (1915–18)* (Rome: Carocci, 2010).

60 Anna Bravo, 'Italian peasant women and the First World War', in Clive Emsley *et al.* (eds.), *War, Peace and Social Change in Twentieth Century Europe* (Milton Keynes: Open University Press, 1989), pp. 102–15; Ermacora, 'Women behind the lines'.

group in villages before the war. But now their number had risen substantially – 36 per cent of all peasant households in Kharkiv province, in what is nowadays the Ukraine, had no adult male worker by 1917. In addition, the *soldatki* soon realised that the authorities were usually reluctant to crack down with severe punishment on their collective actions, even though they invariably threatened to use violence during their protests, and sometimes employed it. In 1914 to 1915, the *soldatki* directed their ire against the ongoing implementation of the Stolypin land reforms, which divided the communal plots of the village community into separate strips of land. In the absence of their husbands, the *soldatki* felt that they would be disadvantaged during this process. In the latter half of the war, they turned against the dramatic inflation in the prices of manufactured household goods and the parallel introduction of fixed prices for agricultural produce, or, in other words, against the scissors crisis brought about by the state. These protests took the form of bazaar riots, with peasant women refusing to sell their produce in market towns for less than the price they deemed appropriate.[61] In the wake of the February Revolution in 1917, these acts of female collective disobedience would evolve – in a moment when the *soldatki* and their husbands were reunited – into spontaneous land seizures. The rise of the *soldatki* and female participation more generally meant that the war 'accelerated the movement of women into male agricultural labour roles and the traditionally patriarchal public sphere of village politics'. Yet leadership positions in the village still remained firmly in male hands, even though the revolution in 1917 brought younger male peasants to the fore, in Viatka province and other regions with an ethnically diverse population – very often those of non-Russian origin.[62]

The third important theme in the changing social fabric of the village community relates to the labour relations between agricultural workers on the one hand and peasant farmers and estate owners on the other. In the early twentieth century, farming in Europe was based on a rather rigid, strictly hierarchical system of dependence on hired labourers, who were boxed in by paternalistic control, legal restrictions to free movement and collective bargaining, and semi-feudal contractual arrangements that undermined the free market, or by a combination of these. In regions with medium-sized family farms, prevalent in many parts of Western and Central Europe, male and female farmhands were living with the peasant family under the same roof in

61 Baker, 'Rampaging soldatki', 138, 143–53, quote on 143; Retish, *Russia's Peasants*, pp. 50–4, 154–6; Emily E. Pyle, 'Peasant strategies for obtaining state aid. A study of petitions during World War I', *Russian History/Histoire Russe*, 24 (1997), pp. 41–64.

62 Retish, *Russia's Peasants*, pp. 48 ff.

what was usually a transitory period of their life cycle, tightly controlled by the farmer and his wife, and in Germany with legislation in place until the revolution in 1918 that made any breach of contract a criminal offence.[63] On the large estates in Eastern and Southern Europe, in Italy, Prussia east of the River Elbe, Russia and Hungary, labourers worked in a variety of different arrangements, from seasonal and daily hire to fixed contracts. Some of these signed up as individuals, others were bound in semi-feudal arrangements in which they contracted the labour of their whole family, and received large parts of their wage as an allowance in kind, usually grain and potatoes.

As working patterns differed widely, and because they were neglected by both contemporary administrators and subsequent historians, it is incredibly difficult to make conclusive statements about the social position of rural labourers during the Great War. Some fairly general observations, however, can be made with regard to the first group, male and female farmhands. As the scarcity of farm labour was a major issue in all countries except the United Kingdom, these farmhands were in high demand, and thus able to increase their wages quite considerably through individual bargaining. For France, one calculation assumes that the annual wage paid to farmhands almost trebled between 1914 and 1920. Yet even despite this considerable rise, many male and female farmhands in France decided to seek even higher wages in the urban munitions industries, as did many of their German and Austrian counterparts, forcing many peasants to leave some land fallow. Thus, the most considerable and enduring consequence of the Great War for this type of labour relations in the countryside was that it further accelerated the flight of farmhands to the cities. In France, about 1.5 million fewer people worked in agriculture in 1921 than had done so in 1911.[64] Some of the more persistent paternalistic attitudes and practices between peasants and farmhands receded during and after the war, as the latter found it much easier to challenge their employers over these issues. But leaving the village for good still appeared to be the preferred option for those farmhands who were seeking a better life, and even during the war there was nothing the authorities could do to stop them.[65]

63 For a fascinating study of these arrangements, see Regina Schulte, *The Village in Court. Arson, Infanticide, and Poaching in the Court Records of Upper Bavaria, 1848–1910* (Cambridge University Press, 1994).

64 Figures in Augé-Laribé and Pinot, *Agriculture*, pp. 115 ff; Hanna, *Your Death*, pp. 193 ff; Ziemann, *War Experiences*, pp. 203–9.

65 Elizabeth Bright Jones, 'A new stage of life? Young farm women's changing expectations and aspirations about work in Weimar Saxony', *German History*, 19 (2001), 549–70, 555 ff.

Labourers working on the big estates had much better prospects for collective bargaining during and immediately after the war, even though manifold regional disparities and different forms of employment ensured that these workers also never evolved into a unified rural working class. A good example for the ways in which peculiar working conditions and contractual arrangements thwarted any calls for collective working-class action are the *Deputatarbeiter* on the estates in Pomerania and other Prussian provinces in the east. They received large parts of their wage as an allowance in kind (*Deputat*), and used much of it for small-scale pig-fattening that yielded some marketable produce. During and after the war, these pigs were a very precious commodity, and their key interest in marketing them was putting the *Deputatisten* firmly in the camp of the agrarian producers. When the socialist trade union for rural workers, the *Deutscher Landarbeiter-Verband* (DLV), decided to take the side of urban labour and to support the requisition of these allowances in the controlled economy, their appeals were bound to fall on deaf ears among the *Deputatarbeiter*.[66] Thus, the economic cleavage between urban consumers and rural producers trumped any potential working-class solidarity.

The scope for collective agency among Italian rural labourers who worked on large, landed estates was much greater than in Germany, or indeed anywhere else in Europe. Since the 1880s, socialist trade unions had been able to agitate and organise Italian rural labourers. In the summer of 1901, a first major strike wave had swept across the landed estates in the country. In its wake, hundreds of local and regional leagues that represented the interests of both sharecroppers and day labourers consolidated across Italy. A congress in late November 1901 founded the *Federterra* as a national trade union of agricultural workers, which soon comprised more members than any industrial union. The socialist labour movement had clearly gained considerable traction in the Italian countryside by 1914. Developments during the war showed considerable regional variation. But even in a socialist stronghold such as the province of Bologna, *Federterra* accepted an agreement with the province prefect and the agrarian employers. It basically suspended collective bargaining and strike action during the war, in return for an official recognition of the union by the estate owners and the use of its facilities as a labour exchange for day workers. Hence, there was no major strike action in the villages of this province from 1915 to 1918. Perhaps paradoxically, the restraint of the reformist socialist trade union during the war strengthened its position. As state officials were keen to

66 Kölling, *Familienwirtschaft*, pp. 216–34, 367.

uphold social peace and to secure the provision of agricultural produce, these corporatist arrangements gave a 'new institutional legitimacy' to the *Federterra*, which it had not enjoyed before the war.[67] Yet, even while direct action of day labourers at the grassroots level had been largely suspended during the war, the estate owners were keen to roll back the progress of the rural labour movement in the post-war years. As in other Italian provinces, the fascist movement made its first advances into the countryside around Bologna in 1921 in attempts to crack down on day labourers and their socialist leagues.[68]

Conclusion

Oswald Sint was the son of a smallholder. Born in 1900 as the youngest of eight children, he grew up in the village of Kartitsch, situated high up in the Austrian Alps at 1,360 metres, in the then rather remote eastern part of the province of Tyrolia. When the war began in August 1914, it made itself felt initially only through the conscription of some adult males. In late September 1914, however, an engineer came to the valley, accompanied by some workers. As the Italian border was in close proximity, they began trench work to defend the region against a potential military invasion. 14-year-old Oswald asked one of the workers whether he could help shovelling, and indeed he could. He and his friends were paid one silver guilder per day shift. That was 'more than very well paid', Oswald reckoned, as so far only strong adult men had received that much for a day's work. When his father had done the most urgent work in the fields, he started doing trench work as well, and by 1916 he had earned enough money to pay off all remaining debt on his small property. In May 1915, a group of men from Bohemia arrived in the village, employed to speed up the trench work. Their Czech language remained alien to Oswald. A general followed shortly after, who explained that all men who volunteered for the *Standschützen*, a reserve formation, would only be deployed within Austria, not at the front. Thirty-five local men and lads did. For a couple of months, the front line came closer, and brought troops to the village who

67 Cardoza, *Agrarian Elites*, pp. 54–7, 68–75, 207, 220–44, quote on p. 229; for a slightly different wartime trajectory in the Lomellina, a region in the northern province of Pavia, see Kölling, *Familienwirtschaft*, pp. 117–58; a fascinating micro-history of the period up until 1914 is Marco Fincardi, 'Zwei landpfarreien im Umbruch. Agrarmodernisierung in der Po-ebene im Zeichen von politischer Konfrontation und Mentalitätswandel', *Journal of Modern European History*, 2 (2004), pp. 208–31.

68 Cardoza, *Agrarian Elites*, pp. 315–27.

were billeted in the farm houses. But even as the military campaign moved further away and left the village in peace, Oswald could not help but be enthralled and captivated by the ongoing operations. He followed the news on the battles in the regional paper. Agitated by the description in a calendar, he penned a poem about 'The Battle of Limanova'. He did not dare to send this poem to a newspaper as he felt it was not well done. But he did so with other reports on wartime events, which were sometimes printed in the *Tiroler Volksbote*, for which his father held a subscription.[69]

The story of Oswald Sint is in many respects indicative of more general developments in the countryside during the First World War. Even in places which were not directly affected by the fighting, the war took away a large proportion of the male workforce, and brought different groups of foreigners – forced labourers, refugees, POWs, urban hoarders – to tightly knit village communities. As many other peasant farmers across Europe, Oswald's father could repay his debt, and in Kartitsch as elsewhere, the war brought money into village communities – through military payments, the black market, state subsidies to soldiers' wives – where it had previously been only a very scarce economic resource. But perhaps the most striking aspect of Oswald Sint's autobiographical narrative of the years from 1914 to 1918 is the way in which he learned to actively engage with the sequence of military events that followed each other in quick succession, and the fact that this engagement widened his intellectual and also political horizon. Oswald Sint's interest in the war was not in any way related to the notion of a jingoistic 'war culture', an interpretation that has appeared in some strands of recent historiography.[70] Like the people in his village and many other peasants across Europe, he noted the detrimental and outright destructive consequences of the war with regret, and his interest in the war did not tap into nationalist ideas. Rather, Sint's example demonstrates what historian Aaron Retish has noted for Russia, the fact that peasants were 'actively engaged in the war effort'. Not only in Tyrolia and in Viatka province, they 'displayed a knowledge of the complexities of the war – news from the front,

69 Sint, *Buibm*, pp. 174 ff, 191–3, 240.

70 Stéphane Audoin-Rouzeau and Annette Becker, *14–18, Understanding the Great War* (New York: Hill & Wang, 2003); for a systematic critique, see Nicolas Offenstadt, 'Der Erste Weltkrieg im Spiegel der Gegenwart. Fragestellungen, Debatten, Forschungsanätze', in Arnd Bauerkämper and Elise Julien (eds.), *Durchhalten! Krieg und Gesellschaft im Vergleich 1914–1918* (Göttingen: Vandenhoeck & Ruprecht, 2010), pp. 54–80; Nicolas Offenstadt, 'À propos d'une notion récente: la "culture de guerre"', online at http://crid1418.org/espace_scientifique/textes/culture_de_guerre.htm (accessed 3 November 2012).

government policies towards the countryside, and who were the leading political figures'.[71]

In that sense, the Great War marked a major caesura in the history of European village communities, as peasants and farmhands fully emerged as a politically active part of their national polities, and learned to frame their economic and political interests in a much broader fashion. An important aspect of this process was realignment in the representation of agrarian interests through pressure groups and parties. In the wake of the Great War, peasants across Europe were able to shake off the patronage of aristocratic landowners in these pressure groups. They deveopled their own voice in the articulation of economic and political demands, and brought a younger generation of genuine peasant leaders to the fore. In many East Central European countries, the founding of peasant parties in the 1920s was a tangible expression of the politicisation of peasant communities during the war. These peasants had learned during this period that 'governments and urban populations depended' on their 'docility and labour', and they raised their voice in the political arena, 'vacillating among resentment, mistrust, despair and rage'.[72] In many European countries, the countryside had been a playing field for populist mobilisation since the late nineteenth century. Yet the impact of the Great War on agrarian economy and society amplified the potential for rural populism on a grand scale.

71 Retish, *Russia's Peasants*, pp. 25 (quote), 60; see Baker, 'Rampaging soldatki', p. 153; Scott J. Seregny, 'Zemstvos, peasants, and citizenship: the Russian adult education movement and World War I', *Slavic Review*, 59 (2000), pp. 290–315; Jan Molenda, 'War, children and youth. The impact of the First World War upon changes in the position of children in the peasant family and community', *Acta Poloniae Historica*, 79 (1999), pp. 161–84.

72 See Joseph Rothschild, *East Central Europe between the Two World Wars* (Seattle, WA and London: University of Washington Press, 1974), pp. 15–18, quote on p. 16; a detailed discussion in Heinz Gollwitzer, 'Europäische Bauerndemokratie im 20. Jahrhundert', in Gollwitzer (ed.), *Europäische Bauernparteien im 20. Jahrhundert* (Stuttgart: Gustav Fischer, 1977), pp. 1–82.

16

Finance

HANS-PETER ULLMANN

'Maximum slaughter at minimum expense' is the basic principle of war finance, as Bertrand Russell allegedly remarked to John Maynard Keynes when he was recruited into the Treasury in 1915. Russell, however, only considered the expenditure side of things.[1] But the states in fact had to take steps to fund goods and services required by the military to create violence and destruction. How did they raise the funds needed to start, fight and end a war? How did they ensure that the sources for funding the war were tapped into as carefully and efficiently as possible? How did they redirect the use of the national product from the future to the present, i.e., from investment into day-to-day expenditure and from private to public consumption?

The twofold redistribution of the national product was achieved by financial incentives and state intervention or by siphoning off buying power from private households and companies. The more successful the state was, the more goods and services were available for war.[2] How this worked out in practice during the war was fundamental in determining both the material resources available to the different states and also the economic deprivation and potential dislocation they faced in mobilising them. The following discussion will focus on the two principal allies of the Central Powers, Germany and Austria-Hungary, and the two financial powerhouses of the Entente, Great Britain and France. It will also consider two neutral countries, one of which became a combatant, the United States, the other of which, the Netherlands, remained neutral throughout. For a global war affected the international financial system as a whole, and thus presented neutral powers

1 William Keith Hancock, *Four Studies of War and Peace in this Century* (Cambridge University Press, 1961), p. 18.
2 Arthur Cecil Pigou, *The Political Economy of War* (London: Macmillan, 1921); Horst Jecht, *Kriegsfinanzen* (Jena: Gustav Fischer, 1938); Horst Mendershausen, *The Economics of War*, 2nd edn (New York: Prentice-Hall, 1943).

(especially those in Europe) with economic challenges that were almost as onerous as those facing the belligerents. In the long run, it also displaced the centre of financial power from Europe, and especially Great Britain, to the United States.

The Central Powers (especially Germany and Austria-Hungary), the Allies (in particular Great Britain, France and the United States) and also neutral states such as the Netherlands, were all faced with the same task.[3] Although they all had access to similar resources, significant dissimilarities come to light when they are examined in greater detail. This applied to the impact of mobilisation on national finances, financing the industrial war effort, demobilisation and return (if possible) to the pre-war financial order, and, last but not least, to the financial legacy of the Great War.

The impact of mobilisation on national finances

Mobilisation for war transformed the peacetime financial systems of the European powers. Being based on the gold standard and gravitating around the London financial market and the Bank of England as its headquarters, the global financial system changed as well.[4] How this transformation was accomplished, the speed, stages and participating actors, and the immediate consequences for the war, all depended on the initial circumstances and measures of mobilisation.

Prior to the First World War, public expenditure in all the major economies both grew outright and also tended to represent a growing proportion of the national product. This reflected an increase in non-military costs as well as the arms race between the major European powers which pushed up military expenditure by approximately 50 per cent between 1908 and 1913 alone. In terms of per capita expenditure, Great Britain topped the league, followed by France and Germany and, further down the list, Austria-Hungary. Military expenditure as a proportion of the national product reveals the defence burden more clearly. It shows Russia with 4.5 per cent (1910 to 1913) in first place, followed by Germany (4.2 per cent), France (4.1 per cent), Great Britain (3.4 per cent), Austria-Hungary (2.8 per cent) and the United States (0.7 per cent).[5]

3 This chapter focuses on the key states in both alliances regarding financing war, as well as telling the story of a neutral severely affected by these developments.

4 Larry Allen, *The Global Financial System 1750–2000* (London: Reaktion Books, 2001).

5 David Stevenson, *Armaments and the Coming of War* (Oxford: Clarendon Press, 1996), pp. 2 ff; Niall Ferguson, *Der falsche Krieg* (Stuttgart: Deutsche Verlags-Anstalt, 1999), pp. 143 ff.

The various countries' financial systems differed in terms of their flexibility in shouldering the burden of growing expenditure.[6] Germany struggled with the fact that the federal structure of the Empire depended on the central institutions of the Reich for funding the army and fleet, while denying it access to the most remunerative taxes, in particular the income tax. Both the federal structure and internal political polarisation blocked any chance of reform or change. Thus, in spite of various financial reforms, the Reich continued to rely on a growing and regressive tax burden on consumption and, as a last resort, on an increase in debt. As municipalities and federal states financed a portion of rising expenditures with credit, the debt ratio rose to 58 per cent, much higher than the central government's 10 per cent ratio.[7] The economically weaker Austro-Hungarian monarchy was confronted with even more serious monetary problems. Both states funded joint affairs, such as the military which made up 96 per cent of the total budget, by customs duties and by a fixed percentage of their budgets. However, they dealt with financing differently. Austria relied more on income taxes, monopolies and consumer taxes, and less on direct taxation. Mainly as a result of rearmament measures, Austria's budget deficit amounted in 1913 to approximately 10 per cent of the budget, or 2 per cent of the national product. The debt ratio reached 73 per cent, whereas Hungary's looked slightly better at 62 per cent.[8]

The Entente states were more centrally governed, although their degrees of financial stability varied. The financial system of Great Britain proved fairly flexible faced with mounting expenditure, thanks to the well-established variable income tax. As people were largely taxed according to their means, indirect taxes on consumption were low and limited to a small number of profitable mass consumer goods. A balanced budget and a debt ratio that dropped to below 26 per cent of the national product both demonstrated the solidity of the financial system.[9] Unlike those of Britain, the finances of France were under more pressure. Frequent budget deficits, which were mostly financed through credit, drove the state debt up to 65 per cent of the national

6 Gerd Hardach, *Der Erste Weltkrieg* (Munich: Deutscher Taschenbuch Verlag, 1973); Hew Strachan, *Financing the First World War* (Oxford University Press, 2007).

7 Hans-Peter Ullmann, *Der deutsche Steuerstaat* (Munich: C. H. Beck, 2005), pp. 56 ff.

8 Josef Wysocki, 'Die österreichische Finanzpolitik', in Adam Wandruszka and Peter Urbanitsch (eds.), *Die Habsburgermonarchie 1848–1918* (Vienna: Verlag der Österreichischen Akademie der Wissenschaften, 1973), vol. I, pp. 68–104; Max-Stephan Schulze, 'Austria-Hungary's economy in World War I', in Stephen Broadberry and Mark Harrison (eds.), *The Economics of World War I* (Cambridge University Press, 2005), pp. 97 ff.

9 Eckart Schremmer, 'Taxation and public finance: Britain, France, and Germany', in Peter Mathias and Sidney Pollard (eds.), *The Cambridge Economic History of Europe* (Cambridge University Press, 1989), vol. VIII, pp. 341 ff.

product. Another reason was a transition phase within the tax system. A modern form of income tax was to supersede the outdated revenue tax. But the reform was politically controversial and not in place by the time war broke out. This necessitated a sharp and regressive turn to consumer and purchase taxes.[10]

The US Government with its federal state system was funded in a similar way to that of the German Reich, in particular through taxes on consumption, customs duties and postal service profits – and from the early twentieth century onwards – through corporation excise and income taxes. At just 2 per cent of the national product, the proportion of federal funding was comparatively low.[11] The same applied to the US Government debt, which amounted to approximately 3 per cent of the national product. In contrast, the financial situation of the central government of the Netherlands was rather more strained. Rising expenditure for infrastructure and education led to budget deficits before the war. These deficits were tackled with increased direct taxes, including the introduction of income tax which somewhat alleviated the pressure on consumer taxes. Owing to the growing national product, the central government's share of the national product dropped only marginally to 6 per cent. The proportion of national debt also decreased by 1913, but was still relatively high at 44 per cent, due to the absorption capacity of the Dutch money market.[12]

Mobilisation measures led to similar results in both belligerent and neutral states. Crises on the stock exchanges and liquidity problems were tackled, and initially the financing of military mobilisation did not pose any insurmountable problems. But bank credits could only be considered a short-term financial solution. They inflated the money supply, failed to absorb purchasing power and insufficiently redirected the national product into public consumption.

In implementing measures of mobilisation, states were on the one hand confronted with similar tasks, while they were influenced by the character of their financial systems on the other hand. Thus, all belligerent countries

10 Henri Truchy, *Les Finances de Guerre de France* (Paris: Presses Universitaires de France, 1926), pp. 1 ff; Pierre-Cyrille Hautcoeur, 'Was the Great War a watershed? The economics of World War I in France', in Broadberry and Harrison, *Economics of World War I*, pp. 183 ff.

11 Charles Gilbert, *American Financing of World War I* (Westport, CT: Greenwood Press, 1970), pp. 45 ff.

12 Marius Jacobus van der Flier, *War Finances in the Netherlands up to 1918* (Oxford: Clarendon Press, 1923), pp. 13 ff; Wantje Fritschy and René van der Voort, 'From fragmentation to unification: public finance, 1700–1914', in Marjolein 'T Hart *et al.* (eds.), *A Financial History of the Netherlands* (Cambridge University Press, 1997), pp. 64–93.

shared both sudden and drastic increases in expenditure due to military mobilisation in the summer of 1914. The additional costs could not be covered by new taxes which needed to be introduced, assessed and then levied, nor could they be funded through loans as the financial markets collapsed when war broke out and stock exchanges had to close. Therefore, bank credits, especially those of central banks, were the only remaining alternative. They increased the money supply, boosted the economy and facilitated a swifter transition from peacetime to wartime economy.[13]

However, financing mobilisation by printing money had the distinct disadvantage of inflating the currency. The European governments therefore felt they had no choice but to revoke pre-war monetary regulations. The gold standard was affected most of all. Prior to the war this had ensured that the money supply could not be increased randomly and that the currency exchange rate remained stable. Provided that gold coins were not circulating as legal tender, the notes issued by the central banks to a certain degree had to be covered by gold and be redeemable in gold. The larger the metal reserves, the more bank notes could be put into circulation. In fact, the central banks had attempted to increase their gold reserves prior to 1914, but this was nowhere near enough to satisfy the huge demand for liquidity triggered by mobilisation and the public panic reaction which followed.[14]

Germany had prepared a number of regulations concerning financial mobilisation that came into force at the beginning of August 1914. They revoked the Reichsbank's obligation to redeem its notes in gold and allowed it to discount bills and treasury bonds of the Reich and classify them as unconditional cover – in addition to gold – for bank notes in circulation. The fact that by these measures a system of autonomous changes in the money supply had replaced the gold standard was deliberately kept quiet. This system facilitated funding for military mobilisation by the Reich taking on short-term debt with the Reichsbank in the form of treasury bills or bonds.[15]

Financial mobilisation in Austria-Hungary followed a similar pattern. The Banking Act of the Austro-Hungarian Bank was suspended. As a result, all regulations concerning cover and convertibility were rendered invalid.

13 Robert Knauss, *Die deutsche, englische und französische Kriegsfinanzierung* (Berlin: Walter de Gruyter, 1923); Rudolf Will, *Die schwebenden Schulden der europäischen Großstaaten* (Tübingen: J. C. B. Mohr, 1921).

14 Barry Eichengreen (ed.), *The Gold Standard in Theory and History* (New York: Methuen, 1985).

15 Konrad Roesler, *Die Finanzpolitik des Deutschen Reiches im Ersten Weltkrieg* (Berlin: Duncker & Humblot, 1967), pp. 35 ff.

Subsequently, the bank was able to grant loans to the state in exchange for treasury bonds or bills and use these as cover for the bank notes in circulation. Thus, with the additional assistance of private banks, military mobilisation was financed rather smoothly. Unlike Germany, which was quite content with a partial moratorium, Austria-Hungary had in place a general payment moratorium. It was extended several times, but was gradually lifted. This gave debtors more time to pay off their maturing liabilities. In order to stabilise credit, Austria-Hungary focused more on immobilising liabilities rather than mobilising assets.[16]

In France, the Bank of France bore the brunt of financial mobilisation and was in an advantageous position when war broke out. Compared even with the Bank of England, the Bank of France possessed large gold and silver reserves and was not subject to any regulations regarding the cover of bank notes. As agreed in 1911, the bank was able to come to the state's aid and advance 2.9 billion francs in return for treasury bonds. This was facilitated by the fact that the bank's currency notes quota doubled and bullion convertibility was no longer compulsory. The run on the banks, leading to a shortage of funds available at the banks in August 1914, triggered a series of moratoria which were extended in the autumn of that year until the end of the war. Coupled with the large numbers of men conscripted, which drained a major proportion of the workforce out of the economy, and the German invasion of economically important parts of northern France, the moratoria caused a gradual economic decline, which persisted longer than in other countries.[17]

The transnational nature of the financial upheaval of 1914 and the collapse of the international system of bill circulation hit all countries, but it hit London especially hard as a global finance centre. Great Britain, therefore, had to tackle the financial crisis and financial mobilisation simultaneously. On the one hand, the government and the Bank of England succeeded in alleviating the liquidity crisis by introducing short-term moratoria and in coming to the aid of ailing bill brokers and banks. In the first year of the war, they simultaneously defended the gold standard and the convertibility of the pound sterling. International confidence in the City depended on this, as did London's current and future position as a global financial centre. On the

16 Eduard März, *Österreichische Bankpolitik in der Zeit der großen Wende 1913–1923* (Munich: R. Oldenbourg Verlag, 1981), pp. 139 ff; Stefan von Müller, *Die finanzielle Mobilmachung Österreichs und ihr Ausbau bis 1918* (Berlin: Leopold Weiß, 1918); Alexander Popovics, *Das Geldwesen im Kriege* (Vienna: Hölder-Pichler-Tempsky, 1925), pp. 41 ff, 86 ff.

17 Kenneth Mouré, *The Gold Standard Illusion* (Oxford University Press, 2002), pp. 27 ff; Truchy, *Finances*, pp. 40 ff.

other hand, the Bank of England shouldered the burden of the financial mobilisation by advancing funds to the government against treasury bills for military expenditure. The suspension of the Bank Act of 1844 enabled the bank to exceed the designated bank note contingency. The government raised further funding by placing treasury bills on the open market, and – unlike other states – through the issuance of currency notes, i.e., state paper money, in smaller denominations.[18]

Although the United States only entered the war alongside the Allies in April 1917, the European states' mobilisation triggered a crisis within the stock exchanges, and banks urgently called for extraordinary support measures. In order to increase the volume of bank notes in circulation, the Federal Reserve Act was modified, and furthermore the treasury issued large amounts of emergency notes. Despite draining considerable gold reserves, the United States retained the gold standard, as did Great Britain at the outset of the war. As the US economy suffered before benefiting from the war in Europe, federal finances fell into deficit and had to be stabilised through higher taxes.

US financial mobilisation in spring 1917, by contrast, proceeded smoothly. The government mostly resorted to Treasury Certificates of Indebtedness, which it placed with banks and trust companies via the Federal Reserve Banks.[19]

The financial system was both international and transnational, in the sense of being a global network. That is why neutrals suffered from the same problems as combatants. The Netherlands felt the financial shock of the outbreak of war, suffering economic collapse and a dramatic increase in the need for liquidity. Banks bore the brunt of the problems, especially the Bank of the Netherlands. Although their notes were well backed by metals, convertibility was restricted as much as possible, gold exports were prohibited and cover was reduced to 20 per cent, heavily boosting the circulation of the notes. These and other measures helped to overcome the liquidity crisis quickly, particularly as the country began to benefit from its neutrality. In order to defend this status, the armed forces were bolstered in numbers and in equipment. These measures were funded by treasury bills monetised by the Bank of the Netherlands.[20]

18 Adam W. Kirkaldy (ed.), *British Finance during and after the War 1914–21* (London: Sir Isaac Pitman & Sons, 1921), pp. 9 ff; E. Victor Morgan, *Studies in British Financial Policy, 1914–25* (London: Macmillan, 1952), pp. 3 ff; George C. Peden, *The Treasury and British Public Policy, 1906–1959* (Oxford University Press, 2000), pp. 73 ff.

19 Gilbert, *American Financing*, pp. 14 ff, 145 ff.

20 Marc Frey, *Der Erste Weltkrieg und die Niederlande* (Berlin: Akademie Verlag, 1998), pp. 56 ff; van der Flier, *War Finances*, pp. 21 ff.

Financing the industrial war effort

Such short-term responses to the financial requirements of the war proved inadequate for a long-term conflict whose outcome depended on mobilising economic resources, as well as military manpower, on a vast scale. The ability of the state to increase taxes, borrow domestic and foreign capital and redirect expenditure from peacetime to wartime output constituted the financial levers behind that effort. But the risk of inflation, which would alter established relations between social groups, let alone absolute shortages that might provoke deep unrest and undermine confidence in the war, were the rocks between which financial policy needed to steer the economic effort of the respective powers. In this sense, wartime finance was one of the key determinants of victory or defeat.

It is impossible to estimate the total cost of that effort, just as it is hard to differentiate between direct, indirect and incidental war costs, or to convert nominal into actual values and national currencies into standard denominations. Existing calculations vary, but serve to indicate the magnitude involved. Between 1914 and 1919, based on contemporary prices, all belligerent states spent slightly under 209 billion dollars on the war, with the Allies accounting for 147 billion and the Central Powers for 62 billion. Germany's expenditure topped the list (47 billion), followed by Great Britain (44 billion), the United States (36 billion), France (28 billion) and Austria-Hungary (13 billion). Based on 1913 prices, war costs amounted to a total of 83 billion dollars: 58 billion for the Allies, 25 for the Central Powers. Great Britain (21 billion) and Germany (20 billion) were more or less neck and neck, followed by the United States (17 billion), France (9 billion) and Austria-Hungary (5 billion). Hence, based on 1913 prices, the war annually devoured 37 per cent of the British national income, and 32, 26, 24 and 16 per cent of that of Germany, France, Austria-Hungary and the United States respectively.[21]

This huge expenditure fundamentally changed the world of public finance and the political decision-making processes inherent in it. The imperative of satisfying an indefinite and unconditional demand replaced that of fiscal solidity. Thus, the line blurred between the ordinary, supposedly balanced state budget and the extraordinary budget which was financed by loans provided that the investments paid for themselves. Most states listed all war expenditure under this latter heading. Classic budgetary procedures

21 Harvey E. Fisk, *The Inter-Ally Debts* (New York: Bankers Trust Co., 1924), pp. 13, 325, 21; with differing numbers because inter-Allied debts were included, Ernest L. Bogart, *War Costs and Their Financing* (New York: D. Appleton and Co., 1921), pp. 82 ff.

disintegrated under such pressure, and under enormous pressure from government and military alike, most wartime legislatures confined themselves to legitimising the war finance system and deciding how to cover the costs.[22]

Taxes or credit were the only available options.[23] The former meant forcibly extracting purchasing power from private households and businesses ultimately to finance the war. If the taxpayers were charged according to their means, the burden was more or less fairly distributed. But there were some obvious disadvantages. For example, the generation waging war and already making considerable sacrifices also was hard pressed financially. In some cases, this made them less keen to support the war. Additionally, higher taxes affected the wartime economy as they siphoned off money which would otherwise have been invested. Ultimately, it was not politically expedient to introduce new taxes in wartime.

The disadvantages of taxes made credit seem more attractive. The state raised the necessary funding by contracting debt with private households, companies or banks. As interest and capital repayment on the loans had to be paid, the burden of financing the war was spread over future generations. More importantly, loans mobilised ready cash or savings so that the large amounts needed could be raised rapidly. The disadvantage of loans was the fact that the costs of the war were merely deferred, since loans entailed interest and capital repayments. Thus, in the end it was not the creditors who bore the burden, but those who paid taxes after the war from which states paid off their debts. Furthermore, it made a difference whether loans were taken out with private households and companies, with banks or abroad. In the first case, especially if it concerned long-term or 'funded' debt, the inflationary effects were less significant. That was not the case regarding short-term bank credits, especially from central banks. They printed new money, meaning that the so-called 'floating debt' entailed a high and unavoidable inflationary potential. Regarding debt in other countries, foreign states made financial demands on delivery of goods and services, and liquidated their holdings abroad, thereby putting a strain on future financial relationships.

Basically, deciding between taxation and credit depended on two issues of how to spread the burden: first, which parts of the population should bear the cost of the war; and, secondly, whether the contribution should be final or temporary. In any case, financing the war transferred purchasing power to the government, while simultaneously rerouting goods and services away from the private sector. The resources which were destroyed in war could only be

22 In a comparative perspective, Strachan, *Financing*, pp. 47 ff. 23 Cf. fn. 2.

replenished from three sources: new domestic production; using up existing stocks or running down capital goods; or imports of goods or capital.[24]

Belligerent and neutral states alike mixed taxation and credit in order to cover war expenditures. However, the level of expenditure as well as the combination of means to cover it varied, with important consequences for the wartime and post-war experiences of the countries concerned. Critically, Germany only funded a small proportion of its war expenditure through taxation.[25] Just as in 1871, its leaders planned to pass the financial burden on to the enemy. Moreover, the tax system was not suitable for raising large sums of money. To maintain the appearance of orderly finances, the government wanted to fund at least the ordinary budget and interest on war loans through taxation, but this turned out to be difficult. In 1916, a modern general tax on turnover was introduced and excess wartime profits (judged against the average profits of the last five peacetime years) were imposed at a very moderate level in order to address charges of 'profiteering'. There was provision as well for individual capital gains tax, later replaced by income tax, and the Reich eventually increased a range of indirect taxes and imposed a consumer tax on coal from 1917 onwards.

None of this amounted to either a stringent or socially equitable regime of wartime taxation. German war finance therefore depended primarily on loans. Up until 1918 the issued nine war loans generated around 97 billion marks (24.6 billion dollars).[26] The money was taken out on five-year treasury notes or ten-year redeemable bonds with 5 per cent interest and issued at a small discount. Grand propaganda campaigns were supposed to ensure that the bonds were fully subscribed and well distributed. This was seen as a gauge of the public's willingness to continue the war. As the bonds served to consolidate floating debt, a cycle of creating money through central bank credits and absorbing money through war loans developed. This worked well up to the fifth loan in autumn 1916. After that, the proceeds from the loans lagged behind the accumulated short-term debts. The fact that Germany was largely cut off from Wall Street both by a US neutrality loaded in favour of the Entente and then by US entry into the war meant that the Reich was deprived of the major alternative source to self-funding its war effort, leading

24 Hans-Peter Ullmann, 'War economy', in Gerhard Hirschfeld *et al.* (eds.), *Brill's Encyclopedia of the First World War* (Leiden: Koninklijke Brill NV, 2012), vol. I, pp. 169–79.

25 Roesler, *Finanzpolitik*, pp. 96 ff, 206 ff; Ullmann, *Steuerstaat*, pp. 88 ff.

26 Ernest L. Bogart, *Direct and Indirect Costs of the Great World War*, 2nd edn (New York: Oxford University Press, 1920), p. 230 (dollars at pre-war rates of exchange).

to greater inflationary pressures than in Entente countries. By November 1918, the national debt in the shape of treasury bills and bonds stood at 51 billion marks; 22 billion were in the Reichsbank portfolio and had expanded the money supply.

Austria-Hungary struggled even more than Germany in financing the war.[27] As its economy was less developed and its financial system weaker, it mustered less funding for fighting the war. Only a fraction originated from taxation. As parliament did not convene until 1917, the government and state bureaucracy had a substantial degree of freedom of action. They made do by increasing existing direct taxes and especially indirect taxes, fees and war surcharges, which were politically easier to enforce. By way of new measures, war profits and coal consumption were both imposed. Yet taxation could not outstrip the devaluation of the currency. As prices rose faster than revenue, the authorities collected less and less in real terms. Ultimately, receipts did not even cover the cost of non-military expenditure and the interest on the debts.

The increasing deficits which amounted to 91 billion crowns therefore had to be financed by loans. Between 1914 and 1918, Austria issued eight war loans and Hungary seventeen, which fetched 51 billion crowns in total (10.6 billion dollars).[28] They matured initially after five years, then after ten or fifteen and later after forty years. At first, they were only floated against treasury notes or after 1916 against bonds, with interest at 5.5 to 6 per cent and at a clear discount. Small subscribers were also welcome as banks offered credits at reasonable terms and conditions. Coupled with the rapidly growing demand of military and civilian agencies as well as by rapidly increasing prices, this credit regime contributed to the inability to fund the floating debt through loans. Therefore, no cycle of creating and absorbing money could develop. Rather, short-term debt with the Austrian-Hungarian Bank and a domestic bank consortium simply carried on uninhibitedly. By the end of the war, the central bank alone had lent Austria 25 and Hungary 10 billion crowns.

In the absence of US capital markets, the only external source of funding for the Central Powers were the European neutral states (Switzerland, Sweden, Denmark and most of all the Netherlands). By the end of the war, Germany had run up 1.6 billion gold marks of debt in the Netherlands alone. Austria-Hungary also borrowed money there as well as taking out small loans in Denmark and Sweden against treasury bills. The Dual Monarchy resorted to

27 März, *Bankpolitik*, pp. 194 ff; Müller, *Mobilmachung*, pp. 157 ff; Wilhelm Winkler, *Die Einkommensverschiebungen in Österreich während des Weltkrieges* (Vienna: Hölder-Pichler-Tempsky, 1930), pp. 68 ff, 157 ff; Schulze, 'Austria-Hungary's economy', pp. 99 ff.

28 Bogart, *Direct and Indirect Costs*, pp. 251 ff (dollars at pre-war rates of exchange).

credit on a larger scale from Germany in order to finance its imports. By the summer of 1918, Austria-Hungary owed its ally 3.5 billion marks.[29]

The Allies, by contrast, not only had access to far greater supplies of international capital (including their own investments in the United States), but also developed a complex, wide-ranging system for managing their reciprocal war debts.[30] Great Britain and the United States developed the so-called 'Dollar-Sterling-Block' in two stages. At first, Great Britain took over the role of a banker for the Allied Powers, a role that passed after 1917 increasingly to the Americans. The growing imports of armaments and other goods along with British loans to the Allies, especially to Russia, put pressure on the exchange rate of the pound against the dollar. The currency problem was only solved on a long-term basis when the United States entered the war, paving the way for loans by the American Treasury. At the end of the war, Great Britain owed 3.7 billion dollars to the United States. Due to growing imports of war materials from the United States, France had to join the Dollar-Sterling-Block, too, and resort to loans from Great Britain. By 1918, France had borrowed 1.7 billion dollars in Great Britain and 2 billion in the United States. Altogether, the Allies were in debt to the United States for 7.1 billion dollars. The fact that Great Britain and France accumulated debts on the one hand, and on the other hand helped their allies to finance the war, complicated the debt relationships between the Allied states. By the end of the war, the inter-Allied war debts had reached a total of 21.6 billion gross or 16.4 billion dollars after offsetting counter debts.[31]

No definitive answer can be given to the question of whether inter-Allied loans made a decisive difference to the outcome of the war. What is beyond doubt is that they contributed to a more integrated economic effort than the Central Powers managed and helped funnel war supplies to the Allied effort. The loans were not monetised, so they did not weaken the wartime domestic purchasing power of the borrowers. Rather, they served to stabilise the exchange rates and brought the Allied states closer together in ways that went beyond finance. More importantly, however, the loans opened the door

29 Marc Frey, 'Deutsche finanzinteressen an den vereinigten staaten und den Niederlanden im Ersten Weltkrieg', *Militärgeschichtliche Mitteilungen*, 53 (1994), pp. 338 ff; Popovics, *Geldwesen*, pp. 120 ff.

30 Fisk, *Debts*; Harold G. Moulton and Leo Pasvolsky, *War Debts and World Prosperity* (Washington, DC: The Brookings Institution, 1932), pp. 25 ff; Martin Horn, *Britain, France, and the Financing of the First World War* (Montreal: McGill-Queen's University Press, 2002), pp. 93 ff.

31 Fisk, *Debts*, p. 345; Moulton and Pasvolsky, *War Debts*, p. 426.

for considerable purchasing of military equipment in the United States and therefore contributed to the Allies' material superiority.[32]

Foreign debt was important to France in funding the war, but domestic loans played the dominant role.[33] The government accessed receptive money and capital markets mainly with treasury bonds. This was bolstered by the fact that the state enjoyed creditors' confidence. Most of the treasury bonds could therefore be placed with the general public and did not have to be placed with banks. From autumn 1914 onwards, the 'Bons du Trésor' were joined by the 'Bons de la Défense Nationale', which matured after between three and twelve months. In fact, they were supposed to be consolidated with war loans, but instead turned into the 'standard instrument for financing war'.[34] The 'Obligations de la Défense Nationale' issued in early 1915 with a maturity of five or ten years were less popular. Even the war loans France issued in the shape of perpetual loans with no fixed maturity terms, but with free repayment and a high interest rate of 5.7 per cent, did not prove as popular as in Germany. The first loan was issued late, namely in November 1915, and was followed by three others in 1916, 1917 and 1918, although they only brought in 24 billion francs. That only accounted for 19 per cent of the total sum of 130 billion francs raised by the government through credit between 1914 and 1918, whereas the short- and medium-term treasury bonds made up about 42 per cent, foreign debt 25 per cent and central bank credit 13 per cent.

Plans to fund a greater proportion of war expenses out of taxation were not put into practice until 1916, when the deficit reached 40 per cent and the debt 125 per cent of the national product. Tax was supposed to cover at least day-to-day expenditures and the interest on the debt. Consequently, the income tax, which had been agreed on in July 1914, was introduced with moderate rates and several consumer taxes were increased. A new wartime profits tax was introduced, which only proved to have any real effect after the war had ended. Therefore, taxation did not have the desired effect. The deficit remained stable at just over 40 per cent of the national product, meaning that France had to take out loans simply to pay interest on its debts.

32 Strachan, *Financing*, pp. 220 ff.

33 Lucien Petit, *Histoire des Finances extérieures de la France pendant la Guerre (1914–1919)* (Paris: Payot, 1929); Truchy, *Finances*; Bertrand Blancheton, *Le Pape et l'empereur* (Paris: Albin Michel, 2001), pp. 87 ff; Hautcoeur, 'Great War', pp. 184 ff; Nicolas Delalande, *Les Batailles de l'Impôt* (Paris: Éditions du Seuil, 2011), pp. 245 ff.

34 Hardach, *Erste Weltkrieg*, p. 176.

Great Britain financed the war through taxation to a greater extent than France, but to a lesser proportion than had been the case in previous wars.[35] The government began with moderate tax increases. Only after 1915 when the deficit hit 43 per cent of the national product did the controversial 'McKenna Rule' plot a course between fiscal orthodoxy and a politically reasonable tax burden. In future, expenditure for peace and interest on state debt would be paid for out of taxation. A comprehensive finance programme was designed especially for this purpose, increasing the standard income tax rate in stages from 5.8 to 30 per cent, while expanding the number of people subject to taxation and imposing a super tax on the rich which drove the top rate up to over 50 per cent. The consumer taxes on luxury foodstuffs were increased several times and – contrary to the traditions of free trade – excise duties were introduced in order to slow down imports; finally, on top of this, an excess profit duty taxed profits above a stipulated peacetime level at an initial rate of 50 per cent, rising to 80 per cent.

Although Great Britain increased its taxes, the revenue only covered a small share of war expenditure and the bulk was financed with credit. By 1917, the Treasury had issued three war loans which were not only accompanied by the usual propaganda, but also offered appealing interest rates varying between 4 and 5.3 per cent in order to attract foreign investors. As the creditors were also able to swap old bonds for new ones, the costs increased considerably. Thus, from 1917 onwards, the government ran up debts against three- to five-year National War Bonds. The time gaps between the war bonds were bridged with treasury bills, while alongside the issue of Exchequer Bonds and National War Bonds, the Ways and Means Advances rose in volume. Hence, between March 1914 and March 1919, the debt increased more than tenfold from 706 million to 7.5 billion pounds, or 128 per cent of the national product. Of the total domestic debt of 6.1 billion, 23 per cent was floating debt, 50 per cent was medium term and just 5 per cent accounted for funded debt.

The United States intended to cover half the war costs with taxes.[36] This was supposed to be made possible by the economic upturn the country was

35 Martin Daunton, *Just Taxes* (Cambridge University Press, 2002), pp. 36 ff; Josiah Stamp, *Taxation during the War* (London: Humphrey Milford, 1932), pp. 23 ff; Jeremy Wormell, *The Management of the National Debt of the United Kingdom, 1900–1932* (London: Routledge, 2000), pp. 63 ff; Kirkaldy, *British Finance*, pp. 124 ff; Morgan, *Studies*, pp. 106 ff; Peden, *Treasury*, pp. 80 ff; Stephen Broadberry and Peter Howlett, 'The United Kingdom during World War I: business as usual?', in Broadberry and Harrison, *Economics of World War I*, pp. 215 ff.

36 Gilbert, *American Financing*, pp. 57 ff, 117 ff; Hugh Rockoff, 'Until it's over, over there: the US economy in World War I', in Broadberry and Harrison, *Economics of World War I*, pp. 315 ff.

experiencing thanks to the growing demand for armaments and other commodities. The government had already increased taxation with its Emergency Revenue Act of 1914 and the Revenue Act of 1916. The War Revenue Acts of 1917 and 1918 especially continued that trend as they concentrated on augmenting direct taxation rather than consumer taxes. Surtaxes were therefore imposed on corporate and personal income taxes. On top of that came an excess profits tax at rates between 20 and 60 per cent. Excise taxes and customs duties also went up. All of these measures pushed up revenue from income and profits taxes from 124 million dollars in 1916 to 2.6 billion dollars in 1919. Thus, the weight shifted away from excise taxes and customs duties which had formed 90 per cent of expenditure before the war, towards income and profits taxes generating 56 per cent of the revenue in 1919.

Although taxation had been increased on a long-term basis, the revenue was nowhere near high enough to cover war expenditure. Starting in May 1917, the United States issued five war loans, four Liberty Loans and one Victory Loan in April 1919. The terms were favourable, aiming to attract as much subscription as possible. The interest rates rose from 3.5 to 4.75 per cent, and other perks were granted, such as tax exemption or conversion privileges. The war loans generated 21.5 billion dollars in total. They were pre-financed to an increasing extent with Anticipation Certificates, in other words floating debts which remained primarily within the banking system and produced considerable inflationary effects. Targeting small savings, after January 1918, five-year War Saving Certificates were issued. They yielded 1.2 billion dollars and although too late and too little, they did siphon off buying power. In total, the debt rose by 24.3 billion dollars from 1916 to 1919, of which 19 billion can be allocated to the non-bank public, 4.1 billion to commercial banks and 0.2 billion to the Federal Reserve Bank.

In the Netherlands, all direct costs to the state on account of war were listed as 'Crisis Expenditure', which added up to 2 billion guilders between 1913 and 1921. It cost 1.4 billion alone just to expand the army and fleet, and to support soldiers' families. The second major item was the maintenance of production and the distribution of food. Large sums of money flowed into financial relief for particular persons or institutions, such as the unemployed or refugees from Belgium and France. The neutral Netherlands covered a comparatively large portion of the additional expenditure through higher taxation. The government imposed extra charges of between 20 and 50 per cent of existing taxes on property and persons, income and capital, as well as on several duties. In addition, highly progressive defence taxes on capital and income were introduced, together with a tax on war profits. As was the case in other states, the weight shifted from consumer to direct taxes. The additional tax revenues kept the deficit down to a relatively low 12 per cent of the national product.

Besides introducing new taxes, the Netherlands also resorted to taking out loans in order to finance the budget deficit. Between December 1914 and December 1918, the government issued five war loans at between 4 and 5 per cent interest and with repayment conditions of between fifteen and forty years. If the loans were not subscribed to in full, there was the risk they would be converted into compulsory loans. They fetched a total of around 1.1 billion guilders. As was the case with the funded debt, the floating debt increased mainly in the form of treasury bills from 13 million guilders in 1913 to 859 million in 1921. Although the state debt of 1.2 billion (1913) rose to 2.9 billion (1918), its 50 to 60 per cent proportion of the national product remained fairly stable in comparison with other countries.

Financing war had far-reaching consequences for the political systems of both the neutral and the belligerent countries. Where parliaments became less important, the executive gained and most of all the military's power and influence grew. The effects on the economy were drastic too. Financing the war helped to transform the economy more or less into a wartime economy with varying transition phases and at times creating a mixture of peacetime and wartime economy. Here and there, however, with production and consumption classed as military necessity, the state considerably increased its influence on the economy.[37] Furthermore, the way in which war was financed influenced the social structures in the belligerent and neutral countries alike. Apart from in the United States and Great Britain, the process of material poverty developed to varying degrees. Poverty led to an increase in social tension as the financial burden was unevenly distributed. Financing the war not only aggravated existing social disparity; it created new tension: between winners and losers of the war, men and women, 'at the front' and 'at home', producers and consumers, town and countryside. At the same time, the perception of social hierarchies changed in wartime. Each social group felt it was financially the most hard done by and that the burden of paying for the war was unfairly distributed. This self-assessment became more intense as the shining counter-image of war profiteers became increasingly evident.

37 Ullmann, 'War economy'.

Demobilisation and the impossible return to the pre-war financial order

Financial demobilisation was no less a transformation than financial mobilisation had been. In the individual states, it was a sluggish and in some cases even a haphazard process, surrounded by political debate. It was also burdened by the illusory assumption that one could and should return to pre-war conditions. Three urgent problems were ubiquitous: first, war funding had to stop; secondly, the money necessary for reconstruction had to be found; and last but not least, thirdly, states had to deal with war debt. Dealing with all three problems was essentially about how to handle the consequences of the war. The question was who would bear the burden at the end of the day. Up until 1920/21, financial demobilisation proceeded in a similar manner, but then the states parted ways.[38]

After war ended, Germany's public finances were in ruins.[39] In addition to the war debt, revenues dwindled as a consequence of the transformation of wartime to peacetime economy and the Treaty of Versailles, additional expenditure for demobilisation, transfer payments to war victims and reparations. Whereas public expenditure in 1910 to 1913 represented 13 per cent of the national income, based on 1913 pricing, it grew in 1919 to 1923 to 38 per cent. Three responses were possible: the first was to raise taxes dramatically in order to pay off state debts and cover the huge expenditure. Without doubt, the price would have been a depression that the young republic could not survive. Secondly, inflationary finance could be continued, as in wartime. Politically, this option was more attractive. It would have jump-started the economy through 'cheap money', but accelerated the devaluation of the currency. Prior to being pushed down that path, the government pursued an attempt at 'relative' stabilisation. If this third option had been a success, it would have halted the devaluation of the currency at around 8 to 10 per cent of its then value and thereby would have avoided hyperinflation.

The financial reform of 1920 pursued this goal, introducing a modern and efficient finance and progressive tax system, and imposing an emergency sacrifice levy to pay off debt, but thereby losing the race against devaluation.

38 Mendershausen, *Economics*, pp. 346 ff; Paul Einzig, *World Finance since 1914* (London: Kegan Paul, Trench, Trubner & Co., 1935); Alberto Alesina, 'The end of large public debts', in Francesco Giavazzi and Luigi Spaventa (eds.), *High Public Debt* (Cambridge University Press, 1988), pp. 34–97.

39 Ullmann, *Steuerstaat*, pp. 97 ff; Niall Ferguson, 'Constraints and room for manoeuvre in the German inflation of the early 1920s', *Economic History Review*, 49 (1996), pp. 635–66; Gerald D. Feldman, *The Great Disorder* (Oxford University Press, 1996); Carl-Ludwig Holtfrerich, *Die deutsche Inflation 1914–1923* (Berlin: Walter de Gruyter, 1980); Martin H. Geyer, *Verkehrte Welt* (Göttingen: Vandenhoeck & Ruprecht, 1998).

The only remaining solution was central bank credits, which raised the national debt to astronomical heights and accelerated hyperinflation.

Only after the occupation of the Ruhr and the currency reform of 1923/24 was it possible to straighten out the financial mess. On the one hand, reform brought an increase in all major taxes, but on the other hand, it reduced the number of employees in the public service and lowered their salaries, and also cut expenditure for buildings, culture, education and social services. The consolidation of public finance made the return to the gold standard in autumn 1924 possible, but at a high social cost.

Financial demobilisation in Germany through inflation and stabilisation put an end to war finance, made reconstruction easier and reduced debt. But that came at a price. Hyperinflation undermined political stability and operated as an unfair tax, rewarding those clever enough to be able to manipulate and profit from devaluation. This 'topsy-turvy world' turned important bourgeois values upside down, destroyed savings, led to dwindling production and the wrong allocation of resources, created surplus capacity and deferred rationalisation of production.

The situation was no different in Austria, one of the new states to emerge from the collapse of the Habsburg monarchy. Established in 1918, the republic was politically unstable, overloaded with debt and, within the confines of the Treaty of Saint-Germain, economically virtually unviable. In an attempt to pay off the debt, a high one-off levy on capital was approved in 1920, but it had little to no effect. In 1922, the budget deficit was at 49 per cent of total expenditure and largely had to be financed by printing money. Hence, circulation of bank notes rose from 4 billion in March 1919 to 3.1 trillion crowns in November 1922, with corresponding growth in inflation. At this point, with the help of the League of Nations, the currency was stabilised, and finances restored to order. To prevent the country from drifting into bankruptcy and dissolving, Austria received a twenty-year loan of 650 million gold crowns. In exchange, the government had to pledge itself in the Geneva Protocol to stop printing money and to establish a new central reserve bank, to permit monitoring by a General Commissioner and introduce rigid savings and deflation policies. Here as well, restoring financial stability came at a price, with high levels of unemployment and a serious deflation crisis. Financial demobilisation was concluded with the Currency Reform of 1925, which introduced the schilling based on the gold standard.[40]

40 März, *Bankpolitik*, pp. 318 ff, 470 ff; Anne Orde, *British Policy and European Reconstruction after the First World War* (Cambridge University Press, 1990), pp. 130 ff.

The question of reparations burdened financial demobilisation in both Germany and Austria. In the peace treaties of Versailles and Saint-Germain, both states committed themselves to payments, the scale of which had not been determined. The demands made on Austria could not be enforced due to its weak economy and finances. They were suspended for twenty years in 1922, and cancelled altogether at the Hague Conference of 1930. The reparation demands made on Germany were a different case. After the republic had made a first payment of 13 billion gold marks, the definitive amount was set in 1921 at 132 billion gold marks or 33 billion dollars. Initially, only the 12 billion A-Bonds and 38 billion B-Bonds had to be repaid annually with interest. The total amount was fixed at 3 billion gold marks or between 5 and 6 per cent of the national product of Germany.

Whether the Weimar Republic could have shouldered the burden remains debatable. Even if the annuities were economically affordable, political factors made it difficult to raise and transfer the sums. Payments soon came to a standstill, and in 1923 the situation ultimately escalated into the occupation of the Ruhr. The Dawes Plan temporarily calmed and depoliticised the reparations problems with lower annuities, regulation of the transfer system, and a massive influx of foreign capital.[41]

The inability to ease the problem of inter-Allied debt by attaching it to the reparations question was a result of the political stance of the United States. The US authorities insisted that war debt, which had grown to 28.3 billion dollars by 1923, should not be offset against demands for reparations. The United States and Great Britain remained the main creditors; France was one of their biggest debtors. Suggestions to scrap debt entirely, to treat them as joint Allied liabilities or divide up payments according to solvency were rejected outright by the United States, which demanded repayment in full. Consequently, no solution could be agreed upon. On the contrary, the problems involved in raising and transferring funds meant on the one hand that the United States had to reduce their demands in bilateral contracts. On the other hand, a payment cycle did in fact develop that included reparations: American capital flowed to Germany, which meant that reparation instalments could be transferred; the recipients in turn used these payments to pay off their debt to the United States. This circulation pattern came to an end in

41 Holtfrerich, *Inflation*, pp. 135 ff; Bruce Kent, *The Spoils of War* (Oxford: Clarendon Press, 1989).

the early 1930s, and the end of reparations also meant the disappearance of the inter-Allied debt question.[42]

The problem of reparations not only affected the Central Powers, but also France. Both government and population intended to shift the onus of the war onto Germany. Only when hopes of being able to do this dwindled did a debate about how to handle the huge debt begin. After all, the French debt amounted to 160 per cent of national product, while simultaneously the rebuilding of the northern departments, devastated by the war, and the provision of support and benefits for war victims had to be financed. There was a plan for the introduction of a capital levy as a fair compromise between those who profited and those who suffered material losses as a result of the war, but since this was politically unfeasible, the only alternative consisted of massive tax increases. While up until 1918, the tax ratio had hovered at around 8 per cent of national product, by the 1920s it rose to between 12 and 16 per cent. The government nevertheless had to continue taking out loans in order to cover the budget deficit; at 159 billion francs between 1919 and 1925, the French debt nearly doubled. As a large portion of that was floating debt which had to be replenished regularly, and because there had been speculation against the franc since 1923, the currency plummeted and could only be stabilised by the financial reform of 1926 at 20 per cent of its pre-war value, bound again to the gold standard. Unlike the Central Powers, which could only regain control over inflation by devaluation, financial demobilisation in France was accompanied by a moderate rate of inflation, which probably eased the economic situation.[43]

Unlike France, the United States, the Netherlands and Great Britain based financial demobilisation on deflation, albeit with varying intensity. American deflationary politics were as simple as they were effective, instigating a series of stabilisation processes by reintroducing the convertibility of the dollar based on its pre-war level. The country had largely remained unscathed by the war, emerged as the main creditor, and after a short transitional period in 1918/19 and a brief crisis in 1920/21, its economy progressed to the 'good times' of the 1920s. That made it possible for the state to master its revenue and spending, all the while curbing inflation. The government was

42 Denise Artaud, *La question des dettes interalliées et la reconstruction de l'Europe (1917–1929)*, 2 vols. (Paris: Librairie Honoré Champion, 1978); Orde, *British Policy*, pp. 146 ff; Fisk, *Debts*, pp. 348 ff; Moulton and Pasvolsky, *War Debts*, pp. 48 ff, 291 ff.

43 Delalande, *Batailles*, pp. 273 ff; Mouré, *Gold Standard*, pp. 50 ff; Dan P. Silverman, *Reconstructing Europe after the Great War* (Cambdridge, MA: Harvard University Press, 1982), pp. 62 ff.

consequently able to reduce its expenditure from 19 billion dollars in 1919 to 4.9 billion in 1921. In the following years, expenditure remained around the 3.2 billion dollar level. At 8 per cent of national product, the state expenditure ratio was four times higher than before the war. This 'displacement effect' was contributed to by expenditures for veterans, as well as those to encourage businesses, expand public works and fund grants-in-aid. As wartime taxes were still in force, revenue after 1920 exceeded expenditure. This triggered a heated debate about whether the surplus should be used for debt retirement or tax reduction. Finally, a compromise was reached. On the one hand, the tax reductions of 1921 and 1924, 1926 and 1928 eased the burden on high earners, but even more on the middle- and lower-income brackets without reversing the shift from indirect to direct taxation. On the other hand, the treasury attempted to fund short-term obligations first of all and reduce debt. As a result, the debt decreased from 26 billion (1919) to 20 billion dollars (1925).[44]

Financial demobilisation in the Netherlands dragged on well into the second half of the 1920s. Certainly prices and costs had risen, and the war had thrown the economy off balance. But the neutral Netherlands had suffered less than other countries. This permitted moderate deflationary politics which did not trigger any major crisis. Expenditure rose dramatically by 1922. There was huge political pressure to replace receding military expenditures with increased spending on housing and education. At the same time, the gap between expenditure and revenue widened, and in 1922 the deficit represented one-third of expenses. Debt therefore continued to grow. At a level of 4.2 billion guilders in 1922, including 1.5 billion in floating debts, debt turned out to be 1.34 billion guilders higher than at the end of the war. This forced radical reforms in 1923 and 1924, drastic cuts in expenditure, the introduction of new taxes and a rise in existing ones. Again, indirect, or consumer, taxation grew faster than direct taxation. At the same time, a portion of the floating debt was consolidated and the funded debt was paid off more quickly. Thus, the 'golden rules of finance', consisting of balanced budgets and loans exclusively reserved for productive investment, were brought back to life. With finances restored to health, the Netherlands reverted to the gold standard in 1924.[45]

44 Paul Studenski and Herman E. Kroos, *Financial History of the United States*, 2nd edn (New York: McGraw-Hill, 1963), pp. 302 ff.

45 Jan Luiten van Zanden, 'Old rules, new conditions, 1914–1940', in Broadberry and Harrison, *Economics of World War I*, pp. 135 ff.

Great Britain had more serious problems with the deflationary effects of demobilisation. In 1919, debts accounted for 130 per cent of national product, and in 1920 and 1921, debt devoured 309 billion pounds or 22 per cent of revenue. The question was how to handle that debt, especially the floating debt, which would be decisive for the distribution of the economic burdens of the war, including the return to the gold standard. In the end, this was only possible through deflationary policies which triggered a major conflict of interest between tax-paying manufacturers on the one hand and rentiers on the other, not to mention the effects on the labour force. The proposal to pay off the debt with a levy on capital or on war wealth was, in this conservative period, as politically impossible as the idea of a general sales tax. In order to service the debt, war taxes continued to be levied and a new corporation tax was introduced. From 1920 to 1921 onwards, public revenue dropped from 1.4 billion to 800 million pounds in 1924 and 1925, due to the fact that the excess profits duty had been revoked, and income and consumer tax rates had been reduced. The government cut down public expenditure even more quickly from 1.7 billion to 796 million, particularly with regard to defence forces and civil services, including education, resulting in a surplus of 430 million pounds. With this, external war commitments and floating debts were reduced. They dropped by 530 million pounds, partly due to conversion. Restructuring finance was an essential step towards stabilising the pound at pre-war levels and returning to the gold standard in 1925.

It is debatable, too, to what extent deflationary demobilisation caused the economic difficulties faced by Britain in the 1920s. The serious depression of 1921 and the comparatively slow economic recovery of Britain, marked by high levels of unemployment in the 1920s, were at least in part a function of the deflationary economic policy adopted to end the wartime financial regime.[46] The repercussions, which culminated in the General Strike of 1926, followed the return to the gold standard as night followed the day. They were part of the story of the social reckoning of financial adjustments to the war in Great Britain. After the General Strike, the burden of retrenchment was placed unequivocally on the shoulders of the working class.

Financial demobilisation following the Great War led to uncertain and therefore temporary stabilisation, not only of public finances, but also of social policy and the political system itself. This was the result of a process of new negotiations concerning post-war social relations and the scope of political power. The outcome was neither a return to, nor a decisive rejection of,

46 Morgan, *Studies*, pp. 95 ff; Daunton, *Taxes*, pp. 60 ff; Wormell, *Management*, pp. 381 ff;

pre-war 'bourgeois Europe', but instead a new unsteady mixture of more state and stronger influence by organised interests.[47]

Public finances played a double role in this process of negotiations and readjusting: on the one hand, they were a key area of politics in which social, economic and political conflicts were battled out in disputes about taxes and debt, or on a more general note, about distributing the burdens of war. On the other hand, public finance reflected the results of those battles and conflicts over the public budget. Rudolf Goldscheid, an Austrian sociologist and pacifist, bluntly highlights this function of public finances and especially the budget in the aftermath of the Great War: 'The state cannot differ much from its budget.' The budget 'is the skeleton of the state stripped of all misleading ideologies'.[48] Transformations of the state as a result of the war were bound to change public finance and its political meaning.

The financial legacy of the Great War

The financial outcome of the war is contradictory in at least three aspects. The first is the relationship between the policies and instruments available to the combatant powers. On the one hand, the similarities stemmed from the homogeneity of fiscal tasks. Each state confronted similar problems: the high expense of war, dwindling revenue and massive deficits. As a result of financial structures, tradition, competition, imitation and the transfer processes between fiscal systems, there were only a limited number of politically realistic fiscal instruments to solve these problems. Every state resorted to a surprisingly similar mixture of taxation and credit; even the types of new taxation and ways of raising public credit were similar. On the other hand, there were substantial differences that were deeply rooted within the idiosyncrasies of different fiscal systems and arose out of particular and divergent political decisions.

This was certainly true of the mixture of taxes and credit. Whereas the neutral Netherlands was able to finance almost half of its additional expenditure caused by the war through taxation, the proportion among the belligerent states looked less favourable. Great Britain managed 26 per cent, the United States around 23 per cent, while Germany remained below 16 per cent,

47 Charles S. Maier, *Recasting Bourgeois Europe. Stabilization in France, Germany and Italy in the Decade after World War I* (Princeton University Press, 1975).

48 Rudolf Goldscheid, 'Staatssozialismus oder staatskapitalismus', in Rudolf Goldscheid and Joseph Schumpeter, *Die Finanzkrise des Steuerstaats* (Frankfurt: Suhrkamp Verlag, 1976), p. 188.

France, was around 15 per cent, and Austria-Hungary amounted to just over one-tenth.[49]

Equally contradictory is the answer to the second question as to whether the methods of financing war were a success or failure. On the one hand, no country failed to raise the necessary funds for war, even if it did cause considerable problems. On the other hand, the price of doing so was extraordinarily high. From an economic perspective, the war was tantamount to the 'economic suicide' of a transnational system of economic and fiscal transactions, as Gerald D. Feldman put it, and this was true, not just for the defeated countries: everyone suffered from a systemic failure. From 100 per cent of 1913 levels, national product shrank by 1918 to 73 per cent in Austria and to 82 per cent in Germany; France even dropped to 64 per cent of pre-war levels. Only in Great Britain and the United States did wartime national product grow by 15 and 13 per cent respectively.[50]

Growth suffered and so did the financial outlook of countries burdened by war debt. In Britain, the debt ratio jumped from 26 to 128 per cent, in France from 65 to 160 per cent, in the United States from 2 to 37 per cent and in the Netherlands from 48 to 60 per cent of the national product. Debt in Germany increased thirtyfold, whereas that of Austria only grew sevenfold, and that of Hungary sixfold, as a result of the low absorption capacity of the money market.[51]

More important than the rising debt was the degree to which this debt could be monetised. This depended on the proportion of floating debt and the volume of money which had been created through the banking system. Whereas the volume of money in Austria-Hungary increased more than twentyfold and almost tenfold in Germany, France saw a fivefold, Britain a two-and-a-half-fold increase, while in the United States the money supply doubled and in the Netherlands it rose three-and-a-half-fold. Coupled with a diminished supply of goods, this led to massive price increases which could only be kept under temporary control through subsidies or rationing measures. This meant in turn that by the end of the war, consumer prices in Austria

49 Theo Balderston, 'War finance and inflation in Britain and Germany, 1914–1918', *Economic History Review*, 42 (1989), pp. 222–44; Rockoff, 'Until it's over', p. 316; Delalande, *Batailles*, p. 249; Schulze, 'Austria-Hungary's economy', p. 99.

50 Stephen Broadberry and Mark Harrison, 'The economics of World War I', in Broadberry and Harrison, *Economics of World War I*, p. 12.

51 Broadberry and Howlett, 'United Kingdom', p. 219; Hautcoeur, 'Great War', p. 186; Herman de Jong, 'Between the devil and the deep blue sea: the Dutch economy during World War I', in Broadberry and Harrison, *Economics of World War I*, p. 155; Ullmann, *Steuerstaat*, p. 98; Schulze, 'Austria-Hungary's economy', p. 102.

had increased approximately sixteenfold, and in Hungary ninefold, since the beginning of the war. In Germany, prices more than doubled, as they did in Great Britain, France and the United States. Only in the Netherlands did the price increase stabilise at the lower level of two-thirds of the 1914 figure.[52] The inflationary spiral of the post-war years made the return to financial stability a pipe dream.

Thirdly, relationships between continuity and discontinuity also proved contradictory.[53] On the one hand, all states, whether belligerent or neutral, reverted to familiar and proven methods of war financing. The better they had functioned before the war, the more successful they were during the war. War left no room for fundamental reforms. In the post-war period, public finances were stabilised through time-proven methods and channels: either through hyperinflation with currency destabilisation or moderate inflation or a more or less sharp deflation. In the end, bringing back the gold standard symbolised a return to an alleged pre-war 'normality', which could never be retrieved.

War finance had fundamentally affected the international currency system, and every country within it. Many countries had left the gold standard during the war and built up their own monetary systems. This was not without consequences. The reinstated gold standard turned out to be unstable and full of disparities, finally collapsing during the world economic crisis of 1931. Attempts to revive a moribund gold standard had only made matters worse; the war had transformed the world financial system, and yet it took thirteen years after the Armistice for everyone to recognise that fact.

There were other structural changes linked to the war. The banks' influence had increased on public spending, especially that of the central banks. On an international level, new institutions came into being, such as the Finance Commission of the League of Nations, which played an important role for several international agreements regulating financial relations between the various states. Last but not least, the weight had shifted in the international financial system and reversed the flow of funds from creditors to debtors. As the European states during the war had not only liquidated substantial portions of their overseas assets, but also taken out considerable loans, the old continent forfeited its position as a creditor. Instead, the United States rose from a debtor to the largest creditor nation, and the dominance of the dollar

52 Winkler, *Einkommensverschiebungen*, pp. 38 ff; Holtfrerich, *Inflation*, pp. 24 ff; Broadberry and Howlett, 'United Kingdom', p. 219; Hautcoeur, 'Great War', pp. 185 ff; Gilbert, *American Financing*, pp. 212 ff; de Jong, *Economy*, p. 158.

53 Niall Ferguson, 'How (not) to pay for the war', in Roger Chickering and Stig Förster (eds.), *Great War, Total War* (Cambridge University Press, 2006), pp. 409–34.

followed suit. All of this may have happened over time, but what the war did was to accelerate the decentralisation of the financial world.

In addition, in the period surrounding the war, fresh approaches were becoming apparent in public finance. This applied to certain taxes, such as the excess profits tax or the general turnover tax. It can be seen as well in the debates about a capital levy. Methods and procedures regarding state debt were changing too. New securitisations were introduced, broader ranges of creditors accessed and alternative methods of debt management pursued. Eventually expenditure, taxes and loans reached a new quantitative dimension which amounted to a qualitative jump. Financing war led ultimately to a 'displacement effect', which increased permanently the proportion of the national economy occupied by the state. That is, services previously provided by the private sector or by local government came under the authority of the central state, with evident financial consequences. At the same time, public debt became an acceptable method of finance, and devaluation proved to be a mechanism for both applying and managing it. The 'fiscal state', which was (and still is) based on a 'dynamic interaction of expenditure, revenue and credit' was a by-product of war.[54]

What Feldman termed the 'economic suicide' of war and its disastrous effects on the pre-war financial order produced long-term consequences of significance. One was the displacement of Europe as the fulcrum of the world economy; a second effect was increasing social and political tensions in countries affected by economic instability in the interwar years, even before the onset of the world economic crisis in 1929. The weakness of parliamentary governments, and the attractiveness of totalitarian alternatives, arose in part out of the exigencies and consequences of war finance.

54 William Mark Ormrod and Richard Bonney (eds.), *Crisis, Revolutions, and Self-Sustained Growth* (Stamford: Paul Watkins, 1999), pp. 1–21; Olivier Feiertag, 'La déroue des monnaies', in Stéphane Audoin-Rozeau and Jean-Jacques Becker (eds.), *Encyclopédie de la Grande Guerre* (Paris: Bayard, 2004), pp. 1163–76.

17

Scientists

ROY MACLEOD

Introduction

It has been said that history is a debate between the present and the past about the future. Nowhere is this sentiment more salient than in the role played by the natural sciences in the Great War, and reciprocally, in the role played by the war in the shaping of modern science, its institutions and its role in the public sphere. The Great War was not the first industrial war, but it was the first to involve all the major industrial nations of the world. And in 2014, we begin to commemorate the outbreak of a war that saw the collapse of three empires, the impoverishment of a fourth, a global redrawing of maps, boundaries and alliances, the rise of a new economic order which in many ways looked to the means and methods of science and technology for what remained of Enlightenment ideals and Utilitarian visions of progress and plenty. Looking forward is to look back, to see the lines of debate with the present just forming. Within four years, the world witnessed unprecedented loss of life and dislocation, but also unprecedented feats of innovation, many of which drew upon and extended pre-war knowledge, but many of which foreshadowed shifts in attitudes towards nationalism and nation-building that were to make an indelible mark on the rest of the twentieth century.

'If we are ever to realize a truly European history of the Great War, we need to go beyond the national boundaries which have dominated historical writing on the subject.' Thus, Jay Winter and Jean-Louis Robert invite us to view wartime London, Paris and Berlin, setting out categories that structure our understanding of stabilities and change.[1] Their call for comparative history is no less relevant to the history of science. To understand how European nations, with competing aims and differing traditions, came to deal with

1 Jay Winter and Jean-Louis Robert (eds.), *Capital Cities at War: Paris, London, Berlin, 1914–1919* (Cambridge University Press, 2007), vol. II, p. 468.

shortages, contrive weapons and produce solutions, requires us to take a comparative view of science, technology and education, and to take a deeper look into the policies that shaped them.

Over the years, literary sources have evoked the war the soldiers fought with coherence, dignity and pathos. But memories of the parts played by science and scientists remain fragmented, fleeting images of hasty improvisation, bombed cities and gassed soldiers. Popular culture representations of the war often mislead – and schoolboy tags, such as the 'chemist's war' – often mask more than they reveal about the complex interaction of materiality and manufacturing, academic disciplines and government departments, laboratories and lecture halls and the dramatic uses and abuses to which the earth's physical environment were made subject. The war, historians have shown, demonstrated both the persistence of tradition and the pressures of modernity. When in January 1917, Emil Fischer – Germany's leading pre-war Nobel prizewinner and chemical *Kulturträger* wrote that 'modern war . . . draws its means from the progress of the sciences', he was saying nothing that military and political leaders on both sides had failed to grasp.[2]

Remarkably, few historians have tried to deal with the implications of scientific mobilisation for our understanding of the conflict and its consequences. As long ago as 1978, the American historian Daniel Kevles observed that 'there is no general history of science in the war', and this remains largely true today. Many secondary accounts of science and technology in the Great War continue to rely on untested generalisations. For example, it has been said that the Allied scientific war was 'reactive', not proactive – responding to new technologies (such as poison gas and submarine warfare) as and when the Germans introduced them. However, the complexity of the Allied 'response' often masks significant differences in the ways in which innovation took place in British, French, German and American industry. Until recently, such fine detail has been locked away in archives, unavailable to scholars. Much of the relevant information produced during the First World War was still 'secret' in the Second; and some of it – in France, for example, and in the former East Germany – is only now being cleared.

While Britain and France honour Rutherford and Marie Curie, in Germany, the list of biographies of wartime scientists is much thinner. Here, too, we may well ask why. As Gerald Feldman observed, although there are many studies

2 Emil Fischer Papers, Bancroft Library, University of California at Berkeley, Emil Fischer to Margarete Oppenheim, 14 December 1917, quoted in Jeffrey Johnson, *The Kaiser's Chemists* (Chapel Hill, NC: University of North Carolina, 1990), pp. 168, 196.

of the German professoriate, surprisingly little attention has been paid to the natural scientists among them. In part, he argues, this seems to have been justified by the assumption that natural scientists are normally 'less articulate about political questions', and therefore perhaps less interesting to historians. Also, he points out, there has been (until recently at least) a 'not entirely unjustified tendency to lump *Naturwissenschaftler* and *Geisteswissenschaftler* together as members of the *Bildungsbürgertum*, in Fritz Ringer's phrase, 'mandarin intellectuals', thus destroying a useful distinction between them.[3] To some extent they did reflect a common class identity, but it is proving of interest to distinguish between and among scholars and scientists in their methods, international connections and disciplinary allegiances. Records of learned societies and universities previously locked away by Archives Acts and Cold War customs are for the first time permitting comparisons by country and by discipline. The result is a shift towards understanding how the experience of the war contributed to the conceptual and institutional development of new disciplines; and how relatively new fields, such as psychology and psychiatry, gained a presence in academic and social space.[4]

Not for the first time in history, of course, would a country's success or failure in the use of natural knowledge lead to new ways of thinking, let alone military victory or defeat. But perhaps for the first time, the Great War created opportunities for the systematic application of a new 'vocabulary of warfare', a new set of professional specialities, a new emphasis on the role of women and minorities, as well as a new politics of science. Max Weber's principle of *Wertfreiheit*, or value-neutrality – and the professional ideals that suffused his memorable *Wissenschaft als Beruf* – delivered as a lecture in 1917 and published in 1919 – would be challenged by the development of closer relations between academia, government, industry and the military. Finally, as we look into the contradictions of precept and practice, once fashionable debates about the origins and conduct of the war dissolve into a more encompassing vision of 'The Great War, 1914–45', in which 'Quatorze-dix-huit' forms but the first instalment in a struggle that would envelop the world again only twenty years later.

3 Gerald Feldman, 'A German scientist between illusion and reality: Emil Fisher, 1909–1919', in Immanuel Geiss and Bernd Jürgen Wendt (eds.), *Deutschland in der Weltpolitik des 19. und 20. Jahrhunderts* (Düsseldorf: Bertelsmann Universitätsverlag, 1973), pp. 341–62.

4 Joanna Bourke, 'Psychology at war, 1914–1945', in Geoffrey C. Bunn *et al.* (eds.), *Psychology in Britain: Historical Essays and Personal Reflections* (Leicester: British Psychological Society, 2001), pp. 133–49.

Not all of these portents were evident in August 1914. Indeed, the war masks yet another step in what David Stevenson calls the 'great acceleration' of the armaments race of the early twentieth century.[5] To grasp how and when these developments took place, it is necessary to understand the war not just as a single semester 'course unit', transmissible in the classroom, but as an evolving struggle whose outcomes were as unexpected as its losses were unfathomable. Into this cauldron leapt the most impressive scientific technologies the world had as yet seen. Over four years, minds and methods were mobilised, *scientifiques* became *savants de guerre*, *Naturwissenschaftler* became *Kriegswissenschaftler*, and British, imperial and American academics became 'scientific soldiers'.[6] Within the British Empire, strong academic and scientific links were formed, and between Britain and France came a marriage of convenience that lasted for decades. Between Britain and America, a 'special relationship' was born, across fields ranging from naval signals and intelligence, to medical and agricultural research, ballistics, aviation and chemical warfare. Among the Allies, the universities became arsenals for research manpower. While in Germany and Austria-Hungary, the universities and the state struggled to develop a collaborative relationship.[7] Both sides saw a rationalisation of the means of warfare through the systematic cooperation of the sciences needed to carry it on.[8]

With such issues in mind, it is useful to borrow Robin Higham's concept of 'military intellectuals' to crystallise a category of scholars and scientists that came to prominence on both sides.[9] The phrase 'scientific intellectuals' was coined by David Edgerton to refer to those in the interwar period who 'spoke and wrote on the social relations of science' – scientists who, in his view, used

5 David Stevenson, *Armaments and the Coming of War: Europe 1904–1914* (Oxford: Clarendon Press, 1996).

6 Bernhard vom Brocke, 'Internationale wissenschaftsbeziehungen und die anfänge einer deutschen auswärtigen kulturpolitik: der professorenaustausch mit Nordamerika', in Bernhard vom Brocke (ed.), *Wissenschaftsgeschichte und Wissenschaftspolitik im Industriezeitalter: Das 'System Althoff' in historischer Perspektive* (Hildesheim: Lax, 1991), pp. 185–242; Bernhard vom Brocke, 'Wissenschaft und militarismus', in William M. Calder III *et al.* (eds.), *Willamowitz nach 50 Jahren* (Darmstadt: Wissenschaftliche Buchgesellschaft, 1985), pp. 649–719.

7 Werner K. Blessing, 'Universität im krieg: erlanger schlüsseljahre im 19. und 20. jahrhundert', in Karl Strobel (ed.), *Die deutsche Universität im 20. Jahrhundert: die Entwicklung einer Institution zwischen Tradition, Autonomie, historischen und sozialen Rahmenbedingungen* (Vierow: SH-Verlag, 1994); Karl Brandi, 'Die Universität im Kriege', in Albrecht Saathoff (ed.), *Göttinger Kriegsgedenkbuch, 1914–1918* (Göttingen: Vandenhoeck & Ruprecht, 1935), pp. 145–52.

8 Feldman, 'German scientist', p. 355.

9 Robin Higham, *The Military Intellectuals in Britain, 1918–1939* (New Brunswick, NJ: Rutgers University Press, 1966), pp. 3–51, 237–48.

their standing as internationalists, universalists and moralists to distance science from war – and to distance war from science.[10] We might broaden the category to include many who saw their duty to their nation as transcending their commitment to 'neutrality' in a process that saw the sciences growing closer than ever to being a political instrument of the nation-state.[11]

In reconstructing the 'scientific war', we can in Britain see three phases. The first – between late 1914 and early 1915 – was dominated by makeshift responses to shortages of key raw materials, and in France to the loss of industrial capacity as its northern regions were occupied.[12] Fears were compounded by Allied outrage at the complicity of German scientists in Germany's advance through Belgium, coupled with anger at what appeared to be Germany's rejection of the conventions of scientific internationalism.[13] A second phase opened in the spring of 1915, with the mobilisation (or what Herbert Mehrtens has called the 'self-mobilisation') of scientists on both sides, early reluctance from the military giving way to government interest in science as an instrument of war. With 1916 came a second mobilisation and on both sides a comprehensive commitment to total war, which in many new ways involved the applications of science. With 1917 came a third phase, in which the United States and US science began to play a major role in what had become a 'war within a war' – a contest among scientists for global leadership in the post-war world.[14] The Armistice was accompanied by Allied attempts to neutralise German science, ironically while letting stand a German industrial base that had almost completely survived the war. The post-war years

10 David Edgerton, 'British scientific intellectuals and the relations of science, technology and war', in Paul Forman and José M. Sanchez-Ron (eds.), *National Military Establishments and the Advancement of Science: Studies in Twentieth Century History* (Dordrecht: Kluwer, 1996), pp. 1–35.

11 See the challenging and pioneering works by Brigitte Schroeder-Gudehus which, after thirty years, surely deserve an English translation: Brigitte Schroeder-Gudehus, *Deutsche Wissenschaft und Internationale Zusammenarbeit, 1914–1928: Ein Beitrag zum Studium kultureller Beziehungen in politischen Krisenzeiten* (Carouge: Imprimerie Dumaret and Golay, 1966) and *Les Scientifiques et la Paix: La Communauté Scientifique Internationale au Cours des Années 20* (Montreal: Les Presses de l'Université de Montréal, 1978). See also Elisabeth Crawford *et al.* (eds), *Denationalizing Science: The Contexts of International Scientific Practice* (Dordrecht: Kluwer Academic Publishers, 1993).

12 Roy MacLeod and Kay MacLeod, 'War and economic development: government and the optical industry in Britain, 1914–18', in Jay Winter (ed.), *War and Economic Development: Essays in Honour of David Joslin* (Cambridge University Press, 1975), pp. 165–204.

13 Roy MacLeod, 'Der wissenschaftliche internationalismus in der krise: die akademien der Alliierten und ihr reaktion auf des Ersten Weltkrieg', in Wolfram Fischer *et al.* (eds.), *Die Preussische Akademie der Wissenschaften zu Berlin, 1914–45* (Berlin: Akademie der Wissenschaften, 2000), pp. 317–49.

14 Robert M. Yerkes (ed.), *The New World of Science* (New York: Century Company, 1920).

saw the creation of an International Research Council and discipline-based International Scientific Union, which for years excluded Germany, and which led inevitably to the replacement of German as a universal scientific language.

Scientific internationalism and national science

First, with the outbreak of fighting, came anger. Thousands of young men on both sides, many fired by patriotism, volunteered when they were not conscripted.[15] Many were science students and graduates, the product of Edwardian Britain's rapidly expanding civic universities, the Facultés des Sciences established by the Third Republic in France and the rapid expansion of universities in Germany.[16] Britain's leading 'scientific intellectuals' were at first reluctant to declare war. Indeed, on 1 August 1914, Sir J. J. Thomson, Director of the Cavendish Laboratory at Cambridge, and Nobel Prize-winner in Physics (1906), sent a collective letter to *The Times*, urging the British Government to resist the impending conflict with Germany. 'We regard Germany as a nation leading the way in the Arts and Sciences', he said, 'with a nation so near akin to our own, and with whom we have so much in common . . . war [would be] . . . a sin against civilization'.[17] Thomson spoke for many Englishmen, including Sir William Ramsay, the Nobel Prize-winning Professor of Chemistry at University College, who had studied in Germany, and who included German chemists among his friends.

A tipping point was reached on 4 October 1914, when ninety-three German scholars – including Germany's leading physicist, Max Planck – signed an 'Appeal to the Civilized World' (*An die Kulturwelt! Ein Aufruf!*). Apparently originating in the Reich Navy Office,[18] the manifesto denied German

15 Anon, 'The waste of brains: young scientists in the fighting line', *The Times*, 24 December 1915, p. 3.

16 Michael Sanderson (ed.), *Universities in the Nineteenth Century* (London: Routledge, 1975). For recent work on 'neutrality' and internationalism, see Rebecka Letervall, Geert Somsen and Sven Widmalm (eds.), *Neutrality in Twentieth-Century Europe: Intersections of Science, Culture, and Politics after the First World War* (London: Routledge, 2012).

17 J.J. Thomson *et al.*, 'Scholars protest against war with Germany', *The Times*, 1 August 1914, p. 6. A careful exposition of the Allied response is Harry Paul, *The Sorcerer's Apprentice: The French Scientist's Image of German Science, 1840–1919* (Gainesville, FL: University of Florida, 1972).

18 Charles McClelland, 'The University of Berlin at its apogée, 1860–1918', in Heinz-Elmar Tenorth (ed.), *Geschichte der Universität unter den Linden, 1810–2010: Biographie einer Institution, Praxis ihrer Disziplinen*, 6 vols. (Berlin: Akademie-Verlag, 2010–12), vol. 1, p. 173.

responsibility for the war, for the invasion of neutral Belgium, and for brutalities against the Belgian population and pledged German scholarship to the Kaiser and the Fatherland. The document was immediately translated into ten languages and distributed across the world.[19] German science and scholarship were deemed to have surrendered the ideals of *Gemeinde* to the aims of *Kriegsgewinnler*. The great majority of signatories were men of letters and lawyers, theologians and philosophers, but twenty-two natural scientists and medical men were among them. Despite protests that some had never seen the document, or had been pressured into signing it, the result, in the words of one German historian, was 'fatal' to the credibility of German academics abroad.[20]

In Britain, already reeling from stories of atrocities in Belgium and the burning of the Louvain University Library, it was taken as a declaration of war. It was, Weber believed, a mistake, certainly in conflict with the spirit of science, and not in Germany's interest. Planck later defended his signature as a matter of military and political necessity. Whether 'necessity' or not, the 'appeal' transcended propaganda. For the last time, Germany had united its enemies. In late October 1914, a letter to *The Times* signed by 120 British scholars set aside their 'real and deep admiration' for German scholarship and science. 'We have many ties with Germany, ties of comradeship, of respect, and of affection. [But] we grieve profoundly that, under the baleful influence of a military system and its lawless dreams of conquest, she whom we honoured now stands revealed as the common enemy of Europe and of all peoples [who] respect the Law of Nations.'[21] In November, Wilhelm Ostwald

19 Klaus Böhme, *Aufrufe und Reden deutscher Professoren im Ersten Weltkrieg* (Stuttgart: Reclam, 1975). For Max Planck, see John Heilbron, *The Dilemmas of an Upright Man: Max Planck as Spokesman for German Science* (Berkeley, CA: University of California Press, 1986). For the Allied reaction, see *The Times*, 21 October 1914, p. 10; Gabriel Petit and Maurice Leudet, *Les Allemands et la Science* (Paris: Felix Alcan, 1916). The manifesto is also cited in Rainald Von Gizycki, 'Centre and periphery in the international scientific community', *Minerva*, 11:4 (1973), pp. 474–94; and in Wolfgang Mommsen, 'German artists, writers and intellectuals and the meaning of war, 1914–1918', in John Horne (ed.), *State, Society and Mobilisation in Europe during the First World War* (Cambridge University Press, 1997), pp. 21–38. There is an English translation of the manifesto in Ralph H. Lutz, *The Fall of the German Empire, 1914–1918* (Palo Alto, CA: Stanford University Press, 1932), vol. 1, pp. 74–8.

20 Hubert Laikto, *Wissenschaft in Berlin von den Anfängen bis zum Neubegnin nach 1945* (Berlin: Dietz, 1987), p. 388.

21 *The Times*, 21 October 1914, p. 10. For a French reaction, see Petit and Leudet, *Les Allemands*. See also Paul Forman, 'Scientific internationalism and the Weimar physicists: the ideology and its manipulation in Germany after World War I', *Isis*, 64 (1973), 151–80, n. 158.

made matters worse by claiming that 'Germany . . . has attained a stage of civilisation far higher than that of all other peoples.' English and French science 'had attained only the degree of cultural development which we ourselves left behind 50 years ago'. 'You ask me what it is that Germany wants. Well, Germany wants to organize Europe.'[22] To the editor of *Nature*, this was not solely an issue of politics; war with Germany now meant war with German science.[23]

The 'Manifesto of the 93' was debated, and later repudiated by some of its signatories (including Max Planck). While it did not explicitly refute the principles of scientific universalism, it was widely taken as contradicting the internationalism of science. Sir William Ramsay, a long-time advocate of German methods, ever ready to use the stick of German superiority to chastise his British colleagues, led the press attack. 'German ideals', he wrote to *Nature* on 8 October 1914, 'are infinitely far removed from the conception of the true man of science; and the methods by which they propose to secure what they regard as the good of humanity are, to all right-thinking men, repugnant'. 'Indeed, it is a common saying that science is international. But we are beginning to revise our verdict', said Ramsay, speaking for his countrymen. The war began with dismay, continued in desperation, and ended with determination to see an end to Germany's hegemony in the scientific world.

Dismay was inevitable for a generation that had, in the previous half-century, witnessed an unprecedented degree of international scientific cooperation. From national congresses held in Germany and Britain in the 1830s, to which foreigners were welcomed, to discipline-based conferences in the 1850s and 1860s, international and trans-European projects flourished in medicine and public health, biology, geography and geology, telegraphy and postal communication. Beneath the surface, however, lay national interests which helped frame competition in the regulation of commerce, trade and navigation, as well as driving the pace of discovery in the fast-moving disciplines of physics, chemistry and medicine. The vision of peace culminating in the establishment of the Nobel Prizes in 1901 was a celebration of internationalism among competing nations. The century that gave conviction to scientific universalism, in respect to the idea that the laws of nature are indifferent to

22 Quoted in Lawrence Badash, 'British and American views of the German menace in World War I', *Notes and Records of the Royal Society of London*, 34 (1979), pp. 91–121.

23 Roy MacLeod, 'The social framework of *nature* in its first fifty years', *Nature*, 224:5218, (1969), pp. 441–6.

national boundaries, also gave fresh impetus to national allegiances, to which scientists were almost universally bound.[24]

Ramsay and Ostwald, who the year before had sat next to each other in Brussels at the International Association of Chemical Societies – founded as a professional gesture of international solidarity as recently as 1911 – were now officially enemies. As were physicists Walther Nernst and Ernest Rutherford, who shared front row seats at the Solvay Physics Conference in Brussels in September 1913. Years of constructive German commitment to academic exchanges were now dismissed as nationalist *Weltpolitik*.[25] Across the Atlantic, Michael Pupin of Columbia University wrote to George Ellery Hale at the California Institute of Technology, 'Science is the highest expression of a civilization', concluding that German science was now wedded to the interests of the German state. 'Allied science is . . . radically different from Teutonic science'. And so it seemed, when Philip Lenard, Professor of Physics at Heidelberg, dismissed the Royal Society of London, which had given him a prize, as the 'supreme academy for all hypocrisy in the world, located on the Thames'. Worse would come, as casualty lists lengthened and hatreds multiplied. The literary propaganda war acquired a ferocity few scientists could match.[26] Ramsay agreed. 'Not merely must the dangerous and insufferable despotism which has eaten like a cancer into the morals of the German nation be annihilated', he wrote in December, 'but all possibility of its resuscitation must be made hopeless. [Germany], in the words of one of its distinguished representatives, must be "bled white"'.[27] 'However the world pretends to divide itself', said Rudyard Kipling, who was soon to lose a son at Loos, there were 'now only two divisions in the world today – human beings and Germans'.[28] Scientific internationalism was neither the first nor the last casualty of the 'war for civilisation'.

A month passed as the opposing armies fought each other to a standstill in France. The war was not going to be over quickly. And it would be a war of artillery. Already, the German army had approached the chemical industry with requests for munitions. By the end of 1914, lines of trenches along the Western Front stretched from Switzerland to the sea. War was no longer to be

24 See Pierre Duhem, *La Science Allemande* (Paris: Hermann & Fils, 1915); with a new introduction by Stanley L. Jaki, *German Science: Some Reflections on German Science and German Virtues* (Chicago: Open Court, 1991).

25 Vom Brocke, 'Internationale wissenschaftsbeziehungen'.

26 Rudyard Kipling, 'Speech at Southgate', *Morning Post*, 22 June 1915, p. 9.

27 Sir William Ramsay, 'Germany's aims and ambitions', *Nature*, 94 (1914), 139.

28 Kipling, 'Speech at Southgate'.

left to the generals. The Royal Society of London, following the Académie des Sciences in Paris, established War Committees in different fields, creating new divisions of labour. A war of position that brought chemistry to the front was soon followed closely by developments in physics, meteorology, oceanography and aeronautics that brought science to the war on the sea and in the air.

1915: the 'makeshift war'

By early 1915, what journalists were calling the 'reasoning war', the British Prime Minister, David Lloyd George, called a 'war of engineers', and soon many academic disciplines were claiming the war as 'theirs'.[29] There were a few attempts to avert a complete breakdown in international scientific relations, but generally those who tried – including Bertrand Russell in Cambridge and G. F. Nicholai in Berlin – suffered ostracism or imprisonment for their conscience. In any case, scientists were far less hesitant in expressing their anger with each other, than their dislike of war. Following Germany's first tactical use of chemical weapons in April 1915, the Belgian and French Academies expelled their German foreign members. The Berlin Academy declined by a narrow margin to retaliate. The Chemical Society of London expelled four, including Nernst and Ostwald, whose doctoral students included A. A. Noyes, who was later to lead American nitrate research, and F. G. Donnan, later Professor of Chemistry at Cambridge. The Royal Society of London, whose Foreign Secretary, Sir Arthur Schuster, was of German birth, narrowly avoided expelling seventeen of its foreign members who came from the Central Powers, but the question was left on the table and was to haunt the scientific community long after the Armistice.[30]

In February 1915, Germany's declaration of unrestricted submarine warfare – with the loss of 115 Allied merchant ships,[31] obliged the British government to enlist the services of Britain's best physicists – the 'chemists in Cockspur Street',

29 See, e.g., June Barrow-Green, 'Cambridge mathematicians' response to the First World War', in David Aubin and Catherine Goldstein (eds.), *The War of Guns and Mathematics: Mathematical Practices and Communities in Allied Countries around World War I* (Washington, DC: American Mathematical Society Press, 2013), pp. 101–66; and William Van der Kloot, 'Mirrors and smoke: AV Hill, his brigands and the science of anti-aircraft gunnery in World War I', *Notes and Records of the Royal Society*, 5:4 (2011), pp. 393–410.

30 Donald S. L. Cardwell, 'Science and World War I', *Proceedings of the Royal Society of London*, A 342 (1975), pp. 447–56; MacLeod, 'Der wissenschaftliche internationalismus', pp. 317–49.

31 Roger Chickering, *Imperial Germany and the Great War, 1914–1918* (Cambridge University Press, 1998), p. 89.

as Lord Curzon endearingly, if misleadingly, referred to Sir Ernest Rutherford, Sir William Bragg and their colleagues at the Admiralty's newly established Board of Invention and Research.[32] Arthur Balfour at the Foreign Office and Winston Churchill (first at the Admiralty and later at the Ministry of Munitions) pioneered closer relations between science and the services.

The 'shell crisis' on the Western Front in the spring of 1915 gave an enormous boost to British scientists trying to persuade the government of their value to the nation. The establishment of a Ministry of Munitions that followed the precedent of French experience also gave momentum to the construction and contracting of British factories for explosives and propellants. The enormous cordite and TNT factory built by the Ministry of Munitions on an immense greenfield site on the English/Scottish border at Gretna – said at the time to be the largest in the world – instantly became 'a byword in war production' when it opened in record time in August 1916.

By mid 1915, Britain's new Ministry of Munitions was regularly appointing Fellows of the Royal Society as advisers, notably to its Munitions Inventions Department.[33] The Allies faced a formidable challenge. In numbers of leading men of science, both sides were about evenly matched in most disciplines, with the singular exception of applied chemistry, where German industrial chemists exceeded those in Britain and France combined. The German chemical industry employed some 1,200 chemists, as many as France and Britain together.[34] Britain was famously dependent upon German imports, as was France. However, as French industry was forced by German invasion to move south, so it began to avail itself of the science faculties of the provincial universities.

In Germany, scientists seem to have 'self-mobilised' at a slower pace. A confident government with a strong army and a prudent industry did not wish or foresee a long war. Fritz Haber began his research on chemical weapons – intended initially to overcome the stalemate of trench warfare – before (and with initial opposition from) the Germany army.[35] While the *Kriegsministerium*

32 Roy MacLeod and Kay Andrews, 'Scientific advice in the war at sea, 1915–17: the Board of Invention and Research', *Journal of Contemporary History*, 6 (1971), pp. 3–40.

33 George Dewar, *The Great Munition Feat, 1914–1918* (London: Constable and Co. Ltd, 1921); Ralph J. Q. Adams, *Arms and the Wizard* (London: Cassell & Co., 1978). See also Roy MacLeod and Jeffrey Johnson (eds.), *Frontline and Factory: Perspectives on the Chemical Industry at War, 1914–1924* (Dordrecht: Springer, Archimedes Series, 2006).

34 Lutz Haber, *The Chemical Industry, 1900–1930* (Oxford: Clarendon Press, 1971).

35 Daniel Charles, *Between Genius and Genocide: The Tragedy of Fritz Haber, Father of Chemical Warfare* (London: Jonathan Cape, 2005); Dietrich Stoltzenberg, *Fritz Haber – Chemist, Nobel Laureate, German, Jew* (Philadelphia, PA: Chemical Heritage Foundation, 2004); see also the standard account by his son Lutz Haber, *The Poisonous Cloud* (Oxford: Clarendon Press, 2002).

established a *Kriegsrohstoff-Abteilung* as early as August 1914, and its Raw Materials Department under Walther Rathenau set about putting Germany on a war footing, the government did not itself begin to foster scientific research until early 1915.

In contrast, by mid 1915, the major institutions of French science were almost totally mobilised, and a small army of academic chemists, physicists and mathematicians were in war work.[36] Gas defence quickly became a speciality of the Paris police, while the École Centrale and the École Supérieure de Physique et de Chimie Industrielles de la Ville de Paris insisted that the army recall its students from the trenches to be trained as explosives works managers. In Germany, where, in this domain, Prussian military tradition inhibited the rapid acceptance of new techniques, academic scientists were slower to gain acceptance. The sudden appearance of chemical weapons on the front in April 1915, following months of secret trials, was an exception. But by the summer of 1915, Germany and the rest of the world saw that chemistry had become a weapon. Gas warfare was steadily refined, from chlorine delivered by clouds and cylinders, to phosgene and mustard gas delivered by shell, with the advice of Berlin-based Kaiser Wilhelm Institutes led by Walther Nernst and Fritz Haber.[37] Both sides had to import sulphur and pyrites. The application of the Haber-Bosch process to the synthesis of ammonia for explosives transformed Germany's prospects of continuing the war.

In the trenches, strategic decisions seldom turned on scientific considerations of topography, let alone logistics; and tactical decisions often seemed to those on the ground as blind to considerations of meteorology and geology. But certain science-based technologies – especially in naval weaponry, geological surveying and trench warfare – fared better.[38] Pre-war German aerodynamics research surfaced in the development of fixed-wing aircraft and in

36 See Elizabeth Fordham, 'The University of Paris during the First World War: some paradoxes'; compare with Thomas Weber, 'British universities in the First World War', in Trude Maurer (ed.), *Kollegen – Kommilitonen – Kämpfer: Europäische Universitäten im Ersten Weltkrieg* (Stuttgart: Steiner, 2006), pp. 91–106, 75–90.

37 *50 Jahre Kaiser-Wilhelm-Gesellschaft und Max- Plank-Gesellschaft zur Förderung der Wissenschaftern, 1911–1961* (Göttingen: Generalverwaltung d. Max-Planck-Gesellschaft z. Förderung d. Wissenschaften e.V., 1961), p. 89; Lothar Burchardt, 'Die Kaiser-Wilhelm-Gesellschaft im Ersten Weltkrieg, 1914–1918', in Rudolf Vierhaus und Bernhard vom Brocke (eds.), *Forschung im Spannungsfeld von Politik und Gesellschaft: Geschichte und Struktur der Kaiser-Wilhelm/Max-Planck-Gesellschaft. Aus Anlass ihres 75-jährigen Bestehens* (Stuttgart: Deutsche Verlags-Anstalt, 1990), pp. 163–96; Jeffrey Johnson, *The Kaiser's Chemists* (Chapel Hill, NC: University of North Carolina Press, 1990).

38 See Guy Hartcup, *The War of Invention: Scientific Developments, 1914–1918* (London: Brasseys Defence Publishers, 1988).

Zeppelin raids on English towns from January 1915. Lessons learned about alloys from 'reverse engineering' work on downed aircraft were not lost on British science.[39] By early 1916, applications of physics and mathematics were making their appearance in new systems of weapons testing, gun control, anti-aircraft prediction, submarine detection and artillery sound ranging. The British army appointed geologists, who studied German military texts on the construction of trenches and use of terrain, which the French refined and perfected.[40] The disease of war in the Mediterranean and the Middle East created new opportunities for British and imperial medical microbiologists and parasitologists from India, Ceylon, Egypt and Australia.[41]

The 'acetone' story, in which laboratory 'biotechnologies' were brought into play to replace traditional forestry and wood distillation, showed the ways in which research, with Admiralty support, solved a key problem in the production of cordite propellant, and launched the career of Chaim Weizmann.[42] French and British scientists established shared lines of communication and research, especially in aviation and chemical munitions, and created common procurement procedures with US banks, industries and government agencies. By 1917, the Allies were sending their hard-won experience of innovation in factory construction, railway and telephone communications, munitions manufacture, military geology, artillery ranging and submarine detection to what a later generation would call the 'arsenal of democracy'. Germany, superior in many sciences at the outset, was hard pressed to keep its best men at work on projects that were likely to have war-winning potential.[43]

By 1916, in France, Russia and Italy, in Britain and her Dominions, and increasingly in the United States as well, the prestige of science had begun to

39 Detief Busse, *Engagement oder Rückzug? Göttingen Naturwissenschaften im Ersten Weltkrieg* (Göttingen: University-Verlag Göttingen, 2008).

40 The discipline of military geology dates from Walter Kranz, 'Militargeologie', *Kriegstech Zeitschrift*, 16 (1913), pp. 464–71, as extended in his *Die Geologie in Ingenieur-baufach* (Stuttgart: F. Enke, 1927). British work is discussed in William B. R. King, 'Geological work on the Western Front', *Geographical Journal*, 54 (1919), pp. 201–21; and King, 'Influence of geology on military operations in Northwest Europe', *Advancement of Science*, 8 (1951), 131–7. US work is discussed by US academics in uniform, Alfred H. Brooks, 'The use of geology on the Western Front', US Geology Survey Professional Paper 128-D (Washington, DC: US Geological Survey, 1920), pp. 85–124; and Whitman Cross, 'Geology in the world war', *Bulletin of the Geological Society of America*, 30 (1919), pp. 165–88.

41 Roy MacLeod (ed.), *The Commonwealth of Science: ANZAAS and the Scientific Enterprise in Australasia, 1888–1988* (Melbourne: Oxford University Press, 1988).

42 Robert Bud, *Uses of Life: A History of Biotechnology* (Cambridge University Press, 1993).

43 Vom Brocke, 'Wissenschaft und Militarismus'.

overcome the 'neglect' that it still experienced in public education and public support. Wartime recognition helped win a case that peacetime rhetoric had failed to establish. As the *Cambridge Magazine* commented:

> The word 'science' [is] on everyone's lips and does yeoman's service in almost every newspaper ... Its very name seems to have suddenly discovered a talismanic power which is somewhat perplexing to those who find their paths menaced by the glare of limelight.[44]

Of all countries in the war, the United States had perhaps most to gain and least to lose from an active participation in the scientific war. Not least for this reason, the Americans saw the expulsion of foreign fellows from academies as a futile gesture, and against the long-term interests of science.[45] Still, as the scientific community was divided into what the American physicist Robert Millikan called 'hostile political camps', the choice was not lost upon Americans and others not yet in the war. Writing to Arthur Schuster in February 1915, George Ellery Hale of the California Institute of Technology, and Foreign Secretary of the US National Academy of Sciences, agreed that German scientists had 'been hypnotized into supporting the murderous policy of their government'.[46] But it was not just a 'question of geography', in the words of the US astronomer W. W. Campbell, 'it is a question of fundamental differences in civilization'.[47]

The fact that many US scientists had studied in Germany, espoused Humboldtian ideals of teaching and research, and even knew German was no guarantee of loyalty to the German professoriate, although experience endorsed their respect for German technology and industry. In early 1916 – fully a year before the United States declared war – Johns Hopkins and Harvard sent scientific and medical missions to England and France to save time before the time had come.[48] Long before US troops began to arrive in the spring and summer of 1917, Ernest Rutherford and his French colleagues were sending details of French and British submarine detection devices – developed at Harwich and Toulon – to US navy scientists at America's submarine base at New London, Connecticut. US scientists were soon arriving in larger numbers, to work with their British and French counterparts in a wide range of

44 Anon, *Cambridge Magazine*, 6, 4 November 1916, p. 76.
45 MacLeod, 'Der wissenschaftliche internationalismus', pp. 317–49.
46 California Institute of Technology Archives, Hale Papers, G. E. Hale to Arthur Schuster, 13 February 1915.
47 Ramsay, 'Germany's aims and ambitions', p. 138.
48 Joseph Ames, 'Science at the front', *The Atlantic Monthly*, 121 (1918), pp. 90–100.

fields, from acoustics to armour and aircraft.[49] By the summer of 1917, members of America's new National Research Council attended meetings in Washington, DC, dressed in military uniform. The US army's Signals Corps had shown signs of becoming a forward-looking scientific service, introducing telephone and wireless communications (and interception) to the craft of command and control. Scientific naval intelligence, famously mediated by Room 40 at the Admiralty, became a staple of wartime legend. With US naval headquarters in the heart of London's West End, the US presence showed signs of becoming permanent. Anglo-American experience in intelligence gathering and assessment was to presage the 'special relationship' of years to come.

1916: the 'pivotal year'

The year 1916 was, in Roger Chickering's phrase, a 'pivotal year'.[50] The land battles of the Somme and Verdun were the most costly ever fought. Germany's military leadership, which had begun to see the value of science in chemical weapons, sound ranging and aviation, looked for convincing means to knock France out of the war. The means was the use of artillery bombardments so intense that, as General Falkenhayn put it, 'not even a mouse could survive'.[51] That, and the Battle of the Somme, which cost both sides over 1 million casualties, were tributes to the new realities, based on the contest of 'materiel' – a *Materialschlacht*. On the Somme, the Allies subjected German trenches to over 1.5 million British shells – mostly high explosive – around the clock for a week. These shells were the product of eighteen months of design and construction at over a dozen new chemical explosive and propellant factories, a tribute to the coordination of a patchwork of public and private firms. As in Britain, the French had recourse to private enterprise in order to achieve munitions output on the required scale. By the end of 1916, both countries were equalling, and in some cases exceeding, German output in chemical explosives and chemical weapons.

To meet this challenge, the German response took the form of the famous Hindenburg Programme, driven by the general who, with Erich Ludendorff, replaced Erich von Falkenhayn in August 1916. During the next three months, Hindenburg called for the total mobilisation of the German economy, to

49 Lawrence Badash, 'British and American views of the German menace in World War I', *Notes and Records of the Royal Society of London*, 34 (1979), pp. 91–121.

50 Chickering, *Imperial Germany*, p. 65.

51 Chickering, *Imperial Germany*, p. 67.

double munitions output and triple the production of artillery. This would require 3 million additional factory workers – all devoted to winning an industrial war based on principles of applied science. Economic mobilisation brought a new agency, the *Kriegsamt* (Supreme War Council), with powers to conscript workers and supervise production. This involved the withdrawal of thousands of soldiers for factory service and the near reorganisation of agriculture and commerce. By August 1917, the programme had failed.[52] Failure was attributed to shortages in manpower and natural resources, industrial resistance and labour friction. But this also revealed the sheer limits of Germany's capacity to mobilise and innovate. With the production of *ersatz* materials Germany's sciences proved highly resilient, but academic scientists had little encouragement to take on war work, which many increasingly resented. In Britain, by contrast, a 'neglect of science' movement united public and press in calling for increased state support of higher education. The establishment of a Department of Scientific and Industrial Research (DSIR),[53] with the intention of putting higher education and industry into a working partnership, was the result – providing a model soon exported to Australia, New Zealand and Canada. By 1917, Germany was in sight of losing the scientific war.

1917: stalemate

Even so, these intimations of mortality were masked by possibly Germany's greatest scientific success, viz., the application of the Haber-Bosch process to capture atmospheric nitrogen for the production of nitrates, which promised to supply both 'guns and butter', and probably enabled Germany to continue fighting for two more years. Nevertheless, by 1917, German agricultural production was suffering, while thanks to convoy techniques and anti-submarine devices, Britain's food imports continued and grew. Thanks to these, Britain could begin to produce more of her own explosives. By the end of 1917, munitions factories were producing 230,000 tons of explosives a year, slightly in excess of the peak of 220,000 tons that would be achieved by Britain in 1943.[54] The sheer supply of explosives gave the Allies far greater scope for action. In June 1917, British and Australian geologists and engineers launched a

52 Feldman, 'German scientist'.

53 Roy MacLeod and E. Kay Andrews, 'The Committee of Civil Research: scientific advice for economic development, 1925–1930', *Minerva*, 7:4 (1969), pp. 423–40.

54 William Hornby, 'Factories and plant', in Sir Keith Hancock (ed.), *History of the Second World War*, UK Civil Series (London: HMSO, 1958), p. 109.

massive mining attack at Messines, the sound of which was heard in London, 220 kilometres away.[55] This gigantic project, kept secret for months, undermined and destroyed 17 kilometres of German lines; in the words of a contemporary, it was 'the most spectacular action of the war'.[56] Geology was visibly in the front lines.

On this, as on many other occasions, scientific successes, left unexploited, failed to bring military victory; indeed in and of themselves, scientific advances could not do so. But with the end of the mining war, with applications of science reflecting progressive degrees of Allied cooperation, there came a farsighted interest in asking what might happen after the war. Among the Allies, a 'second mobilisation' took place in 1917, reflecting a growing belief that traditional military operations alone could not determine the outcome. The alternative was '*la guerre intégrale*', total war, in which every group in society not already mobilised would be brought into play. In France and England, the Académie des Sciences and the Royal Society did their part in pushing a campaign to create an Allied 'scientific alliance'. Both Britain and France strengthened their delegations to the United States, to US procurement agencies, and to cooperative work in submarine and anti-submarine detection, military aviation, natural resources and nitrate production.

America's entry into the war brought closer cooperation with the US Academy of Sciences, and soon with its newly formed 'war committee', the National Research Council, which focused enthusiasm among US scientists for the Allied cause. Leading US universities began to plan courses in 'military geology' for the next academic year. In September 1917, William Campbell, director of the Lick Observatory, recalling the imperialising pronouncements of Ostwald two years earlier, announced his conclusion that German scientists were no better than enemy soldiers: 'Germany, the most scientific of nations, has prostituted science to the base ambition of "Deutschland über Alles".'[57] In October 1917, Russell Chittenden of Yale agreed; writing to Hale, he said, 'at first I could not believe that the reports coming to me were true, but it is now perfectly clear that the men of science . . . have lost what I should call their scientific common sense'.[58]

55 Roy MacLeod, '"*Kriegsgeologen* and practical men": military geology and modern memory 1914–1918', *British Journal of the History of Science*, 28 (1995), pp. 427–50.

56 See George A. Kiersch, 'Engineering geosciences and military operations', *Engineering Geology*, 49 (1998), p. 124.

57 William Wallace Campbell, 'International cooperation in science', 15 September 1917, Halle Papers.

58 California Institute of Technology, Hale Papers, Russell Chittenden to George Hale, 3 October 1917.

With a rejection of German scientific leadership came an argument that German science was not what it was made out to be, and that even the German language had lost its moral authority to be the language of science. The practical response was more explicit. By late 1917, hundreds of American chemists had been recruited to a Chemical Warfare Service and America's chemical industry had laid plans to take on massive explosives and chemical weapon production.[59] US science was fully 'over there'.

1918

The new DSIR, which began work in July 1916, began to build bridges between the universities and industry,[60] while the Medical Research Council began joint projects with academics.[61] By 1918, Britain had become a gigantic military-academic-industrial complex, co-opting and managing much of the nation's scientific workforce.[62] By 1918, at least half of Britain's scientists who remained in civilian life were doing war work. Imperial College London, as Hannah Gay has reminded us, 'did not see the war so much in terms of service, duty, sacrifice or glory, but rather as something that was perhaps unnecessary, and that was being conducted inefficiently and irrationally. If more attention were paid to science, the country would be better off.'[63] It was a lesson Winston Churchill never forgot.[64]

The Kaiser Wilhelm Institutes turned their attention to many war projects, but Germany's main scientific war efforts remained based in industry. A

59 MacLeod and Johnson, *Frontline and Factory*.

60 Roy MacLeod and Kay Andrews, 'The origins of the DSIR: reflections on ideas and men, 1915–16', *Public Administration*, 48:1 (1970), pp. 23–48.

61 For the medical history of the war, see Ian Whitehead, *Doctors in the Great War* (London: Leo Cooper, 1999); Mark Harrison, 'The medicalization of war – the militarization of medicine', *Social History of Medicine*, 9 (1996), pp. 267–76; Roger Cooter *et al.* (eds.), *Medicine and Modern Warfare* (Amsterdam: Rodopi, 1998) and *War, Medicine and Modernity* (Stroud: Sutton, 1999); Wolfgang Eckart and Christophe Gradmann (eds.), *Die Medizin und der Erste Weltkrieg* (Pfaffenweiler: Centaurs-Verlag, 1996).

62 Everett Mendelsohn, 'Science, technology and the military', in Jean-Jacques Salomon (ed.), *Science, War and Peace* (Paris: Economica, 1989), p. 54.

63 The Imperial College student magazine *Phoenix* conveyed this ambivalence. For example, 'Our country first – and then back to the college' was a rallying cry in the March 1915 issue. In the same issue there was a copy of Rupert Brooke's sonnet, 'If I should die . . .' together with other war poetry. See Hannah Gay, *Imperial College London, 1907–2007: Higher Education in Science and Technology in Twentieth-Century Britain* (London: Imperial College, 2007).

64 Stephen W. Roskill, *Hankey, Man of Secrets* (London: Collins, 1970), vol. 1, pp. 244–5.

generation of top-flight advisers served Bayer and BASF.[65] But there was no comparable effort to encourage university scientists to 'self-enlist' like their British and French counterparts.[66] Germany's scientists, it is suggested, had generally remained in their libraries and laboratories protesting against expenditure cuts,[67] while French, British and US scientists dropped their research to fight a war that required less theory than application. The French Government easily called upon the laboratories of the École Normale, the Institut Pasteur, the Institut Curie and the École Supérieure de Physique et de Chimie Industrielles de la Ville de Paris – their proximity to the weapons testing grounds at St Cloud and Vincennes bringing special advantages.[68] By early 1915, science graduates were being withdrawn from the front to run the explosives factories of the Service des Poudres and civilian factories relocated to Brittany and the Rhône.[69] Provincial Faculties of Science drew into a productive circle, with colleagues from Bordeaux, Lyon and Toulouse. Private industry – including Schneider in Le Creusot, with their own scientific staffs – responded so well that, by the beginning of 1918, France was meeting its shell quotas, and in some munitions, outpacing Germany. By the Armistice, Paris – like Berlin and London – was a city of science at war.[70]

In early 1917, the German Government established a Kaiser Wilhelm Stiftung für Kriegstechnische Wissenschaft (KWKW), which openly credited the British with having in the DSIR a better designed system of military-scientific industrial cooperation. Although it had the support of leading scientists, including Emil Fischer, Walther Nernst and Fritz Haber, by the time it came into operation, it was too late.[71] Flushed with the success of the German offensive of March 1918, Fritz Haber congratulated his colleagues on their success:

> The relationship between the army and the exact sciences: before the war, it was incomplete. The general lived in the penthouse, so to speak, and greeted the scholar who lived in the same house, but a deeper connection did not

65 Jeffrey Johnson and Roy MacLeod, 'War work and scientific self-image', in Rüdiger vom Bruch and Brigitte Kaderas (eds.), *Wissenschaften und Wissenschaftspolitik – Bestandsaufnahmen zu Formationen, Brüchen und Kontinuitäten im Deutschland des 20. Jahrhunderts* (Berlin: Akademie Verlag, 2002), pp. 169–79.

66 MacLeod and Johnson, *Frontline and Factory*. 67 Busse, *Engagement oder Rückzug?*

68 The Americans were quick to note and praise the French example. See George Burgess, 'Applications of science to warfare in France', *Scientific Monthly*, 5:19 (1917), pp. 289–97.

69 Patrice Bret, 'Managing chemical expertise: the laboratories of the French artillery and the *Service des Poudres*', in MacLeod and Johnson, *Frontline and Factory*, pp. 203–20.

70 See Winter and Robert, *Capital Cities at War*.

71 Manfred Rasch, 'Science and the military: the Kaiser Wilhelm Foundation for Military-Technical Science,' in MacLeod and Johnson, *Frontline and Factory*, pp. 179–203.

> exist. The industrialist in the house served him as mediator, a relationship conditioned by the clear subordination of techniques to tactics before the war. Today things are different.[72]

But 'things' would be 'different' in unexpected ways. The devastation wrought by the Allied counter-attack saw science moving swiftly during the coming months, working towards the anticipated Allied spring campaign of 1919. Then, it was said, Churchill, Minister of Munitions, had contemplated sending fleets of bombers and gas weapons against German cities, to force an unconditional surrender. The sudden end of fighting in November 1918 caught scientists, like many others, by surprise. Some echoed the sentiments of George Ellery Hale, that the war had been 'the greatest chance we ever had to advance research', and were disappointed that the end had come before US science could demonstrate its full potential. Only an Armistice, it seemed, could stay the hand of science.[73]

Looking ahead

The war produced many changes in science and its relationship to society. First, Allied scientists were anxious to preserve the sense of superiority that military and economic victory had given them.[74] Would it not be ironic, as G. A. Miller asked in August 1918, if 'the Allies would win the war in a military sense only to find ourselves dominated by German knowledge and German science?' In Britain and the United States, the war had 'democratised' the professional scientist, and encouraged the notion that the disciplines of natural and social science in fact comprised a 'community', with shared values, methods and ethos. As Hyman Levy, the British physicist, put it, 'the war fostered . . . a new sense of solidarity . . . it was the occasion for the birth of the scientific profession'.[75] Especially in North America, Britain and Australia, the war coincided with the rise of the 'scientific worker' – from psychologists who applied theories about IQ testing to officer selection, to chemists who saw an opportunity for professional advancement.[76] The war accelerated what

72 Fritz Haber, 'To the Bunsen Society for Applied Physical Chemistry, April 1918', *Chemiker-Zeitung*, 42 (1918), p. 197.

73 Burgess, 'Applications of science', pp. 289–97 and 'The scientific work which our government is carrying on and its influence upon the nation', *The Scientific Monthly*, 19 (1924), pp. 113–15.

74 George A. Miller, 'Scientific activity and the war', *Science*, 48 (1918), pp. 117–18.

75 Hyman Levy, *Modern Science* (London: Hamish Hamilton, 1939), p. 95.

76 Robert M. Yerkes, 'The role of psychology in the war', in Yerkes (ed.), *Science in the Great War* (New York: Century Company, 1920).

Durkheim called the 'accommodation' of newer groups previously outside the settled order of the professions, and gave them 'social space'. A new 'class interest' emerged among wartime scientists, and associations were created to advance their 'pay and prospects'.[77] A. P. Rowe, then a young scientist at the National Physical Laboratory in London, who later featured in Britain's radar war, put it squarely: 'I can now have all the money I want, within reason.'[78] It proved to be so again for his generation in 1939 to 1945.

At the same time, the war gave new depth and meaning to the relationship between science and the military.[79] There had been much misunderstanding, and the relationship remained incomplete. Scientists were given problems to solve, rather than being asked to suggest what the problems were. But this was a problem that foreshadowed fuller engagement.[80] As the war contributed to their popularity and self-esteem, few Allied scientists feared a loss of independence. Francis Bacon once wrote: 'It is a strange desire to seek power and to lose liberty.' But that danger, if real, was not yet felt. The war had demonstrated that, while battles might not be won by science, without science, they might be lost.[81]

A war that brought European governments, industries and academia into a closer relationship was one which Americans keenly observed. US science seized the day, and brought a new energy to the Allied effort. The US army took to Europe some of America's leading chemists and physicists, including Karl Compton, later president of MIT, and Augustus Trowbridge, Professor of Physics at Princeton and later head of the Rockefeller Foundation's programme in Europe. Trowbridge and Compton, Rutherford and Bragg were among the first to make scientific cooperation a feature of the Anglo-American relationship.[82] When victory came, it was heralded as a victory for Allied science. Nationalism had undermined the prestige of the German professor.[83]

77 Kay Andrews and Roy MacLeod, 'The contradictions of professionalism: scientists, trade unionism and the First World War', *Social Studies of Science*, 9 (1979), pp. 1–32.

78 Albert P. Rowe, *If the Gown Fits* (Melbourne University Press, 1969).

79 David Edgerton, 'Science and war', in Robert Olby *et al.* (eds.), *The Companion to the History of Modern Science* (London: Routledge, 1990), p. 941.

80 MacLeod and Andrews, 'Origins of the DSIR'.

81 See Guy Hartcup, *The War of Invention* (London: Brasseys Defence Publishers, 1988).

82 On Conant, see: James B. Hershberg, *Conant: Harvard to Hiroshima and the Making of the Nuclear Age* (New York: Knopf, 1993); and James Conant, *Modern Science and Modern Man* (New York: Doubleday Anchor Books, 1955). See also Roy MacLeod, 'Secrets among friends: the Research Information Service and the "special relationship" in Allied scientific information and intelligence, 1916–18', *Minerva*, 37:3 (1999), pp. 201–33; Cooter *et al.*, *War, Medicine and Modernity*.

83 Fritz Ringer, *The Decline of the German Mandarins* (Cambridge, MA: Harvard University Press, 1969).

The victors paid tribute to the virtues of internationalism, but without prejudice to the role that Allied scientists were certain to play the next time Europe went to war.[84] As Basil Liddell Hart wrote in 1924:

> In seeking to estimate the nature of the next great war, the course of our thought must inevitably reflect the progress of scientific invention. This development, whether for good or ill, is the supreme factor in modern civilization and is affecting the organization and mentality of national communities in such measure that it is only reasonable to suppose that the methods of war will reflect the ever-changing face of civil life.[85]

If war offered science such opportunities, had it a future as an objective, Weberian value-free agent of benefit to humanity? On this, the scientific community was far from unanimous. In Britain, J. B. S. Haldane saw merit in the use of chemical weapons, on the grounds that they did less harm than high explosives.[86] Leading scientists were caught between conscience and obligation.[87] Few criticised the wartime applications of science-based knowledge – more often, it was a question of which side, or which group on either side, had solved a given problem first, or better.[88] The moral argument was turned on its head, in the interests of efficiency. This was the subtext of Haldane's *Daedalus*, the 'cunning craftsman'. Daedalus made wings both for himself and his son Icarus. Icarus flew too near the sun, and so fell to his death, but Daedalus lived to fight another day.

Fritz Haber remained committed to the uses of science in war, whatever the political consequences. Few scientists followed Russell or Einstein in becoming pacifists. However, there were passive conscripts. Max Born, who studied with J. J. Thomson in Cambridge before the war, recalls being stationed with a detachment of physicists, outside Berlin, whose task was to improve sound-ranging techniques; they did what they were asked to do,

84 James Conant, *My Several Lives: Memoirs of a Social Inventor* (New York: Harper and Row, 1970).

85 Basil H. Liddell-Hart, 'The next Great War', *Journal of the Royal Engineers* (March 1924), p. 90.

86 John B. S. Haldane, *Daedalus, or Science and the Future: A Paper Read to the Heretics, Cambridge, on February 4th, 1923* (London: Kegan Paul, 1923).

87 John Heilbron, *The Dilemmas of an Upright Man: Max Planck as Spokesman for German Science* (Berkeley, CA: University of California, 1986).

88 Kay Andrews and Roy MacLeod, 'The social relations of science and technology, 1914–1939', in Carlo Cipolla (ed.), *The Fontana Economic History of Europe: The Twentieth Century*, vol. v, *The Twentieth Century* (Glasgow: Fontana/Collins, 1976), Pt I, pp. 301–35.

he says, but actually preferred to do 'some real science when time allowed'.[89] The result was Born's first book, on the dynamics of crystal lattices, and research that later led to his Nobel Prize.

On the other hand, wartime experience made 'normal' a range of activities that might have earlier been regarded as interruptions seldom asked. In November 1916, Winston Churchill had impatiently chided his Cabinet colleagues: 'A hiatus exists between inventors who know what they could invent, if they only knew what was wanted, and the soldiers who know, or ought to know, what they want, and would ask for it if they only knew how much science could do for them.'[90] By 1918, the 'reasoning war' was not confined to what Sir Douglas Haig called the 'mechanical contrivances' of the battlefield.[91] On both sides, new knowledge came from the miseries of trench warfare, and from managing the most complex lines of production, supply and distribution the world had ever seen.[92] Germany began the war with a science base that was in many ways superior to that of France and Britain. Germany failed to develop its potential until the war was well underway, and then, if Max Weber is correct, misunderstood its function and mismanaged its resources. By contrast, the Americans and British gave their scientists rank, authority and access to High Command. The war encouraged their use of interdisciplinary, problem-solving approaches, and models of coordination and cooperation. Victory favoured those who, whatever their specialisation, were best at joining in the solution of common problems.[93]

The war was never merely a 'chemists' war'.[94] In Europe and the United States, civilian applications emerged in a range of disciplines, from orthopaedics to meteorology, aviation to photography, wireless to industrial psychology. Geologists found new sources of oil and water, physicists designed

89 Max Born, *My Life: Recollections of a Nobel Laureate* (London: Taylor & Francis, 1978); Nancy Greenspan, *The End of the Certain World: The Life and Science of Max Born* (New York: Basic Books, 2005).

90 Winston Churchill, 'The greater application of mechanical power to the prosecution of an offensive on land', November 1916, Cabinet Office, Appendix, 'Mechanical power in the offensive', in Churchill, *The World Crisis* (London: Thornton Butterworth, 1927), vol. III, App. V, para. 15.

91 Field Marshal Sir Douglas Haig, 'Final despatch', *London Gazette*, 8 April 1919, pp. 4,693–712.

92 Roy MacLeod, 'The "arsenal" in the Strand: Australian chemists and the British Munitions Effort, 1916–19', *Annals of Science*, 46:1 (1989), pp. 45–67; 'The chemists go to war: the mobilization of civilian chemists and the British war effort, 1914–1918', *Annals of Science*, 50 (1993), pp. 455–81; and 'Sight and sound on the Western Front: surveyors, scientists and the "battlefield laboratory", 1915–1918', *War and Society*, 18:1 (2000), pp. 23–46.

93 Johnson and MacLeod, 'War work'.

94 Anon, 'Science and the munitions of war', *Nature*, 95 (1915), pp. 562–4.

acoustic devices, geographers drew artillery maps, biologists developed disinfectants and psychologists treated shell shock. The war marked a permanent shift away from a view of war as a distraction from civilian science. A warfare state had emerged as both client and customer. For Lewis Mumford, the war marked the consummation of the 'neo-technic age'.[95]

War service had also given scientists a new profile. In Germany, its institutions reeling from defeat and economic crisis, the professions struggled to regain their prestige and purpose; but among the Allies, victory seemed to endorse everything the scientists had promised. When called upon, they had produced 'winning weapons'. They had become national heroes. Thus, Frederick Lindemann, later Lord Cherwell, won the admiration of Churchill.[96] Science had a new prominence in political life, which scientific establishments were quick to exploit.[97] In Britain, thanks to the war, the natural sciences were given a greater role in secondary and higher education.[98] In the United States, if 'Better Living through Chemistry' was a phrase waiting to be coined, the chemical profession was quick to market it. Between 1920 and 1932, twice as many students studied science in the United States as between 1860 and 1920.[99] Reporting to the US National Academy of Sciences on its wartime work, Robert Yerkes, the Yale psychologist and zoologist, proudly entitled his book, *The New World of Science* (1920), a brave new world whose vernacular language would be English.[100]

At Versailles, Woodrow Wilson reflected on the circumstances before him:

> We must take, so far as we can, a picture of the world into our minds. Is it not a startling circumstance for one thing that the great discoveries of science, that the quiet study of men in laboratories, that the thoughtful developments

95 Lewis Mumford, *Technics and Civilization* (New York: Harcourt-Brace, 1934).

96 Adrian Fort, *Prof: The Life of Frederick Lindemann* (London: Jonathan Cape, 2004), p. 62.

97 MacLeod and MacLeod, 'Social relations'.

98 See Anon, 'The neglect of science', *The Times*, 7 March 1916, pp. 28–33; Ray Lankester, *The Neglect of Science*, pamphlet (London: 1916). Following intense public debate, the British Government convened several enquiries into the scientific health of the nation. These culminated in to a committee chaired by Sir J. J. Thomson, whose recommendations concerning the promotion of science in secondary schools were widely accepted. See 'Committee on the Neglect of Science', *Chemical News*, 30 November 1917, pp. 267–91; and the *Report of the Committee to Enquire into the Position of Natural Science in the Educational System of Great Britain*, 19 February 1918, *Parliamentary Papers* [CD 9011], pp. 471–556. Their implications for the universities are explored in Zuoyue Wang, 'The First World War, academic sciences and the "two cultures": educational reforms at the University of Cambridge', *Minerva*, 32:2 (1995), pp. 107–27.

99 MacLeod and MacLeod, 'Contradictions of professionalism'.

100 Sir Douglas Haig, 'Final despatch'.

> which have taken place in quiet lecture rooms, have now been turned to the destruction of civilization? . . . the enemy whom we have just overcome had at its seats of learning some of the principal centres of scientific study and discovery, and used them in order to make destruction sudden and complete; and only the watchful, continuous cooperation of men can see to it that science, as well as armed men, is kept within the harness of civilization.[101]

When Fritz Haber was awarded the Nobel Prize in 1918 – for his pre-war work on atmospheric nitrogen – the act suggested to some a return to an idealised discourse about pure science. But a deeper reading of sources behind the Nobel Committee shows that this award was more about power than principle – about the changing roles of nation-states.[102] In 1927, Julian Benda deplored the fact that, in preferring nation to reason, many intellectuals, scientists among them, had contributed to the violence of conflict. Bertrand Russell saw warfare implicit in the nature – and nurture – of science itself – contrary imaginations that required a new politics. The mandarins of German science, epitomised by Max Planck, were adroit in defending their role as *Kulturträger*, and avoiding the labels of defeat. But if they had not lost the war for Germany, the war had been at the cost of German science. Max Weber feared a cataclysmic *Krise der Wissenschaft* – a crisis in cultural assumptions, professional confidence and epistemological certainty. The best hope lay in a future calling of '*Weltfreiheit*' or value-neutrality[103] – a concept that concerned the young Karl Popper in Vienna.[104] Many looked for new ways of re-expressing the values of science – from the scientific humanism of George Sarton, to the idealism of Arthur Eddington, and the science-as-socialism of J. D. Bernal.[105] By the 1930s, it could be asked whether scientists had a special social responsibility to match their new prestige and power. But by the

101 Woodrow Wilson, *Addressing the Second Plenary Session of the Peace Conference, January 1919, in US State Department, Papers relating to the Foreign Relations of the United States: The Peace Conference* (Washington, DC: Government Printing Office, 1942–7), vol. III, p. 179.

102 Frederick G. Cottrell, 'Les relations scientifiques internationales', *Review Scientifique* (Paris), 59:1 (1921), pp. 37–41.

103 See Max Weber, 'Wissenschaft als beruf', translated as 'Science as a vocation', in Bernard Barber and Walter Hirsch (eds.), *The Sociology of Science* (New York: The Free Press of Glencoe, 1962).

104 Karl Popper, *Unended Quest: An Intellectual Autobiography* (London: Fontana, 1976).

105 For Sarton, see Lewis Pyenson, *The Passion of George Sarton: A Modern Marriage and Its Discipline* (Philadelphia, PA: American Philosophical Society, 2007). For Eddington, see Matthew Stanley, 'Mysticism and Marxism: A. S. Eddington, Chapman Cohen, and political engagement through science popularization', *Minerva*, 46:2 (2004), pp. 181–94. For Bernal, see Andrew Brown, *J. D. Bernal: The Sage of Science* (Oxford University Press, 2005); and Roy MacLeod, 'The world, the flesh and the devil: a vision revisited', Bernal Lecture, Birkbeck College London, June 2008.

outbreak of the Great War again in 1939, few doubted that science would play a decisive role, not only in winning the conflict, but in asserting the values of science as the values of democracy.[106] By 1945, science had acquired an ideology and a politics of its own.[107] Today, this message underlies the history of science and scientists in the Great War. If we are to read it correctly, we must revisit those four years when scientists across the world chose to serve the political order they had helped to create.

106 See David Hollinger, 'The defense of democracy and Robert K. Merton's formulation of the scientific ethos', *Knowledge and Society*, 4 (1983), pp. 1–15 and 'Science as a weapon in *kulturkampfe* in the United States during and after World War Two', *Isis*, 82 (1995), pp. 400–54, reprinted in Ronald L. Numbers and Charles E. Rosenberg (eds.), *The Scientific Enterprise in America: Readings from Isis* (University of Chicago Press, 1996).

107 The contradictions are well summarised in Jerome Ravetz, *Scientific Knowledge and its Social Problems* (Oxford: Clarendon Press, 1971) (reprinted with new Introduction, London: Transaction Press, 1996) and *The Merger of Knowledge with Power: Essays in Critical Science* (London: Mansell, 1990).

18

Blockade and economic warfare

ALAN KRAMER

Introduction

As is well known, a large part of the German population suffered severe hunger during the First World War, with disastrous consequences for morale and health. In March 1915, bread had to be rationed, and long queues formed outside bakeries. The cost of feeding a family went up, according to one estimate, by 50 per cent from June 1914 to June 1915.[1] By this time, as General Groener recalled, it was impossible to ignore the 'growing threats to the food supply of the population and the army'.[2] Many food items were no longer affordable for working-class families. The social-democratic daily newspaper in Hamburg remarked on 3 August: 'It is the naked, sad truth today that countless families of the men who spill their blood for the fatherland have not been able to buy a piece of meat for weeks on end, nor eggs or butter.'[3]

Even potatoes, which Germany grew in vast quantities, were rationed and limited in 1916 to four pounds per person per week.[4] By winter that year all the main foods were rationed.[5] Women in the cities, who were in the front line of the food shortages, began to stage spontaneous hunger demonstrations in October 1915.[6] The police in Berlin noted several downward shifts in morale as

1 Volker Ullrich, *Kriegsalltag. Hamburg im ersten Weltkrieg* (Cologne: Prometh Verlag, 1982), p. 40.
2 Wilhelm Groener, *Lebenserinnerungen. Jugend, Generalstab, Weltkrieg* (Göttingen: Vandenhoeck & Ruprecht, 1957), p. 332.
3 *Hamburger Echo*, 3 August 1915, cited in Ullrich, *Kriegsalltag*, p. 39.
4 Ullrich, *Kriegsalltag*, pp. 40–3.
5 Avner Offer, *The First World War: An Agrarian Interpretation* (Oxford: Clarendon Press, 1991), p. 28.
6 Belinda J. Davis, *Home Fires Burning: Food, Politics, and Everyday Life in World War I Berlin* (Chapel Hill, NC: University of North Carolina Press, 2000). The best treatment of the themes of everyday life, food supply, hunger, and the social and political repercussions in urban Germany is the exemplary study by Roger Chickering, *The Great War and Urban Life in Germany. Freiburg, 1914–1918* (Cambridge University Press, 2007).

prices rose and staple foods became scarce in the course of 1915.[7] In early 1916, women gathered in towns in the Ruhr to demand improved distribution of potatoes and fats; the following spring there were widespread riots, with hungry women and children looting shops and markets.[8] Groener noted in his diary in February 1916 that the War Minister, 'in a very pessimistic mood over the food crisis, reported to General Headquarters that we will have to give up soon'.[9]

The hunger was at its worst in the winter of 1916/17 – the 'turnip winter', when the unusually wet autumn ruined the potato crop; swede turnips (or rutabaga) became the substitute, neither nutritious nor palatable. Rations fell that winter on average below 1,150 calories, well below minimum requirements.[10] By the end of the war, hundreds of thousands of civilians had died from diseases related to hunger and malnutrition. German accounts after the war estimated 700,000 or even 800,000 deaths; Jay Winter, whose demographic history of the war is the standard work, estimates that it was more like '478,500 excess civilian war-related deaths in Germany'.[11] Many of the victims succumbed to diseases which were already present in the population, but posed a greater risk in wartime, such as tuberculosis, from which 160,000 more people died from 1914 to 1919 than would be expected in peacetime.[12] Some 180,000 died from the influenza epidemic in 1918. Infant mortality, by contrast, fell markedly.[13] This chapter does not attempt to recalculate the figure for total civilian mortality, but whichever estimate is used, it was clearly a very high number, just over or somewhat under 1 per cent of the 1913 population of 67 million.

The mass hunger has traditionally been attributed to what is widely called the British hunger blockade. The blockade raises a number of questions of historical methodology.

7 Report of the Berlin chief of police, 18 September 1915, in Wolfdieter Bihl (ed.), *Deutsche Quellen zur Geschichte des Ersten Weltkrieges* (Darmstadt: Wissenschaftliche Buchgesellschaft, 1991), doc. 69, p. 146. Cf. *ibid.*, police reports from Charlottenburg (later a suburb of Berlin) in February and March, and Berlin in *ibid.*, docs. 44 and 49.

8 Anna Roerkohl, *Hungerblockade und Heimatfront. Die kommunale Lebensmittelversorgung in Westfalen während des Ersten Weltkrieges* (Stuttgart: Steiner, 1991), pp. 127–31.

9 Groener, *Lebenserinnerungen*, p. 332.

10 Roerkohl, *Hungerblockade*, p. 321. Chickering, *The Great War and Urban Life*, has an evocative description of the 'loathsome' turnip, pp. 269–71.

11 Gustavo Corni, 'Food supplies', in Gerhard Hirschfeld *et al.* (eds.), *Brill's Encyclopedia of the First World War* (Leiden and Boston: Brill, 2012); Roerkohl, *Hungerblockade*, p. 312; and Charles Paul Vincent, *The Politics of Hunger. The Allied Blockade of Germany, 1915–1919* (Athens, Ohio and London: Ohio University Press, 1985), p. 145, using German sources from immediately after the war, cite the figure 800,000, although the latter admits the figure may be too high; Jay Winter and Jean-Louis Robert, *Capital Cities at War. Paris, London, Berlin 1914–1919* (Cambridge University Press, 1997), vol. 1, p. 517, n. 34.

12 Roerkohl, *Hungerblockade*, p. 309.

13 Roerkohl, *Hungerblockade*, pp. 312–13.

First, we have to liberate our perspective from the narrow focus on the British blockade of Germany. It was not an exclusively British but an Allied policy, executed also by the French, Russian, and later the Italian and American fleets, directed also at Austria-Hungary, Turkey and Bulgaria. It was of great importance to the French Government: in Clemenceau's War Cabinet the Minister for the Blockade was one of its six members.[14] In fact, both sides attempted to blockade the other. Germany tried to cut off supplies reaching the Entente through naval warfare; submarine warfare was merely the most extreme and lethal variant of this strategy.

Secondly, blockades, whether imposed by surface or submarine fleets, were part of broader economic warfare, as had been employed in various forms in the Napoleonic Wars and the American Civil War. Economic warfare means all the measures designed to weaken the enemy's economy. It involved preventing imports of goods capable of being used in the war effort, above all munitions and raw materials used in munitions production, but it included food and ultimately everything likely to sustain the armed forces and the economy that provisioned them, thus targeting also the enemy civilian population. Economic warfare further entailed attacks on the enemy's financial system and his transport and communications infrastructure at home and abroad. That included denying access to the vital international credit system and the blocking or expropriation of enemy-owned assets.

Economic warfare is a part of strategy, and in the years before 1914 it was the British Government's main strategic approach to the impending threat of European war. The government rejected the idea of 'sending a continental-scale army' to France and preferred to apply economic pressure on Germany by naval blockade. In hindsight, British military intervention with its land army in August 1914 appears inevitable. That was not how contemporaries saw it. As late as 31 July, the commitment of the army on the continent was an open question. The navy was Britain's main armed force, the guarantor of its Empire and its globally oriented economy, and protector of its imports of cheap food and raw materials. Unlike Germany, Britain's status as a great power rested on its navy, not its army. Britain's small professional army, essentially a colonial police force, would require much time and money to transform it into a continental-scale army. It was Kitchener, when he became War Minister in August 1914, who persuaded the Cabinet to reverse its strategic thinking, and turn Britain into a 'nation in arms', to raise a mass

14 Clinton L. Rossiter, *Constitutional Dictatorship. Crisis Government in Modern Democracies* (Princeton University Press, 1948), pp. 110–11.

army to fight in France. By spring 1915, when the Liberal government collapsed, Lloyd George insisted that Britain had to adopt a policy of total war. That meant abandoning traditional British liberal *laissez-faire* economic policies in favour of the 'New Liberalism' of Lloyd George and Winston Churchill: state intervention.[15] This, too, had repercussions for the type of economic warfare to be waged. Blockade, therefore, was not only a long-term strategy to stifle the enemy's economy: it was also a feasible and necessary measure during the build-up of the mass army.

The Admiralty was aware of the central role of the international system of credit and globalised financial transactions, and Germany's vulnerability to disruption of the global credit system.[16] Such disruption would, and indeed did, occur at the outset of war without the intervention of the Royal Navy, and it threw the entire global economy into a crisis. In addition, as from 1905 the Naval Intelligence Department worked on plans for blockade and economic warfare, including the seizure of indirect shipments via neutral ports. This 'would doubtless inflict in the end considerable losses on Germany ... But the effect would take time to produce'.[17] Essentially this remained the view of those who favoured economic warfare, that it would be a slow-acting strategy.[18]

The Admiralty continued to discuss blockade strategy in the years before 1914, traditionally conceived as a close blockade of the enemy's ports and coastline. Recent innovations such as torpedoes, mines and submarines, and powerful new coastal artillery, however, presented great risks to even the best-armoured warships. A conference in the Admiralty on 9 December 1913 decided that a submarine blockade of German ports would be the best option, but when the war broke out the navy had too few suitable submarines. So the Admiralty settled on distant blockade, preventing ships bound for or from Germany from traversing the North Sea via the English Channel and between Scotland and Norway. In international law, this was technically not a 'blockade', because enemy ports were not blocked; in practice it was one. For many in the Royal Navy, blockade was a 'defensive means to an offensive end, to bring the German fleet to battle; it was not primarily an end in itself'. Opinion in the Admiralty on the potential of economic warfare to bring sufficient

15 David French, *British Economic and Strategic Planning 1905–1915* (London: Routledge, 1982), pp. 1–2.

16 Nicholas A. Lambert, *Planning Armageddon. British Economic Warfare and the First World War* (Cambridge, MA and London: Harvard University Press, 2012), p. 123.

17 Offer, *First World War*, p. 227, quoting from a memorandum of 1905.

18 Lambert, *Planning Armageddon*, p. 3, bravely puts forward the argument that the Admiralty had a 'plan for *fast*-acting economic pressure', but the evidence is not convincing.

pressure to bear on Germany was divided. Some thought a blockade would bring German industry to a halt and starve its people, but the decision-makers were sceptical; by 1909 the Admiralty had disbanded the Trade Division, 'the navy's "think-tank" on blockade'.[19] One group of experts, among them the young marines lieutenant Maurice Hankey and the Director of Naval Intelligence, Captain Charles Ottley, continued to argue that the German economy was vulnerable to blockade. In a 'protracted war', Ottley wrote in 1908, 'the mills of our sea-power (though they would grind the German industrial population slowly perhaps) would grind them "exceedingly small" – grass would sooner or later grow in the streets of Hamburg and wide-spread dearth and ruin would be inflicted'.[20] Others were less enthusiastic about what appeared to be a passive strategy, and favoured schemes for an aggressive naval strategy, such as amphibious operations to invade German territory.

The differences between the 'economic' and the 'battle' planners were more tactical than in principle. First Sea Lord Sir John (Jackie) Fisher himself embodied both perspectives, being in favour of economic warfare, but he also yearned for the offensive to destroy the German navy, and even declared an interest in various half-baked schemes such as an amphibious operation on the Baltic Sea coast of Pomerania to land an army to capture Berlin. Hankey, too, advocated amphibious operations.[21]

The army and the Foreign Office rejected the 'economist' doctrine. Acknowledging Germany's dependence on imports of food and essential materials, they assumed that a blockade would be ineffective, for Germany would continue to trade through neutral neighbours. This may explain why the Foreign Office argued for the Declaration of London (1909), which protected neutral shipping rights: it backed the army's continental strategy. In the end, after a campaign by the Conservative opposition, supported by navy personnel, the British Government refused to ratify the Declaration.[22]

This allowed the government freedom of action. Immediately the war began, it thus decided on a strategy of distant blockade. Given Britain's fundamentally global orientation, with its imports and exports crossing the world's oceans, the ultimate goal was to deny that global option to Germany both by locking its main battle fleet into its home ports, and by blocking its

19 Hew Strachan, *The First World War*, vol. 1, *To Arms* (Oxford University Press, 2001), pp. 393–400.

20 Sir C. L. Ottley to R. McKenna, 5 December 1908, quoted in Offer, *First World War*, p. 232.

21 Strachan, *To Arms*, pp. 402, 442, 255.

22 Offer, *First World War*, pp. 275–81, 288–93.

trade access to global markets.[23] This would require patience. Churchill, First Lord of the Admiralty, certainly had a long-term view. He wrote: '*We* sit still in the steady cold blooded game & can I think keep it up indefinitely. Doom has fallen upon Prussian military arrogance. Time & determination are all that is needed.'[24] Blockade policy essentially went through three phases: 'restricted blockade until March 11, 1915; unrestricted blockade after the British Order in Council of that date announced the intention of preventing goods of any kind from entering or leaving Germany; and unrestricted blockade with American collaboration after the United States entered the war'.[25]

Certainly, Allied economic warfare was effective so far as German commercial shipping was concerned. Within a week of the outbreak of war the German merchant fleet had been banished from the oceans. Of its 1,500 ships 245 had been captured, 1,059 were locked up in neutral ports and 221 were restricted to plying the Baltic.[26] Two features of these initial actions should be clarified. First, they were not measures of the blockade, but broader economic warfare. They went together with the swift action of the Royal Navy, the morning after the British ultimatum to Berlin expired, to cut Germany's telegraph cables with the rest of the world.[27] This made it far more difficult for German merchants and banks to communicate with overseas suppliers.

Secondly, Germany was not the only victim. The Austro-Hungarian fleet also ceased to trade. Germany and Austria together had about 2,500 ships with a transport capacity of 3.5 million tons, which were stuck in their own ports, interned, sequestered or sunk. Likewise, the Russian navy and merchant fleets, blockaded by the Central Powers, were confined to the Black Sea and the Baltic Sea, leaving open only the routes from the Arctic ports and Vladivostok and in transit via Sweden.[28] In turn, the Russian navy blockaded the Bosporus, and, despite the presence of two German warships, *Goeben* and

23 Strachan, *To Arms*, p. 442.

24 Churchill to Col. Seely, 20 September 1914, in Martin S. Gilbert, *Winston S. Churchill*, vol. III, *Companion*, Pt I, *Documents July 1914–April 1915* (London: Heinemann, 1972), p. 125.

25 David Stevenson, 'Introduction', in Kenneth Bourne and D. Cameron Watt (gen. eds.), *British Documents on Foreign Affairs: Reports and Papers from the Foreign Office Confidential Print*, Pt II – *From the First to the Second World War*, Series H – David Stevenson (ed.), *The First World War, 1914–1918*. vol. V, *Blockade and Economic Warfare, I: August 1914–July 1915* (N. pl.: University Publications of America, 1989), p. xvii.

26 Lambert, *Planning Armageddon*, p. 212.

27 Paul Kennedy, 'Imperial cable communications and strategy, 1870–1914', *English Historical Review*, 86 (1971), 752.

28 Lucien Petit, *Histoire des finances extérieures de la France pendant la Guerre (1914–1919)* (Paris: Payot, 1929), p. 37.

Breslau, it established superiority in the Black Sea that effectively cut off the supply of coal from Turkish ports to Constantinople.[29]

The blockade and the neutrals

Yet the effective loss of the Central Powers' merchant fleet did not automatically mean the end of their international trade: they could trade with neighbouring neutral states, and make use of neutral ships and merchants. British policy was therefore not only to blockade Germany, but also exercise some form of control over the seaborne trade of neutral states which might re-export cargoes to Germany. That affected the commercial rights of neutral states. The diplomatic archives are full of papers recording the neutral states' complaints about interference with their lucrative trade, and the British attempts to stop war supplies reaching Germany, while not antagonising the neutrals to the extent that they might join the enemy.[30]

The initial list of 'absolute contraband' of August 1914, i.e., forbidden cargoes, included arms, explosives, warships, aircraft and other items for use in war. 'Conditional contraband' included goods such as food and fuel, if they were destined for the armed forces. In the autumn of 1914, the British Government expressly did not intend to starve the German civil population.[31] The Netherlands government agreed not to export to Germany overseas food, hay, straw, leather, coal, fuel, oil, motor vehicles, medicines, ammunition and gunpowder, and sodium nitrate.[32] The lists were refined in the autumn of 1914, and an extensive list of 23 December 1914 included further ingredients of explosives.[33] At the insistence of the Foreign Office, the food blockade had been lifted since late autumn 1914, also in order not to antagonise the United States, which shipped greatly increased quantities of grain and other foodstuffs to neutral ports for re-export to Germany. Only after

29 Paul G. Halpern, 'The war at sea', in Hew Strachan (ed.), *The Oxford Illustrated History of the First World War* (Oxford University Press, 1998), pp. 113–14.

30 Archibald Colquhoun Bell, *A History of the Blockade of Germany and of the Countries Associated with her in the Great War Austria-Hungary, Bulgaria, and Turkey, 1914–1918* (London: HMSO, 1961). Bell describes in some detail the legal and diplomatic complexities of the first Order in Council of 20 August 1914, the pressure of public opinion and of the French government for a more stringent policy to stop the enemy's supplies, and conflicts with the United States over its exports of copper and cotton, pp. 40–50.

31 Bell, *A History of the Blockade*, pp. 16, 59, and App. II, p. 722; Lambert, *Planning Armageddon*, p. 226.

32 *British Documents*, vol. v, doc. 6, enclosure in doc. 5, the Netherlands Minister to Sir Edward Grey, 27 September 1914, p. 4.

33 *Ibid.*, doc. 16, 'List of articles to be treated as absolute contraband under the Royal Proclamations of October 18 and December 1914', pp. 12–13.

Germany had declared the seas around the British Isles to be a 'military area' (the first phase of unrestricted submarine warfare) in February 1915 did Britain announce its Order in Council of 11 March as an act of retaliation, to impose a ban on all goods of German origin or destination.[34] The French Government made a parallel announcement.

The British Government was soon aware that Germany was using the neutral states for the import of contraband. Thus US exports to Sweden showed a sudden, enormous expansion in the war, at the same time as US trade with Germany dropped. US trade returns showed that exports increased from 1.1 million dollars in January 1914 to 9.9 million dollars in the same month in 1915, and from 700,000 dollars in February 1914 to 13.7 million dollars in February 1915; US exports to Germany decreased from 34.4 million in January 1914 to 6.4 million dollars in January 1915, and from 24 million to 4.9 million dollars between February 1914 and February 1915. Imports of maize into Sweden in early 1915 had increased 900 per cent over the corresponding months in 1914.[35] While the Foreign Office was afraid of affronting Sweden in case it endangered the Russian transit trade or even joined the war as an enemy, Admiralty staff were deeply frustrated at the failure to prosecute the blockade effectively. The head of the Admiralty trade division, Captain Webb, protested in a note to the First Lord in June 1915: 'Sweden is the principal offender, and the chief source of supply for Germany at present, and goods are flowing through her ports in enormous quantities.'[36]

In view of the great increase in the export of copper (essential in munitions production) from the United States, Britain put pressure on the neutrals to agree not to export it to Germany and Austria; copper was placed on the list of absolute contraband (along with aircraft, barbed wire, explosives, iron ore, rubber, etc.) on lists of 23 December 1914 and 11 March 1915.[37] Despite complaints from some US exporters, agreements were reached between the United Kingdom and the United States, including direct agreements, such as that with the rubber manufacturers not to export any rubber or tyres from the United States, except to the British Empire, France and Russia.[38]

34 Lambert, *Planning Armageddon*, pp. 366–9.

35 *British Documents*, vol. v, doc. 123, Memorandum to Swedish Minister, 10 May 1915, pp. 152–5. On Sweden, see Lambert, *Planning Armageddon*, pp. 392–408.

36 Lambert, *Planning Armageddon*, p. 407.

37 *British Documents*, vol. v, doc. 36, Royal Proclamations of December 23, 1914 and March 11, 1915, pp. 42–4.

38 *Ibid.*, doc. 57, Rubber Agreement, 29 March 1915, p. 65.

It proved to be easier to block the supply of physical goods and reach agreements on import levels than to prevent British banks from providing credit to German companies. This was still an issue in May 1915 (and possibly even in 1916), indicating the difficulty of making the transition from free trade liberalism to interventionist economic warfare. The government was reluctant to interfere with London's powerful financial sector.[39]

The French Government was even more worried than the British about supplies reaching Germany via the neutrals. They demanded a declaration that 'all articles that could possibly be used for munitions – cotton included – would be treated as contraband'.[40] Partly through blockade evasion and stocks in the Netherlands, Germany was evidently still able to import a great deal of nitrates in early 1915; Britain had to admit that 17,261 tons out of the total of 79,241 tons of manures, guano and nitrates imported by Germany from the Netherlands from January to March 1915 had come from Britain; it was only 1,649 tons in the corresponding period in 1914.[41] At an Allied conference in Paris in June 1915 to discuss the neutral states' evasion of contraband agreements, the French expressed their anger at the level of British exports to continental Europe that were allegedly reaching Germany; to the chagrin of the British, they possessed good statistical evidence to corroborate their accusations. The French proposed limiting neutral imports to their pre-war levels, a solution that Lloyd George had proposed in 1912.[42] Agreements were thereafter reached above all with the Netherlands, Denmark and Sweden, in which Britain allowed them to import similar quantities of essential items as before the war.

In the course of 1915, Allied economic warfare began to become more effective in stifling German direct imports and exports. Germany's exports to the United States declined from 238 million francs in April to June 1914 to 40 million francs in the same period in 1915 – a spectacular reduction of 83 per cent, far higher than the 42 per cent reduction in the first quarter of 1915.[43] Until the change in policy in

39 *Ibid.*, doc. 131, Report by Cornhill Committee, 14 May 1915, pp. 189–92; Lambert, *Planning Armageddon*, pp. 355–61. Owing to the destruction of records, Lambert is unable to quantify the extent, but he claims it was 'substantial and even critical'. This indicates the need for research in German sources.

40 Bell, *A History of the Blockade*, p. 45.

41 *British Documents*, vol. v, doc. 153, papers communicated by Restriction of Enemy's Supplies Committee, 27 May 1915, pp. 217–21.

42 Lambert, *Planning Armageddon*, pp. 428–9; Offer, *First World War*, p. 306 (on Lloyd George).

43 *British Documents*, vol. vi, *Blockade and Economic Warfare, II: July 1915–January 1916* (N. pl.: University Publications of America, 1989), docs. 94 and 95, Lord Bertie (Paris) to Sir Edward Grey, 24 September 1915, and enclosure, memorandum from French customs on German exports, pp. 120–2.

March 1915, the British did not attempt to stop German exports via neutrals, because this was not provided for without a formal close blockade. Thereafter, the Royal Navy was empowered to stop all goods going to or coming from Germany; in legal terms, the Foreign Office conceded: 'Although the word blockade was not used in the Order [in Council], the state of affairs produced by it is in effect a blockade.'[44]

However, US exports to the neutrals were still alarmingly high from the Allied perspective: there were significant increases in US exports of important commodities to Denmark, Norway, Sweden and Holland. The decrease in exports from New York to Germany, from 90.7 million from August 1913 to September 1914 to 5.8 million dollars in the same period in 1914/15 (almost 85 million dollars), was almost exactly matched by the increase in exports to Denmark, Norway and Sweden from 20 million to 104 million dollars.[45] By mid 1915, the British Government was forced to realise that the blockade policy was not working properly; Germany was obtaining significant imports via the neutrals. The Board of Trade even doubted whether the German economy faced any serious shortages;[46] that, however, was based on ignorance of the real situation. Nevertheless, US exports of cotton, essential for the manufacture of explosives, directly to Germany and indirectly via neutral ports, had increased to 5.9 million bales in the period January to July 1915 from 3.7 million bales in the corresponding period in 1914. Against the objections of Foreign Secretary Sir Edward Grey, who feared friction with Washington, the Cabinet decided on 14 July to declare cotton contraband.[47]

Another headache for the Allies was the redirection of trade patterns by the neutrals adjacent to Germany, who sold their own produce to Germany and imported food from overseas instead. While the Netherlands met their promise to Britain to end the transit trade, nothing was done at first to stop the vast increase in the export of home-produced food to Germany. The Dutch thus exported between three and five times more cheese, butter, eggs, potatoes and meat in 1915 compared with 1913; practically all Dutch food exports went to Germany. In the first half of 1916, 5 million gold marks' worth of food arrived daily from the Netherlands, which made up the gap with imported food. Without such food imports from the neutrals, German

44 *Ibid.*, doc. 217, memorandum Foreign Office 28 December 1915, pp. 367–78.
45 *Ibid.*, docs. 120 and 121 (enclosure), Sir C. Spring-Rice to Sir Edward Grey, 1 October 1915, pp. 154–61.
46 Lambert, *Planning Armageddon*, pp. 431–2.
47 Lambert, *Planning Armageddon*, pp. 438–9.

Chancellor Theobald von Bethmann Hollweg confessed to a secret meeting of politicians, Germany would have been defeated in early 1916.[48] By the autumn, however, the British had persuaded the Dutch to accept limits on their exports to Germany, and by February 1917 Britain was taking roughly half of Dutch native foodstuff exports. The policy of 'starving Germany', i.e., 'keeping from her foodstuffs and raw materials', was beginning to bite.[49] Dutch imports were lower in 1916 than 1911 to 1913 for almost every commodity, except oil and cotton; imports of fertiliser were remarkably below the normal. Germany received a larger share of Dutch exports than before war, but less than 1915.[50]

Germany's resumption of unlimited submarine warfare in February 1917 imperilled Dutch overseas trade, and above all the entry of the United States into the war in April tightened the screw further on the adjacent neutrals. After intense consultations with British officials and a visit to Washington by Foreign Secretary Arthur Balfour, the US Government decided to emulate British measures of economic warfare; from July 1917 until the end of the war, the United States implemented a virtually total trade embargo on the Netherlands. In 1918, Dutch food exports to Germany dwindled to nothing.[51]

Germany's position before the war

Had German experts not foreseen such developments? In the period 1912 to 1914 the Reich Department of the Interior produced several memoranda on the question of Germany's food security. As a result of increased agricultural productivity (the hectare yield for rye almost doubled between 1899 and 1909), Germany was held to be in a position to feed itself in case of war.[52] However, Admiral Alfred von Tirpitz and the Reich Navy Office questioned that judgement.[53] Tirpitz had long been warning that Germany was vulnerable to blockade. Correctly, he pointed out (in 1907) that agriculture:

48 Marc Frey, 'Trade, ships, and the neutrality of the Netherlands in the First World War', *International History Review*, 19:3 (1997), p. 547; Lambert, *Planning Armageddon*, p. 475.

49 *British Documents*, vol. VIII, *Blockade and Economic Warfare, IV: November 1916 – November 1918*, docs. 50–1, Townley to Balfour, report by Francis Oppenheimer (British commercial attaché at The Hague) 14 February 1917, pp. 98–100.

50 *British Documents*, vol. VIII, doc. 53, report by A. Akers-Douglas, 7 March 1917, pp. 140–1, 147–8.

51 Frey, 'Trade', pp. 552–4, 561.

52 Arnulf Huegel, *Kriegsernährungswirtschaft Deutschlands während des Ersten und Zweiten Weltkrieges im Vergleich* (Konstanz: Hartung-Gorre, 2003), p. 13.

53 Huegel, *Kriegsernährungswirtschaft*, p. 13.

> depended heavily on fodder and fertilizer imports, and that demand would increase in wartime, while production would fall ... Although eastern Europe was the most important source of imported grain, the shipments arrived by sea through the western seaports ... [Yet] Germany's railways did not have sufficient capacity to carry grain from the east to replace the grain imported by sea.[54]

The latter point was also true: 74 per cent of Germany's imports came by sea, directly or indirectly.[55] Even Russian grain usually came by ship. However, Tirpitz – like many historians – was ignoring the obvious: if Germany went to war with Russia, where exactly were the imports from 'Eastern Europe' going to come from?

In any case, however, the proportion of food that Germany had to import was relatively low. Pre-war German estimates ranged from 10 to 20 per cent. A group of German experts appointed at the outbreak of war to study Germany's food situation, the Eltzbacher commission, published its findings in December 1914 that Germany imported 20 per cent of its food by calorific value (including imported fodder), 20 per cent of its animal protein and 42 per cent of fats.[56] There is no good reason to doubt these figures, but the historian Roger Chickering estimates 25 per cent of food was imported; C. P. Vincent and Belinda Davis state it was at least one-third.[57] When war began, official experts were optimistic. The Eltzbacher commission was confident that since Germans had in the years before the war become accustomed to consuming 59 per cent more calories and 44 per cent more protein than were required, it was merely a matter of changing nutrition habits, and the deficit due to the blockade could be overcome. Germany could thus 'withstand a war lasting for many years'.[58]

Did the blockade cause the shortage of food?

For many historians it was self-evident that the blockade caused hunger in Germany. This has had a long tradition, going back to Britain's official historian of the blockade, A. C. Bell, who argued that Germany's high civilian

54 Offer, *First World War*, p. 341.

55 Offer, *First World War*, p. 335, based on a study by the Reich Navy Office of January 1907.

56 Paul Eltzbacher (ed.), *Die deutsche Volksernährung und der englische Aushungerungsplan. Eine Denkschrift* (Braunschweig: Vieweg, 1914), pp. 62–3. Offer, *First World War*, p. 25, cites the English edition, *Germany's Food. Can it Last?* (1915).

57 Roger Chickering, *Imperial Germany and the Great War, 1914–1918* (Cambridge University Press, 1998, 2004), p. 41; Vincent, *Politics of Hunger*, p. 20; Davis, *Home Fires*, p. 22.

58 Eltzbacher, *Die deutsche Volksernährung*, pp. 64, 195.

death toll was caused by the campaign. Bell in turn had taken the German attribution of deaths to the blockade, computed just after the war at a time of quivering nationalist hatred, at face value.[59] Davis ultimately ascribes the cause of the hunger in Germany to the blockade, although she rightly refers also to inequalities in the rationing system. The blockade, she writes, was creating hardship in Germany by the end of 1914; it curtailed imports of wheat and animal feed.[60] C. P. Vincent claimed that 'there is no question that the vast increase in civilian mortality after 1914 was largely attributable to the blockade'.[61] Eric Osborne argues even more pointedly that the 'British blockade' (he ignores the Allies) caused hunger, and was 'the greatest factor behind the Allied victory over Germany':

> In the age of total warfare, the blockade destroyed the German domestic front and rendered the country incapable of continuing the conflict. The lack of sufficient food was one of the greatest factors in the collapse of the German home front . . . The consequences of the blockade were enormous and it had a great impact on Germany's war effort . . . It also had crippling effects on the morale of the people, a vital aspect of total warfare.[62]

While there is no doubt that the blockade had a serious effect, most historians have not assessed its impact: they have merely asserted it. Without a transnational approach, utilising both Allied and German sources, and without international comparison, such claims can be neither verified nor disproved. The analysis of basic economic data may provide some illumination.

More rational economic historians have challenged some of these assumptions. Avner Offer argued that while the German people ate less during the war, and suffered sometimes from hunger, Germany did not starve.[63] The economic historians Broadberry and Harrison bluntly state that:

> there might still be plenty of food, but it was in the wrong place. The farmers preferred to eat it themselves than sell it for a low return . . . There was still enough food for everyone to have enough to eat; the localized shortages that began to spread were famines that arose from the urban society's loss of entitlement, not from the decline in aggregate availability.[64]

59 Bell, *History of the Blockade*, pp. 672–4. 60 Davis, *Home Fires*, p. 22.
61 Vincent, *Politics of Hunger*, p. 145.
62 Eric W. Osborne, *Britain's Economic Blockade of Germany 1914–1919* (London: Frank Cass, 2004), pp. 4, 182.
63 Offer, *First World War*, pp. 46–53.
64 Stephen Broadberry and Mark Harrison, 'The economics of World War I: an overview', in Broadberry and Harrison (eds.), *The Economics of World War I* (Cambridge University Press, 2005), p. 19. Their comment is clearly intended to apply to Germany, in addition to those other countries that suffered severe problems with food supply.

That view is too crude, since there were real falls in food production. Even had imported fertiliser been available, production would have fallen: the area of land under cultivation fell over the course of the war, by 32.3 per cent for wheat, 23 per cent for rye and 31.3 per cent for potatoes.[65] After all, two-thirds of the male labour force in agriculture, the strongest and most skilled part, disappeared into the army.[66] Women, children, old men and prisoners of war were unable to compensate for the lack of labour. The army also requisitioned large numbers of horses, depriving farms of their vital draught animals.

One prime example of the need for dispassionate analysis of economic data is the question of fats. Fats are vitally important in the diet, especially for physically demanding labour: 'In 1917', Osborne writes, 'the Germans procured 5,181 tons of fats from imports through the blockade. During the first ten months of 1918, this figure was only 1,928 tons.'[67] This implies that 5,181 tons was a significant amount, but it breaks down to only 77 grams per person per year, or 0.21 grams per day. In 1917, the fat ration was 100 grams per week for normal consumers, in 1918 – 70 grams.[68] The blockade thus made very little difference to the drop from 1917 to 1918. Since total annual consumption of animal and vegetable fats before the war was almost 2.6 million tons,[69] the imports of 1917 were almost invisible amounts that would comfortably fit on the head of a pin. The problem lay elsewhere.

Towards the end of the nineteenth century, Germany had become ever more dependent on imports for its supply of fats and oils, having replanted almost all the oil-seed growing farmland with sugar beet. In the last two years before the war, Germany's consumption of fats and oils amounted to 1,680,000 tons, of which 1,460,000 tons were for human and animal nutrition, the rest being for technical purposes. (The discrepancy with the above figure of 2.6 million tons is probably because the latter included the raw material, the former only the refined product.) Germany's domestic production accounted for 1,105,000 tons. In particular, 97 per cent of vegetable fats and oils were imported in 1912 to 1913. The main sources for oil-seed plants were the tropics, mainly the British

65 Roerkohl, *Hungerblockade*, p. 31. These figures are for Westphalia, but there is no reason to assume it was very different elsewhere.

66 Offer, *First World War*, p. 62.

67 Osborne, *Britain's Economic Blockade*, p. 182. According to a German source from the 1920s, German imports of fats (which means butter, vegetable oils and fats, and margarine) may have been even lower – 3,767 tons in 1917. August Skalweit, *Die deutsche Kriegsernährungswirtschaft* (Berlin: Deutsche Verlags-Anstalt, 1927), quoted in Albrecht Ritschl, 'The pity of peace: Germany's economy at war, 1914–1918 and beyond', in Broadberry and Harrison, *Economics of World War I*, p. 58, Table 2.13.

68 Huegel, *Kriegsernährungswirtschaft*, p. 329.

69 Eltzbacher, *Die deutsche Volksernährung*, p. 62.

and French African colonies, Argentina, Egypt, India, the Dutch East Indies and China. India alone provided 70 to 80 per cent of rapeseed.[70]

This might appear to be German globalisation in a fit of absent-mindedness, but it was a rational calculation by the Reich that the economy stood to gain from the growing global division of labour. Tariffs on the import of oil-seeds, starting in 1885, applied only partly to manufactured oils, and were not high enough to encourage domestic production. To facilitate the German oil refineries, tariffs on oil-seeds were reduced, which made it even less attractive for German farmers to grow oil-seed. The German refineries became very efficient and competed with other countries such as Britain and Holland.[71]

Yet the German expert in the field in the 1920s, Riebel, wrote of the 'English-French blockade' which deprived Germany of its imports of oil-seeds and manufactured oil and fats. This was not thoughtlessness. He knew where the imports came from. What contemporary German experts and generations of historians have repeatedly called 'blockade' was not blockade at all: it was the Allies' refusal to sell their own resources to the enemy. 'Blockade' expressed for German writers a common assumption about the past war and the future: it was unfair and immoral, in their view, that the Allies used their control of global resources to defeat Germany. In future, Germany would have to ensure self-sufficiency to compensate for its enemies' maritime superiority. That is exactly what some experts counselled at the end of the war, anticipating the later debates that were to culminate in the Nazi policy of autarky.[72]

A key question, therefore, is where Germany's food imports came from. Germany imported 2,545,959 tons of wheat in 1913, it produced 4,655,956 tons, and it exported 538,349 tons. Of the imports, 519,518 tons came from Russia, or one-fifth. 1,005,864 tons came from the United States; 446,605 tons from Argentina, which remained neutral during the war. 318,571 tons came from Canada, and 94,933 tons from Romania. In 1912, 2,297,422 tons of wheat were imported, of which Russia supplied one-quarter.[73]

Traditionally, rye was the most important bread grain in Germany, producing dark bread. Germany produced so much rye – over 12 million tons in 1913 – that it was a net exporter: it imported 352,542 tons and exported 934,463 tons.[74]

70 Kurt Riebel, *Die Versorgung Deutschlands mit tierischen und pflanzlichen Oelen und Fetten. Ein Vergleich mit der Vorkriegszeit* (Diss. Heidelberg, 1926), p. 7.

71 Riebel, *Die Versorgung Deutschlands*, pp. 30–4.

72 Cf. Riebel, *Die Versorgung Deutschlands*, p. 62, and preface, p. v.

73 Kaiserliches Statistisches Amt (ed.), *Statistisches Jahrbuch für das Deutsche Reich* (*SJDR*) (Berlin: Puttkammer & Mühlbrecht, 1914), p. 183, also for the following table.

74 *SJDR* 1914, pp. 43, 182.

Germany imported about 6 million tons of animal fodder per year before the war.[75] A great deal of this came from Russia – for example, almost half the total of 1,414,256 tons of bran.[76]

The conclusion is inescapable: not the blockade but going to war against its main suppliers drastically reduced food imports.

The shortage of food should moreover be placed in the context of the distortions caused by the war economy and the power structure. The army had first priority in the distribution of food; in the retrospective judgement of German medical experts the soldiers were in the main not affected by serious nutrition deficiencies.[77] Other privileged groups were the food producers: farmers had access to all the food they needed; finally, the wealthy always had enough money to buy food on the black market. That left about two-thirds of civilian society which went short of food as from 1915. But the incompetence of the state's food policy also contributed to the misery. At the very start of the war, in an attempt to keep down the cost of living, the authorities imposed maximum prices for food, but this had the effect of inducing farmers to withhold their produce from normal markets and sell it privately to wealthier customers. The prime example of this was the great pig massacre of 1915: on the recommendation of the Eltzbacher commission (discussed above), the Reich Food Office decided that pigs were competing with humans in the consumption of grain, so the order was given to slaughter 9 million pigs. In principle, the decision was motivated by rational science. However, farmers continued illegally to feed their animals grain and potatoes, and sell pork on the black market.[78]

The great increase in agricultural yields in the two decades before 1914 had been the result of the growing application of scientific methods, farm mechanisation, and above all the input of artificial fertilisers. Germany had to import all of its saltpetre (sodium nitrate) from Chile. Yet this was only one of three major classes of artificial fertilisers, phosphates and potassium being the other two; of the latter Germany possessed large deposits (in Alsace-Lorraine and Stassfurt), and the former was derived from steel production.[79] Much of the increased production of grain and potatoes went into animal feed.

75 Offer, *First World War*, p. 63. 76 *SJDR* 1914, p. 199.

77 Dr Paul Musehold, 'Ernährung. I. Die Ernährung des Feldheeres', in Otto von Schjerning (ed.), *Handbuch der Ärztlichen Erfahrungen im Weltkriege 1914/1918*, vol. VII, *Hygiene* (Leipzig: Barth, 1922), p. 100.

78 Chickering, *Imperial Germany*, p. 42.

79 Hans-Ulrich Wehler, *Deutsche Gesellschaftsgeschichte*, vol. III, *Von der 'Deutschen Doppelrevolution' bis zum Beginn des Ersten Weltkrieges 1849–1914* (Munich: C. H. Beck, 1995), p. 698.

The historic shift in the nature of the German diet towards high meat consumption was to pose a severe problem. By 1911, per capita consumption was 52.3 kilograms of meat per year, outdone only by Australians (111.6 kilograms per year) and Americans (54.4 kilograms).[80] Max Rubner, the nutritionist, had long been arguing against the consensus view that meat eating was healthy. Addressing the Reichstag in December 1914, Rubner stated that although many were now in fear of the blockade that might starve Germany into defeat, he was optimistic that if Germans switched to a low-meat, low-fat diet, and agriculture switched from meat and dairy production to the growing of pulses and grains, the nutrition import deficit could be almost entirely made good.[81]

Supplies other than food

The distortions of the war economy were not restricted to food. Two of the most important industrial products, iron and coal, were also seriously affected. Iron production depends on the availability primarily of iron ore and coal, both of which Germany had in abundance. However, Germany's output of iron and steel fell to 61 per cent of its 1913 level in 1916, and by the end of the war it was only 53 per cent.[82] Some historians suggest that this, too, was the result of the blockade, which is nonsensical.[83] Before the war, Germany was a net exporter of coal, with reserves that lasted beyond the end of the twentieth century. Germany had even greater resources during the war because of the capture of the iron ore areas of French Lorraine, the coal of the Pas de Calais and the Belgian coal mines. Yet German coal production also fell, and it was in short supply for the food-processing industry and for domestic consumers, who often lacked fuel for hot water, heating and cooking. The causes were the shortage of labour, which could not be entirely made up by prisoners of war and foreign labour, the shortage of investment and the shortage of pit props because of the demand for timber in construction at the front.

Oil was fast becoming a crucial source of mobility in the war. Germany had to import 90 per cent of its requirements, from Austrian Galicia and Romania (together 27 per cent), and the rest mainly from the United States.[84] Romania's

80 Corinna Treitel, 'Max Rubner and the biopolitics of rational nutrition', *Central European History*, 41 (2008), p. 9.

81 Treitel, 'Max Rubner', pp. 19–20. 82 Ritschl, 'The pity of peace', p. 49, Table 2.5.

83 Osborne, *Britain's Economic Blockade*, p. 183. He estimates German iron production in 1918 to be 9,208 tons (sic).

84 Rainer Karlsch and Raymond G. Stokes, *'Faktor Öl'. Die Mineralölwirtschaft in Deutschland 1859–1974* (Munich: C. H. Beck, 2003), p. 93.

entry into the war in August 1916 offered Germany the opportunity to gain control of its valuable oil wells, but in November to December, as the Central Powers closed in, the British deployed a group of engineers under the command of Colonel John Norton-Griffiths to destroy the oil installations and make them unproductive for as long as possible. Oil rigs and refineries at Ploesti and almost all other oilfields were blown up, boreholes plugged and stocks of oil burned. It took German engineers until the end of 1917 to make repairs and reach half the previous production, which was still not fully restored at the end of the war. The daring exploits of Norton-Griffiths, the greatest single act of economic warfare in the war, had deprived the Central Powers of 4 million tons of oil; considering the total available to them during the war was 6.5 million tons, this was a remarkable feat that has gone almost unnoticed in mainstream history.[85]

Did the blockade cause the decline in German trade?

The blockade clearly impeded the flow of imports and exports, with varying degrees of efficiency that depended on the ingenuity of neutral shippers and the resolve of the Allies in the application of pressure on the neutrals. By 1918, Germany's imports fell catastrophically to less than 39 per cent of their pre-war value, and only one-fifth of their pre-war volume.[86] Yet the blockade was not the only reason for the decline in German trade.

The incarceration of the German merchant fleet immediately denied Germany many essentials, such as the direct supply of Chilean saltpetre, and blockade policy aimed to stop indirect supplies from December 1914.[87] Saltpetre was essential not only as a fertiliser, but also for the manufacture of explosives, and Germany was Chile's most important market, taking over 30 per cent of sales of nitrates. Allied demand took up the slack, mainly for the manufacture of explosives, and Chilean exports recovered in 1915.[88]

The following table shows that there was another impediment to German imports.

85 Karlsch and Stokes, *'Faktor Öl'*, p. 107; David Stevenson, *With Our Backs to the Wall. Victory and Defeat in 1918* (London: Allen Lane, 2011), p. 225. See full report by Norton-Griffiths, 22 January 1917, at the National Archives CAB/24/6 (online).

86 Offer, *First World War*, p. 61.

87 'List of articles to be treated as absolute contraband under the Royal Proclamations of October 18 and December 1914', 23 December 1914, *British Documents*, vol. v, doc. 16, pp. 12–13.

88 Bill Albert, *South America and the First World War. The Impact of the War on Brazil, Argentina, Peru and Chile* (Cambridge University Press, 1988), p. 46. Table with figures on nitrate production, exports and prices on p. 97.

Table 18.1 *Germany: balance of trade, 1913–1918*

	Billion marks at current prices			Billion marks at constant prices (i.e., gold marks)		
	Exports	Imports	Balance	Exports	Imports	Balance
1913	10.1	10.8	–0.7	10.1	10.8	–0.7
1914	7.4	8.5	–1.1	7.5	8.5	–1.0
(Aug.–Dec.)	1.4	2.1	–0.7	1.5	2.1	–0.6
1915	3.1	7.1	–4.0	2.5	5.9	–3.4
1916	3.8	8.4	–4.6	2.9	6.4	–3.5
1917	3.5	7.1	–3.6	2.0	4.2	–2.2
1918	4.7	7.1	–2.4	2.8	4.2	–1.4
Aug. 1914 to Dec. 1918	16.5	31.8	–15.3	11.7	22.8	–11.1

Source: Albrecht Ritschl, 'The pity of peace: Germany's economy at war, 1914–1918 and beyond', in Stephen Broadberry and Mark Harrison (eds.), *The Economics of World War I* (Cambridge University Press, 2005), Table 2.7, p. 50; and Gerd Hardach, *Der Erste Weltkrieg 1914–1918* (Munich: Deutscher Taschenbuch Verlag, 1973), Table 6, p. 42.

A country that wishes to import goods has to pay for them through exports, gold or by liquidating foreign assets. A growing deficit in the balance of trade and in the balance of payments usually causes currency devaluation, until foreign creditors no longer take the risk of accepting the importer's currency and stop sending their goods. By far Germany's largest export market before the war was Britain, to which Germany exported in 1913 goods to the value of 1,438 million marks. Next was Austria-Hungary, with 1,104 million marks, followed by Russia, with 880 million, and France, with 789 million marks. The crucial point is that more than half of Germany's exports, 5.7 billion marks out of 10 billion, went to countries with which Germany was at war by 1917.[89]

Germany's exports fell even more disastrously, to about 25 per cent of the pre-war level. Going to war against one's customers was half the cause.[90] The blockade accounted for the other half. At the end of 1915, the British Foreign Office was able to report that the navy had managed to reduce German and Austrian exports to the United States by a substantial amount, from 124 million dollars in the seven months from March to September 1914 to only 22 million

89 *SJDR* 1914, p. 258.

90 This elementary point seems to have escaped those who have hitherto written on the blockade and the war economy; cf. Ritschl, 'The pity of peace', p. 52.

dollars in the same period in 1915. The figures for September showed that over 92 per cent of German exports to the United States had been stopped.[91]

The German response

Import substitution is the standard response to shortages, and Germany was able to increase the production of many industrial and agricultural goods which were previously imported. The prime example is raw materials for fertiliser.

The blockade is often thought to have adversely affected agricultural production by depriving it of fertilisers, notably, as we have seen, Chilean saltpetre. Shortly before the war, however, the chemist Fritz Haber had developed a process for the fixation of atmospheric nitrogen to produce ammonia; Carl Bosch, at the Badische Anilin- und Sodafabrik (BASF), turned Haber's process into industrial production, and by July 1914 was producing the equivalent of 6,000 tons of nitrogen in the form of ammonium sulphate. After the government provided finance, guaranteeing high profits to BASF, annual output soon increased to 200,000 tons of nitrogen. Together with another process invented before the war to manufacture calcium cyanamide, by the end of 1915 industry was producing 90 per cent of the nitrogen for explosives, and 70 per cent of the demand for agriculture.[92] A second factory was built, at a projected cost of 60 million marks, at Leuna near Merseburg, to produce 3,000 tons of ammonia per month for fertiliser, using the Haber process.[93] So the result was success for import substitution.

Pre-war surveys by Germany's Naval Office and the Interior Ministry had found that stocks of imported raw materials, especially rubber and non-ferrous metals, held by firms in the Ruhr would last for only three months on average. The position turned out to be more favourable, with import substitution (for example, nickel mined in Germany, albeit at a higher cost), exploitation of the resources of occupied territory, the halting of exports and home consumption, and the build-up of certain strategic stocks before the war.[94] The stocks of rubber (together with those discovered in Belgium)

91 *British Documents*, vol. VI, doc. 217, Memorandum Foreign Office 28 December 1915, pp. 367–78.

92 Strachan, *To Arms*, pp. 1026–7.

93 Report by Captain (Res.) Julius Bueb, War Labour Office in the Prussian War Ministry to the War Ministry, 22 April 1916, in Helmut Otto and Karl Schmiedel (eds.), *Der erste Weltkrieg. Dokumente* (Berlin: Militärverlag der DDR, 1983), doc. 62, pp. 170–3.

94 Strachan, *To Arms*, pp. 1018–20.

turned out to be relatively large.[95] Production of non-ferrous metals trebled during the war.[96]

International comparisons

In Austria-Hungary, the food situation was even worse than in Germany, especially in Vienna and the Alpine districts. Yet the Habsburg monarchy had been virtually self-sufficient in food, a net exporter of livestock and in some years also of grain.[97] The problem was that Hungary imported Serbian grain as cattle-fodder, so here, too, it was war against a supplier nation rather than blockade which interrupted food imports. Essentially, Austria went hungry because of Hungary. The Hungarian half of the Empire simply refused to continue to send food to Austria. The blockade was virtually irrelevant. Austria's descent into hunger ended with starvation diets of 700 calories per day for civilians. Some 400,000 civilians died in the Empire, or about 1 per cent of the population. Not even the thorough exploitation of occupied Serbia and Romania alleviated Austria's hunger; the occupation of wealthy north-eastern Italy after Caporetto in late 1917 provided only temporary respite, although it caused mass hunger among the Italians under the occupation; and the prospect of gaining the rich resources of the Ukraine in the occupation in 1918 proved to be a chimera.

The comparison with Russia demonstrates the illogicality of the hunger-blockade thesis. Here, food shortages in the cities were a critical problem by 1916; the calorific value of the diet of unskilled workers declined by 25 per cent, and the infant mortality rate doubled.[98] The reasons were the collapse of the transport system under the impact of the war, the shortage of labour in the countryside owing to conscription, the army's appropriation of horses and the failure of the state's rationing system. Yet Russia had had a significant grain surplus before the war, and was a major exporter of food. The blockade of the Black Sea impeded the export of grain, which should have been available to feed domestic consumers, but this surplus was soon eaten up by the millions of refugees and soldiers; in addition, peasants preferred to

95 Otto Goebel, *Deutsche Rohstoffwirtschaft im Weltkrieg* (Stuttgart: Deutsche Verlagsanstalt, 1930), p. 16.

96 Ritschl, 'The pity of peace', p. 47 and Table 2.5, p. 49.

97 Max-Stephan Schulze, 'Austria-Hungary's economy in World War I', in Broadberry and Harrison, *Economics of World War I*, p. 91; Stevan K. Pavlowitch, *Serbia. The History behind the Name* (London: Hurst, 2002), p. 81.

98 Orlando Figes, *A People's Tragedy. A History of the Russian Revolution* (New York: Viking, 1996), p. 300.

consume increased amounts of grain, meat and butter rather than sell it to the inefficient state which they no longer trusted.[99] In any case, the blockade of Russia was not perfect: it still managed to export 2 million tons of grain to France in 1916.[100]

Italy, as a neutral and as from May 1915 an Entente power, had access to global supplies. Yet the health of the population was greatly affected by the war, and excess civilian mortality amounted to 546,450, or 1.4 per cent, a higher rate than that in Germany.[101] This was partly due to the incompetence of the Italian state in ensuring equitable food distribution, by the reappearance of epidemics of malaria, tuberculosis (from which 121,000 died in 1917 and 1918) and other diseases, and by the state's deliberate flouting of health and safety measures to prevent workers falling victim to increasingly dangerous and toxic working environments in war production. The impact of the little-known naval war in the Mediterranean was considerable: more than one-quarter of Allied shipping was sunk in the Mediterranean, 3.7 million tons out of 12.5 million tons in total. To some extent this curtailed Italy's imports, but it was not as import-dependent as Britain, nor did submarine warfare pose such a grave threat. Credits extended by Britain and the United States enabled Italy to import increasing quantities of grain and meat. The high civilian mortality rate was thus not caused by a decline in the availability of food. Certainly, there were periodic local shortages, such as in 1917 in Turin, provoking the workers there, who had been hostile to the war from the start, to express their opposition in strikes and bread riots. There were moments of anxiety, such as in Calabria for a week in summer 1917 when submarines sank grain ships bound for Naples. But the rural population never suffered from a lack of flour for bread and pasta, vegetables, eggs or

99 Pater Gatrell, 'Poor Russia, poor show: mobilising a backward economy for war, 1914–1917', in Broadberry and Harrison, *Economics of World War I*, pp. 256–9.

100 Petit, *Histoire des finances extérieures*, pp. 20–1. Lambert argues with some justification that the British Government's decision to launch the Dardanelles offensive was partly motivated by the desire to reopen the trade route. Success would have allowed Russian wheat to be exported, thus reducing rising bread prices in Britain. *Facing Armageddon*, pp. 334–8. As David Stevenson shows, however, broader geostrategic considerations were at stake: *1914–1918. The History of the First World War* (London: Allen Lane, 2004), p. 117.

101 Mario Isnenghi and Giorgio Rochat, *La Grande Guerra, 1914–1918* (Florence: Scandicci, 2000), pp. 301–2. Mortara calculated excess war-related civilian mortality for the period 1915–18 of 606,407 compared with the period 1911–13 (p. 140). The increase may have been largely due to the severity of the influenza outbreak (p. 213), which apparently accounted for 274,041 deaths in 1918. Giorgio Mortara, *La Salute pubblica in Italia durante e dopo la guerra* (Bari, Laterza and New Haven, CT: Yale University Press, 1925), pp. 466–7.

chickens, and were even able to purchase sugar and coffee, luxuries previously rare on the peasant table. On the whole, Italian society benefited from slightly increased nutrition. Not even the rate of infant mortality rose: it was 4.07 per cent in the years 1911 to 1913, changing to 4.10, 4.09, 4.05 and 4.14 per cent in 1914, 1915, 1916 and 1917 respectively. Only in 1918 was there a substantial increase, to 4.81 per cent, which must have been connected with the influenza epidemic.[102]

The mortality rate of the civilian population was similarly high in France (600,000 or 1.5 per cent), which may be partly explained by the poor conditions in the occupied departments, and by the serious rise in infant mortality. In 1913, 109 children per 1,000 births had died in their first year, and 110 in 1914; that figure rose to 143 in 1915, the highest level in the war. This indicates that although sufficient food was available, many nursing mothers now had to work, often in physically demanding, dangerous or toxic conditions, thus impairing the welfare of infants. Infant mortality fell to 125 and 126 in 1916 and 1917, and rose in the last year of war to 140, which may have been caused by the influenza epidemic, before falling back in 1919 to 122.[103]

The high death rate in France disguises several more positive trends: unemployment virtually disappeared, and the demand for labour in war industries and agriculture was insatiable, so ill-health through dire poverty was probably overcome. The remarkable success of French agriculture in responding to wartime needs meant that food rationing was not introduced until as late as June 1918.[104]

The success of the Allies in maintaining the supply of wheat, cotton and chemicals illustrates how decisive was Allied control of global resources.

Before the war France imported 15 million quintals (1 French quintal = 100 kilograms) of wheat out of its total consumption of 95 million quintals, from Algeria, Tunisia, Russia, Germany, Argentina, Australia, the United States and Romania. Domestic production fell from 88 million quintals in 1913 to 58 million in 1916, and 40 million in 1917. But the shortfall was met by the United States and Argentina. In 1916, even Russia supplied 2 million

102 Piero Melograni, *Storia politica della Grande guerra, 1915–1918* (Milan: Mondadori, 1998), pp. 307–11, 332–5; Luigi Einaudi, *La condotta economica e gli effetti sociali della guerra italiana* (Bari: Laterza, 1933), pp. 179–84, 186 (credits and imports); Mortara, *La Salute pubblica*, pp. 466–7 (infant mortality).

103 Michel Huber, *La Population de la France pendant la guerre* (Paris: Presses Universitaires de France; New Haven, CT: Yale University Press, 1931), table 'Mortalité infantile dans les 77 départements', p. 288.

104 Leonard V. Smith *et al.*, *France and the Great War, 1914–1918* (Cambridge University Press, 2003), p. 67.

quintals, and Canada and Australia each sent almost 9 million. In 1918, total wheat imports fell to 12 million, the bulk of which came from the United States and Argentina.[105]

Two-thirds of France's 2.5 million quintals of cotton were imported from the United States. The majority of the cotton-consuming industries were in the invaded territories, so demand for raw cotton dropped, but the need for cotton for the manufacture of explosives and ammunition was so great that it reached 2.5 million quintals in 1917, 85 per cent from the United States.[106] Imports of chemicals, which previously came above all from Germany, were replaced by Britain, the United States and some other countries.[107]

German economic warfare

Of German intentions before 1914 there could be no doubt. They were no less ruthless than the British. Count Helmut von Moltke, the revered victor of the German wars of unification, wrote in 1880 to the Swiss international lawyer Johann Caspar Bluntschli:

> The greatest good deed in war is its speedy ending, and every means to that end, so long as it is not plain reprehensible, must be open to choose. In no way can I state myself in agreement with the Declaration of St. Petersburg that the sole justifiable measure in war is 'the weakening of the enemy's military power, etc.' No, all the resources of the enemy government must be attacked, its finances, railways, food supplies, even its prestige.[108]

Germany, which was not lacking in foreign assets before the war, tried to translate them into economic warfare. In July 1915, the British consul-general at New York reported that a US entrepreneur closely connected with the Deutsche Bank was attempting to buy up companies that had munitions contracts with the Entente, such as Bethlehem Steel, Remington and Winchester; German interests were rumoured to have made an offer of $22 million for Union Metallic Cartridge Co.[109]

While these attempts to gain foreign assets failed, the invasions in 1914 brought rich territories under German control. The ten occupied departments of northern France accounted for 20 per cent of wheat grown in France,

105 Petit, *Histoire des finances extérieures*, pp. 20–1.
106 Petit, *Histoire des finances extérieures*, p. 25.
107 Petit, *Histoire des finances extérieures*, p. 32.
108 First published in 1880, cited in Otto Koellreutter, 'Kriegsrecht und Völkerrecht', *Zeitschrift für Völkerrecht*, 10 (1917/18), pp. 494–5.
109 *British Documents*, vol. v, doc. 226, Broderick to Scott, 17 July 1915, pp. 312–13.

30 per cent of its output of linen and clothing, 60 per cent of its steel, 74 per cent of its coal, and 92 per cent of its iron.[110] Not content with having exploited the coal and industrial production of Belgium, in 1917 to 1918 the German occupation proceeded to dismantle the most valuable industrial equipment, machines, motors and machine tools, and transport them to Germany along with stocks of metals and raw materials. This continued until the last weeks of the war, culminating in the pillage of the iron and steel plants of Charleroi and Liège.[111] Allied economic warfare was thus partly offset by German exploitation of these resources.

In turn, the devastation of French economic resources during the German retreats of 1917 and 1918 was not only intended to hold up the Allied advance; the deliberate destruction in October 1918 of the northern French coal mines in the area east of Lens to Valenciennes was designed to make the production of coal impossible for 'five to six years', by blowing up the works above ground and the shafts, and flooding the mines underground.[112]

German naval policy in the years before 1914, which often appears to have been a systematic attempt to challenge British naval supremacy, was less well thought through and less consistent than often assumed. Some, starting with the top naval enthusiast Kaiser Wilhelm II, assumed that the German navy would wage cruiser warfare against British merchant ships on the high seas; others wanted to deploy the mass of the fleet against a part of the British navy, detached by some deceptive manoeuvre, destroy it, and thus even up the balance between the two fleets. Submarine warfare had only a subordinate place in planning when the war started.

Germany's own colonial Empire was too scattered to provide a proper network of coaling and communications for a global presence or even be defended, but in the Far East, Maximilian Graf von Spee, commander of the German East Asiatic squadron, in agreement with the Admiralty Staff, saw the opportunity for cruiser warfare to cause serious disruption to trade by destroying British merchant ships. It would also divert British warships away from the North Sea, opening up new possibilities. The tactic was in principle rational, and there were spectacular initial successes. *Karlsruhe* captured or

110 Gaston Jèze, *The War Expenditure of France*, published as first part of *The War Finance of France* (New Haven, CT: Yale University Press, 1927), pp. 73–4.

111 Sophie de Schaepdrijver, *La Belgique et la Première Guerre mondiale* (Brussels: Peter Lang, 2004), pp. 216–17.

112 Report by the military chief of mines to Quartermaster General II General von Hahndorff, 17 October 1918, in Otto and Schmiedel, *Der erste Weltkrieg*, doc. 134, pp. 326–7.

sank eighteen merchant ships by October 1914; *Emden* bombarded Madras, sank a Russian cruiser and a French destroyer at Penang, and had captured or sunk twenty-three vessels, before being destroyed by the Australian cruiser *Sydney* in November 1914. The East Asiatic squadron then escaped across the Pacific to South American waters. After defeating a poorly led British attack at Coronel (Chile) in November, Maximilian Graf von Spee took a rash decision to raid the Falkland Islands, where British battle cruisers imposed a crushing defeat on 8 December, sinking almost the entire squadron, including the renowned *Gneisenau* and *Scharnhorst*. The Falkland Islands battle was 'the most decisive naval engagement of the war', as Hew Strachan writes, and it meant the end of the German cruiser threat to Allied shipping. By January 1915, only 273,000 tons, or 2 per cent of British merchant ships, had been sunk.[113] Ultimately, the German navy lacked the military and economic resources to wage cruiser warfare. It resorted to submarine warfare by default.

In January 1915, Admiral Hugo von Pohl, Chief of Admiralty Staff, argued in a memorandum to the Kaiser that owing to the failure of the land war hitherto a new strategy was imperative. German naval warfare had not managed to do any significant damage to British sea power; German torpedo boats could not reach the British blockade vessels, and neither submarines nor mines had produced the expected results. Raids on the British east coast had been a political success, but had made little military impact. Nothing had been able to lure the British fleet into a trap. The German naval strategy of not putting its main fleet at risk of destruction was playing into British hands in the long term. Pohl therefore insisted that the High Seas Fleet should be prepared for action: submarine and mine warfare should be energetically pursued to impose a blockade around British coasts to cut its vital nerves, its commerce.[114] The result was the decision for the first round of 'unrestricted submarine warfare', in which the enemy's merchant ships would be destroyed without warning, commencing on 22 February 1915.[115] After the sinking of *Lusitania* in May with the loss of 1,198 lives including 128 US citizens, the Kaiser prohibited attacks on passenger ships, and in September U-boat warfare in the waters around the British Isles was suspended.

113 Strachan, *To Arms*, pp. 466–80.

114 Memorandum by the Chief of Admiralty Staff, Admiral Hugo von Pohl, 7 January 1915, in Otto and Schmiedel, *Der erste Weltkrieg*, doc. 35, pp. 117–21.

115 Order by Admiral Gustav Bachmann on behalf of Admiralty Staff, 18 February 1915, in Otto and Schmiedel, *Der erste Weltkrieg*, doc. 36, pp. 122–3.

In planning the second phase of unrestricted U-boat warfare, which was to begin on 1 February 1917, the new Chief of Admiralty Staff, Admiral Henning von Holtzendorff, argued that by destroying 600,000 tons of Allied and neutral shipping per month, 'at least two-fifths of neutral shipping would be deterred from sailing to Britain'. He calculated that after five months British maritime traffic would decline by 39 per cent; economics and the 'psychological impact of panic and terror' would mean that 'England would not be able to tolerate this'.[116]

The policy meant that all ships en route for the United Kingdom, whether Allied or neutral, would be sunk without warning. German experts calculated Britain's wheat consumption at 141,500 tons per week, and that it would lose 114,300 tons per week. With reserves already low, supplies would run out within three months. Prices would rise steeply, there would be a crisis in the balance of payments, widespread hunger and riots; Britain would be forced to sue for peace. The effect would not only be felt on the home front. Ludendorff, who keenly supported the Admiralty's plans, expected that the success of the U-boat campaign would swing the military situation back in Germany's favour. It would reduce the supply of munitions, bringing relief to the German armies on the Western Front. 'We must', he said, 'spare the troops a second Somme'.[117]

In the first six months of the campaign, the predictions came true: in the first four months an average of 629,862 tons of shipping were destroyed, in the next two, an average of 506,069 tons.[118] The British navy was convinced that catastrophe was looming. The First Sea Lord, Admiral Sir John Jellicoe, said in April 1917 that the Germans 'were winning', and at the War Cabinet he warned that 'disaster is certain to follow'. Churchill was later to write: 'The U-boat was rapidly undermining not only the life of the British islands, but the foundations of the Allies' strength; and the danger of their collapse in 1918 began to loom black and imminent.'[119]

116 Covering letter by Chief of Admiralty Staff Admiral von Holtzendorff on the memorandum 'On the necessity of unrestricted U-boat warfare' to the Chief of General Staff of the army, Field Marshal von Hindenburg, 22 December 1916, in Otto and Schmiedel, *Der erste Weltkrieg*, doc. 85, pp. 213–15.

117 Minutes of meeting between Chancellor von Bethmann Hollweg, Chief of Army General Staff Field Marshal von Hindenburg, and First Quartermaster General, General Ludendorff, on the opening of unrestricted U-boat warfare, 9 January 1917, in Otto and Schmiedel, *Der erste Weltkrieg*, doc. 88, pp. 222–4.

118 Holger Herwig, 'Total rhetoric, limited war. Germany's U-boat campaign, 1917–1918', in Roger Chickering and Stig Förster (eds.), *Great War, Total War. Combat and Mobilization on the Western Front, 1914–1918* (Cambridge University Press, 2000), pp. 192–200.

119 Both cited in Herwig, 'Total rhetoric', p. 192.

The expectation of British collapse was premature. A bundle of measures was taken that demonstrated the resilience of the British navy and society. To overcome the scepticism of Jellicoe, who fatalistically believed nothing could be done to defeat the German submarines, Lloyd George had to browbeat the Admiralty to introduce the convoy system with warship escorts. It proved highly effective, and the number of sinkings by U-boats dropped. Of the 16,693 convoy ships that departed for or from the United Kingdom, only 102 were torpedoed; 99.1 per cent arrived safely.[120] Other measures were import substitution, food rationing, the substitution of wheat by other foodstuffs, a big increase in the area of land cultivated for grain, vegetables and potatoes, and the introduction of a more efficient command economy than in Germany, including a 'food controller' who regulated the sale of 85 per cent of the food consumed. Moreover, Britain still had access to the vast resources of North America: virtually inexhaustible credit and ample grain.[121]

The paradoxical result was that Britain, which was to a far greater extent dependent on imported food (about 58 per cent of its calories in the years 1909 to 1913) than Germany, ended the war with its population better fed and healthier than in 1914, while Germany suffered widespread hunger.[122] Overall, however, 600,000 civilians died in the United Kingdom in excess of the peacetime mortality rate, or about 1.3 per cent, a higher rate than Germany.[123] This is explained partly by the influenza epidemic, with 200,000 victims, and respiratory diseases such as bronchitis and tuberculosis which were connected with the general wartime conditions (war work, poor housing) rather than with nutrition.

Ludendorff's hope that U-boat warfare would relieve pressure on the Western Front was dashed. So successful was the Entente response to German economic warfare that Groener wrote in November 1917 that the U-boat campaign was making no impact on the warfare of the British and French: 'On the contrary, they have more munitions and guns at their disposal than ever.'[124]

120 Lance E. Davis and Stanley L. Engerman, *Naval Blockades in Peace and War. An Economic History since 1750* (Cambridge University Press, 2006), p. 187.

121 Herwig, 'Total rhetoric', pp. 200–2. See above all Jay Winter, *The Great War and the British People*, 2nd edn (Basingstoke: Palgrave Macmillan, 2003), pp. 103–53.

122 Offer, *First World War*, p. 81.

123 Table 'Military and civilian losses', in *Brill's Encyclopedia of the First World War*, pp. 732–3. Although his thesis is that civilian mortality declined in the war, Winter does not provide overall figures for excess civilian mortality in *The Great War and the British People*.

124 General Groener, letter of 3 November 1917, in Otto and Schmiedel, *Der erste Weltkrieg*, doc. 108, pp. 270–1.

Conclusion

Did economic warfare win the war? The food situation in Germany in late 1918 was somewhat better than the previous year, and civilian morale played no part in the decision taken by the German High Command to end the war. The Allies won the war on the battlefield. At the end of the war Allied superiority in logistics was crushing, and German logistical weakness was manifesting itself in crucial areas, as the shortage of lubricants, petrol and rubber was seriously affecting the mobility of the German army. The end of the supply of these imported raw materials was within sight: as the Bavarian Crown Prince and army group commander Rupprecht admitted in mid October 1918: 'There is a lack of fuel for the lorries, and if the Austrians abandon the alliance and we don't get any more petrol from Romania, our air force will be grounded within two months.'[125] Not only was the cohesion of the army disappearing, as Ludendorff feared at the end of September: it was facing a threat to its freedom of manoeuvre. An army that is paralysed is in peril of complete disintegration. While the German army did not starve, for the Austro-Hungarian and Turkish armies hunger and the shortage of uniforms were a major factor in their capitulation.

Economic warfare, which targeted the entire enemy economy and its resources, including the civilian population, represented a step on the road to total warfare in the twentieth century. It was not against the letter of international law, still less the tradition of warfare, but it was contrary to the spirit of international law which was to protect civilians from war. The economic war waged by the Central Powers had little chance of threatening the Allies' command of global resources, except briefly in 1917. Their blockade of Russia was one factor in the downfall of the tsarist Empire, alongside several more important ones. The Central Powers were able to use the adjacent neutral states to obtain essential imports, but with sharply declining quantities as from mid 1916. Their strongest asset to challenge the Allies was their command of the labour, industry, agriculture and finances of occupied Belgium, northern France, north-eastern Italy, Romania, Serbia, Poland, Lithuania and the Ukraine. These resources, although smaller than Allied global resources, were of considerable value, and it remains a task of research to assess their value.

125 Commander of Army Group Crown Prince Rupprecht, Field Marshal Crown Prince Rupprecht von Bayern, to Chancellor Prince Max von Baden, 18 October 1918, in Otto and Schmiedel, *Der erste Weltkrieg*, doc. 135, pp. 327–9.

Allied economic warfare meant securing access to global resources. Their denial was one of the causes of the reduction in German food supply, along with several other endogenous causes within Germany, notably the disruption of agriculture through the shortages of labour and draught animals, a reduction of land under cultivation, and the shortage of coal to transport and process food. Taken together, blockade and the broader measures of economic warfare probably contributed half of the exogenous effect on German food supply; endogenous factors probably accounted for far greater declines in food availability. The long-term shortages of key industrial raw materials and oil, partly caused by the blockade, partly by the Central Powers' declining ability to pay for imports, but mostly by their enemies' ownership of the resources, were more decisive in shifting the military balance than shortages of food.

PART IV

*

THE SEARCH FOR PEACE

Introduction to Part IV

GERD KRUMEICH

This section concerns the multiple forms of the search for peace. From the very beginning and throughout the world war, all the belligerents insisted that they were sincerely seeking peace, a lasting peace opening the way to the pacification of the world. This stance of seeking peace through total war was sufficiently incoherent as to be discredited as simply a part of war propaganda. At the same time, the movements and initiatives of varying kinds which were authentically pacifist in character were split, crippled and dispersed.

Our international and transnational approach enables us to see at what level the diplomacy of the combatant powers tried throughout the war to convince civilians and soldiers, as well as neutrals, of the profoundly pacifist character of their nation's investment in war. And yet this claim hardly rang true when set against war aims and the exigencies of victory leading to the domination of the vanquished. It was in the context of this contradiction that the peace initiative of the Vatican came undone. The Pope's ability to act as an honest broker was put in doubt by enemy propaganda of both sides. Was he not the '*Papa boche*' in French or the 'top German'? Did he not have '*ultramontaine*' tendencies detested by the German authorities? And given the total material and moral investment of the combatants in the war, what other outcome was possible than the destruction of the forces of one side or the other? Furthermore, the world had never seen a peace constructed by a tribunal, which did not even admit the vanquished to take part in the discussion of the terms of the future peace. And that inevitably meant that the war was not ended by the treaties of 1919 and 1920, and that the European diplomatic equilibrium, maintained for 200 years and more, had now been shattered to pieces. Consequently, there emerged new wars of domination, of ethnicities, revolution and counter-revolution, independence and more. They were partly the result of these treaties which completed the destruction of the old international order.

In this section, a number of studies written by scholars of transnational and comparative history enable us to see the paradoxical character of the struggle for domination through the idea of peace during and after the war. Never before 1914 had so many actors on so many levels focused on the same two questions: how to stop the war and how to prevent another war like it from breaking out in the future? Throughout the world, actors on many levels worked at bringing about a durable peace which would transform the world. This 'Wilsonian' hope is evident in the Kienthal and Zimmerwald socialist conferences, where men and women of different ideological stances worked to form a transnational peace effort. The same was true of the international women's movement, dedicated to forging a peace without a tilt towards any one nation. The International Women's League for peace and freedom met at The Hague in 1915 to do just that. These groups were certainly in the minority during the war, but registered a hope that would not go away.

We know that all these efforts came to naught. Future research needs to uncover the evolution of what we understand as mental frameworks or *mentalités* which led to the destruction of the grand principle of peace central to European culture: the belief that war was considered as a form of politics, but that the task of politics was to find a way to construct a durable peace, a peace of consent among all parties. To find out more about the sources of that failure is the task that awaits future scholars in this field.

19
Diplomacy

GEORGES-HENRI SOUTOU

Introduction

It is widely believed that we know everything about the diplomatic history of the First World War. That is not the case. Most documents have been accessible only since the end of the 1960s or 1970s, at a time when interest in the topic, which had been rekindled at the beginning of the 1960s by the 'Fischer Controversy' about German war aims, had been superseded by the new emphasis on research on the cultural, social and psychological aspects of the war.[1] Therefore. there is still a lot to be, if not really discovered, at least explained and put into proper perspective.

We need to follow three main strands: relations and negotiations inside both camps, with the neutrals, and between the two opposing groups. We should note here that, although there was a lively diplomatic exchange among allies in both camps, and with the neutrals, for the first time in a European conflict no open negotiations took place between the belligerents during the war (apart from technicalities about prisoner exchanges, application of the Hague Conventions and so on). This significant break in a longstanding European tradition of intra-war diplomacy was of course one of the consequences of the new form of war, escalating to 'total' and global warfare. It was also the consequence of a new level of hatred: the adversary must not

Helen McPhail translated this chapter from French into English.

1 Fritz Fischer's book, *Griff nach der Weltmach. Die Kriegszielpolitik des kaiserlichen Deutschlands 1914–1918* (Düsseldorf: Droste Verlag, 1961), which underlined the very extensive war aims of the Reich during the Great War as well as its responsibility for its outbreak, aroused tremendous controversy at the time of its publication. The account of this can be found in Jacques Droz, *Les causes de la Première Guerre mondiale* (Paris: Le Seuil, 1973).

For a new historiographical current, cf. Antoine Prost and Jay Winter, *Penser la Grande Guerre. Un essai d'historiographie* (Paris: Le Seuil, 2004); and Wolfgang J. Mommsen, *Der Grosse Krieg und die Historiker. Neue Wege der Geschichtsschreibung über des ersten Weltkrieg* (Essen: Klartext Verlag, 2002).

only be vanquished – he must be crushed. Hence, also, vastly expanded war aims in a conflict which largely came to resemble a modern ideological crusade. It must be recognised that the Great War was not only about acquiring territories, it was also about political beliefs, juridical norms, economic interests, within but also outside Europe, in a world still largely dominated by the major European powers.

But even without any real diplomatic exchanges between the two sides, we have to address two important and relevant aspects: the (largely competitive and mutually influenced) definition of war aims on both sides; and the secret and complex peace feelers and clandestine diplomacy which took place during the war. They failed; but they were meaningful, and understanding why they failed helps us towards a better perspective into what actually happened during the war and at the peace conferences.

Forging the War Alliance against the Central Powers and the rejection of wartime negotiations (1914–1916)

The Allies (or the Entente as they were usually called at the time) were from the beginning fully convinced that German power would have to be sharply reduced. As early as 5 September 1914, in the London Declaration, Great Britain, France and Russia committed themselves to exclude any separate peace and, when the time would come, to put forward commonly agreed peace terms. Instead of the imperfect and uneven combination of the Franco-British Entente and the Franco-Russian alliance as war broke out, there was now a common agreement binding all three countries. As early as the end of September (after victory on the Marne), the French Government decided that the war would be prosecuted beyond the liberation of French territory and until 'the end of Prussian militarism', meaning in reality a deep transformation of Germany, if not the outright end of the Reich.

By early autumn 1914, and again through the spring of 1915, the Russians and the French agreed that each country would support the aims of its ally: specifically, at the end of the war France would deal with the Rhineland as it would see fit; and Russia would do the same in the Prussian part of Poland. Thus, the two more closely involved Allies (British contribution at this stage was still limited) agreed quite early to coordinate their war aims. During 1915, Russian ambitions in the Balkans and the Straits strained the alliance, but, as we shall see, the three countries were able to agree and thus to maintain, at least outwardly, their unity; the British and the French were of course not enthusiastic about Russian aims against Turkey.[2]

But unity was of the essence, because Berlin naturally tried to break the enemy alliance, starting with the country deemed to be least able to resist the stress of a great war: Russia. As early as November 1915, Berlin tried to open a channel of secret negotiations with Russia through various intermediaries. But, despite rather encouraging suggestions (the situation would revert more or less to the status quo of 1914, thus retaining the major part of Poland and the Baltic provinces), Tsar Nicholas refused three times (June, July and August 1915) to follow suit: beyond the fact that he was basically true to his word, Russia stood to gain more if it stayed in the Alliance; or so it seemed at the time. An important result was that Berlin, still realising that a negotiated settlement on the basis of the status quo with Russia was the only way out of a very difficult geostrategic situation, began nonetheless in the autumn of 1915 to discuss with Vienna the possibility of taking Poland away from Russia, thus fatally precluding any possible agreement with Imperial Russia (the Romanovs could not contemplate the loss of Poland).

One must not forget that the linchpin of the case which the Allies were making, in international law and also in their propaganda towards their own public and the neutrals, was the invasion and occupation of Belgium by the Reich. Belgian neutrality had been guaranteed in 1839 by the great European powers, all of them now at war. It was the violation of Belgian neutrality which propelled an initially quite reluctant United Kingdom into the war. It was that violation which allowed the Allies to capture the moral high ground of the 'war for justice'. That is why the Germans tried to bring Belgium out of the war: at the end of 1915 and beginning of 1916, they repeatedly tried to make a deal with King Albert I. Belgium would be evacuated and restored, but would enter a customs union and a military alliance with Germany. But the Allies learned about those contacts and urgently convinced the Belgians to break them off, with the promise of a full restoration of Belgium (Declaration of Sainte-Adresse, 14 February 1916). They were of course fully decided not to let Berlin, even in the guise of an economic and military alliance, control the very important Belgian economy, but they had every interest in retaining the defence of Belgian integrity as their best justification for war.

Up to a point, the same applied to Serbia. After all, it was the country on behalf of which war had started in the first place. The defence of little Serbia

2 Georges-Henri Soutou, 'La France et les marches de l'est, 1914–1919', *Revue Historique*, 578 (1978), pp. 341–88.

was also a good argument for the Allies in the ongoing propaganda war. In the case of Serbia, there were many alerts: in December 1914, the Austrians tried to conclude a separate peace with Serbia. During the summer of 1915, the Allies were struck by the lack of activity of the Serbian army, and they feared some secret deal with the Austro-Germans. In Paris, some suspected that the Serbians were reacting that way because they feared the consequences, for their territorial integrity and their aspirations, of the London treaty with Italy in April, and the ongoing negotiations between the Allies and Bulgaria and Romania. And once again, at the time of the great Austrian-German-Bulgarian offensive in October 1915, the Allies feared a Serbian defection. That is why, in different instances from May to December 1915, they promised the Serbs in writing that their interests would be taken into account in these negotiations and that, in exchange for a return to the 1912 frontier with Bulgaria, Serbia would get access to the Adriatic and Bosnia-Herzegovina. But in each instance the French went beyond that, indicating, but only verbally, that Serbia would be allowed to incorporate Croatia. This support for the Yugoslav idea was not at all obvious in Paris, up until 1919, because of the fear of precluding any possibility of a separate peace with Vienna, and also because the French did not want to antagonise Italy, which had its own agenda in the Adriatic.

But this lukewarm support of the Serbs, made even more difficult because of the need at the same time to win over Italy, Bulgaria and Romania, which adopted opposing aims, shows that it was essential for Paris to keep Serbia in the war. Not so much for strategic reasons (at the end of 1915 the defeated Serbian army had been virtually written off by the Allies) as for political and propaganda ones. As for Belgium, the Allies were fighting for justice and international law, for the independence of small countries. But many of those agreements or promises, especially when they came to collide with other promises made to neutrals which the Allies were wooing, such as Italy, Bulgaria or Romania, were to complicate things until and including the peace treaties, when the Allies, having tied themselves in knots, had some trouble untying themselves.[3]

But at another level the Allies were progressively getting their act together. The new French Premier, Aristide Briand, who succeeded the rather ineffectual René Viviani in October 1915, decided to pursue the war much more vigorously and to coordinate the Allies much more effectively at all levels

3 Georges-Henri Soutou, 'La France et la crainte d'une paix de compromise entre la Serbie et les puissances centrals, 1914–1918', *Aspects de l'histoire des rapports diplomatico-stratégiques*, Cahier no. 13 (Paris: Centre d'Histoire de la Défense, 2000).

(military, political, economic). Thus, at the Rome conference in February 1916, the Allies instituted a regular military council and a political one, which convened for the first time in March. And an inter-Allied economic conference was held in Paris in June. Even if these coordinating efforts were still a far cry from the high level of quasi-integrated cooperation the Allies would achieve by 1918, they were undisputedly making progress. At the same time, the British, who had introduced conscription in 1916, became increasingly involved in the war and displaced the Russians as the major allies of France. The war had been at first basically a Franco-Russian business; it was now a Franco-British one.[4]

The Central Powers 1914–1915

The Central Powers had less trouble in getting organised. After all, the main relationship, between Berlin and Vienna, could be dealt with within the framework of the usual bilateral relations, and the two general staffs collaborated fairly easily. And war aims on both sides were not too difficult to reconcile. Turkey signed a secret treaty with Berlin as early as 2 August, and joined the war on 1 November 1914, the delay being used in order to allow two powerful German battle cruisers to reach the Turkish Straits, and for the Turks to complete their preparation for war. Turkey was not geographically linked to Austria-Hungary and Germany, which was a problem, but the entry of Bulgaria (encouraged by promises made to her at the expense of Serbia) in the war on their side in October 1915 solved it. Berlin was decidedly the leader, and the major provider of war material and troop reinforcements when necessary (the Austrians benefited from them against Italy and Romania) or military advisers (as in the case of Turkey, where German officers could be found in all staffs down to division level). Nevertheless, recent historiography tends to go beyond a Eurocentric view and to underline the specific role of the Ottoman Empire in the origins of the First World War and during the war itself. Many pieces of an otherwise complicated puzzle fall into place when

4 Georges-Henri Soutou, 'Comment la coopération économique franco-britannique fut favorisée par la bataille de Verdun (mai 1916)', in Claude Carlier and Guy Pedroncini (eds.), *La Bataille de Verdun* (Paris: Economica, 1997); Georges-Henri Soutou, 'Relations internationals, tentatives de paix et buts de guerre en 1916', in Centre de Recherche de l'Historial de la Grande Guerre, *La Bataille de la Somme dans la Grande Guerre*, Actes du Colloque des 1er, 2, 3, 4 juillet 1996 (Péronne: Centre de Recherche de l'Historial de la Grande Guerre, 2000).

one considers Turkey and its strategy against Russia and against the British in the Middle East.[5]

But for long-term preparations the relationship between Germany and Austria-Hungary was less successful. Berlin was very well aware that, beyond the war, the relationship with Vienna would be essential to reinforce Germany's security in the future, which was the major war aim for the majority of German leaders (a security of course expansively calibrated), apart from those who were more influenced by the pan-Germanic agenda. Shortly after the outbreak of the war, Chancellor Bethmann Hollweg had devised the concept of a Central European economic union, based foremost on Germany and Austria, in order to achieve German dominance in the region under the guise of trade agreements and without too many or too big annexations, which could turn out to be counterproductive (*vide* Alsace-Lorraine). In August 1915, the then Chief of Staff, Falkenhayn, went even further: the only way to discourage the Allies would be to conclude there and then a strong political, military and economic alliance with Vienna. In exchange, Germany would let Austria incorporate Russian Poland (the 'Austro-Polish solution'). On 13 November 1915, Berlin offered to start negotiations with Vienna on the establishment of close political, military and economic links. Economic negotiations began immediately. They became quickly bogged down in a series of difficulties and contradictions. The Austrians stalled, because the Austro-Hungarian *Ausgleich* had to be renewed in 1917, with important economic and customs aspects, and they wanted to solve them before dealing in earnest with Berlin. In addition, they perfectly realised what the Germans were aiming at, and they did not want to become satellised. And the idea of a 'Germanic' solidarity with the Reich was abhorrent to them, and ran, as they told Berlin, directly against the whole notion and tradition of the Habsburg Empire.

The Germans themselves were deeply divided over the advisability of a customs union with Austria: it might excite retaliation by other countries, which were more important markets for Germany than Austria. And they quickly had second thoughts about Poland: they could not count upon Austria to ensure security against Russia, with which it would in that case share a very long border, and an influx of Slavs into the Dual Monarchy would endanger its 'Germanic' character, and Berlin's influence. Hence a new plan, devised in Berlin in February 1916: Russian Poland would become autonomous, but

5 Sean McMeekin, 'The war of the Ottoman succession', *Historically Speaking*, 13:1 (2012), pp. 2–4.

would be closely linked to the Reich politically, militarily and economically. The Austrians were predictably furious, but, after acrimonious exchanges, had to comply: on 5 November 1916, Berlin and Vienna announced through a common declaration the creation of the resurrected Polish State, and Austria would control with Berlin its foreign policy (but not its military one, which would depend on Germany in the framework of what was in all practical terms a German protectorate over Poland). As for the trade and customs union between Germany and Austria, negotiations went on in a desultory way, but were never completed. The Austrians no longer had any incentive, and many circles in Germany had always been rather tepid. After an auspicious start, German-Austrian relations soured, even more from 1917 onwards with the growing difficulty for the Austrian Empire to sustain the war, and with ever-more difficult exchanges with Berlin, as we shall see, about the advisability and possibility of a negotiated settlement of the war.[6]

At the same time, the difficult German-Austrian relationship had an important side effect: it started the ball of national independence for dominated nations rolling. In 1916, the Allies, which included a multi-ethnic Russian Empire, were still very far from putting the liberation of 'oppressed nationalities' on their agenda. This momentous development in European history was not started by the Allies, contrary to a frequent belief, but by the Germans, which of course had a strong interest in weakening the Russian Empire, since they had renounced the hope of concluding a separate peace with it.

1915–1916: towards a long war and the wooing of the neutrals

As early as the end of 1914, it became evident that the war would not limit itself to a short spasmodic clash, a sort of cleansing of the European atmosphere, after which a new European balance would be established, but along traditional lines. In the search for ways to overcome the stalemate, both camps tried of course to win over the neutrals and to enrol new allies. A major prize in this search was Italy, which had been allied with the Central Powers before the war, but had stayed neutral in 1914 because its partners had not been the victims of an unprovoked attack. The Germans tried hard to bring in Italy on their side, but, despite strenuous efforts, they were unable to bring the

6 Georges-Henri Soutou, *L'Or et le Sang. Les buts de guerre économique de la Première Guerre mondiale* (Paris: Fayard, 1989).

Austrians to make the necessary concessions (particularly Trieste and the Trentino region). But, in Italy, although many would have preferred to remain neutral, a vocal part of public opinion and a majority of the ruling circles wanted to use the opportunity to achieve the nationalist agenda of annexing the Italian-speaking parts of Austria and expanding towards the Balkans and the Mediterranean. The French and the British were in a better situation to oblige: under the Treaty of London, 26 April 1915, Italy would receive Trieste, the Trentino region, the Adriatic islands, part of the Dalmatian coastline and part of Turkish Anatolia. (The treaty was in principle secret, but many features were quickly more or less known.) Shortly thereafter, Italy entered the war.[7]

But some of those promises (particularly towards the Adriatic) collided with what was, as we saw, also promised at about the same time to the Serbs. This was to lead to great difficulties in 1918 and 1919 and France, not wishing to antagonise either country, tried unsuccessfully to mediate between the two. And, decidedly tying themselves in knots, the Allies tried in 1915 to bring Bulgaria onto their side, but unsuccessfully, as we saw, by promising Sofia a good part of Macedonia (which Serbia had conquered during the Second Balkan War against Bulgaria in 1913). They were more successful with Romania, which in August 1916 was promised Transylvania, Bukovina and the Banat, and which therefore entered the war on the side of the Allies. It might have been a grave menace to the Central Powers, but they did react very fast and the Romanians were severely defeated after about one month. But the promises made to Bucharest in 1916 would reverberate at the peace conferences in 1919 and 1920, their more or less complete translation in the peace treaties would lead after that to severe problems with Hungary and Russia, which were still evident after 1945. As was often the case, hastily cobbled agreements reached under the pressure of the Great War were to haunt Europe for a long time to come, because the principles of the European Concert (permanent contact with all major powers, self-restraint, balance, refusal to put national issues above the need for stability) had been discarded in 1914.

Another botched attempt to enlist a strategically important neutral, in this case Greece (the most direct road to Belgrade and Central Europe started in Salonica, along the River Vardar), was also to have lasting consequences. In October 1915, the English and French landed troops in Salonica, despite

7 Frédéric Le Moal, *La France et l'Italie dans les Balkans 1914–1919. Le cententieux adriatique* (Paris: L'Harmattan, 2006).

the fact that Greece was neutral, to open a front against the Bulgarians. But King Constantine, who was accused by the French of leaning towards the Central Powers, then dismissed Prime Minister Venizelos, who was in favour of abandoning neutrality and joining the Allies. In 1916, the Allies exerted the utmost pressure on the king. However, the situation was not clarified, Constantine remaining neutral. Finally, the Allies forced him to abdicate in June 1917 and reinstated Venizelos. These very untidy developments, with many serious incidents, revealed deep differences between Paris and London, which all along had been anxious not to appear to put too much pressure on Athens. Moreover, the whole issue put into question the Allied stance of defending the rights of the neutrals against the Central Powers: in the Greek case, the Allies lost the moral high ground.[8]

Obviously, a very important neutral was the United States, which was courted by both sides at least as a possible purveyor of important commodities, foodstuff and industrial imports. President Wilson stressed neutrality, believing that responsibilities in the outbreak of the war were evenly divided between both camps. Until 1917, there were constant tensions between Washington and both sides: with the Allies because of the ever-more severe blockade of Germany, which quickly banned more and more types of exports to the Central Powers (even non-lethal ones) and were very adverse to the trade interests of the neutrals; with the Germans, because they engaged in their own kind of blockade of the British Isles, using their submarines and sinking increasing numbers of neutral ships, including US ones. The acceptability of both types of blockade in terms of international law was in fact highly disputable. We should also add that, until his re-election in 1916, the American President was very anxious not to antagonise one or other part of a still fragmented population, in terms of different national origins.[9]

At the same time, Wilson was from the very beginning convinced that Britain and France, from a liberal and democratic point of view, were closer to the United States than the Central Powers. A negotiated peace in Europe would be the best outcome, but if one side had to win, then an Allied victory would be more in the interest of the United States. On top of that, an important but unofficial financial conduit in the private sector had already been established in October 1914 between Washington and London. The sudden beginning of the war had left the US economy and its banking system

8 Yannis G. Mourélos, *L'intervention de la Grèce dans la Grande Guerre* (Athens: Collection de l'Institut français d'Athènes, 1983).

9 Lloyd E. Ambrosius, *Woodrow Wilson and the American Diplomatic Tradition* (Cambridge University Press, 1987).

in a dangerous situation, all the more so because the Federal Reserve System was due to be actually introduced in November, with the looming possibility of panic in the financial markets. The British Government, at the request of Washington, induced the City to provide help, and thus the crisis was averted. And afterwards the Allies were able, owing to their huge investments in the United States, to borrow much more than the Germans could, and they were also able, due to their (relative if not total) mastery of the sea lanes, to carry the purchased goods much more easily across the Atlantic. If the United States were militarily and politically neutral, they were not so at the economic level.[10]

The British, much more than the French, who could not reconcile themselves with the sort of moral equivalence with which President Wilson appeared to consider both camps, were keen on nurturing the relationship with Washington, if only to prevent the United States from opposing the Allied blockade more actively or restricting financial and trade facilities for the Allies. That is largely the reason why they tried to persuade President Wilson to support US mediation to end the war, probably without believing that such a goal could be achieved. And the American President was himself not keen to engage in mediation, because at that time, he still did not want his country to be involved, with all the responsibilities such involvement would entail, in the peace-making process and in any new organisation which, it was felt increasingly in different quarters, was bound to be created after the war, in order to ensure the peace.

But Colonel House, Wilson's personal adviser, who had already undertaken an information trip around European capitals in 1915, and who was more in favour of the Entente than the President, was convinced that, because of the attacks of German submarines against neutral shipping, ultimately the United States would not be able to avoid entering the war on the Allied side. And he was authorised to undertake a new trip to Europe at the beginning of 1916. The result was a memorandum, signed by House and the British Foreign Secretary Grey and approved by the President, according to which Wilson would offer his mediation if the Allies were to become stuck in a difficult military situation. He would then suggest that Belgium should be restored, Alsace-Lorraine given back to France and Constantinople transferred to Russia. In exchange, the Germans would get some Allied colonies. If Germany were to refuse those conditions, then the United States would 'probably' enter the war on the Allied side. But the Allies were not really

10 Soutou, *L'Or et le Sang*, pp. 117–39.

ready to content themselves with those results: when in May 1916 Wilson offered to implement the memorandum, London refused, which proves that the real aim of the exercise had been to humour Washington and to bring the Americans to soften their stand with respect to the Allies.[11]

But on 12 December 1916, after the very disquieting outcome of the Anglo-French offensive on the Somme (for the first time the German army and industry realised that they had reached their limits) and after the entry of German and Austrian troops into Bucharest, Berlin and Vienna made a peace overture. Berlin was much more serious than was realised at the time, and the peace plan was not just a propaganda ploy: the Germans were basically ready to go back to the status quo of 1914 in the West, limiting their gains to the East, at the expense of a weakening Russia. Actually, the majority of the ruling classes and of the general population were keener to achieve gains in the East than in the West. It would roll back the much feared Russian Empire, and provide more opportunities for colonisation than heavily populated Western Europe. And the new resources and power bases gained in the East would be enough to establish a definitive secure position for Germany.

Wilson reacted to the Austro-German note by proposing his mediation on 18 December: the belligerent countries should state their war aims and a peace conference would be convened, chaired by Wilson himself. The Germans answered privately and tried to obfuscate the issues, refusing, as did the Austrians, to state their war aims. The Allies answered publicly on 10 January 1917. They rejected the US offer of mediation, but they stated their aims: evacuation and restoration of Belgium and Serbia, return of Alsace-Lorraine to France and partition of the Austro-Hungarian Empire according to nationalities (they were still far from really wanting that – it was more a means to put pressure on Vienna). They alluded to 'security guarantees' (actually a coded expression to cover a special status for the Rhineland, either neutralisation or permanent occupation by French troops). And they accepted the idea of a League of Nations, along the concept defended by Wilson. The French, furious at Wilson's intervention, would have preferred a sterner answer, but the British were more astute and suggested putting what were actually very tough Allied aims (as we shall see) in a more or less Wilsonian wording. They were right: three months later, on 4 April 1917, the United States entered the war on the side of the Allies (but as an Associated Power, retaining its own

11 Victor H. Rothwell, *British War Aims and Peace Diplomacy 1914–1918* (Oxford University Press, 1971), pp. 33–6; Arthur S. Link, *Wilson: Confusions and Crises 1915–1916* (Princeton University Press, 1964), pp. 110 ff.

agenda, not as a new ally). President Wilson had hesitated for a long time, but the launching of 'all-out submarine warfare' by Berlin in January 1917 convinced him that a German victory would be more irreconcilable with his own views for the post-war world than an Allied one.

1914–1916: Escalation of war aims and the end of the Concert of Europe

Surprisingly, there were no real negotiations, apart from some inconclusive soundings, before 1917, and even then there were no official negotiations but only secret ones, through intermediaries and mostly under the form of peace feelers, despite the heavy toll and the huge expenses incurred by the combatants. This can be explained through two related phenomena. The first was the collapse of the Concert of Europe, which had begun already before the war, for some historians with the Morocco crises of 1905 and 1911, for others with the Balkan wars in 1912 and 1913. That meant the collapse of a whole system of relations and practices (restraint, systematic multilateral consultations and so on) devised to prevent, defuse or localise crisis. And, secondly, there were the quite ambitious peace aims which were defined very early after the start of the war in most belligerent countries, and which went on escalating – escalation on one side justifying of course escalation on the other. No return to the status quo seemed possible to the ruling circles before 1917, not even a form of status quo plus. More prudent, some groups and individuals (not necessarily pacifist) imagined a negotiated settlement with a return, basically, to the situation in 1914, but they could not make themselves heard before 1917.

On 9 September 1914, Chancellor Bethmann Hollweg inspired a document, known today as the 'September Programme'. It alluded to possible annexations in the East and at the expense of Belgium and France. But the full scope of Germany's defeat in the Battle of the Marne was not yet known in Berlin. Anyway, territorial aspects were not the main thrust of that document: its actual recipients were the different authorities in charge of preparing the trade and economic clauses of the future peace. Bethmann Hollweg was just envisioning the possible outcome of the war, to clarify what he believed at the time to be the general background of a peace everyone in Berlin saw as very near, the framework of what became quite early on his major war aim: a customs and economic union in Central Europe, linking Germany, Austria, Belgium and Poland, which was to be separated from Russia (later on, as we saw, when it was realised that the war would last, the Chancellor was ready to renounce that objective). This project (usually described at the time by the expression 'Mitteleuropa', which held considerable historic and cultural appeal for the Germans), despite its economic content, had basically a political and geostrategic aim. It was perfectly understood by the German Government that, at the economic level, the plan made little sense: Germany was doing only 4 per cent of its trade with Austria; its major markets were outside Mitteleuropa. And most economic circles were against it. But it was seen as the perfect lever to control Central Europe, indirectly, through its economy. Thus, it would be possible to establish security in the future against the Allies without resorting to problematic annexations. For Bethmann Hollweg it was also an instrument to contain the dangerous annexationist fantasies of the Emperor and the military. The Central European customs union was to remain until 1918 the major and only permanent war aim of Berlin. It was seen as the only practical way to ensure that Austria-Hungary would remain linked to Berlin after the war, with Poland and (if possible) Belgium.

For the most realistic leaders in Berlin, as early as 1915 and apart from a short period of renewed optimism when Russia left the war, it was understood that a clear-cut victory on all fronts with grandiose spoils of war was out of the question. The most that could be hoped for was a relative victory, or some sort of stalemate, which could bring the Allies to have to accept the realisation of the Mitteleuropa.

As for territorial gains, as early as 1915, Berlin became very uncertain. It was realised that only a separate peace with one of the enemies could ensure victory over the others. As we saw, Berlin did try to negotiate with Belgium and Russia in 1915. But, already at the beginning of 1916, it became evident that the way to a separate peace was closed, because the Allies were minded to put an end to a situation of German hegemony over Europe and to reduce vastly German power at all levels (political, military, economic). Berlin, also encouraged by the inability of the Western Allies to push the Germans back, and by the great and mounting difficulties of Russia, then returned to more ambitious aims: it was understood that Belgium, Poland and the Baltic countries would become German protectorates, closely controlled by Berlin at the political, military and economic level.

Beyond their purely national goals, the Allies naturally had a certain concept of post-war Europe. In London, reflections were initially not far developed; nonetheless, it was certain that Belgian independence must be re-established. Beyond that, it was decided that German power must be reduced, particularly in military and naval terms, as well as clearing the Reich out of Africa and containing German influence in the Middle East. Britain did not specify its objectives until the end of 1916. They increasingly included the determination, ever-more resolute as the war continued, to weaken Germany decisively. On this point, contrary to everything which has been claimed, there was deep agreement between Paris and London; but London was less optimistic than Paris over the possibility of weakening Germany at the geopolitical heart of Mitteleuropa: the essential element was to guarantee Western Europe (France, Belgium, the Netherlands) and the Middle East against German supremacy. As for Central and Eastern Europe, London was less sure than Paris that it would be possible to remove German influence, and proved very cautious over national movements. At least until 1918, Britain was strongly inclined to maintain the Austro-Hungarian Empire. The lasting weakening of Germany was above all to be achieved through a form of commercial and permanent economic discrimination, prolonging the wartime blockade to some extent, even in attenuated form. This last point would be rapidly forgotten with the post-war economic crisis and the necessity, in British eyes, of bringing Germany back into the commercial world.

In general terms, however, Great Britain had hardened its position in 1916. After a phase of hesitation following the disappointments of the Battle of the Somme, in the autumn, when the Liberal Prime Minister Asquith considered the possibility of a negotiated compromise peace with the Reich, a conspiracy between the Conservatives and Lloyd George brought the latter as head of the government on 6 December 1916. From then on it was understood that war would be waged to the end, in particular with the support of the United States, whose entry into the war appeared imminent and who were counted on to achieve the British objectives, at the price of sharing with them the management of world affairs in the post-war era. But there was less optimism in London than in Paris. In London, it was thought that it would not be possible to prevent the Reich from gathering around it the European heartland, Mitteleuropa, with Austria, Poland and Romania. What in return appeared essential to British eyes was to control coastlines, to prevent Germany from having any outlet to the world's oceans, thus to chase it out of Belgium, Africa and the Middle East. The liberation of Belgium, the destruction of the Ottoman Empire and the broad development of the British presence in the Middle East – at that moment, these were London's main objectives. At times these clashed with aims in Paris, which also wished to establish a presence in the Middle East, in particular in Syria and Lebanon; but France lacked the capacity, in any form, to send to this region the 1.5 million soldiers available to the British Empire at the end of the war. The outcome was that the Sykes–Picot Agreement of 1916, in which the two nations broadly shared the Middle East between them (France concentrating on modern Syria and Lebanon, Great Britain on modern Iraq), was reconsidered in 1917 – at France's expense. Britain courted the Arabs, and provided the necessary encouragement to rise up against Turkey, while at the same time, she proclaimed the Balfour Declaration, with the objective of creating a Jewish National Home in Palestine.[12]

France also accorded the greatest importance to the economic weakening of Germany, although the French governmental objectives were, in the immediate view, largely territorial: it was very quickly understood that, apart of course from the recuperation of Alsace-Lorraine, the left bank of the Rhine would at the very least be occupied permanently by France, or perhaps established as an independent state separate from the Reich. Some authorities and publicists thought that it might even be annexed to France. Paris also counted on Russia taking control of substantial territories to the East; depending on the circumstances, the Reich would see its unity weakened or even questioned.

In October 1915, Briand replaced Viviani in Paris as Prime Minister. Briand was to lead the war much more vigorously than his predecessor, and the war aims question was to be specified precisely, in particular after the defensive victory of Verdun in June 1916 and the promising start of the Somme offensive in July. On 7 October, there was a very important governmental meeting at the Elysée palace, presided over by Poincaré, who in the matter of war aims was notably more active and ambitious than the more cautious Briand. After a final ministerial deliberation in Council, Briand set out the French objectives in a letter on 12 January 1917 to Paul Cambon, the French ambassador to London.

It was understood that at the right moment, apart of course from the return of Alsace-Lorraine, France would annex the Saarland. As for the Rhineland, internal divergences within the government had prevented any possibility of reaching a choice among three options: annexation, simple military occupation, or separation from the Reich and the constitution in the Rhineland of one or two states as a French political, economic and military protectorate. But in any case France must win recognition from its Allies for complete freedom of

12 For this passage in full, cf. Soutou, *L'Or et le Sang*; Soutou, 'La France et les marches de l'est'; David Stevenson, *French War Aims against Germany 1914–1919* (Oxford University Press, 1982); Christopher Andre and A. Kanya-Forstner, *France Overseas. The Great War and the Climax of French Imperial Expansion* (London: Thames & Hudson, 1981); Rothwell, *British War Aims*; Marian Kent, *Oil and Empire. British Policy and Mesopotamian Oil 1900–1920* (London: Macmillan, 1976); Jukka Nevakivi, *Britain, France and the Arab Middle East 1914–1920* (London: Athlone Press, 1969).

action in settling the question to its benefit at the moment of the peace. The justifications evoked for the Rhineland were of course strategic, but also historic (the Rhine had been the French frontier during the revolution and the Empire), national (the Rhinelanders were closer to the French than to the Prussians) and even ideological: for historical reasons the Rhinelanders were inclined to adopt the French Republican model, and to promote this cause with the rest of Germany, against 'Prussian militarism'. Apart from the Saarland and perhaps the Rhineland, Germany should cede the other provinces, in particular to Russia, and even its unity potentially could be placed in doubt.

French political and administrative thinking was divided over Luxembourg, as shown by the internal debates during the preparation of instructions to Paul Cambon on 12 January 1917. Some wished to reunite the Grand Duchy with Belgium, to obtain in exchange a close political, military and economic union between the two countries. Others (the majority, it seems) wished to achieve the annexation, pure and simple, of Luxembourg with France.

This ensemble of goals was the consequence not so much of a genuine imperialist determination as of an obsession with security, in the face of a Germany whose power and dynamism were feared. This security was understood by the French authorities in two ways: strategic security of course, hence the wish to control the Rhine in one way or another; but also economic security, to the extent that security as understood in the twentieth century was henceforward inseparable from industrial power. But the addition to the French steel sector of that of Lorraine, the Saarland and Luxembourg, would set the French steel industry on a level with the British and not far behind Germany, instead of the difference of nearly 1:4 between the French and German steel industries of pre-war days. A major expansion in French industry could therefore be counted on, whatever other measures were taken to reduce Germany's economic power.

In fact, in particular under the influence of Clémentel, Minister for Trade and Industry from 1915 until the end of the war, and sustained by an entire elite from the industrial world (the great corps of state engineers, so characteristic of modern France), the government would formulate a vast project for the development of the French economy. This project addressed a concern present in some circles before the war, about the relative shrinking of the French economy in the world and the nation's inadequate industrialisation. French heavy industry and banking, which had considerable links with the German and Austrian economies before 1914, and which were therefore, with a few exceptions, in favour of a return to economic exchanges with the central empires after the war, were against these governmental projects, supported by small and medium-sized industries, far more affected by German competition.

This project for economic expansion was based on a developed strategy; apart from the steel manufacturing effects of the return of Alsace-Lorraine and control of the Saarland and Luxembourg, there was the wish to enter into customs unions with Belgium and Italy, in order to bring Western Continental Europe under French economic influence. Further, there was an understanding with Britain, both for joint management of the major raw materials from overseas, in order to avoid them being dependent on market forces alone, and for the drastic reduction of German economic power.

The beginnings of realisation of this programme began in June 1916 at the meeting in Paris of an inter-Allied economic conference, with agreement on inter-Allied collaboration during and after the war and the assurance of efficient supervision of the major global raw materials (which would give them a degree of pressure on Germany). Further, the Reich would be subject to a prolonged period of trade discrimination after the war. In the end, the Belgians, Italians and Russians, anxious not to compromise the resumption of their economic relations with Germany after the war, did not ratify the recommendations of the Paris economic conference. But Britain, which in 1916, fearing German economic power, was largely ready to abandon its traditional liberalism, continued until 1919 to sustain the propositions of the Allied economic conference, which it had moreover helped to inspire, and of which some elements would even emerge in the Treaty of Versailles. The Franco-British wartime project to reduce the economic power of their German rival was much stronger than is often realised.

True, other politicians defended more moderate ideas, such as Caillaux, Painlevé and Briand (although the latter only from 1917), but, as is well known, they could not make themselves heard. After the hesitations of 1917, Clemenceau returned to a very firm programme, including on the economic level, aimed at weakening Germany permanently. The only option which he did not support was the reopening of the matter of German unity (although he retained an energetic policy to control the Rhineland). Furthermore, the French leaders were increasingly determined to annex Luxembourg and to link Belgium and Italy closely with France, politically, militarily and economically. A Western Europe would thus be reconstructed under French leadership.[13]

13 Soutou, 'Les marches de l'est'.

As can be seen, Britain and France also held a very unilateral vision of the future Europe. It was evident that neither the German model, nor the British or French models, envisaged the reconstruction of a balanced and genuinely pacified Europe. In effect, Europeans appeared incapable of proposing a viable model for the reconstruction of Europe. The political wisdom of which the continent had given proof since 1815 was nowhere to be seen.

1917: secret negotiations, as the last chance for a European Europe?

As we have noted, it is crucial to recognise that during the Great War, in contrast with all the previous great European conflicts, no official negotiations took place between the belligerents: total warfare imposed its own logic. There were, however, public proposals of negotiation from the Central Powers (on 12 December 1916) and certain neutrals, such as the United States (on 18 December) and the Holy See. Numerous secret negotiations looked at potential solutions which could not be announced publicly.

In 1917, the year when all the nations at war suffered a lowering of morale, peace was perhaps not far away. Three years of war, the social and political repercussions of the Russian Revolution and, in France, the disappointment following the setback in the Nivelle offensive in April, had created a general lassitude. Germany had its first significant industrial strikes, France its mutinies in June, Austria-Hungary entered into the crisis, which would lead to its gradual dissolution in the following year.

The additional factor was the entrance of the United States into the war in April 1917. The immediate influence of Wilson, through the immediate weight of US economic power and its financial aid to the Allies, and the prospect of a serious military contribution from 1918, forced the warring nations to take Wilsonian principles into account in their definition of war aims. Hitherto, Berlin, like the Allies, had pursued a traditional style policy of power, defined by the Cabinets in the most rigorous secrecy and with little or no consideration of public opinion. The Allies signed multiple secret accords among themselves, with the Serbians, Italians and Romanians, in particular to plan in advance how to divide up the ruins of the German, Austrian and Turkish empires. From this point it would be necessary, in defining the war aims, to refer at least formally to principles capable of being publicly announced: public opinion had to be sought to support the war aims.

The Reichstag, after the failure of the all-out submarine warfare proclaimed in January 1917, which brought the United States into the war, voted in July for a 'peace resolution' that rejected 'annexations by force'; they envisaged a peace which would be based on the status quo in the West, and in the East on a military, political and economic protectorate of the Reich over the Baltic nations and Poland, but without annexation. The Allies interpreted this 'peace resolution', wrongly, as a purely propaganda manoeuvre; in fact at that moment it represented the true orientation of the German leaders, who despite the reluctance of the High Command were aware of the Reich's strategic impasse.

In Paris, following the revelation by the Russian revolutionaries of February 1917 of the secret accords concluded between France and the Tsar, the Chamber sat in secret committee at the beginning of June to discuss war aims; this was the only such occasion during the entire war. The resolution voted at the end of the debate rejected 'all thought of conquest', but reaffirmed 'the defeat of Prussian militarism' and the need to 'obtain lasting guarantees of peace'. Close study of the debates shows that the deputies had wished in this way to reject the aim of an annexation of the Rhineland, but to keep open the possibility either of occupying it permanently, or even of detaching it from the Reich. Of the three options – envisaged by the government since the summer of 1916, it should be remembered – only annexation pure and simple was henceforward dismissed, for it no longer corresponded to the new spirit created by the US entry into the war and the Russian Revolution. It must be stressed, however, that the government, supported by a majority of deputies, still saw the need to have a Rhineland policy as such.

Further, the military impasse, the February Revolution in Russia, and the social and political difficulties in the two camps would, for the first time since the outbreak of the war, lead certain figures in authority to consider seriously the possibility of a negotiated peace, not imposed by victory, or at least defined from a position of strength. In great secrecy, there was discussion of peace on several occasions, much more seriously than has often been noted. Joseph Caillaux in France and Lord Lansdowne in Great Britain – to cite only the most trenchant stances at the time – favoured a negotiated peace and the abandonment of the previously proclaimed aim of a victorious peace. In Russia, after the October Revolution Lenin proposed the opening of negotiations with a view to a peace 'without annexations or indemnities'. At the end of December 1917, in fact, he opened negotiations with the Central Powers alone, which would end with the Treaty of Brest-Litovsk in March 1918.

The best-known affair, but no doubt not the most important, was the negotiation attempted by Emperor Charles of Austria-Hungary (who had succeeded Franz-Joseph in October 1916) aimed at the Allies through the mediation of his brother-in-law Sixtus von Bourbon Parma in March 1917.

The Austrian Emperor was not thinking so much of a separate peace as of a process of negotiation initiated by Vienna with which Berlin would have to associate itself in order to avoid remaining isolated. Charles was ready to cede Austrian Poland to the Reich, which would then retrocede Alsace-Lorraine to France, with the aim of unblocking the peace process. His attempt collapsed for two reasons: he refused to make any of the territorial concessions that were demanded (Trieste), and the French, in any case very distrustful and fearing an Austro-German manoeuvre, considered that the return of Alsace-Lorraine would be insufficient: the status of the Rhineland must also be modified – a matter which Charles was naturally not in a position to discuss.

More important were four closely intertwined matters: soundings with Germany from Briand (Prime Minister until March 1917), from December 1916 to March 1917; soundings with Austria-Hungary from Painlevé (Minister for War between March and September 1917, then Prime Minister from September to November of that year); the famous Briand-Lancken affair in the spring and summer of 1917; and the 'peace offensive' of the Foreign Secretary, Kühlmann, in September.

Let us deal with these in turn. In December 1916, Briand, apparently doubting the timeliness of the extended war aims which were under discussion in Paris at that time, established a secret contact with Berlin through the intermediary of Professor Haguenin, director of the press and information bureau in the French embassy in Berne, and Count Kessler, an intimate of Wilhelm II, who communicated directly with Bethmann Hollweg. During a series of conversations which continued until March, the two men very delicately discussed the possibility of resolving the Alsace-Lorraine problem, through either autonomy within the Reich or the return of part of the territory to France, with condominium status for the remainder. In exchange, France would grant Germany economic and military guarantees in Alsace-Lorraine (free access to iron ore and demilitarisation) and an economic rapprochement with the Reich after the war; further, Paris would give up the British proposal for the formation of an anti-German bloc after the war. The fall of Briand in March, and Poincaré's determination to maintain the Nivelle offensive of April 1917 despite the strategic disarray following the Russian Revolution and America's entry into the war, brought these soundings to an end. Still somewhat mysterious, they nonetheless reveal a serious divergence at the heart of the French Government in the spring of 1917. Some, including Poincaré, continued to seek a decisive victory in order to realise the extended programme of war aims, as defined since the preceding autumn; this was the reason for the continuation of the Nivelle offensive against objections from part of the government and some of the most senior military leaders. But other responsible figures apparently envisaged the possibility of a negotiated peace; their view was supported by the setback of the Nivelle offensive.

Throughout the spring and summer of 1917, Painlevé maintained various contacts with Vienna. During these contacts, either a separate peace with Austria or a general peace was envisaged, but in the latter case using Vienna to bring pressure to bear on Berlin. With Austria's support, France would recover Alsace-Lorraine. In exchange, the integrity of Austria would be guaranteed (on condition of reform to provide more space for its Slav population, so that it would cease to be a Germanic power allied to Germany). Germany would be compensated for the loss of Alsace-Lorraine by colonial concessions (Indochina and the Congo).

Vienna took these suggestions very seriously. It was even envisaged that the Minister for Foreign Affairs, Czernin, would meet Painlevé in Switzerland. Informed at the beginning of September, Kühlmann, the German Foreign Secretary, also took the soundings seriously. He realised how far Austria was tempted to follow them up, and decided to counter-attack immediately. He had a secret offer sent to London: the Reich declared itself ready to re-establish the integral independence of Belgium. Belgium was by now even more clearly the nerve-point of peace soundings, since Pope Benedict XV's solemn appeal on 1 August to the belligerents to make peace. The only stipulation was the restoration of Belgium. Kühlmann thought that under these conditions Britain would be inclined to make peace and would force France to follow suit: the Reich could always recover at the expense of Russia. Kühlmann's offer was very serious: Berlin would never be closer to accepting a negotiated peace. The British Cabinet studied the Berlin offer at the end of September, and decided to reject it, against Lloyd George's objections. The majority of the Cabinet considered that if the Reich managed to strengthen itself in the East at the expense of Russia, it would renew hostilities a few years later in the West, in much better conditions.

At the same moment, the news broke out of the secret contacts undertaken some months earlier by Briand, now outside the government, and Lancken, head of the German civil administration in Belgium and close to the Emperor. According to Briand, on this occasion the possibility of integral Belgian re-establishment and the restitution of Alsace-Lorraine were considered in exchange for economic concessions. It has often been thought that Briand had been manoeuvred by Lancken in this affair. This is not certain, and on certain points these soundings recall the Haguenin-Kessler soundings. In any case, Painlevé (then Prime Minister) and Lloyd George discussed the affair on

25 September, and they are known to have taken it very seriously. But the British Conservatives in London and Poincaré in Paris united to bring the plan down, judging that it was no more than a German trap.

In the following weeks, the situation changed again, considerably. Encouraged by the perspective of an imminent separate peace with Russia, German aims hardened. In France, Clemenceau's accession to power in November put an end to any perspective other than victory. Britain followed the same evolution, despite two final secret attempts on its part to separate Austria from Germany in December 1917 and March 1918. Further, London only then undertook to demand the return of Alsace-Lorraine to France at the time of peace negotiations.

In April 1918, an allusion by the Austrian Minister for Foreign Affairs, Czernin, to the secret mission of Sixtus von Bourbon Parma in 1917 provoked a very strong reaction from Clemenceau ('Count Czernin was lying'). In this climate, and in the context of struggle against the 'defeatist plots', Briand and Painlevé themselves had to justify their attempts the previous year, when Joseph Caillaux was arrested for defeatism. Further, the very tough treaties imposed by the Central Powers on Russia (the Treaty of Brest-Litovsk) and Romania (Treaty of Bucharest) in March and May 1918 made the general atmosphere less than favourable for peace soundings. By then, the Europeans had lost the last chance of settling the conflict between them, before the effective entry of the United States into the war and into the circle of powers determining the peace. This was the beginning of the end of the era of European worldwide predominance.[14]

1917: The search for a new European Concert: either peace through collective security, or peace through revolution

After the period of 1914 to 1916 when the belligerents could not envisage anything less than a peace through victory, the common feature in the various

14 For this passage in full: Soutou, 'Les marches de l'est'; 'Briand et l'Allemagne au tournant de la guerre (septembre 1916–janvier 1917)', in *Media in Francia. Recueil de mélanges offert à Karl Ferdinand Werner* (Maulévrier: Hérault, 1989); 'Paul Painlevé und die Möglichkeit eines Verhhandlungsfriedens im Kriegsjahr 1917', in Walther L. Bernecker and Volker Dotterweich (eds.), *Deutschland in den internationalen Beziehungen des 19. und 20. Jahrhunderts* (Munich: Ernst Vögel, 1996); and Stevenson, *French War Aims*; Rothwell, *British War Aims*; Guy Pedroncini, *Les négociations secrètes pendant la grande guerre* (Paris: Flammarion, 1969); Wolfgang Steglich, *Der Friedensappell Papst Benedikts XV vom 1. August 1918 und die Mittelmächte* (Wiesbaden: Steiner, 1970); Nathalie Renoton-Beine, *La colombe et les tranchées. Les tentatives de paix de Benoît XV pendant la Grande Guerre* (Paris: Cerf, 2004).

secret negotiations in 1917 was the return to less radical aims. Now the objective was one of a rebalancing (with everyone naturally trying to improve the situation from their own point of view) within the tradition of European diplomacy and was not incompatible with the restoration of the classic European Concert. Furthermore, the peace feelers of 1915 to 1916 aimed at separate peace negotiations or the disabling of an adversary, in order to force on the other enemies very harsh terms. In 1917, the possibility of a general negotiation was back on the agenda. A new Congress of Vienna was conceivable once more. The failure of peace attempts in 1917 once again posed the fundamental problem as to what would be the organisation of the post-war international system? In this questioning, the paradigms of the European Concert, as established in 1815, were left behind.

A new concept, that of 'collective security', was now opposed to the 'Concert of the European Great Powers'. The small powers were increasingly dissatisfied with a system which barely admitted their voice into the debate, no more indeed than the foreign 'nationalities' had in Austria or Russia. Yet these two states were pillars of the Concert of Europe, which they used specifically to support national claims, in the name of 'balance' between the powers. The effect was to make the satisfaction of national claims dependent on the agreement – the concert – of the great European powers.

Collective security was also a reaction to the permanent alliances of peacetime, which ended up bringing war into being in 1914, through an apparently inexorable mechanism, a situation which had made a profound impression at the time. In particular, the Franco-Russian Alliance of 1891 to 1893 (secret and automatically engaged) had appeared to many in July 1914 to be heavy with consequences. Indeed, the leaders themselves were sometimes convinced of this even if they could not say so publicly.

In reaction, the idea emerged that from now on security must be established *with* the potential adversary, by taking him into the diplomatic system, not *against* him, by means of bilateral alliances which to some extent defined the adversarial relationship. This new philosophy inspired President Wilson and the creation in 1919 of the League of Nations which he had called for during the war. Furthermore, many informed observers, reflecting on the different crises and wars in the Balkans, the pogroms in Russia, the recurrent massacres in the Ottoman Empire, and the tensions and crises which they led to in the international system, had come to the view that the reconstruction of Europe around the nation-state model was necessary, since the old dynastic multi-ethnic empires no longer met the needs of the modern world.

These new states, it was immediately evident, would be liberal and democratic, on Western European lines. After all, the war was also ideological and reflected the opposition between the liberal democratic regimes of France and Britain (and the United States, after the exit of Russia from the war), and the Central Powers, still largely traditional, aristocratic, scarcely democratic – undoubtedly constitutional, but not parliamentary. This opposition was fundamental, and was repeated time and again in speeches and propaganda. For example, from the outset the French (the government, and also the fighting forces) considered that they were defending a democratic republican order against 'Prussian militarism' and the Kaiser. After victory over the Central Powers and the establishment of a new international system, the different states would lead a democratic external policy, breaking away from former elite styles: no more 'Cabinet policy', no more secret diplomacy, no more bilateral treaties or secret agreements, no more combinations of great powers at the expense of smaller ones – but a public form of diplomacy open to all nations, respecting their equality in international law, based on treaties ratified by elected assemblies ('open covenants openly arrived at', as Wilson declared in his Fourteen Points of January 1918).

This model of international 'democratic' politics is not a reconstruction by historians: it was very fully understood as such by the activists of the time, as shown, for example, in Wilson's speeches and writings.[15] We observe in passing that this form of politics, profoundly liberal in inspiration, was neither new in 1919 nor invented by Wilson alone; it dated back to the very origins of US diplomacy, which from the outset had wished to break with the traditional methods of European diplomacy.[16] The peace of 1919, a judicial, moral, abstract peace, was also, in a way, the end-point of the Enlightenment.

The system's mode of functioning would be 'collective security': there should be no more patterns of antagonistic alliances, largely considered as the first cause of the disaster of 1914. Instead, there would be regional accords of collective security, specifically including potential adversaries. In 1919 this would be grounded initially in a League of Nations Pact, which required treaties to be deposited with that organisation and compatible with its dispositions, under which an alliance could not take effect until the Council of the League had approved it. This was the end to automatic alliances and secret commitments.

15 Arthur S. Link (ed.), *The Papers of Woodrow Wilson*, 4 vols. (Princeton University Press, 1956–65).

16 Marc Bellissa, 'La diplomatie américaine et les principes du droit des gens (1774–1787)', *Revue d'Histoire Diplomatique*, 111:1 (1997), pp. 3–20.

At the same time, an alternative model appeared in Europe: Leninism, triumphant in Russia. On 15 March 1917, Nicholas II had abdicated in the aftermath of violent riots in Petrograd (the February Revolution, according to the old Orthodox calendar), due primarily to Russian exhaustion in a war that was too hard and too long for the country in its state of relative backwardness. From that moment, two powers coexisted: the provisional government, led by a liberal bourgeoisie with little national representation, and the soviets of workers and soldiers, more socialist in tendency, with at their head the Petrograd Soviet, a veritable counter-power, much more left-leaning, particularly after Lenin's return to Petrograd on 16 April. The return was encouraged by the Germans, who saw in it the means of accelerating Russia's departure from the war. The provisional government wished to keep Russia in the war on the side of the Allies, whose programme of liberal democracy it shared. The Petrograd Soviet, without any doubt closer to the population on this point, called for immediate peace. The failure of the final Russian offensive in July meant the end of the provisional government, while the army disintegrated. On 7 November, Lenin and the Bolsheviks seized power by force, certainly without the active support of the majority of the population. A provisional assembly, elected on the old suffrage and immediately dissolved in December 1918, gave only one-quarter of its seats to the Bolsheviks. But two of Lenin's immediate decisions were popular: immediate peace and land for the peasants. The Allies did not recognise this new regime – which did not bother Lenin, who followed a revolutionary policy and thought he could reach the peoples of the central empires and the Allied nations over the heads of their leaders on the theme of an immediate peace 'without annexations or indemnity'. This would transform the war into a revolution, according to the process that had unfolded in Russia, starting with Germany, the heart of European capitalism. Not recognised by the Allies, he then negotiated the Peace of Brest-Litovsk with the Central Powers. Lenin judged that saving the regime in Russia was the most urgent factor, even at the price of serious economic and territorial concessions. But in the long term he did not reject the installation everywhere of the 'dictatorship of the proletariat'; the creation of communist society, peaceable after the suppression of 'class' contradictions, and worldwide in character. With this revolutionary world programme, Russia (the new regime had also immediately nationalised foreign-owned assets and repudiated tsarist debts) was excluded for a long period from the political, moral, cultural and economic European arena, even though many active political minorities considered that the only way in which to avoid the repetition of war was to adopt the programme of the worldwide communist revolution. For these groups, wars were a consequence of capitalism, and they would vanish together.

Spring 1918: Germany reshapes Europe? Brest-Litovsk and Bucharest

For a while, from the October Revolution to the setback in the Ludendorff offensives in March to May 1918, the Germans were able to believe that their victory was within reach. At the territorial level, from autumn 1917, with the defeat of Russia, the following dynamic could be seen to emerge in Berlin: return to the *status quo ante* in the West, which the Allies, weary of war, would finally end up by accepting, while, in the East, on the ruins of the Russian Empire, Germany would establish political, military and economic protectorates in Poland, Ukraine, the Baltic countries, Finland and Romania. This part of the plan was briefly realised by the Treaties of Brest-Litovsk on 3 March 1918 with Russia and of Bucharest on 7 May with Romania, which without any doubt represented the peak of German ambitions during the First World War. Unquestionably, these were very harsh treaties: Romania became a political and economic protectorate of the Central Powers, Russia lost Poland, Finland, the Baltic states and, more serious still, Ukraine, as all these regions were to become protectorates of the Reich.

But the situation gave rise to radically divergent analyses in Berlin. For the military leaders, the peace treaties in the East would enable the return to the offensive in the West and give them the chance to win the war before the mass arrival of US troops. This was indeed the aim of the series of offensives which began at the end of March on the Western Front. Victory there would make it possible to establish definitively a vast independent ensemble closely controlled by Berlin, from the Ukraine to Belgium, as a permanent feature of German power after the war. As for Bolshevik Russia, there was no question of Germany cooperating with it; the only possibility was to weaken it as much as possible.

For the civilian leaders, on the other hand, there was no possibility of constructing such an independent geopolitical space. It would never be recognised by the Allies and would in any case be inadequate for the demands of the German economy. In their thinking, total victory was an illusion; what they had to do was to play the cards they held with a view to peace negotiations; the best possible conditions at the time must be obtained, in particular to prevent the Allies from depriving Germany of its colonies and subjecting it to permanent economic discrimination. From this point of view, the treaties concluded in the East were provisional and subject to revision when general peace was achieved.

Moreover, in May 1918, Berlin embarked on fresh negotiations with the Russians, against the advice of the military leaders who sought rather to extend the German occupation zone into Russia. The result of these negotiations was the Treaty of Berlin on 27 August, which came down to a considerable revision of the Treaty of Brest-Litovsk: the Germans accepted the prospect of an imminent return of the Ukraine to Russia and the settlement of reciprocal financial obligations in a way that was reasonably favourable to the Russians. Above all, the treaty of 27 August prepared close economic cooperation between the two nations. Furthermore, Berlin and the Bolsheviks came to an agreement to collaborate, potentially militarily, against the White Russians and against Allied intervention in Russia. Evidently, the military theorists were losing ground. This was indeed understood more clearly after the great military defeats of August. But the 'victory' of the civil authorities came too late: the harsh conditions of the treaties of Brest-Litovsk and Bucharest had instantly destroyed any hope that the Allies might still have held of reaching a negotiated compromise peace with the Reich: henceforward, the only acceptable peace would be victorious and imposed. If not, it was thought, Germany, strengthened by the downfall of the Russian Empire and, it was imagined, potentially supported by the Bolsheviks, would regain the ascendant.

1918: Wilsonism and New Diplomacy

Wilson thought at first that responsibility for the outbreak of the war was shared between the Allies and Germany. But, in 1916, as he began to realise that the United States could not stay definitively outside the conflict, he gradually abandoned this fundamentally isolationist view and adopted a much more active internationalist view of America's role in the world. This was generally qualified as the 'Open Door doctrine' (rejection of exclusive zones of political and economic influence as the protected hunting ground for any specific power). With increasing clarity, he was to defend a new vision of international relations, breaking with the secret diplomacy of the traditional European Concert. An open diplomacy, peoples' right to self-determination, freedom of the seas, disarmament – here was the policy that Wilson would defend from then on with increasing firmness, in the name of a worldwide expansion of the values of US political and economic liberalism. He was adopting what could be called the 'Atlantic' policy, no longer isolationist, recommended to him, against the majority of public opinion and the industrialists of America's heartlands, but in the great economic interests of the East Coast and in particular of Wall Street, very close to the City of London and looking forward to close collaboration with the Allies in the post-war world.

Joining the war on the side of the Allies in April 1917 did not modify Wilson's major lines of thought. Immediately rejecting the ensemble of secret agreements concluded between the Allies since the beginning of the war, he was to reassert the 'Open Door' against their exclusive and traditional territorial and economic objectives. He refused to describe himself as an 'ally', but only as an 'associate' of London and Paris. This enabled him – and this was new – to present war aims based on principles that were clearly comprehensible to public opinion and which would be heard as clearly as possible even within the Central Powers. It also allowed him to retain full independence in relation to the Allies and, in universalist language, to promote a worldwide opening for the economic and political values of liberalism wholly in line with the interests of an America which already represented more than one-third of global industrial activity.

Of all the war leaders, only Wilson, in his Fourteen Points of 8 January 1918, raised himself to the level of general principles based essentially on the rejection of secret diplomacy, permanent peacetime alliances and expressions of economic discrimination (which he considered as being the true causes of the war), the extension of the political and economic principles of liberal democracy to the whole of Europe, and the management of the international system as part of a League of Nations. In general terms, Wilson proclaimed the global validity of 'The American Way of Life', in other words democracy and free enterprise, which was in fact his primordial war aim ('to make the world safe for Democracy'). The response in public opinion, on both sides, was at the time truly remarkable.

In his speech of 8 January, Wilson began by reasserting the great principles of open diplomacy, freedom of the seas and economic non-discrimination. But the rest of his speech was more cautious than has sometimes been thought; although it recognised the right to self-determination, it also acknowledged history, and strategic and economic equilibrium. Belgium would be restored, Poland re-established, Alsace-Lorraine returned to France; but neither Austria-Hungary nor Turkey would be dissolved, merely reformed, on the basis of equal rights for their various populations. The frontiers of Italy and the Balkan states would take account of economic and strategic needs. This meant that the break with the principles of the pre-1914 Concert of Europe was not total.

As far as Germany was concerned, Wilson was extremely cautious; there was no question at that moment of imposing a change of regime on Germany; the US President was still convinced that the Reich would remain the leading power in continental Europe, with strong influence over Central and Eastern Europe. This was inevitable in his view, and acceptable on the condition that Berlin accepted the international rules of Wilsonian thinking. In January 1918, Wilson still considered that the democratisation of Germany was not the essential condition for peace with the Reich. For him, there was no question of excluding Germany from the international economic and political order after the war.

It is understandable that the British – and above all the French – allies, who were pursuing far more radical territorial and economic objectives against the Reich and had no intention of accepting this new international order after the war, were very far from satisfied with the Fourteen Points, which were finally directed almost as much against their own plans as against those of the Central Powers. But the hardening of Wilson after the events of the spring of 1918 would finally allow a convergence between the war aims of the Allies and the United States – not total, but sufficient to win the war and impose the treaties of 1919.[17]

The spring of 1918 was when the dialectic of war aims on both sides became visible. The Germans had concluded very tough treaties with the East partly because they feared the punitive political and economic plans of the Allies in prospect for the post-war era; but in return these treaties convinced the Allies, and in particular Wilson, of the comprehensive and irredeemably imperialist nature of German policies. Their attitude hardened further. From that time on, the Allies and Wilson were in agreement in thinking that a profound change of regime and individuals had to be imposed on Germany, an immediate democratisation, as a condition of peace; it was not possible to accept, as Wilson had hitherto been inclined to do, a simple adherence of the Wilhelmine Reich to the international principles of Wilsonian diplomacy.

Furthermore, it would no longer be a question of accepting implicitly, as Washington and London had done to date, any control, even indirect, of Germany over Mitteleuropa. The geopolitical power of the Reich had to be cut back drastically, and on this point Wilson subsequently supported the theories of the British and above all of the French. As a means of pressure

17 Apart from Soutou, *L'Or et le Sang*, cf. the biography of Wilson by Link, *Wilson*; and Lawrence E. Gelfand, *The Inquiry. American Preparation for Peace 1917–1919* (Westport, CT: Greenwood Press, 1976).

essential to force Germany to democratise itself and accept the new international order, the 'economic weapon' was essential. That weapon was Allied control of the world's main raw materials and the possibility of imposing forms of economic and commercial discrimination on the Reich. Wilson now accepted the principle of the 'economic weapon', which he had previously rejected.

Furthermore, Wilson, contrary to his previous position expressed in the Fourteen Points, was now convinced that Austria-Hungary had to be eliminated and the demands for independence of subject minorities supported. He persuaded Lloyd George of this without difficulty, but found Clemenceau much more difficult to convince. In effect, and contrary to currently accepted opinion, the French Government was initially not at all in favour of the break-up of Austria-Hungary and the constitution of small nations in Central and Eastern Europe, based on the nationality principle. There was fear in Paris that Austria, reduced to its German-speaking population, would immediately rejoin the Reich, and more generally that Germany would easily dominate a Central–Eastern Europe split up in this way. Paris would have preferred to keep Austria-Hungary (the French Government was still secretly trying to save it in October 1918) with the establishment of an enlarged Poland, including Lithuania and part of Ukraine. It was hoped that these conditions would make it possible to contain Germany. Wilson's new policy was only accepted with difficulty in Paris, and efforts were then made to initiate the creation of states as powerful as possible, at the cost of their ethnic cohesion. As a result, in the winter of 1919, France played an essential role in the definition of Polish and Czechoslovakian frontiers, despite ethnographic contradictions, and with the fundamental concern of building as powerful a set of barriers as possible against Germany. On this point, the treaties of 1919 and 1920 effectively ratified French policy during the winter of 1919.

Of course the agreement between French, British and Americans, although deeper since the spring of 1918, was far from total. Clemenceau continued, discreetly but firmly, to pursue the separate French aims far beyond Wilsonian principles: the new frontier with Germany would not be that of 1815, but that of 1790, that is including the largest part of the Saarland; the Rhineland would be detached from the Reich and in one way or another would come under French control; Luxembourg would become a republic closely linked to France.

But above all the British and French disagreed with Wilson on a fundamental point: for them, the political and economic organisation of the world after the war (the League of Nations and the economic accords among Allies) must exclude Germany, even democratised, for a very long time. For Wilson, on the other hand, as soon as that country had reformed itself and adhered to the international principles of Wilsonianism, Germany had to be welcomed without hesitation into the new international community arising out of the war. In particular, Wilson did not accept the idea, which was firmly defended in Paris and also in London, that Germany must be subject to lasting economic and commercial discrimination after the war. For Wilson, such discrimination could only be temporary, and must cease as soon as Berlin bowed to the new political and economic world order.[18]

National self-determination as new European paradigm, and its limits

The principle of nationalities, that is the radical challenge to multi-national states based on a historical and dynastic legitimacy in the name of the right to self-determination (democratic and national legitimacy), was very present during the war. Indeed, it was one of the essential stakes of the conflict, but in a much more complex way than is generally realised. The nationality principle served to justify the aspiration of some nationalities (or more exactly of groups which spoke in their name) to form themselves into independent states, using the opportunity of the war. We think here first of the Polish National Committee, founded in August 1917 by Dmowski, and the National Council of Czech Countries, founded in June 1916 by Masaryk and Bénès. These two organs played a considerable part in achieving Allied acceptance of the concept of Polish and Czechoslovak independence and to bring them (very gradually, as we shall see) to commitment to this independence in their war aims.[19] But it must also be seen that the claims of these two bodies, although based on the 'modern' and 'democratic' principle of nationalities, in fact equally reflected claims to legitimacy which were above all historical in nature. Dmowski's Greater Poland would have included many Lithuanians and Ukrainians; it took its inspiration largely from the history of Poland in the seventeenth century. The same could be said of the Czechoslovakia of Bénès

18 Apart from the works cited above, cf. Jean-Baptiste Duroselle, *Clemenceau* (Paris: Fayard, 1988).

19 In particular, for the action of the Polish National Committee towards France, see Georges-Henri Soutou (also ed.), Ghislain de Castelbajac and Sébastien de Gasquet, *Recherches sur la France et le problème des Nationalités pendant la Première Guerre mondiale (Pologne, Lithuanie, Ukraine)* (Paris: Presses de l'Université de Paris-Sorbonne, 1995), particularly pp. 63–97.

and Masaryk. Further, these claims were by no means universally supported by the interested parties: in Poland, Pilsudski, Dmowski's rival who triumphed in the struggle for power at the end of the war, held more moderate ideas. Further, it must not be thought that before 1917 or even 1918 all Poles and all Czechs favoured the Allied cause: some thought it possible to reach understanding with Austria, even, in the case of Poland, with Germany, at least temporarily and tactically. This was, with nuances, Pilsudski's position. Finally, the question of relations with Russia was complex, even for many Poles; as in Czech lands, there existed a Russophile current that was fairly strongly opposed to the Western-inclined orientations of Bénès and Masaryk.

The principle of nationality also of course served well to justify the war aims of certain belligerents (Alsace-Lorraine for France, the irredentist provinces for Italy, Croatia and Slovenia for Serbia). But it was also, much more ambiguously, a means to weaken the cohesion of the multi-national adversary, by arousing centrifugal movement; the German policy towards the Russian Empire is very relevant in this respect. There was also a historical dynamic which meant that sometimes, a policy of this kind, using national divisions and starting as a simple diversionary manoeuvre, would ultimately have long-term consequences unforeseen at the outset.

On this point, it is important to stress the decisive importance of Germany's role in ethnic liberation in Poland and Russia, a little-known and essential fact. This is crucial for an understanding of the post-war period: in this region, Germany was not only the occupier, but also, facing Russia, the liberator. In effect, from the beginning of the war, Berlin upheld the rights of foreign nationalities. It began as a secret service manoeuvre, extending as far as the Caucasus, to weaken Russia in the war.[20] Initially a purely tactical manoeuvre, it created a movement. In this respect, German policy became strategically important in 1916, when Berlin understood that it would not be possible to reach agreement with the Tsar over a separate peace. From this point on, there were no more arrangements to be agreed. The foreign nationality card had to be played to the end, to prepare a radical reduction of the Russian Empire and substitute German influence for Russian domination throughout the region from the Vistula to the Dniepr.[21]

The broad stages of this policy were as follows: on 5 November 1916, the Austro-German declaration proclaimed the formation of a Polish state; during

20 Wolfdieter Bihl, *Die Kaukasus-Politik der Mittelmächte* (Vienna: Böhlau Verlag, 1975).
21 On all of this, cf. Fischer, *Griff nach der Weltmacht*.

the summer of 1917, the beginning of the process of creating Baltic states, with councils representing the population (even if the German element was over-represented in these councils); on 9 February 1918, the conclusion of a separate peace treaty with the Ukraine at Brest-Litovsk, a return to recognition of Ukrainian independence.

All this upset the situation. The Reich naturally had second thoughts and counted firmly on developing economic and military ties with the new states, which would at times have been handed to German princes. In this case, Berlin would have exercised strong influence, genuine informal control. But some of the independence-seeking leaders least open to challenge, who were in no case collaborators or Germanophiles (Pilsudski in Poland, Gabrys in Lithuania, Pietlura in the Ukraine) were not mistaken: they understood that despite German afterthoughts the Berlin proposals constituted a stage which they could turn to their benefit. For a short time at least, they were in step with Germany, without illusions but decisively looking to the future of their independent countries.

This was particularly true in that until 1918 the Allies remained very cautious over the nationality principle, contrary to general belief, and despite certain vague declarations. The territorial promises made by the French and British to the countries which they wished to take into the war on their side should not be confused with the adoption of the nationality principle as such, as the axis of their war aims. Of course the defection of the Russian ally in 1917 was a real problem for Paris. Again, contrary to what is often believed, it is not possible to draw the conclusion from this that in Eastern Europe France would henceforward use the foreign nationalities for additional support. This was obviously not possible at the time of the Franco-Russian Alliance: if Austria-Hungary, the Ottoman Empire and even Germany could be weakened by encouragement of their minority nationalities to win their independence, the Russian Empire itself had millions of ethnic foreigners. Before 1917, the question therefore could not be openly addressed. Paris was very cautious on this point, and in October 1918 Clemenceau would still try to rescue an Austria-Hungary (certainly largely reduced) so that Germany could not lay hands on Austria. In fact, the nationality principle in the strict sense was not genuinely at the heart of French concerns during the war – it was used only as an instrument of policy. The essential point was to build a counterbalance in Eastern Europe to German power. For this reason, in 1919 France would support the constitution of a Poland embracing numerous minority populations, and multi-ethnic Czechoslovakia and a Yugoslavia, behind the discourse of 'oppressed nationalities'.

But it must be repeated that it was only in 1918 that the Allies – and still with great reservations and second thoughts and under pressure from Wilson – adopted the nationality principle, as (up to a certain point) the axis of their peace policy. Britain was barely interested in nationalities; it thought that inevitably the whole of Central and Eastern Europe would be controlled by the central empires and Russia, in proportions dependent on the outcome of the war. According to a geopolitical vision expressed from this time by Mackinder, who was listened to closely by certain of Lloyd George's counsellors, Great Britain was primarily concerned with the coastlines of Europe and the Middle East and not with Central and Eastern Europe.[22] France was to follow Wilson, but remained more reticent than is generally believed today. In consequence, at the end of June 1918, Paris recognised Czechoslovakia in principle; but this recognition was imposed by the Chamber of Deputies under pressure from the radical-socialists, warm partisans of the nationalities principle, on an unwilling Clemenceau. Again, in October and November 1918, at the moment of the armistices, Paris tried to save Austria-Hungary – for it was feared that if these countries ceased to exist, the Austrian part would immediately reunite with Germany.[23] As for Serbia, in the autumn of 1918, to avoid clashing with Italy, the government hesitated to uphold the 'Yugoslav' claims fundamentally.[24]

For Poland, whose independence had been recognised by Russia after the February Revolution, Paris became more strongly engaged. The creation of a Polish army in June 1917 and a speech by Prime Minister Alexandre Ribot in August 1917 saluting the reconstitution and independence of Poland prove this point. But it was not until after Brest-Litovsk, when all hope of bringing Russia back into the war had vanished, that Paris took the final step. On 3 June 1918, after three months of negotiations, Paris obtained from the British and the Italians – initially very reluctant – a declaration of the official recognition on the principle of the creation of an independent Polish state with access to the

22 For British policy, cf.: Rothwell, *British War Aims*; and Soutou, *L'Or et le Sang*.

23 Louis-Pierre Laroche, 'L'affaire Dutasta: les dernières conversations diplomatiques pour sauver l'empire des Habsbourg', *Revue d'Histoire Diplomatique*, 1 (1994), pp. 51–76.

24 On the very complex game of France in 1918–19 towards Yugoslavia (Paris preferred a Yugoslav state clearly run by the Serbs, who it was judged would be firmer in the face of Germany, and more acceptable for Italy than a more authentic 'Yugoslav' state in which Croats and Slovenes, in direct rivalry with Rome, would have played a more important role), cf. François Grumel-Jacquignon, *La Yougoslavie dans la stratégie française de l'Entre-deux-guerres (1918–1935)* (Brussels: Peter Lang, 1999).

sea. But even then, Paris did not adhere strictly to the nationality principle: it was decided to favour a Greater Poland, as envisaged by Dmowski and the Polish National Committee, including Lithuania and Ukraine, so as to constitute a counterbalance against Germany, without too much concern for true lines of nationality.

Where Russia's other foreign nationals were concerned, Clemenceau's government showed great caution. They had no wish to weaken Russia, even Lenin's Russia, in the face of Germany; at certain moments (before Brest-Litovsk), it was thought possible to reach a *modus vivendi* with Lenin, on condition of not appearing to want the disintegration of Russia; after Brest-Litovsk, when it was decided to support the Whites, there was also no question of recognising the foreign nationalities, since the Whites had conclusively decided to reconstitute imperial unity. As for Ukraine, no one in Paris believed in the reality of its right to independence: simply it was conceded that it was moving away from Moscow, while anarchy or Bolshevism reigned in Russia, and that the movement for Ukrainian independence was entirely relative. As far as the Baltic countries were concerned, it was not until the end of December 1918 that the Clemenceau government agreed to recognise them, under pressure from Wilson and the Chamber. In fact, the creation of the Baltic states was contrary to the vision in Paris of Russia, or alternatively of Greater Poland, and constituted a sprinkling of states along the German frontiers, that is to say exactly what Clemenceau did not want.

In other words, Clemenceau and the diplomatic and military personnel (with numerous missions in place, in particular in Ukraine) showed themselves very cautious; there was no move towards recognition of nationalities except under pressure from Wilson and the radical-socialists in the Chamber; but the latter made it very clear that there was no question of applying the nationalities question absolutely, except in a modulated form. There was a wish to constitute viable states against Germany, or which appeared as such in 1918 and 1919, such as Czechoslovakia, a powerful Poland, a Serbia or a Romania vastly strengthened by the peace treaties. The fundamental idea in these circles was that the French influence would rely on the new nations. This represented, in part, the ideology of the radical left of the pre-war period, its distrust of the Russian Empire and its determination to break with the Concert of the European Great Powers, and the realist acknowledgement that Russia, the traditional ally in reserve, was for the moment out of the game. As we have seen, recognition of the nationality principle remained very limited, restricted as it was by considerations of political opportunity and geostrategic balance.[25] This was very marked for the French, it was present with the British, and Wilson himself was cautious for longer than is recognised. Certain of his collaborators, like the Secretary of State Robert Lansing, were openly sceptical: how is it possible, they asked, to define in Central Europe, in such mixed populations, sufficiently clear national lines for the construction of stable nations?

The Armistice: the beginning of the end, or the end of the beginning?

Liberated in the East by the Peace of Brest-Litovsk, Germany launched a series of offensives in the West in the hope of decisive victory before the large-scale arrival of US troops. But the Allies rallied after some very difficult moments, and the French and British finally established a unified command. From that moment on, they had considerable superiority in terms of numbers and *matériel* and, with powerful aviation and a new army and tanks, they could finally lead a very mobile war. From August, the much-weakened German armies retreated steadily, while the Army of the East in Salonica took action and forced Bulgaria to conclude an armistice on 29 September. There was nothing more to prevent the Allied armies from advancing the length of the Danube up to Germany. Germany was therefore defeated – and defeated on the ground: the numbers in the line melted away under the force of the offensives.

Faced with the threat of the collapsing front line, Ludendorff thought up a skilful manoeuvre. As long as the German troops were still on enemy soil, and without waiting for the now foreseeable catastrophe, a carefully managed exit from the war would be achieved through an equally controlled transformation of the Reich. On 29 September 1918, when the Bulgarian armistice was announced, Ludendorff declared to the government that an armistice demand must be addressed to the Allies, but – and herein lay the skill – on the basis of the Fourteen Points proclaimed by President Wilson on 8 January 1918 (that is, on the basis of two essential German interests, the right to self-determination and non-discrimination in economic and commercial matters). Furthermore, added Ludendorff, a new Chancellor must be named at the head of the Reich and install a parliamentary regime; until then, the Chancellor had depended

25 Cf. Georges-Henri Soutou (ed.), *Recherches sur la France et le problème des Nationalités pendant la Première Guerre mondiale* (Paris: Presses de l'Université de Paris-Sorbonne, 1995).

uniquely on the Emperor – now he would be answerable to the Reichstag. The purpose of this second proposal was to win the sympathy of Wilson, who since the spring had increasingly insisted on the need to end the authoritarian nature of the Reich. It was also designed to try to reduce the rise in popular discontent, apparent since the previous year and which was eventually to end in revolution, in Berlin and in the capitals of the Reich's states, on 7 to 9 November. Ultimately, its aim – and it must be stated immediately that this goal was achieved, with the greatest consequences as a result – was to shield the military establishment from its responsibilities in the eyes of public opinion: in essence, it was the military who had led the war, at least since 1916, but it would be for the civilians to negotiate the Armistice and then the peace.

This sudden move by Ludendorff naturally came like a thunderbolt for the government, parliament and public opinion, carefully misled by the military headquarters, who continued to evoke the victories of the spring and early summer. After the great successes of the treaties of Brest-Litovsk with the Russian Bolsheviks in March and with Romania in May, they imagined that peace was within their grasp. But Ludendorff attracted attention: on 3 October, Prince Max von Baden, known for his liberalism, became Chancellor and in the summer of 1917 formed a government representing the majority in the Reichstag (social-democrats, liberals, Catholics of the *zentrum*). Very logically, the domestic reforms followed at the speed of a forced march: electoral reform in Prussia on 24 October (the primordial element for any democratisation of the Reich) and, on 28 October, reform which transformed the imperial constitution into a parliamentary monarchy.

The second element in Ludendorff's manoeuvre, the international gambit, was launched by the new Max von Baden government on 4 October with the demand to open negotiations for an armistice. But the manoeuvring continued: the Germans did not officially address the ensemble of the Allies and 'associates' (recalling that the United States were not legally linked with France and Great Britain), but only President Wilson. Hoping to forestall the harsher aims of Paris and London, Germany wished to conclude the Armistice on the basis of the Fourteen Points. These would enable the undoubtedly German territories to remain within the Reich, its unity immune to challenge. It is clear that although Wilsonianism had hitherto opposed the broad war aims followed by Berlin, it could constitute a guarantee for the future of defeated Germany: its loss of territory would be limited and dislocation and economic subjection prevented.

Furthermore, the right to self-determination would prevent the surrender of Poland and the Baltic States to Russia. In these circumstances it was clear that the Reich would certainly continue to exercise a profound influence, even if indirect, on these countries. Max von Baden's entire strategy at the end of the war and during the Armistice negotiations therefore consisted in trying to press Wilson, in the name of the Fourteen Points, to halt the much more aggressive plans of the French and the British. This strategy was to be partly successful, for at the moment of the Armistice of 11 November 1918, the Reich indeed won the guarantee that the peace would be established on the basis of the Fourteen Points – but only in part, because Wilson had considerably hardened his attitude towards Germany since the spring. It took time for Berlin to grasp this fact. It certainly forced the Reich into a much tougher Armistice than Berlin had anticipated, including in particular the evacuation not only of Belgium and northern France, but also of Alsace-Lorraine and the left bank of the Rhine. In addition, it required a greater degree of democratisation in the German constitution than had initially been envisaged, but it also required the Allies to recognise the Fourteen Points, as the basis of the future peace. They accepted this on 4 November, after a month of resistance. It should be remembered that, in January 1918, Paris and London had taken great care to avoid committing themselves formally to the Fourteen Points; for Wilson it was 'now or never' for them to be forced into acceptance. French diplomacy was immediately faced with many problems: it would not be possible to question the structure of the Reich in the peace treaty directly, and the experts feared that a democratised Germany would in the end be even more centralised than the old Empire, with its structures still largely federal.

Furthermore, the Fourteen Points would limit reparations to the 'restoration' of the invaded regions. They did not, for example, cover pensions which, after such a war, must be agreed for the wounded and the families of the dead. Still less did they deal with the total cost of the war, or even a 'war indemnity' (as France had had to pay after 1871). This was contrary to traditional European practice, and much less extensive than Paris and London had initially planned to inflict on Germany. And above all, the notes exchanged between Berlin and Washington through 5 November indicated that 'the peace would be based' on the Fourteen Points. For Berlin, in its defeat, this was a certain guarantee – but it would prove less effective than the initial German hopes.

Finally, the Reich signed a very tough Armistice on 11 November 1918, at Rethondes in the Forest of Compiègne. Germany had to hand over considerable quantities of weaponry and rolling stock, and its war fleet had to be given up; it was subsequently sunk by its crews at Scapa Flow, off the north of Scotland. Unable to resume operations, Germany now saw its military defeat confirmed. In addition, it had to evacuate Belgium and the north of France, which it had occupied since 1914, as well as Alsace-Lorraine and the left bank of the Rhine, which was immediately occupied by Allied troops. Finally, the rigorous blockade imposed on the Reich would remain in force, strangling the German economy; indeed (apart from humanitarian food deliveries), it continued in essentials until July 1919. In order to maintain pressure on Germany, the Armistice, which was concluded for one month only, was renewable each month. In the practical preparation of the clauses of the Armistice, the British and French had undoubtedly achieved a hardening of its conditions, as we shall see, but the Germans had built up their illusions on Wilson's determination to put the Reich beyond any capacity for harm, and had underestimated the fundamental unity of its adversaries.

Meanwhile, in the Middle East, the Moudros Armistice on 31 October had brought the war with Turkey to an end, and the Allies occupied the Straits. But it was Britain which dominated the situation in this theatre of operations, which would later lead to serious friction with France. London had committed 1 million men to the Middle East, and France a single regiment: but the great ambitions developed in Paris for this region since the beginning of the war were immediately compromised.

On 3 November, the Armistice of Villa Giusti was signed between the Italian General Staff and General Staff of an Austria-Hungary which no longer existed since its disintegration a few days earlier. This meant that Italy controlled large stretches of South-East Europe on the borders of Austria and in the Balkans. In 1919 and throughout the interwar years, France would have to take account of this in relation to the Adriatic, the Balkans and the Danube regions – much more so than was initially realised in Paris, and certainly much more than it would have wished.

The situation, in fact, was far from totally satisfactory for France: in effect, since the autumn of 1917, the British and the Americans had been playing a growing role in the war in military but also economic terms. France, despite its undeniable victory, carried relatively less weight than at the outbreak of the war. The Rethondes Armistice was obviously very satisfactory for the French in some ways – the immediate return of Alsace-Lorraine, occupation of the Rhineland – but, as we have seen, Paris had been forced to accept the basic line of the Fourteen Points. This severely restricted the potential accomplishment of longer-term French objectives: permanent military occupation, even annexation, of the Rhineland; permanent economic control in Germany; and the potential break-up of the Reich, or at least its transformation into a loose confederation. And in the Balkans, above all in the Middle East, the situation at the end of the war was not exactly what the French leaders had hoped for. Taking the armistices as a whole, and not only the Rethondes agreement, as too often happens, the French position as victor was weaker than it appeared, and certainly less strong than that of Britain.

Wilson wanted to create a new international system, substituting itself for a Concert of Europe which in his eyes had been no more than the selfish instrument of the great European powers and an essential part of the process which had led to war in 1914. This was the whole point of the remarkable parallel negotiations led by Wilson in October 1918, with the Germans on one side and the Allies on the other, to gain world recognition for his Fourteen Points as the foundation for the future peace – while Paris and London continued to think more traditionally, in terms of a new European balance designed to subjugate the Reich. The only problem with this was that the French wanted an active geopolitical equilibrium, with the Allies permanently engaged in the whole of the continent to control Germany, while the British wanted a quasi-automatic equilibrium in Europe which would release them from direct engagement and allow them to return to what was essential in their eyes, in other words the Empire and the world. The realisation of such an equilibrium obviously required that France should not be too powerful, even if it was wrong to think (as the French frequently thought in the 1920s, 1930s and even the 1940s) that, after 11 November 1918, London was committed to just a single idea: the reduction of French power.

These fundamental disagreements were clear and broke out immediately after the Armistice. As a result, the French and the British succeeded in having a clause included in the Armistice to maintain the German blockade. All of the world understood that this would affect the future, since Paris and London wished to subject the post-war Reich to permanent economic discrimination, for which the continuing blockade would be the ideal instrument. But immediately after the Armistice, the Americans prepared to return to supplying Germany once more; this would initially be under 'humanitarian' cover, but the re-establishment of Germany in the global liberal and economic frame as soon as possible was clearly part of their thinking. Given that the United States were then alone in having the material resources available and a currency which had not devalued against the gold standard, their point of view was obviously crucial, and from the beginning of 1919 the British fell in with this. The French were isolated with their projects of 'organised liberalism' and permanent inter-Allied economic entente, designed equally to facilitate the reconstruction of France and the permanent weakening of Germany.

The situation was even clearer in the geopolitical domain. Analysis of the negotiations in October and early November between the Allies' military and political authorities, over the military clauses of the future Armistice, show the relevant second thoughts clearly: the French wanted their occupation to extend right up to the Rhine, and even the bridgeheads at Cologne, Coblenz and Mainz, while the British did not wish it to go beyond the limits of Alsace-Lorraine. The reason given was their fear of seeing the Germans reject an excessively harsh Armistice, but in fact the internal English documents show clearly that the real fear was of seeing the French settle permanently into the Rhineland – a fear enhanced by the concept of the 'military frontier on the Rhine' that the French leaders had no hesitation in defending. Clemenceau gave his de facto support; his opposition to Foch on this point was not so much concern with the basis, contrary to what has sometimes been said, as the fact that he judged this question to be one of political power and not a matter for the military authorities.

It will be noted, in addition, that after 11 November 1918 Great Britain had realised its essential war aims: Belgium was evacuated and would be restored; and Germany was decisively weakened and deprived of its fleet, the main threat to Britain. A radically new European equilibrium would be established, which the British expected to manage in line with their own ideas. France was certainly victorious, but weakened; it would recover Alsace-Lorraine and enter the Rhineland, but all its other objectives (definitive status of the left bank of the Rhine, the status of Germany, the question of the Saarland and Luxembourg, reparations, the economic reorganisation of Western Europe) remained hanging on the future peace treaty. France considered that it held moral capital in relation to its Allies: 'yesterday soldier of God, today soldier of Humanity, France will always be the soldier of the Ideal', as Clemenceau proclaimed in his magnificent speech to the Chamber on 11 November 1918. Contrary to frequent thinking, this was not false; Lloyd George and Wilson recognised France's losses and wanted to see its security assured, with German hegemony over Europe eliminated once and for all. But they were not yet ready to accept all French demands, which in their eyes would risk compromising the new international system that they wished to establish – and which in particular would have fostered the German wish for revenge. Weakened by the loss of 1.3 million men and innumerable war-disabled men, entire regions ruined, despite its considerable military strength in 1918, France was in no state to impose its will: after the Armistice, France would need to negotiate craftily to keep the greatest number of possible options open.[26]

In addition, the Armistice did not resolve everything, particularly in Eastern Europe. Although the Rethondes text, once again very political in its terms, stipulated that the Reich renounce the treaties of Brest-Litovsk and Bucharest (Article XV), Article XII imposed on Germany the obligation to remain in the territories which before the war had belonged to Russia (therefore the Baltic states and Ukraine) until the Allies judged otherwise, 'taking into account the internal situation of these territories'. Of course it was a matter for the Allies to stop the Bolsheviks settling in on the heels of the retreating Germans, but the consequence was that until the spring of 1919 it was German troops who continued to hold the eastern boundaries of Europe and the Baltic states. Lenin accused the 'capitalist' powers, the Reich and the Allies, of anti-Soviet complicity, and historiography has sometimes – excessively – tended to stress this collusion as fact.[27] But until they received the text of the treaty, on 7 May, which was an unpleasant shock for the Germans, Berlin was convinced that in the name of European defence against Bolshevism, the Reich could continue to play a leading role in Eastern Europe and thus remain a great power. This should be emphasised: after the Armistice, the Reich, going through what was certainly a difficult phase, still considered itself a great power. The full measure of the defeat was not grasped until the Treaty of Versailles. This psychological gap obviously had the greatest consequences for the immediate rejection of a *Diktat* that was unexpected and for which they were unprepared, however odd this might seem in hindsight. The Germans had genuinely expected to be treated in Wilsonian fashion, in conformity with the notes exchanged with Washington before 11 November, which was only very partially the case.[28]

Furthermore, from 1918, the Allies were fundamentally divided over Bolshevik Russia, even though they had sent troops there from March of that year. Initially, despite Brest-Litovsk, this intervention was designed to attempt the reconstitution of an Eastern Front against the Reich. After 11 November, the motivation was obviously strictly anti-Bolshevik. But the

26 For this passage in full, cf. Pierre Renouvin, *L'armistice de Rethondes* (Paris: Gallimard, 1968), pp. 210–12.

27 Arno J. Mayer, *Politics and Diplomacy of Peacemaking: Containment and Counterrevolution at Versailles, 1918–1919* (New York: Knopf, 1967).

28 Georges-Henri Soutou, 'La France et l'Allemagne en 1919', in Jean-Marie Valentin *et al.* (eds.), *La France et L'Allemagne entre les deux guerres mondiales* (Presses Universitaires de Nancy, 1987).

Allies were not fundamentally in agreement. Wilson wanted the Russians to be able to decide for themselves, without external intervention – and although US troops had been sent to Vladivostok, this was essentially in order to watch the Japanese there, whose imperialism he distrusted. Lloyd George was above all preoccupied with the fastest possible recovery of British trade with Russia. Clemenceau had a more complex vision, based on a French policy of intervention which, in one form or another, was to continue until the summer of 1920 and which had as its objective the reconstruction of a powerful and democratic Russian federation. This new Russia would break with tsarism as much as with Bolshevism, but its democratic reforms and federal organisation could enable it to retain the foreign territories within its borders and maintain the former geopolitical area of tsarist Russia. It would constitute a counterweight against Germany, the primordial French obsession.

Nor was there agreement over the treatment of Germany. Wilson and Lloyd George counted above all on the calming virtues of democracy, which could not fail to penetrate rapidly a Reich relieved of its princely houses and noble aristocracy, hitherto very powerful, and which would make it possible to bring Germany into the new liberal world order. On this point Clemenceau was much more sceptical. In addition, the British and Americans were strongly opposed to any annexation, or even to any prolonged French presence in the Rhineland, in order to avoid creating an Alsace-Lorraine situation in reverse and to avoid disrupting reconciliation with Germany immediately on its departure. On this point, Clemenceau was very cautious, although he was in fact more active than was acknowledged in the Rhineland. Moreover, on 16 February 1919, he declared to the Commission for Foreign Affairs in the Senate that the Rhineland would be constituted as an independent state, occupied, and linked to France by a customs union: 'in fact, one would occupy it until the country was disposed to reunite with France'.[29] Without going into details here, we should be clear that he was fully informed of what was happening in this region, and that he allowed the military and the secret services to sustain the Rhineland autonomists – it is important to distinguish them here from the separatists, in whom the French secret services did not believe. The goal was the promotion of an autonomous Rhineland, separate from Prussia, in a decentralised Germany; and this policy was pursued despite the setback of the Dorten attempt in May 1919. For Clemenceau, matters must not be hurried, but should be sensitive and prompt, and should not prevent any development if the Rhinelanders truly wished it. At the same time, the

29 Soutou, 'La France et les marches de l'est', p. 384.

French High Commissioner in the Rhine territories, Tirard, was directed to promote the French democratic model in the Rhineland. Clemenceau's Rhineland policy was thus located at two levels: first, a cultural and 'republican' influence on Germany overall, apart from the Rhineland; but if the Rhinelanders wished for a broader autonomy in relation to Berlin, France would not prevent them.[30] All possibilities thus remained open, and Clemenceau could reconcile his undoubted liberalism and rejection of annexations with his determination to improve French security.[31] Paris would pursue this policy until 1924. This divergence from the Anglo-Saxon attitude would subsequently be a heavy burden on France's foreign policy.

The Allies were also not in agreement over Germany unity. For the British and Americans, there could be no question of reopening the question, while the French were much more ambivalent. Ideas often raised in secret among the leaders, and much more openly among experts and publicists during the war (to transform the Reich into a vague confederation, or at least reconsider Bismarckian unity with its tendency to centralisation), were in the ascendant in Paris at the time of the Armistice. The will to reconsider the structures of the Reich is clear. However, these ideas were not truly picked up again subsequently by the French Government. In particular, Clemenceau was convinced that German unity was solid and that France had to abandon its illusions on this point (the Reich was not going to dissolve itself overnight). However, the French position in 1919 was more complex and nuanced than has been recognised, particularly since between the centralised Reich and its complete dissolution lay a full range of possible intermediate solutions – a confederation evoking the German past, or 'federalism', that is greater autonomy in relation to Berlin. In particular, Clemenceau took a considerable interest in Bavaria which, it was thought, might detach itself from Berlin.[32]

Finally, it should be added that in the autumn of 1918 the French Government had a clear geopolitical vision of the role of Central and Eastern Europe. This vision was much stronger than that of the British, and much less obsessed

30 Pierre Jardin, 'La politique rhénane de Paul Tirard (1920–1923)', *Revue d'Allemagne*, 21:2 (1989), pp. 208–16.

31 Cf. George-Henri Soutou, 'The French peacemakers and their home front', in Manfred B. Boemecke *et al.* (eds.), *The Treaty of Versailles. A Reassessment after 75 Years* (Cambridge University Press, 1998).

32 On these questions, cf. Georges-Henri Soutou, 'La France et la Bavière, 1866–1949', in Bayerischer Staatsarchiv and Archives Nationales, *France Bayern* (Paris: Biro, 2006); and 'La France et le problème de l'unité et du statut international du Reich, 1914–1924', *Le statut international de l'Allemagne. Des traités de Westphalie aux accords '2+4'*, studies collected by Georges-Henri Soutou and Jean-Marie Valentin, *Études Germaniques*, 59:4 (2004), pp. 745–93.

with the ideology of the human right to self-determination than that of the Americans. The first objective, paradoxically, was to avoid Germany gaining any benefit from the right to self-determination by absorbing Austria at the moment when the other parts of the Empire were achieving independence; the vote in the Austrian Parliament in November 1918 in favour of rejoining Germany shows that this was a genuine problem. And, realising that the Russian Revolution and the end of Austria-Hungary meant the end of any counterbalance to the Reich in Eastern Europe, Foch and the French military missions in Central and Eastern Europe played a determining role in settling the frontiers of the new states. These were conceived much more to enable them to form an 'eastern barrier' against Germany than according to ethnographic considerations or linked to rights to independence. In addition, economic penetration into these regions was actively being planned, to eradicate German influence.[33] It should be added that in the Balkan and Danube regions of Europe in 1918 to 1919 and, subsequently, the real problem for France was not so much Germany or the Anglo-Saxons, but Italy![34]

Conclusion

In slightly modifying Clausewitz's best-known quotation, one could say that: 'Peace is the continuation of war by other means.' This formula can certainly be accurately applied to the period that began on 11 November 1918 and which was to end with the signing of the treaties of 1919 to 1920. Theoretically, an armistice is a suspension of hostilities, which does not bring a state of war to an end, but opens the way to negotiations, and which remains politically neutral. In fact, the Armistice of 1918 prejudged the consideration of a certain number of questions essential to the future peace. Moreover, the same could be said of the other armistices agreed in the autumn of 1918 with Bulgaria, Turkey and Austria-Hungry, no doubt less well known, but also extremely important. It was a matter of armistice agreements that were not purely military, but were politico-military in nature; hence the importance of this period during which the Great War was halted, but the peace treaties were still awaited. At the same time, it was seen to have come about as the result of the very rapid military end of the war together with the rapid rise in strength of the war

33 Georges-Henri Soutou, 'L'impérialisme du pauvre: la politique économique du gouvernment française en Europe centrale et orientale de 1918 à 1929', *Relations internationales*, 7 (1976), 219–39.

34 Frédéric Le Moal, *La France et l'Italie dans les Balkans 1914–1919. Le contentieux adriatique* (Paris: L'Harmattan, 2006).

aims of the different warring nations. The denouement pushed aside the issue that everyone had in mind at the beginning of the war: a swift, 'clean sweep', followed by general negotiation in traditional style to establish a new European equilibrium, but without any fundamental break with the 'Concert of Powers' established since 1815. This would not happen.

This politicisation of the armistices, and in particular that of Rethondes, relates to two essential factors. First of all, it was what all the belligerents, on both sides, wanted: Germans, Americans, British, French – all wished to contribute some clauses to the text of the Armistice to bring them fundamentally into line politically with the peace negotiations ahead, in order to achieve the war aims that they had defined since 1914 or 1917. Furthermore, these negotiations did not take place at all as initially expected. An inter-Allied conference in London at the beginning of December 1918 had settled the location for the Peace Conference (Paris, which meant that France would preside over the discussions) and the broad lines of the programme, generally following the proposals of French diplomacy. First, the preliminaries for peace would be established among the Allies, that is the broad lines of the various treaties to be concluded, then the conquered powers would be invited to negotiate the details. This was altogether in line with the usual practice (no different from the way in which matters were organised in 1814 and 1815, a precedent constantly recalled in the French notes after the Armistice); but as the discussions among the Allies were much more difficult and lengthy than anticipated, they only came to an end in April 1919. And the text to which they gave birth in no way consisted of simple preliminaries. Here was a complete instrument of 439 articles touching on virtually every aspect of life in the Reich. It was delivered to the Germans on 7 May and they were required to sign on 28 June. Suddenly, there were no preliminaries, and matters remained under 'Armistice' conditions, an essential point, until 28 June 1919 – even, in fact, until the Versailles Treaty took effect on 10 January 1920. This meant that the Armistice was no simple period of parenthesis: for fourteen months it governed Europe, and it set certain subsequent developments in place irreversibly.

It has been established that neither the British nor the French models for the post-war period made it possible to envisage the reconstruction of a well-balanced and truly pacified Europe. The Europeans appeared incapable of proposing a viable model for European reconstitution. The continent's political wisdom, visible since 1815, appeared to be extinct. Only Wilson had a concept with room for all, including the defeated, on condition that they democratised and accepted the new facts of the international liberal order proposed by Washington. But in order to function, the US model, apart of course from suiting first the now worldwide economic and financial interests of the United States, presupposed Washington's active participation in international affairs – which, as we know, was not to be the case after 1919. Further, this liberal ideological model presupposed the acceptance of liberalism throughout Europe which, with a few exceptions, was also not to be the case in post-war Central and Eastern Europe. In addition, the Wilsonian approach was universal and abstract, and did not adequately take into account the historic complexities of European equilibrium. Seen from 1918, and still more in 1919, the ambiguities, frustrations and resentments raised by the peace settlement led not to the calming of Europe, but to the next phase of a 'Thirty Years War'.

20

Neutrality

SAMUËL KRUIZINGA

Introduction

At the outbreak of war in August 1914, the majority of the world's nations did not belong to either belligerent bloc. On 11 November 1918, only a handful of states remained neutral: Norway, Sweden, Denmark, the Netherlands, Switzerland and Spain in Europe, and Mexico, Chile and Argentina in South America. All the other sovereign nations of the world had joined or, at the very least, severed diplomatic relations with one of the warring parties, most of them – by far – of their own accords. Moreover, the nations that did remain neutral saw their *rights* as non-belligerents frequently violated. Prior to 1914, an elaborate – but by no means definitive – body of international law had been created, whose primary function was to delineate neutral rights in wartime. However, these rights were challenged by both the Allies and the Central Powers, as they felt that they gave their enemies an undue advantage or denied them key 'belligerent rights'. Finally, during the war neutrality lost its moral connotation. As both sets of belligerents recast the conflicts in terms of an epic, and perhaps final, struggle for universalistic principles such as *civilization* or *Kultur*, the neutrals were increasingly perceived as too spineless to act in their own interest, or too self-absorbed to see a bigger picture than their immediate safety.[1]

The dwindling number of neutrals, the loss of the neutral moral high ground and, most of all, the lack of respect for their legal rights has prompted historians to view the First World War as a period during which neutrality, as it had emerged out of international conferences and attempts to codify international law, 'declined': during the war neutrals were unable to force respect for their rights, so after the war traditional neutrality was replaced by a

1 Maartje Abbenhuis, 'Too good to be true? European hopes for neutrality before 1914', in Herman Amersfoort and Wim Klinkert (eds.), *Small Powers in the Age of Total War, 1900–1940* (Leiden: Brill, 2011), p. 26.

new concept of non-belligerency cast in the framework of Wilsonian internationalism and collective security.[2]

In this chapter, I wish to sidestep the issue of whether neutrality, in a legal or moral sense, declined or transformed during the Great War. The rules and regulations, and the different interpretations of their meaning and legality, and the disputed morality of neutrality were but two aspects of that difficult-to-grasp concept that, in the words of Neville Wylie – writing about Second World War-era neutrality – 'continues to defy simplistic categorisation'.[3] In this chapter, I wish to focus on neutrality not from the standpoint of international rights or morality, but as a guideline foreign policy. Instead of focusing on decline or transformation, my aim is to discover why some countries could and did remain neutral, while others could or did not. In other words: under what conditions was neutrality a viable base for foreign policy during the First World War?

This chapter is based on evidence gathered by many others, to whom I am deeply indebted. In it, I have tried to include the most up-to-date views on countries that tried, at one point or another and for variable amounts of time and equally varied reasons, to remain neutral. For reasons of practicality, I have omitted all countries which were not fully sovereign in the conduct of their foreign policy: states under military occupation, colonies, or dependencies do not figure in my account, nor do mini- and microstates unable to pursue an independent foreign policy (such as Liechtenstein or Monaco).

Neutrality abandoned

The number of belligerents at the war's end was significantly higher than in August 1914. A multitude of explanations has been given as to why this is the case. The most cynical of these points to the fact that aspiring belligerents were in it for material or even immaterial gains: money, territory, 'Great Power status'. Others name cultural factors such as nationalism, militarism, Social Darwinism and imperialism as the ultimate culprits. Others look at the

2 Nils Ørvik, *The Decline of Neutrality, 1914–1941: With Special Reference to the United States and the Northern Neutrals*, 2nd edn (London: Frank Cass & Co., 1971 [1953]); Stephen C. Neff, *The Rights and Duties of Neutrals: A General History* (Manchester University Press, 2000). See also Johan den Hertog and Samuël Kruizinga, 'Introduction', in Hertog and Kruizinga (eds.), *Caught in the Middle. Neutrals, Neutrality and the First World War* (Amsterdam: Aksant, 2011), pp. 1–14.

3 Neville Wylie, 'Victors or actors? European neutrals and non-belligerents, 1939–1945', in Neville Wylie (ed.), *European Neutrals and Non-Belligerents during the Second World War* (Cambridge University Press, 2002), p. 26.

role of governing elites or lobby groups in bringing their countries into war, sometimes over the objections of a large part of their population. And finally some look at commercial, religious or other ties linking neutrals to a certain belligerent bloc, easing their way into war.[4] In the following three sections, I have grouped together countries based on what I believe – on the basis of the most recent literature – their *ultima movens* to be in forgoing their neutrality.

This overview is neither exhaustive nor complete, but will serve to paint in broad strokes the reasons why neutrality as a foreign policy option failed these countries at one point or another during the war. In my view, the main reasons were:

(i) the fear that non-belligerency would seriously and permanently limit the freedom of action of a neutral state, especially in the area of recouping past losses or realising irredentist ideals (see 'Belligerent or irrelevant', below);
(ii) the notion that non-belligerency would preclude a country having influence in redressing the international system after the war (see 'Fighting for the future', below);
(iii) the immediate and grave danger neutrality posed to a country if it did not join the war (see 'Economic belligerency', below).

Belligerent or irrelevant

Italy declared its neutrality on 4 August, despite having been a party to the Triple Alliance since its inception in 1882. However, the value of that membership had been steadily declining since the start of the twentieth century. First and foremost, Franco-Italian rivalries over North Africa had ended and given way to a remarkable *rapprochement*. Moreover, Austrian incursions into the Balkans had raised the spectre of an Austrian dominance in the Adriatic Sea. The Italian Government of August 1914, headed by Antonio Salandra, therefore had little intention of joining the Austrians in their conflict with Serbia. Furthermore, its army was not ready for combat, being embroiled in a protracted colonial conflict in Libya, while the navy could not possibly hold its own against the Franco-British Mediterranean fleets. Finally, the majority of Italians would not have consented to joining the Triple Alliance partners in war. Many Catholics, influenced by the Holy See, wished Italy to remain neutral, while others might

4 Richard F. Hamilton and Holger H. Herwig, *Decisions for War, 1914–1917* (Cambridge University Press, 2004), pp. 1–23; Glenn E. Torrey, 'The Balkans: Serbia, Bulgaria, Romania, and Greece', in Robin Higham and Dennis Showalter (eds.), *Researching World War I. A Handbook* (Westport, CT: Greenwood Press, 2003), pp. 202–26.

support war but not on Austria's side: after all, the Habsburg Empire still held significant swathes of territory which many considered Italian. The Italian Government therefore made it known to Germany and Austria-Hungary that it did not feel itself obligated to join the war effort. After the Battle of the Marne broke the spell of Austro-German invincibility, Salandra, together with his Foreign Minister Sidney Sonnino, began planning an intervention on the side of Austria's enemies. They were afraid that by remaining neutral, they might lose any opportunity of obtaining any Austrian territories. After the start of the Dardanelles campaign, joining the Allies also seemed to offer Italy the opportunity to cement its burgeoning Great Power status by acquiring territory in Asia Minor. For Salandra and Sonnino, it became a question of *when* Italy would join the Allies, not *if*. They hoped to dictate the moment of intervention, so that Italy's armed forces were optimally prepared and its actions would have the most effect on the war, so that Italy could demand maximum compensations.[5]

However, fear of Austro-German economic or military reprisals caused the Italian Government to conduct simultaneous negotiations with the Central Powers. These were dragged out by the Italian negotiators on purpose and were never meant to result in Italy joining the Central Powers' cause. Moreover, Italy's intent on joining the Allies is obvious from the fact that, in negotiating the Pact of London of 26 April 1915 – whereby Italy promised to declare war on Austria within one month – the Italian delegation compromised on a number of key issues. After 26 April, one obstacle remained: the majority of the Italian Parliament, although not keen on Austria, seemed to support continued neutrality over war. However, an irredentist press campaign, which furthermore stressed the need for Italy to join the war effort or risk becoming an 'effeminate' second-rate power, succeeded in creating a popular interventionist movement. Swayed by the war crowds during the *Radiosomaggismo* ('radiant May'), the Italian Chamber voted on 20 May 1915 to declare war on Austria, effective 23 May.[6]

5 Jean-Jacques Becker, 'War aims and neutrality', in John Horne (ed.), *A Companion to World War I* (Chichester: Wiley-Blackwell, 2010), p. 207; Brunello Vigezzi, 'La neutralité de l'Italie en 1870, 1913, 1939 (et en 1948)', in Jukka Nevakivi (ed.), *Neutrality in History / La Neutralité dans l'Histoire* (Helsinki: SHS/FHS, 1993), pp. 63–74; Holger Afflerbach, 'Vom bündnispartner zum kriegsgegner. Ursachen und folgen des italienischen kriegseintrits im Mai 1915', in Johannes Hürter and Gian Enrico Rusconi (eds.), *Der Kriegseintritt Italiens im Mai 1915* (Munich: R. Oldenbourg Verlag, 2007), pp. 53–61.

6 Italy's reliance on German markets and investments delayed its declaration of war against Germany for almost a full year. William A. Renzi, 'Italy's neutrality and entrance into the Great War', *American Historical Review*, 73:5 (1968), pp. 1414–32; William A. Renzi,

Romania, like Italy, was a member of the Triple Alliance when war broke out in July 1913, having joined in 1883. And although Romania's king, Carol I Hohenzollern-Sigmaringen, strongly supported the Central Powers, his ministry, led by Ion I. C. Brătianu, and indeed the majority of Romanians, did not. Their enmity was mostly directed towards Austria-Hungary, which was seen as the oppressor of the large Romanian minority in Transylvania and a strong – but tacit – supporter of Romania's enemies during the Balkan wars. Opposition of the king and the fluid nature of the Eastern Front precluded speedy intervention on the side of the Allies, however. All this seemed to change when Carol died in October 1914 and was succeeded by his pro-Allied nephew Ferdinand, while Russia's invasion of Hungary proceeded full steam ahead. As the press clamoured for Romania to take up arms against Austria and reclaim its lost provinces, Brătianu and his Cabinet moved cautiously. First, he negotiated with Russia to secure for his country a promise that Romania would be entitled to Transylvania in case of Austrian dismemberment. Secondly, he waited, just as Salandra had done, for the most opportune moment to intervene. However, unlike Italy, that momentum seemed to have waned after Russia was driven out of Hungary and the Central Powers took the initiative. Strategically, Romanian intervention seemed, for the moment at least, out of the question. Fearful of the Central Powers' reprisals, Brătianu negotiated several trade agreements with them, especially concerning transit of military goods and the sale of oil and grain. Meanwhile, the Romanian Government assured Russia that intervention would come, provided the Allies were in a position to support it militarily and thereby provide the maximum amount of security. In the summer of 1916, the Allies pressed Brătianu to support Russia's Brusilov offensive, threatening to renege on their earlier promise to allow the Romanians to partake fully in the division of Austrian territory after the Allied victory. Brătianu agreed, and rallied his Cabinet by stating that Romania's intervention would

In the Shadow of the Sword. Italy's Neutrality and Entrance into the Great War, 1914–1915 (New York: Peter Lang, 1987). For a local view of the effects of 'Radiant May', see Sean Brady, 'From peacetime to wartime: the Sicilian province of Catania and Italian intervention in the Great War, June 1914–September 1915', in James E. Kitchen *et al.* (eds.), *Other Combatants, Other Fronts. Competing Histories of the First World War* (Newcastle upon Tyne: Cambridge Scholars Publishing, 2011), pp. 3–28. For an overview of Italian negotiations with the Central Powers and the Allies during her period of neutrality, see: Cedric J. Lowe, 'Britain and Italian intervention, 1914–1915', *Historical Journal*, 12:3 (1969), pp. 533–48; and Leo Valiani, 'Italian-Austro-Hungarian negotiations 1914–1915', *Journal of Contemporary History*, 1 (1966), pp. 113–36; Alberto Monticone, *Deutschland und die Neutralität Italiens, 1914–1915* (Wiesbaden: Steiner, 1982).

deny the Austrians a victory that would reduce his country to a client state. After promises of support from both the Russian and the Salonica armies, Romania declared war on Austria-Hungary on 27 August 1916.[7]

Whereas the Central Powers' defeat was, in the end, deemed essential to secure both Italian and Romanian territorial concessions and future security, the reverse seemed to be true for Bulgaria. The country had, in contrast to Romania, emerged defeated from the Second Balkan War and had extensive scores to settle with its neighbours, most notably Serbia. Prime Minister Vasil Radoslavov even applied for formal membership of the Triple Alliance on 16 July 1914, hoping that Austria would defeat Serbia and Bulgaria could lay claim to the Macedonian territories that after 1913 had been incorporated into Serbia. However, the Austrians refused, as they still held hope that the conflict could be localised. Meanwhile, cooler heads prevailed in Bulgaria, arguing that the army needed more time to recover. Even after the proclamation of neutrality, the Austrophile Radoslavov tried his very best to aid the Central Powers' war effort by allowing his army staff to aid Macedonian guerrillas fighting the Serbian army. After the Ottoman entry into the war, the value of Bulgaria to both belligerent blocs increased exponentially, and both sides tried to tempt the Radoslavov government by offering it parts or even all of Macedonia. However, the Allied powers could hardly dismantle Serbia, while Germany and Austria had little compunction in carving it up. Moreover, Russia's defeats disheartened the Russophile elements of the Bulgarian population, while – as in Italy and Romania – fear reigned that remaining neutral for too long would deprive the country of a say in the remaking of the map of Europe. Austria-Hungary and Germany moreover enticed the Ottoman Empire to give up parts of Thrace (lost during the Second Balkan War) and furnished the chronically cash-strapped country with sizeable loans. The failure of the Dardanelles offensive sealed the deal,

7 Valeriu Florin Dobrinescu, 'Les neutralités de la Roumanie de 1914 à 1916 et de 1939 à 1940; etude comparative', in Nevakivi, *Neutrality in History*, pp. 101–4; Glenn E. Torrey, 'Rumania and the belligerents 1914–1916', *Journal of Contemporary History*, 1 (1966), pp. 171–91, later reprinted in his *Romania and World War I. A Collection of Studies* (Iaşi, Oxford and Portland: The Center for Romanian Studies, 1998), pp. 9–28. Torrey's 'Romanian historiography on the First World War', *Military Affairs*, 46:1 (1982), pp. 25–8 contains an interesting overview of (older) Romanian-language works on the country's neutrality and belligerency. See also Rudolf Dinu, 'Romania's way from neutrality to war. An analysis regarding the evolution of Romanian foreign policy, 1912–1916', in Christophe Prochasson and Florin Ţurcanu (eds.), *La Grande Guerre. Histoire et mémoire collective en France et en Roumanie* (Bucharest: New Europe College – Institut d'études avancées, 2010), pp. 9–17.

and on 6 September 1915, Bulgaria signed a five-year alliance treaty with the Central Powers, engaging the Serbian armies on 11 October.[8]

Greece's road to the First World War was equally fuelled by dreams of a national homeland for all its nationals, but lead through undeclared civil war. After a military coup d'état in 1907, a Liberal Party dreaming of the *Megali Idea* ('Great Idea') of creating a Greater Greece encompassing, among other things, Macedonia and Asia Minor, came to power. Led by Prime Minister Eleftherios Venizelos, this faction was opposed by a faction combining conservative, reactionary and military elements, led by King Constantine, the brother-in-law of Wilhelm II. After the outbreak of war, Venizelos argued for intervention on the side of the Allies, hoping thus to participate in the dismantlement of the Ottoman Empire. Constantine argued against, hoping – among other things – that the struggle over foreign policy would provide him and his supporters with an opportunity to reverse some of the political reforms made after the 1907 coup. The conflict came to a head when Venizelos offered Bulgaria Greek territory in the hope of preventing them from joining the Allies (in exchange for secret promises of Asia Minor gains after the war) and, later, he wanted Greece to join the Allied campaign in the Dardanelles. Constantine dismissed Venizelos, but he returned after his party won the ensuing elections. Once Bulgaria joined the Central Powers and invaded Serbia, Venizélos argued that this activated a treaty signed between Belgrade and Athens after the Second Balkan War, whereby they promised each other assistance in the case of an attack by Bulgarian forces. He therefore supported the arrival of a Franco-British army in Salonica sent in October 1915 to assist the Serbian army. However, the high-handed attitude of General Maurice Sarrail of the 'Salonica army' towards the Greek population, Allied military failures and pro-German propaganda eroded Venizelos's pro-Allied majority. In order to salvage the situation, he announced in August 1916 that the conflict between the king and himself was irreparable and established a rival republic in Salonica, splitting the country into two hostile camps. In December 1916, open hostility broke out between Allied troops and Greek military units loyal to Constantine, creating

8 Richard C. Hall, *Bulgaria's Road to the First World War* (New York: Columbia University Press, 1996), pp. 286–308; Wolfgang-Uwe Friedrich, *Bulgarien und die Mächte, 1913–1915. Ein Beitrag zur Weltkriegs- und Imperialismusgeschichte* (Stuttgart: Steiner, 1985), pp. 133–279. An overview of recent literature, mostly in Bulgarian, can be found in Richard C. Hall, 'Bulgaria in the First World War', *The Historian. A Journal of History*, 73:2 (2011), pp. 300–16. This new literature does not challenge the (largely compatible) older views of both Hall himself and Friedrich on Bulgaria's reasons for belligerency.

fear that the king would ally himself with the Central Powers. The Allies, however, hesitated to support Venizelos in an armed struggle against the king. Russia and Italy feared Greek designs in Asia Minor conflicting with their own territorial ambitions, while Britain advised against deposing of a king, fearing this would cast the Allied cause in an inherently anti-monarchical light. In the end, the Allies reached a compromise, issuing an ultimatum that the king should leave Greece in order to prevent military action and a blockade of royalist territory. On 12 June, the king abdicated, saving his country from civil war and ensuring its entry into the war under the guidance of Venizelos.[9]

Fighting for the future

There has been a long and arduous debate among historians as to the nature of US neutrality.[10] Some state that America's neutrality was slanted from the beginning, with Washington turning a blind eye to Allied infractions of international law in pursuing economic warfare. US interest in an Allied victory is usually explained by way of economics – the United States supplied munitions, raw materials, food and financial services to the Allies at great profit – or by focusing on the key decision-makers in Washington, who were supposedly, for various reasons, strongly pro-Allied. Nowadays, most if not all researchers agree that US policy disproportionately benefited the Allies, but some deny allegations that this policy was illegal or that meaningful alternatives existed due to America's geographic and ideological distance from the Central Powers.[11]

At the outbreak of war, most Americans believed it to be highly undesirable for the United States to enter the war. The United States was a country of

9 George B. Leontaritis, *Greece and the Great Powers, 1914–1917* (Thessaloniki: Institute for Balkan Studies, 1974); and *Greece and the First World War. From Neutrality to Intervention, 1917–1918* (New York: Columbia University Press, 1990), pp. 3–39.

10 Some key works are Arthur S. Link, *Wilson: The Struggle for Neutrality, 1914–1915* (Princeton University Press, 1960); and Ernest R. May, *The World War and American Isolation, 1914–1917* (Cambridge, MA: Harvard University Press, 1959). These claim that US President Woodrow Wilson's administration was, until 1917, strictly neutral. Ross Gregory, *The Origins of American Intervention in the First World War* (New York: W. W. Norton, 1971) and Patrick Devlin, *Too Proud to Fight: Woodrow Wilson's Neutrality* (New York: Oxford University Press, 1975) assert that Wilson tried to remain neutral, but as the war intensified the breakdown of international law made this impossible. John W. Coogan, *The End of Neutrality: The United States, Britain, and Maritime Rights, 1899–1915* (Ithaca, NY: Cornell University Press, 1981) asserts that US neutrality had a strong pro-British bias, as did Wilson and many of his closest advisers. Current historiography tends to view Coogan's thesis as on the extreme side, but generally correct.

11 Robert W. Tucker, *Woodrow Wilson and the Great War: Reconsidering America's Neutrality, 1914–1917* (Charlottesville, VA: University of Virginia Press, 2007), pp. 72–89.

immigrants who still were bound to their motherland on the old continent, which was now tearing itself apart. Neutrality seemed to equal national unity. Moreover, the American executive, most of all President Woodrow Wilson, hoped to use his country's resources to force belligerents to the negotiating table and mitigate some of the effects of war and, perhaps, even broker a peace which would form the basis of a new world order, based on international law. This would also safeguard US interests by reducing the global risk of conflict and the possibility of unwanted European meddling in New World affairs. Wilson and many of his inner circle, including his trusted adviser 'Colonel' Edward M. House, however, believed that the German system of government and its methods in waging war were an impediment to such an 'American' peace. Interestingly, they did not feel that their anti-German stance was at odds with neutrality. They felt that, as the most powerful neutral, the United States was the trustee of international law and should judge the belligerents according to their adherence to it. A 'neutral' or 'impartial' view of the situation, at least when filtered through the eyes of the legal advisers, deemed British violations of neutral rights insignificant in comparison to the broader German threat to US interests and global peace.[12] However, during 1914 to 1916, Wilson was unwilling to declare war over German infractions, even when they directly affected US interests – such as the torpedoing of the *Lusitania* by a German submarine. First of all, his administration still hoped for either a negotiated settlement or at the very least to pressure Germany into renouncing illegal warfare methods. Moreover, the US military was hardly prepared for conflict and its most experienced units were stationed along the border with unstable Mexico. Finally, many Americans still believed in neutrality; intervention on the side of the Allies would not only have estranged German-Americans, but also many in the South, the traditional power base of Wilson's Democratic Party, whose cotton trade with Germany had been made impossible by the Allied blockade.[13]

12 For a dissenting view, see John A. Thompson, *Woodrow Wilson* (London: Longman for Pearson Education, 2002), pp. 108–9. On Bryan and Lansing, see Daniel M. Smith, 'Robert Lansing and the formation of American neutrality policies, 1914–1915', *Mississippi Valley Historical Review*, 43:1 (1956), pp. 63–5; Kendrick A. Clements, 'Woodrow Wilson and World War I', *Presidential Studies Quarterly*, 34:1 (2004), pp. 65–7.

13 Benjamin Coates, '"Upon the neutral rests the trusteeship of international law". Legal advisers and American unneutrality', in Hertog and Kruizinga, *Caught in the Middle*, pp. 35–51; Robert H. Zieger, *America's Great War: World War I and the American Experience* (Oxford: Rowman & Littlefield, 2000), pp. 30–42. See for more details on heated Anglo-American exchanges regarding the Allied blockade of Germany, Nicholas A. Lambert, *Planning Armageddon. British Economic Warfare and the First World War* (Cambridge, MA and London: Harvard University Press, 2012), pp. 232–78.

However, Wilson did begin to see US intervention in the war as increasingly inevitable in the long run, especially when the German declaration of unrestricted U-boat warfare seemed to confirm his worst suspicions as to what a world in which the Central Powers were victorious would look like. After trying one last time to offer the belligerent parties mediation for a 'peace without victory' based on 'American principles' and 'American policies', Wilson felt he was out of options: a peace based on 'American principles' and compatible with his particular interpretation of neutrality was not possible without a 'regime change' in Germany, brought about by its defeat. Public opinion was swayed by the embarrassing Zimmermann Telegram, which suggested that Germany could pose, via a Mexican proxy, a direct threat to the continental United States. More importantly, several US ships were sunk, creating uproar and helping Wilson shepherd a declaration of war on Germany, or rather the German *Government*, through Congress, which became official on 6 April.[14] A number of Latin American and Caribbean states, as well as African Liberia, followed the United States' example by severing relations with or declaring war on the Central Powers out of sympathy for US war aims or economic or political dependence on Washington.[15]

The Ottoman Empire's fatal decision to join the war has stirred up almost as much controversy as that of the United States.[16] Many believe that the Ottoman Empire's Young Turk leadership, above all Defence Minister Enver Pasha, were in thrall by German military prowess, had been bought by German money or were consumed by petty revanchism. However, recent scholarship offers an alternative explanation: the decision sprung out of their belief that it was in the Empire's best interest to join with a Great Power in an

14 Jennifer D. Keene, 'The United States', in Horne, *Companion to World War I*, pp. 508–12. To underline the fact that the United States' chief issue was with the political and military leadership of the German Empire, Washington did not enter the war against Austria-Hungary until 7 December 1917, mostly to prop up Italy after the defeat at Caporetto, and never against Bulgaria or the Ottoman Empire.

15 Bolivia (13 April 1917), Costa Rica (21 September), Ecuador (7 November), Guatemala (27 April), Honduras (17 May), Nicaragua (19 May), Peru (6 October) and Uruguay (7 October) severed relations with (one of the) Central Powers. Guatemala (23 April 1918), Nicaragua (8 May), Costa Rica (23 May) and Honduras (19 July) subsequently declared war, as did Haïti (12 July). Liberia had declared war on Germany on 4 August 1918. El Salvador, finally, never declared war on Germany, but did open its ports for US naval ships, proclaiming itself to be a 'friendly neutral'. See Olivier Compagnon, '1914–1918: the death throes of civilisation. The elites of Latin America face the Great War', in Jenny Macleod and Pierre Purseigle (eds.), *Uncovered Fields. Perspectives in First World War Studies* (Leiden: Brill, 2004), pp. 279–95.

16 Hamit Bozarslan, 'The Ottoman Empire', in Horne, *Companion to World War I*, provides a summary on pp. 495–6.

alliance, which would bring military security and financial stability *after* the war. (Russia was widely suspected of trying to gain control of the Empire's capital and thereby secure the strategically important waterways between the Black Sea and the Mediterranean, and Britain and France enjoyed extensive financial concessions within the country and were thus unlikely to support a financially and economically independent Empire.) As alliance partners, the Central Powers were therefore much more attractive, all the more because large parts of both the Ottoman army and navy were dependent on the many German advisers in-country at the war's outbreak. Unwilling to cripple the military now that the Empire's neighbours were mobilising, the Ottoman leadership signed a secret treaty promising to declare war on Russia in exchange for a lasting strategic and economic alliance. However, the Ottoman executive reneged on their promise, continually postponing the moment of intervention and even going so far as to attempt renegotiation on the basis of an alliance without any military obligations on the part of the Ottomans. Throughout August to October 1914, German pressure for an immediate Ottoman attack on Russia mounted as the Austrian front seemed to buckle. Germany threatened to withhold any further financial assistance and recall its military personnel (including the Liman von Sanders mission, the crews of the *Goeben* and *Breslau*, and the engineers upgrading the fortresses of Constantinople) vital to the Ottoman mobilisation, even going so far as to threaten the prospect of a separate peace with Russia bought with promises of Ottoman territory. Unwilling to forgo the prospect of a permanent alliance with Germany and fearing that continued neutrality would directly threaten its existence, the Ottoman Empire declared war on Russia on 29 October 1914.[17]

China's decision for war was likewise taken with an eye to the post-war future. Initially, the politically unstable country had opted for neutrality, as it was in no position to fight anyone and feared that the European powers who had settlements in-country would start fighting each other on its soil once it joined one of the two blocs. The situation changed drastically, however, when Japan was requested by Britain to honour its treaty obligations and attack German shipping and naval bases in the Pacific. One of these bases was Qingdao in China's Shantong province, which was leased to Berlin in 1898 for a period of ninety-nine years. Faced with the prospect of Qingdao permanently falling into Japanese hands, serving as a forward base to

17 Mustafa Aksakal, *The Ottoman Road to War in 1914. The Ottoman Empire and the First World War* (Cambridge University Press, 2008), pp. 3–15, 122, 153–65, 186–94.

increase its influence in Shantong and possibly Mongolia, the overarching object of China's foreign policy then became to obtain an invitation to a conference settling all outstanding territorial questions in the East, or possibly even the peace conference at the war's end. At first, it was hoped that it could attain this objective by remaining neutral and enlisting the diplomatic assistance of the Western Allies (and support against Japan) by sending large labour battalions to France. After Japan issued its Twenty-One Demands late in April 1915 without interference from Britain, France or Russia, it became evident that this strategy was failing. Joining the war was increasingly seen as an absolute condition for any say at the negotiating table at the war's end. However, Japan blocked China's joining the Allies precisely because it did not want China to attend any such conference which would presumably have broad powers to decide on territorial questions, and since China was dependent on Japan for several key loans, it could not alienate its Eastern rival. Beijing's chance came after the United States severed diplomatic relations with Germany in February 1917 and urged others to do the same: a request the Allies could hardly ignore. A declaration of war, delayed by revolutionary Russian activity along its border and internal political strife, was issued on 14 August 1917.[18] China thereby followed the example set by Siam, now known as Thailand. Its declaration of war on the Central Powers on 22 July 1917 was mainly motivated by the desire to argue for the amendment of the nineteenth-century treaties imposed on it by Britain and France limiting its sovereignty at the peace conference.[19]

Economic belligerency

The United States, the Ottoman Empire, China and Siam became belligerents almost reluctantly and in order to influence the post-war order. Portugal, by stark contrast, was neutral despite itself. On 4 August 1914, the British Government informed its Portuguese counterpart that it would not call for Portuguese assistance under the terms of the 1386 Anglo-Portuguese Treaty. London argued that the fragile republican government of the Iberian country,

18 Hiroshi Momose, 'Neutrals and Japan in the First World War', in Nevakivi, *Neutrality in History*, pp. 136–42; Stephen G. Craft, 'Angling for an invitation to Paris. China's entry into the First World War', *International History Review*, 16:1 (1994), pp. 1–24; Guoqi Xu, *Strangers on the Western Front. Chinese workers in the Great War* (Cambridge, MA: Harvard University Press, 2011), pp. 10–37.

19 Stephen Lyon Wakeman Greene, *Absolute dreams. Thai Government under Rama VI, 1910–1925* (Bangkok: White Lotus Press, 1999), pp. 102–13.

its vulnerable economy and its decrepit army would probably not survive belligerency. The Portuguese neutrality proclamation, made on 7 August 1914, reflected its dual position as both a non-belligerent and Britain's ally, by stating that while the country was not currently at war with anyone, it would honour any and all existing treaty obligations. This state of affairs neither satisfied Portuguese interventionists – who feared the country would be reduced to a client state to Britain if it did not enter the war on its own accord and that their colonies might be bartered away in the peace settlement – and neutralists – who shared London's assessment of the country's poor capacity to wage war. Interestingly, the British government apparently reversed its position on 10 October 1914, formally requesting Portuguese intervention so that its army could send its French-built field guns to the Western Front. The request was vetoed by French army command, as it possessed neither the ammunition to fire them nor the space to store them until it did. The aborted intervention swung power in the hands of the Portuguese neutralists, which in turn provoked a revolution by their political enemies on 14 May 1915. Portugal's curious neutrality, pursued against the wishes of the majority of its new political leaders, endured, however, for a little under a year. Britain and France still opposed active Portuguese belligerence, since they reaped plenty of benefits from Portuguese aid without it, under the terms of the old alliance. Portuguese troops aided the Allies in Africa, the Royal Navy used Portuguese harbours at its pleasure, and Portuguese armaments factories worked full-time to provide the Allies with as much as they could spare. This changed when Britain's eye fell on the seventy-odd German and Austrian ships which had fled to neutral Lisbon at the outbreak of war. As Portugal was dependent on British tonnage for carrying most of its foreign trade and on City loans to keep its fragile economy afloat, London pressured Portugal to commandeer the 242,000 tons of Central Powers' ships lying idle in its ports. As Britain needed its own ships elsewhere, shortages increased and on 23 February 1916, Portuguese troops stormed and subsequently commandeered the Austrian and German ships. Germany considered this to be an act of aggression and declared war on Portugal on 9 March, more as a warning to other neutrals and to satiate public opinion than for any other reason.[20]

20 Filipe Ribeiro de Meneses, *Portugal 1914–1926. From the First World War to Military Dictatorship* (Bristol: HiPLAM, 2004), pp. 1–31; Nuno Severiano Teixeira, *L'entrée du Portugal dans la Grande Guerre. Objectifs nationaux et stratégies politiques* (Paris: Economica / Institut de Stratégie Comparée, 1998), pp. 173–366.

For the former Portuguese colony of Brazil, economics were also paramount in deciding between non-belligerency and war. Brazil declared herself to be neutral at war's outbreak, as did all other Latin American countries. Just like in the United States, the countries' diverse immigrant populations were a deciding factor in opting for neutrality. The war ruptured some of the vital links between Latin America and Europe, causing Latin American businesses and governments to look to the United States for alternative outlets for their products and investments in finance, public utilities and the railways. Moreover, the European war made Washington's call for more unity and cooperation in the New World all the more attractive. Brazil, therefore, followed the US lead by severing relations with Germany in April 1917, followed in June by Uruguay. However, the two republics were distrustful of each other, and strong but unfounded rumours of German agitation in the south of Brazil caused Uruguay not to declare war, although it was a de facto belligerent, even sending medical teams to Allied armies in France. Brazil had no such compunctions and declared war on the Central Powers on 26 October 1917, a move partly designed to end British economic warfare against German interests in the country.[21]

Neutrality lost

The fact that countries, first and foremost the United States, opted for belligerency instead of neutrality changed the course of the war. Similarly, the fact that in August 1914 the neutrality of Belgium was violated, transformed the nature of the conflict from a continental European to a truly global war. Belgium's neutrality was forfeit the moment the German army planners decided to use the country as a shortcut to Paris. Tellingly, the same day German troops crossed over into Belgian territory, Chancellor Theobald von Bethmann Hollweg apologised for the violation of international law which was made necessary by 'dire necessity'. Later that day, however, in a final telephone call to British ambassador Edward Goschen before he was to leave

21 Antonio O. Saldanha da Gama, 'The European war and the Brazilian decision to enter the war', *Acta International Commission for Military History*, 10 (1983), pp. 186–90; Philip A. Dehne, *On the Far Western Front. Britain's First World War in South America* (Manchester University Press, 2009), pp. 171–81; Bill Albert with Paul Henderson, *South America and the First World War. The Impact of the War on Brazil, Argentina, Peru and Chile* (Cambridge University Press, 1988), pp. 18–19, 45, 369–70. Interestingly, Brazilian belligerence did not mean the end of British meddling in her economic affairs. In fact, Brazil was the only co-belligerent where Britain maintained the Statutory Black List. See Emily Rosenberg, 'Anglo-American economic rivalry in Brazil during World War I', *Diplomatic History*, 2:2 (1978), pp. 131–52.

the country, Bethmann Hollweg expressed his exasperation that the British Empire would wage global warfare against Germany over a 'scrap of paper', the 1839 treaty signed guaranteeing Belgian neutrality. Both the Chancellor's apology and his later outburst served to paint Germany as untrustworthy and callous as regards the rights of small nations.[22]

But it is doubtful that invoking the image of 'gallant little Belgium' would have had the same propagandistic effect if she had followed the example of the very first country whose neutrality was violated. In the early morning of 2 August 1914, a large German invasion force crossed into neutral Luxembourg's government, occupying strategically important railway links to and from Belgium and France. And although Grand Duchess Maria Adelheid officially protested against the German invasion – and even blocked an advancing column of Germans using her own car – the government offered no further resistance, as the 315-men national militia was in no condition to stop the German advance. Moreover, by choosing to remain in the country instead of electing exile and making no attempt to link up with Germany's enemies, Luxembourg earned the scorn of the Allies: the country was never offered the same explicit guarantee received by Belgium that after Allied victory its independence would be fully restored.[23]

A third neutrality violated by belligerents during the war was that of Albania, a country freshly created out of the First Balkan War and a model of instability. In September 1915, rebel factions ousted Prince Wilhelm zu Wied – appointed by the Great Powers to lead the fledgling nation – in early September 1914. Thereafter, factional strife increased as belligerents (and even neutral Italy) interfered, hoping to push the country into an alliance with one of them, or at the very least control a significant portion of its territory. The country remained neutral, as each side was unwilling or unable to escalate its efforts into a full-blown invasion. This ended when Italy declared war on Austria in May 1915, after which Albania became the subject of a four-pronged invasion as each of the interested parties swooped in to establish a firm foothold.[24]

22 Sophie de Schaepdrijver, *De Groote Oorlog. Het koninkrijk België tijdens de Eerste Wereldoorlog* (Antwerp and Amsterdam: Atlas, 1997), pp. 98, 139–41. This book was also published in French as *La Belgique et la première Guerre mondiale* (Brussels: Archives & Musée de la Littérature, 2004). See also her 'Belgium', in Horne, *Companion to World War I*, pp. 386–403, esp. 386–7.

23 Hans A. Schmitt, 'Violated neutrals: Belgium, the dwarf states, and Luxemburg', in Hans A. Schmitt (ed.), *Neutral Europe between War and Revolution 1917–23* (Charlottesville, VA: University Press of Virginia, 1988), pp. 217–26.

24 Marvin Benjamin Fried, 'The cornerstone of Balkan power projection: Austro-Hungarian war aims and the problem of Albanian neutrality, 1914–1918', *Diplomacy and Statecraft*, 23:3 (2012), pp. 425–45.

Neutrality maintained

Perhaps the fates of Belgium, Luxembourg and Albania helped to inspire Daniel Frey, a Swiss scholar, to posit a novel, three-level analysis of neutrality, which serves as the basis of the next three sections of this chapter. The first of these three levels concerns the external conditions necessary for a successful neutrality policy, such as geography, the nature of the conflict and the international system (see 'External conditions'). In the case of Belgium, simple geography and German military planning – deeply embedded in preventing the strategic nightmare of a two-front war – made neutrality impossible. The second level concerns the external credibility of neutrality: whether neutral states can project an image of indifference as to the outcome of a conflict (see 'The image of indifference'). Luxembourg failed in this category to project an even-handed neutrality by offering only token resistance to invasion and apparently resigning itself to German dominance. The third level, finally, deals with the compatibility of neutrality with the other policies of a neutral state (see 'Neutrality and national policy'). Albania's factions, for example, could not agree on important aspects of foreign policy and conspired with outside forces, creating a situation in which it was impossible to remain neutral. It must be noted that Frey felt that his three dimensions would be quite hard to operationalise and, even then, might be mutually interdependent. However, the value of his approach lies exactly in these apparent flaws. Neutrality, as we shall see, is not easily maintained, once divorced from a purely legalistic standpoint, whereby neutrality is reduced to a set of rules one either does or does not abide by. Moreover, its successful implementation and operation depends on a number of factors, some of which a neutral has influence over and others which are the province of the belligerents or are determined by the shape of the international economy, accidents of geography or the shifting nature of the various fronts.[25]

External conditions

A country's geographic location was an important deciding factor in whether a country could remain neutral. The Netherlands occupied a strategic position at the German army's left flank and prohibited any Allied strikes at the Ruhr or Antwerp. Inversely, Dutch neutrality denied Germany submarine or air bases

25 Daniel Frey, 'Dimensionen neutraler Politik: Ein Beitrag zur Theorie der Internationalen Beziehungen' (PhD thesis, University of Geneva, 1969), pp. 18–19, 206.

from which to strike at Britain.[26] Danish and Swedish neutrality denied complete control over the Baltic Sea to either the Allies or the Central Powers. Sweden, finally, of all the European neutrals occupied by far the most sheltered position, even more so than Spain. Moreover, and crucially, it formed an important link in the transit trade between the Western Allies and Russia, since the Black Sea was closed off by Ottoman belligerence and the northern port of Archangel was closed by ice during most of the year.[27] The non-European neutrals Argentina, Mexico and Chile, finally, obviously enjoyed the geographic advantage of being far away from the front lines.

A further essential precondition for successful neutrality was that its existence, in theory at least, could benefit *all* belligerents. Neutrals, for example, could serve a useful function by keeping certain diplomatic channels between the belligerents open. Since the belligerents had withdrawn their own diplomatic staff from the countries with which they were now at war, neutrals temporarily took care of their interests. The Spanish legation in Portugal, Romania and Italy, for example, served in this capacity for the German and Austro-Hungarian governments, while Spanish diplomats in Germany, Turkey, Persia and occupied Belgium watched after French affairs.[28] Moreover, the neutrals facilitated low-level contacts between the belligerents. The Dutch Government in 1917 arranged talks between members of the British and German governments – although they never met face to face, Dutch Foreign Minister John Loudon functioning as a go-between – which resulted in an exchange of wounded POWs via Dutch territory.[29] The Swiss and Danish governments inspected POW camps in Eastern Europe and aided Red Cross workers there, while the US Government played a key role in establishing the Committee for the Relief of Belgium, a role taken over after 1917 by the Dutch and Spanish governments.[30] Additionally,

26 Maartje Abbenhuis, *The Art of Staying Neutral. The Netherlands in the First World War, 1914–1918* (Amsterdam University Press, 2006), pp. 26–35.

27 Patrick Salmon, *Scandinavia and the Great Powers 1890–1940* (Cambridge University Press, 1997), pp. 11, 131; Olof Åhlander, *Staat, Wirtschaft und Handelspolitik. Schweden und Deutschland 1918–1921* (Lund: Esselte Studium, 1983), pp. 50–4.

28 Francisco J. Romero Salvadó, *Spain 1914–1918. Between War and Revolution* (London and New York: Routledge, 1999), p. 75.

29 Suzanne Wolf, 'Guarded Neutrality. The Internment of Foreign Military Personnel in the Netherlands during the First World War' (PhD thesis, University of Sheffield, 2008), pp. 224–46. The Swiss Government had, through the intermediary of the Red Cross and Pope Benedict XV, managed to conclude a similar exchange agreement between the German and French governments in 1915.

30 On Danish involvement in the care for POWs, see Bent Blüdnikow, 'Denmark during the First World War', *Journal of Contemporary History*, 24:4 (1989), pp. 683–703. For Switzerland, see Frédéric Yerly, 'Grande guerre et diplomatie humanitaire. La mission

neutral territory offered the belligerents an excellent opportunity to spy on each other. Especially those neutrals contiguous to Germany, notably Switzerland and the Netherlands, became hotbeds of international intrigue.[31]

The neutrals could also provide important economic, financial and transportation services to the belligerents. Norway and the Netherlands were in possession of sizeable merchant fleets capable of partly relieving the transport difficulties of warring states. Owing to their control of the sea and most of the globe's bunker coal deposits, the Allies reaped by far the greatest economic benefits during the war. The Central Powers – conscious of their ever-greater isolation – hoped, however, that they could maintain an economic foothold in neutral countries significant enough that, after the war, they could function as their links to overseas markets. That is why, even when the Allies and the United States forced neutral tonnage into their service in 1917 to 1918, Germany stimulated neutral shipbuilding by increasing steel exports.[32] Neutrals also produced important raw materials and/or finished products which were of great benefit to the belligerents. Sweden, for example, produced iron ore and timber, Norway had a large fishing and whaling industry, Denmark and the Netherlands produced great quantities of agricultural produce, and Switzerland possessed a sizeable armaments industry. The belligerents vied for access to neutral markets not only to buy much-needed goods, but also – with an eye to both the immediate and the eventual post-war future – to safeguard existing and possibly create additional outlets for their own trade to (help) pay for the mounting costs of war.[33] Neutral trade with belligerents, especially the Central Powers, was extremely lucrative: Danish farmers, for example, who seized on this opportunity, became known as the 'Gulash-barons', as much for their wealth as for their attempts to emulate the manners of the old-money aristocracy – which, to the delight

catholique Suisse en faveur des prisonniers de guerre (1914–1918)', *Vingtième Siècle. Revue d'histoire*, 58:1 (1998), pp. 13–28; and Pierre Du Bois, 'L'action humanitaire de la Suisse durant la Première Guerre mondiale', *Revue d'Allemagne et des pays de langue allemande*, 28:3 (1996), pp. 377–89. US and subsequent Dutch and Spanish diplomatic efforts on behalf of the Belgian population are detailed in Johan den Hertog, 'The Commission for Relief in Belgium and the political diplomatic history of the First World War', *Diplomacy and Statecraft*, 21:4 (2010), pp. 593–613.

31 Hubert P. van Tuyll van Serooskerken, *The Netherlands and World War I. Espionage, Diplomacy and Survival* (Leiden: Brill, 2001), pp. 163–4, 169–70.

32 Marc Frey, 'The neutrals and World War One', *Defence Studies*, 3 (2000), p. 14.

33 Olav Riste, *The Neutral Ally. Norway's Relations with Belligerent Powers in the First World War* (Oslo: Universitetsforlaget, 1965), pp. 42–3; Salmon, *Scandinavia*, pp. 24, 118–19; Herman Amersfoort and Wim Klinkert, 'Introduction. Small states in a big world', in Amersfoort and Klinkert, *Small Powers*, p. 14.

of many a cartoonist, often spectacularly backfired. All the money earned also strengthened neutral financial institutes, which were besieged by both Allied and Central Powers representatives for loans. For the latter, the neutral European banks acquired more importance as Britain extended her control over telegraphic communication, censored telegraphic transactions and monopolised the New York money market in 1915 to 1916.[34]

It has been suggested, both during and after the war, that neutrals missed an opportunity to take more direct control over their fates, improve respect for their legal rights, lessen the effects of the war on their countries and perhaps even to mitigate or end the conflict by mediation by not working together. Several efforts to create a 'third bloc' of neutral states had been attempted, but they all failed. Perhaps as a possible alternative to entering the war, the British Foreign Office developed a plan in early August to create a 'ring' of neutral powers around Germany, militarily supported by Britain, to contain the war and prevent an invasion of France.[35] Around the same time, the Belgian Government proposed to its Dutch counterpart to enter in a defensive military alliance as a deterrent to possible German aggression.[36] However, the German ultimatum to and subsequent invasion of Belgium put an end to both plans. Finally, the Swedish Government proposed on 1 August to form a defensive and offensive alliance with Norway. The alliance was meant to ensure that Norway and Sweden would not join or be forced into opposing camps, but would also function as a powerful counterweight to pressure from either side – especially to Britain, whom the Swedish Government felt would try to send its navy into the Baltic through Norwegian or Swedish territorial waters. Norway declined to bind itself to any offensive action, but on 8 August the two countries issued a proclamation that the war would not cause the two countries to be on opposite sides.[37]

A further sign of Scandinavian solidarity was the meeting of the foreign ministers of Norway, Sweden and Denmark on 18 to 19 December 1914 in Malmö, Sweden. The practical consequences of such meetings, which were scheduled regularly throughout the war, were, however, limited: the political differences between the different Scandinavian governments, most notably the socialist-liberal coalition in power in Denmark and the conservative Swedes, and lingering fears in Norway and Sweden about possible Swedish hegemonistic designs, made that impossible. Moreover, the countries could

34 Hew Strachan, *Financing the First World War* (Oxford University Press, 2004), pp. 161–6.
35 Lambert, *Planning Armageddon*, pp. 205–6.
36 Abbenhuis, *Art of Staying Neutral*, p. 65.
37 Riste, *Neutral Ally*, p. 37; Salmon, *Scandinavia*, p. 127.

not manage to alleviate their economic woes by increasing inter-Scandinavian trading, since most of the goods they required could not be offered by the others, although especially during 1917 to 1918 some successes were recorded. The biggest result that came out of the top-level Scandinavian meetings was that through diplomatic cooperation – by issuing the same notes to belligerents infringing on neutral rights, for example, and debating the role of Scandinavia in the post-war future – the foundation was laid for more extensive cooperation after 1918.[38]

There were several attempts at convening a neutral conference to discuss even more intensive cooperation or to protest against specific elements of the war, most notably the British blockade and German U-boat warfare. At different points during 1914 to 1917, the US Government was asked to organise, or at the very least attend, such a conference. But every time Washington declined, pointing out that the geographical distance between them meant that the European neutrals had less freedom of action, making concerted action difficult at best. Moreover, the State Department felt that convening a neutral conference during the war would be dangerous, as 'any position taken by such a conference during the war would be considered, not upon its merits, but as it affected one side or the other'.[39] Finally, and perhaps most importantly, it seems likely that Washington was simply unwilling to dilute any of its attempts to negotiate or impose an 'American' peace on the belligerents. Since the United States refused to take the lead, the Netherlands and Switzerland declined to combine forces with the Scandinavians, deeming neutral *démarches* without US backing useless, even dangerous.[40]

Interestingly, just after breaking off diplomatic relations with Germany on 3 February 1917, the US Government suggested that all the neutrals do the same. This final attempt at creating a neutral counterweight to belligerent – specifically German – aggression was enthusiastically embraced by some South American neutrals (see above), but their European counterparts replied using almost the same language as Washington had done earlier. They pointed out that the result of any political action they might take would have much more dramatic consequences for them than for the United

38 Karen Gram-Skjoldager and Øyvind Tønnesson, 'Unity and divergence: Scandinavian internationalism, 1914–1921', *Contemporary European History*, 17:3 (2008), pp. 305–6, 315–17.

39 Bryan to Wilson, 10 May 1915, cited in Marc Frey, *Der Erste Weltkrieg und die Niederlande: ein neutrales Land im politischen und wirtschaftlichen Kalkül der Kriegsgegner* (Berlin: Akademie Verlag, 1998), p. 111.

40 Frey, 'The neutrals and WWI', pp. 6–9; Coates, 'Upon the neutral', p. 43; Patrick Salmon, 'British attitudes towards neutrality in the twentieth century', in Nevakivi, *Neutrality in History*, pp. 122–3.

States, since they were within striking range of German arms, whereas Washington was not.[41]

The image of indifference

Neutrality could potentially benefit both sides, but only when neutrals made sure the advantages were as evenly spread as possible. First of all, the European neutrals had to present a believable defensive force and strategy, in order to show that they were willing and capable of offering real resistance to attack. If they did not, one of the belligerents might judge the costs of attacking a neutral and so creating a new front so lowered as to negate any rewards reaped from continued neutrality. The problem, however, was that the belligerents possessed military capabilities far in excess of anything the neutrals could offer. They tried to solve the dilemma by showing themselves capable of defending their country in view of those odds in different ways.[42]

The European countries closest to the fronts (the Netherlands, Switzerland and Denmark) had reinforced key points in their defensive systems with modern fortifications. The fortresses of Amsterdam, Copenhagen and the Swiss Alps served as national redoubts which would be held at all cost in case of invasion and would serve as a staging ground for counter-attacks, to be coordinated with the enemies of the invading party. Moreover, the European neutrals made sure that they cultivated contact within different levels of both belligerent camps' military and governmental circles. By sharing key information regarding their own defensive preparations and even some of what they knew of the other camps' strengths and weaknesses, neutral army commanders and politicians attempted to reinforce the idea that they were well prepared for any event, especially, of course, an attack from the other side. In other cases, however, they created doubt and confusion by spreading rumours and false reports, causing, for example, one side to overestimate the forces their enemy had available to assist a neutral in case of invasion. Moreover, by constantly reinforcing the idea of the value of a country's neutrality to key figures in belligerent countries – either directly or via their legations – they were able to create internal resistance to demands of military 'hawks' arguing for invasion of neutral territory. Finally, pointing

41 Thomas A. Bailey, *The Policy of the United States toward the Neutrals, 1917–1918* (Gloucester, MA: Peter Smith, 1942, repr. 1966), pp. 20–2.
42 Salmon, *Scandinavia*, p. 29.

out the dangers posed by one of the belligerent blocs was a useful argument in obtaining (additional) weapons or ammunition.[43]

However, there were also key differences in the defensive plans of Denmark, Switzerland and the Netherlands, which betray different strategic and political conceptions of defence. Denmark, for example, never fully mobilised its army during the war. The Danish Government in power during the war consisted of a coalition of so-called radical liberals and social-democrats, who saw limited value in an all-out defence against invasion. They felt that such a defence would only lead to senseless loss of Danish lives. Danish army and navy command disagreed. They stuck to the operational plan devised in 1909, calling for a fighting retreat from Jutland to protect the full mobilisation of forces for the Copenhagen Fortress in times of invasion. But during the war, conflicts between the military and the civilian government – who frustrated the full execution of the 1909 scheme – caused workable relations to break down and, as one Danish military historian concludes, Denmark had to rely on other factors to deter potential invaders. This was already clear to the Danish Government in August 1914. Germany – as Sweden – feared a British naval sortie into the Baltic via the Great Belt, which separates the Danish islands Sjælland (Zealand) and Fyn (Funen) and connects the Kattegat to the Baltic Sea. Since the Copenhagen Convention of 1857, the Belt was an international waterway, so Denmark would not be obliged by international law to fight any fleet steaming the Belt. On 5 August, however, the German Government demanded that Denmark mine the Belt. The demand caused a government crisis in Denmark, as some ministers argued for refusing the German demand (which would mean war with the Central Powers), while others feared that acquiescing could result in a conflict with the Allies. King Christian X intervened in support of compliance, but further German demands for more mines and preferential treatment of German navy vessels would be refused. Denmark's neutrality policy thereafter had a distinctly pro-German slant, as the country was especially vulnerable to German invasion, but the king, the Foreign Minister and business elites managed to convincingly communicate the reasons for the mining and other seemingly pro-German acts to the Allies.[44]

43 Amersfoort and Klinkert, 'Introduction', pp. 12–13.

44 Michael Clemmesen, *The Danish Armed Forces 1909–1918. Between Politicians and Strategic Reality* (Copenhagen: Royal Danish Defence College, 2007), pp. 33–9; Hans Branner, 'The August 1914 mine-laying crisis', in Michael Epkenhans and Gerhard P. Groß (eds.), *The Danish Straits and German Naval Power 1905–1918* (Potsdam: Militärgeschichtliches

Switzerland fully mobilised its 220,000-member militia forces when war broke out and moved them along the border to counter any attempts by French or German forces to outflank each other via Swiss terrain. Once the fronts had stabilised in November 1914, most of the militia was sent home again, although the size of the army kept fluctuating. In 1918, reacting to social and economic pressure, there were only 20,000 troops under the colour, although some units were again called up in response to widespread unrest in November 1918. Perhaps because Switzerland enjoyed both a more defensible geography and the advantage of an internationally recognised neutrality, Swiss politicians left the army to its own devices. Swiss army generals, for example, strategised with counterparts from both belligerent camps to counter any invasions by their enemies.[45]

This was in sharp contrast to the Danish, but also the Dutch situation. The Netherlands Government felt that neutrality would be best safeguarded by a close watch on its borders and making sure any and all infractions of its territorial integrity, however small, could and would be dealt with. In order to do so, the army kept its 200,000-men army mobilised throughout the war. Moreover, Dutch interpretation of strict neutrality left no room for high-level contacts with belligerent armies, as in Switzerland. The Netherlands Government vowed to only seek outside help in case of actual invasion, and considered planning beforehand a danger to neutrality which would, if the belligerents found out, *invite* instead of *prevent* invasion.[46]

It is still a matter of historical debate whether a neutral military deterrent really had any effect. Proponents point to the fact that the military situation on the

Forschungsamt, 2010), pp. 97–106. See for the struggle between German 'hawks' (especially in the *Kriegsmarine*) and the 'doves' of the Foreign Office on the question of Danish neutrality Udo Dobers, 'Die deutsch-dänischen politischen Beziehungen im Spätsommer 1914. Untersuchung eines Sektors der deutschen Außenpolitik bei Ausbruch des Ersten Weltkrieges' (PhD thesis, University of Hamburg, 1972).

45 Max Mittler, *Der Weg zum Ersten Weltkrieg: Wie neutral war die Schweiz? Kleinstaat und europaïscher Imperialismus* (Zürich: Verlag Neuer Zürcher Zeitung, 2003), pp. 595–899; Antoine Saküle, 'L'armée suisse (1914–1918): forces et difficultés', in Jules Maurin and Jean-Charles Jauffret, *La Grande Guerre 1914–1918: 80 ans d'historiographie et de représentations. Colloque international – Montpellier 20–21 novembre 1998* (Presses de l'Université de Montpellier, 2002), pp. 265–80. For more information on Swiss operational war planning before and during the war, see Hans-Rudolf Fuhrer, *Die Schweizer Armee im ersten Weltkrieg. Bedrohung. Landesverteidigung, Landesbefestigung* (Zürich: NZZ Verlag: 2000).

46 Wim Klinkert, 'Threatened neutrality: Holland between the German army and the British navy', in Epkenhans and Groß, *Danish Straits*, pp. 139–54. See also the forthcoming essay collection by Klinkert: *Neutrality Defended. The Netherlands Prepares for War, 1900–1925* (Leiden: Brill, 2013).

Western Front meant that even the smaller neutral armies would be formidable foes for whatever forces the belligerents could scramble for an invasion, a position enhanced by a skilfully executed campaign of (mis)information. They also note that most invasion plans prepared by the belligerents (such as 'Scheme S' for a British invasion of the southern Netherlands, 'Case J' for a German invasion of Jutland and German naval operations in Danish waters) were specifically designed for situations in which a neutral was attacked by another party: a German attack on Holland in the case of the first, and British incursions though Denmark towards the Kiel Canal in the second example. Real offensive plans did exist (for example, the French army 'Plan H' for a strike at Germany through Switzerland in the winter of 1915/16), but mainly in response to rumours that a neutral country might choose sides after all.[47]

Detractors, however, argue that other factors might have played a much more important role in upping the benefits of neutrality to the belligerents, mainly economics. As mentioned in the previous section, access to neutral (financial) markets could potentially have huge benefits to both sets of belligerents. As part of their economic warfare campaigns, the Allies and the Central Powers tried their best to profit as much as possible from trade with neutrals, while simultaneously denying their enemies that same benefit. For neutrals, the danger was that giving in too much to the economic demands of one side could lead to accusations of un-neutral behaviour.

However, the problem with which many of the neutrals were faced was the fact that Britain controlled all oceanic trade routes and could deny them access to badly needed supplies such as foodstuffs, fertiliser and cotton at will. The British Government used this weapon to pressure the neutrals, especially those contiguous to Germany, to stop all transit trade. The Netherlands was the earliest target of this strategy, since the River Rhine provided Germany's chief industrial areas with easy access to the sea via the Dutch port of Rotterdam. However, the Dutch Government had signed a free-trade agreement with Germany and feared that giving in to British demands would force it into a serious conflict with the Central Powers. Literally caught between 'the devil and the deep blue sea', the Dutch Government found itself paralysed. However, fearing that an

47 Wim Klinkert, 'Fall K. German offensive plans against the Netherlands 1916–1918' and C. Paulin, 'German war plans against Denmark 1916–1918', in Amersfoort and Klinkert, *Small Powers*, pp. 85–117, 119–34. See for 'Plan H' Hans Rudolf Ehrbahr, *Schweizerische Militärpolitik im Ersten Weltkrieg. Die militärischen Beziehungen zu Frankreich vor dem Hintergrund der schweizerischen Außen- und Wirtschaftspolitik 1914–1918* (Bern: Verlag Stämpfli & Cie, 1976), pp. 87–144.

Anglo-Dutch conflict over contraband trade would ruin the small neutral country and damage the Allied cause in the eyes of other neutrals – most notably the United States – British diplomats in the Netherlands conspired with key figures from the Dutch governmental circles and an influential community of bankers and businessmen, who came up with a solution that would preserve Dutch neutrality and protect British interests. They founded the Netherlands Overseas Trust Company (NOT), a private organisation that would guarantee the home consumption of any goods declared by the British to be contraband. This guaranteed that the Netherlands would be able to import much-needed goods from overseas without compromising the burgeoning British blockade of the Central Powers. As NOT was not in any way (formally) connected with the government, Prime Minister P. W. A. Cort van der Linden and his Cabinet could disavow knowledge of or complicity in any actions of NOT vis-à-vis Germany. The NOT agreement of December 1914 was in July 1915 supplemented with a voluntary rationing agreement. Moreover, in 1916, the British Government and NOT negotiated a trading agreement between Dutch farmers and the Allied governments limiting agricultural exports to Germany.[48]

The Allies hoped that other neutral countries could be induced to create NOT-like institutions. The Swiss Government was willing to entertain such a suggestion, but demanded a greater level of oversight than its Dutch counterpart, for fear that Allied pressure on a purely private company (the *Société Suisse de Surveillance*, set up in October 1915) would cause it to favour French-speaking Swiss over their German-speaking counterparts. The Swiss were on the one hand more dependent on the Allies than were the Dutch, since their access to the sea could be completely controlled by the Allies (especially after the Italian declaration of war). On the other hand, they managed to negotiate with both parties from a position of relative strength, as Germany did not protest the Swiss Government's official involvement in the negotiations and the Allies allowed some goods to pass the blockade in order to be bartered for much-needed coal and iron for Swiss industries. This strength

48 Samuël Kruizinga, 'Government by committee: Dutch economic neutrality and the First World War', in Kitchen *et al.*, *Other Combatants, Other Fronts*, pp. 99–124, and 'NOT neutrality. The Dutch Government, the Netherlands Overseas Trust Company, and the Entente blockade of Germany, 1914–1918', in Hertog and Kruizinga, *Caught in the Middle*, pp. 85–104; Frey, *Erste Weltkrieg*, pp. 110–203, 232–330; Herman de Jong, 'Between the devil and the deep blue sea: the Dutch economy during World War I', in Stephen Broadberry and Mark Harrison (eds.), *The Economics of World War I* (Cambridge University Press, 2005), pp. 137–68.

derived partly from both sides' dependence on Swiss munitions and machine works, the secure knowledge of Swiss neutrality and Swiss relative military strength.[49]

In Denmark, the government initially remained aloof, just as the Dutch had done. They stood by while British Government officials negotiated trade and home consumption agreements with the pre-existing *Industriråd* (Industrial Council) and the *Grosserer Societet* (Merchants' Guild) representing most of Danish industry, in November 1915, and informal agreements with several farmers' organisations regarding agricultural export in 1915 and early 1916. However, the Danish executive began to fear that these private negotiations would endanger neutrality, as the council and the guild seemed more concerned with protecting their British markets than Danish neutrality. Foreign Minister Erik Scavenius therefore intervened in March 1916, annulling a recent trade treaty and forcing Danish participants to consider German demands from a wider political standpoint. This had remarkable success, as Britain recognised the tremendous amount of military pressure Berlin could apply to the Danes.[50]

In Norway, there was no NOT-like institution. As Norwegian industry specialised in a few major sectors, so-called 'branch agreements' were created with each of these sectors regarding imports and exports. Moreover, the British traded tonnage from the large Norwegian merchant fleet for coal, and thereby set a precedent followed from 1916 onwards by the Netherlands and Denmark. In addition to these private agreements, the government negotiated a sharp curb to fish and pyrite exports to Germany with the Allies in 1916. Germany was not in an economic position to pressure

49 David Daniel Driscoll, 'Anglo-Swiss Relations 1914–1918 with Special Reference to the Allied Blockade of the Central Powers' (PhD thesis, University of London, 1968); Heinz Ochsenbein, *Die verlorene Wirtschafsfreiheit 1914–1918. Methoden ausländischer Wirtschafskontrollen über die Schweiz* (Bern: Verlag Stämpfli & Cie, 1971); Marjorie Farrar, 'Le système de blocus suisse (1914–1918): les interactions de la diplomatie, de la stratégie et des priorités intérieures', *Revue d'histoire moderne et contemporaine*, 21:4 (1974), pp. 591–622; Pierre Luciri, *Les sources de la neutralité économique suisse. Les accords secrets de Berlin des 26 mars et 5 août 1915, l'arrangement du 22 septembre 1915 instituant la Société suisse de surveillance* (Lausanne: Institut universitaire de hautes études internationales, 1976). The effects of economic war on Swiss companies in different sectors of Swiss industry and the service sectors are treated in Roman Rossfeld and Tobias Straumann (eds.), *Der vergessene Wirtschaftskrieg. Schweizer Unternehmen im Ersten Weltkrieg* (Zürich: Chronos Verlag, 2008).

50 For negotiations with Britain, see Tage Kaarsted, *Great Britain and Denmark 1914–1920* (Odense University Press, 1979), pp. 99–104; Eli F. Heckscher *et al.*, *Sweden, Norway, Denmark and Iceland in the World War* (New Haven, CT and London: Yale University Press and Oxford University Press, 1930), pp. 419–20.

the Norwegians, and increasing U-boat sinkings only solidified the pro-Allied economic slant of Norwegian neutrality.[51]

Sweden, finally, refused to discuss her export regulations with the British, and she also declined to provide them with statistics. There were agreements with shipping lines, but in general economic warfare was conducted on a piecemeal basis – that is, ships destined for Sweden were frequently held up or their cargoes were brought to the prize court. Swedish exports of raw materials continued unencumbered to Germany, as the Allies could not risk the country closing Russia's lifeline to the West. But when Russia started to pull out of the war and food shortages increased, popular discontent forced a change of government to one more amenable to coming to economic and tonnage agreements with the Allies.[52]

Neutrality and national policy

Institutions like the NOT and military arrangements such as Denmark's kowtowing to German military might were hardly neutral in the legal sense of the word. However, the belligerents seemed to have accepted them, even though formal protests were lodged. The German Government seemed to have accepted the necessity of economic agreements between neutrals and the Allies: without NOT, for example, the Netherlands would have been included in the blockade and therefore not been able to produce an agricultural surplus which could be exported to the Central Powers. Moreover, the NOT businessmen had demanded that certain luxury goods from the Indies could still be sold via the Netherlands to Germany. Finally, Berlin took advantage of the creation of wartime private organisations and companies encompassing all-important Dutch bankers, businessmen and farmers to negotiate loan agreements and fixed prices, which eased their own financial woes. However, Berlin carefully watched the arrangements and was not above applying some economic pressure of its own when it felt that NOT

51 Riste, *Neutral Ally*, pp. 91–4; Paul G. Vigness, *The Neutrality of Norway in the World War* (Stanford University Press, 1932), pp. 47–50.

52 Steven Koblik, *Sweden: The Neutral Victor. Sweden and the Western Powers 1917–1918. A Study of Anglo-American-Swedish Relations* (Stockholm: Läromedelsförlagen, 1972), pp. 15–32. German-Swedish negotiations are detailed in Justus-Andreas Grohmann, *Die deutsch-swedische Auseinandersetzung um die Fahrstrassen des Öresunds im Ersten Weltkrieg* (Boppard am Rhein: H. Boldt, 1974), pp. 114–52, 169–70; Anglo-Swedish negotiations in Brian J. C. McKercher and Keith E. Neilson, 'The triumph of unarmed forces: Sweden and the Allied blockade of Germany, 1914–1917', *Journal of Strategic Studies*, 7:2 (1984), pp. 178–99.

and its sister organisations had gone too far in appeasing the Allies. Likewise, Britain accepted the military arrangements made by Denmark with Germany, as she simply lacked the military force to apply similar pressure. Here, too, Denmark had to walk a fine line between necessary (and thus acceptable) and *excessive* accommodation.[53]

However, in Holland as well as in Denmark, neutrality itself was accepted by the vast majority of the population as the right and necessary foreign policy. Both their governments were acutely aware that their geostrategic position, compounded by the fact that both had extensive colonial empires to consider, made joining one of the blocs a very perilous adventure. Moreover, for many citizens of neutral countries, neutrality retained its positive self-image: they saw themselves as possessing cooler heads and a higher morality than the belligerents, whose mission to 'save the world' was seen as self-serving and hypocritical.[54] However, even in the countries that arguably practised a neutrality closest to the letter of international law, the Netherlands – who had created a strict barrier between the government and NOT – and Switzerland – whose neutrality was guaranteed by international treaty and its own federal constitution – neutrality and domestic policy could be at odds.

In January 1916, Switzerland was rocked by the *Obersten-Affäre* (the 'Colonels' Affair'). Two senior intelligence officers of the Swiss army were discovered to have been supplying the German and Austrian military attachés with information about French and Russian troop movements. At first, Swiss army command tried to hush the affair by transferring the offending officers away from the intelligence section, but when a Francophone Swiss newspaper broke the news, it caused a huge outcry both among French-speaking Swiss – who saw their worst fears of a supposed pro-German bias within the military confirmed – and the Allies. To prevent the affair from spiralling out of control, the Swiss Federal Council decided that the case should be heard before a military court. Interestingly, the officers were found not guilty of treason (no Swiss military secrets were passed on) and Chief of Staff Theophil Sprecher von Bernegg, ultimately responsible, was not relieved of his duties. But perhaps most revealing is Sprecher's witness statement of 29 February 1916: '[A]s on the one hand we have to accept that our rights as a neutral are violated

53 Frey, 'The neutrals and WWI', pp. 16–24. See also his 'Die Niederlande als transatlantische vermittler, 1914–1920', in Ragnhild Fiebif-von Hase and Jürgen Heideking (eds.), *Zwei Wege in die Moderne: Aspekte der deutsch-amerikanischen Beziehungen 1900–1918* (Trier: Wissenschaftlicher Verlag, 1998), pp. 177–98.

54 Denmark, for example, had no realistic hope of reacquiring the territory lost in the Second Schleswig War of 1864.

and restricted whenever it suits the belligerent, we also need not be too obsequious and strict in the observation of our duties.'[55]

His views were taken to the extreme by Dutch supreme commander C. J. Snijders. He argued that maintaining a close 'neutrality watch' along the borders of his country to punish any infraction was sapping his troop strength and diminishing his capacity to defend the country. This was compounded by his government's refusal to enter into preliminary talks with the belligerents to discuss operational plans in case of invasion. Under these conditions, he argued in 1917 to 1918, his country was essentially undefendable against attack. In his view, defending neutrality and defending his country had come to be at odds. Snijders was, like Sprecher, not fired, indicating that in neutral countries the question posed by those two military men – whether the rules of neutrality actually protected the neutral country – did not have a ready solution.[56]

In Spain, a dilemma of a different sort surfaced. There, not unlike in Greece, the war highlighted pre-existing sharp divides within the country. This crisis was deepened by the economic impact of the war, made worse by the fact that the country had to deal with over 40,000 Spanish migrant workers returning home. As, once again, in Greece, a virulent debate over foreign policy exacerbated the sharp debate – which one researcher has dubbed 'the moral equivalent . . . of civil war' – between two opposing groups. One, catholic, conservative and monarchic in outlook, supported the Central Powers, who were seen as bulwarks of the monarchy, authority, a hierarchical social order, discipline and religious devoutness. The other, a wide but disparate coalition of anti-clerical forces, saw the Allies as defenders of religious and political freedom and models of the future social, cultural and economic modernisation they hoped Spain would emulate. This group was also supported by many in Catalonia, who felt economic, cultural, familial and linguistic ties to France. Although proponents of both groups argued for entering the war and discussed among themselves the best moment to do so, the very fact that Spain was so fundamentally divided precluded choosing a side, because doing so would cause massive unrest and probably a civil war. Moreover, many felt that neutrality was Spain's only true option, even in spite of their sympathies

55 Paul Moeyes, 'Neutral tones. The Netherlands and Switzerland and their interpretation of neutrality 1914–1918', in Amersfoort and Klinkert, *Small Powers*, pp. 72–4 (citation on p. 73). Cf. H. R. Fuhrer, 'Die oberstenaffäre', in Hans-Rudolf Fuhrer and Paul M. Strässle (eds.), *General Ulrich Wille: Vorbild den einen – Feindbild den anderen* (Zürich: Verlag Neue Zürcher Zeitung, 2003), pp. 359–408.

56 Abbenhuis, *Art of Staying Neutral*, pp. 243–7, Tuyll, *The Netherlands and WWI*, pp. 110–21.

for either belligerent bloc: the country's inherent economic and military weakness precluded active involvement.[57]

Mexico's neutrality was similarly default, since it was in the throes of an *actual* civil war. From 1910 until 1919, one political faction after another gained power, often with the (secret) backing of Britain, Germany or the United States, who hoped thereby to better protect their existing investments or to gain more influence in the future. After 1914, Germany began pondering the possibility of US belligerence on the Allied side and therefore stepped up its activities in Mexico, hoping to either create a base of operations in case of a US declaration of war or to stir up so much trouble that Washington would be too preoccupied to enter the European battlefields. A proxy war ensued in which American, German, and, although with far less success, British interests squared off, with domestic Mexican concerns thrown into the mix. In the end, Mexico remained divided during the war: its neutrality was therefore by default.[58]

In Sweden, there was only one 'war party': the so-called activists (*aktivisterna*). They urged Sweden to take up arms alongside Germany, but did so for a variety of reasons. Some saw Sweden as the primary exponent of the Nordic Teutons, and urged 'Germania's favourite, most fair-haired daughter' to join her racial relations in a struggle for civilisation. Others dreaded an Allied victory over the Central Powers which would give Russian 'eastern barbarity' predominance in the Baltic Sea, which was especially troubling considering they held the Åland Islands. And some dreamed that aiding Germany would mean a return to Swedish predominance in Scandinavia, albeit under German aegis.[59] The activists used sexual and Social Darwinian imagery to

57 Gerald H. Meaker, 'A civil war of words: the ideological impact of the First World War on Spain, 1914–1918', in Schmitt, *Neutral Europe*, pp. 1–65; Jean-Marc Delaunay, '1914. Les espagnols et la guerre', in Jean-Jacques Becker and Stéphane Audoin-Rouzeau (eds.), *Les sociétés européennes et la guerre de 1914–1918: actes du colloque organisé à Nanterre et à Amiens du 8 au 11 décembre 1988* (Paris: Université Paris X-Nanterre, Centre d'Histoire de la France contemporaine, 1990), pp. 117–34; Romero Salvadó, *Spain 1914–1918*, pp. 9–16, 165–73; Romero Salvadó, 'The Great War and the crisis of liberalism in Spain, 1916–1917, *Historical Journal*, 36:4 (2003), pp. 893–914; Romero Salvadó, 'Fatal neutrality: pragmatism or capitulation? Spain's foreign policy during the Great War', *European History Quarterly*, 33:3 (2003), pp. 291–316.

58 Friedrich Katz, *The Secret War in Mexico. Europe, the United States, and the Mexican Revolution* (University of Chicago Press, 1981), pp. 253–524; Michael C. Meyer, 'The Mexican-German conspiracy of 1915', *The Americas*, 23:1 (1966), pp. 76–89.

59 Inger Schuberth, *Schweden und das Deutsche Reich im Ersten Weltkrieg. Die Aktivistenbewegung 1914–1918* (Bonn: Röhrscheid, 1981). See for German attempts to politically support the Swedish activists Wilhelm M. Carlgren, *Neutralität oder Allianz. Deutschlands Beziehungen zu Schweden in den Anfangsjahren des ersten Weltkrieges* (Stockholm: Almqvist & Wiksel, 1962), pp. 73–5.

portray belligerent countries as strong and masculine, while neutrality was denounced as weak and feminine, just as the interventionist press in Italy had done during 'radiant May'. In their social conservatism and a certain measure of pro-Germanism, the activists found some support with the government of Hjalmar Hammarskjöld and King Gustav V. But this influence was largely cancelled out by liberal and social-democratic resistance to 'adventurism' in foreign policy, support for further democratisation and a more even-handed neutrality policy. Hammarskjöld's resignation, the sobering influence of press reports on the horrors of war and a realistic reorientation of diplomatic efforts following British economic measures severely reduced – but never completely extinguished – the activist movement.[60]

In far-away Chile, finally, the country was as divided as Spain. Here, too, a faction centred on church and army supported the Central Powers, and liberals of many colours and creeds advocated the cause of the Allies. However, the situation was made more complex by the existence of large groups of German immigrants, who in 1916 had created a powerful lobby group, the Deutsch-Chilenischen Bund (German-Chilean League). Moreover, distrust of her Latin American neighbours Peru and Bolivia, who had joined with the United States after 1917, and a US-led campaign against German economic influence in Chile led to a massive wave of anti-Americanism.[61] Argentina's neutrality was similarly influenced by anti-Allied feeling. Argentina had been dependent on British markets and finance for a long time, and the country might have joined her neighbours to the north throwing in her lot with the Allies, as German submarines had harassed Argentine shipping and, in September 1917, an intercepted telegram from the German minister in Buenos Aires, Count Carl von Luxburg, became public in which he derided his host country's Foreign Minister as 'a notorious ass' and recommended that all Argentine ships be 'sunk without a trace'. However, in

60 Lina Sturfelt, 'From parasite to angel. Narratives of neutrality in the Swedish popular press during the First World War', in Hertog and Kruizinga, *Caught in the Middle*, pp. 110–14; Steven Koblik, 'Sweden, 1917: between reform and revolution', in Schmitt, *Neutral Europe*, p. 115. On the Swedish monarchy's support for the Central Powers, see Franklin D. Scott, 'Gustav V and Swedish attitudes toward Germany, 1915', *Journal of Modern History*, 39:2 (1967), pp. 113–18.

61 Fredrick B. Pike, *Chile and the United States, 1880–1962; the Emergence of Chile's Social Crisis and the Challenge to United States Diplomacy* (Notre Dame, IN: University of Notre Dame Press, 1963), pp. 88–91. On the enduring German influence in Chile, see Stefan Rinke, 'Ein pickelhaube macht noch keinen Preußen: preußisch-deutsche militärberater, militärethos und modernisierung in Chile, 1886–1973', in Sandra Carreras (ed.), *Preußen und Lateinamerika: Im Spannungsfeld von Commerz, Macht und Kultur* (Münster: LIT-Verlag, 2004), pp. 259–84.

October 1916, Hipólito Yrigoyen had come to power on an anti-British, anti-globalisation platform. Despite the economic dependence on British markets and finance, since the start of the war many had felt the oppressive side-effect of this dependence as Britain had begun an aggressive campaign of economic warfare against German interests in Argentina. The callous way in which this campaign was waged so infuriated the populace that Yrigoyen's neutrality policy went virtually uncontested: Argentina's agricultural surplus thereby formed a vital bargaining chip.[62]

Conclusions

Why did some countries manage to stay neutral, while others opted for or were forced into belligerency? This seemingly simple question has spawned a mountain of literature in dozens of languages. Mostly, in countries that remained neutral, the national historiography has focused on the question of whether this feat was due to successful leadership which steered the neutral ship of state in an even course between Allied Scylla and German Charybdis, or whether external circumstances, such as the specific nature of the conflict or the policies of the belligerents, made for such a tranquil sea that smooth sailing was all but assured. In countries that opted for belligerency, historians ask 'why', but also 'who': who was ultimately responsible for changing course from peace to war. Debates are especially heated if belligerency is seen as contrary to the wishes or interests of the majority of the population (such as in Italy, where historians note that many urging for war in 1915 also supported the fascists in the 1920s) or did not have the desired effects (such as in the Ottoman Empire, where belligerency designed to save the country ended up destroying it).[63] Interestingly, in countries whose neutrality was violated, there is little or no discussion about the reasons why: Belgium and Luxembourg were 'in the way' and therefore had no hope of maintaining their neutrality.

In this chapter, I have tried to draw some conclusions from a very disparate and, more importantly, very 'national' historiography on neutrality during the

62 Philip Dehne, 'Britain's global war and Argentine neutrality', in Hertog and Kruizinga, *Caught in the Middle*, pp. 67–83; Dehne, *On the Far Western Front. Britain's First World War in South America* (Manchester University Press, 2009), pp. 160–71; Robert Gravil, 'The Anglo-Argentine connection and the war of 1914–1918', *Journal of Latin American Studies*, 9:1 (1977), pp. 55–89; Joseph S. Tulchin, *Argentina and the United States. A Conflicted Relationship* (Boston: Twayne, 1990), pp. 36–8.

63 Renzi, *In the Shadow of the Sword*, p. 264.

First World War. First of all: the countries that opted for belligerency were led into the war by governments or governing elites believing that remaining neutral deprived them of a vital chance to shape their own future, instead of it being decided *for* them in a fashion that threatened vital national interests. Interestingly, my findings show that the original belligerents – try as they might – could only (and not even in all cases) influence the *timing*, but not the *direction* of intervention.[64]

The countries whose neutrality was violated by the belligerents were victims of geography and, to a lesser degree, strategy. The fate of Belgium and Luxembourg was decided the moment German war planners concluded that their sovereignty was a necessary sacrifice for the speedy victory over France, without which the country would fall victim to the Russian 'steam-roller'. Albania was a country created to prevent war: its territory was coveted by so many that giving it to one would invite invasion by the other. This objective was already failing in 1914 when war broke out.

A select group of states opted to remain neutral. Their governments believed that belligerency would be far too dangerous and/or would provide too few benefits. In most countries, only fringe groups argued for intervention, but in others pre-existing ideological, linguistic and ethnic divides were deepened by war and neutrality – the only course on which they did not disagree. The twin examples of Spain, where the 'civil war of words' descended in the 1920s and 1930s into *actual* civil war and fascist dictatorship, and Switzerland, which forged a unique 'neutral' national identity for the Francophone and German-speaking parts of the nation, illustrate that the choice for neutrality could have long-term consequences.[65]

However, simply declaring oneself neutral was not enough. Since internationally recognised rules and regulations on the rights and duties of neutrals were inconsistent at best, non-existent at worst, neutrals and belligerents had to constantly negotiate a (constantly shifting) modus vivendi. The outcome of this modus vivendi was determined by a number of key factors:

(i) Geographical circumstances form a significant deterrent against attack. As the neutrality of Belgium and Luxembourg was a victim of geography, it stands to reason that in other cases, geography worked to maintain it.

64 Lothar Höbelt, 'Der Balkan und die strategie der Entente', in Jürgen Angelow (ed.), *Der Erste Weltkrieg auf dem Balkan* (Berlin: be.bra Wissenschaft Verlag, 2011), pp. 57–73.

65 Mittler, *Weg zum Ersten Weltkrieg*, pp. 662–6.

(ii) The benefits of neutrality are (perceived to be) spread as evenly as possible given the military and economic circumstances.
(iii) Neutrals work to maximise the costs of a (possible) attack, while minimising the penalty associated with their neutrality to each belligerent.

Finally, this chapter shows that the way in which the modus vivendi was negotiated between neutrals and belligerents varied considerably. First of all, the benefits of their neutrality might be perceived differently by different belligerents, or even different factions within belligerent countries. Moreover, neutrals had to react to rapidly changing circumstances which could render some of the benefits of their neutrality moot. Finally, neutrals had to decide *how* they best presented their 'case' to the belligerents. This constant renegotiation, and not the supposed 'decline' of international law, is the essence of First World War neutrality.

21
Pacifism

MARTIN CEADEL*

Definitions

Still a recently minted word in 1914, 'pacifism' became embedded in most major languages when the world conflict brought views about war to the forefront of political life. The price, however, was a deepening uncertainty as to its primary meaning, which even now is not fully resolved. To delineate the scope of this chapter, it is necessary to identify the three senses in which the word was used during the Great War. In descending order of rigour, these were: first, the absolute rejection of military force, most dramatically expressed as a conscientious refusal to be conscripted; secondly, the progressive belief that political reforms could ultimately abolish war, most notably expressed in liberal demands for a League of Nations, radical demands for democratic control of foreign policy, and socialist demands for the overthrow of capitalism and imperialism; and, thirdly, simple war-aversion, as expressed in strikes and mutinies motivated by material factors rather than by any belief in the reformability of the international system.

In 1901, Émile Arnaud of France's Ligue international de la paix et de la liberté had coined *'le Pacifisme'* to describe the full range of ideas that the peace movement had been promoting as an articulate political minority for just over a century. He had done so to provide an alternative to *'le Fédéralisme'*, the narrower programme to which some activists such as Jacques Novicow were then trying to restrict that movement.[1] Unlike 'paxism', which G. H. Perris of Britain's International Arbitration and Peace Association had been promoting

* I am grateful to Isabel Holowaty for bibliographical assistance.

1 Arnaud first used it in an article in *L'Indépendence belge* in August 1901, immediately reprinted it in *États-Unis d'Europe: Journal de la Ligue internationale de la paix et de la liberté*, 1 (August 1901), and used it on the platform of the Universal Peace Congress at Glasgow the following month: see *Proceedings of the 10th Universal Peace Congress, St Andrew's Hall, Glasgow, 10–13 September 1901* (London: 1901), pp. 82–90.

since 1897,[2] the new word caught on. In Britain, 'pacifism', sometimes rendered by etymological purists as 'pacificism', was first used in peace journals in the autumn of 1903, and reached the country's principal newspaper *The Times* two years later. It did not appear in the first edition of the *Concise Oxford Dictionary*, published in 1911, but made it into the 1914 version's *addendum*.

The peace movement, for whose ideas Arnaud had been seeking a snappily inclusive label, had emerged in Britain in the aftermath of the French Revolution and had been institutionalised into peace associations in both the United States and Britain at the end of the Napoleonic Wars, spreading gradually and on a smaller scale into Europe in subsequent decades. It was united by its belief in the achievability of 'peace' of a more profound and enduring kind than the truce between armed and watchful states for which governments settled on realist grounds. But from the outset, this idealistic movement to transform the international system by abolishing the institution of war had two distinct wings, absolutist and reformist. Absolutists, a minority even among English-speaking peace activists and even rarer among those of other countries, inherited their approach from Christian sects such as the Mennonites and Quakers. They rejected all military force, and sought to abolish war through conscientious objection. Their policy was sometimes described as 'non-resistance', although in domestic politics this term had the confusingly contrasting implication of obedience to governmental authority.[3] The reformists, a majority in all peace movements, were inspired by Enlightenment ideas of the irrationality of war. They sought to abolish it by a variety of political reforms, although until any of these bore fruit they accepted the legitimacy of military force unless used in either an aggressive or a reactionary way. There was no agreed term for a reformist, although 'peace advocate of defensive war' was used in 1846 by the US pacifist Elihu Burritt.[4]

Arnaud's neologism of 1901 thus filled a linguistic void, being particularly useful as a label for the reformist majority of peace activists, although in also covering the absolutist minority it could cause confusion. Its meaning was further complicated by the First World War in two somewhat contradictory ways. First, it began the long-term process whereby, particularly in the English-speaking world, the narrower, absolutist sense took over as the primary meaning: this was because conscientious objectors proved controversial out of all proportion to their tiny numbers. Secondly, in the short term it extended

2 Martin Ceadel, *Semi-Detached Idealists: The British Peace Movement and International Relations, 1854–1945* (Oxford University Press, 2000), p. 147.

3 See, e.g., *The Times*, 3 July 1817, p. 3.

4 E. Burritt diary, 30 October 1846: New Britain Public Library, Connecticut.

the word beyond the peace movement to those thought to be obstructing the war effort even though they offered no dissenting critique of international relations: for example, worker unrest linked to war-weariness was sometimes reported in the press under headlines such as 'Pacifist Strikes'.[5]

This chapter will cover pacifism in all three senses, although it will offer only cursory treatment of the third, which is essentially a matter of morale rather than of belief in the possibility of abolishing war. Applying the term to absolutists presents few problems, since this is now pacifism's primary English-language meaning. Reformists continue to present a labelling challenge for those writing about peace activism: for example, Lawrence S. Wittner favours 'peace-oriented non-pacifist'; and David Cortright uses 'pragmatic pacifist';[6] but following a suggestion by A. J. P. Taylor,[7] the term preferred here is '*pacificist*' (italicised to minimise visual confusion with 'pacifist'). For the merely war-weary, the description 'anti-war' will be used.

Determinants

An account of these three kinds of pacifism across the main combatant nations risks coming across as a bewildering series of discrete micro-histories in which obscure groups and individuals bulk too large. To demonstrate that there was in fact an underlying pattern, it will be now be shown how pacifism of each type was determined by particular conditions, which meant that its development during 1914 to 1918 was to a considerable extent predictable on the basis of previous history.

The absolute variety has most commonly surfaced when compulsory military service has been imposed on Christian sects that object to it; and how states have handled this confrontation has to a considerable extent been shaped by the sects with which they first had to deal. Britain's formative experience came after the Society of Friends, better known as the Quakers, adopted a policy of non-resistance in 1661. By both developing a respected social position as an unthreatening minority and submitting to seizures of their property rather than hire a substitute or pay a fine when called for militia service, the Quakers convinced public opinion that theirs was a principled belief which any Christian could adopt, rather than a sectarian peculiarity that could be bought off by

5 See, e.g., *The Times*, 6 September 1918, p. 8.

6 Lawrence S. Wittner, *Toward Nuclear Abolition* (Stanford University Press, 2003), p. 14; David Cortwright, *Peace: A History of Movements and Ideas* (Cambridge University Press, 2008), pp. 14–15, 30–1.

7 Alan J. P. Taylor, *The Trouble Makers* (London: H. Hamilton, 1957), n. 51.

special treatment. In 1796, the first pacifist texts by non-Quakers were published in London; and in 1816 non-Quaker Christians combined with Quakers to establish the world's first enduring national peace association, the (London) Peace Society. Respect for Quakerism helps to explain why, when Britain belatedly introduced conscription in 1916 (militia service having become a dead letter after the 1830s), it alone made statutory provision for exemption from all compulsory service and not just from bearing arms.

Sects other than the Quakers mostly accepted some form of alternative service, the most important in continental Europe being the Mennonites, whom the Habsburg regime allowed to serve in medical units and the Russians in forestry camps. Experience of this majority Mennonite attitude made the other states allowing for conscientious objection during 1914 to 1918 – New Zealand, the United States and Canada – offer exemption only from combatant service and only to historic peace sects. But some sects presented greater difficulties: after Nazarene objectors made converts among serving soldiers in Hungary, the Habsburg regime revoked their exemption in 1875 and repressed them; and Russia's uncompromising Dukhubors were first harried by the tsarist regime and then driven into exile in Canada in 1895.[8]

Pacifism of the reformist variety has been generated by the right combination of optimism (about the reformability of international relations) and pessimism (about the risk of embroilment in war), which has in turn depended both on a state's geography and on its political culture.[9]

Britain has had comparatively the world's strongest peace movement because of its semi-secure geostrategic position and its semi-liberal political culture. Insularity and the Royal Navy provided sufficient security to permit some optimism about the international system and even to convince some Britons, notably the free-trade campaigner, liberal politician and *pacificist* Richard Cobden, that 'no foreign politics' was a viable option. But there remained some risk of invasion and blockade, which is why British governments had traditionally striven to keep the ports across the English Channel in friendly hands by paying due attention to the European balance of power; and in addition overseas colonies needed defending.

The United States had provided the world's first peace associations, because its war of 1812 had ended before the Napoleonic Wars: in August 1815, a pacifist society was founded in New York; and a *pacificist* one was formed in Boston

8 Peter Brock, *Against the Draft: Essays on Conscientious Objection from the Radical Reformation to the Second World War* (University of Toronto Press, 2006), pp. 143–4, 156–60.

9 This analysis is developed more fully in Martin Ceadel, *Thinking about Peace and War* (Oxford University Press, 1987), ch. 7.

four months later. In 1828, a national association, the American Peace Society, was established; and in 1838, William Lloyd Garrison created the New England Non-Resistance Society, whose anarcho-pacifist rejection of a slave-holding polity was to influence Tolstoy. But the high degree of security enjoyed by America after settling its border dispute with Canada meant that a significant amount of potential pacifist sentiment began to leak away into simple isolationism, one historian noting of the decades following its civil war: 'So much peace was there that the peace movement in the United States kept alive only with difficulty.'[10] By contrast, in semi-secure Britain most idealists worked hard to abolish war because they feared that Britain would be sucked into any major conflict: even Cobden came to see the need for arbitration treaties.

British peace activists also benefited from a liberal, protestant, commercial culture which entrenched free speech, voluntarism and free trade; which integrated the labour movement into national life; and which legitimised what A. J. P. Taylor called 'trouble-making'[11] criticism of the government's foreign and defence policies. In 1857, Cobden brought down Palmerston's government in the House of Commons over its aggressive behaviour towards China, although the 'peace party' lost the ensuing general election.[12] Protectionism and conscription became political impossibilities, despite the growing economic and military challenges to Britain and its Empire. The country's political rulers when the First World War broke out were the liberals, the self-styled party of peace, retrenchment and reform: indeed, the failure of some of its ministers and many of its backbenchers to understand the geopolitical case for standing by France against Germany explains why the Liberal government failed to secure any deterrent value out of its willingness to do so on 4 August 1914. The German violation of Belgian neutrality provided a conveniently moralistic and *pacificist* reason to support British intervention that belatedly satisfied most liberals and also a majority in the labour movement. Although the crusading impulse was not unknown in Britain, as progressive enthusiasm for fighting Russia in 1854 had shown, it faced stronger political checks than in the United States, where the generally bellicose response to a manufactured crisis with Britain over the Venezuelan border in 1895 to 1896 shocked a young Norman Angell, later the best-selling author of *The Great Illusion* (London: Heinemann, 1910), but then a would-be settler in California, into writing for the first time

10 Robert H. Ferrell, 'The peace movement', in Alexander DeConde (ed.), *Isolation and Security* (Durham, NC: Duke University Press, 1957), p. 92.
11 See above, n. 8. 12 Ceadel, *Semi-Detached Idealists*, pp. 57–9.

about political irrationality.[13] Britain's liberal idealism tempered by conservative realism provided a political climate in which peace activists, although subjected to hostility when they refused to support the Crimean War, the occupation of Egypt and the Boer Wars, were regarded by their opponents as deluded more than treacherous.

On the maritime fringes of Northern Europe, the Low Countries and Scandinavia shared enough of Britain's geographical and cultural predispositions to produce *pacificism* of a similar kind. But the heartland of continental Europe was militarily insecure; and the political culture of Catholic, Lutheran or Orthodox countries was less conducive to individualistic moral dissent. In consequence, peace activism either eschewed trouble making or was linked to the far left.

Admittedly, a substantial number of *pacificist* associations had been created in Europe, sometimes under British influence; from 1889 a series of Universal Peace Congresses were held almost annually in different cities; and from 1892 an International Peace Bureau operated in Berne as a coordinating secretariat. But such associations rarely if ever criticised their own governments, believing that international conflicts should be arbitrated and a European federation created only after their particular country had achieved national and even imperial fulfilment – an assumption captured in the title of Sandi E. Cooper's wide-ranging study of European peace activism between 1815 and 1914: *Patriotic Pacifism*. In the short term, their 'pacifism' involved little more than rejecting Social Darwinist ideas of an eternal inter-state struggle for mastery.

The only peace advocates potentially deviating from patriotism were the socialist parties affiliated to the Second International. This last had been created in 1889, and from 1907 had been discussing a possible general strike against war. It believed that its peace campaign had stopped the First Balkan War of 1912 from escalating; and as late as 29 July 1914, when an enthusiastic public meeting in Brussels followed a surprisingly harmonious meeting of the International Socialist Bureau, it assumed that it was doing the same in respect of the Austro-Serbian crisis.[14] However, socialist *pacificism* suffered from two difficulties. First, a labour movement sufficiently alienated from its country to consider not defending it tended also to be organisationally weak, the same being even truer of the anarchists who operated even further towards the extremist fringe. Secondly, even if socialists were convinced that

13 Martin Ceadel, *Living the Great Illusion: Sir Norman Angell, 1872–1967* (Oxford University Press, 2009), pp. 56–62.

14 George Haupt, *Socialism and the Great War: The Collapse of the Second International* (Oxford: Clarendon Press, 1972), pp. 203–15.

overthrowing capitalism could alone produce lasting peace, the process itself might not be peaceful: revolutionary violence or even exploiting a war for political purposes might prove a temptation, which muddied the message of peace.

France had more *pacificist* associations than any other continental country: as Roger Chickering noted in a perceptive comparative addendum to his important study of its German counterpart, the French peace movement 'was, organizationally at least, an impressive phenomenon'. Yet its members 'perceived no conflict between their patriotism and their pacifism' and 'championed tenaciously what they held to be the welfare of their country' in crises such as those with Germany over Morocco. The peace movement had close links with radicalism, the country's strongest and most pro-republic political tendency, which suspected the professional army of monarchist leanings, and was therefore 'responsive to arrangements, such as arbitration, which would minimize the influence of soldiers in political councils'. Moreover, for a nation which cherished an imperial role yet was falling behind the neighbour that had stripped it of Alsace-Lorraine in the Franco-Prussian War of 1870–1 'championing the substitution of law and justice for armed power in international politics . . . could both pave the way for the return of the provinces through arbitral decree and unburden itself of the costs of an armed peace, thereby freeing the country to accomplish its mission overseas'. Likewise, France's peace movement saw a future European federation as an extension of the country's republican values. Admittedly, an insurrectionist strand within the SFIO, the united Socialist Party created in 1905, did not want the workers to defend the state. But from 1912 its most vocal anti-militarist, Gustave Hervé, defected to an ultra-patriotic position. And although the SFIO leader Jean Jaurès was involved in the Second International's peace efforts, and for that reason was assassinated in Paris on 31 July 1914, he advocated a citizen army and had a conception of international relations that was 'much the same as the bourgeois pacifists'.[15]

Elsewhere, peace associations suffered from the even greater weakness of constitutional and economic liberalism. In Austria-Hungary, where there were 'severe restrictions on rights of association, assembly, and free speech', the Austrian Peace Society established in 1891 by Bertha von Suttner, the aristocratic author two years previously of *Die Waffen Nieder*, was confined to 'a thin stratum of the upper bourgeoisie and liberal aristocracy'. It failed to

15 Roger Chickering, *Imperial Germany and a World without War* (Princeton University Press, 1975), pp. 339, 349–50, 353, 359.

condemn its government's annexation of Bosnia-Herzegovina in 1908, and was 'moribund' by June 1914 when its founder died.[16] Those who defied the state such as the anarchist Rudolf Grossman – whose radicalisation had taken place in New York and London[17] – were exceptional individuals.

Likewise, Italy's best-known peace activist, Ernesto Moneta of the Lombard Peace Union, came out in enthusiastic support of his country's aggressive war against the Ottoman Empire to seize Libya in 1911.[18] In Russia, the movement associated with the Universal Peace Congresses was 'largely absent'; and although a peace association was created in Moscow in 1909, it was 'a pale echo' of counterparts elsewhere.[19] When Russia's system of conscription was reformed in 1912, the followers of the idiosyncratic intellectual Leo Tolstoy, a former soldier who had become a no-force Christian anarcho-pacifist, and some liberals in the Duma, called for a conscience clause, but were too weak to prevail. When Japan opened itself to Western ideas as a modernising, state-strengthening strategy after the Meiji Restoration of 1868, it imported not only conscription, but some Christianity and socialism and with them a very small amount of pacifism. Yet this last proved 'alien to the people's outlook', and was for that reason ultra cautious: there were thus only two known conscientious objectors during Japan's war of 1904 to 1905 with Russia; and one of them was talked out of going through with his protest by the country's leading pacifist, who travelled through the night to do so.[20]

In Germany, with its geostrategic sensitivity to encirclement by France and Russia, its cult of the strong state and its industrial development, militarism was stronger than peace sentiment. Liberalism had been suborned by Bismarck, who delivered national unification and tariffs to the middle classes instead of constitutionalism and free trade. The peace movement 'can best be

16 Solomon Wank, 'The Austrian peace movement and the Habsburg ruling elite, 1906–1914', in Charles Chatfield and Peter van den Dungen (eds.), *Peace Movements and Political Cultures* (Knoxville, TN: University of Tennessee Press, 1988), p. 42; Richard R. Laurence, 'The peace movement in Austria, 1867–1914', in Solomon Wank (ed.), *Doves and Diplomats: Foreign Offices and Peace Movements in Europe and America in the Twentieth Century* (Westport, CT: Greenwood Press, 1978), p. 27.

17 Richard R. Laurence, 'Rudolf Grossman and anarchist militarism in Austria before World War 1', *Peace and Change*, 14 (1989), pp. 155–75.

18 Sandi E. Cooper, *Patriotic Pacifism: Waging War on War in Europe, 1815–1914* (New York: Oxford University Press, 1991), pp. 173–4; Brock, *Against the Draft*, ch. 10; Alberto Castelli, 'Between patriotism and pacifism: Ernesto Teodore Moneta and the Italian conquest of Libya', *History of European Ideas*, 36 (2010), pp. 324–9.

19 Joshua A. Sanborne, *Drafting the Russian Nation: Military Conscription, Total War, and Mass Politics, 1905–1925* (DeKalb, IL: Northern Illinois University Press, 2003), p. 183; Linda H. Edmondson, *Feminism in Russia, 1900–17* (Stanford University Press, 1984), p. 158.

20 Brock, *Against the Draft*, ch. 13.

understood as the inheritance of Germany's attenuated liberal tradition'[21] and appeared alien to many Germans, as symbolised by the fact that the co-founder in 1892 and acknowledged leader of the German Peace Society, Alfred Fried, was an Austrian Jew. Historians have recognised the country's inhospitability towards pacifism: having written a dissertation on its pre-1914 peace activism, such as it was, Roger Chickering realised that he had failed to explain 'why the opposition to the peace movement was so widespread in Germany', and so re-oriented the published version away from the activists themselves and towards those 'features in the German political system that accounted for the fact ... that peace movement was significantly weaker in Germany than elsewhere'.[22] But the peace cause had one potential asset in Germany: the strains of rapid industrialisation were such that a Marxist party, the SPD, became the largest grouping in the Reichstag after the 1912 elections. Despite its contempt for bourgeois pacifism, it was prepared to discuss a strike against war to be organised through the Second International; and it mounted peace demonstrations in July 1914.

Pacifism in the merely anti-war sense has been less a function of geography and culture than of a state's inability to maintain public support for its defence effort. It has thus appeared when total war has exacerbated military incompetence, administrative inefficiency, economic weakness, political restiveness, social conflict or ethnic disunity, and has thus particularly affected states unable to draw on a broad base of constitutional consent. The pre-1914 militarist expectation, particularly in authoritarian states, that war would be a state-integrating experience proved to be one of the worst political predictions in modern history. Pacifism in this loose yet politically important sense turned out, paradoxically, to be strongest where the genuine peace movement was weakest.

Pacifism (absolute) and conscientious objection

As an absolutist ideology that might in principle affect the average citizen's willingness to fight, pacifism existed only in Britain, some of its Dominions and the United States during 1914 to 1918. Even here it remained small-scale, although it was subsequently talked up as part of the understandable reaction against the First World War. And even here the majority of absolute pacifists belonged to Christian sects too small to influence the war effort unless their

21 James D. Shand, 'Doves among the eagles: German pacifists and their government during World War I', *Journal of Contemporary History*, 10 (1975), p. 95.

22 Chickering, *Imperial Germany*, pp. vi–xii.

special treatment caused resentment in wider society. In all other combatant countries, conscientious objection 'was the path chosen only by a few obscure and harmless religious sectaries and a handful of eccentric radicals',[23] whose fate depended largely on how much time the local military authorities wanted to waste on trying to enforce conformity.

Ironically, given their role in making conscientious objection comprehensible to British society, an increasing number of Quakers had by the late nineteenth century become somewhat detached from their peace testimony, although in reaction against this acculturation a number of their younger colleagues had experienced a fundamentalist 'renaissance', in some cases under the influence of socialist or Tolstoyan ideas.[24] The First World War exposed this division: 33.6 per cent of Quaker males of military age served in the armed forces; and one senior Quaker, who refused to condemn those joining the army, privately admitted 'it was a good thing there were not too many pacifists, as that might seriously undermine the strength of the Allies and lead to a German victory'. But 44.5 per cent claimed a conscientious objection; and the Friends' Service Committee, an official body created in May 1915 to help Quakers of military age, proved one of the most intransigent peace organisations, giving encouragement to absolutist conscientious objectors. Most Quakers sought a humanitarian middle way: their best-remembered response to the First World War, albeit an unofficial one because it could be interpreted as compromising their peace testimony, was the Friends' Ambulance Unit organised by Philip Baker (later Noel-Baker), who was himself a *pacificist*.[25]

In parallel with these developments within the Society of Friends, the (London) Peace Society lost its vitality in the late nineteenth century, and, although reaffirming its pacifism when the war broke out, did not act on it, merely asking its dwindling band of members on 5 August 1914 'to hold themselves in check'. Its president, the liberal politician J. A. Pease, chose to remain in the government, and proffered his resignation 'not because my peace principles have altered a tittle but because I might be regarded as being in a false position', the Peace Society accepting it in order to 'hold an absolutely detached

23 Peter Brock and Nigel Young, *Pacifism in the Twentieth Century* (New York: Syracuse University Press, 1999), p. 62.

24 The authoritative account is Thomas C. Kennedy, *British Quakerism 1860–1920: The Transformation of a Religious Community* (Oxford University Press, 2001).

25 John Rae, *Conscience and Politics: The British Government and the Conscientious Objector to Military Service 1916–1919* (Oxford University Press, 1970), p. 73; Ceadel, *Semi-Detached Idealists*, pp. 190–1.

outlook'. The chairman of its committee resigned when the society declined to sponsor its own 'military ambulance'; and his successor, a lawyer, implicitly endorsed the war effort. He published a pamphlet calling for the execution of the Kaiser and his family and for the repatriation of all Germans in Britain, and condemning those 'professed Pacifists' unable to 'recognize any distinction between the idea of conduct for the individual in ... the "Sermon on the Mount", and that incumbent on the Rulers of States to whose peoples they stand in a fiduciary relation'.[26] Only after Herbert Dunnico, a Baptist minister and member of the Independent Labour Party (ILP), became its secretary in January 1916 did the Peace Society become involved in the campaign for a negotiated peace; and by then, on the eve of its centenary, it had in practice been superseded by two new pacifist associations, the Fellowship of Reconciliation and the No-Conscription Fellowships.

Some British Christians accepted that in political terms their country's cause might be just, but nonetheless doubted whether it was theologically permissible. Following an intense and mainly Quaker gathering at Llandudno, on 25 to 30 September 1914, convened by the medical missionary Henry Hodgkin, a more ecumenical gathering was convened at Cambridge in the last four days of the year, with the assistance of Ebenezer Cunningham, a local mathematics don and devout Congregationalist. A majority of the 130 present adopted a statement to the effect that Christians were 'forbidden to wage war', being called instead 'to a life of service for the enthronement of love in personal, social, commercial and national life'. They thereby constituted the Fellowship of Reconciliation (FoR), which soon appointed a full-time secretary, held a number of meetings in churches, and in June 1915 acquired a horse-drawn caravan in which the preacher Maude Royden toured the Midlands in a 'Pilgrimage of Peace'. But after a mob at Hinckley burnt the caravan and terrified its occupants, the FoR decided after 'some divergence of opinion' to avoid 'indiscriminate propaganda'. When conscription was introduced, it pointed its members towards alternative service. This new quietism caused some activists to set up small rival groupings, but appealed to thoughtful, mainly middle-class Christians troubled by war but not wishing to confront those who thought differently from them. The FoR acquired a membership of 6,983 by the Armistice, although its public impact was negligible.[27]

26 Herbert Sefton-Jones, *German Crimes and Our Civil Remedy* (London and New York: John Lane, 1916), pp. 8, 16–18; Ceadel, *Semi-Detached Idealists*, pp. 192–4.

27 Jill Wallis, *Valiant for Peace: A History of the Fellowship of Reconciliation 1914 to 1989* (London: Fellowship of Reconciliation, 1991), Pt I.

A second and more conspicuous pacifist organisation was created almost simultaneously to cater for that minority of socialists who interpreted their creed as requiring the refusal to kill. These were mostly found in the ILP, which differed from the Labour Party, to which it was affiliated, in opposing the war. In November 1914, Fenner Brockway, editor of the ILP paper *Labour Leader*, asked readers determined to resist conscription, should it be introduced, to declare themselves. Their response led to the creation of the No-Conscription Fellowship (NCF), which declared 'human life to be sacred' and therefore refused to 'assume the responsibility of inflicting death'.[28] An attempt by socialist *pacificists* to delete this explicitly absolutist formulation was defeated at the NCF's first national convention in November 1915, by which time it was claiming 5,000 military-age male members. After conscription was introduced, the NCF became a welfare organisation for conscientious objectors with 'no equivalent in any other belligerent country from 1914 to 1918'.[29]

Although passed by a government which since May 1915 had included Conservatives, the Military Service Acts of January and May 1916 (for bachelors and married men respectively) contained provisions for 'conscientious objection' (a legal concept familiar from the Vaccination Act of 1898) that were generous in two ways. First, they in principle allowed exemption not only from bearing arms, but also from both non-combatant service in the army and alternative civilian service. Secondly, they applied not only to members of historic peace churches, but to those holding religious or ethical objections to all war. The numbers claiming to be conscientious objectors turned out to be small: only around 16,500, a mere 0.33 per cent of those recruited voluntarily or compulsorily. The tribunals established to assess their claims were once much criticised, but are now recognised to have done a creditable job in difficult circumstances.[30] Four-fifths of those claiming an objection were awarded some kind of exemption; and approximately two-thirds of objectors accepted their tribunal's ruling. That 4,486 rejected what they had been offered reflected an unanticipated disagreement about whether the unconditional exemption allowed in the legislation should be reserved for exceptional cases. The tribunals

28 Thomas C. Kennedy, *The Hound of Conscience: A History of the No-Conscription Fellowship, 1914–1919* (Fayetteville, AR: University of Arkansas Press, 1981), p. 51.

29 Kennedy, *Hound of Conscience*, p. 52.

30 Tribunals are vilified in John W. Graham, *Conscription and Conscience: A History 1916–1919* (London: Allen & Unwin, 1922); and David Boulton, *Objection Overruled* (London: McGibbon & Kee, 1967), but treated more sympathetically in Rae, *Conscience and Politics* (the source of the statistics given here) and James McDermott, *British Military Service Tribunals, 1916–1918: 'A Very Much Abused Body of Men'* (Manchester University Press, 2011).

mostly thought so, which was why they granted it to only 350 objectors, almost all of them Quakers. Yet under the influence of the NCF and the Friends' Service Committee, a larger minority of objectors than expected sought unconditional exemption.

In the early months of conscription, the almost 6,000 'conchies' inducted into the army suffered some harsh treatment when they refused to wear uniform, as most did; and a few were taken to France where disobedience in the face of the enemy triggered a death sentence. But the army was instructed not to carry out such sentences, and as early as 22 May 1916 decided that such objectors should be handed over to the civil authorities, although this did not stop the NCF winning a public-relations victory the following month when as a result of military confusion thirty-four recalcitrant members of the Non-Combatant Corps were sentenced to death at Boulogne before being quickly reprieved.[31] Objectors who were then transferred to civil prisons had their cases reviewed by a central tribunal, which showed flexibility in declaring all but 313 of them to have genuinely conscientious motives. Most of these reviewed objectors showed a reciprocal flexibility in agreeing to undertake non-military work of national importance under the aegis of the Home Office. After February 1918, when men in formerly protected occupations such as mining were called up, many of those determined not to fight decided not to go before a tribunal, but to announce their conscientious scruples only when inducted into the army. In particular, 50 per cent of conscientious objectors from the Lanarkshire coalfields chose this path into civilian work under the Home Office scheme.[32]

Only 985 absolutists refused any type of alternative service; but they attracted public attention out of all proportion to their numbers because they included a number of high-profile idealists, such as Fenner Brockway and his fellow ILP activist Clifford Allen. The most famous of all was the saintly, Eton-and-Balliol-educated, Tolstoy-influenced Quaker-convert Stephen Hobhouse, who had refused his tribunal's requirement that he serve in the Friends' Ambulance Unit and whose prison sufferings were publicised in a book ostensibly by his mother, but in fact ghost-written by the philosopher Bertrand Russell, an activist in the NCF.[33] By November 1917, such publicity obliged the government to release Hobhouse and other medically unfit absolutists, albeit as part of a package deal whereby all conscientious objectors were to be disfranchised for

31 Kennedy, *Hound of Conscience*, pp. 142–6. 32 Rae, *Conscience and Politics*, p. 69.

33 Jo Vellacott, *Bertrand Russell and the Pacifists in the First World War* (Brighton: Harvester Press, 1980), pp. 210–13.

five years.[34] By stoically enduring during 1916 to 1917 the consequences of their refusal to serve, the absolutist elite of objectors demonstrated powerfully that pacifism could involve courage and sacrifice.

Even so, Brockway, Allen and Hobhouse were atypically attractive figures. Some absolutists demonstrated dogmatism more than saintliness, such as Bert Brocklesby, a Methodist who 'had an absolute conviction that he was being guided by God and no one was going to change the way he thought'.[35] The commonest type of objector was characterised by 'literal biblicism, sectarian withdrawal, [and] apocalyptic expectations',[36] with the Christadelphians alone providing at least 1,176 objectors. This one sect was thus nearly as numerous as the grand total of 1,191 socialists, most of them ILP members, known to the NCF, although in some industrial towns where pacifist feeling was strong, such as Huddersfield, the number of political objectors may have matched that of religious ones.[37] Some socialists hoped that their defiance of the Military Service Acts would advance not just the pacifist cause but also the wider socialist one, an expectation which proved mistaken: after the two Russian revolutions, the work of socialists who had not renounced force, both Brockway and Allen 'lost heart in the usefulness' of their absolutism, and concluded that the 'Socialist Movement has first claim on us' in future, rather than the pacifist movement.[38]

Two British Dominions had attracted the attention of British pacifists in the years before the war. Alarmed by Japan's defeat of Russia in 1904 to 1905, Australia and New Zealand had both introduced compulsory military training for adolescents in 1909 without provision for conscientious objection, sparking some protests. Australia, which had developed pacifist as well as *pacificist* associations following the Boer Wars, narrowly rejected conscription in two referendums in 1916 and 1917: it and South Africa were the only First World War combatants to rely entirely on volunteering.[39] New Zealand legislated for conscription in 1916, exempting only recognised sects (Quakers, Christadelphians and Seventh-Day Adventists), and doing so only from combatant service. As a settler society that required its citizens to pull together, it was intolerant towards

34 Rae, *Conscience and Politics*, pp. 221–3.

35 Will Ellsworthy-Jones, *We Will Not Fight: The Untold Story of the First World War's Conscientious Objectors* (London: Aurum Press, 2007), p. 269.

36 Rae, *Conscience and Politics*, pp. 71, 76.

37 Cyril Pearce, *Comrades in Conscience: The Story of an English Community's Opposition to the Great War* (London: Francis Bourle, 2001), p. 182.

38 Martin Gilbert, *Plough My Own Furrow: The Life of Lord Allen of Hurtwood* (London: Longmans, 1965), pp. 108–9.

39 Malcolm Saunders and Ralph Summy, *The Australian Peace Movement: A Short History* (Canberra: Peace Research Centre, Australian National University, 1986), pp. 13–23.

those whom it regarded as shirkers, and imprisoned a significant number of religious, socialist, Irish and Maori objectors, not all of whom were pacifists. The 2,600 men released at the end of the war lost the vote for ten years.[40]

In the United States, absolutism had lost some of its vitality after many of its adherents – even those in the New England Non-Resistance Society – had endorsed the northern cause in the Civil War. In that conflict, members of historic peace sects had been exempted from combatant service, the absence of unconditional exemption reflecting the prominence among America's pacifists of the Mennonites. The outbreak of European war in 1914 drew some socialists and socially minded Christians towards pacifism for the first time. Jessie Wallace Hughan, a schoolteacher, socialist and Unitarian, formed an Anti-Enlistment League in May 1915, which by the time it was wound up on US entry into the war in April 1917 had collected 3,500 pacifist pledges. She also joined the US branch (established in November 1915) of the FoR, as did Norman Thomas (a Presbyterian pastor who later led the Socialist Party), A. J. Muste (a Congregationalist minister who later became the country's best-known pacifist and labour activist) and John Nevin Sayre (a theology lecturer and Episcopalian rector), who all parted company with their congregations on account of their pacifism.[41] When the United States joined the war, it passed a Selective Service Act whose provision for conscientious objection was no advance on the Civil War. Not belonging to a pacifist sect, Norman Thomas's brother Evan, who took an absolutist position, was imprisoned, being chained in a standing position for nine hours a day.[42] 64,693 claims of conscientious objection were made – a mere 0.023 per cent, of the 2.81 million men inducted into the armed services – of which 58,830 were accepted. Even sectarians thus exempted had first to undergo a medical examination and then, if deemed fit as 20,873 were, to enter an army camp, where such pressure was placed on them not to avail themselves of their certificate of exemption from combatant service that four-fifths gave in. (By contrast, in Britain only 22 of the first 400 conscientious objectors gave in, as the NCF proudly pointed out.) Of

40 David Grant, *Out in the Cold: Pacifists and Conscientious Objectors in New Zealand during World War II* (Auckland, NZ: Reed Methuen, 1986), pp. 18–19.

41 S. H. Bennett, *Radical Pacifism: The War Resisters League and Gandhian Nonviolence in America. 1915–1963* (New York: Syracuse University Press, 2003), pp. 2–16; Jo A. Robinson, 'A. J. Muste and ways to peace', in Charles Chatfield (ed.), *Peace Movements in America* (New York: Schocken Books, 1973), pp. 81–95; Bernard K. Johnpoll, *Pacifist's Progress: Norman Thomas and the Decline of American Socialism* (Chicago, IL: Quadrangle Books, 1970), pp. 13–20; Charles F. Howlett, 'John Nevin Sayre and the International Fellowship of Reconciliation', *Peace and Change*, 15 (1990), pp. 123–49.

42 William A. Swanberg, *Norman Thomas: The Last Idealist* (New York: Charles Scribner, 1976), pp. 66–9.

the fewer than 4,000 Americans who used their certificates, about one-third eventually accepted non-combatant service. In June 1918, the army agreed to 'furlough' the remaining absolutists from their camps in order to undertake civilian agricultural or relief work. By then, both the army and the White House had issued orders pragmatically recognising the 'conscientious scruples' of sincere non-sectarians for whom the Selective Service Act had failed to cater, 450 of whom had ended up in military prisons. But as late as September 1918, a Harvard-educated social worker of secular views who had become a civil-liberties campaigner, Roger Baldwin, refused his army medical because he was 'opposed' both 'to the use of force to accomplish any end, however good' and to 'any service whatsoever designed to help prosecute the war', and was sentenced to a year's imprisonment.[43] Even so, such absolutists, religious or political, had considerably less public impact than in Britain, because, according to the *doyen* of historians of international pacifism Peter Brock, 'most American objectors sought a viable compromise with the state at war'.[44]

Like the United States, Canada experienced a small-scale drift of socially conscious intellectuals towards pacifism as a result of the war: its emblematic figure was the Oxford-educated future progressive MP for Winnipeg, J. S. Woodsworth, who eventually resigned from the Methodist ministry on this issue in June 1918. In August 1917, it introduced conscription with a muddled mixture of leniency and harshness. Mainly on occupational grounds it exempted, from any form of service, a half of those called up, including many sectarians employed in agriculture, and thereby also largely avoided a confrontation with French Canadians. But on conscientious grounds it exempted – merely from combatant service – certain established sects (Mennonites, Quakers, Hutterites and Dukhobors), thereby causing problems both for their unrecognised counterparts, such as the Bible Students, and for unaffiliated pacifists. Canada's solution was to allow army commanders to allocate those conscientious objectors whom they deemed sincere to non-combatant duties, and to threaten only the residual recalcitrants with prison: those incarcerated numbered about 130.[45]

43 Robert C. Cottrell, *Roger Nash Baldwin and the American Civil Liberties Union* (New York: Columbia University Press, 2000), p. 81.

44 Horace C. Peterson and Gilbert C. Fite, *Opponents of War 1917–1918* (Madison, WI: University of Wisconsin Press, 1957), p. 120; Charles Chatfield, *For Peace and Justice: Pacifism in America 1914–1941* (Knoxville, TN: University of Tennessee Press, 1971), pp. 68–71; Kennedy, *Hound of Conscience*, p. 139; Brock and Young, *Pacifism*, p. 57.

45 Thomas P. Socknat, *Witness against War: Pacifism in Canada, 1900–1945* (University of Toronto Press, 1987), ch. 3; Peter Brock and Thomas P. Socknat (eds.), *Challenge to Mars: Essays on Pacifism from 1918 to 1945* (University of Toronto Press, 1999), ch. 12.

Outside the English-speaking world there was little absolutism during the First World War. In Russia, 'there was not the faintest possibility of a non-revolutionary pacifist movement surviving', although when the poet Maksimilian Voloshin refused to fight in 1916 out of respect for the harmony of all creation, he was let off on medical grounds.[46] Mennonites were additionally offered work in ambulance units in 1914, which they mostly carried out in a patriotic spirit. Members of other small sects claiming a conscientious objection, including Molokans, Malevantsy and Tolstoyans, faced military courts if they could not persuade their commanders to assign them to non-combatant duties, and received a wide variety of sentences. In May 1917, the provisional government issued a list of 837 non-Mennonite sectarians tried for refusing to bear arms 'on grounds of conscience' since the outbreak of war: although considerably increased from pre-war rates of objection to conscription, it was an exiguous number in a country where the army had by then expanded from 2.7 to 6.9 million men.[47] However, in January 1919, the Bolsheviks, their sympathy for groups that had defied tsarism temporarily trumping their atheistic authoritarianism, introduced a provision for total exemption from military service on religious grounds, although it proved unworkable and remained a dead letter.[48]

France produced very few absolute pacifists. Only one of its Mennonites, Pierre Kennel, made such a stand, escaping to Switzerland where he also had citizenship.[49] A study of primary-schoolteachers reveals that 'only seven ... lost their jobs for pacifist action over the course of the war' – and this moreover on a broad definition of pacifism that includes mere support for a negotiated peace.[50] A study of female socialists concludes that only one of them 'opposed the war from its outset': the seamstress Louise Saumoneau.[51] A few who went into the army subsequently refused to fight on Christian-pacifist grounds, including Jean Paganon and Lucien Gross, who were imprisoned, and Émile Bonnet and Pastor Guitton, who were put in psychiatric hospitals; and a schoolteacher with Tolstoyan opinions, Paul Savigny, was shot after deserting for pacifist reasons.[52] The novelist Romain Rolland, who

46 Edmondson, *Feminism in Russia*, p. 159; Brock and Young, *Pacifism*, pp. 59–60.

47 Brock, *Against the Draft*, ch. 19. 48 Sanborn, *Drafting the Russian Nation*, pp. 192–9.

49 Brock and Young, *Pacifism*, pp. 60–1.

50 Mona L. Siegel, *The Moral Disarmament of France: Education, Pacifism, and Patriotism, 1914–1940* (Cambridge University Press, 2004), pp. 30, 42–9.

51 Charles Sowerwine, *Sisters or Citizens: Women and Socialism in France since 1876* (Cambridge University Press, 1982), p. 165.

52 Michel Auvray, *Objecteurs, insoumis, déserteurs: Histoire des réfractaires en France* (Paris: Stock/2, 1983), pp. 161–2.

chose to remain in Switzerland for the duration, criticised the war's autocratic origins, its propaganda excesses and the view that Germany was solely responsible in his controversial essay, 'Au-dessus de la mêlée'; but it was not until the 1920s that he endorsed the non-violent methods, until that point 'astonishingly' ignored in France, which had been 'employed among Anglo-Saxons by the thousands of "conscientious objectors"' in those countries and were now being adopted by Gandhi in India.[53]

In Germany there was no significant pacifist movement. Mennonites succumbed to the dominant culture and mostly agreed to bear arms, although in West Prussia about a third sought and were granted non-combatant duties in 1914. The Seventh-Day Adventists also rallied to the flag, with many securing work as medical orderlies; and although some dissenters formed a splinter group that rejected even this, it comprised only 2 per cent of the sect. Likewise, Bible Christians (Jehovah's Witnesses), initially cooperative, produced some absolutists by 1916 to 1917, but only perhaps fifty in all. Socialist or anarchist objectors could be counted on the fingers of one hand. The army, whose rules specifically stated that conscience provided no excuse for refusing military orders, humanely referred some such religious or political absolutists to psychiatrists, but probably shot others.[54] In Italy, 'where hitherto no pacifist tradition of any kind existed', the only three known conscientious objectors – a Bible Christian, a Tolstoyan and a humanist – served long prison sentences and were threatened with mental asylums. In Hungary, Nazarene objectors were imprisoned or executed.[55] Elsewhere, the fate of such objectors as there were remains obscure.

This chapter focuses of course on combatant countries, but must note in passing that Northern-European neutrals had their own pacifists: Norway exempted religious objectors to military service even before the war; Denmark introduced alternative civilian service in 1917; and the Netherlands fined or imprisoned a number of anarcho-pacifist objectors.[56]

Pacificism

As an ideology that could shape war aims and peace terms in and after 1914, the reformist version of pacifism existed on a broader geographical base than its

53 Norman Ingram, 'Romain Rolland the problem of peace', in Chatfield and Dungen, *Peace Movements*, pp. 146–7.

54 Brock, *Against the Draft*, ch. 18.

55 Brock and Young, *Pacifism*, pp. 60–1.

56 Brock and Young, *Pacifism*, p. 61.

absolutist counterpart. Admittedly, British and US progressives took the lead with ideas of international organisation and popular accountability. But the Dutch peace movement used its country's neutrality to facilitate the emergence of a feminist strand of *pacificism*; and the most powerful non-absolutist challenges to war efforts came from socialists in countries such as Russia and Germany where *pacificism* had hitherto been weak.

The outbreak of war presented the reformist majority of the peace movement with two problems. First, it had to acknowledge that the dominant pre-1914 peace idea, international arbitration, had failed, thereby discrediting many existing peace associations. Secondly, unlike absolute pacifists (unless they recanted), *pacificists* had to decide whether or not to support their governments. Most did so, arguing that, being fought to defeat militarism and even to end war, the conflict was in the interests of peace in the long term rather than merely of the balance of power in the short term. The liberals who soon came up with a scheme for a League of Nations and the radicals who began demanding that democratic principles should constrain any peace settlement put some political pressure on combatant governments, particularly at the conclusion of the conflict. In general, however, they caused them few worries.

More concerning for the political authorities were *pacificists* who opposed the war. No state was prepared to recognise as conscientious objectors those who rejected only particular conflicts. Fortunately for the authorities, outright non-absolutist defiance of the war effort was largely confined to the far left, although there was a significant amount of tacit dissent, couched as disingenuous or half-hearted support. *Pacificist* activity went through three phases. In 1914 to 1915, innovative ideas – feminist, liberal and radical – were expounded by new organisations in the teeth of complaints that they were distracting from the military struggle. The stalemate that had become apparent by 1916 produced a growing number of calls for peace negotiations, although these were often hard to interpret: some *pacificists* stipulated armistice terms that made an end to the fighting very unlikely; others by contrast were prepared to accept peace at almost any price; and between these two groups lay many who were simply ignorant of the difficulties involved in reconciling the war aims that each combatant state had developed in order to justify the sacrifices already made. In 1917 to 1918, the revolutions in Russia and the entry of the United States into the war – events which in military terms cancelled each other out – significantly boosted the liberal, radical and socialist strands of *pacificism*, although they subsided for the duration of the Ludendorff offensive.

The international peace movement was taken by surprise by the sudden worsening of the European crisis brought about by Russia's general mobilisation of 30 July 1914. As late as 31 July, British delegates (including Henry Hodgkin) set off for Constance for the following day's scheduled launch of the World Alliance for Promoting International Peace and Friendship through the Churches, an organisation intended to improve Anglo-German relations. And on the same day the International Peace Bureau met in Brussels to discuss the crisis, the German delegates were departing on the last train before their own country invaded Belgium. The Universal Peace Congress, arranged for September in Vienna, was cancelled. Established *pacificist* associations mostly rallied behind their governments. As Emily Hobhouse, who remarkably managed to enter Germany and interview its Foreign Minister, put it to Jane Addams: 'Most of the Peace Societies don't want Peace – they want victory.'[57] They were superseded by new bodies created by feminists, liberals, radicals and socialists.

Women, with a ready-made international network from their suffrage campaigns, had the further advantage as nurturers and non-combatants of being able to call for peace without being accused either of behaviour inappropriate to their sex or of cowardice. Thus, suffragists from both sides of the conflict, Emmeline Pethick-Lawrence from England and the Hungarian émigrée Rosika Schwimmer, could tour the United States together in the autumn of 1914 calling for mediation by neutrals. Liberal *pacificists* dropped arbitration in favour of a League of Nations, the adoption of this goal by President Woodrow Wilson in May 1916 forcing all governments to take it seriously. Radical *pacificists* called for the post-war settlement to be based on democratic principles and therefore to eschew annexations and indemnities, a slogan that gained increasing resonance as the strains of war increased and labour movements – which enjoyed unprecedented political leverage everywhere in the first industrial war – became critical of prolonging the conflict for acquisitive rather than defensive purposes. However, left-wing socialists who coalesced in the Zimmerwald movement began to criticise this view, arguing that only a socio-economic transformation could bring peace. Indeed, it was to proclaim the superiority of socialist *pacificism* over its radical counterpart that a distinctive communist International emerged.

Having cut their organisational teeth on suffragism or social work, the minority of women who opposed the war became indispensable to the peace

57 Hobhouse to Addams, 5 July 1915, cited in David S. Patterson, *Negotiated Peace: Women's Activism and Citizen Diplomacy in World War I* (New York: Routledge, 2008), p. 95.

movement. For example, in Britain, Catherine Marshall worked first for Norman Angell's Neutrality League and then for the No-Conscription Fellowship, while across the Atlantic Frances Witherspoon and Tracy Mygatt gave legal help to conscientious objectors.[58] Female-only initiatives were also made. A Women's Peace Army was launched in Australia.[59] And as a result of Pethick-Lawrence and Schwimmer's visit, the Chicago social worker Jane Addams, who had become an absolute pacifist, created a Woman's Peace Party in January 1915, which took up the continuous-mediation call and soon became 'the most vibrant entity in the American peace movement'.[60] It supported the decision to hold an International Congress of Women in The Hague on 28 to 30 April 1915. Neutral Holland's first woman doctor, Aletta Jacobs, had wanted a replacement for the biennial suffragist conference scheduled for Berlin but cancelled by local feminists, and was persuaded by the British secretary of the International Woman Suffrage Alliance, Chrystal Macmillan, to focus it on peace as well as on the vote. This was not the first international women's gathering since the outbreak of war: a meeting of twenty-eight female socialist *pacificists* had taken place in Berne on 25 March 1915, six months before its much better-known male counterpart in Zimmerwald. But the Hague congress was the first to attract publicity: despite government obstruction which limited the British delegation to three, 1,136 delegates attended an event that was careful to make clear it was 'not a "Stop the War" or "Peace at any Price" demonstration', but a call for mediation by neutrals and for a female say in the terms of any peace.[61] They included Anita Augspurg and Lida Gustava Heymann from Munich, who had denounced a 'men's war' fought between 'men's states' and were shortly to be banned by the German authorities from public agitation.[62] The women's congress overshadowed the Central Organization for a Durable Peace, which had been convened by the Dutch Anti-War Council in the same city on 7 to 10 April, and had a similar purpose.[63] An International Committee of Women for Permanent Peace was created, which sent envoys to European leaders, and in turn spawned various national sections. In France, which like Russia had not

58 Ceadel, *Living the Great Illusion*, p. 154; Jo Vellacott, *From Liberal to Labour with Women's Suffrage: The Story of Catherine Marshall* (Montreal: McGill-Queen's University Press, 1993), pp. 359–61; Frances H. Early, *A World without War: How US Feminists and Pacifists Resisted World War* (New York: Syracuse University Press, 1997), p. 5.

59 Leslie C. Jauncey, *The Story of Conscription in Australia* (Melbourne: Macmillan, 1968), pp. 105–6.

60 Patterson, *Negotiated Peace*, p. 152.

61 *Concord*, July–August 1915, pp. 199–200.

62 Richard J. Evans, *The Feminist Movement in Germany 1894–1933* (London: Sage Publications, 1976), pp. 218–22.

63 Organisation Centrale pour une paix durable, *Compte Rendu de la Réunion Internationale 7–10 avril 1915, La Haye* (The Hague: Organisation Centrale pour une paix durable, 1915).

been represented at The Hague, Gabrielle Duchêne, a wealthy feminist and philanthropist, established one, although it had no more than 'half a dozen members', like a socialist rival.[64] A British section formed on 30 September 1915, which prudently dropped the word 'peace' and simply called itself the Women's International League, was the most substantial, although being organised on sex rather than ideological lines in a country with a significant absolute-pacifist minority, it suffered from periodic internal disagreements about the legitimacy of military sanctions.

Liberal and radical *pacificism* emerged most strongly in Britain during the early months of the war. The country already had two small *pacificist* associations with similar names, which both soon became as moribund as the Peace Society. The older, the artisan-based International Arbitration League, had been created in 1870 as the Workmen's Peace Committee in order to keep Britain out of the Franco-Prussian War; and as late as 4 August 1914 it favoured neutrality. Thereafter, however, it supported what it deemed 'above and before all things a war against militarism', and recognised that 'a distinction should be made between pacifists who hold the extreme doctrine of non-resistance and those who do not'. It claimed the right to share the label 'pacifist' with the opponents of the war, and resented the efforts of 'some pacifists to rule us out of the household of faith'. But it soon recognised that this was a losing linguistic battle: in 1917 its president, the Lib-Lab MP Thomas Burt, claimed to be 'a peace man', despite his support for the war, although 'not a pacifist in the narrow improper sense in which the word is now used'. The other society, the International Arbitration and Peace Association, had been established in 1880 to make practical recommendations for resolving disputes between states, but had recently fallen under socialist influence. It was paralysed by indecision when Britain entered the war, pulping the August 1914 edition of its journal *Concord* and printing a non-committal edition two months later, before endorsing the war in November.

What fatally wounded both British arbitration societies was less their support for the war than their failure to cater for the widespread assumption by progressives that an international political organisation was now required. Shocked not only by war in Europe, but by the fact that their own party had taken them into it, Liberals were serious in wanting it to be a war that would end war, and soon identified a League of Nations as the best instrument for achieving this. In May 1915, they founded a new organisation, the League of

64 Lorraine Coons, 'Gabrielle Duchêne: feminist, pacifist, reluctant bourgeoise', *Peace and Change*, 24 (1999), p. 123.

Nations Society, which kept a low profile for two years. But after the United States entered the war under a president committed to a League, it began a public campaign and expanded from 400 to 2,000 members. The League idea having entered the political mainstream in 1917 to 1918, realists attempted to hijack it for their own purposes, calling for the wartime alliance to become the basis of the proposed League – an anti-German move that most members of the League of Nations Society disliked. When at its annual meeting on 14 June 1918 the 'jingoes were defeated by the cranks',[65] in the approving words of the novelist Virginia Woolf who attended with her husband and fellow 'crank' Leonard, a separate League of Free Nations Association was created, although when the imminent end of the war made their disagreement irrelevant, the two bodies merged as the League of Nations Union.

Some radical neutralists on the liberal left and in the Labour Party continued to have doubts about British intervention even after Germany's violation of Belgian neutrality. As early as 10 August 1914, Ramsay MacDonald (who had resigned as Labour leader), C. P. Trevelyan (who had resigned from the Liberal government), E. D. Morel (who was about to forfeit a Liberal parliamentary candidacy) and Norman Angell (by then an independent publicist admired for leading the neutrality campaign of 28 July to 4 August) created the Union of Democratic Control (UDC), issuing a private circular implicitly blaming the war on 'the old control of foreign policy by a narrow clique and the power of armament organizations', calling for parliamentary accountability and proposing to campaign on this theme as soon as 'the country is secure from danger'. Exposed by the *Morning Post* exactly a month later, they explained that the UDC was not a 'stop-the-war' organisation, but stood for certain principles that should govern any peace settlement whenever it came, particularly that any territorial transfer should be subject to a plebiscite. Yet its leaders were understood to regard British intervention as a blunder; and initially they indeed believed that the public would soon arrive at the same conclusion, Angell claiming that the UDC would be supported by 'scores of millions in England'.[66] But ironically for those invoking democracy, they had underestimated public support for the government. By implying both that Britain bore some responsibility for its outbreak and that there might be a compromise peace, the UDC was thought by many to be disingenuous in its claim not to oppose the war: indeed, although Angell's wartime writings

65 Anne O. Bell (ed.), *Diaries of Virginia Woolf*, 5 vols. (New York: Harcourt, 1977–84), vol. 1, pp. 157–8.

66 Ceadel, *Living the Great Illusion*, p. 173. See also Marvin Swartz, *The Union of Democratic Control in British Politics during the First World War* (Oxford: Clarendon Press, 1971).

insisted that he wanted Germany to be defeated, he later gave the game away by describing himself as 'an outlaw, an opponent of the war'.[67] In March 1916, the UDC was instrumental in creating a Peace Negotiations Committee, of which Herbert Dunnico became secretary, although it denied wanting either 'to end the war at any price' or to 'embarrass the government'. By the autumn of the following year, the committee had gathered 221,617 signatures for its petition calling for an exploration of possible peace terms.[68] It was during 1917 to 1918, as in the case of the League of Nations Society, that the UDC found wider favour. Following the abdication of the Tsar, the Petrograd Soviet of Workers' and Soldiers' Deputies called for a peace 'without annexations and indemnities', and tried to organise an international socialist conference at Stockholm in support of this goal: understandably, UDC took this as an endorsement of its policies. After visiting Russia for the British Government, Arthur Henderson (MacDonald's successor as Labour leader) also backed the Stockholm conference, and in August 1917 left the War Cabinet over this issue. Thereafter, the pro- and anti-war wings of the Labour Party sank their differences and united in support of the UDC's approach to a post-war settlement. The UDC thereby acquired considerable political influence, which was to last until 1924.

Socialist *pacificism* had been emerging as a distinct strand in Britain before 1914, with Keir Hardie of the ILP being the co-proposer at the Second International of the strike against war, which he regarded as having at least propaganda value. But it remained only one of the strands of thinking that made the ILP oppose the war, the others being the socialist pacifism of Allen and Brockway, which appealed to a small but vocal minority, and the radical *pacificism* of MacDonald, which, as just noted, came to be widely supported within the British labour movement.

It was the Russian Bolsheviks who gave the biggest boost to socialist *pacificism*. Like the Trudoviks, the Social Democrats as a whole had held out against the patriotic mood in August 1914 by abstaining in the vote for war credits. Lenin prudently moved to Switzerland, where in September 1915 he took part in a conference of socialist opponents of the war at Zimmerwald. In demanding 'a peace without annexations or war indemnities', the Zimmerwald Conference initially seemed to be endorsing the UDC's approach rather than proposing an explicitly socialist alternative. But at its next meeting, at Kienthal in April 1916, the Zimmerwald movement made clear its contempt not only for 'bourgeois' peace ideas like compulsory arbitration and disarmament, but also for the

67 Ceadel, *Living the Great Illusion*, pp. 220–1, 226.
68 Ceadel, *Semi-Detached Idealists*, pp. 223–4.

radical demand for 'the so-called democratization of foreign policy',[69] and insisted that socialist revolution was essential. Not all Russian socialists were quite so dismissive of other strands of *pacificism*, however: the Petrograd Soviet was in March 1917 to accept the UDC line, as already noted.

In France, the *pacificist* associations supported a war that seemed unequivocally defensive, as symbolised by Émile Arnaud's joining up at the age of 50 and winning a *Croix de guerre*. Because of its growing association with a refusal to bear arms, the word he had coined was starting to seem anti-patriotic, so Theodore Ruyssen of the Association de la paix par le droit started to promote '*Juripacifisme*' in its place, so as to emphasise the law-and-order approach long adopted by French peace associations. This approach was by 1918 adapted into support for a League of Nations, albeit one with its own military forces capable of enforcing a peace settlement.[70] The SFIO rallied to the *union sacrée*, so socialist *pacificism* remained weak in France. Some protestant areas in the south and industrial towns in the north-east held protest meetings early in the war;[71] but sustained dissent was mainly confined to the anarcho-syndicalist far left, a number of whom fled abroad: for example, the co-secretaries of the Féderation communiste anarchiste, Henri Combes and Edouard Boudot, went to Britain.[72]

In the United States, a few *pacificists* had held out against the crusading fervour of US foreign policy as it began to flex its newly industrialised muscles from the mid 1890s – for example, the biologist and president of Stanford University David Starr Jordan, who condemned the seizure of the Philippines – although they were 'ridiculed or even hanged in effigy' for doing so.[73] The peace movement was financially boosted by the creation in 1910 of both the Carnegie Endowment for International Peace (funded by the Scottish-born steel magnate Andrew Carnegie who had also subsidised both of Britain's arbitration associations)[74] and the American Peace Foundation (the brainchild of the wealthy Boston bookseller Edwin Ginn). But the real basis of

69 Olga H. Gankin and Harold H. Fisher, *The Bolsheviks and the World War: The Origin of the Third International* (Stanford University Press, 1940), pp. 326–32, 407–22.

70 Michael Clinton, 'Coming to terms with "pacifism": the French case, 1901–1918', *Peace and Change*, 26 (2011), pp. 14–16.

71 Richard Cobb, 'France and the coming of war', in Robert J. W. Evans and Hartmut Pogge von Strandmann (eds.), *The Coming of the First World War* (Oxford: Clarendon Press, 1988), pp. 140–1.

72 Auvray, *Objecteurs*, p. 160.

73 David S. Patterson, *Toward a Warless World: The Travail of the American Peace Movement 1887–1914* (Bloomington, IN: Indiana University Press, 1976), p. 69; Patterson, *Negotiated Peace*, p. 333.

74 Ceadel, *Semi-Detached Idealists*, pp. 129, 144.

US *pacificism* at the outbreak of war in Europe was less the country's peace associations and more its constitutionalism, legalism, populism, isolationism, turbulent industrial relations and small but influential socialist movement. In the years before 1914, many Americans 'had come to believe in a democratic League modeled after their own nation – a federal union'.[75] Even former Republican President (and future Chief Justice) William Howard Taft favoured a scheme of compulsory arbitration by a world court that was so utopian as to create 'a feeling of dizziness' in Britain's internationalists,[76] although he moderated his position as president of the League to Enforce Peace, which was created in June 1915 and adopted a policy close to that of Britain's League of Nations Society. At the first annual meeting of the League to Enforce Peace, on 27 May 1916, President Woodrow Wilson committed himself to a League of Nations, although he favoured a more organic and less legalistic version than Taft.[77] Three-time Democratic presidential candidate William Jennings Bryan was noted not only for his populist attacks on financiers, but also for his peace rhetoric, although Norman Angell considered 'pacifism of the Bryan kind' too moralistic and sentimental.[78] Woodrow Wilson's Secretary of State Bryan negotiated an arbitration treaty with Britain, but resigned in 1915 because he believed that Wilson's demands of Germany after it sank the *Lusitania* were excessive. Much of the opposition to US 'preparedness' for war rested on isolationism, particularly in the Midwest; but some was *pacificist*, intended to bring the European war to an end. David Starr Jordan's was a case in point. More famously, the motor manufacturer Henry Ford, who believed that 'German-Jewish bankers' had caused the war, not only opposed 'preparedness', but took up the neutral-mediation cause, chartering a 'peace ship' in November 1915 to take activists to Europe, where the following February in a Stockholm hotel they established a Neutral Conference for Continuous Mediation, run, after a falling out with Rosika Schwimmer, by Louis Lochner of the Chicago Peace Society. Likewise, the Anti-Preparedness Committee, which was established in December 1915 and re-branded itself as the American Union against

75 Warren F. Kuehl, *Seeking World Order: The United States and International Organization to 1920* (Nashville, TN: Vanderbilt University Press, 1969), p. 171.

76 Alfred Zimmern, *The League of Nations and the Rule of Law 1918–1935* (London: Macmillan, 1936), pp. 123–4. See also Stephen Wertheim, 'The league that wasn't: American designs for a legalist-sanctionist League of Nations and the intellectual origins of international organization, 1914–1920', *Diplomatic History*, 35 (2011), 797–835.

77 Laurence W. Martin, *Peace without Victory: Woodrow Wilson and the British Liberals* (New Haven, CT: Yale University Press, 1958); Peter Yearwood, *The Guarantee of Peace: The League of Nations in British Policy 1914–1925* (Oxford University Press, 2009).

78 Ceadel, *Living the Great Illusion*, p. 137.

Militarism in April 1916, contained a core of socialist *pacificists*, including Crystal Eastman.[79]

Once America entered the conflict in April 1917, the League to Enforce Peace largely welcomed the decision, as did the American Peace Society, while other activists, such as David Starr Jordan, accepted the war more reluctantly. Those who continued to oppose it faced severe repression: in May many arrests were made of 'Wobblies' (members of the militant union International Workers of the World, which also spearheaded *pacificist* opposition to the war in Australia[80]), socialists and anarchists for opposing the Selective Service Act; and an Iowa man received a year's imprisonment merely for donating 25 cents and applauding the speeches at an anti-conscription meeting.[81] Some liberals thought Wilson's conception of a League was too focused on a guarantee of the status quo, and created a League of Free Nations Association in the summer of 1918, although they did not launch it publicly until the Armistice. (Very confusingly, therefore, the same name was adopted for the internationalist movement's progressive wing in the United States as had been used by its conservative wing in Britain.)

The German Peace Society 'carefully refrained from any criticism of Germany's role in the events leading up to the war', although this did not prevent the official harassment that drove Alfred Fried to Switzerland at the end of 1914. Ludwig Quidde, who took over as chairman, refused to criticise the violation of Belgian neutrality and accepted the legitimacy of universal conscription. After a new organisation of liberal intellectuals, the Bund Neues Vaterland, which included the feminist Helen Stoecker, began to criticise annexationists in the summer of 1915, it found itself 'totally suppressed by early 1916' as part of the Chancellor's drive to prevent any public discussion of war aims.[82]

Only Germany's decentralised structure of military rule and its concern for its international image enabled some women to attend the Hague congress, as already noted. Its main opposition to war came from the far left that eventually emerged within the SPD. The party initially regarded the war as defensive and voted for war credits, although one deputy, the future co-founder of the German Communist Party Karl Liebknecht, broke ranks as early as December 1914, after visiting occupied Belgium, and opposed them. In February 1915, he was drafted into the army, albeit in a works battalion rather than a combatant one, in an

79 Chatfield, *For Peace and Justice*, pp. 22–7.
80 Jauncey, *Conscription in Australia*, p. 105.
81 Peterson and Fite, *Opponents of War*, pp. 24, 36.
82 Shand, 'Doves among the eagles', pp. 96–8; Karl Holl, *Ludwig Quidde (1858–1941): Eine Biographie* (Düsseldorf: Droste Verlag, 2007).

attempt to stop him expressing his socialist-*pacificist* views outside the Reichstag. Unlike most British absolutists, Liebknecht donned his uniform and served three short tours of military duty.[83] But he sent a defiant message, which Lenin greatly liked, to the Zimmerwald Conference calling for 'civil war, not civil peace', and urging an 'international class war for peace'. Although in calling for further strife in the short term this viewpoint was not calculated to appeal to those for whom peace was the principal goal, it had gained some ground within the left wing of the SPD, causing the party to split; and on 1 May 1916 Liebknecht was arrested and imprisoned for telling demonstrators in Berlin: 'Down with the War! Down with the government!'[84] Thereafter, Germany's socialist *pacificists* had to cope with increased repression as well as their internal divisions over whether to call for peace or for insurrection.

'Pacifism' of the anti-war kind

'Pacifism' arising from the material strains of war rather than from an idealistic approach to international relations could be found in most combatant states; but it most acutely affected authoritarian regimes. From the outset, and in all countries, some resistance to the war effort was unprincipled. For example, those few Frenchmen who failed to report for military duty included Bretons who could not read the state language and vagrants from Normandy who were in some cases too drunk to know war had broken out.[85] Farmers' fears of a labour shortage and trade unions' fears of skilled-labour dilution played their part in the defeat of conscription in the Australian referendums. The British Government's fear of nationalist resistance stopped it extending conscription to Ireland. And in all probability many of America's estimated 171,000 draft evaders were motivated by simple self-interest.[86]

In time, the demands of war produced material grievances even among those who had previously acquiesced. In well-functioning states, such grievances could to a considerable extent be compartmentalised: for example, when on Christmas Day 1915 skilled workers in Glasgow heckled Britain's Minister of Munitions, Lloyd George – a fact which the Scottish ILP journal

83 I am grateful to Professor Nicholas Stargardt for this information.

84 Roger Chickering, *Imperial Germany and the Great War, 1914–1918* (Cambridge University Press, 1998), p. 156.

85 Cobb, 'France and the coming of war', pp. 142–3.

86 Charles Chatfield, *For Peace and Justice: Pacifism in America 1914–1941* (Knoxville, TN: University of Tennessee Press, 1971), p. 69.

Forward was suppressed for revealing[87] – they were criticising his policy of dilution, but not the war as such. Likewise, the wartime franchise reform that nearly trebled the British electorate was not forced on the government by the need to maintain popular support.

Sometimes, however, the strains of war became connected with demands for peace. Famously, in France, Nivelle's suicidal offensive of April 1917 provoked army mutinies in which, as his successor Pétain soon became convinced, 'pacifist propaganda' from anarchist groups played a part.[88] But, because the country's political institutions and war aims were generally still accepted, a change in military leadership and outlook, determined repression and censorship eventually restored order without mishap to the state.

In countries in which both the regime and its military goals were contentious, protests were much harder to compartmentalise. In Germany, where the blockade caused inflation and food shortages, by the autumn of 1915 'poor consumers on the streets, simultaneously empowered and frustrated by the question of affordable food, began to threaten the state with a call for peace at any price', according to a study of Berlin.[89] Such protests soon became connected with demands for constitutional concessions to compensate the masses for their sacrifices: on May Day 1916, demonstrators in the German capital carried placards calling for 'Bread, Freedom and Peace'; and after Liebknecht's imprisonment for addressing them, many factory workers went on strike. The anti-war agenda had become even more apparent by the time a major wave of strikes erupted across the country in January 1918.[90] Although German socialists offered a *pacificist* analysis in which capitalism was argued to be the cause of war as well as of want, most strikers were influenced by deprivation rather than by ideology. Similarly, in Russia by the summer of 1917: 'The appeal of the Bolsheviks lay in their programme of "peace, land, and bread".'[91] This slogan cannily linked the food shortages in Russia's cities and the desire of its peasantry to own the soil they tilled with an end to the fighting, although the indictment of capitalism and imperialism that was packaged up with it added little value. Likewise, the 'Women's Revolt' that was endemic in Bulgaria by May 1918 was caused by starvation, not by the socialist-*pacificist*

87 *Forward*, 1 January 1916.

88 John Williams, *Mutiny 1917* (London: Heinemann, 1962), p. 121.

89 Belinda J. Davis, *Home Fires Burning: Food, Politics, and Everyday Life in World War I Berlin* (Chapel Hill, NC: University of North Carolina Press, 2000), p. 75.

90 Chickering, *Imperial Germany*, pp. 156, 160.

91 Geoffrey Hosking, *A History of the Soviet Union* (London: Fontana Press, 1985), p. 46.

agitation that accompanied it.[92] The exploitation of material grievances had a major political impact during 1917 to 1918; but only by stretching the word to the limit can anti-war sentiment of this kind be classified as 'pacifism'.

Conclusion

The various varieties of pacifism had little impact on the war itself, though rather more on the politics of the two decades that followed. The absolutist variety was both numerically negligible and dominated by religious sectarianism during 1914 to 1918. Yet, with the reputation of conscientious objectors rising retrospectively as that of the Great War plummeted, absolute pacifism was to reach an all-time pinnacle of broader-based support in the late 1930s, before Hitler's actions all but killed it. Reformist pacifism gave rise to demands both for a peace without annexations and for a League of Nations to which wartime politicians had to pay heed. Yet *pacificism*, most notably in the form of commitment to the Genevan ideal, was to peak in the mid 1930s, before the League's failure over Abyssinia in 1936 tipped the balance of thinking about international relations sharply back towards realism. The anti-war 'pacifism' of material grievance had much the greatest short-term impact, especially in countries too illiberal to allow an authentic peace movement to flourish even as a safety valve: by exploiting it, Lenin, much more an opportunistic revolutionary than a principled *pacificist*, took his country out of the conflict in March 1918 – the most significant achievement during the war to which the label 'pacifist' can plausibly be applied. Yet dislike of warfare was to become particularly apparent during the formation and life of the French veterans' movement, the outpouring of anti-war literature of 1928 to 1930 and the Munich crisis of 1938, before public opinion accepted that appeasement was not working. As regards the First World War, what remains remarkable is not the degree of opposition of whatever kind to fighting it, but the degree of support for seeing it through to the bitter end.

92 Richard J. Crampton, *Bulgaria* (Oxford University Press, 2007), p. 215.

22

Drafting the peace

HELMUT KONRAD

Introduction

In 1918, as the First World War, generally considered the *Ur*-catastrophe of the twentieth century, was drawing to a close and its outcome was no longer in doubt, the creation of a new order for Europe, indeed for the world, became the central issue of the day, especially for the victorious powers. Peace treaties needed to be established that, on the one hand, would satisfy the war aims of the victors, but that, on the other, would also guarantee a long-lasting peace and prevent further wars, especially those of the magnitude of the war of 1914 to 1918.

A full century earlier, the Napoleonic Wars, stemming from the French Revolution, had forced a new order upon Europe, which was formalised at the Congress of Vienna. Of course, the circumstances at that time were clearly different. First of all, it really was just a question of Europe. Secondly, the losers sat as equals at the negotiating table. And, thirdly, a 'top-down' decision could be made, a pact between leaders; for neither political parties nor parliaments, let alone 'the people', were major participants. Nationalism was still in its infancy, and the social question was not yet a vital political concern. Information could not yet travel easily and rapidly, and spatial and social mobility were still minimal. Thus, it was possible to spread a kind of net over the entire continent that kept conflict in check and that for decades limited the interests that had to be balanced to those of the dominant groups.

The balance of power between the ruling houses, the reconciliation of interests within the aristocracy between St Petersburg and Paris, and between Berlin and Istanbul was soon challenged by the phenomena accompanying industrialisation, especially mobility, the decline in illiteracy, new forms of communication and nationalism. But the measures taken in Vienna to

Harvey Mendelsohn translated this chapter from German into English.

promote the restoration of the Ancien Régime withstood the pressures of the new age for an astonishingly long time. The pre-modern structures endured, at least on the surface, while underneath a social transformation was completing its course, as became stunningly evident in the revolutions of 1848.

If 1815 witnessed the restoration of the old order, at the end of the First World War an entirely new order had emerged. In the course of a century, changes had taken place that were so dramatic that the preconditions for arranging a peace settlement were scarcely comparable to those existing 100 years earlier. Most of these changes were linked with the contradictory project of modernity.

Science had made great strides in many areas of life. Weights and measures were standardised, and new systems of rules were developed in various domains. The first metropolises strikingly displayed the new types of mobility. Medicine and technology were the guiding disciplines; the world seemed to be subject to calculation, and nature itself seemed to be becoming more subject to human control. The tempo of these changes awakened great hopes for the future, but also anxiety and uncertainty. The feeling of belonging and (pseudo-) scientifically based fantasies of superiority offered protection and security in the form of definitions of 'us' and 'others'. While questions of belonging had long been settled in terms of religion or of who ruled the territory one lived in, the power of definition was now assumed by language. One was no longer a 'Bohemian', but a Czech or a German, no longer a 'Carinthian', but a German or a Slovene, depending on one's so-called 'mother tongue', that is to say, the language preferred for use in everyday communication.

Europe was the centre and motor of this ambivalent development, and the decades before 1914 can rightly be called a European era. The world was becoming smaller at an accelerating rate, as men, goods, capital, services and, above all, information, circulated ever-more quickly, and politically, economically and culturally most of the globe was ruled or at least dominated by Europe. The First World War fundamentally altered this situation. It laid bare the darker aspects of modernisation, its accompanying depersonalisation, and the destructive potential of its new technologies, which threatened not only people's physical existence, but also their psychological balance. And in the thunder of combat (or in the fog of the gas fumes), it burst asunder the dominant role of the Old Continent. The broken pieces it left in its wake had to be reassembled into a new order.

It was abundantly clear, moreover, that this task would not be limited to Europe. The war had become a world war, which, on the one hand, brought troops from all over the world to the European theatres of operations, and, on the other, was literally fought on other continents, as well. Accordingly, more than Europe was at stake: it was essential to create some form of order throughout the entire world. The nature of the war, which had involved the entire population of the combatant countries, and the fact that, ultimately, its outcome was decided at least as much on the home fronts as on the battlefields gave rise to new representations of the enemy that were widely disseminated by the new media. Thus, it was no longer only territorial claims and issues of power that were at stake; the situation was seen in terms of good and evil, of black and white. Many saw the war in an ideological perspective and thought it should result in the defeat of the evil side, whose challenge to the good and whose overweening and unjustified aspirations to power had unleashed the war and which thus now had to bear sole responsibility for the war. This is also the deeper cause of the notion of war guilt, which was formulated for the first time in history at Versailles, and although it pertained chiefly to Germany, it extended to all of its allies, as well. The defeated countries, Germany above all, were shocked and appalled by the victors' contention 'that Germany, on account of its "aggression" in the year 1914, was guilty of a crime and was *solely* responsible for the [resulting] unparalleled mass deaths and immense destruction'.[1]

Such language was not included even in the Treaty of Brest-Litovsk, which the Russians were constrained to sign. Although the harshness of its basic elements was not surpassed in any of the subsequent treaties, in negotiating Brest-Litovsk the victors and the vanquished at least sat together at one table, and the proceedings included no moral assessment of the war or of the warring parties. Thus, at Paris new norms were in fact introduced: exclusion of the defeated countries from the discussions and a moral condemnation of the defeated states and their political system, without, moreover, any recognition of the structural transformations which had begun in the autumn of 1918.

The Treaty of Brest-Litovsk

Beginning in December 1917, an armistice had been in effect along the battle line known (from the German perspective) as the 'Eastern Front'. Romania had already signed it on 9 December, and Russia followed suit on 15 December. The peace negotiations of Brest-Litovsk began on 22 December, and at the request of the Russians they were held in public. 'The representatives of

1 Gerd Krumeich, 'Nationalsozialismus und Erster Weltkrieg. Eine Einführung', in Gerd Krumeich (ed.), *Nationalsozialismus und Erster Weltkrieg* (Essen: Klartext Verlag, 2010), p. 11.

the new Russia thereby were able to exploit the conference table to make revolutionary propaganda.'[2] Germany, on the other hand, spoke of the right of self-determination for Poland, Lithuania and Courland (Latvia), as well as of an independent Ukraine, which it saw as a source of raw materials for the German munitions industry and, above all, as a source of grain for the starving population of the Habsburg monarchy. Russia insisted on a peace without annexation or monetary payments, while the Central Powers called for voluntary separation of the repressed peoples. On 28 December, the two sides agreed on a ten-day pause in the proceedings.

By the time they reconvened on 8 January 1918, the internal political situation had changed, especially in Vienna. A revolutionary mood had gripped Austria-Hungary, and a few days later Vienna was crippled by strikes. On 18 January, the strike affected Budapest, too, and ten days later half a million people stopped working in the German Empire, as well. In the Habsburg monarchy, a total of 700,000 workers were on strike. In its naval port, Cattaro (Kotor), the 6,000 sailors there raised red flags and disarmed their officers.[3] The flames of revolution seemed truly to be spreading to the main power bases of the Central Powers, and thus at Brest-Litovsk Trotsky played for time.

After their defeat in the election for a constitutional convention, the Bolsheviks bloodily suppressed democratic demands and transferred power to the councils (soviets) on '19 January 1918, marking no more and no less than a definitive break between the Bolsheviks and the democratic majority of the European workers' movement'.[4] But Trotsky's tactic of drawing out the peace proceedings in order to strengthen the Central European revolutions was frustrated by Lenin's conviction that, whatever the cost, peace had to be established in order to secure the Bolsheviks' hold on power within Russia. On 10 February, Trotsky broke off the negotiations in Brest-Litovsk. The Germans responded on 16 February with a forty-eight-hour ultimatum and on 18 February resumed fighting, but there was no functioning Russian army to oppose them. Finally, in the face of the existential threat to the Soviets' only recently established domination, Lenin was able to impose his decision to accept Germany's peace conditions. But the latter had hardened in the meantime. Now the Russians not only had

2 Heinrich August Winkler, *Geschichte des Westens. Die Zeit der Weltkriege 1914–1945* (Munich: C. H. Beck, 2011), p. 72.

3 Richard G. Plaschka, *Cattaro-Prag. Revolte und Revolution. Kriegsmarine und Heer im Feuer der Aufstandsbewegungen vom 1. Februar an 28. Oktober 1918* (Graz: Böhlau Verlag, 1963).

4 Winkler, *Geschichte des Westens*, p. 74.

to give up the entire Baltic region and Finland, but also had to recognise the independence of the Ukraine, with which Germany had signed a separate peace on 10 February and whose mineral wealth and agricultural output would now be available to the Central Powers.

The Bolsheviks gave in to the pressure and on 3 March 1918 signed the peace treaty. 'It was a brutal Diktat.'[5] Russia lost about one-quarter of its European territory, 73 per cent of its iron industry and coal mines, one-quarter of its railroad network[6] and 60 million people; about one-third of the total population of the Tsarist Empire henceforth lived outside of Russia.

The Central Powers treated Romania just as ruthlessly. With the Peace of Bucharest on 7 May 1918, Romania had to relinquish Dobruja, which was divided between Bulgaria and the victors. Furthermore, the Central Powers obtained the right to exploit the oil fields and Romania had to sell its agricultural surplus to the victors.

Three days after the signing, at their 7th party congress, the Bolsheviks approved the conditions of the peace treaty. But they did not obtain the pause they had hoped for in order to consolidate their power at home. On 9 March, British troops landed at Murmansk to give support to the Bolsheviks' opponents. The ensuing bloody civil war and further interventions proved to be decisive in the following years. It is not entirely without justification that Heinrich August Winkler characterised the Bolshevik regime of terror as 'to date the most radical counter-scheme to the normative project of the West'.[7] Russian modernisation, although oriented towards the Western paradigm (for example, in the change of calendar), excluded the liberal, democratic developments in the West and took up where the French Revolution had left off in 1794.

The counter-model

One of the men whose ideas shaped the peace settlement after the great bloodletting of the war years was without a doubt the US President, Woodrow Wilson. 'Although he had campaigned in 1916 on a platform of keeping the country neutral, Wilson brought the United States into the war in April 1917. He was convinced that he was doing the right

5 Winkler, *Geschichte des Westens*, p. 77.
6 Wolfdieter Bihl, *Österreich-Ungarn und die Friedensschlüsse von Brest-Litowsk* (Vienna, Cologne and Graz: Böhlau Verlag, 1970), p. 118.
7 Winkler, *Geschichte des Westens*, p. 82.

thing.'[8] Above all, he was convinced that a lasting peace settlement could be established on the basis of the Fourteen Points he presented to both houses of the US Congress on 8 January 1918. Some of the points were clear and completely accepted among the Allies. This was especially true of Point 7:

> Belgium, the whole world will agree, must be evacuated and restored without any attempt to limit the sovereignty which she enjoys in common with all other free nations. No other single act will serve as this will serve to restore confidence among the nations in the laws which they have themselves set and determined for the government of their relations with one another. Without this healing act the whole structure and validity of international law is forever impaired.[9]

Point 8, the return of Alsace-Lorraine to France, could also be seen as a common concern of the Allies. And the same is true of Point 14, the plan to work towards the creation of a 'general association of nations' which would mutually guarantee 'political independence and territorial integrity'.[10] But Point 1, the renunciation of any form of secret diplomacy, was a naive dream. And Points 2 through to 4, which called for liberal, free-trade policies and a reduction in armaments, did not find favour in all quarters.

The Africans and Asians who had risked their lives in the war to fight for democracy might have had problems with Point 5:

> A free, open-minded, and absolutely impartial adjustment of all colonial claims, based upon a strict observance of the principle that in determining all such questions of sovereignty, the interests of the populations concerned must have equal weight with the equitable claims of the government whose title is to be determined.[11]

Point 6 pertaining to Russia had to remain ambiguous due to the moment in time when it was proclaimed, namely a few weeks after the October Revolution. Points 9 through to 13, concerning the creation of new boundaries in Europe and the Near East, awakened many hopes but were based on totally false premises. What, in fact, were 'clearly recognizable lines of nationality'? What was meant by the 'freest opportunity of autonomous development'?[12] To promise the Serbians access to the sea and, simultaneously, to promote

8 Margaret Macmillan, *Paris 1919: Six Months that Changed the World* (New York: Random House, 2003), p. 4.

9 Macmillan, *Paris 1919*, p. 496.

10 Macmillan, *Paris 1919*, p. 495.

11 Macmillan, *Paris 1919*, p. 496.

12 Macmillan, *Paris 1919*, p. 496.

'international guarantees of the political and economic independence and territorial integrity of the several Balkan states'[13] was self-contradictory.

In line with European thinking of the time, Wilson's conception of a nation was based solely on linguistic considerations. He paid no heed to mobility within the multi-ethnic states, and other forms of identity such as religion were subordinated to language. Accordingly, there were no Jews, but also no 'Bohemians' (with differing mother tongues). Language boundaries for him were definite, specifiable lines on the map. The fact that the right of self-determination ceased to apply when it came to the colonies and (understandably) to the soon-to-be defeated enemy powers weakened the proclamation's moral force.

Freedom of the seas, free trade, the economic and political dominance of the Allies – these were Wilson's primary concerns. Rights were established at the level of states, not of individual people. In this regard, the legacy of 1815 can still be clearly seen. Nevertheless, it was precisely the lack of clarity in the Fourteen Points and the possibility of different ways of reading them, as well as the expression itself of 'self-determination', which exercised a huge fascination. Just who the 'self' was in that expression remained unclear. (In any case, it was not the individual person.) Nor was what 'nation' meant defined. Hopes were thereby awakened that could not withstand the pressures of reality.

The war's end

The hopes of the Central Powers that the end of the war on two fronts was sure to bring quick successes on the Western Front were rapidly disappointed. Their offensive remained stalled. Likewise, Ukrainian grain never reached the capital of the Austro-Hungarian monarchy, and expectations of relief for the hungry were disappointed. The home front, scene of the sacrifices of an exhausted population, played as decisive a role as the military front in bringing about the end of the war. 'Hunger as a weapon of war was etched more deeply in the memory of people in Germany in the winter of 1918–1919 than during the war years.'[14]

In 1918, the internal situation facing the Central Powers had become as decisive a factor in undermining their war effort as were events on the

13 Macmillan, *Paris 1919*, p. 496.

14 Hew Strachan, *Der Erste Weltkrieg. Eine neue illustrierte Geschichte* (Munich: C. Bertelsmann, 2006), p. 394.

battlefield. Moreover, in Berlin and Vienna, as well as in the other large cities of these two allies, Wilson's Fourteen Points were 'very rightly interpreted as a call for a democratic revolution'.[15] To be sure, in the minds of many the conception of a revolution went beyond a matter of gaining greater democracy. The Russian model was attractive, not least because the Soviets' radical exit from the war had made possible the return of many war prisoners. Revolution and the end of war were thereby seen as closely connected. Austria's efforts to make a separate peace in 1918 failed miserably. The so-called 'Sixtus Affair'[16] was ultimately a fiasco and yoked the Habsburg monarchy definitively to Imperial Germany until the war's end.

By the second half of the year 1918, the Central Powers could no longer think of achieving a 'victorious peace'. Their chief concern was, therefore, to create the preconditions for an armistice and for the best possible terms at the peace settlement. These were thought to lie in the overthrow of the old aristocratic order in the Habsburg monarchy, but also in granting greater autonomy to the various 'nations' in the multi-ethnic state. The 'Peoples' Manifesto' (*Völkermanifest*)[17] came much too late, however, and, above all, did not take into account the influence of the Czech exiles in the United States, an influence further strengthened by the existence of the Czech Legion in Russia. From the time of the establishment of the Czechoslovakian National Council in 1916, Tomáš Masaryk and Edvard Beneš aimed at an independent state of Bohemia, Moravia and Slovakia. By the middle of May 1918, such a state had already taken shape on paper in the Pittsburgh Agreement between the exile groups, with an autonomous administration foreseen for the Slovaks.[18] The fact that Wilson had not yet made the destruction of the Habsburg monarchy a point of his programme was the result of tactical considerations, namely in order not to push Austria even closer to Germany. The influence of the Czech exiles in the United States on shaping the post-war order has, however, long been acknowledged. Moreover, what the Czechs and Slovaks had already actually achieved was not something that could be denied to the southern Slavs, whose interests, to be sure, clashed with those of the Italians,

15 Winkler, *Geschichte des Westens*, p. 88.

16 Robert A. Kann, *Die Sixtusaffäre und die geheimen Friedensverhandlungen Österreich-Ungarns im Ersten Weltkrieg* (Vienna: Böhlau Verlag, 1966).

17 Helmut Rumpler, 'Die Sixtusaktion und das Völkermanifest Kaiser Karls. Zur Strukturkrise des Habsburgerreiches 1917/18', in Karl Bosl (ed.), *Versailles – St. Germain – Trianon. Umbruch in Europa vor fünfzig Jahren* (Munich: R. Oldenbourg Verlag, 1971), pp. 112–13.

18 Winkler, *Geschichte des Westens*, p. 90.

who had been induced to enter the war by the territorial rewards promised to them in the Treaty of London.

The Ottoman Empire, whose collapse was likewise imminent as a result of the war, was the object of the often conflicting interests of the Allies, and the problems resulting from its break-up persisted throughout the twentieth century. Since by autumn of 1918, at the latest, the victory of the Allies was no longer in any doubt, their principal concern in the months around the end of the war was how to balance their respective interests, which, in fact, diverged dramatically. They agreed on the need to put an end to the 'old' systems in Germany and Austria, which, in any case, were beginning to change in the last weeks of the war in response to internal pressures. In Germany, the Social Democrats and the bourgeois parties were united in thinking that democratisation would, on the one hand, lay the basis for milder peace conditions, and, on the other, deprive a potential Bolshevik revolution of mass support. In Austria, political changes came even earlier, and far-reaching concessions regarding the so-called 'national question' were already announced. Massive political change in Germany, however, was decisively accelerated in the end by revolutionary actions, above all the sailors' revolt in Kiel. Meanwhile, in Austria, without waiting for the war to end, the individual nationalities declared their separation from the state before the 'Austrian Revolution'[19] forced the transformation of the remainder state into a democratic republic – in this case, too, through popular unrest.

All of this, however, came too late to make a difference. The interests of the victorious Allies were too clearly spelled out, and the outlines of the future disposition of power were too firmly settled in their minds, even though there were still major differences to be worked out. Their focus was not going to be on the establishment of an ideal post-war order, but rather on questions of power and influence. Wilson himself was primarily interested in creating a League of Nations, as well as setting up a *cordon sanitaire*, a ring of states to contain revolutionary Russia. On this latter point, he was supported by Britain, which, however, looked with suspicion on French efforts to weaken Germany's position in Europe for the foreseeable future. Beyond this French effort to secure hegemony on the continent, there was also tension between the British and French concerning the colonies and the crumbling Ottoman Empire. Finally, Italy considered herself a victor and sought to exert

19 Otto Bauer, *Die österreichische Revolution* (Vienna: Verlag Wiener Volksbuchhandlung, 1923). It was this book which first introduced the notion of revolution into the discussion of the fall of the Habsburg monarchy.

dominance in the Adriatic, in disregard of the claims of the new southern Slav state, but supported by the Treaty of London. In sum, even before the peace negotiations began, the positions of the victorious powers were not harmoniously aligned; in fact, they were full of contradictions and potential conflicts.

Versailles

'The peace treaties were the principal legacy of the war. The struggle over their acceptance was the main subject of post-war international politics and proved to be similarly decisive in the internal politics of the successor nations.'[20] The war had been fought, as the French formulated it before the Armistice, 'in order to achieve results'.[21] Above all, 'it was Belgium and France which had suffered. They wanted compensation for past injustice and security for the future.'[22] The peace treaty should, on the one hand, put an end to military activity and, on the other, hinder wars in the future through the existence of a new world. But there was also the matter of compensation, which was put forward by those countries where the battles had actually taken place. To this was added the human toll, both physical and psychological, the care of the dependents, and much more as well.

The peace treaties thus had to establish new boundaries, forestall further wars through disarmament and the reduction in the size of standing armies, and deal with the material damages caused by the war. All this, it was decided, would come exclusively at the cost of the losers, and it could be done with all the more justification if it were possible to make an unambiguous judgement concerning the question of war guilt.

The Paris Peace Conference began in January 1919 and lasted until January 1920, when it was succeeded by a permanent conference of the Allied ambassadors. 'The Conference produced five peace treaties: with Germany, in Versailles, on 29 June 1919; with Austria, in Saint-Germain-en-Laye, on 10 September; with Bulgaria, in Neuilly, on 27 November; with Hungary, at the Trianon, on 4 June 1920; and with Turkey, in Sèvres, on 10 August 1920.'[23] The treaty with Germany was undoubtedly the most important; for it was not only the model for the others, but also anticipated their content (for example, forbidding Austrian incorporation into Germany – the *Anschlussverbot*).

20 David Stevenson, *1914–1918. Der Erste Weltkrieg* (Düsseldorf and Zürich: Artemis und Winkler Verlag, 2006), p. 595.

21 Stevenson, *1914–1918*, p. 595.

22 Strachan, *Der Erste Weltkrieg*, p. 397.

23 Stevenson, *1914–1918*, p. 596.

Overcoming Wilson's objections, the victorious European powers were able to impose their own views of how the peace conference should be conducted. There were in fact 'preliminary meetings which excluded the public, the less important among the participating countries, and the adversaries, on the grounds, in part, that their governments could not be considered legitimate. Instead, the basic substance of the peace proposals was to be determined by the High War Council (later called the "Council of Ten"), membership in which was limited to the Great Powers.'[24] Nevertheless, the conference formally opened in proper form with a plenary session at which were seated the representatives of the governments of all thirty-two participating states, consisting of the Entente Cordiale, that is to say, Great Britain and France, the powers 'associated' with them like the United States and Japan, 'additional members of the British Empire', i.e., Canada, Australia, New Zealand, South Africa and India, as well as the new states like Poland and Czechoslovakia, and, as a late-joining ally, Romania. Russia was not represented, despite great efforts to bring a non-revolutionary representative to the table. To be sure, the really important decisions were made by the Council of Four (the United States, Great Britain, France and Italy).

The conflicts between the respective goals of the French and the Anglo-Saxons quickly became apparent. France pursued its intention to occupy the left bank of the Rhine and advocated a large Polish state, whereas Britain strove for a 'balance of power'[25] in order to prevent too great a French dominance on the continent. 'Wilson was fully committed to an appropriate punishment of Germany (and made little distinction between the fallen imperial state and the new regime). He was, however, unwilling to compromise any more than was absolutely necessary concerning the principle of the self-determination of peoples that he had so vigorously proclaimed, and for this reason alone could not give in to French pressure.'[26] Thus, the conflicts among the four main personalities (Wilson, Lloyd George, Clemenceau and Orlando) quickly became apparent. Clemenceau wanted to exclude any possibility of a strong Germany posing a threat in the future, and Lloyd George was mainly concerned with eliminating the Germans as competitors on the world market, and therefore with matters pertaining to the colonies and the size of the German navy.

24 Klaus Schwabe, 'Das Ende des Ersten Weltkriegs', in Gerhard Hirschfeld *et al.* (eds.), *Enzyklopädie Erster Weltkrieg* (Paderborn: Ferdinand Schöningh, 2004), p. 295.

25 Winkler, *Geschichte des Westens*, p. 175.

26 Winkler, *Geschichte des Westens*, p. 175.

The struggles over the treaty finally ended with a compromise among the victorious powers. Germany's western boundary was pushed eastwards, with Alsace-Lorraine being returned to France without a plebiscite being held. The Saarland was placed under the aegis of the League of Nations for fifteen years, and then the population would decide on its final disposition. The Rhineland remained in Germany, but was demilitarised. In addition, the Allies were to hold several bridgeheads on the Rhine's right bank. Belgium obtained the district of Eupen-Malmedy. In the east, Germany's territorial losses were much more dramatic. The Grand Duchy of Posen (Poznan) was given to Poland, as was Upper Silesia. In order for it to obtain access to the sea, Poland also received a large portion of West Prussia, which resulted in East Prussia being cut off from the rest of Germany. Danzig became a 'Free City' under the supervision of a League of Nations' commissioner. Memelland was also to be administered by the Entente. A plebiscite led to the division of North Schleswig between Denmark and Germany, and in Masuria (in the southern part of East Prussia) the population voted to remain in Germany.

Wilson's Fourteen Points really should have supported the unification of Germany and the German-speaking part of Austria, since all the nations of the fallen Dual Monarchy had flown into the arms of their respective 'mother countries'. The great majority of the Austrian population did in fact wish this to happen, as several regional polls made clear, but the Allies simply could not accept a measure that would have added 6 million people to Germany's population. This was the reason for Article 80 of the Treaty of Versailles, forbidding German annexation of Austria (the *Anschlussverbot*), which was to have a lasting influence on post-war politics.

'As a result of the peace treaty Germany gave up a seventh of its territory and tenth of its population, and it lost its colonies as well.'[27] It also lost one-third of its coal and three-quarters of its mineral resources. And it had to hand over still more wealth in the form of reparations. In addition, it was forced to reduce its armed forces: the army was limited to 100,000 men, and the navy to 15,000, all of whom had to be professional soldiers. Submarines, military aircraft, tanks and weapons for gas warfare were all forbidden to Germany. Finally, the ocean-going fleet had to be surrendered, but this was rendered unnecessary by the fact that the Germans had already scuttled their own warships.

Emotionally, the most upsetting element of the settlement for Germany was undoubtedly the question of war guilt. Even decades later, it was still the

27 Winkler, *Geschichte des Westens*, p. 176.

subject of vigorous scholarly controversy.[28] Article 231 stated that Germany was the instigator of the war and therefore was responsible for all the damages and losses suffered by its military opponents as a result of the war that was forced upon them. The expression 'sole guilt' was not used, but this is how it was interpreted in Germany, and this perception led to stronger protests than all of the other provisions, even though the latter were extremely burdensome. Germany, moreover, did not sit at the negotiating table, whereas even in Brest-Litovsk the victors and the defeated had sat down together, although, certainly, there the terms dictated to the loser were more severe than at Versailles. These two points, war guilt and exclusion from the negotiations, were not decisive on the material level, yet they were very disturbing on the emotional level and were experienced as traumas well into the Weimar Republic. They smoothed the way for the perception among part of the

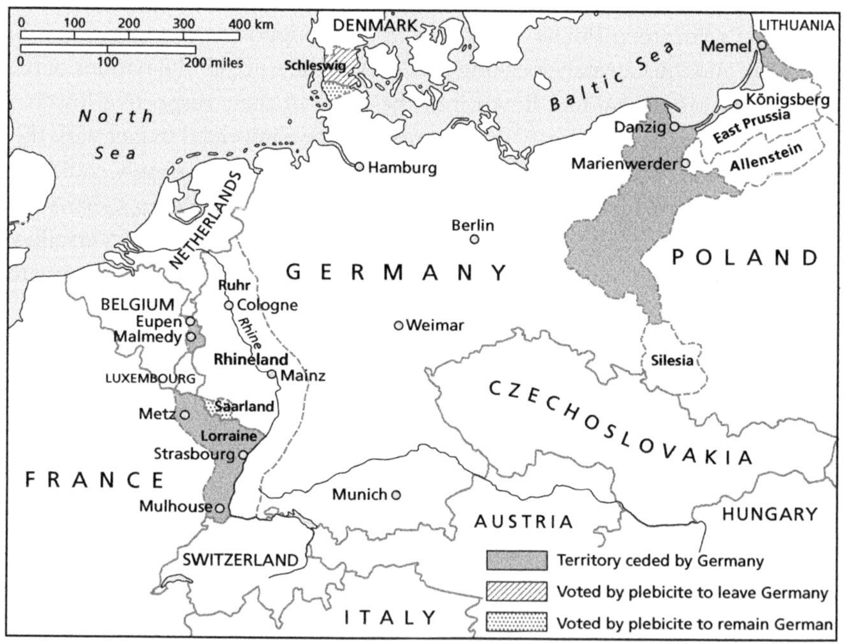

Map 22.1 Territory ceded by Germany in Versailles settlement

28 Fritz Fischer, *Der Griff nach der Weltmacht. Die Kriegszielpolitik des Kaiserlichen Deutschland 1914–1918* (Düsseldorf: Droste Verlag, 1961).

population that Versailles was a 'shameful peace', and they offered fertile ground for the revanchist politics of the National Socialists.

The internal negotiations between the victorious powers at Versailles were overshadowed by two conflicts which were only very indirectly related to their work on the treaty. The first involved Italy, whose claim to Dalmatia and Fiume[29] raised the basic question of what criteria should be used in concluding the peace: Wilson's announced ideal of national self-determination or the superior power the victorious states were intent on exerting? Wilson supported the resistance of the southern Slavs, even though he had already agreed to Italy's demand that the frontier should be the Brenner pass between Bolzano and Innsbruck. Meanwhile, in the Far East, Great Britain and France had offered Japan major concessions as the price of its entering the war. Wilson, however, refused to go along with these, not least because of his defence of the right of self-determination for the Chinese. In this connection, there also existed an unspoken claim of the 'white man's' right to exercise power. 'An article submitted by the Japanese to the group working on the creation of the League of Nations, which affirmed the principle of the equality of all races, was likewise rejected.'[30] Both of these conflicts delayed agreement on the treaty with Germany and made it clear how thin was the ice on which the negotiating partners were skating.

On 7 May 1919, the German delegation at Versailles was handed a draft of the peace conditions. This first meeting of the Germans with the representatives of the victors was a disaster right from the start. 'None of the German diplomats had noticed, apparently, until this moment, what a dreadful public speaker Brockdorff-Rantzau was.'[31] And the fact that during his first speech he remained sitting while Clemenceau had stood up in order to address his remarks to the delegation was an additional source of irritation. The sharp rejection of the notion of German war guilt and the charges of inhuman cruelty directed against the Allies further worsened the negotiating climate. Accordingly, the compromises that still remained in the treaty were truly minimal.

In Germany, the tide of rejection was at first very strong, and it did not abate even with the two revisions concerning the Rhineland and Upper Silesia. It was clear, certainly, that there was no alternative. 'On 22 June the National Assembly agreed to sign the peace treaty by a majority of 237 to 138 votes, with

29 Klaus Schwabe (ed.), *Quellen zum Friedensschluss von Versailles* (Darmstadt: Wissenschaftliche Buchgesellschaft, 1997), p. 17.

30 Schwabe, *Versailles*, p. 17.

31 Charles L. Mee, *The End of Order. Versailles 1919* (New York: E. P. Dutton, 1980), p. 214.

6 abstentions, with reservations concerning the questions of war guilt and war crimes. The response came quickly – in the form of an ultimatum to sign the treaty within 24 hours without reservations.'[32] On 28 June 1919, sitting in the Hall of Mirrors at Versailles, where forty-eight years earlier the German Empire had been established, the Germans, under the leadership of the Foreign Minister Hermann Müller, placed their signatures on the treaty. With all its short- and long-term consequences, with all the anticipations and rejections it incorporated, the model for the subsequent treaties was now established.

Saint-Germain

The First World War, at least formally, was a consequence of the Habsburg monarchy's declaration of war against Serbia. The shots fired at Sarajevo, which killed the successor to the Austrian throne, and Vienna's ultimatum to Belgrade (which was largely complied with), formed the basis for a war which fundamentally changed the world, and most especially 'Zwischeneuropa' – 'the Europe in between'.[33]

The Habsburg monarchy was already an anachronism for decades before the war. As early as 1848, Engels had observed that 'the Austrian monarchy, the patchwork of territories amassed by inheritance and by theft, that organized muddle of the ten languages and nations, that unplanned conglomeration of the most contradictory customs and laws'[34] was at last beginning to fall apart. He was right on the mark with his description of the state's structure, though not in his prediction of its life expectancy. 'Kakania' (as it was nicknamed), which was often described as a 'prison of peoples', long maintained its structure intact, even into the war years. Disloyalty was uncommon, and it was not only the severe court-martial sentences which kept the number of troops going over to the enemy low. 'Respect for the

32 Winkler, *Geschichte des Westens*, p. 179.

33 The notion of 'Zwischeneuropa' has appeared sporadically since 1916, when it was introduced in the *Zeitschrift für Erdkunde zu Berlin*, Heft 3 (1916), pp. 177 ff. Most recently it has been reintroduced into discussion by Helmut Konrad and Monika Stromberger as an alternative to the politically charged notion of 'Mitteleuropa'. See Konrad and Stromberger, 'Der kurze Traum von Selbstständigkeit. Zwischeneuropa', in Walter L. Bernecker and Hans Werner Tobler (eds.), *Die Welt im 20. Jahrhundert bis 1945* (Vienna: Mandelbaum Verlag, 2010), pp. 76–7.

34 Karl Marx and Friedrich Engels, *Werke*, 43 vols. (Berlin: Dietz-Verlag, 1956–90), vol. IV, p. 504.

army persisted in broad sectors – even among internal political opponents – for a surprisingly long time.'[35]

It was the homecoming prisoners of war who first created the potential for serious unrest, and they bore 'a strong social, not a nationalist accent'.[36] The Entente, too, thought that the Austro-Hungarian monarchy, once it was democratised within and its external borders were corrected, would remain intact. The Fourteen Points were formulated from this point of view, despite America's strong backing of the Czechs, and in the Empire itself they were read as a guarantee of its continued existence. The Habsburg monarchy differed from the other multi-ethnic states, above all in its lack of a dominant 'national' (that is to say, linguistic) group. Among the at least eleven nationalities, the Germans constituted only 24 per cent of the total population, and the Magyars only 20 per cent. They were surpassed by the Slavic groups, which together made up 47 per cent. Even in the 'Austrian half of the Empire', the German-speaking population was only about a little over one-third of the total. And the Magyars, likewise, failed to constitute the majority of those living in the Hungarian half of the Empire.[37]

In the autumn of 1918, hunger on the home front, the growth of revolutionary sentiments and the dissolution of the imperial state made continued prosecution of the war impossible. Indeed, the army in the field 'was ever more openly accused of prolonging the war'.[38] Emperor Karl finally decided, much too late to save the monarchy, to ask for an armistice, the conditions for which were transmitted on 2 November and signed on 3 November 1918. The war was over for the Austro-Hungarian monarchy, and it ceased to exist as a state. Moreover, twelve days previously, even the German-speaking deputies had already constituted 'German Austria' as a state.[39] New states had emerged which were to assume their definitive form at Saint-Germain.

The Austrian delegation travelled to Paris as early as May 1919, but it was not admitted to the proceedings. The team of delegates drew on individuals

35 Richard G. Plaschka *et al.*, *Innere Front. Militärassistenz, Widerstand und Umsturz in der Donaumonarchie 1918* (Munich: R. Oldenbourg Verlag, 1974), vol. I, p. 12.

36 Holm Sundhaussen, 'Von der Multiethnizität zum Nationalstaat. Der Zerfall "Kakaniens" und die staatliche Neuordnung im Donauraum am Ende des Ersten Weltkrieges', in Holm Sundhaussen and Hans-Joachim Torke (eds.), *1917–1918 als Epochengrenze?* (Wiesbaden: Harrassowitz, 2000), p. 83.

37 Sundhausen and Torke, *1917–1918*, pp. 80–1.

38 Manfried Rauchensteiner, '"Das neue jahr machte bei uns einen traurigen Einzug." Das ende des Großen Krieges', in Helmut Konrad und Wolfgang Maderthaner (eds.), . . . *der Rest ist Österreich. Das Werden der Ersten Republik* (Vienna: Carl Gerold's Sohn, 2008), vol. I, p. 41.

39 Heinz Fischer, 'Vorwort', in Konrad and Maderthaner, . . . *der Rest ist Österreich*, p. 7.

from all those parts of the Habsburg monarchy which, on the one hand, included a German-speaking population, but which, on the other, were claimed by the new states which already existed by this date (and which, despite participating in the war as parts of Austria, were accorded the status of victorious powers). The Treaty of Saint-Germain was biased in important respects through the decisions made at Versailles. In any event, simultaneously with the Austrian peace treaty, a treaty was signed with Czechoslovakia guaranteeing the rights of minorities, namely of the 'Germans' and 'Slovaks' in the new Czech Republic.

Austria's contention that in 1914 it did not yet really exist as a state and was only one among a number of successor states of a defeated empire fell on deaf ears. Czechs, Slovaks, Romanians, Italians, Croats and Slovenians who lived under the monarchy were victors, and the German-speaking population and the Magyars were the only losers. The Austrians' desire to obtain a national treaty instead of a peace treaty could not be realised in 1919, and it was only thirty-six years later, on the basis of similar arguments, that this goal was achieved.

On 2 September 1919, the Austrian delegation in Saint-Germain was presented with the treaty, which was finally signed eight days later by Karl Renner. In drawing Austria's northern boundary, the treaty, disregarding the right to national self-determination, employed the old frontiers of the crown lands. Thus, all of Bohemia, Moravia, Silesia and even a few communities in Northern Austria were given to Czechoslovakia, thereby bestowing on the latter a German-speaking minority of as many as 3 million people. Galicia went to Poland; South Tirol, Welsch Tirol and the Carinthian Canal Valley went to Italy, as did Istria. Bukovina was given to Romania. Dalmatia, Lower Styria, the Miess Valley and Seeland were promised to the new state of Serbia, Croatia and Slovenia (Yugoslavia). A plebiscite was set for Lower Carinthia south of the Drau, the result of the so-called 'Carinthian Defensive Battle' ('Kärntner Abwehrkampfs'). The West Hungarian counties went to Austria (with the exception of the county of Sopron/Ödenburg, which joined Hungary after a later plebiscite). The use of the name 'German Austria' (Deutsch-Österreich) was forbidden, and the prohibition against Austria joining Germany stated in the Versailles Treaty was reconfirmed. The army was reduced to 10,000 professional soldiers, and Austria was obliged to pay reparations. Altogether, only two-thirds of the German-speaking population of the Austria of the old Habsburg monarchy resided in the new state. Within the country itself many long doubted its viability, and incorporation into Germany seemed to be the only hope for the future, a hope that was realised exactly two decades later under dramatically altered circumstances.[40]

Trianon

When the Hungarian delegation was invited to Paris at the end of 1919, after the conclusion of the treaty with Austria, the essential decisions had already been taken at Versailles and Saint-Germain; and they also reflected the political reality in Hungary's northern and southern regions. Hungary, like Austria, was accorded a peace treaty, but not a treaty creating a nation-state. And it, too, had to accept the burden of war guilt. This, however, was not the central concern of the Hungarian population, and the same may be said of the articles regarding reparations and the restrictions placed on the size of the army and on armaments.

The overwhelming concern of the Hungarians was the establishment of the nation's new boundaries, and this has continued to be the case for the entire period up to the present. The Magyars, an ethnicity without a great 'brother country' beyond the frontiers of the Habsburg Empire, were much more strongly drawn to nationalism as an instrument of internal cohesion. This was all the more important in Hungary – as opposed to Germany and Austria – inasmuch as the revolutionary experiment at the end of the war actually took on a concrete form there. In Germany, the revolutionary forces were able to take power for just a short period, and at that only regionally, with strong support in only a few cities; and in Austria, the strong Social Democratic movement quickly domesticated the revolution and used the councils or soviets as extra-parliamentary reinforcement of their own domination of the parliament itself. In Hungary, by contrast, a revolution really occurred. In March 1919, Béla Kun proclaimed the creation of the 'Federated Hungarian Soviet Socialist Republic', which for just about half a year was able to hold its ground against stiff resistance. Kun, who had become a Bolshevik while a Russian prisoner of war, followed the revolutionary path all the way to the end. The experiment of rule by the soviets failed in Hungary, in part because of Austria's refusal to follow suit, but also because of the military intervention of Romania, whose forces reached as far as Budapest and compelled Kun to take flight. Miklós Horthy, who headed the conservative, nationalistic counter-regime established in Szeged, entered Budapest as victor

40 Helmut Konrad (ed.), *Sozialdemokratie und 'Anschluss'. Historische Wurzeln – Anschluss 1918 und 1938 – Nachwirkungen* (Vienna: Europa Verlag, 1978).

in November 1919. The 'red' terror was followed by a 'white' terror directed against communists and socialists; it also displayed strong anti-Semitic tendencies. In March 1920, Horthy became 'regent' in a monarchy without a king.

The traumatic internal political disruptions of this period could be mastered only through the establishment of clearly defined external enemies. Hungarians believed that they had been sacrificed and been bequeathed a country without friends and without allies. The territorial determinations of the Treaty of Trianon were tailor-made to encourage this belief. According to its terms, Hungary lost Slovakia and the Carpathian Ukraine to the Czechoslovakian Republic; the western Hungarian counties to Austria; Croatia, Slavonia, Prekmurje, Batshcka and part of the Banat to the new Yugoslavian state; and Transylvania and the remainder of the Banat to Romania. Poland received a small region, as well, and Fiume, too, was separated from Hungary (and was itself destined to traverse a very difficult period).

As a result of all these changes, from 1920 onwards 3 million Hungarians lived outside of the Hungarian state. Minor, partially contested border revisions did little to alter the situation. Moreover, Hungary's population still included 800,000 members of minority groups (Germans, Slovaks, Romanians, Croatians, Serbs and Slovenians). The Trianon immediately became a dramatic site of memory, and still today, on numerous Hungarian automobiles and even in semi-official contexts, one can see depictions of the country in which ethnic boundaries are displayed rather than the actual international frontier. Even scholarly discussions about Hungarian emigration[41] are full of nationalistic discourse, whereas, for example, the Slovakian discussions seek to establish a more nuanced picture.[42]

Hungarian schoolchildren in the interwar years learned that Hungary is surrounded only by Hungarians, because there is a significant Hungarian population in all neighbouring countries. They lived with the watchword 'Nem, nem, Soha!' ('No, no, never!') and saw the national flag constantly flying at half-mast. To a much greater degree than Saint-Germain or even Versailles in the cases, respectively, of Austria and Germany, the Trianon remained the central focal point of Hungarian self-understanding into the twenty-first century. Trianon-Hungary – as opposed to the 'Lands of the Crown of St Stephen', or at least as opposed to a 'language union' – persisted

41 Laszlo Bolos, *The Road to the Dictated Peace* (Cleveland, OH: Apard Puiblishing Co., 1999).

42 Marian Hronský, *The Struggle for Slowakish and the Treaty of Trianon* (Bratislava: VEDA Publishing House of the Slovak Academy of Science, 2001).

as the hated counter-image of what Hungary ought to be. As late as 1999, it was argued that 'according to the census of 1910, 54.5% of the population of Hungary was Hungarian. The minorities in Historic Hungary numbered 45.5%. After Trianon, in the successor states, the number of minorities grew to 54.2%.[43] And only 20% of the new Hungarian borders were natural borders; 60% of them took no account of linguistic borders.'[44]

Horthy built his dominant position on this negative image of the Treaty of Trianon, together with the negative image of the 'Judeo-Bolsheviks' as the nation's enemies. Accordingly, after the Treaty of Trianon this anachronistic state – which introduced no land reform, retained exalted privileges for the nobility, was formally a monarchy, rejected liberalism and maintained an 'ethnic-national' definition of who was a genuine Hungarian – was in conflict with all of its neighbouring states.

Neuilly

Bulgaria's decision to enter the war on the side of the Central Powers was not something that could have been foreseen long in advance. In the First Balkan War, Bulgaria, Serbia, Greece and Montenegro had wrested Macedonia from the Ottoman Empire. The dispute over the division of the spoils led to the Second Balkan War between Bulgaria, on the one side, and Serbia, Greece and (later) Romania on the other. Bulgaria's defeat led to its loss of Macedonia and the flight of over 100,000 people from Macedonia to Bulgaria. The resulting economic problems compelled Bulgaria to borrow funds from abroad, and when the French refused to lend it money, Germany quickly agreed to do so in the summer of 1914. Macedonia constituted a problem both domestically, as the immigrants confronted a Macedonian elite in Bulgaria, and in the realm of foreign relations and military matters, where the 'loss' of Macedonia was an important factor. These were Bulgaria's two main concerns on the eve of entering the war. Thus, in terms of economic as well as territorial issues, the Central Powers were more suitable allies.

> The war began well for Bulgaria. Alliance with the Ottoman empire meant the gain of some territory in Thrace, the defeat of Serbia meant Romania in 1916–17 placed some of the Dobruja under Bulgarian control. The fact that Bulgaria was in occupation of former enemy territory meant that Sofia, like

43 Bolos, *Road to Dictated Peace*, p. 417. 44 Bolos, *Road to Dictated Peace*, p. 431.

> Berlin, saw little reason to contemplate peace. It also meant that, like its counterparts in Berlin and Vienna, the government in Sofia refused to take sufficient account of the growing social problems affecting the country.[45]

The main problem was provisioning the civilian population, but the army, too, faced a similar problem. Bulgaria, in fact, suffered in this respect even more than its allies. In addition, almost 39 per cent of the adult male population was serving in the military, more than in any of the other combatant countries, and their lack was felt in both agriculture and manufacturing. The supply of horses was also insufficient, since so many were being used by the army. Accordingly, Sofia experienced its first severe food shortages as early as 1916. By 1918, the situation had become hopeless: food and clothing were almost entirely lacking. As a result, desertions increased, especially during the harvest months, when soldiers, after their home leave, simply disappeared instead of returning to the front. In September, the front collapsed.

With the army in complete disarray, Tsar Ferdinand stepped down from the throne at the beginning of October. The war was lost, and malnutrition weakened resistance against the Spanish flu, which in this case, too, killed almost more people than the war did. Already a week before the Tsar abdicated, Bulgaria had sued for an armistice. Internally, the country was politically divided, but in the post-war years the conservative forces were stronger than the radical left.

The peace treaty with Bulgaria was concluded on 27 November 1919 in Neuilly-sur-Seine. In it Bulgaria had to guarantee that the frontier with Romania would once again conform to the one drawn after its defeat in the Second Balkan War. It also had to give up access to the Aegean Sea, for Western Thrace came under the administration of the Entente, and therefore indirectly fell to Greece. Furthermore, Bulgaria lost several small areas to the new Yugoslavian state. Following the examples of the preceding treaties, its army was limited to 20,000 professional soldiers, and reparations were imposed. The latter, however, were reduced in 1923 and eliminated altogether in 1932. The treaty provided for a population exchange between Greece and Bulgaria, a 'convention concerning a mutual and freely chosen emigration', which led to the departure of 50,000 Bulgarians from Greece and 40,000 Greeks from Bulgaria. A total of more than 100,000 refugees, mainly from Macedonia, Thrace and Dobruja entered the country, intensifying the existing

45 Richard J. Crampton, 'Deprivation, desperation and degradation: Bulgaria in defeat', in Peter Liddle and Hugh Cecil (eds.), *At the Eleventh Hour. Reflections, Hopes and Anexieties at the Closing of the Great War 1918* (Barnsley: Pen and Sword Books, 1998).

social problems. All the same, Bulgaria managed to break out of its international isolation and to enter the League of Nations already in 1920. Many of those who had fled to Bulgaria subsequently emigrated overseas.

From Sèvres to Lausanne

In no other region of the world did the First World War and the peace treaties create a greater re-orientation and a greater, long-term potential for conflict than in those areas that until 1918 had constituted the 'Ottoman Empire . . . a structure that had survived the bygone era to which it belonged'.[46] The 'sick man of the Bosporus' had, for a variety of reasons, rejected the modernisation process of the second half of the nineteenth century and had fallen behind the other Great Powers in the areas of foreign policy, military technology and the economy, as well as social development. Even the population was declining. From being a player in world politics, it had become the stage on which the other powers sought to pursue their conflicting geopolitical ambitions. Moreover, its geographic position was of the greatest strategic importance. Russia was pushing in the direction of the Bosporus and the Dardanelles in order to secure an ice-free route to the world's seas, and with the building of the Suez Canal Britain had shortened decisively the distance of the sea route to India. Military and political control of the region was thus of the highest priority.

The long-delayed efforts to bring about modernisation were accelerated for the first time with the putsch led by the Young Turks in 1908. The latter, however, did not share a common programme. They included both secular centralisers who pushed for a strong state, on the one hand, and, on the other, liberal proponents of decentralisation who were especially concerned to work out an arrangement with the non-Muslim groups. In 1909, after a counter-putsch by the sultan and then his removal from the throne, the Ottoman Empire became a constitutional monarchy in which the military, which shared the political views of the centralist Young Turks, had the main say both on the road to war and during the war itself. The state was restructured as a secular entity, but it was not possible to provide it with a unified, 'nation'-creating identity – neither on the basis of religion (Muslim, Jewish, Christian) nor of language or ethnicity. Even in Anatolia, many Armenians and Kurds lived alongside the Turks, and the European states within the realm included

46 David Fromkin, *A Peace to End All Peace, the Fall of the Ottoman Empire and the Creation of the Modern Middle East* (New York: Henry Holt & Co., 2009), p. 33.

Greeks, Romanians, Albanians, Macedonians and still others. Added to these were large portions of the Arab world. The mixture was more complex than that of the Habsburg monarchy, and even more heterogeneous. In addition to all this, the Empire's geographic situation made it one of the main crossroads of the interests of the Great Powers. Consequently, in this case the victors were not able to impose upon the losers the same sort of conditions that they could at Saint-Germain or the Trianon (and to a degree also at Versailles).

The Ottoman Empire entered the war in November 1914 on the side of the Central Powers, a choice based on the actions of Russia and Great Britain. The British had annexed Cyprus and declared Egypt and Kuwait to be their protectorates; and Russia (like, moreover, its new ally, the Habsburg monarchy) was a competitor in the Balkans with a vital strategic interest in obtaining access to the Mediterranean from the Black Sea. The war in the Caucasus, which also influenced the Armenian tragedy, went poorly, and after the Treaty of Brest-Litovsk, which did not bar the Ottoman Empire from continuing the fight against Russia, it went no better. Only Gallipoli could be counted an Ottoman victory. In the Arab world, the conflict quickly passed from a test of strength into a matter of the enemy dividing the spoils. The British had occupied Baghdad in March 1917, and in the autumn of 1918 Arab troops pushed north from Egypt, alongside the British. An armistice was concluded on 30 October 1918.

Already during the war an agreement had been signed concerning Palestine. Since Jerusalem was a holy place for more than one religion, the city and its symbolic power had to be protected by treaty. France considered itself to be the defender of the Catholics, especially those living in Lebanon. Russia saw itself as the protector of the Orthodox population, and Britain sought to represent the interests of the Jewish population, which numbered about 24,000 after the first waves of immigration to Palestine (a number which quickly grew larger). The Sykes-Picot Agreement of January 1916 foresaw a division of the Near East between a French sphere of influence and a British one, with Jerusalem and the surrounding territory to be internationalised and administered by France, Britain and Russia. By the time of the October Revolution, at the latest, the plan was already obsolete. In the Balfour Declaration of 2 November 1917, the British Foreign Minister promised the creation of a 'national homeland' for the Jewish people, one which, however, would not diminish the rights of the other inhabitants of Palestine. After the war, mandates were created in the Near East under the auspices of the League of Nations, but in practice they were really French (in the case of Lebanon and Syria) and British (in the case of Palestine, Jordan and Iraq) zones of influence.

Jewish emigration increased rapidly following the war, and conflicts with the Arab population of Palestine became bloody from 1919 on.

The decisive factor in the peace process, though, was time. It took no less than twenty months to turn the ceasefire into a peace treaty, and almost a year-and-a-half went by before the victorious powers, meeting in London and San Remo in the first half of 1920, could reach an agreement in principle concerning the key points of the treaty. In the meantime, however, the region had undergone dramatic changes: to the north in the Caucasus, in Anatolia itself and, above all, in the Arab portions of the defunct Ottoman Empire. The peace treaty was finally signed in Sèvres on 10 August 1920.

At the end of the war, Britain had over 1 million soldiers stationed in the former Ottoman Empire. They oversaw the defeated armies as they sank their weapons into the swamps, but since by the summer of 1919 only one-third of the British troops remained in the country, the process could henceforth be only partially supervised. The most important development in the Caucasus was the creation of several independent countries (Armenia, Georgia and Azerbaijan). The main concern of the Allies, however, especially of Churchill, was support of the 'Whites' in the conflict with the Bolsheviks, but in the summer of 1919, the British troops withdrew from the region. To the south, 'where the present Turkish borders run with those of Syria, Iraq and Iran, lay the area imprecisely known as Kurdistan, where British officials thought of sponsoring another of their protectorates'.[47] The area was promised to the French in the Sykes-Picot Agreement, but in 1919 they had no presence there. The British efforts ended, however, in an uprising of the various Kurdish groups against the recent meddling by outsiders in their affairs.

Even within Turkey itself, it was unclear who was in charge. The British and French controlled Constantinople, the British fleet dominated the coast, and the means of communication and transport were in the hands of the victors. The Sultan had only limited power, and the Young Turks staged a putsch against him. He was ready to agree to all the victors' demands, but the country was not under his control. Meanwhile, General Mustafa Kemal, who had distinguished himself in Gallipoli, was creating a new Turkish army in eastern Anatolia. Turkish anxieties were awakened in May 1919 when Wilson and Lloyd George decided to support the Greeks against the Italians in the islands and in Anatolia. Given 'Moslem Turkish hatred of the two large Christian populations in their midst – Greeks and Armenians'[48] – this move

47 Fromkin, *A Peace to End All Peace*, pp. 404–5.
48 Fromkin, *A Peace to End All Peace*, p. 407.

strengthened Kemal and his supporters in their opposition to the victors. In February 1920, the newly formed Turkish army defeated a French unit in southern Anatolia, making it completely clear to the victorious powers that a new player had arrived on the scene.

The situation was even more complex in the south, in the regions of the old empire where the majority of the inhabitants were Arab. The French had concentrated their power in Lebanon and along the Syrian coast. Syria's interior was formally ruled by King Faisal, who resided in Paris during the peace conference, but effectively power was shared among a number of influential Arab families. A unified Arab nationalism did not yet exist, and the Arabs were divided in their objectives. 'Those from communities like Jerusalem denounced Zionism in Palestine; those from Baghdad complained of the British in Mesopotamia; and the Syrians wanted to expel the French from their seacoast and from Lebanon.'[49] The notion of Pan-Arabism was still a long way off, and King Faisal derived his power from the presence in Damascus of the British, who, however, withdrew in 1919. The French goals were clear: dominance in Lebanon and Syria's existence as a state dependent on the French. Faisal's support within the Arab world, however, was contingent upon his success in resisting France's efforts to assert its control over Syria. Thus, although he was supported by the French, he had at the same time to keep them at a distance. Finally, an agreement was reached with Clemenceau that Syria would become independent, but that it would draw exclusively on French 'advisers'.

It was amidst these difficult circumstances that the definitive decisions concerning the peace treaty were eventually reached, initially in London, then in San Remo, and finally in Sèvres. The principal outcome was the division of the region into English and French spheres of influence. The British received Palestine and Mesopotamia; Arabia was to remain independent but ruled by monarchs who would follow London's directives; and Egypt and the Gulf coast were already under British control. Lebanon and Syria were assigned to the French sphere of influence. Iraq would be a mandate of the League of Nations, with independence as a medium-range goal.

The Aegean islands, European Turkey and Smyrna, along with Western Anatolia, were given to the Greeks, with the understanding that in five years a plebiscite would be held in Western Anatolia. The area around the Dardenelles came under international administration, and the status of Constantinople was tied to Turkish treatment of the Christian minorities.

49 Fromkin, *A Peace to End All Peace*, p. 409.

Armenia was to become independent, and the Kurds were to be granted autonomy. Turkish finances were to be administered jointly by Britain, France and Italy. In August 1920, the Sultan's plenipotentiaries signed the peace treaty in Sèvres, but peace itself was not thereby established – neither at home nor abroad. Internally, there were major conflicts of interest, for example, between the Kurds and the Armenians. Whereas the Armenians sat at the negotiating table in Paris, the Kurds were excluded. An independent Kurdistan, going beyond autonomy, was in fact considered, but was made dependent on it being demonstrated that the majority of Kurds wanted such a state.

The harshness of the peace provisions had several grounds: the strategic and geopolitical goals of Britain and France; the Armenian genocide; and also the defeat of the British at Gallipoli, which remained a sore spot. Finally, the centuries-old threat to Europe, to the 'Christian West', posed by the Ottoman Empire, the so-called 'Turkish threat', still evoked a strong emotional response; and thus the goal of seeing all of Europe once again lying outside of Turkish domination was indirectly a motive, at least for handing over the European portion of Turkey to the Greeks. 'The Treaty of Sèvres did not signal the beginning of a new era guided by the idea of the self-determination of peoples, but rather a return to the zenith of European imperialism.'[50] It was the last of the treaties concluded in the Parisian suburbs and also the only one that never actually went into effect; for the Turkish National Assembly did not ratify it. Those who signed it at Sèvres were called 'traitors to the fatherland', and Kemal manoeuvred politically and militarily to change it.

Despite all of Turkey's conflicts with the Bolsheviks, it signed a pact of mutual assistance with Russia, which ultimately led to their dividing Armenia between them. Furthermore, the Greek army intervened twice, in January and March 1921, and was defeated each time. In October 1920, France concluded a treaty with Turkey which amounted to a separate peace. Italy, too, moved closer to the Turkish regime.

In January 1921, the Great National Assembly, sitting in Ankara, produced a constitution, which also spelled out the nation's territorial claims. It 'included Turkey's renunciation of all Arab territories, but also the claim to full sovereignty over all regions in which there existed a Turkish majority'.[51] This laid the basis for an advance against the Greek army, and in September

50 Winkler, *Geschichte des Westens*, pp. 190–1.

51 Ulrike Freitag, 'Unter imperialer Herrschaft. Vorderasien und Nordafrika', in Bernecker and Tobler (eds), *Die Welt im 20. Jahrhundert*, p. 288.

1922 Turkish troops stood before Smyrna, which fell on 12 September. 'The onward-rushing Turkish troops drove the fleeing Greek soldiers and civilians into the sea; and it was far from all of them who were able to board ships and boats and thus reach the nearby Greek islands of Chios and Mytilene.'[52] Smyrna went up in flames in a fire presumably set by the Turkish troops.

Since the Allies persisted in considering the Sultan's regime in Istanbul as the country's legal representative, the National Assembly decided on 1 November to abolish the Sultanate, thereby definitively bringing to a close the history of the Ottoman Empire. Mustafa Kemal and the Great National Assembly now claimed to be the country's sole representatives, and they set about refashioning Turkey. Thus, after two years, the Treaty of Sèvres was already a dead letter. At a conference in Lausanne, which began in December 1922 and lasted beyond the middle of 1923, the treaty was substantially altered, and the frontier between Greece and Turkey was redrawn.

The main concern of the Peace Treaty of Lausanne, signed on 24 July 1923, was the creation of new boundaries. The Straits of the Dardanelles came under international administration and were demilitarised. Neither a state of Kurdistan nor a state of Armenia was established, since the Turkish re-conquests had created new facts on the ground. In contrast, the 'League of Nations mandates for the Arab provinces (Iraq, Palestine and Trans-Jordan going to the British, and Syria and Lebanon going to the French)'[53] were reconfirmed.

By the beginning of 1923, however, Greece and Turkey had agreed not only on an exchange of prisoners of war, but also on a massive population exchange. About 1.5 million Greeks and 400,000 Turks were resettled. The exchange encompassed 'almost in their entirety the Muslim population of Greece and the Greek Orthodox population of Turkey (except for the Greeks in Istanbul and the Turks in Western Thrace)'.[54] The Treaty of Lausanne gave its blessing to the plan. Adding this population exchange to the one provided for in the Treaty of Neuilly between Bulgaria and Turkey, we see that as a result of the First World War millions of people were resettled just along the boundaries of Europe and Asia Minor in order to achieve ethnic and religious homogeneity. The politics of 'ethnic cleansing' was thereby introduced in twentieth-century practice, and seven decades later it reappeared in several dramatic follow-up experiments, particularly in the Balkans.

52 Winkler, *Geschichte des Westens*, p. 192.

53 Freitag, 'Unter imperialer Herrschaft', p. 289.

54 Winkler, *Geschichte des Westens*, p. 192.

An ambivalent outcome

A Peace to End All Peace[55] is the expression chosen by David Fromkin for his account of the collapse of 'the Ottoman Empire and the creation of the modern Middle East'. The history of this region of the world, which Fromkin recounts up to the present day, justifies his title even if it indirectly minimises the significance of earlier periods. Yet, all things considered, were the treaties which ended the First World War peace treaties which actually made peace impossible? Are Versailles, Saint-Germain, Trianon, Neuilly and Sèvres symbolic sites of failure? One cannot answer this question in a completely unequivocal manner. It is clear that the treaties were compromise solutions which realised few of the idealistic preconceptions that originally swirled around them. In the end, they did not give rise to a group of self-determined 'national states' with minimal military forces, united through free trade and agreements for the solution of international conflicts. Nor did the spark of revolution spread throughout the industrialised world, rendering national borders meaningless in the face of the overarching unity of the working class.

To the contrary. Although in Paris even the minor victorious countries and those late in joining the Allies had a seat at the negotiating table, the decisions were ultimately determined by the political interests of the Great Powers. In Europe, the right of self-determination was subordinated to questions of power and security and to economic interests. Outside of Europe, the right of self-determination was not even a subject of discussion. The old ideology of 'The White Man's Burden'[56] gave way only slightly in the case of Japan, which was one of the victors, and not at all when it came to the colonies and Dominions, which had shared the costs of the war and paid a heavy toll in blood. It was simply taken for granted that they would continue to bear the colonial yoke.

Still, even if Wilson's Fourteen Points had been more fully realised in practice, a fundamental problem would have remained unsolved: securing rights at the level of nations, not just at that of individuals. From the perspective of human rights, the treaties would have had to establish the 'self' in 'the right of self-determination' – in other words, come to grips with the decision of where an individual feels he or she belongs, of how he defines his identity – at the level of the individual person. There certainly existed

55 That is the title of David Fromkin's book.

56 The poem by Rudyard Kipling was first published in 1899 and relates specifically to the United States and the Philippines.

models for this approach. The Moravian agreement of 1905, for example, had based rights such as the language one could use in the courts or in school on the individual level, thereby abandoning the territorial principle,[57] a change which found theoretical support in the writings of Karl Renner.[58] This way of thinking, dating from before the First World War, pointed beyond the rather simple territorial concepts expressed in the 1919 to 1923 treaties; the latter recalled, rather, the solutions agreed upon at the Congress of Vienna, which, it must be said, were still considered the only feasible ones available in the Balkans even late into the twentieth century. The equation of nation and language is more than problematic, and if it is used to legitimate the establishment of political boundaries, then the kind of failures we have seen, ranging from Paris to the Dayton Accords, are inevitable.

When it came to translating their ideas into practice, the Bolsheviks likewise often left theory behind. Events in Finland and the Baltic countries transpired 'out of sight for the people in the western metropoles'.[59] The Finns did reach an understanding with Lenin near the very end of 1917 that they could separate from Russia, but the October Revolution engulfed Helsinki, too. In a bloody war, the 'Whites', with the help of Germany, defeated the 'Reds', and in 1919 the Finns were in a difficult position, having soured their relations with both the Western powers and the Bolsheviks. The annexation of East Karelia was to remain only a dream, and it was not until October 1920 that the Russo-Finnish border was definitively established.

Initially, for a period Russia really did try to honour the right of self-determination within its borders, although with scarcely adequate means, since, in practice, mobility and urbanisation were major constraints on Stalin's territorial principle. In external matters, however, its policies, like those of other countries, were driven primarily by strategic considerations and a desire to maintain the status of a major power. In dealing with Finland, Armenia and Central Asia, its concerns were power, influence and security.

Thus, both models, the Western and the Bolshevik, were completely and persistently shaped by self-interest. All the same, this is what made it possible to create, for the middle term, at least, a reasonably 'just' peace. Moreover,

57 Lukáš Fasora, *Der Mährische Ausgleich von 1905. Möglichkeiten und Grenzen für einen nationalen Ausgleich in Mitteleuropa* (Brno: Vyzkum.stred.pro dejini, 2006).

58 Rudolf Springer (= Karl Renner), *Der Kampf der österreichischen Nationen um den Staat* (Vienna and Leipzig: Deuticke Verlag, 1902). According to the author, national – in other words, linguistic – rights should be based on the interests of individual persons and not on a principle of territoriality.

59 Konrad and Stromberger, 'Zwischeneuropa', p. 61.

most people had truly had enough of war. The great numbers of casualties, of the maimed and of the psychologically damaged – these sent a clear message. It was not only the pacifists who adopted the slogan 'War on war!' Another war seemed unthinkable: images of destruction and annihilation had been seared into the minds of the survivors. The pacifist Ernst Friedrich published images of this kind in 1924 in his book *Krieg dem Kriege! Guerrre à la Guerre! War against War! Oorlog aan den Oorlog!*[60] The public was shocked by the unimaginable examples of mutilation it contained, all of which were brought together and displayed in his anti-war museum in Berlin, a museum later destroyed by the Nazis.

And yet, too many questions remained unanswered. Too many conflicts remained unresolved, and to these new ones were added. Considering the situation just within Europe, a number of factors rendered the peace a fragile one:

- Germany ('undefeated in the battlefield') offered fertile ground for the legend of the 'stab in the back', for the thirst for revenge and for labelling the Treaty of Versailles a 'shameful peace'. The Weimar Republic was able to contain the spread of these notions at least until the global economic crisis, but then they helped the National Socialists in garnering support for their policies.
- Italy mourned its 'lost victory', seeing itself disadvantaged as a nation, one which, moreover, was sharply divided politically and socially. From the trenches of Isonzo there emerged numerous groups of men ready to employ violence to advance their jingoistic and anti-democratic ideas, and they furnished the basis of the *Fasci di Combattimento* (the early members of the Fascist Party).
- In 'Zwischeneuropa',[61] the creation of a chain of independent states did not diminish the number of ethnic minorities; instead, it simply reversed the hierarchies between the new majority populations and the old ones, which now found themselves occupying the position of minorities. From the Baltic Sea to the Adriatic, the new states – after brief democratic interludes – all became dictatorships, except for the Czech Republic.
- Russia's separate path, which led to its isolation and, at least partially as a result of that, to Stalin's despotic rule, diminished the world of free

60 Ernst Friedrich, *Krieg dem Kriege* (Munich: Deutsche Verlagsanstalt, 1924, 2004).
61 Konrad and Stromberger, 'Zwischeneuropa', pp. 54–79.

trade and thereby destabilised the market-based economies of the industrialised countries.

The sources of future conflicts, moreover, could also be clearly discerned far beyond the borders of Europe:

- Japan, which during the war had gone from being a 'debtor nation to a creditor nation',[62] was present in Paris, it is true, as a victorious power; and it did obtain Shandong as well as the former German South Seas colonies. Yet, even though it was a founding member of the League of Nations, it soon found itself isolated. 'As the only non-Western great power, Japan demanded that the preamble of the clause establishing the League of Nations contain a declaration of the equality of all peoples, regardless of their race',[63] but a unanimous decision on this question could not be reached. On the other hand, it should be noted that Japan's fantasies of superiority over its neighbours, especially Korea and China, stood in contradiction to its desire that the major powers should set aside racial prejudice and deal with each other as equals.
- The unresolved colonial problems were simply left to be dealt with at a later time. The colonial powers spoke about self-determination, but in those lands under their control or in their zones of influence they refused to offer any form of self-determination and often suppressed any attempts to achieve it, thereby setting the stage for numerous wars and conflicts later in the twentieth century.
- Palestine and, in fact, the entire Near East – encompassing not just the 'special case of Palestine',[64] but also Syria, Lebanon and Trans-Jordan – were politically organised, it is true, but by no means stabilised.

Treaties, especially when a large number of parties are involved in the negotiations, are necessarily compromises, and the compromises reached at Paris were primarily devoted to settling the conflicting claims within the victorious camp. The losers were not even seated at the negotiating table. What, then, can be counted among their positive achievements? It may certainly be said that, at the very least, in spite of all the critical objections raised about the League of Nations, a genuine effort was made to use it as a means of maintaining peace at a global level, and with the signing of the Treaty of Versailles the League of Nations was effectively established, since its

62 Sepp Lienhart, 'Ein halbes Jahrhundert Imperialismus. Japan', in Bernecker and Tobler, *Die Welt im 20. Jahrhundert*, p. 171.

63 Lienhart, 'Japan', p. 172.

64 Freitag, 'Unter imperialer Herrschaft', p. 300.

creation was a part of the treaty. In 1920, the League of Nations protocols were ratified, and it could take up its work. The fact that the United States never became a member and that at different moments Germany, Italy, Japan and Russia all lacked member status permanently weakened the organisation. Still, associated organisations such as the International Labour Organization, to which all the members of the League of Nations belonged, quickly agreed upon and implemented very positive measures designed to halt any further estrangement between wage labour and capital throughout the world. In the beginning, the actual effect of these efforts may have been small, but they nevertheless established the principle that the spiritual, physical and moral well-being of the individual person should be considered a political objective. Moreover, it was in this context that the notion of the rights of man received one of its earliest formulations. This was also the period of the creation of a number of associated organisations and of the International Court of Justice, all of which made significant contributions in the course of the twentieth century.

The further course of history, the readiness of nations to turn to violence in the subsequent decades, and, finally, the catastrophe of the Second World War with its still unimaginable number of victims and its genocide(s) – makes it seem in retrospect that the results of the peace treaties were among the preconditions for these subsequent disasters. But the treaties should be judged in light of the conditions in which they were forged. In other words, they were fragile compromises in which the victors brushed aside the concerns of the losers, devoting their energy to jockeying for power among themselves and placing national interests above the common good. All the same, they were at least attempts to come to terms with the traumatic experience of the First World War, using the tools of diplomacy in the service of achieving strategic objectives. The main goal, however, that of making wars of this dimension impossible in the future through mutual commitments and guarantees, was not achievable, given the limited room for manoeuvre available in 1919, and given, as well, the world views and values of the leading participants.

23

The continuum of violence

ROBERT GERWARTH

Introduction

In the second volume of his often overlooked masterpiece, *November 1918*, the acclaimed German novelist Alfred Döblin ended his narrative on a sombre note: a war-mongering monster – half human, half beast – raises its head in the heart of Europe, its hairy arms tearing apart the paper-thin 'wall of pergament which the world of peace has erected around itself'.[1] Döblin was not the only eminent contemporary writer who believed that the peace established on the Western Front by the Armistice of 11 November 1918 was at best precarious. His Austrian colleague, Joseph Roth, had already published a prophetic novel, *The Spider's Web*, about the post-war upheavals in Central Europe a few years earlier: the protagonist of his novel, Lieutenant Theodor Lohse, was one of the many demobilised officers of the defeated Central Powers, for whom defeat in the Great War served as a major source of political mobilisation against the post-war peace. Forced to earn a meagre living as a private tutor in the household of a wealthy Jewish businessman, Lohse soon despaired over his loss of professional prestige, the perceived national humiliation caused by military collapse, and the hostility with which his own family greeted his return from the battlefields of Flanders:

> They couldn't forgive Theodor for having failed – he who had twice been mentioned in despatches – to die a hero's death as a lieutenant. A dead son would have been the pride of the family. A demobilised lieutenant, a victim of the revolution, was a burden to his womenfolk ... He could have told his sisters that he was not responsible for his own misfortune; that he cursed the revolution and was gnawed by hatred for the socialists and the Jews; that he

1 Alfred Döblin, *November 1918: Eine deutsche Revolution*, vol. II, *Heimkehr der Fronttruppen* (repr. Frankfurt am Main: S. Fischer, 2008).

> bore each day like a yoke across his bowed neck and felt himself trapped in his epoch as in some sunless prison.'[2]

The only escape route from the 'sunless prison' of a meaningless existence was the possibility of continuing the war through paramilitary activity – an activity that offered structure and purpose when it was most needed. Lohse joined one of the many paramilitary organisations that mushroomed in post-war Europe and which symptomatically stood for a major problem facing most of the continent in the years immediately after 1918: the absence of peace.

With the benefit of hindsight, most historians today would agree with the assessments of perceptive contemporary novelists such as Döblin or Roth. If anything, the cessation of hostilities on the Western Front was atypical for interwar Europe as violent upheavals, pogroms and civil wars remained a characteristic feature of post-war Europe's everyday life. Violence was particularly intense in the vast territories of the defeated dynastic land empires – the Habsburg, Romanov and Ottoman empires – whose disappearance from the map provided the space for the emergence of new and often nervously aggressive nation-states.[3] Those who fought in the name of these new nation-states sought to determine or defend their real or imagined borders through force and strove to create ethnically or religiously homogenous communities. The birth of these new nation-states in East-Central Europe and the Baltic region was generally most violent in those regions where national and social revolutions overlapped. For herein lay one of the peculiarities of the 'wars after the war'[4]: in the exposure of Eastern and Central Europe to two currents of revolution, the revolutions of national self-determination and the social revolutions for the redistribution of power, land and wealth. Despite regional variations in the intensity of violence and its causes, hardly any territories east of the River Elbe remained unaffected. An extensive arc of post-war violence stretched from Finland and the Baltic states through Russia and Ukraine, Poland, Austria, Hungary, Germany, all the way through the Balkans into Anatolia, the Caucasus and the Middle East, with newly founded

2 Joseph Roth, *The Spider's Web* (New York: Overlook Press, 2003), pp. 4–6.

3 Michael A. Reynolds, *Shattering Empires: The Clash and Collapse of the Ottoman and Russian Empires* (Cambridge and New York: Cambridge University Press, 2011); Alexander V. Prusin, *The Lands Between, Conflict in the East European Borderlands, 1870–1992* (Oxford and New York: Oxford University Press, 2010), pp. 72–97; Piotr Wróbel, 'The seeds of violence: the brutalization of an East European region, 1917–1921', *Journal of Modern European History*, 1 (2003), pp. 125–49.

4 Peter Gatrell, 'Wars after the war: conflicts, 1919–1923', in John Horne (ed.), *Blackwell Companion to the First World War* (Oxford: Blackwell, 2010), pp. 558–75.

Czechoslovakia under President Tomas Masaryk remaining an exceptional island of peace.[5]

What was new about the post-war conflicts was that they occurred after a century in which European states had more or less successfully managed to assert their monopoly on legitimate violence, in which national armies had become the norm and in which the fundamentally important distinction between combatants and non-combatants had been codified (even if it was frequently breached in practice). The post-war conflicts that erupted in 1918 reversed that trend. In the absence of functioning states, militias of various political persuasions assumed the role of the national army for themselves (often against armed opposition from other groups), while the lines between friends and foes, combatants and civilians, were far less clearly demarked than they had been during the Great War. Not since the Thirty Years' War had a series of inter-connected civil wars been as messy and deadly as now, as civil wars overlapped with revolutions, counter-revolutions and border conflicts between states without clearly defined frontiers or internationally recognised governments. German freebooters fought with (and against) Latvian and Estonian nationalists, Russian Whites and Reds clashed throughout the region, while Polish, Ukrainian and Lithuanian armed bands fought over ill-defined borders. Other flashpoints of armed conflict included Fiume, Western and Eastern Anatolia, the Caucasus, Upper Silesia, the Burgenland and the former Ottoman lands in what only now became known as the 'Middle East'. The death toll of the short period under investigation in this chapter – the years between the Great War's official end in 1918 and the Treaty of Lausanne in 1923 – was extraordinary: including those killed in the Russian civil war, well over 4 million people lost their lives as a result of civil wars or inter-ethnic struggles, not counting the millions of expellees and refugees who fled the havoc unleashed in Eastern and Central Europe.

Despite these horrific effects on Europe's 'post-war' societies, the conflicts of the years after 1918 have not attracted nearly as much scholarly attention as

5 Recent literature on some of these conflicts discussed include: Serhy Yekelchyk, *Ukraine: Birth of a Modern Nation* (Oxford and New York: Oxford University Press, 2007); Reynolds, *Shattering Empires*; Michael A. Reynolds, 'Native sons: post-imperial politics, Islam, and identity in the North Caucasus, 1917–1918', *Jahrbücher fur Geschichte Osteuropas*, 56 (2008), pp. 221–47; John Paul Newman, 'Post-imperial and post-war violence in the South Slav lands, 1917–1923', *Contemporary European History*, 19 (2010), pp. 249–65; Julia Eichenberg, 'The dark side of independence: paramilitary violence in Ireland and Poland after the First World War', *Contemporary European History*, 19 (2010), pp. 231–48; Ryan Gingeras, *Sorrowful Shores: Violence, Ethnicity, and the End of the Ottoman Empire, 1912–1923* (Oxford University Press, 2009); Tim Wilson, *Frontiers of Violence: Conflict and Identity in Ulster and Upper Silesia, 1918–1922* (Oxford University Press, 2010).

the events on the Western Front over the previous four years. For decades they were belittled by Western observers as in Churchill's famous words 'wars of the pygmies'[6] and have only recently for the first time become the subject of systematically comparative research.[7] What dominated the overwhelmingly nation-centric research agenda of previous decades was not so much an interest in the origins and phenomenology of post-war violence, but the search for the roots of fascism in Italy and National Socialism in Germany.[8] The escalation of an even more devastating conflict than the First World War after 1939 convinced many that the Great War had unleashed furies that could not be contained by the peace treaties of Paris. The 'brutalisation thesis', famously developed in George Mosse's 1990 classic *Fallen Soldiers*, essentially suggested that the totalisation process at work in the First World War generated a brutalisation both of war and society by establishing new and unprecedented levels of acceptable violence which prepared the way for, and were only surpassed by, the horrors of the Second World War, during which the number of killed civilians exceeded that of combatants.[9]

Recent empirical scholarship has, however, cast doubt on the explanatory value of the 'brutalisation thesis', notably because the trench experience itself does not account for why the world of politics was brutalised in *some* of the former combatant states post-1917/18, but not in others.[10] After all, there was no fundamental difference in the war experiences of Allied soldiers and those of the Central Powers – except for the outcomes of the war. The brutalising moment, it could be argued, lay not so much in the war itself, but in the transitional period from war to peace.

6 Churchill as quoted in: Norman Davies, *White Eagle, Red Star: The Polish-Soviet War, 1919–20*, 2nd edn (London: Pimlico, 2004), p. 21.

7 Robert Gerwarth and John Horne (eds.), *War in Peace: Paramilitary Violence after the Great War* (Oxford and New York: Oxford University Press, 2012). A notable exception is Sven Reichardt, *Faschistische Kampfbünde. Gewalt und Gemeinschaft im italienischen Squadrismus und in der deutschen SA* (Cologne, Weimar and Vienna: Böhlau Verlag, 2002).

8 A classic example is: Nigel H. Jones, *Hitler's Heralds: The Story of the Freikorps, 1918–1923* (London: John Murray, 1987).

9 George L. Mosse, *Fallen Soldiers: Reshaping the Memory of the World Wars* (Oxford and New York: Oxford University Press, 1990). Similar arguments were made for the case of Italy – see: Adrian Lyttleton, 'Fascism and violence in post-war Italy: political strategy and social conflict', in Wolfgang J. Mommsen and Gerhard Hirschfeld (eds.), *Social Protest, Violence and Terror* (London: Macmillan, 1982), here pp. 262–3.

10 See, e.g., Benjamin Ziemann, *War Experiences in Rural Germany, 1914–1923* (Oxford and New York: Berg, 2007); Dirk Schumann, 'Europa, der Erste Weltkrieg und die nachkriegszeit: eine kontinuität der gewalt?', *Journal of Modern European History*, 1 (2003), pp. 24–43. See, too: Antoine Prost and Jay Winter (eds.), *The Great War in History: Debates and Controversies, 1914 to the Present* (Cambridge and New York: Cambridge University Press, 2005).

Building on this hypothesis, this chapter seeks to explain the geography and different levels of violence in 'post-war' Europe through a combination of three factors. The first of these factors was undoubtedly the Russian Revolution, both as a game-changer in international politics and as a fantasy that mobilised anti-revolutionary forces well beyond those countries where a triumph of Bolshevism was probable.[11]

A second factor that explains the uneven distribution of post-war violence lies in the mobilising power of defeat (or, in the case of Italy, the perception of a 'mutilated victory') in 1918 on the one hand, and the internally appeasing power of victory on the other.[12] For while in the victorious states of Europe (except Italy) and their empires (except Ireland, India, Egypt and Korea) there was no substantial increase in political violence post-1918,[13] the same cannot be said about the vanquished. There may have been a 'fear of brutalisation' in Britain or France, but violence at home remained exceptional, whereas none of the defeated states of the Great War managed to return to pre-war levels of domestic stability and internal peace.[14]

The third major factor for the upsurge in violence after 1918 was the abrupt break-up of Europe's land empires and the inability of the successor states to agree on borders with their neighbours. Within the national revolutions that occurred throughout the 'shatter-zones' of Europe's land empires,[15] the intensity of post-war violence also appears to have depended on the strength and perceived legitimacy of the state to which the former combatants returned. Where the state monopoly of violence was successfully upheld,

11 Robert Gerwarth and John Horne, 'Bolshevism as fantasy: fear of revolution and counter-revolutionary violence, 1917–1923', in Gerwarth and Horne, *War in Peace*. On Italy: Emilio Gentile, 'Paramilitary violence in Italy: the rationale of fascism and the origins of totalitarianism', in Gerwarth and Horne, *War in Peace*.

12 Robert Gerwarth and John Horne, 'Vectors of violence: paramilitarism in Europe after the Great War, 1917–1923', *Journal of Modern History*, 83 (2011), pp. 489–512, 3.

13 On the white settler societies post 1918, see: Stephen Garton, 'Demobilization and empire: nationalism, empire nationalism and soldier citizenship in settler society dominions after World War I', *Journal of Contemporary History* (forthcoming); on African combatants and the lack of brutalisation, see: Richard Fogarty and David Killingray, 'The brutalization thesis revisited: demobilization in British and French Africa at the end of the First World War', *Journal of Contemporary History* (forthcoming). On Ireland and paramilitarism, see: David Leeson, *The Black and Tans: British Police and Auxiliaries in the Irish War of Independence, 1920–21* (Oxford and New York: Oxford University Press, 2011).

14 On Britain: Jon Lawrence, 'Forging a peaceable kingdom: war, violence, and fear of brutalization in post-First World War Britain', *Journal of Modern History*, 75 (2003), pp. 557–89. On France: John Horne, 'Defending victory: paramilitary politics in France, 1918–26', in Gerwarth and Horne, *War in Peace*.

15 The term 'shatter zone' was first used by Donald Bloxham, *The Final Solution: A Genocide* (Oxford University Press, 2009), p. 81.

violence carried out by non-state actors was unlikely. The potential for a peaceful exit from the first total war of the twentieth century also partly depended on the ability of states to reintegrate veterans into civilian life, either through material or symbolic compensation (the latter of which proved much easier in the victor states of the Great War).[16]

Obviously, these three factors should not blind one to the importance of local traditions and conditions, often deriving from much older conflicts, which shaped the violence that emerged after the war. The *chetnik* tradition of guerrilla warfare in the Balkans,[17] the pre-war revolutionary tensions in Russia[18] or the physical force tradition of Irish republicanism are cases in point.[19] Yet, taken together, the overarching factors mentioned above – revolution, defeat and imperial collapse / national 'rebirth' – help to explain why and how predominantly paramilitary violence became both a possibility and a grim reality at this critical juncture in modern history.

The Russian Revolution and the fear of a European civil war

Is it wrong to emphasise the Russian Revolution – after all a geographically isolated event in the midst of a global war that affected *all* major European societies – as one of the major factors in the brutalisation of interwar European politics? A similar question, asked with very different intentions, triggered the notorious *Historikerstreit* of the late 1980s when it was raised by the conservative German historian Ernst Nolte.[20] Nolte implicitly sought to attribute blame for the rise of the Nazis and the Holocaust on the Bolsheviks who had allegedly first introduced 'Asiatic' practices of extreme violence that were then copied by Hitler's movement. Stripped of these polemical and misleading undertones, however, the question of the place of '1917' in the history of

16 On international debates about veterans' welfare, see the instructive book by Julia Eichenberg, *Kämpfen für Frieden und Fürsorge: Polnische Veteranen des Ersten Weltkriegs und ihre internationalen Kontakte, 1918–1939* (Munich: R. Oldenbourg Verlag, 2011).

17 John Paul Newman, 'Serbian integral nationalism and mass violence in the Balkans 1903–1945', *Tijdschrift voor Geschiedenis*, 124 (2011), pp. 448–63.

18 Peter Holquist, 'Violent Russia, deadly marxism? Russia in the epoch of violence, 1905–1921', *Kritika*, 4:3 (2003), pp. 627–52.

19 Owen McGee, *The IRB: The Irish Republican Brotherhood from the Land League to Sinn Féin* (Dublin: Four Courts Press, 2005).

20 Ernst Nolte, 'Die vergangenheit, die nicht vergehen will. Eine Rede, die geschrieben, aber nicht gehalten werden konnte', *Frankfurter Allgemeine Zeitung*, 6 June 1986. On the subsequent debate, see: Ernst Reinhard Pieper (ed.), *Historikerstreit: Die Dokumentation der Kontroverse um die Einzigartigkeit der nationalsozialistischen Judenvernichtung* (Munich and Zurich: Piper, 1987).

political violence in Europe is perfectly legitimate and important, particularly when the focus is less on the rise of National Socialism and more on the immediate effects of the revolution on both Russia and the rest of Europe in the years 1917 to 1923.

In Russia, as elsewhere, the Great War had prepared the stage for a potential brutalisation of society. According to official estimates, Russia suffered some 7 million casualties (including those who had died as POWs or who were still held by the Germans at the time of Russia's exit from the conflict in early 1918) out of a total of 15 million men who had been mobilised for war against Germany and her allies.[21] The immediate effects of war were most keenly felt in the western border regions of the Romanov Empire, which constituted the conflict's eastern frontline zones and their hinterland. In addition to the countless military and civilian casualties in this region, more than 6 million people fled these borderlands, were evacuated or were expelled during the war.[22]

Yet although the borderlands were in deep crisis before 1917, it was the Bolshevik seizure of power that set different political factions across the Empire on the course of almost inevitable collision.[23] As Peter Gatrell has argued convincingly, the outbreak of civil war in Russia was indeed predictable once the Bolsheviks had come into power. As the Bolshevik leadership was well aware, their ambition to unleash class war would invite stubborn resistance from those 'propertied classes' that Lenin knew were poised to offer 'frantic resistance'.[24]

The revolution and subsequent civil war not only continued a process of suffering, but also (and more importantly) extended the battle zone into Russia proper. For Russia and the majority of its population, the revolution of 1917 and the subsequent civil war thus constituted perhaps more immediately life-changing events than the Great War itself, largely because violence was now both internalised and universalised. Over the following years, up to 5 million people were recruited into the Red Army (of whom more than 700,000 died), and roughly 1 million men were drafted into the White Armies where casualty rates may have been as high as 225,000. In addition, up to

21 William G. Rosenberg, 'Paramilitary violence in Russia's civil wars, 1918–1921', in Gerwarth and Horne, *War in Peace*, p. 25.

22 Joachim Tauber (ed.), 'Über den Weltkrieg hinaus. Kriegserfahrungen in Ostmitteleuropa 1914–1921', *Nordost-Archiv*, 17 (2008); Peter Gatrell, *A Whole Empire Walking. Refugees in Russia During World War I* (Bloomington, IN: Indiana University Press, 1999), pp. 3–5; Werner Benecke, *Die Ostgebiete der zweiten polnischen Republik. Staatsmacht und öffentliche Ordnung in einer Minderheitenregion 1918–1939* (Cologne: Böhlau Verlag, 1999), pp. 27–40.

23 Dietrich Beyrau, 'Brutalization revisited: the case of Russia', *Journal of Contemporary History* (forthcoming).

24 Gatrell, 'Wars after the war'.

1.3 million people perished as a result of Bolshevik repression and pacification measures, and up to 100,000 in consequence of the White terror. Disease wiped out up to an estimated further 2 million, including 280,000 Red Army soldiers.[25]

Nearly everywhere in the former territories of the Romanov Empire, the civil war was unimaginably brutal and devoid of normative moral restraints.[26] Although violence was indiscriminate, Jews were targeted particularly often and throughout the former Romanov lands.[27] Fanned by the comparatively strong Jewish representation in the Russian Revolution, anti-Bolshevik movements were quick to stigmatise the 1917 Revolution as the result of a Jewish conspiracy.[28] It was first used for propaganda purposes by the 'White' Russian forces as they tried to orchestrate resistance against the Bolsheviks who otherwise had much more appealing promises ('land, bread, liberation') to offer to new recruits.[29] The anti-Judeo-Bolshevik card gave the 'Whites' at least something popular to identify with and it quickly led to outbreaks of anti-Semitic violence throughout the former Romanov Empire. In Kaunas and other Lithuanian towns, Jews were harassed, their shop windows smashed and Yiddish inscriptions painted over.[30] In Western Russia and Ukraine, the situation was even worse as Jews bore the murderous hatred of anti-Bolshevism. Between June and December alone, some 100,000 of them were murdered, notably by members of General Anton Denikin's 'Volunteer Army'. Denikin's men, however, were not alone in singling out Jews for murder: Ukrainian and Polish nationalist forces and various peasant armies also participated in the slaughter of Jews, usually in alcohol-fuelled pogroms of which 934 were recorded in Ukraine alone in 1919.[31]

It did not take long before the notion of Jews as the main 'beneficiaries' of Bolshevism spread beyond the Russian borders. The fact that a relatively high

25 Estimates on the number of victims in: Nikolaus Katzer, *Die weiße Bewegung in Russland* (Cologne: Böhlau Verlag, 1999), p. 293.

26 Rosenberg, 'Russia's civil wars', here p. 21. For concrete examples, see: Orlando Figes, *A People's Tragedy: The Russian Revolution, 1891–1924* (London: Jonathan Cape, 1996).

27 Oleg Budnitskii, *Russian Jews between the Reds and Whites, 1917–1920* (Philadelphia, PA: University of Pennsylvania Press, 2011).

28 Budnitskij, *Jews between Reds and Whites*.

29 Norman Cohn, *Warrant for Genocide: The Myth of the Jewish World Conspiracy and the Protocols of the Elders of Zion* (London: Serif, 1996).

30 Tomas Balkelis, 'Turning citizens into soldiers: Baltic paramilitary movements after the Great War', in Gerwart and Horne, *War in Peace*, p. 136.

31 On the infamous 1918 pogrom in Lwów, e.g., see: William W. Hagen, 'The moral economy of ethnic violence: the pogrom in Lwów, November 1918', *Geschichte und Gesellschaft*, 31 (2005), pp. 203–26.

number of Jews played prominent roles in the subsequent Central European revolutions of 1918/19 – Rosa Luxemburg in Berlin, Kurt Eisner in Munich, Bela Kun in Hungary, Victor Adler in Vienna – seemed to make such accusations plausible, even for observers in Britain and France. One in three contemporary French newspapers, for instance, attributed the Bolshevik Revolution to Jewish influence.[32] And in Britain, Winston Churchill wrote his infamous 1920 article attributing blame for the Continental European revolutions to the Jews:

> From the days of Spartacus-Weishaupt to those of Karl Marx, and down to Trotsky (Russia), Bela Kun (Hungary), Rosa Luxemburg (Germany), and Emma Goldman (United States), this world-wide revolutionary conspiracy for the overthrow of civilization and for the reconstitution of society on the basis of arrested development, of envious malevolence, and impossible equality, has been steadily growing . . . It has been the mainspring of every subversive movement during the Nineteenth Century; and now at last this band of extraordinary personalities from the underworlds of the great cities of Europe and America have gripped the Russian people by the hair of their heads and have become practically the undisputed masters of the enormous empire. There is no need to exaggerate the part played in the creating of Bolshevism and in the actual bringing about of the Russian Revolution by these international and for the most part atheistic Jews. It is certainly a very great one; it probably outweighs all others.[33]

Such views were further fuelled by the broad international circulation of the forged *Protocols of the Elders of Zion* which was translated into Western European languages from 1919 onwards. Its exposure as a forgery in 1921 did not reverse its enormous impact on the counter-revolutionary imagination. Yet the unholy marriage of anti-Semitism and anti-Bolshevism produced very different results in different European settings. It was only east of the River Rhine (and more dramatically east of the River Elbe) that anti-'Judeo-bolshevism' would lead to the pogroms and mass murders of Jews that became such a stark and gruesome feature of European history until 1945.

Yet despite the particular prominence of Jews among the victims of counter-revolutionary violence, the civil war in Russia affected people of all ages, social groups and both sexes. There were several reasons for the eruption of the particularly unrestrained and indiscriminate violence of the civil war. Apart

32 Léon Poliakov, *The History of Anti-Semitism* (Philadelphia, PA: University of Pennsylvania Press, 2003), vol. IV, pp. 274–6.

33 Winston Churchill, 'Zionism versus Bolshevism', *Illustrated Sunday Herald*, 8 February 1920.

from ideological motivations for fighting an existential war against broadly defined internal enemies, the disintegration of the former Empire (and attempts to regain territories insisting on their independence such as Poland, the Baltic States, Ukraine or the Caucasus) amplified the potential for ultra-violence. The already extreme situation was made worse through the wrenching scarcity of foodstuffs and material deprivation which beset almost the entire population of the former Russian Empire. The chronic shortages in essential goods, caused by dislocations of war, depletion of reserves and distribution problems which escalated dramatically after 1917, led to a raw struggle for collective and individual survival. The famine of 1921 to 1922 affected between 22 and 30 million people. Famine deaths in the Volga region and the Ukraine are estimated at about 1 million each. Some authors even claim a total of 5 million.[34] From 1917 onwards, hungry bands of deserters terrorised the countryside, prompting the mobilisation of various peasant self-defence groups. For many now caught in the unrestrained violence of civil war, the inability of any regime to bring security only escalated self-mobilisation in local bands and ever-more brutal forms of resistance as well as reciprocal and emulatory violence.

Within the complex amalgam of violent actors in post-revolutionary Russia, two groups in particular stood out in sheer size and by claiming to be the heir to the collapsed Russian imperial army as the sole legitimate bearer of arms: the Red Army and its 'White' adversaries. Even before the Red Army was officially formed, the so-called Red Guards, paramilitary volunteer formations consisting primarily of factory workers, soldiers and sailors, challenged the state's monopoly on legitimate violence in the waning days of the Romanov Empire before being reorganised into the Red Army in 1918.[35] The Red Guards – soon to be copied by Finnish, Estonian, Ukrainian, Hungarian and Austrian revolutionaries – stood symptomatically for a new type of ideologically motivated violent actor. What we witness in this period, first in Russia and then throughout Europe, is the emergence of new political personnel – revolutionary and counter-revolutionary in both a social and a political or national sense – which tried to implement ideas that were not in themselves new, but which now became the object of prolonged armed conflict. From 1917 to 1918, revolutionary politics were no longer dominated by the lawyers, intellectuals and trade-union officials of the pre-1914 era. Instead, power, and

34 Frank Golczewski (ed.), *Geschichte der Ukraine* (Göttingen: Vandenhoeck & Ruprecht, 1993), p. 206.

35 Rex Wade, *Red Guards and Workers' Militias in the Russian Revolution* (Palo Alto, CA: Stanford University Press, 1984).

more especially the levers of violent action, had passed to new figures, who depended on their radicalism of both rhetoric and action for their authority.[36]

On the extreme right, too, the immediate post-war years witnessed the emergence of a new political culture of the armed group, not only in Russia, but largely inspired by its example. Yet their political aims were often more vaguely defined than those of their communist counterparts which – at least in theory – strove for the realisation of the proletarian utopia set out in the writings of Marx and Lenin. The Russian 'White' forces, by contrast, were less bound by theory and anything but united in their goals – a fact that contributed to their ultimate defeat. The major leaders of the Whites – Admiral Aleksandr Kolchak in the East, General Anton Denikin in the North Caucasus and the Don region, General Piotr Wrangel in the Crimea – never formed a coherent movement under unified military command. In Siberia and Southern Russia, self-styled 'Atamans' like Grigory Semenov or Roman von Ungern-Sternberg also acted independently. Although sanctioned by the Whites, their 'Whiteness' came from the fact that they were fiercely anti-Bolshevik or 'anti-Red', a colour that now covered a broad spectrum of loosely allied enemies of class revolution.[37]

In Ukraine in particular, the civil war between Whites and Reds gained further complexity through the involvement of further violent actors as the growing chaos and lawlessness in the countryside led to the emergence of a large peasant self-defence movement. The movement assumed the historical name of the Cossacks whose state had disappeared in Ukraine by the early nineteenth century, but who lived on in popular memory as symbols of past prosperity and freedom. They were soon joined by other stakeholders such as Nestor Makhno, a peasant anarchist, who concentrated his 40,000-strong Black Army in the Southern Steppe. Yet whatever the colour of the flag under which the overwhelmingly illiterate peasant warriors were fighting – red, white, green or black – ideology seemed to have mattered less than survival under dangerous and bewildering conditions in which the ruling political regimes changed several times per year.[38]

36 Martin Conway and Robert Gerwarth, 'Revolution and counterrevolution', in Donald Bloxham and Robert Gerwarth, *Political Violence in Twentieth-Century Europe* (Cambridge and New York: Cambridge University Press, 2011).

37 Katzer, *Weisse Bewegung*.

38 Serhy Yekelchyk, 'Bands of nation-builders? Insurgency and ideology in the Ukranian Civil War", in Gerwarth and Horne, *War in Peace*. For a survey of peasant insurgencies in Ukraine during 1918–20, see Andrea Graziosi, *The Great Soviet Peasant War: Bolsheviks and Peasants, 1917–1933* (Cambridge, MA: Harvard Ukrainian Research Institute, 1996), pp. 11–37.

The Bolshevik Revolution and the subsequent civil war across the former imperial Russian territories quickly interacted with revolutionary and counter-revolutionary movements further afield, either as a beacon of hope for those longing for violent socio-economic and political change or as the nightmarish vision of a rise of the uneducated masses.

One of the most extreme cases was Finland, a country which (with no more than 1,500 volunteers fighting on the Russian or German side between 1914 and 1918) had been a non-combatant in the Great War. Despite the lack of 'brutalisation' through war, Finland experienced one of the bloodiest civil wars of the entire period: over 36,000 people – 1 per cent of the overall population – died within the six months of the civil war in 1918, making it one of the deadliest civil wars in twentieth-century history.[39] For a long time, historians saw the Finnish case merely as an extension of the Russian civil war, yet here (as elsewhere), the threat of a Bolshevik takeover was more imagined than real. The often alleged 'Russian involvement' in the Finnish civil war was actually quite marginal, with no more than 5 to 10 per cent of those fighting against General Carl Mannerheims' White Army being Russian volunteers. And even if Bolshevik-inspired Red Guards had carried out the coup d'état in Helsinki in January 1918 and thereby triggered the civil war, it was the more moderate Finnish Social Democrats that almost immediately assumed control of the revolutionary movement which was ultimately suppressed with the extreme violence typical of civil wars fought between members of the same local communities.[40]

The case that (at least initially) seemed to follow the Russian model most closely was that of the short-lived Hungarian Soviet Republic (March to August 1919) under Béla Kun, which copied the Russian Red Guards in an attempt to safeguard the gains of the revolution before being overthrown by a joint Romanian-Czechoslovak military intervention and replaced by Miklos Horthy's counter-revolutionary regime, a regime that used extreme violence to avenge the crimes of the so-called 'Red Terror'.[41]

39 Pertti Haapala and Marko Tikka, 'Revolution, civil war and terror in Finland in 1918', in Gerwarth and Horne, *War in Peace*, pp. 71–83.

40 On the Finnish civil war in English: Anthony Upton, *The Finnish Revolution, 1917–18* (Minneapolis, MN: University of Minnesota Press, 1980); Risto Alapuro, *State and Revolution in Finland* (Berkeley, CA: University of California Press, 1988); Tuomas Hoppu and Pertti Haapala (eds.), *Tampere 1918: A Town in the Civil War* (Tampere, Finland: Tampere Museums, 2010); Jason Lavery, 'Finland 1917–19: three conflicts, one country', *Scandinavian Review*, 94:3 (2006), pp. 1–6; Evan Mawdsley, *The Russian Civil War* (London: Birlin, 2000), pp. 27–9.

41 On Hungary, see the innovative new works by Bela Bodo, 'The White Terror in Hungary, 1919–1921: the social worlds of paramilitary groups', *Austrian History Yearbook*, 42 (2011),

Even in those countries where the likelihood of a Bolshevik takeover was marginal – as in Germany or Austria – the successful consolidation of power by a determined revolutionary minority of Russian Bolsheviks quickly injected a powerful new energy into politics and triggered the emergence of determined counter-revolutionary forces, for whom the violent repression of revolution, and more especially of revolutionaries, constituted their overriding goal. Not dissimilar to the situation in the late eighteenth century when Europe's horrified ruling elites feared a Jacobin 'apocalyptic' war, many Europeans after 1917 suspected that Bolshevism would spread to 'infect' the rest of the old world, prompting violent mobilisation and action against the perceived menace. What was characteristic of that menace everywhere in Europe was the seemingly faceless nature of that threat to the established order: from anonymous crowds that assaulted bourgeois notions of property to female snipers and Jewish-Bolshevik world conspiracies.[42] Such abstract fears were fuelled by news about Bolshevik atrocities, many of them real, others exaggerated, which spread quickly in Western Europe. In July 1918, the worst fears of Bolshevik brutality and lawlessness seemed to be confirmed when the German ambassador to Moscow, Count Mirbach, was murdered inside the Embassy. Soon after, news broke that the ex-Tsar and his family had been executed. Fear of 'Russian conditions' resulted in authoritarian measures, from strengthened policing to laws of exception, but also in a right-wing counter-mobilisation that bred charismatic leaders and apocalyptic visions of its own.[43]

In these armed subcultures, ex-officers brutalised by the war joined forces with members of a younger generation, who compensated for their lack of combat experience by often surpassing the war veterans in terms of radicalism, activism and brutality. For many of these young officer cadets and nationalist students, who had come of age in a bellicose atmosphere saturated with tales of heroic bloodshed but had missed out on their first-hand experience of the 'storms of steel', the militias appear to have offered a welcome opportunity to live a romanticised warrior existence. Together, they formed

pp. 133–63. See, too: Robert Gerwarth, 'The Central European counter-revolution: paramilitary violence in Germany, Austria and Hungary after the Great War', *Past & Present*, 200 (2008), pp. 175–209.

42 Robert Gerwarth and John Horne, 'Bolshevism as fantasy: fear of revolution and counter-revolutionary violence, 1917–1923', in Gerwarth and Horne, *War in Peace*. On the Flintenweiber in the German and Baltic context, see Klaus Theweleit, *Male Fantasies*, trans. Stephan Conaway, 2 vols. (Minneapolis, MN: University of Minnesota Press, 1987).

43 Jones, 'How the war came home'.

explosive subcultures of ultra-militant masculinity in which brutal violence was an acceptable, if not desirable, form of political expression. In addition, large numbers of unemployed ex-soldiers and landless labourers were attracted by the prospect of theft, plunder, rape, extortion or simply by the opportunity to settle scores with neighbours of different ethnicity without fear of state reprisals. Action, not ideas, was the defining characteristic of these groups. They were driven forward not by a revolutionary vision of a new politics, but by a common rhetoric of the creation of 'new orders' and an interlocking series of social antipathies.

The mobilising power of defeat

On 31 October 1918, the commander of the Adriatic-based Habsburg fleet, Miklos Horthy, sent a final telegram to his Emperor, Charles I, assuring him of his 'unshakable loyalty'. Minutes later, he surrendered the flagship of his fleet, the SMS *Viribus Unitis*, to the new South Slav state (the future Yugoslavia) releasing the Czech, Croatian, Polish and German-Austrian sailors and officers around him into an uncertain future as post-imperial subjects. For Horthy himself, however, the war was by no means over. Once fighting between the major combatants of the Great War had ended, he soon found another project: the cleansing of his native Hungary from those forces which had allegedly caused the Habsburgs' defeat and the break-up of their Empire.[44]

In this respect, Horthy's reaction to the situation of late 1918 was not fundamentally different from that of 37-year-old Brigadier Mustafa Kemal, who – roughly at the same time – returned from the lost Palestinian front to Istanbul. In 1926, when he was already known as Atatürk and President of the Turkish Republic, he recalled his arrival in the defeated Ottoman Empire's capital as the beginning of his 'mission' to transform the 'Turkic core' of the Empire into a Turkish nation-state. He would achieve this 'mission' through a series of violent conflicts and, after halting a Greek advance into Anatolia, the largest expulsion of civilians before the Second World War.[45]

Both examples highlight a second factor that helps to explain the uneven geography of post-war violence in Europe: the mobilising power of defeat. Defeat should be seen not just in terms of the balance of power, but also as

44 Thomas Sakmyster, *Hungary's Admiral on Horseback: Miklos Horthy, 1918–1944* (New York: Columbia University Press, 1994).

45 Gingeras, *Sorrowful Shores*.

a state of mind (including the refusal to acknowledge the reversal) which Wolfgang Schivelbusch has termed a 'culture of defeat'.[46] The state had played a central role during the Great War in organising and endorsing the mass deployment of violence by millions of European men and it was also the state (in close cooperation with the military leadership) that was in charge of demobilisation, both militarily and culturally (by legitimising, reabsorbing or neutralising the violence of war once the conflict was over). Where the state had been defeated, however, either in reality or in perception (as with nationalist circles in Italy), it was more difficult for the state to play this role; indeed, it may have done precisely the opposite, exacerbating violence and generalising it to a host of groups and individuals who chose to take it on themselves to redress defeat and national humiliation.

The nature of the homecoming in a context of victory or defeat was thus an important variable as individual testimonies from November 1918 confirm. In explaining their refusal to demobilise (or desire to remobilise) and their determination to continue their soldierly existence after November 1918, paramilitary activists across Central Europe frequently invoked the horrors of returning from the front in 1918 to an entirely hostile world of upheaval, a perception triggered by both the temporary collapse of military hierarchies and public order.[47]

The prominent Carinthian *Heimwehr* activist, Hanns Albin Rauter, who returned to Graz at the end of the war, for example, emphasised his first contact with the homefront as an eye-opener: 'When I finally arrived in Graz, I found that the Communists had taken the streets.' Confronted by a group of communist soldiers, 'I pulled my gun and I was arrested. This was how the *Heimat* welcomed me.' Being arrested by soldiers of lower rank reinforced Rauter's perception of having returned to a 'world turned upside down', a

46 Wolfgang Schivelbusch, *The Culture of Defeat: On National Trauma, Mourning, and Recovery* (New York: Metropolitan Books, 2003).

47 On the deterioration of the relationship between home front and war front in the later stages of the war, see: Richard G. Plaschka *et. al.* (eds.), *Innere Front: Militärassistenz, Widerstand und Umsturz in der Donaumonarchie 1918*, 2 vols. (Munich: R. Oldenbourg Verlag, 1974); Mark Cornwall, *The Undermining of Austria-Hungary: The Battle for Hearts and Minds* (New York: Macmillan, 2000); Manfred Rauchensteiner, *Der Tod des Doppeladlers: Österreich-Ungarn und der Erste Weltkrieg* (Graz: Verlag Styria, 1993). That the revolution was brought about by men who had not served at the front was a common accusation made by right-wing veterans. See, e.g.: private papers of Ernst Rüdiger Starhemberg, 'Aufzeichnungen' (Oberösterreichisches Landesarchiv, Linz), p. 21. On Germany: Richard Bessel, *Germany after the First World War* (Oxford and New York: Oxford University Press, 1993).

world in which hitherto unquestionable norms and values, social hierarchies, institutions and authorities had suddenly become obsolete.[48]

Experiences in Budapest and Munich were not dissimilar. Upon arrival in Hungary from the front in the late autumn of 1918, the Hussar officer Miklós Kozma was one of many war veterans 'welcomed' by disorderly crowds shouting abuse at the returning troops as well as by ordinary soldiers physically attacking their officers. In Kozma's account, revolutionary activists always appeared as an effeminate 'dirty crowd', a crowd 'that has not washed in weeks and has not changed their clothes in months; the smell of clothes and shoes rotting on their bodies is unbearable.'[49] Ex-officers in neighbouring Bavaria echoed such impressions. The future Austrian Vice-Chancellor and *Heimwehr* activist, Eduard Baar von Baarenfels, for example, reported back to Austria from revolutionary Munich how he had witnessed jewellery shops being plundered, and officers being disarmed and insulted. The revolution, Baarenfels insisted, had 'washed up the worst scum from the deepest depths of hell' – people who were now freely roaming the streets of Central European capital cities.[50]

What Baarenfels, Kozma and many others described was a nightmare that had haunted Europe's conservative establishment since the French Revolution, a nightmare that – ever since the Bolshevik takeover in Russia in 1917 and the Central Powers' defeat in the autumn of 1918 – appeared to have become a reality. They refused to accept that military defeat had caused the collapse of the Central European empires, creating national variants of the 'stab-in-the-back' legend,[51] and regarded the Armistice as an intolerable insult to their honour as 'militarily undefeated' officers. As the war veteran and infamous *Freikorps* leader, Manfred von Killinger, expressed in a letter to his family: 'I have made a promise to myself, Father. Without armed struggle, I have handed over my torpedo boat to the enemies and watched my flag

48 Rauter Papers, NIOD (Amsterdam), Doc. I 1380, H, 2. On the 'world turned upside down', see: Martin H. Geyer, *Verkehrte Welt: Revolution, Inflation und Moderne. München, 1914–1924* (Göttingen: Vandenhoeck & Ruprecht, 1998).

49 Miklós Kozma, *Makensens Ungarische Husaren: Tagebuch eines Frontoffiziers, 1914–1918* (Berlin and Vienna: Verlag für Kulturpolitik, 1933), p. 459.

50 Eduard Baar von Baarenfels, 'Erinnerungen (1947)', Österreichisches Staatsarchiv, MS B/120:1, here pp. 10–13. See, too: Anita Korp, 'Der Aufstieg vom Soldaten zum Vizekanzler im Dienste der Heimwehr: Eduard Baar von Baarenfels' (MA thesis, University of Vienna, 1998).

51 For Austria, see: Oswald Überegger, *Erinnerungskriege. Der Erste Weltkrieg, Österreich und die Tiroler Kriegserinnerung in der Zwischenkriegszeit* (Innsbruck: Universitätsverlag Wagner, 2011); on Germany, see: Boris Barth, *Dolchstoßlegenden und politische Desintegration. Das Trauma der deutschen Niederlage im Ersten Weltkrieg 1914–1933* (Düsseldorf: Droste Verlag, 2003).

go down. I have sworn to take revenge against those who are responsible for this.'[52] Confronted with public unrest and personal insults, the future *Heimwehr* leader, Ernst Rüdiger von Starhemberg, came to a similar conclusion when he expressed his 'burning desire to return to my soldier's existence as soon as possible, to stand up for the humiliated Fatherland'. Only then, 'the shame of a gloomy present' could be forgotten.[53]

As a consequence of such common perceptions, paramilitary subcultures of the right shared important characteristics, at least in Central Europe. In Germany, Austria and Hungary, the leading figures involved in setting up and running paramilitary organisations of the right were junior ex-officers (mostly lieutenants and captains, occasionally colonels) from middle- or upper-class backgrounds, such as Hanns Albin Rauter, Ernst-Rüdiger Starhemberg, Eduard Baar von Baarenfels, Beppo Römer, Gerhard Roßbach, Franz von Epp, István Hejjas, Pál Prónay and Gyula Osztenburg, who had been educated and trained in the military academies of the late Habsburg and Hohenzollern empires.[54] In Hungary, it was not only Gyula Gömbös's powerful veterans' organisation MOVE (Hungarian National Defence Union) or the Union of Awakening Hungarians, but also the much more sizeable Hungarian National Army that was dominated by former combat officers. Of the 6,568 volunteers who followed Horthy's initial recruitment call of 5 June 1919 for the formation of the counter-revolutionary National Army, almost 3,000 were former army and cavalry officers and an additional 800 men were officers from the semi-military border guards, the *Gendarmerie*. Many of the activists in all three countries came from rural backgrounds and notably from the border regions where notions of embattled ethnicity were much more real than they were in larger cities such as Budapest, Vienna or Berlin. In the case of Hungary, the large influx of refugees from Transylvania further contributed to the radicalisation of the atmosphere in Budapest, a capital city already militarised by the experiences of revolution and temporary occupation by Romanian forces.[55]

52 Manfred von Killinger, *Der Klabautermann. Eine Lebensgeschichte*, 3rd edn (Munich: Eher, 1936), p. 263.

53 Starhemberg, 'Aufzeichnungen', pp. 20–2.

54 See, too, the very detailed autobiographical account of this education in: Ernst Heydendorff, 'Kriegsschule 1912–1914', in Heydendorff papers, Österreichisches Staatsarchiv, Vienna, B 844/74.

55 Béla Kelemen, *Adatok a szegedi ellenforradalom és a szegedi kormány történetéhez* (Szeged: Szerzö Kiadása, 1923), pp. 495–6. For Austria: Walter Wiltschegg, *Die Heimwehr: Eine unwiderstehliche Volksbewegung?* (Munich: R. Oldenbourg Verlag, 1985), pp. 274–80. For Germany, see: Gerwarth, 'Central European Counter-revolution'.

Figure 24.1 French cameraman surrounded by Chinese workers.
Chinese labor corps workers gathering around a French cameramen near Oudezeele, Nord–Pas-de-Calais, France, June 1918.

Figure 24.2 Frank Hurley, *The raid*.
This image is also titled *Going over the Top* and *An Episode after the Battle of Zonnebeke*. It is a composite photograph of twelve negatives taken during training sessions of Australian troops in autumn 1917 and presented to the public at a very successful exhibition at Grafton Galleries, London, in May 1918. Like other photographers of the time, Hurley, whose pictures helped build the Anzac legend, was convinced that his composites were the only possible means to represent adequately the complex and multidimensional battlefield action of modern war, and thereby to pay tribute to the

Figure 24.3 Ivor Castle, *The Battle of Vimy Ridge*.
Composite photograph showing the successful Canadian attack on Vimy Ridge on 9 April 1917, at an exhibition of the Canadian War Records Section at Grafton Galleries, London, July 1917. The picture, measuring 6.10 m × 3.35 m, was probably the biggest war photograph of the time.

Figure 24.4 José Simont, *La charge mécanique*.
This image, published in *L'illustration* on 18 May 1918, shows British tanks dispersing elements of a German infantry division at Cachy, Somme, France. The tank, in this drawing the British Mark A Whippet, became an important visual trademark of modern war and an important propaganda motif highlighting the growing material and technological superiority of the Allies, thereby reassuring soldiers and civilians alike.

Figure 24.5 Crowds cheering Allied generals.
This image shows Marshal Joffre leaving the Hôtel Crillon after having met General Pershing in Paris in June 1917. Masses of people pressing in and eagerly trying to get a glimpse of military leaders, the stars of another age, were a common propaganda theme that aimed to highlight the 'unwavering' popular support of the war.

Figure 24.6 Narrow-gauge train transporting shells during the Battle of the Somme.
This image shows 220 mm shells en route to the front near Le Quesnel on the Somme on 10 July 1916. Photos like this one showed off Allied industrial and logistical capabilities and made the point that the Allies were well able to effectively organise the war effort.

Figure 24.7 Indian troops on double-decker buses.

This image taken in Northern France was published in *L'Illustration* on 6 February 1915. The imagery of industrial war, symbolised by the unendings column of motor cars in this picture is complemented here by the comforting message the presence of Allied combatants from all over the world sent to the peoples of the Entente: the whole world was siding with them in the fight against Germany.

Figure 24.8 Landing of Russian troops in Marseille.
This photo shows Russian infantrymen from the First Brigade disembarking at Marseille in April 1916. The arrival of Russian soldiers who had travelled around the globe from Moscow via Asia, the Pacific Ocean, the Suez Canal and the Mediterranean, and who paraded through Saigon, Singapore and Colombo (Sri Lanka) on the way, was a major propaganda event. It underlined the close ties between the Allies and the efficiency of their global cooperation, unmatched and undisrupted by the Central Powers.

Figure 24.9 Wreck of German Zeppelin exhibited in Salonica.
This photo showed the wreck of German zeppelin LZ 85 shot down on 5 May 1915 during a raid on Salonica, reconstructed and exhibited near the White Tower in that city. Booty and destroyed enemy weaponry were on display in every major city, and in particular in every capital city, in all belligerent countries.

Figure 24.10 Execution of Jules Brillant of the French 362nd Infantry Regiment.
This soldier was shot for dereliction of duty at Conchy-les-Pots, on 26 August 1916. This snapshot was taken covertly by a French soldier, a serious offence against military law that would not have been possible without the complicity of at least some of his comrades. It shows troops marching by the dead body, which was an integral part of the execution 'ceremony'. After the war, these men 'shot at dawn' became a powerful symbol of the arbitrary and unlimited power of the High Command during the war.

LE MIROIR 5

SUR LES LIGNES DE VAUQUOIS : L'ÉPOUVANTAIL

(Droits réservés.)

Les Allemands n'ont jamais pu reprendre le corps de cet officier observateur

Aux approches du petit village, riant naguère, seuls quelques arbres dressent des bras de catastrophe sur la campagne désolée. L'un d'eux, dans ses branches déchiquetées par les balles et les éclats d'obus, tend vers le ciel un épouvantail sinistre : c'est le cadavre d'un officier observateur allemand qui fut tué là, à son poste. Pendant trois semaines, les soldats ennemis, en dépit d'efforts répétés, et qui leur valurent des pertes sérieuses, ne purent jamais reprendre le corps de leur chef.

Figure 24.11 The body of a German officer in a tree.
This man's body, hanging in a tree near Vauquois in the Meuse, was published in *Le Miroir* on 9 May 1915. This photograph was entitled 'The Scarecrow'. Its publication shows that not all pictures of war circulating in the press were sanitised. On the contrary, there were some disturbingly grotesque representations of violence. A photograph of a dead French soldier in an analogous position would probably not have appeared, in part because of self-censorship among photographers.

Sixième année. — N° 150. Le Numéro : 25 centimes. DIMANCHE 8 Octobre 1916.

LE MIROIR

PUBLICATION HEBDOMADAIRE, 18, Rue d'Enghien, PARIS

LE MIROIR paie n'importe quel prix les documents photographiques relatifs à la guerre, présentant un intérêt particulier.

APRÈS UN DUEL A MORT ENTRE UN FRANÇAIS ET UN ALLEMAND DEVANT COMBLES

L'offensive qui devait nous donner Combles les a mis face à face dans une tranchée bouleversée. Comme les guerriers de jadis, ils ont lutté corps à corps de toute leur vigueur, de toute leur haine, jusqu'à la mort.

Figure 24.12 Bodies of French and German soldiers in a trench.
This scene, near Combles on the Somme, appeared in *Le Miroir* on 8 October 1916. Photographs like this one were not distributed through official sources. There is an ambiguity in the image. On the one hand, it seems to support the notion of fighting to the death, and killing the hated invader. On the other hand, the image has a certain peaceful air, as if the two men were sleeping close to each other. This appeared on the cover page of *Le Miroir*, which (as the caption above the picture states) was prepared 'to pay any price for war pictures of particular value'. This enabled it to publish visual representations of modern warfare that were at odds with official propaganda.

Figure 24.13 Russian soldiers fleeing in disarray.
Appearing in *L'Illustration*, on 8 September 1917, this picture, like the next one (Figure 24.14) is part of a series of eight photographs taken by G. H. Mewes, correspondent of the *Daily Mirror*. It is one of the very few pictures of panicking soldiers during the war.

Figure 24.14 Allied officer attempting to restore order in Russia.
From *L'Illustration*, 8 September 1917. The officer on the right appears to be a member of a group of several British officers the photographer, G. H. Mewes, was accompanying on their mission.

Figure 24.15 Poster addressing Canadian Jews to aid the war effort.
The message in this Canadian post is this: 'The Jews the world over love liberty, have fought for it and will fight for it. Britain expects every son of Israel to do his duty. Enlist with the infantry reinforcements for overseas.' The man whose bonds are about to be cut by a British soldier says: 'You have cut my bonds and set me free – now let me help you set others free!' The three men above this scene are Jewish Members of Parliament in London. Before 1917, hatred of the Tsarist oppression of Jews had to be reduced in order to persuade Jews in Canada to join up.

Figure 24.16 Mobilising the French colonies: subscription to war bonds.
This image of a scene in Bondoukou, Ivory Coast, was published in *L'Illustration* on 3 June 1916. Note the charcoal drawing of Abel Faivre's famous poster 'Pour la France – versez votre or!' ('For France – hand over your cash') on the left. This was one of the iconic war bond images of the conflict, and reached French Africa too.

Figure 24.17 Hungarian war loan poster.
This design by Mihály Bíró accompanied this message: 'We defend our homeland with arms and money. Subscribe to the war loan', 1917. Already before the war Bíró was known for his social protest posters. After the defeat of the Central Powers, he became a leading propaganda artist for the short-lived Hungarian Soviet Republic.

Figure 24.18 Dutch postcard on mobilisation.
This shows a Dutch soldier willing to do his duty in order to defend his country. At the outbreak of the war, European neutrals like Switzerland and the Netherlands mobilized in order to prevent any encroachment on their territory. As they never fully demobilised during the war, these neutral states remained on a war footing.

Figure 24.19 Women's Batallion of Death.
This image shows women in uniform from Petrograd relaxing, drinking tea and eating, in front of their tents. The presence of a cameraman in the photograph shows the media value of the formation in revolutionary Russia of women's units in June 1917. The hope was that such images would have a positive psychological impact on men's morale. Only one such women's formation, the First Women's Battalion of Death, saw combat against the Central Powers.

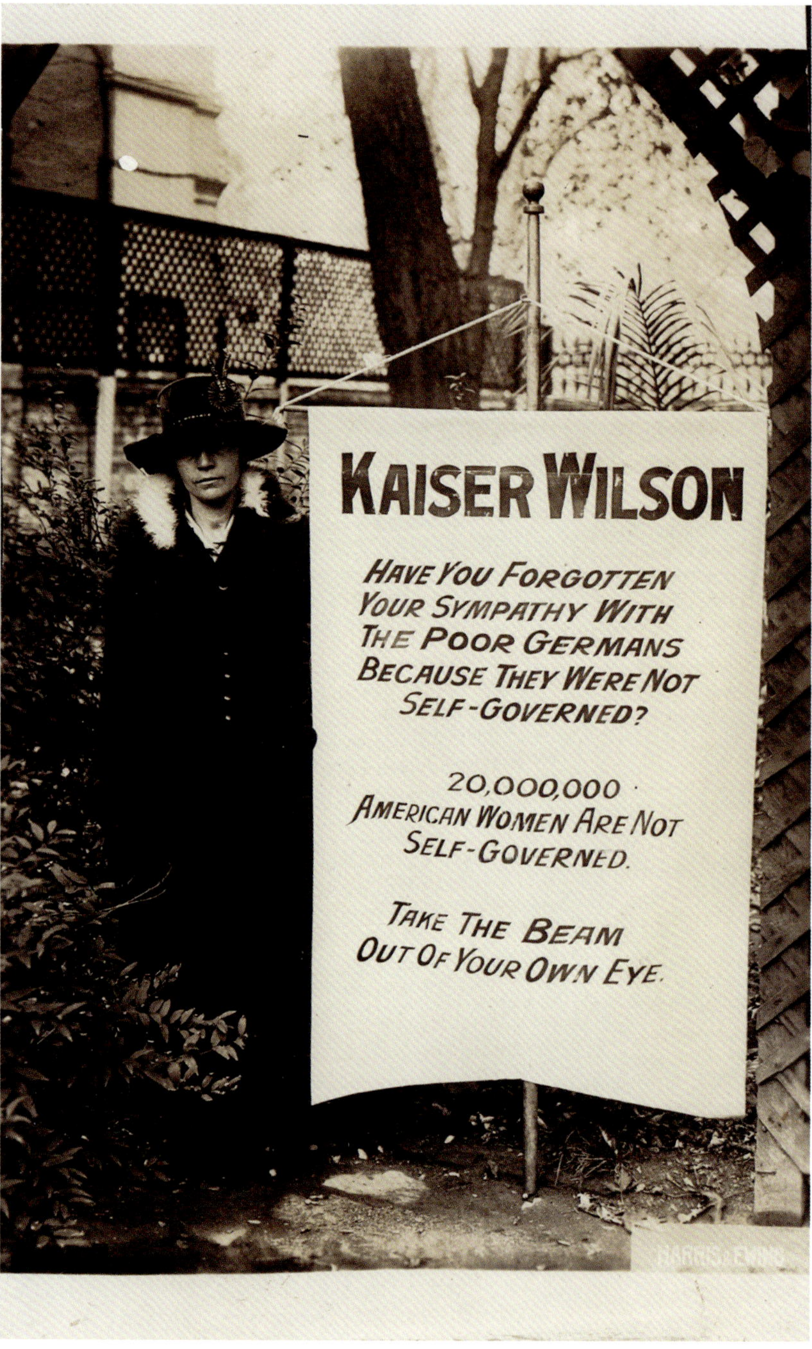

Figure 24.20 Suffragette picketing in front of the White House, 1917.
During the war years, suffragettes picketed in front of the White House with posters like this one, comparing President Wilson to Kaiser Wilhelm II. American women got the vote in 1918.

Figure 24.21 Rice riots in Japan, 1918.
This image shows Suzuki Shoten burned down during the rice riots in Japan, 11 August 1918. Suzuki Shoten was a Kobe-based trading company that had expanded considerably during the war years, and whose main office was ransacked in a wave of unrest that erupted in Japan from July to September 1918. The rice riots were triggered by massive increases in rice prices that were part of a war-related inflationary spiral the state failed to control.

Figure 24.22 Poster with Swiss ration cards during the First World War.
The belligerent states were not alone in suffering from hardship and shortages of all kinds during the war. Neutral states like the Netherlands, Switzerland and Sweden were also challenged by the necessity to fix the prices of certain commodities and by the rationing of foodstuffs in order to provide for their people. In Switzerland, this meant rationing bread and flour in October 1917, butter in March 1918, and cheese and milk in June and July 1918, respectively.

Figure 24.23 German currency: a bill for one billion Marks.
This thousand Reichsmark banknote dating from December 1922 was converted into a one billion Reichsmark banknote during the period of hyperinflation. Whereas at the beginning of the war one American dollar was worth 4.2 Reichsmarks, the value of the mark dropped during the war years to half its pre-war value. However, worse was yet to come. Just before the currency reform of November 1923, one dollar was worth an incredible 4.2 trillion Reichsmarks.

Figure 24.24 Antiseptic creams to prevent the spread of venereal diseases among German soldiers.
This wooden box contained antiseptic creams whose purpose was to prevent the spread of venereal disease among German soldiers. All armies developed a pragmatic approach to this problem. Prostitutes were told exactly what they needed to avoid infection, where they could get it, and what would happen if they failed to use the prophylactic kits sold to them at cost price. They would be severely punished. The prostitute was held responsible for both her hygiene and that of her client.

Figure 24.25 Parisian women reading the decree on the introduction of Daylight Saving, June 1916.
Germany and its allies were the first to introduce summertime on 30 April/1 May 1916. France and Britain followed suit six weeks later, on 14/15 June, while Russia and the US waited until 1917 and 1918, respectively.

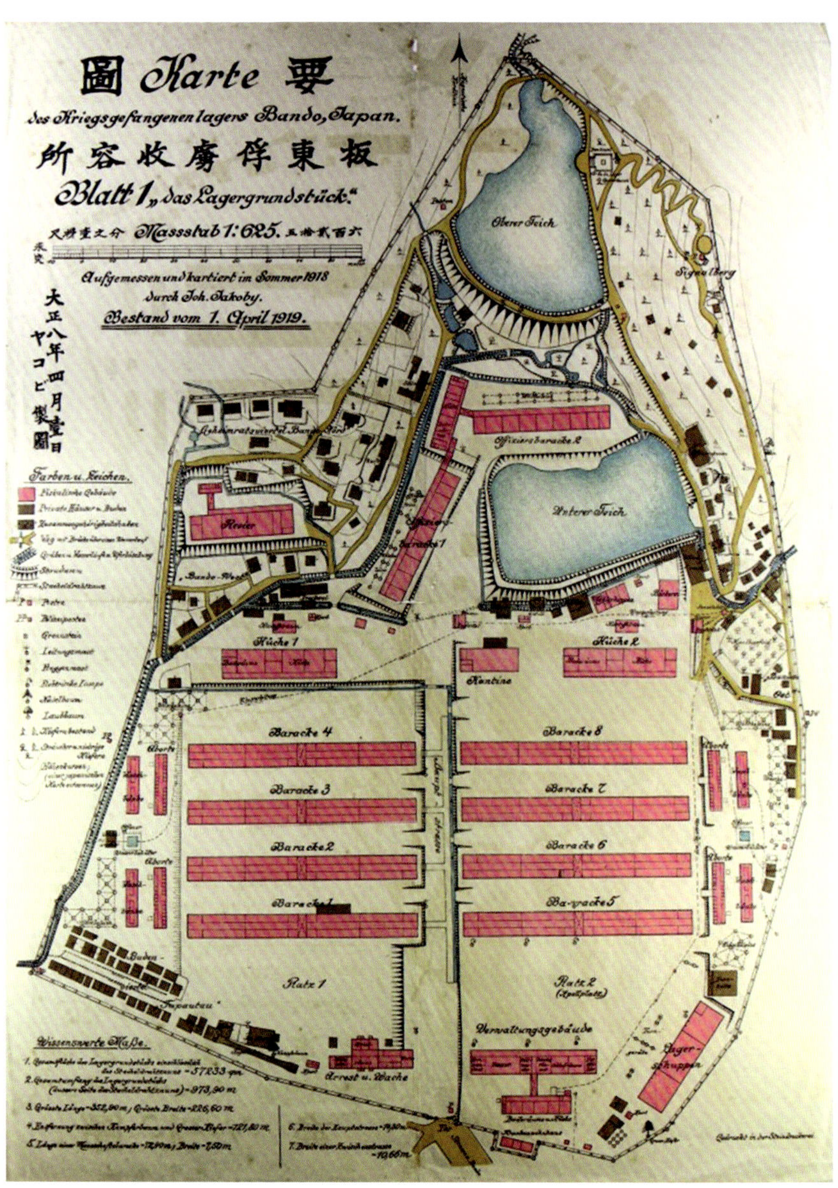

Figure 24.26 Hand-drawn map of German POW camp, Japan.
This map shows the camp near Bandō on 1 April 1919. It was drawn by POW Johannes Jakoby.

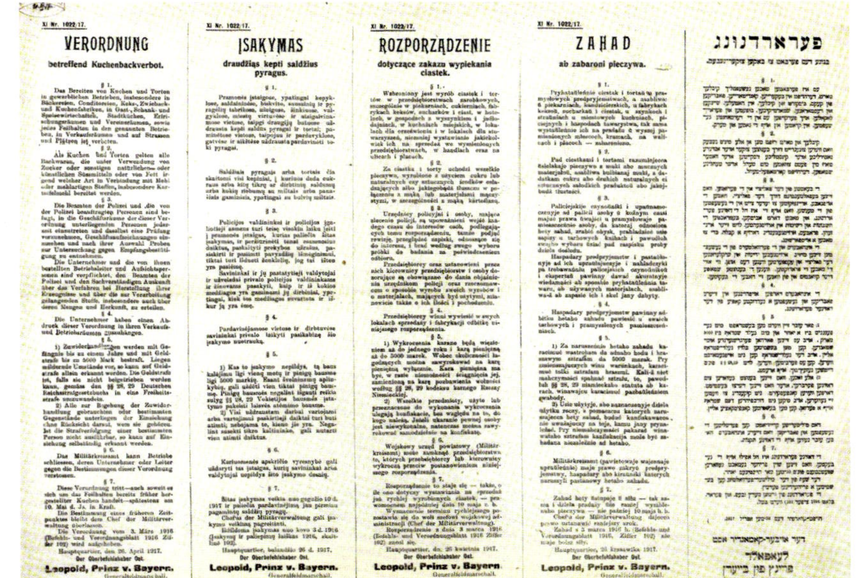

XI Nr. 1022/17.

VERORDNUNG

betreffend Kuchenbackverbot.

Leopold, Prinz v. Bayern.

XI Nr. 1022/17.

ĮSAKYMAS

draudžiąs kepti saldžius pyragus.

Leopold, Prinz v. Bayern.

XI Nr. 1022/17.

ROZPORZĄDZENIE

dotyczące zakazu wypiekania ciastek.

Leopold, Prinz v. Bayern.

XI Nr. 1022/17.

ZAHAD

ab zabaroni pieczywa.

Leopold, Prinz v. Bayern.

פעראָרדנונג

Figure 24.27 Multi-lingual ban on making and selling all baked goods on the Eastern Front.
This poster, dated 26 April 1917, is in German, Polish, Lithuanian, Belorussian, and Yiddish. Here was the bureaucratic logic of occupation, informing the administration of the 'military state' of Ober Ost, the German eastern command, in large parts of what are today the Baltic States, Poland, and Belorussia.

Figure 24.28 Photographic data on the occupied population collected by German troops, Russian Poland, 1915.
The collection of anthropometric and photographic data facilitated the creation of various types of identity cards or permits which allowed people under occupation to circulate. Everywhere this logic gained ground. France, for instance, introduced an obligatory ID for foreigners living within its borders in April 1917. This was the end of the pre-1914 world of travel without passports.

Figure 24.29 Hanging of civilians.
Bulgarian troops executed these people near Niš, in south-eastern Serbia in 1917. Three years earlier, French and Belgian civilians suffered severely from reprisals and other acts of repression, many of which constituted war crimes at the time. On sectors of the Eastern Front, the situation was as bad or worse. The number of civilians executed by the Austro-Hungarian army in Galicia and Serbia alone is estimated to be 60,000.

Figure 24.30 Caricature of Clemenceau as 'the soldier on the home front'.
This cartoon appeared in *Le rire rouge* on 16 February 1918. Georges Clemenceau, French Prime Minister since November 1917, embodied a policy of unconditional warfare that earned him the title of 'father of victory'. The caricature refers to his crackdown on what he saw as pacifist or 'defeatist' tendencies of all kinds. Trials of political opponents such as former Prime Minister Joseph Caillaux or former Minister of the Interior Louis Malvy on charges of high treason bore witness to Clemenceau's resolution to destroy any and all opposition to seeing the war through to the end.

Figure 24.31 Caricature of popular aspirations for democratisation in wartime Germany. This cartoon on the new fashion in beards (for which read constitutional reform) appeared in the satirical review *Kladderadatsch* on 29 July 1917. Barber Michel, a popular figure representing the German national character, says, looking at the Teutonic knight's beard: 'At first, the new moustache-trainer "all equal under the law" might be a little uncomfortable. But they will get used to it.' The caricature refers approvingly to pressures for constitutional reform which emerged in 1917.

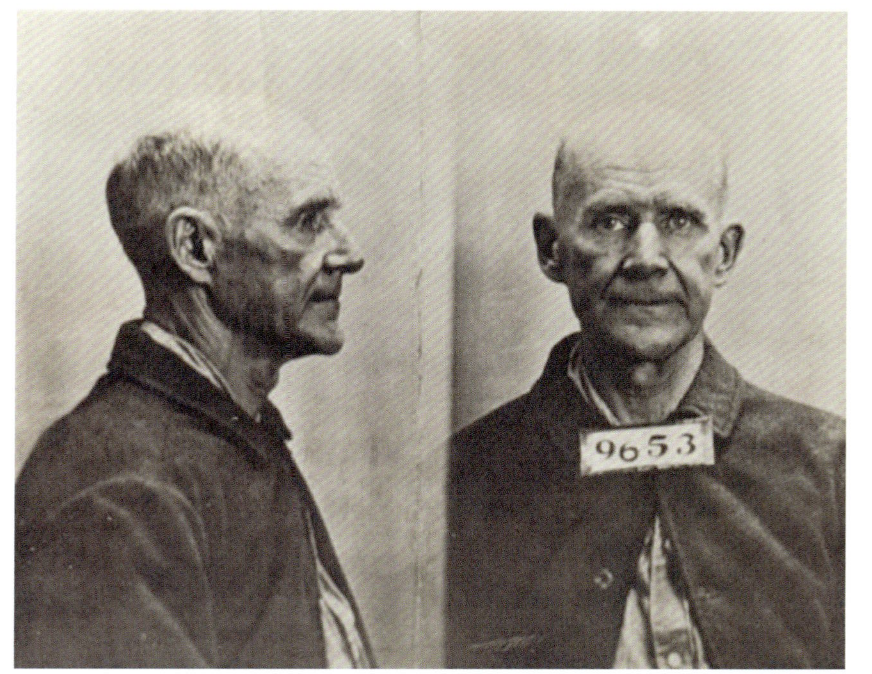

Figure 24.32 Mugshots of Eugene V. Debs.
American socialist leader and anti-war activist, Debs was an outspoken critic of American entry into the war and of the military draft system. He was arrested on 30 June 1918 and tried under the Espionage Act of 1917. He was sentenced to ten years in prison on 18 November 1918: that is, after the end of the war.

Figure 24.33 Car with Russian revolutionaries.
This photograph shows soldiers in Petrograd travelling on the footboard of motor cars with red flags affixed to their bayonets, 1917. Military control of Petrograd was the decisive step in the Bolshevik seizure of power in November 1917.

Figure 24.34 Japanese lithograph on Siberian intervention.

This print glorified the Battle of Ussuri, a victory over Bolshevik forces in Siberia on 24 August 1918. In this battle, Japanese, French, Czechoslovak and White Russian troops defeated Red Army units near Khabarovsk, Russia. The illustration shows the moment when a Japanese hero, Captain Konomi, is killed at close range by enemy troops. Note that the 'Bolsheviks' look like German soldiers of 1914, wearing the 'Pickelhaube' helmet. One interpretation is that Japanese leaders feared that German and Austrian prisoners of war might

The situation in Italy was somewhat different, notably because the country was not defeated in the Great War. Instead it suffered – at least in the eyes of Italian nationalists – a 'mutilated victory'. Such widespread perceptions were largely the result of exaggerated expectations at the war's end. The dissolution of the Austro-Hungarian Empire, the expansion of Italy's borders to the Brenner Pass and Istria and a seat at the victors' table in Paris had been seen as fitting compensation for half a million dead and millions wounded or permanently mutilated, but the post-war rejection of Italy's claim to Dalmatia (and the ongoing quarrel over Fiume) frustrated those with maximalist expectations. Paramilitary groups of the right, such as the *Arditi* or Mussolini's *Fasci di combattimento*, were united in the belief that Italy had been betrayed at the Paris Peace Conference by its own allies, who had refused to grant full recognition of Italy's territorial claims despite the fact that Italy had suffered more casualties in the war than Britain. Such beliefs merged with fears of Bolshevik Revolution, notably after several post-war socialist victories in the local elections of Northern and Central Italy as well as in the Po valley.[56] In an escalating whirlwind of domestic violence, 172 socialists were killed in 1920 alone, as were ten members of the Popular Party, four fascists and fifty-one police officers. During the 1921 general elections, violence increased further: on election day alone (15 May), twenty-eight people died and 104 were injured.[57]

Defeat (or the perception of a 'mutilated victory') and the fear (or reality) of revolution created the climate for violent clashes between movements of different political creeds, but the geography and intensity levels of violence also depended on a third factor: ethnic conflicts in the shatter zones of Europe's land empires.

Imperial collapse and inter-ethnic violence

If the Bolshevik Revolution and the subsequent civil war had spread fears of a European class war, and the defeat of the Central Powers had undermined the legitimacy and viability of Europe's land empires (and in some cases, that of their successor states), the idea of creating ethnically homogeneous nation-states proved to be yet another important source of post-war violence in much of Europe at the end of the Great War. This was especially the case where claims for national independence were opposed by other ethnic groups.

56 Gentile, 'Paramilitary violence in Italy', p. 89.
57 Gentile, 'Paramilitary violence in Italy', p. 91.

All national movements in the former land empires took inspiration from US President Woodrow Wilson's promise, manifested in the famous 'Fourteen Points' of January 1918, that the allegedly suppressed nations of East-Central Europe should have an opportunity for 'autonomous development'.[58] But while the slogan of 'self-determination' provided a powerful rallying cry for the mobilisation of anti-imperial emotions and personnel, the nascent national movements of Eastern Europe quickly encountered opposition from various camps. In Estonia and Latvia, where national movements seized the opportunity of the Bolshevik coup to declare their independence, the legitimacy of the new national assemblies was swiftly called into question by local Bolsheviks, the Estonian 'Military-Revolutionary Committee' (VRK) and the Latvian 'Executive Committee' who could count on strong leftist support from the workers of Tallinn and Riga, leading to months of terror and counter-terror.[59] The situation became more confusing in the spring, when a German offensive led to the occupation of all of Latvia, Estonia, Belorussia and Ukraine, only to be reversed when the German war effort collapsed in November that year and was followed by a Red Army advance towards Minsk and Vilnius.[60] In Poland, too, the attempt to restore a powerful nation-state in the heart of Europe encountered severe problems: by the spring of 1919, Josef Pilsudki's reorganised Polish armed forces were engaged on four fronts: in Upper Silesia against strong German volunteer forces, in Teschen/Teshyn against the Czechs, in Galicia against Ukrainian forces and against the Soviets threatening to invade from the West.[61]

In the conquered and re-conquered territories, notably in the Baltic region and in Ukraine, a bewildering complexity of violent actors emerged: from 'red', 'white', 'green' and 'black' armies to German *Freikorps* (who were

58 To what extent the late European empires were indeed 'people's prisons' remains a controversial question to this day; recent scholarship has emphasised the Habsburg Empire in particular as an evolving civil society rather than as a decrepit polity doomed to dissolution by the forces of centrifugal nationalism. See Jonathan Kwan, 'Nationalism and all that: reassessing the Habsburg monarchy and its legacies', *European History Quarterly*, 41 (2011), 88–108.

59 Alexander V. Prusin, *The Lands Between: Conflict in the East European Borderlands, 1870–1992* (Oxford University Press, 2010), pp. 74 ff; Aviel Roshwald, *Ethnic Nationalism and the Fall of Empires: Central Europe, Russia and the Middle East, 1914–1923* (London: Routledge, 2001).

60 On the German occupation of 'Ober-Ost', see: Vejas Gabriel Liulevicius, *War Land on the Eastern Front: Culture, National Identity and German Occupation in World War I* (Cambridge University Press, 2000).

61 Julia Eichenberg, 'Soldiers to civilians, civilians to soldiers: Poland and Ireland after the First World War', in Gerwarth and Horne, *War in Peace*; Wróbel, 'Seeds of violence'; Wilson, *Frontiers of Violence*.

particularly active in Latvia in the spring of 1919) and a large variety of anti-Bolshevik 'homeguards' such as the Lithuanian Riflemen Union, the Latvian Aizsargi or the Estonian Kaitseliit (with over 100,000 members in 1919).[62] It was not until 1920 that a degree of stability returned to the region. Following successful counter-attacks against the Red Army in Latvia and Poland – commemorated in Latvian and Polish nationalist folklore as the 'miracles' of the Daugava and Vistula rivers – Lenin's dream of recapturing the former tsarist Empire under the red flag temporarily faltered. In February, July and August 1920, the Soviet Government signed peace treaties with Estonia, Lithuania and Latvia renouncing territorial claims in the Baltic region while the last German *Freikorps* fighters left Latvia and Estonia in October after a crushing defeat at the gates of Riga.[63] A few months later, in 1921, the Soviet-Polish Treaty of Riga confirmed Poland as one of the winners of the post-war conflicts, assigning western Belorussia, East Galicia and Volhynia to Warsaw's direct control.[64] Only Romania, which had entered the war late on the Entente's side, managed to secure similarly sizeable territories (Bessarabia and the Bukovina) after prolonged fighting with the Red Army.[65]

The fates of East and Central European national projects in this period thus differed considerably – from victory and territorial expansion for the 'Little Entente States' (Czechoslovakia, Romania and Yugoslavia) and Poland, to frustrated hopes for Lithuania and Belorussia, to 'national catastrophes' for Bulgaria and Hungary – both of which suffered severe territorial losses in the peace treaties of Trianon and Neuilly. The outcomes of the war and the post-war conflicts set the tone for inter-state relations and also prepared the ground for new waves of violence in the region. In the Balkans, and notably in areas such as Macedonia and Kosovo, Serbian and pro-Yugoslav paramilitary groups, emboldened by victory in the Great War, played an important role as para-state actors, shoring up the territorial gains made during the war and violently suppressing those opposing them. These groups competed with, and were opposed by, revisionist forces such as the Internal Macedonian Revolutionary Organization (IMRO, the largest paramilitary group in the region), the pro-Albanian Kačak movement or the Croatian 'Ustashe' (whose

62 Balkelis, 'Turning citizens into soldiers'.

63 Bernhard Sauer, 'Vom "mythos des ewigen soldatentum": der feldzug deutscher soldaten im Baltikum im jahre 1919', *Zeitschrift fuer Geschichtswissenschaft*, 43 (1993), pp. 869–902.

64 Davies, *White Eagle*.

65 Glenn E. Torrey, *Romania and World War I: A Collection of Studies* (Oxford and Portland: Romanian Studies Centre, 1998).

BULGARIA
Black Sea
Adrianople
(Edirne)
Midia
Bosporus
Constantinople
Rodosto
(Tekirdağ)
Izmit
Kavala
Dedeagatch
Keshan
Sea of Marmara
Salonica
Samothrace
Bandirma
Mudania
Bursa
Biga
Imbros
Chanak
Lemnos
Kum
Kale
Inönü
Eskisehir
Dardanelles
GREECE
Aegean Sea
Kûtahya
Mitylene
Lesbos
TURKEY
Manisa
Dumlupiner
Afionkarahissar
Smyrna
(Izmir)
Athens
Denizli
Dodecanese
Islands
Rhodes
Crete
Greece in 1914
Bulgarian territory ceded to Greece in 1919
Turkish territory occupied by Greece in 1919 with British encouragement
Turkish advances against Greek occupation
0 50 100 150 200 km
0 50 100 miles

Map 23.1 The Turkish war of independence, 1918–22

members cooperated with IMRO in 1934 in the assassination of the Yugoslav King Alexander Karadjordjević).[66]

The fate of territorial dismemberment also affected another defeated state of the Great War: the Ottoman Empire, which lost all of its Middle Eastern possessions and was threatened in Western Anatolia by an initially successful Greek advance into Asia Minor shortly after the Ottoman defeat in October 1918, as well as an Armenian insurgency in the East.[67] What the Young Turks and nationalist historians in Turkey to this day refer to as the 'War of Liberation' (*İstiklâl Harbi*, 1919 to 1923) was in essence a form of violent nation-state formation that represented a continuation of wartime ethnic un-mixing and exclusion of Ottoman Christians and Armenians from Anatolia – a process that began long before the proclamation of a Turkish nation-state on 29 October 1923.[68] Here, as elsewhere, the nation-building process came at a high price, paid in particular by the minorities of the country. When Smyrna was re-conquered by Turkish troops in 1922, some 30,000 Greek residents were massacred and many more expelled in what became the largest population transfer in European history before the Second World War. All in all, some 70,000 people died violent deaths in Turkey during the decade after the war's end, while approximately 900,000 Ottoman Greeks and 400,000 Greek Turks were forcibly resettled in a 'homeland' most of them had never visited before.[69]

Legacies

By late 1923, the levels of violence in Europe had decreased significantly. After the end of the Franco-Belgian occupation of the Ruhr, the termination of the

66 John Paul Newman, 'The origins, attributes, and legacies of paramilitary violence in the Balkans', in Gerwarth and Horne, *War in Peace*.

67 John Keegan, *The First World War* (New York: Vintage, 1998), p. 415; Erik-Jan Zürcher, 'The Ottoman Empire and the Armistice of Moudros', in Hugh Cecil and Peter H. Liddle (eds.), *At the Eleventh Hour: Reflections, Hopes, and Anxieties at the Closing of the Great War, 1918* (London: Leo Cooper, 1998), pp. 266–75.

68 Erik-Jan Zürcher, *The Unionist Factor: The Rôle of the Committee of Union and Progress in the Turkish National Movement 1905–1926* (Leiden: Brill, 1984); Paul Dumont, 'The origins of Kemalist ideology', in Jacob M. Landau (ed.), *Atatürk and the Modernization of Turkey* (Boulder, CO: Westview Press, 1984), pp. 25–44; Sabri M. Akural, 'Ziya Gökalp: The Influence of his Thought on Kemalist Reforms' (PhD thesis, Indiana University, 1979); M. Şükrü Hanioğlu, 'Garbcilar: their attitudes toward religion and their impact on the official ideology of the Turkish Republic', *Studia Islamica*, 86 (1997), pp. 133–58.

69 There are no reliable statistics on the post-war Kurdish massacres, but the approximate numbers are: 5,000 deaths in 1921, 15,000 deaths in 1925, 10,000 deaths in 1930 and 40,000 deaths in 1938. See Robert Gerwarth and Ugur Umit Ungor, 'Imperial apocalypse: the collapse of the Ottoman and Habsburg empires and the brutalization of the successor states', *Journal of Contemporary History* (forthcoming).

Russian and Irish Civil Wars and the conclusion of the Lausanne Treaty which specifically aimed 'to bring to a final close the state of war which has existed in the East since 1914', Europe experienced a period of tentative political and economic stability that would last until the Great Depression.

Yet what did not disappear altogether in 1923 was the wider culture of violent rhetoric, uniformed politics and street fighting. Paramilitarism remained a central feature of interwar European political cultures, and it included movements as diverse as the German storm troopers or SA, the Italian *squadristi*, the legionaries of the Romanian Iron Guard, the Hungarian Arrow Cross, the Croation *Ustasha*, or Leon Degrelle's Rexist movement in Belgium and the Croix de Feu in France. While none of these movements would have gained its subsequent importance without the Great Depression, its roots frequently lay in the upheavals of the immediate post-war period. In the case of Italian fascism and German National Socialism, but also in Atatürk's new Turkey or in the Baltic dictatorships of Smetona, Ulmanis and Päts, paramilitary movements contributed strongly to their establishment and were often held up as the origin of the new 'paramilitary states'. In the Italian case, Mussolini's Fascist Party was particularly outspoken about its paramilitary past and future: the regulations for members' conduct published by the semi-official *Il Popolo d'Italia* on 8 October 1922 stated that the Fascist Party 'is still a militia' and that all its members 'must abide by the Fascist Militia's special laws of honour and military discipline'.[70] However, as many former paramilitary leaders (notably in the case of the demise of the SA in Nazi Germany in 1934) had to learn the hard way, this did not prevent the new political leadership from ridding itself of its paramilitary activists once they were seen as no longer useful.

A second, even more important, legacy of the immediate post-war period was the perceived need to cleanse communities of their alien elements before a utopian new society could emerge, to root out those who were perceived to be harmful to the balance of the community. This belief constituted a powerful component of the common currency of radical politics and action in Europe between 1917 and the later 1940s, particularly in those countries frustrated with the outcomes of both the Great War and the post-war conflicts. Whatever its manifold political expressions, this politics of the purified community was a prominent element of peasant dreams, workers' ambitions and bureaucratic models of a People's Community. As such, it provides an important key for understanding the cycles of violence that characterised so many violent upheavals in Europe in the three decades after 1917.

70 Gentile, 'Paramilitary violence in Italy', p. 93.

A third (very long-term) legacy can be identified in the non-European world where paramilitarism remained the exception, at least in the immediate post-war period. However, many of the leaders of post-1945 decolonisation movements experienced the political discourses (and broken promises) of 1918 as something formative, regardless of whether they took inspiration from the Wilsonian discourse on democratic self-determination or the Communist (Third) International's promise of support for colonial struggles against 'imperialist powers'.[71] While this did not lead to the same kind of escalating violence as it did in the colonial world post 1945, the seeds of protracted conflict were sown in the years immediately following the Great War.[72]

Conclusions

Three decisive and often mutually reinforcing factors contributed to the manifold paramilitary conflicts post 1918. Although there can be little doubt that the sheer scale and effects of mass armed combat in the First World War *did* prepare the stage for the post-war conflicts, the geographically uneven spread of post-war violence in Europe cannot be explained by the trench experience itself. One of the factors that did contribute to post-war mobilisation was the Russian Revolution (and subsequent civil war), as well as the ideological counter-revolution that this generated internationally. As has been suggested in this chapter, the largely fantastic fear of a Bolshevik appropriation of the entire old world exerted a powerful influence on the political imagination of Europeans from the very moment Lenin came to power in Russia. Partly propaganda and partly a genuine concern for those who had more to lose than their chains, Bolshevism quickly became synonymous with the elusive threats and underhand enemies that menaced European post-war societies. The morbid fantasy of encirclement by nihilistic forces of disorder inspired conservative and counter-revolutionary politics across Europe, but it played out in different ways, depending on what has been highlighted here as the second dependent variable in explaining post-war conflicts: victory or defeat. Where victory in the Great War had strengthened the state and its

71 Erez Manela, *The Wilsonian Moment: Self-Determination and the International Origins of Anticolonial Nationalism* (New York: Oxford University Press, 2007).

72 Important studies on this include David M. Anderson and David Killingray (eds.), *Policing and Decolonization: Politics, Nationalism, and the Police, 1917–65* (Manchester University Press, 1992); Thomas R. Mockaitis, *British Counterinsurgency, 1919–60* (Basingstoke: Macmillan, 1990); Peter Sluget, *Britain in Iraq: Contriving King and Country* (New York: Columbia University Press, 2007).

institutions, anti-Bolshevik mythology also served to stabilise the existing system by rallying those prepared to defend it against 'chaos'. In the defeated states of Europe, by contrast, anti-Bolshevism helped to explain why the war had been lost, why the old regimes disappeared and why chaos ruled over much of Eastern and Central Europe. Anti-Bolshevism – usually coupled with anti-Semitism – gave paramilitary responses a direction and a goal; it helped to make the illusive enemy identifiable, drew on familiar resentments against the urban poor, the Jews and disorder more generally.

The extent of chaos and violence in East-Central and South-Eastern Europe depended – thirdly – on the degree of state collapse in the shatter zones of the multi-ethnic dynastic Ottoman, Habsburg and Romanov empires and the strength of those movements attempting to create ethnically homogenous nation-states under the banner of 'self-determination'. Violence thus remained a variable that depended largely on the circumstances in which it occurred. If many paramilitaries of different political, religious or ethnic beliefs and identities shared fantasies of violently imposing New Orders, they differed markedly in their ability to act independently and to succeed in implementing their aims. In the largely stateless borderlands of post-revolutionary Russia, Ukraine or the Baltic region, the fantasies turned into reality on a massive scale, while in the former territories of pre-1918 Hungary, 'red' and 'white' paramilitary groups were able to enact large-scale terror campaigns against real or perceived enemies. Further west, however, the opportunities for independent political action were much more limited. The circumstances and opportunities for violent action were to change over the coming decades, but the underlying logic – born in the immediate aftermath of the Great War – remained the same: the aim was no longer militarily to defeat an opposing army and to impose one's conditions (however harsh) on the vanquished, as had been the case during the Great War, but to annihilate those who stood in the way of the creation of new utopian societies.

24

Visual essay: War and the state

ARNDT WEINRICH

The media revolution of the early twentieth century was already well under way when the First World War broke out in 1914. Still, the impact of total war on its acceleration can hardly be overestimated. For the first time in history, millions of individual lives in Europe and beyond were irreversibly altered by the necessities of global war. This turbulence created a global mass market for visual representations of the war that could explain or at least help convey a sense of what was going on on the battlefields, where relatives and friends of millions of people faced death and mutilation. All civilian and military leaders at war rapidly understood that they had to make every effort to control public opinion on the war. The wartime state of exception, in Carl Schmitt's term, provided them with different means to that end, among them propaganda and censorship.[1]

The struggle of the state for hegemony as much in the realm of public representation of the war as in every other sphere of mobilisation is at the heart of this photographic chapter. Using different sets of images, I illustrate the extension of state authority, but also the limits of its power. While the First World War marked the emergence and the apotheosis of the modern national

1 This chapter builds upon numerous works on the history of photography and more generally of media during the twentieth century and the First World War in particular. The ideas it develops are inspired by readings of among others: Caroline Brothers, *War and Photography. A Cultural History* (London and New York: Routledge, 1997); Jane Carmichael, *First World War Photographers* (London and New York: Routledge, 1989); Anton Holzer, *Die andere Front. Fotografie und Propaganda im Ersten Weltkrieg* (Darmstadt: Primus Verlag, 2007); Anton Holzer, *Das Lächeln der Henker. Der unbekannte Krieg gegen die Zivilbevölkerung 1914–1918* (Darmstadt: Primus Verlag, 2008); Gerhard Paul (ed.), *Das Jahrhundert der Bilder. 1900 bis 1949* (Göttingen: Vandenhoeck & Ruprecht, 2009); Gerhard Paul, *Krieg der Bilder – Bilder des Krieges. Visualisierung des modernen Krieges* (Paderborn: Ferdinand Schöningh, 2004); Ute Daniel (ed.), *Augenzeugen. Kriegsberichterstattung vom 18. zum 21. Jahrhundert* (Göttingen: Vandenhoeck & Ruprecht, 2006); Joëlle Beurier, *Images et violence 1914–1918. Quand Le Miroir racontait la Grande Guerre* (Paris: Nouveau Monde Editions, 2007).

state, the conflict also undermined the legitimacy of the German, Austrian, Russian and Ottoman empires. They collapsed outright in the final stages of the war. Even the victorious states, though, went through periods of crisis, in which the legitimacy of their regimes were by no means unquestioned. The exercise of at times uncontrolled power during the First World War was a precedent many people wanted never to repeat.

The photographs of the war that exist by the tens of thousands in public and private archives and libraries all over the world have essentially two origins. On the one hand, there are pictures and film material taken by official war photographers and cameramen, such as the first military stock photography agency that came into being during the First World War – the staff of the French Section photographique de l'Armée and the Section Cinématographique de l'Armée founded both in 1915. Along with their counterparts in the other belligerent armies, they were responsible for satisfying the public's ever growing demand for 'authentic' pictures from the war zone (Figure 24.1). Their official mission in the propaganda war was to present a patriotic, sanitised version of what was going on at the front. The Australian war photographer Frank Hurley and the Canadian William Ivor Castle provided iconic (though false) representations of attacking Allied forces (Figures 24.2 and 24.3), and their work reveals much about the interplay of propaganda and photography. Neither of the two pictures shows a real battle scene. They created composite pictures, assembled of several – in Hurley's case, twelve – negatives taken on different occasions (in particular during training and manoeuvres), and were thus mock or fictional images. The technique of creating the composite photographs, very popular (though not uncontroversial) among Anglo-Saxon war photographers, simply reflects how difficult it was to capture the drama of battlefield action, once combat began and when the troops' primary aim was to expose themselves as little as possible. There are very, very few shots of combat while it was happening on any front, and they are not as dramatic or as transparent as Hurley's and Castle's hyper-realistic canvases.

The obstacles to 'real' photography help to explain why all sides relied on artists to visualise the war and to portray the 'heroic' struggle of their own troops. Figure 24.4 shows one rather typical specimen of these war scenes. The drawing of José Simont features several British Mark A Whippet tanks engaging and dispersing German troops near Cachy (in the Somme sector) in April 1918. This image is a fine example of the way in which the search for drama and action overrode considerations of the truth value of the photographs. The Whippet actually had its crew compartment at the rear and not – as suggested in Figure 24.4 – at the front end of the vehicle; thus the whole scene betrays the ignorance and the artistic licence of its creator, sitting well behind the front lines.

When not trying to describe combat, with what images did the official photographers provide the press and thereby the home front? If we leave aside the legions of pictures displaying one's own (always spirited) soldiers tending to everyday activities and all those photographs relating to the enemy and the destruction brought about by artillery, three sets of images stand out. First, there are the shots of political and, more importantly, military leaders, who were depicted as faithful, resolute and reliable servants of the nation. They epitomised the state's ability successfully to wage modern war; it was therefore crucial to present them positively in the public arena. The personality cult that developed around figures like Paul von Hindenburg, Georges Clemenceau, Belgium's King Albert and other military leaders (Figure 24.5) was by no means invariant over time; military failure mattered. But the striking resilience of elite profiling highlights the fact that even after years of inconclusive fighting and right until the end many people continued to believe in the legitimacy and the ability of the state to organise for modern war and to see the effort through to victory.

The second set of visual motifs prominent among official photographs focused on the efficiency of state-run mobilisation of resources. Numerous representations of hardware, of military logistics and the output of the sinews of war aimed at reassuring the public that however complex the organisation of industrial war might appear, the state and both its military and industrial leadership had mastered it. It is hardly surprising that huge stacks of high-calibre shells, narrow-gauge railway trains supplying heavy artillery with ammunition, or more generally motorised supply columns became the visual trademark of the first industrial world war (Figure 24.6). On the Allied side, multiple images presented their global supply network of men and materiel. There was an abundance of pictures of colonial troops being moved to different theatres of war (Figure 24.7). In addition, we find photographs of different logistical feats such as the transport of Russian troops from Moscow via Siberia, Ceylon, the Suez Canal and the Mediterranean to Marseille (Figure 24.8). There were images of the Chinese Labour Corps crossing the Pacific, North America and the Atlantic to get to Europe. And their presence in France showed what the Central Powers were unable to match or to disrupt.

The real hardware of war, however, were the modern and increasingly sophisticated weapons systems. They constitute the third body of visual motifs provided in abundance by official photographers. Images of mighty railway guns, battleships, military aircrafts of all kinds and tanks that were increasingly displayed in the press were intended to show off one's own military strength and reassure soldiers and civilians alike. Captured weapons constituted a trump card in the war of propaganda that all sides were all too happy to exploit. After all, what could illustrate the superiority of one's own weaponry better than booty or enemy aircraft brought down by hostile fire (Figure 24.9)?

Due to the increased portability and affordability of roll film cameras, professional photographers were by no means alone in transmitting visual representations of the war. It is the soldiers themselves to whom we owe the bulk of our photographic archives. The pictures they took, mostly snapshots showing comrades and more generally life behind the frontlines, have a distinctively private character, and only exceptionally convey the realities of combat, military discipline and hardships.

When they do, however, probe beneath the surface of official discourse, they shed considerable light on different features of the war. Consider, for instance, this image of the execution of a French soldier (Figure 24.10), whose body is afterwards presented to the troops on parade to remind them of their duties and the gruesome consequences of failing to fulfil them. While pictures like this one could not be published during the war, others were. In fact, the distinction between private amateur pictures and published official photographs is artificial. In order to fill the demand for spectacular pictures, illustrated magazines particularly in France turned to amateur photographers whom they invited to send in their photographs for publication. The magazine that went furthest in this regard was *Le Miroir*, which throughout the war organised a monthly contest for the best 'authentic' amateur photograph. As a consequence, it was able to publish pictures whose depiction of violence was at odds with the prevailing official discourse (Figures 24.11 and 24.12). Contrary to common belief, censors did not try to protect the public on the home front from gruesome representations of violence, as long as the taboo of showing pictures of one's own dead or badly wounded soldiers was respected. And if they decided to intervene, they were not sure of succeeding. Such was the case of a *Daily Mirror* reportage on the crisis of the Russian army in 1917 that the French periodical *L'Illustration* decided to reprint (Figures 24.13 and 24.14). Just a few months after the French mutinies of 1917, the publication of pictures showing troops fleeing and acting to restore order was considered totally inappropriate by military censors. *L'Illustration* was asked to take out the pictures, which it said it would do, not without publicly contesting the censorship's decision. However, the decision of French authorities to seize this number in the army zone indicates that the journal did in fact not react fast enough. In other words, journalists at times preferred to risk sanctions rather than to withdraw pictures they considered sensational.

In the context of an expanding mass market, the state was thus only to a limited extent able to control the public representations of the war. And yet the mainstream press in all combatant countries embraced the official discourse of national unity and patriotic mobilisation for the duration of the war; clearly this tendency arose more out of self-censorship and self-mobilisation, and less out of fear of the censor.

Alongside state mobilisation came the mobilisation of civil society, the subject of the third volume of *The Cambridge History of the First World War*. Certainly, the wartime state came to permeate every aspect of social life, but this expansion went side by side with the work of voluntary groups to ensure that the war effort was run as efficiently as possible. Soldiers had to be recruited, at least initially in countries like the United Kingdom, where there was no conscription until 1916 (Figure 24.15). The belligerents' financial resources had to be mobilised (Figures 24.16 and 24.17). Propaganda posters created a modern visual language of mobilisation that all combatants shared.

The general mobilisation of men for military service went relatively smoothly – not only in the countries at war, but also – and this tends to be overlooked – in the neutral Netherlands and Switzerland, where there was also a degree of militarisation of social life (Figure 24.18) Although no other country followed the lead of the Russian Provisional Government, in recruiting women for fighting units (the famous Battalion of Death, Figure 24.19), many women served in the military as nurses or in other support roles. More importantly, there was a consensus about the need to facilitate the use of more female labour than ever before in heavy industry, where they replaced volunteers and conscripts. On the whole, the mobilisation of women during the war led to an unprecedented incursion of women into the public sphere, and reinforced claims for women's suffrage (Figure 24.20).

A distinctive feature of the state's control over the national economy was the rationing of food and raw materials and price controls for certain goods. Images of people queuing up for food are part of the collective imagery of the war in many combatant countries. But it should not be forgotten that elsewhere food provision was a serious issue, too. The 1918 rice riots in Japan were unprecedented and still remain unparalleled in modern Japanese history in terms of scope and violence (Figure 24.21). In effect all belligerents suffered in one way or the other from the massive disruption of international trade and inflation caused by the First World War. Even in (some) neutral countries, the state had to intervene to ensure that market distortions due to the war did not undermine the nation's food supply (Figure 24.22). In many places, that effort failed. A black-market economy flourished, especially among the Central Powers. The Armistice did not end the material misery of daily life in the defeated countries, and in some respects, things got worse, especially in light of the continuing Allied blockade lifted only on 28 June 1919. There were many reasons for hyperinflation (Figure 24.23), but its consequences were devastating. Destroying a sense of the future as secure, destroying savings and impoverishing those on fixed incomes, like the retired and the elderly, the dizzying price spiral sapped people's trust in the ability of the state to guarantee the value of its currency, or to secure the future of their children. How could any state claim legitimacy when it could not feed its own people?

Food provision was not the only issue on which the state focused. Public health was of equal importance. After all, venereal diseases constituted a threat to the combat strength of their army. As an abstentionist discourse proved ineffective, military authorities had to accept that soldiers' sexuality was beyond their control, and they had to adopt a pragmatic approach to this matter. The creation of military brothels was as much part of that policy as the instruction of soldiers and prostitutes alike, in the use of prophylactic creams and kits that were handed to them in order to minimise the risk of infection (Figure 24.24).

These examples, far from being exhaustive, reflect the pervasiveness of the state in the lives of civilians and soldiers, and of the state's attempts to optimise the war effort. Consider too the first introduction of the daylight saving time in 1916 (Figure 24.25): even Chronos had to serve the purposes of the waging of war.

To be effective, the state required accurate information and, where necessary, the power to control the substantial population flows of mobilised men and women, the wounded, prisoners of war, refugees, internees, foreign workers and the like. The thousands of camps put up in the war zones and on the home front appeared to be the solution to the organisational challenges of securing and supplying this flow of men, women and animals (Figure 24.26).

The right of the state to restrict liberties, to incarcerate and ultimately to put to death those who failed to accept its authority, stands out as the most drastic feature of state power during the Great War. Above (Figure 24.10), we have already seen the ultimate punishment meted out to soldiers. Military justice was rigorous and provided capital punishment for an entire range of offences, although capital sentences were rarely carried out, in particular in the German army. Enemy civilians under occupation, or elsewhere entire ethnic groups said to be hostile to the country they lived in, suffered most from the extension of the power of the state. At times restrictions imposed by the state were absurd: consider the ban on baking cake that the German Commander-in-Chief on the Eastern Front signed in April 1917 (Figure 24.27). Still, when German authorities collected anthropometric and photographic data on the population of occupied territories, and treated these people as groups to be organised or moved, they set a dangerous precedent for what would come twenty-five years later in the Second World War (Figure 24.28). Alongside often summary executions for sabotage and espionage (Figure 24.29), these images highlight the extent to which the occupying state tended to consider occupied populations as an asset at its disposal.

In the case of the Armenian population in Anatolia, genocide was the outcome (see Volume I, Chapter 24 – 'Visual essay: global war'). And yet the Armenians were Ottoman subjects. The regime treated them as enemy aliens, a threat to the existence of a regime under siege. That was why the Turkish ruling triumvirate moved to deport and eliminate them as a people.

The perimeter of state action was neither the same in all belligerent countries nor invariant over time. Furthermore, there was considerable conflict as to whether the military or civilian leadership should have the last word on matters of strategic importance. While everywhere the military was relatively free as far as the operational conduct of the war was concerned, it was subject to parliamentary and governmental control in other domains, in particular in the case of France. Whereas the civilian authorities abdicated most of their responsibilities to the military at the beginning of the war, they contested the military's predominance as the war dragged on. Different parliamentary commissions and in particular the French Senate's Commission de l'Armée proved in that context highly efficient in reining in the general staff and in organising the war effort. The fact that it was a civilian, George Clemenceau, who came to be the embodiment of the French nation at war and later on of victory (Figure 24.30), reflects better than anything else the active part of the parliamentary regime in the waging of the war. Certainly, the French example stands out. We should not, however, underestimate the extent to which similar developments took place in other countries, too.

Faced with the necessities of mobilising the entire population, Austria was the only major power that declined to recall the legislature in the first year of the war and only did so in 1917, when the cracks in the legitimacy of the state had become all too apparent. All the other powers, including the Hungarian part of the Habsburg Empire, understood that there had to be some kind of forum for public opinion and an outlet for popular complaints. The socialist and liberal-dominated German Reichstag, for instance, although weak constitutionally, did not only vote for the war credits, but throughout the war raised concerns about the mistreatment of soldiers and the harshness of military justice. The Reichstag even passed legislation leading to the softening of the military penal code. Its 'peace resolution' of 1917 defied government and High Command alike.

The military retained considerable power everywhere. Nevertheless, the enormous sacrifices made by the population during the First World War made a considerable difference. Thereafter, the state had to draw its legitimacy from the people. Constitutional reform or at least the promise of constitutional reform was indispensable for securing the adhesion of public opinion to the war effort and their loyalty to the state (Figure 24.31).

Where the link between government and governed was missing or had eroded, the state faced growing contestation. Opposition movements, initially limited in their capacity to express themselves in public, grew more important the longer the war dragged on. Some were opposed to the war on principle; others to the murderousness and endlessness of it; others still saw the war as the springboard to revolution. Opposition figures such as the US socialist leader Eugene Debs (Figure 24.32), the German independent socialists Karl Liebknecht and Rosa Luxemburg, and the philosopher Bertrand Russell were sent to prison. In the second half of the war, when the stalemate at the front seemed unbreakable, such measures did not stop the erosion of faith in the state and doubts about its ability fairly to distribute the burden of war. Strike movements erupted all across Europe. Finally, when the prospect of victory vanished first in Russia, and later on in Austria-Hungary and Germany, the revolutions of February and November 1917 and November 1918 swept away states that had failed to meet the challenges of total war (Figure 24.33), resulting in chaos and, for some parts of Europe, in civil war. Where some states – at least temporarily – ceased to function, other powers stepped in to maintain order and/or to push their own imperialist agenda. This holds true as much for the remnants of the Ottoman Empire as for the Russian Empire, which saw several foreign interventions, among them the occupation of virtually all of Siberia in 1918 to 1920 by British, US and Japanese forces (Figure 24.34).

Some subject populations refused to accept their subordination to imperial rule. There was violence in Ireland, Egypt, Palestine, India, China and Korea; it was suppressed, but signalled an ominous future. Domestically, social strife persisted throughout Southern, Central and Eastern Europe. The wars after the war proved that the Armistice was not the end of the fighting.

In general, the new powers and financial claims on the population established in wartime set new standards of state power. This was true in democracies like Britain and France, as well as in authoritarian regimes. Historians have argued that the emergence and subsequent rule of communist and fascist regimes must be seen in part as the extension and expansion of the wartime state of exception. In the Soviet Union, the state of exception became the norm. There the state remained on a wartime footing until 1945. To varying degrees, most of the combatant states did not fully demobilise after the First World War. The photographic archive of the period is an essential source for the transformations of state power in the era of total war.

Bibliographical essays

1 Heads of state and government

Jean-Jacques Becker

One place to start is to consider the bibliography following Volume I, Chapter 2, on 1914 and the outbreak of the war. In addition, there are many and diverse works to consider on the themes of this chapter. It would be wise to consult initially Pierre Renouvin, *La crise européenne et la première guerre mondiale. Peuples et civilisations*, 4th edn (Paris: Presses Universitaires de France, 1962). This book is still important fifty years after its initial publication. In addition, there is much of value in the following works: François Lagrange (ed.), *Inventaire de la Grande Guerre* (Paris: Universalis, 2005); Stéphane Audoin-Rouzeau and Jean-Jacques Becker (eds.) *Encyclopédie de la Grande Guerre 1914–1918* (Paris: Bayard, 2004); Antonio Gibelli (ed.), *La prima guerra mondiale*, Italian edn (Rome: Einaudi, 2007); Gerhard Hirschfeld, Gerd Krumeich and Irina Renz (eds.), *Enzyklopädie Erster Weltkrieg* (Paderborn: Ferdinand Schöningh, 2003); François Cochet and Rémy Porte (eds.), *Dictionnaire de la Grande Guerre (1914–1918)* (Paris: Robert Laffont, 2008); Jean-Jacques Becker, *Dictionnaire de la Grande Guerre* (Brussels: André Versaille éditeur, 2008); Holger Herwig and Neil Heyman, *Biographical Dictionary of World War I* (Wesport, CT: Greenwood Press, 1982); Stephen Pope and Elizabeth-Ann Wheal (eds.), *The Dictionary of the First World War* (New York: St Martin's Press, 1995).

Various national histories offer essential interpretations and documents on numerous heads of state during the war and their vicissitudes. On Germany, see: Roger Chickering, *Das Deutsche Reich und der Erste Weltkrieg* (Munich: C. H. Beck, 2002); Roger Chickering, *Imperial Germany and the Great War* (Cambridge University Press, 1998); Raymond Poidevin, *L'Allemagne de Guillaume II à Hindenburg (1900–1933)* (Paris: Éditions Richelieu, 1972); Golo Mann, *Wilhelm II* (Munich: Scherz Verlag, 1964); Isabel V. Hull, *The Entourage of Kaiser Wilhelm II, 1888–1918* (Cambridge University Press, 1982); John C. G. Röhl, *The Kaiser and His Court: Wilhelm II and the Government of Germany* (Cambridge University Press, 1994); and Isabel V. Hull, *Absolute Destruction: Military Culture and the Practices of War in Imperial Germany* (Ithaca, NY: Cornell University Press, 2006).

On Austria-Hungary, see: Jean-Paul Bled, *François-Joseph* (Paris: Fayard, 1987); Mark Cornwall, *Undermining of Austria-Hungary: The Battle for Hearts and Minds* (New York: St Martin's Press, 2000); and two collections of essays edited by Cornwall: *Last*

Years of Austria-Hungary: A Multi-National Experiment in Early Twentieth-Century Europe (University of Exeter Press, 2002); and *Last Years of Austria-Hungary: Essays in Political and Military History, 1908–1918* (University of Exeter Press, 1990). On Franz-Joseph, see Steven Beller, *Francis Joseph. Profiles in Power* (London: Longman, 1996); Lothar Höbelt, *Franz Joseph I: Der Kaiser und sein Reich: eine politische Geschichte* (Vienna: Böhlau Verlag, 2009); and John Van der Kiste, *Emperor Francis Joseph: Life, Death and the Fall of the Habsburg Empire* (Stroud, UK: Sutton, 2005).

On the Balkans, see: Jonathan Gumz, *The Resurrection and Collapse of Empire in Habsburg Serbia, 1914–1918* (Cambridge University Press, 2009); and George B. Leontartis, *Greece and the First World War: From Neutrality to Intervention, 1917–1918* (New York: Columbia University Press, 1990). For general surveys, see: Georges Castellan, *Histoire des Balkans* (Paris: Fayard, 1991); and Catherine Durandin, *Histoire des Roumains* (Paris: Fayard, 1995). On a particular point, there is a useful article by David J. Dutton, 'The Balkan campaign and French war aims in the Great War', *English Historical Review*, 94:370 (1979), pp. 97–113.

On Belgium, there is: Laurence van Ypersele, *Le roi Albert, histoire d'un mythe* (Ottignies: Éditions Quorum, 1995); and Sophie van Schaepdrijver, *La Belgique et la Première Guerre Mondiale* (Berlin: Peter Lang, 2004).

On China, see: Marie-Claire Bergère, *Sun Yat-sen*, trans. Janet Lloyd (Stanford University Press, 1998); Harold Z. Schiffrin, *Sun Yat-sen, Reluctant Revolutionary* (Boston: Little, Brown & Co., 1980); Jonathan Clements, *Wellington Koo* (London: Haus Publishing, 2008); and for a general survey – Jean Chesneaux, Francoise le Barbier and Marie-Claire Bergere, *China from the 1911 Revolution to Liberation*, trans. Paul Auster and Lydia Davis (New York: Pantheon Books, 1977). On the Ottoman Empire, see: Jean-Pierre Derrienic, *La Moyen-Orient au XXe siècle* (Paris: Armand Colin, 1980); David Fromkin, *A Peace to End All Peace: Creating the Modern Middle East 1914–1922* (New York: Henry Holt & Co., 1989); M. Şükrü Hanioğlu, *Preparation for a Revolution: The Young Turks, 1902–1908* (Oxford University Press, 2001); Yves Ternon, *Empire ottoman: Le déclin, la chute, l'effacement* (Paris: Edition du Félin, 2002).

On the United States, see: David M. Kennedy, *Over Here: The First World War and American Society* (New York: Oxford University Press, 1980); John Milton Cooper, *Woodrow Wilson: A Biography* (New York: Vintage, 2011); and his *Breaking the Heart of the World: Woodrow Wilson and the Fight for the League of Nations* (New York: Cambridge University Press, 2001).

On France, see: Nicolas Beaupré, *1914, les Grandes Guerres* (Paris: Éditions Belin, 2012); Jean-Jacques Becker, 'L'impact de la Grande Guerre sur les familles politiques françaises', in *Les familles politiques en Europe occidentale au XXe siècle* (Rome: École française de Rome, 2000); and Fabienne Bock, *Un parlementarisme de guerre. I914–1919* (Paris: Éditions Belin, 2002). This book is fundamental and unfortunately unmatched in the international literature.

On Italy, see: Serge Berstein and Pierre Milza, *L'Italie contemporaine* (Paris: Armand Colin, 1995); Mario Isnenghi, *La Première guerre mondiale* (Paris and Florence: Casterman-Giunti, 1993); Roy Pryce, 'Italy and the outbreak of the First World War', *Cambridge Historical Journal*, 11:2 (1954), pp. 219–27; Mario Isnenghi, *Grande guerra: uomini e luoghi del '15–18* (Turin: UTET, 2008); and Giorgio Rochat, *Italia nella prima guerra mondiale: problemi di interpretazione e prospettive di ricerca* (Milan: Feltrinelli, 1976).

On Portugal, see: Nuno Severiano Teixeira, *L'entrée du Portugal dans la Grande Guerre, objectifs nationaux et stratégies politiques* (Paris: Economica, 1998).

On Britain, the following are useful: Trevor Wilson, *The Myriad Faces of War: Britain and the Great War* (Cambridge: Polity Press, 1986); David Stevenson, *With Our Backs to the Wall: Victory and Defeat in 1918* (London: Allen Lane, 2011); Gary Sheffield and John Bourne (eds.), *Douglas Haig: War Diaries and Letters, 1914–1918* (London: Weidenfeld & Nicolson, 2005); George H. Cassar, *Asquith as War Leader* (London: Hambledon Press, 1994); Zara Steiner, *Britain and the Origins of the First World War* (New York: St Martin's Press, 1977).

On Russia: the classics, Marc Ferro, *La révolution russe de 1917*, 3rd edn (Paris: Flammarion, 1989); and Hélène Carrère d'Encausse, *Nicolas II, la transition interrompue* (Paris: Hachette littératures, 2012). Of importance are: Peter Holquist, *Making War, Forging Revolution: Russia's Continuum of Crisis, 1914–1921* (Cambridge, MA: Harvard University Press, 2002); and Joshua Sanborn, *Drafting the Russian Nation: Military Conscription, Total War, and Mass Politics, 1905–1925* (DeKalb, IL: Northern Illinois University Press, 2003).

2 Parliaments

Dittmar Dahlmann

There is no comprehensive and comparative history of parliaments during the First World War and for some countries not even a monograph or an article. Here are some leads for individual national cases.

For Russia, Sergei S. Oldenburg, *Last Tsar. Nicholas II. His Reign and His Russia* (Gulf Breeze, FL: Academic International Press, 1978), vol. IV provides a general overview; Manfred Hildermeier, *Die russische Revolution 1905–1921* (Frankfurt am Main: Suhrkamp, 1989) deals with home policy during the war; Michael F. Hamm, 'Liberal politics in wartime Russia. An analysis of the Progressive Bloc', *Slavic Review*, 33 (1974), pp. 453–68; and Thomas Riha, 'Miliukov and the Progressive Bloc in 1915. A study in last chance politics', *Journal of Modern History*, 32 (1960), pp. 16–24 put their emphasis on the Constitutional Democrats; the article by V. Ju. Černjaev, 'Pervaja mirovaja vojna i perspektivy demokratičeskogo preobrazovanija Rossijskoj Imperii', in Nikolaj N. Smirnov *et al.* (eds.), *Rossija i pervaja mirovaja vojna. Materialy meždunarodnogo naučnogo Kollokviuma* (St Petersburg: DB, 1999), pp. 189–201 discusses the chances for a democratic development in the Russian Empire during the war.

For Austria, Berthold Sutter and Ernst Bruckmüller, 'Der Reichsrat, das Parlament der westlichen Reichshälfte Österreich-Ungarns (1861–1918)', in Ernst Bruckmüller (ed.), *Parlamentarismus in Österreich* (Vienna: öbv und hpt, 2001), pp. 60–109 deal with the history of the Austrian Parliament; and Lothar Höbelt, 'Parlamente der europäischen Nachbarn II: Die Vertretung der Nationalitäten im Wiener Reichsrat', in Dittmar Dahlmann and Pascal Trees (eds.), *Von Duma zu Duma. Hundert Jahre russischer Parlamentarismus* (Göttingen: V & R Unipress, 2009), pp. 339–59 discusses the national minorities in the Reichsrat.

For Germany, readers should consult the multi-volume Constitutional History by Ernst Rudolf Huber, *Deutsche Verfassungsgeschichte seit 1789*, vol. 3, *Bismarck und das Reich* (Stuttgart: Kohlhammer, 1988), chs. 15–17; vol. 4, *Struktur und Krisen des Kaiserreichs* (1982), chs. 2 and 4; as well as vol. v, *Weltkrieg, Revolution und Reichserneuerung 1914–1919* (1992). An insightful book on the Reichstag during the war is Ernst-Albert Seils,

Weltmachtstreben und Kampf für den Frieden. Der deutsche Reichstag im Ersten Weltkrieg (Frankfurt am Main: Peter Lang, 2011). Wolfgang J. Mommsen's two books on Wilhelmine Germany: *Bürgerstolz und Weltmachtstreben. Deutschland unter Wilhelm II. 1890–1918* (Berlin: Propyläen-Verlag, 1995); and *Der Erste Weltkrieg. Anfang vom Ende des bürgerlichen Zeitalters* (Frankfurt am Main: Fischer Taschenbuch Verlag, 2004) offer a thorough and insightful history of Germany during the war.

For France, Fabienne Bock's book *Un parlementarisme de guerre, 1914–1919* (Paris: Éditions Belin, 2002) is essential, as is the article by Jean-Jacques Becker on France, in Gerhard Hirschfeld, Gerd Krumeich and Irina Renz (eds.), *Brill's Encyclopedia of the First World War* (Leiden and Boston: Brill, 2012). See, too, Inge Saatmann, *Parlament, Rüstung und Armee in Frankreich 1914/18* (Düsseldorf: Droste Verlag, 1978).

For Britain, there are three important contributions: John Turner, *British Politics and the Great War. Coalition and Conflict 1915–1918* (New Haven, CT and London: Yale University Press, 1992); Catriona Pennell, *A Kingdom United. Popular Responses to the Outbreak of the First World War in Britain and Ireland* (Oxford University Press, 2012); and Adrian Gregory, *The Last Great War. British Society and the First World War* (Cambridge University Press, 2008). Kurt Kluxen, 'Die Umformung des parlamentarischen Regierungssystems in Großbritannien beim Übergang zur Massendemokratie', in Kluxen, *Parlamentarismus* (Cologne: Suhrkamp, 1976) surveys the development of the British Parliament in the age of mass democracy.

For the United States, see: David M. Kennedy, *Over Here. The First World War and American Society* (New York: Oxford University Press, 1980); and Robert H. Ferrell, *Woodrow Wilson and World War I, 1917–1921* (New York: Harper & Row Publishers, 1985) also deals with the Houses of Congress during the war.

For Japan, see: Frederick R. Dickinson, *War and National Reinvention. Japan in the Great War, 1914–1919* (Cambridge, MA and London: Cambridge University Press, 1999). Hans H. Baerwald, *Japan's Parliament: An Introduction* (Cambridge University Press, 1974) provides much of use on the Japanese Parliament.

3 Diplomats

David Stevenson

David Stevenson, *The First World War and International Politics* (Oxford University Press, 1986) remains the most up-to-date diplomatic history of the war. Zara S. Steiner (ed.), *The Times Survey of Foreign Ministries of the World* (London: Times Books, 1982) is invaluable on foreign ministry organisation, and Markus Mosslang and Torstan Riotte (eds.), *The Diplomats' World: A Cultural History of Diplomacy, 1815–1914* (Oxford: German Historical Institute London and Oxford University Press, 2008) on the social milieu. Matthew S. Anderson, *Rise of Modern Diplomacy* (London: Longman, 1993) provides a longer-term context.

Luigi Albertini, *The Origins of the War of 1914*, Engl. edn, 3 vols. (Oxford University Press, 1952–7) remains unsurpassed on pre-1914 diplomacy. William Mulligan, *The Origins of the First World War* (Cambridge University Press, 2010) is an up-to-date synthesis that emphasises diplomatic aspects. Zara S. Steiner, *The Foreign Office and Foreign Policy, 1898–1914*

(Cambridge University Press, 1969), was the starting point for the new work on officials, and Thomas G. Otte, *The Foreign Office Mind: The Making of British Foreign Policy, 1865–1914* (Cambridge University Press, 2011), is an essential supplement to it. For other countries, see: M. B. Hayne, *The French Foreign Office and the Origins of the First World War, 1898–1914* (Oxford University Press, 1993); Peter Jackson, 'Tradition and adaptation: the social universe of the French Foreign Ministry in the era of the First World War', *French History*, 24 (2010), pp. 164–96; Paul G. Lauren, *Diplomats and Bureaucrats: The First Institutional Responses to Twentieth-Century Diplomacy in France and Germany* (Stanford University Press, 1976); Lamar Cecil, *The German Diplomatic Service, 1871–1914* (Princeton University Press, 1976); William D. Godsey, Jr, *Aristocratic Redoubt: The Austro-Hungarian Foreign Office on the Eve of the First World War* (West Lafayette, IN: Purdue University Press, 1999); G. Bolsover, 'Isvolsky and the reform of the Russian Ministry of Foreign Affairs', *Slavonic and Eastern European Review*, 63:1 (1985), pp. 21–40; Warren F. Ilchman, *Professional Diplomacy in the United States, 1789–1939: A Study in Administrative History* (University of Chicago Press, 1961); Elmer Pilschke, *US Department of State: A Reference History* (Westport, CT: Greenwood Press, 1999); and Ian Nish, *Japanese Foreign Policy, 1869–1942: Kasumigaseki to Miyakezaku* (London: Routlege & Kegan Paul, 1977). Among the more informative of the foreign ministers' memoirs are Edward Grey, *Twenty-Five Years, 1892–1916*, 2 vols. (London: Hodder & Stoughton, 1925); Sergei Sazonov, *Fateful Years: The Reminiscences of Serge Sazonov* (London: Cape, 1928); and Walter W. Goetz (ed.), *Die Erinnerungen des Staatssekretärs Richard von Kühlmann* (Munich: Bayerische Akademie der Wissenschaften, 1952). Maurice Paléologue, *An Ambassador's Memoirs, 1914–17* (London: Hutchinson, 1973) is atmospheric but for use with caution; Algernon G. Lennox (ed.), *The Diary of Lord Bertie of Thame, 1914–18* (New York: G. H. Doran, 1924) is gossipy. For biographies of diplomats, see: Keith A. Hamilton, *Bertie of Thame: Edwardian Ambassador* (Woodbridge: Boydell, 1990); Marina Soroka, *Britain, Russia, and the Road to War: The Fateful Embassy of Count Alexsandr Benckendorff, 1903–16* (Farnham: Ashgate, 2011); and Reinhard R. Doerries, *Imperial Challenge: Ambassador Count von Bernstorff and German-American Relations, 1908–1917* (Chapel Hill, NC and London: University of North Carolina Press, 1989).

Studies of diplomacy during the war are fewer. Roberta M. Warman, 'The erosion of foreign office influence in the making of foreign policy, 1916–1918', *Historical Journal*, 15 (1972), pp. 133–59 is useful. Victor H. Rothwell, *British War Aims and Peace Diplomacy 1914–1918* (Oxford: Clarendon Press, 1971) and David Stevenson, *French War Aims against Germany 1914–1919* (Oxford University Press, 1982) contain useful material. On peace feelers, see: Guy Pedroncini, *Les négociations secrètes pendant la Grande Guerre* (Paris: Flammarion, 1969). Arno J. Mayer, *Political Origins of the New Diplomacy, 1917–1918* (New Haven, CT: Yale University Press, 1959) surveys the international debate on 'secret diplomacy' in 1917 to 1918.

On peacemaking, Margaret O. MacMillan, *Peacemakers: the Paris Peace Conference of 1919 and its Attempt to End War* (London: John Murray, 2003); Michael L. Dockrill and Zara S. Steiner, 'The Foreign Office at the Paris Peace Conference in 1919', *International History Review*, 2 (1980), pp. 55–86; Stevenson, *French War Aims*; and Inga Floto, *Colonel House in Paris: A Study of American Policy at the Paris Peace Conference, 1919* (Aarhus: Universitetsforlaget i Aarhus, 1973), all discuss the diplomats' role.

The journals *Diplomacy and Statecraft*, *The International History Review*, *Relations Internationales* and *Revue d'Histoire diplomatique* all publish articles of relevance.

4 Civil-military relations

Stig Förster

The historical literature on civil-military relations is rich and varied. But there is not a single book on civil-military relations during the First World War that deals with this specific topic on a comparative basis. Hence this chapter constitutes something of an experiment. The facts related here have been cobbled together from many publications. Extremely helpful was the following outstanding handbook on the Great War: Hirschfeld *et al.*, *Enzyklopädie Erster Weltkrieg*.

For many years the problem of militarism stood at the centre of studies on civil-military relations. But this debate has somewhat run its course, as the concept of militarism proved to be too narrow and too one-sided. Moreover, the term 'militarism' is burdened with political ideology. Modern research has become more differentiated and therefore largely abandoned the concept of militarism. For an overview of the nevertheless interesting debate on militarism, see: Volker R. Berghahn, *Militarism. The History of an International Debate, 1861–1979* (Leamington Spa: Berg, 1981).

Publications on the First World War fill whole libraries. The same is true for the national history of some of the powers involved. Very few historians, if any, can keep abreast with the enormous amount of literature. It would mean asking too much to expect a comprehensive report on all the publications in the field. Under these circumstances, the following bibliographical remarks limit themselves to the literature quoted in this chapter.

On Clausewitz

There is an excellent English translation of Clausewitz's most famous book: Carl von Clausewitz, *On War*, edited and translated by Michael Howard and Peter Paret (Princeton University Press, 1976).

Among the many analyses of Clausewitz's thoughts, a classic but by now outdated, is: Raymond Aron, *Penser la guerre, Clausewitz*, 2 vols. (Paris: Gallimard, 1976).

Ludendorff's pamphlet does not really aim to do justice to Clausewitz, but is more concerned with arguing for the establishment of military dictatorship in modern warfare. Needless to say, Ludendorff regarded himself as being the only person in Germany capable of running the war effort: Erich Ludendorff, *Der totale Krieg* (Munich: Ludendorffs Verlag, 1935).

An interesting and intelligent interpretation is provided by: Panajotis Kondylis, *Theorie des Krieges: Clausewitz – Marx – Engels – Lenin* (Stuttgart: Steiner, 1988).

The case studies

On France

The two classic studies are: Jean-Jacques Becker, *Les Français dans la Grande Guerre* (Paris: Éditions Richelieu, 1972); and Jean-Baptiste Duroselle, *La France et les Français, 1914–1920* (Paris: Éditions Richelieu, 1972). Of the two, Becker has perhaps the more modern approach.

Useful and far-reaching interpretations are contained in: Patrick Fridenson (ed.), *The French Home Front, 1914–1918* (Providence, RI: Berg, 1992). The most exhaustive study on the role of French Parliament during the war is provided by Fabienne Bock, *Un parlementarisme de guerre. Recherches sur le fonctionnement de la IIIème République pendant la Grande Guerre*, 3 vols. (Paris: Éditions Belin, 2002).

On the United Kingdom

There exist many excellent studies on Britain during the Great War. The following books are all useful, but put different emphases in their interpretations: John M. Bourne, *Britain and the Great War, 1914–1918* (London: Edward Arnold, 1989); David French, *British Economy and Strategic Planning, 1905–1915* (London: Allen & Unwin, 1982); David French, *British Strategy and War Aims, 1914–1916* (London: Allen & Unwin, 1986); Peter Simkins, *Kitchener's Army. The Raising of the New Armies, 1914–1916* (Manchester University Press, 1988); Wilson, *Myriad Faces of War*; Jay M. Winter, *The Great War and the British People* (London: Macmillan, 1985).

A controversial but nevertheless thought-provoking analysis is provided by Niall Ferguson, *The Pity of War: Explaining World War I* (London: Penguin, 1998).

There is also an interesting and well-written book on radical opposition to the war and its suppression in Britain and Germany: Francis L. Carsten, *War against War. British and German Radical Movements in the First World War* (London: Batsford Academic and Educational, 1982).

On Italy

There are not too many books on Italy during the Great War. But some of them are quite good: Howard James Burgwyn, *The Legend of the Mutilated Victory. Italy, the Great War, and the Paris Peace Conference, 1915–1919* (Westport, CT: Greenwood, 1993); Mario Isnenghi, *Il mito della grande guerra* (Bologna: Il Mulino, 1997).

An excellent overview over the history of Italy is certainly: Volker Reinhard, *Geschichte Italiens. Von der Spätantike bis zur Gegenwart* (Munich: C. H. Beck, 2003).

On Russia

Research on the history of Russia during the First World War has long suffered from difficulties of gaining access to Soviet archives. Nevertheless, there are some impressive studies: Dominic C. B. Lieven, *Russia and the Origins of the First World War* (London: Macmillan, 1983); Hugh Seton-Watson, *The Russian Empire, 1801–1917* (Oxford University Press, 1967); Norman Stone, *The Eastern Front, 1914–1917* (London: Hodder & Stoughton, 1975); Allan K. Wildman, *The End of the Russian Imperial Army: The Old Army and the Soldiers' Revolt, March to April 1917* (Princeton University Press, 1980); and Wildman, *The End of the Russian Imperial Army II: The Road to Soviet Power and Peace* (Princeton University Press, 1987).

On Japan

The Pacific War has overshadowed research on Japan's role in the First World War. Hence only a few useful books on that topic have been published. Among the best are: Frederick

R. Dickinson, *War and National Reinvention. Japan in the Great War, 1914–1919* (Cambridge, MA and London: Cambridge University Press, 1999); and Richard Storry, *A History of Modern Japan* (London: Penguin, 1960).

On the United States

Unsurprisingly, much research has been done on the role of the United States in the Great War. Among the many good books on that subject, perhaps the most outstanding are: Edward M. Coffman, *The War to End All Wars. The American Military Experience in World War I* (Madison, WI: University of Wisconsin Press, 1986); David M. Kennedy, *Over Here. The First World War and American Society* (New York: Oxford University Press, 1980); Robert H. Zieger, *America's Great War. World War I and the American Experience* (Lanham, MD: Rowman & Littlefield, 2000).

On the plight of 'enemy aliens' in the United States, see the impressive volume by Jörg Nagler, *Nationale Minoritäten im Krieg. 'Feindliche Ausländer' und die amerikanische Heimatfront während des Ersten Weltkrieges* (Hamburg: Hamburger Edition, 2000).

For a path-breaking study on the history of the army, which also provides a good analysis of the Great War from a US perspective, see Russell F. Weigley, *History of the United States Army* (Bloomington, IN: Indiana University Press, 1967).

On the Ottoman Empire

Publications on the Ottoman Empire in the First World War are limited. But much has been done in recent years. A classic is Alan Palmer, *The Decline and Fall of the Ottoman Empire* (London: John Murray, 1992).

An exhaustive, albeit a little overenthusiastic, analysis of the Ottoman army is provided by Edward J. Erickson, *Ordered to Die. A History of the Ottoman Army in the First World War* (London: Greenwood Press, 2001).

Research on the German military mission in the Ottoman Empire has accelerated. We now also have two excellent biographies on two of the most prominent German officers in Ottoman service: Jehuda L. Wallach, *Anatomie einer Militärhilfe. Die preussisch-deutschen Militärmissionen in der Türkei, 1835–1919* (Düsseldorf: Droste Verlag, 1976); Holger Afflerbach, *Falkenhayn. Politisches Denken und Handeln im Kaiserreich* (Munich: R. Oldenbourg Verlag, 1994); Carl Alexander Krethlow, *Generalfeldmarschal Colmar Freiherr von der Goltz Pascha. Eine Biographie* (Paderborn: Ferdinand Schöningh, 2012).

On Austria-Hungary

Taking into account the importance of Austria-Hungary to the Great War, it is astonishing that for a long time little research on this topic was forthcoming. Especially Austrian historians, over the years, were not too interested in the final war of the Empire. This has now been remedied. The most complete analysis of Austria-Hungary in that period, although at times (especially regarding the origins of the war) somewhat apologetic, is: Manfred Rauchensteiner, *Der Tod des Doppeladlers. Österreich-Ungarn und der Erste Weltkrieg*, 2nd edn (Graz: Verlag Styria, 1994). Very useful, particularly on the relationship between Germany and Austria-Hungary, is Holger H. Herwig, *The First World War. Germany and Austria-Hungary, 1914–1918* (London: Edward Arnold, 1997).

There are also several good articles on aspects of the role of Austria-Hungary, among them: Günther Kronenbitter, '"Nur los lassen". Österreich-Ungarn und der Wille zum Krieg', in Johannes Burkhardt, Josef Becker, Stig Förster and Günther Kronenbitter, *Lange und kurze Wege in den Ersten Weltkrieg. Vier Augsburger Beiträge zur Kriegsursachenforschung* (Munich: Ernst Vögel, 1996), pp. 159–87; Max-Stephan Schulze, 'Austria-Hungary's economy in World War I', in Stephen Broadberry and Mark Harrison (eds.), *The Economics of World War I* (Cambridge University Press, 2005), pp. 77–111; Graydon A. Tunstall, Jr, 'Austria-Hungary', in Richard F. Hamilton and Holger H. Herwig (eds.), *The Origins of World War I* (Cambridge University Press, 2003), pp. 112–49.

On Imperial Germany

Civil-military relations in Germany during the war have long attracted much attention among historians. After all, it was Ludendorff's 'silent dictatorship' that seemed to provide the most striking example of overbearing military power. Yet, in recent years historians have become a little more cautious in asserting all-out military rule in the case of Imperial Germany. See: Roger Chickering, *Imperial Germany and the Great War, 1914–1918* (Cambridge University Press, 1998); Stig Förster, 'Ein militarisiertes Land? Zur gesellschaftlichen Stellung des Militärs im Deutschen Kaiserreich', in Bernd Heidenreich and Sönke Neitzel (eds.), *Das Deutsche Kaiserreich, 1890–1914* (Paderborn: Ferdinand Schöningh, 2011), pp. 157–74.

The more traditional line is provided by: Robert B. Asprey, *The German High Command at War. Hindenburg and Ludendorff and the First World War* (New York: W. Morrow, 1991); Martin Kitchen, *The Silent Dictatorship. The Politics of the German High Command under Hindenburg and Ludendorff, 1916–1918* (London: Croom Helm, 1976).

Recently, a new academic – but somewhat conventional – biography of Ludendorff appeared: Manfred Nebelin, *Ludendorff. Diktator im Ersten Weltkrieg* (Munich: Siedler Verlag, 2010).

A more differentiating view may be found in the biographical sketch by: Markus Pöhlmann, 'Der "moderne Alexander" im Maschinenkrieg. Erich Ludendorff, 1865–1937', in Stig Förster, Markus Pöhlmann and Dierk Walter (eds.), *Kriegsherren der Weltgeschichte. 22 historische Porträts* (Munich: C. H. Beck, 2006), pp. 268–85.

On the military coup in German East Africa, see the prize-winning book by Tanja Bührer, *Die Kaiserliche Schutztruppe für Deutsch-Ostafrika. Koloniale Sicherheitspolitik und transkulturelle Kriegführung, 1885 bis 1918* (Munich: R. Oldenbourg Verlag, 2011).

5 Revolution

Richard Bessel

The classic histories of revolution during the First World War focused on the great political revolutions in Russia and Germany. These revolutions generated a vast literature, but one in which the war appeared largely as a backdrop, with the (party) politics of revolution at the fore. Nevertheless, a number of studies, focusing primarily on individual states, offer insight into the relationship between the war and revolution.

For Russia, the pioneering study by Norman Stone, *The Eastern Front 1914–1917*, remains important in this regard; and the more recent panoramic studies by Richard Pipes, *The Russian Revolution* (New York: Knopf, 1990), and by Orlando Figes, *A People's Tragedy: The Russian Revolution, 1891–1924* (London: Jonathan Cape, 1996) offer much information and insight into the relationship of war and revolution in Russia. Of great significance for this theme is the path-breaking study by Peter Gatrell, *A Whole Empire Walking: Refugees in Russia in World War I* (Bloomington, IN: Indiana University Press, 1999), together with Holquist, *Making War, Forging Revolution*; and Eric Lohr, *Nationalizing the Russian Empire: The Campaign against Enemy Aliens during World War I* (Cambridge, MA: Harvard University Press, 2003). On the collapse of the Russian army, see Wildman, *The End of the Russian Imperial Army* and *The End of the Russian Imperial Army II*.

For Germany, the revolution of 1918 was intensively debated during the 1960s and 1970s, but those investgations concentrated essentially on the politics of revolution rather than the war. For insight into the relationship of war and revolution, good places to start remain the classic studies by Gerald D. Feldman, *Army, Industry and Labor in Germany, 1914–1918* (Princeton University Press, 1966), and by Jürgen Kocka, *Facing Total War, German Society, 1914–1918* (Leamington Spa and Cambridge, MA: Berg and Harvard University Press, 1984). Unexcelled for its discussion of the effects of the war on German (rural) society is Benjamin Ziemann, *War Experiences in Rural Germany 1914–1923* (Oxford: Berg, 2006). Alexander Watson, *Enduring the Great War. Combat, Morale and Collapse in the German and British Armies, 1914–1918* (Cambridge University Press, 2008) offers a very perceptive discussion of the attitudes of German soldiers and the collapse of 1918. Also informative is Jeffrey R. Smith, *A People's War: Germany's Political Revolution, 1913–1918* (Lanham, MD: University Press of America, 2007).

For Austria-Hungary, there is less work available in English, although Herwig, *First World War: Germany and Austria-Hungary* offers a useful account. A very detailed, blow-by-blow account of the end of Austria-Hungary's war and the end of Austria-Hungary from a military perspective may by found in Richard G. Plaschka, Horst Haselsteiner and Arnold Suppan, *Innere Front. Militärassistenz, Widerstand und Umsturz in der Donaumonarchie 1918* (Munich: R. Oldenbourg Verlag, 1974), and a solid overview is available in Manfried Rauchensteiner, *Der Tod des Doppeladlers. Österreich-Ungarn und der Erste Weltkrieg* (Graz: Verlag Styria, 1993). A perceptive recent study of the effects of the war in Vienna is offered by Maureen Healy, *Vienna and the Fall of the Habsburg Empire: Total War and Everyday Life in World War I* (Cambridge University Press, 2004).

For France, the classic text on the 1917 mutinies remains Guy Pedroncini, *Les Mutineries de 1917*, 3rd edn (Paris: Presses Universitaires de France, 1996). An overview of the crises of 1917 may be found in Leonard V. Smith, Stéphane Audoin-Rouzeau and Annette Becker, *France and the Great War* (Cambridge University Press, 2003), pp. 113–45.

On the collapse of the Ottoman Empire, see: Ryan Gingeras, *Sorrowful Shores: Violence, Ethnicity, and the End of the Ottoman Empire, 1912–1923* (Oxford University Press, 2009); and Michael A. Reynolds, *Shattering Empires: The Clash and Collapse of the Ottoman and Russian Empires* (Cambridge University Press, 2011).

On the global aspects of the relationship between war and revolution, see: Evez Manela, *The Wilsonian Moment: Self-Determination and the International Origins of Anticolonial Nationalism* (New York: Oxford University Press, 2007); and Aviel Roshwald, *Ethnic*

Nationalism and the Fall of Empires: Central Europe, Russia and the Middle East, 1914–1923 (London: Routledge, 2001).

6 Combat and tactics

Stéphane Audoin-Rouzeau

The modalities of combat during the Great War have long fascinated military historians, and more recently, this subject has attracted social and cultural historians as well. Within this immense bibliography, I draw particular attention to these recent approaches, in particular those published in English.

In order to place the study of combat and tactics in a general framework, these works are fundamental: John Keegan, *The First World War* (London: Hutchinson, 1998); and Hew Strachan, *European Armies and the Conduct of War* (London: Allen & Unwin, 1983).

On combat and tactics outside of the Western Front, there is much to learn from these important studies: Norman Stone, *The Eastern Front, 1914–1917*; Giorgo Rochat, 'The Italian Front, 1915–1918', in John Horne (ed.), *A Companion to World War I* (Chichester: Wiley-Blackwell, 2010), pp. 82–96; and Mark Thompson, *The White War. Life and Death on the Italian Front, 1915–1919* (London: Faber, 2008).

On combat on the Western Front, on which so much of the literature focuses, these works are useful: Michel Goya, *La chair et l'acier. L'invention de la guerre moderne (1914–1918)* (Paris: Tallandier, 2004); Gerhard Hirschfeld, Gerd Krumeich and Irina Renz (eds.), *Scorched Earth. The Germans on the Somme, 1914–1918* (Barnsley: Pen and Sword Books, 2009); Bruce Gudmundsson, *Stormtroop Tactics: Innovation in the German Army, 1914–1918* (London: Praeger, 1989); Eric Leed, *No Man's Land: Combat and Identity in World War I* (Cambridge University Press, 1979); Tim Travers, *The Killing Ground. The British Army, the Western Front and the Emergence of Modern Warfare, 1900–1918* (London: Unwin Hyman, 1987).

The battles of the Somme and Verdun, so central to the military history of the war, and so heavy in terms of human costs, are well treated in: John Keegan, *The Face of Battle. A Study of Agincourt, Waterloo and the Somme* (London: Cape, 1976), in particular for its central chapter on the Battle of the Somme; Robin Prior and Trevor Wilson, *The Somme* (New Haven, CT: Yale University Press, 2005); Gary Sheffield, *The Somme* (London: Cassell, 2003).

The appearance and deployment of new weapons have attracted the attention of: Lutz Haber, *The Poisonous Cloud. Chemical Warfare in the First World War* (Oxford: Clarendon Press, 1986); Olivier Lepick, *La Grande Guerre chimique, 1914–1918* (Paris: Presses Universitaires de France, 1998); Lee Kennett, *The First Air War, 1914–1918* (New York, Free Press, 1991); John Morrow, *The Great War in the Air: Military Aviation from 1909 to 1921* (Washington DC: Smithsonian Institution Press, 1993).

On the subject of close combat, see: Stéphane Audoin-Rouzeau, *Les armes et la chair. Trois objets de mort en 1914–1918* (Paris: A. Colin, 2009); Joanna Bourke, *An Intimate History of Killing. Face to Face Killing in Twentieth Century Warfare* (London: Granta Books, 1999). Useful on many facets of the history of the Great War; Antoine Prost, 'Les limites de la brutalisation. Tuer sur le front occidental, 1914–1918', *Vingtième Siècle. Revue d'histoire*, 81 (2004), pp. 5–20. This article presents a different point of view from that of Audoin-Rouzeau and Bourke.

How soldiers endured the war, how they held out, has attracted considerable attention from these scholars, among others: Stéphane Audoin-Rouzeau, *Men at War. National Sentiment and Trench Journalism in France during the First World War* (Leamington Spa: Berg, 1992); John Horne, 'De la guerre de mouvement à la guerre de positions: les combattants français', in Horne *et al.* (eds.), *Vers la guerre totale. Le tournant de 1914–1915* (Paris: Tallandier, 2010), pp. 75–91; John Horne, 'Entre expérience et mémoire: les soldats français de la Grande Guerre', *Annales. Histoire, sciences sociales*, 60:5 (2005), pp. 903–19; Stéphane Audoin-Rouzeau and Annette Becker, *1914–1918. Understanding the Great War* (London: Profile, 2002), especially chapter 2; John Fuller, *Troop Morale and Popular Culture in the British and Dominion Armies, 1914–1918* (Oxford University Press, 1990); Richard Holmes, *Tommy. The British Soldier on the Western Front* (London: Harper Collins, 2004); Tony Ashworth, *Trench Warfare, 1914–1918. The Live and Let Live System* (London: Macmillan, 1980); Watson, *Enduring the Great War*. This is a remarkable comparative study, raising doubts about Wilhlem Deist's interpretation of the German army's performance in 1918. Another innovative essay is that of Anne Duménil, 'De la guerre de mouvement à la guerre de positions: les combattants allemands', in Horne, *Vers la guerre totale*, pp. 53–75.

Resistance and rebellion constitute a subject in and of itself in the historiography of the Great War. These subjects are at the heart of these discussions of combat and wartime violence: Nicolas Werth, 'Les déserteurs en Russie: violence de guerre, violence révolutionnaire et violence paysanne (1916–1921)', in Stéphane Audoin-Rouzeau, Annette Becker, Christian Ingrao and Henry Rousso (eds.), *La violence de guerre, 1914–1945* (Brussels: Complexe, 2002), pp. 99–116; Leonard V. Smith, *Between Mutiny and Obedience. The Case of the French Fifth Division during World War I* (Princeton University Press, 1994). Smith's is the best study on the French mutinies of 1917. See as well this comparative work, with primary emphasis on France: Nicolas Offenstadt, *Les fusillés de la Grande Guerre et la mémoire collective (1914–1919)* (Paris: Odile Jacob, 1999).

On the psychological consequences of combat in 1914 to 1918, see Jay Winter (ed.), 'Shell-shock', special issue of *Journal of Contemporary History*, 35:1 (2000).

The publications of the writings of former soldiers provide an immense source on the history of combat. To approach the writings of French veterans recalling their experience on the battlefield, see: Leonard V. Smith, *The Embattled Self. French Soldiers' Testimony of the Great War* (Ithaca, NY: Cornell University Press, 2007); and Antoine Prost, *In the Wake of War. 'Les anciens combattants' and French Society, 1914–1933* (Oxford: Berg, 1992).

7 Morale

Alexander Watson

Morale has attracted much scholarly interest. Older studies of soldiers' motivations in combat and the battlefield dynamics of the First World War have been joined by newer works analysing how military institutions, propaganda and the relationship between front and home all shaped troops' morale. There have been detailed examinations of disciplinary systems, officership, *esprit de corps*, army religion and rear-line recreations. Recent research has drawn on Foucauldian and psychoanalytic theory, psychology and sociology to illuminate why and how soldiers endured the stresses of active service. The literature is particularly well developed for the British and, to a lesser extent, German, armies. Investigation of morale in the forces of other nations and empires has begun, but is not yet as far advanced.

There are a number of general studies worthy of attention. Ashworth, *Trench Warfare 1914–1918*, is a sociological examination of the dynamics of trench warfare. Hugh Cecil and Peter H. Liddle (eds.), *Facing Armageddon. The First World War Experienced* (London: Leo Cooper, 1996) is an essay collection which includes short studies on morale in a number of armies, including the little-studied Ottoman and Italian militaries. Keegan, *The Face of Battle*, is a classic study of why soldiers fight and how armies motivate them on the battlefield. Watson, *Enduring the Great War*, is a comparative study examining individual psychological coping strategies, as well as military institutional means of upholding morale.

On particular armies and morale, see: Jennifer D. Keene, *Doughboys, the Great War, and the Remaking of America* (Baltimore, MD and London: John Hopkins University Press, 2001); Richard Lein, *Pflichterfüllung oder Hochverrat? Die tschechischen Soldaten Österreich-Ungarns im Ersten Weltkrieg* (Vienna and Berlin: Lit, 2011); Wencke Meteling, *Ehre, Einheit, Ordnung. Preußische und französische Städte und ihre Regimenter im Krieg, 1870/71 und 1914–1919* (Baden-Baden: Nomos, 2010); Wildman, *The End of the Russian Imperial Army*, 2 vols. Wildman's is a pioneering study of the disintegration of the Tsar's army in 1914 to 1917; Benjamin Ziemann, *Front und Heimat. Ländliche Kriegserfahrung im südlichen Bayern 1914–1923* (Essen: Klartext Verlag, 1997). Ziemann provides an examination of Bavarian soldiers' war experiences, concentrating on discipline and the rhythms of front life to explain their endurance.

On training and discipline, a good place to start is: Michael Howard, 'Men against fire: expectations of war in 1914', *International Security* 9 (1984), pp. 41–57. This is a helpful introduction to European military professionals' pre-war attitudes to morale. On discipline, see: Cathryn Corns and John Hughes-Wilson, *Blindfold and Alone. British Military Executions in the Great War* (London: Cassell, 2001, 2002); Christoph Jahr, *Gewöhnliche Soldaten. Desertion und Deserteure im deutschen und britischen Heer 1914–1918* (Göttingen: Vandenhoeck & Ruprecht, 1998). Jahr's book is a systematic and illuminating comparative analysis of desertion and punishment in the German and British armies. See also Offenstadt, *Les fusillés de la Grande Guerre*.

More general works on morale and the character of the armies include: Plaschka *et al.*, *Innere Front*. This is one of the few scholarly studies of the wartime Habsburg army. Its focus is on home units, however, not those at the front. See also Smith, *Between Mutiny and Obedience*.

On cohesion, see John Baynes, *Morale. A Study of Men and Courage. The Second Scottish Rifles at the Battle of Neuve Chapelle 1915* (London: Leo Cooper, 1967, 1987). This is a classic study of British professional soldiers' combat motivations, stressing particularly the importance of *esprit de corps*. Additional insights may be gained from consulting Timothy Bowman, *The Irish Regiments in the Great War. Discipline and Morale* (Manchester University Press, 2003); and David French, *Military Identities. The Regimental System, the British Army, and the British People, c. 1870–2000* (Oxford University Press, 2005).

On support, start with Rachel Duffett, *The Stomach for Fighting. Food and the Soldiers of the Great War* (Manchester University Press, 2012). Then consult Fuller, *Troop Morale and Popular Culture*. This is a comprehensive examination of how the British army supported its troops behind the lines.

On leadership, there is a substantial scholarship. Among the important works are: Istvan Deák, *Beyond Nationalism. A Social and Political History of the Habsburg Officer Corps, 1848–1918* (Oxford University Press, 1990); and Gary Sheffield, *Leadership in the Trenches. Officer-Man Relations, Morale and Discipline in the British Army in the Era of the First World War* (Basingstoke: Macmillan, 2000).

On citizen-soldiers, their families, religious practices and patriotism, there is much recent scholarship. A striking example is Michael Roper, *The Secret Battle. Emotional Survival in the Great War* (Manchester University Press, 2009). Influenced by psychoanalytic theory, this work highlights the importance of family links for British soldiers' morale. On religion, one place to start is Michael Snape, *God and the British Soldier. Religion and the British Army in the First and Second World Wars* (London and New York: Routledge, 2005). This is a thorough examination of how Christian belief and clergy influenced British troops and their army during the two world wars.

On patriotism and national sentiment, see Audoin-Rouzeau, *Men at War 1914–1918*. This is an investigation of French soldiers' wartime attitudes and combat motivation based on the study of trench newspapers. Audoin-Rouzeau stresses the importance of the bond between home and front. Helen B. McCartney, *Citizen Soldiers. The Liverpool Territorials in the First World War* (Cambridge University Press, 2005), is a rare study of volunteer soldiers set in their local community. See, too, Joshua Sanborn, *Drafting the Russian Nation. Military Conscription, Total War, and Mass Politics, 1905–1925* (Dekalb, IL: Northern Illinois University Press, 2003).

On psychological warfare, see: Cornwall, *Undermining of Austria-Hungary*. Here is an impressive investigation of the military propaganda campaigns in Russia and Italy in 1917 to 1918. It is insightful too on the physical and psychological collapse of the Habsburg military on the Italian Fronts in the final months of the war.

On the German army's attempts to guide and motivate its troops through propaganda, see Anne Lipp, *Meinungslenkung im Krieg. Kriegserfahrungen deutscher Soldaten und ihre Deutung 1914–1918* (Göttingen: Vandenhoeck & Ruprecht, 2003).

8 Mutiny

Leonard V. Smith

Mutiny has long been a subject of historical interest, but generally along certain well-defined paths. Military historians have studied the 'cautionary tale' aspects of mutiny, from the point of view of how to prevent a military machine from malfunctioning. More recently, social historians have been interested in mutinies as a form of strike. Others have resisted this approach, on the basis that soldiers and sailors are not workers and war is not production – quite the reverse. The question of mutinies and 'politics' remains open, and at times contentious. The comparative study of the myriad forms of mutiny in the Great War is a promising field for future research.

On mutiny and the articulation of the wartime state, these are useful: Ian F. W. Beckett, 'The Singapore Mutiny of February 1915', *Journal of the Society of Army Historical Research*, 62 (1984), pp. 132–53. This is a thorough narrative account. See too Christine Doran, 'Gender matters in the Singapore Mutiny', *Sojourn: Journal of Social Issues in Southeast Asia*, 17 (2002), pp. 76–93. Here is a fine analysis particularly of the aftermath, according to gender.

W. F. Elkins, 'Revolt of the British West India Regiment', *Jamaica Journal*, 11 (1978), pp. 72–5, brings to light a little-known but interesting episode. Douglas Gill and Gloden Dallas, *The Unknown Army* (London: Verso, 1985) is a book which situates mutinies in the British army according to traditions of labour history. Robert B. Haynes, *A Night of Violence: The Houston Riot of 1917* (Baton Rouge, LA: Louisiana State University Press, 1976) is an engaging, narrative account without much connection to broader currents beyond the United States and African-American history. Benjamin Isitt, 'Mutiny from Victoria to Vladivostok, December 1918', *Canadian Historical Review*, 87 (2006), pp. 223–64 is a lively account of a little-known episode.

On French mutinies, André Loez, *14–18, les refus de la guerre: une histoire des mutins* (Paris: Gallimard, 2010), is an up-to-date but sometimes derivative and ideologically constrained study. Guy Pedroncini, *Les Mutineries de 1919* (Paris: Presses Universitaires de France, 1967) was a seminal work. It is very pro-Pétain, but groundbreaking, the first to use archival sources. See as well Smith, *Between Mutiny and Obedience*, for a French social history approach to military experience during the Great War. For the contextualisation of the mutinies within the broader history of the French army during the war, see Leonard V. Smith, 'Remobilizing the citizen-soldier through the French army mutinies of 1917', in John Horne (ed.), *State, Society, and Mobilization during the First World War* (Cambridge University Press, 1997), pp. 144–59.

David Woodward, 'Mutiny at Cattaro, 1918: insurrection in the Austro-Hungarian fleet on February 1st', *History Today*, 26 (1976), pp. 804–10 is a narrative account of a little-known but intriguing incident.

On the relative absence of mutinies in the British forces, see Sheffield, *Leadership in the Trenches*. This is traditional military history, well informed by current approaches.

On the parallel theme of mutiny and the destruction of the wartime state, a good place to start is Deák, *Beyond Nationalism*. This is an important work which at times waxes nostalgic, but remains highly insightful. John Bushnell, *Mutiny amid Repression: Russian Soldiers in the Revolution of 1905–1906* (Bloomington, IN: Indiana University Press, 1990) is excellent on the evolution of authority in the Old Regime Russian army. Daniel Horn, *The German Naval Mutinies of World War I* (New Brunswick, NJ: Rutgers University Press, 1968) is a thoughtful narrative history. For a more up-to-date work which situates mutiny in the context of the current historiography of war and violence, see Mark Jones, 'Violence and Politics in the German Revolution of 1918–19' (PhD Diss., European University Institute, Florence, 2011).

On the Czech Legion, by one of the architects of the Cold War, we have: George F. Kennan, 'The Czechoslovak Legion', *Russian Review*, 16 (1957), 3–16. Ivan Volgyes, 'Hungarian prisoners of war in Russia, 1916–1919', *Cahiers du Monde russe et soviétique*, 14 (1973), pp. 54–85 removes Hungarians from the shadow of the Czech Legion. John Albert White, *The Siberian Intervention* (Princeton University Press, 1950) is a very durable account that admirably covers the role of the Czech Legion.

On the chaotic situation in Russia, a sure guide is Wildman, *End of the Russian Imperial Army*. See too for an excellent overview Elise Kimmeling Wirthschafter, *From Serf to Russian Soldier* (Princeton University Press, 1990).

On the topic of mutiny and the building of the post-war state, a good place to start is Richard Bessel, *Germany after the First World War* (Oxford: Clarendon Press, 1993). This is a general account, excellent on the transition from war to peace. See too Vladimir Brovkin,

'On the internal front: the Bolsheviks and the Greens', *Jahrbücher für Geschichte Osteuropas*, 39 (1989), pp. 541–68. This article argues for the importance of the 'Greens'. Robert Gerwarth, 'The Central European counter-revolution: paramilitary violence in Germany, Austria and Hungary after the Great War', *Past and Present*, 200 (2008), pp. 175–209 is a transnational account of a transnational phenomenon and is an important contribution to rethinking the whole question of mutiny and violence. These ideas are developed further in Robert Gerwarth and John Horne, 'Vectors of violence: paramilitarism in Europe after the Great War, 1917–1923', *Journal of Modern History*, 83 (2011), pp. 489–512. Here too is a reconfiguration of the entire question of 'cultural demobilization'.

For the opposite, see Klaus Theweleit, *Male Fantasies*, trans. Stephan Conaway, 2 vols. (Minneapolis, MN: University of Minnesota Press, 1987–9). This is a bizarre but often brilliant psycho-history of the *Freikorps* focused on gender anxieties.

On the Ottoman and post-Ottoman part of the story, Ryan Gingeras, *Sorrowful Shores: Violence, Ethnicity, and the End of the Ottoman Empire, 1912–1923* (Oxford University Press, 2009) illustrates the true complexity of the question in the context of present-day approaches. A sympathetic, highly detailed account of the transition to Atatürk's regime is Andrew Mango, *Atatürk: The Biography of the Founder of Modern Turkey* (Woodstock, NY: Overlook Press, 1999).

On violence in the context of the Russian Revolution, see Nicolas Werth, 'Les déserteurs en Russie: violence de guerre, violence révolutionnaire et violence paysanne (1916–1922)', in Audoin-Rouzeau *et al.*, *La Violence de guerre*, pp. 99–116. This essay focuses on peasant soldiers. Nicolas Werth, 'Un état contre son peuple: violence, repressions, terreurs en Union soviétique', in Stéphane Courtois *et al.* (eds.), *Le Livre Noir du communisme* (Paris: Robert Laffont, 1997), pp. 48–163 is a comprehensive, post-Soviet, highly anti-Bolshevik account. See also Donald Raleigh, *Experiencing Russia's Civil War: Politics, Society, and Revolutionary Culture in Saratov, 1917–1922* (Princeton University Press, 2002), which situates 'Greens' in the setting of broad rural issues. Raleigh is more sceptical than Werth as to their importance.

Mark von Hagen, *Soldiers in the Proletarian Dictatorship: The Red Army and the Soviet Socialist State, 1917–1930* (Ithaca, NY: Cornell University Press, 1990), provides an effective explanation of how military and political structures built each other.

9 Logistics

Ian Brown

Logistics is critically important to the conduct of military operations and shoddy logistic planning is a handicap that will cripple even the most tactically sophisticated armies. Despite this, the historical study of logistics is largely ignored, overwhelmed by the plethora of studies covering tactics, operations and strategy. Glamour sells and logistics simply lacks glamour. For most historical periods, one can generally uncover a single volume that covers the topic in some depth, but the total number of works on military logistics, for all periods, would take up significantly less shelf-space than the number covering just the Battle of the Somme. With this in mind, anyone interested in studying logistics must be willing to dig information out of the pages of works that have little or nothing to do with the subject.

General logistics

There are a handful of works that cover logistics over an extended time frame (amounting to more than a single war or campaign). Van Creveld's work is the one that broke the groundwork for the historical study of military logistics. Unfortunately, he essentially skips the First World War and jumps from the nineteenth century into the Second World War. John Lynn's edited volume rectifies the oversight and must be read in conjunction with van Creveld's work as it expands brilliantly on a number of topics and provides considerable additional context. Thompson's work is also useful; he does cover the First World War briefly, but the work is most useful in covering a number of non-traditional twentieth-century campaigns.

Here are full bibliographical references: Martin van Creveld, *Supplying War: Logistics from Wallenstein to Patton* (Cambridge University Press, 1977); John A. Lynn (ed.), *Feeding Mars: Logistics in Western Warfare from the Middle Ages to the Present* (Boulder, CO: Westview Press, 1993); Julian Thompson, *The Lifeblood of War, Logistics in Armed Conflict* (London: Brassey's Defence Publishers, 1991).

First World War logistics and transportation

It is impossible to study First World War logistics without also considering transportation: the two are linked. The difficulties inherent in moving things a century ago – cumbersome packaging materials and the requirement that manpower move almost everything on and off of the means of transportation ensures this. Further, the fact that two of the Great Powers involved in the fighting in Western Europe fielded armies at the ends of an overseas supply line means that one cannot divorce transportation and logistics. Those interested in the concept of maritime power should read Kennedy's work and particularly Keith Neilson's chapter therein entitled 'Reinforcements and supplies from overseas: British strategic sealift in the First World War'. Fayle first tried to put some numbers to the scope of Britain's pre-war maritime dominance, but Lambert's recently published work shows it to have been even more pronounced than Fayle understood. If one is curious about just how vastly shipping changed over the course of the twentieth century, then Cudahy's work provides a very useful overview. On land, railways were and remain the most economical way to move large quantities of materiel over significant distances. There are numerous works that study railways, but most do not also consider logistic questions. Wolmar's work is extremely useful in this regard, covering the entire period from the middle of the nineteenth century through the twentieth, with extensive coverage of the First World War and providing the most useful single volume on railways and warfare. In terms of the First World War specifically, Brown examines how the British Expeditionary Force (BEF) managed to expand its infrastructure in France to support a continental commitment and Zabecki provides excellent additional context for examining some of the logistic lessons of 1918. Heniker's volume of the official history remains invaluable, and *Statistics of the Military Effort of the British Empire during the Great War* is an extraordinary resource for anyone who is looking for numbers.

Works to consult are: Ian M. Brown, *British Logistics on the Western Front, 1914–1919* (Westport, CT: Praeger, 1998); Brian J. Cudahy, *Box Boats: How Container Ships Changed the World* (New York: Fordham University Press, 2006); W. J. K. Davies, *Light Railways of the First World War: A History of Tactical Rail Communication on the British Battlefronts, 1914–1918*

(Newton Abbot: David and Charles, 1967); Charles Ernest Fayle, *The War and the Shipping Industry* (London: Oxford University Press, 1927); Paul G. Halpern, *A Naval History of World War I* (Annapolis, MD: Naval Institute Press, 1994); James A. B. Hamilton, *Britain's Railways in World War I* (London: Allen & Unwin, 1967); Alan M. Heniker, *Transportation on the Western Front, 1914–18* (London: HMSO, 1937); Paul Kemp, *Convoy Protection: The Defence of Seaborne Trade* (London: Arms and Armor Press, 1993); Greg Kennedy (ed.), *The Merchant Marine in International Affairs, 1850–1950* (London: Frank Cass, 2000); Nicholas A. Lambert, *Planning Armageddon: British Economic Warfare and the First World War* (Cambridge, MA: Harvard University Press, 2012); Edwin A. Pratt, *British Railways and the Great War: Organisation, Efforts, Difficulties and Achievements*, 2 vols. (London: Selwyn and Blount, 1921); Kaushik Roy, 'From defeat to victory: logistics of the campaign in Mesopotamia, 1914–1918', *First World War Studies*, 1:1 (2010), pp. 35–55; War Office, *Statistics of the Military Effort of the British Empire during the Great War, 1914–1920* (London: HMSO, 1922); Christian Wolmar, *Engines of War: How Wars Were Won and Lost on the Railways* (New York: Public Affairs, 2010); and David Zabecki, *The German 1918 Offensives: A Case Study in the Operational Level of War* (London: Routledge, 2006).

Official histories, government records, service and branch histories

Most official histories cover logistic and administrative issues sparingly, preferring to focus on tactical and operational issues. All should be examined, including Second World War studies, although logistic information can be deeply buried.

See the following: Jonathan B. A. Bailey, *Field Artillery and Firepower* (Annapolis, MD: Naval Institute Press, 2004); Henry Eccles, *Logistics in the National Defense* (Harrisburg, PA: Stackpole, 1959); James E. Edmonds, *Military Operations: France and Belgium, 1914–1919*, 14 vols. (London: HMSO, 1922–48); John W. Fortescue, *The Royal Army Service Corps: A History of Transportation and Supply in the British Army*, 2 vols. (Cambridge University Press, 1931); John Starling and Ivor Lee, *No Labour, No Battle: Military Labour during the First World War* (Stroud, UK: Spellmount, 2009); US Department of the Army, Historical Division, *United States Army in the World War 1917–1919*, 17 vols. (Washington, DC: Center of Military History, 1948).

Other histories

There is a plethora of works available covering the First World War. Some less well-known but extremely useful studies include biographies of administrators such as Sir John Cowans and George Goethals. Grieves's work is a must-read for anyone with even a passing interest in how the BEF overcame its supply crisis during the Battle of the Somme. Nicholson offers an autobiographical account of the service in France in an administrative position. Chickering and Förster's compilation includes chapters that cover or touch significantly on logistics, although the value of the work is in its breadth. Finally, Avner Offer provides a fascinating look at the kind of strategic decision-making that impacts logistics, and David Stevenson's new volume is a brilliant look at the war's climactic year covering a wealth of topics, including logistics, in a brilliantly integrated manner.

These are the works to consult: Desmond Chapman-Huston and Owen Rutter, *General Sir John Cowans: The Quartermaster-General of the Great War* (London: Hutchinson, 1924); Roger Chickering and Stig Förster (eds.), *Great War, Total War: Combat and Mobilization on the Western Front, 1914–1918* (Washington, DC: German Historical Institute and Cambridge University Press, 2000); Keith Grieves, *Sir Eric Geddes: Business and Government in War and Peace* (Manchester University Press, 1989); W. N. Nicholson, *Behind the Lines: An Account of Administrative Staffwork in the British Army 1914–1918* (London: The Strong Oak Press with Tom Donovan Publishing, n.d., first published by Jonathan Cape, 1939); Avner Offer, *The First World War: An Agrarian Interpretation* (Oxford: Clarendon Press, 1989); David Stevenson, *With Our Backs to the Wall: Victory and Defeat in 1918* (Cambridge, MA: Belknap Press, 2011); Phyllis A. Zimmerman, *George W Goethals and the Reorganization of the US Army Supply System, 1917–1918* (College Station, TX: Texas A&M University Press, 1992).

10 Technology and armaments

Frédéric Guelton

The historiography of the Great War, written in successive waves, frequently has addressed technical questions with military implications. Nonetheless, this literature has limitations, in particular in treating the links and interactions between war and technology, but also between technology and strategy, tactics, the economy and so on. It neglects the role of men as actors, obstacles or accelerators of technological changes, defenders or adversaries of their introduction into armed forces.

In contrast, the historian is confronted with a wide array of research and micro-historical publications on each army, weapons system or article. These studies are intrinsically interesting, but lack contextualisation, and are limited in their utility due to their positivism. This applies to French and German scholarship, but happily there is more nuanced research in the Anglo-Saxon world.

These constraints limit this bibliography, presented in three parts. The first considers works with a wider time horizon than just the Great War. The second focuses on the war period, broadly conceived. The third presents works on the specific links between war, a service arm and technology.

General studies on war and technology

First, here are important works with a wider time horizon than just the Great War. Some have chapters on the war, some place the war in a broader context, as their titles indicate. Let us start with John Fuller and Charles Frederick, *Armament and History, A Study of the Influence of Armament on History from the Dawn of Classical Warfare to the Second World War* (London: Eyre & Spottiswoode, 1946, Da Capo Press, 1998). A classic work, dated perhaps, but important due to the clarity of its argument and the originality of its approach. Stephen Biddle, *Military Power: Explaining Victory and Defeat in Modern Battle* (Princeton University Press, 2004), p. 352, a key study focusing on recourse to technology, in producing new weapons; on industrial production, or arms used; and on their deployment, or organisation.

These are additional contributions: Max Boot, *War Made New: Technology, Warfare and the Course of History: 1500 to Today* (New York: Gotham Books, 2006); Stephen Chiabotti (ed.), *Tooling for War, Military Transformation in the Industrial Age* (Proceedings of the

Sixteenth Military History Symposium of the United States Air Force Academy, Chicago: Imprint, 1996); François Crouzet, *De la supériorité de l'Angleterre sur la France. L'économique et l'imaginaire,* XVIIe – XXe *siècle* (Paris: Perrin, 1985), p. 596; in English, *Britain Ascendant: Comparative Studies in Franco-British Economic History* (Cambridge University Press, 1990); Paul, M. Kennedy, 'Arms-races and the causes of war, 1850–1945', in Kennedy, *Strategy and Diplomacy, 1870–1945* (London: Eight Studies, 1983), pp. 163–77; Jean Kogej, *Economie et technologie, 1880–1945* (Paris: Ellipses, 1996); William H. McNeil, *The Pursuit of Power. Technology, Armed Force and Society since A.D. 1000* (University of Chicago Press, 1982); Pierre Pascallon (ed.), *La Guerre technologique en débat* (Paris: L'Harmattan, 2010); Christian Potholm, *Winning at War: Seven Keys to Military Victory throughout History* (Lanham, MD: Rowman & Littlefield, 2010); Philip Pugh, *The Cost of Sea Power. The Influence of Money on Naval Affairs from 1815 to the Present Day* (London: Conway Maritime Press, 1986); George Raudzens, 'War-winning weapons: the measurement of technological determinism in military history', *Journal of Military History*, 54 (1990), pp. 403–33; Martin L. van Creveld, *Supplying War: Logistics from Wallenstein to Patton* (Cambridge University Press, 1980, 2004); and his *Technology and War, from 2000 BC to the Present* (London and New York: Free Press, 1989, 1991).

General works on the Great War and technology

The works cited here deal directly with the First World War. Most have clear chronologies and avoid focusing on only one weapon, category or technology: Guy Hartcup, *The War of Invention; Scientific Developments, 1914–18*, 1st edn (London: Brassey's Defence Publishers, 1988), p. 226. One of the most complete treatments of the use of science and technology by the belligerents is David G. Herrmann, *The Arming of Europe and the Making of the First World War* (Princeton University Press, 1997), which is a study with much of interest to say on arms production and the road to war. Dennis Showalter, 'Mass warfare and the impact of technology', in Chickering and Förster, *Great War, Total War*. In chapter 4, the author discusses the links between technology and national armies. Other chapters are useful, in particular, chapter 5 on the chemical war, chapter 11 on strategic bombing, and chapters 17 and 20 on economic and financial questions.

There is useful material as well in the following works: Bill Rawling, *Survivre aux tranchées, l'armée canadienne et la technologie, 1914–1918* (Outremont, Québec: Éditions Athéna, 2004); Claude Carlier and Guy Pedroncini (eds.), *1916 L'Émergence des armes nouvelles, actes du colloque* (Paris: Économica, Hautes Études militaires 4, 1997); CERMA, Cahiers d'études et de recherches du musée de l'Armée, *1904–1914 de la guerre pensée à la guerre sur le terrain, techniques, tactiques, pratiques* (Paris: Musée de l'Armée, DRHAP, No. 5, 2004); François Crouzet, 'Recherches sur la production d'armements en France, 1815–1913', *Revue historique*, 509 (1974), pp. 45–84; and by the same author, 'Remarques sur l'industrie des armements en France du milieu du XIXe siècle à 1914', *Revue historique*, 510 (1974), pp. 409–22; Antulio J. Echevarria, 'The "cult of the offensive" revisited: confronting technological change before the Great War', *Journal of Strategic Studies*, 25:1 (2002), pp. 199–214; Michael Epkenhans, 'Grossindustrie und schlachtflottenbau, 1897–1914', *Militärgeschichtliche Mitteilungen*, 22:1 (1988), pp. 65–140; Gerhard Schneider, *Der Erste Weltkrieg als erste industrialisierter Krieg* (Schwalbach am Taurus: Wochenschau-Verlag, 2003); Gerd Hardach, 'Mobilisation industrielle en 1914–1918, production, planification, idéologie', in Patrick

Fridenson and Jean-Jacques Becker (eds.), '1914–1918, L'autre front', *Cahier du Mouvement social*, 2 (1977), 82–101; Holger H. Herwig, 'The dynamics of necessity, German military policy during the First World War', in Allan R. Millet and Murray Williamson (eds.), *Military Effectiveness*, vol. 1, *The First World War* (Boston, MA: Unwin Hyman, 1989), pp. 80–115; Hubert C. Johnson, *Breakthrough! Tactics, Technology and the Search for Victory on the Western Front in World War I* (Novato, CA: Presidio Press, 1994); Gerd Krumeich, *Armaments and Politics in France on the Eve of the First World War. The Introduction of Three-Year Conscription, 1913–1914* (Leamington Spa: Berg, 1984); Hans Linnenkohl, *Vom Einzelschuß zur Feuerwalze: Der Wettlauf zwischen Technik und Taktik im Ersten Weltkrieg* (Bonn: Bernhard und Graefe, 1996); Jonathan Shimshoni, 'Technology, military advantage, and World War I: a case for military entrepreneurship', *International Security*, 15:3 (1990–1), pp. 187–215; Dennis, E. Showalter, 'Army and society in imperial Germany: the pain of modernization', *Journal of Contemporary History*, 18:4 (1983), pp. 583–618; Tim Travers, *How the War Was Won: Command and Technology in the British Army on the Western Front, 1917–1918* (London: Routledge, 1992); and by the same author *The Killing Ground*; Clive Trebilcock, 'Legends of the British armaments industry, 1890–1914: a revision', *Journal of Contemporary History*, 5:4 (1970), pp. 3–19; Michael D. Wallace, 'Arms races and escalation: some new evidence', *Journal of Conflict Resolution*, 23:1 (1979), pp. 3–16.

Some other essential works on the Great War and technology

This list is limited to indicate some important works in a well-populated field: Anthony Saunders, *Weapons of the Trench War, 1914–1918* (Stroud, UK: Sutton, 2000); David J. Childs, *A Peripheral Weapon? The Production and Employment of British Tanks in the First World War* (Westport, CT: Greenwood Press, 1999); John Ellis, *The Social History of the Machine-Gun* (Baltimore, MD: Johns Hopkins University Press, 1975); Holger H. Herwig, *'Luxury' Fleet, The Imperial German Navy, 1888–1918* (London: Prometheus Books, 1987); Lee Kennett, *La première guerre aérienne, 1917–1918* (Paris: Economica, 2005); Olivier Lepick, *La Grande Guerre chimique, 1914–1918* (Paris: Presses Universitaires de France, 1998); Jon Tetsuro Sumida, *In Defence of Naval Supremacy: Finance, Technology and British Naval Policy, 1889–1914* (London: Routledge, 1993); Gary E. Weir, 'Building the Kaiser's navy', in *The Imperial Naval Office and German Industry in the von Tirpitz Era 1890–1919* (Annapolis, MD: Naval Institute Press, 1992).

11 Prisoners of war

Heather Jones

Until the 1990s, the historiography of prisoners of war in the Great War was not well developed. Captivity in the Western powers had been largely ignored since 1939, overshadowed by the experience of the Second World War, while captivity on the Eastern Front had been predominantly researched in terms of how prisoners of war had engaged with communism. East German, Hungarian and Soviet historians had looked at the role of prisoners in the rise of communism post 1917, while Austrian historians had considered how repatriated prisoners had supported socialist and communist movements. However, in the 1990s with the fall of the Berlin wall and access to new source materials, as well as the advent of cultural history, interest in prisoners of war grew. In particular, a number of new monographs were published that showed the extent to which captivity was central to the war and which challenged the idea that prisoners were largely well treated in the conflict, a myth that stemmed from an over-reliance in some interwar histories on officers' accounts of life in officers' camps. However, much of the new historiography on prisoners of war is in German and French; English language studies remain under-represented in the field.

Among the key pioneering works from the new historiography on prisoners is Odon Abbal, *Soldats Oubliés: Les prisonniers de guerre français* (Bez-et-Esparon: Études et Communication éditions, 2001). This is a detailed study of the experience of prisoners from a region of the south of France who were captured by Germany. The same author has written 'Un combat d'aprés-guerre: le statut des prisonniers', *Revue du Nord*, 80:325 (1998), pp. 405–16, an excellent discussion of the post-war campaign by French ex-prisoners to be treated the same as veterans who had not been captured. See also his 'Santé et captivité: le traitement des prisonniers français dans les hopitaux allemands', in *Actes du Colloque 'Forces Armées et société'* (Montpellier: Centre d'histoire militaire et d'études de défense nationale, 1987), pp. 273–83, and 'Le Maghreb et la Grande Guerre: les camps d'internement en Afrique du Nord', in Jean-Charles Jouffret (ed.), *Les Armes et la Toge, Mélanges offerts à André Martel* (Montpellier: Centre d'histoire militaire et d'études de défense nationale, 1997), pp. 623–35. Annette Becker, *Oubliés de la Grande Guerre: humanitaire et culture de guerre, 1914–1918: populations occupées, déportés civils, prisonniers dc guerre* (Paris: Noêsis, 1998), is an outstanding study of French prisoners of war and civilian internees in Germany as well as in the German-occupied zones of France, which pioneered the cultural history of prisoners of war and revealed the extent of prisoner mistreatment in Germany. Becker argues aspects of Great War captivity pointed to developments that would occur in the Second World War.

Additional scholarship includes: Sylvie Caucanas, Rémy Cazals and Pascal Payen (eds.), *Les Prisonniers de Guerre dans l'Histoire. Contacts entre peuples et cultures* (Toulouse: Privat, 2003); and Gerald H. Davis, 'Prisoners of war in twentieth century war economies', *Journal of Contemporary History*, 12 (1977), pp. 623–34. This is a key attempt to analyse the impact of prisoner labour from an economic perspective. It is particularly valuable on the Eastern Front. See also his 'National Red Cross societies and prisoners of war in Russia, 1914–1918', *Journal of Contemporary History*, 28:1 (1993), pp. 31–52.

Uta Hinz, *Gefangen im Großen Krieg. Kriegsgefangenschaft in Deutschland, 1914–1921* (Essen: Klartext Verlag, 2006), is the first detailed monograph study of the treatment of prisoners of war of all nationalities in Germany during the Great War. Hinz argues that only limited radicalisation of captivity occurred, driven by labour needs. Robert Jackson, *The Prisoners 1914–1918* (London: Routledge, 1989), is an overview of prisoners' experiences based solely on sources from the Imperial War Museum. Heather Jones, *Violence against Prisoners of War in the First World War: Britain, France and Germany, 1914–1920* (Cambridge University Press, 2011), is the first study to compare violence against prisoners in captivity in Germany, France and Britain and the first to highlight the significance of prisoner-of-war labour companies working for captor armies at or near the front. See also her 'Imperial captivities: colonial prisoners of war in Germany and the Ottoman empire, 1914–1918', in Santanu Das (ed.), *Race, Empire and First World War Writing* (Cambridge University Press, 2011), pp. 177–8. This chapter highlights the mistreatment of prisoners of war after the siege of Kut-al-Amara and explores the role of 'race' as a factor in determining captivity experience in Germany in the Great War. See also Alan Kramer, 'Prisoners in the First World War', in Sibylle Scheipers (ed.), *Prisoners in War* (Oxford University Press, 2010).

An essential work is Alon Rachamimov, *POWs and the Great War. Captivity on the Eastern Front* (Oxford and New York: Berg, 2002). This is a key study that examines how Austro-Hungarian prisoners understood their national identity and the first study to use censorship records of prisoners' letters. Rachamimov argues that Great War captivity was closer to nineteenth-century practices than 1939 to 1945.

Hannes Leidinger, 'Gefangenschaft und Heimkehr: Gedanken zu Voraussetzungen und Perspektiven eines neuen Forschungsbereiches', *Zeitgeschichte* (Austria), 25:11–12 (1998), pp. 333–42, is a valuable article that sets out the historiographical transition that has occurred in the study of prisoners of war on the Eastern Front since the fall of communism. See, too: Verena Moritz, *Zwischen allen Fronten. Die russischen Kriegsgefangenen in Österreich im Spannungsfeld von Nutzen und Bedrohung, 1914–1921*, published PhD dissertation (Vienna: University of Vienna, 2001); and Reinhard Nachtigal, *Kriegsgefangenschaft an der Ostfront 1914 bis 1918* (Frankfurt am Main: Peter Lang, 2005). This is an excellent overview of captivity on the Eastern Front during the war. In the same field, Reinhard Nachtigal, *Russland und seine österreichisch-ungarischen Kriegsgefangenen (1914–1918)* (Remshalden: Verlag Bernhard Albert Greiner, 2003) – a detailed, comprehensive and well-researched study of the treatment of Austro-Hungarian prisoners of war in Russia. See also his three articles: 'Seuchen unter militärischer aufsicht in Rußland: das Lager Tockoe als Beispiel für die behandlung der Kriegsgefangenen 1915/16', *Jahrbücher für Geschichte Osteuropas*, 48 (2000), 363–87; 'Seuchenbekämpfung als Probleme der russischen Staatsverwaltung: Prinz Alexander von Oldenburg und die Kriegsgefangenen der Mittelmächte', *Medizinhistorisches Journal*, 39 (2004), pp. 135–63; and 'The repatriation and reception of returning prisoners of war, 1918–22', *Immigrants and Minorities*, 26:1/2 (2008), pp. 157–84.

See as well Jochen Oltmer (ed.), *Kriegsgefangene im Europa des Ersten Weltkriegs* (Paderborn: Ferdinand Schöningh, 2006). This is a valuable collection of essays by a selection of leading prisoner-of-war experts. A general work on this subject is Rüdiger Overmans (ed.), *In der Hand des Feindes. Kriegsgefangenschaft von der Antike bis zum Zweiten Weltkrieg* (Cologne, Weimar, Vienna: Böhlau Verlag, 1999). See also the same author's '"Hunnen" und "Untermenschen" – deutsche und russisch/sowjetische Kriegsgefangenschaftserfahrungen im Zeitalter der Weltkriege', in Bruno Thoss and Hans-Erich Volkmann (eds.), *Erster Weltkrieg – Zweiter Weltkrieg. Ein Vergleich: Krieg, Kriegserlebnis, Kriegserfahrung in Deutschland* (Paderborn: Ferdinand Schöningh, 2002), pp. 335–65. This is an important, innovative chapter that sets out the differences between captivity in Germany and Russia in the two world wars.

Further research in different national contexts is available in: Rainer Pöppinghege, *Im Lager unbesiegt. Deutsche, englische und französische Kriegsgefangenen-Zeitungen im Ersten Weltkrieg* (Essen: Klartext Verlag, 2006); Giovanna Procacci, *Soldati e prigionieri italiani nella Grande guerra* (Turin: Bollati Boringhieri, 2000); Kai Rawe, *'... wir werden sie schon zur Arbeit bringen!' Ausländerbeschäftigung und Zwangsarbeit im Ruhrkohlenbergbau während des Ersten Weltkrieges* (Essen: Klartext Verlag, 2005); Richard B. Speed III, *Prisoners, Diplomats and the Great War: A Study in the Diplomacy of Captivity* (New York and London: Greenwood Press, 1990). Adopting a diplomatic history approach, this book is nevertheless a good general overview of the treatment of prisoners of war in multiple belligerent states. Mark Spoerer, 'The mortality of Allied prisoners of war and Belgian civilian deportees in

German custody during World War I: a reappraisal of the effects of forced labour', *Population Studies*, 60:2 (2006), pp. 121–36, is a key study that uses statistical analysis to correlate death rates for prisoners by nationality with length of time in captivity. It shows that British prisoners had a very high death rate in Germany given that the majority of them spent only a short time overall in captivity. See, too, Matthew Stibbe (ed.), *Captivity, Forced Labour and Forced Migration in Europe during the First World War* (London: Routledge, 2009). Still useful is Samuel R. Williamson Jnr and Peter Pastor (eds.), *Essays on World War One: Origins and Prisoners of War* (New York: Columbia University Press, 1983). This is a book that pioneered the study of prisoner-of-war treatment on the Eastern Front and which gives a good political overview.

On surrender and on prisoner killing on the battlefield, see: Bourke, *An Intimate History of Killing*; Brian Feltman, 'The British treatment of prisoners of war on the Western Front', *War in History*, 17 (2010), pp. 435–58; Ferguson, *The Pity of War*; Niall Ferguson, 'Prisoner taking and prisoner killing in the age of total war: towards a political economy of military defeat', *War in History*, 11:2 (2004), pp. 148–92. Ferguson's is an interesting article that uses economic history methodologies applied to surrender patterns to discuss the impact surrender had upon the outcome of the war. See, too, Jahr, *Gewöhnliche Soldaten*; Edgar Jones, 'The pyschology of killing: the combat experience of British soldiers during the First World War', *Journal of Contemporary History*, 41 (2006), pp. 229–46. Watson, *Enduring the Great War*, contains a very valuable discussion as to why German units surrendered in 1918, arguing that junior officers were key to this process.

For official interwar sources, see: Hans Weiland and Leopold Kern (eds.), *In Feindeshand: Die Gefangenschaft im Weltkriege in Einzeldarstellungen*, 2 vols. (Vienna: Bundesvereinigung der ehemaligen österreischischen Kriegsgefangenen, 1931). This is an Austrian-based attempt to write an interwar global history of prisoners of war in the Great War. Although it attempts to be objective, this study tends to focus on German speakers' experiences. See also: Wilhelm Doegen, *Kriegsgefangene Völker*, vol. 1, *Der Kriegsgefangenen Haltung und Schicksal in Deutschland, Bearbeitet in verbindung mit Theodor Kappstein und hrsg. im amtlichen Auftrage des Reichswehrministeriums* (Berlin: D. Reimer, 1919 [1921]). This is a very pro-German history, but one which had access to the Prussian military archives later destroyed in the Second World War and thus contains key information and statistics.

On escapes, see Simon P. Mackenzie, 'The ethics of escape: British officer POWs in the First World War', *War in History*, 15:1 (2008), pp. 1–16.

12 War economies

Barry Supple

The underlying elements of mobilisation for a war of unprecedented scale are presented in: Kevin D. Stubbs, *Race to the Front: The Material Foundations of Coalition Strategy in the Great War* (London: Praeger, 2002); and Roger Chickering and Stig Förster, *Great War, Total War: Combat and Mobilization on the Western Front, 1914–1918* (Cambridge University Press, 2000).

Useful summary views of the varied economic issues and aspects of the war are contained in: Gerald Feldman, 'Mobilizing economies for war', in Jay Winter, Geoffrey Parker and Mary R. Habeck (eds.), *The Great War and the Twentieth Century* (New Haven, CT: Yale

University Press, 2000); and the essay on the changing historiography of the economic aspects of the war in 'Businessmen, industrialists, and bankers: how was the economic war waged?', in Jay Winter and Antoine Prost (eds.), *The Great War in History: Debates and Controversies, 1914 to the Present* (Cambridge University Press, 2005).

A somewhat more elaborate treatment of the economics of the war, covering individual countries as well as international and general topics, is Stephen Broadberry and Mark Harrison, *Economics of World War I* (Cambridge University Press, 1998), which deals analytically as well as empirically with its economic processes and macroeconomic features.

A contrast, from an earlier period, is the vast (132-volume) *Economic and Social History of the World War*, published by the Carnegie Endowment for International Peace from the early 1920s. Much of its empirical detail is overwhelming, and the quality is uneven, but it remains an invaluable repository of information concerning the sources for and details of government control and economic activity and outcomes – both generally and in individual countries (those peripheral to the war as well as the principal combatants). Two examples of particularly useful studies are: the volumes on the collapse of the Russian economy and society – Michael T. Florinsky, *The End of the Russian Empire* (Oxford and New Haven, CT: Yale University Press, Carnegie Endowment for International Peace, Economic and Social History of the World War, 1931); and on the control mechanism adopted in the United Kingdom – Edward M. H. Lloyd, *Experiments in State Control at the War Office and the Ministry of Food* (Oxford: Clarendon Press, 1924). In each case there are various volumes on the relevant country.

The Carnegie series also deals at length with particular aspects of economic activity – for example, in Fayle, *The War and the Shipping Industry*.

A vital perspective on the international financial and therefore economic impact of the war can be found in Barry Eichengreen, *Golden Fetters: The Gold Standard and the Great Depression, 1919–1939* (Oxford University Press, 1992). This can be compared with the dire warnings about the economic costs of international war in Norman Angell's early classic *The Great Illusion: A Study of the Relation of Military Power in Nations to Their Economic and Social Advantage* (London: Heinemann, 1910). Another distinctive perspective on the con-iflict is Avner Offer, *The First World War, An Agrarian Interpretation* (Oxford: Clarendon Press, 1989).

Demographic aspects of the war and its impact on civilian life in various countries are considered in Winter, *The Great War and the British People*; Jay Winter and Jean-Louis Robert (eds.), *Capital Cities at War: London, Paris, Berlin, 1914–1919* (Cambridge University Press, 1997); Kocka, *Facing Total War*; Fridenson, *French Home Front*; and David M. Kennedy, *Over Here: The First World War and American Society* (New York: Oxford University Press, 2004).

Mechanisms of market control and industrial policies are discussed in E. M. H. Lloyd's volume on experiments in state control (already cited); Feldman, *Army, Industry, and Labor*; John F. Godfrey, *Capitalism at War: Industrial Policy and Bureaucracy in France, 1914–1918* (Leamington Spa: Berg, 1987); Gerd Hardach, 'Industrial mobilization in 1914–1918: production, planning and ideology', in Fridenson, *French Home Front*; and Chris J. Wrigley, *David Lloyd George and the British Labour Movement: Peace and War* (Hassocks: Harvester, 1976).

The impact of the war in individual countries is considered in some of the foregoing publications. In addition, general national perspectives are also available in: Chickering, *Imperial Germany and the Great War, 1914–1918*; Peter Gatrell, *Russia's First World War: An*

Economic and Social History (Harlow: Pearson Longman, 2005); and Kathleen Burk (ed.), *War and the State: The Transformation of British Government, 1914–1919* (London: Allen & Unwin, 1982). A contrast to the established interpretation of Germany's ultimate wartime economic frailty can be found in Niall Ferguson, *The Pity of War* (New York: Basic Books, 1999).

Adaptations of business structures and associations are considered in various of the foregoing national studies, and can be supplemented by Keith Middlemas, *Politics in Industrial Society: The Experience of the British System since 1911* (London: Andre Deutsch, 1979).

Examples of contemporaneous discussion by economists of the implications of the wartime experience for the role of the state are: Arthur C. Pigou, *The Political Economy of War* (London: Macmillan, 1921); and John M. Clark, 'The basis of wartime collectivism', *American Economic Review*, 7:4 (1917), pp. 772–90. An example of official consideration of such issues is in the 'Final report of the committee on commercial and industrial policy after the war' (Cd. 9035, 1918, XIII).

Comparisons of the impact of the two world wars of the twentieth century are in Broadberry and Harrison, *Economics of World War I* and Alan S. Milward, *The Economic Effects of the Two World Wars on Britain* (London: Macmillan, 1984).

13 Workers

Antoine Prost

The story of workers during the war was a central focus for the historians of the 1970s to 1980s. Léopold H. Haimson helped to organise international research on strikes which was presented in two very extensive volumes, partly quantitative: one written with Charles Tilly, *Strikes, Wars and Revolutions in an International Perspective* (Cambridge and Paris: Cambridge University Press and Éditions de la MSH, 1989); the other edited together with Giulio Sapelli, *Strikes, Social Conflict and the First World War. An International Perspective* (Milan: Feltrinelli, 1992). Jay Winter has similarly edited comparative collective works: with Richard Wall, *The Upheaval of War. Family, Work and Welfare in Europe 1914–1918* (Cambridge University Press, 1988); and with Jean-Louis Robert, *Capital Cities at War. London, Paris, Berlin 1914–1919* (Cambridge University Press, 1997). But the first systematic comparison is John Horne's book, derived from his doctoral thesis: *Labour at War. France and Britain 1914–1918* (Oxford: Clarendon Press, 1991).

Comparisons are sometimes weakened by lack of precision in their concepts. The contributions from economists assembled by Broadberry and Harrison, *Economics of World War I*, do not suffer from this drawback, but are much less substantial than the works cited above. Finally, we should draw attention to a general article: Carmen J. Sirianni, 'Workers' control in the era of the First World War. A comparative analysis of the European experience', *Theory and Society*, 9:1 (1980), pp. 29–88.

National studies are variable. The case of Britain has been the subject of several works, including particularly James Hinton, *The First Shop Steward's Movement* (London: Allen & Unwin, 1973), analysed by Alastair Reid in his contribution 'Dilution, trade unionism and the state in Britain during the First World War', in Steven Tolliday and Jonathan Zeitlin (eds.), *Shop Floor Bargaining and the State* (Cambridge University Press, 1985), pp. 46–74. Other studies relocate the history of the workers in that of society as a whole. Leading works in this tradition include Bernard Waites, *A Class Society at War. England 1914–1918* (Leamington Spa: Berg, 1987); Arthur Marwick, *The Deluge. British Society and the First World War*, 2nd edn (London: Macmillan, 1991); and Chris Wrigley, *David Lloyd George and the British Labour Movement. Peace and War* (Hassock and New York: Harvester and Barnes & Noble, 1976).

The same global perspective reappears in the two essential works on Germany: Jürgen Kocka, *Facing Total War. German Society 1914–1918* (Leamington Spa and Cambridge MA: Berg and Harvard University Press, 1984); and Gerald D. Feldman, *Army Industry and Labor in Germany, 1914–1918* (Oxford and Providence: Berg, 1992; 1st edn – Princeton University Press, 1966). To these can be added monographs on cities, such as Sean Dobson, *Authority and Upheaval in Leipzig, 1910–1920* (New York: Columbia University Press, 2001); and Mary Nolan, *Social-Democracy and Society. Working-Class Radicalism in Düsseldorf, 1890–1920* (Cambridge University Press, 2002).

For France, apart from the pioneering articles gathered by Patrick Fridenson (ed.), *1914–1918: l'autre front* (Paris: Éditions Ouvrières, 1977) (*Cahier du Mouvement social* no. 2), the only extensive work is the thesis by Jean-Louis Robert on workers and the conditions of working life in the Paris region during the war. Parts of this major work are published in his book, *Les Ouvriers, la Patrie et la Révolution. Paris 1914–1918* (Besançon: Annales littéraires de l'Université de Besançon no. 392, série historique no. 11, 1995). This book highlights the factual narrative aspects of his work, leaving out the important socio-anthropological approach which governs his *these d'état*.

Peter Gatrell, *Russia's First World War: A Social and Economic History* (Harlow: Pearson/ Longman, 2005), gives the general framework of Russian developments. The Petrograd workers have been covered by David Mandel in his two books, *The Petrograd Workers and the Fall of the Old Regime: From the February Revolution to the July Days, 1917*, and *The Petrograd Workers and the Soviet Seizure of Power: From the July Days to July 1918* (London: Macmillan, 1983 and 1984). Those of Moscow have been covered by Diane P. Koenker, *Moscow Workers and the 1917 Revolution* (Princeton University Press, 1981). We should not overlook the books by Haimson already cited.

The bibliography for Italy is thinner. We have the contributions published by Haimson, and the collective work edited by Giovanna Procacci, *Stato e classe operaia in Italia durante la primo guerre mondiale* (Milan: Franco Angeli, 1983). For Austria-Hungary, as well as Francis L. Carsten's *Revolutions in Central Europe, 1918–1919* (London: Temple Smith, 1972), we should mention the article by Hans Hauptmann, 'Vienna: a city in the years of radical change', in Chris Wrigley (ed.), *Challenges of Labour. Central and Western Europe 1917–1920* (London and New York: Routledge, 1993), pp. 87–104.

Finally, the development of gender studies has brought us some original works on female labour: Angela Woollacott, *On Her Their Lives Depend. Munition Workers in the Great War* (Berkeley, CA: University of California Press, 1994); Laura Lee Downs, *Manufacturing Inequality: Gender Division in the French and British Metalworking Industries, 1914–1939* (Ithaca, NY: Cornell University Press, 1995); French translation: *L'inégalité à la chaîne. La division sexuée du travail dans l'industrie métallurgique en France et en Grande-Bretagne* (Paris: A. Michel, 2002); or Ute Daniel, *The War from Within, German Working-Class Women in the First World War* (Oxford and New York: Berg, 1997).

14 Cities

Stefan Goebel

The urban history of total war is an emerging field of historical enquiry, bringing into dialogue urban studies with military history. For an introduction to the historiography, see Stefan Goebel and Derek Keene, 'Towards a metropolitan history of total war: an introduction', in Goebel and Keene (eds.), *Cities into Battlefields: Metropolitan Scenarios, Experiences and Commemorations of Total War* (Farnham: Ashgate, 2011), pp. 1–46. Some of the most innovative works in this field have appeared in the series *Studies in the Social and Cultural History of the Great War*, in particular Jay Winter and Jean-Louis Robert (eds.), *Capital Cities at War: Paris, London, Berlin 1914–1919*, 2 vols. (Cambridge University Press, 1997–2007), a polygraph produced by a team of scholars from Britain, France, Germany and the United States. While the first volume charts the social relations of sacrifice, labour, incomes, consumption and health, volume II takes the reader on a virtual tour of metropolitan sites from the railway stations to the cemeteries.

Jean-Louis Robert, the French co-editor, is the leading expert on wartime Paris and its revolutionary workers. A digest of his unpublished 1989 thesis appeared under the title *Les Ouvriers, la Patrie et la Révolution: Paris 1914–1919* (Paris: Les Belles Lettres, 1995). Another collaborator in the *Capital Cities* project published subsequently a history of British society during the Great War: Adrian Gregory, *The Last Great War: British Society and the First World War* (Cambridge University Press, 2008) is a general survey, but with a strong urban focus.

Arguing that 'total war requires total history', Roger Chickering has produced a magisterial history of a German town: *The Great War and Urban Life in Germany: Freiburg, 1914–1918* (Cambridge University Press, 2007) covers (nearly) everything from civic administration to the smells and sounds of the wartime city. Less comprehensive but equally significant is Healy, *Vienna and the Fall of the Habsburg Empire*. Although not narrowly a work of gender history, Healy's book is especially attentive to the gendering of urban life in wartime. Martin Geyer's study of Munich, *Verkehrte Welt: Revolution, Inflation und Moderne, München 1914–1924* (Göttingen: Vandenhoeck & Ruprecht, 1998), focuses on the experience of a 'world turned upside down' in the era of inflation. He departs from the conventional periodisation, choosing 1924 as his cut-off point. Taken together, these works transcend the divide between social and cultural history, pointing towards a more integrative mode of historical research into cities at war.

Urban communities

The wartime fragmentation of urban society has received a great deal of attention from scholars. Traditionally, historians have focused on social classes, notably the working conditions and wages of labourers – for instance, Mary Nolan, *Social Democracy and Society: Working-Class Radicalism in Düsseldorf, 1890–1920* (Cambridge University Press, 1981). More recently, historians inspired by the cultural turn have highlighted the transformation of class conflict during the war. Belinda J. Davis analyses the reconfiguration of older social categories in patterns of gender and consumption in her study *Home Fires Burning: Food, Politics, and Everyday Life in World War I Berlin* (Chapel Hill, NC: University of

North Carolina Press, 2000). Similarly, Tyler Stovall, *Paris and the Spirit of 1919: Consumer Struggles, Transnationalism, and Revolution* (Cambridge University Press, 2012), charts how class antagonism was channelled into a consumer struggle spearheaded by women.

Social relations in occupied cities became dangerously strained, as Antoon Vrints's study of public violence and street politics in Antwerp shows: *Het theater van de straat: Publiek geweld in Antwerpen tijdens de eerste helft van de twintigste eeuw* (Amsterdam University Press, 2011). Compare this with the multi-ethnic and multi-religious cities of Eastern and South-Eastern Europe and Asia Minor where the war became a catalyst for the uprooting of entire communities. A number of important studies have adopted a longer-term perspective, placing the experience of the Great War within a broader historical context from the late nineteenth century to the end of the Second World War: Ulrike von Hirschhausen, *Die Grenzen der Gemeinsamkeit: Deutsche, Letten, Russen und Juden in Riga 1860–1914* (Göttingen: Vandenhoeck & Ruprecht, 2006); Christoph Mick, *Kriegserfahrung in einer multiethnischen Stadt: Lemberg 1914–1947* (Wiesbaden: Harrassowitz, 2010); Mark Mazower, *Salonica: City of Ghosts: Christians, Muslims and Jews 1430–1950* (London: Harper Perennial, 2005).

Propaganda spectacles and the media

The symbiosis between war propaganda and popular culture, which became a salient mark of the Great War, was pioneered in the large cities and rooted in urban civic culture. Indispensable is Winter and Robert, *Capital Cities at War*, vol. II, which contains chapters on metropolitan entertainments, exhibitions, schools and universities. Healy, *Vienna*, too, is pertinent to the study of the propaganda spectacle and media representation. The connections between war, theatre and the city are explored in: Martin Baumeister, *Kriegstheater: Großstadt, Front und Massenkultur 1914–1918* (Essen: Klartext Verlag, 2005); and Jan Rüger, 'Laughter and war in Berlin', *History Workshop Journal*, 67 (2009), pp. 23–43.

A comparative study of the public sphere in London and Berlin (with an emphasis on press censorship and rumours) is offered by Florian Altenhöner, *Kommunikation und Kontrolle: Gerüchte und städtische Öffentlichkeiten in Berlin und London 1914/1918* (Munich: R. Oldenbourg Verlag, 2008). His findings should be compared to Jovana Knežević, 'Reclaiming their city: Belgraders and the combat against Habsburg propaganda through rumours, 1915–18', in Goebel and Keene, *Cities into Battlefields*, pp. 101–18, who follow Healy's lead.

Commemorations

The 'memory boom' in historical studies has produced a number of works on urban forms of commemoration. Ken S. Inglis, 'Entombing unknown soldiers: from London and Paris to Baghdad', *History & Memory*, 5:2 (1993), pp. 7–31, focuses on the national war memorials in capital cities, while Mark Connelly, *The Great War, Memory and Ritual: Commemoration in the City and East London, 1916–1939* (Woodbridge: Boydell, 2002), examines commemorations at the neighbourhood level. Others have charted commemorative cityscapes, for instance the historical geographer Yvonne Whelan, *Reinventing Modern Dublin: Streetscape, Iconography and the Politics of Identity* (University College Dublin Press, 2003). A comparative approach, contrasting Paris and Berlin, is adopted by Élise Julien, *Paris, Berlin: La mémoire de la guerre 1914–1933* (Presses Universitaires de Rennes, 2009).

A yawning gap in the literature is the lack of studies of colonial cities at war, which Abigail Jacobson's lone *From Empire to Empire: Jerusalem between Ottoman and British Rule* (New York: Syracuse University Press, 2011) cannot fill.

15 Agrarian society

Benjamin Ziemann

The agrarian economy and rural society during the Great War are a much-neglected topic even for most of the major belligerent European countries, let alone neutral countries such as Switzerland, Spain or the smaller countries of the Balkans. For many countries, the respective volumes produced for the Carnegie Endowment on Peace in the 1920s for its series on the economic and social history of the war are still the state of the art or at least the major source of core information. For Austria-Hungary, compare Hans Loewenfeld-Russ, *Die Regelung der Volksernährung im Kriege* (Vienna: Holder, 1926); for France, Michel Augé-Laribé and Pierre Pinot, *Agriculture and Food Supply in France during the War* (New Haven, CT: Yale University Press, 1927); for Germany, Friedrich Aereboe, *Der Einfluß des Krieges auf die landwirtschaftliche Produktion in Deutschland* (Stuttgart: Deutsche Verlags-Anstalt, 1927); and for Italy, Arrigo Serpieri, *La guerra e le classi rurali italiane* (Rome: Laterza, 1930).

The most notable exception from this poor state of historiographical debate is Russia, where peasants were part and parcel of a seminal regime transformation in 1917, and for which Anglo-Saxon historians have produced a number of excellent studies on wartime social change in the countryside. Peter Gatrell, *Russia's First World War. A Social and Economic History* (Harlow: Longman, 2005) offers an accessible general account of economy and society in Russia during the war. A trailblazing study of the food economy in Russia is Lars T. Lih, *Bread and Authority in Russia, 1914–1921* (Berkeley, CA: University of California Press, 1992). The three most important regional studies on social transformation in the countryside are Holquist, *Making War, Forging Revolution*; Aaron Retish, *Russia's Peasants in Revolution and Civil War. Citizenship, Identity, and the Creation of the Soviet State, 1914–1922* (Cambridge University Press, 2008); and Sarah Badcock, *Politics and the People in Revolutionary Russia. A Provincial History* (Cambridge University Press, 2007). Highly pertinent is also the forthcoming book-length study by Mark Baker on Kharkiv province, some aspects of which have been previously released in article form.

Germany is comparatively well covered by two regional studies in English. There is an emphasis on agrarian politics and the Catholic Centre Party in the study by Robert G. Moeller, *German Peasants and Agrarian Politics, 1914–1924. The Rhineland and Westphalia* (Chapel Hill, NC and London: University of North Carolina Press, 1986). A study of social relations for both peasants at the home front and rural soldiers in southern Bavaria is Ziemann, *War Experiences in Rural Germany*. Some primary evidence on German rural soldiers and their relatives is documented in the source collection by Bernd Ulrich and Benjamin Ziemann (eds.), *The German Soldiers of the Great War. Letters and Eyewitness Accounts* (Barnsley: Pen & Sword Books, 2010).

The French historians of the Annales school have produced trailblazing books on medieval and early modern village societies in the Hexagon, yet on the First World

War we only have the older study by Henri Gerest, *Les populations rurales du Montbrisonnais et la Grande Guerre* (Saint Étienne: Centre d'Études Foréziennes, 1977). Key data are presented in the relevant sections of Michel Gervais, Marcel Jollivet and Yves Tavernier, *La fin de la France paysanne, de 1914 à nos jours*, vol. IV, *Histoire de la France rurale* (Paris: Seuil, 1976), pp. 44–55, 165–91, 531–42. The best English-language account of French society during the Great War, including chapters on popular sentiment, society and economy in the countryside, is still Jean-Jacques Becker, *The Great War and the French People* (Leamington Spa: Berg, 1985). For a fascinating study of the personal relationship between a French smallholder who served at the front and his wife, based on their war letters, see Martha Hanna, *Your Death Would Be Mine. Paul and Marie Pireaud in the Great War* (Cambridge, MA: Havard University Press, 2009). Changing social relations and social conflicts in the Italian countryside are covered in English language by two regional studies: Anthony L. Cardoza, *Agrarian Elites and Italian Fascism. The Province of Bologna, 1901–1926* (Princeton University Press, 1982); and Frank M. Snowden, *Violence and Great Estates in the South of Italy. Apulia, 1900–1922* (Cambridge University Press, 1986). The best comparative discussion of peasant parties in interwar Europe remains the edited collection by Heinz Gollwitzer (ed.), *Europäische Bauernparteien im 20. Jahrhundert* (Stuttgart: G. Fischer, 1977).

16 Finance

Hans-Peter Ullmann

Comparative studies on financing the First World War are rare. The analysis by Robert Knauss, *Die deutsche, englische und französische Kriegsfinanzierung* (Berlin: Walter de Gruyter, 1923), is still recommended reading. *Financing the First World War* (Oxford University Press, 2007) by Hew Strachan is one of the more recent works which must be mentioned. Alain Plessis, 'Financer la guerre', in Stéphane Audoin-Rouzeau and Jean-Jacques Becker (eds.), *Encyclopédie de la Grande Guerre* (Paris: Bayard, 2004), pp. 479–93, and Georges-Henri Soutou, 'Comment a été financée la guerre', in Paul-Marie de la Gorce (ed.), *La Première Guerre mondiale* (Paris: Flammarion, 1991), vol. I, pp. 281–97, provide a brief overview. Reference should also be made to the relevant passages in the books by Gerd Hardach, *Der Erste Weltkrieg* (Munich: Deutscher Taschenbuch Verlag, 1973), pp. 151 ff; and Niall Ferguson, *Der falsche Krieg* (Stuttgart: Deutsche Verlags-Anstalt, 1999), pp. 143 ff, 296 ff.

Important studies on the theory of war finance were published at the time of the two world wars, for example by Pigou, *Political Economy of War*; Horst Jecht, *Kriegsfinanzen* (Jena: Gustav Fischer, 1938); and Horst Mendershausen, *The Economics of War*, 2nd edn (New York: Prentice-Hall, 1943).

Estimates of war costs differ considerably. The most reliable surveys are those by Ernest L. Bogart, *Direct and Indirect Costs of the Great World War*, 2nd edn (New York: Oxford University Press, 1920); and also *War Costs and their Financing* (New York: D. Appleton and Co., 1921); and Harvey E. Fisk, *The Inter-Ally Debts* (New York: Bankers Trust Co., 1924).

Regarding inter-ally war debts, work published between the wars should be highlighted, especially that of Fisk, *Inter-Ally Debts*, and Harold G. Moulton and Leo Pasvolsky, *War Debts and World Prosperity* (Washington, DC: The Brookings Institution, 1932). From among more recent studies, Martin Horn, *Britain, France, and the Financing of the First World War* (Montreal: McGill-Queen's University Press, 2002) is recommended.

Public finances in the neutral and belligerent states have been researched in varying depth. Brief overviews can be found in selected articles in the book by Broadberry and Harrison, *Economics of World War I*. The studies on the various countries compiled by the Carnegie Endowment for International Peace and which were published (from 1911 to 1941) as part of eighteen national studies are still of interest. A general overview is available in Carnegie Endowment for International Peace (ed.), *Summary of Organization and Work 1911–1941* (Washington, DC: Carnegie Endowment for International Peace, 1941).

An in-depth study about the German Reich was written by Konrad Roesler in *Die Finanzpolitik des Deutschen Reiches im Ersten Weltkrieg* (Berlin: Duncker & Humblot, 1967). Hans-Peter Ullmann provides a short overview, *Der deutsche Steuerstaat* (Munich: C. H. Beck, 2005), pp. 88 ff.

Eduard März's relevant chapters on Austria-Hungary, *Österreichische Bankpolitik in der Zeit der großen Wende 1913–1923* (Munich: R. Oldenbourg Verlag, 1981) contain valuable information. Regarding less recent studies, Alexander Popovics, *Das Geldwesen im Kriege* (Vienna: Hölder-Pichler-Tempsky, 1925), and Wilhelm Winkler, *Die Einkommensverschiebungen in Österreich während des Weltkrieges* (Vienna: Hölder-Pichler-Tempsky, 1930) deserve mentioning.

There are numerous studies of varying quality on Great Britain. Essential early studies are: Adam W. Kirkaldy (ed.), *British Finance during and after the War 1914–21* (London: Sir Isaac Pitman & Sons, 1921); and E. Victor Morgan, *Studies in British Financial Policy, 1914–25* (London: Macmillan, 1952). An in-depth study of the Treasury is George C. Peden, *The Treasury and British Public Policy, 1906–1959* (Oxford University Press, 2000); on taxation, Martin Daunton, *Just Taxes* (Cambridge University Press, 2002); and on debt, Jeremy Wormell, *The Management of the National Debt of the United Kingdom, 1900–1932* (London: Routledge, 2000).

Among older studies about France, Henri Truchy, *Les Finances de Guerre de France* (Paris: Presses Universitaires de France, 1926) is essential, together with Gaston Jèze, *Les dépenses de guerre de la France* (Paris: Presses Universitaires de France, 1926). Lucien Petit, *Histoire des Finances extérieures de la France pendant la Guerre (1914–1919)* (Paris: Payot, 1929) examines foreign debt; Nicolas Delalande, *Les Batailles de l'Impôt* (Paris: Éditions du Seuil, 2011) examines tax policy.

Recommended literature on the United States are Charles Gilbert, *American Financing of World War I* (Westport, CT: Greenwood Press, 1970), as well as Paul Studenski and Herman E. Kroos, *Financial History of the United States*, 2nd edn (New York: McGraw-Hill, 1963). Michael Edelstein provides interesting comparisons with later wars in 'War and the American economy in the twentieth century', in Stanley L. Engerman and Robert E. Gallman (eds.), *The Cambridge Economic History of the United States*, vol. III (Cambridge University Press, 2000), pp. 329–405.

Among studies on the Netherlands particularly useful are: Marius Jacobus van der Flier, *War Finances in the Netherlands up to 1918* (Oxford: Clarendon Press, 1923); and Wantje Fritschy and René van der Voort, 'From fragmentation to unification: public finance, 1700–1914', in Marjolein 'T Hart, Joost Jonker and Jan Luiten van Zanden (eds.), *A Financial History of the Netherlands* (Cambridge University Press, 1997), pp. 64–93.

Research on the financial consequences of the First World War is extensive. The following provide an initial overview: Derek H. Aldcorft, *Die zwanziger Jahre* (Munich: Deutscher Taschenbuch Verlag, 1978); Charles S. Maier, *Recasting Bourgeois Europe* (Princeton University Press, 1975); and Dan P. Silverman, *Reconstructing Europe after the Great War* (Cambridge, MA: Harvard University Press, 1982). Gerald D. Feldman wrote an important study of inflation in Germany, *The Great Disorder* (Oxford University Press, 1996). Kenneth Mouré, *The Gold Standard Illusion* (Oxford University Press, 2002), informs us about the moderate inflation in France. Recommended literature on the deflationary politics in the United States, Great Britain and the Netherlands are: Studenski and Kroos, *Financial History*; Daunton, *Taxes*; and Jan Luiten van Zanden, 'Old rules, new conditions, 1914–1940', in Broadberry and Harrison, *Economics of World War I*, pp. 135 ff. The best overview on reparations can be found in Bruce Kent's *The Spoils of War* (Oxford: Clarendon Press, 1989). On the inter-ally war debts, see Denise Artaud, *La question des dettes interalliées et la reconstruction de l'Europe (1917–1929)*, 2 vols. (Paris: Librairie Honoré Champion, 1978). On inter-Allied coordination on all economic and financial issues, see John Godfrey, *Capitalism at War. Industrial Policy and Bureaucracy in France 1914–1918* (Leamington Spa: Berg, 1987). He offers much of interest on profits in chapter 7.

17 Scientists

Roy MacLeod

Only in the last decade can we see the emergence of comparative, international studies that will help calibrate the relative effects of continuities and change in science across cultures and societies at war. That is one goal. Another is to compare the effects of war on the different sciences, on different methods and mentalities, and on the ways in which institutions either recognise or fail to confront the ethical challenges that modern warfare increasingly presents. With these questions and much else that still forms 'work in progress', a start to understanding the changing roles of science, technology, government, industry and statecraft in the Great War can be made with the following sources.

Science and internationalism

The roles of 'scientific internationalism' and 'internationalism in science' have been studied extensively. For France, the history of national scientific competition was given a fresh start with Harry W. Paul, *The Sorcerer's Apprentice: The French Scientist's Image of German Science 1840–1919* (Gainesville, FL: University of Florida Press, 1972), with an emphasis that continues through Christophe Prochasson and Anne Rasmussen, *Au Nom de la Patrie: Les Intellectuals et la Première Guerre Mondiale (1910–1919)* (Paris: Éditions La

Découverte, 1996). In recent years, the growing interest in the politics of scientific non-combatants has been caught by Rebecka Lettevall, Geert Somsen and Sven Widmalm (eds.), *Neutrality in Twentieth Century Europe; Intersections of Science, Culture and Politics after the First World War* (London: Routledge, 2011). The largely Anglocentric account of wartime science that appears in Donald S. L. Cardwell, 'Science and World War I', *Proc. Royal Society of London*, A 342 (1975), pp. 447–56, has been revised and updated in Jon Agar, *Science in the Twentieth Century and Beyond* (London: Polity, 2012). An account of 'military intellectuals' can be found in Roy MacLeod, 'The scientists go to war: revisiting precept and practice, 1914–1919', *Journal of War and Culture Studies*, 2:1 (2009), pp. 37–51. Parts of the present chapter appeared originally in this issue, and acknowledgement is made to the publishers, *Intellect*, of Bristol.

Scientists militant

The lives of individual scientists caught up in the war have had less coverage, but at greater depth. Important examples are John Heilbron, *The Dilemmas of an Upright Man: Max Planck as Spokesman for German Science* (Berkeley, CA: University of California, 1986) and his *Ernest Rutherford and the Explosion of Atoms* (Oxford University Press, 2003) and John Campbell, *Rutherford: Scientist Supreme* (Christchurch: AAS Publications, 1999). An engaging account of academic and industrial chemists can be found in Gerald D. Feldman, 'A German scientist between illusion and reality: Emil Fischer, 1909–1919', in Imanuel Geiss and Bernd Jurgen Wendt (eds.), *Deutschland in der Weltpolitik des 19. und 20. Jahrnhunderts* (Düsseldorf: Bertelsmann Universitätsverlag, 1973), pp. 341–62. For the tragedy of Fritz Haber, see Margit Szöllösi-Janze, *Fritz Haber: 1868–1934: Eine Biographie* (Munich: C. H. Beck, 1998); Dietrich Stoltzenberg, *Fritz Haber: Chemist, Nobel Laureate, German, Jew* (Philadelphia, PA: Chemical Heritage Press, 2004); and Daniel Charles, *Between Genius and Genocide: The Tragedy of Fritz Haber, Father of Chemical Warfare* (London: Jonathan Cape, 2005).

For insight into Italy, see Judith R. Goodstein, 'The rise and fall of Vito Volterra's world', *Journal of the History of Ideas*, 45 (1984), pp. 607–17. For Russia, the scholar must begin with the life of General V. N. Ipat'ev, the central figure in wartime explosives, for whom there is no major biography. A start could be made with Lewis H. Siegelbaumn, *The Politics of Industrial Mobilization in Russia, 1914–17: A Study of the War-Industries Committees* (New York: St Martin's Press, 1983). See also Alexei Kojevikov, 'The Great War, the Russian Civil War and the invention of big science', *Science in Context*, 15:2 (2002), pp. 239–75. Remarkably, Alexander Vucinich's classic two-volume work on *Science in Russian Culture* (Stanford University Press, 1963, 1970) gives only a few pages to science during the war, while Loren Graham's *Science in Russia and the Soviet Union* (Cambridge University Press, 1993) almost entirely neglects the war. Possibly access to fresh archives in Moscow and St Petersburg will remedy this neglect.

For France, the list of scientists would include Marie Curie, for work with X-rays, but also many less well-known figures, such as M. G. A. Koehler, Marius-Daniel Marqueyrol, Henri Muraour, Gabrielle Bertrand and Charles Moureu, as well as noteworthy politicians like Albert Thomas, the socialist Minister of Munitions and Minister of Armament, who was (1915 to 1917) the Parisian counterpart of David Lloyd George, but whose work with science and industry has been far less appreciated. In

Germany, a similar role was played by Walther Rathenau, student of chemistry and physics, and first Director of the Raw Materials Department of the Kriesgsministerium, whose wartime life remains incompletely studied. But see: David Felix, *Walther Rathenau and the Weimar Republic* (Baltimore, MD: Johns Hopkins University Press, 1971); and Shulamit Volkov, *Walther Rathenau: Weimar's Fallen Statesman* (New Haven, CT: Yale University Press, 2012).

Wartime states and scientific mobilisation

The role of leading national institutions in the scientific war has yet to be fully explored, but a fine start for Germany was made a generation ago by the prodigiously productive Bernhard vom Brocke, whose work spans a generation. Of particular interest to the history of wartime science are his 'Wissenschaft und Militarismus', in William M. Calder III *et al.* (eds.), *Wilamowitz nach 50 Jahren* (Darmstadt: Wissenschaftliche Buchgesellschaft, 1985), pp. 649–719; 'Die Kaiser-Wilhelm-Gesellschaft im Ersten Weltkrieg (1914–1918)', in Bernhard vom Brocke and R. Vierhaus (eds.), *Forschung im Spannungsfeld von Politik und Gesellschaft: Geschichte und Structure der Kaiser-Wilhelm/Max Planck Gesellschaft* (Stuttgart: Deutsche Verlags-Anstalt, 1990), pp. 163–98; and 'Internationale Wissenschaftsbeziehungen und die Anfänge einer deutschen auswärtigen Kulturpolitk: der Professorenaustausch mit Nordamerika', in Bernhard vom Brocke (ed.), *Wissenschaftsgeschichte und Wissenschaftspolitik im Industriezeitalter: Das 'System Althoff' in historischer Perspektive* (Hildesheim: Lax, 1991), pp. 185–242.

Britain's scientific mobilisation has been studied by Donald S. L. Cardwell, and by Roy MacLeod, 'The chemists go to war: the mobilisation of civilian chemists and the British war effort, 1914–1918', *Annals of Science*, 50 (1993), pp. 455–81. On the history of French institutions, and their relationships with America and the Allies, see 'Le sabre et l'eprouvette: l'Invention d'une science de guerre, 1914–39', in *14–18–Aujourdhui*, 6 (2003), pp. 45–64. Articles in this issue discuss the ways in which by 1918 the 'French miracle' in the application of science to armaments, gas weapons, tanks and aeroplanes saved the government and restored the fortunes of France. The French story is brought to an international audience, in keeping with the tendencies of our time, in Danielle M. E. Fauque, 'French chemists and the international reorganisation of chemistry after World War I', *Ambix: Journal of the Society for the History of Alchemy and Chemistry*, 58:2 (2011), pp. 116–35.

On the much shorter US story of wartime government and military science, one can begin with Benedict Crowell, *America's Munitions, 1917–1918*, 2 vols. (Washington, DC: US Government Printing Office, 1920), closely followed by Crowell and Robert Forrest Wilson, *The Armies of Industry I: Our Nation's Manufacture for a World in Arms, 1917–18* (New Haven, CT: Yale University Press, 1921). Daniel J. Kevles, *The Physicists: The History of a Scientific Community in Modern America* (New York: Knopf, 1978) has a seminal chapter on U physicists in the Allied cause, and argues controversially that in the so-called 'Chemist's War', physics was more important than chemistry, as submarines were a greater threat than gas or explosives. A well-used survey of US science at war since the American Revolution which sees the significance of scientific and technological mobilisation in the First World War as a harbinger of things to come is Alex Roland, 'Science and war', *Osiris*, 2nd series (1), (1985), 247–72.

The sciences at war

Discipline-specific histories have much to offer the student of military science, whether the focus is government, academic or industrial. In chemistry, students might begin with Germany and with Lutz Haber, *The Chemical Industry, 1900–1930: International Growth and Technological Change* (Oxford: Clarendon Press, 1971), technically extended and morally deepened by his *The Poisonous Cloud*. Both have been set in context by Jeffrey Johnson, *The Kaiser's Chemists: Science and Modernization in Imperial Germany* (Chapel Hill, NC: University of North Carolina, 1990), and by the international authors in Roy MacLeod and Jeffrey Johnson (eds.), *Frontline and Factory: Comparative Perspectives on the Chemical Industry at War, 1914–1924* (Dordrecht: Springer, 2006). To date, this work has not been superseded.

For wartime physics and the applied sciences, among the best introductions to be found is David Cahan, 'Werner Siemens and the origin of the physickalisch-technische reichsanstalt, 1872–1887', *Historical Studies in the Physical Sciences*, 12:2 (1981), pp. 253–84. He explores similar issues at length in his *An Institute for an Empire: The Physikalisch-Technische Reichsanstalt, 1871–1918* (Cambridge University Press, 1989). Developments in the physical sciences are also described in Paul Forman and José Sanchez-Ron (eds.), *National Military Establishments and the Advancement of Science and Technology: Studies in 20th Century History* (Dordrecht: Kluwer, 1996), including essays by Helge Kragh, 'Telephone technology and its interaction with science and the military, ca 1900–1930', pp. 37–67, and Michael Eckert, 'Theoretical physicists at war: Sommerfeld students in Germany and as emigrants', pp. 69–87. Comparative themes are developed in Michael Heidelberger, 'Weltbildveränderungen in der modernen Physik vor dem Ersten Weltkrieg', in Rüdiger vom Bruch and Brigitte Kaderas (eds.), *Wissenschaften und Wisssenschaftspolitik* (Stuttgart: Steiner, 2002), pp. 84–96. A comparative study of mathematics, based primarily on France, is soon to appear as David Aubin and Catherine Goldstein (eds.), *The War of Guns and Mathematics: Mathematical Practices and Communities in Allied Countries around World War I* (Washington, DC: American Mathematical Society, 2012). This contains a useful essay by June Barrow-Green, 'Cambridge mathematicians' responses to the First World War', pp. 101–66, which complements William Van der Kloot's recent 'Mirrors and smoke: A. V. Hill, his brigands, and the science of anti-aircraft gunnery in World War I', *Notes and Records of the Royal Society*, 65 (2011), pp. 393–410.

For the wartime role of psychiatry and psychology, see Volker Roelcke, 'Die Entwicklung der Psychiatrie zwischen 1880 und 1932: Theoriebildung, Institutionen, Interaktionen mit zeitgenössischer Wissenschafts und Sozialpolitik', in Rüdiger vom Bruch und Brigitte Kaderas, *Wissenschaften und Wisssenschaftspolitik* (Stuttgart: Steiner, 2002), pp. 109–24; and Joanna Bourke, 'Psychology at war, 1914–1945', in Geoffrey C. Bunn, A. D. Lovie and G. D. Richards (eds.), *Psychology in Britain: Historical Essays and Personal Reflections* (Leicester: British Psychological Society, 2001), pp. 133–49.

Centre and periphery

During the last two decades, the history of wartime science in Britain, France and Germany has begun to attract increasing attention on a regional basis. Archival sources are being tapped to show how extensive levels of activity were not confined exclusively to the metropolitan centres. In Germany, an important step in this direction was taken by Peter Borscheid, *Naturwissenschaft, Staat und Industrie in Baden (1848–1914)* (Stuttgart: Ernst Klett, 1976), and today continues in Karl Strobel (ed.), *Die deutsche Universität im 20. Jahrhundert* (Vierow bei Greifswald: SH Verlag, 1994), with essays by Rüdiger vom Bruch on Berlin, Werner K. Blessing on Erlangen, and Notker Hammerstein on Frankfurt. More recently, a new milestone has been set by Trude Maurer (ed.), *Kollegen – Kommilitonen – Kämpfer: Europäische Universitäten im Ersten Weltkrieg* (Stuttgart: Steiner, 2006). Studies in local university and commercial archives in regional Australia, Canada, the United States and France, especially in relation to the discovery, exploitation and use of raw materials, are likely to be similarly fruitful. In many ways, the history of the Great War, once focused on political and economic history, and later on social and cultural history, is beginning to converge with current trends in environmental and material history – as befits a subject with global bearing.

18 Blockade and economic warfare

Alan Kramer

A comprehensive guide to the literature published before 2000 is in Eugene L. Rasor, 'The war at sea', in Robin D. S. Higham and Dennis E. Showalter (eds.), *Researching World War I: A Handbook* (Westport, CT: Greenwood Press, 2003), pp. 315–44.

Published sources

Kenneth Bourne and D. Cameron Watt (gen. eds.), *British Documents on Foreign Affairs: Reports and Papers from the Foreign Office Confidential Print*, Pt II: *From the First to the Second World War*, Series H: David Stevenson (ed.), *The First World War, 1914–1918*, vol. v – *Blockade and Economic Warfare, I: August 1914–July 1915*; vol. vi – *Blockade and Economic Warfare, II, July 1915–January 1916*; vol. vii – *Blockade and Economic Warfare, III, January–October 1916*; vol. viii – *Blockade and Economic Warfare, IV, November 1916–November 1918* (N. pl.: University Publications of America, 1989).

The very extensive US collection of documents, US Department of State, *Papers Relating to the Foreign Relations of the United States*, is now available online at http://digicoll.library.wisc.edu/cgi-bin/FRUS. For research on the diplomacy between the United States, the other neutrals and the belligerents, this is an essential source.

Archibald Colquhoun Bell, *A History of the Blockade of Germany and of the Countries Associated with Her in the Great War Austria-Hungary, Bulgaria, and Turkey, 1914–1918* (London: HMSO, 1961) was first published in 1937, but only for government use. Lambert claims that it 'remained a confidential document until 1961' (Lambert, *Planning Armageddon*, p. 13). In fact, it was not kept secret; the legal deposit libraries in the United Kingdom and Ireland received copies of the 1937 version, and it was even published in 1943 in an abridged version in German translation, under the title *Die englische Hungerblockade im Weltkrieg 1914–15* (Essen: Essener Verlagsanstalt, 1943). Although it provides a wealth of detail, the lack of references and its circumlocutory style tend to make the work opaque and reduce its usefulness for the modern scholar.

The legal and moral implications are discussed from the German viewpoint in Johannes Bell, Walter Schücking and B. Widmann (eds.), *Das Werk des Untersuchungsausschusses der Verfassunggebenden deutschen Nationalversammlung und des deutschen Reichstages*, 3rd series, *Völkerrecht im Weltkrieg*, vol. IV, *Der Gaskrieg, der Luftkrieg, der Unterseebootkrieg, der Wirtschaftskrieg* (Berlin: Deutsche Verlagsgesellschaft für Politik und Geschichte, 1927). This restates the wartime belief that Germany had a clear conscience, for its own submarine warfare was imposed on it by 'England', which had the intention of reducing Germany to defeat by starvation. U-boat warfare was thus a legitimate reprisal in international law. Rejecting the Allied allegation that submarine warfare was an atrocity responsible for the deaths of civilians at sea, it held that the blockade was responsible for killing 750,000 civilians in Germany.[1]

Historical interpretations

Gerd Krumeich's essay, 'Le blocus maritime et la guerre sous-marine', in Horne, *Vers la Guerre Totale*, pp. 175–90, is an eloquent introduction to the mentalities and culture of the blockade, exploring how it matched perfectly with the obsessive belief in Germany, ever since 1900, that it was 'encircled' by a world of enemies who were determined to deny its 'place in the sun'. Both the blockade and U-boat warfare marked decisive steps towards total war against civilians.

Avner Offer, *The First World War: An Agrarian Interpretation* (Oxford: Clarendon, 1991) is the standard work on the topic, with a largely convincing argument, based on research in British and German sources.

In Lance E. Davis and Stanley L. Engerman, *Naval Blockades in Peace and War. An Economic History since 1750* (Cambridge University Press, 2006) chapter 5, 'International law and naval blockades during World War I', pp. 159–237, the strong point is the collection of statistics, especially on German sinkings of Allied ships and on imports to the United Kingdom and Germany. However, it is unreliable in detail, with several factual errors. The discussion of the historiography, while to some extent useful, omits several relevant works and is restricted to English-language material. The heavy emphasis on food supply obscures the importance of other goods, and there is little indication that economic warfare involved states other than Germany, Britain and the United States. The conclusion that the blockade accounted for about one-quarter of the food shortages in Germany is a reasonable guess, but is not backed with evidence.

Nicholas A. Lambert, in *Planning Armageddon. British Economic Warfare and the First World War* (Cambridge, MA: Harvard University Press, 2012), argues that previous generations of historians were wrong in assuming that blockade 'must be a slow-acting weapon' and have 'overlooked evidence suggesting that the Admiralty developed a *fast*-acting plan for economic pressure'. Like Offer, Lambert shows that the Admiralty devoted considerable thought to economic warfare before and during the war, and that it understood the central role of the international system of credit and globalised

1 Gerd Krumeich, 'Le blocus maritime et la guerre sous-marine', in John Horne (ed.), *Vers la Guerre Totale. Le Tournant de 1914–1915* (Paris: Tallandier, 2010), pp. 175–90, here p. 178.

financial transactions. However, the evidence for the 'fast-acting plan' is not convincing. The book is nevertheless a mine of information on the inter-departmental battles over economic warfare, before and during the war, as well as Admiralty infighting. In particular, the Foreign Office was sceptical of its value, and the Board of Trade, as a redoubt of 'free trade ideals and laissez-faire economics', opposed interference in the market. Unfortunately, the book promises more than it can deliver. Among its overstated claims is the title: Lambert ends the story with the decision in February 1916 to establish the Ministry of Blockade, with the stated intention of enforcing blockade policy. By omitting the decisive stages of the period from early 1916 to late 1918, it tells the story of the failure of economic warfare. Moreover, by ignoring the effects of the policy in Germany, it misses the opportunity to assess its impact. As a study of the bureaucratic and political struggle within the British administration in the first eighteen months of the war, the book is a considerable achievement, but Lambert is unable to sustain his initial melodramatic arguments.

The best book on the hunger in Germany is Anna Roerkohl, *Hungerblockade und Heimatfront. Die kommunale Lebensmittelversorgung in Westfalen während des Ersten Weltkrieges* (Stuttgart: Steiner, 1991). Although it is a case study of Westphalia, this area not only contained some of Germany's prime industries and coal mines, it was also a large agricultural producer. Many of Roerkohl's careful judgements can be applied equally to the rest of Germany. Despite the title, she rejects the simplistic thesis that the blockade caused starvation.

David Stevenson provides a deft account of the high politics of the topic in the chapter 'Naval warfare and blockade' in his *1914–1918. The History of the First World War* (London: Allen Lane, 2004) (in the United States entitled *Cataclysm: The First World War as Political Tragedy*).

The economic history of the war is well analysed from a global perspective by Gerd Hardach, *The First World War 1914–1918*, vol. 2, *History of the World Economy in the Twentieth Century* (London: Penguin, 1977; first published in German in 1970). It is still unsurpassed.

The essays by Albrecht Ritschl (Germany) and Stephen Broadberry and Peter Howlett (the United Kingdom) in Broadberry and Harrison (eds), *Economics of World War I*, provide useful further perspectives.

19 Diplomacy

Georges-Henri Soutou

The printed sources on diplomacy during the First World War are not very numerous. We can start with: André Scherer and Jacques Grunewald (eds.), *L'Allemagne et les problèmes de la paix pendant la Première Guerre mondiale* (Paris: Presses Universitaires de France, 1962–78); Arthur S. Link (ed.), *The Papers of Woodrow Wilson* (Princeton University Press, 1956–65); and, in preparation, Ministère des Affaires étrangères, *Documents diplomatiques français, 1914–1918* (Brussels: Peter Lang, 1999, 2002–4).

We note here only the most significant works, which help readers through their substantial references. Recent archive-based studies concerning the internal relations of each of the two camps are few in number, and should be developed in future. Of significance are: Wolfgang Steglich, *Bündnissicherung oder Verständigungsfrieden. Untersuchungen zu dem Friedensangebot der Mittelmächte vom 12. Dezember 1916* (Göttingen: Musterschmidt, 1958); Georges-Henri Soutou (ed.), *Recherches sur la France et le problème des nationalités pendant la Première Guerre mondiale* (Paris: Presses de l'Université de Paris-Sorbonne, 1995); and the same author's 'La France et la crainte d'une paix de compromis entre la Serbie et les puissances centrales, 1914–1918', *Aspects de l'histoire des rapports diplomatico-stratégiques*, Cahier no. 12 (CEHD, 2000); Yannis G. Mourélos, *L'intervention de la Grèce dans la Grande Guerre* (Athens: Collection de l'Institut français d'Athènes, 1983); and Frédéric Le Moal, *La France et l'Italie dans les Balkans 1914–1919. Le contentieux adriatique* (Paris: L'Harmattan, 2006).

Studies of the soundings, peace attempts and secret negotiations between the two camps are more numerous. However, we still lack more synthesised studies, evaluating the relative importance of the different (and numerous) attempts and their interactions – here are two promising subjects for research. In the meantime, consult: Pedroncini, *Les négociations secrètes*; Nathalie Renoton-Beine, *La colombe et les tranchées. Les tentatives de paix de Benoît XV pendant la Grande Guerre* (Paris: Cerf, 2004); Wolfgang Steglich, *Der Friedensappell Papst Benedikts XV vom 1. August 1917 und die Mittelmächte* (Wiesbaden: Steiner, 1970); Georges-Henri Soutou, 'Briand et l'Allemagne au tournant de la guerre (septembre 1916-janvier 1917)', in *Media in Francia. Recueil de mélanges offert à Karl Ferdinand Werner* (Paris: Hérault-Éditions, 1989); and the same author's 'Paul Painlevé und die möglichkeit eines vehrhandlungsfriedens im kriegsjahr 1917', in Walther L. Bernecker and Volker Dotterweich (eds.), *Deutschland in den internationalen Beziehungen des 19. und 20. Jahrhunderts* (Munich: Ernst Vögel, 1996). See Jean-Claude Allain, Joseph Caillaux, vol. II, *L'Oracle, 1914–1944* (Paris: Imprimerie Nationale, 1982), on the very controversial role of Joseph Caillaux, which makes it possible to see the fragile and still controversial distinction in historiography between peace soundings and defeatism, and between action by a political leader in the setting of his responsibilities and accusation of treason, in the obsessive context of the epoch.

Concerning war aims: the controversy aroused by Fritz Fischer's book, *Griff nach der Weltmach. Die Kriegszielpolitik des kaiserlichen Deutschlands 1914–1918* (Düsseldorf: Droste Verlag, 1961), focused on the fact that he studied German goals without enquiring into those of the Allies, thus ruling out any evaluation of the effect of reciprocal escalation, of interaction between the two sides, although this did indeed occur. Now we have fairly numerous works on the principal warring nations: Georges-Henri Soutou, 'La France et les marches de l'est, 1914–1919', *Revue Historique* (October–December 1978); and the same author's *L'Or et le Sang. Les buts de guerre économique de la Première Guerre mondiale* (Paris: Fayard, 1989). This book in fact concerns war aims in general. See, too, Stevenson, *French War Aims*; Gitta Steinmeyer, *Die Grundlagen der französischen Deutschlandpolitik 1917–1919* (Stuttgart: Klett-Cotta, 1979); Rothwell, *British War Aims*; and Christopher Andrews and A. S. Kanya-Forstner, *France Overseas. The Great War and the Climax of French Imperial Expansion* (London: Thames & Hudson, 1981).

One subject has still received insufficient coverage: the interactions between diplomacy, war aims, internal politics, propaganda, psychological warfare, the cultural and social stakes of the game, extending into the international domain the new axes of research (politics, society, culture). One should start with: Antoine Prost and

Jay Winter, *Penser la Grande guerre. Un essai d'historiographie* (Paris: Le Seuil, 2004); and Wolfgang J. Mommsen, *Der Grosse Krieg und die Historiker. Neue Wege der Geschichtsschreibung über den ersten Weltkrieg* (Essen: Klartext Verlag, 2002). However, in *L'Or et le Sang*, Soutou made a determined effort to study the internal and external politics over the question, limited but central, of economic war aims. And we should cite too on this subject a collected work which is unfortunately difficult to find: Jean-Jacques Becker and Stéphane Audoin-Rouzeau (eds.), *Les sociétés européennes et la guerre de 1914–1918* (Paris: Université de Paris X Nanterre, 1990).

On the other hand, the Armistice of 11 November 1918 at Rethondes (far less the others, with Bulgaria, Turkey and Austria-Hungary!) together with the preparations for the Treaty of Versailles, has been the subject of an abundant bibliography. See the following: Pierre Renouvin, *L'armistice de Rethondes* (Paris: Gallimard, 1968); and his *Le traité de Versailles* (Paris: Flammarion, 1969); Jean-Jacques Becker, *Le traité de Versailles* (Paris: Presses Universitaires de France, 2002); Harold Nicolson, *Peace Making 1919* (New York: Constable, 1974); Eberhard Kolb, *Der Frieden von Versailles* (Munich: C. H. Beck, 2005); Klaus Schwabe (ed.), *Quellen zum Friedensschluss von Versailles* (Darmstadt: Wissenschaftliche Buchgesellschaft, 1997); Manfred F. Boemecke, Gerald D. Feldman and Elisabeth Glaser (eds.), *The Treaty of Versailles. A Reassessment after 75 Years* (Cambridge University Press, 1998); Macmillan, *Peacemakers*; Klaus Schwabe, *Woodrow Wilson, Revolutionary Germany and Peacemaking 1918–1919* (Chapel Hill, NC: University of North Carolina Press, 1985); Arno J. Mayer, *Politics and Diplomacy of Peacemaking: Containment and Counter-Revolution at Versailles, 1918–1919* (New York: Knopf, 1967); Gerd Krumeich and Silke Fehlemann (eds.), *Versailles 1919, Le Traité de Versailles vu par ses contemporains* (Paris: Alvik, 2003); Pierre Ayçoberry, Jean-Paul Bled and Istvan Hunyadi (eds.), *Les conséquences des traités de paix de 1919–1920 en Europe centrale et sud-orientale* (Strasbourg University Press, 1987); and David Fromkin, *A Peace to End All Peace: The Fall of the Ottoman Empire and the Creation of the Modern Middle East* (New York: Henry Holt & Co., 1989).

It was in fact to a large extent the end of the First World War which gave it its full meaning, in the long-term development of Europe and the international system. I have attempted some reflections in this sense in my book *L'Europe de 1815 à nos jours, 'Nouvelle Clio'* (Paris: Presses Universitaires de France, 2007).

20 Neutrality

Samuël Kruizinga

Neutrality during the First World War has been the subject of many national studies, but most of them have been written in that country's native language. This is the root cause of the fact that more general reviews of the subject, or even comparative studies, are very rare. Great debates or schools of thought on the subject are therefore never to be found, although each national historiography of neutrality features (implicitly or explicitly) a discussion on whether a country's neutrality either could have been maintained or, when it was, whether this was due to internal or external factors.

Two essay collections explicitly deal with neutrality during the First World War: Johan den Hertog and Samuël Kruizinga (eds.), *Caught in the Middle. Neutrals, Neutrality and the First World War* (Amsterdam: Aksant, 2011); and Hans A. Schmitt (ed.), *Neutral Europe between War and Revolution 1917–23* (Charlottesville, VA: University Press of Virginia, 1988). The first is very much a mixed bag of articles dealing with subjects ranging from diplomacy to cultural history; the second deals mostly (but not exclusively) with the effects of revolutionary movements in neutral countries. Both contain a number of English-language articles on neutrality (usually from the perspective of a single country), but neither made any serious attempt at synthesis. The same can be said for Herman Amersfoort and Wim Klinkert (eds.), *Small Powers in the Age of Total War, 1900–1940* (Leiden: Brill, 2011), which contains a number of essays dealing primarily with military aspects of neutrality. Richard F. Hamilton and Holger H. Herwig, *Decisions for War, 1914–1917* (Cambridge University Press, 2004), contains a number of chapters in which the authors try to explain, in a fashion very similar to my chapter in this book (Chapter 20), why countries decided to enter the war. The chapters on Greece, the Balkans and Italy are excellent. Finally Jukka Nevakivi (ed.), *Neutrality in History / La Neutralité dans l'Histoire* (Helsinki: SHS/FHS, 1993), pp. 135–44 devotes several short chapters to case studies of First World War neutrality in both legal theory and practice.

Several more general surveys on the First World War also include a chapter on neutrality: Jean-Marc Delauney, 'Les neutres européens', in Stéphane Audoin-Rouzeau and Jean-Jacques Becker (eds.), *Encyclopédie de la Grande Guerre, 1914–1918* (Paris: Bayard, 2004), pp. 855–66; Henning Hoff, 'Neutrale staaten', in Gerhard Hirschfeld, Gerd Krumeich and Irina Rentz (eds.), *Enzyklopädie Erster Weltkrieg*, 2nd edn (Paderborn: Ferdinand Schöningh, 2004), pp. 736–7; Jean-Jacques Becker, 'War aims and neutrality', in Horne, *A Companion to World War I*, pp. 202–16. These chapters provide brief overviews of the countries that remained neutral during the war and their main activities to either remain neutral or promote peace.

Works on the general history of neutrality also have a definite bearing on the First World War era – in fact, they treat it as somewhat of a watershed. Nils Ørvik, *The Decline of Neutrality, 1914–1941: With Special Reference to the United States and the Northern Neutrals*, 2nd edn (London: Frank Cass & Co., 1971 [1953]), sees neutrality under serious threat during the First World War. According to him, small neutrals were too weak to enforce their rights vis-à-vis the belligerent blocs, while larger neutrals could not stand by idly in the 'war to end all wars' lest the world be remade without them. At the end of the war, according to Ørvik, neutrality as it had developed during the eighteenth to nineteenth centuries was done for, although he concedes that it made a remarkable comeback during the Second World War. For a rebuttal of Ørvik, see the introduction by Samuël Kruizinga and Johan den Hertog in their *Caught in the Middle*.

Daniel Frey, 'Dimensionen neutraler Politik. Ein Beitrag zur Theorie der Internationalen Beziehungen' (PhD thesis, University of Geneva, 1969) has attempted to create a theory of political neutrality which is worthwhile, but remains largely untested (although my chapter in this book is a first attempt). Efraim Karsh, *Neutrality and Small States* (London and New York: Routledge, 1990) takes a different, but equally theoretical, approach by attempting to explain why neutrality works well for small countries and what strategies they can employ to enhance their security and safeguard their neutrality. His aims are somewhat similar to Frey, but his model is simpler and exclusively geared towards small neutrals. Stephen C. Neff, *The Rights and Duties of Neutrals: A General History* (Manchester University Press, 2000) provides an excellent overview of the history of the legal concept of neutrality.

Finally, only four works of which I am aware compare the neutral experience of different countries. Marc Frey, 'The neutrals and World War One', *Defence Studies*, 3 (2000), pp. 3–39 is an admirable overview of the war history of the 'northern neutrals': the Netherlands, Denmark, Norway and Sweden. Especially the section on economic history is useful. Patrick Salmon, *Scandinavia and the Great Powers 1890–1940* (Cambridge University Press, 1997) compares, on pp. 118–68, Danish, Norwegian and Swedish neutrality (and the war history of Finland), based on an impressive amount of primary and secondary sources in each of these countries' languages. Finally, Paul Moeyes's article, 'Neutral tones. The Netherlands and Switzerland and their interpretation of neutrality 1914–1918', which can be found in *Small Powers in the Age of Total War* (pp. 57–84), features an interesting comparison between the different 'neutralities' that animated both the Dutch and the Swiss approach to the belligerents during the First World War. Finally, Harm Anton Smidt, 'Dutch and Danish agricultural exports during the First World War', *Scandinavian Economic History Review*, 44:2 (1996), pp. 140–60, highlights the role of Dutch and Danish elites in determining trade policy during the war, which formed an important determinant of a neutral country's relationship vis-à-vis the belligerents.

21 Pacifism

Martin Ceadel

Although they have been supplemented by recent work, most notably in *Peace and Change: A Journal of Peace Research*, the foundations of our knowledge of pacifism were laid some decades ago. For an explanation as to why attitudes have differed so markedly from country to country, see Martin Ceadel, *Thinking about Peace and War* (Oxford University Press, 1987). For peace movements before 1914, see in particular Sandi E. Cooper, *Patriotic Pacifism: Waging War on War in Europe, 1815–1914* (New York: Oxford University Press, 1991).

In respect of pacifism in the absolute sense, the leading scholar has been Peter Brock, who updated his 1970 overview of twentieth-century developments in collaboration with Nigel Young: the chapter 'Patterns of conscientious objection: WWI' in their *Pacifism in the Twentieth Century* (New York: Syracuse University Press, 1999) is the best survey. For Britain, John Rae, *Conscience and Politics: The British Government and the Conscientious Objector to Military Service 1916–1919* (London: Oxford University Press, 1970) and Thomas C. Kennedy, *The Hound of Conscience: A History of the No-Conscription Fellowship, 1914–1919* (Fayetteville, AR: University of Arkansas Press, 1981) have become classics, their nearest counterparts for North America being: H. C. Peterson and Gilbert C. Fite, *Opponents of War 1917–1918* (Madison, WI: University of Wisconsin Press, 1957); Charles Chatfield, *For Peace and Justice: Pacifism in America 1914–1941* (Knoxville, TN: University of Tennessee Press, 1971); and Thomas P. Socknat, *Witness against War: Pacifism in Canada, 1900–1945* (Toronto University Press, 1987).

Seminal studies focusing on reformist pacifism in this period are: Henry Winkler, *The League of Nations Movement in Great Britain, 1914–1919* (New Brunswick, NJ: Rutgers University Press, 1952); Gertrude Bussey and Margaret Tims, *The Women's International League for Peace and Freedom* (London: Allen & Unwin, 1965); Warren F. Kuehl, *Seeking World Order: The United Sates and International Organization to 1920* (Nashville, TN: Vanderbilt University Press, 1969); Marvin Swartz, *The Union of Democratic Control in British Politics during the First World War* (Oxford: Clarendon Press, 1971); and Keith Robbins, *The Abolition of War: The 'Peace Movement' in Britain, 1914–1919* (Cardiff: University of Wales Press, 1976). More recent is Martin Ceadel, *Semi-Detached Idealists: The British Peace Movement and International Relations 1854–1945* (Oxford University Press, 2000).

Many general histories of defeated states provide accounts of pacifism in the merely anti-war sense, as in more detail do: Francis L. Carsten, *War against War: British and German Radical Movements in the First World War* (London: Batsford Academic and Educational, 1982); Michel Auvray, *Objecteurs, insoumis, déserteurs: Histoire des réfractaires en France* (Paris: Stock/2, 1983); and Belinda J. Davies, *Home Fires Burning: Food, Politics, and Everyday Life in World War I Berlin* (Chapel Hill, NC: University of North Carolina Press, 2000). Leonard V. Smith has an interesting approach to the pacifism of the 5th French Infantry Division, which was against the High Command, but not against the war. See his *Between Mutiny and Obedience: The Case of the French Fifth Infantry Division During World War I* (Princeton University Press, 1994).

22 Drafting the peace

Helmut Konrad

Owing to the abundance of the source material and to the wide spectrum of issues involved, the bulk of writings on the peace treaties still consists of specialised accounts devoted entirely to a single treaty, viewed from the perspective of the country or countries directly involved in that particular one. Pride of place in this regard goes to the Treaty of Versailles, the basic book on which is Margaret Macmillan's thoroughly detailed account, *Paris 1919. Six Months that Changed the World* (New York: Random House, 2002). Versailles is also the focal point in the collective volume by Manfred M. Boemke, Gerald D. Feldman and Elisabeth Glaser, *The Treaty of Versailles. A Reassessment after 75 years* (Cambridge University Press, 2006).

Even big surveys like Heinrich August Winkler's *Geschichte des Westens. Die Zeit der Weltkriege 1914–1945* (Munich: C. H. Beck, 2011) and David Stevenson's *Cataclysm. The First World War as Political Tragedy* (New York: Basic Books, 2004) devote a disproportionate amount of attention to Versailles in their discussions of the treaties, although they both offer good overviews of the end of the war and of the consequences of the First World War in general. An excellent introduction to the complex problems raised by the treaties taken as a whole is provided by Klaus Schabe in 'Das ende des Ersten Weltkriegs', his contribution to the big *Enzyklopädie Erster Weltkrieg*, 2nd edn, edited by Hirschfeld *et al.*

An entirely different perspective is offered by David Fromkin in his outstanding study, *A Peace to End All Peace. The Fall of the Ottoman Empire and the Creation of the Modern Middle East*, 2nd edn (New York: Henry Holt & Co., 2009), where he offers a penetrating analysis of events in the vast region from the Balkans to Afghanistan (including North Africa as well) during the period following the Great War.

Numerous works have been written about the effect on Central Europe (or 'Zwischeneuropa') of the treaties of Saint-Germain and the Trianon. For the Austrian peace treaty, which Manfried Rauchensteiner knows better than anyone else, see his *Der Tod des Doppeladlers. Österreich-Ungarn und der Erste Weltkrieg*, 2nd edn (Graz, Vienna and Cologne: Böhlau Verlag, 1994), and, more recently, in the collective volume edited by Helmut Konrad and Wolfgang Maderthaner, *. . . der Rest ist Österreich. Das Werden der Ersten Republik* (Vienna: Carl Gerolds Sohn, 2008), vol. 1.

The most significant recent writing on the Treaty of the Trianon has primarily been the work of Slovakian historians, most recently Marian Hronský in *The Struggle for Slovakia and the Treaty of Trianon* (Bratislava: VEDA Publishing House of the Slovak Academy of Science, 2001). The Hungarian literature on the subject takes a narrower approach and is still strongly nationalistic; see, for example, Laszlo Boto, *The Road to the Dictated Peace* (Cleveland, OH: Arpad Publishing Co., 1999).

Just how traumatic the consequences of the peace treaties were for the history of the affected states in the subsequent years, especially in Hungary and Germany, is shown in exemplary fashion in the volume edited by Gerd Krumeich, *Nationalsozialismus und Erster Weltkrieg* (Essen: Klartext Verlag, 2010), which traces the political aftershocks of the peace treaties. On this subject, see also the book by Thomas Lorenz, *Die Weltgeschichte ist das Weltgericht. Der Versailler Vertrag im Diskurs und Zeitgeist der Weimarer Republik* (Frankfurt and New York: Campus Verlag, 2008).

An attempt to set the peace treaties as a whole within the framework of the hopes, expectations and disappointments of the affected parties has been undertaken by Jay Winter in chapter 2 of his book *Dreams of Peace and Freedom in the Twentieth Century* (New Haven, CT: Yale University Press, 2006). In this connection, see also the debates in chapter 4 of Jay Winter (ed.), *The Legacy of the Great War. Ninety Years on* (Columbia, MO: University of Missouri Press, 2009).

23 The wars after the war

Robert Gerwarth

The literature on violent conflicts in Europe after the Great War has proliferated in recent years, both in terms of regional studies and synthetic pan-European surveys.

General histories of the post-war period

An excellent short general introduction to the subject is offered in Peter Gatrell, 'War after the war: conflicts, 1919–1923', in John Horne (ed.), *Blackwell Companion to the First World War* (Oxford: Blackwell, 2010), pp. 558–75. See also the collected essays on European post-war paramilitarism edited by Robert Gerwarth and John Horne (eds.), *War in Peace: Paramilitary Violence after the Great War* (Oxford University Press, 2012) and the survey provided by Alexander V. Prusin, *The Lands Between: Conflict in the East European Borderlands, 1870–1992* (Oxford University Press, 2010), pp. 71–97.

For an international history of the post-war period, see Zara S. Steiner, *The Lights that Failed: European International History 1919–1933* (Oxford University Press, 2004).

The brutalisation debate

Following the classic study by George Mosse, *Fallen Soldiers: Reshaping the Memory of the World Wars* (Oxford University Press, 1990), various scholars have suggested that the 'totalisation' process at work in the First World War generated a 'brutalisation' both of war and society by establishing new and unprecedented levels of acceptable violence. Historians associated with the Historial de la Grande Guerre, the history museum established at Péronne in the Somme in 1992, have been particularly prominent in reflecting on the transformation of violence occasioned by the First World War, for example in: Jean-Jacques Becker, Jay M. Winter, Gerd Krumeich, Annette Becker and Stéphane Audoin-Rouzeau (eds.), *Guerre et cultures 1914–1918* (Paris: Colin, 1994). See also Audoin-Rouzeau and Becker, *Understanding the Great War*. Other historians, such as Michael Geyer ('The militarization of Europe 1914–1945', in John R. Gillis (ed.), *The Militarization of the Western World* (New Brunswick, NJ: Rutgers University Press, 1989), pp. 65–102), have used the concept of the 'militarisation' of European society in this period to account for the ways in which the organisation of violence permeated societies, which in turn destabilised the post-war period.

For critical engagements with the brutalisation thesis, see Dirk Schumann, 'Europa, der Erste Weltkrieg und die Nachkriegszeit: eine Kontinuität der Gewalt?', *Journal of Modern European History* (2003), pp. 24–43.

The Russian Revolution / Russian Civil War

For surveys on the Russian Revolution and the subsequent civil war, see: Steve A. Smith, *The Russian Revolution: A Very Short Introduction* (Oxford University Press, 2002); Rex A. Wade, *The Russian Revolution, 1917* (Cambridge University Press, 2005); Sheila Fitzpatrick, *The Russian Revolution*, 2nd edn (Oxford University Press, 2001); Figes, *A People's Tragedy*; and Nikolaus Katzer, *Die Weiße Bewegung in Rußland. Herrschaftsbildung, praktische Politik und politische Programmatik im Bürgerkrieg* (Cologne: Böhlau Verlag, 1999). On the psychological effects of the revolution on counter-revolutionary mobilisation, see Robert Gerwarth and John Horne, 'Bolshevism as fantasy: fear of revolution and counter-revolutionary violence, 1917–1923', in Gerwarth and Horne, *War in Peace*. A major single-volume study on the psychological effects of the Bolshevik Revolution on Europe and the wider world, however, remains to be written.

Imperial collapse

A very good survey is offered in Roshwald, *Ethnic Nationalism*. See also Reynolds, *Shattering Empires*. More regional studies include work on the Balkans such as John Paul Newman, 'Post-imperial and post-war violence in the South Slav Lands, 1917–1923', *Contemporary European History*, 19 (2010), pp. 249–65; or comparative work on Poland and Ireland as in

Julia Eichenberg, 'The dark side of independence: paramilitary violence in Ireland and Poland after the First World War', *Contemporary European History*, 19 (2010), pp. 231–48; and in Tim Wilson, *Frontiers of Violence: Conflict and Identity in Ulster and Upper Silesia, 1918–1922* (Oxford University Press, 2010). The shattering Ottoman Empire is receiving renewed interest, for example in Gingeras, *Sorrowful Shores*.

Index

Cumulative index for Volumes I, II, and III.